SAM

7th Edition

Anthropology

CAROL R. EMBER

Hunter College of the City University of New York
Human Relations Area Files

MELVIN EMBER

Human Relations Area Files

PRENTICE HALL, *Englewood Cliffs, New Jersey* 07632

Library of Congress Cataloging-in-Publication Data

EMBER, CAROL R.
    Anthropology / Carol R. Ember, Melvin Ember. — 7th ed.
      p.   cm.

    Includes bibliographical references and index.
    ISBN 0-13-038183-7
    1. Anthropology.   I. Ember, Melvin.   II. Title.
GN25.E45   1993   92-27559
301—dc20   CIP

Acquisitions Editor: Nancy Roberts
Production Editor: Mary Anne Shahidi
Copy Editor: Elizabeth Gregory
Interior Design: Lisa Domingues
Cover Design: Jerry Votta
Art Director: Florence Dara Silverman/Anne Bonanno
Page Layout: Gail Collis
Photo Researcher: Tobi Zausner
Photo Editor: Lorinda Morris-Nantz
Prepress Buyer: Kelly Behr
Manufacturing Buyer: Mary Ann Gloriande
Supplements Editor: Sharon Chambliss
Editor-in-Chief: Charlyce Jones Owen
Editorial Assistant: Pat Naturale
Marketing Manager: Tracy Augustine
Cover Art: Funk/The Image Bank

 © 1993, 1990, 1988, 1985, 1981, 1977, 1973 by Prentice-Hall, Inc.
A Simon & Schuster Company
Englewood Cliffs, New Jersey 07632

Printed in the United States of America
10 9 8 7 6 5 4 3 2 1

ISBN 0-13-038183-7

Prentice-Hall International (UK) Limited, *London*
Prentice-Hall of Australia Pty. Limited, *Sydney*
Prentice-Hall Canada Inc., *Toronto*
Prentice-Hall Hispanoamericana, S.A., *Mexico*
Prentice-Hall of India Private Limited, *New Delhi*
Prentice-Hall of Japan, Inc., *Tokyo*
Simon & Schuster Asia Pte. Ltd., *Singapore*
Editora Prentice-Hall do Brasil, Ltda., *Rio de Janeiro*

Contents

iii

PART FOUR
Culture and Anthropology in the Modern World

Preface

For us, the challenges of research and of textbook-writing are similar. Both build on current knowledge, and both generate new questions to be investigated: What do we think we know, and what do we need to know? In addition, our research and the textbook sometimes stimulate each other. So, for example, when we realized that theories about why human societies universally have marriage had not been tested, we thought of research we could do ourselves. We decided to do a cross-species study (described in the chapter on marriage and the family), in which we could test theories by examining variation across birds and mammals, some of which have the functional equivalent of marriage.

Our recent cross-cultural research on war and peace has led us to think about how our knowledge of possible causes of war and peace may suggest policies that would minimize the risk of war. Our experience with war and peace issues also prompted us to look at research on other global social problems. Do the results in these other areas also imply possible solutions? We think the answer is yes, and we therefore decided to include an extensive discussion of these issues in our textbook.

We do so in the last chapter, titled "Explaining and Solving Social Problems," which is almost entirely new to this edition. We focus on AIDS, disasters, homelessness, crime, family violence, and war.

This is not the first time we have added a new chapter. For the 3rd edition we added a chapter on "Sex and Culture," and in the 4th edition we added a chapter on "Explanation and Evidence." Just as in this edition, we did so because we thought that a new chapter was warranted by the level of interest in the discipline or the amount of research available.

This edition also has a great deal of additional new material; most of the chapters have been considerably revised in the light of recent research. We hope our readers will like what we have added; we welcome comments and suggestions. One measure of how much we have added is the fact that more than 160 references are new to this edition. In the next section, we briefly describe the various chapters and the major changes in them.

As always, the book goes beyond description. We are not only interested in *what* humans are like. We are also interested in *why* humans are the way they are, why they got to be that way and why they vary. When there are alternative explanations, we try to communicate the necessity to evaluate them both on logical grounds and on the basis of the available evidence. The chapter on "Explanation and Evidence" is designed to help students distinguish between theory and evidence and to see how explanations can be and have been tested. In the substantive chapters, we note when the available evidence is not clear or is still lacking. We will be pleased if we succeed in helping students understand that no idea, including those put forward in textbooks, should be accepted simply on authority.

Throughout the book, we try to encourage appreciation of other peoples and their cultures. We think the best way to do so is to examine how characteristic traits may be adaptations to different life conditions. If people understood why others are different, they might be more tolerant.

Overview of the Seventh Edition

In what follows below, we briefly indicate what is covered in each chapter and what are the major changes in this edition.

Chapter 1, which is Part One, introduces the student to anthropology. We discuss what we think is special and distinctive about anthropology in general, and about each of its subfields in particular, and how each of the subfields is related to other disciplines such as biology, psychology, and sociology. We also discuss the usefulness of anthropology in the modern world.

Chapter 2, which begins Part Two ("Human Evolution: Biological and Cultural"), discusses evolutionary theory as it applies to all forms of life, including humans. We discuss how natural selection may operate on behavioral traits, and how cultural evolution differs from biological evolution. We have updated our discussion of DNA and RNA, and we now discuss the human genome project and the ethical issues posed by the possibility of genetic engineering.

Chapter 3 describes the nonhuman primates now living and their variable adaptations, as background for understanding the evolution of primates in general and humans in particular. After describing the various species, we discuss some possible

explanations of how the primates differ—in body and brain size, size of social group, and female sexuality. The chapter ends with a discussion of the distinctive or unusual features of humans.

Chapter 4 begins with the emergence of the early primates and ends with what we know about the Miocene apes, one of whom (known or unknown) was ancestral to the bipedal hominids. The chapter now discusses the relative dating of specimens on the basis of stratigraphy and biostratigraphy.

Chapter 5 starts with the emergence of the first bipedal hominids, the australopithecines. Before getting to the available fossil evidence, we first discuss trends in, and possible explanations of, the distinctive developments in the hominid line— the emergence of bipedalism, the expansion of the brain, and the reduction of the face, teeth, and jaws. We discuss the latest research on dental development and the duration of dependency in the australopithecines. We have extensively revised our discussion of the robust australopithecines because of new research on their size and dietary adaptation. And we discuss the latest research and thinking on the controversy over big-game hunting and the use of fire by *Homo erectus*.

Chapter 6 discusses the transition between *Homo erectus* and *Homo sapiens* and the emergence of modern-looking humans. We have added material on thermoluminescence dating and electron spin resonance dating. In keeping with our global purview, we discuss fossil and archeological materials from many areas of the world, not just Europe and the Near East.

Chapter 7 is considerably revised. It brings the discussion of human biological evolution into the present, dealing with biological variation in living human populations. Revisions include a new introduction, an extended discussion of types of natural selection, a greater emphasis on the interaction of culture and genes, and updated discussions of interpopulation variation in height, lactase deficiency, and sickle-cell anemia.

Chapter 8 deals with the emergence of broad-spectrum collecting and settled life, and the domestication of plants and animals, in various parts of the world. Our discussion mainly focuses on the possible causes and consequences of these developments.

Chapter 9, the final chapter in Part Two, discusses the rise of civilization in a number of areas of the world and the various theories that have been offered to explain the development of state-type political systems.

Chapter 10, which begins Part Three ("Cultural Variation"), discusses the concept of culture. We first try to convey a feeling for what culture is, before dealing more explicitly with the concept and some assumptions about it. We discuss the fact that individual behavior varies in all societies and how such variation may be the beginning of new cultural patterns.

Chapter 11 discusses the various kinds of theoretical orientation or approach in cultural anthropology, in more or less historical sequence. This chapter now includes a section on interpretive approaches.

Chapter 12 discusses explanation and evidence in cultural anthropology, but we like to think it provides a general introduction to all kinds of scientific research in anthropology. We consider how all knowledge is tentative, and how explanations are evaluated on the basis of evidence. We discuss why theories cannot be proven in any absolute sense and how we try to test them by collecting objective evidence that could possibly falsify their implications. We discuss what it means to evaluate test results statistically and why relationships or associations that are probably true may always have exceptions. Finally, we discuss the advantages and disadvantages of the various research strategies in cultural anthropology.

In most of the chapters in Part Three, we try to convey the range of cultural variation in the domain discussed with ethnographic examples from all over the world. Wherever we can, we discuss possible explanations of why societies may be similar or different in regard to some aspect of culture. If anthropologists have no explanation as yet for some kind of variation, we say so. But if we have some idea of the kinds of conditions that may be related to a particular kind of variation, even if we do not know yet why they are related, we discuss that too. If we are to train students to go beyond what we know now, we have to tell them what we do not know, as well as what we think we know.

Chapter 13 deals with language and culture. We discuss how linguists discover the unconscious rules of a language, how they determine that different languages may have a common ancestry, and how other aspects of culture may influence language and thought. There is a revised and updated discussion of child language, and we now discuss the implications of the symbolic as well as vocal ability of parrots.

Chapter 14 discusses how societies vary in getting their food, and how such variation seems to affect other kinds of cultural variation discussed later in the book—including variation in economic systems, social stratification, and political life. The discussion of environmental restraints on food-getting has been considerably revised.

Chapter 15 on economic systems discusses how societies vary in the ways they allocate resources (what is "property" and what ownership may mean), convert or transform resources through labor into usable goods, and distribute and perhaps exchange goods and services. There is a revised discussion of the possible effects of risk and uncertainty on the degree and kinds of sharing.

Chapter 16 discusses variation in degree of social stratification and how the various forms of social inequality (rank, class, caste, slavery) may develop.

Chapter 17 discusses how and why sex differences and sexual behavior, and attitudes about them, vary cross-culturally. The chapter now discusses the concept of gender, and variation in what has been called gender stratification. In the section on division of labor by gender, we now discuss how traditional calculations of contribution to subsistence did not pay sufficient attention to the activities necessary to prepare food for eating.

Chapter 18 discusses variation in marriage and family. There is now an extended and revised discussion of economic transactions at marriage; and we have updated the sections on incest taboos and polyandry in the light of recent research.

Chapter 19, on marital residence and kinship, now reverses the descriptions of kinship terminology, dealing first with the type of system most students are familiar with, the Inuit (Eskimo) system. We also now discuss how people in a society with descent groups may be named in a way that does not depend upon which descent group they belong to.

Chapter 20, on associations (nonkin and nonterritorial groups), now has an extended and revised discussion of "secret societies," which includes material on the women's society called Sande in West Africa.

Chapter 21, on political life, now includes an extended discussion of the sphere of life we call politics (how political decisions are made). We particularly focus on cross-cultural variation in degree of participation in the political process. We also discuss the latest cross-cultural findings on the possible causes of war and peace.

Chapter 22 discusses psychological differences between and within societies, and psychological similarities across societies. We now discuss the findings of recent cross-cultural research on adolescence.

Chapter 23, on religion and magic, now discusses how humans may create religions in response to certain needs or conditions, including the need for intellectual understanding, guilt and projection, anxiety and uncertainty, and the need for community. There are new discussions of trances, shamanism, ergot poisoning and hallucinations; and we have shortened the section on ways of dealing with the supernatural.

Chapter 24, on the arts, incorporates a revised definition of what constitutes the arts. The chapter also has a new introduction.

Chapter 25, on culture change, has a new discussion of how culture change may be adaptive. We have also updated the discussion of the Mundurucú.

Chapter 26 ("Explaining and Solving Social Problems") is almost entirely new. We begin with an updated discussion of applied anthropology, but we mostly discuss the study of global social problems, and how understanding their possible causes may suggest possible solutions. As noted above, we focus on AIDS, disasters, homelessness, crime, family violence, and war.

The book concludes with an Epilogue that we hope students will read, because it deals with the effects of the modern world on anthropology and the continuing and new challenges for anthropological research.

Features of the Book

Readability. We derive a lot of pleasure from trying to describe research findings, especially complicated ones, in ways that introductory students can understand. Thus, we try to minimize technical jargon, using only those terms students must know to appreciate the achievements of anthropology and to take advanced courses. We think readability is important not only because it may enhance the reader's understanding of what we write, but also because it should make learning about anthropology more enjoyable! When new terms are introduced, which of course must happen sometimes, they are set off in boldface type and defined right away. A glossary at the back of the book serves as a convenient reference for the student.

References. Because we believe firmly in the importance of evidence, we think it essential to tell our readers, both professional and student, what our conclusions are based on. Usually the basis is published research. References to the relevant studies are provided in complete footnotes, and a complete bibliography is also provided at the end of the book.

Summaries and Suggested Readings. In addition to the overview provided at the beginning of each chapter, there is a detailed summary at the end of the chapter that will help the student review the major concepts and findings discussed. Suggested readings are included to provide general or more extensive references on the subject matter of the chapter.

Supplements

An instructor's edition, a study guide for students, and a test item file are available for this edition. The instructor's edition, prepared by Alex Cohen and Dennis Werner, includes suggested discussion topics and ideas for students' essays or projects. The study guide and test item file were written by James Matlock and Dennis Werner. The study guide is designed to help students review the important points of the text and test themselves for understanding. A test item file of multiple-choice and fill-in questions is also availbale to the instructor, either on floppy disks—available for IBM computers—or through a Telephone Test Preparation Service, which the instructor can call toll free to have Prentice Hall prepare tests.

Acknowledgments

We thank Daniel Strouthes for retrieving most of the library materials we needed to revise the book for this edition. We thank a number of people at Prentice Hall for various kinds of help, including Nancy Roberts, editor for anthropology, Mary Anne Shahidi, for seeing the manuscript through the production process, and Tobi Zausner for photo research.

We are grateful to a number of people, including a few who wish to remain anonymous, for agreeing to review our chapters and make suggestions. These reviewers include: Katharine Milton, University of California-Berkeley; Alan Mann, University of Pennsylvania; C. Loring Brace, University of Michigan; Jeffery W. Froehlich, University of New Mexico; Robert Eckhardt, Pennsylvania State University-University Park; Francis E. Johnston, University of Pennsylvania; Gary M. Feinman, University of Wisconsin-Madison; Stephen A. Kowalewski, University of Georgia; William L. Coleman, University of North Carolina-Greensboro; Robert Dirks, Illinois State University; Susan Ward, Old Dominion University; W. Penn Handwerker, Humboldt State University; Vernon R. Dorjahn, University of Oregon; Rae Lesser Blumberg, University of California-San Diego; Martin Ottenheimer, Kansas State University; Michael R. Rhum, Northern Illinois University; Carolyn Edwards, University of Massachusetts-Amherst; Donald Hill, State University of New York College-Oneonta; Susan Wadley, Syracuse University; Norris Johnson, University of North Carolina; Barry Hewlett, Tulane University; Philip Silverman, California State University-Bakersfield; and Luther P. Gerlach, University of Minnesota.

We thank all of you, named and unnamed, who gave us advice.

CAROL R. EMBER AND MELVIN EMBER

1

What Is Anthropology?

Anthropology defines itself as a discipline of infinite curiosity about human beings. But this definition—which comes from the Greek *anthropos* for "man, human" and *logos* for "study"—is not complete. Anthropologists do seek answers to an enormous variety of questions about humans. They are interested in discovering when, where, and why humans appeared on the earth, how and why they have changed since then, and how and why modern human populations vary in certain physical features. Anthropologists are also interested in how and why societies in the past and present have varied in their customary ideas and practices.

But a definition of anthropology as the study of human beings is not complete, for according to such a definition anthropology would appear to incorporate a whole catalog of disciplines: sociology, psychology, political science, economics, history, human biology, and perhaps even the humanistic disciplines of philosophy and literature. Needless to say, the many other disciplines concerned with humans would not be happy to be regarded as sub-

FIGURE 1–1
The four major subdisciplines of anthropology (in bold letters) may be classified according to subject matter (physical or cultural) and according to the period with which each is concerned (distant past versus recent past and present).

Characteristics of Concern		Distant Past	Recent Past and Present
Physical		Human Evolution **PHYSICAL ANTHROPOLOGY**	Human Variation
Cultural	L A N G U A G E	Historical Linguistics **LINGUISTICS**	Descriptive or Structural Linguistics
	O T H E R	Cultural History **ARCHEOLOGY**	Cultural Variation **ETHNOLOGY** (Cultural Anthropology)

branches of anthropology. After all, most of them have been separate disciplines longer than anthropology, and each considers its own jurisdiction to be somewhat distinctive. There must, then, be something unique about anthropology—a reason for its having developed as a separate discipline and for its having retained a separate identity over the last 100 years.

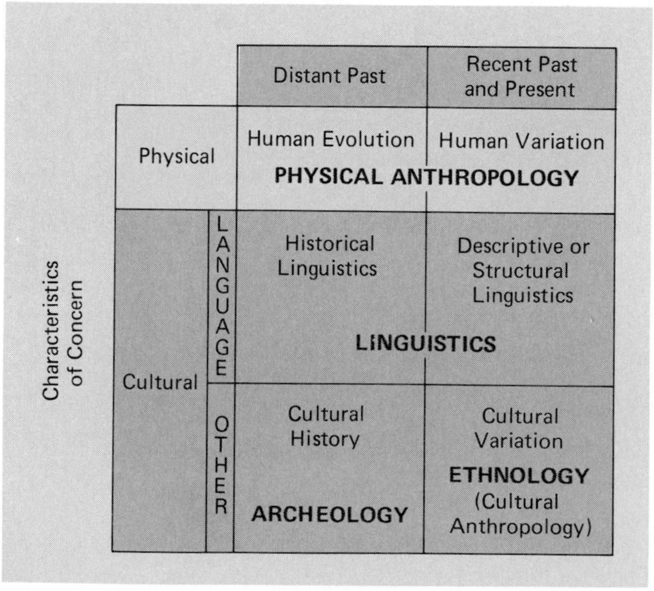

The Scope of Anthropology

Anthropologists are generally thought of as individuals who travel to little-known corners of the world to study exotic peoples, or who dig deep into the earth to uncover the fossil remains or the tools and pots of people who lived long ago. These views, though clearly stereotyped, do indicate how anthropology differs from other disciplines concerned with humans: anthropology is broader in scope (geographically and historically) than these other fields of study. Anthropology is concerned explicitly and directly with all varieties of people throughout the world, not only those close at hand or within a limited area. It is also interested in people of all periods. Beginning with the immediate ancestors of humans who lived a few million years ago, anthropology traces the development of humans until the present. Every part of the world that has ever contained a human population is of interest to anthropologists.

Anthropologists have not always been as broad and comprehensive in their concerns as they are today. Traditionally, they concentrated on non-Western cultures and left the study of Western civilization and similarly complex societies, with their recorded histories, to other disciplines. In recent years, however, this general division of labor among the disciplines has begun to disappear. Now anthropologists can be found at work in cities of the industrial world, as well as in remote villages of the non-Western world.

What induces the anthropologist to choose so broad a subject for study? In part, he or she is motivated by the belief that any suggested generalization about human beings, any possible explanation of some characteristic of human culture or biology, should be shown to apply to many times and places of human existence. If a generalization or explanation does not prove to apply widely, we are entitled or even obliged to be skeptical about it. The skeptical attitude, in the absence of persuasive evidence, is our best protection against accepting ideas about humans that are wrong.

For example, when American educators discovered in the 1960s that black schoolchildren rarely drank milk, they assumed that lack of money or education was the cause. But evidence from anthropology suggested a different explanation. Anthropologists had known for years that in many parts of the world where milking animals are kept, people do not drink fresh milk; rather, they sour it before they drink it, or they make it into cheese. Why this is so is now clear. Many people lack an enzyme, lactase, that is necessary for breaking down lactose, the sugar in milk. Such people cannot digest milk properly, and drinking it will make them sick, causing bloating, cramps, stomach gas, and diarrhea. Recent studies indicate that milk intolerance is found in many parts of the world.[1] The condition is common in adulthood among Orientals, southern Europeans, Arabs and Jews, West Africans, Inuit (Eskimos), and North and South American Indians, as well as American blacks! Because anthropologists are acquainted with human life in an enormous variety of geographical and historical settings, they are often able to correct or clarify beliefs and practices generally accepted by their contemporaries.

The Holistic Approach

In addition to the worldwide as well as historical scope of anthropology, another distinguishing feature of the discipline is its **holistic** or multi-faceted approach to the study of human beings. Anthropologists not only study all varieties of people; they also study many aspects of human experience. For example, when describing a group of people he or she has studied, an anthropologist might discuss the history of the area in which the people live, the physical environment, the organization of family life, the general features of their language, the group's settlement patterns, political and economic systems, religion, and styles of art and dress.

[1]Gail G. Harrison, "Primary Adult Lactase Deficiency: A Problem in Anthropological Genetics," *American Anthropologist*, 77 (1975): 812–35.

In the past, individual anthropologists tried to be holistic and cover all aspects of the subject. Today, as in many other disciplines, so much information has been accumulated that anthropologists tend to specialize in one topic or area. Thus, one anthropologist may investigate the physical characteristics of our prehistoric ancestors. Another may study the biological effect of the environment on a human population over time. Still another will concentrate on the customs of a particular group of people. Despite this specialization, however, the discipline of anthropology retains its holistic orientation in that its many different specialties, taken together, describe many aspects of human existence, both past and present, on all levels of complexity.

The Anthropological Curiosity

Thus far we have described anthropology as being broader in scope, both historically and geographically, and more holistic in approach than other disciplines concerned with human beings. But this statement again implies that anthropology is the all-inclusive human science. How, then, is anthropology really different from these other disciplines? We suggest that anthropology's distinctiveness may lie principally in the kind of curiosity it arouses.

Anthropologists are concerned with many types of questions: Where, when, and why did people first begin living in cities? Why do some peoples have darker skin than others? Why do some languages contain more color terms than other languages? Why, in some societies, are men allowed to be married to several women simultaneously? Although these questions seem to deal with very different aspects of human existence, they have at least one thing in common: they all deal with *typical characteristics* of particular populations. The typical characteristic of a people might be relatively dark skin, a language having many color terms, or the practice of having several wives. In fact, it could be almost any human trait or custom. This concern with typical characteristics of populations is perhaps the most distinguishing feature of anthropology. Thus, for example, where economists might take our monetary system for granted and study how it operates, anthropologists ask why *only some* societies during the last few thousand years used money. In short, anthropologists are curious about the typical characteristics of human populations—how and why such populations and their characteristics have varied—throughout the ages.

Fields of Anthropology

Different anthropologists may concentrate on different typical characteristics of societies. Some are concerned primarily with *biological* or *physical* characteristics of human populations; others are interested principally in what we call *cultural* characteristics. Hence, there are two broad classifications of subject matter in anthropology: **physical** (biological) **anthropology** and **cultural anthropology.** Physical anthropology is one major field of anthropology. Cultural anthropology is divided into three major subfields—archeology, linguistics, and ethnology. Ethnology, the study of recent cultures, is often referred to by the parent name, cultural anthropology.

Physical Anthropology

There are two distinct sets of questions that physical anthropology seeks to answer. The first set includes questions about the emergence of humans and their later evolution (this is the focus called **human paleontology** or **paleoanthropology**). The second set includes questions about how and why contemporary human populations vary biologically (the focus referred to as **human variation**).

In order to reconstruct human evolution, human paleontologists search for and study the buried, hardened remains or impressions—known as **fossils**—of humans, prehumans, and related animals. Paleontologists working in East Africa, for instance, have excavated the fossil remains of humanlike beings who lived more than 3 million years ago. These findings have suggested the approximate dates when our ancestors began to develop two-legged walking, very flexible hands, and a larger brain.

In attempting to clarify evolutionary relationships, human paleontologists may use not only the fossil record but also geological information on the succession of climates, environments, and plant and animal populations. Moreover, when recon-

Paleontologist Richard Leakey holding fossilized skulls of early humans.

structing the past of humans, paleontologists are also interested in the behavior and evolution of our closest relatives among the mammals—the prosimians, monkeys, and apes, which, like ourselves, are members of the order of **Primates.** (Those anthropologists, psychologists, and biologists who specialize in the study of primates are called **primatologists.**) Species of primates are observed in the wild and in the laboratory. One especially popular subject of study is the chimpanzee, which bears a close resemblance to humans in behavior and physical appearance, has a similar blood chemistry, and is susceptible to many of the same diseases.

From primate studies, physical anthropologists try to discover those characteristics that are distinctly human, as opposed to those that might be part of the primate heritage. With this information, they may be able to infer what our prehistoric ancestors were like. The inferences from primate

Nadine Peacock, a biological anthropologist, studied reproduction and health among the Efe-Ituri Pygmies of Zaire.

studies are checked against the fossil record. The evidence from the earth, collected in bits and pieces, is correlated with scientific observations of our closest living relatives.

In short, physical anthropologists piece together bits of information obtained from a number of different sources. They construct theories that explain the changes observed in the fossil record and then attempt to evaluate these theories by checking one kind of evidence against another. Human paleontology thus overlaps a great deal with disciplines such as geology, general vertebrate (and particularly primate) paleontology, comparative anatomy, and the study of comparative primate behavior.

The second major focus of physical anthropology—the study of human variation—investigates how and why contemporary human populations differ in physical or biological characteristics. All living people belong to one species, *Homo sapiens,* for all can successfully interbreed. Yet there is

much that varies among human populations. The investigators of human variation ask such questions as these: Why are some peoples taller than others? How have human populations adapted physically to their environmental conditions? Are some peoples, such as Inuit (Eskimos), better equipped than other peoples to endure cold? Does darker skin pigmentation offer special protection against the tropical sun?

To better understand the biological variations observable among contemporary human populations, physical anthropologists use the principles, concepts, and techniques of three other disciplines: human genetics (the study of human traits that are inherited); population biology (the study of environmental effects on, and interaction with, population characteristics); and epidemiology (the study of how and why diseases affect different populations in different ways). Research on human variation, therefore, overlaps with research in other fields. Those who consider themselves physical anthropologists, however, are concerned most with human populations and how they vary biologically.

Cultural Anthropology

To an anthropologist, the term **culture** generally refers to the customary ways of thinking and behaving of a particular population or society. The culture of a social group, therefore, is composed of its language, general knowledge, religious beliefs, food preferences, music, work habits, taboos, and so forth. **Archeology, anthropological linguistics,** and **ethnology,** the subdisciplines we consider next, are all directly concerned with human culture. Thus, they can be grouped under the broad classification of cultural anthropology.

Archeology. The archeologist seeks not only to reconstruct the daily life and customs of peoples who lived in the past but also to trace cultural changes and to offer possible explanations of those changes. This concern is similar to that of the historian, but the archeologist reaches much farther back in time. The historian deals only with societies possessing written records and is therefore limited to the last 5000 years of human history. But human societies have existed for more than a million years, and almost all in the last 5000 years did not have writing. For all those past societies lacking a written record, the archeologist serves as historian. Lacking written records for study, archeologists must try to reconstruct history from the remains of human cultures. Some of these remains are as grand as the Mayan temples discovered at Chichén Itzá in Yucatán, Mexico. More often they are as ordinary as bits of broken pottery, stone tools, and even garbage heaps.

Most archeologists deal with **prehistory,** the time before written records. However, there is a specialty within archeology, called **historical archeology,** that studies the remains of recent peoples who left written records. This specialty, as its name implies, employs the methods of archeologists *and* the methods of historians to study recent societies for which we have both archeological and historical information.

In trying to understand how and why ways of life have changed through time in different parts of the world, archeologists collect materials from sites of human occupation. Usually, these sites must be unearthed. On the basis of materials they have collected and excavated, they then ask various questions: Where, when, and why did the distinctive human characteristic of toolmaking first emerge? Where, when, and why did agriculture first develop? Where, when, and why did people first begin to live in cities?

To collect the data they need in order to suggest answers to these and other questions, archeologists use techniques and findings borrowed from a number of other disciplines, as well as what they may infer from anthropological studies of recent and contemporary cultures. For example, to guess where to dig for evidence of early toolmaking, archeologists rely on geology to tell them where sites of early human occupation are likely (because of erosion and uplifting) to be found close to the existing surface of the earth. (The evidence available today indicates that the earliest toolmakers lived in East Africa.) To infer when agriculture first developed, archeologists date the relevant excavated materials by a process originally developed by chemists. And to try to understand why cities first emerged, archeologists may need information from historians, geographers, and others about how recent and contemporary cities may relate economically and politically to their hinterlands. If we can discover what recent and contemporary cities have in common, perhaps we can speculate on why cities developed originally. Archeologists can then test these speculations. Thus, archeologists use information from the present and recent past in trying to understand the distant past.

Anthropological Linguistics. A second branch of cultural anthropology is linguistics, the study of languages. As a science, the study of languages is somewhat older than anthropology. The two disciplines became closely associated in the early days of anthropological fieldwork, when anthropologists enlisted the help of linguists to study unwritten languages. In contrast with other linguists, then, anthropological linguists are interested primarily in the history and structure of formerly unwritten languages.

Like physical anthropologists, linguists are interested both in changes that have taken place over time and in contemporary variation. Some anthropological linguists are concerned with the emergence of language and also with the divergence of languages over thousands of years. The study of how languages change over time and how they may be related is known as **historical linguistics.** Anthropological linguists are also interested in how contemporary languages differ—especially in the way they differ in construction. This focus of linguistics is generally called **structural (or descriptive) linguistics.** The study of how language is used in actual speech is called **sociolinguistics.**

In contrast with the human paleontologist and archeologist, who have physical remains to help them reconstruct change over time, the historical linguist is dealing only with languages—and usually unwritten ones at that. (Writing is only about 5000 years old, and the vast majority of languages before and since have not been written.) Because an unwritten language must be heard in order to be studied, it does not leave any traces once its speakers have died off. Linguists interested in reconstructing the history of unwritten languages must begin in the present, with comparisons of contemporary languages. On the basis of these comparisons, they may draw inferences about the kinds of change in language that may have occurred in the past and that may account for similarities and differences observed in the present. The historical linguist typically asks such questions as these: Did two or more contemporary languages diverge from a common ancestral language? If they are related, how far back in time did they begin to differ?

Unlike the historical linguist, the descriptive (or structural) linguist is typically concerned with discovering and recording the principles that determine how sounds and words are put together in speech. For example, a structural description of a particular language might tell us that the sounds *t* and *k* are interchangeable in a word without causing a difference in meaning. In the islands of American Samoa, one could say *Tutuila* or *Kukuila* as the name of the largest island and everyone, except perhaps the visiting anthropologist, would understand that the same island was being mentioned.

The sociolinguist is interested in determining how people speak differently in various social contexts. In English, for example, we do not address everyone we meet in the same way. "Hi, Joe" may be the customary way a person greets a friend. But the same person would probably feel uncomfortable addressing a doctor by first name; instead, he or she would probably say "Good morning, Dr. Smith." Such variations in language use, which are determined by the social status of the persons being addressed, are significant for the sociolinguist.

Ethnology. Ethnologists seek to understand how and why peoples today and in the recent past differ in their customary ways of thinking and acting. Ethnology, then, is concerned with patterns of thought and behavior, such as marriage customs, kinship organization, political and economic systems, religion, folk art, and music, and with the ways in which these patterns differ in contemporary societies. Ethnologists also study the dynamics of culture—that is, how various cultures develop and change. In addition, they are interested in the relationship between beliefs and practices within a culture. Thus, the aim of ethnologists is largely the same as that of archeologists. However, ethnologists generally use data collected through observation and interviewing of living peoples. Archeologists, on the other hand, must work with fragmentary remains of past cultures, on the basis of which they can only make inferences about the actual customs of prehistoric peoples.

One type of ethnologist, the **ethnographer,** usually spends a year or so living with, talking to, and observing the people whose customs he or she is studying. This fieldwork provides the data for a detailed description (an **ethnography**) of many aspects of the customary behavior and thought of those people. The ethnographer not only tries to describe the general patterns of their life but also may suggest answers to such questions: How are economic and political behavior related? How may the customs of people be adapted to environmental conditions? Is there any relationship between beliefs about the supernatural and beliefs or practices in the natural world? In other words, the ethnographer depicts the way of life of a particular group of people and may also suggest explanations for some of the customs he or she has observed.

Because so many cultures have undergone extensive change in the recent past, it is fortunate that another type of ethnologist, the **ethnohistorian,** is prepared to study how the ways of life of a particular group of people have changed over time. Ethnohistorians investigate written documents (which may or may not have been produced by anthropologists). They may spend many years going through documents, such as missionary accounts, reports by traders and explorers, and government records, to try to establish the cultural changes that have occurred. Unlike ethnographers, who rely mostly on their own observations, ethnohistorians rely on the reports of others. Often, they must attempt to piece together and make sense of widely scattered, and even apparently contradictory, information. Thus, the ethnohistorian's research is very much like that of the historian, except that the ethnohistorian is usually concerned with the history of a people who did not themselves leave written records. The ethnohistorian tries to reconstruct the recent history of a people and may also suggest why certain changes in their way of life took place.

With the data collected and analyzed by the ethnographer and ethnohistorian, the work of a third type of ethnologist, the **cross-cultural researcher,** can be done. The cross-cultural researcher is interested in discovering why certain cultural characteristics may be found in some societies but not in others. Why, for example, do some societies have plural marriages (one spouse of one sex and two or more spouses of the other sex), circumcision of adolescent boys, or belief in a high god or supreme being? In testing possible answers to such questions, cross-cultural researchers use data from samples of cultures to try to arrive at general explanations of cultural variation.

All types of cultural anthropologists may be interested in many aspects of customary behavior and thought, from economic behavior to political behavior to styles of art, music, and religion. Thus, cultural anthropology overlaps with disciplines that concentrate on some particular aspect of human existence, such as sociology, psychology, economics, political science, art, music, and comparative religion. The distinctive feature of cultural anthropology is its interest in how all these aspects of human existence vary from society to society, in all historical periods and in all parts of the world.

The Usefulness of Anthropology

For many centuries, the idea of traveling to the moon was only a dream. Yet in 1969 the dream became a reality when a U.S. Air Force officer gingerly planted his space boot in the moon dust. As the moon shot demonstrates, we know a great deal about the laws of nature in the physical world. If we did not understand so much, the technological achievements we are so proud of would not be possible.

In comparison, we know little about people, about how and why they behave as they do. When we consider the great number of social problems facing us, the importance and relevance of continuing research in cultural anthropology and the other social sciences become evident. Since social problems such as violence in the streets and wars between nations are products of human behavior, we need to find out what conditions produce those problems. Once we gain such understanding, we may be able to change the conditions and so solve the problems.

That anthropology and other sciences dealing with humans began to develop only relatively recently is not in itself a sufficient reason for our knowing so little. Why, in our quest for knowledge of all kinds, did we wait so long to study ourselves? Leslie White has suggested that in the history of science those phenomena most remote from us and least significant as determinants of human behavior were the first to be studied. The reason for this, he suggests, is that humans like to think of themselves as citadels of free will, subject to no laws of nature. Hence there is no need to see ourselves as objects to be explained.[2] Even today, society's unwillingness to accept the notion that human behavior is objectively explainable is reflected in the popularity of astrology as a determining factor in human behavior. It is highly improbable that the stars could account for human behavior when there are no known mechanisms by which they could influence people. Yet as long as such far-removed and improbable "causes" can pass for explanations, more reasonable explanations will not be sought, much less tested.

The belief that it is impossible to account for human behavior scientifically, either because our actions and beliefs are too individualistic and complex or because human beings are understandable only in otherworldly terms, is a self-fulfilling idea.

[2]Leslie A. White, "The Expansion of the Scope of Science," in Morton H. Fried, ed., *Readings in Anthropology*, 2nd ed., vol. 1 (New York: Thomas Y. Crowell, 1968), pp. 15–24.

!Kung at a feast in the Kalahari Desert. Their sharing, as well as other customs, may be an adjustment to their environment.

We cannot discover principles explaining human behavior if we neither believe there are such principles nor bother to look for them. The result is ensured from the beginning: those who do not believe in principles of human behavior will be reinforced by their finding none. If we are to increase our understanding of human beings, we first have to believe it is possible to do so.

Anthropology is useful, then, to the degree that it contributes to our understanding of human beings. In addition, it is useful because it helps us to avoid misunderstandings between peoples. If we can understand why other groups are different from ourselves, we might have less reason to condemn them for behavior that appears strange to us. We may then come to realize that many differences among peoples are products of physical and cultural adaptations to different environments.

For example, someone not very knowledgeable about the !Kung[3] of the Kalahari Desert of south-

ern Africa might decide that those people are savages. The !Kung wear little clothing, have few possessions, live in meager shelters, and enjoy none of our technological niceties. But let us reflect on how a typical North American community might react if it awoke to find itself in an environment similar to that in which the !Kung live. The people would find that the arid land makes both agriculture and animal husbandry impossible, and they might have to think about adopting a nomadic existence. They might then discard many of their material possessions so that they could travel easily, in order to take advantage of changing water and wild food supplies. Because of the extreme heat and the lack of extra water for laundry, they might find it more practical to be almost naked than to wear clothes. They would undoubtedly find it impossible to build elaborate homes. For social security, they might start to share the food brought into the group. Thus, if they survived at all, they might end up looking and acting far more like the !Kung than like typical North Americans.

Physical differences, too, may be seen as results of adaptations to the environment. For exam-

[3]The exclamation point in the word !*Kung* signifies one of the clicking sounds made with the tongue by speakers of the !Kung language.

The shuttle Challenger, shown here, blew up after launch in January 1986. Its failure was in part due to human errors in decision making. If we understood human behavior as well as we understand the physical universe, the shuttle Challenger may not have failed.

ple, in our society we admire people who are tall and slim. However, if these same individuals were forced to live above the Arctic Circle, they might wish they could trade their tall, slim bodies for short, compact ones, since stocky physiques appear to conserve body heat more effectively and may therefore be more adaptive in cold climates.

Exposure to anthropology might help to alleviate some of the misunderstandings that arise between people of different cultural groups from subtle causes operating below the level of consciousness. For example, different cultures have different conceptions of the gestures and interpersonal distances that are appropriate under various circumstances. Arabs consider it proper to stand close enough to other people to smell them.[4] Judging from the popularity of deodorants in our culture, Americans seem to prefer to keep the olfactory dimension out of interpersonal relations. When someone comes too close, we may feel he or she is being too intimate. However, we should remember that this person may only be acting according to a culturally conditioned conception of what is proper in a given situation. If our intolerance for others results in part from a lack of understanding of why peoples vary, then the knowledge accumulated by anthropologists may help lessen that intolerance.

Knowledge of our past may also bring both a feeling of humility and a sense of accomplishment. If we are to attempt to deal with the problems of our world, we must be aware of our vulnerability, so that we do not think the problems will solve themselves. But we also have to think enough of our accomplishments to believe we can find solutions to our problems.

It may be that much of the trouble people get themselves into is a result of their feelings of self-importance and invulnerability—in short, their lack of humility. Knowing something about our evolutionary past may help us to understand and accept our place in the biological world. Just as for any other form of life, there is no guarantee that any particular human population, or even the entire human species, will perpetuate itself indefinitely. The earth changes, the environment changes, and humanity itself changes, so that what survives and flourishes in the present might not do so in the future.

Yet our vulnerability should not make us feel powerless. There are many reasons to feel confident about the future. Consider what we have accomplished so far. By means of tools and weapons fashioned from sticks and stones, we were able to hunt animals larger and more powerful than ourselves. We discovered how to make fire and we learned to use it to keep ourselves warm and to cook our food. As we domesticated plants and animals, we gained greater control over our food supply and were able to establish more permanent settlements. We mined and smelted ores to fashion more durable tools. We built cities and irrigation systems, monuments and ships. We made it possible to travel from one continent to another in a single day. We conquered various illnesses and prolonged human life.

In short, human beings and their cultures have changed considerably over the course of history. Some human populations— though different ones at different times—have been able to adapt to changing circumstances. Let us hope that humans continue to adapt to the challenges of the present and the future.

[4]Edward T. Hall, *The Hidden Dimension* (Garden City, NY: Doubleday, 1966), pp. 144–53.

SUMMARY

1. Anthropology is literally the *study of human beings.* It differs from other disciplines concerned with people in that it is broader in scope. It is concerned with humans in all places of the world (not simply those places close to us), and it traces human evolution and cultural development from millions of years ago to the present day.

2. Another distinguishing feature of anthropology is its holistic approach to the study of human beings. Not only do anthropologists study all varieties of people, they also study all aspects of those peoples' experiences.

3. Anthropologists are concerned with identifying and explaining typical characteristics of particular human populations. Such a characteristic might be any human trait or custom.

4. Physical anthropology is one of the major fields of the discipline. Physical anthropology studies the emergence of humans and their later physical evolution (the focus called human paleontology). It also studies how and why contemporary human populations vary biologically (the focus called human variation).

5. The second broad area of concern to anthropology is cultural anthropology. Its three subfields—archeology, anthropological linguistics, and ethnology—all deal with aspects of human culture—that is, with the customary ways of thinking and behaving of a particular society.

6. Archeologists seek not only to reconstruct the daily life and customs of prehistoric peoples but also to trace cultural changes and offer possible explanations of those changes. Therefore, archeologists try to reconstruct history from the remains of human cultures.

7. Anthropological linguists are concerned with the emergence of language and with the divergence of languages over time (a subject known as historical linguistics). They also study how contemporary languages differ, both in construction (structural or descriptive linguistics) and in use in actual speech (sociolinguistics).

8. The ethnologist seeks to understand how and why peoples of today and the recent past differ in their customary ways of thinking and acting. One type of ethnologist, the ethnographer, usually spends a year or so living with, talking to, and observing the customs of a particular population. Later, he or she may prepare a detailed report of the group's behavior, which is called an ethnography. Another type of ethnologist, the ethnohistorian, investigates written documents to determine how the ways of life of a particular group of people have changed over time. A third type of ethnologist—the cross-cultural researcher—studies data collected by ethnographers and ethnohistorians for a sample of cultures and attempts to discover which explanations of particular customs may be generally applicable.

9. Anthropology may help people to be more tolerant. Anthropological studies can show us why other people are the way they are, both culturally and physically. Customs or actions of theirs that appear improper or offensive to us may be adaptations to particular environmental and social conditions.

10. Anthropology is also valuable in that knowledge of our past may bring us both a feeling of humility and a sense of accomplishment. Like any other form of life, we have no guarantee that any particular human population will perpetuate itself indefinitely. Yet, knowledge of our achievements in the past may give us confidence in our ability to solve the problems of the future.

SUGGESTED READING

AKMAJIAN, A., DEMERS, R. A., AND HARNISH, R. M. *Linguistics: An Introduction to Language and Communication,* 2nd ed. Cambridge, MA: M.I.T. Press, 1984. A survey of many of the kinds of research on language and communication.

FAGAN, B. M. *People of the Earth: An Introduction to World Prehistory,* 6th ed. Glenview, IL: Scott, Foresman and Company, 1989. A survey of world prehistory, describing what we know from archeology about hunters and gatherers, farmers, and cities and civilizations in all areas of the world.

HARRISON, G. A., TANNER, J. M., PILBEAM, D. R., AND BAKER, P. T. *Human Biology: An Introduction to Human Evolution, Variation, Growth, and Adaptability,* 3rd ed. Oxford: Oxford University Press, 1988. A survey of research and recent developments in the study of human evolution, human genetics and variation, human growth and constitution, and human adaptability.

KONNER, M. *The Tangled Wing: Biological Constraints on the Human Spirit.* New York: Harper & Row, Pub., 1982. A biological anthropologist discusses the biological and cultural roots of human behavior and emotions.

2

Evolution

Astronomers estimate that the universe has been in existence for some 15 billion years. To make this awesome history more understandable, Carl Sagan has devised a calendar that condenses this span into a single year.[1] Using as a scale twenty-four days for every billion years and one second for every 475 years, Sagan moves from the "Big Bang," or beginning of the universe, on January 1 to the origin of the Milky Way on May 1. September 9 marks the beginning of our solar system and September 25 the origin of life on earth. At 10:30 in the evening of December 31, the first humans appear. Sagan's compression of history provides us with a manageable way to compare the short span of human existence with the total time span of the universe: human beings have been around for only about ninety minutes out of a twelve-month period! In this book, we are concerned with what has happened in the last few hours of the year.

Some 70 million years ago, the first primates may have appeared. They are believed to be ancestral to all living primates, including monkeys, apes, and humans. The early primates may or may not have lived in trees, but they had flexible digits and could grasp things. Later (about 35 million years ago) they began to be replaced by the first monkeys and apes. Some 20 million years after the appearance of monkeys and apes, the immediate apelike ancestors of humans probably emerged. About 100,000 years ago, "modern" humans evolved.

How do we account for the biological and cultural evolution of humans? The details of the emergence of primates and the evolution of humans and their cultures will be covered in subsequent chapters. In this chapter, we focus on how the modern theory of evolution developed and how it accounts for change over time.

The Evolution of Evolution

According to the Judeo-Christian view of history, the world was only a few thousand years old. An eminent calculator of biblical events, Archbishop Ussher, even set the date of creation at pre-

cisely 4004 B.C. That was the year God was supposed to have created Adam and, from Adam's rib, Eve. Man and woman, fashioned in God's image, were seen as "little lower than the angels." Given such a view, the acceptance of the theory of *evolution*—the idea that different species developed, one from another, over long periods of time—was impossible.

The dominant Western view of the seventeenth and eighteenth centuries also held that God and all His creations were locked into a natural hierarchy. This hierarchy was defined and perpetuated by the theological doctrine of the scale of nature, also called the chain of being.[2] It placed humans above rocks, plants, and animals and below spiritual beings. Although the scale of nature placed humans close to apes, people were not shocked, for each creature in the chain of being was said to have been created separately by God's divine art. The physical resemblances between human and ape were thus the result of separate acts of divine creation.

Belief in the scale of nature was accompanied by the conviction that an animal species could not become extinct. The notion of extinction threatened people's trust in God; it was unthinkable that a whole group of God's creations could simply disappear. The irony is that although the doctrine of the scale of nature delayed an evolutionary theory, its concept of an order of things in nature encouraged comparative anatomical studies and thus provided a stimulus for the development of the idea of evolution.

Early in the eighteenth century, an influential scientist, Carolus Linnaeus (1707–1778), classified plants and animals in a *systema naturae*, which placed humans in the same order (Primates) as apes and monkeys. Linnaeus did not suggest an evolutionary relationship between humans and apes; he mostly accepted the notion that all **species** were created by God and fixed in their form. Not surprisingly, then, Linnaeus is often viewed as an anti-evolutionist. But Linnaeus's hierarchical classification scheme, in descending order going from kingdom to class, order, genus, and species, pro-

[1]Carl Sagan, "A Cosmic Calendar," *Natural History,* December 1975, pp. 70–73.

[2]See Loren C. Eiseley, "The Dawn of Evolutionary Theory," in Loren C. Eiseley, *Darwin's Century: Evolution and the Men Who Discovered It* (Garden City, NY: Doubleday, 1958); reprinted in Louise B. Young, ed., *Evolution of Man* (New York: Oxford University Press, 1970), p. 10.

The giraffe's long neck is adaptive for eating tree leaves high off the ground. Giraffes with short necks would not be favored by natural selection.

vided a framework for the idea that humans, apes, and monkeys had a common ancestor.[3]

Others did not believe species were fixed in their form. According to Jean Baptiste Lamarck (1744–1829), acquired characteristics could be inherited and therefore species could evolve; individuals who in their lifetime developed characteristics helpful to survival would pass those characteristics on to future generations, thereby changing the physical makeup of the species. For example, Lamarck explained the long neck of the giraffe as the result of successive generations of giraffes stretching their necks to reach the high leaves of trees. The stretched muscles and bones of the necks were somehow transmitted to the offspring of the neck-stretching giraffes, and eventually all giraffes came to have long necks. Erasmus Darwin (1731–1802), grandfather of the celebrated Charles Darwin and a contemporary of Lamarck, also believed in the inheritance of acquired characteristics as a way of explaining evolutionary changes in life forms. But because Lamarck and later biologists failed to produce evidence to support the hypothesis that acquired characteristics can be inherited, this explanation of evolution is now generally dismissed.[4]

By the nineteenth century some thinkers were beginning to accept evolution, although a number of leading scientists were trying to refute it.[5] Sir Charles Lyell, in his *Principles of Geology* (1830–1833), questioned the biblical conception of the earth's creation, but nonetheless rejected the idea that species could evolve. With respect to the earth, Lyell suggested that it was constantly being shaped and reshaped by natural forces that had been operating since the beginning of time. But his view of species was entirely different. Lyell believed that a species became extinct because it had a predetermined end. It was then replaced by another of God's creations. For Lyell, natural law applied to the earth, but not to the plant and animal species living on earth. Georges Cuvier (1769–1832) was another leading opponent of evolution. Cuvier's theory of **catastrophism** proposed that a series of catastrophes accounted for changes in the fossil record. Cataclysms and upheavals such as Noah's flood had killed off previous sets of living creatures, which each time were replaced by new creations.

The Theory of Natural Selection

After studying changes in plants, fossil animals, and varieties of domestic and wild pigeons, Charles Darwin (1809–1882) rejected the notion that each species was created independently. The results of his investigations pointed clearly, he thought, to the evolution of species through change. More than that, they pointed to a mechanism—**natural selection**—that might explain how

[3]Eiseley, "The Dawn of Evolutionary Theory," in Young, ed., *Evolution of Man*, pp. 13–15; and Ernst Mayr, *The Growth of Biological Thought: Diversity, Evolution, and Inheritance* (Cambridge, MA: The Belknap Press of Harvard University Press, 1982), pp. 171–75, 340–41.

[4]Mayr, *The Growth of Biological Thought*, pp. 339–60.
[5]Ernst Mayr, "The Nature of the Darwinian Revolution," *Science*, June 2, 1972, pp. 981–89.

evolution took place. While Darwin was completing the work necessary to support his theory, he was sent a manuscript by Alfred Russell Wallace, a naturalist who had independently reached conclusions about the evolution of species that matched his own. In 1858, the two men presented the astonishing theory of natural selection to their colleagues at a meeting of the Linnaean Society of London.[6]

In 1859, when Darwin published *The Origin of Species*, he wrote, "I am fully convinced that species are not immutable; but that those belonging to what are called the same genera are lineal descendants of some other and generally extinct species, in the same manner as the acknowledged varieties of any one species."[7] His conclusions outraged those who believed in the biblical account of creation. Evolutionary evidence was sufficiently convincing to make some people interpret the Bible metaphorically or figuratively, but the fundamentalists who worshiped the literal word of "The Book" would not compromise their beliefs. The result was years of bitter controversy.

Until 1871 (when *The Descent of Man* was published), Darwin avoided stating categorically that humans were descended from nonhuman forms, but the implications of his theory were clear. People began immediately to take sides. In June 1860, at the annual meeting of the British Association for the Advancement of Science, Bishop Wilberforce saw an opportunity to attack the Darwinists. Concluding his speech, he faced Thomas Huxley, one of the Darwinists' chief advocates, and inquired, "Was it through his grandfather or his grandmother that he claimed descent from a monkey?" Huxley responded,

If . . . the question is put to me would I rather have a miserable ape for a grandfather than a man highly endowed by nature and possessing great means and influence and yet who employs those faculties and that influence for the mere purpose of introducing ridicule into a grave scientific discussion—I unhesitatingly affirm my preference for the ape.[8]

[6]Mayr, *The Growth of Biological Thought*, p. 423.
[7]Charles Darwin, "The Origin of Species," in Young, ed., *Evolution of Man*, p. 78.
[8]Quoted in Ashley Montagu's introduction to Thomas H. Huxley, "Man's Place in Nature," in Young, ed., *Evolution of Man*, pp. 183–84.

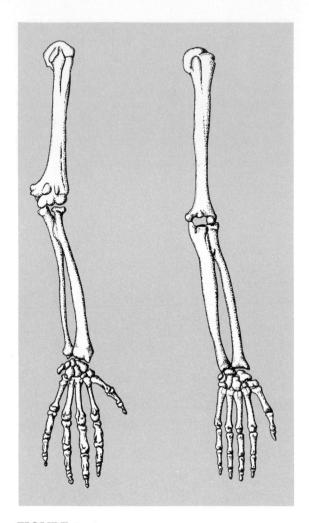

FIGURE 2–1
The idea that chimpanzees and humans descend from a common ancestor is suggested by anatomical similarities, such as in their forelimbs. Chimpanzee forelimb skeleton (left); human forelimb skeleton (right).

One of the most famous confrontations between evolutionists and their critics occurred at the 1927 Scopes trial in Tennessee. John Scopes, defended by the renowned lawyer Clarence Darrow, was convicted of teaching evolution. Scopes's opponents won the court decision, but the real victors were the proponents of Darwin's theory. The wide publicity given the trial and the discussion it generated greatly increased the public's awareness and understanding of evolution—if not its total acceptance. Even recently people have protested the teaching of evolution and requested equal treatment for the biblical story of creation.

Darwin was not the first person to view the creation of new species as evolutionary, but he was the first to provide a comprehensive, well-documented explanation for the way evolution had occurred. He pointed out that each species is composed of a great variety of individuals, some of which are better adapted to their environment than others. The better-adapted individuals generally produce more offspring over generations than the poorer-adapted. Thus, over time natural selection results in increasing proportions of individuals with advantageous traits.

When we say that certain traits are advantageous, we mean that they result in greater reproductive success in a particular environment. The phrase *particular environment* is very important. Even though a species may become better adapted to a particular environment over time, we cannot say that one species adapted to its environment is "better" than another species adapted to a different environment. For example, we may like to think of ourselves as better than the other animals, but humans are clearly less adapted than fish for living underwater, bats for catching flying insects, and raccoons for living on suburban garbage.

Changes in a species can be expected to occur as the environment changes or as some members of the species move into a new environment. With environmental change, different traits become adaptive. The forms of the species that possess the more adaptive traits will become more frequent, whereas those forms whose characteristics make continued existence more difficult or impossible in the modified environment will eventually become extinct. According to Wallace's theory as originally presented, environmental difficulties would mean that

those forming the least numerous and most feebly organized variety would suffer first, and, were the pressure severe, must soon become extinct. . . . the parent species would next suffer, would gradually diminish in numbers, and with a recurrence of similar unfavorable conditions might also become extinct. The superior variety would then alone remain. . . .[9]

[9]Alfred Russell Wallace, "On the Tendency of Varieties to Depart Indefinitely from the Original Type," *Journal of the Proceedings of the Linnaean Society*, August 1858; reprinted in Young, ed., *Evolution of Man*, p. 75.

Consider how the theory of natural selection would explain why giraffes became long-necked. Originally, the necks of giraffes varied in length, as happens with virtually any physical characteristic in a population. During a period when food was scarce, those giraffes with longer necks who could reach higher tree leaves might be better able to survive and suckle their offspring, and thus they would leave more offspring than shorter-necked giraffes. Eventually, the shorter-necked giraffes would diminish in number and the longer-necked giraffes would increase. The resultant population of giraffes would still have variation in neck length, but on the average would be longer-necked than earlier forms.

Because the process of evolution occurs mainly in small, nearly imperceptible gradations over many generations, it is difficult to observe directly. Nevertheless, because some life forms reproduce rapidly, it is possible to observe some examples of natural selection operating over relatively short periods in changing environments.

Within the last 150 years in England, for example, scientists have been able to observe natural selection in action. When certain areas of the country became heavily industrialized, the pale bark of trees in those regions became coated with black soot. Light-colored moths, formerly well adapted to blend with their environment, became clearly visible against the sooty background of the trees and were easy prey for birds. Darker moths, previously at a disadvantage against the light bark, were now better adapted for survival. Their dark color became an advantage, and subsequently the darker moths became the predominant variety in industrial regions. This evolution has recently been reversed. With the decline in industrial pollutants, light-colored moths have begun to regain their old advantage.

Another well-known example of natural selection is the acquired resistance of houseflies to the insecticide DDT. When DDT was first used to kill insects, beginning in the 1940s, several new, DDT-resistant strains of housefly evolved. In the early DDT environment, many houseflies were killed. But the few that survived were the ones that reproduced—and their resistant characteristics became common to the housefly populations. To the chagrin of medical practitioners, similar resistances develop in bacteria. A particular antibi-

The light-colored moth is more visible to predators than the dark-colored moth on a dark tree trunk. When trees in England became coated with black soot from industrial pollution, natural selection favored dark-colored moths.

otic may lose its effectiveness after it comes into wide use because new, resistant bacterial strains emerge. These new strains will become more frequent than the original ones because of natural selection.

The theory of natural selection answered many questions, but it also raised at least one whose answer eluded even Darwin. The appearance of a beneficial trait may assist the survival of an organism, but what happens when the organism reproduces by mating with members that do not possess this new variation? Will not the new adaptive trait eventually disappear if subsequent generations mate with individuals that lack this trait? Darwin knew variations were transmitted through heredity, but he could not explain the source of new variations and the mode of inheritance. Gregor Mendel's pioneering studies in the science of genetics provided the foundation for the answers, but his discoveries were not widely known until 1900.

Heredity

Gregor Mendel's Experiments

Mendel (1822–1884), a monk and amateur botanist who lived in what is now Czechoslovakia, bred several varieties of pea plants and made detailed observations of their offspring. He chose as breeding partners plants that differed by only one observable trait: tall plants were crossed with short ones, and yellow ones with green, for example.

When the pollen from a yellow pea plant was transferred to a green pea plant, Mendel observed a curious phenomenon: all of the first-generation offspring bore yellow peas. It seemed that the green trait had disappeared. But when seeds from this first generation were crossed, they produced both yellow and green pea plants in a ratio of three yellow to one green pea plant (see Figure 2–2). Apparently, Mendel reasoned, the green trait had not been lost or altered; the yellow trait was simply **dominant** and the green trait was **recessive.** Mendel observed similar results with other traits. Tall-

FIGURE 2–2

When Mendel crossed a plant having two genes for yellow peas (YY) with a plant having two genes for green peas (yy), the peas for each offspring were yellow but carried one gene for yellow and one gene for green (Yy). The peas were yellow because the gene for yellow is dominant over the recessive gene for green. Crossing the first generation yielded three yellow pea plants for each green pea plant.

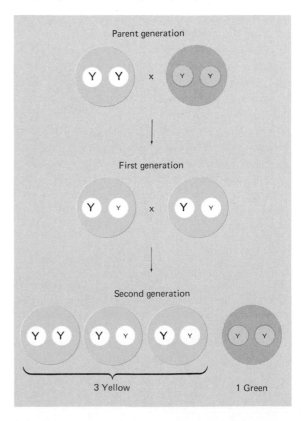

ness dominated shortness, and the factor for smooth-skinned peas dominated the factor for wrinkled ones. In each cross, the three-to-one ratio appeared in the second generation. Self-fertilization, however, produced different results. Green pea plants always yielded green pea plants, and short plants always produced short plants.

From his numerical results, Mendel concluded that some yellow pea plants were pure for that trait, whereas others also possessed a green factor. That is, although two plants might both have yellow peas, one of them might produce offspring with green peas. In such cases, the genetic makeup, the **genotype,** differed from the observable appearance, or **phenotype.**

Genes: The Conveyors of Inherited Traits

Mendel's units of heredity were what we now call **genes.** He concluded that these units occurred in pairs for each trait, and that offspring inherited one unit of the pair from each parent. Today we call each member of a gene pair or group an **allele.** If the two genes, or alleles, for a trait are the same, the organism is **homozygous** for that trait; if the two genes for a characteristic differ, the organism is **heterozygous** for that trait. A pea plant that contains a pair of genes for yellow is homozygous for the trait. A yellow pea plant with a dominant gene for yellow and a recessive gene for green, although phenotypically yellow, has a heterozygous genotype. As Mendel demonstrated, the recessive green gene can reappear in subsequent generations. But Mendel knew nothing of the composition of genes or the processes that transmit them from parent to offspring. Many years of scientific research have yielded much of the missing information.

The genes of higher organisms (not including bacteria and primitive plants such as green-blue algae) are located on ropelike bodies called **chromosomes** within the nucleus of every one of the organism's cells. Chromosomes, like genes, usually occur in pairs. Each allele for a given trait is carried in the identical position on corresponding chromosomes. The two genes that determined the color of Mendel's peas, for example, were opposite each other on a pair of chromosomes.

Mitosis and Meiosis. The body cells of every plant or animal carry chromosome pairs in a number appropriate for its species. Humans have twenty-three pairs, or a total of forty-six chromosomes, each carrying many times that number of genes. Each new body cell receives this number of chromosomes during cellular reproduction, or **mitosis,** as each pair of chromosomes duplicates itself.

But what happens when a sperm cell and an egg cell unite to form a new organism? What prevents the human baby from receiving twice the number of chromosomes characteristic of its species—twenty-three pairs from the sperm and twenty-three pairs from the egg? The process by which the reproductive cells are formed, **meiosis,** ensures that this will not happen. Each reproductive cell contains *half* the number of chromosomes appropriate for the species. Only one member of each chromosome pair is carried in every egg or sperm. At fertilization, the human embryo normally receives twenty-three separate chromosomes from its mother and the same number from its father, which add up to the twenty-three pairs.

DNA. As we have said, genes are located on chromosomes. Each gene carries a set of instructions encoded in its chemical structure. It is from this coded information carried in genes that a cell makes all the rest of its structural parts and chemical machinery. It appears that in most living organisms, heredity is controlled by the same chemical substance, **DNA** (deoxyribonucleic acid). An enormous amount of recent research has been directed toward understanding DNA—what its structure is, how it duplicates itself in reproduction, and how it conveys or instructs the formation of a complete organism.

One of the most important keys to understanding human development and genetics is the structure and function of DNA. In 1953, biologist James Watson, with British chemist Francis Crick, proposed that DNA is a long, two-stranded molecule shaped like a double helix[10] (see Figure 2–3). Genetic information is stored in the linear sequences of the bases; different species have different sequences and every individual is slightly different from every other individual. Notice that in the DNA molecule each base always has the same opposite base (adenine and thymine are paired, as are cy-

---

[10]Bruce Alberts, Dennis Bray, Julian Lewis, Martin Raff, Keith Roberts, and James D. Watson, *Molecular Biology of the Cell* (New York: Garland Publishing, 1983), p. 185.

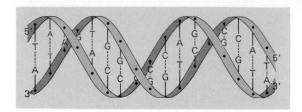

FIGURE 2–3

The DNA molecule consists of two spiral sugar-phosphate strands. The strands are linked by the nitrogenous bases adenine (A), guanine (G), thymine (T), and cytosine (C). When the DNA molecule reproduces, the bases separate and the spiral strands unwind. Each original strand serves as a mold along which a new complementary chain is formed. *(From "A DNA Operator-Repressor System" by Tom Maniatis and Mark Ptashne. Copyright © 1976 by Scientific American, Inc. All rights reserved.)*

tosine and guanine). The importance of this is that each strand carries the same information so that when the double helix unwinds each strand can form a template for a new strand of complementary bases.[11] Because DNA stores the information required to make up the cells of an organism, it has been called the language of life. As George and Muriel Beadle put it,

the deciphering of the DNA code has revealed our possession of a language much older than hieroglyphics, a language as old as life itself, a language that is the most living language of all—even if its letters are invisible and its words are buried deep in the cells of our bodies.[12]

Once it was understood that genes are made of DNA, concerted efforts were begun to map DNA sequences and their locations on the chromosomes of different organisms. A project known as the human genome project set out recently to assemble a complete genetic map for humans. Much progress has already been made, but it will take many years and an enormous amount of research to finish this project.[13]

Messenger RNA. DNA stores the information to make cells, but it does not directly affect the formation of cells. One type of ribonucleic acid (RNA), messenger RNA (mRNA), is copied from a portion of DNA and moves outside the cell nucleus to direct the formation of proteins. Proteins are the building blocks of the body and determine the shape and the structure of cells. Messenger RNA is like DNA in that it has a linear sequence of bases attached to a sugar-phosphate backbone, but it is slightly different chemically. One difference is that messenger RNA has the base uracil instead of the base thymine. Messenger RNA also has a different sugar-phosphate backbone and is single- rather than double-stranded. Messenger RNA is formed when a double-stranded DNA molecule unwinds and forms a template for the mRNA. After a section of DNA is copied, the RNA releases from the DNA, leaves the nucleus, and the double-helix of the DNA is re-formed.[14]

Sources of Variability

Natural selection proceeds only when individuals within a population vary. There are two genetic sources of variation: genetic recombination and mutation.

Genetic Recombination

The distribution of traits from parents to children varies from one offspring to another. Brothers and sisters, after all, do not look exactly alike, nor does each child resemble 50 percent of the mother and 50 percent of the father. This variation occurs because when a sperm cell or an egg is formed, the single member of each chromosome pair it receives is a matter of chance. Each reproductive cell, then, carries a *random assortment* of chromosomes and their respective genes. At fertilization, the egg and sperm that unite are different from every other egg carried by the mother and every other sperm carried by the father. A *unique* offspring is thus produced by a shuffling of the parents' genes. One cause of this shuffling is the random **segregation** or sorting of chromosomes in meiosis: an individual could conceivably get any of the possible assortments of the paternal and maternal chromosomes. Another cause of the shuffling of parental genes is **crossing-over,** the exchange of sections of chromo-

---

[11]Ibid., pp. 99–103.

[12]George Beadle and Muriel Beadle, *The Language of Life* (Garden City, NY: Doubleday, 1966), p. 216.

[13]J. Claiborne Stephens, Mark L. Cavanaugh, Margaret I. Gradie, Martin L. Mador, and Kenneth K. Kidd, "Mapping the Human Genome: Current Status," *Science*, October 12, 1990, pp. 237–50.

[14]Alberts et al., *Molecular Biology of the Cell*, pp. 107–11.

somes between one chromosome and another.[15] Thus, after meiosis the egg and sperm do not receive just a random mixture of complete paternal and maternal chromosomes; because of crossing-over they also receive chromosomes in which some of the sections may have been replaced.

The traits displayed by each organism are not simply the result of combinations of dominant and recessive genes, as Mendel had hypothesized. In humans, most traits are influenced by the activity of many genes. Skin color, for example, is the result of several inherited characteristics. A brownish shade results from the presence of a pigment known as *melanin;* the degree of darkness in the hue depends largely on the amount of melanin present and how it is distributed in the layers of the skin. Another factor contributing to the color of all human skin is the blood that flows in blood vessels located in the outer layers of the skin. Humans carry at least five different genes for the manufacture of melanin, and many other genes for the other components of skin hue. In fact, almost all physical characteristics in humans are the result of the concerted action of many genes. Some traits are sex-linked. The X chromosome, which together with the presence or absence of a Y chromosome determines sex, may also carry the gene for hemophilia or the gene for color blindness. The expression of these two characteristics depends on the sex of the organism.

These processes of genetic recombination ensure that variety is achieved, and genetic variation within a species is essential for the operation of natural selection. Evolution and genetic variation, then, are inseparable.

At any given moment, the major source of variability in a population is genetic recombination. Ultimately, however, the major source of the variability on which natural selection proceeds is mutation. This is because mutation replenishes the supply of variability, which is constantly being reduced by the selective elimination of less-fit variants.

Mutation

A **mutation** is a change in the DNA sequence. Such a change produces an altered gene. The majority of mutations are thought to occur because of occasional mismating of the chemical bases that make up DNA. Just as a typist will make errors in copying a manuscript, so will DNA, in duplicating itself, occasionally change its code.[16] A mutation will result from such an error.

Mutations are sometimes lethal. Tay-Sachs disease, for example, is caused by two recessive mutant genes. Its effects are blindness, severe retardation, and death by the age of three or four. An organism with both recessive mutant genes for a given harmful trait will probably die before it can reproduce—and often before it is born. But the trait can be passed on by individuals who are heterozygous for the recessive gene.

We can discuss the relative merits or disadvantages of a mutant gene *only* in terms of the physical, cultural, and genetic environment of that gene.[17] Galactosemia, for example, is caused by a recessive mutant gene and usually results in mental retardation and blindness. But it can be prevented by dietary restrictions begun at an early age. In this instance, the intervention of human culture counteracts the mutant gene and allows the afflicted individual to lead a normal life. Thus, some cultural factors can modify the effects of natural selection by helping to perpetuate a harmful mutant gene. People with the galactosemia trait who are enabled to function normally can reproduce and pass on one of the recessive genes to their children. Without cultural interference, natural selection would prevent such reproduction. Usually, natural selection acts to retain only those mutations that aid survival.

Even though mutations are not usually adaptive, those that are will multiply in a population relatively quickly, by natural selection. As Theodosius Dobzhansky has suggested:

Consistently useful mutants are like needles in a haystack of harmful ones. A needle in a haystack is hard to find, even though one may be sure it is there. But if the needle is valuable, the task of finding it is facilitated by setting the haystack on fire and looking for the needle among the ashes. The role of the fire in this parable is played in biological evolution by natural selection.[18]

[16]Beadle and Beadle, *The Language of Life,* p. 123.
[17]Theodosius Dobzhansky, *Mankind Evolving: The Evolution of the Human Species* (New Haven: Yale University Press 1962), pp. 138–40.
[18]Ibid., p. 139.

[15]Ibid., p. 842.

The Origin of Species

One of the most controversial aspects of Darwin's theory was the suggestion that one species could, over time, evolve into another. **Speciation,** or the development of a new species, does not happen suddenly. Nor is it the result of one or two mutations in the history of a single family.

Speciation may occur if one subgroup of a species finds itself in a radically different environment. In the subgroup's adaptation to the new environment, enough genetic changes may occur to result in a new variety, or **race.** Races, however, are not separate species. They are simply slight variants of a single species that can interbreed. As Dobzhansky explains, "Perhaps there is no recorded instance of intermarriage between some races, say of Eskimos with Papuans, but Eskimos as well as Papuans do interbreed with other races; channels, however tortuous, for gene exchange exist between all human races."[19]

But a species usually cannot breed successfully with a different species. Generally, the genetic makeup of separate species is so different that reproduction is impossible. If members of different species did mate, it is unlikely that the egg would be fertilized, or, if it were, that the embryo would survive. If birth did occur, the offspring would either die or be infertile. What is the explanation for this differentiation? How does one group of organisms become so unlike another group having the same ancestry that it forms a totally new species?

Speciation may occur if the populations become so separated from each other geographically that gene exchanges are no longer possible. In adapting to their separate environments, the two populations may undergo enough genetic changes to prevent them from interbreeding. Numerous factors can prevent the exchange of genes. Two species living in the same area may breed at different times of the year, or their behavior during breeding—their courtship rituals—may be distinct. The difference in body structure of closely related forms may in itself bar interbreeding. Geographic barriers may also prevent interbreeding.

Once species differentiation does occur, the evolutionary process cannot be reversed; the new species can no longer mate with other species related to its parent population. Humans and gorillas, for example, have the same distant ancestors, but their evolutionary paths have diverged irreversibly.

Natural Selection of Behavioral Traits

Until now we have discussed how natural selection might operate to change a population's physical traits, such as the color of moths or the neck length of giraffes. But natural selection can also operate on the behavioral characteristics of populations. Although this idea is not new, it is now receiving more attention. The approaches called **sociobiology**[20] and **behavioral ecology**[21] involve the application of evolutionary principles to the behavior of animals. (Behavioral ecology is interested in how all kinds of behavior relate to the environment; sociobiology is particularly interested in social organization and social behavior.) The typical behaviors of a species are assumed to be adaptive and to have evolved by natural selection. For example, why do related species exhibit different social behaviors even though they derive from a common ancestral species?

Consider the lion, as compared with other cats. Although members of the cat family are normally solitary creatures, lions live in social groups called *prides.* Why? George Schaller has suggested that lion social groups may have evolved primarily because group hunting is a more successful way to catch large mammals in open terrain. He has observed that not only are several lions more successful in catching prey than are solitary lions, but several lions are more likely to catch and kill large and dangerous prey such as giraffes. Then too, young cubs are generally safer from predators when in a social group than when alone with their mothers. Thus, the social behavior of lions probably evolved primarily because it provided selective

---

[19]Ibid., p. 184.

[20]David P. Barash, *Sociobiology and Behavior* (New York: Elsevier, 1977).

[21]J. R. Krebs and N. B. Davies, eds., *Behavioural Ecology: An Evolutionary Approach,* 2nd ed. (Sunderland, MA: Sinauer Associates, 1984).

Prides of lions who live in open country are more successful in catching large animals than are solitary lions. This social behavior probably evolved because it provided selective advantages in the lions' open-country environment.

advantages in the lions' open-country environment.[22]

The sociobiological approach has aroused controversy because it assumes that genes are important determinants of human behavior. For exam-

ple, all human societies have marriage and the family, the prohibition of incest, and a division of roles between males and females. Sociobiologists contend that these universal behaviors may have some genetic basis in the human species; otherwise, why would they be universal? Many anthropologists and other social scientists are critical of this idea. They say that cultural behavior is learned, and that some behavior may be universal because it has been learned universally. (In the

[22]George B. Schaller, *The Serengeti Lion: A Study of Predator Prey Relations* (Chicago: University of Chicago Press, 1972), cited in Edward O. Wilson, *Sociobiology* (Cambridge, MA: The Belknap Press of Harvard University Press, 1975), p. 504.

Mountain lions live in wooded environments and hunt individually.

chapter titled "Schools of Thought in Cultural Anthropology," we discuss the controversy over sociobiology in more detail.)

The Evolution of Culture

Whether much or any of human cultural behavior can be explained by heredity, there is no question that culture has evolved. We became tool-users and tool-makers. We began to grow plants and animals for food. We built cities and complex political systems. Can these and other cultural changes be explained by natural selection even if cultural behavior has no genetic component? To answer this question, we must remember that the operation of natural selection requires three conditions. First, natural selection requires variation upon which to operate. Second, there must be differential reproduction, that is, differences in reproductive success. And third, there must be a mechanism for duplicating adaptive traits. Do these three requirements apply to cultural behavior? How is cultural evolution like or unlike biological evolution?

In biological evolution, variability comes from genetic recombination and mutation. In cultural evolution, it comes from recombination of learned behaviors and from invention.[23] Cultures are not closed or reproductively isolated, as species are. A species cannot borrow genetic traits from another species, but a culture can borrow new things and behaviors from other cultures. The custom of growing corn, which has spread from the New World to many other areas, is an example of this phenomenon. As for the requirement of differential reproduction, it does not matter whether the trait in question is genetic or learned or both. As Henry Nissen has emphasized, "behavioral incompetence leads to extinction as surely as does morphological disproportion or deficiency in any vital organ. Behavior is subject to selection as much as

"We humans have been around almost forty years now, son. We must be doin' something right." (© 1977 Punch/Rothco)

bodily size or resistance to disease."[24] Finally, although learned traits are obviously not passed to offspring through genetic inheritance, parents who exhibit adaptive behavioral traits are more likely to "reproduce" those traits in their children, who may learn them by imitation or by parental instruction. Children and adults may also copy adaptive traits they see in people outside the family.

Thus, even though biological and cultural evolution are not the same, it seems reasonable to assume that natural selection may generally operate on learned cultural behavior as well as on genes.

Biological and cultural evolution in humans may not be completely separate processes.[25] As we will discuss, some of the most important biological features of humans—such as two-legged walking and relatively large brains—may have been favored by natural selection because our ancestors

[23]Donald T. Campbell, "Variation and Selective Retention in Socio-Cultural Evolution," in Herbert Barringer, George Blankstein, and Raymond Mack, eds., *Social Change in Developing Areas: A Re-Interpretation of Evolutionary Theory* (Cambridge, MA: Schenkman, 1965), pp. 19–49.

[24]Henry W. Nissen, "Axes of Behavioral Comparison," in Anne Roe and George Gaylord Simpson, eds., *Behavior and Evolution* (New Haven: Yale University Press, 1958), pp. 183–205.

[25]For recent discussions and illustrations of biological and cultural evolution, see Robert Boyd and Peter J. Richerson, *Culture and the Evolutionary Process* (Chicago: University of Chicago Press, 1985); and William H. Durham, *Coevolution: Genes, Culture, and Human Diversity* (Stanford, CA: Stanford University Press, 1991).

made tools (a cultural trait). Conversely, the cultural trait of informal and formal education may have been favored by natural selection because humans have a long period of immaturity (a biological trait).

As long as the human species continues to exist and the social and physical environment continues to change, there is no reason to suppose that natural selection of biological and cultural traits will cease. However, as humans learn more and more about genetic structure they will become more and more capable of curing genetically caused disorders and even altering the way evolution proceeds. Today, genetic researchers are capable of diagnosing genetic defects in developing fetuses, and parents can and do decide often whether to terminate a pregnancy. Soon genetic engineering will probably allow humans to "fix" defects and even try to "improve" the genetic structure of a growing fetus. Whether and to what extent humans should alter genes will undoubtedly be the subject of continuing debate.

SUMMARY

1. If we think of the history of the universe in terms of twelve months, the history of humans would take up only about one-and-a-half hours of this period. Although the universe is some 15 billion years old, modern humans have existed for about 100,000 years.

2. Ideas about evolution took a long time to take hold because they contradicted the biblical view of events. But from 1745 to 1830, a great deal of evidence became available that suggested that evolution was a viable theory. A number of thinkers during this period, including Lamarck and Erasmus Darwin, began to discuss evolution and how it might occur. Lamarck's suggested mechanism of the inheritance of acquired characteristics is not generally accepted today.

3. Charles Darwin and Alfred Wallace proposed the mechanism of natural selection to account for the evolution of species. Those organisms best adapted to a particular environment produce the most offspring over time.

4. In the process of natural selection, changes in species can be expected to occur as the environment changes or as some members of a species move into a new environment. Natural selection can also operate on the behavioral or social characteristics of populations.

5. Mendel's and subsequent research in genetics and our understanding of the structure and function of DNA and mRNA help us to understand the mechanisms by which traits may be passed from one generation to the next.

6. Natural selection depends upon variation within a population. The two sources of biological variation are genetic recombination and mutation.

7. Speciation—the development of a new species—may occur if one subgroup becomes separated from other subgroups. In adapting to different environments, these subpopulations may undergo enough genetic changes to prevent interbreeding, even if they reestablish contact. Once species differentiation occurs, the evolutionary process cannot be reversed.

8. Humans are a product of the interaction of biological and cultural evolution. Culturally, traits are transmitted by learning and imitation. Cultural evolution is more subject to conscious human control and change than biological evolution. Still, both types of evolution may be subject to natural selection.

SUGGESTED READING

BONNER, J. T. *The Evolution of Culture in Animals.* Princeton: Princeton University Press, 1980. A biologist describes the similarities, differences, and interactions of genetic and cultural evolution, and traces the human capacity for culture back into early biological evolution.

BOYD, R., AND RICHERSON, P. J. *Culture and the Evolutionary Process.* Chicago: University of Chicago Press, 1985. The authors develop mathematical models to analyze how biology and culture interact, under the influence of evolutionary processes.

CAPLAN, A. L. *The Sociobiology Debate: Readings on Ethical and Scientific Issues.* New York: Harper & Row, Pub., 1978. A collection of frequently cited papers dealing with the historical background, ethical issues, and scientific concerns of the discipline of sociobiology.

CHIRAS, D. D. *Human Biology: Health, Homeostasis, and the Environment.* St. Paul, MN: West Publishing Company, 1991. An introductory textbook in human biology. See chapters 3–5 for a survey of cell biology and how genes work.

DOBZHANSKY, T. *Mankind Evolving: The Evolution of the Human Species.* New Haven: Yale University Press, 1962. A classic demonstration that the mechanisms of evolution, primarily natural selection, are still active.

DURHAM, W. H. *Coevolution: Genes, Culture, and Human Diversity.* Stanford, CA: Stanford University Press, 1991. A discussion of the evolution of culture that considers how theory and research point to the interaction of genes and culture in human populations.

MAYR, E. *The Growth of Biological Thought: Diversity, Evolution, and Inheritance.* Cambridge, MA: The Belknap Press of Harvard University Press, 1982. A history of ideas that discusses the successful and unsuccessful attempts to understand problems in the study of evolution.

3

The Living Primates

The goal of primatology, the study of primates, is to understand how different primates have adapted anatomically and behaviorally to their environments. The results of such studies may help us to understand the behavior and evolution of the human primate.

But how can living primates such as chimpanzees tell us anything about humans or the primates that were our ancestors? After all, each living primate species has its own history of evolutionary divergence from the earliest primate forms. And contrary to what some believe, the monkeys and apes we see in zoos and films are not our ancestors. All living primates, including humans, evolved from earlier primates that are now extinct. Nonetheless, by observing how humans and other primates differ from and resemble each other, we may be able to infer how and why humans may have diverged from the other primates.

In conjunction with fossil evidence, anatomical and behavioral comparisons of living primates may help us reconstruct what early primates were like. For example, those traits characteristic of most of the living primates (such as living or sleeping in trees) may have been characteristic of our primate ancestors. Such an inference can be checked against the fossil record. Anatomical and behavioral differences may also point by analogy to the life-styles of extinct primates. For example, if we know that modern primates that swing through the trees have a particular kind of shoulder bone structure, we can infer that similar fossil bones probably belonged to an animal that also swung through the trees. Differing adaptations of living primates may also suggest why certain divergences occurred in primate evolution. If we know what traits belong to humans, and humans alone, this knowledge may suggest why the line of primates that led to humans branched away from the line leading to chimpanzees and gorillas.

In this chapter, we first examine the common features of the living primates. Next we introduce the different animals that belong to the order Primates, focusing on the distinctive characteristics of each major type. Then we discuss possible explanations of some of the varying adaptations exhibited by the different primate species. We close with a look at the traits that make humans different from all other primates. The purpose of this chapter is to help us understand more about humans. There-fore, we emphasize the features of primate anatomy and behavior that perhaps have the greatest bearing on human evolution.

The order Primates is divided into two suborders: the **prosimians** (literally, premonkeys) and the **anthropoids.** The prosimians include lemurs and lorises. The anthropoid suborder includes tarsiers, monkeys, the lesser apes (gibbons, siamangs), the great apes (orangutans, gorillas, chimpanzees), and humans. Figure 3–1 shows a simplified classification of the surviving primates.

Common Primate Traits

All primates belong to the class Mammalia, and they share all the common features of mammals. Except for humans, their bodies are covered with hair or fur, which provides insulation. And even humans have some hair in various places, though perhaps not for insulation. Mammals are *warm blooded;* that is, their body temperature is more or less constantly warm and usually higher than that of the air around them. Almost all mammals give birth to live young that develop to a considerable size within the mother and are nourished by suckling from the mother's mammary glands. The young have a relatively long period of dependence on adults after birth. This period is also a time of learning, for a great deal of adult mammal behavior is learned rather than instinctive. Play is a learning technique common to mammal young and is especially important to primates, as we shall see later in this chapter.

In addition to their mammalian features, the primates have a number of physical and social traits that set them apart from other mammals.

Physical Features

No one of the primates' physical features is unique to primates; animals from other orders share one or more of the characteristics described below. But the complex of all these physical traits *is* unique to primates.[1]

Many skeletal features of the primates reflect an **arboreal** (tree-living) existence. All primate

[1]Our discussion of common primate traits is based largely on J. R. Napier and P. H. Napier, A *Handbook of Living Primates* (New York: Academic Press, 1967).

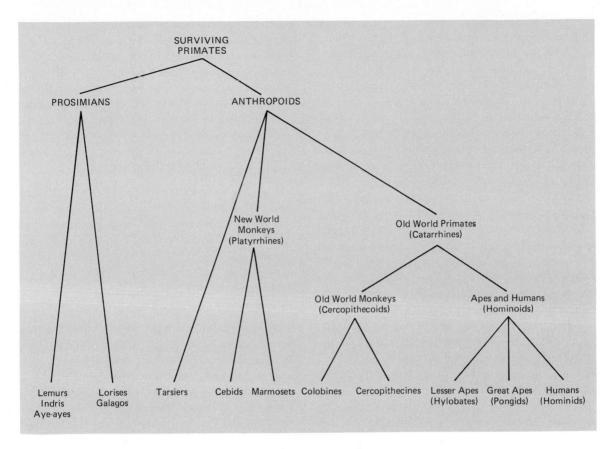

FIGURE 3–1 A Simplified Classification of the Surviving Primates

hind limbs are structured principally to provide support, but the "feet" in most primates can also grasp things. Some primates—orangutans, for instance—can suspend themselves from their hind limbs. The forelimbs are especially flexible, built to withstand both pushing and pulling forces. Each of the hind limbs and forelimbs has one bone in the upper portion and two bones in the lower portion (with the exception of the tarsier). This feature is little changed since the time of our earliest primate ancestors. It has remained in modern primates (although many other mammals have lost it) because the double bones give great mobility for rotating arms and legs. Another characteristic structure of primates is the clavicle, or collarbone. The clavicle also gives primates great freedom of movement, allowing them to move the shoulders both up and down and back and forth. Although humans obviously do not use this flexibility for arboreal activity, they do use it for other activities. Without a clavicle we could not throw a spear or a ball; no

fine tools could be made, no doorknobs turned, if we did not have rotatable forearms.

Primates generally are **omnivorous;** that is, they eat all kinds of food, including insects and small animals as well as fruits, seeds, leaves, and roots. The teeth of primates reflect this omnivorous diet. The chewing teeth—the **molars** and **premolars**—are very unspecialized, particularly in comparison with those of other groups of animals, such as the grazers. The front teeth— the **incisors** and **canines**—are often quite specialized, principally in the lower primates. For example, in many prosimians the slender, tightly packed lower incisors and canines form a "dental comb" the animals use in scraping hardened gum (which is a food for them) from tree trunks.[2]

Primate hands are extremely flexible. All pri-

[2]Simon K. Bearder, "Lorises, Bushbabies, and Tarsiers: Diverse Societies in Solitary Foragers," in Barbara Smuts et al., eds., *Primate Societies* (Chicago: University of Chicago Press, 1987), p. 14.

mates have **prehensile** (grasping) hands, which can be wrapped around an object. Primates have five digits on both hands and feet (in some cases, one digit may be reduced to a stub), and their nails, with few exceptions, are broad and flat, not clawlike. This structure allows them to grip objects; the hairless, sensitive pads on their fingers, toes, heels, and palms also help them to grip. Many primates have **opposable thumbs**—a feature that allows an even more precise and powerful grip.

Vision is extremely important to primate life. Compared with other mammals, primates have a relatively larger portion of the brain devoted to vision rather than smell. Primates are characterized by stereoscopic or depth vision. Their eyes are directed forward, rather than sideways as in other animals—a trait that allows them to focus on an object (insects or other food, or a distant branch) with both eyes at once. Most primates also have color vision. By and large, these tendencies are more developed in anthropoids than in prosimians.

Another important primate feature is a large brain relative to body size. That is, primates generally have larger brains than animals of similar size, perhaps because their survival depends upon an enormous amount of learning, as we discuss later. In general, animals with large brains seem to grow up slower and live longer.[3] The slower an animal grows up and the longer it lives, the more it can learn.

Finally, the primate reproductive system sets this order of animals apart from other mammals. In most primate species, males have a pendulous penis that is not attached to the abdomen by skin (a trait shared by a few other animals, including bats and bears). Females in most primate species have two mammary glands, or breasts, on the chest (a few prosimians have multiple nipples). The uterus is usually constructed to hold a single fetus, not a litter as with most other animals. This reproductive system can be seen as emphasizing quality over quantity—an adaptation possibly related to the dangers of life in the trees.[4] Primate infants gener-

ally tend to be relatively well developed at birth, although humans, apes, and some monkeys have helpless infants. Most infant primates, except for humans, can cling to their mothers from birth. Primates typically take a long time to mature. For example, the rhesus monkey is not sexually mature until about three years of age, the chimpanzee not until about age nine.

Social Features

For the most part, primates are social animals. And just as physical traits such as grasping hands and stereoscopic vision may have developed as adaptations to the environment, so may many patterns of social behavior. For most primates, particularly those that are **diurnal** (active during the day), group life may be crucial to survival, as we will see later in this chapter.

Dependency and Development in a Social Context. Social relationships begin with the mother and other adults during the fairly long dependency period of primates. (For the dependency period in primates—the infancy and juvenile phases—see Figure 3–2.) The prolonged dependency of infant monkeys and apes probably offers an evolutionary advantage in that it allows infants more time to observe, note, and learn the complex behaviors es-

Most primates, like these Barbary apes (macaques) on Gibraltar, are very social.

[3]Alison F. Richard, *Primates in Nature* (New York: W. H. Freeman & Company Publishers, 1985), pp. 22ff.

[4]Robert D. Martin, "Strategies of Reproduction," *Natural History*, November 1975, p. 50. The opossum, which is not a primate but which lives in trees and still has many babies at a time, is a marsupial and has a pouch in which to keep the babies when they are very young.

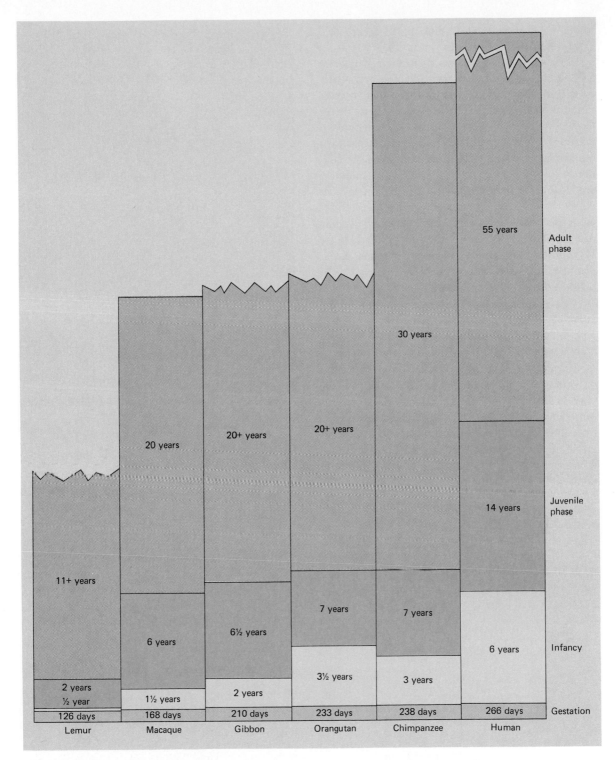

FIGURE 3–2 Primate Age Spans

(Adapted and reprinted with permission of Macmillan Publishing Co., Inc., from The Evolution of Primate Behavior, Second Edition, by Alison Jolly, p. 292. Copyright © 1985 by Alison Jolly.)

sential to survival, while enjoying the care and protection of mature adults.

Primates without a warm, social relationship with a mother or another individual do not appear to develop appropriate patterns of social interaction. In a series of classic experiments with rhesus monkeys, Harry Harlow investigated the effects of maternal neglect and isolation on offspring.[5] He found that as a result of either inadequate mothering or isolation from other infants, some monkeys are unable to lead normal social lives. They develop aberrant sexual activities and may even become juvenile delinquents. Harlow mated socially deprived female monkeys with well-adjusted males. When these females gave birth, their behavior was not at all motherly, and they often rejected their babies entirely. Their abnormal behavior was offered as evidence that mothering is more than instinctive. These experiments underline the importance of maternal care and attention for monkeys and, as a corollary, for humans.

In many primate groups the mother is not the only individual providing care to the dependent young. Among gray langur monkeys, the birth and subsequent rearing of a new baby absorb the attention of most female members of the troop.[6] And in some primate species, the father may expend as much time caring for infants as the mother.[7]

Primates at Play. Harlow's investigations have provided other information about social learning in young primates. The experiments that showed the importance of maternal care to baby rhesus monkeys also revealed that play is another crucial ingredient of normal development during the dependency period. Just as monkeys raised without mothers showed abnormal behavior as adults, so did monkeys raised with mothers but lacking peers to play with. In fact, when some of the monkeys raised without mothers were allowed a regular playtime with peers, many of them behaved more nor-

A flower may be beautiful to us, but to a gorilla it may be food.

mally. Subsequent work has supported Harlow's findings.[8]

Play is important for learning.[9] Play provides practice for the physical skills necessary or useful in adulthood. For example, young monkeys racing through the trees at top speed are gaining coordination that may save their lives if they are chased by predators later on. Play is also a way of learning social skills, particularly in interacting and communicating with other members of the group. Some dominance relationships seem to be established partly through the rough-and-tumble games

[5] H. F. Harlow et al., "Maternal Behavior of Rhesus Monkeys Deprived of Mothering and Peer Association in Infancy," *Proceedings of the American Philosophical Society*, 110 (1966): 58–66.

[6] Nancy A. Nicolson, "Infants, Mothers, and Other Females," in Smuts et al., eds., *Primate Societies*, p. 339.

[7] See J. Patrick Gray, *Primate Sociobiology* (New Haven: HRAF Press, 1985), pp. 144–63, for a discussion of research that attempts to explain the variation among primates in the degree of male parental care.

[8] Anne E. Russon, "The Development of Peer Social Interaction in Infant Chimpanzees: Comparative Social, Piagetian, and Brain Perspectives," in Sue Taylor Parker and Kathleen Rita Gibson, eds., *"Language" and Intelligence in Monkeys and Apes: Comparative Developmental Perspectives* (New York: Cambridge University Press, 1990), p. 379.

[9] Phyllis Jay Dohlinow and Naomi Bishop, "The Development of Motor Skills and Social Relationships among Primates through Play," in Phyllis Jay Dohlinow, ed., *Primate Patterns* (New York: Holt, Rinehart & Winston, 1972), pp. 321–25.

that older juveniles play, where winning depends on such factors as size, strength, and agility. These qualities, or the lack of them, may influence the individual's status throughout adult life. (Other factors also help determine an individual's status. For instance, the mother's status has been shown to be very important in some primates.)[10]

Learning from Others. We know that primates, nonhuman and human, learn many things in social groups. Among humans, children often imitate others and adults often deliberately teach the young. In English we say, "Isn't it cute how Tommy 'apes' his father?" But do apes (and monkeys) imitate others, or do they just learn to do similar things whether or not a model is observed? There is controversy among researchers as to how much imitation versus independent learning occurs in nonhuman primates. Even more arguable is whether deliberate teaching occurs among nonhuman primates.[11]

Some field workers have suggested that chimpanzees may learn by imitation to use tools. For example, Jane Goodall cites an occasion when a female with diarrhea picked up a handful of leaves to wipe her bottom. Her two-year-old infant watched closely, and then twice picked up leaves to wipe its own clean behind.[12] Termite "fishing" (using a grass stalk to withdraw termites from a termite mound) is probably the best known example of chimpanzee tool-use. Immature chimpanzees in the wild have been observed to watch attentively and pick up stalks while others are "fishing." And mothers let their infants hold on to the stalks while the mothers "fish." But some observers do not think these reports provide clear evidence of imitation or teaching. Even though the mother lets the infant hold on to the "fishing" stalk, the infant is doing the activity with her, not watching it and then independently repeating it later.[13]

Primates can learn from direct teaching, but they learn mostly by imitation and trial-and-error.

[10]D. S. Sade, "Some Aspects of Parent–Offspring and Sibling Relationships in a Group of Rhesus Monkeys, with a Discussion of Grooming," *American Journal of Physical Anthropology*, 23 (1965): 1–17; and Glenn Hausfater, Jeanne Altmann, and Stuart Altmann, "Long-Term Consistency of Dominance Relations among Female Baboons," *Science*, August 20, 1982, pp. 752–54.

[11]Elisabetta Visaberghi and Dorothy Munkenbeck Fragaszy, "Do Monkeys Ape?" in Parker and Gibson, eds., *"Language" and Intelligence in Monkeys and Apes*, p. 265; Michael Tomasello, "Cultural Transmission in the Tool Use and Communicatory Signaling of Chimpanzees," in ibid., pp. 304–5.

[12]Jane van Lawick-Goodall, *In the Shadow of Man* (Boston: Houghton Mifflin, 1971), p. 242.

[13]Visaberghi and Fragaszy, "Do Monkeys Ape?" pp. 264–65.

The Various Primates

Now that we have discussed the common features of primates, let us turn to the different primates living in the world today, focusing on some of the ways in which they vary.

Prosimians

The prosimians resemble other mammals more than the anthropoid primates do. For example, the prosimians depend much more on smell for information than do anthropoids. Also in contrast with the anthropoids, they typically have more mobile ears, whiskers, longer snouts, and relatively fixed facial expressions. The prosimians also exhibit many traits shared by all primates, including grasping hands, stereoscopic vision, and enlarged visual centers in the brain. There are three theories suggesting why these traits were favored by natural selection in the evolution of the early primates. One theory stresses the importance of tree dwelling and of eating plant foods (fruits, leaves, seeds) in the trees. A second theory suggests that the early primates hunted insects on slender branches close to the ground. A third theory combines elements of the first two, hypothesizing that the earliest primates ate plant foods as well as insects located on the slender ends of tree branches. We discuss these theories in the next chapter.

Lemurlike Forms. Lemurs and their relatives, the indris and the aye-ayes, are found only on two island areas off the southeastern coast of Africa: Madagascar and the Comoro Islands. These primates range in size from the rat-sized mouse lemur to the four-foot-long indri. Members of the lemur group usually produce single offspring, although twins and even triplets are common in some species. Many of the species in this group are **quadrupeds** (animals that move on all fours), and walk on all fours in the trees as well as on the ground. Some species, such as the indris, use their hind limbs alone to push off from one vertical position to another in a mode of locomotion called **vertical clinging and leaping.** Lemurs are mostly vegetarians, eating fruit, leaves, bark, and flowers. Many lemur species, particularly those that are **nocturnal** (active during the night), are solitary during their active hours. Other lemur species live in small family groups, and still others are much more social, living in groups ranging from four or five members to as many as sixty. The group-living lemurs are very communicative and announce their whereabouts and intentions to other lemurs through a wide range of gestures, sounds, and smells.[14] An unusual feature of the lemurlike primates is that females often dominate males, particularly over access to food. In most primates, and in most other mammals, female dominance is rarely observed.[15]

Lorislike Forms. Representatives of this group are found in both Southeast Asia and sub-Saharan Africa. All are nocturnal and arboreal. They eat fruit, tree gum, and insects, and usually give birth to single infants.[16]

There are two major subfamilies, the lorises and the galagos (bushbabies), and they show wide behavioral differences. Bushbabies are quick, active animals that hop between branches and tree trunks in the vertical-clinging-and-leaping pattern. On the ground they often resort to a kangaroolike hop. Lorises are much slower, walking sedately along branches hand over hand in the quadrupedal fashion. Because they are nocturnal, the lorises and their relatives are difficult to observe in their natural habitats. But with the use of search lights and technical aids such as radio tracking, field researchers have learned a good deal about their behavior. For example, we now know that among bushbabies, females, particularly mothers and young adult daughters, stay together in small groups, whereas the males disperse. Newborns are born in nests or hollows of trees (which related females may share) and mothers return to nurse them regularly. A few days after birth, a mother may carry her infant in her mouth to nearby trees, "parking" it while she feeds.[17]

---

[14]G. A. Doyle and R. D. Martin, eds., *The Study of Prosimian Behavior* (New York: Academic Press, 1979); and Ian Tattersall, *The Primates of Madagascar* (New York: Columbia University Press, 1982).

[15]Alison F. Richard, "Malagasy Prosimians: Female Dominance," in Smuts et al., eds., *Primate Societies*, p. 32.

[16]Bearder, "Lorises, Bushbabies, and Tarsiers," p. 13.

[17]Pierre Charles-Dominique, *Ecology and Behaviour of Nocturnal Primates*, trans. R. D. Martin (New York: Columbia University Press, 1977), p. 258. See also Robert D. Martin and Simon K. Bearder, "Radio Bush Baby," *Natural History*, October 1979, pp. 77–81; and Bearder, "Lorises, Bushbabies, and Tarsiers," pp. 18-22.

Anthropoids

The anthropoid suborder includes humans, apes, monkeys, and tarsiers. Most anthropoids share several traits in varying degree. They have rounded brain cases; reduced, nonmobile outer ears; and relatively small, flat faces instead of muzzles. They have highly efficient reproductive systems, including a placenta that is formed more fully than in any prosimian. They have highly dextrous hands.[18] We shall discuss four major groups of anthropoids: tarsiers, the monkeys of the New World (Central and South America), the monkeys of the Old World (Africa, Asia, and Europe), and the apes and humans.

Tarsiers. The nocturnal, tree-living tarsiers, found now only on the islands of the Philippines and Indonesia, are the only primates that depend completely on animal foods. They are usually insect-eaters, but they sometimes capture and eat other small animals. They are well equipped for night vision, possessing enormous eyes, extraordinary eyesight, and enlarged visual centers in the brain. The tarsiers get their name from their elongated tarsal bones (the bones of the ankle), which give them tremendous leverage for their long jumps. Tarsiers are very skilled at vertical clinging and leaping. Recent studies indicate that tarsiers live in family groups composed of a mated pair and their offspring. Like some higher primates, male and female tarsiers sing together each evening to advertise their territories.[19]

Most primatologists now classify tarsiers as anthropoids for several reasons. For example, compared with prosimians, tarsiers have larger and more highly developed brains, shorter snouts, and eyes that are closer together and protected by bony orbits.[20]

New World Monkeys. The New World monkeys are called **platyrrhines** (broad noses) to distinguish them from the **catarrhines** (downward-facing

New World monkeys, like this Mexican spider monkey, are completely arboreal. No Old World monkeys have prehensile or grasping tails, but many New World monkeys do.

noses)—the Old World monkeys, apes, and humans. Besides the shape of the nose and position of the nostrils, a number of other anatomical features distinguish the New World monkeys from the catarrhines. The New World species have three premolars, whereas the Old World species have two. Some New World monkeys have a prehensile (grasping) tail; no Old World monkeys do. All the New World monkeys are completely arboreal, with different species occupying higher or lower levels in the trees. They vary a lot in diet and in the size of their groups. Their food ranges from insects to nectar and sap to fruits and leaves.[21]

There are two main families of New World monkeys: marmosets and cebid monkeys. The marmosets are quite small, have claws instead of fingernails, and give birth to twins who mature in about two years. Perhaps because twinning is so common and the infants have to be carried, mar-

[18]Napier and Napier, *A Handbook of Living Primates,* pp. 32–33.

[19]John MacKinnon and Kathy MacKinnon, "The Behavior of Wild Spectral Tarsiers," *International Journal of Primatology,* 1 (1980): 361–79.

[20]Robert D. Martin, "Ascent of the Primates," *Natural History,* March 1975, pp. 52–61; and Frederick S. Szalay and Eric Delson, *Evolutionary History of the Primates* (New York: Academic Press, 1979), p. 189.

[21]Richard, *Primates in Nature,* pp. 164–65.

moset mothers cannot take care of them alone. Fathers and older siblings have often been observed carrying infants. Indeed, males may do more carrying than females. Marmoset groups may contain a mated pair (monogamy) or a female mated to more than one male (polyandry). The marmosets, like other very small primates, obtain a large portion of their protein requirements from insects.[22] Cebids are generally larger than marmosets, take about twice as long to mature, and tend to bear only one offspring at a time.[23] The cebids are very variable in size, group composition, and diet. For example, squirrel monkeys weigh about two pounds, whereas woolly spider monkeys weigh more than sixteen pounds. Some cebids have small groups with one male–female pair, others have groups of up to fifty individuals. Some of the smallest cebids have a diet including leaves, insects, flowers, and fruits, while other cebids are mostly fruit-eaters with secondary dependence on seeds, leaves, or insects.[24]

Old World Monkeys. The Old World monkeys, or **cercopithecoids,** are related more closely to humans than to New World monkeys. They have the same number of teeth as apes and humans.

The Old World monkey species are not as diverse as their New World cousins, but they live in a greater variety of habitats. Some live both in trees and on the ground. Others, such as the gelada baboon, are completely **terrestrial,** or ground-living. Macaques are found both in tropical jungles and on snow-covered mountains, and they range from the Rock of Gibraltar to Africa to northern India, Pakistan, and Japan. There are two major subfamilies of Old World monkeys.

COLOBINE MONKEYS This group includes Asian langurs, the African colobus monkeys, and several other species. These monkeys live mostly in trees and their diet consists principally of leaves. Their digestive tracts are equipped to obtain maximum nutrition from a high-cellulose diet; they have pouched stomachs, which provide a large surface area for breaking down plant food, and very large intestinal tracts.

One of the most noticeable features of colobines is the flamboyant color typical of newborns. For example, in one species dusky gray mothers give birth to brilliant orange babies.[25] Observational studies suggest that the colobines are also unusual among the primates (except for humans) in that mothers let other group members take care of their infants shortly after birth. But males who are not members of the group are dangerous for infants, since males trying to enter and take over a group have been observed to kill infants. Although this may suggest that a one-male group is the typical group structure, there does not appear to be a typical pattern for a given species. When more than one site of a species has been studied, both one-male and multi-male groups have been found.[26]

CERCOPITHECINE MONKEYS This subfamily of monkeys includes more terrestrial species than any other subfamily. Many of these species are characterized by a great deal of **sexual dimorphism** (the sexes look different): the males are larger and have longer canines, and are more aggressive than females. Cercopithecines depend more on fruit than do colobines. They are also more capable of surviving in arid and seasonal environments.[27] Pouches inside the cheeks allow cercopithecines to take food away for later digestion. An unusual physical feature of these monkeys is the *ischial callosities*, or callouses, on their bottoms—an adaptation that enables them to sit comfortably in trees or on the ground for long periods of time.[28]

[22]Anne Wilson Goldizen, "Tamarins and Marmosets: Communal Care of Offspring," in Smuts et al., eds., *Primate Societies*, p. 34. See also John F. Eisenberg, "Comparative Ecology and Reproduction of New World Monkeys," in Devra Kleiman, ed., *The Biology and Conservation of the Callitrichidae* (Washington, DC: Smithsonian Institution, 1977), pp. 13–22; and R. W. Sussman and W. G. Kinzey, "The Ecological Role of the Callitrichidae: A Review," *American Journal of Physical Anthropology*, 64 (1984): 419–49.

[23]Eisenberg, "Comparative Ecology and Reproduction of New World Monkeys," pp. 15–17.

[24]John G. Robinson, Patricia C. Wright, and Warren G. Kinzey, "Monogamous Cebids and Their Relatives: Intergroup Calls and Spacing," in Smuts et al., eds., *Primate Societies*, pp. 44–53; Carolyn Crockett and John F. Eisenberg, "Howlers: Variations in Group Size and Demography," in ibid., pp. 54–68; John G. Robinson and Charles H. Janson, "Capuchins, Squirrel Monkeys, and Atelines: Socioecological Convergence with Old World Primates," in ibid., pp. 69–82.

[25]Sarah Blaffer Hrdy, *The Langurs of Abu: Female and Male Strategies of Reproduction* (Cambridge, MA: Harvard University Press, 1977), p. 18.

[26]Ibid., pp. 18–19.

[27]J. R. Napier, "Paleoecology and Catarrhine Evolution," in J. R. Napier and P. H. Napier, eds., *Old World Monkeys: Evolution, Systematics, and Behavior* (New York: Academic Press, 1970), pp. 80–82.

[28]Linda Marie Fedigan, *Primate Paradigms: Sex Roles and Social Bonds* (Montreal: Eden Press, 1982), p. 11.

Recent studies of baboons and macaques suggest that closely related females form the core of a local group, or *troop*. In large groups, which are common among rhesus monkeys, many social behaviors seem to be determined by degree of biological relatedness. For example, an individual is more likely to sit next to, groom, or help an individual who is closely related maternally.[29] Moreover, a closely related subgroup is likely to stay together when a large troop divides.[30]

The Hominoids: Apes and Humans. The **hominoid** group includes three separate families: the lesser apes (gibbons and siamangs), the great apes or **pongids** (orangutans, gorillas, and chimpanzees), and humans or **hominids.** Several characteristics distinguish the hominoids from the other primates. Their brains are relatively large, especially the areas of the cerebral cortex associated with the ability to integrate data. The hominoids have several skeletal and muscular traits that point toward their common ancestry. All have fairly long arms, short and broad trunks, and no tails. Their blood proteins show many similarities, too. This blood likeness is particularly strong among chimpanzees, gorillas, and humans. For this reason, primatologists think chimpanzees and gorillas are evolutionarily closer to humans than are the lesser apes and orangutans, who probably branched off at some earlier point.

GIBBONS AND SIAMANGS The agile gibbons and their close relatives, the siamangs, are found in the jungles of Southeast Asia. The gibbons are small, weighing only about eleven to fifteen pounds. The siamangs are somewhat larger—no more than twenty-five pounds. Both are mostly fruit-eaters, although they also eat leaves and insects. They are spectacular **brachiators** (arm swingers), with long arms and fingers that let them swing hand over hand through the trees.[31] A gibbon can move more than thirty feet in a single forward swing.

C. R. Carpenter's pioneering studies of gibbons told us a great deal about the animal's social behavior,[32] and more recent field studies have told us more.[33] Gibbons and siamangs live in small family groups consisting of an adult pair, who appear to mate for life, and one or two immature offspring. When the young reach adulthood, they are driven from home by the adults. There is little sexual dimorphism—males and females do not differ in size and appearance—nor is there any clear pattern of dominance by either sex. These lesser apes are also highly territorial; an adult pair advertises its territory by singing and defends it by chasing others away.

ORANGUTANS Orangutans survive only on the islands of Borneo and Sumatra. Unlike gibbons and siamangs, they are clearly recognizable as males or females. Not only do males weigh almost twice as much as females (up to 200 pounds), but they have large cheek pads, throat pouches, beards, and long hair.[34] Like gibbons and siamangs, orangutans are primarily fruit-eating and arboreal. They are the heaviest of the arboreal primates, and perhaps for this reason they move slowly and laboriously through the trees. They are unusual among the higher primates in living basically solitary lives, except for mothers and their young. There are different ideas about the solitary habit of orangutans. One is that there may be insufficient food in any one tree or home range to support more than a single adult orangutan (a pretty large animal, as animals go). To obtain sufficient food each day without having to travel over a huge area, orangutans may therefore live alone rather than in groups.[35] Another idea is that animals live in groups when they are subject to heavy predation; the large size of orangutans may make them immune to attacks from most animals, so liv-

[29]Ibid., pp. 123–24.

[30]Phyllis C. Lee, "Home Range, Territory and Intergroup Encounters," in Robert A. Hinde, ed., *Primate Social Relationships: An Integrated Approach* (Sunderland, MA: Sinauer Associates, 1983), p. 231.

[31]Holger Preuschoft, David J. Chivers, Warren Y. Brockelman, and Norman Creel, eds., *The Lesser Apes: Evolutionary and Behavioural Biology* (Edinburgh: Edinburgh University Press, 1984).

[32]C. R. Carpenter, "A Field Study in Siam of the Behavior and Social Relations of the Gibbon (*Hylobates lar*)." *Comparative Psychology Monographs*, 16, 5 (1940): 1–212.

[33]See, for example, David John Chivers, *The Siamang in Malaya* (Basel, Switzerland: Karger, 1974); and David J. Chivers, ed., *Malayan Forest Primates: Ten Years' Study in Tropical Rain Forest* (New York: Plenum, 1980).

[34]H. D. Rijksen, *A Fieldstudy on Sumatran Orang Utans* (Pongo Pygmaeus Abelii Lesson 1827): *Ecology, Behaviour and Conservation* (Wageningen, The Netherlands: H. Veenman and Zonen B. V., 1978), p. 22.

[35]Biruté M. F. Galdikas, "Orangutan Adaptation at Tanjung Puting Reserve: Mating and Ecology," in David A. Hamburg and Elizabeth R. McCown, eds., *The Great Apes* (Menlo Park, CA: Benjamin/Cummings, 1979), pp. 220–23.

"Maybe you're descended from a lemur, but I'm not descended from any lemur." *(Drawing by W. Miller; © 1972 The New Yorker Magazine, Inc.)*

ing alone may be a viable option.[36] A third idea, which on the face of it seems opposite to the second, is that living alone may be an adaptation to heavy predation by humans. The orangutan's best defense against humans with guns may be to hide alone in the trees.[37]

GORILLAS   Gorillas are found in lowland areas of western equatorial Africa and in the mountain areas of Zaire, Uganda, and Rwanda.[38] Unlike the other apes, they are mostly leaf-eaters; about 86 percent of the gorilla diet consists of leaves, shoots, and stems.[39] Gorillas are by far the largest

of the surviving apes. In their natural habitats, adult males weigh up to 450 pounds and females up to 250 pounds. (Gorillas in zoos are generally even heavier, because of their inactive lives.) To support the weight of massive chests, gorillas travel mostly on the ground on all fours in a form of locomotion known as **knuckle walking:** they walk on the thickly padded middle joints of their fingers. Gorillas' arms and legs, especially those of the young, are well suited for climbing. (As adults, their heavier bodies make climbing more precarious.)[40] They sleep on the ground or in tub-shaped nests they make from nonfood plants each time they bed down.[41]

Gorillas tend to live in groups consisting of a dominant male (a silverback), other adult males,

[36]Dorothy L. Cheney and Richard W. Wrangham, "Predation," in Smuts et al., eds., *Primate Societies,* p. 236.

[37]Rijksen, *A Fieldstudy on Sumatran Orang Utans,* p. 321.

[38]Dian Fossey, *Gorillas in the Mist* (Boston: Houghton Mifflin, 1983), p. xvi.

[39]D. Fossey and A. H. Harcourt, "Feeding Ecology of Free-ranging Mountain Gorilla *(Gorilla gorilla beringei),*" in T. H. Clutton-Brock, ed., *Primate Ecology: Studies of Feeding and Ranging Behaviour in Lemurs, Monkeys and Apes* (London: Academic Press, 1977), p. 426.

[40]George Schaller, *The Mountain Gorilla: Ecology and Behavior* (Chicago: University of Chicago Press, 1963). See also Schaller's *The Year of the Gorilla* (Chicago: University of Chicago Press, 1964).

[41]Fossey, *Gorillas in the Mist,* p. 47.

adult females, and immature offspring. Both males and females, when mature, seem to leave the groups into which they were born. The silverback male is very much the center of attention; he acts as the main protector of the group and the leader in deciding group movements.[42]

CHIMPANZEES   Because they are more sociable and easier to find and "adopt," chimpanzees have been studied far more than gorillas. Recent studies have noted that chimpanzees exhibit many gestures and postures similar to ours in behavioral situations common to both species. A good part of our information about chimpanzees in the wild comes from studies by Jane Goodall at Gombe National Park in Tanzania.[43]

Although they are primarily fruit-eaters, chimpanzees show many similarities to their close relatives, the gorillas. Both are arboreal and terrestrial. Like gorillas, chimpanzees are good climbers, especially when young, and they spend many hours in the trees. But they move best on the ground, and when they want to cover long distances they come down from the trees and move by knuckle walking. Occasionally, they stand and walk upright, usually when they are traveling through tall grass or are trying to see long distances. Chimpanzees sleep in tree nests that they carefully prepare anew—complete with a bunch of leaves as a pillow—each time they bed down.

Chimpanzees are only slightly sexually dimorphic. Males weigh a little more than 100 pounds on the average, females somewhat less. However, males have longer canines. For quite some time, it was thought that chimpanzees ate only plant food. However, studies at Gombe Park have shown that not only do they eat insects, small lizards, and birds, but they actively hunt and kill larger animals.[44] They have been observed hunting and eating a range of animals that includes monkeys, young baboons, and bushbucks in addition to smaller prey such as lizards and birds. Of course, this diet reflects the prey available at Gombe and

may not be an accurate representation of the chimpanzee diet in general. Prey is caught mostly by the males, which hunt either alone or in small groups. It is then shared with (or perhaps scrounged by) as many as fifteen other chimpanzees in friendly social gatherings that may last up to nine hours.[45]

Chimpanzee social groups persist over time in a home range. Individual members come together and drift apart depending upon the availability of food. The very large social groups observed in parks such as Gombe may be the result of humans having given them food there.[46]

HOMINIDS   The hominoids we call hominids now include only one species—modern humans. Humans have many distinctive characteristics that set them apart from other anthropoids and other hominoids. These traits will be discussed later in this chapter and also throughout much of the rest of the book.

Explanations of Variable Primate Adaptations

Thus far we have discussed the common features of primates and introduced the different primates that survive in the world today. Now let us examine possible explanations, suggested by recent research, of some of the ways in which the surviving primates vary.

Body Size

The different surviving primates vary enormously in body size, ranging from the 2 or so ounces of the average gray mouse lemur to the 350 pounds of the average male gorilla. What accounts for this sizable variation?

Three factors seem to be important—the time of day the species is active, where it is active (in the trees or on the ground), and the kinds of food eaten.[47] All the nocturnal primates are small, probably because small animals make less noise and

---

[42]A. H. Harcourt, "The Social Relations and Group Structure of Wild Mountain Gorillas," in Hamburg and McCown, eds., The Great Apes, pp. 187–92.

[43]Jane Goodall, "My Life among Wild Chimpanzees," National Geographic, August 1963, pp. 272–308; and van Lawick-Goodall, In the Shadow of Man.

[44]Geza Teleki, "The Omnivorous Chimpanzee," Scientific American, January 1973, pp. 32–42.

[45]Ibid., pp. 35–41.

[46]Michael Patrick Ghiglieri, The Chimpanzees of Kibale Forest: A Field Study of Ecology and Social Structure (New York: Columbia University Press, 1984), pp. 174–75.

[47]T. H. Clutton-Brock and Paul H. Harvey, "Primate Ecology and Social Organization," Journal of Zoology, London, 183 (1977): 8–9.

therefore are more likely to avoid predators that hunt in the dark by sound. Among the primates active during the day, the arboreal ones tend to be smaller than the terrestrial ones. One reason may be the amount of weight that can be supported by small tree branches, where foods such as fruits are mostly located: small animals can go out to small branches more safely than large animals. Also, ground dwellers might be bigger because large size is a protection against predation. Finally, species such as the gorilla that eat mostly leaves tend to be heavier than species that eat mostly fruits and seeds (for example, chimpanzees). The food of leaf-eaters is relatively low in energy, and so leaf-eaters have to consume a lot of food. They also need large stomachs and intestines to extract the nutrients they need, and a bigger gut in turn requires a bigger skeleton and body.[48]

Relative Brain Size

Larger primates usually have larger brains. But larger animals of all types generally have larger brains. So primatologists are more interested in relative brain size, that is, the ratio of brain size to body size.

Perhaps because human primates have the largest brain relatively of any primate, we tend to think a larger brain is "better." However, a large brain does have "costs." From an energy perspective, the development of a large brain requires a great deal of metabolic energy; therefore it should not be favored by natural selection unless the benefits outweigh the costs.[49]

Fruit-eating primates tend to have relatively larger brains than leaf-eating primates. This may be due to natural selection in favor of more capacity for memory, and therefore relatively larger brains, in fruit-eaters. Leaf-eaters may not need as much memory, because they depend on food that is more readily available in time and space, and therefore they may not have to remember where food might be found. In contrast, fruit-eaters may need greater memory and brain capacity because

their foods ripen at different times and in separate places that have to be remembered to be found.[50] The brain requires large supplies of oxygen and glucose. Since leaf-eating primates do not have as much glucose in their diets as fruit-eating primates, they may also not have the energy reserves to support relatively large brains.[51]

Group Size

Primate groups vary in size from a few individuals, as with gibbons, to the 100 or so individuals in some Old World monkey troops.[52] What factors might account for such variation?

Nocturnal activity is not only an important predictor of small body size; it also predicts small group size. Nocturnal primates feed either alone or in pairs.[53] John Terborgh has noted that most nocturnal predators hunt by sound, and so a nocturnal animal might best avoid attack by being silent.[54] Groups are noisy, and therefore nocturnal animals might be more likely to survive by living alone or in pairs.

On the other hand, a large group might provide advantages in the daytime. The more eyes, ears, and noses a terrestrial group has, the quicker a would-be predator might be detected—and perhaps avoided—and a larger group would have more teeth and strength to frighten or mob a predator that actually attacked.[55]

But this line of reasoning would lead us to expect that all diurnal terrestrial species would have large groups. Yet not all do so. So there must be other factors operating. One seems to be the amount and density of food. If food resources occur in small amounts and in separate places, only small

[48]Alison Jolly, *The Evolution of Primate Behavior*, 2nd ed. (New York: Macmillan, 1985), pp. 53–54.
[49]Sue Taylor Parker, "Why Big Brains Are So Rare," in Sue Taylor Parker and Kathleen Rita Gibson, eds., *"Language" and Intelligence in Monkeys and Apes: Comparative Developmental Perspectives* (New York: Cambridge University Press, 1990), p. 130.

[50]Katharine Milton, "Distribution Patterns of Tropical Plant Foods as an Evolutionary Stimulus to Primate Mental Development," *American Anthropologist*, 83 (1981): 534–48; T. H. Clutton-Brock and Paul H. Harvey, "Primates, Brains and Ecology," *Journal of Zoology, London*, 190 (1980): 309–23.
[51]Katharine Milton, "Foraging Behaviour and the Evolution of Primate Intelligence," in Richard W. Bryne and Andrew Whiten, eds., *Machiavellian Intelligence: Social Expertise and the Evolution of Intellect in Monkeys, Apes, and Humans* (Oxford: Clarendon Press, 1988), pp. 285-305.
[52]Jolly, *The Evolution of Primate Behavior*, p. 119.
[53]Clutton-Brock and Harvey, "Primate Ecology and Social Organization," p. 9.
[54]John Terborgh, *Five New World Primates: A Study in Comparative Ecology* (Princeton: Princeton University Press, 1983), pp. 224–25.
[55]Jolly, *The Evolution of Primate Behavior*, p. 120.

Some primates, such as the white-handed gibbons of southeast Asia, live in small groups. The olive baboons of Kenya live in large groups.

groups could get enough to eat; if food occurs in large patches, there would be enough to support large groups.[56] An additional factor may be competition over resources. One suggestion is that substantial but separated patches of resources are likely to be fought over, and therefore individuals living in larger groups might be more likely to obtain access to them.[57]

Distinctive Human Traits

We turn now to some of the features that distinguish us—humans—from the other primates. Although we like to think of ourselves as unique, many of the traits we discuss here are at the extreme of a continuum that can be traced from the prosimians through the apes.

Physical Traits

Of all the primates, only humans consistently walk erect on two feet. Gibbons, chimpanzees, and gorillas may stand or walk on two feet some of the time, but only for very short periods. All other primates require thick, heavy musculature to hold their heads erect; this structure is missing in hu-

mans, for our heads are more or less balanced on top of our spinal columns. A dish-shaped pelvis (peculiar to humans), straight lower limbs, and arched, nonprehensile feet are all related to human **bipedalism.** Because we are fully bipedal, we can carry objects without impairing our locomotor efficiency. (In Chapter 5 we consider the effects bipedalism may have had on such diverse traits as toolmaking, prolonged infant dependency, and the division of labor by sex.) Although many primates have opposable thumbs that enable them to grasp and examine objects, the greater length and flexibility of the human thumb allow us to handle objects with more firmness and precision.

The human brain is large and complex, particularly the **cerebral cortex,** the center of speech and other higher mental activities. The brain of the average adult human measures more than 1300 cubic centimeters, compared with 525 cubic centimeters for the gorilla, the primate with the next largest brain. The frontal areas of the human brain are also larger than those of other primates, so that humans have more prominent foreheads than monkeys or gorillas. Human teeth reflect our completely omnivorous diet and are not very specialized, which may reflect the fact that we use tools and cooking to prepare our food. Many other primates have long lower canines, which are accommodated by a space in the upper jaw; in humans, the canines both look and act very much like inci-

[56]Ibid., p. 122.
[57]Richard W. Wrangham, "An Ecological Model of Female-Bonded Primate Groups," *Behaviour*, 75 (1980): 262–300.

"I'm walking upright! By God, this calls for a drink or something!" *(Ross, courtesy of Saturday Review)*

sors, and there are no spaces between the teeth. The human jaw is shaped like a parabolic arch, rather than a U shape as in the apes, and is composed of relatively thin bones and light muscles. Humans have chins; other primates do not. Humans are relatively hairless; other primates are not.

One other distinctive human trait is the sexuality of human females, who may engage in intercourse at any time throughout the year; most other primate females engage in sex periodically.[58] (Humans are also unusual among the primates in having male–female bonding.[59] Later, in the chapter on marriage and the family, we discuss some theo-ries suggesting why male–female bonding, which in humans we call "marriage," may have developed.) It used to be thought that more or less continuous female sexuality may be related to male–female bonding. However, comparative research on mammals and birds contradicts this idea. Those mammals and birds that have more frequent sex are not more likely to have male–female bonding.[60]

Why then does human female sexuality differ from that of most other primates? One suggestion is that more or less continuous female sexuality became selectively advantageous in humans after male–female bonding developed in conjunction with local groups consisting of at least several adult males and adult females.[61] More specifically, the combination of group living *and* male–female bonding—a combination unique to humans among the primates—may have favored a switch

---

[58]Female pygmy chimpanzees engage in sexual intercourse nearly as often as human females. See Nancy Thompson-Handler, Richard K. Malenky, and Noel Badrian, "Sexual Behavior of *Pan paniscus* under Natural Conditions in the Lomako Forest, Equateur, Zaire," in Randall L. Susman, ed., *The Pygmy Chimpanzee: Evolutionary Biology and Behavior* (New York: Plenum, 1984), pp. 347–66.

[59]By male–female bonding we mean that at least one of the sexes is "faithful," i.e., typically has intercourse with just one opposite-sex partner throughout at least one estrus or menstrual cycle or breeding season. Note that the bonding may not be monogamous; an individual may be bonded to more than one individual of the opposite sex. See Melvin Ember and Carol R. Ember, "Male–Female Bonding: A Cross-Species Study of Mammals and Birds," *Behavior Science Research*, 14 (1979): 37–41.

[60]Melvin Ember and Carol R. Ember, "Male–Female Bonding," p. 43; see also Carol R. Ember and Melvin Ember, "The Evolution of Human Female Sexuality: A Cross-Species Perspective," *Journal of Anthropological Research*, 40 (1984): 203–4.

[61]Ember and Ember, "The Evolution of Human Female Sexuality," p. 207.

from the common higher-primate pattern of periodic female sexuality to the pattern of more or less continuous female sexuality. Such a switch may have been favored in humans because periodic (rather than continuous) female sexuality would undermine male–female bonding in multi-male/multi-female groups.

Field research on nonhuman primates strongly suggests that males usually attempt to mate with any females ready to mate. If the female (or females) a male was bonded to was not interested in sex at certain times, but other females in the group were, it seems likely that the male would try to mate with those other females. Frequent "extra-marital affairs" might jeopardize the male–female bond, which would presumably reduce the reproductive success of both males and females. Hence natural selection may have favored more or less continuous sexuality in human females if humans already had the combination of group living (and the possibility of "extramarital affairs") and marriage. If bonded adults lived alone, as in gibbons, noncontinuous female sexuality would not threaten bonding, because "extramarital" sex would not be likely to occur. Similarly, seasonal breeding would also pose little threat to male–female bonds, because all females would be sexually active at more or less the same time.[62]

So, since the combination of group living and male–female bonding occurs only in humans, that combination of traits may explain why continuous female sexuality developed in humans.

Behavioral Abilities

In comparison with other primates, a much greater proportion of human behavior is learned and culturally patterned. As with many physical traits, we can trace a continuum in the learning abilities of all primates. The great apes, including orangutans, gorillas, and chimpanzees, are probably about equal in learning ability.[63] Old and New World monkeys do much less well in learning tests, and surprisingly gibbons perform more poorly than most monkeys.

Toolmaking. The same kind of continuum is evident in inventiveness and toolmaking. There is no evidence that any nonhuman primates except great apes use tools, although several species of monkeys use "weapons"— branches, stones, or fruit dropped onto predators below them on the ground. Chimpanzees both fashion and use tools in the wild. They strip leaves from sticks and then use the sticks to "fish" termites from their mound-shaped nests. They use leaves to mop up termites, to sponge up water, or to wipe themselves clean.

One example of chimpanzee tool use suggests planning. In Guinea, West Africa, observers watched a number of chimpanzees crack oil palm nuts with two stones. The "platform" stone had a hollow depression; the other stone was used for pounding. The observers assumed that the stones had been brought by the chimpanzees to the palm trees, since no stones like them were nearby and the chimps were observed to leave the pounding stone on top of or near the platform stone when they were finished.[64]

In captivity, chimpanzees have been observed to be inventive toolmakers. One mother chimpanzee was seen examining and cleaning her son's teeth, using tools she had fashioned from twigs. She even extracted a baby tooth he was about to lose.[65]

Humans have usually been considered the only toolmaking animal, but observations such as these call for modification of the definition of toolmaking. If we define toolmaking as adapting a natural object for a specific purpose, then at least some of the great apes are toolmakers too. As far as we know, though, humans are unique in their ability to use one tool to make another. In the words of Goodall, "the point at which tool-using and tool-making, as such, acquire evolutionary significance is surely when an animal can adapt its ability to manipulate objects to a wide variety of purposes, and when it can use an object spontaneously to solve a brand-new problem that without the use of a tool would prove insoluble."[66]

Language. Only humans have spoken, symbolic language. But, as with toolmaking abilities, the

---

[62]Ibid., pp. 208–9.
[63]Duane M. Rumbaugh, "Learning Skills of Anthropoids," in L. A. Rosenblum, ed., *Primate Behavior* (New York: Academic Press, 1970), 1: 52–58.

[64]Observation by Sugiyama, cited by Jolly, *The Evolution of Primate Behavior*, p. 53.
[65]"The First Dentist," *Newsweek*, March 5, 1973, p. 73.
[66]van Lawick-Goodall, *In the Shadow of Man*, p. 240.

Koko, a gorilla, can understand 2,000 English words, but she cannot speak them. She uses a special computer that "speaks" words when she touches signs for them on the monitor.

line between human language and the communications of other primates is not as sharp as we once thought. In the wild, vervet monkeys make different alarm calls to warn of different predators. Observers playing back tape recordings of these calls found that monkeys responded to them differently, depending upon the call. If the monkeys heard an "eagle" call they looked up; if they heard a "leopard" call they ran high into the trees.[67]

Common chimpanzees are also communicative, using gestures and many vocalizations in the wild. Researchers have used this "natural talent" to teach chimpanzees symbolic language in experimental settings. Beatrice T. and R. Allen Gardner raised a female chimpanzee named Washoe and trained her to communicate with startling effectiveness by means of American Sign Language hand gestures.[68] After a year of training, she was able to associate gestures with specific activities. For example, if thirsty, Washoe would make the signal for "give me" followed by the one for "drink." As she learned, the instructions grew more detailed. If all she wanted was water, she would merely signal for "drink." But if she craved soda pop, as she did more and more, she prefaced the drink signal with the sweet signal—a quick touching of the tongue with her fingers. Later, the Gardners had even more success in training four other chimpanzees, who were taught by fluent deaf users of American Sign Language.[69]

A common chimpanzee named Sarah has been taught to read and write with plastic symbols; her written vocabulary is 130 "words."[70] She can perform complex tasks such as simultaneously putting an apple in a pail and a banana in a dish on written command—a feat that requires an understanding of sentence structure as well as words. A chimpanzee named Lana became so proficient in a symbolic language called Yerkish that she scored 95 on some tests in comprehension and sentence completion after six months of training.[71]

Bonobos or pygmy chimpanzees have recently provided strong evidence that they understand simple grammatical "rules," very much like two-year-old humans. Pointing to graphic symbols for different particular meanings, a bonobo named Kanzi regularly communicated sequences of types of symbols; for example, he would point to a symbol for a verb ("bite") and then point to a symbol for an object ("ball," "cherry," "food").[72]

[67]Robert M. Seyfarth, Dorothy L. Cheney, and Peter Marler, "Monkey Response to Three Different Alarm Calls: Evidence of Predator Classification and Semantic Communication," *Science*, November 14, 1980, pp. 801–3.

[68]R. Allen Gardner and Beatrice T. Gardner, "Teaching Sign Language to a Chimpanzee," *Science*, August 15, 1969, pp. 664–72.

[69]Beatrice T. Gardner and R. Allen Gardner, "Two Comparative Psychologists Look at Language Acquisition," in K. E. Nelson, ed., *Children's Language* (New York: Halsted Press, 1980), 2: 331–69.

[70]Ann James Premack and David Premack, "Teaching Language to an Ape," *Scientific American*, October 1972, pp. 92–99.

[71]Duane M. Rumbaugh, Timothy V. Gill, and E. C. von Glaserfeld, "Reading and Sentence Completion by a Chimpanzee (Pan)," *Science*, November 16, 1973, pp. 731–33.

[72]Patricia Marks Greenfield and E. Sue Savage-Rumbaugh, "Grammatical Combination in *Pan paniscus*: Processes of Learning and Invention in the Evolution and Development of Language," in Parker and Gibson, eds., *"Language" and Intelligence in Monkeys and Apes*, pp. 540–78.

Other Human Traits. Although many primates are omnivores, eating insects and small reptiles in addition to plants (some even hunt small mammals), only humans have hunted very large animals. Also, humans are one of the few primates that are completely terrestrial. We do not even sleep in trees, as many other ground-living primates do. Perhaps our ancestors lost their perches when the forests receded, or cultural advances such as weapons or fire may have eliminated the need to seek nightly shelter in the trees. In addition, as we have noted, we have the longest dependency period of any of the primates, requiring extensive parental care for up to twenty years or so.

Finally, humans are unlike almost all other primates in having a division of labor by sex in food-getting (and food-sharing) in adulthood. Among nonhuman primates, both males and females forage for themselves after infancy. In humans, there is more sex-role specialization, perhaps because men, unencumbered by infants and small children, were freer to hunt and chase large animals. We consider the possible causes and consequences of a sexual division of labor among humans in the chapter on sex and culture.

Having examined our distinctive traits and the traits we share with other primates, we need to ask what selective forces may have favored the emergence of primates, and then what forces may have favored the line of divergence leading to humans. These questions are the subjects of the next two chapters.

SUMMARY

1. Although no living primate can be a direct ancestor of humans, we do share a common evolutionary history with the other surviving primates. Studying the behavioral and anatomical features of our closest living relatives may help us make inferences about primate evolution. Studying distinctive human traits may help us understand why the line of primates that led to humans branched away from the line leading to chimpanzees and gorillas.

2. No one trait is unique to primates. However, primates do share the following features: two bones in the lower part of the leg and in the forearm, a collarbone, flexible prehensile (grasping) hands, stereoscopic vision, a relatively large brain, only one (or sometimes two) offspring at a time, long maturation of the young, and a high degree of dependence on social life and learning.

3. The order Primates is divided into two suborders: the prosimians and the anthropoids. Compared to the anthropoids, prosimians depend more on smell for information. They have mobile ears, whiskers, longer snouts typically, and relatively fixed facial expressions. The anthropoids are subdivided into tarsiers, New World monkeys, Old World monkeys, and hominoids (pongids or apes, and hominids or humans). Anthropoids have rounded brain cases; reduced, nonmobile outer ears; and relatively small, flat faces instead of muzzles. They have highly dextrous hands.

4. The anthropoid apes consist of the lesser apes (gibbons and siamangs) and the great apes (orangutans, gorillas, and chimpanzees).

5. Along with the gorilla, the chimpanzee has blood chemistry remarkably similar to that of humans, as well as anatomical and behavioral similarities to humans. Wild chimpanzees have been seen to create and use tools, modifying a natural object to fulfill a specific purpose. High conceptual ability is also demonstrated by both the chimpanzee's and the gorilla's facility in learning sign language.

6. Variable aspects of the environment, differences in activity patterns, and variation in diet may explain many of the traits that vary in the primates. Nocturnal primates tend to be small and to live alone or in very small groups. Among diurnal species, the arboreal primates tend to be smaller and to live in smaller social groups than terrestrial primates. Fruit-eaters have relatively larger brains.

7. The differences between humans and the other anthropoids show us what makes humans distinctive as a species. Humans are totally bipedal: they walk on two legs and do not need the arms for locomotion. The human brain is the largest and most complex, particularly the cerebral cortex. In contrast to females of almost all other primates, human females may engage in sexual intercourse at any time throughout the year. Offspring have a proportionately longer dependency stage. And in comparison with other primates, more human behavior is learned and culturally patterned. Spoken, symbolic language and the use of tools to make other tools are uniquely human behavioral traits. Humans also generally have a division of labor in food-getting (and food-sharing) in adulthood.

SUGGESTED READING

GRAY, J. P. *Primate Sociobiology.* New Haven: HRAF Press, 1985. A survey and discussion of empirical studies that tested 396 possible explanations, mostly derived from sociobiological theory, of many aspects of variation in primate behavior.

JOLLY, A. *The Evolution of Primate Behavior,* 2nd ed. New York: Macmillan, 1985. A discussion of research and theory on variable primate adaptations.

PARKER, S. T., AND GIBSON, K. R., eds. *"Language" and Intelligence in Monkeys and Apes: Comparative Developmental Perspectives.* New York: Cambridge University Press, 1990. A volume of twenty papers that apply frameworks from human developmental psychology and evolutionary biology to comparative studies of primate abilities.

RICHARD, A. F. *Primates in Nature.* New York: W. H. Freeman & Company Publishers, 1985. A discussion of how primate behavior has been shaped by environmental factors.

SMUTS, B. B., CHENEY, D. L., SEYFARTH, R. M., WRANGHAM, R. W., AND STRUHSAKER, T. T., eds. *Primate Societies.* Chicago: University of Chicago Press, 1987. An extensive review, by some fifty primatologists, of primate species that have been studied in the wild.

4

Primate Evolution: From Early Primates to Hominoids

The story of primate evolution is still fragmentary and tentative, and it will probably always be so. Paleontologists have to make judgments based on incomplete evidence about what happened in evolutionary history, where and when events occurred, and why they happened the way they did. Inferences about evolution are based on a number of kinds of information—fossilized bones and teeth from extinct biological forms; indicators of ancient environments and climates discovered by geologists; and comparisons of the anatomical, physiological, molecular, and behavioral characteristics of living animals. But even though paleontological inferences will always be tentative, some are supported more strongly by the available evidence than others. A particular judgment based on one kind of evidence can be checked against other kinds of evidence. In this way, some conclusions come to be discarded and others tentatively accepted.

In the next two chapters we describe the main features of current theory and evidence about primate evolution, from the origin of primates to the origin of humans. In this chapter we deal with that part of the story before the emergence of definite humans. When, where, and why did the early primates emerge, and how and why did they diverge? Our overview covers the period from about 70 million years ago to the end of the Miocene, about 5 million years ago.

Interpreting the Fossil Record

How can paleontologists know about what may have happened millions of years ago? There is no written record from that period from which they can draw inferences. But we do have another kind of evidence for primate evolution: the fossil record. And we have ways of "reading" the record left by fossils and of telling how old fossils are.

What Are Fossils?

A **fossil** may be an impression of an insect or leaf on a muddy or other surface that now is stone. Or it may consist of the actual hardened remains of an animal's skeletal structure. It is this second type of fossil—bone turned to stone—that has given

paleontologists the most information about primate evolution.

When an animal dies, the organic matter that made up its body quickly begins to deteriorate. The teeth and skeletal structure are composed largely of inorganic mineral salts, and soon they are all that remains. Under most conditions, these parts eventually deteriorate too. But once in a great while conditions are favorable for preservation—for instance, when volcanic ash, limestone, or highly mineralized ground water is present to form a high-mineral environment. If the remains are buried under such circumstances, the minerals in the ground may become bound into the structure of the teeth or bone, hardening and thus making them less likely to deteriorate.

What Can We Learn from Fossils?

Paleontologists can tell a great deal about an extinct animal from its fossilized bones or teeth, but reading the fossil record is not easy. For one thing, the very formation of a fossil depends a good deal on chance; the fossil record contains remains of only a small proportion of all the animals and plants that ever lived. Chance also plays a large role in the discovery of fossils, although paleontologists often know on the basis of geological evidence where fossils of a particular age might be found. Rock that was laid down millions of years ago will be visible only if uplift reveals it or erosion has removed what was laid down over it. In addition, fossils are often fragmented or damaged, and judgments about what the organism looked like may be based on one or just a few pieces. Although we can tell the age of a fossil with some accuracy, methods of dating are not always exact enough for the paleontologist to determine whether a fossil is older than, contemporaneous with, or more recent than other fossils. For this reason too, evolutionary lines are difficult to trace.

A further complication is an artificial one: the problem of **taxonomy,** or classification. Over the period that paleontologists have been discovering primate remains, different assumptions have guided scientists in making judgments about the taxonomic status of fossils. Even when paleontologists agree in theory, they often have honest differences of opinion about the status of a fossil. After all, we cannot conclude without doubt that two similar

TABLE 4–1 An Overview of Human Evolution: Biological and Cultural

TIME (YEARS AGO)	GEOLOGIC EPOCH	FOSSIL RECORD (FIRST APPEARANCE)	ARCHEOLOGICAL PERIODS (OLD WORLD)	MAJOR CULTURAL DEVELOPMENTS (FIRST APPEARANCE)
			Bronze Age	Cities and states; social inequality; full-time craft specialists
5500 (3500 B.C.)				
			Neolithic	Domesticated plants and animals; permanent villages
10,000 (8000 B.C.)				
			Mesolithic	Broad-spectrum food collecting; increasingly sedentary communities; many kinds of microliths
14,000 (12,000 B.C.)	Pleistocene	Earliest humans in New World		
			Upper Paleolithic	Cave paintings; female figurines; many kinds of blade tools
40,000				
		Modern humans *Homo sapiens sapiens*	Middle Paleolithic	Religious beliefs (?); burials; Mousterian tools
200,000		Neandertal *Homo sapiens*		
300,000		Earliest *Homo sapiens* (?)		
700,000				Acheulian tools
1,500,000		*Homo erectus*		
1,800,000			Lower Paleolithic	Hunting and/or scavenging; seasonal campsites; Oldowan tools
2,000,000	Pliocene	*Homo habilis*		
				Earliest stone tools
		Earliest hominids *Australopithecus*		
5,000,000				
	Miocene	Diversification of apes *Sivapithecus*		
22,500,000		*Dryopithecus* *Proconsul*		
29,000,000		Earliest apes (?) Propliopithecids,		
32,000,000	Oligocene	e.g., *Aegyptopithecus* Earliest anthropoids Parapithecids, e.g., *Apidium*		
38,000,000				
50,000,000	Eocene	*Amphipithecus* *Tetonius*		
53,500,000				
65,000,000	Paleocene			
70,000,000	Late Cretaceous	Earliest primates *Purgatorius*		

Source: Geological dates from W. A. Berggren and J. A. Van Couvering, "The Late Neocene: Biostratigraphy, Geochronology and Paleoclimatology of the Last 15 Million Years in Marine and Continental Sequences," *Palaeogeography, Palaeoclimatology, Palaeoecology,* 16 (1974): 13–16, 165.

fossil forms belonged to separate species, because we cannot know whether or not they interbred.

Despite all these problems, fossils do provide a wealth of information. In studying primate evolution, paleontologists ask two basic questions as they examine an animal fossil: What was the animal's means of food-getting? And what was its means of locomotion? Often the answers to both questions can be determined from a few fragments of bone or teeth.

Much of the evidence for primate evolution comes from teeth, which along with jaws are the most common animal parts to be preserved as fossils. Animals vary in *dentition,* the number and kinds of teeth they have, their size, and their arrangement in the mouth. Dentition provides clues to evolutionary relationships because animals with similar evolutionary histories often have similar teeth. Dentition also suggests the relative size of an animal and often offers clues about its diet.

Paleontologists can tell much about an animal's posture and locomotion from fragments of its skeleton. They can often judge whether the animal was a brachiator and whether it walked on all fours (quadrupedalism) or upright (bipedalism). The bone structure also tells much about the soft tissues. The form and size of muscles can be estimated by marks found on the bones to which the muscles were attached. Finally, fragments of the skull or vertebrae provide clues about the proportions and structure of the brain and spinal cord. From such evidence, scientists can tell whether areas of the brain associated with vision, or smell, or memory were large or small.

Dating Fossils

Scientists use different methods to estimate the age of a fossil, depending on the conditions present in the deposit where the fossil was found or in the fossil itself. There are two main approaches to dating fossils.[1] The first, **relative dating,** is used to determine the age of a specimen or deposit relative to another specimen or deposit. The second type, **chronometric** or **absolute dating,** is used to measure the actual age of a specimen or deposit.

Relative Dating Methods. The earliest and still the most commonly used method of relative dating is based on **stratigraphy,** the study of how different rock formations and fossils are laid down in successive layers or strata. Older layers are generally deeper or lower than more recent layers. To establish a stratigraphic sequence for the relative dating of new finds, the most suitable indicator-fossils are from animals (fauna) and plants (flora) that spread widely over short periods of time, or that died out fairly rapidly, or that evolved rapidly. Different animals and plants are used as indicators of relative age in different areas in the world. In Africa, elephants, pigs, and horses have been particularly important in establishing the stratigraphic sequences. Once the stratigraphy of an area is established, the relative age of two different fossils in the same or different sites is indicated by the associated flora and fauna.[2]

Major transitions in flora and fauna define the epochs and larger units of geologic time (periods and eras). The dates of the boundaries between such units are estimated by absolute dating, described below.

If a site has been disturbed, stratigraphy will not be a satisfactory way of determining relative age. For instance, remains from different periods may be washed or blown together by water or wind. Or a landslide may superimpose an earlier on a later layer. Still, it may be possible using chemical methods to estimate the relative age of the objects found in a disturbed site.

Three of the chemical methods used to date fossil bones relatively are the fluorine, uranium, and nitrogen tests (sometimes known as the F–U–N trio).[3] All are based on the same general principle: bones and teeth undergo a slow transformation in chemical composition when they remain buried for long periods, and this transformation reflects the mineral content of the groundwater in the area in which they are buried. Fluorine is one mineral present in groundwater; therefore, the older a fossil is, the higher its fluorine content will be. Uranium, like fluorine, is also present in

[1]Kenneth P. Oakley, "Analytical Methods of Dating Bones," in Don Brothwell and Eric Higgs, eds., *Science in Archaeology* (New York: Basic Books, 1963), pp. 24–34.

[2]Richard G. Klein, *The Human Career: Human Biological and Cultural Origins* (Chicago: The University of Chicago, 1989), pp. 1–12.
[3]Oakley, "Analytical Methods of Dating Bones," p. 26.

groundwater, and so the longer bones or teeth remain in the ground, the greater their uranium content. The proportions are reversed for nitrogen: the older the fossil is, the smaller the amount of nitrogen present in it. Thus, older bones have relatively higher concentrations of fluorine and uranium, and less nitrogen, than recent bones.

But a possible problem arises with the F–U–N tests because the mineral content of bones reflects the mineral content of the groundwater in the area. A 30-million-year-old fossil from a high-mineral area may have the same fluorine content as a 50-million-year-old fossil from a low-mineral site. So these chemical relative-dating methods cannot be used to find the relative ages of specimens from widely separated sites. The F–U–N tests are restricted then to specimens from the same site or from neighboring sites.

Each of the chemical relative-dating methods, used alone, can give only tentative evidence. But when the three methods are combined and confirm—that is, corroborate—one another, they are quite effective. Of the three methods we have discussed, the uranium test is by far the most reliable when used alone. It is not strictly a relative-dating method. There seems to be some consistency in the increase in radioactivity with age, even in bones from different deposits. The uranium test has another distinct advantage over the other tests: because uranium is radioactive, measuring the radioactivity does not require the destruction of any part of the sample in testing.

Chronometric or Absolute Dating Methods. Radiocarbon or carbon[14] (^{14}C) dating is perhaps the most popularly known method of determining the absolute age of a specimen. But it is not used to study early phases in primate evolution, for one important reason: the **half-life,** or rate of deterioration, of ^{14}C is relatively short. This means that radiocarbon dating is not usually accurate for anything more than 40,000 years old—and the primate paleontologist is interested in fossils as early as the late **Cretaceous** period, over 65 million years ago! The **potassium-argon** and **fission-track** methods are currently more useful for studying primate evolution.

POTASSIUM-ARGON (K-AR) DATING   [40]K, a radioactive form of potassium, decays at an established rate and forms argon ([40]Ar). Since the half-

life of [40]K is a known quantity, the age of a material containing potassium can be measured by the amount of [40]K compared to the amount of [40]Ar it contains.[4] Radioactive potassium's ([40]K's) half-life is very long—1330 million years. This means that K-Ar dating may be used to date samples from 5,000 years old up to 3 billion years old.

The K-Ar method is used to date potassium-rich minerals in rock, not the fossils that may be found in the rock. A very high temperature, such as occurs in a volcanic event, drives off any original argon in the material. Therefore, the amount of argon that accumulates afterward from the decay of radioactive potassium is directly related to the amount of time since the volcanic event. This type of dating has been extremely useful in east Africa where volcanic events have occurred frequently since the Miocene.[5] If the material to be dated is not rich in potassium, or the area did not experience any high-temperature events, other methods of absolute dating are required.

FISSION-TRACK DATING   The fission-track method is another means of determining the absolute age of fossil deposits.[6] Like the K-Ar method, it dates minerals contemporaneous with the deposit in which fossils are found and it also requires the prior occurrence of a high-temperature event. But the kinds of samples it can be used to date—such as crystal, glass, and many uranium-rich minerals—include a much wider variety than those that can be dated by the K-Ar method. The age range of fission-track dating, like that of K-Ar dating, is quite extensive—20 years to 5 billion years.[7]

How does it work? This method is basically the simplest of all the methods discussed here. It entails counting the number of paths, or tracks, etched in the sample by the fission (explosive division) of uranium atoms as they disintegrate. Scientists know that U-238, the most common uranium

[4]W. Gentner and H. J. Lippolt, "The Potassium-Argon Dating of Upper Tertiary and Pleistocene Deposits," in Brothwell and Higgs, eds., *Science in Archaeology*, pp. 72–84.

[5]Klein, *The Human Career: Human Biological and Cultural Origins*, pp. 15–17.

[6]Robert L. Fleischer et al., "Fission-Track Dating of Bed I, Olduvai Gorge," *Science*, April 2, 1965, pp. 72–74.

[7]Robert L. Fleischer and Howard R. Hart, Jr., "Fission-Track Dating: Techniques and Problems," in W. A. Bishop and J. A. Miller, eds., *Calibration of Hominid Evolution* (Toronto: University of Toronto Press, 1972), p. 474.

isotope, decays at a slow, steady rate. This decay takes the form of spontaneous fission, and each separate fission leaves a scar or track on the sample, which can be seen when chemically treated through a microscope. To find out how old a sample is, one counts the tracks, then measures their ratio to the uranium content of the sample.

The fission-track method has been used to date Bed I at Olduvai Gorge in Tanzania, East Africa (where some early hominids were found).[8] It was able to corroborate earlier K-Ar estimates that the site dated back close to 2 million years. That the K-Ar and fission-track methods use different techniques and have different sources of error makes them effective as checks on each other. When the two methods support each other, they provide very reliable evidence.

In later chapters, we discuss other methods of relative and absolute dating that are used for more recent finds.

The Emergence of Primates

With a rudimentary understanding of the kinds of information fossils provide and of the methods of dating that allow scientists to tell the age of fossils, we can look at, and suggest answers to, some major questions about primate evolution. When did the earliest primates appear? What were they like, and what kind of animal did they evolve from? Where did they live? What was their environment like? And which of their traits seem to have been favored by that environment?

The Earliest Primates

Finds made by two paleontologists in eastern Montana in 1964 suggest that some very early primates may have existed as far back as the Late Cretaceous period—some 70 million years ago. Molars from two species (one from the Cretaceous period, the other from the Paleocene) of the genus *Purgatorius* show some primate characteristics.[9] The earlier of these species is very old indeed. It

The primates probably evolved from a creature like this tree shrew, which has claws rather than nailed fingers, a long snout, and eyes on the sides of its head.

was contemporaneous with at least six species of dinosaurs. In fact, this specimen was recovered from the same site that contained the skeleton of a *triceratops*—a large horned dinosaur of the late Cretaceous—now mounted in the American Museum of Natural History in New York City.

Both of these earliest primate finds illustrate how much of the paleontologist's work depends on inference. *Purgatorius* may have been a primate, but it is impossible to tell for sure. The Cretaceous specimen consists of only one tooth found with fauna dating from that period. Because the tooth has some characteristics like those found in the teeth of some later Paleocene primates, some paleontologists think it represents a very early primate form. Fossil finds from later primates (that lived in the middle **Paleocene** epoch, about 60 million years ago) are much more abundant; several genera have been identified. The earliest *Purgatorius* remains consist only of teeth, but we have some skeletal parts of the later primates.

Paleocene and early Eocene archaic primates have been found in both Europe and North America. Several different particular species have been found in both areas. How could a nonbird species be found on two different continents? The answer to this puzzle, and to many similar puzzles in fossil distributions, is provided by the **continental-drift theory**.[10] At one time, about 180 million years ago, the continents were not separated as they are today. Instead, they formed a single superconti-

[8]Fleischer et al., "Fission-Track Dating of Bed I, Olduvai Gorge."

[9]L. Van Valen and R. E. Sloan, "The Earliest Primates," *Science*, November 5, 1965, pp. 743–45; and Frederick S. Szalay, "The Beginnings of Primates," *Evolution*, 22 (1968): 19–36.

[10]A. Hallam, "Alfred Wegener and the Hypothesis of Continental Drift," *Scientific American*, February 1975, pp. 88–97.

nent; the rest of the earth was covered by sea. Continental drift has since broken up that supercontinent. But even after the primates emerged, until about 60 million years ago, North America and Europe were connected in the vicinity of Greenland.[11] Only in relatively recent times (geologically speaking) have the continents moved far enough apart so that the intervening seas could block gene flow between related populations.

The Environment

During the late Cretaceous and early Paleocene, many new mammal forms began to appear—so many that this time is known as the beginning of the *age of mammals.* Larger reptiles such as dinosaurs were dying out, and at the same time many new and different mammal forms were branching out from the more primitive Cretaceous ones. Paleontologists think primates evolved from one of these *radiations,* or extensive diversifications, probably from **insectivores** (the order or major grouping of mammals, including modern shrews and moles, that is adapted to feeding on insects).

These changes in the earth's population may have been favored by the environmental changes that marked the end of the Cretaceous period and the beginning of the Paleocene. Shifts in climate, vegetation, and fauna signal the beginning of every major epoch, and many important changes were taking place at this time.

The climate of the Cretaceous period was almost uniformly damp and mild. Around the beginning of the Paleocene epoch, both seasonal and geographic fluctuations in temperature began to develop. At this time the climate became much drier in many areas, and vast swamplands disappeared. With changes in climate came changes in vegetation. During the Cretaceous period, the first deciduous (not evergreen) trees and flowering plants were emerging.

The new kinds of plant life opened up sources of food and protection for new animal forms. They created new habitats. Important to primate evolution was the Late Cretaceous forest. The new deciduous plant life provided an abundant food supply for insects. The result was that insects proliferated in both number and variety, and this led in turn to an increase in insectivores—the mammals that ate the insects. The insectivores were very adaptable, for they took advantage of many different habitats—underground, in water, on the ground, and above ground—the woody habitat of bushes, shrubs, vines, and trees.

It is this last adaptation that may have been the most important to primate evolution. The woody habitat had been exploited only partially in earlier periods. But sometime during the Late Cretaceous period, several different kinds, or *taxa,* of small animals, one of which may have been the archaic primate, began to take advantage of this habitat.

What May Have Favored the Emergence of Primates?

Why did the primates emerge? The traditional view of primate origins has been called the *arboreal theory.* According to this view, the primates evolved from insectivores that took to the trees.

Different paleontologists emphasized different possible adaptations to life in the trees. In 1912, G. Elliot Smith suggested that taking to the trees favored vision over smell. Searching for food by sniffing and feeling with the snout might suit terrestrial insectivores, but vision would be more useful in an animal that searched for food in the maze of tree branches. With smaller snouts and the declining importance of the sense of smell, the eyes of the early primates would have come to face forward. Frederic Wood Jones emphasized changes in the hand and foot. He thought that tree climbing would favor grasping hands and feet, with the hind limbs becoming more specialized for support and propulsion. In 1921, Treacher Collins suggested that the eyes of the early primates came to face forward not just because the snout got smaller. Rather, he thought that three-dimensional binocular vision would be favored because an animal jumping from branch to branch would be more likely to survive if it could accurately judge distances across open space.[12] In 1968, Frederick Sza-

---

[11]Malcolm C. McKenna, "Was Europe Connected Directly to North America Prior to the Middle Eocene?" in T. Dobzhansky, M. K. Hecht, and W. C. Steere, eds., *Evolutionary Biology* (New York: Appleton-Century-Crofts, 1972), 6: 179–88.

[12]Alison F. Richard, *Primates in Nature* (New York: W. H. Freeman & Company Publishers, 1985), p. 31; and Matt Cartmill, "Rethinking Primate Origins," *Science,* April 26, 1974, pp. 436–37.

lay suggested that a shift in diet—from insects to seeds, fruits, and leaves—might have been important in the differentiation of primates from insectivores. Lower-cusped, bulbous teeth, better for chewing tough husks and fruits, are an identifying feature of the earliest primates (indeed the *only* identifying feature where no skull or bone fossils have been found).[13]

Arboreal theory still has some proponents, but in 1974 Matt Cartmill highlighted some crucial weaknesses in the theory.[14] He argued that tree living is not a good explanation for many of the primate features because there are a number of living mammals that dwell in trees but seem to do very well without primatelike characteristics. One of the best examples, he says, is the tree squirrel. Its eyes are not front-facing, its sense of smell is not reduced in comparison with other rodents, it has claws rather than nails, and it lacks an opposable thumb. Yet these squirrels are very successful in the trees: they can leap accurately from tree to tree, they can walk over or under small branches, they can go up and down vertical surfaces, and they can even hang from their hind legs to get food below them. Furthermore, other animals have some primate traits but do not live in trees or do not move around in trees as primates do. For example, carnivores such as cats, hawks, and owls have forward-facing eyes, and the chameleon (a reptile) and some Australian marsupial mammals that prey on insects in bushes and shrubs have grasping hands and feet.

Cartmill thinks, then, that some factor other than moving about in trees may account for the emergence of the primates. He proposes that the early primates may have been basically insect-eaters, and that three-dimensional vision, grasping hands and feet, and reduced claws may have been selectively advantageous for hunting insects on the slender vines and branches that fill the undergrowth of tropical forests. Three-dimensional vision would allow the insect hunter to gauge the prey's distance accurately. Grasping feet would allow the predator to move quietly up narrow supports to reach the prey, which could then be grabbed with the hands. Claws, Cartmill argues,

would make it difficult to grasp very slender branches. And the sense of smell would have become reduced, not so much because it was no longer useful, but because the location of the eyes at the front of the face would leave less room for a snout.

Robert Sussman's theory builds on Cartmill's *visual predation theory* and on Szalay's idea about a dietary shift.[15] Sussman accepts Cartmill's point that the early primates were likely to eat and move about mostly on small branches. This would explain why the early primates would have had nails rather than claws (as do squirrels) and grasping hands and feet. If an animal is moving mostly on small, slender branches and hardly ever travels on large trunks and branches (as do squirrels), grasping hands and feet and reduced claws or nails would be advantageous. Sussman also accepts Szalay's point that the early primates probably ate the new types of plant food (flowers, seeds, and fruits) that were beginning to become abundant at the time, as flowering trees and plants spread throughout the world. But Sussman asks an important question: If the early primates ate mostly plant foods rather than speedy insects, why did they become more reliant on vision than on smell? Sussman suggests it was because the early primates were probably nocturnal (as many prosimians still are): if they were to locate and manipulate small food items at the ends of slender branches in dim light, they would need improved vision.

We still have very little fossil evidence of the earliest primates. When additional fossils become available we may be better able to evaluate the various explanations that have been suggested for the emergence of primates.

The Early Primates: What They Looked Like

From the clues provided by fossils, comparative anatomy, physiology, behavior, and our knowledge of the Paleocene and Eocene environments, we can put together a composite sketch of

[13]Szalay, "The Beginnings of Primates," pp. 32–33.
[14]Cartmill, "Rethinking Primate Origins," pp. 436–43.

[15]Robert W. Sussman, *The Ecology and Behavior of Free-ranging Primates* (New York: Macmillan, forthcoming). See also Robert W. Sussman and Peter H. Raven, "Pollination by Lemurs and Marsupials: An Archaic Coevolutionary System," *Science,* May 19, 1978, pp. 734–35.

what early primates must have been like. In general, the primates of the Paleocene epoch seem to have looked a little like the mice and rats of today.

Although there is debate about whether the earliest primates lived in the trees, later primates in the **Eocene** epoch (from 53.5 to 38 million years ago) were apparently doing so, judging from their anatomy. Vertical clinging and leaping was probably a common method of locomotion. Eocene prosimians not only moved around the way modern prosimians do; some also looked quite a bit like living prosimians. Through the evolutionary process of natural selection, their eyes became located closer to the front of the face and their snout was reduced. Digits became longer and were specialized for grasping. The importance of vision is apparent in a 50-million-year-old fossilized skull of the Eocene primate *Tetonius* that contains imprints of different parts of the brain.[16] The brain has large occipital and temporal lobes—the regions associated with perception, integration, and visual memory.

All primates did not adapt in the same way to life in the trees. There was a great deal of diversity among all mammals during the Paleocene and Eocene epochs, and the primates were no exception. Evolution seems to have proceeded rapidly during those years.

The Emergence of Anthropoids

The anthropoids of today—monkeys, apes, and humans—are the most successful living primates and include well over 150 species. Unfortunately, the fossil record documenting the emergence of the anthropoids is extremely spotty, and there is virtually no record of the Old World forms (the catarrhines) in the two areas where they are most abundant today—the rain forests of sub-Saharan Africa and Southeast Asia.[17] The oldest primate thought by some paleontologists to be an anthropoid (*Amphipithecus*) appears to have lived in what is now Burma between 44 and 40 million

years ago.[18] Undisputed remains of early anthropoids date from a somewhat later period (the Early Oligocene, after 38 million years ago) in the Fayum area southwest of Cairo, Egypt.

The Fayum Oligocene Anthropoids

The Fayum today is an uninviting area of desert badlands, but during the **Oligocene** epoch (38 to 22.5 million years ago) it was a tropical rain forest quite close to the shores of the Mediterranean Sea. The area had a warm climate, and it contained many rivers and lakes. The Fayum, in fact, was far more inviting than the northern continents at that time, for the climates of both North America and Eurasia were beginning to cool during the Oligocene. The general cooling seems to have resulted in the virtual disappearance of primates from the northern areas, at least for a time.

Two main types of anthropoid have been found in the Fayum. The monkeylike **parapithecids** had three premolars, as do most prosimians and the New World monkeys. They were generally quite small, weighing under three pounds. Their relatively small eye sockets suggest that they were not nocturnal. And their teeth suggest that they ate mostly fruits and seeds. One of the parapithecids, *Apidium,* was probably an arboreal, quadrupedal leaper.[19] There is still disagreement among paleontologists as to whether or not the parapithecids preceded or followed the split between the New World monkeys (platyrrhines) and the Old World monkeys and apes (catarrhines). In any case, the parapithecids are the most primitive known anthropoids.[20]

The other type of anthropoid found in the Fayum, the **propliopithecids,** had apelike teeth. For example, in contrast with the parapithecids, who had three premolars, the propliopithecids had only two premolars, just like modern apes, humans, and Old World monkeys. *Aegyptopithecus,* the best-known propliopithecid, probably moved

---

[16]Leonard Radinsky, "The Oldest Primate Endocast," *American Journal of Physical Anthropology,* 27 (1967): 358–88.

[17]John G. Fleagle and Richard F. Kay, "The Paleobiology of Catarrhines," in Eric Delson, ed., *Ancestors: The Hard Evidence* (New York: Alan R. Liss, 1985), p. 25.

[18]Russell L. Ciochon, Donald E. Savage, Thaw Tint, and Ba Maw, "Anthropoid Origins in Asia? New Discovery of *Amphipithecus* from the Eocene of Burma," *Science,* August 23, 1985, pp. 756–59.

[19]Fleagle and Kay, "The Paleobiology of Catarrhines," p. 30.

[20]Fleagle, *Primate Adaptation & Evolution* (San Diego: Academic Press, 1988), pp. 334–35, 341.

Reconstruction of Aegyptopithecus.

around quadrupedally in the trees, weighed about thirteen pounds, and ate mostly fruit. Although its teeth and jaws are apelike, the rest of *Aegyptopithecus*'s skeleton is similar to that of the modern South American howler monkey.[21] Because the propliopithecids lack the specialized characteristics of living Old World monkeys and apes (catarrhines), but share the dental formula of the catarrhines, it is thought that the propliopithecids were primitive catarrhines, ancestral to both the Old World monkeys and the hominoids (apes and humans).[22]

The Miocene Anthropoids: Monkeys, Apes, and Hominids(?)

During the **Miocene** epoch (22.5 to 5 million years ago), monkeys and apes clearly diverged in appearance, and numerous kinds of apes appeared in Europe, Asia, and Africa. In the Early Miocene, the temperatures were considerably warmer than the temperatures in the Oligocene. From Early to

Late Miocene conditions became drier.[23] We can infer that late in the Miocene (between about 8 and 5 million years ago) the direct ancestor of humans (the first hominid) may have emerged in Africa. The inference about *where* hominids emerged is based on the fact that undisputed hominids lived in East Africa after about 5 million years ago. The inference about *when* hominids emerged is based not on fossil evidence but on comparative molecular and biochemical analyses of modern apes and humans. One of the Miocene apes (known or unknown) was ancestral to hominids, and so our discussion here deals mostly with the *proto-apes* (anthropoids with some apelike characteristics) and the apes of the Miocene.

Early Miocene Proto-apes. Most of the fossils from the Early Miocene (about 22 to 15 million years ago) are described as proto-apes. They have been found mostly in Africa. The one best known is *Proconsul africanus.*[24]

Proconsul africanus was much larger than any of the anthropoids of the Oligocene, about three times the weight of *Aegyptopithecus* and about the size of a modern baboon. Most paleontologists now agree that *Proconsul* was definitely a hominoid, but quite unlike any ape living today. Like the Oligocene anthropoids, it was quadrupedal and mostly a fruit-eater (judging from its skeletal anatomy and teeth). But, unlike the Oligocene anthropoids, *Proconsul* was probably arboreal *and* terrestrial (again judging from its skeleton). It had elbow and shoulder joints like a chimpanzee, a wrist like a monkey, and a lower backbone like a gibbon.[25] Some paleontologists think that *Proconsul* may have been ancestral to apes and humans.[26]

Compared with the Oligocene anthropoids, the Early Miocene proto-apes were quite diverse. They ranged in size from that of the modern gibbon (about 10 pounds) to that of the modern chimpanzee (about 100 pounds). And in contrast with the Oligocene anthropoids, who appear to have been arboreal quadrupeds, some of the Early Miocene species, such as *Proconsul,* appear to have

[21]Fleagle and Kay, "The Paleobiology of Catarrhines," pp. 25, 30.

[22]Fleagle, *Primate Adaptation & Evolution,* p. 339. See also J. G. Fleagle and R. F. Kay, "New Interpretations of the Phyletic Position of Oligocene Hominoids," in Russell L. Ciochon and Robert S. Corruccini, eds., *New Interpretations of Ape and Human Ancestry* (New York: Plenum, 1983), p. 205.

[23]Fleagle, *Primate Adaptation & Evolution,* p. 363.

[24]Fleagle and Kay, "The Paleobiology of Catarrhines," p. 31.

[25]Ibid.; and David Pilbeam, "The Descent of Hominoids and Hominids," *Scientific American,* March 1984, pp. 84–96.

[26]Fleagle, *Primate Adaptation & Evolution,* p. 374.

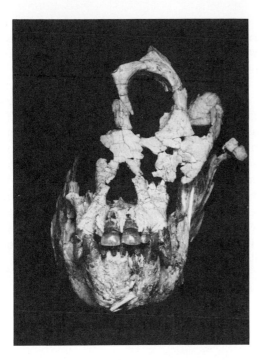

Remains of a *Sivapithecus sivalensis*.

Most paleontologists divide the Middle and Late Miocene apes into two groups: **Dryopithecus,** found primarily in Europe, and **Sivapithecus,** found primarily in western and southern Asia.[29] The genus *Dryopithecus* is known mostly from its teeth, which strongly resemble the teeth of the Early Miocene *Proconsul.* Judging from the dryopithecines' teeth—which consist of small to medium incisors and relatively small molars and premolars with thin enamel—their owners probably ate relatively soft foods (fruits, leaves, and young plants). The dryopithecines disappear from the fossil record after about 9 million years ago, perhaps because climates became cooler and habitats less forested in the areas where they lived.[30]

Most species of *Sivapithecus* were larger than earlier dryopithecines; some sivapithecines were as large as a present-day male orangutan or a female gorilla.[31] Compared with the dryopithecines' teeth, the sivapithecines' molars and premolars are relatively larger (adjusting for differences in body size) and more thickly enameled, and their canines are somewhat reduced.[32] Many paleontologists think that these apes with their thickly enameled teeth were probably adapted to habitats and had diets that were different from the dryopithecines'. The thick enamel and large molars suggest that sivapithecines depended more on hard foods such as seeds. Such a diet would be possible because the sivapithecines lived in open woodlands and grasslands—habitats where seeds would be plentiful. Such habitats became more common in the world after the Early Miocene.[33]

It is still very difficult to identify the evolutionary lines leading from Miocene apes to modern apes and humans. Only the orangutans have been linked to the later Miocene ape genus, *Sivapithecus.*[34]

been terrestrial at least some of the time; others appear to have been arboreal brachiators (moving through the trees by swinging from the arms rather than by walking on all fours).

Later Miocene Apes. The hominoids that lived 14 to 8 million years ago have been classified as apes (rather than proto-apes), even though they did not look completely like modern apes. They ranged from gibbonlike to gorillalike in size; one of them, **Gigantopithecus,** weighed over 600 pounds. Just like the Early Miocene anthropoids, the later Miocene apes included some arboreal and some terrestrial forms, and some of the arboreal ones were brachiators.[27] Most of the ape fossils from the later Miocene have been found in Europe and Asia. At the end of the Early Miocene, continental drift had moved Africa and Arabia into contact with Eurasia, allowing the migration of African hominoids (and other animals) into the rest of the Old World.[28]

[27]Fleagle and Kay, "The Paleobiology of Catarrhines," pp. 25–32.

[28]Pilbeam, "The Descent of Hominoids and Hominids," p. 91.

[29]Fleagle, *Primate Adaptation & Evolution,* p. 382.

[30]David Pilbeam, "Recent Finds and Interpretation of Miocene Hominoids," *Annual Review of Anthropology,* 8 (1979): 345–46.

[31]Fleagle, *Primate Adaptation & Evolution,* pp. 382–85.

[32]Pilbeam, "Recent Finds and Interpretation of Miocene Hominoids," pp. 346–47.

[33]M. Pickford, "Sequence and Environments of the Lower and Middle Miocene Hominoids of Western Kenya," in Ciochon and Corruccini, eds., *New Interpretations of Ape and Human Ancestry,* pp. 436–37.

[34]Fleagle, *Primate Adaptation & Evolution,* pp. 388–90.

The Place of the Miocene Hominoids in Hominid Evolution

Who or what are hominids, and how do they differ from other hominoids? The hominid family comprises modern humans, their ancestors, and other extinct bipedal hominoids. The family includes at least two genera: **Homo** (including modern humans) and **Australopithecus** (a genus of hominids that lived during the Pliocene and Pleistocene epochs). In general, hominids are characterized by a number of identifying traits. (The earliest ones may not have had all of these traits, but later ones did.) They are bipeds. They have an enlarged brain. Their face is relatively small and relatively nonprotruding. And their teeth are small and arranged on jaws that are parabolic in shape (viewed from above or below), rather than U-shaped as in the apes.

Not so long ago, many paleontologists thought that the Miocene ape **Ramapithecus** (now classified by most as a sivapithecine) was a good candidate for consideration as the first hominid and direct ancestor of the undisputed hominids who lived some millions of years later. The idea that *Ramapithecus* was a hominid was based primarily on the resemblance of its cheek teeth and jaws (the only fossil remains available at the time) to those of the definitely bipedal australopithecines who lived 3 to 4 million years ago in East Africa. Assuming that *Ramapithecus* was ancestral to the hominid line and that it emerged about 14 million years ago, many paleontologists used to think that the split between hominids and apes must have occurred before about 15 million years ago. But biochemical and genetic comparisons of various living primates as well as recent fossil finds in Pakistan and Turkey have persuaded most paleontologists that the split between hominids and apes probably occurred more recently.

In 1966, on the basis of biochemical comparison of blood proteins in the different surviving primates, Vincent Sarich and Allan Wilson estimated that gibbons diverged from the other hominoids about 12 million years ago, orangutans 10 million years ago, and the other apes (gorillas and chimps) from hominids only 4.5 million years ago. These estimates depended on the assumption that the more similar in chemistry the bloods of different primates are (for instance, chimpanzees and humans), the closer those primates are in evolutionary time. In other words, the more similar the bloods of related species, the more recently they diverged.[35]

Subsequent comparative studies of the living primates, employing a variety of techniques (including comparisons of their DNA), have confirmed the probable recency of the hominid divergence from chimpanzees and gorillas. The DNA comparisons place the split somewhat earlier than the Sarich and Wilson estimate, but not by much: the DNA comparisons suggest that the common ancestor of chimpanzees and hominids lived 6 to 8 million years ago, while gorillas diverged about 2 million years earlier.[36]

Most paleontologists are now persuaded that the hominid–ape split probably occurred in the later part of the Miocene. A major reason they are now so persuaded is that recent fossil finds in Pakistan and Turkey (skull finds more complete than just teeth and jaws) suggest that sivapithecines were not very hominidlike.[37] As we noted above, sivapithecines are now thought to be ancestral to orangutans.

So what does the available evidence tell us about where and when hominids first emerged? Unfortunately, the answer is nothing as yet. For we still do not have any definitely hominid fossils in Africa from the Late Miocene (8 to 5 million years ago)—the presumed place and time hominids emerged.[38] And definitely hominid fossils dating from the Late Miocene have not been found anywhere else as yet. So all we know definitely now is that primates with undisputably hominid characteristics lived 3 to 4 million years ago in East Africa. We turn to these undisputed hominids in the next chapter.

[35]Vincent M. Sarich and Allan C. Wilson, "Quantitative Immunochemistry and the Evolution of the Primate Albumins: Micro-Component Fixations," *Science*, December 23, 1966, pp. 1563–66; Vincent M. Sarich, "The Origin of Hominids: An Immunological Approach," in S. L. Washburn and Phyllis C. Jay, eds., *Perspectives on Human Evolution* (New York: Holt, Rinehart & Winston, 1968), 1: 99–121; and Roger Lewin, "Is the Orangutan a Living Fossil?" *Science*, December 16, 1983, pp. 1222–23.

[36]Adalgisa Caccone and Jeffrey R. Powell, "DNA Divergence among Hominoids," *Evolution*, 43 (1989): 925–42.

[37]Lewin, "Is the Orangutan a Living Fossil?" See also Fleagle, *Primate Adaptation & Evolution*, pp. 384–85, 390–91.

[38]Pilbeam, "The Descent of Hominoids and Hominids," p. 88.

SUMMARY

1. We cannot know for sure how primates evolved. But fossils, a knowledge of ancient environments, and an understanding of comparative anatomy and behavior give us enough clues so that we have a tentative idea of when, where, and why primates emerged and diverged.

2. There are two main approaches to dating fossils. Relative-dating methods—using stratigraphy and associated fauna and flora, and certain chemical tests within sites—tell whether one find is about the same age (or older or younger) than another find. Absolute tests, such as potassium-argon and fission-track dating, give the approximate age of a fossil or deposit.

3. The surviving primates—prosimians, New World monkeys, Old World monkeys, apes, and humans—are thought to be descendants of small, originally terrestrial insectivores.

4. Changes in climate during the Late Cretaceous favored the extensive development of deciduous forests and their understories of bushes, shrubs, and vines. Many of the flowering trees and plants emerged during this period. The early primates probably began to exploit these forests, which provided a largely untapped habitat with many new food resources. The earliest primates may have emerged some 70 million years ago.

5. The traditional view of primate evolution is that arboreal (tree) life would have favored many of the common primate features, including distinctive dentition, greater reliance on vision over smell, three-dimensional binocular vision, and grasping hands and feet. A second theory proposes that some of the distinctive primate characteristics were selectively advantageous for hunting insects on the slender vines and branches that filled the undergrowth of forests. A third theory suggests that the distinctive features of primates (including reliance more on vision than on smell) were favored because the early primates were nocturnal feeders on flowers, fruits, and seeds, which they had to locate on slender branches in dim light.

6. Undisputed remains of early anthropoids unearthed in Egypt date from the Early Oligocene (after 38 million years ago). They include the monkeylike parapithecids and the propliopithecids, who had apelike teeth.

7. During the Miocene epoch, which began about 22 million years ago, monkeys and apes clearly diverged and numerous kinds of apes appeared in Europe, Asia, and Africa. The Miocene proto-apes and apes were very diverse in size, ranging from about 10 pounds to as much as 600 pounds. Unlike the Oligocene anthropoids, who all appear to have been arboreal quadrupeds, some of the Miocene apes were at least partly terrestrial and others were arboreal brachiators. The two main groups of apes in the Middle and Late Miocene were the dryopithecines (with thin-enameled cheek teeth) and the sivapithecines (with larger and more thickly enameled cheek teeth).

8. The fossil record does not yet tell us who the first hominid was, but biochemical and genetic analyses of modern apes and humans suggest that the hominid–ape split occurred during the Late Miocene (after about 8 million years ago). Since undisputed hominids lived in East Africa after about 4 million years ago, the first hominid probably emerged in Africa.

SUGGESTED READING

ANDREWS, P., AND STRINGER, C. *Human Evolution: An Illustrated Guide.* London: British Museum, 1989. A brief introduction to primate and human evolution, illustrated by reconstructions in color of many fossil finds.

CIOCHON, R. L., AND CORRUCCINI, R. S., eds. *New Interpretations of Ape and Human Ancestry.* New York: Plenum, 1983. A large volume of papers on the ancestry of apes and humans. Topics discussed include the timing and geographic location of the ape–human divergence and the possible reasons for that divergence.

CIOCHON, R. L., AND FLEAGLE, J. G., eds. *Primate Evolution and Human Origins.* Hawthorne, NY: Aldine de Gruyter, 1987. A collection of many of the most important articles on primate evolution and human origins that were published over the last twenty years.

FLEAGLE, J. G. *Primate Adaptation & Evolution.* San

Diego: Academic Press, 1988. A textbook that examines the comparative anatomy, behavioral ecology, and paleontology of humans and their nearest relatives. Chapters 9–14 are particularly relevant to this chapter.

PILBEAM, D. "The Descent of Hominoids and Hominids." *Scientific American,* March 1984, pp. 84–96. A discussion of the divergence of apes from Old World monkeys and the later divergence of humans from apes.

SZALAY, F. S., AND DELSON, E. *Evolutionary History of the Primates.* New York: Academic Press, 1979. A detailed analysis, extensively illustrated, of the primate fossil record, with interpretations of phylogeny, adaptations, and morphology. Advanced level.

5

Early Hominids and Their Cultures

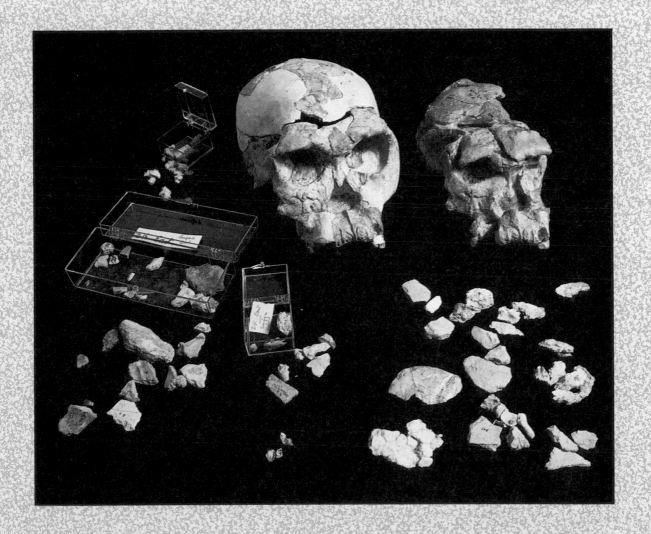

Undisputed bipedal hominids lived in East Africa about 4 million years ago. These hominids, and others who lived in East and South Africa until 2 million years ago, are generally classified in the genus *Australopithecus.* And some East African hominids that are nearly 2 million years old are classified in our own genus, *Homo.* In this chapter we discuss what we know or suspect about the emergence and relationship of the australopithecines and *Homo.* We also discuss the life-styles or cultures of the hominids from about 4 million until about 300,000 years ago, when the first members of our own species (*Homo sapiens*) may have emerged.

Trends in Hominid Evolution

Perhaps the most crucial change in early hominid evolution was the development of bipedal locomotion, or walking on two legs. We now know from the fossil record that other important physical changes—including the expansion of the brain, modification of the female pelvis to allow bigger-brained babies to be born, and reduction of the face, teeth, and jaws—did not occur until about 2 million years after the emergence of bipedalism. Other human characteristics—including an extended period of infant and child dependency and more meat-eating—may also have developed after that time.

Bipedalism

We do not know whether bipedalism developed quickly or gradually, since the fossil record for the period between 8 and 4 million years ago is very skimpy. We do know that many of the Miocene anthropoids, judging from the skeletal anatomy, were capable of assuming an upright posture. For example, brachiation (arm swinging through the trees) puts an animal in an upright position; so does climbing up and down trees with the use of grasping hands and feet. It is also likely that the proto-hominids were capable of occasional bipedalism, just like many modern monkeys and apes.[1]

As we noted at the end of the last chapter, definitely bipedal hominids apparently emerged first in Africa. The physical environment in Africa was changing from tropical forest to more open country.[2] The proto-apes flourished at the very beginning of the Miocene epoch, when lush tropical rain forests were the predominant habitat. Somewhat later in the Miocene, about 16 to 11 million years ago, a drying trend set in that continued into the Pliocene. Gradually the African rain forests, deprived of intense humidity and rainfall, gave way mostly to **savannas** (grasslands) and scattered deciduous woodlands. The tree-dwelling primates did not completely lose their customary habitats, since some forest areas remained, and natural selection continued to favor the better-adapted tree dwellers in those forest areas. But the new, more open country probably favored characteristics adapted to ground living in some primates as well as other animals. In the evolutionary line leading to humans, these adaptations included bipedalism.

So what in particular may have favored the emergence of bipedal hominids? There are several possible explanations for this development. One idea is that bipedalism was adaptive for life amid the tall grasses of the savannas because an erect posture may have made it easier to spot ground predators as well as potential prey.[3] This theory does not adequately account for the development of bipedalism, however. Baboons and some other Old World monkeys also live in savanna environments, yet although they can stand erect, and occasionally do so, they have not evolved fully bipedal locomotion.

Other theories stress the importance of freeing the hands. If some hand activity is critical while an animal is moving, selection may favor bipedalism because it frees the hands for other activities at the same time. What hand activities might have been so critical?

Gordon Hewes has suggested that carrying food in the hands was the critical activity—if it were necessary to carry food from one locale to another, moving about only on the hind limbs would

---

[1]M. D. Rose, "Food Acquisition and the Evolution of Positional Behaviour: The Case of Bipedalism," in David J. Chivers, Bernard A. Wood, and Alan Bilsborough, eds., *Food Acquisition and Processing in Primates* (New York: Plenum, 1984), pp. 509–24.

[2]John Napier, "The Antiquity of Human Walking," *Scientific American,* April 1967, pp. 56–66.

[3]Kenneth Oakley, "On Man's Use of Fire, with Comments on Tool-Making and Hunting," in S. L. Washburn, ed., *Social Life of Early Man* (Chicago: Aldine, 1964), p. 186.

TABLE 5–1 An Overview of Human Evolution: Biological and Cultural

TIME (YEARS AGO)	GEOLOGIC EPOCH	FOSSIL RECORD (FIRST APPEARANCE)	ARCHEOLOGICAL PERIODS (OLD WORLD)	MAJOR CULTURAL DEVELOPMENTS (FIRST APPEARANCE)
			Bronze Age	Cities and states; social inequality; full-time craft specialists
5500 (3500 B.C.)			——————	
			Neolithic	Domesticated plants and animals; permanent villages
10,000 (8000 B.C.)			——————	
			Mesolithic	Broad-spectrum food collecting; increasingly sedentary communities; many kinds of microliths
14,000 (12,000 B.C.)	Pleistocene	Earliest humans in New World	——————	
			Upper Paleolithic	Cave paintings; female figurines; many kinds of blade tools
40,000			——————	
		Modern humans *Homo sapiens sapiens*	Middle Paleolithic	Religious beliefs (?); burials; Mousterian tools
200,000		Neandertal *Homo sapiens*		
300,000		Earliest *Homo sapiens* (?)	——————	
700,000				Acheulian tools
1,500,000		*Homo erectus*		
1,800,000	——————		Lower Paleolithic	Hunting and/or scavenging; seasonal campsites; Oldowan tools
2,000,000	Pliocene	*Homo habilis*	——————	
		Earliest hominids *Australopithecus*		Earliest stone tools
5,000,000	——————			
	Miocene	Diversification of apes *Sivapithecus* *Dryopithecus* *Proconsul*		
22,500,000	——————			
		Earliest apes (?) Propliopithecids, e.g., *Aegyptopithecus*		
29,000,000				
32,000,000	Oligocene	Earliest anthropoids Parapithecids, e.g., *Apidium*		
38,000,000	——————			
	Eocene	*Amphipithecus* *Tetonius*		
50,000,000				
53,500,000	——————			
	Paleocene			
65,000,000	——————			
	Late Cretaceous	Earliest primates *Purgatorius*		
70,000,000				

Source: Geological dates from W. A. Berggren and J. A. Van Couvering, "The Late Neocene: Biostratigraphy, Geochronology and Paleoclimatology of the Last 15 Million Years in Marine and Continental Sequences," *Palaeogeography, Palaeoclimatology, Palaeoecology,* 16 (1974): 13–16, 165.

Early hominids probably lived in an environment much like the Serengeti Park in Tanzania, East Africa (shown here).

have been adaptive.[4] Hewes emphasized the importance of carrying hunted or scavenged meat, but many paleontologists now question whether early hominids hunted or even scavenged.[5] However, the ability to carry any food to a place safe from predators may have been one of the more important advantages of bipedalism. C. Owen Lovejoy has suggested that food carrying might have been important for another reason. If males provisioned females and their babies by carrying food back to a home base, the females would have been able to conserve energy by not traveling around

and therefore might have been able to produce and care for more babies.[6] Thus, whatever the advantages of food carrying, the more bipedal a proto-hominid was, the more it might reproduce.

Bipedalism might also have been favored by natural selection because the freeing of the hands would allow proto-hominids to use, and perhaps even make, tools that they could carry as they moved about. Consider how advantageous such tool use might have been. Sherwood Washburn has noted that some contemporary ground-living primates dig for roots to eat, "and if they could use a stone or a stick they might easily double their food supply."[7] David Pilbeam also suggests why tool use by the early savanna dwellers may have appreciably increased the number and amount of

[4]Gordon W. Hewes, "Food Transport and the Origin of Hominid Bipedalism," *American Anthropologist,* 63 (1961): 687–710.
[5]Pat Shipman, "Scavenging or Hunting in Early Hominids: Theoretical Framework and Tests," *American Anthropologist,* 88 (1986): 27–43; Erik Trinkaus, "Bodies, Brawn, Brains and Noses: Human Ancestors and Human Predation," in M. H. Nitecki and D. V. Nitecki, eds., *The Evolution of Human Hunting* (New York: Plenum, 1987), p. 115.

[6]C. Owen Lovejoy, "The Origin of Man," *Science,* January 23, 1981, pp. 341–50.
[7]Sherwood Washburn, "Tools and Human Evolution," *Scientific American,* September 1960, p. 63.

plant foods they could eat: in order to be eaten, many of the plant foods in the savanna probably had to be chopped, crushed, or otherwise prepared with the aid of tools.[8] In the new open-country habitat, tools may also have been used to kill and butcher animals for food. Without tools, primates in general are not well equipped physically for regular hunting. Their teeth and jaws are not sharp and strong enough, and their speed afoot is not fast enough. So the use of tools to kill and butcher game might have enlarged even further the potential supply of food available in the environment.

Finally, tools may have been used as weapons against predators, which would have been a great threat to the relatively defenseless ground-dwelling proto-hominids. As Milford Wolpoff notes, "faced with a predator, a hominid who knew how to use a club for defense but did not have one available was just as dead as one to whom the notion never occurred."[9] In Wolpoff's opinion, it was the advantage of carrying weapons *continuously* that was responsible for transforming occasional bipedalism to completely bipedal locomotion.

But some anthropologists question the idea that tool use and toolmaking may have favored bipedalism. They point out that our first evidence of stone tools appears at least a million years *after* the emergence of bipedalism. So how could toolmaking be responsible for bipedalism? Wolpoff suggests an answer. Even though bipedalism appears to be at least a million years older than stone tools, it is not unlikely that proto-hominids used tools made of wood and bone, neither of which would be as likely as stone to survive in the archeological record. Moreover, unmodified stone tools present in the archeological record might not be recognizable as tools.[10]

All theories about the origin of bipedalism are, of course, speculative. We do not yet have direct evidence that any of the factors we have discussed were actually responsible for bipedalism. Any or all of these factors—being able to see far, carrying food back to a home base, carrying tools that included weapons—may explain the transformation of an occasionally bipedal proto-hominid to a completely bipedal hominid.

Expansion of the Brain

The first definitely bipedal hominids, the australopithecines, had relatively small cranial capacities, ranging from about 380 to 530 cubic centimeters (cc)—not much larger than that of chimpanzees. But around 2 million years ago, half a million years after stone tools appear, some hominids classified as members of our genus, *Homo*, had cranial capacities of about 750 cc. *Homo erectus* of about 1 million years ago had a cranial capacity of about 1000 cc. Modern humans average slightly more than 1300 cc.

Since the australopithecines were quite small, the later increase in brain size might have been a result of later hominids' bigger bodies. When we correct for body size, however, it turns out that brain size increased not only absolutely but also relatively after 2 million years ago. Between about 4 and 2 million years ago, relative brain size remained just about the same. Only in the last 2 million years has the hominid brain doubled in relative size (and tripled in absolute size).[11]

What may have favored the increase in brain size? Many anthropologists think that the increase is linked to the emergence of stone toolmaking between 2.5 and 2 million years ago. The reasoning is that stone toolmaking was important for the survival of our ancestors, and therefore natural selection would have favored bigger-brained individuals because they had motor and conceptual skills that enabled them to be better toolmakers. According to this view, the expansion of the brain and more and more sophisticated toolmaking would have developed together. Other anthropologists think that the expansion of the brain may have been favored by other factors, such as warfare, hunting, longer life, and language.[12]

[8]David Pilbeam, *The Ascent of Man* (New York: Macmillan, 1972), p. 153.

[9]Milford H. Wolpoff, "Competitive Exclusion among Lower Pleistocene Hominids: The Single Species Hypothesis," *Man*, 6 (1971): 602.

[10]M. H. Wolpoff, "*Ramapithecus* and Human Origins: An Anthropologist's Perspective of Changing Interpretations," in Russell L. Ciochon and Robert S. Corruccini, eds., *New Interpretations of Ape and Human Ancestry* (New York: Plenum, 1983), p. 666.

[11]Henry M. McHenry, "The Pattern of Human Evolution: Studies on Bipedalism, Mastication, and Encephalization," *Annual Review of Anthropology*, 11 (1982): 160–61.

[12]Ibid., p. 162.

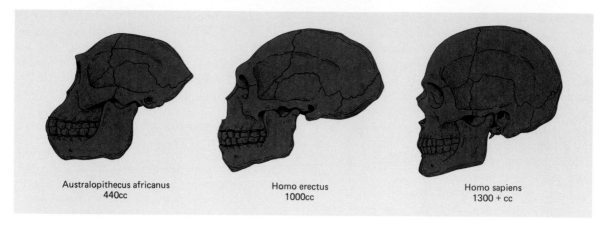

FIGURE 5-1

Comparison of the estimated cranial capacities in *Australopithecus africanus*, *Homo erectus*, and *Homo* sapiens, demonstrating the expansion of the brain in hominid evolution. *(Estimated cranial capacities from Ian Tattersall, Eric Delson, John Van Couvering, eds.,* Encyclopedia of Human Evolution and Prehistory. *New York: Garland Publishing, 1988, pp. 80, 263, 268.)*

Whatever the factors selecting for bigger brains, natural selection also favored the widening of the female pelvis to allow larger-brained babies to be born. But there was probably a limit to how far the pelvis could widen and still be adapted to bipedalism. Something had to give, and that something was the degree of physical development of the human infant at birth: the human infant is born with cranial bones so plastic that they can overlap. Because birth takes place before the cranial bones have hardened, the human infant with its relatively large brain can pass through the opening in the mother's pelvis.

Reduction of the Face, Teeth, and Jaws

As in the case of the brain, substantial changes in the face, teeth, and jaws do not appear in hominid evolution until after about 2 million years ago. The australopithecines all have cheek teeth that are very large relative to their estimated body weight. The australopithecines' diet may have been especially high in plant foods,[13] including small, tough objects such as seeds, roots, and tubers. The australopithecines also have relatively large faces that project forward below the eyes, and

thick jawbones. It is particularly in the *Homo* forms that we first see reductions in the size of the face, smaller cheek teeth, and smaller jaws.

Changes Not Firmly Dated

The fossil evidence, which we discuss shortly, suggests when (and in which hominids) changes occurred in brain size and in the face, teeth, and jaws. Other changes in the evolution of hominids cannot as yet be confidently dated with regard to time and particular hominid. For example, we know that modern humans are relatively hairless compared with the other surviving primates. But we do not know when hominids became relatively hairless, because fossilized bones do not tell us whether their owners were hairy. On the other hand, we suspect that most of the other characteristically human traits have developed after the brain began to increase in size (during the evolution of the genus *Homo*). These changes include the extension of the period of infant and child dependency, the scavenging and hunting of meat, the development of a division of labor by sex, and the sharing of food.

One of the possible consequences of brain expansion was the lessening of maturity at birth, as we have noted. That babies were born more immature may at least partially explain the lengthening of the period of infant and child dependency in

[13]David Pilbeam and Stephen Jay Gould, "Size and Scaling of Human Evolution," *Science*, December 6, 1974, p. 899.

hominids. Compared with other animals, we spend not only a longer proportion of our life span, but also the longest absolute period, in a dependent state. Prolonged infant dependency has probably been of great significance in human cultural evolution. According to Dobzhansky,

it is this helplessness and prolonged dependence on the ministrations of the parents and other persons that favors . . . the socialization and learning process on which the transmission of culture wholly depends. This may have been an overwhelming advantage of the human growth pattern in the process of evolution.[14]

It used to be thought that the australopithecines had a long period of infant dependency, just like modern humans, but recent research suggests that the early australopithecines followed an ape-like pattern of development, judging by the way their teeth apparently developed. Thus, prolonged maturation may be relatively recent, but just how recent is not yet known.[15]

Although some use of tools for digging, defense, scavenging, or hunting may have influenced the development of bipedalism, full bipedalism may have made possible more efficient toolmaking and consequently more efficient scavenging and hunting. As we shall see, there are archeological signs that early hominids may have been scavenging and/or hunting animals at least as far back as Lower Pleistocene times. We have fairly good evidence that *Homo erectus* was butchering and presumably eating big game after a million years ago. Whether or not the big game were hunted is not yet clear.

But whenever hominids began to hunt regularly, the development of hunting, combined with longer infant and child dependency, may have fostered a division of labor by sex. The demands of nursing might have made it difficult for women to hunt. Certainly, it would have been awkward, if not impossible, for a mother carrying a nursing child to chase animals. Alternatively, if she left the child at home, she would not have been able to travel very far to hunt. Since the men would have been freer to roam farther from home, they probably became the hunters. While the men were away hunting, the women may have gathered wild plants within an area that could be covered in a few hours.

The division of labor by sex may have increased the likelihood of food-sharing. If men primarily hunted and women primarily gathered plant foods, the only way each sex could obtain a complete diet would have been to share the results of their respective labors.

What is the evidence that the physical and cultural changes we have been discussing occurred during the evolution of the hominids? We shall now trace the sequence of known hominid fossils and how they are associated with the development of bipedalism, brain expansion, and reduction of the face, jaws, and teeth. We also trace the sequence of cultural changes in toolmaking, scavenging and hunting, and other aspects of cultural development.

Australopithecines: The Earliest Definite Hominids

Fossil finds from Hadar, in the Afar triangle of Ethiopia, and Laetoli, Tanzania, clearly show that bipedal hominids lived in East Africa between 4 and 3 million years ago. At Laetoli, more than fifty hardened humanlike footprints about 3.6 million years old give striking confirmation that the hominids there were fully bipedal. But their bipedalism does not mean that these earliest definite hominids were completely terrestrial. Studies of the skeletal remains at Hadar suggest that the hominids there spent part of the time in trees, possibly feeding, sleeping, and/or avoiding predators. All of the australopithecines, including the later ones, seem to have been capable of climbing and moving in trees.[16]

The hominids at Hadar and Laetoli are classified by some paleontologists as belonging to the

[14]Theodosius Dobzhansky, *Mankind Evolving: The Evolution of the Human Species* (New Haven: Yale University Press, 1962), p. 196.

[15]Timothy G. Bromage and M. Christopher Dean, "Reevaluation of the Age at Death of Immature Fossil Hominids," *Nature*, 317 (1985), October 10, pp. 525–27; B. Holly Smith, "Dental Development in *Australopithecus* and Early *Homo*," *Nature*, 323 (1986), September 25, pp. 327–30.

[16]Randall L. Susman, Jack T. Stern, Jr., and William L. Jungers, "Locomotor Adaptations in the Hadar Hominids," in Eric Delson, ed., *Ancestors: The Hard Evidence* (New York: Alan R. Liss, 1985), pp. 184–92. See also Rose, "Food Acquisition and the Evolution of Positional Behaviour."

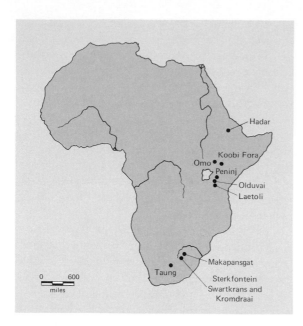

FIGURE 5-2 Location of Major
Australopithecus **and** *Homo* **Sites in East and South Africa**

species ***Australopithecus afarensis.*** Other paleontologists do not think that these hominids should be placed in a separate species, because of their resemblances to the later hominid species ***Australopithecus africanus,*** which lived between about 3 and 2 million years ago. And then there were the robust australopithecines who lived between 2 and 1 million years ago. Some paleontologists classify all the robust specimens, from East as well as South Africa, as ***Australopithecus robustus.*** But most paleontologists think that the East and South African specimens belonged to two different species; the East African species is called ***Australopithecus boisei*** and the South African species is called A. *robustus.* Current thinking, then, divides the genus *Australopithecus* into two, three, or four species.[17]

Our own genus is *Homo.* Which of the australopithecines was ancestral to *Homo?* Here there is considerable controversy, as we shall see. Whatever the ancestry of *Homo,* fossils so classified date from about 2 million years ago.

[17]Niles Eldredge and Ian Tattersall, *The Myths of Human Evolution* (New York: Columbia University Press, 1982), pp. 131–41.

Raymond Dart's Taung Child

In 1925, Raymond Dart, professor of anatomy at the University of Witwatersrand in Johannesburg, South Africa, presented the first evidence that an erect bipedal hominid existed in the Pliocene epoch. As he separated bones from a matrix of material found in Taung, South Africa, Dart realized he was looking at more than the remains of an ape. He described the experience:

On December 23, [1924,] the rock parted. I could view the face from the front, although the right side was still embedded. The creature that had contained this massive brain was no giant anthropoid such as a gorilla. What emerged was a baby's face, an infant with a full set of milk teeth and its permanent molars just in the process of erupting.[18]

By the teeth Dart identified the fossil as the remains of a five- to seven-year-old child (although recent analysis by electron microscope suggests that the child was no more than three and a half[19]). He named the specimen *Australopithecus africanus,* which means "southern ape of Africa." Dart was certain the skull was that of a bipedal animal. He based his conclusion on the fact that the ***foramen magnum,*** the hole in the base of the skull through which the spinal cord passes en route to the brain, faced downward, indicating that the head was carried directly over the spine. (In monkeys and apes, this passageway is near the back of the skull, in a position more appropriate to a less erect head posture.) Furthermore, the Taung child's incisors and canine teeth were short, and therefore definitely more human than apelike.

Dart's conclusion met with widespread skepticism and opposition. Not the least of the problems was that scientists at the time believed hominids had originated in Asia. But there were probably other reasons: Dart had found only one fossil; it was an infant rather than an adult; and no other hominid fossils had yet been found in Africa. Other australopithecines were not found until the 1930s, when Robert Broom recovered some fossils from Sterkfontein in South Africa. Dart's and

[18]Raymond Dart, "*Australopithecus africanus:* The Man-Ape of South Africa," *Nature,* 115 (1925): 195.
[19]Bromage and Dean, "Re-evaluation of the Age at Death of Immature Fossil Hominids," pp. 525–27; Smith, "Dental Development in *Australopithecus* and Early *Homo,*" pp. 327–30.

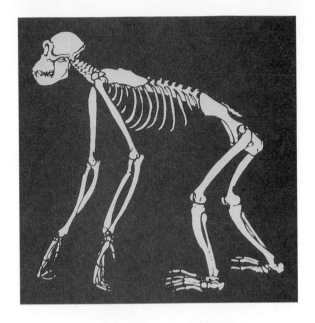

Broom's conclusions did not begin to be accepted until after 1945, when Le Gros Clark, a professor of anatomy at Oxford, supported the hominid status of their finds.[20]

Australopithecus africanus

Since the Taung child's discovery nearly seventy years ago, the remains of hundreds of other australopithecines have been unearthed. From this abundant evidence a fairly complete picture of *A. africanus* can be drawn: "The brain case is rounded with a relatively well-developed forehead. Moderate brow ridges surmount a rather projecting face."[21] The estimated cranial capacity for the various finds from Taung and Sterkfontein is between 428 and 485 cc. In contrast, modern humans have a cranial capacity of between 1000 and 2000 cc.[22] *A. africanus* was quite small: the adults were only about 3.5 to 4.5 feet tall and weighed about 45 to 90 pounds.[23]

A. africanus retained the large chinless jaw of the ape, but some of its dental features were similar to those of modern humans—broad incisors and short canines. Though the premolars and molars were larger than in modern humans, their form was quite similar. Presumably, function and use were also similar.

The broad, bowl-shaped pelvis, which is very similar to the human pelvis in form and in areas for muscle attachments, provides additional evidence for bipedalism. In both *A. africanus* and modern humans, the pelvis curves back, carrying the spine and trunk erect. In contrast, the ape's pelvis does not curve back; the spine and trunk are carried foward.

The shape of the curve of the australopithecine spine also suggests that these hominids walked erect. The bottom part of the vertebral column forms a curve, causing the spinal column to be S-shaped (seen from the side). This **lumbar curve** and the S-shaped spinal column are found only in hominids. Analysis of hip-joint and femoral-bone fossils also indicates that the australopithecines

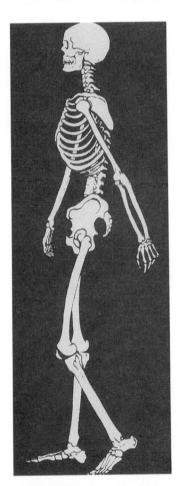

Chimpanzee and human skeletons. The chimpanzee's pelvis does not curve back (as it does in humans), but carries the spine and trunk forward.

[20]Eldredge and Tattersall, *The Myths of Human Evolution*, pp. 80–90.
[21]Pilbeam, *The Ascent of Man*, p. 107.
[22]Ralph Holloway, "The Casts of Fossil Hominid Brains," *Scientific American*, July 1974, pp. 106–15.
[23]Frederick S. Szalay and Eric Delson, *Evolutionary History of the Primates* (New York: Academic Press, 1979), p. 504.

walked fully upright, and that at least the later ones walked with the same direct, striding gait observed in modern humans.[24]

Australopithecus afarensis

Do the finds of Hadar and Laetoli, dated between 4 and 3 million years ago, represent a species of *Australopithecus* different from *A. africanus*? Some paleontologists think yes; they classify the Hadar and Laetoli hominids as *Australopithecus afarensis*. Other paleontologists think that the finds labeled *afarensis* by some are not different enough from *africanus* to merit a separate species designation. The paleontologists who think that *A. afarensis* was a separate species go not only by its apparent earlier dating; they also think that the finds they designate as *afarensis* are different in some anatomical features.

The candidates for *A. afarensis* status come from two separate excavations.[25] Remains from at least fourteen hominids were unearthed at Laetoli, Tanzania. Although the remains there consisted largely of teeth and jaws, there is no question that the Laetoli hominids are bipedal, since it was at the Laetoli site that the now famous trail of footprints was found. Two hominids walking erect and side by side left their tracks in the ground 3.6 million years ago! The remains of at least thirty-five individuals have been found at Hadar, Ethiopia. The Hadar finds are quite remarkable for their completeness. Whereas paleontologists often find just parts of the cranium and jaws, many parts of the rest of the skeleton were also found at Hadar. For example, paleontologists found 40 percent of the skeleton of a female hominid they named Lucy after the Beatles' song "Lucy in the Sky with Diamonds."[26] An analysis of Lucy's pelvis indicates clearly that she was a bipedal walker;[27] but she probably also climbed a lot in the trees, judging

Mary Leakey's expedition discovered these two sets of fossilized footprints from 3.6 million years ago. The adults who left them were clearly upright walkers.

by her leg bones and joints which are not as large proportionately as in modern humans.[28]

Dating of the hominid remains at Laetoli suggests that the hominids there lived between 3.8 and 3.6 million years ago.[29] Although Lucy and

[24]C. Owen Lovejoy, Kingsbury Heiple, and Albert Bernstein, "The Gait of *Australopithecus*," *American Journal of Physical Anthropology*, 38 (1973): 757–79.

[25]Donald C. Johanson and Tim D. White, "A Systematic Assessment of Early African Hominids," *Science*, January 26, 1979, pp. 321–30; and Tim D. White, "Les Australopithèques," *La Recherche*, November 1982, pp. 1258–70.

[26]Donald C. Johanson and Maitland Edey, *Lucy: The Beginnings of Humankind* (New York: Simon & Schuster, 1981), pp. 17–18.

[27]C. Owen Lovejoy, "Evolution of Human Walking," *Scientific American*, November 1988, pp. 118–25.

[28]William L. Jungers, "Relative Joint Size and Hominoid Locomotor Adaptations with Implications for the Evolution of Hominid Bipedalism," *Journal of Human Evolution*, 17 (1988): 247–65.

[29]Johanson and White, "A Systematic Assessment of Early African Hominids," p. 321.

the other hominids at Hadar were once thought to be about as old as those at Laetoli, recent dating suggests that they are somewhat younger—less than 3.2 million years old. Lucy probably lived 2.9 million years ago.[30]

Those paleontologists, such as Donald Johanson and Tim White, who believe the Laetoli and Hadar hominids should be given the separate species name A. *afarensis* base their decision primarily on some features of the skull, teeth, and jaws that they believe are more apelike than those of the later hominids previously classified as A. *africanus*. For example, the incisors and canines of the Laetoli and Hadar hominids are rather large, their tooth rows converge slightly at the back of the jaw, and the palate (roof of the mouth) is flat and narrow. The A. *afarensis* skull tends also to have a crest at the lower back.[31]

In some other respects, the Laetoli and Hadar fossils resemble A. *africanus*. Like A. *africanus*, individuals are quite small. Lucy, for example, was about 3.5 feet tall, and the largest individuals at these sites, presumably males, were about 5 feet tall.[32] The brains of the Laetoli and Hadar hominids also tend to be small: cranial capacity is estimated at 415 cc, just slightly less than that of A. *africanus*.[33]

Australopithecus robustus and boisei

Paleontologists may disagree about whether A. *afarensis* is separate from A. *africanus*. But there is little disagreement that at least one other australopithecine species—*Australopithecus robustus*, existed between about 2 and 1 million years ago. "Robust" australopithecines were found first in South Africa, and later in East Africa. As we noted above, the East and South African "robust" australopithecines are sometimes classified together as A. *robustus*; however, the later "robust" East African finds are often classified separately as *Australopithecus boisei*. In contrast to A. *africanus*, the

A reconstruction of what *Australopithecus africanus* might have looked like.

"robust" australopithecines in general had larger molars and premolars but smaller incisors and canines, more massive muscle attachments for chewing, and well-developed cranial crests and ridges.[34] In addition, the "robust" australopithecines are estimated to have cranial capacities of about 530 cc., which is somewhat greater than in A. *africanus*.[35]

It used to be thought that the "robust" australopithecines were substantially bigger than the other australopithecines (hence the use of the word "robust" in the name). But recent calculations suggest that these australopithecines were not substantially different in body weight or height as compared with the other australopithecines. The robustness is primarily in the skull and jaw, most strikingly in the teeth. The back teeth are more than two times larger than expected in hominids their size.[36]

In 1954, John T. Robinson proposed that A. *africanus* and A. *robustus* had different dietary adaptations, *africanus* being an omnivore (dependent on meat and plants) and *robustus* a vegetarian.

[30]Roger Lewin, "Fossil Lucy Grows Younger, Again," *Science*, January 7, 1983, pp. 43–44.

[31]Tim D. White, Donald C. Johanson, and William H. Kimbel, "*Australopithecus africanus*: Its Phyletic Position Reconsidered," *South African Journal of Science*, 77 (1981): 445–70; and Johanson and White, "A Systematic Assessment of Early African Hominids."

[32]Bernard G. Campbell, *Humankind Emerging*, 4th ed. (Boston: Little, Brown, 1985), p. 202.

[33]McHenry, "The Pattern of Human Evolution," p. 161.

[34]Szalay and Delson, *Evolutionary History of the Primates*, p. 504.

[35] Ralph L. Holloway, "'Robust' Australopithecine Brain Endocasts: Some Preliminary Observations," in Frederick E. Grine, ed., *Evolutionary History of the "Robust" Australopithecines* (New York: Aldine de Gruyter, 1988), pp. 97–105.

[36]Henry M. McHenry, "New Estimates of Body Weight in Early Hominids and Their Significance to Encephalization and Megadontia in 'Robust' Australopithecines," in Grine, ed., *Evolutionary History of the "Robust" Australopithecines*, pp. 133–48; William L. Jungers, "New Estimates of Body Size in Australopithecines," in ibid., pp. 115–25.

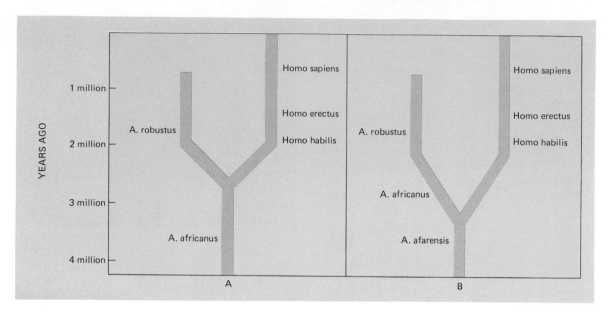

FIGURE 5-3 The Two Current Models of Human Evolution

(Adapted from Tim D. White, "Les Australopithèques, La Recherche, November 1982, p. 1266.)

Robinson's view was hotly debated for many years, but recent evidence tends to support it. Comparisons of microscopic tooth wear on *africanus* and *robustus* teeth as well as on living primates suggest that the patterns on the teeth of *robustus* specimens are consistent with chewing mostly on hard objects such as seeds. In contrast, the wear on the teeth of *africanus* tends to be similar to the wear in primates whose diets consist primarily of soft fruits and leaves.[37]

Was *A. robustus* adapted then to a drier, more open environment than *A. africanus*? This is a possibility, but the evidence is somewhat controversial. At any rate, most paleontologists think that *robustus* died out shortly after 900,000 years ago[38] and therefore could not be ancestral to our own genus, *Homo*.[39]

Two Current Models of Human Evolution

Currently, there are a number of models of human evolution. We show two models in Figure 5–3 to illustrate the agreements and disagreements among paleontologists. Those paleontologists who classify the Hadar and Laetoli hominids as a separate australopithecine species (*A. afarensis*) propose the model of human evolution shown in part B of Figure 5–3. They think that it was *A. afarensis*, not *A. africanus*, that was ancestral to the *Homo* line. Paleontologists who think that the Hadar and Laetoli hominids should be classified as *A. africanus* think that *africanus* was ancestral to the *Homo* line (see part A of Figure 5–3). The main points of disagreement, then, concern when the *Homo* line first diverged and which species of *Australopithecus* was ancestral to that line. Some paleontologists say that it is not yet possible to decide whether *A. afarensis* and/or *A. africanus* was ancestral.[40] There is considerable agreement among paleontologists about other aspects of early hominid evolution: (1) there were at least two separate

[37]Richard F. Kay and Frederick E. Grine, "Tooth Morphology, Wear and Diet in *Australopithecus* and *Paranthropus* from Southern Africa, in Grine, ed., *Evolutionary History of the "Robust" Australopithecines*, pp. 427–47.

[38]Frederick E. Grine, "Evolutionary History of the 'Robust' Australopithecines: A Summary and Historical Perspective," in Grine, ed., *Evolutionary History of the "Robust" Australopithecines*, pp. 515–16.

[39]C. Stringer, "Evolution of a Species," *Geographical Magazine*, 57 (1985): 601–7.

[40]Trinkaus, "Bodies, Brawn, Brains and Noses," p. 110.

hominid lines between 3 and 1 million years ago; (2) the robust australopithecines were not ancestral to modern humans but became extinct after a million years ago; and (3) *Homo habilis* (and successive *Homo* species) were in the direct ancestral line to modern humans.

Early Species of *Homo*

Hominids with a brain absolutely and relatively larger than that of the australopithecines appear about 2 million years ago. These hominids, classified in our own genus, *Homo*, are generally called **Homo habilis** after the fossils found in East Africa and named by Louis Leakey, Phillip Tobias, and John Napier. (As we will see, less than half a million years later a larger-brained species, *Homo erectus*, appears in East Africa.) Apparently, the robust australopithecines were contemporaneous with both *Homo habilis* and *Homo erectus* in East Africa[41] (see Figure 5–4). Compared with the australopithecines, *Homo habilis* was slightly larger and had a significantly larger brain (ranging from 600 to 800 cc) and more rounded brain case.[42]

Stone tools found at a number of sites in East Africa are at least 2 million years old.[43] Some anthropologists surmise that *Homo habilis*, rather than the australopithecines, made those tools. After all, *H. habilis* had the greater brain capacity. But the fact of the matter is that none of the earliest stone tools have been found to be directly associated with fossils, and so it is impossible as yet to know who made them. We turn now to those tools and what archeologists guess about the life-styles of their makers, the hominids (whoever they were) who lived between about 2 and 1.5 million years ago.

[41]Noel T. Boaz, "Hominid Evolution in Eastern Africa during the Pliocene and Early Pleistocene," *Annual Review of Anthropology*, 8 (1979): 73, 78.

[42]Ibid., p. 77; and N. T. Boaz, "Morphological Trends and Phylogenetic Relationships from Middle Miocene Hominoids to Late Pliocene Hominids," in Ciochon and Corruccini, eds., *New Interpretations of Ape and Human Ancestry*, pp. 714–15.

[43]Glynn Ll. Isaac, "The Archaeology of Human Origins: Studies of the Lower Pleistocene in East Africa, 1971–1981," in Fred Wendorf and Angela E. Close, eds., *Advances in World Archaeology* (Orlando, FL: Academic Press, 1984), 3: 7–8.

Early Hominid Cultures

Tool Traditions

Regularly patterned tools are considered by some to be archeological signs of culture because *culture* is conventionally defined as learned and shared patterns of behavior, thought, and feeling. Therefore, tools made according to a standard pattern and found in different places presuppose some culture. The earliest patterned stone tools found so far come from Hadar, Ethiopia, and may be 2.4 million years old.[44] More securely dated stone tools have been found in Omo, Ethiopia, from about 2 million years ago.[45] These early tools were apparently made by striking a stone with another stone, a technique known as **percussion flaking.** Both the sharp-edged flakes and the sharp-edged cores (the pieces of stone left after flakes are removed) were used as tools. If the stone has facets removed from only one side of the cutting edge, we call it a **unifacial tool.** If the stone has facets removed from both sides, we call it a **bifacial tool.**

What were these tools used for? What do they tell us about early hominid culture? Unfortunately, little can be inferred about life-styles from the earliest tool sites because little else is found with the tools. In contrast, finds of later tool assemblages at Olduvai Gorge in Tanzania have yielded a rich harvest of cultural information.

The Olduvai site was uncovered accidentally in 1911 when a German entomologist chasing a butterfly followed it into the gorge and found a number of fossil remains. Beginning in the 1930s, Louis and Mary Leakey patiently searched the gorge for clues to the evolution of early humans. Of the Olduvai site, Louis Leakey wrote,

[It] is a fossil hunter's dream, for it shears 300 feet through stratum after stratum of earth's history as through a gigantic layer cake. Here, within reach, lie countless fossils and artifacts which but for the faulting and erosion would have remained sealed under thick layers of consolidated rock.[46]

[44]Roger Lewin, "Ethiopian Stone Tools Are World's Oldest," *Science*, February 20, 1981, pp. 806–7.

[45]Isaac, "The Archaeology of Human Origins," pp. 7–8.

[46]L. S. B. Leakey, "Finding the World's Earliest Man," *National Geographic*, September 1960, p. 424.

The oldest cultural materials from Olduvai (Bed I) date from Lower Pleistocene times. The stone *artifacts* (things made by humans) include bifacial and unifacial core tools and sharp-edged flakes. Flake tools predominate. The kind of tool assemblage found in Bed I and to some extent in later (higher) layers is referred to as **Oldowan** (see Figure 5–4).[47]

Life-Styles

Archeologists have speculated about the possible life-styles of early hominids from Olduvai and other sites. Some of these speculations come from analysis of what can be done with the tools, microscopic analysis of wear on the tools, and examination of the marks the tools make on bones; other speculations are based on what is found with the tools.

Nicholas Toth and Peter Jones have experimented with what can be done with Oldowan tools. The flakes appear to be very versatile: they can be used for slitting the hides of animals, dismembering animals, and whittling wood into sharp-pointed sticks (wooden spears or digging sticks). The larger stone tools (choppers and scrapers) can be used to hack off branches or perform rough butchery.[48] None of the early flaked stone

[47]J. Desmond Clark, *The Prehistory of Africa* (New York: Praeger, 1970), p. 68.

[48]Reported in Isaac, "The Archaeology of Human Origins," pp. 11–13.

FIGURE 5-4 Oldowan Tools from Bed I, Olduvai Gorge

Numbers 1, 2, minimally chipped flakes; 3, modified chunks with utilized notches; 4, 5, bifacially worked choppers; 6, flake scrapers; 7, proto-hand axes; 8, unifacial choppers. *(From* The Prehistory of Africa *by J. Desmond Clark. Copyright © 1970 in London, England, by J. Desmond Clark. Reprinted by Praeger Publishers, New York.)*

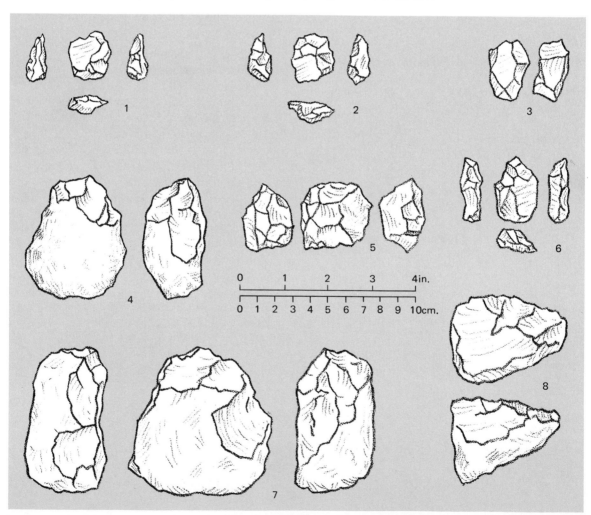

tools can plausibly be thought of as a weapon. So, if the toolmaking hominids were hunting or defending themselves with weapons, they had to have used wooden spears, clubs, or unmodified stones as missiles. Later Oldowan tool assemblages also include stones that were flaked and battered into a rounded shape. The unmodified stones and the shaped stones might have been lethal projectiles.[49]

Experiments may tell us what can be done with tools, but of course they do not tell us what was actually done with them. Other techniques, such as microscopic analysis of the wear on tools, are more informative. Lawrence Keeley has analyzed the kind of "polish" that develops on tools with different uses, and has shown that at least some of the early tools were used for cutting meat, cutting or whittling wood, and cutting plant stems.[50]

There seems to be no question that some hominids shortly after 2 million years ago were cutting up animal carcasses for meat. But were they scavenging meat (taking meat from carcasses that other animals had killed)? Or were they themselves hunting and killing the animals? Based on her analysis of cut marks on bone from Bed I in Olduvai Gorge, Pat Shipman suggests that scavenging, not hunting, was the major meat-getting activity of the hominids living there between 2 and 1.7 million years ago. For example, cut marks made by stone tools usually (but not always) overlie teeth marks made by carnivores, which suggests that the hominids were often procuring the meat of animals killed and partially eaten by predators. However, the fact that the cut marks were sometimes made first suggests to Shipman that the hominids were also sometimes the hunters.[51] On the other hand, prior cut marks may indicate only that the hominids scavenged before carnivores had a chance to!

The artifact and animal remains from Bed I and the lower part of Bed II at Olduvai suggest a few other things about the life-styles of the hominids there. First, it seems that the hominids moved around during the year; most of the sites in what is now the Olduvai Gorge appear to have been used only in the dry season, judging from an analysis of the kinds of animal bones found there.[52] Second, whether or not the early Olduvai hominids were hunters or more likely scavengers, they apparently exploited a wide range of animals. Although most of the bones are from medium-sized antelopes and wild pigs, even large animals such as elephants and giraffes seem to have been eaten.[53] It is clear then that the Olduvai hominids scavenged and/or hunted for meat, but we cannot tell yet how important meat-eating was in their diet.

There is also no consensus yet about how to characterize the Olduvai sites. In the 1970s, there was a tendency to think of these sites (which contain tools and animal bones) as home bases to which hominids (presumably male) brought meat to share with others (perhaps mostly nursing mothers and young children). In short, the scenario involved a home base, a division of labor by sex, and food sharing. But archeologists now are not so sure; the sites might just have been places where hominids ate, not stayed. (After all, we don't live in restaurants!) But the fact that mostly limb bones from food animals are found together with tools at the sites suggests that the hominids deliberately brought scavenged or hunted meat to these places.[54] So the evidence from Olduvai does not necessarily indicate a scenario of home base, division of labor by sex, and food sharing; on the other hand, it does not rule out such a scenario.

Homo erectus

Until the mid 1970s, the available fossil finds in Java and China suggested that **Homo erectus** was not more than about 700,000 years old. But in 1975 near Lake Rudolf in Kenya, Richard Leakey's team found a *Homo erectus* cranium that was 1.6 to 1.3 million years old. Thus, the evidence now suggests that *Homo erectus* may have emerged

---

[49]Ibid., p. 13.
[50]Reported in ibid.
[51]Pat Shipman, "Scavenging or Hunting in Early Hominids," 27–43. For the idea that scavenging may have been an important food-getting strategy even for proto-hominids, see Frederick S. Szalay, "Hunting-Scavenging Protohominids: A Model for Hominid Origins," Man, 10 (1975): 420–29.

[52]John D. Speth and Dave D. Davis, "Seasonal Variability in Early Hominid Predation," Science, April 30, 1976, pp. 441–45.
[53]Glynn Isaac, "The Diet of Early Man: Aspects of Archaeological Evidence from Lower and Middle Pleistocene Sites in Africa," World Archaeology, 2 (1971): 289.
[54]Isaac, "The Archaeology of Human Origins," pp. 31–32, 61–68.

Reconstruction of the skull and head of *Homo erectus,* Java type.

in East Africa, rather than in Asia as previously thought.[55]

The Discovery in Java and Later Finds

In 1891, Eugene Dubois, a Dutch anatomist digging in Java, found what he called **Pithecanthropus erectus,** meaning "erect ape man." (We now refer to this hominid as *Homo erectus.*) The discovery was not the first humanlike fossil found—Neandertals, which we discuss in the next chapter, were known many years earlier. But no one was certain, not even Dubois himself, whether the fossil he found in Java was an ape or a human.

[55]R. E. F. Leakey, "An Overview of the East Rudolf Hominidae," in Yves Coppens, F. Clark Howell, Glynn Ll. Isaac, and Richard E. F. Leakey, eds., *Earliest Man and Environments in the Lake Rudolf Basin* (Chicago: University of Chicago Press, 1976), pp. 476–83; and G. H. Curtis, R. Drake, T. E. Cerling, and J. Hampel, "Age of the KBS Tuff in the Koobi Fora Formation, East Rudolf, Kenya," *Nature,* 258 (1975): 395–98.

The actual find consisted of a cranium and a thighbone. For many years it was thought that the fragments were not even from the same animal. The skull was too large to be that of a modern ape but was smaller than that of an average human, having a cranial capacity between the average ape's 500 cc and the average modern human's 1300+ cc. The thighbone, however, matched that of a modern human. Did the two fragments in fact belong together? The question was resolved many years later by fluorine analysis. As we saw in Chapter 4, the amount of fluorine that accumulates in bones increases the longer the bones lie in the earth. If fossils from the same deposit contain the same amount of fluorine, they are the same age; if they contain different amounts, fluorine analysis can establish their relative ages. The skull fragment and thighbone found by Dubois were tested for fluorine content and found to be the same age.

A discovery by G. H. R. von Koenigswald in the mid 1930s, also in Java, not only confirmed Dubois's earlier speculations and extended our knowledge of *Homo erectus*'s physical characteristics, but also gave us a better understanding of this early human's place in time. Since then many more *H. erectus* fossils have been found in Java. Although the absolute dating is problematic, the Java finds are thought to be not more than 1 million years old.[56]

Between the times of Dubois's and von Koenigswald's discoveries, Davidson Black, a Canadian anatomy professor teaching in Peking (now Beijing), China, set out to investigate a large cave at nearby Zhoukoudian where a fossilized tooth had been found. Confident that the tooth came from a hitherto unknown hominid genus, he obtained funds to excavate the area extensively. After two years of excavation, he and his colleagues found a skull in limestone whose owner was dubbed **Peking man.** Black died in 1934, and his work was carried on by Franz Weidenreich. The original finds at Zhoukoudian were lost during the Japanese invasion of China in December 1941. Fortunately, Weidenreich had sent casts of the fossils to the United States.

We now know from a large number of finds that *Homo erectus* was the first hominid species to be widely distributed in the Old World. The first finds date from about 1.6 million years ago in East Africa, later ones from about 1 million years ago in Asia. *Homo erectus* may also have spread to Europe. However, some anthropologists think that the finds in Europe thought to be *Homo erectus* are actually early examples of *Homo sapiens*, just like some of the finds in southern Africa and the Near East that were also previously thought to be *Homo erectus*.[57]

Physical Characteristics of *Homo erectus*

The *Homo erectus* skull generally was long, low, and thickly walled, with a flat frontal area and prominent brow ridges. Compared to the aus-

tralopithecines, *Homo erectus* had relatively small teeth. The brain was larger than that found in any of the australopithecines but smaller than the average brain of a modern human.[58] *Homo erectus* had a prominent, projecting nose, in contrast to the australopithecines' flat, nonprojecting noses.[59] From the neck down, *Homo erectus* was practically indistinguishable from *Homo sapiens*. The size of the long bones indicates that a *Homo erectus* male was about 5.5 to 6 feet tall.

The remains from Peking are perhaps 500,000 years more recent than the remains from Java. Some researchers think that *H. erectus* evolved over time in ways that are consistent with the general trends in hominid evolution. For example, the Peking specimens had higher and less sloping foreheads, and their cranial capacity was about 1054 cc, compared with the 900 cc average for the Java specimens.[60] *Homo erectus* from Peking also had a shorter, rounder palate than the Java forms. Thus, the Peking *erectus* face resembled more closely the modern human face (but the jaw did not have a chin); and the teeth in the Peking jaw were smaller than those of the australopithecines and the Java *erectus* specimens.[61]

Homo erectus Cultures

The archeological finds of tools and other cultural artifacts dating from 1.6 million years ago to about 300,000 to 100,000 years ago are assumed to have been produced by *Homo erectus*. But we do not usually have fossils associated with these materials. Therefore it is possible that some of the tools during this period were produced by hominids other than *Homo erectus*, such as australopithecines earlier and *Homo sapiens* later. Since the so-called Acheulian tool assemblages dating from 1.5 million years ago to more than a million years later are very similar to each other, and since *Homo*

---

[56]G. Philip Rightmire, *The Evolution of* Homo Erectus: *Comparative Anatomical Studies of an Extinct Human Species* (Cambridge: Cambridge University Press, 1990), pp. 12–14.

[57]Milford H. Wolpoff and Abel Nkini, "Early and Early Middle Pleistocene Hominids from Asia and Africa," in Delson, ed., *Ancestors*, pp. 202–5. See also G. P. Rightmire, "The Tempo of Change in the Evolution of Mid-Pleistocene *Homo*," in Delson, ed., *Ancestors*, pp. 255–64.

[58]Ian Tattersall, *Man's Ancestors* (London: John Murray, 1970), pp. 51–54.

[59]Robert G. Franciscus and Erik Trinkaus, "Nasal Morphology and the Emergence of *Homo erectus*," *American Journal of Physical Anthropology*, 75 (1988): 517–27.

[60]Wu Rukang and Lin Shenglong, "Peking Man," *Scientific American*, June 1983, p. 90.

[61]Perhaps the best evidence is for the change in brainsize, but Rightmire, *The Evolution of* Homo Erectus, pp. 191–201, does not find the other differences statistically significant.

A collection of Acheulian handaxes and cleavers found in Olduvai Gorge, Tanzania, that are about 100,000 years old.

erectus is the only hominid that spans the entire period, it is conventionally assumed that erectus was responsible for most if not all of the Acheulian tool assemblages we describe below.[62]

The Acheulian Tool Tradition

A stone toolmaking tradition known as the **Acheulian,** after the site at St. Acheul, France, where the first examples were found, is generally associated with Homo erectus. This tradition appears first in East Africa about 1.5 million years ago,[63] and it persists in later times when Homo sapiens was on the scene. Acheulian stone-tool assemblages have a wide variety of small and large tools, including small flakes (which may have been used for butchering) and large bifacial implements such as the so-called hand axes (which may have been used for digging or pounding). The predominance of hand axes and other bifacial tools particularly characterizes the Acheulian tradition.[64]

Big-Game Eating

Some of the Acheulian sites have produced evidence of big-game eating. F. Clark Howell, who excavated the sites at Torralba and Ambrona, Spain, found a substantial number of elephant remains and unmistakable evidence of human presence in the form of tools. Howell suggests that

Homo erectus at those sites used fire to frighten elephants into muddy bogs, from which they would be unable to escape.[65] To hunt elephants in this way, these hominids would have had to plan and work cooperatively in fairly large groups.

But do these finds of bones of large and medium-size animals, in association with tools, tell us that Homo erectus definitely was a big-game hunter? Some archeologists who have reanalyzed the evidence from Torralba think that the big game may have been scavenged. Because the Torralba and Ambrona sites are near ancient streams, many of the elephants could have died naturally—their bones accumulating in certain spots because of the flow of water.[66] Thus, whether Homo erectus hunted big game at Torralba and Ambrona is debatable; all we can be sure of, as of now, is that the people there seem to have consumed big game and probably hunted smaller game.

Control of Fire

Since Homo erectus was the first hominid to be found throughout the Old World and in areas with freezing winters, most anthropologists presume that H. erectus had learned to control fire, at least for warmth. There is archeological evidence of fire in some early sites, but fires can be natural events. Thus, whether fire was under deliberate control by H. erectus is much more difficult to establish.

Suggestive but not conclusive evidence of the deliberate use of fire comes from Kenya in East Africa and is over 1.4 million years old.[67] More persuasive, but still not definite, evidence of human control of fire, dating from nearly 500,000 years ago, comes from the cave at Zhoukoudian in China where H. erectus fossils have been found.[68] In that cave are thousands of splintered and charred animal bones, apparently the remains of

[62]David W. Phillipson, African Archaeology (Cambridge: Cambridge University Press, 1985), p. 55.

[63]Phillipson, African Archaeology, p. 32.

[64]Richard G. Klein, The Human Career: Human Biological and Cultural Origins (Chicago: University of Chicago Press, 1989), p. 210.

[65]F. Clark Howell, "Observations on the Earlier Phases of the European Lower Paleolithic," in Recent Studies in Paleoanthropology. American Anthropologist, special publication, April 1966, pp. 111–40.

[66]Richard G. Klein, "Reconstructing How Early People Exploited Animals: Problems and Prospects," in Nitecki and Nitecki, eds., The Evolution of Human Hunting, pp. 11–45; and Lewis R. Binford, "Were There Elephant Hunters at Torralba?" in ibid., pp. 47–105.

[67]Isaac, "The Archaeology of Human Origins," pp. 35–36.

[68]Klein, The Human Career, p. 171.

meals. There are also layers of ash, suggesting human control of fire.

But recent analysis raises questions about these finds. The most serious problem is that human remains, tools, and ash rarely occur together in the same layers. In addition, there are no hearths at the site. Fires can spontaneously occur with heavy accumulation of organic matter, so clear evidence of human control of fire is not definitely attested. Even the inference that humans brought the animals to the cave for butchering is just possibly a correct guess. Throughout the cave there is evidence of hyenas and wolves and they, not the humans, may have brought many of the animal parts to the cave.[69]

Better evidence of the deliberate use of fire comes from Europe somewhat later. Unfortunately, the evidence of control of fire at these European sites is not associated with *H. erectus* fossils, so the link between deliberate use of fire and *H. erectus* cannot be definitely established yet. The lack of clear evidence does not of course mean that *H. erectus* did not use fire. After all, *H. erectus* did move into cold areas of the world, and it is hard to imagine how that could have happened without the deliberate use of fire.

Fire would be important not only for warmth; cooking would also be possible. The control of fire was a major step in increasing the energy under human control. Cooking made all kinds of possible food (not just meat) more safely digestible and therefore more usable. Fires would also have kept predators away, a not inconsiderable advantage given that there were a lot of them around.

Campsites

Acheulian sites were usually located close to water sources, lush vegetation, and large stocks of herbivorous animals. Some camps have been found in caves, but most were in open areas surrounded by rudimentary fortifications or windbreaks. Several African sites are marked by stony rubble brought there by *Homo erectus*, possibly for the dual purpose of securing the windbreaks and providing ammunition in case of a sudden attack.[70]

The presumed base campsites display a wide variety of tools, indicating that the camp was the center of many group functions. More specialized sites away from camp have also been found. These are marked by the predominance of a particular type of tool. For example, a butchering site in Tanzania contained dismembered hippopotamus carcasses and rare heavy-duty smashing and cutting tools. Workshops are another kind of specialized site encountered with some regularity. They are characterized by tool debris and are located close to a source of natural stone suitable for toolmaking.[71]

A camp has been excavated at the Terra Amata site near Nice, on the French Riviera, which is presumed to be a *Homo erectus* site. (But since we do not have any associated human bones, archeologists cannot be sure that *H. erectus*, rather than early forms of *H. sapiens*, occupied the site.) The camp appears to have been occupied in the late spring or early summer. (The season is indicated by analysis of pollen found in fossilized human feces.) The excavator describes stake holes driven into the sand, paralleled by lines of stones, presumably marking the spots where the people constructed huts of roughly thirty by fifteen feet (Figure 5–5). A basic feature of each hut was a central hearth that seems to have been protected from drafts by a small wall built just outside the northeast corner of the hearth. The evidence suggests that the Terra Amata occupants gathered seafood such as oysters and mussels, did some fishing, and hunted in the surrounding area. Judging from the animal remains, they obtained both small and large animals but mostly got the young of larger animals such as stags, elephants, boars, rhinoceroses, and wild oxen. Some of the huts contain recognizable toolmakers' areas, scattered with tool debris; occasionally, the impression of an animal skin shows where the toolmaker actually sat.[72]

The cultures of early hominids are traditionally classified as Lower Paleolithic or early Stone Age. In the next chapter, we discuss the emergence of *Homo sapiens* and cultural developments in the Middle and Upper Paleolithic periods.

[69]Lewis R. Binford and Chuan Kun Ho, "Taphonomy at a Distance: Zhoukoudian, 'The Cave Home of Beijing Man'?" *Current Anthropology*, 26 (1985): 413–42.

[70]J. Desmond Clark, *The Prehistory of Africa*, pp. 94–95.

[71]Ibid., pp. 96–97.

[72]Henry de Lumley, "A Paleolithic Camp at Nice," *Scientific American*, May 1969, pp. 42–50.

FIGURE 5–5 A Reconstruction of the Oval Huts Built at Terra Amata

These huts were approximately thirty by fifteen feet. *(From "A Paleolithic Camp at Nice" by Henry de Lumley. Copyright © 1969 by Scientific American, Inc. All rights reserved.)*

SUMMARY

1. The drying trend in climate that began about 16 to 11 million years ago diminished the African rain forests and gave rise to grasslands. This change reduced the habitats for tree dwellers and created selective pressures for terrestrial adaptation—pressures that favored bipedalism.

2. One of the crucial changes in early hominid evolution was the development of bipedalism. There are several theories for this development: it may have increased the emerging hominid's ability to see predators and potential prey while moving through the tall grasses of the savanna; by freeing the hands for carrying, it may have facilitated transferring food from one place to another; and finally, tool use, which requires free hands, may have favored two-legged walking.

3. Other important physical changes—including the expansion of the brain, modification of the

female pelvis to allow bigger-brained babies to be born, and reduction of the face, teeth, and jaws—did not begin until about 2 million years after the emergence of bipedalism. By that time (about 2 million years ago) hominids had come to depend to some extent on scavenging and possibly hunting meat.

4. Undisputed hominids dating back to between 4 and 3 million years ago have been found in East Africa. These definitely bipedal hominids are now generally classified in the genus *Australopithecus*. Some East African hominids nearly 2 million years old are classified as *Homo habilis*, an early species of our own genus, *Homo*.

5. The earliest patterned stone tools date back 2.5 to 2 million years. We do not yet know who made them. These tools were made by striking a stone with another stone to remove sharp-edged flakes. Both the flakes and the sharp-edged cores were used as tools. This early tool tradition is named Oldowan.

6. *Homo erectus,* with a larger brain capacity than *Homo habilis,* emerged about 1.6–1.3 million years ago. The earliest *erectus* finds are from East Africa. *H. erectus* specimens date back about 1 million years in Asia. The tools and other cultural artifacts from about 1.5 million to about 300,000 years ago were probably produced by *Homo erectus;*

Acheulian is the name given to the tool tradition of this period. Acheulian tools include both small flake tools and large tools, but hand axes and other bifacial tools are characteristic. Although it is presumed that *H. erectus* had learned to use fire to survive in areas with cold winters, there is no definite evidence of the control of fire by *H. erectus.* There is evidence in some sites of big-game eating—but whether or not *H. erectus* hunted those animals has been debated.

SUGGESTED READING

GRINE, F. G., ed. *Evolutionary History of the "Robust" Australopithecines.* New York: Aldine de Gruyter, 1988. A great deal of controversy has surrounded the "robust" australopithecines. In a 1987 workshop, participants from many different fields were asked to summarize recent knowledge of this group of australopithecines.

ISAAC, G. L. "The Archaeology of Human Origins: Studies of the Lower Pleistocene in East Africa, 1971–1981." In F. Wendorf and A. E. Close, eds., *Advances in World Archaeology.* Orlando, FL: Academic Press, 1984, 3: 1–87. A thoughtful review of what we know, suspect, and do not know about hominid life 2 million years ago.

JOHANSON, D., AND EDEY, M. *Lucy: The Beginnings of Humankind.* New York: Simon & Schuster, 1981. A popular and personal book about the history of recent paleontological research on early hominid evolution in East Africa.

LEAKEY, R. E. *The Making of Mankind.* New York: Dutton, 1981. A popular book, beautifully illustrated, describing human evolution, both biological and cultural. Chapters 1–5 and 7–8 are particularly relevant to this chapter.

PHILLIPSON, D. W. *African Archaeology.* Cambridge: Cambridge University Press, 1985. A summary and interpretation of the archeological evidence in Africa and what it tells us about human history from its beginnings to historic times. Chapters 2 and 3 are particularly relevant to this chapter.

RIGHTMIRE, G. P. *The Evolution of* Homo Erectus: *Comparative Anatomical Studies of an Extinct Human Species.* Cambridge: Cambridge University Press, 1990. A review of the anatomical features of *H. erectus* and how they changed over time.

6

The Emergence
of Homo sapiens
and Their Cultures

Humans who looked very much like people living now appeared at least 50,000 years ago and probably earlier. How do we know that they looked like modern people? Obviously only by skeletal remains. One paleontologist, Chris Stringer, characterizes the modern human as having "a domed skull, a chin, small eyebrows [brow ridges] and a rather puny skeleton."[1] Some of us might not like to be called "puny," but most modern humans are definitely puny compared with *Homo erectus* (and even with earlier forms of our own species, *Homo sapiens*). In this chapter we discuss the fossil evidence for the transition from *Homo erectus* to modern humans, which may have begun 500,000 years ago. We also discuss what we know archeologically about the cultures of *Homo sapiens* who lived from about 150,000 to between 14,000 and 10,000 years ago.

The Transition from *Homo erectus* to *Homo sapiens*

Most anthropologists agree that *Homo erectus* evolved into *Homo sapiens*. But there is disagreement about how and where the transition occurred. There is also disagreement about how to classify some fossils from 500,000 to about 200,000 years ago that have a mixture of *Homo erectus* and *Homo sapiens* traits.[2] A particular fossil might be called *Homo erectus* by some anthropologists and "archaic" *Homo sapiens* by others. And, as we shall see, still other anthropologists see so much continuity between *Homo erectus* and *Homo sapiens* that they think it is completely arbitrary to call them different species; according to these anthropologists, *H. erectus* and *H. sapiens* may just be earlier and later varieties of the same species.

The fossils with mixed traits have been found in Africa, Europe, and Asia. For example, a specimen from the Broken Hill mine in Zambia, central Africa, dates from about 200,000 years ago. Its mixed traits include a cranial capacity of over 1200 cc (well within the range of modern *Homo sapiens*) together with a low forehead and large brow ridges,

which are characteristic of earlier *Homo erectus* specimens.[3] Other fossils with mixed traits have been found at Bodo, Hopefield, Ndutu, Elandsfontein, and Rabat in Africa; Heidelberg, Bilzingsleben, Petralona, Arago, Steinheim, and Swanscombe in Europe; and Dali and Solo in Asia.

Neandertals and Other Definite *Homo sapiens*

There may be disagreement about how to classify the mixed-trait fossils from 500,000 to 200,000 years ago, but there is hardly any disagreement about the fossils that are less than 200,000 years old. Nearly all anthropologists agree that they were definitely *Homo sapiens*. Mind you, these early definite *Homo sapiens* did not look completely like modern humans. But they were not so different from us either, not even the ones called Neandertals, after the valley in Germany where the first evidence of them was found.

Somehow, through the years the Neandertals have become the victims of their cartoon image, which usually misrepresents them as burly and more ape than human. Actually, they might go unnoticed in a cross section of the world's population today.

In 1856, three years before Darwin's publication of *The Origin of Species*, a skullcap and other fossilized bones were discovered in a cave in the Neander Valley (*tal* is the German word for valley) near Düsseldorf, Germany. The fossils in the Neander Valley were the first that scholars could tentatively consider as an early hominid. (The fossils classified as *Homo erectus* were not found until later in the nineteenth century, and the fossils belonging to the genus *Australopithecus* were not found until the twentieth century.) After Darwin's revolutionary work was published, the Neandertal find aroused considerable controversy. A few evolutionist scholars, such as Thomas Huxley, thought that the Neandertal was not that different from modern humans. Others dismissed the Neandertal as irrele-

[1]C. Stringer, "Evolution of a Species," *Geographical Magazine*, 57 (1985): 601–7.
[2]Ibid.

[3]G. Philip Rightmire, "*Homo sapiens* in Sub-Saharan Africa," in Fred H. Smith and Frank Spencer, eds., *The Origins of Modern Humans: A World Survey of the Fossil Evidence* (New York: Alan R. Liss, 1984), p. 303.

TABLE 6–1 An Overview of Human Evolution: Biological and Cultural

TIME (YEARS AGO)	GEOLOGIC EPOCH	FOSSIL RECORD (FIRST APPEARANCE)	ARCHEOLOGICAL PERIODS (OLD WORLD)	MAJOR CULTURAL DEVELOPMENTS (FIRST APPEARANCE)
			Bronze Age	Cities and states; social inequality; full-time craft specialists
5500 (3500 B.C.)			————————	
			Neolithic	Domesticated plants and animals; permanent villages
10,000 (8000 B.C.)			————————	
			Mesolithic	Broad-spectrum food collecting; increasingly sedentary communities; many kinds of microliths
14,000 (12,000 B.C.)	Pleistocene	Earliest humans in New World	————————	
			Upper Paleolithic	Cave paintings; female figurines; many kinds of blade tools
40,000			————————	
		Modern humans *Homo sapiens sapiens*	Middle Paleolithic	Religious beliefs (?); burials; Mousterian tools
200,000		Neandertal *Homo sapiens*		
300,000		Earliest *Homo sapiens* (?)	————————	
700,000 1,500,000 1,800,000		*Homo erectus*	Lower Paleolithic	Acheulian tools
				Hunting and/or scavenging; seasonal campsites; Oldowan tools
2,000,000	Pliocene	*Homo habilis*	————————	
		Earliest hominids *Australopithecus*		Earliest stone tools
5,000,000		————————		
	Miocene	Diversification of apes *Sivapithecus*		
22,500,000		*Dryopithecus* *Proconsul*		
29,000,000 32,000,000		Earliest apes (?) Propliopithecids, e.g., *Aegyptopithecus*		
	Oligocene	Earliest anthropoids Parapithecids, e.g., *Apidium*		
38,000,000		————————		
50,000,000	Eocene	*Amphipithecus* *Tetonius*		
53,500,000		————————		
	Paleocene			
65,000,000		————————		
70,000,000	Late Cretaceous	Earliest primates *Purgatorius*		

Source: Geological dates from W. A. Berggren and J. A. Van Couvering, "The Late Neocene: Biostratigraphy, Geochronology and Paleoclimatology of the Last 15 Million Years in Marine and Continental Sequences," *Palaeogeography, Palaeoclimatology, Palaeoecology,* 16 (1974): 13–16, 165.

vant to human evolution; they saw it as a pathological freak, a peculiar, disease-ridden individual. However, similar fossils turned up later in Belgium, Yugoslavia, France, and elsewhere in Europe, which meant that the original Neandertal find could not be dismissed as an oddity.[4]

The dominant reaction to the original and subsequent Neandertal-like finds was that the Neandertals were too "brutish" and "primitive" to have possibly been ancestral to modern humans. This view prevailed in the scholarly community until well into the 1950s. A major proponent of this view was Marcellin Boule, who claimed between 1908 and 1913 that the Neandertals would not have been capable of complete bipedalism. Since the 1950s, however, a number of studies have disputed Boule's claim, and it is now generally agreed that the skeletal traits of the Neandertals are completely consistent with bipedalism. Perhaps more important, when the much more ancient australopithecine and *Homo erectus* fossils were accepted as hominids in the 1940s and 1950s, anthropologists realized that the Neandertals did not look that different from modern humans—despite their sloping foreheads, large brow ridges, flattened braincases, large jaws, and nearly absent chins.[5] After all, they did have larger brains than modern humans on the average.[6]

It took almost 100 years to accept the idea that Neandertals were not that different from modern humans and therefore should be classified as *Homo sapiens neanderthalensis*. But, as we shall see, there is still debate over whether the Neandertals in western Europe were ancestral to modern-looking people who lived later in western Europe, after about 40,000 years ago. In any case, Neandertals lived in other places besides western Europe. A large number of fossils from central Europe (Yugoslavia, Czechoslovakia, Hungary) strongly resemble those from western Europe, although some

features, such as a projecting midface, are less pronounced.[7] Neandertals have also been found in southwestern Asia (Israel, Iraq) and Central Asia (Uzbekistan). One of the largest collections of Neandertal fossils comes from Shanidar Cave in the mountains of northeastern Iraq, where Ralph Solecki unearthed the skeletons of nine individuals.[8]

The Neandertals have received a great deal of scholarly and popular attention, probably because they were the first premodern humans to be found. But we now know that other premodern *Homo sapiens*, some perhaps older than Neandertals, lived elsewhere in the Old World—in East, South, and North Africa as well as in Java and China.[9] These other premodern but definite *Homo sapiens* are sometimes considered Neandertal-like, but more often they are named after the places where they were found (as indeed the original Neandertal was). For example, the cranium from China called *Homo sapiens daliensis* was named after the Chinese county (Dali) in which it was found in 1978.[10]

Middle Paleolithic Cultures

The period of cultural history associated with the Neandertals is traditionally called the Middle Paleolithic in Europe and the Near East and dates from about 300,000 years ago to about 40,000 years ago.[11] For Africa, the term *Middle Stone Age* is used instead of *Middle Paleolithic*. The tool assemblages from this period are generally referred to as *Mousterian* in Europe and the Near East, and as *post-Acheulian* in Africa.

[4]Frank Spencer, "The Neandertals and Their Evolutionary Significance: A Brief Historical Survey," in Smith and Spencer, eds., *The Origins of Modern Humans*, pp. 1–50.

[5]Erik Trinkaus, "Pathology and the Posture of the La Chapelle-aux-Saints Neandertal," *American Journal of Physical Anthropology*, 67 (1985): 19–41.

[6]Spencer, "The Neandertals and Their Evolutionary Significance," p. 20.

[7]Fred H. Smith, "Fossil Hominids from the Upper Pleistocene of Central Europe and the Origin of Modern Humans," in Smith and Spencer, eds., *The Origins of Modern Humans*, p. 187.

[8]Erik Trinkaus, "Western Asia," in Smith and Spencer, eds., *The Origins of Modern Humans*, pp. 251–53.

[9]See various chapters in Smith and Spencer, eds., *The Origins of Modern Humans*.

[10]Wu Xinzhi and Wu Maolin, "Early *Homo sapiens* in China," in Wu Rukang and John W. Olsen, eds., *Paleoanthropology and Paleolithic Archaeology in the People's Republic of China* (Orlando, FL: Academic Press, 1985), pp. 91–106.

[11]Lawrence Guy Straus, "On Early Hominid Use of Fire," *Current Anthropology*, 30 (1989): 488–91.

Tool Assemblages

The Mousterian. The **Mousterian** type of tool complex is named after the tool assemblage found in a rock shelter at Le Moustier in the Dordogne region of southwestern France. Compared with an Acheulian assemblage, a Mousterian tool assemblage has a greater proportion of flake tools, with large bifacial tools occurring rarely. Although many flakes struck off from a core were used "as is," the Mousterian is also characterized by flakes that were often altered or "retouched" by striking small flakes or chips from one or more edges (see most of the tools in Figure 6–1).[12]

[12]Richard G. Klein, *The Human Career: Human Biological and Cultural Origins* (Chicago: University of Chicago Press, 1989), pp. 291–96.

Toward the end of the Acheulian period, a technique developed that enabled the toolmaker to produce flake tools of a predetermined size instead of simply chipping flakes away from the core at random. In this **Levalloisian** method, the toolmaker first shaped the core and prepared a "striking platform" at one end. Flakes of predetermined and standard sizes could then be knocked off. Although some Levallois flakes date from as far back as 400,000 years ago, they are found more frequently in Mousterian tool-kits.[13]

Although the tool assemblages in particular sites may be characterized as Mousterian, one site may have more or fewer scrapers, points, and so forth, than another site. A number of archeologists

[13]Ibid., pp. 421–22.

FIGURE 6-1 A Typical Mousterian Tool Kit

A Mousterian tool kit emphasized sidescrapers (1-4), notches (5), points (6), and denticulates (7). How these stone artifacts were actually used is not known, but the points may have been joined to wood shafts, and denticulates could have been used to work wood. The tools illustrated here are from Mousterian sites in western Europe. *(Source: "Ice-Age Hunters of the Ukraine" by Richard G. Klein. Copyright © 1974 by Scientific American, Inc. All rights reserved.)*

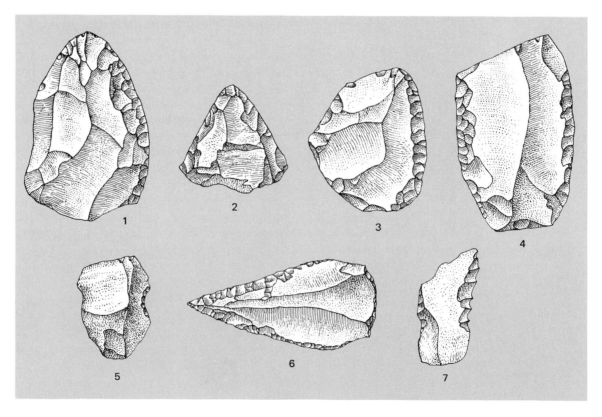

have suggested possible reasons for this variation. For example, Sally and Lewis Binford suggested that different activities may have occurred in different sites: some sites may have been used for butchering and other sites may have been base camps. Hence the kinds of tools found in different sites should vary.[14] And Paul Fish has suggested that some sites may have more tools produced by the Levalloisian technique because larger pieces of flint were available.[15]

The Post-Acheulian in Africa. Like Mousterian tools, many of the post-Acheulian tools in Africa during the Middle Stone Age were struck off prepared cores in the Levalloisian way. The assemblages consist mostly of various types of flake tools. A well-described sequence of such tools comes from the area around the mouth of the Klasies River on the southern coast of South Africa.

This area contains rock shelters and small caves in which early and later *Homo sapiens* lived. The oldest cultural remains in one of the caves may date back 120,000 years.[16] These earliest tools include parallel-sided flake blades (probably used as knives), pointed flakes (possibly spearpoints), burins or gravers (chisellike tools), and scrapers. Similar tools discovered at another South African site, Border Cave, may have been used almost 200,000 years ago.[17]

Homesites

Most of the excavated Middle Paleolithic homesites in Europe and the Near East are located in caves and rock-shelters. The same is true for the excavated Middle Stone Age homesites in sub-Saharan Africa. We might conclude, therefore, that Neandertals and other early *Homo sapiens* lived mostly in caves or rock-shelters. But that conclusion could be incorrect. Caves and rock-

shelters may be overrepresented in the archeological record because they are more likely to be found than sites originally in the open but now hidden by thousands of years of **sediment.** Sediment is the dust, debris, and decay that accumulates over time; when we dust the furniture and vacuum the floor, we are removing sediment.

Still we know that many early *Homo sapiens* lived at least part of the year in caves. This was true, for example, along the Dordogne River in France. The river gouged deep valleys in the limestone of that area. Below the cliffs are rock-shelters with overhanging roofs and deep caves, many of which were occupied during the Middle Paleolithic. Even if the inhabitants did not stay all year, the sites do seem to have been occupied year after year.[18]

Quite a few homesites of early *Homo sapiens* were in the open. In Africa, open-air sites were located on floodplains, at the edges of lakes, and by springs.[19] Many open-air sites have been found in Europe, particularly eastern Europe. The occupants of the well-known site at Moldova in western Russia lived in river-valley houses framed with wood and covered with animal skins. Mammoth bones surrounding the remains of hearths were apparently used to help hold the animal skins in place. Even though the winter climate near the edge of the glacier nearby was cold at that time, there would still have been animals to hunt because the plant food for the game was not buried under deep snow.

The hunters probably moved away in the summer to higher land between the river valleys. In all likelihood, the higher ground was grazing land for the large herds of animals the Moldova hunters depended on for meat. In the winter river-valley sites archeologists have found skeletons of wolf, arctic fox, and hare with their paws missing. These animals probably were skinned for pelts that were made into clothing.[20]

[14]Sally R. Binford and Lewis R. Binford, "Stone Tools and Human Behavior," *Scientific American,* 220 (April 1969): 70–84.

[15]Paul R. Fish, "Beyond Tools: Middle Paleolithic Debitage Analysis and Cultural Inference," *Journal of Anthropological Research,* 37 (1981): 377.

[16]Karl W. Butzer, "Geomorphology and Sediment Stratigraphy," in Ronald Singer and John Wymer, *The Middle Stone Age at Klasies River Mouth in South Africa* (Chicago: University of Chicago, 1982), p. 42.

[17]David W. Phillipson, *African Archaeology* (Cambridge: Cambridge University Press, 1985), pp. 61–62.

[18]For the controversy about whether the inhabitants of the Dordogne Valley lived in their homesites year-round, see Lewis R. Binford, "Interassemblage Variability: The Mousterian and the 'Functional' Argument," in Colin Renfew, ed., *The Explanation of Culture Change: Models in Prehistory* (Pittsburgh: University of Pittsburgh Press, 1973).

[19]Richard G. Klein, "The Ecology of Early Man in Southern Africa," *Science,* July 8, 1977, p. 120.

[20]Richard G. Klein, "Ice-Age Hunters of the Ukraine," *Scientific American,* June 1974, pp. 96–105.

Food-Getting

How early *Homo sapiens* got their food probably varied with their environments. In Africa they lived in savanna and semiarid desert. In western and eastern Europe they had to adapt to cold; during periods of increased glaciation, much of the environment was steppe grassland and tundra.

The European environment during this time was much richer in animal resources than the tundra of northern countries is today. Indeed, the European environment inhabited by Neandertals abounded in game, both big and small. The tundra and alpine animals included reindeer, bison, wild oxen, horses, mammoths, rhinoceroses, and deer, as well as bears, wolves, and foxes.[21] Some European sites have also yielded bird and fish remains. For example, people in a summer camp in northern Germany apparently hunted swans and ducks and fished for perch and pike.[22] Little, however, is known about the particular plant foods the European Neandertals may have consumed; the remains of plants are unlikely to survive thousands of years in a nonarid environment.

In Africa too, early *Homo sapiens* varied in how they got food. For example, we know that the people living at the mouth of the Klasies River in South Africa ate a great deal of shellfish, as well as meat from small grazers such as antelopes and large grazers such as eland and buffalo.[23] But archeologists disagree about how the Klasies River people got their meat when they began to occupy the caves in the area.

Richard Klein thinks they hunted large as well as small game. Klein speculates that since the remains of eland of all ages have been found in Cave 1 at this site, the people there probably hunted the eland by driving them into corrals or other traps, where animals of all ages could be killed. Klein thinks that buffalo were hunted differently. Buffalo tend to charge attackers, which would make it difficult to drive them into traps. Klein believes that since bones from mostly very young and very old buffalo are found in the cave, the hunters were able to stalk and kill only the most vulnerable animals.[24]

Lewis Binford thinks the Klasies River people hunted only small grazers and scavenged eland and buffalo meat from the kills of large carnivores. He argues that sites should contain all or almost all of the bones from animals that were hunted. According to Binford, since more or less complete skeletons are found only from small animals, the Klasies River people were not at first hunting all the animals they used for food.[25]

Funeral Rituals?

Some Neandertals were deliberately buried. At Le Moustier, the skeleton of a boy fifteen or sixteen years old was found with a beautifully fashioned stone ax near his hand. Near Le Moustier, graves of five other children and two adults, apparently interred together in a family plot, were discovered. These finds, along with one at Shanidar Cave in Iraq, have aroused speculation about the possibility of funeral rituals.

The evidence at Shanidar consists of pollen around and on top of a man's body. Pollen analysis suggests that the flowers included ancestral forms of modern grape hyacinths, bachelor's buttons, hollyhocks, and yellow flowering groundsels. John Pfeiffer has speculated about this find as follows:

A man with a badly crushed skull was buried deep in the cave with special ceremony. One spring day about 60,000 years ago members of his family went out into the hills, picked masses of wild flowers, and made a bed of them on the ground, a resting place for the deceased. Other flowers were probably laid on top of his grave; still others seem to have been woven together with the branches of a pinelike shrub to form a wreath.[26]

Do we know this? Not really. All we know for sure is that there was pollen near and on top of the body. It could have gotten there because humans

---

[21]François Bordes, "Mousterian Cultures in France," *Science*, September 22, 1961, pp. 803–10.

[22]Thomas C. Patterson, *The Evolution of Ancient Societies: A World Archaeology* (Englewood Cliffs, NJ: Prentice Hall, 1981).

[23]Phillipson, *African Archaeology*, p. 63.

[24]Richard G. Klein, "The Stone Age Prehistory of Southern Africa," *Annual Review of Anthropology*, 12 (1983): 38–39.

[25]Lewis R. Binford, *Faunal Remains from Klasies River Mouth* (Orlando, FL: Academic Press, 1984), pp. 195–97. To explain the lack of complete skeletons of large animals, Klein (see previous footnote) suggests that the hunters butchered the large animals elsewhere and could carry home only small sections of them.

[26]John E. Pfeiffer, *The Emergence of Man*, 3rd ed. (New York: Harper & Row, Pub., 1978), p. 155.

put flowers in the grave, or it could have gotten there for other, even accidental reasons.

The Emergence of Modern Humans

Cro-Magnon humans, who appear in western Europe about 35,000 years ago, were once thought to be the earliest specimens of modern humans, or *Homo sapiens sapiens.* (The Cro-Magnons are named after the rock-shelter in France where they were first found in 1868.[27]) But we now know that modern-looking humans appear earlier outside of Europe. As of now, the oldest known fossils classified as *Homo sapiens sapiens* come from Africa. Some of these fossils, discovered in one of the Klasies River Mouth caves, are possibly as old as 100,000 years.[28] Other modern-looking fossils of about the same age have been found in Border Cave in South Africa, and a find at Omo in Ethiopia may be an early *Homo sapiens sapiens.*[29] Remains of anatomically modern humans found at two sites in Israel (Skhul and Qafzeh), which used to be thought to date back 40,000 to 50,000 years, may be 90,000 years old.[30] There are also anatomically modern human finds in Borneo (Niah) from about 40,000 years ago and in Australia (Lake Mungo) from about 30,000 years ago.[31]

These modern-looking humans differed from the Neandertals and other early *Homo sapiens* in that they had higher, more bulging foreheads, thinner and lighter bones, smaller faces and jaws, chins (the bony protuberances that remain after projecting faces recede), and slight bone ridges (or

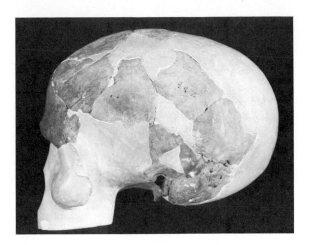

Reconstruction of early *homo sapiens sapiens* from Border Cave in South Africa, dating from 50,000 to 100,000 years ago.

no ridges at all) over the eyes and at the back of the head.

Theories about the Origins of Modern Humans

Two theories about the origins of modern humans continue to be debated among anthropologists. One, which can be called the *single-origin* theory, suggests that modern humans emerged in just one part of the Old World and then spread to other parts, superseding Neandertals and other premodern *Homo sapiens.* The second theory, which can be called the *continuous-evolution* theory, suggests that modern humans emerged gradually in various parts of the Old World, becoming the varieties of humans we see today.[32]

According to the single-origin theory, most of the Neandertals and other premodern *Homo sapiens* did not evolve into modern humans. Rather, according to this view, most Neandertals became extinct after 35,000 years ago because they were replaced by modern humans. The presumed place of origin of the first modern humans has varied over the years as new fossils have been discovered.

[27]C. B. Stringer, J. J. Hublin, and B. Vandermeersch, "The Origin of Anatomically Modern Humans in Western Europe," in Smith and Spencer, eds., *The Origins of Modern Humans,* p. 107.

[28]Singer and Wymer, *The Middle Stone Age at Klasies River Mouth in South Africa,* p. 149.

[29]Günter Bräuer, "A Craniological Approach to the Origin of Anatomically Modern *Homo sapiens* in Africa and Implications for the Appearance of Modern Europeans," in Smith and Spencer, eds., *The Origins of Modern Humans,* pp. 387–89, 394; and Rightmire, "*Homo sapiens* in Sub-Saharan Africa," p. 320.

[30]H. Valladas, J. L. Joron, G. Valladas, O. Bar-Yosef, and B. Vandermeersch, "Thermoluminescence Dating of Mousterian 'Proto-Cro-Magnon' Remains from Israel and the Origin of Modern Man," *Nature,* 331 (1988), 18 February, pp. 614–16.

[31]Stringer, Hublin, and Vandermeersch, "The Origin of Anatomically Modern Humans in Western Europe," p. 121.

[32]For arguments supporting the "single-origin" theory, see the chapters by Günter Bräuer, F. Clark Howell, and C. B. Stringer et al., in Smith and Spencer, eds., *The Origins of Modern Humans.* For arguments supporting the "continuous-evolution" theory, see the chapters by C. L. Brace et al., David W. Frayer, Fred H. Smith, and Milford H. Wolpoff et al., in the same volume.

In the 1950s the source population was presumed to be the Neandertals in the Near East, who were referred to as "generalized" or "progressive" Neandertals. Later, when earlier *Homo sapiens sapiens* were found in Africa, some anthropologists postulated that modern humans emerged first in Africa and then moved to the Near East and from there to Europe and Asia. Single-origin theorists postulate that the originally small population of *Homo sapiens sapiens* had some biological and/or cultural advantage that allowed them to spread and replace the premodern *Homo sapiens.*

According to the continuous-evolution theory, *Homo erectus* populations in various parts of the Old World gradually evolved into anatomically modern-looking humans. To the theorists espousing this view, the "transitional" or "archaic" *Homo sapiens* and the Neandertals and other definite *Homo sapiens* represent phases in the gradual development of more "modern" anatomical features. Indeed, as we have noted, some of these theorists see so much continuity between *Homo erectus* and modern humans that they classify *Homo erectus* as *Homo sapiens erectus.*

To explain why human evolution would proceed gradually and in the same direction in various parts of the Old World, many continuous-evolution theorists point to cultural improvements in cutting-tool and cooking technology that occurred all over the Old World. These cultural improvements may have relaxed the prior natural selection for heavy bones and musculature in the skull. The argument is that unless many plant and animal foods were cut into small pieces and thoroughly cooked (in hearths or pits that were efficient thermally), they would be hard to chew and digest. Thus people previously would have needed robust jaws and thick skull bones to support the large muscles that enabled them to cut and chew their food. But robust bone and muscle would no longer be needed after people began to cut and cook more effectively.[33]

The single-origin and continuous-evolution theories are not the only possible interpretations of the available fossil record. There is also the intermediate interpretation that there may have been some replacement of one population by another, some local continuous evolution, and some interbreeding between early modern humans (who spread out of Africa) and some of the populations they encountered in North Africa, Europe, and Asia.[34] As we discuss in the chapter on human variation, although modern humans are all *Homo sapiens sapiens*, human populations vary in physical features perhaps mostly because natural selection favors different features in different environments.

Dating Skeletal and Archeological Remains of Modern Humans

Radiocarbon Dating. Radiocarbon dating (discussed briefly in Chapter 4) is a reliable method for dating remains up to 30,000 to 40,000 years old. Radiocarbon dating is based on the principle that all living matter possesses a certain amount of a radioactive form of carbon (carbon[14], or ^{14}C). Radioactive carbon, produced when nitrogen[14] is bombarded by cosmic rays, is absorbed from the air by plants and then ingested by animals that eat the plants. After an organism dies, it no longer takes in any of the radioactive carbon. Carbon 14 decays at a slow but steady pace and reverts to nitrogen 14. (By *decays* we mean that the ^{14}C gives off a certain number of beta radiations per minute.) The rate at which the carbon decays is known: [14]C has a half-life of 5730 years. In other words, half of the original amount of ^{14}C in organic matter will have disintegrated 5730 years after the organism's death; half of the remaining ^{14}C will have disintegrated after another 5730 years; and so on. After about 30,000 to 40,000 years, the amount of ^{14}C remaining in the organic matter is too small to permit reliable dating.

To discover how long an organism has been dead (to determine how much ^{14}C is left in the organism and therefore how old it is), we count the number of beta radiations given off per minute per gram of material. Modern ^{14}C emits about 15 beta radiations per minute per gram of material, but ^{14}C that is 5730 years old emits only half this amount (the "half-life" of ^{14}C) per minute per gram. So if a sample of some organism gives off 7.5 radiations a minute per gram, which is only half the amount

[33]Erik Trinkaus, "The Neandertals and Modern Human Origins." *Annual Review of Anthropology,* 15 (1986): 193–218.

[34]Ibid., p. 210.

given off by modern ^{14}C, the organism must be 5730 years old.[35]

As a test of its accuracy, radioactive-carbon dating was used to judge the age of parts of the Dead Sea Scrolls and some wood from an Egyptian tomb, the dates of which were already known from historical records. The results based on ^{14}C analysis agreed very well with the historical information.

The ^{14}C method is not accurate for samples more than 30,000 to 40,000 years old because beyond that range very few radioactive emissions are occurring and a low count does not make for a reliable estimate of age. A new dating technique (using a linear accelerator) allows researchers to assess the actual amount of ^{14}C, not just its radioactive emissions, in some material; this method provides a way to date specimens up to 100,000 old.[36]

Thermoluminescence Dating. Many minerals emit light when they are heated ("thermoluminescence"), even before they become "red hot." This "cold light" comes from the release under heat of "outside" electrons trapped in the crystal structure. *Thermoluminescence dating*[37] makes use of the principle that if an object is heated at some point to a high temperature (as when clay is baked to form a pot), it will release all the trapped electrons it held previously. Over time, the object will continue to trap electrons from radioactive elements (such as ^{40}K, thorium, and uranium) around it. The amount of thermoluminescence that is emitted when the object is heated during testing allows researchers to calculate the age of the object, if it is known what kind of radiation the object has been exposed to in its surroundings (for example, the surrounding soil in which a clay pot is found).

Thermoluminescence dating is well suited to samples of ancient pottery, brick, tile, or terra cotta which were originally heated to a high temperature when they were made. This method can also be applied to burnt flint tools, hearth stones, lava or lava-covered objects, meteorites and meteor craters.[38]

Electron Spin Resonance Dating. **Electron spin resonance dating** is a technique that, like thermoluminescence dating, measures trapped electrons from surrounding radioactive material. But the method in this case is different. The material to be dated is exposed to varying magnetic fields and a spectrum of the microwaves absorbed by the tested material is obtained. Since no heating is required for this technique, electron spin resonance is especially useful for dating organic material such as bone and shell which decompose if heated.[39]

Upper Paleolithic Cultures

The period of cultural history in Europe, the Near East, and Asia known as the Upper Paleolithic dates from about 40,000 years ago to the period known as the Mesolithic (about 14,000 to about 10,000 years ago, depending on the area). In Africa, the cultural period comparable to the Upper Paleolithic is known as the Later Stone Age and begins around the same time. (To simplify terminology, we use the term *Upper Paleolithic* in referring to cultural developments in all areas of the Old World during this period.)

In many respects, life-styles during the Upper Paleolithic were similar to life-styles before. People were still mainly hunters and gatherers and fishers who probably lived in highly mobile bands. They made their camps out in the open (in skin-covered huts) and in caves and rock-shelters. And they continued to produce smaller and smaller stone tools.

But the Upper Paleolithic is also characterized by a variety of new developments. One of the most striking is the emergence of art—painting on cave walls and stone slabs, and the carving of decorative objects and personal ornaments out of bone, antler, shell, and stone. (Perhaps for this as well as other purposes, people began to obtain materials from distant sources.) Since more archeological sites date from the Upper Paleolithic than from any previous period, and since some Upper Paleolithic sites seem larger than any before, many archeologists think that the human population increased considerably during the Upper Paleo-

[35]Frank Hole and Robert F. Heizer, *An Introduction to Prehistoric Archeology*, 3rd ed. (New York: Holt, Rinehart & Winston, 1973), pp. 252–54.

[36]Klein, *The Human Career*, p. 22.

[37]M. J. Aitken, *Thermoluminescence Dating* (London: Academic Press, 1985), pp. 1–4.

[38]Ibid., pp. 191–202.

[39]Ibid., pp. 4, 211–13.

FIGURE 6-2

Here we see the type of mammoth-bone shelters constructed about 15,000 years ago on the East European Plain. Often mammoth skulls formed part of the foundation for the tusk, long bone, and wooden frame, covered with hide. As many as 95 mammoth mandibles were arranged around the outside in a herringbone pattern. Ten men and women could have constructed this elaborate shelter of 258 square feet in six days, using 46,000 pounds of bone. *(Source: National Geographic, October 1988, used with permission.)*

lithic.[40] And new inventions, such as the bow and arrow, the spear-thrower, and tiny replaceable blades that could be fitted into handles, appear for the first time.[41]

Homesites

As was the case in the known Middle Paleolithic sites, most of the Upper Paleolithic remains that have been excavated were situated in caves and rock-shelters. In southwestern France, some groups seem to have paved parts of the floor of the shelter with stones. Tentlike structures were built in some caves, apparently to keep out the cold.[42] Some open-air sites have also been excavated. The site at Dolni Vestonice in Czechoslovakia, dated to around 25,000 years ago, is one of the first for which there is an entire settlement plan.[43]

The settlement seems to have consisted of four tentlike huts, probably made from animal skins, with a great open hearth in the center. Around the outside were mammoth bones, some rammed into the ground, which suggests that the huts were surrounded by a wall. All told, there were bone heaps from about 100 mammoths. Each hut probably housed a group of related families—about 20 to 25 people. (One hut was approximately twenty-seven by forty-five feet and had five hearths distributed inside it, presumably one for each family.) With 20 to 25 people per hut, and assuming that all four huts were occupied at the same time, the population of the settlement would have been 100 to 125. Up a hill from the settlement was a fifth and different kind of hut. It was dug into the ground, and contained a bake oven and more than 2300 small, fired fragments of animal figurines. There were also some hollow bones that may have been musical instruments. Another interesting feature of the settlement was a burial find, of a woman with a disfigured face. She may have been a particularly important personage, since her face was found engraved on an ivory plaque near the central hearth of the settlement down the hill.

Tools: The Blade Technique

Upper Paleolithic toolmaking appears to have its roots in the Mousterian and post-Acheulian traditions, since flake tools are found in many Upper

[40]Randall White, "Rethinking the Middle/Upper Paleolithic Transition," *Current Anthropology,* 23 (1982): 169–75.

[41]Lawrence Guy Straus, Comment on ibid., *Current Anthropology,* 23 (1982): 185–86.

[42]Patterson, *The Evolution of Ancient Societies.*

[43]Bohuslav Klima, "The First Ground-Plan of an Upper Paleolithic Loess Settlement in Middle Europe and Its Meaning," in Robert J. Braidwood and Gordon R. Willey, eds., *Courses toward Urban Life: Archaeological Consideration of Some Cultural Alternatives,* Viking Fund Publications in Anthropology, no. 32. (Chicago: Aldine, 1962), pp. 193–210.

FIGURE 6-3
One way to remove blades from a core is to hit them with a punch. The object being struck is the punch, which is made of bone or horn. *(Source: Brian M. Fagan, In the Beginning, Boston: Little, Brown, p. 195.)*

Paleolithic sites. Numerous blade tools have also been uncovered. Blades were found in Middle Paleolithic assemblages as well, but they were not widely used until the Upper Paleolithic. In the **blade** technique of toolmaking, a core is prepared by shaping a piece of flint with a hammerstone into a pyramidal or cylindrical form. Then a series of blades, more than twice as long as they are wide, are struck off (see Figure 6–3).

The Upper Paleolithic period is also noted for the production of large numbers of bone and antler tools. The manufacture of these implements may have been made easier by the development of many varieties of burins. **Burins,** or gravers, are chisellike stone tools used for carving; bone and antler needles, awls, and projectile points could be produced with them.[44] Burins have been found in

Middle and Lower Paleolithic sites but are present in great number and variety only in the Upper Paleolithic. **Pressure flaking** also appeared during the Upper Paleolithic. In the traditional percussion method, used since Oldowan choppers were first made at least 2 million years before, the core was struck with a hammerstone to knock off the flake. In pressure flaking, small flakes were struck off by pressing against the core with a bone, wood, or antler tool probably made with a burin. Pressure flaking gave the toolmaker greater control in the shaping of the tool.

As time went on, all over the Old World smaller and smaller blade tools were produced. The very tiny ones, called **microliths,** were often hafted or fitted into handles, one blade at a time or several blades together, to serve as spears, adzes, knives, and sickles. The hafting required the inventing of a way to trim the blade's back edge so that it would be blunt rather than sharp. In this way the blades would not split the handles into which they might be inserted; the blunting would also prevent the users of an unhafted blade from cutting themselves.[45]

Some archeologists think that the blade technique was adopted because it made for more economical use of flint. André Leroi-Gourhan of the Musée de l'Homme in Paris calculated that with the old Acheulian technique, a two-pound lump of flint yielded sixteen inches of working edge and produced only two hand axes. If the more advanced Mousterian technique were used, a lump of equal size would yield two yards of working edge. The Upper Paleolithic blade technique, however, yielded twenty-five yards of working edge.[46] With the same amount of material, a significantly greater number of tools could be produced. Getting the most out of a valuable resource may have been particularly important in areas lacking large flint deposits.

Jacques Bordaz believes that the evolution of toolmaking techniques, which continually increased the amount of usable edge that could be gotten out of a lump of flint, was significant because people could then spend more time in regions where flint was unavailable:

[44]Jacques Bordaz, *Tools of the Old and New Stone Age* (Garden City, NY: Natural History Press, 1970) p. 68.

[45]Phillipson, *African Archaeology*, p. 58.
[46]Bordaz, *Tools of the Old and New Stone Age*, p. 68.

Hunters and gatherers can only carry a limited amount of material with them during their seasonal migrations and hunting expeditions. With more efficient methods of knapping flint, their range could be extended farther and for longer periods of time into areas where flint was locally unavailable, of poorer quality, or difficult in access.[47]

Another reason for adopting the blade toolmaking technique may have been that it made for easy repair of tools. For example, the cutting edge of a tool might consist of a line of razorlike microliths set into a piece of wood. The tool would not be usable if just one of the cutting edge's microliths broke off or was chipped. But if the user carried a small prepared core of flint from which an identical-sized microlith could be struck off, the tool could be repaired easily by replacing the lost or broken microlith. A spear whose point was lost could be repaired similarly. Thus, the main purpose of the blade toolmaking technique may not have been to make more economical use of flint, but rather to allow easy replacement of damaged blades.[48]

How Were the Tools Used?   Ideally, the study of tools should reveal not only how the implements were made but also how they were used. One way of suggesting what a particular tool was used for in the past is to observe the manner in which similar tools are used by members of recent or contemporary societies, preferably societies with subsistence activities and environments similar to those of the ancient toolmakers. This method of study is called reasoning from **ethnographic analogy.** The problem with such reasoning, however, is obvious: we cannot be sure that the original use of a tool has not changed. For example, just because we use an implement called a toothbrush on our teeth does not mean that a much later society will also use it on teeth. When selecting recent or contemporary cultures that may provide the most informative and accurate comparisons, we should try to choose

those that derive from the ancient culture we are interested in. If the cultures being compared are historically related—prehistoric and recent Pueblo cultures in the southwestern United States, for example—there is a greater likelihood that both groups used a particular kind of tool in similar ways and for similar purposes.

Another way of suggesting what a particular kind of tool was used for in the past is to compare the visible and microscopic wear marks on the prehistoric tools with the wear marks on similar tools made and experimentally used by contemporary researchers. The idea behind this approach is that different uses leave different wear marks. A pioneer in this research was S. A. Semenov, who recreated prehistoric stone tools and used them in a variety of ways to find out which uses left which kinds of wear marks. For example, by cutting into meat with his re-created stone knives, he produced a polish on the edges that was like the polish found on blades from a prehistoric site in Siberia. This finding led Semenov to infer that the Siberian blades were probably also used to cut meat.[49]

Inventions for Killing.   During the Upper Paleolithic, and probably for the first time, spears were shot from a spear-thrower rather than thrown with the arm. We know this because bone and antler **atlatls** (the Aztec word for "spear-thrower") have been found in some sites. A spear propelled off a grooved board could be sent through the air with increased force, causing it to travel farther and hit harder, and with less effort by the thrower. The bow and arrow was also used in various places during the Upper Paleolithic; and harpoons, used for fishing and perhaps for reindeer hunting, were invented at this time.

Art

The earliest discovered traces of art are beads and carvings, and then paintings, from Upper Paleolithic sites. We might expect that early artistic efforts were crude, but the cave paintings of Spain

---

[47]Ibid., p. 57.

[48]We thank Robert L. Kelly (personal communication) for bringing this possibility to our attention. See also J. Desmond Clark, "Interpretations of Prehistoric Technology from Ancient Egyptian and Other Sources. Part II: Prehistoric Arrow Forms in Africa as Shown by Surviving Examples of the Traditional Arrows of the San Bushmen," *Paleorient*, 3 (1977): 136.

[49]S. A. Semenov, *Prehistoric Technology*, trans. M. W. Thompson. (Bath, England: Adams & Dart, 1970), p. 103. For a more recent discussion of research following this strategy, see Lawrence H. Keeley, *Experimental Determination of Stone Tool Uses: A Microwear Analysis* (Chicago: University of Chicago Press, 1980).

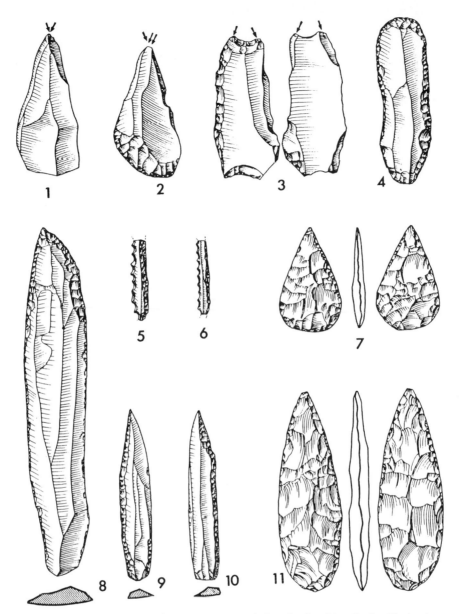

Upper Paleolithic tool kit from Hungary and Czechoslovakia. Burin (1), burin-scraper (2), multiple burin (3), end-scraper on retouched blade (4), denticulated backed bladelets (5, 6), pointed retouched blade (8), gravette points (9, 10), bifacial points (7, 11). *(Source: Francois Bordes,* The Old Stone Age, *trans. J. E. Anderson. New York: World University Library, 1968).*

and southern France show a marked degree of skill. So do the naturalistic paintings on slabs of stone excavated in southern Africa. Some of those slabs appear to have been painted as much as 28,000 years ago, which suggests that painting in Africa is as old as painting in Europe.[50]

[50]Phillipson, *African Archaeology,* p. 73.

Peter J. Ucko and Andrée Rosenfeld have identified three principal locations of paintings in the caves of western Europe: (1) in obviously inhabited rock-shelters and cave entrances—art as decoration or "art for art's sake"; (2) in "galleries" immediately off the inhabited areas of caves; and (3) in the inner reaches of caves, whose difficulty of access has been interpreted by some as a sign

"And if you take the place, you'll not just be getting a splendid, roomy home. You'll also be making a very sound investment in contemporary art." (© 1975 Punch ROTHCO)

that magical-religious activities were performed there.[51]

The subjects of the paintings are mostly animals. The paintings rest on bare walls, with no backdrops or environmental trappings. Perhaps, like many contemporary peoples, Upper Paleolithic men and women believed that the drawing of a human image could cause death or injury. If that were indeed their belief, it might explain why human figures are rarely depicted in cave art. Another explanation for the focus on animals might be that these people sought to improve their luck at hunting. This theory is suggested by evidence of chips in the painted figures, perhaps made by spears thrown at the drawings. But if hunting magic was the chief motivation for the paintings, it is difficult to explain why only a few show signs

of being speared. Perhaps the paintings were inspired by the need to increase the supply of animals. Cave art seems to have reached a peak toward the end of the Upper Paleolithic period, when herds of game were decreasing.

Another interpretation of Upper Paleolithic cave art has been suggested by Leroi-Gourhan. On the basis of a statistical analysis of the types of paintings and their locations within each of sixty-six caves, he concluded that choice of subject and placement of the paintings were not haphazard or arbitrary but probably had some symbolic significance. For example, female animals were usually located in the central chambers of the caves and were associated with what may be considered female signs—enclosed circles. Male animals, located at the entrances and back portions of the caves, were associated with presumably male signs—dots and barbed symbols.[52]

The particular symbolic significance of the cave paintings in southwestern France is more explicitly revealed, perhaps, by the results of a more recent, statistical study.[53] The data suggest that the animals portrayed in the cave paintings were mostly the ones that the painters preferred for meat and for materials such as hides. For example, wild cattle (bovines) and horses are portrayed more often than we would expect by chance, probably because they were larger and heavier (meatier) than the other animals in the environment. In addition, the paintings mostly portray animals that the painters may have feared the most because of their size, speed, natural weapons such as tusks and horns, and unpredictability of behavior. That is, mammoths, bovines, and horses are portrayed more often than deer and reindeer. Thus, the paintings are consistent with the idea that "the art is related to the importance of hunting in the economy of Upper Paleolithic people."[54] Consistent with this idea, according to the investigators, is the fact that the art of the cultural period follow-

[51]Peter J. Ucko and Andrée Rosenfeld, *Paleolithic Cave Art* (New York: McGraw-Hill, 1967).

[52]André Leroi-Gourhan, "The Evolution of Paleolithic Art," *Scientific American,* February 1968, pp. 58–70.

[53]Patricia C. Rice and Ann L. Paterson, "Cave Art and Bones: Exploring the Interrelationships," *American Anthropologist,* 87 (1985): 94–100. For similar results of a study of cave art in Spain, see Patricia C. Rice and Ann L. Paterson, "Validating the Cave Art–Archeofaunal Relationship in Cantabrian Spain," *American Anthropologist,* 88 (1986): 658–67.

[54]Rice and Paterson, "Cave Art and Bones," p. 98.

Upper Paleolithic cave painting in France.

ing the Upper Paleolithic seems also to reflect how people got their food. But in that period, when food-getting no longer depended on the hunting of large game (because they were becoming extinct), the art no longer focused on portrayals of animals.

Upper Paleolithic art was not confined to cave paintings. Many shafts of spears and similar objects were decorated with figures of animals. Alexander Marshack has an interesting interpretation of some of the engravings made during the Upper Paleolithic. He believes that as far back as 30,000 B.C., hunters may have used a system of notation, engraved on bone and stone, to mark the phases of the moon. If this is true, it would mean that Upper Paleolithic people were capable of complex thought and were consciously aware of their environment.[55] In addition, figurines representing the human female in exaggerated form have been found at Upper Paleolithic sites. Called *Venuses*, these women are portrayed with broad hips and large breasts and abdomens. It has been suggested

that the figurines may have been an ideal type, or an expression of a desire for fertility.

What the Venus figurines symbolized is still controversial. As is usually the case in current scholarly controversies, there is little or no evidence available now that might allow us to accept or reject a particular interpretation. But not all controversies in anthropology continue because of lack of evidence. Sometimes a controversy continues because there is some (usually disputed) evidence on all sides! This is the case with the controversy to which we now turn—whether there were people in the Americas prior to 12,000 years ago.

The Earliest Humans and Their Cultures in the New World

So far in this chapter we have dealt only with the Old World—Africa, Europe, and Asia. What about the New World—North and South America? How long have humans lived there, and what were their earliest cultures like?

[55]Alexander Marshack, *The Roots of Civilization* (New York: McGraw-Hill, 1972).

Because only *Homo sapiens* fossils have been found in North and South America, migrations of humans to the New World had to have taken place sometime after the emergence of *Homo sapiens*. But exactly when these migrations occurred is subject to debate, particularly about when *H. sapiens* got to areas south of Alaska. Some anthropologists think there are indications of humans south of Alaska well before 12,000 years ago. Other anthropologists see no good evidence of a human presence south of Alaska until after 12,000 years ago. Obviously, the opposing positions in this debate cannot both be correct.

The anthropologists who think that humans were present south of Alaska in the Americas before 12,000 years ago point to a number of presumably older finds—including human skeletal remains and various "artifacts," such as bone and stone "tools," at a number of sites all over the New World. But the dating of these finds is not accepted by many archeologists. So, for example, the supposedly old skeletal remains may not be very old, and some of the tools may be intrusions from more recent periods. In addition, some of the things thought to be tools may not have been made by humans; rather, these scattered, usually single pieces of stone and bone may have been fractured by natural fires and geological processes. Perhaps the most telling criticism of the idea of an ancient occupation of the Americas south of Alaska is that archeologists have not yet found any tool kits (assemblages of different tools) that are undisputably more than 12,000 years old. (In contrast, we know that Australia was occupied more than 30,000 years ago, because anthropologists have found tool kits there that are definitely that old.) As of now, then, the evidence available does not unquestionably confirm a human presence in the New World south of Alaska prior to 12,000 years ago.[56] However, new sites continue to be excavated and the finds debated, so our understanding of when humans entered and spread into the New World may change.

If there is disagreement about when people entered and spread into the New World, there is almost unanimous consensus on where and how they entered the New World. They probably came into North America from Siberia, walking across the land that bridged what is now the Bering Strait between Siberia and Alaska. This "land bridge" existed because the ice sheets that partly covered the high latitudes of the world contained so much of the world's water (they were thousands of feet thick in some places) that the Bering Strait was dry land. Since then the glaciers have mostly melted, and the Bering "bridge" has been covered by a higher sea level.

According to comparative linguists Morris Swadesh and Joseph Greenberg, there were three waves of migration into the New World.[57] First came the speakers of a language that diverged over time into most of the languages found in the New World; the speakers of these related languages came to occupy all of South and Central America as well as most of North America. Next came the ancestors of the people who speak languages belonging to the Nadené family, which today includes Navaho and Apache in the southwestern United States as well as the several Athapaskan languages of northern California, coastal Oregon, northwestern Canada, and Alaska. Finally, perhaps 4,000 years ago, came the ancestors of the Inuit (Eskimo) and Aleut (the latter came to occupy the islands southwest of Alaska and the adjacent mainland).

The tool assemblages from the earliest definite sites of human occupation are quite similar to one another. Most of the sites investigated by archeologists are *kill sites*, where game had been slaughtered and then butchered. Most occur along ancient lakes or creeks, where the animals probably came to drink, or at the bases of cliffs, over which herds were probably stampeded.

Archeological remains of these apparently earliest New World hunters have been found in a number of places in the United States, Mexico, and Canada. One of these places was just south of the furthest reaches of the last glaciation, the area east of the Rockies known as the High Plains. This

---

[56]Roger C. Owen, "The Americas: The Case against an Ice-Age Human Population," in Smith and Spencer, eds., *The Origins of Modern Humans*, pp. 517–63. See also Dena F. Dincauze, "An Archaeo-Logical Evaluation of the Case for Pre-Clovis Occupations," in Fred Wendorf and Angela E. Close, eds., *Advances in World Archaeology* (Orlando, FL: Academic Press, 1984), 3: 275–323. For the view that humans were south of Alaska earlier than 12,000 years ago, see William N. Irving, "Context and Chronology of Early Man in the Americas," *Annual Review of Anthropology*, 14 (1985): 529–55.

[57]Cited in Owen, "The Americas," pp. 524–25.

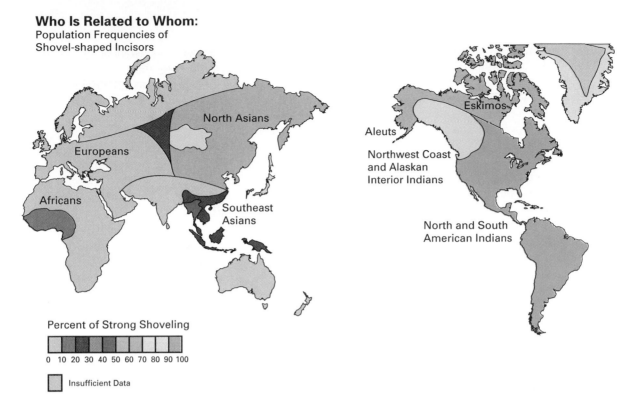

Who Is Related to Whom:
Population Frequencies of Shovel-shaped Incisors

North Asians

Europeans

Africans

Southeast Asians

Eskimos

Aleuts

Northwest Coast and Alaskan Interior Indians

North and South American Indians

Percent of Strong Shoveling

0 10 20 30 40 50 60 70 80 90 100

Insufficient Data

FIGURE 6-4

Inuit (Eskimos) and Aleuts, speakers of Nadené languages, and the other Native American language groups differ in the frequency of shovel-shaped incisors. These genetic differences seem to reflect three waves of migration into the New World. *(Adapted from Christy G. Turner II, "Telltale Teeth," Natural History, January 1987, p. 8.)* *(Courtesy of Natural History Magazine.)*

area abounded with mammoths (huge elephants, now extinct), bison, wild camels, and wild horses. The mammoth was one of the principal game animals beginning about 12,000 years ago. The tools found with mammoth kills are known as the *Clovis complex,* which includes the Clovis projectile point as well as stone scrapers and knives and bone tools. The Clovis projectile point is large and leaf-shaped, flaked on both sides. It has a broad groove in the middle, presumably so that the point could be attached to a wooden spear shaft.[58]

The mammoth disappeared about 10,000 years ago (for possible reasons, see Chapter 8), and the major game animal became the now extinct large, straight-horned bison. The hunters of that bison used a projectile point called the Folsom point, which was somewhat smaller than the Clovis point. Since tools are also found with many other kinds of animal remains, including wolf, turtle, rabbit, horse, fox, deer, and camel, the bison

Examples of North American points, probably used as spear points. The smallest is a Folsom point; the largest is a Clovis point.

[58]Joe B. Wheat, "A Paleo-Indian Bison Kill," *Scientific American,* January 1967, pp. 44–47.

hunters obviously depended on other animals as well.[59] In the Rio Grande valley, the Folsom toolmakers characteristically established a base camp on low dune ridges overlooking both a large pond and broad, open grazing areas. If we assume that the pond provided water for the grazing herds, the people in the camp would have been in an excellent position to watch the herds.[60]

As the climate of the American Southwest became drier, the animals and the cultural adaptations changed somewhat. About 9,000 years ago the smaller modern bison replaced the earlier straight-horned variety.[61] Base camps began to be located farther from ponds and grazing areas and closer to streams. If the ponds were no longer reliable sources of water during these drier times, the animals probably no longer frequented them—which would explain why the hunters had to change the sites of their base camps. Not that much is known about the plant foods these people may have exploited, but on the desert fringes plant gathering may have been vital. In Nevada and Utah, archeologists have found milling stones and other artifacts for processing plant food.[62]

The Olsen-Chubbuck site, a kill site excavated in Colorado, shows the organization that may have been involved in the hunting of bison.[63] In a dry gulch dated to 6500 B.C. were the remains of 200 bison. At the bottom were complete skele-

tons and at the top, completely butchered animals. This clearly suggests that hunters deliberately stampeded the animals into a natural trap—an arroyo, or steep-sided dry gully. The animals in front were probably pushed by the ones behind into the arroyo. Joe Wheat estimates that the hunters may have obtained 55,000 pounds of meat from this one kill! Judging from recent Plains Indians, who could prepare bison meat to last a month, and estimating that each person would eat a pound a day, the kill at the Olsen-Chubbuck site could have fed more than 1,800 people for a month. The hunters must have been highly organized not only for the stampede itself but also for butchering. It seems that the enormous carcasses had to be carried to flat ground for that job. In addition, the 55,000 pounds of meat and hides had to be carried back to camp.[64]

Although big game may have been most important on the High Plains, other areas show different adaptations. For example, people in woodland regions of what is now the United States seem to have depended more heavily on plant food and smaller game. In some woodland areas, fish and shellfish may have been a vital part of the diet.[65] And in some areas, the lower Illinois River valley being one example, people who depended on game and wild vegetable foods managed to get enough such food to live in permanent villages of perhaps 100 to 150 people.[66]

In recent and modern times too, the peoples of the world have varied culturally. In the next chapter we discuss how they vary physically.

[59]J. D. Jennings, *Prehistory of North America* (New York: McGraw-Hill, 1968), pp. 72–88.

[60]W. James Judge and Jerry Dawson, "Paleo-Indian Settlement Technology in New Mexico," *Science,* June 16, 1972, pp. 1210–16.

[61]Wheat, "A Paleo-Indian Bison Kill."

[62]Brian M. Fagan, *People of the Earth: An Introduction to World Prehistory*, 6th ed. (Glenview, IL: Scott, Foresman and Company, 1989), p. 221.

[63]Wheat, "A Paleo-Indian Bison Kill."

[64]Ibid.

[65]Fagan, *People of the Earth*, p. 227.

[66]Ibid.

SUMMARY

1. Most anthropologists agree that *Homo erectus* began to evolve into *Homo sapiens* after about 500,000 years ago. But there is disagreement about how and where the transition occurred. The mixed traits of the transitional fossils include large cranial capacities (well within the range of modern humans) together with low foreheads and large brow ridges (which are characteristic of *Homo erec-*

tus specimens). The earliest definite *Homo sapiens,* who did not look completely like modern humans, appeared after about 200,000 years ago.

2. Premodern *Homo sapiens* have been found in many parts of the Old World—in Africa and Asia as well as in Europe. Some of these *Homo sapiens* may have lived earlier than the Neandertals of Europe, who were the first premodern humans to be found. There is still debate over whether the Neandertals in western Europe became extinct, or survived and were ancestral to the modern-looking people who lived in western Europe after about 40,000 years ago.

3. The period of cultural history associated with the Neandertals is traditionally called the Middle Paleolithic in Europe and the Near East and dates from after about 300,000 to about 40,000 years ago. For Africa, the term *Middle Stone Age* is used. The assemblages of flake tools from this period are generally referred to as *Mousterian* in Europe and the Near East, and as *post-Acheulian* in Africa.

4. How early *Homo sapiens* got their food probably varied with their environments. Small animals and birds were hunted, large animals were hunted and/or scavenged, and in some places the people seem also to have fished. Little is known about the plant foods that may have been collected, because the remains of plants are unlikely to survive over thousands of years.

5. Some Mousterian sites show signs of intentional burial.

6. Fossil remains of fully modern-looking humans have been found in Africa, the Near East, Asia, and Australia, as well as in Europe. The oldest of these fossils have been found in South Africa.

7. Two theories about the origins of modern humans continue to be debated among anthropologists. One, which can be called the *single-origin* theory, suggests that modern humans emerged in just one part of the Old World (the Near East and, more recently, Africa have been the postulated places of origin) and spread to other parts of the Old World, superseding Neandertals and other premodern *Homo sapiens*. The second theory, which can be called the *continuous-evolution* theory, suggests that modern humans emerged gradually in various parts of the Old World, becoming the varieties of humans we see today.

8. The period of cultural history known as the Upper Paleolithic (in Europe, the Near East, and Asia) or the Later Stone Age (in Africa) dates from about 40,000 years ago to about 14,000 to 10,000 years ago. In many respects, life-styles were similar to life-styles before. People were still mainly hunters and gatherers and fishers who probably lived in highly mobile bands. They made their camps out in the open and in caves and rock-shelters. And they produced smaller and smaller stone tools.

9. The Upper Paleolithic is also characterized by a variety of new developments: the emergence of art, population growth, and new inventions such as the bow and arrow, the spear-thrower, and microliths—tiny replaceable stone blades that could be fitted into handles.

10. Investigators attempt to determine the functions of ancient tools by observing modern cultures with similar technologies and by making and using the tools themselves.

11. Only *Homo sapiens* remains have been found in the New World. The prevailing opinion is that humans migrated to the New World over a land bridge between Siberia and Alaska in the area of what is now the Bering Strait. But when this occurred is subject to debate. The evidence now available does not unquestionably confirm a human presence south of Alaska prior to about 12,000 years ago.

SUGGESTED READING

FAGAN, B. M. *People of the Earth: An Introduction to World Prehistory*, 6th ed. Glenview, IL: Scott, Foresman and Company, 1989. Chapters 5–8 of this book survey the fossil and archeological evidence on *Homo sapiens* in different parts of the world.

LEAKEY, R. E. *The Making of Mankind.* New York: Dutton, 1981. A popular, beautifully illustrated book describing human evolution, both biological and cultural. Chapters 9–11 are particularly relevant to this chapter.

SMITH, F. H., AND SPENCER, F., eds. *The Origins of Modern Humans: A World Survey of the Fossil Evidence.* New York: Alan R. Liss, 1984. Theories about the origins of *Homo sapiens* have traditionally emphasized developments in Europe because most of the fossil evidence available comes from Europe. This volume of papers reflects a shift away from that bias: five of the ten chapters discuss the *Homo sapiens* fossils discovered in Africa, various parts of Asia, and Australia.

TRINKAUS, E., ed. *The Emergence of Modern Humans: Biocultural Adaptations in the Later Pleistocene.* Cambridge: Cambridge University Press, 1989. Physical anthropologists and archeologists review and debate what is known and not known about the Neandertals and the transition to modern humans.

WENKE, R. J. *Patterns in Prehistory: Humankind's First Three Million Years,* 3rd ed. New York: Oxford University Press, 1990. A summary of cultural development that focuses on why various crucial changes may have occurred. Chapter 4 is particularly relevant to this chapter.

7
Human Variation

In the preceding chapter, we discussed the emergence of people like ourselves, *Homo sapiens sapiens*. Just as the cultures of those human beings differed in some respects, so do the cultures of peoples in recent times, as we will see in the chapters that follow. But anthropologists are also concerned with how recent human populations physically resemble or differ from each other, and why.

In any given human population, individuals vary in external features such as skin color or height and in internal features such as blood type or susceptibility to a disease. If you measure the frequencies of such features in different populations, you will typically find differences from one population to another. So, for example, some populations are typically darker in skin color than other populations.

Why do these physical differences exist? They may be purely the product of differences in genes. Or they may be purely the product of environmental factors (physical and cultural). Or they may be the product of environmental factors *and* genetic differences. That is, the environment (including the social or cultural environment) may influence the frequencies of physical traits in different populations.

We turn first in this chapter to the factors that may singly or jointly produce the varying frequencies of physical traits in different human populations. Then we discuss a number of specific differences in external and internal characteristics and how they might be explained. Finally, we close with a critical examination of the concept of race, and whether or not it is relevant to the study of human variation.

Factors in Human Variation

Natural Selection

Mutations, or changes in the chemistry of a gene, are the ultimate source of all genetic variation. Since different genes make for greater or lesser chances of survival and reproduction, natural selection results in more favorable genes becoming more frequent in a population over time. How adaptive a gene or trait is depends on the environment; what is adaptive in one environment may not be adaptive in another. For example, in the chapter on evolution, we discussed the advantage dark moths had over light moths when certain areas of England became industrialized. Predators could not easily see the darker moths against the soot-covered trees, and these moths soon outnumbered the lighter variety. Similarly, human populations live in a great variety of environments, and so we would expect natural selection to favor different genes and traits in those different environments. As we shall see, variation in skin color and body build are among the many features that may be at least partly explainable by natural selection.

The type of natural selection in the moth example is called *directional* selection because a particular trait seems to be positively favored. But natural selection can also be *normalizing*; genes that arise by mutation may be harmful and therefore will be removed by natural selection.[1] The two types of selection just discussed assume that natural selection will either favor or disfavor genes. However, there is also the possibility of *balancing* selection.[2] This occurs when a heterozygous combination of alleles is positively favored even though a homozygous combination is disfavored. Later in this chapter, we discuss a trait that apparently involves balancing selection—sickle-cell anemia—which is found in persons of West African ancestry, among other populations.

Natural selection does not account for variation in frequencies of neutral traits, or traits that do not seem to confer any advantages or disadvantages on their carriers. The sometimes different and sometimes similar frequencies of neutral traits in human populations may result, then, from genetic drift or gene flow.

Genetic Drift

The term **genetic drift** is used to refer to various random processes that affect gene frequencies in small, relatively isolated populations. Genetic

---

[1]G. A. Harrison, J. M. Tanner, D. R. Pilbeam, and P. T. Baker, *Human Biology: An Introduction to Human Evolution, Variation, Growth, and Adaptability*, 3rd ed. (Oxford: Oxford University Press, 1988), pp. 209–12.
[2]William H. Durham, *Coevolution: Genes, Culture, and Human Diversity* (Stanford, CA: Stanford University Press, 1991), pp. 122–23.

drift is also known as the *Wright effect,* after the geneticist Sewall Wright who first directed attention to this process. Over time in a small population, genetic drift may result in a neutral or nearly neutral gene becoming more or less frequent just by chance.[3]

One variety of genetic drift, called the founder principle, occurs when a small group recently derived from a larger population migrates to a relatively isolated location.[4] If a particular gene is absent just by chance in the migrant group, the descendants are likely also to lack that gene, assuming that the group remains isolated. Similarly, if all members of the original migrant group just by chance carried a particular gene, their descendants would also be likely to share that gene.

Gene Flow

Gene flow is the process whereby genes pass from one population to another population through mating and reproduction. Unlike the other processes of natural selection and genetic drift, which act generally to differentiate populations, gene flow tends to work in the opposite direction: it tends to decrease variation. Two populations at opposite ends of a region may have different frequencies of a particular gene. But the populations located between them have an intermediate gene frequency, because of gene flow between them. The variation in gene frequency from one end of the region to the other is called a *cline.* In Europe, for example, there is a cline in the distribution of blood-type B, which gradually diminishes in frequency from east to west.[5]

Gene flow may occur between distant as well as close populations. Long-range movements of people, to trade or raid or settle, may result in gene flow. But they do not always do so, at least not to any substantial degree. A group may move to a new place but refuse to interbreed with the natives of that area. In the United States, for example, the Amish of Pennsylvania have tried to remain isolated. Nevertheless, some marriages have occurred between Amish and non-Amish people, and reproduction has introduced new genes into the Amish gene pool.[6]

Influence of the Physical Environment

Natural selection may favor certain genes because of certain physical environmental conditions, as in the case of the moths in England. But the physical environment can sometimes produce variation even in the absence of genetic change. As we shall see, climate may influence the way the human body grows and develops, and therefore some kinds of human variation may be explainable largely as a function of environmental variation. Moreover, access to certain nutrients and exposure to certain diseases may vary from one physical environment to another, which may also influence how one population varies physically as compared with another. But the influence of the physical environment might be modified by the social or cultural environment.

Influence of the Social or Cultural Environment

Culture may allow humans to modify their environments, which may lessen the likelihood of genetic adaptation. For example, the effects of cold may be modified by the culture traits of living in houses, harnessing energy to create heat, and clothing the body to insulate it. Iron deficiency may be overcome by the culture trait of cooking in iron pots. If a physical environment lacks certain nutrients, people may get them by the culture trait of trading for them; trading for salt has been common in world history. Culture can also influence the direction of natural selection. As we shall see, the culture of dairying seems to have increased the frequency of genes that allow adults to digest milk.[7]

In the section that follows, we discuss some aspects of human (physical) variation for which we

[3]Harrison et al., *Human Biology,* pp. 205–6.
[4]Ibid., pp. 205–8.
[5]Ibid., pp. 198–200.

[6]Laura Newell Morris, "Gene Flow," in Laura Newell Morris, ed., *Human Populations, Genetic Variation, and Evolution* (San Francisco: Chandler, 1971), p. 302. See also W. F. Bodmer and L. L. Cavalli-Sforza, *Genetics, Evolution, and Man* (San Francisco: W. H. Freeman & Company Publishers, 1976), pp. 403–6.
[7]See Durham, *Coevolution: Genes, Culture, and Human Diversity,* pp. 154–225, for an extensive discussion of the relationship between genes and culture.

have explanations that involve one or more of the factors discussed above.

Physical Variation in Human Populations

The most noticeable physical variations among populations are those that are on the surface—body build, facial features, skin color, and height. No less important are those variations that are internal, such as variation in susceptibility to different diseases and differences in the ability to produce certain enzymes.

We begin our survey with some physical features that appear to be strongly linked to variation in climate, particularly variation in temperature, sunlight, and altitude.

Body Build and Facial Construction

Scientists have suggested that the body build of many birds and mammals may vary according to the temperature of the environment in which they live. Bergmann and Allen, two nineteenth century naturalists, suggested some general rules for animals, but it was not until the 1950s that researchers began to examine whether these rules applied to human populations.[8] **Bergmann's rule** describes what seems to be a general relationship between body size and temperature: the slenderer populations of a species inhabit the warmer parts of its geographical range, and the more robust populations inhabit the cooler areas.

The studies by D. F. Roberts of variations in the mean body weights of people living in regions with widely differing temperatures have provided support for Bergmann's rule.[9] Roberts discovered that the lowest body weights were found among residents of areas with the highest mean annual temperatures, and vice versa. For example, where

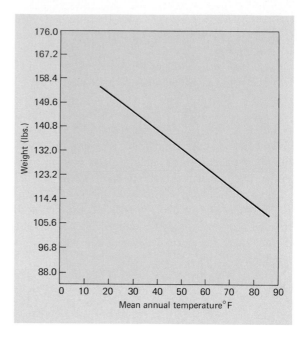

FIGURE 7-1

Graph demonstrating the relationship of mean body weight in a population to the mean annual temperature of the area in which the population is located. The graph supports the application of Bergmann's rule to human populations, suggesting that the lower the mean annual temperature, the higher the mean body weight of the population. *(Source: After Stanley M. Garn, Human Races, 3rd ed., 1971. Courtesy of Charles C Thomas, Publisher, Springfield, Illinois.)*

the mean annual temperatures are 70° to 82° F., people weigh, on the average, only 110 to 120 pounds. Populations with average weights over 140 pounds live where the temperature averages 40° F (See Figure 7–1).

Allen's rule refers to another kind of variation in body build among birds and mammals: protruding body parts (e.g., limbs) are relatively shorter in the cooler areas of a species' range than in the warmer areas. Research comparing human populations tends to support Allen's rule.[10]

The rationale behind these theories is that the long-limbed, lean body type often found in tropical regions provides more surface area in relation to body mass and thus facilitates the dissipation of body heat. In contrast, the chunkier, shorter-limbed body type found among the residents of cold regions promotes retention of body heat be-

[8]Joel M. Hanna, Michael A. Little, and Donald M. Austin, "Climatic Physiology," in Michael A. Little and Jere D. Haas, eds., *Human Population Biology: A Transdisciplinary Science* (New York: Oxford University Press, 1989), pp. 133–36; Harrison et al., *Human Biology*, pp. 504–7.

[9]D. F. Roberts, "Body Weight, Race, and Climate," *American Journal of Physical Anthropology*, 2 (1953): 553–58. Cited in Stanley M. Garn, *Human Races*, 3rd ed. (Springfield, IL: Charles C Thomas, 1971), p. 73. See also D. F. Roberts, *Climate and Human Variability*, 2nd ed. (Menlo Park, CA: Cummings, 1978).

[10]Ibid.

These Samburu men in northern Kenya have the long-limbed, lean body type that is often found in equatorial regions. Such a body type provides more surface area in relation to body mass and thus may facilitate the dissipation of body heat.

cause the amount of surface area relative to body mass is lessened. The build of the Inuit appears to exemplify Bergmann's and Allen's rules. Their relatively large bodies and short legs may be adapted to the cold temperatures in which they live.

It is not clear whether differences in body build between populations are due solely to natural selection of different genes under different conditions of cold or heat. Some of the variation may be induced during the life span of individuals.[11] Alphonse Riesenfeld has provided experimental evidence that extreme cold can affect body proportions during growth and development. Rats raised under conditions of extreme cold generally show changes that resemble characteristics of humans in cold environments. These cold-related changes include long-bone shortening consistent with Allen's rule.[12]

Like body build, facial structure may be af-

fected by environment. Riesenfeld found that the facial width of rats increased in cold temperatures and their nasal openings grow smaller.[13] Because the rats raised in cold environments were genetically similar to those raised in warmer environments, we can confidently conclude that environment, not genes, brought about these changes in the rats. How much the environment directly affects variation in the human face is not yet clear. We do know that variation in climate is associated with facial variation. For example, people living in the humid tropics tend to have broad, short, flat noses, whereas people living in climates with low humidity (with cold or hot temperatures) tend to have long, thin noses. A relatively narrow nose may be a more efficient humidifier of drier air than a broad nose.[14]

[11]Harrison et al., *Human Biology*, p. 505.

[12]Alphonse Riesenfeld, "The Effect of Extreme Temperatures and Starvation on the Body Proportions of the Rat," *American Journal of Physical Anthropology*, 39 (1973): 427–59.

[13]Ibid., pp. 452–53.

[14]J. S. Weiner, "Nose Shape and Climate," *Journal of Physical Anthropology*, 4 (1954): 615–18; A. T. Steegman, Jr., "Human Adaptation to Cold," in Albert Damon, ed., *Physiological Anthropology* (New York: Oxford University Press, 1975), pp. 130–66.

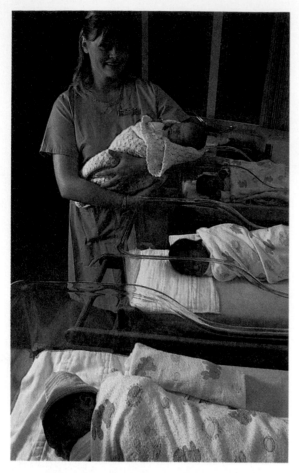

Natural selection seems to favor darker skin color in areas close to the equator.

Skin Color

Human populations obviously differ in average skin color. Many people consider skin color the most important indicator of racial distinction and sometimes treat others differently solely on this basis. But anthropologists, in addition to being critical of racial discrimination, also note that skin color is not a good indicator of racial or geographical ancestry. For example, extremely dark skin is found most commonly in Africa. However, there are natives of southern India whose skin is as dark as, or darker than, that of many Africans. Yet these people are not closely related to Africans, either genetically or historically.

How can we explain the wide range of skin colors among the peoples of the world? The color of a person's skin depends on both the amount of

dark pigment or melanin in the skin and the amount of blood in the small blood vessels of the skin.[15] Despite the fact that there is still much to understand about the genetics of skin color, we do have some theories that may partially account for variation in skin color.

The amount of melanin in the skin seems to be related to the climate in which a person lives. **Gloger's rule** states that populations of birds and mammals living in warm, humid climates have more melanin (and therefore darker skin, fur, or feathers) than do populations of the same species living in cooler, drier areas. On the whole, this association with climate holds true for people as well as for birds and other mammals.

The populations of darker-skinned humans do live mostly in warm climates (although all residents of warm climates do not have dark skins). Dark pigmentation seems to have at least one specific advantage in tropical climates. Melanin protects the sensitive inner layers of the skin from the sun's damaging ultraviolet rays; therefore, dark-skinned people living in sunny areas are safer from sunburn and skin cancers than light-skinned people. Dark skin may also confer a number of other important biological advantages in tropical environments, such as greater resistance to tropical diseases.[16]

What, then, might be the advantages of light-colored skin? Presumably, there must be some benefits; otherwise, through the process of natural selection, human populations would all tend to have more or less dark skin. Although light-skinned people are more susceptible to sunburn and skin cancers, the ultraviolet radiation that light skin absorbs also facilitates the body's production of vitamin D. Vitamin D helps the body incorporate calcium and thus is necessary for the proper growth and maintenance of bones. Too much vitamin D, however, can cause illness. Thus, the light-colored skin of people in temperate latitudes maximizes ultraviolet penetration, perhaps ensuring production of sufficient amounts of vitamin D for good health,

[15]Harrison et al., *Human Biology,* pp. 308–10.
[16]Anthony P. Polednak, "Connective Tissue Responses in Negroes in Relation to Disease," *American Journal of Physical Anthropology,* 41 (1974): 49–57. See also Richard F. Branda and John W. Eaton, "Skin Color and Nutrient Photolysis: An Evolutionary Hypothesis," *Science,* August 18, 1978, pp. 625–26.

whereas the darker skin of people in tropical latitudes minimizes ultraviolet penetration, perhaps thereby preventing illness from too much vitamin D.[17] Light skin may also confer another advantage in colder environments: it is less likely to be damaged by frostbite.[18]

Adaptation to High Altitude

Oxygen constitutes 21 percent of the air we breathe at sea level. At high altitudes, the percentage of oxygen in the air is the same, but because the barometric pressure is lower, we take in less oxygen with each breath.[19] We breathe more rapidly, our hearts beat faster, and all activity is more difficult. This leads to discomfort and a condition known as **hypoxia,** or oxygen deficiency.

Since high altitude presents such difficulties for many human beings, how is it that populations numbering in the millions can live out their lives, healthy and productive, at altitudes of 6,000, 12,000, or even 17,000 feet? Populations in the Himalayas and the Andes seem to have adapted to their environments, and do not display the symptoms suffered by low-altitude dwellers when exposed to high altitudes. Moreover, high-altitude dwellers have also come to terms physiologically with extreme cold, deficient nutrition, strong winds, rough countryside, and intense solar radiation.[20]

The early studies of Andean high-altitude dwellers found that they differed in certain physical ways from low-altitude dwellers. Compared to low-altitude dwellers, high-altitude Andean Indians had larger chests and greater lung capacity, as well as more surface area in the capillaries of the lungs (which was believed to facilitate the transfer of oxygen to the blood).[21] It seemed to the early researchers that genetic changes had allowed the Andeans to maximize their ability to take in oxygen at the lower barometric pressure of their high-altitude environment.

However, recent research has cast some doubt on this conclusion. It appears now that other populations living at high altitudes do not show the Andean pattern of physical differences. In the Himalayas, for example, low-altitude dwellers and high-altitude dwellers do not differ in chest size or lung size, even though both groups show similar lung functioning.[22]

Thus, current research does not suggest that high-altitude living requires biological adaptations that are purely genetic. In fact, some evidence suggests that humans who grow up as children in a high-altitude environment may adapt to hypoxia during their lifetimes, as they grow up. For example, Peruvians who were born at sea-level, but who grew up at high altitudes, developed the same amount of lung capacity as people who spent their entire lives at high altitudes.[23] As with other traits that have been studied, it appears that genetic predispositions can often be modified by life experiences.

Height

Studies of identical twins and comparisons of the height of parents and children suggest that heredity plays a considerable role in determining height,[24] so genetic differences presumably play a significant role in determining population differences in average height. But if average height can increase dramatically in a few decades, as in Japan between 1950 and 1980 and in many other countries in recent times,[25] environmental influences are also likely to be important.

Human populations vary considerably in average height. The Dutch of Europe are among the tallest populations in the world on average, the Mbuti Pygmies of Zaire in central Africa among

[17]W. Farnsworth Loomis, "Skin-Pigment Regulation of Vitamin-D Biosynthesis in Man," *Science*, August 4, 1967, pp. 501–6.

[18]Peter W. Post, Farrington Daniels, Jr., and Robert T. Binford, Jr., "Cold Injury and the Evolution of 'White' Skin," *Human Biology*, 47 (1975): 65–80.

[19]William A. Stini, *Ecology and Human Adaptation* (Dubuque, IA: Wm. C. Brown, 1975), p. 53.

[20]Richard B. Mazess, "Human Adaptation to High Altitude," in Damon, ed., *Physiological Anthropology*, p. 168.

[21]Lawrence P. Greksa, and Cynthia M. Beall, "Development of Chest Size and Lung Function at High Altitude," in Little and Haas, eds., *Human Population Biology*, p. 223.

[22]Ibid., p. 226.

[23]A. Roberto Frisancho, and Lawrence P. Greksa, "Development Responses in the Acquisition of Functional Adaptation to High Altitude," in Little and Haas, eds., *Human Population Biology*, p. 204.

[24]Phyllis B. Eveleth, and James M. Tanner, *Worldwide Variation in Human Growth*, 2nd ed. (Cambridge: Cambridge University Press, 1990), pp. 176–79.

[25]Ibid., pp. 205–6.

the shortest.[26] Since weight is related to height (heavier people are likely to be taller), and since weight is related to mean annual temperature (Bergmann's rule), some of the population variation in height would appear to involve adaptation to heat and cold.[27] However, other factors besides heat and cold must also be operating, since tall and short peoples can be found in most areas of the world.

Many researchers think that undernutrition and disease lead to reduced height and weight. In many parts of the world, children in higher social classes are taller on the average than children in lower social classes,[28] and this difference is more marked in economically poorer countries[29] (where the wealth and health differences between the classes are particularly large). During times of war and undernutrition, children's stature often decreases. For example, in Germany during World War II, the stature of children 7–17 years of age declined as compared with previous time periods, despite the fact that stature had generally increased over time.[30]

More persuasive evidence for the effect of undernutrition and disease comes out of studies of the same individuals over time (these are called "longitudinal" studies). For example, Reynaldo Martorell found that children in Guatemala who had frequent bouts of diarrhea were on the average over an inch shorter at age seven than children without frequent diarrhea.[31] Although malnourished or diseased children can catch up later in their growth, follow-up research on Guatemalan children suggests that if stunting occurs before three years of age, stature at age eighteen will still be reduced.[32]

A more controversial set of studies links a very different environmental factor to variation in height in human populations. The factor at issue is stress (physical and emotional) in infancy.[33] Contrary to the view that any kind of stress is harmful, it appears that some presumably stressful experiences in infancy are associated with greater height and weight. Experimental studies with rats provided the original stimulus for the studies investigating the possible effect of stress on height. The experiments showed that rats physically handled ("petted") by the experimenters grew to be longer and heavier than rats not petted. Researchers originally thought that this was because the petted rats had received "tender loving care." But someone noticed that the petted rats seemed terrified (they urinated and defecated) when petted by humans, which suggested that the petting might have been stressful. It turned out in subsequent studies that even more obviously stressful experiences such as electric shock, vibration, and temperature extremes also produced rats with longer skeletons (as compared with unstressed rats).

Many cultures have customs for treating infants that could be stressful, including circumcision, branding of the skin with sharp objects, piercing the nose, ears, or lips for the insertion of ornaments, molding and stretching the head and limbs for cosmetic purposes, vaccination, and separating the baby from its mother right after birth. In cross-cultural comparisons, it seems that these stressful practices *if practiced before two years of age* predict greater adult height; males are on the average two inches taller in such societies. (It is important to note that the stresses being discussed are short in duration and do not constitute prolonged stress or abuse.)

Even though the researchers tried to control for nutritional differences, it is possible that the differences in height were due to other differences

---

[26]Barry Bogin, *Patterns of Human Growth* (Cambridge: Cambridge University Press, 1988), pp. 105–6.

[27]Harrison et al., *Human Biology*, p. 300.

[28]Ibid., p. 198.

[29]Rebecca Huss-Ashmore and Francis E. Johnston, "Bioanthropological Research in Developing Countries," *Annual Review of Anthropology*, 14 (1985): 482–83.

[30]Harrison et al., *Human Biology*, pp. 385–86.

[31]R. Martorell, "Interrelationships between Diet, Infectious Disease and Nutritional Status," in L. Greene and F. E. Johnston, eds., *Social and Biological Predictors of Nutritional Status, Physical Growth and Neurological Development* (New York: Academic Press, 1980), pp. 81–106.

[32]Reynaldo Martorell, Juan Rivera, Haley Kaplowitz, and Ernesto Pollitt, "Long-Term Consequences of Growth Retardation during Early Childhood," paper presented at the VIth International Congress of Auxology, September 15–19, 1991, Madrid.

[33]Thomas K. Landauer and John W. M. Whiting, "Infantile Stimulation and Adult Stature of Human Males," *American Anthropologist*, 66 (1964): 1007–28; S. Gunders and J. W. M. Whiting, "Mother–Infant Separation and Physical Growth," *Ethnology*, 7 (1968): 196–206; J. Patrick Gray and Linda D. Wolfe, "Height and Sexual Dimorphism of Stature among Human Societies," *American Journal of Physical Anthropology*, 53 (1980): 446–52; Thomas K. Landauer and John W. M. Whiting, "Correlates and Consequences of Stress in Infancy," in Ruth H. Munroe, Robert L. Munroe, and Beatrice B. Whiting, eds., *Handbook of Cross-Cultural Human Development* (New York: Garland Press, 1981), pp. 361–65.

between the societies. More persuasive evidence may be forthcoming from an experimental study conducted in Kenya.[34] The researchers there arranged for a randomly selected sample of children to be vaccinated before they were two years old. (Other children were vaccinated soon after they were two.) At seven years of age the two groups of children were compared with respect to height. Consistent with the cross-cultural evidence on the possible effect of stress on height, the children vaccinated before the age of two were significantly taller than the children vaccinated later. Since the children vaccinated before the age of two were selected *randomly* for early vaccination, it is unlikely (although not impossible) that nutritional or other differences between the two groups may account for the difference between them in height.

In several areas of the world, people have recently been getting taller. For example, between World Wars I and II, the average height of males in the United States increased by two inches.[35] As mentioned earlier, Japan since World War II shows the same trend.

What accounts for this recent trend toward greater height? Several factors may be involved. Some researchers think that it may be the result of improved nutrition and lower incidence of infectious diseases.[36] But it might also be that infant stress has increased as a result of giving birth in hospitals, which usually separate babies from mothers and also subject the newborns to medical tests including the taking of blood. And various kinds of vaccinations have also become more common in infancy.[37]

Any of the genetic and environmental factors (singly and in combination) discussed in this section may affect human size. Further research is needed to determine which factors are the most important.

Susceptibility to Infectious Diseases

Certain populations seem to have developed inherited resistances to certain infectious diseases. That is, populations repeatedly decimated by certain diseases in the past now have a high frequency of genetic characteristics that minimize the effects of these diseases. As Arno Motulsky has pointed out, if there are genes that protect people from dying when they are infected by one of the diseases prevalent in their area, these genes will tend to become more common in succeeding generations.[38]

A field study of the infectious disease myxomatosis in rabbits supports this theory. When the virus responsible for the disease was first introduced into the Australian rabbit population, more than 95 percent of the infected animals died. But among the offspring of animals exposed to successive epidemics of myxomatosis, the percentage of animals that died from the disease decreased from year to year. The more epidemics the animals' ancestors had lived through, the smaller the percentage of current animals that died of the disease. Thus, the data suggested that the rabbits had developed a genetic resistance to myxomatosis.[39]

Infectious diseases seem to follow a similar pattern among human populations. When tuberculosis first strikes a population that has had no previous contact with it, the disease is commonly fatal. But some populations seem to have inherited a resistance to death from tuberculosis. For example, the Ashkenazi Jews in America (those whose ancestors came from central and eastern Europe) are one of several populations whose ancestors survived many years of exposure to tuberculosis in the crowded European ghettos where they had previously lived. Although the rate of tuberculosis infection is identical among American Jews and non-Jews, the rate of tuberculosis mortality is significantly lower among Jews than among non-Jews in this country.[40] After reviewing other data on this subject, Motulsky thinks it likely "that the present relatively high resistance of Western populations to tuberculosis is genetically conditioned through natural selection during long contact with the disease."[41]

We tend to think of measles as a childhood disease that kills virtually no one. And we now have a vaccine against it. But when first intro-

[34]Landauer and Whiting, "Correlates and Consequences of Stress in Infancy," p. 369.

[35]Stini, *Ecology and Human Adaptation*, p. 3.

[36]Eveleth and Tanner, *Worldwide Variation in Human Growth*, p. 205.

[37]Thomas K. Landauer, "Infantile Vaccination and the Secular Trend in Stature," *Ethos*, 1 (1973): 499–503.

[38]Arno Motulsky, "Metabolic Polymorphisms and the Role of Infectious Diseases in Human Evolution," in Morris, ed., *Human Populations, Genetic Variation, and Evolution*, p. 223.

[39]Ibid., p. 226.

[40]Ibid., p. 229.

[41]Ibid., p. 230.

duced into populations, the measles virus can kill large numbers of people. In 1949, the Tupari Indians of Brazil numbered about 200 people. By 1955, two-thirds of the Tupari had died of measles introduced into the tribe by rubber gatherers in the area.[42] Large numbers of people died of measles in epidemics in the Faroe Islands in 1846, in Hawaii in 1848, in the Fiji Islands in 1874, and among the Canadian Inuit quite recently. It is possible that where mortality rates from measles are low, populations have acquired a genetic resistance to death from this disease.[43]

Some researchers suggest that nongenetic factors may be more important than genetic factors in differential resistance to infectious disease. For example, cultural practices more than genetic susceptibility may explain the epidemics of measles among the Yanomamö Indians of Venezuela and Brazil. The Yanomamö frequently visit other villages. That together with the nonisolation of sick individuals promoted a very rapid spread of the disease. Many individuals were sick at the same time, so there were not enough healthy people to feed and care for the sick; mothers down with measles could not even nurse their babies. Thus, cultural factors may increase exposure to a disease and worsen its effect on a population.[44]

Sickle-Cell Anemia

Another biological variation is an abnormality of the red blood cells known as **sickle-cell anemia,** or **sicklemia.** This is a condition in which the red blood cells assume a crescent (sickle) shape when deprived of oxygen, instead of the normal (disk) shape. The sickle-shaped red blood cells do not move through the body as readily as normal cells, which causes more oxygen deficiency and damage to the heart, lungs, brain, and other vital organs. In addition, the red blood cells tend to "die" more rapidly, which also worsens the anemia.[45]

It is now known that sickle-cell anemia is caused by a variant of the genetic instructions for hemoglobin, the protein that carries oxygen in the red-blood cells.[46] Individuals who have sickle-cell anemia have inherited the same allele (Hb S) from both parents and are therefore homozygous for that gene. Individuals who receive this allele from only one parent are heterozygous; they have one Hb S allele and one allele for normal hemoglobin (Hb A). Heterozygotes will generally not show the full-blown symptoms of sickle-cell disease, although in some cases a heterozygous individual may have a mild case of anemia. A heterozygous person of course has a 50 percent chance of passing on the sickle-cell allele to a child. And if the child mates with another person who is also a carrier of the sickle-cell allele, the statistical probability is that 25 percent of their children will develop sickle-cell anemia. Without advanced medical care, most individuals with two Hb S alleles are unlikely to live more than a few years.[47]

Why has the allele for sickle-cell persisted in various populations? Since people with sickle-cell anemia do not usually live to reproduce, we would expect a reduction in the frequency of Hb S to near-zero through the process of *normalizing* selection. But the sickle-cell allele occurs fairly often in some parts of the world, particularly in the wet tropical belt of Africa (where frequencies may be between 20 and 30 percent) and in Greece, Sicily, and southern India.[48]

Since the sickle-cell gene occurs in these places much more often than expected, researchers in the 1940s and the 1950s began to suspect that heterozygous individuals (who carry one Hb S allele) might have a reproductive advantage in a malarial environment.[49] If the heterozygotes were more resistant to attacks of malaria than the homozygotes for normal hemoglobin (who get the Hb A allele from both parents), the heterozygotes would be more likely to survive and reproduce, and therefore the recessive Hb S allele would persist at a higher than expected frequency in the population. This kind of outcome is an example of *balancing* selection.

[42]Ibid., p. 233.

[43]Ibid.

[44]James V. Neel et al, "Notes on the Effect of Measles and Measles Vaccine in a Virgin-Soil Population of South American Indians," *American Journal of Epidemiology*, 91 (1970): 418–29.

[45]Durham, *Coevolution: Genes, Culture, and Human Diversity*, pp. 105–7.

[46]Ibid.

[47]Ibid., p. 107.

[48]Harrison et al., *Human Biology*," p. 231.

[49]For a review of the early research, see Durham, *Coevolution: Genes, Culture, and Human Diversity*, pp. 123–27. The particular form of malaria that is being discussed is caused by the species *Plasmodium falciparum*.

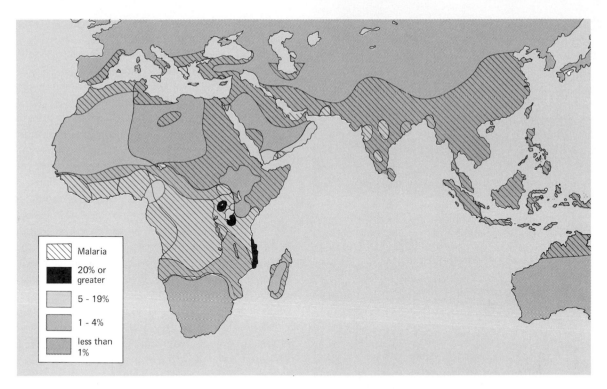

FIGURE 7-2 Geographical Distribution of Sicklemia and Its Relationship to the Distribution of Malaria

(Source: Adapted from Physical Anthropology: A Perspective, *by John Buettner-Janusch. © 1973 By John Wiley & Sons, Inc. Reprinted by permission of John Wiley & Sons, Inc.)*

A number of pieces of evidence support the "malaria theory." First, geographical comparisons show that the sickle-cell allele tends to be found where the incidence of malaria is high (see Figure 7–2). Second, as land in the tropics is opened to yam and rice agriculture, the incidence of the sickle-cell allele also increases. The reason seems to be that malaria, carried principally by the *Anopheles gambiae* mosquito, becomes more likely as tropical forest gives way to more open land where mosquitos can thrive in warm, sunlit ponds. Indeed, even among peoples of similar cultural backgrounds, the incidence of the sickle-cell allele increases with greater rainfall and surpluses of water. Third, children who carry the sickle-cell allele tend to have fewer malarial parasites in their bodies and are more likely to survive.[50] The sickling trait does not necessarily keep people from contracting malaria, but it greatly decreases the rate of mortality from malaria—and in evolutionary terms, the overall effect is the same.[51]

Lactase Deficiency

When American educators discovered that black schoolchildren very often did not drink milk, they assumed that lack of money or of education was the reason. These assumptions provided the impetus for establishing the school milk programs prevalent around the country.

However, it now appears that after infancy many people lack an enzyme, lactase I, that is necessary for breaking down the sugar in milk, lactose, into simpler sugars that can be absorbed into the bloodstream.[52] Thus, a person without lactase cannot digest milk properly, and drinking it may cause bloating, cramps, stomach gas, and diarrhea. A

[51]Motulsky, "Metabolic Polymorphisms and the Role of Infectious Diseases in Human Evolution," p. 238.
[52]Durham, *Coevolution: Genes, Culture, and Human Diversity,* p. 230.

[50]Ibid., pp. 124–45.

Milking a cow in Barnstable, Massachusetts. Natural selection may favor production of the enzyme lactase, a genetic way of making milk digestible in dairying populations far from the equator.

A Masai woman milking a cow in Kenya. Natural selection may favor the souring of milk, a cultural way of making it digestible in dairying populations close to the equator.

study conducted in Baltimore among 312 black and 221 white children in grades 1 through 6 in two elementary schools indicated that 85 percent of the black children *and* 17 percent of the white children were milk-intolerant.[53]

More recent studies indicate that lactose intolerance is frequent in adults in many parts of the world.[54] The condition is common in Southeast and East Asia, India, the Mediterranean and the Near East, sub-Saharan Africa, and among Native North and South Americans.

What accounts for adult intolerance of milk? Part of the answer is that some people do not inherit the ability to make lactase I and digest lactose. (We still need to understand why selection would favor this genetic inability in some populations but not in others.) In the late 1960s Simoons and McCracken noted a relationship between lactose absorption and dairying (raising cows for milk). They suggested that with the advent of dairying, individuals with the genetic ability to produce lactase in adulthood would have greater reproductive success, and hence dairying populations would come to have a high proportion of individuals with the ability to break down lactose.[55]

But people in some dairying societies do not produce lactase in adulthood. Rather, they seem to have developed a cultural solution to the problem of lactase deficiency: they transform their milk into cheese, yogurt, sour cream, and other milk products that are low in lactose. To make these low-lactose products, people separate the lactose-rich whey from the curds, or treat the milk with a bacterium (*Lactobacillus*) that breaks down the lactose, thus making the milk product digestible by a lactase-deficient person.[56]

So why in some dairying societies did natural selection favor a biological solution (the production in adulthood of the enzyme lactase) rather than the cultural solution? William Durham has collected evidence that natural selection may favor the biological solution in dairying societies further from the equator. The theory is that lactose behaves biochemically like vitamin D, facilitating the absorption of calcium—but only in people who produce lactase so that they can absorb the lactose. Because people in more temperate latitudes are not exposed to that much sunlight, particularly in the winter, and therefore make less vitamin D in their skin, natural selection may have favored the lactase way of absorbing dietary calcium.[57] In other words, natural selection may favor

[53]Jane E. Brodey, "Effects of Milk on Blacks Noted," *New York Times*, October 15, 1971, p. 15.

[54]Durham, *Coevolution: Genes, Culture, and Human Diversity*, pp. 233–35.

[55]Robert D. McCracken, "Lactase Deficiency: An Example of Dietary Evolution," *Current Anthropology*, 12 (1971): 479–500; see also references to the work of F. J. Simoons as referred to in Durham, *Coevolution: Genes, Culture, and Human Diversity*, pp. 240–41.

[56]McCracken, "Lactase Deficiency, p. 480.

[57]Durham, *Coevolution: Genes, Culture, and Human Diversity*, pp. 263–69.

lactase production in adulthood, as well as lighter skin, at higher latitudes (where there is less sunlight).

This is an example of how culture may influence the way natural selection favors some genes over others. Without dairying, natural selection may not have favored the genetic propensity to produce lactase.

The Concept of Race

Fortunately, internal variations such as lactase deficiency have never caused tensions among peoples—perhaps because such differences are not immediately obvious. Unfortunately, the same cannot be said for some of the more obvious external human differences.

Race and Racism

For as long as any of us can remember, countless aggressive actions—from fistfights to large-scale riots and countrywide civil wars—have stemmed from tension and misunderstandings among various "races." "The race problem" has become such a common phrase that most of us take the concept of race for granted, not bothering to consider what it does, and does not, mean.

The word **race** is used in a variety of ways. Consider, for example, what we mean when we refer to the "human race." Obviously, that phrase is supposed to include *all* people and does not have anything to do with the usual meaning of race. The "Aryan race" was supposed to be the group of blond-haired, blue-eyed, white-skinned people whom Hitler wanted to dominate the world, to which end he attempted to destroy as many members of the "Jewish race" as he could. But who are the Aryans? Technically, Aryans are any people, including the German-speaking Jews in Hitler's Germany, who speak one of the Indo-European languages. The Indo-European languages include such disparate modern tongues as Greek, Spanish, Hindi, Polish, French, Icelandic, German, Gaelic, and English, and many Aryans speaking these languages have neither blond hair nor blue eyes. Similarly, the Jewish race does not exist in anthropological terms, since all kinds of people may be Jews, whether or not they descend from the ancient Near Eastern population that spoke the He-

brew language. There are light-skinned Danish Jews and darker Jewish Arabs. One of the most orthodox Jewish groups in the United States is based in New York City and is composed entirely of African Americans.

Nevertheless, most people in this country do identify themselves with a "racial" group, most often one of the three races most commonly recognized: the Caucasoid (white), Negroid (black), and Mongoloid (yellow and red). Many people think that certain biological traits are characteristic of each race. Another frequent belief is that although the races have become "adulterated" through miscegenation (marriage and breeding between different races), some individuals still exist who typify the "pure" Caucasoid, Negroid, and Mongoloid types. The inaccuracy of such a classification should be obvious. Although many Caucasoids have straight hair and light skin, some have curly or quite frizzy hair and rather dark skin. Not all Negroids have wide noses or thick lips. And many people do not easily fit into any of the three major racial types at all.

But racial stereotypes persist—largely because of the ease with which such obvious traits as skin color can be recognized and used to classify people. In itself, this tendency to attribute certain biological factors to all members of a supposed race, while inaccurate, is not disturbing. What is disturbing is the frequent association of the race concept with racism.

Race concepts have often been, and still are, used by certain groups to justify their exploitation of other groups. Discrimination against African Americans is an example of how racism is linked to inaccurate concepts of race. Most of the people who tried to justify the virtual elimination of black civil rights did so because of a belief in blacks' inherent (genetic) inferiority to whites. In fact no such inferiority has been demonstrated. This racist outlook may be a remnant of slavery days, when white slaveholders assumed that their servants were inferior—and tried to convince the slaves that they were—in order to perpetuate the system.

The Arbitrariness of the Concept of Race

The major difficulty with the race concept is its arbitrariness. The number of races into which the world's population can be divided depends on who is doing the classifying, because each classifier may use different traits as the basis for the classification. Any variable traits—such as skin color, blood type, and hair, nose, and lip shape—could be considered when developing a racial classification. But unfortunately for the classifiers, many of these traits do not vary together. Even the supposedly distinguishing features of a Mongoloid person—the so-called Mongoloid spot, a dark patch of skin at the base of the spine that disappears as the person grows older; shovel-shaped incisor teeth; and the epicanthic fold, a bit of skin overlapping the eyelid—are not limited to people traditionally classified as Mongoloid. Southern Africa's Bushmen have epicanthic folds, for example, and Caucasoids can have Mongoloid spots.

Thus, since the number of races in each classification of peoples depends on the traits used in the classification, and since many anthropologists base their classifications on different traits, there is no right or wrong number of races. William Boyd says there are five races, Carleton Coon recognizes nine, and Joseph Birdsell counts thirty-two.[58]

Racial taxonomies in anthropology typically involve the identification of both geographical races and local races. A geographical race is a set of at least once-neighboring populations that has certain distinctive trait frequencies. Thus, the traditional trio of races (Negroid, Mongoloid, Caucasoid) would be considered geographical. Stanley Garn identifies a total of nine geographical races: European-Caucasoid and Western Asiatic; Northern Mongoloid and Eastern Asiatic; African-Negroid; (South Asian) Indian; Micronesian; Melanesian; Polynesian; (Native) American; and (Native) Australian.[59] A local race is like a Mendelian population: it is a breeding population, or local group, whose members usually interbreed. Garn identifies approximately thirty-two local races.[60]

Anthropologists not only disagree on the number of races into which people can be classified; many would argue that the concept of race is not particularly useful scientifically. Racial categories hardly ever correspond to the variations in human

biology we want to explain. For example, populations classified as belonging to the same "race" may differ considerably in height, skin color, and body build. In addition, "racial" differences explain only a small percentage of the known genetic differences among humans. R. C. Lewontin estimates that only about 6 percent of genetic diversity can be explained by "racial" differences.[61] Racial taxonomies, then, may hinder rather than facilitate the study of human variation.

Racial and Cultural Variation: Is There a Relationship?

Many persons hold the racist viewpoint that the biological inferiority of certain races is reflected in the supposedly primitive quality of their cultures. Racists refuse to recognize that the facts of history very often contradict their theories.

Race and Civilization. Many of today's so-called underdeveloped nations—primarily in Asia, Africa, and South America—had developed complex and sophisticated civilizations long before Europe reached beyond a simple level of technology or tribal organization. The advanced societies of the Shang dynasty in China, the Mayans in Mesoamerica, and the African empires of Ghana, Mali, and Songhay were all founded and developed by nonwhites.

Between 1523 and 1028 B.C., China had a complex form of government, armies, metal tools and weapons, and production and storage facilities for large quantities of grain. The early Chinese civilization also had a form of writing and elaborate religious rituals.[62] From A.D. 300 to 900, the Mayans were a large population with a thriving economy. They built many large and beautiful cities, in which were centered great pyramids and luxurious palaces.[63] According to legend, the West African civilization of Ghana was founded during the second century A.D. By A.D. 770 (the time of the Sonniki rulers), Ghana had developed two capital cities—one Muslim and the other non-Muslim—

[58]Theodosius Dobzhansky, *Mankind Evolving: The Evolution of the Human Species* (New Haven: Yale University Press, 1962), p. 266.
[59]Garn, *Human Races*, pp. 152–67.
[60]Ibid., pp. 169–79.

[61]R. C. Lewontin, "The Apportionment of Human Diversity," in Theodosius Dobzhansky, ed., *Evolutionary Biology* (New York: Plenum, 1972), pp. 381–98.
[62]L. Carrington Goodrich, *A Short History of the Chinese People*, 3rd ed. (New York: Harper & Row, 1959), pp. 7–15.
[63]Michael D. Coe, *The Maya* (New York: Praeger, 1966), pp. 74–76.

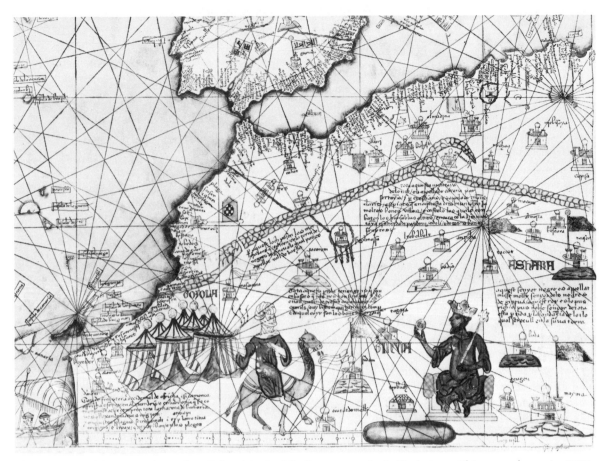

The Western African Kingdom of Mali flourished while Europe was in its Dark Ages. This map, drawn in 1375, shows an Arab trader coming to bargain with Mali's ruler. The writing says, "This Negro Lord is called Musa Mali, Lord of the Negroes of Guinea. So abundant is the gold which is found in his land that he is the richest and most noble King in all the land."

each with its own ruler and both supported largely by Ghana's lucrative gold market.[64]

Considering how recently northern Europeans developed civilizations, it seems odd that some whites should label Africans, South American Indians, and others backward in terms of historical achievement, or biologically inferior in terms of capacity for civilization. But racists, both white and nonwhite, choose to ignore the fact that many populations have achieved remarkable advances in civilization. Most significant, racists refuse to believe that they can acknowledge the achievements of another group without in any way downgrading the achievements of their own.

Race, Culture, and Infectious Disease. Although biological variations cannot set fixed limits on the development of a particular culture, they may strongly influence it. Earlier, we discussed how continued exposure to epidemics of infectious diseases, such as tuberculosis and measles, can cause succeeding generations to acquire a genetic resistance to death from such diseases. But on a short-term basis, differential susceptibility to disease may have affected the outcome of contact between different societies.[65] A possible example of this is the rapid defeat of the Aztecs of Mexico by Cortez and his conquistadores. In 1520, a member of Cortez's army unwittingly transmitted smallpox

[64]Elizabeth Bartlett Thompson, *Africa, Past and Present* (Boston: Houghton Mifflin, 1966), p. 89.

[65]William H. McNeill, *Plagues and Peoples* (Garden City, NY: Doubleday Anchor, 1976).

to the Indians. The disease spread rapidly through the population, killing at least half of the Indians, who were thus at a considerable disadvantage in their battling with the Spanish.[66]

Outbreaks of smallpox repeatedly decimated many Native American populations in North America a century or two later. In the early nineteenth century, the Massachusetts and Narragansett Indians, with populations of 30,000 and 9,000, respectively, were reduced by smallpox to a few hundred members. Extremely high mortality rates were also noted among the Crow, the Blackfoot, and other Native American groups during the nineteenth century. The germ theory alone cannot explain these epidemics. Once the European settlers realized how susceptible the natives were to smallpox, they purposely distributed infected blankets to them. Motulsky calls the spread of smallpox "one of the first examples of biological warfare."[67]

Race and Intelligence. Perhaps the most controversial aspect of the racial distinctions made among people is the relationship sometimes supposed between race and intelligence.

In the nineteenth century, European white supremacists attempted to find scientific justification for what they felt was the genetically inherited mental inferiority of blacks. They did this by measuring skulls. It was believed that the larger the skull, the greater the cranial capacity and the bigger (hence, also better) the brain.

Interest in skull measurement was first aroused by a number of separate researchers in different parts of Europe who tried to determine the relative intelligence of round-headed versus narrow-headed individuals. Not surprisingly, their results were generally either inconclusive or contradictory. Paul Broca held that round-headed Frenchmen were superior in intelligence to narrow-headed Frenchmen, while Otto Ammon concluded that the city of Baden's more intelligent residents had narrow heads. The Italian Livi concluded that southern Italians with round heads were of superior intelligence.

Although the skull-measuring mania quickly disappeared and is no longer considered seriously as a way to measure intelligence, the actions of these

"We don't consider ours to be an underdeveloped country so much as we think of yours as an overdeveloped country." (Courtesy of *Saturday Review*, January 10, 1970.)

men paved the way for other attempts to justify racism. Other, more insidious, and often more powerful, "facts" may be used to demonstrate the presumed intellectual superiority of white people—namely, statistics from intelligence tests.

The first large-scale intelligence testing in this country began with our entry into World War I. Thousands of draftees were given the so-called Alpha and Beta IQ tests to determine military assignments. Later, psychologists arranged the test results according to race and found what they had expected—blacks scored consistently lower than whites. This was viewed as scientific proof of the innate intellectual inferiority of blacks and was used to justify further discrimination against blacks, both in and out of the army.[68]

Otto Klineberg's subsequent statistical analyses of IQ-test results demonstrated that blacks from northern states scored higher than blacks from the

[66]Motulsky, "Metabolic Polymorphisms and the Role of Infectious Diseases in Human Evolution," p. 232.
[67]Ibid.

[68]Otto Klineberg, *Negro Intelligence and Selective Migration* (New York: Columbia University Press, 1935); and Otto Klineberg, ed., *Characteristics of the American Negro* (New York: Harper & Brothers, 1944).

South. Although dedicated racists explained that this was due to the northward migration of innately intelligent blacks, most academics attributed the result to the influence of superior education and more stimulating environments in the North. When further studies showed that northern blacks scored higher than southern whites, the better-education-in-the-North theory gained support—but again racists insisted such results were due to northward migration by all innately intelligent whites.

As a further test of his conclusions, Klineberg gave IQ tests to black schoolgirls born and partly raised in the South who had spent varying lengths of time in New York City. He found that the longer the girls had been in the North, the higher their average IQ. In addition to providing support for the belief that blacks are not inherently inferior to whites, these findings suggested that cultural factors can and do influence IQ scores, and that IQ is not a fixed quantity but can be raised by contact with an improved environment.

The controversy about race and intelligence was fueled in 1969 by Arthur Jensen. He showed that although the IQ scores of American blacks overlapped considerably with the IQ scores of whites, the average score for blacks was 15 points lower than the average for whites. Jensen also presented evidence of a considerable genetic component in IQ scores; he suggested that approximately 80 percent of a person's IQ score is genetically determined. His evidence came from comparisons of the IQ scores of identical twins with those of other pairs of biological relatives (parent and child, first cousins, and so forth). For example, identical twins (with presumably the same genes) have more similar IQ scores even when reared apart than do nonidentical twins and siblings reared together.[69] The problem is not with Jensen's findings, but with how we are to interpret them. Since IQ scores presumably have a large genetic component, the lower average score for blacks implies to some that blacks are genetically inferior to whites. But others contend that the evidence presented by Jensen implies no such thing.

The critics of the genetic interpretation point

It is hoped that we will create a society in which everyone is given the same opportunity to develop as he or she chooses, regardless of race.

to at least two problems. First, there is the issue of exactly what IQ tests measure. There is widespread recognition now that IQ tests are probably not accurate measures of "intelligence" because they are probably biased in favor of the subculture of those who construct the tests. That is, many of the questions on the test refer to things that white, middle-class children are more familiar with, thus giving such children an advantage.[70] So far, no one has come up with a "culture-fair" or bias-free test. There is more agreement that although the IQ test may not measure "intelligence" well, it may predict scholastic success or how well a child will do in the primarily white-oriented school system.[71]

A second major problem with a purely genetic interpretation of the Jensen results is that many studies also show that IQ scores can be influenced by environment. Economically deprived children, whether black or white, will generally score lower than affluent white or black children. And training of children with low IQ scores clearly improves their test scores.[72] More dramatic evidence is provided by Sandra Scarr and her colleagues. Black

[69]Arthur Jensen, "How Much Can We Boost IQ and Scholastic Achievement?" *Harvard Educational Review*, 29 (1969): 1–123.

[70]M. W. Smith, "Alfred Binet's Remarkable Questions: A Cross-National and Cross-Temporal Analysis of the Cultural Biases Built into the Stanford-Binet Intelligence Scale and Other Binet Tests," *Genetic Psychology Monographs*, 89 (1974): 307–34.

[71]Theodosius Dobzhansky, *Genetic Diversity and Human Equality* (New York: Basic Books, 1973), p. 11.

[72]Ibid., pp. 14–15.

children adopted by well-off white families have IQ scores above the average for whites. And those "blacks" with more European ancestry do not have higher IQ scores.[73] So, the critics argue, the average difference between blacks and whites in IQ cannot be attributed to presumed genetic differences. For all we know, the 15-point average difference may be due completely to differences in environment or to test bias.

The geneticist Theodosius Dobzhansky has reminded us that conclusions about the causes of different levels of achievement on IQ tests cannot be drawn until both black and white people have equal opportunities to develop their potentials. He stressed the need for an open society operating under the democratic ideal, where every person is given an equal opportunity to develop whatever gifts or aptitudes he or she possesses and chooses to develop.[74]

The Future of Human Variation

Laboratory fertilization, subsequent transplantation of the embryo, and successful birth have been accomplished with humans and nonhumans. Cloning—the exact reproduction of an individual from cellular tissue—has been achieved with frogs. And genetic engineering—the substitution of some genes for others—is increasingly practiced in nonhuman organisms. Indeed, genetic engineering may soon be used in humans to eliminate certain disorders that are produced by defective genes.

What are the implications of such practices for the genetic future of humans? Will it really be possible someday to control the genetic makeup of our species? If so, will the effects be positive or negative?

It is interesting to speculate on the development of a "perfect human." Aside from the serious ethical question of who would decide what the perfect human should be like, there is the serious biological question of whether such a development might in the long run be detrimental to the human species, for what is perfectly suited to one physical or social environment may be totally unsuited to another. And the collection of physical, emotional, and intellectual attributes that might be "perfect" in the late twentieth century might be inappropriate in the twenty-first.[75] Even defects such as the sickle-cell trait may confer advantages under certain conditions, as we have seen.

In the long run, the perpetuation of genetic variability is probably more advantageous than the creation of a "perfect" and invariable human being. In the event of dramatic changes in the world environment, absolute uniformity in the human species might be an evolutionary dead end. Such uniformity might lead to the extinction of the human species if new conditions favored genetic or cultural variations that were no longer present in the species. Perhaps our best hope for maximizing our chances of survival is to tolerate, and even encourage, the persistence of many aspects of human variation, both biological and cultural.[76]

[73]Research by Sandra Scarr and others reported in Robert Boyd and Peter J. Richerson, *Culture and the Evolutionary Process.* Chicago: The University of Chicago Press, 1985, p. 56.
[74]Dobzhansky, *Mankind Evolving*, p. 243.

[75]J. B. S. Haldane, "Human Evolution: Past and Future," in Glenn L. Jepsen, Ernst Mayr, and George Gaylord Simpson, eds., *Genetics, Paleontology, and Evolution* (New York: Atheneum, 1963), pp. 405–18.
[76]George Gaylord Simpson, *The Meaning of Evolution* (New York: Bantam, 1971), pp. 297–308.

SUMMARY

1. Physical variation from one human population to another (variation in the frequencies of physical traits) is the result of one or more of the following factors: natural selection, genetic drift, gene flow, the influence of the physical environment, and the influence of the social or cultural environment.

2. Some physical variations in human populations involve genetic variation; other variations, including body build, facial construction, and skin color, may be adapted mostly to variation in climate. Still other variations, such as the ability to make lactase, may be adapted partially to variation in cultural environment.

3. The major problem with the concept of race is its arbitrariness. The number of races in the world population depends on who is doing the classifying, because each classifier may use different traits as the basis for classification. Racial classifiers identify both geographical and local races. A geographical race is a set of at least once-neighboring populations that has certain distinctive trait frequencies. A local race is a breeding population—that is, a local group whose members usually interbreed. Race concepts have often been, and still are, used by some groups to justify discrimination against other groups.

4. Perhaps the most controversial aspect of racial discrimination is the relationship supposed between race and intelligence. Attempts have been made to show, by IQ tests and other means, the innate intellectual superiority of one race to another. But there is doubt that IQ tests measure intelligence fairly. Since there is evidence that IQ scores are influenced by both genes and environment, conclusions about the causes of differences in IQ scores cannot be drawn until the people being compared have equal opportunities to develop their potentials.

SUGGESTED READING

BODMER, W. F., AND CAVALLI-SFORZA, L. L. *Genetics, Evolution, and Man.* San Francisco: W. H. Freeman & Company Publishers, 1976. An exhaustive, nonmathematical introduction to the principles and findings of research on human genetics.

DOBZHANSKY, T. *Mankind Evolving: The Evolution of the Human Species.* New Haven: Yale University Press, 1962. A now-classic introduction to the interaction between cultural and biological components of human evolution. Keeping the technical details and vocabulary of genetics to a minimum, Dobzhansky discusses natural selection and biological fitness in human populations.

DURHAM, W. H. *Coevolution: Genes, Culture, and Human Diversity.* Stanford, CA: Stanford University Press, 1991. Intended as an update of Dobzhansky's *Mankind Evolving,* this book discusses recent theory and research on how the interaction of genes and culture helps determine human diversity.

FRISANCHO, A. R. *Human Adaptation: A Functional Interpretation.* Ann Arbor: University of Michigan Press, 1981. A survey of research on human adaptations to heat, cold, humidity, high altitude, solar radiation, under- and over-nutrition, and the Westernization of dietary habits.

HARRISON, G. A., TANNER, J. M., PILBEAM, D. R., AND BAKER, P. T. *Human Biology: An Introduction to Human Evolution, Variation, Growth, and Adaptability,* 3rd ed. Oxford: Oxford University Press, 1988. A survey of research and recent developments in the study of human evolution, human genetics and variation, human growth and constitution, and human adaptability.

LOEHLIN, J. C., LINDZEY, G., AND SPUHLER, J. N. *Race Differences in Intelligence.* San Francisco: W. H. Freeman & Company Publishers, 1975. A balanced discussion of the relative effects of genes and environment on observed differences in average IQ score among racial-ethnic groups in the United States.

OVERFIELD, T. *Biologic Variation in Health and Illness: Race, Age, and Sex Differences.* Menlo Park, CA: Addison-Wesley, 1985. A survey of research on biological variation in humans and how it relates to health and illness.

8

Origins of Food Production and Settled Life

Toward the end of the period known as the Upper Paleolithic, which we know best archeologically for Europe, people seem to have gotten most of their food from hunting the available migratory herds of large animals, such as wild cattle, antelope, bison, and mammoths. These hunter-gatherers were probably highly mobile in order to follow the migrations of the animals. Beginning about 14,000 years ago, people in some regions began to depend less on big-game hunting and more on relatively stationary food resources such as fish, shellfish, small game, and wild plants. Salt- and freshwater food supplies may have become more abundant in many areas after the glaciers withdrew. As the ice melted, the level of the oceans rose and formed inlets and bays where crabs, clams, and sea mammals could be found. In some areas, particularly Europe and the Near East, the exploitation of local and relatively permanent resources may account for an increasingly settled way of life. The cultural period in Europe and the Near East during which these developments took place is called the **Mesolithic,** or the Middle Stone Age.[1] Other areas of the world show a similar switch to what is called *broad-spectrum* food collecting, but they do not always show an increasingly settled lifestyle.

We see the first evidence of a changeover to food production—the cultivation and domestication of plants and animals—in the Near East about 8000 B.C. This shift has been called the "Neolithic revolution," and it occurred, probably independently, in a number of other areas as well. There is evidence of cultivation some time after 6800 B.C. in the lowland plains of Southeast Asia (what is now Malaysia, Thailand, Cambodia, and Vietnam), North and South China about 6000 B.C., and in sub-Saharan Africa after 3000 B.C. In the New World, there appear to have been a number of places of original cultivation and domestication. The highlands of Mesoamerica (about 7000 B.C.) and the central Andes around Peru (about 4500 B.C.) were probably the most important in terms of food plants used today.

In this chapter, we discuss what is believed about the origins of food production and settled life (**sedentarism**)—how and why people in different places may have come to cultivate and domesticate plants and animals and to live in permanent villages. Agriculture and a sedentary life did not necessarily go together. In some regions of the world, people began to live in permanent villages before they cultivated and domesticated plants and animals, whereas in other places people planted crops without settling down permanently. Much of our discussion focuses on the Near East and Europe, the areas we know best archeologically for the developments leading to food production and settled life. As much as we can, however, we try to indicate how data from other areas appear to suggest patterns different from, or similar to, those in Europe and the Near East.

Preagricultural Developments

Europe

After about 10,000 years ago in Europe, the glaciers began to disappear. With their disappearance came other environmental changes: the melting of the glacial ice caused the oceans to rise; and as the seas moved inland, the waters inundated some of the richest fodder-producing coastal plains, creating islands, inlets, and bays. Other areas, particularly in Scandinavia, were opened up for human occupation as the glaciers retreated and the temperatures rose.[2] The cold, treeless plains (**tundras**) and grasslands eventually gave way to dense mixed forests, mostly birch, oak, and pine, and the mammoths became extinct. The warming waterways began to abound with fish and other aquatic resources.[3]

Archeologists believe these environmental changes induced some populations in Europe to alter their food-getting strategies. The disappearance of the tundras and grasslands meant that hunters could no longer obtain large quantities of meat simply by remaining close to large migratory herds of animals, as they probably did during Upper Pa-

[1]Lewis R. Binford, "Post-Pleistocene Adaptations," in Stuart Struever, ed., *Prehistoric Agriculture* (Garden City, NY: Natural History Press, 1971), p. 27. Originally published in Sally R. Binford and Lewis R. Binford, eds., *New Perspectives in Archaeology* (Chicago: Aldine, 1968).

[2]Desmond Collins, "Later Hunters in Europe," in Desmond Collins, ed., *The Origins of Europe* (New York: Thomas Y. Crowell, 1976), pp. 88–125.

[3]Chester S. Chard, *Man in Prehistory* (New York: McGraw-Hill, 1969), p. 171.

TABLE 8-1 An Overview of Human Evolution: Biological and Cultural

TIME (YEARS AGO)	GEOLOGIC EPOCH	FOSSIL RECORD (FIRST APPEARANCE)	ARCHEOLOGICAL PERIODS (OLD WORLD)	MAJOR CULTURAL DEVELOPMENTS (FIRST APPEARANCE)
			Bronze Age	Cities and states; social inequality; full-time craft specialists
5500 (3500 B.C.)			————	
			Neolithic	Domesticated plants and animals; permanent villages
10,000 (8000 B.C.)			————	
			Mesolithic	Broad-spectrum food collecting; increasingly sedentary communities; many kinds of microliths
14,000 (12,000 B.C.)	Pleistocene	Earliest humans in New World	————	
			Upper Paleolithic	Cave paintings; female figurines; many kinds of blade tools
40,000			————	
		Modern humans *Homo sapiens sapiens*	Middle Paleolithic	Religious beliefs (?); burials; Mousterian tools
200,000		Neandertal *Homo sapiens*		
300,000		Earliest *Homo sapiens* (?)	————	
700,000				Acheulian tools
1,500,000		*Homo erectus*		
1,800,000		————	Lower Paleolithic	Hunting and/or scavenging; seasonal campsites; Oldowan tools
2,000,000	Pliocene	*Homo habilis*	————	
				Earliest stone tools
		Earliest hominids *Australopithecus*		
5,000,000		————		
	Miocene	Diversification of apes *Sivapithecus* *Dryopithecus*		
22,500,000		———— *Proconsul*		
29,000,000		Earliest apes (?) Propliopithecids, e.g., *Aegyptopithecus*		
32,000,000	Oligocene	Earliest anthropoids Parapithecids, e.g., *Apidium*		
38,000,000		————		
50,000,000	Eocene	*Amphipithecus* *Tetonius*		
53,500,000				
	Paleocene			
65,000,000		————		
70,000,000	Late Cretaceous	Earliest primates *Purgatorius*		

Source: Geological dates from W. A. Berggren and J. A. Van Couvering, "The Late Neocene: Biostratigraphy, Geochronology and Paleoclimatology of the Last 15 Million Years in Marine and Continental Sequences," *Palaeogeography, Palaeoclimatology, Palaeoecology,* 16 (1974): 13–16, 165.

leolithic times. Even though there were deer and other game around, the density of animals per square mile had decreased, and it had become difficult to stalk and kill animals sheltered in the thick woods. Thus, in many areas of Mesolithic Europe people seemed to have turned from a reliance on big-game hunting to the intensive collecting of wild plants, mollusks, fish, and small game to make up for the extinction of the mammoths and the northward migration of the reindeer.

The Maglemosian Culture of Northern Europe. Some adaptations to the changing environment can be seen in the cultural remains of the settlers in northern Europe who are called **Maglemosians.** Their name derives from the peat bogs (*magle mose* in Danish means "great bog") where their remains have been found.

To deal with the new, more forested environment, the Maglemosians made stone axes and adzes to chop down trees and form them into various objects. Large timbers appear to have been split for houses; trees were hollowed out for canoes; and smaller pieces of wood were made into paddles. The canoes presumably were built for travel and perhaps for fishing on the lakes and rivers that abounded in the postglacial environment.

We do not know to what extent the Maglemosians relied on wild plant foods, but there were a lot of different kinds available, such as hazelnuts. We do know many other things about the Maglemosians' way of life. Although fishing was fairly important, as suggested by the frequent occurrence of bones from pike and other fish as well as fishhooks, these people apparently depended mainly on hunting for food. Game included elk, wild ox, deer, and wild pig. In addition to many fishing implements and the adzes and axes previously mentioned, the Maglemosians' tool kit included the bow and arrow. Some of their tools were ornamented with finely engraved designs. Ornamentation independent of tools also appears in amber and stone pendants and small figurines such as the head of an elk.[4]

Like the Maglemosian finds, many of the European Mesolithic sites are along lakes, rivers, and oceanfronts. But these sites probably were not in-habited year-round, since there is evidence that at least some groups moved seasonally from one place of settlement to another, perhaps between the coast and inland areas.[5] Finds such as **kitchen middens** (piles of shells) that centuries of Mesolithic seafood eaters had discarded, and remains of fishing equipment, canoes, and boats, indicate that Mesolithic people depended much more heavily on fishing than had their ancestors in Upper Paleolithic times.

The Near East

Cultural developments in the Near East seem to have paralleled those in Europe.[6] Here too there seems to have been a shift from mobile big-game hunting to the utilization of a broad spectrum of natural resources. There is evidence that people subsisted on a variety of resources, including fish, mollusks, and other water life; wild deer, sheep, and goats; and wild grains, nuts, and legumes.[7] The increased utilization of stationary food sources such as wild grain may partially explain why some people in the Near East began to lead more sedentary lives during the Mesolithic.

Even today, a traveler passing through the Anatolian highlands of Turkey and other mountainous regions in the Near East may see thick stands of wild wheat and barley growing as densely as if they had been cultivated. Wielding flint sickles, Mesolithic people could easily have harvested a bountiful crop from such wild stands. Just how productive these resources can be was demonstrated in a field experiment duplicating prehistoric conditions. Using the kind of flint-blade sickle a Mesolithic worker would have used, researchers were able to harvest a little over two pounds of wild grain in an hour. A Mesolithic family of four, working only during the few weeks of the harvest season, probably could have reaped more wheat and barley than they needed for the entire year.[8]

The amount of wild wheat harvested in the

[4]Grahame Clark, *The Earlier Stone Age Settlement of Scandinavia* (Cambridge: Cambridge University Press, 1975), pp. 101–61.

[5]Erik B. Petersen, "A Survey of the Late Paleolithic and the Mesolithic of Denmark," in S. K. Kozlowski, ed., *The Mesolithic in Europe* (Warsaw: Warsaw University Press, 1973), pp. 94–96.
[6]Binford. "Post-Pleistocene Adaptations," pp. 45–49.
[7]Kent V. Flannery, "The Origins of Agriculture," *Annual Review of Anthropology,* 2 (1973): 274.
[8]Jack R. Harlan, "A Wild Wheat Harvest in Turkey," *Archaeology,* 20, no. 3 (June 1967): 197–201.

Reconstruction of a Mesolithic sickle with an end-to-end row of stone blades.

Foundation of a Natufian house in Israel from 9600 years ago.

experiment prompted Kent Flannery to conclude, "Such a harvest would almost necessitate some degree of sedentism—after all, where could they go with an estimated metric ton of clean wheat?"[9] Moreover, the stone equipment used for grinding would have been a clumsy burden to carry. Part of the harvest would probably have been set aside for immediate consumption, ground, and then cooked either by roasting or boiling. The rest of the harvest would have been stored to supply food for the remainder of the year. A grain diet, then, could have been the impetus for the construction of roasters, grinders, and storage pits by some Mesolithic people, as well as for the construction of solid, fairly permanent housing. Once a village was built, people may have been reluctant to abandon it. We can visualize the earliest preagricultural settlements clustered around such naturally rich regions, as archeological evidence indeed suggests they were.

The Natufians of the Near East.
Eleven thousand years ago the **Natufians,** a people living in the area that is now Israel and Jordan, inhabited caves and rock-shelters and built villages on the slopes of Mount Carmel in Israel. At the front of their rock-shelters they hollowed out basin-shaped

depressions in the rock, possibly for storage pits. Examples of Natufian villages are also found at the Eynan site in Israel.

Eynan is a stratified site containing the remains of three villages in sequence, one atop another. Each village consisted of about fifty circular *pit houses.* The floor of each house was sunk a few feet into the ground, so that the walls of the house consisted partly of earth, below ground level, and partly of stones, above ground level. Pit houses had the advantage of retaining heat longer than houses built above ground. The villages appear to have had stone-paved walks; circular stone pavements ringed what seem to be permanent hearths; and the dead were interred in village cemeteries.

The tools suggest that the Natufians harvested wild grain intensively. Sickles recovered from their villages have a specific sheen, which experiments have shown to be the effect of flint striking grass stems, as the sickles would have been used in the cutting of grain. The Natufians are the earliest Mesolithic people known to us to have stored surplus crops. Beneath the floors of their stone-walled houses they constructed plastered storage pits. In addition to wild grains, the Natufians exploited a wide range of other resources.[10] The remains of many wild animals are found in Natufian sites; they appear to have concentrated on hunting ga-

---

[9] Kent V. Flannery, "The Origins and Ecological Effects of Early Domestication in Iran and the Near East," in Struever, ed., *Prehistoric Agriculture,* p. 59. Originally published in Peter J. Ucko and G. W. Dimbleby, eds., *The Domestication and Exploitation of Plants and Animals* (Chicago: Aldine, 1969).

[10] James Mellaart, "Roots in the Soil," in Stuart Piggott, ed., *The Dawn of Civilization* (London: Thames & Hudson, 1961), pp. 41–64.

zelle, which they would take by surrounding whole herds.[11]

The Natufians show many differences from food collectors of earlier periods. Not only was food collection based on a more intensive use of stationary resources like wild grain, but the archeological evidence suggests increasing social complexity. Communities are somewhat larger and more permanent, population densities are higher, and burial patterns suggest more social differences between people,[12] not unlike trends among food collectors in other areas.[13]

Other Areas

People in other areas in the world also shifted from hunting big game to collecting many types of food before they apparently began to practice agriculture. The still-sparse archeological record suggests that such a change occurred in Southeast Asia, which may have been one of the important centers of original plant and animal domestication. The faunal remains in inland sites there indicate that many different sources of food were being exploited from the same base camps. For example, at these base camps we find the remains of animals from high mountain ridges as well as lowland river valleys; birds and primates from nearby forests; bats from caves, and fish from streams. The few coastal sites indicate that many kinds of fish and shellfish were collected, and that animals such as deer, wild cattle, and rhinoceros were hunted.[14] As in Europe, the preagricultural developments in Southeast Asia probably were responses to changes in the climate and environment, including a warming trend, more moisture, and a higher sea level.[15]

In Africa too the preagricultural period was marked by a warmer, wetter environment (after about 5500 B.C.). The now-numerous lakes, rivers, and other bodies of water provided fish, shellfish, and other resources that apparently allowed people to settle more permanently than they had before. For example, there were lakes in what is now the southern and central Sahara desert, where people hunted hippopotamuses and crocodiles and fished. This pattern of broad-spectrum food collecting seems also to have been characteristic of the areas both south and north of the Sahara.[16]

At about the same time in the Americas, people were beginning to exploit a wide variety of wild food resources, just as they were in Europe, Asia, and Africa. For example, evidence from Alabama and Kentucky shows that by about 5000 B.C., people had begun to collect freshwater mussels as well as wild plants and small game. In the Great Basin of what is now the United States, people were beginning to spend a longer and longer period each year collecting the wild resources around and in the rivers and glacial lakes.[17]

Why Did Broad-Spectrum Collecting Develop?

It is apparent that the preagricultural switch to broad-spectrum collecting was fairly common throughout the world. Climate change may have been partly responsible for the exploitation of new sources of food. For example, the worldwide rise in sea level may have increased the availability of fish and shellfish. Changes in climate may have also been partly responsible for the decline in the availability of big game, particularly the large herd animals. It has been suggested that another possible cause of that decline was human activity, specifically overkilling of some of these animals. The evidence suggesting overkill is that the extinction in the New World of many of the large Pleistocene animals, such as the mammoth, may have coincided with the movement of humans from the Ber-

---

[11]Donald O. Henry, *From Foraging to Agriculture: The Levant at the End of the Ice Age* (Philadelphia: University of Pennsylvania Press, 1989), pp. 214–15.

[12]Ibid., pp. 38–39, 209–10.

[13]James A. Brown and T. Douglas Price, "Complex Hunter-Gatherers: Retrospect and Prospect," in T. Douglas Price and James A. Brown, *Prehistoric Hunter-Gatherers: The Emergence of Cultural Complexity* (Orlando, FL: Academic Press, 1985), pp. 435—41.

[14]Chester Gorman, "The Hoabinhian and After: Subsistence Patterns in Southeast Asia during the Late Pleistocene and Early Recent Periods," *World Archaeology*, 2 (1970): 315–16.

[15]Kwang-Chih Chang, "The Beginnings of Agriculture in the Far East," *Antiquity*, 44, no. 175 (September 1970): 176. See also Gorman, "The Hoabinhian and After," pp. 300–19.

[16]J. Desmond Clark, *The Prehistory of Africa* (New York: Praeger, 1970), pp. 171–72.

[17]Thomas C. Patterson, *America's Past: A New World Archaeology* (Glenview, IL: Scott, Foresman and Company, 1973), p. 42.

ing Strait region to the southern tip of South America.[18]

But the overkill hypothesis has been questioned on the basis of bird as well as mammal extinctions in the New World. An enormous number of bird species also became extinct during the last few thousand years of the North American Pleistocene, and it is difficult to argue that human hunters caused those extinctions. Since the bird extinctions occurred simultaneously with the mammal extinctions, it is likely that most or nearly all the extinctions were due to climatic and other environmental changes.[19]

The decreasing availability of big game may have stimulated people to exploit new food resources. But they may have turned to a broader spectrum of resources for another reason—population growth. As Mark Cohen has noted, hunter-gatherers were "filling up" the world, and they may have had to seek new and possibly less desirable sources of food.[20] (We might think of shellfish as more desirable than mammoths, but only because we don't have to do the work to get such food. An awful lot of shellfish have to be collected, shelled, and cooked to produce the animal protein obtainable from one large animal.) Consistent with the idea that the world was filling up around this time is the fact that not until after 30,000 years ago did hunter-gatherers begin to move into deserts, polar regions, and possibly tropical forests.[21] Some researchers theorize that those environments would not have been habitats of choice, so they probably would not have been exploited until the rest of the world was filled up (see Figure 8–1).

Broad-spectrum collecting may have involved exploitation of new sources of food, but that does not necessarily mean that people were eating better. Even a higher population density does not mean that resources were more plentiful; it means only that more people lived there, not that they were better nourished. Consistent with the notion that broad-spectrum collecting may not have been associated with improved nutrition is the apparent fact that height declined during the Mesolithic by as much as two inches in many parts of the Old World (Greece, Israel, India, and northern and western Europe).[22] This decline may have been a result of decreasing nutrition, but it could also be that natural selection for greater height was relaxed because more leverage for throwing projectiles (such as spears) was not as favored as before the decline of big-game hunting. (Greater limb bone length, and therefore greater height, would mean that you could throw a spear with more force and farther.)[23] In other areas of the world, such as Australia and what is now the midwest United States, skeletal evidence also suggests a decline in the general level of health with the rise of broad-spectrum collecting.[24]

Broad-Spectrum Collecting and Sedentarism

Does the switch to broad-spectrum collecting explain the increasingly sedentary way of life we see in various parts of the world in preagricultural times? The answer seems to be yes and no. In some areas of the world—some sites in Europe, the Near East, Africa, and Peru—settlements became more permanent. In other areas, such as the semiarid highlands of Mesoamerica, the switch to broad-spectrum collecting was not associated with increasing sedentarism. Even after the highland Mesoamericans began to cultivate plants, they still did

[18]Paul S. Martin, "The Discovery of America," *Science*, March 9, 1973, pp. 969–74.

[19]Donald K. Grayson, "Pleistocene Avifaunas and the Overkill Hypothesis," *Science*, February 18, 1977, pp. 691–92. See also three articles in Paul S. Martin and Richard G. Klein, eds., *Quaternary Extinctions: A Prehistoric Revolution* (Tucson: University of Arizona Press, 1984): Larry G. Marshall, "Who Killed Cock Robin?: An Investigation of the Extinction Controversy," pp. 785–806; Donald K. Grayson, "Explaining Pleistocene Extinctions: Thoughts on the Structure of a Debate," pp. 807–23; and R. Dale Guthrie, "Mosaics, Allelochemics and Nutrients: An Ecological Theory of Late Pleistocene Megafaunal Extinctions," pp. 259–98.

[20]Mark Nathan Cohen, *The Food Crisis in Prehistory: Overpopulation and the Origins of Agriculture* (New Haven: Yale University Press, 1977), pp. 12, 85.

[21]Ibid., p. 85; and Fekri A. Hassan, *Demographic Archaeology* (New York: Academic Press, 1981), p. 207. For the view that hunter-gatherers were very unlikely to have lived in tropical forests prior to agriculture, see Robert C. Bailey, Genevieve Head, Mark Jenike, Bruce Owen, Robert Rechtman, and Elzbieta Zechenter, "Hunting and Gathering in Tropical Rain Forest: Is It Possible?" *American Anthropologist*, 91 (1989): 59–82.

[22]Mark Nathan Cohen, *Health and the Rise of Civilization* (New Haven: Yale University Press, 1989), pp. 112–13.

[23]David W. Frayer, "Body Size, Weapon Use, and Natural Selection in the European Upper Paleolithic and Mesolithic," *American Anthropologist*, 83 (1981): 57–73.

[24]Cohen, *Health and the Rise of Civilization*, pp. 113–15.

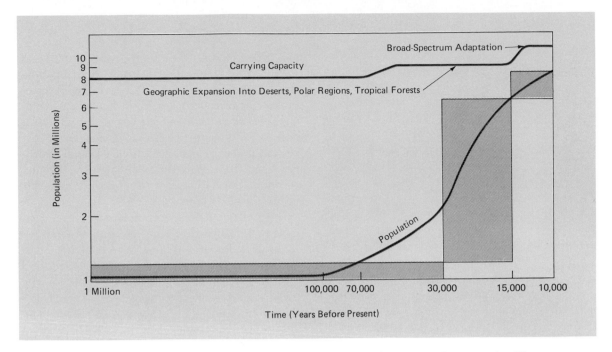

FIGURE 8-1 Reconstructed Increases in World Population and Carrying Capacity for Humans during the Pleistocene

(Redrawn from Demographic Archaeology, *Fekri A. Hassan, 1981, p. 207.)*

not live in permanent villages.[25] Why the difference? It would seem that it is not simply the switch to broad-spectrum collecting that accounts for increasing sedentarism in many areas. Rather, judging from a comparison of settlements on the Peruvian coast, the more permanent settlements seem to have been located nearer (within three and a half miles) to most, if not all, of the diverse food resources exploited during the year. The community that did not have a year-round settlement seems to have depended upon more widely distributed resources. What accounts for sedentarism may thus be the nearness[26] or the high reliability and yield[27] of the broad-spectrum resources, rather than the broad spectrum itself.

[25]Kent V. Flannery, "The Origins of the Village as a Settlement Type in Mesoamerica and the Near East: A Comparative Study," in Ruth Tringham, ed., *Territoriality and Proxemics* (Andover, MA: Warner Modular Pub., 1973), R1, pp. 1–31.

[26]Thomas C. Patterson, "Central Peru: Its Population and Economy," *Archaeology*, 24 (1971): 318–19.

[27]Gregory A. Johnson, "Aspects of Regional Analysis in Archaeology," *Annual Review of Anthropology*, 6 (1977): 488–89. See also David R. Harris, "Settling Down: An Evolutionary Model for the Transformation of Mobile Bands into Sedentary Communities," in J. Friedman and M. J. Rowlands, eds., *The Evolution of Social Systems* (London: Duckworth, 1977), pp. 401–17.

Sedentarism and Population Growth

Although some population growth undoubtedly occurred throughout the hunting and gathering phase of world history, some anthropologists have suggested that populations would have increased dramatically when people began to settle down. The evidence for this suggestion comes largely from a comparison of recent nomadic and sedentary !Kung populations.

The settling down of a previously nomadic group may reduce the spacing between births.[28] Nomadic !Kung have children spaced four years apart on the average; in contrast, recently sedentarized !Kung have children about three years apart. Why might birth spacing change with settling down? There are several possibilities.

The spacing of children far apart can occur in a number of ways. One way, if effective contraceptives are not available, is prolonged sexual absti-

[28]Robert Sussman, "Child Transport, Family Size, and the Increase in Human Population Size during the Neolithic," *Current Anthropology*, 13 (April 1972): 258–67; and Richard B. Lee, "Population Growth and the Beginnings of Sedentary Life among the !Kung Bushmen," in Brian Spooner, ed., *Population Growth: Anthropological Implications* (Cambridge, MA: M.I.T. Press, 1972), pp. 329–42.

The !Kung of the Kalahari Desert on the move. Spacing births an average of four years apart helps to ensure that a woman will not have to carry more than two children at a time.

nence after the birth of a child, which is common in recent human societies. Another possible way is abortion or infanticide.[29] Nomadic groups may be motivated to have children farther apart because of the problem of carrying small children. Carrying one small child is difficult enough; carrying two might be too burdensome. Thus, sedentary populations presumably could have their children spaced more closely because carrying children would not always be necessary.

Although some nomadic groups may have deliberately spaced births by abstinence or infanticide, there is no evidence that such practices explain why four years separate births among nomadic !Kung. There may be another explanation, involving an unintended effect of how babies are fed. Nancy Howell and Richard Lee have suggested that the presence of baby foods other than mother's milk may be responsible for the decreased birth spacing in sedentary agricultural !Kung groups.[30] It is now well established that the longer a mother nurses her baby without supplementary foods, the longer the mother is unlikely to start ovulating again. Nomadic !Kung women have little to give their babies in the way of soft digestible food, and the babies depend largely on mother's milk for two to three years. But sedentary !Kung mothers can give their babies soft foods such as cereal (from cultivated grain) and milk from domesticated animals. Such changes in feeding practices may shorten birth spacing by shortening the interval between birth and the resumption of ovulation. In preagricultural sedentary communities, it is possible that baby foods made from wild grains might have had the same effect. For this reason alone, therefore, populations may have grown even before people started to farm or herd.

Another reason sedentary !Kung women may have more babies than nomadic !Kung women has to do with the ratio of body fat to body weight. It is suspected by some investigators that a critical minimum of fat in the body may be necessary for ovulation. A sedentary !Kung woman may have more fatty tissue than a nomadic !Kung woman, who walks many miles daily to gather wild plant foods and who may be carrying a child around with her. Thus, sedentary !Kung women might resume ovulating sooner after the birth of a baby and so may be likely to have more closely spaced children. If some critical amount of fat is necessary for ovulation, that would explain why in our own society women who have little body fat (long-distance runners, gymnasts, ballet dancers) often do not ovulate regularly.[31]

Mesolithic Technology

Technologically, Mesolithic cultures did not differ radically from Upper Paleolithic cultures. (*Mesolithic*, like the term *Upper Paleolithic*, properly applies only to cultural developments in the Old World. However, we use the term *Mesolithic* here for some general preagricultural trends.) The trend toward smaller and lighter tools continued. *Microliths*, small blades half an inch to two inches long, which were made in late Upper Paleolithic times, were now used in quantity. In place of the one-piece flint implement, Mesolithic peoples in Europe, Asia, and Africa equipped themselves with composite tools—that is, tools made of more than one material.

Microliths could be fitted into grooves in bone or wood to form arrows, harpoons, daggers, and

[29]For some examples of societies that have practiced infanticide, see Harris, "Settling Down," p. 407.

[30]Nancy Howell, *Demography of the Dobe !Kung* (New York: Academic Press, 1979); and Richard B. Lee, *The !Kung San: Men, Women, and Work in a Foraging Society* (Cambridge: Cambridge University Press, 1979).

[31]Rose E. Frisch, "Fatness, Puberty, and Fertility," *Natural History*, October 1980, pp. 16–27; and Howell, *Demography of the Dobe !Kung.*

sickles. A sickle, for example, was made by inserting several microliths into a groove in a wooden or bone handle. The blades were held in place by resin. A broken microlith could be replaced like a blade in a modern razor. Besides being adaptable for many uses, microliths could be made from many varieties of available stone; Mesolithic people were no longer limited to flint. Since they did not need the large flint nodules to make large core and flake tools, they could use small pebbles of flint to make the small blades.[32]

The Domestication of Plants and Animals

Neolithic means *"of the new stone age"*; the term originally signified the cultural stage in which humans invented ground-stone tools and pottery. However, we now know that both characteristics were present in earlier times, so we cannot define a Neolithic state of culture on the basis of these two criteria. At present, archeologists generally define the Neolithic in terms of the presence of domesticated plants and animals. In this type of culture, people began to produce food rather than merely collect it.

The line between food collecting and food producing occurs when people begin to plant crops and to keep and breed animals. How do we know when this transition occurred? In fact, archeologically we do not see the beginning of food production. We can see signs of it only after plants and animals show differences from their wild varieties. When people plant crops, we refer to the process as *cultivation*. It is only when the crops cultivated and the animals raised are different from wild varieties that we speak of plant and animal **domestication.**

How do we know, in a particular site, that domestication occurred? Domesticated plants have characteristics different from those of wild plants of the same types. For example, wild grains of barley and wheat have a fragile **rachis** (the seed-bearing part of the stem), which shatters easily, releasing the seeds. Domesticated grains have a tough rachis, which does not shatter easily.

[32]S. A. Semenov, *Prehistoric Technology*, trans. M. W. Thompson (Bath, England: Adams & Dart, 1970), pp. 63, 203–4.

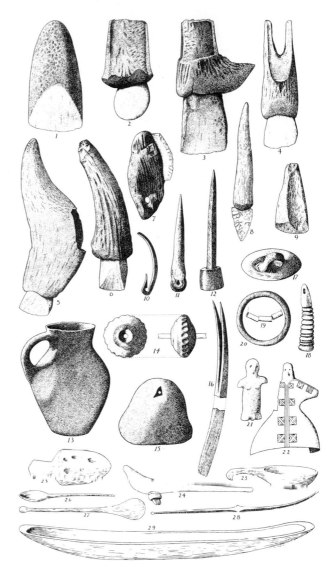

Neolithic implements from Switzerland, including axes (1–5, 24), chisels made of stone and bone (6, 9), awls made of bone (11, 12), flint knives (7, 8), weaving implements made of clay and bone (14–16), and ornaments (18–22). (Courtesy of the American Museum of Natural History)

How did the domesticated plants get to be different from the wild varieties? Artificial or human selection, deliberate or accidental, obviously was required. Consider why the rachis of wheat and barley may have changed. As we said, when wild grain ripens in the field, the seed-bearing part, or rachis, shatters easily, scattering the seed. This is selectively advantageous under wild conditions, since it is nature's method of propagating the species. Plants with a tough rachis, therefore, have only a slight chance of reproducing themselves under natural conditions, but are more desirable for planting. When humans arrived with sickles and flails to collect the wild stands of grain, the seeds harvested probably contained a higher proportion of tough-rachis mutants, since these could best withstand the rough treatment of harvest processing. If planted, the harvested seeds would be more likely to produce tough-rachis plants. If in each successive harvest seeds from tough-rachis plants were less likely to be lost, tough-rachis plants would come to predominate.[33]

Domesticated species of animals also differ from the wild varieties. For example, the horns of wild goats in the Near East are shaped differently from those of domesticated goats.[34] But differences in physical characteristics may not be the only indicators of domestication. Some archeologists believe that imbalances in the sex and age ratios of animal remains at sites suggest that domestication had occurred. For example, at Zawi Chemi Shanidar in Iraq, the proportion of young to mature sheep remains was much higher than the ratio of young to mature sheep in wild herds. One possible inference to be drawn from this evidence is that the animals were domesticated, the adult sheep being saved for breeding purposes while the young were eaten. (If mostly young animals were eaten, and only a few animals were allowed to grow old, most of the bones found in a site would be from the young animals that were killed regularly for food.)[35]

Domestication in the Near East

For some time most archeologists have thought that the Fertile Cresent, the arc of land stretching up from Israel and the Jordan Valley through southern Turkey and then downward to the western slopes of the Zagros Mountains in Iran, was one of the earliest centers of plant and animal domestication. We know that several varieties of domesticated wheat were being grown there after about 8000 B.C., as were barley, lentils, and peas. And there is evidence that goats, sheep, pigs, cattle, and dogs were being raised at about the same time. Let us turn to two of the early Neolithic sites in the Near East to see what life there may have been like after people began to depend on domesticated plants and animals for food.

Ali Kosh. At the stratified site of Ali Kosh in what is now southwestern Iran, we see the remains of a community that starts out about 7500 B.C. living mostly on wild plants and animals. Over the next two thousand years, until about 5500 B.C., we see agriculture and herding becoming increasingly important. And after 5500 B.C. we see the appearance of two innovations—irrigation and the use of domesticated cattle—that seem to stimulate a minor population explosion during the following millennium.

From 7500 to 6750 B.C., the people at Ali Kosh cut little slabs of raw clay out of the ground to build small multi-room structures. The rooms excavated by archeologists are small too, seldom more than seven by ten feet, and there is no evidence that the structures were definitely houses where people actually spent time or slept. Instead they may have been storage rooms. On the other hand, house rooms of even smaller size are known in other areas of the world, so it is possible that the people at Ali Kosh in its earliest phase were actually living in those tiny unbaked "brick" houses. There is a bit of evidence that the people at Ali Kosh may have moved for the summer (with their goats) to the grassier mountain valleys nearby, which were just a few days' walk away.

We have a lot of evidence about what the people at Ali Kosh ate. They got some of their food from cultivated emmer wheat and a kind of barley, and a considerable amount from domesticated goats. We know the goats were domesticated because wild goats do not seem to have lived in the area. Also, virtually no bones from elderly goats were found in the site, which suggests that the goats were domesticated and herded, rather than hunted. Moreover, it would seem from the horn cores found in the site that mostly young male goats were eaten, which suggests that the fe-

[33]Daniel Zohary, "The Progenitors of Wheat and Barley in Relation to Domestication and Agricultural Dispersal in the Old World," in Ucko and Dimbleby, eds., *The Domestication and Exploitation of Plants and Animals,* pp. 47–66.
[34]Kent V. Flannery, "The Ecology of Early Food Production in Mesopotamia," *Science,* March 12, 1965, p. 1252.
[35]Ibid., p. 1253. For the view that a high proportion of immature animals does not necessarily indicate domestication, see Stephen Collier and J. Peter White, "Get Them Young? Age and Sex Inferences on Animal Domestication in Archaeology," *American Antiquity,* 41 (1976): 96–102.

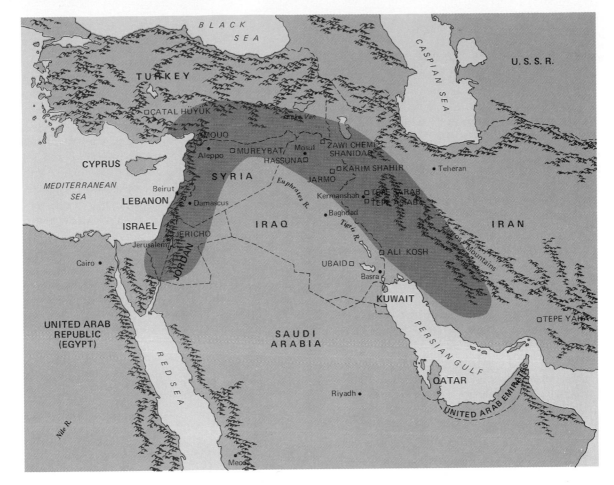

FIGURE 8-2 Early Agricultural Settlements in the Near East.
Modern cities are represented by a dot. The darker color indicates the area known as the Fertile Crescent.

males were kept for breeding and milking. But with all these signs of deliberate food production, there is an enormous amount of evidence (literally tens of thousands of seeds and bone fragments) that the people at the beginning of Ali Kosh depended mostly on wild plants (legumes and grasses) and wild animals (including gazelles, wild oxen, and wild pigs). They also collected fish, such as carp and catfish, and shellfish, such as mussels, as well as waterfowl that visited the area during part of the year.

The flint tools used during this earliest phase at Ali Kosh were varied and abundant. Finds from this period include tens of thousands of tiny flint blades, some only a few millimeters wide. About 1 percent of the chipped stone found by archeologists was **obsidian,** or volcanic glass, which came from what is now eastern Turkey, several hundred miles away. Thus, the people at Ali Kosh during

its earliest phase definitely had some kind of contact with people elsewhere. This contact is also suggested by the fact that the emmer wheat they cultivated did not have a wild relative in the area.

From 6750 to 6000 B.C., the people increased their consumption of cultivated food plants: 40 percent of the seed remains in the hearths and refuse areas are now from emmer wheat and barley. The proportion of the diet coming from wild plants is much reduced, probably because the cultivated plants have the same growing season and grow in the same kind of soil as the wild plants. Grazing by the goats and sheep that were kept may also have contributed to the reduction of wild plant foods in the area and in the diet. The village may or may not have gotten larger, but the multi-room houses definitely had. The rooms are now larger than ten by ten feet. The walls are much thicker, and the clay-slab bricks are now held together by a mud mortar. Also, the walls now often have a coat of smooth mud plaster on both sides. The stamped-mud house floors were apparently covered with rush or reed mats (you can see the imprints of them). There were courtyards with domed brick ovens and brick-lined roasting pits. Understandably, considering the summer heat in the area, none of the ovens found by the archeologists was inside a house.

Even though the village probably contained no more than 100 individuals, it participated in an extensive trading network. Seashells were probably obtained from the Persian Gulf, which is some distance to the south; copper may have come from what is now central Iran; obsidian was still coming from eastern Turkey; and turquoise somehow made its way from what is now the border between Iran and Afghanistan. Some of these materials were used as ornaments worn by both sexes—or so it seems from the remains of bodies found buried under the floors of houses.

After about 5500 B.C., the area around Ali Kosh begins to show signs of a much larger population, apparently made possible by a more complex agriculture employing irrigation and plows drawn by domesticated cattle. In the next thousand years, by 4500 B.C., the population of the area probably tripled. This population growth was apparently part of the cultural developments that culminated in the rise of urban civilizations in the Near East,[36] as we will see in the next chapter.

Population growth may have occurred in the area around Ali Kosh but did not continue in all areas of the Near East after domestication. For example, one of the largest early villages in the Near East, 'Ain Ghazal (on the outskirts of what is now Amman, Jordan), suffered a decline in population and standard of living over time, perhaps because the environment around 'Ain Ghazal could not permanently support a large village.[37]

Catal Hüyük. On a wind-swept plateau in the rugged, mountainous region of southern Turkey stand the remains of a mud-brick town. It is known as Catal Hüyük—*Hüyük* being the Turkish word for a mound formed by a succession of settlements, one built on top of another.

About 5600 B.C., Catal Hüyük was an adobe town. Some 200 houses have been excavated, and they are interconnected in pueblo fashion. The inhabitants decorated the walls of the houses with imaginative murals and their shrines with symbolic statuary. The murals depict what seem to be religious scenes and everyday events. Archeologists peeling away frescoes found layer upon layer of murals, indicating that old murals were plastered over to make way for fresh paintings. Several rooms are believed to have been shrine rooms. They contain many large bull murals and clay bull figurines, and have full-sized clay heads of cattle on the walls.

Surviving walls from a building in Catal Huyuk, a Neolithic settlement in southern Turkey.

[36]Frank Hole, Kent V. Flannery, and James A. Neely, *Prehistory and Human Ecology of the Deh Luran Plain*, Memoirs of the Museum of Anthropology, no. 1 (Ann Arbor: University of Michigan, 1969).
[37]See Alan H. Simmons, Ilse Köhler-Rollefson, Gary O. Rollefson, Rolfe Mandel, and Zeidan Kafafi, "'Ain Ghazal: A Major Neolithic Settlement in Central Jordan," *Science,* April 1, 1988, pp. 35–39.

Other "shrine room" murals depict scenes of life and death, painted in red and black, respectively. Clay statuettes of a pregnant woman and of a bearded man seated on a bull have also been found in these rooms.

Farming was well advanced at Catal Hüyük. Lentils, wheat, barley, and peas were grown in quantities that produced a surplus. Archeologists were astonished at the richly varied handicrafts, including beautifully carved wooden bowls and boxes, that the people of the town produced. These people also had obsidian and flint daggers, spearheads, lance heads, scrapers, awls, and sickle blades. Bowls, spatulas, knives, ladles, and spoons were made from bone. The houses contained belt hooks, toggles, and pins carved from bone. Evidence also suggests that men and women wore jewelry fashioned from bone, shell, and copper and that they used obsidian mirrors.[38]

Since Catal Hüyük is located in a region with few raw materials, the town evidently depended upon exchange with other areas to secure the rich variety of materials it used. Shells were procured from the Mediterranean, timber from the hills, obsidian from fifty miles away, and marble from western Turkey.

Domestication in Southeast Asia, China, and Africa

A number of areas in the world other than the Near East appear to have been early centers of independent plant and animal domestication. One such area, which may have been a center of domestication almost as early as the Near East, was mainland Southeast Asia. The dates of the earliest cultivation there are not clear. Some plants found in Spirit Cave in northwest Thailand date from about 6800 B.C., but these specimens are not clearly distinguishable from wild varieties. They may have been wild, or they may have been cultivated but not yet changed in appearance.

Most of the early cultivation in mainland Southeast Asia seems to have occurred in the plains and low terraces around rivers, although the main subsistence foods of early cultivators were probably the fish and shellfish in nearby waters. The first plants to be domesticated were probably not cereal

grains, as in the Near East. Indeed, some early cultivated crops may not have been used for food. Bamboo and a variety of bottle gourd, for example, were probably grown for use as containers. However, other plants were probably grown to be eaten: herbs, roots and tubers such as taro and yams, fruits, beans, and water chestnuts.[39]

The earliest evidence of cereal cultivation outside the Near East dates from China. Late in the sixth millenium B.C. in North China there were sites where foxtail millet was cultivated. Storage pits, storage pots, and large numbers of grinding stones suggest that millet was an important item in the diet. Judging from the wild-animal bones and the hunting and fishing tools that have been found, people still depended on hunting and fishing somewhat, even though domesticated pigs (as well as dogs) were present. In South China archeologists have found, dating from about the same time, a village by the edge of a small lake where people cultivated rice, bottle gourds, water chestnuts, and the datelike fruit called jujube. The people in South China also raised water buffalo, pigs, and dogs. And, as in the North China sites, they got some of their food from hunting and fishing.[40]

Some plants and animals were domesticated first in Africa, but there probably was not only one center of domestication. Most of the early domestications probably occurred in the wide and broad belt of woodland-savanna country south of the Sahara and north of the equator.[41] Among the cereal grains, sorghum was probably first domesticated in the central or eastern part of this belt, bulrush millet and a kind of rice (different from Asian rice) in the western part, and finger millet in the east. In what we now call West Africa, groundnuts (peanuts) and yams were domesticated.[42] Some of

[38]James Mellaart, "A Neolithic City in Turkey," *Scientific American*, April 1964, pp. 94–104.

[39]Chang, "The Beginnings of Agriculture in the Far East," pp. 175–85.

[40]K. C. Chang, "In Search of China's Beginnings: New Light on an Old Civilization," *American Scientist*, 69 (1981): 148–60.

[41]Jack R. Harlan, J. M. J. De Wet, and Ann Stemler, "Plant Domestication and Indigenous African Agriculture," in Jack R. Harlan, Jan M. J. De Wet, and Ann B. L. Stemler, eds., *Origins of African Plant Domestication* (The Hague: Mouton, 1976), p. 13.

[42]J. W. Purseglove, "The Origins and Migrations of Crops in Tropical Africa," in Harlan, De Wet, and Stemler, eds., *Origins of African Plant Domestication*, pp. 291–309; Jack R. Harlan and Ann Stemler, "The Races of Sorghum in Africa," in Harlan, De Wet, and Stemler, eds., *Origins of African Plan Domestication*, p. 472.

these domestications are estimated to have occurred after about 3000 B.C.[43] In addition to these
domesticated plants, the ass, cat, and guinea fowl
may also have been first domesticated in Africa.[44]

Domestication in the New World

In the New World, evidence of independent domestication of plants comes from at least three areas: Mexico, South America, and the eastern
United States. Possibly the first plants to be domesticated in the New World were members of the cu-
curbit family; they included a variety of the bottle
gourd, summer squash, and pumpkins. Although
probably not an important source of food anywhere,
the woody bottle gourd could have been used as a
water jug or cut into bowls. People may also have
made musical instruments and art objects out of the
bottle gourd. It is difficult to establish exactly when
and where the New World variety of bottle gourd
was first domesticated. Some suspect it is native to
Africa and floated to the New World like a runaway
buoy.[45] Fragments and seeds of bottle gourd do date
from as far back as 7400 B.C. in Oaxaca, Mexico.
Summer squash was probably domesticated in Mexico between 7400 and 6700 B.C.[46]

Although the origins of maize (corn) are controversial, an early domesticated form dating from
about 5000 B.C. has been found in Tehuacán,
Mexico. Until 1970, the most widely accepted
view was that maize was cultivated from a now-extinct "wild maize" that had tiny cobs topped by
small tassels. Now other views are considered: that
maize was domesticated from teosinte, a tall, wild
grass that still grows widely in Mexico, or that it
resulted from a cross between a perennial variety of
teosinte and a wild corn.[47]

People who lived in Mesoamerica (Mexico
and Central America) are often credited with the
invention of planting maize, beans, and squash to-

Corn evolved in the Tehuacán Valley of central Mexico from tiny wild corncobs, about 7000 years ago, to
modern corn, about 3500 years ago. Shown here are
some of the varieties of corn grown today.

gether in the same field. This planting strategy
provides a number of important advantages. Maize
takes nitrogen from the soil; beans, like all legumes, put nitrogen back into the soil. The maize
stalk provides a natural pole for the bean plant to
twine around, and the low-growing squash can
grow around the base of the tall maize plant. Beans
supply people with the amino acid, lysine, that is
missing in maize. Thus, maize and beans together
provide all the essential amino acids that humans
need to obtain from food. Whether teosinte was or
was not the ancestor of maize, it may have provided the model for this unique combination since
wild runner beans and wild squash occur naturally
where teosinte grows.[48]

There are hints that plant cultivation began in
South America almost as early as in Mexico. The
first crops cultivated on the Peruvian coast were
gourds, squash, lima beans, and possibly cotton.
Around 4,500 years ago, chili peppers, achira (a

[43]J. Desmond Clark, "Prehistoric Populations and Pressures Favoring Plant Domestication in Africa," in Harlan, De
Wet, and Stemler, eds., Origins of African Plant Domestication,
p. 87.

[44]Clark, The Prehistory of Africa, pp. 202–6.

[45]Charles B. Heiser, Jr., Of Plants and People (Norman:
University of Oklahoma Press, 1985), p. 21.

[46]Kent V. Flannery, "The Research Problem," in Kent V.
Flannery, ed., Guila Naquitz: Archaic Foraging and Early Agriculture in Oaxaca, Mexico (Orlando, FL: Academic Press, 1986),
pp. 6–8.

[47]Ibid.

[48]Ibid., pp. 8–9.

starchy root crop), jack beans, and guava were added. The root crops manioc and sweet potato may have been first domesticated in South America, or, less likely, in Mexico.[49]

Many of the plants grown in North America—such as corn, beans, and squash—were apparently introduced from Mesoamerica. However, at least two plants were probably domesticated independently in North America—sunflowers and a now-extinct variety of sumpweed. Both plants, members of the same biological family, contain seeds that are highly nutritious: they have a high fat and protein content. Sumpweed is an unusually good source of calcium, rivaled only by greens, mussels, and bones. It would also have been a very good source of iron (better than beef liver) and thiamine. Both plants may have been cultivated in the area of Kentucky, Tennessee, and southern Illinois beginning around 1500 B.C., prior to the introduction of maize.[50]

On the whole, domestic animals were less important economically in the New World than they were in many parts of the Old World. The animals domesticated in the New World included dogs, muscovy ducks, turkeys, guinea pigs, alpacas, and llamas. But the central Andes was the only area where animals were a significant part of the economy.[51] Guinea pigs, ducks, and turkeys were raised for food, alpacas mainly for their fur, and llamas for transporting goods. Animal domestication in the New World differed from that in the Old World because different wild species were found in the two hemispheres. The Old World plains and forests were the homes for the wild ancestors of the cattle, sheep, goats, pigs, and horses we know today. In the New World, the Pleistocene herds of horses, mastodons, mammoths, and other large animals were long extinct, allowing few opportunities for domestication of large animals.

Although there is evidence from Mexico and other parts of the Americas that cultivation was under way between the fifth and third millennia B.C., permanent villages were probably not established in Peru until about 2500 B.C. and in areas of Mesoamerica until about 1500 B.C.[52] Archeologists once thought that settled village life followed as a matter of course as soon as people had learned to domesticate plants. But evidence from the arid highlands of Mesoamerica contradicts this, and the reason may be that in highland Mesoamerica resources were widely distributed and relatively scarce in the dry season. Richard MacNeish suggests, for example, that the early cultivators depended mostly on hunting during the winter and on seed collecting and podpicking in the spring. In addition to their food-collecting activities, in the summer they planted and harvested crops such as squash, and in the fall they collected fruit and harvested the avocados they had planted. These varied activities seem to have required people to spend most of the year in small groups, gathering into larger groups only in the summer and only in moister areas.[53]

Why Did Food Production Develop?

We know that an economic transformation occurred in widely separate areas of the world beginning after about 10,000 years ago, as people began to domesticate plants and animals. But why did domestication occur? And why did it occur independently in a number of different places within

[49]Barbara Pickersgill and Charles B. Heiser, Jr., "Origins and Distribution of Plants Domesticated in the New World Tropics," in Charles A. Reed, ed., Origins of Agriculture (The Hague: Mouton, 1977), pp. 825–27.

[50]Richard A. Yarnell, "Domestication of Sunflower and Sumpweed in Eastern North America," in Richard I. Ford, ed., The Nature and Status of Ethnobotany, Anthropological Papers, Museum of Anthropology, no. 67 (Ann Arbor: University of Michigan, 1978), pp. 289–300. See also Nancy B. Asch and David L. Asch, "The Economic Potential of Iva annua and Its Prehistoric Importance in the Lower Illinois Valley," in Ford, ed., The Nature and Status of Ethnobotany, pp. 301–42.

[51]Robert J. Wenke, Patterns in Prehistory: Humankind's First Three Million Years, 2nd ed. (New York: Oxford University Press, 1984), pp. 350, 397–98.

[52]Flannery, "The Origins of the Village as a Settlement Type in Mesoamerica and the Near East," p. 1. However, there is evidence that there could have been permanent communities as far back as 6000 B.C. in central Mexico, near what is now Mexico City; see Christine Niederberger, "Early Sedentary Economy in the Basin of Mexico," Science, January 12, 1979, pp. 131–42.

[53]Richard S. MacNeish, "The Evaluation of Community Patterns in the Tehuacán Valley of Mexico and Speculations about the Cultural Processes," in Ruth Tringham, ed., Ecology and Agricultural Settlements (Andover, MA: Warner Modular Publications, 1973), R2, 1–27. Originally published in Peter J. Ucko, Ruth Tringham, and G. W. Dimbleby, eds., Man, Settlement and Urbanism (London: Duckworth; Cambridge, MA: Schenkman, 1972).

a period of a few thousand years? (Considering that people depended only on wild plants and animals for millions of years, the differences in exactly when domestication first occurred in different parts of the world seem small.) There are many theories of why food production developed; most have tried to explain the origin of domestication in the area of the Fertile Crescent.

Gordon Childe's theory, popular in the 1950s, was that a drastic change in climate caused domestication in the Near East.[54] According to Childe, the postglacial period was marked by a decline in summer rainfall in the Near East and North Africa. As the rains supposedly decreased, people were forced to retreat into shrinking pockets, or *oases*, of food resources surrounded by desert. The lessened availability of wild resources provided an incentive for people to cultivate grains and domesticate animals, according to Childe.

Robert Braidwood criticized Childe's theory for two reasons. First, Braidwood believed that the climate changes may not have been as dramatic as Childe had assumed, and therefore the "oasis incentive" may not have existed. Second, the climatic changes that occurred in the Near East after the retreat of the last glaciers had probably occurred at earlier interglacial periods too, but there had never been a similar food-producing revolution before. Hence, according to Braidwood, there must be more to the explanation of why people began to produce food than simply changes in climate.[55]

Braidwood's archeological excavations in the Near East indicated to him that domestication began in regions where local plants and animals were species that could be domesticated. Wild sheep, goats, and grains were found in areas with the oldest farming villages. Braidwood and Gordon Willey claimed that in addition, people did not undertake domestication until they had learned a great deal about their environment and until their culture had evolved far enough for them to handle such an undertaking: "Why did incipient food production not come earlier? Our only answer at the moment

is that culture was not ready to achieve it."[56] As Braidwood had written earlier,

there is no need to complicate the story with extraneous "causes." . . . Around 8,000 B.C. the inhabitants of the hills around the fertile crescent had come to know their habitat so well that they were beginning to domesticate the plants and animals they had been collecting and hunting. . . . From these "nuclear" zones cultural diffusion spread the new way of life to the rest of the world.[57]

But most archeologists now think we should try to explain why people were not "ready" earlier to achieve domestication. Both Lewis Binford and Kent Flannery have suggested that *some change* in external circumstances, not necessarily environmental, must have induced or favored the changeover to food production.[58] As Flannery points out, there is no evidence of a great economic incentive for hunter-gatherers to become food producers. In fact, as we shall see in the chapter on food-getting, some contemporary hunter-gatherers may actually obtain adequate nutrition with far *less* work than many agriculturalists. So what might push food collectors to become food producers?

Binford and Flannery thought that the incentive to domesticate animals and plants may have been a desire to reproduce what was wildly abundant in the most bountiful or optimum hunting and gathering areas. Because of population growth in the optimum areas, people might have moved to surrounding areas containing fewer wild resources. It would have been in those marginal areas that people turned to food production in order to reproduce what they used to have.

The Binford-Flannery model seems to fit the archeological record in the Levant (the southwestern part of the Fertile Crescent), where population increase did precede the first signs of domestication.[59] But as Flannery admits, in some regions,

[54]Cited in Gary A. Wright, "Origins of Food Production in Southwestern Asia: A Survey of Ideas," *Current Anthropology*, 12 (1971): 453–54.

[55]Robert J. Braidwood, "The Agricultural Revolution," *Scientific American*, September 1960, p. 130.

[56]Robert J. Braidwood and Gordon R. Willey, "Conclusions and Afterthoughts," in Robert J. Braidwood and Gordon R. Willey, eds., *Courses toward Urban Life: Archeological Considerations of Some Cultural Alternatives*, Viking Fund Publications in Anthropology, no. 32 (Chicago: Aldine, 1962), p. 342.

[57]Braidwood, "The Agricultural Revolution," p. 134.

[58]Binford, "Post-Pleistocene Adaptations," pp. 22–49; and Flannery, "The Origins and Ecological Effects of Early Domestication in Iran and the Near East," pp. 50–70.

[59]Wright, "Origins of Food Production in Southwestern Asia," p. 470.

such as southwestern Iran, the optimum hunting-gathering areas do not show population increase before the emergence of domestication.[60]

The Binford-Flannery model focuses on population pressure in a small area as the incentive to turn to food production. Mark Cohen theorizes it was population pressure on a global scale that explains why so many of the world's peoples adopted agriculture within the span of a few thousand years.[61] He argues that hunter-gatherers all over the world gradually increased in population so that by about 10,000 years ago the world was more or less filled with food collectors. Thus people could no longer relieve population pressure by moving to uninhabited areas. To support their increasing populations, they would have had to exploit a broader range of less desirable wild foods; that is, they would have had to switch to broad-spectrum collecting, or they would have had to increase the yields of the most desirable wild plants by weeding, protecting them from animal pests, and perhaps deliberately planting the most productive among them. Cohen thinks that people might have tried a variety of these strategies but would generally have ended up depending on cultivation because that would have been the most efficient way to allow more people to live in one place.

Recently, some archeologists have returned to the idea that climatic change (not the extreme variety that Childe envisaged) might have played a role in the emergence of agriculture. It seems clear from the evidence now available that the climate of the Near East about 13,000 to 12,000 years ago became more seasonal: the summers got hotter and drier than before and the winters became colder. These climatic changes may have favored the emergence of annual species of grain which archeologically we see proliferating in many areas of the Near East.[62] People like the Natufians intensively exploited the seasonal grains, developing an elaborate technology for storing and processing the grains and giving up their previous nomadic existence to do so. The transition to agriculture may have occurred when sedentary foraging no longer provided sufficient resources for the population. This could have happened because sedentarization led to population increase and therefore resource scarcity,[63] or because local wild resources became depleted after people settled down in permanent villages.[64] In the area of Israel and Jordan where the Natufians lived, some of the people apparently turned to agriculture, probably to increase the supply of grain, while other people returned to nomadic food collection because of the decreasing availability of wild grain.[65]

Change to a more seasonal climate might also have led to a shortage of certain nutrients for food collectors. In the dry seasons certain nutrients would have been less available. For example, grazing animals get lean when grasses are not plentiful, and so meat from hunting would have been in short supply in the dry seasons. Although it may seem surprising, some recent hunter-gatherers have starved when they had to rely on lean meat. If they could have somehow increased their carbohydrate or fat intake, they might have been more likely to get through the periods of lean game.[66] So, it is possible that some wild-food collectors in the past thought of planting crops to get them through the dry seasons when hunting, fishing, and gathering did not provide enough carbohydrates and fat for them to avoid starvation.

Consequences of the Rise of Food Production

We do not know for sure that population pressure was responsible (at least partially) for plant and animal domestication. But we do know that population growth accelerated after the rise of food production (see Figure 8–3). There were other

[60]Flannery, "The Research Problem," pp. 10–11.
[61]Mark N. Cohen, "Population Pressure and the Origins of Agriculture," in Reed, ed., *Origins of Agriculture*, pp. 138–41. See also Cohen, *The Food Crisis in Prehistory*, p. 279.
[62]Roger Byrne, "Climatic Change and the Origins of Agriculture," in Linda Manzanilla, ed., *Studies in the Neolithic and Urban Revolutions*, British Archaeological Reports International Series 349 (Oxford, 1987), pp. 21–34; referred to in Mark A. Blumler and Roger Byrne, "The Ecological Genetics of Domestication and the Origins of Agriculture," *Current Anthropology*, 32 (1991): 23–35. See also Henry, *From Foraging to Agriculture*, pp. 30–8; and Joy McCorriston and Frank Hole, "The Ecology of Seasonal Stress and the Origins of Agriculture in the Near East," *American Anthropologist*, 93 (1991): 46–69.

[63]Henry, *From Foraging to Agriculture*, p. 41.
[64]McCorriston and Hole, "The Ecology of Seasonal Stress."
[65]Henry, *From Foraging to Agriculture*, p. 54.
[66]John D. Speth and Katherine A. Spielmann, "Energy Source, Protein Metabolism, and Hunter-Gatherer Subsistence Strategies," *Journal of Anthropological Archaeology*, 2 (1983): 1–31.

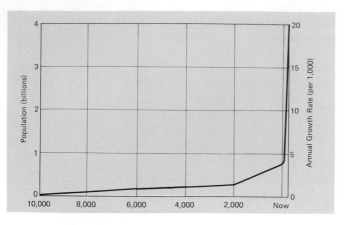

FIGURE 8-3 Population Growth Since 10,000 Years Ago

(Adapted from "The History of the Human Population," by Ansley J. Coale. Copyright © by Scientific American, Inc. All rights reserved.)

consequences too. Paradoxically, perhaps, health seems to have declined. Material possessions, though, became more elaborate.

Accelerated Population Growth

As we have seen, settling down (even before the rise of food production) may have increased the rate of human population growth. But population growth definitely accelerated after the emergence of farming and herding, possibly because the spacing between births was reduced further and therefore fertility (the number of births per mother) increased. Increased fertility may have been advantageous because of the greater value of children in farming and herding economies; there is evidence from recent population studies that fertility rates are higher where children contribute more to the economy.[67] Not only may parents desire more children to help with chores; the increased work load of mothers may also (but inadvertently) decrease birth spacing. The busier a mother is, the less frequently she may nurse and the more likely her baby will be given supplementary food by baby-sitters such as older siblings.[68]

Less frequent nursing[69] and greater reliance on food other than mother's milk may result in an earlier resumption of ovulation after the birth of a baby. (Farmers and herders are likely to have animal milk to feed to babies, and also cereals that have been transfomed by cooking into soft, mushy porridges.) Therefore the spacing between births may have decreased (and the number of births per mother may have increased) when mothers got busier after the rise of food production.

Declining Health

Although the rise of food production may have led to increased fertility, this does not mean that health generally improved. In fact, it appears that health may often have declined with the transition to food production. Although the two trends may seem paradoxical, rapid population growth can occur if each mother gives birth to a large number of babies, even if many of them die early because of disease or poor nutrition.

The evidence that health may have declined after the rise of food production comes from studies of the bone and teeth of some prehistoric populations, before and after the emergence of food production. Nutritional and disease problems are indicated by such features as incomplete formation of tooth enamel, nonaccidental bone lesions (incompletely filled in bone), reduction in stature, and decreased life expectancy. Many of the studied prehistoric populations that relied heavily on agriculture seem to show less adequate nutrition and higher infection rates than populations living in the same areas prior to agriculture. Some of the agricultural populations are shorter and had lower life expectancies.[70]

[67]Benjamin White, "Demand for Labor and Population Growth in Colonial Java," *Human Ecology*, 1, no. 3 (March 1973): 217–36. See also John D. Kasarda, "Economic Structure and Fertility: A Comparative Analysis," *Demography*, 8, no. 3 (August 1971): 307–18.

[68]Carol R. Ember, "The Relative Decline in Women's Contribution to Agriculture with Intensification," *American Anthropologist*, 85 (1983): 285–304.

[69]Melvin Konner and Carol Worthman, "Nursing Frequency, Gonadal Function, and Birth Spacing among !Kung Hunter-Gatherers," *Science*, February 15, 1980, pp. 788–91.

[70]Anna Curtenius Roosevelt, "Population, Health, and the Evolution of Subsistence: Conclusions from the Conference," in Mark Nathan Cohen and George J. Armelagos, eds., *Paleopathology at the Origins of Agriculture* (Orlando, FL: Academic Press, 1984), pp. 559–84. See also Mark Nathan Cohen and George J. Armelagos, "Paleopathology at the Origins of Agriculture: Editors' Summation," in the same volume, pp. 585–602; and Mark N. Cohen, "The Significance of Long-Term Changes in Human Diet and Food Economy," in Marvin Harris and Eric B. Ross, eds., *Food and Evolution: Toward a Theory of Human Food Habits* (Philadelphia: Temple University Press, 1987), p. 269–73.

The reasons for a decline in health in those populations are not yet clear. Greater malnutrition can result from an overdependence on a few dietary staples that lack some necessary nutrients. Overdependence on a few sources of food may also increase the risk of famine because the fewer the staple crops, the greater the danger to the food supply posed by a weather-caused crop failure. But some or most nutritional problems may be the result of social and political organization, particularly the rise of different socioeconomic classes of people and unequal access, between and within communities, to food and other resources.[71]

As we will see in the next chapter, social stratification or considerable socioeconomic inequality seems to develop frequently after the rise of food production. The effects of stratification and political dominance on the general level of health may be reflected in the skeletal remains of prehistoric native Americans who died in what is now Illinois between A.D. 950 and 1300 (the period spanning the changeover in that region from hunting and gathering to agriculture). The agricultural people living in the area of Dickson's Mounds (burial sites named after the doctor who first excavated them) were apparently in much worse health than their hunter-gatherer ancestors. But curiously, archeological evidence suggests they were still also hunting and fishing. A balanced diet was apparently available, but who was getting it? Possibly it was the elite at Cahokia (110 miles away, where perhaps 30,000 people lived) who were getting most of the meat and fish. The individuals near Dickson's Mounds who collected the meat and fish may have gotten luxury items such as shell necklaces from the Cahokia elite, but many of the people buried at Dickson's Mounds were clearly not benefiting nutritionally from the relationship with Cahokia.[72]

The Elaboration of Material Possessions

In the more permanent villages that were established after the rise of food production, houses became more elaborate and comfortable, and construction methods improved. The materials used in construction depended upon whether timber or stone was locally available or whether a strong sun could dry mud bricks. Modern architects might find to their surprise that bubble-shaped houses were known long ago in Neolithic Cyprus. Families in the island's town of Khirokitia made their homes in large, domed, circular dwellings shaped like beehives and featuring stone foundations and mud-brick walls. Often, to create more space, the interior was divided horizontally and the second floor was propped firmly on limestone pillars.

Sizable villages of solidly constructed, gabled wood houses were built in Europe on the banks of the Danube and along the rims of Alpine lakes.[73] Many of the gabled wooden houses in the Danube region were long, rectangular structures that apparently sheltered several family units. In Neolithic times these longhouses had doors, beds, tables, and other furniture that closely resembled those in our society. We know the people had furniture because miniature clay models have been found at their sites. Several of the chairs and couches seem to be models of padded and upholstered furniture with wooden frames, indicating that Neolithic European artisans were creating fairly sophisticated furnishings.[74] Such furnishings are the result of an advanced tool technology put to use by a people who, because they were staying in one area, could take time to make furniture.

For the first time, apparel made of woven textile appeared. This development was not simply the result of the domestication of flax (for linen), cotton, and wool-growing sheep. These sources of fiber alone could not produce cloth. It was the development by Neolithic society of the spindle and loom for spinning and weaving that made textiles possible. True, textiles can be woven by hand without a loom, but to do so is a slow and laborious process, impractical for producing garments.

[71]Roosevelt, "Population, Health, and the Evolution of Subsistence"; and Cohen and Armelagos, "Paleopathology at the Origins of Agriculture."

[72]Alan H. Goodman and George J. Armelagos, "Disease and Death at Dr. Dickson's Mounds," *Natural History*, September 1985, p. 18. See also Alan H. Goodman, John Lallo, George J. Armelagos, and Jerome C. Rose, "Health Changes at Dickson Mounds, Illinois (A.D. 950–1300)," in Cohen and Armelagos, *Paleopathology at the Origins of Agriculture*, p. 300.

[73]Grahame Clark and Stuart Piggott, *Prehistoric Societies* (New York: Knopf, 1965), pp. 240–42.
[74]Ibid., p. 235.

Reconstruction of lake dwellings in Switzerland during the Neolithic.

The pottery of the early Neolithic was similar to the plain earthenware made by some Mesolithic groups, and included large urns for grain storage, mugs, cooking pots, and dishes. To improve the retention of liquid, potters in the Near East may have been the first to glaze the earthenware's porous surface. Later, Neolithic ceramics became more artistic. Designers shaped the clay into graceful forms and painted colorful patterns on the vessels.

It is probable that virtually none of these architectural and technological innovations could have occurred until humans became fully sedentary. Nomadic hunting and gathering peoples would have found it difficult to carry many material goods, especially fragile items such as pottery. It was only when humans became fully sedentary that these goods would have provided advantages, enabling villagers to cook and store food more ef-fectively and to house themselves more comfortably.

There is also evidence of long-distance trade in the Neolithic, as we have noted. Obsidian from southern Turkey was being exported to sites in the Zagros Mountains of Iran and to what are now Israel, Jordan, and Syria in the Levant. Great amounts of obsidian were exported to sites about 190 miles from the source of supply; more than 80 percent of the tools used by residents of those areas were made of this material.[75] Marble was being sent from western to eastern Turkey, and seashells from the coast were traded to distant inland regions. Such trade suggests a considerable amount of contact among various Neolithic communities.

About 3500 B.C., cities first appeared in the Near East. These cities had political assemblies, kings, scribes, and specialized workshops. The specialized production of goods and services was supported by surrounding farming villages, which sent their produce to the urban centers. A dazzling transformation had taken place in a relatively short time. Not only had people settled down, but they had also become "civilized," or urbanized. (The word *civilized* literally means to make "citified."[76]) Urban societies seem to have developed first in the Near East, and somewhat later around the eastern Mediterranean, in the Indus Valley of northwest India, in northern China, and in Mexico and Peru. In the next chapter we turn to the rise of these earliest civilizations.

[75]Colin Renfrew, "Trade and Culture Process in European Prehistory," *Current Anthropology*, 10 (April–June 1969): 156–57; 161–69.
[76]*Webster's New World Dictionary*, Third College Edition (New York: Webster's New World, 1988).

SUMMARY

1. In the period prior to the emergence of plant and animal domestication (which in regard to Europe and the Near East is called the Mesolithic period) there seems to have been a shift in many areas of the world to less dependence on big-game hunting and greater dependence on what is called broad-spectrum collecting. The broad spectrum of available resources frequently included aquatic resources such as fish and shellfish, a variety of wild plants, and a wide variety of smaller game. Climatic changes may have been partially responsible for the change to broad-spectrum collecting.

2. In some sites in Europe, the Near East, Africa, and Peru, the switch to broad-spectrum collecting seems to be associated with the development of more permanent communities. In other areas, such as the semiarid highlands of Mesoamerica, the switch was not associated with the development of more permanent villages. In that area,

permanent settlements may have emerged only after the domestication of plants and animals.

3. The shift to the cultivation and domestication of plants and animals has been referred to as the Neolithic revolution, and it occurred, probably independently, in a number of areas. To date the earliest evidence of domestication comes from the Near East about 8000 B.C. Other centers of domestication in the Old World include Southeast Asia after about 6800 B.C., North and South China about 6000 B.C., and sub-Saharan Africa after 3000 B.C. In the New World, evidence for independent domestication comes from the highlands of Mexico (about 7000 B.C.), Peru (about 4500 B.C.), and the U.S. Midwest (about 1500 B.C.).

4. Theories about why food production originated are still quite controversial, but most archeologists think that certain conditions must have pushed people to switch from collecting to producing food. Some possible causal factors include (1) population growth in regions of bountiful wild resources (which may have pushed people to move to marginal areas where they tried to reproduce their former abundance); (2) global population growth (which filled most of the world's habitable regions and may have forced people to utilize a broader spectrum of wild resources and to domesticate plants and animals); and (3) the emergence of hotter and drier summers and colder winters (which may have favored sedentarization near seasonal stands of wild grain; population growth in such areas may have forced people to plant crops and raise animals to support themselves).

5. Regardless of why food production originated, it seems to have had important consequences for human life. Populations generally increased substantially *after* plant and animal domestication. Even though the early cultivators were not all sedentary, sedentarism did increase with greater reliance on agriculture. Somewhat surprisingly, some prehistoric populations that relied heavily on agriculture seem to have been less healthy than prior populations that relied on hunting and gathering. In the more permanent villages that were established after the rise of food production, houses and furnishings became more elaborate, and people began to make textiles and paint pottery. These villages have also yielded evidence of increased long-distance trade.

SUGGESTED READING

COHEN, M. N. *The Food Crisis in Prehistory: Overpopulation and the Origins of Agriculture.* New Haven: Yale University Press, 1977. An extensive review of archeological evidence, from the Old and New Worlds, suggesting that the origins of agriculture in most areas may be linked to the general tendency of human populations to increase.

COHEN, M. N., AND ARMELAGOS, G. J., eds. *Paleopathology at the Origins of Agriculture.* Orlando, FL: Academic Press, 1984. A volume of papers, covering nearly all regions of the world, that review the existing skeletal and paleopathological data on changes in human health associated with the transition from food collection to food production.

HARRIS, M., AND ROSS, E. B., eds. *Food and Evolution: Toward a Theory of Human Food Habits.* Philadelphia: Temple University Press, 1987. A collection of papers on why human populations may vary in what they eat.

HENRY, D. O. *From Foraging to Agriculture: The Levant at the End of the Ice Age.* Philadelphia: University of Pennsylvania Press, 1989. An examination and discussion of theories about the origin of agriculture, with particular reference to the areas bordering the eastern Mediterranean.

PRICE, T.D., AND BROWN, J. A., eds. *Prehistoric Hunter-Gatherers: The Emergence of Cultural Complexity.* Orlando, FL: Academic Press, 1985. A volume of papers by archeologists on the beginnings of social complexity among hunter-gatherers. The scope is global; most of the chapters deal comparatively or cross-archeologically with the various adaptations of hunter-gatherers in the past.

WENKE, R. J. *Patterns in Prehistory: Humankind's First Three Million Years,* 3rd ed. New York: Oxford University Press, 1990. Chapter 6 is an up-to-date review of what is known and what is controversial about the origins of food production and settled life.

9

Origins of Cities and States

From the time agriculture first developed until about 6000 B.C., people in the Near East lived in fairly small villages. There were few differences in wealth and status from household to household, and there was apparently no governmental authority beyond the village. There is no evidence that these villages had any public buildings or craft specialists, or that one community was very different in size from its neighbors. In short, these settlements had none of the characteristics we commonly associate with "civilization."

But sometime around 6000 B.C. in parts of the Near East—and at later times in other places—a great transformation in the quality and scale of human life seems to have begun. For the first time, we can see evidence of differences in status among households. Communities began to differ in size and to specialize in certain crafts. There are signs that some political officials had acquired authority over several communities, that what anthropologists call "chiefdoms" had emerged.

Somewhat later, by about 3500 B.C., we can see many, if not all, of the conventional characteristics of **civilization:** the first inscriptions or writing; cities; many kinds of full-time craft specialists; monumental architecture; great differences in wealth and status; and the kind of strong, hierarchical, and centralized political system we call the state.

This type of transformation has occurred many times and in many places in human history. The most ancient civilizations arose in the Near East around 3500 B.C., in northwestern India after 2500 B.C., in northern China around 1650 B.C., in the New World (Mexico and Peru) a few hundred years before the time of Christ, and in tropical Africa around the same time.[1] At least some of these civilizations evolved independently of the others—for example, those in the New World and those in the Old World. Why did they do so? What conditions favored the emergence of centralized, state-like political systems? What conditions favored the

establishment of cities? (We ask this last question separately, because archeologists are not yet certain that all the ancient state societies had cities when they first developed centralized government.) In this chapter, we discuss some of the things archeologists have learned or suspect about the growth of ancient civilizations. Our discussion focuses primarily on the Near East and Mexico because archeologists know the most about the sequences of cultural development in these two areas.

Archeological Inferences about Civilization

The most ancient civilizations have been studied by archeologists rather than historians because those civilizations evolved before the advent of writing. How do archeologists infer that a particular people in the preliterate past had social classes, cities, or centralized government?

As we have noted, it appears that the earliest Neolithic societies were *egalitarian*: people did not differ much in wealth, prestige, or power. Some later societies show signs of social inequality. One kind of evidence of inequality in an ancient society is provided by burial finds. Archeologists generally assume that inequality in death reflects inequality in life, at least in status and perhaps also in wealth and power. Thus, we can be fairly sure that a society had differences in status if only some people were buried with special objects, such as jewelry or pots filled with food. And we can be fairly sure that high status was assigned at birth rather than achieved in later life if we find noticeable differences in children's tombs. For example, some (but not all) child burials from as early as 5500 to 5000 B.C. at Tell es-Sawwan in Iraq, and from about 800 B.C. at La Venta in Mexico, are filled with statues and ornaments suggesting that some children had high status from birth.[2] But burials indicating differences in status do not necessarily mean a society had significant differences in wealth. It is only when archeologists find other substantial differences, as in house size and furnishings, that we can

[1]Robert J. Wenke, *Patterns in Prehistory: Humankind's First Three Million Years,* 3rd ed. (New York: Oxford University Press, 1990). See also Graham Connah, *African Civilizations: Precolonial Cities and States in Tropical Africa, an Archaeological Perspective* (Cambridge: Cambridge University Press, 1987); and Elman R. Service, *Origins of the State and Civilization: The Process of Cultural Evolution* (New York: W. W. Norton & Co., Inc., 1975), p. 5.

[2]Kent V. Flannery, "The Cultural Evolution of Civilizations," *Annual Review of Ecology and Systematics,* 3 (1972): 399–426.

TABLE 9–1 An Overview of Human Evolution: Biological and Cultural

TIME (YEARS AGO)	GEOLOGIC EPOCH	FOSSIL RECORD (FIRST APPEARANCE)	ARCHEOLOGICAL PERIODS (OLD WORLD)	MAJOR CULTURAL DEVELOPMENTS (FIRST APPEARANCE)
			Bronze Age	Cities and states; social inequality; full-time craft specialists
5500 (3500 B.C.)			————————	
			Neolithic	Domesticated plants and animals; permanent villages
10,000 (8000 B.C.)			————————	
			Mesolithic	Broad-spectrum food collecting; increasingly sedentary communities; many kinds of microliths
14,000 (12,000 B.C.)	Pleistocene	Earliest humans in New World	————————	
			Upper Paleolithic	Cave paintings; female figurines; many kinds of blade tools
40,000			————————	
		Modern humans *Homo sapiens sapiens*	Middle Paleolithic	Religious beliefs (?); burials; Mousterian tools
200,000		Neandertal *Homo sapiens*		
300,000		Earliest *Homo sapiens* (?)	————————	
700,000				Acheulian tools
1,500,000		*Homo erectus*		
1,800,000	————————		Lower Paleolithic	Hunting and/or scavenging; seasonal campsites; Oldowan tools
2,000,000	Pliocene	*Homo habilis*	————————	
		Earliest hominids *Australopithecus*		Earliest stone tools
5,000,000	————————	Diversification of apes *Sivapithecus* *Dryopithecus*		
	Miocene			
22,500,000	————————	*Proconsul* Earliest apes (?)		
29,000,000		Propliopithecids, e.g., *Aegyptopithecus*		
32,000,000	Oligocene	Earliest anthropoids Parapithecids, e.g., *Apidium*		
38,000,000	————————			
50,000,000	Eocene	*Amphipithecus* *Tetonius*		
53,500,000	————————			
	Paleocene			
65,000,000	————————			
70,000,000	Late Cretaceous	Earliest primates *Purgatorius*		

Source: Geological dates from W. A. Berggren and J. A. Van Couvering, "The Late Neocene: Biostratigraphy, Geochronology and Paleoclimatology of the Last 15 Million Years in Marine and Continental Sequences," *Palaeogeography, Palaeoclimatology, Palaeoecology,* 16 (1974): 13–16, 165.

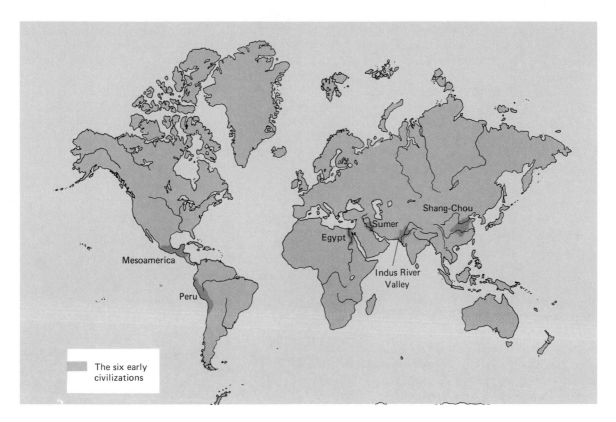

FIGURE 9-1 Six Early Civilizations

(Adapted from Origins of the State and Civilization: The Process of Cultural Evolution, by Elman R. Service. By permission of W. W. Norton & Company, Inc. Copyright © 1975 by W. W. Norton & Company, Inc.)

be sure the society had different socioeconomic classes of people.

Some archeologists think that states first evolved around 3500 B.C. in Greater Mesopotamia, the area now shared by southern Iraq and southwestern Iran. Archeologists do not always agree on how a state should be defined, but most seem to agree that hierarchical and centralized decision making affecting a substantial population is the key criterion. Other characteristics are usually, but not always, found in these first states. Such states usually have cities with a substantial proportion of the population not involved directly in the collection or production of food (which means that people in cities are heavily dependent on people elsewhere); full-time religious and craft specialists; public buildings; and often an official art style. There is a hierarchical social structure topped by an elite class from which the leaders are drawn. The government tries to claim a monopoly on the use of force.

(Our own state society says that citizens do not have the right "to take the law into their own hands.") The state uses its force or threat of force to tax its population and to draft people for work or war.[3]

How can archeologists tell, from the information provided by material remains, whether a society was a state or not? This depends in part on what is used as the criterion for a state. For example, Henry Wright and Gregory Johnson define a state as a centralized political hierarchy with at least three levels of administration.[4] But how might archeologists infer that such a hierarchy ex-

[3]Ibid. See also Charles L. Redman, *The Rise of Civilization: From Early Farmers to Urban Society in the Ancient Near East* (San Francisco: W. H. Freeman & Company Publishers, 1978), pp. 215–16.

[4]Henry T. Wright and Gregory A. Johnson, "Population, Exchange, and Early State Formation in Southwestern Iran," *American Anthropologist*, 77 (1975): 267.

isted in some area? Wright and Johnson suggest that the way settlement sites differ in size is one indication of how many levels of administration there were in an area.

During the early Uruk period (just before 3500 B.C.) in what is now southwestern Iran, there were some fifty settlements that seem to fall into three groups in terms of size.[5] There were about forty-five small villages; three or four "towns"; and one large center, Susa. These three types of settlements seem to have been part of a three-level administration hierarchy, since many small villages could not trade with Susa without passing through a settlement intermediate in size. Because a three-level hierarchy is Wright and Johnson's criterion of a state, they think a state had emerged in the area by early Uruk times.

Evidence from the next period, middle Uruk, suggests more definitely that a state had emerged. This evidence takes the form of clay seals that were apparently used in trading.[6] *Commodity sealings* were used to keep a shipment of goods tightly closed until it reached its destination, and *message sealings* were used to keep track of goods sent and received. The clay seals found in Susa include many message seals and *bullae* (clay containers that served as bills of lading for goods received). The villages, in contrast, had few message seals and bullae. This finding suggests that Susa administered the regional movement of goods and that Susa was the "capital" of the state.

Let us turn now to the major features of the cultural sequences leading to the first states in southern Iraq.

Cities and States in Southern Iraq

Farming communities older than the first states have not been found in the arid lowland plains of southern Iraq—the area known as Sumer, where some of the earliest cities and states developed. Perhaps silt from the Tigris and Euph-

rates rivers has covered them. Or, as has been suggested, Sumer may not have been settled by agriculturalists until people learned how to drain and irrigate river-valley soils otherwise too wet or too dry for cultivation. At any rate, small communities depending partially on agriculture had emerged in the hilly areas north and east of Sumer early in the Neolithic. Later, by about 6000 B.C., a mixed herding-farming economy developed in those areas.

The Formative Era

Elman Service calls the period from about 5000 to 3500 B.C. the *formative era*, for it saw the coming together of many changes that seem to have played a part in the development of cities and states. Service suggests that with the development of small-scale irrigation, lowland river areas began to attract settlers. The rivers provided not only water for irrigation but also mollusks, fish, and water birds for food. And they provided routes by which to import needed raw materials, such as hardwood and stone, that were lacking in the region of Sumer.

We see a number of changes during this period that suggest an increasingly complex social and political life. We see differences in status reflected in the burial of statues and ornaments with children. We see different villages specializing in the production of different goods—pottery in some, copper and stone tools in others.[7] We see the building of temples in certain places that may have been centers of political as well as religious authority for several communities.[8] Some anthropologists think that chiefdoms, each having authority over a number of villages, had developed by this time.[9]

Sumerian Civilization

By about 3500 B.C., there were a number of cities in the area of Sumer. Most were enclosed in a fortress wall and surrounded by an agricultural area. Shortly after the first forms of writing appeared—about 3000 B.C.—all of Sumer was unified under a single government. After that time,

[5]The discussion in the remainder of this section draws from ibid., pp. 269–74. See also Gregory A. Johnson, "The Changing Organization of Uruk Administration on the Susiana Plain," in Frank Hole, ed., *Archaeology of Western Iran* (Washington DC: Smithsonian Institution Press, 1987), pp. 107–39.
[6]Ibid., pp. 271–72.

[7]Flannery, "The Cultural Evolution of Civilizations."
[8]Service, *Origins of the State and Civilization*, p. 207.
[9]Ibid.; and Flannery, "The Cultural Evolution of Civilizations."

Partially restored ziggurat, or temple tower, in what was the Sumerian city of Ur, in 2100 B.C.

Ruins of temples and other buildings in the Mayan city of Tikal (Guatemala).

Sumer became an empire. It had great urban centers. Imposing temples, commonly set on artificial mounds, dominated the cities. (In the city of Warka the temple mound was about 150 feet high.) The empire was very complex. It included an elaborate system for the administration of justice, codified laws, specialized government officials, a professional standing army, and even sewer systems in the cities. Among the many specialized crafts were brickmaking, pottery, carpentry, jewelry making, leatherworking, metallurgy, basketmaking, stonecutting, and sculpture. Sumerians learned to construct and use wheeled wagons, sailboats, horse-drawn chariots, and spears, swords, and armor of bronze.[10]

As economic specialization developed, social stratification became more elaborate. Sumerian documents describe a system of social classes: nobles, priests, merchants, craftworkers, metallurgists, bureaucrats, soldiers, farmers, free citizens, and slaves. Slaves were common in Sumer; they were often captives, brought back as the spoils of war.

We see the first evidence of writing around 3000 B.C. The earliest Sumerian writings were in the form of ledgers containing inventories of items stored in the temples and records of livestock or other items owned or managed by the temples. Sumerian writing was wedge-shaped, or **cuneiform,** formed by pressing a stylus against a damp clay tablet. For contracts and other important documents,

the tablet was fired to create a virtually permanent record. (Egyptian writing, or **hieroglyphics,** appeared about the same time. Hieroglyphics were written on rolls woven from papyrus reeds, from which our word *paper* derives.)

Cities and States in Mesoamerica

Cities and states emerged in Mesoamerica (Mexico and Central America) later than they did in the Near East. The later appearance of civilization in Mesoamerica may be linked to the later emergence of agriculture in the New World, as we saw in the last chapter, and possibily to the near-absence of large animals like cattle and horses that could be domesticated.[11] We will focus primarily on the developments that led to the rise of the city-state of Teotihuacán, which reached its height shortly after the time of Christ. Teotihuacán is located in a valley of the same name, which is the northeastern part of the larger Valley of Mexico.

The Formative Period

The formative period in the area around Teotihuacán (1000–300 B.C.) was characterized initially by small, scattered farming villages on the hilly slopes just south of the Teotihuacán Valley.

[10]This description of Sumerian civilization is based on Samuel Noel Kramer, *The Sumerians: Their History, Culture, and Character* (Chicago: University of Chicago Press, 1963).

[11]Jared Diamond, "The Accidental Conqueror," *Discover,* December 1989, pp. 71–76.

There were probably a few hundred people in each hamlet, and each of these scattered groups was probably politically autonomous. After about 500 B.C., there seems to have been a population shift to settlements on the valley floor, probably in association with the use of irrigation. Between about 300 and 200 B.C. we see the emergence of small "elite" centers in the valley, each of which had an earth or stone raised platform. Residences or small temples of poles and thatch originally stood on these platforms. That some individuals, particularly those in the elite centers, were buried in special tombs supplied with ornaments, headdresses, carved bowls, and a good deal of food indicates the presence of some social inequality.[12] The various elite centers may indicate the presence of a number of chiefdoms.

The City and State of Teotihuacán

About 150 years before the time of Christ, no more than a few thousand people lived in scattered villages in the Teotihuacán Valley. In A.D. 100 there was a city of 80,000. By A.D. 500, well over 100,000 people, or approximately 90 percent of the entire valley population, seem to have been drawn or coerced into Teotihuacán.[13]

The layout of the city of Teotihuacán shows a tremendous amount of planning. This suggests that from its beginning, the valley may have been politically unified under a centralized state. Mapping has revealed that the streets and most of the buildings are laid out in a grid pattern. The grid follows a basic modular unit of fifty-seven square meters. Residential structures are often squares of this size, and many streets are spaced according to multiples of the basic unit. Even the river that ran through the center of the city was channeled to conform to the grid pattern. Perhaps the most outstanding feature of the city is the colossal scale of its architecture. Two pyramids dominate the metropolis, the so-called Pyramid of the Moon and the Pyramid of the Sun. At its base the latter is as big as the great Pyramid of Cheops in Egypt. At the height of its power, the metropolis of Teotihuacán encompassed a larger area than imperial Rome.[14]

The thousands of residential structures built after A.D. 300 follow a standard pattern. Narrow streets separate the one-story buildings, each of which has high, windowless walls. Patios and shafts provide interior light. The layout of rooms suggests that each building consisted of several apartments; more than 100 people may have lived in one of these apartment compounds. There is variation from compound to compound in the size of rooms and the elaborateness of interior decoration, suggesting considerable variation in wealth.[15]

At the height of its power (A.D. 200–500), much of Mesoamerica seems to have been influenced by Teotihuacán. Archeologically, this is suggested by the extensive spread of Teotihuacán-style pottery and architectural elements. Undoubtedly, large numbers of people in Teotihuacán were engaged in production for, and the conduct of, long-distance trade. Perhaps 25 percent of the city's population worked at various specialized crafts, including the manufacture of projectile points and cutting and scraping tools from volcanic obsidian. Teotihuacán was close to major deposits of obsidian, which was apparently in some demand over much of Mesoamerica. Judging from materials found in graves, there was an enormous flow of foreign goods into the city, including precious stones, feathers from colorful birds in the tropical lowlands, and cotton.[16]

The City of Monte Albán

Teotihuacán was probably not the earliest city-state in Mesoamerica: there is evidence of political unification somewhat earlier, about 500 B.C., in the Valley of Oaxaca in southern Mexico, with the city of Monte Albán at its center. Monte Albán presents an interesting contrast to Teotihuacán. Whereas Teotihuacán seems to have completely dominated its valley, containing almost all

[12]Mary W. Helms, *Middle America* (Englewood Cliffs, NJ: Prentice Hall, 1975), pp. 34–36, 54–55. See also William T. Sanders, Jeffrey R. Parsons, and Robert S. Santley, *The Basin of Mexico: Ecological Processes in the Evolution of a Civilization* (New York: Academic Press, 1979).

[13]Wenke, *Patterns in Prehistory: Humankind's First Three Million Years*, 2nd ed. (New York: Oxford University Press, 1984), p. 368; and René Millon, "Teotihuacán," *Scientific American*, June 1967, pp. 38–48.

[14]Millon, "Teotihuacán," pp. 38–44.

[15]René Millon, "Social Relations in Ancient Teotihuacán," in Eric R. Wolf, ed., *The Valley of Mexico: Studies in Pre-Hispanic Ecology and Society* (Albuquerque: University of New Mexico Press, 1976), pp. 215–20.

[16]Helms, *Middle America*, pp. 61–63.

Ruins at Monte Albán.

its inhabitants and craftspeople, Monte Albán did not. The various villages in the Valley of Oaxaca seem to have specialized in different crafts, and Monte Albán did not monopolize craft production. After the political unification of the valley, cities and towns other than Monte Albán remained important: the population of Monte Albán grew only to 30,000 or so. Unlike Teotihuacán, Monte Albán was not an important commercial or market center, it was not laid out in a grid pattern, and its architecture was not that different from other settlements in the valley in which it was located.[17]

Monte Albán did not have the kinds of resources that Teotihuacán had. It was located on top of a mountain in the center of the valley, far from either good soil or permanent water supplies that could have been used for irrigation. (Even finding drinking water must have been difficult.) No natural resources for trade were nearby, nor is there much evidence that Monte Albán was used as a ceremonial center. Because the city was at the top of a steep mountain, it is unlikely that it could have been a central marketplace for valleywide trade.

Why, then, did Monte Albán rise to become one of the early centers of Mesoamerican civilization? Richard Blanton suggests it may have originally been founded in the late formative period (500–400 B.C.) as a neutral place where representatives of the different political units in the valley could reside to coordinate activities affecting the whole valley. Thus Monte Albán may have been like the cities of Brasília, Washington, DC, and Athens, all of which were originally founded in "neutral," nonproductive areas. Such a center, lacking obvious resources, would not, at least initially, threaten the various political units around it. Later it might become a metropolis dominating a more politically unified region, as Monte Albán came to do in the Valley of Oaxaca.[18]

[17]Richard E. Blanton, "The Rise of Cities," in Jeremy A. Sabloff, ed., *Supplement to the Handbook of Middle American Indians* (Austin: University of Texas Press, 1981), 1: 397. See also Joyce Marcus, "On the Nature of the Mesoamerican City," in Evon Z. Vogt and Richard M. Leventhal, eds., *Prehistoric Settlement Patterns: Essays in Honor of Gordon R. Willey* (Albuquerque: University of New Mexico Press, 1983), pp. 195–242.

[18]Richard Blanton, "The Origins of Monte Albán," in C. Cleland, ed., *Cultural Continuity and Change* (New York: Academic Press, 1976), pp. 223–32; and Blanton, *Monte Albán: Settlement Patterns at the Ancient Zapotec Capital* (New York: Academic Press, 1978).

Other Centers of Mesoamerican Civilization

In addition to Teotihuacán and Oaxaca, there were other Mesoamerican state societies, which developed somewhat later. For example, there are a number of centers with monumental architecture, presumably built by speakers of Mayan languages, in the highlands and lowlands of modern-day Guatemala and the Yucatán Peninsula of modern-day Mexico. Judging from surface appearances, the Mayan centers do not appear to have been as densely populated as Teotihuacán or Monte Albán. But it is now evident that the Mayan centers were more densely populated and more dependent on intensive agriculture than was once thought.[19] And recent translations of Mayan picture writing indicate a much more developed form of writing than previously thought.[20] It is apparent now that Mayan urbanization and cultural complexity were underestimated because of the dense tropical forest that now covers much of the area of Mayan civilization.

The First Cities and States in Other Areas

So far we have discussed the emergence of cities and states in southern Iraq and Mesoamerica whose development is best, if only imperfectly, known archeologically. But other state societies probably arose more or less independently in many other areas of the world as well. We say "independently" because such states seem to have emerged without colonization or conquest by other states.

Almost at the same time as the Sumerian Empire, the great dynastic age was beginning in the Nile Valley in Egypt. The Old Kingdom, or early dynastic period, began about 3100 B.C. with a capital at Memphis. The archeological evidence from the early centuries is limited, but most of the population appears to have lived in largely self-sufficient villages. Many of the great pyramids and palaces were built around 2500 B.C.[21]

In the Indus Valley of northwestern India, a large state society had developed by 2300 B.C. This Harappan civilization did not have much in the way of monumental architecture, such as pyramids and palaces, and it was also unusual in other respects. The state apparently controlled an enormous territory—over a million square kilometers. There was not just one major city but many, each built according to a similar pattern and with a municipal water and sewage system.[22]

The Shang dynasty in northern China (1750 B.C.) has long been mentioned as the earliest state society in the Far East. But recent research suggests that an earlier one, the Xia dynasty, may have emerged in the same general area by 2200 B.C.[23] In any case, the Shang dynasty had all the earmarks of statehood: a stratified, specialized society; religious, economic, and administrative unification; and a distinctive art style.[24]

In South America, state societies may have emerged after 200 B.C. in the area of modern-day Peru.[25] In sub-Saharan Africa by A.D. 800, the western Sudan had a succession of city-states. One of them was called Ghana, and it became a major source of gold for the Mediterranean world.[26] And in North America there is some evidence that a complex chiefdom (and possibly a state-level society) existed in the area around St. Louis by A.D. 1050. Huge mounds of earth 100 feet high mark the site there called Cahokia.[27]

Theories about the Origin of the State

We have seen that states developed in many parts of the world. Why did they evolve when and where they did? A number of theories have been

---

[19]B. L. Turner, "Population Density in the Classic Maya Lowlands: New Evidence for Old Approaches," *Geographical Review*, 66, no. 1 (January 1970): 72–82. See also Peter D. Harrison and B. L. Turner II, eds., *Pre-Hispanic Maya Agriculture* (Albuquerque: University of New Mexico Press, 1978).

[20]Stephen D. Houston, "The Phonetic Decipherment of Mayan Glyphs," *Antiquity*, 62 (1988): 126–35.

[21]Wenke, *Patterns in Prehistory*, 2nd ed., p. 289.

[22]Ibid., pp. 305–20.

[23]K. C. Chang, "In Search of China's Beginnings: New Light on an Old Civilization," *American Scientist*, 69 (1981): 148–60.

[24]Kwang-Chih Chang, *The Archaeology of Ancient China* (New Haven: Yale University Press, 1968), pp. 235–55.

[25]Wenke, *Patterns in Prehistory*, 2nd ed., p. 404.

[26]Brian M. Fagan, *People of the Earth: An Introduction to World Prehistory*, 6th ed. (Glenview, IL: Scott, Foresman and Company, 1989), pp. 428–30.

[27]Melvin L. Fowler, "A Pre-Columbian Urban Center on the Mississippi," *Scientific American*, August 1975, pp. 92–101.

proposed. We will consider the ones that have been discussed frequently by archeologists.[28]

Irrigation

Irrigation seems to have been important in many of the areas in which early state societies developed. Irrigation made the land habitable or productive in parts of Mesoamerica, southern Iraq, the Nile Valley, and other areas. It has been suggested that the labor and management needed for the upkeep of an irrigation system leads to the formation of a political elite (the overseers of the system), who eventually become the governors of the society.[29] Proponents of this view believe that both the city and civilization were outgrowths of the administrative requirements of an irrigation system.

Critics note that this theory does not seem to apply to all areas where cities and states may have emerged independently. For example, in southern Iraq, the irrigation systems serving the early cities were generally small in scale and probably did not require extensive labor and management. Large-scale irrigation works were not constructed until after cities had been fully established.[30] Thus, irrigation could not have been the main stimulus for the development of cities and states in Sumer. Even in China, for which the irrigation theory was first formulated, there is no evidence of large-scale irrigation as early as Shang times.[31]

Although large-scale irrigation may not always have preceded the emergence of the first cities and states, even small-scale irrigation systems could have resulted in unequal access to productive land and so may have contributed to the development of a stratified society.[32] In addition, irrigation sys-

Irrigated rice fields in modern China.

tems may have given rise to border and other disputes between adjacent groups, thereby prompting people to concentrate in cities for defense and stimulating the development of military and political controls.[33] Finally, as Robert Adams and Elman Service both suggest, the main significance of irrigation—either large- or small-scale—may have been its intensification of production, a development that in turn may have indirectly stimulated craft specialization, trade, and administrative bureaucracy.[34]

Population Growth, Circumscription, and War

Robert Carneiro suggests that states may emerge because of population growth in an area that is physically or socially limited. Competition and warfare in such a situation may lead to the subordination of defeated groups, who are obliged to pay tribute and to submit to the control of a more powerful group.[35] Carneiro illustrates his theory by describing how states may have emerged on the northern coast of Peru.

After the people of that area first settled into

[28]For a more complete review of the available theories, see various chapters in Ronald Cohen and Elman R. Service, eds., *Origins of the State: The Anthropology of Political Evolution* (Philadelphia: Institute for the Study of Human Issues, 1978).

[29]Karl Wittfogel, *Oriental Despotism: A Comparative Study of Total Power* (New Haven: Yale University Press, 1957).

[30]Robert M. Adams, "The Origin of Cities," *Scientific American*, September 1960, p. 153. See also Henry T. Wright, "The Evolution of Civilizations," in David J. Meltzer, Don D. Fowler, and Jeremy A. Sabloff, eds., *American Archaeology Past and Future* (Washington DC: Smithsonian Institution Press, 1986), pp. 323–65.

[31]Paul Wheatley, *The Pivot of the Four Quarters* (Chicago: Aldine, 1971), p. 291.

[32]Adams, "The Origin of Cities," p. 153.

[33]Robert McC. Adams, *Heartland of Cities: Surveys of Ancient Settlement and Land Use on the Central Floodplain of the Euphrates* (Chicago: University of Chicago Press, 1981), p. 244.

[34]Ibid., p. 243; and Service, *Origins of the State and Civilization*, pp. 274–75.

[35]Robert L. Carneiro, "A Theory of the Origin of the State," *Science*, August 21, 1970, pp. 733–38. See also William T. Sanders and Barbara J. Price, *Mesoamerica* (New York: Random House, 1968), pp. 230–32.

an agricultural village life, population grew at a slow, steady rate. Initially, new villages were formed as population grew. But in the narrow coastal valleys—blocked by high mountains, fronted by the sea, and surrounded by desert—this splintering-off process could not continue indefinitely. The result, Carneiro suggests, was increasing land shortage and warfare between villages as they competed for land. Since the high mountains, the sea, and the desert blocked any escape for losers, the defeated villagers had no choice but to submit to political domination. In this way, chiefdoms may have become kingdoms as the most powerful villages grew to control entire valleys. As chiefs' power expanded over several valleys, states and empires may have been born.

Carneiro notes that physical or environmental circumscription may not be the only kind of barrier that gives rise to a state. Social circumscription may be just as important. People living at the center of a high-density area may find that their migration is blocked by surrounding settlements just as effectively as it could be by mountains, sea, and desert.

Marvin Harris suggests a somewhat different form of circumscription. He argues that the first states with their coercive authority could emerge only in areas that permitted intensive grain agriculture (and the possibility of high food-production) and were surrounded by areas that could *not* support intensive grain agriculture. So people in such areas might put up with the coercive authority of a state because they would suffer a sharp drop in living standards if they moved away.[36]

Carneiro suggests that his theory applies to many areas besides the northern coast of Peru, including southern Iraq and the Indus and Nile valleys. While there were no geographical barriers in areas such as northern China or the Mayan lowlands on the Yucatán Peninsula, the development of states in those areas may have been the result of social circumscription. Carneiro's theory seems to be supported for southern Iraq, where there is archeological evidence of population growth, cir-

cumscription, and warfare.[37] And there is evidence of population growth prior to the emergence of the state in the Teotihuacán Valley.[38]

But population growth does not necessarily mean population pressure. For example, the populations in the Teotihuacán Valley and the Oaxaca Valley apparently did increase prior to state development, but there is no evidence that they had even begun to approach the limits of their resources. More people could have lived in both places.[39] Nor is population growth definitely associated with state formation in all areas where early states arose. For example, according to Wright and Johnson, there was population growth long before states emerged in southwestern Iran, but just prior to their emergence the population apparently declined.[40]

In addition, Carneiro's circumscription theory leaves an important logical question unanswered: Why would the victors in war let the defeated populations remain and pay tribute? If the victors wanted the land so much in the first place, why wouldn't they try to exterminate the defeated and

[36]Marvin Harris, *Cultural Materialism: The Struggle for a Science of Culture* (New York: Random House, 1979), pp. 101–2. See also Wenke, *Patterns in Prehistory*, 3rd ed.

[37]T. Cuyler Young, Jr., "Population Densities and Early Mesopotamian Urbanism," in P. J. Ucko, R. Tringham, and G. W. Dimbleby, eds., *Man, Settlement and Urbanism* (Cambridge, MA: Schenkman, 1972), pp. 827–42.

[38]Sanders and Price, *Mesoamerica*, p. 141.

[39]Richard E. Blanton, Stephen A. Kowalewski, Gary Feinman, and Jill Appel, *Ancient Mesoamerica: A Comparison of Change in Three Regions* (New York: Cambridge University Press, 1981), p. 224. For the apparent absence of population pressure in the Teotihuacán Valley, see Elizabeth Brumfiel, "Regional Growth in the Eastern Valley of Mexico: A Test of the 'Population Pressure' Hypothesis," in Kent V. Flannery, ed., *The Early Mesoamerican Village* (New York: Academic Press, 1976), pp. 234–50. For the Oaxaca Valley, see Gary M. Feinman, Stephen A. Kowalewski, Laura Finsten, Richard E. Blanton, and Linda Nicholas, "Long-Term Demographic Change: A Perspective from the Valley of Oaxaca, Mexico," *Journal of Field Archaeology*, 12 (1985): 333–62.

[40]Wright and Johnson, "Population, Exchange, and Early State Formation in Southwestern Iran," p. 276. However, Carneiro argues otherwise, that there was population growth just prior to the emergence of the state in southwestern Iran—see Robert L. Carneiro, "The Circumscription Theory: Challenge and Response," *American Behavioral Scientist*, 31 (1988): 506–8. Whether or not population declined, Frank Hole has suggested that climate change around that time may have forced local populations to relocate, some to centers that became cities; see his "Environmental Shock and Urban Origins," in Mitchell S. Rothman and Gil Stein, eds., *Chiefdoms and Early States in the Near East: The Organizational Dynamics of Complexity*, in press.

occupy the land themselves, which has happened many times in history?

Local and Long-Distance Trade

It has been suggested that trade was a factor in the emergence of the earliest states.[41] Wright and Johnson have theorized that the organizational requirements of producing items for export, redistributing the items imported, and defending trading parties would foster state formation.[42]

Does the archeological evidence support the theory that trade played a crucial role in the formation of the earliest states? In southern Iraq and the Mayan lowlands, long-distance trade routes may indeed have stimulated bureaucratic growth. In the lowlands of southern Iraq, as we have seen, people needed wood and stone for building, and they traded with highland people for these items. In the Mayan lowlands, the development of civilization seems to have been preceded by long-distance trade: farmers in the lowland regions traded with faraway places in order to obtain salt, obsidian for cutting blades, and hard stone for grinding tools.[43] In southwestern Iran, long-distance trade did not become very important until after Susa became the center of a state society, but short-distance trade may have played the same kind of role in the formation of states. The situation in other areas is not yet known.

The Various Theories: An Evaluation

Why do states form? As of now, no one theory seems to fit all the known situations. The reason may be that different conditions in different places may have favored the emergence of centralized government. After all, the state, by definition, implies an ability to organize large populations for a collective purpose. In some areas, this purpose may have been the need to organize trade with local or far-off regions. In other cases, the state may have emerged as a way to control defeated populations in circumscribed areas. In still other instances, a combination of factors may have fostered the development of the state type of political system.[44] It is still not clear what specific conditions led to the emergence of the state in each of the early centers. But since the question of why states formed is a lively focus of research today, more satisfactory answers may come out of ongoing and future investigations.

---

[41]Karl Polanyi, C. M. Arensberg and Harry W. Pearson, eds., *Trade and Market in the Early Empires* (New York: Free Press, 1957), pp. 257–62; and William T. Sanders, "Hydraulic Agriculture, Economic Symbiosis, and the Evolution of States in Central Mexico," in Betty J. Meggers, ed., *Anthropological Archeology in the Americas* (Washington, DC: Anthropological Society of Washington, 1968), p. 105.

[42]Wright and Johnson, "Population, Exchange, and Early State Formation in Southwestern Iran," p. 277.

[43]William L. Rathje, "The Origin and Development of Lowland Classic Maya Civilization," *American Antiquity*, 36 (1971): 275–85.

[44]For a discussion of how political dynamics may play an important role in state formation, see Elizabeth M. Brumfiel, "Aztec State Making: Ecology, Structure, and the Origin of the State," *American Anthropologist*, 85 (1983): 261–84.

SUMMARY

1. Archeologists do not always agree on how a state should be defined, but most seem to agree that hierarchical and centralized decision making affecting a substantial population is the key criterion. Most states have cities with public buildings, full-time craft and religious specialists, an official art style, and a hierarchical social structure topped by an elite class from which the leaders are drawn. Most states maintain power with a monopoly on the use of force. Force or the threat of force is used by the state to tax its population and to draft people for work or war.

2. Early state societies arose within the Near East in what is now southern Iraq and southwestern Iran. Southern Iraq, or Sumer, was unified under a single government just after 3000 B.C. It had writing, large urban centers, imposing temples, codified laws, a standing army, wide trade net-

works, a complex irrigation system, and a high degree of craft specialization.

3. Probably the earliest city-state in Mesoamerica developed around 500 B.C. in the Valley of Oaxaca, with a capital at Monte Albán. Somewhat later, in the northeastern section of the Valley of Mexico, Teotihuacán developed. At the height of its power (A.D. 200–500), the city-state of Teotihuacán appears to have influenced much of Mesoamerica.

4. City-states arose early in other parts of the New World: in Guatemala, the Yucatán Peninsula of Mexico, Peru, and possibly near St. Louis. In the Old World, early states developed in Egypt, the Indus Valley of India, northern China, and in West Africa.

5. There are several theories of why states arose. The irrigation theory suggests that the administrative needs of maintaining extensive irrigation systems may have been the impetus for state formation. The circumscription theory suggests that states emerge when competition and warfare in circumscribed areas lead to the subordination of defeated groups, who are obliged to submit to the control of the most powerful group. Theories involving trade suggest that the organizational requirements of producing exportable items, redistributing imported items, and defending trading parties would foster state formation. Which is correct? At this point, no one theory is able to explain the formation of every state. Perhaps different organizational requirements in different areas all favored centralized government.

SUGGESTED READING

BLANTON, R. E., KOWALEWSKI, S. A., FEINMAN, G., AND APPEL, J. *Ancient Mesoamerica: A Comparison of Change in Three Regions.* New York: Cambridge University Press, 1981. A comparison and analysis of cultural development, and particularly the development of states, in three regions of Mesoamerica—the Valley of Oaxaca, the Valley of Mexico, and the eastern (Mayan) lowlands.

COHEN, R., AND SERVICE, E. R., eds. *Origins of the State: The Anthropology of Political Evolution.* Philadelphia: Institute for the Study of Human Issues, 1978. A collection of theoretical and empirical papers on the possible origins of states.

SANDERS, W. T., PARSONS, J. R., AND SANTLEY, R. S. *The Basin of Mexico: Ecological Processes in the Evolution of a Civilization.* New York: Academic Press, 1979. A description of a long-term archeological project that investigated the evolution of civilization in the Valley of Mexico from 1500 B.C. to A.D. 1500, particularly as reflected in the history of its settlement.

SERVICE, E. R. *Origins of the State and Civilization: The Process of Cultural Evolution.* New York: W. W. Norton & Co., Inc., 1975. A survey of prehistoric and some historic state societies. An attempt is made to evaluate some theories of the origin of the state.

WENKE, R. J. *Patterns in Prehistory: Humankind's First Three Million Years,* 3rd ed. New York: Oxford University Press, 1990. Chapters 7–15 provide an up-to-date review of what is known and what is controversial about the origins of cities and states around the world.

10

The Concept
of Culture

We all consider ourselves to be unique individuals with a set of personal opinions, preferences, habits, and quirks. Indeed, all of us *are* unique individuals, and yet most of us share the feeling that it is wrong to eat dogs, the belief that bacteria or viruses cause illness, the habit of sleeping on a bed. There are many such feelings, beliefs, and habits that we share with most of the people who live in our society. We hardly ever think about the ideas and customs we share, but they constitute what anthropologists refer to as North American "culture."

We tend not to think about our culture because it is so much a part of us that we take it for granted. If and when we become aware that other peoples have different feelings from ours, different beliefs, and different habits, we begin to think of how we share certain ideas and customs. We would never even think of the possibility of eating dog meat if we were not aware that people in some other societies commonly do so. We would not realize that our belief in germs was cultural if we were not aware that people in some societies think that illness is caused by witchcraft or evil spirits. We could not become aware that it is our custom to sleep on beds if we were not aware that people in many societies sleep on the floor or ground. It is only when we compare ourselves with people in other societies that we become aware of cultural differences and similarities. This is, in fact, the way that anthropology as a profession began; when Europeans began to explore and move to faraway places, they were forced to confront the sometimes striking facts of cultural variation.

Attitudes That Hinder the Study of Cultures

Many of the Europeans who first came to those faraway places were revolted or shocked by customs they observed. Such reactions are not surprising. People commonly feel that their own customary behaviors and attitudes are the correct ones, that people who do not share those patterns are immoral or inferior. But our own customs and ideas may appear bizarre or barbaric to an observer from another society. Hindus in India, for example, would consider our custom of eating beef both primitive and disgusting. In their culture, the cow

is a sacred animal and may not be slaughtered for food. Even our most ordinary customs—the daily rituals we take for granted—might seem thoroughly absurd when viewed from the perspective of a foreign culture. A visitor to our society might justifiably take notes on certain strange behaviors that seem quite ordinary to us, as the following extract shows:

The daily body ritual performed by everyone includes a mouth-rite. Despite the fact that these people are so punctilious about the care of the mouth, this rite involves a practice which strikes the uninitiated stranger as revolting. It was reported to me that the ritual consists of inserting a small bundle of hog hairs into the mouth, along with certain magical powders, and then moving the bundle in a highly formalized series of gestures. In addition to the private mouth-rite, the people seek out a holy-mouth man once or twice a year. These practitioners have an impressive set of paraphernalia, consisting of a variety of augers, awls, probes, and prods. The use of these objects in the exorcism of the evils of the mouth involves almost unbelievable ritual torture of the client. The holy-mouth man opens the client's mouth and, using the above mentioned tools, enlarges any holes which decay may have created in teeth. Magical materials are put into these holes. If there are no naturally occurring holes in the teeth, large sections of one or more teeth are gouged out so that the supernatural substance can be applied. In the client's view, the purpose of these ministrations is to arrest decay and to draw friends. The extremely sacred and traditional character of the rite is evident in the fact that the natives return to the holy-mouth man year after year, despite the fact that their teeth continue to decay.[1]

We are likely to protest that to understand the behaviors of a particular society—in this case our own—the observer must try to find out more about why the people in that society say they do things. For example, the observer might find out that periodic visits to the "holy-mouth man" are for medical, not magical, purposes. Indeed, the observer, after some questioning, might discover that the "mouth-rite" has no sacred or religious connotations whatsoever. The anthropological attitude that a society's customs and ideas should be described objectively and understood in the context of that society's problems and opportunities is called **cultural relativism.** Because this attitude

[1]Horace Miner, "Body Rituals among the Nacirema," *American Anthropologist*, 58 (1956): 504–5 (reproduced by permission of the American Anthropological Association from the *American Anthropologist*, 58: 504–5, 1956).

We are told that brushing our teeth will prevent cavities. So how come we still get them?

fosters empathy and understanding, it is humanistic; because it requires impartial observation and involves an attempt to test possible explanations of customs, the attitude of cultural relativism is also scientific.

In general, cultural relativism is impeded by two different but commonly held attitudes. The first is the tendency toward negative evaluation, which usually results from ethnocentrism; the second is the tendency toward positive evaluation, which often takes the form of a naive yearning for the simple life of the "noble savage."

Ethnocentrism

The person whose vision is limited strictly to his or her own needs and desires is generally ineffective in dealing with other people. We call such an individual egocentric, and we would be sorry to have such a person for a psychiatrist. The person who judges other cultures solely in terms of his or her own culture is **ethnocentric**. (This attitude is called **ethnocentrism.**) Not only are such people ill equipped to do anthropological work, but they may be unable to recognize and deal with social problems in their own society.

Because we are ethnocentric about many things, it is often difficult to criticize our own customs—some of which might be shocking to a member of another society. Here a grandfather in China, very much the center of his family, presents a sharp contrast to an elderly American man, who spends a lot of his time alone.

For example, an ethnocentric North American would view as barbaric the ceremonies that initiate adolescent boys into manhood in many societies. These ceremonies often involve hazing, difficult tests of courage and endurance, and painful circumcision. The ethnocentric North American would be unable to understand why anyone would willingly endure such hardships merely to be publicly accepted as an adult. However, the same type of ethnocentric thinking would make it difficult for such a person to question the North American custom of confining young children to little cages called cribs and playpens, a practice that observers from another society might consider cruel. Ethnocentrism, then, hinders our understanding of the customs of other people and, at the same time, keeps us from understanding our own customs. If we think that everything we do is best, we are not likely to ask why we do what we do or why "they" do what "they" do.

The "Noble Savage"

Whenever we are weary of the complexities of civilization, we may long for a way of life that is "closer to nature" or "simpler" than our own. For instance, a young North American whose parent is holding two or three jobs just to provide his or her family with bare necessities might briefly be attracted to the life-style of the !Kung of the Kalahari Desert. The !Kung share their food and therefore are often free to engage in leisure activities during the greater part of the day. They obtain all their food by hunting animals and gathering wild plants. Since they have no facilities for refrigeration, sharing a freshly killed animal is clearly more sensible than hoarding rotten meat. Moreover, as it turns out, the sharing provides a kind of social-security system for the !Kung. If a hunter is unable to catch an animal on a certain day, he can obtain food for himself and his family from someone else in his band. Conversely, at some later date the game he catches will provide food for the family of some other unsuccessful hunter. This system of sharing also ensures that persons too young or too old to help with the collecting of food will still be fed. However, the food-sharing system of the !Kung is a solution to the problems posed by their

special environment and is not necessarily a practical solution to problems in our own society. Moreover, other aspects of !Kung life would not appeal to many North Americans. For example, when the nomadic !Kung decide to move their camps, the women must carry all the family possessions, substantial amounts of food and water, and all young children below age four or five. This is a sizable burden to carry for any distance. And since the !Kung travel about 1500 miles in a single year,[2] it is unlikely that most North American women would find the !Kung way of life enviable in all respects.

The point is not that we should avoid comparing our culture with others, but that we should not romanticize other cultures. Most of the customs of other societies probably are, or were, appropriate to their environments, just as most of our customs probably are, or were, appropriate to our own environment. Cultural relativism asks that all customs of a society be viewed objectively, not ethnocentrically or romantically.

Does cultural relativism mean that the actions of another society, or of our own, should not be judged? Does our insistence on objectivity mean that anthropologists should not make moral judgments about the cultural phenomena they observe and try to explain? Not really. Anthropologists do make judgments, and some try to change behavior they think is harmful. But judgments need not and should not preclude objectivity. Our goal in research is to strive for accurate description and explanation in spite of any judgments we might have. In the chapter on explanation and evidence, we discuss some procedures that scientists, including anthropologists, employ to minimize the possibility that their own expectations will affect their observations and tests of explanations.

We have tried so far in this chapter to convey intuitively what culture is, and we have discussed attitudes that hinder or bias the study of cultures. Now let us turn to what seem to be the defining features of culture for most anthropologists.

[2]Richard B. Lee, "Population Growth and the Beginnings of Sedentary Life among the !Kung Bushmen," in Brian Spooner, ed., *Population Growth: Anthropological Implications* (Cambridge, MA: M.I.T. Press, 1972), pp. 329–42.

Defining Features of Culture

In everyday usage, the word *culture* refers to a desirable quality we can acquire by attending a sufficient number of plays and concerts and trudging through several miles of art galleries. The anthropologist, however, has a different definition, as Ralph Linton explains:

[*Culture*] refers to the total way of life of any society, not simply to those parts of this way which the society regards as higher or more desirable. Thus culture, when applied to our own way of life, has nothing to do with playing the piano or reading Browning. For the social scientist such activities are simply elements within the totality of our culture. This totality also includes such mundane activities as washing dishes or driving an automobile, and for the purposes of cultural studies these stand quite on a par with "the finer things of life." It follows that for the social scientist there are no uncultured societies or even individuals. Every society has a culture, no matter how simple this culture may be, and every human being is cultured, in the sense of participating in some culture or other.[3]

Culture, then, refers to innumerable aspects of life. Some anthropologists think of culture as the rules or ideas behind behavior.[4] Most anthropologists think of culture as including the learned behaviors as well as the beliefs, attitudes, values, and ideals that are characteristic of a particular society or population.

Culture Is Commonly Shared

If only one person thinks or does a certain thing, that thought or action represents a personal habit, not a pattern of culture. For a thought or action to be considered cultural, it must be commonly shared by some population or group of individuals. Even if some behavior is not commonly practiced, it is cultural if most people think it is appropriate. The idea that marriage should involve only one man and only one woman is cultural in our society. Most North Americans share this idea and act accordingly when they marry. The role of president or prime minister is not widely shared—after all, there is only one such person at a time—but the role is cultural because most inhabitants of a country with such a position agree that it should exist, and its occupant is generally expected to exhibit certain behaviors. We usually share many values, beliefs, and behaviors with our families and friends (although anthropologists are not particularly concerned with this type of cultural group). We commonly share cultural characteristics with segments of our population whose ethnic or regional origins, religious affiliations, and occupations are the same as or similar to our own. We have certain practices, beliefs, and feelings in common with most North Americans. And we share certain characteristics with people beyond our society who have similar interests (such as rules for international sporting events) or similar roots (as do the various English-speaking nations).

When we talk about the commonly shared customs of a society, which constitute the central concern of cultural anthropology, we are referring to a *culture*. When we talk about the commonly shared customs of a group within a society, which are a central concern of sociology, we are referring to a **subculture**. And when we study the commonly shared customs of some group that includes different societies, we are talking about a phenomenon for which we do not have a single word (only compound phrases including the word *culture*). So, for example, we refer to *Western culture* (the cultural characteristics of societies in or derived from western Europe) and the *culture of poverty* (the presumed cultural characteristics of poor people the world over).

We must remember that even when anthropologists refer to something as cultural, there is always individual variation, which means that not everyone in a society shares a particular cultural characteristic of the society. For example, it is cultural in our society for adults to live apart from parents. But this does not mean that all adults in our society do so, nor that all adults wish to do so. The custom of living apart from parents is considered cultural because most adults practice that custom. As Edward Sapir noted fifty years ago, in every society studied by anthropologists—in the simplest as well as the most complex—individuals

---

[3]Ralph Linton, *The Cultural Background of Personality* (New York: Appleton-Century-Crofts, 1945), p. 30.

[4]See, for example, Dorothy Holland and Naomi Quinn, eds., *Cultural Models in Language and Thought* (Cambridge: Cambridge University Press, 1987), p. 4.

do not *all* think and act the same.[5] As we discuss below, individual variation is the source of new culture.[6]

Culture Is Learned

Not all things shared generally by a population are cultural. The typical hair color of a population is not cultural. Nor is eating. For something to be considered cultural, it must be learned as well as shared. A typical hair color (unless dyed) is not cultural because it is genetically determined. Humans eat because they must, but what and when and how they eat is learned and varies from culture to culture. North Americans do not think dogs are edible, and indeed the idea of eating dogs horrifies us. But in China, as in some other societies, dog meat is considered delicious. In our society, many people consider a baked ham to be a holiday dish. However, in several societies of the Middle East, including those of Egypt and Israel, eating the meat of a pig is forbidden by sacred writings.

To some extent, all animals exhibit learned behaviors, some of which may be shared by most individuals in a population and may therefore be considered cultural. However, different animal species vary in the degree to which their shared behaviors are learned or are instinctive. The sociable ants, for instance, despite all their patterned social behavior, do not appear to have much, if any, culture. They divide their labor, construct their nests, form their raiding columns, and carry off their dead, all without having been taught to do so and without imitating the behavior of other ants. In contrast, much of the behavior of humans appears to be culturally patterned.

We are increasingly discovering that our closest biological relatives—the monkeys and the apes—learn a wide variety of behaviors. Some of their learned responses are as basic as those involved in maternal care; others are as frivolous as the taste for candy. Some of these learned behaviors when shared could be described as cultural. For example, as we discuss in more detail in the chapter on language and culture, vervet monkeys learn to use a certain call in the presence of circling eagles, who prey on the monkeys. The call seems to mean "Watch out—there are eagles around!" Its meaning seems to be shared or understood by the group, since they all respond similarly when one individual sounds the call.

The proportion of an animal's life span occupied by childhood seems to reflect the degree to which the animal depends upon learned behavior for survival. Monkeys and apes have relatively long childhoods compared with other animals. Humans have by far the longest childhood of any animal, reflecting our great dependence on learned behavior. Although humans may acquire much learned behavior by trial and error and imitation, as do monkeys and apes, most human learned behavior is probably acquired with the aid of spoken, symbolic language.

Language. All people known to anthropologists, regardless of their kind of society, have had a complex system of spoken, symbolic communication, what we call *language*. Language is *symbolic* in that a word or phrase can represent what it stands for *whether or not that thing is present.*

This symbolic quality of language has tremendous implications for the transmission of culture. It means that a human parent can tell a child that a snake, for example, is dangerous and should be avoided. The parent can then describe the snake in great detail—its length, diameter, color, texture, shape, and means of locomotion. The parent can also predict the kinds of places where the child is likely to encounter snakes and explain how the child can avoid them. Should the child encounter a snake, then, he or she will probably recall the symbolic word for the animal, remember as well the related information, and so avoid danger. If symbolic language did not exist, the parent would have to wait until the child actually saw a snake and then, through example, show the child that such a creature is to be avoided. Without language we could not transmit or receive information symbolically, and thus would not be heir to so rich and varied a culture.

To sum up, we may say that something is cultural if it is a learned behavior, belief, attitude, value, or ideal generally shared by the members of a group. Traditionally, anthropologists have usually been concerned with the cultural characteristics of a **society,** by which they mean a group of

[5]Edward Sapir, "Why Cultural Anthropology Needs the Psychiatrist," *Psychiatry,* 1 (1938): 7–12; cited by Pertti J. Pelto and Gretel H. Pelto, "Intra-Cultural Diversity: Some Theoretical Issues," *American Ethnologist,* 2 (1975): 1.

[6]Pelto and Pelto, "Intra-Cultural Diversity," pp. 14–15.

people who occupy a particular territory and speak a common language not generally understood by neighboring peoples.[7] Hence, when an anthropologist speaks about *a* culture, he or she is usually referring to that set of learned and shared beliefs, values, and behaviors generally characteristic of a particular society. But now that we have defined what is cultural, we must ask a further question: How does an anthropologist go about deciding which particular behaviors, values, and beliefs of individuals are cultural?

Describing a Culture

Individual Variation

Describing a particular culture might seem relatively uncomplicated at first: you simply observe what the people in that society do and then record their behavior. But consider the substantial difficulties you might encounter in doing this. How would you decide which people to observe? And what would you conclude if each of the first dozen people you observed or talked to behaved quite differently in the same situation? Admittedly, you would be unlikely to encounter such extreme divergence of behaviors. Yet there would tend to be significant individual variation in the actual behaviors observed, even when individuals were responding to the same generalized situation and conforming to cultural expectations.

To better understand how an anthropologist might make sense of diverse behaviors, let us examine this diversity as it exists at a professional football game in the United States.

When people attend a football game, various members of the crowd behave differently while

"The Star-Spangled Banner" is being played. As they stand and listen, some people remove their hats; a child munches popcorn; a former soldier stands at attention; a teenager searches the crowd for a friend; and the two head coaches take a final opportunity to intone secret chants and spells designed to sap the strength of the opposing team. Yet despite these individual variations, most of the people at the game respond in a basically similar manner: nearly everyone stands silently, facing the flag. Moreover, if you go to a number of football games, you will observe that many aspects of the event are notably similar. Although the plays used will vary from game to game, the rules of the game are never different, and although the colors of the uniforms vary for each team, the players never appear on the field dressed in swimsuits.

Although the variations in individual reactions to a given stimulus are theoretically limitless, in fact they tend to fall within easily recognizable limits. The child listening to the anthem may continue to eat popcorn, but will probably not do a rain dance. Similarly, it is unlikely that the coaches will react to that same stimulus by running onto the field and embracing the singer. Variations in behavior, then, are confined within socially acceptable limits, and it is part of the anthropologist's goal to find out what these limits are. He or she may note, for example, that some limitations on behavior have a practical purpose: a spectator who disrupts the game by wandering onto the field would be required to leave. Other limitations are purely traditional. In our society it is considered proper for a man to remove his overcoat if he becomes overheated, but others would undoubtedly frown upon his removing his trousers even if the weather was quite warm. Using such observations, the anthropologist attempts to discover the customs and the ranges of acceptable behavior that characterize the society under study.

By focusing on the range of customary behavior, discovered by observing or asking about individual variation, the anthropologist is able to describe cultural characteristics of a group. For example, an anthropologist interested in describing courtship and marriage in our society would initially encounter a variety of behaviors. The anthropologist may note that one couple prefers to go to a concert on a first date, whereas another couple chooses to go bowling; some couples have very

---

[7]Note that by this definition, societies do not necessarily correspond to nations. There are many nations, particularly the "new" ones, that have within their boundaries different peoples speaking mutually unintelligible languages. By our definition of society, such nations are composed of many different societies and cultures. Also, by our definition of society, some societies may even include more than one nation. For example, we would have to say that Canada and the United States form a single society because both groups generally speak English, live next to each other, and share many common beliefs, values, and practices. That is why we refer to "North American culture" in this chapter. Not everyone would agree Canada and the United States form a single society; some would prefer to consider the United States and Canada two different societies because they are separate political entities.

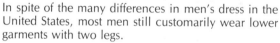
In spite of the many differences in men's dress in the United States, most men still customarily wear lower garments with two legs.

long engagements and others never become engaged at all; some couples emphasize religious rituals in the marriage ceremony but others are married by civil authorities; and so on. Despite this variability, the anthropologist, after further observation and interviewing, might begin to detect certain regularities in courting practices. Although couples may do many different things on their first and subsequent dates, they nearly always arrange the dates by themselves, they try to avoid their parents when on dates, they often manage to find themselves alone at the end of a date, they put their lips together frequently, and so forth. After a series of more and more closely spaced encounters, a man and woman may decide to declare themselves publicly as a couple, either by announcing that they are engaged or by revealing that they are living together or intend to do so. Finally, if the two of them decide to marry, they must in some way have their union recorded by the civil authorities.

In our society a person who wishes to marry cannot completely disregard the customary patterns of courtship. If a man saw a woman on the street and decided he wanted to marry her, he could conceivably choose a quicker and more direct form of action than the usual dating procedure. He could get on a horse, ride to the woman's home, snatch her up in his arms, and gallop away with her. In Sicily, until recently such a couple would have been considered legally married, even if the woman had never met the man before or had no intention of marrying. But in our society, any man who acted in such a fashion would be arrested and jailed for kidnapping and would probably have his sanity challenged. Such behavior would not be acceptable in our society. Although individual behaviors may vary, most social behavior falls within culturally acceptable limits.

Cultural Constraints

A primary limit on the range of the individual behavior variations is the culture itself. The noted French sociologist Émile Durkheim stressed that culture is something *outside* us exerting a strong coercive power on us. We do not always feel the constraints of our culture because we generally conform to the types of conduct and thought it requires. Yet when we do try to oppose cultural constraints, their strength becomes apparent.

Cultural constraints are of two basic types, *direct* and *indirect*. Naturally, the direct constraints are the more obvious. For example, if you wear clothing that is atypical of our culture, you will probably be subject to ridicule and a certain amount of social isolation. But if you choose to wear only a scanty loincloth, you will receive a stronger, more direct cultural constraint—arrest for indecent exposure.

Although indirect forms of cultural constraint are less obvious than direct ones, they are no less effective. Durkheim illustrated this point when he wrote, "I am not obliged to speak French with my fellow-countrymen, nor to use the legal currency, but I cannot possibly do otherwise. If I tried to escape this necessity, my attempt would fail miserably."[8] In other words, if Durkheim had decided he

would rather speak Serbo-Croatian than French, nobody would have tried to stop him. But no one would have understood him either. And although he would not have been put into prison for trying to buy groceries with Icelandic money, he would have had difficulty convincing the local merchants to sell him food.

In a series of experiments on conformity, Solomon Asch revealed how strong cultural constraints can be. Asch coached the majority of a group of college students to give deliberately incorrect answers to questions involving visual stimuli. A "critical subject," the one student in the room who was not so coached, had no idea that the other participants would purposely misinterpret the evidence presented to them. Asch found that in one-third of the experiments, the critical subject *consistently* allowed his own correct perceptions to be distorted by the obviously incorrect statements of the others. And in another 40 percent of the experiments, the critical subject yielded to the opinion of the group some of the time.[9]

The existence of social or cultural constraints, however, is not necessarily incompatible with individuality. Cultural constraints are usually exercised most forcefully around the limits of acceptable behavior. Thus, there is often a broad range of behavior within which individuals can exercise their uniqueness. And individuals do not always give in to the wishes of the majority. In the Asch experiments, many individuals (one-fourth of the critical subjects) consistently retained their independent opinions in the face of complete disagreement with the majority.

Ideal versus Actual Cultural Patterns

Every society has ideas about how people in particular situations ought to behave. In everyday terms we speak of these ideas as *ideals*; in anthropology we refer to them as *ideal cultural patterns*. These patterns tend to be reinforced through cultural constraints. However, we all know that people do not always behave according to the standards they express. If they did, there would be no need for direct or indirect constraints. Some of our ideal patterns differ from actual behavior because the ideal is outmoded—that is, based on the way a

[8]Émile Durkheim, *The Rules of Sociological Method*, 8th ed., trans. Sarah A. Soloway and John H. Mueller, ed. George E. Catlin (New York: Free Press, 1938 [originally published 1895]), p. 3.

[9]Solomon Asch, "Studies of Independence and Conformity: A Minority of One against a Unanimous Majority," *Psychological Monographs*, 70 (1956): 1–70.

society used to be. (Consider the ideal of "free enterprise"—that industry should be totally free of governmental regulation.) Other ideal patterns may never have been actual patterns and may represent merely what people would like to see as correct behavior.

To illustrate the difference between ideal and actual culture, consider the idealized belief, long cherished in North America, that doctors are selfless, friendly people who choose medicine as their profession because they feel a call to serve humanity, and who have little interest in either money or prestige. Of course, many physicians do not measure up to this ideal. Nevertheless, the continued success of television programs that portray the average North American M.D. as a paragon of virtue indicates that the ideal of the noble physician is still very much a part of our culture.

How to Discover Cultural Patterns

There are two basic ways in which an anthropologist can discover cultural patterns. When dealing with customs that are overt or highly visible within a society—for example, our custom of sending children to school—the investigator can determine the existence of such practices and study them with the aid of a few knowledgeable persons. When dealing with a particular sphere of behavior that encompasses many individual variations, or when the people studied are unaware of their pat-

Just as in a public elevator, North Americans customarily face front while they wait. Here people are waiting to get into the Washington Monument.

tern of behavior, the anthropologist should collect information from a sample of individuals in order to establish what the cultural pattern is.

One example of a cultural pattern that most people in a society are not aware of is how far apart people stand when they are having a conversation. Yet there is considerable reason to believe that unconscious cultural rules govern such behavior. These rules become obvious when we interact with people who have different rules. We may experience considerable discomfort when another person stands too close (indicating too much intimacy) or too far (indicating unfriendliness). Edward Hall reports that Arabs customarily stand quite close to others—close enough, in fact, to be able to smell the other person. In interactions between Arabs and North Americans, then, the Arabs will move closer at the same time the North Americans back away.[10]

If we wanted to arrive at the cultural rule for conversational distance between casual acquaintances, let us say, we could study a sample of individuals from a society and determine the *modal response,* or *mode.* The mode is a statistical term that refers to the most frequently encountered response in a given series of responses. So, for the North American pattern of casual conversational distance, we would plot the actual distance for a number of observed pairs of people. Some pairs may be 2 feet apart, some 2.5, and some 4 feet apart. If the observer counts the number of times every particular distance is observed, these counts provide what we call a *frequency distribution.* The distance with the highest frequency is the modal pattern. Very often the frequency distribution takes the form of a *bell-shaped curve,* as shown in Figure 10–1. There the characteristic measured is plotted on the horizontal axis (in this case, the distance between conversational pairs) and the number of times each distance is observed (its frequency) is plotted on the vertical axis. If we were to plot how a sample of North American casual conversational pairs is distributed, we would probably get a bell-shaped curve that peaks at around 3 feet.[11] Is it any wonder, then, that we sometimes speak of keeping others "at arm's length"?

[10]Edward T. Hall, *The Hidden Dimension,* (Garden City, NY: Doubleday, 1966), pp. 159–60.
[11]Ibid., p. 120.

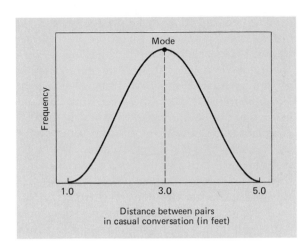

FIGURE 10-1 Frequency Distribution Curve

Frequency distributions may be calculated on the basis of behaviors exhibited or responses given by all the members of a particular population. However, to save time, the anthropologist can rely on data obtained from a representative sample of persons, called a **random sample.** The members of this sample would be selected randomly from the society or community—that is, all individuals would have an equal chance of being chosen. If a sample is random, it will probably include examples of all frequent variations of behavior exhibited within the society or community in roughly the proportions in which they occur.

Since it is relatively easy to make generalizations about public aspects of a culture, such as how football players behave during a game, random sampling is often not necessary. But in dealing with aspects of culture that are private or unconscious, such as how far people stand from each other when talking, the investigator may have to observe or interview a random sample of people if he or she is to generalize correctly about cultural patterns. The reason is that most people are not aware of others' private behavior and thoughts, nor are they aware of unconscious cultural patterns.

Although we may be able to discover by interviews and observation that a behavior, thought, or feeling is widely shared within a society, how do we establish that something commonly shared is learned, so that we can call it cultural? Establish-ing that something is or is not learned may be difficult. Since children are not reared apart from adult caretakers, the behaviors they exhibit as part of their genetic inheritance are not clearly separated from those they learn from others around them. We suspect that particular behaviors and ideas are learned if they vary from society to society. And we suspect purely genetic determinism when particular behaviors or ideas are found in all societies. For example, as we will see in the chapter on language, children the world over seem to acquire language at about the same time, and the structure of their early utterances seems to be similar. These facts suggest that human children are born with an innate grammar. However, although early-childhood language seems similar the world over, the particular languages spoken by adults in different societies show considerable variability. This variability suggests that particular languages have to be learned. Similarly, if the courtship patterns of one society differ markedly from those of another, we can be fairly certain that those courtship patterns are learned and therefore cultural. Of course, anthropologists may sometimes err in their presumption that a particular behavior, thought, or feeling is cultural.

Some Assumptions About Culture

Culture Is Generally Adaptive

There are some cultural behaviors that, if carried to an extreme, would decrease the chances of survival of a particular society. For example, certain tribes in New Guinea view women as essentially unclean and dangerous individuals with whom physical contact should be as limited as possible. Suppose the men in one such tribe decided to avoid sex with women completely. Clearly, we would not expect such a society to survive for long. Although this example may appear extreme, it indicates that customs that diminish the survival chances of a society are not likely to persist. Either the people clinging to those customs will become extinct, taking the customs with them, or the customs will be replaced, thereby possibly helping the people to survive. By either process, *maladaptive* customs (those that diminish the chances of sur-

The Indians who lived hundreds of years ago at Mesa Verde, Colorado, built their villages in inaccessible places, presumably as an adaptation to the need to defend themselves against attack.

vival and reproduction) are likely to disappear. Those customs of a society that enhance survival and reproductive chances are *adaptive* and are likely to persist. Hence, we assume that if a society has survived to be described in the annals of anthropology (the "ethnographic record"), much if not most of its cultural repertoire is adaptive, or was at one time.

When we say that a custom is adaptive, however, we mean it is adaptive only with respect to a specific physical and social environment. What may be adaptive in one environment may not be adaptive in another. Therefore, when we ask why a society may have a particular custom, we are really asking if that custom makes sense as an adaptation to that society's particular environmental conditions.

Many cultural behaviors that would otherwise appear incomprehensible to us may be understandable as a society's response to its environment. For example, we might express surprise at certain societies' postpartum sex taboos that prohibit women from engaging in sexual intercourse until their two-year-olds are ready to be weaned. But in the tropical areas where such taboos exist, they may represent a people's means of adjusting to their physical environment. If there were no such taboo and a mother had another baby soon, she could no longer continue to nurse the older baby. Without its mother's milk, the older child might succumb to **kwashiorkor,** a severe protein-deficiency disease that is common in those tropical areas. The taboo, then, may serve to give infants a better chance to survive.[12] Thus, a long postpartum sex taboo may be an adaptive custom in certain tropical countries. In nontropical areas where kwashiorkor is not a problem, the same taboo may not be advantageous.

Just as culture represents an adjustment to the physical environment and to biological demands, it may also represent an adjustment to the social environment—that is, to neighboring peoples. For example, we do not know for sure why the Hopi Indians of what is now the state of Arizona began building their settlements on the tops of mesas. They must have had strong reasons for doing so, because there were many difficulties in building on such sites—the problem of hauling water long distances to the settlements, for instance. It is possible that the Hopi chose to locate their villages on mesa tops for defensive reasons when Athapaskan-speaking groups of Indians (the Navaho and Apache) moved into the Hopi area. In other words, the Hopi may have adjusted their living habits to their social environment.

A given custom represents one society's adaptation to its environment; it does not represent all possible adaptations. Different societies may choose different means of adjusting to the same situation. Thus, among some Native South American Indian societies where people's diets are low in protein, there is no long postpartum sex taboo, but induced abortion is reported to be a common practice. This practice may serve the same function of spacing out live births and thereby preventing too early weaning of children. The Hopi Indians, when suddenly confronted by the Navaho and Apache, clearly had to take some action to protect themselves. But instead of deciding to build their

---

[12]John W. M. Whiting, "Effects of Climate on Certain Cultural Practices," in Ward H. Goodenough, ed., *Explorations in Cultural Anthropology* (New York: McGraw-Hill, 1964), pp. 511–44.

settlements on easily defended mesa tops, they could conceivably have developed a standing army.

Why a society develops a particular response to a problem, rather than some other possible response, always requires explanation. The choice may depend largely on whether a particular response is possible, given the existing cultural repertoire. For example, in the Hopi case a standing army would not have been a likely response to the problem of invaders because the Hopi economy probably could not have supported any large group of full-time specialists such as soldiers. As we shall see later in the chapter on food-getting, full-time specialists have to be fed by the regular production of more food than the people involved in food production generally need, and such a level of food production was not found among the Hopi. The strategy of moving their villages to easily defended mesa tops may have been the easiest option, given the Hopi economy.

Although we may assume that societies surviving long enough to be described have generally had adaptive culture traits, this does not mean that *all* culture traits are adaptive. Some traits—such as clothing styles and rules of etiquette—may be neutral in terms of adaptation. That is, they may have no direct relationship to biological needs or environmental conditions at the present time. Consider, for example, the buttons and incompletely closed seam at the end of a man's suit jacket sleeve. This style does not appear to have any adaptive value now. In the past, when there was no central heating in buildings, the style may have been quite adaptive, enabling the wearer to close the sleeves tightly about the wrist. Neutral traits may once have had adaptive consequences, or they may never have had any.

We must remember that a society is not forced to adapt its culture to changing environmental circumstances. First, even in the face of changed circumstances, people may choose not to change their customs. For example, the Tapirapé of central Brazil did not alter their customs limiting the number of births, even though they suffered severe population losses after contact with Europeans and their diseases. The Tapirapé population fell to fewer than 100 people from over 1000. Clearly they were on the way to extinction, yet they continued to value small families. Not only did they believe a woman should have no more than three

children, but they took specific steps to achieve this limitation. They practiced infanticide if twins were born, if the third child was of the same sex as the first two children, and if the possible fathers broke certain taboos during pregnancy or in the child's infancy.[13]

Of course, it is also possible that a people will behave maladaptively even if they try to alter their behavior. After all, although people may alter their behavior according to what they perceive will be helpful to them, what they perceive to be helpful may not prove to be adaptive.

Culture Is Mostly Integrated

When we hear of an unfamiliar cultural pattern, our natural response is to try to imagine how that pattern would work in our own society. We might wonder, for example, what would happen if North American women adopted a long postpartum sex taboo—say, one year of abstinence after the birth of a baby. Such a question is purely whimsical, for the customs of one culture cannot easily be grafted onto another culture. A long postpartum sex taboo presupposes a lack of effective birth-control methods, but our society already has many such methods. Moreover, a long postpartum sex taboo could conceivably affect a number of important aspects of our culture, such as the idea that a happy marriage is a sexy one. The point is that with such a taboo imposed on it, our culture would no longer be the same. Too many aspects of the culture would have to be changed to accommodate the new behavior. This is so because our culture is mostly integrated.

In saying that a culture is mostly *integrated*, we mean that the elements or traits that make up that culture are not just a random assortment of customs but are mostly adjusted to or consistent with one another. One reason anthropologists believe that culture tends to be integrated is that culture is generally adaptive. If certain customs are more adaptive in particular settings, then those "bundles" of traits will generally be found associated under similar conditions. For example, the !Kung, as we have mentioned, subsist by hunting wild ani-

[13]Charles Wagley, "Cultural Influences on Population: A Comparison of Two Tupi Tribes," in Patricia J. Lyon, ed., *Native South Americans: Ethnology of the Least Known Continent* (Boston: Little, Brown, 1974), pp. 377–84.

mals and gathering wild plants. They are also nomadic, have very small communities, have low population densities, share food within their bands, and have few material possessions. As we will see later, these cultural traits usually occur together when people depend on hunting and gathering for their food.

A culture may also tend to be integrated for psychological reasons. The traits of a culture—attitudes, values, ideals, and rules for behavior—are stored, after all, in the brains of individuals. Research in social psychology has suggested that people tend to modify beliefs or behaviors that are not cognitively or conceptually consistent with other information.[14] We do not expect cultures to be completely integrated, just as we do not expect individuals to be completely consistent. But if a tendency toward cognitive consistency is generally found in humans, we might expect that at least some aspects of a culture would tend to be integrated for this reason.

How this pressure for consistency works is not hard to imagine. Children, for example, seem to be very good at remembering *all* the things their parents said. If they ask for something and the parents say no, they may say, "But you said I could yesterday." This pressure for consistency may even make parents change their minds! Of course, not everything one wants to do is consistent with the rest of one's desires, but there surely is pressure from within and without to make it so.

Humans are also capable of rational decision making: they can often, if not usually, figure out that certain things are not easy to do because of other things they do. For example, if society has a long postpartum sex taboo, we might expect that most people in the society could figure out that it would be easier to observe the taboo if husband and wife did not sleep in the same bed. Or, if people drive on the left side of the road (as in England), it is easier and less dangerous to drive a car whose steering wheel is on the right, because that placement allows you to judge more accurately how close you are to cars coming at you from the opposite direction.

Consistency or integration of culture traits may also be produced by less conscious psychological processes. As we discuss in the chapters on psychology and culture, religion and magic, and the arts, people may generalize (transfer) their experiences from one realm of life to another. For example, where children are taught it is wrong to express anger toward family and friends, it turns out that folktales parallel the child rearing: anger and aggression in the folktales tend to be directed only toward strangers, not toward family and friends. It seems as if the expression of anger is too frightening (or maladaptive) to be expressed close to home, even in folktales.

The tendency for a culture to be integrated, then, may be cognitively and emotionally, as well as adaptively, induced.

Culture Is Always Changing

When you examine the history of a society, it is obvious that its culture has changed over time. Some of the shared behaviors, beliefs, and values that were common at one time are modified or replaced at another time. In North American society, we only have to consider our attitudes toward sex and marriage to realize that a lot of our culture has changed recently. The impetus for change may come from within the society or from without. From within, the unconscious or conscious pressure for consistency will produce culture change if enough people adjust old behavior and thinking to new. Change can also occur if people try to invent better ways of doing things. Michael Chibnik suggests that people who confront a new problem conduct mental or small "experiments" to decide how to behave. These experiments may give rise to new cultural traits.[15]

A good deal of culture change may be stimulated by changes in the external environment. For example, if people move into an arid area, they will have to either give up farming or develop a system of irrigation. In the modern world, changes in the social environment are probably more frequent stimuli for culture change than changes in the physical environment. Many North Americans, for example, started to think seriously about conserving energy, and about using sources of energy other than oil, only after oil supplies from the

[14]Roger Brown, *Social Psychology* (New York: Free Press, 1965), pp. 549–609.

[15]Michael Chibnik, "The Evolution of Cultural Rules," *Journal of Anthropological Research*, 37 (1981): 256–68.

Near East were curtailed in 1973 and 1974. Different societies have often affected each other, and a significant amount of culture change that has occurred in the last few hundred years has been due to the colonial expansion of Western societies into other areas of the world. Native Americans, for instance, were forced to alter their life-styles drastically when they were driven off their lands and confined to reservations. In the chapter on culture change, we discuss the major patterns of culture change in the modern world.

If we assume that cultures are more than random collections of behaviors, beliefs, and values—that they tend to be adaptive, integrated, and changing—then the similarities and differences between them should be understandable. That is, we can expect that similar circumstances within or outside the culture will give rise to, or favor, similar cultural responses. Although we may assume that cultural variation is understandable, the task

of discovering which particular circumstances favor which particular patterns is a large and difficult one. In the chapters that follow, we hope to convey the main points of what anthropologists think they know about aspects of cultural variation, and what they do not know. We frequently describe particular cultures to illustrate aspects of cultural variation. When we do so, the reader should understand that the culture described is probably not the same now, since the sources of our material always refer to some previous time.[16]

[16]Indeed, some of the cultures we refer to may have been quite different before as well as after the time referred to. For example, the !Kung hunter-gatherers of southern Africa probably were not only hunter-gatherers in the past. There is evidence that the !Kung of the Kalahari Desert have switched from hunting and gathering to herding animals, and back again, many times in the past. See Carmel Schrire, "An Inquiry into the Evolutionary Status and Apparent Identity of San Hunter-Gatherers," *Human Ecology,* 8 (1980): 9–32.

SUMMARY

1. Despite very strong individual differences, the members of a particular society closely agree in their responses to certain phenomena because they share common beliefs, attitudes, values, ideals, and behaviors, which constitute their culture.

2. The anthropological attitude that a society's customs and ideas should be studied objectively and understood in the context of that society's culture is called cultural relativism. In general, cultural relativism is impeded by two different but commonly held attitudes: first, the tendency toward negative evaluation, or ethnocentrism; second, the tendency toward positive evaluation, which often takes the form of a naive yearning for the simple life of the "noble savage."

3. Culture may be defined as the learned behaviors, beliefs, attitudes, values, and ideals generally shared by the members of a group.

4. The size of the group within which cultural traits are shared can vary from a particular society or a segment of that society to a group that transcends national boundaries. When anthropologists refer to a culture, they are usually referring to the cultural patterns of a particular society—that is, a particular territorial population speaking a language not generally understood by neighboring territorial populations.

5. A defining feature of culture is that it is learned. Although other animals exhibit some cultural behavior, humans are unusual in the number and complexity of the learned patterns they transmit to their young. And they have a unique way of transmitting their culture: through spoken, symbolic language.

6. Anthropologists seek to discover the customs and ranges of acceptable behavior that constitute the culture of a society under study. In doing so, they focus on general or shared patterns of behavior rather than on individual variations. When dealing with practices that are highly visible, or with beliefs that are almost unanimous, the investigator can rely on observation or on a few knowledgeable persons. With less obvious behaviors or attitudes, the anthropologist must collect information from a sample of individuals. The mode of a frequency distribution can then be used to express the cultural pattern.

7. Every society develops a series of ideal cultural patterns that represent what most members of the society believe to be the correct behavior in particular situations. A society's ideal cultural patterns, however, do not always agree with its actual cultural patterns.

8. One important factor that limits the range of individual variation is the culture itself, which acts directly or indirectly as a constraint on behavior. The existence of cultural constraints, however, is not necessarily incompatible with individuality.

9. Several assumptions are frequently made about culture. First, culture is generally adaptive to the particular conditions of its physical and social environment. What may be adaptive in one environment may not be adaptive in another. Some cultural traits may be neutral in terms of adaptation, some may merely have been adaptive in the past, and still others may be maladaptive. Second, culture is mostly integrated, in that the elements or traits that make up the culture are mostly adjusted to or consistent with one another. Third, culture is always changing.

SUGGESTED READING

FREILICH, M., ed. *The Meaning of Culture.* Lexington, MA: Xerox, 1972. Several different views of culture are presented. See chapters 7–21.

GOLDE, P., ed. *Women in the Field: Anthropological Experiences,* 2nd ed. Berkeley: University of California Press, 1986. A group of papers dealing in general with women's experiences as field anthropologists and in particular with their unique problems as women in a male-dominated profession.

HALL, E. T. *The Hidden Dimension.* Garden City, NY: Doubleday, 1966. An evocative discussion of the unconscious quality of much of culture, focusing on how use of space is culturally patterned.

KROEBER, A. L. *The Nature of Culture.* Chicago: University of Chicago Press, 1952. A collection of papers on the nature of culture by a distinguished pioneer in North American anthropology.

SPINDLER, G. D., ed. *Being an Anthropologist: Fieldwork in Eleven Cultures.* New York: Holt, Rinehart & Winston, 1970. A series of reports by thirteen anthropologists describing how they and their families adapted to life in eleven different cultural situations. The papers are case studies in which both subjective problems of field study and methodological problems and techniques are discussed.

WERNER, O., AND SCHOEPFLE, G. M. *Systematic Fieldwork. Volume 1: Foundations of Ethnography and Interviewing.* Newbury Park, CA: Sage Publications, 1987. A detailed presentation and discussion of the methods used to discover patterns of culture on the basis of fieldwork.

11

Schools of Thought in Cultural Anthropology

Anthropologists have been going to live in other societies for nearly a hundred years. At first, there were only a few such hardy (some would say foolhardy) souls. But their number slowly increased over the years as more and more individuals became interested in the challenge of spending a year or so in some usually distant place, without the comforts of home, to learn how some other people lived and thought. The idea was to add to our knowledge so that we might someday come to understand how human cultural behavior could vary so much and yet be so much the same at different times and in different places.

Close to 2,000 different societies have now been described to some extent in the literature of anthropology. This enormous wealth of information constitutes our data bank of cultural variation. If we are to understand how and why cultures differ and are similar, we must do more than simply inspect this mass of information. We must have ideas about what we should look for. Just as a photographer must aim and focus a camera in order to capture a scene, so an anthropologist must focus on what he or she considers important in order to describe, and possibly explain, some particular aspect of culture. Even the most thorough observer must concentrate on certain aspects of life and neglect others.

Which aspects of life an individual anthropologist concentrates on usually reflects his or her theoretical orientation, subject interest, or preferred method of research. A *theoretical orientation* is a general attitude about how cultural phenomena are to be explained. In this chapter we describe some of the major theoretical orientations that have existed in cultural anthropology. We also describe some recent schools of thought that identify themselves in terms of subject interests or methods of research. The members of our profession do not always fit neatly into one of the categories we identify here. Nevertheless, such general labels as *interpretive anthropologist, functionalist, cultural ecologist,* and *hypothesis-tester* do provide us with a way to discuss the different interests and styles of explanation exhibited by cultural anthropologists.

Theoretical Orientations

In anthropology, as in any discipline, there is continual ebb and flow of ideas. One theoretical ori-

entation will arise and may grow in popularity until another is proposed in opposition to it. Often, one orientation will capitalize on those aspects of a problem a previous orientation has ignored or played down. In our survey of the orientations that have developed since the emergence of cultural anthropology as a professional discipline, we will use an approximate historical sequence. As we discuss each school of thought, we will indicate what kinds of information or phenomena it emphasizes (if it does) as explanatory factors. Some of these orientations have passed into history by now; others continue to attract adherents.

Early Evolutionism

In the early years of anthropology, the prevailing view was that culture generally develops (or evolves) in a uniform and progressive manner. It was thought that most societies pass through the same series of stages, to arrive ultimately at a common end. The sources of culture change were generally assumed to be embedded within the culture from the beginning, and therefore the ultimate course of development was thought to be internally determined. Two nineteenth-century anthropologists whose writings exemplified the theory that culture generally evolves uniformly and progressively were Edward B. Tylor (1832–1917) and Lewis Henry Morgan (1818–1889).

Tylor maintained that culture evolved from the simple to the complex, and that all societies passed through three basic stages of development: from savagery through barbarism to civilization.[1] "Progress" was therefore possible for all. To account for cultural variation, Tylor and other early evolutionists postulated that different contemporary societies were at different stages of evolution. According to this view, the "simpler" peoples of the day had not yet reached "higher" stages. Thus, simpler contemporary societies were thought to resemble ancient societies. The more advanced societies, on the other hand, testified to cultural evolution by exhibiting what Tylor called *survivals*—traces of earlier customs that survive in present-day cultures. The making of pottery is an example of a survival in the sense used by Tylor. Earlier peoples made their cooking pots out of clay; today we gen-

[1]Edward B. Tylor, *Primitive Culture* (New York: Harper Torchbooks, 1958 [originally published 1871]).

erally make them out of metal because it is more durable. But we still prefer dishes made out of clay.

Tylor believed there was a kind of psychic unity among all peoples that explained parallel evolutionary sequences in different cultural traditions. In other words, because of the basic similarities common to all peoples, different societies often find the same solutions to the same problems independently. But Tylor also noted that cultural traits may spread from one society to another by simple **diffusion**—the borrowing by one culture of a trait belonging to another as the result of contact between the two.

Another nineteenth-century proponent of uniform and progressive cultural evolution was Lewis Henry Morgan. A lawyer in upstate New York, Morgan became interested in the local Iroquois Indians and defended their reservation in a land-grant case. In gratitude, the Iroquois "adopted" Morgan.

In his best-known work, *Ancient Society*, Morgan postulated several sequences in the evolution of human culture. For example, he speculated that the family evolved through six stages. Human society began as a "horde living in promiscuity," with no sexual prohibitions and no real family structure. Next was a stage in which a group of brothers was married to a group of sisters and brother-sister matings were permitted. In the third stage, group marriage was practiced, but brothers and sisters were not allowed to mate. The fourth stage, which supposedly evolved during barbarism, was characterized by a loosely paired male and female who still lived with other people. Then came the husband-dominant family, in which the husband could have more than one wife simultaneously. Finally, the stage of civilization was distinguished by the monogamous family, with just one wife and one husband who were relatively equal in status.[2]

Morgan believed that family units became progressively smaller and more self-contained as human society developed. However, his postulated sequence for the evolution of the family is not supported by the enormous amount of ethnographic data that has been collected since his time. For example, no recent society that Morgan would call savage indulges in group marriage or allows broth-

[2]Lewis Henry Morgan, *Ancient Society* (Cambridge, MA: Harvard University Press, Belknap Press, 1964 [originally published in 1877]).

Before containers were made of metal and plastic, people used pots made of clay for storage and cooking. The making of clay pots, such as the one shown here from the American southwest, survives today mostly as an art form.

er-sister mating. (In the chapter on marriage and the family, we discuss how recent cultures have varied in regard to marriage customs.)

Karl Marx was struck by the parallels between Morgan's evolutionism and his own theory of history. Marx and his co-worker, Friedrich Engels, devised a theory in which the institutions of monogamy, private property, and the state were assumed to be chiefly responsible for the exploitation of the working classes in modern industrialized societies. Marx and Engels extended Morgan's evolutionary scheme to include a future stage of cultural evolution in which monogamy, private property, and the state would cease to exist and the "communism" of primitive society would once more come into being.

The evolutionism of Tylor, Morgan, and others of the nineteenth century is largely rejected today. For one thing, their theories cannot satisfactorily account for cultural variation—why, for instance, some societies today are in "upper savagery" and others in "civilization." The "psychic unity of mankind" or "germs of thought" that were postulated to account for parallel evolution cannot also account for cultural differences. Another weakness in the early-evolutionist theories is that they cannot explain why some societies have regressed or even become extinct. And finally, although other societies may have progressed to "civilization," some of them have not passed through all the stages. Thus, early-evolutionist theory cannot explain the details of cultural evolution and variation as anthropology now knows them.

Historical Particularism

The beginning of the twentieth century brought the end of evolutionism's reign in cultural anthropology. Its leading opponent was Franz Boas (1858–1942), whose main disagreement with the evolutionists involved their assumption that universal laws governed all human culture. Boas pointed out that these nineteenth-century individuals lacked sufficient data (as did Boas himself) to formulate many useful generalizations. Boas almost single-handedly trained the first generation of American anthropologists, including (among others) Alfred Kroeber, Robert Lowie, Edward Sapir, Melville Herskovits, Ruth Benedict, Clark Wissler, E. Adamson Hoebel, and Margaret Mead.[3]

Boas stressed the apparently enormous complexity of cultural variation, and perhaps because of this complexity he believed it was premature to formulate universal laws. He felt that single cultural traits had to be studied in the context of the society in which they appeared. In 1896, Boas published an article entitled "The Limitation of the Comparative Method of Anthropology,"[4] which dealt with his objections to the evolutionist approach. In it, he stated that anthropologists should spend less time developing theories based on insufficient data. Rather, they should devote their energies to collecting as much data as possible, as quickly as possible, before cultures disappeared (as so many had already done, after contact with foreign societies). He asserted that only after this body of data was gathered could interpretations be made and theories proposed.

[3]L. L. Langness, *The Study of Culture* (San Francisco: Chandler and Sharp, 1974), p. 50.
[4]Reprinted in Franz Boas, *Race, Language, and Culture* (New York: Macmillan, 1940), pp. 270–80.

Franz Boas

Boas expected that if a tremendous quantity of data was collected, the laws governing cultural variation would emerge from the mass of information by themselves. According to the method he advocated, the essence of science is to mistrust all expectations and to rely only on facts. However, the "facts" that are recorded, even by the most diligent observer, will necessarily reflect what that individual considers important. Collecting done without some preliminary theorizing, without ideas about what to expect, is meaningless, for those facts that are most important may be ignored while irrelevant ones may be recorded. Although it was appropriate for Boas to criticize previous "armchair theorizing," his concern with an infinite number of local details did not encourage a belief that it might be possible to explain the major variations in culture that anthropologists observe.

Diffusionism

In the late nineteenth and early twentieth centuries, while the cultural evolutionism of Tylor and Morgan was still popular, diffusionism began to take hold among anthropologists in several parts of the world. The two main schools with a diffusionist viewpoint were the British and the German-Austrian.

The main spokesmen for the British school of diffusionism were G. Elliot Smith, William J. Perry, and W. H. R. Rivers. Smith and Perry stated that most aspects of higher civilization were developed in Egypt (which was relatively advanced culturally because of its early development of agriculture) and were then diffused throughout the world as other peoples came in contact with the Egyptians.[5] The British diffusionists thought that the independent parallel evolution of a particular cultural trait in two widely removed areas of the world was extremely rare. People, they believed, are inherently uninventive and invariably prefer to borrow the inventions of another culture rather than develop ideas for themselves. This viewpoint was never widely accepted, and it has now been abandoned completely.

Inspired by Fredrick Ratzel, Fritz Graebner and Father Wilhelm Schmidt led the German-Austrian diffusionist school, which also held that people borrow from other cultures because they are basically uninventive themselves. Graebner and Schmidt suggested that cultural traits can diffuse as a group, as well as singly, over great distances.[6] In contrast to Smith and Perry of the British school, who assumed that all cultural traits originated in one place (Egypt) and filtered out to cultures throughout the world, the German-Austrian school suggested the existence and diffusion of a number of different cultural complexes (*Kulturkreise*).[7] However, like the British diffusionists, the *Kulturkreis* school provided little documentation for the historical relationships it assumed.

A separate American diffusionist school of thought, led by Clark Wissler and Alfred Kroeber (both students of Boas), also arose about this time. It was similar in method to the German-Austrian school but more modest in its claims. The American diffusionists attributed the characteristic features of a culture area to a geographical *culture center*, where the traits were first developed and from which they then diffused outward. This theory led Wissler to formulate his age-area principle: if a given trait diffuses outward from a single culture center, it follows that the most widely distributed traits found to exist around such a center must be the oldest traits.[8]

Although most anthropologists today acknowledge the spread of traits by diffusion, few try to account for most aspects of cultural development and variation in terms of diffusion. For one thing, the diffusionists dealt only in a very superficial way with the question of how cultural traits are transferred from one society to another. The failing was a serious one, since one of the things we want to explain is why a culture accepts or rejects or modifies a trait that one of its neighbors has. Also, even if it could be demonstrated how and why a trait diffused outward from a cultural center, we would still be no closer to an explanation of how or why the trait developed within that center in the first place.

Functionalism

Bronislaw Malinowski (1884–1942) lived among the natives of the Trobriand Islands during World War I. He immersed himself in the language and customs of the natives in order to view the world from their perspective and to better understand their culture. This practice is known as the **participant-observer** approach to anthropological fieldwork.

Malinowski's theoretical orientation, **functionalism,** assumes that all cultural traits serve the needs of individuals in a society.[9] That is, the function of a culture trait is its ability to satisfy some *basic* or *derived need* of the members of the group. The basic needs include nutrition, reproduction, bodily comfort, safety, relaxation, movement, and growth. Some aspects of the culture satisfy these basic needs. In doing so, they give rise to derived needs that must also be satisfied. For example, culture traits that satisfy the basic need for food give rise to the secondary, or derived, need for cooperation in food collection or production.

[5]Marvin Harris, *The Rise of Anthropological Theory: A History of Theories of Culture* (New York: Thomas Y. Crowell, 1968), pp. 380–84; Langness, *The Study of Culture,* pp. 50–53.
[6]Ibid.
[7]Ibid.

[8]Langness, *The Study of Culture,* pp. 53–58; Harris, *The Rise of Anthropological Theory,* pp. 304–77.
[9]Bronislaw Malinowski, "The Group and the Individual in Functional Analysis," *American Journal of Sociology,* 44 (1939): 938–64.

Bronislaw Malinowski, during his fieldwork among the Trobriand Islanders (1915–1918), talks to Togu-guà, a sorcerer and informant.

Societies will in turn develop forms of political organization and social control that guarantee the required cooperation.

The major objection to Malinowski's functionalism is that it cannot readily account for cultural variation. The needs he identified—such as the need for food—are all more or less universal: all societies must deal with them if they are to survive. Thus, while the functionalist approach may tell us that all societies engage in food-getting, it cannot tell why different societies have different food-getting practices. In other words, functionalism does not explain why certain specific cultural patterns arise to fulfill a need that might be fulfilled just as easily by any of a number of alternative possibilities.

Structural Functionalism

Like Malinowski, Arthur Reginald Radcliffe-Brown, a British social anthropologist (1881–1955), based his theory of human social behavior on the concept of functionalism. But unlike Malinowski, Radcliffe-Brown felt that the various aspects of social behavior maintain a society's social structure rather than satisfying individual needs. The social structure of a society is the total network of its existing social relationships.[10]

[10]A. R. Radcliffe-Brown, *Structure and Function in Primitive Society* (London: Cohen & West, 1952).

An example of Radcliffe-Brown's structural-functionalist approach is his analysis of the ways different societies deal with the tensions that are likely to develop among people related through marriage. To reduce potential tension between in-laws, he suggests, societies do one of two things. They may develop strict rules forbidding the persons involved ever to interact face to face (as do the Navaho, for example, in requiring a man to avoid his mother-in-law). Or they may allow mutual disrespect and teasing between the in-laws. Radcliffe-Brown suggests that avoidance is likely to occur between in-laws of different generations, whereas disrespectful teasing is likely between in-laws of the same generation.[11] Both avoidance and teasing, he suggests, are ways to avoid real conflict and help maintain the social structure. (American mother-in-law jokes may also help relieve tension.)

A major problem of the structural-functional approach is that it is difficult to determine whether a particular custom is in fact functional in the sense of contributing to the maintenance of the social system. In biology, the contribution an organ makes to the health or life of an animal can be assessed by removing it. But we cannot subtract a cultural trait from a society to see if the trait really does contribute to the maintenance of that group. It is conceivable that certain customs within the society may be neutral or even detrimental to its maintenance.

We cannot assume that all of a society's customs are functional merely because the society is functioning at the moment. And even if we are able to assess whether a particular custom is functional, this theoretical orientation fails to deal with the question of why a particular society chooses to meet its structural needs in a particular way. A given problem does not necessarily have only one solution. We still must explain why one of several possible solutions is chosen.

Psychological Approaches

In the 1920s, some American anthropologists began to study the relationship between culture and personality. While there are varying opinions about how the culture-and-personality school got started, the writings of Sigmund Freud and other

[11]Ibid., pp. 92–93.

Margaret Mead

psychoanalysts were undoubtedly influential. Edward Sapir, one of Boas's earliest students, reviewed a number of psychoanalytic books and seems to have influenced two other students of Boas—Ruth Benedict and Margaret Mead—who became early proponents of a psychological orientation.[12]

In *Patterns of Culture,* Benedict argued not only that cultures are patterned but also that different cultures could be characterized in terms of different personality types. In contrast to Benedict, Mead did not attempt to describe cultures in terms of personality types. But for Mead as well as Benedict, culture and personality were strongly linked. After studying three different societies in New Guinea, Mead suggested that each of those societies had a different pattern of sex differences in personality. In other words, men and women were different psychologically in the three societies, and the differences were not the same across the three societies. If the women in one could act like the men in another, Mead concluded that culture, not biology, was mainly responsible for personality differences between the sexes. Although many of Benedict's and Mead's assertions were later challenged, the research of these two women aroused a great deal of interest in personality and culture and in anthropology generally.

In seminars at Columbia University in the 1930s and 1940s, Ralph Linton, an anthropologist, and Abram Kardiner, a psychoanalyst, developed a number of important ideas for culture-and-personality studies. Kardiner suggested that in every culture there is a *basic personality* that is produced by certain shared cultural experiences. In other words, just as a child's later personality may be shaped by his or her earlier experiences, so the personality of adults in a society should be shaped by common cultural experiences. These shared experiences derive from the society's **primary institutions,** which have to do with the customary ways of making a living, the customary composition of the family, and the customs of child rearing. The basic personality structure, in turn, gives rise to the aspects of culture, called **secondary institutions,** which are created to satisfy and reconcile the needs and conflicts that constitute the basic personality structure. These institutions—which include ritual, religion, and folklore—are considered secondary because they presumably stem from the basic personality structure.[13]

Not all psychological anthropologists use Kardiner's entire scheme. But most assume that there is a set of typical personality characteristics in a society, whether they call it "basic personality," "national character," or "modal personality." And most accept Kardiner's assumption that the typical personality is produced by certain aspects of cultural experience, particularly the customs of child rearing.

During World War II and shortly thereafter, the culture-and-personality orientation was applied to complex societies. Most of these studies of national character attributed the apparent personality traits of different nations to aspects of child rearing. For example, three different studies suggested that adult Japanese were compulsive because of the

[12]Langness, *The Study of Culture,* pp. 85–93; Philip K. Bock, *Continuities in Psychological Anthropology: A Historical Introduction* (San Francisco: W. H. Freeman and Company Publishers, 1980), pp. 57–82.

[13]Abram Kardiner, with Ralph Linton, *The Individual and His Society* (New York: Columbia University Press, 1939), pp. 471–87.

strict toilet training they received as children.[14] Similarly, the manic-depressive swings in emotion believed to be common among Russians were attributed by Geoffrey Gorer and John Rickman to the practice in Soviet nurseries of swaddling infants from birth.[15] (Swaddling involves wrapping cloth strips around an infant's body to keep arms and legs immobile.) This was considered to cause anger and frustration in the infant that were later expressed in the adult as manic-depressive behavior.

Unfortunately, because it was wartime, the investigators working on Japanese compulsiveness were unable to do any fieldwork. The anthropologists studying Russian character were also forced to use indirect research methods. Later, when researchers were able to obtain firsthand data from more representative samples of subjects, they discovered that the conclusions of the earlier studies were not always reliable. For example, it was found that the toilet-training practices of the Japanese were not particularly strict. In other words, the early studies of national character had been crude attempts to use methods of social science to substantiate *subjective* generalizations about personality differences between complex societies.

As time went on, the focus of the psychological approach changed. While retaining their interest in Freudian theories and the relation between child training and adult personality, some anthropologists began to investigate the possible determinants of variation in child-training practices. For example, in a comparative study, Herbert Barry, Irvin Child, and Margaret Bacon suggested that the future food supply in herding and agricultural societies is best ensured by adherence to an established routine, since mistakes may jeopardize a year's food supply. In most hunting and fishing societies, however, mistakes will affect only the daily food supply. Therefore, adherence to routine is not so essential, and individual initiative may be encouraged. As the investigators predicted, the cross-cultural evidence indicates that agricultural socie-

ties are apt to stress obedience and responsibility in their child training, whereas hunting and fishing societies tend to emphasize independence and self-reliance.[16]

In addition to exploring the determinants of different patterns of child training, some studies have elaborated on Kardiner's suggestion that personality traits and processes may account for cross-cultural associations between one cultural pattern and another. The argument in these studies is that certain culture traits produce certain psychological characteristics, which in turn give rise to other culture traits. Such a mediating influence of personality is suggested, for example, by the work of John Whiting and Irvin Child on cultural explanations of illness.[17] They suggest that severe punishment for aggression in childhood (a cultural characteristic) may lead to an exaggerated preoccupation with aggression in adulthood (a psychological characteristic), which may in turn predispose adults to believe that aggressive behavior causes illness (a cultural characteristic).

To generalize about the psychological approach to cultural anthropology, then, we may say that it tries to understand how psychological factors and processes may help to explain cultural practices.

Later Evolutionism

The evolutionary approach to cultural variation did not die with the nineteenth century. In the 1930s, Leslie A. White attacked the Boasian emphasis on historical particularism and championed the evolutionist orientation.

Though quickly labeled a neo-evolutionist, White rejected the term, insisting that his approach did not depart significantly from the theories adopted in the nineteenth century. What White did add to the classical evolutionist approach was a conception of culture as an energy-capturing system. According to his "basic law" of cultural evolution, "other factors remaining constant, *culture evolves as the amount of energy harnessed per capita per year is increased or as the effi-*

[14]Ruth Benedict, *The Chrysanthemum and the Sword* (Boston: Houghton Mifflin, 1946); Geoffrey Gorer, "Themes in Japanese Culture," *Transactions of the New York Academy of Sciences,* 5 (1943): 106–24; and W. LaBarre, "Some Observations on Character Structure in the Orient: The Japanese," *Psychiatry,* 8 (1945): 326–42.

[15]Geoffrey Gorer and John Rickman, *The People of Great Russia: A Psychological Study* (New York: Chanticleer, 1950).

[16]Herbert Barry III, Irvin L. Child, and Margaret K. Bacon, "Relation of Child Training to Subsistence Economy," *American Anthropologist,* 61 (1959): 51–63.

[17]John W. M. Whiting and Irvin L. Child, *Child Training and Personality: A Cross-Cultural Study* (New Haven: Yale University Press, 1953).

ciency of the instrumental means of putting the energy to work is increased."[18] In other words, a more advanced technology gives humans control over more energy (human, animal, solar, and so on), and cultures expand and change as a result.

White's orientation has been criticized for the same reasons that the ideas of Tylor and Morgan were. In describing what has happened in the evolution of human culture, he assumes that cultural evolution is determined strictly by conditions (preeminently technological ones) inside the culture. That is, he explicitly denies the possibility of environmental, historical, or psychological influences on cultural evolution. The main problem with such an orientation is that it cannot explain why some cultures evolve while others either do not evolve or become extinct. Thus, White's theory of energy capture as the mechanism of cultural evolution sidesteps the question of why only some cultures are able to increase their energy capture.

Julian H. Steward, another later evolutionist, divides evolutionary thought into three schools: unilinear, universal, and multilinear.[19] Steward feels that Morgan and Tylor are examples of the unilinear approach to cultural evolution—the classical nineteenth-century orientation that attempts to place particular cultures on the rungs of a sort of evolutionary ladder. Universal evolutionists such as Leslie White, on the other hand, are concerned with culture in the broad sense, rather than with individual cultures. Steward classified himself as a multilinear evolutionist—one who deals with the evolution of particular cultures and only with demonstrated sequences of parallel culture change in different areas.

Steward was concerned with explaining specific cultural differences and similarities. Consequently, he was critical of White's vague generalities and his disregard of environmental influences. White, on the other hand, asserted that Steward fell into the historical-particularist trap of paying too much attention to particular cases.

Marshall Sahlins and Elman Service, who were students and colleagues of both White and Steward, combined the views of these two individuals by recognizing two kinds of evolution—specific and general.[20] **Specific evolution** refers to the particular sequence of change and adaptation of a particular society in a given environment. **General evolution** refers to a general progress of human society, in which higher forms (having higher energy capture) arise from and surpass lower forms. Thus, specific evolution is similar to Steward's multilinear evolution, and general evolution resembles White's universal evolution. Although this synthesis does serve to integrate both points of view, it does not give us a way of explaining why general evolutionary progress has occurred. But unlike the early evolutionists, some of the later evolutionists did suggest a mechanism to account for the evolution of particular cultures—namely, adaptation to particular environments.

Structuralism

Claude Lévi-Strauss has been the leading proponent of an approach to cultural analysis called **structuralism.** Lévi-Strauss's structuralism differs from that of Radcliffe-Brown. Whereas Radcliffe-Brown concentrated on how the elements of a society function as a system, Lévi-Strauss concentrates more on the origins of the systems themselves. He sees culture, as expressed in art, ritual, and the patterns of daily life, as a surface representation of the underlying structure of the human mind. Consider, for example, how he tries to account for what anthropologists call a *moiety system.* Such a system is said to exist if a society is divided into two large intermarrying kin groups (each called a *moiety*—probably derived from the French world *moitié,* meaning "half"). Lévi-Strauss says that moiety systems reflect the human mind's predisposition to think and behave in terms of *binary oppositions* (contrasts between one thing and another).[21] Clearly, a moiety system involves a binary opposition: you are born into one of two groups and you marry someone in the other. The problem with Lévi-Strauss's explanation of moieties is that he is postulating a constant—the human mind's supposed dualism—to account for a cultural feature that is not universal. Moiety systems are

[18]Leslie A. White, *The Science of Culture: A Study of Man and Civilization* (New York: Farrar, Straus & Cudahy, 1949), pp. 368–69.
[19]Julian H. Steward, *Theory of Culture Change,* (Urbana: University of Illinois Press, 1955).

[20]Marshall D. Sahlins and Elman R. Service, *Evolution and Culture* (Ann Arbor: University of Michigan Press, 1960).
[21]Claude Lévi-Strauss, *The Elementary Structures of Kinship,* rev. ed., trans. James H. Bell and J. R. von Sturmer, ed. Rodney Needham (Boston: Beacon Press, 1969), p. 75.

Claude Lévi-Strauss

found in only a relatively small number of societies, so how could something that is universal explain something else that is not?

Lévi-Strauss's interpretations of cultural phenomena (which tend to be far more involved and difficult to follow than the example just described) have concentrated on the presumed cognitive processes of people—that is, the ways in which people supposedly perceive and classify things in the world around them. In studies such as *The Savage Mind* and *The Raw and the Cooked*, he suggests that even technologically simple groups often construct elaborate systems of classification of plants and animals, not only for practical purposes but also out of a need for such intellectual activity.[22]

Structuralism has not only influenced thinking in France; Britain too has been receptive. But the British structuralists, such as Edmund Leach, Rodney Needham, and Mary Douglas, do not follow Lévi-Strauss in looking for panhuman or universal principles in the human mind. Rather, they concentrate on applying structural analysis to particular societies and particular social institutions.[23] For example, Mary Douglas discusses an argument that took place in her home over whether soup is an "appropriate" supper. She suggests that meals (in her household and in culturally similar households) have certain structural principles. They have contrasts: hot and cold, bland and spiced, liquid and semi-liquid; and various textures. They must incorporate cereals, vegetables, and animal protein. Douglas concludes that if the food served does not follow these principles, it cannot be considered a meal![24]

Some structuralist writings have been criticized for their concentration on abstruse, theoretical analysis at the expense of solid, ethnological observation and evidence. For example, it is not always clear how Lévi-Strauss has derived a particular structuralist interpretation, and in the absence of any systematically collected supporting evidence, the reader must decide whether or not the interpretation seems plausible. Thus, Lévi-Strauss's studies have come to be regarded by many as vague and untestable, as self-contained intellectual constructs with little explanatory value. Moreover, even if there are some universal patterns that underlie cultural phenomena, such universals or constants cannot explain cultural differences.

Ethnoscience

Lévi-Strauss's structuralist approach involves intuitively grasping the rules of thought that may underlie a given culture. An ethnographic approach known as **ethnoscience** attempts to derive these rules from a logical analysis of ethnographic data that are kept as free as possible from contamination by the observer's own cultural biases.

[22]Claude Lévi-Strauss. *The Savage Mind*, trans. George Weidenfeld and Nicolson, Ltd. (Chicago: University of Chicago Press, 1966 [first published in French, 1962]); and Lévi-Strauss, *The Raw and the Cooked*, trans. John and Doreen Weightman (New York: Harper & Row, Publishers, 1969 [first published in French, 1964]).

[23]Sherry B. Ortner, "Theory in Anthropology since the Sixties," *Comparative Studies in Society and History*, 26 (1984): 126–66.
[24]Mary Douglas, *Implicit Meanings: Essays in Anthropology*, (London: Routledge and Kegan Paul, 1975.)

The approach of ethnoscience is similar to that of Lévi-Strauss insofar as both are influenced by the methodology of descriptive linguistics, but there the similarity ends. Rather than collecting data according to a predetermined set of anthropological categories, the ethnoscientist seeks to understand a people's world from their point of view. Utilizing what he or she has discovered about them through studying their language, and particularly the words they use to describe what they do, the ethnoscientist tries to formulate the rules that generate acceptable behavior in the culture. The rules in question are believed to be comparable to the grammatical rules that generate the correct use of language.

Many ethnoscientists think that if we can discover the rules that generate correct cultural behavior, we can explain much of what people do and why they do it. Probably individuals do generally act according to the conscious and unconscious rules they have internalized. However, we still need to understand why a particular society has developed the particular cultural rules it has. Just as a grammar does not explain how a language came to be what it is, so the ethnoscientific discovery of a culture's rules does not explain why those rules developed.

Cultural Ecology

It is only relatively recently that anthropologists have begun to take seriously the influence of environment on culture. Julian Steward was one of the first to advocate the study of **cultural ecology**—the analysis of the relationship between a culture and its environment. Steward felt that the explanation for some aspects of cultural variation could be found in the adaptation of societies to their particular environments. But rather than merely hypothesize that the environment did or did not determine cultural variation, Steward wished to resolve the question empirically—that is, he wanted to carry out investigations to substantiate his viewpoint.[25]

However, Steward felt that cultural ecology must be separated from biological ecology (the study of the relationships between organisms and their environment). Later cultural ecologists such as Andrew Vayda and Roy Rappaport wish to incorporate principles of biological ecology into the study of cultural ecology in order to make a single science of ecology.[26] In their view, cultural traits, just like biological traits, can be considered adaptive or maladaptive. Cultural ecologists assume that cultural adaptation involves the mechanism of natural selection—the more frequent survival and reproduction of the better-adapted. Environment, including the physical and social environment, affects the development of culture traits in that "individuals or populations behaving in certain different ways have different degrees of success in survival and reproduction and, consequently, in the transmission of their ways of behaving from generation to generation."[27]

Consider how culture and environment may interact among the Tsembaga, who live in the interior of New Guinea.[28] The Tsembaga are horticulturists, living mainly on the root crops and greens they grow in home gardens. They also raise pigs. The pigs are seldom eaten; instead, they serve other useful functions. They keep residential areas clean by consuming garbage, and they help prepare the soil for planting by rooting in it. Small numbers of pigs are easy to keep; they run free all day, returning at night to eat whatever substandard tubers are found in the course of their owners' harvesting of their daily rations. Thus pigs, which require a minimum of maintenance, serve the Tsembaga both as janitors and as cultivating machines.

But problems arise when the pig herd grows large. Often there are not enough substandard tubers, and then the pigs must be fed human rations. Also, although a small number of pigs will clean up yards and soften the soil in the gardens, a large herd is likely to intrude upon garden crops. Pigs can even break up communities. If one person's pig invades a neighbor's garden, the garden owner of-

[25]Julian H. Steward, "The Concept and Method of Cultural Ecology," in Steward, *Theory of Culture Change*, pp. 30–42.

[26]Andrew P. Vayda and Roy A. Rappaport, "Ecology: Cultural and Noncultural," in James H. Clifton, ed., *Introduction to Cultural Anthropology* (Boston: Houghton Mifflin, 1968), pp. 477–97.

[27]Ibid., p. 493.

[28]See Roy A. Rappaport, "Ritual Regulation of Environmental Relations among a New Guinea People," *Ethnology*, 6 (1967): 17–30.

Sometimes you can have too many pigs. A pig feast solves this problem and maintains or creates close ties between groups. Here we see preparations for a pig feast on the island of Tanna in the New Hebrides.

ten retaliates by killing the offending pig. In turn, the dead animal's owner may kill the garden owner, the garden owner's wife, or one of his pigs. As the number of such feuds increases, people begin to put as much distance as possible between their pigs and other people's gardens.

Rappaport suggests that to cope with the problem of pig overpopulation, the Tsembaga have developed an elaborate cycle of rituals that involves the slaughter of large numbers of surplus pigs. The pigs can then be distributed in the form of pork—a valuable commodity—to friends and to ancestors (who, the Tsembaga believe, will grant them strength and courage in return). Thus, this cultural practice of ritual pig feasts can be viewed as a possible adaptation to environmental factors that produce a surplus pig population.

The cultural ecologist tries to explain cultural variation by suggesting how a particular trait is adaptive in a particular physical and/or social environment. In applying this orientation to a specific society, the ecologist may be subject to the same kind of criticism that has been directed at the structural functionalist. Just as the structural func-

tionalist may not be able to show that a particular custom is functional, so the ecologist who is analyzing a specific society may not be able to show that a particular custom is adaptive. With regard to the Tsembaga, for example, it is hard to know whether their ritual pig feasts are more adaptive than other possible solutions to the problem of pig overpopulation. Might it be more adaptive to slaughter and eat pigs regularly so that pig herds never get too large?

Without being able to contrast the effects of alternative solutions, a cultural ecologist studying a single society may find it difficult to obtain evidence that a custom already in place is more adaptive than other possible solutions to the problem.

Political Economy

Like cultural ecology, the school of thought known as political economy assumes that external forces explain the way a society changes and adapts. But it is not the natural environment, or social environment in general, that is central to the approach of political economy. What is central is the social and political impact of those powerful state societies (principally Spain, Portugal, Britain, and France) that transformed the world by colonialism and imperialism and fostered the development of a worldwide economy or world-system.[29]

Some of the earliest figures associated with the political economy approach (in anthropology) were trained at Columbia University when Julian Steward was a professor there. For those students, Steward's cultural ecology was insufficiently attentive to recent world history. For example, Eric Wolf and Sidney Mintz argued that the communities they studied in Puerto Rico developed as they did because of colonialism and the establishment of plantations to supply sugar and coffee to Europe and North America.[30] And Eleanor Leacock, who studied the Montagnais-Naskapi Indians of Labrador, suggested that their system of family hunting territories was not an old characteristic, present before European contact, but developed instead out of the Indians' early involvement in the European-introduced fur trade.[31]

Central to the later intellectual development of political economy in anthropology are the writings of two political sociologists, André Frank and Immanuel Wallerstein. Frank suggested that the development of a region (Europe, for example) depended on the suppression of development or underdevelopment of other regions (the New World, Africa). He argued that if we want to understand why a country remains underdeveloped, we must understand how it is exploited by developed nations.[32] Frank is concerned with what happened in the underdeveloped world. Wallerstein is more concerned with how capitalism developed in the privileged countries and how the expansionist requirements of the capitalist countries led to the emergence of the world-system.[33]

The political economy or world-system view has inspired many anthropologists to study history more explicitly, and to explore the impact of external political and economic processes on local events and cultures in the underdeveloped world. In the past, when anthropologists first started doing fieldwork in the far corners of the world, they could imagine that the cultures they were studying (or reconstructing) could be investigated as if those cultures were more or less isolated from external influences and forces. In the modern world, such isolation hardly exists. The political economy approach has reminded us that the world, every part of it, is interconnected for better or worse.

Sociobiology

The idea that natural selection can operate on the behavioral or social characteristics of populations (and not just on their physical traits) is shared by cultural ecology and another, more recent theoretical orientation called **sociobiology.** Developed mainly by biologists, particularly those who have concentrated on the social insects, the sociobiological orientation involves the application of biological evolutionary principles to the social behavior of animals, including humans. Sociobiology has aroused a lot of controversy in cultural anthropology. Why there is so much controversy may become clear if we ask how the sociobiological orientation differs from that of cultural ecology.

Although both orientations assume the importance of natural selection in cultural evolution, they differ in at least three respects. First, cultural ecology focuses mostly on what biologists would call **group selection:** cultural ecologists talk mostly about how a certain behavioral or social characteristic may be adaptive for a group or society in a given environment. In contrast, sociobiology focuses mostly on what biologists call **individual selection:** sociobiologists talk mostly about how a certain characteristic may be adaptive for an indi-

[29]Ortner, "Theory in Anthropology since the Sixties," pp. 141–42.

[30]William Roseberry, "Political Economy," *Annual Review of Anthropology*, 17 (1988): 163; see also Eric R. Wolf, "San José: Subcultures of a 'Traditional' Coffee Municipality," in Julian H. Steward, Robert A. Manners, Eric R. Wolf, Elena Padilla Seda, Sidney W. Mintz, and Raymond L. Scheele, *The People of Puerto Rico* (Urbana: University of Illinois Press, 1956), pp. 171–264; and Sidney W. Mintz, "Canamelar: The Subculture of a Rural Sugar Plantation Proletariat," in *The People of Puerto Rico*, pp. 314–417.

[31]Roseberry, "Political Economy," p. 164; see also Eleanor Leacock, "The Montagnais 'Hunting Territory' and the Fur Trade," *American Anthropological Association*, Memoir 78, (1954): 1–59.

[32]Roseberry, "Political Economy," p. 166; see also André Gunder Frank, *Capitalism and Underdevelopment in Latin America: Historical Studies of Chile and Brazil* (New York: Monthly Review Press, 1967).

[33]Roseberry, "Political Economy," pp. 166–67; see also Immanuel Wallerstein, *The Modern World-System* (New York: Academic Press, 1974).

vidual in a given environment.[34] Second, according to the sociobiologist, natural selection operates *only* on genes (the chemical transmitters of heredity); to the cultural ecologist, natural selection operates on behavior, whether or not it is purely genetically determined.[35] A third and probably the most controversial difference between cultural ecology and sociobiology has to do with the relative importance each assigns to genetic determinants of social behavior. Cultural ecologists (like most cultural anthropologists) would say that social behavior in humans is determined only very loosely by genes, that inherited characteristics may allow for the expression of certain behaviors but do not determine exactly what is done. Thus, most cultural anthropologists would say that although human culture could not have evolved in the absence of some genetically determined characteristics (such as a large brain or the mouth and throat anatomy required for spoken language), the varieties of culture observed in the human species are mainly learned. In contrast, sociobiologists suggest that behavior, including the social behavior of humans, is the product of both genetic and environmental influences.[36]

As in any controversy, the opposing points of view about sociobiology can be exaggerated. Contrary to what some critics say, most sociobiologists do not deny that human behavior can be modified by learning or experience.[37] And contrary to what some sociobiologists say, most social scientists do not deny that there must be genetic potentials for behavior. Thus, much of the controversy over the possible application of sociobiology to human behavior may be unnecessary. To be sure, when we

are dealing with a universal or near-universal human behavior, it is difficult to discover whether it is universal because of the universality of certain genes or because of the universality of certain learning experiences (or perhaps both). Instead of arguing fruitlessly, what we need is empirical research that tests alternative explanations of universals and variables in human behavior.

The sociobiological and other approaches may generate different predictions, only some of which may be supported by empirical research. When we eventually have the results of such research, we may be more entitled to draw specific conclusions about the environmental and/or genetic determinants of human behavior.

Interpretive Approaches

Over the last 30 years or so, writers in the field of literary criticism have influenced the development of a variety of "interpretive" approaches in cultural anthropology, particularly with respect to ethnography.[38]

Clifford Geertz popularized the idea that a culture is like a literary text that can be analyzed for meaning, as the ethnographer interprets it. According to Geertz, ethnographers choose to interpret the meaning of things in their field cultures that are of interest to themselves. Then they try to convey their interpretations of cultural meaning to people of their own culture. Thus, according to Geertz, the ethnographer is a kind of selective inter-cultural translator.[39]

Some anthropologists think that interpretation is the only achievable goal in cultural anthropology, because they do not believe it is possible to describe or measure cultural phenomena (and other things involving humans) in objective or unbiased ways.[40] Scientific anthropologists do not agree. To be sure, interpretive ethnographies might provide insights. But we do not have to be-

[34]William Irons, "Natural Selection, Adaptation, and Human Social Behavior," in Napoleon A. Chagnon and William Irons, eds., *Evolutionary Biology and Human Social Behavior: An Anthropological Perspective* (North Scituate, MA: Duxbury, 1979), pp. 10–12. For a mathematical model and a computer simulation suggesting that group selection is likely in cultural evolution, see Robert Boyd and Peter J. Richerson, "Group Selection among Alternative Evolutionarily Stable Strategies," *Journal of Theoretical Biology*, 145 (1990): 331–42.

[35]William H. Durham, "Toward a Coevolutionary Theory of Human Biology and Culture," in Chagnon and Irons, eds., *Evolutionary Biology and Human Social Behavior*, pp. 39–40.

[36]Napoleon Chagnon and William Irons, "Prologue," in Chagnon and Irons, eds., *Evolutionary Biology and Human Social Behavior*, p. xvi.

[37]David P. Barash, *Sociobiology and Behavior* (New York: Elsevier, 1977), pp. 40–41; and Martin A. Etter, "Sahlins and Sociobiology," *American Ethnologist*, 5 (1978): 160–68.

[38]James Clifford, "Introduction: Partial Truths," in James Clifford and George E. Marcus, eds., *Writing Culture: The Poetics and Politics of Ethnography* (Berkeley: University of California Press, 1986), p. 3.

[39]George E. Marcus and Michael M. J. Fischer, *Anthropology as Cultural Critique: An Experimental Moment in the Human Sciences* (Chicago: University of Chicago Press, 1986), pp. 26–29.

[40]For discussion of this position, see Marcus and Fischer, *Anthropology as Cultural Critique*, pp. x, 180–81.

lieve what an interpretation suggests, no matter how eloquently it is stated. (We are rarely given objective evidence to support an interpretation.) Scientific researchers have developed many techniques for minimizing bias and increasing the objectivity of measurement. Thus, interpretive anthropologists who deny the possibility of scientific understanding of human behavior and thinking may not know how much has been achieved so far by scientific studies of cultural phenomena, which we try to convey in the chapters that follow.

As Dan Sperber has suggested, the task of interpretation in cultural anthropology is clearly different from the task of explanation.[41] The goal of interpretation is to convey intuitive understanding of human experience in a *particular* culture (intuitive in the sense of not requiring conscious reasoning or systematic methods of inquiry). Thus the interpretive ethnographer is like a novelist (or literary critic). In contrast, the goal of explanation is to provide general and causal understanding of cultural phenomena (causal in the sense of mechanisms that account for why something comes to be shared in a population, and general in the sense of applying to a number of similar cases).

Does one goal (interpretation versus explanation) preclude or invalidate the other? We do not think so. We share Sperber's view that interpretation and explanation are not opposed goals: they just are different kinds of understanding. Indeed, an intuitive interpretation described in causal and general terms might turn out, when scientifically tested, to be a plausible explanation!

Subject and Method Orientations

Cultural anthropologists do not come only in the varieties so far described. There are still other kinds who do not define themselves in terms of theoretical orientations or where they would look for explanations. Rather, they define their approaches in terms of subject interests or preferred methods of research.

Most subject orientations focus on conventionally distinguished aspects of culture, which usually furnish the chapter titles in a textbook such as this one. So there are cultural anthropologists who identify themselves as *economic anthropologists* or *political anthropologists*, who are interested mostly in economic and political organization, respectively. Other subject orientations crosscut the conventionally distinguished aspects of culture. One such orientation is *cognitive anthropology*, which is interested in the ways people think and perceive in different societies—how they make economic decisions, how they think about male and female roles, how they classify plants and animals.[42] The various subject orientations are not mutually exclusive. A particular anthropologist might be interested in a number of subject areas. For example, there are investigators who would call themselves cognitive economic anthropologists.

Some cultural anthropologists have method rather than subject or theoretical orientations. They think of themselves *mostly* as ethnographers or ethnohistorians or cross-cultural researchers. We discuss these three types of research more fully toward the end of the next chapter.

The Hypothesis-Testing Orientation

An increasing number of contemporary cultural anthropologists would explicitly deny that they prefer any particular theoretical orientation, subject interest, or method of research. Rather, they think of themselves as having a *hypothesis-testing* orientation. That is, they think of themselves as being interested mostly in trying to explain cultural phenomena. Any type of theory might be considered and a variety of research methods might be employed by such anthropologists. Their major goal is to test possible explanations because they believe that any explanation should be exposed to the possibility of being falsified by some set of systematically collected data. In the absence of such a test, these anthropologists would say that we are entitled or even obliged to be skeptical about the validity of any suggested explanation.

To those with a hypothesis-testing orienta-

---

[41]Dan Sperber, *On Anthropological Knowledge: Three Essays* (Cambridge: Cambridge University Press, 1985), p. 34.

[42]For examples of some recent research in cognitive anthropology, see Dorothy Holland and Naomi Quinn, eds., *Cultural Models in Language and Thought* (Cambridge: Cambridge University Press, 1987).

tion, the plausibility or persuasiveness of an explanation cannot be considered a sufficient reason to accept it; the explanation must still be tested and supported. And even if it is supported, there still may be grounds for skepticism. According to this orientation, then, all knowledge is uncertain and therefore subject to increasing or decreasing confirmation as new tests are made. If this is true—and it may be uncomfortable to acknowledge—it means that we will never arrive at absolute truth. On the other hand—and this is encouraging—we should be able to achieve a more and more reliable understanding if we keep testing our theories.

SUMMARY

1. Which aspects of life an individual anthropologist concentrates on usually reflects his or her theoretical orientation, subject interest, or preferred method of research.

2. A theoretical orientation is usually a general attitude about how cultural phenomena are to be explained.

3. The prevailing theoretical orientation in anthropology during the nineteenth century was based on a belief that culture generally evolves in a uniform and progressive manner; that is, most societies were believed to pass through the same series of stages, to arrive ultimately at a common end. Two proponents of this early theory of cultural evolution were Edward B. Tylor and Lewis Henry Morgan.

4. During the early twentieth century the leading opponent of evolutionism was Franz Boas, who rejected the way in which early evolutionists had assumed that universal laws governed all human culture. Boas stressed the importance of collecting as much anthropological data as possible, from which the laws governing cultural variation would supposedly emerge by themselves.

5. The diffusionist approach, popular in the late nineteenth and early twentieth centuries, was developed by two main schools—the British and the German-Austrian. In general, diffusionists believed that most aspects of high civilization had emerged in culture centers from which they then diffused outward.

6. Functionalism as an approach to anthropology was proposed by Bronislaw Malinowski. It holds that all culture traits serve the needs of individuals in a society; that is, the function of a culture trait is its ability to satisfy some basic or derived need of the members of the group.

7. Unlike the functional approach of Malinowski, the structural-functional approach of A. R. Radcliffe-Brown assumes that the various aspects of social behavior maintain a society's social structure—its total network of social relationships—rather than satisfying individual needs.

8. The psychological orientation of anthropology, which began in the 1920s, seeks to understand how psychological factors and processes may help us explain cultural practices.

9. In the 1930s, the evolutionary approach to cultural development was revived by Leslie A. White, who proposed that "culture evolves . . . as the efficiency of the instrumental means of putting . . . energy to work is increased." Anthropologists such as Julian H. Steward, Marshall Sahlins, and Elman Service have also presented evolutionary viewpoints in recent times.

10. Claude Lévi-Strauss has been the leading proponent of structuralism. Essentially, Lévi-Strauss sees culture, as it is expressed in art, ritual, and the patterns of daily life, as a surface representation of the underlying patterns of the human mind.

11. Whereas Lévi-Strauss's approach involves intuitively grasping the rules of thought that may underlie a given culture, an ethnographic approach known as ethnoscience attempts to derive these rules from a logical analysis of data—particularly the words people use to describe their activities. In this way, the ethnoscientist tries to formulate the rules that generate acceptable behavior in a given culture.

12. Cultural ecology seeks to understand the relationships between cultures and their physical and social environments. Cultural ecologists ask how a particular culture trait may be adaptive in its environment.

13. The theoretical orientation called political economy focuses on the impact of external political and economic processes, particularly as con-

nected to colonialism and imperialism, on local events and cultures in the underdeveloped world. The political economy approach has reminded us that every part of the world is interconnected for better or worse.

14. Sociobiology is a theoretical orientation that involves the application of biological evolutionary principles to the social behavior of animals, including humans.

15. Interpretive approaches consider cultures as texts to be analyzed for their meaning. The ethnographer is thus like a novelist or literary critic.

16. Some cultural anthropologists define their approaches in terms of subject interests, such as economics, politics, or cognition.

17. Some cultural anthropologists identify themselves in terms of a method of research ranging from ethnography to ethnohistory to cross-cultural research.

18. Finally, there are cultural anthropologists who do not follow any particular theoretical orientation or prefer any particular subject matter or method of research. These anthropologists think of themselves as having a hypothesis-testing orientation.

SUGGESTED READING

HARRIS, M. *The Rise of Anthropological Theory: A History of Theories of Culture.* New York: Thomas Y. Crowell, 1968. A critical review of the history of anthropological theory from 1750 to the 1960s. The author discusses the social context of, and the personalities involved in, the different theoretical orientations.

LANGNESS, L. L. *The Study of Culture,* rev. ed. Novato, CA: Chandler and Sharp, 1987. A survey of the history of theory in the study of culture. Significant theorists and their concepts and concerns are the main focus. The book also describes how the development of culture theory has been linked to developments in other disciplines.

MANNERS, R. A., AND KAPLAN, D., eds. *Theory in Anthropology: A Sourcebook.* Chicago: Aldine, 1968. A massive compilation of readings representing the leading theoretical orientations of the past.

STOCKING, G. W., JR., ed. *History of Anthropology,* vols. 1–6. Madison, WI: University of Wisconsin, 1983–1989. A series of edited volumes on various topics in the history of anthropology, including the beginnings of fieldwork in anthropology (vol. 1, *Observers Observed: Essays on Ethnographic Fieldwork*) and romantic motives that may have driven people to become anthropologists (vol. 6, *Romantic Motives: Essays on Anthropological Sensibility*).

12

Explanation and Evidence

An important part of any discipline is description. A cultural anthropologist who goes to study a group of people tries to describe how the people live. How do they get food? How do they organize labor? How do they marry? The traditional goal of fieldwork is to arrive at accurate answers to such descriptive questions. But as important as accurate description is, it is not the ultimate goal of anthropology. Anthropologists want to understand—to know *why* people have certain traits or customs, not just that they *do* have them. As difficult as the *how* and *what* questions are to answer, the *why* questions are even harder. *Why* questions deal with explanations, which are harder to generate and harder to evaluate. In science, to understand is to explain, and so the major goal of science is to arrive at trustworthy explanations.[1]

This chapter is concerned largely with scientific understanding—what it means to explain, and what kinds of evidence are needed to evaluate an explanation. We also discuss the various types of research that are conducted in cultural anthropology, from ethnography and ethnohistory to cross-cultural comparisons.

Explanations

An **explanation** is an answer to a *why* question. But there are many types of explanation, some more satisfying than others. For example, suppose we ask why a society has a long postpartum sex taboo. We could guess that the people in that society *want* to abstain from sex for a year or so after the birth of a baby. Is this an explanation? Yes, because it does suggest that people have a *purpose* in practicing the custom; it therefore partly answers the *why* question. But such an explanation would not be very satisfying because it does not specify what the purpose of the custom might be. How about the idea that people have a long postpartum sex taboo because it is their tradition? Yes, that too is an explanation, but it is not satisfactory for a different reason: it is a *tautology*, which means that the thing to be explained (the taboo) is being explained by itself, by its prior existence. To explain something in terms of tradition is to say that

people do it because they already do it, which is not very informative. What kinds of explanations are more satisfactory, then? In science, there are two kinds of explanation that researchers try to achieve—associations and theories.

Associations

One way of explaining something (an observation, an action, a habit, a custom) is to say how it conforms to a general principle or relationship. So to explain why the water left out in the basin froze last night, we say that it was quite cold last night and that water freezes at 32° F. The statement that water solidifies (becomes ice) at 32 degrees is a statement of a relationship or association between two **variables**—things or quantities that vary. In this case, variation in the state of water (liquid versus solid) is related to variation in the temperature of the air (above versus below 32° F). The truth of the relationship is suggested by repeated observations. In the physical sciences, such relationships are called **laws** when they are accepted by almost all scientists. We find such explanations satisfactory because they allow us to predict what will happen in the future or to understand something that has happened regularly in the past. In the social sciences, associations are usually stated probabilistically: we say that two or more variables *tend* to be related in a predictable way, which means that there are usually some exceptions. For example, to explain why a society has a long postpartum sex taboo, we can point to the association (or correlation) that John Whiting found in a worldwide sample of societies: those societies with apparently low-protein diets tend to have long postpartum sex taboos.[2] We call the relationship between low protein and the sex taboo a **statistical association,** which means that the observed relationship is unlikely to be due to chance.

Even though laws and statistical associations explain by relating what is to be explained to other things, we want to know more—why those laws or associations exist. Why does water freeze at 32° F? Why do societies with low-protein diets tend to have long postpartum sex taboos? Therefore, scientists try to formulate theories that will explain the ob-

[1]Carl G. Hempel, *Aspects of Scientific Explanation* (New York: Free Press, 1965), p. 139.

[2]John W. M. Whiting, "Effects of Climate on Certain Cultural Practices," in Ward H. Goodenough, ed., *Explorations in Cultural Anthropology* (New York: McGraw-Hill, 1964), pp. 511–44.

served relationships (laws and statistical associations).[3]

Theories

Theories—explanations of laws and statistical associations—are more complicated than the observed relationships they are intended to explain. It is difficult to be very precise about what a theory is. By way of example, let us return to the question of why some societies have long postpartum sex taboos. We have already seen that a known statistical association can be used to help explain it: generally (but not always), if a society has a low-protein diet, it will have a long postpartum sex taboo. But most people would ask additional questions. Why does a low-protein diet explain the taboo? What is the mechanism by which a society with such a diet develops the custom of a long postpartum sex taboo? A theory is intended to answer such questions. In the chapter on the concept of culture, we briefly discussed John Whiting's theory that a long postpartum sex taboo may be an adaptation to certain conditions. Particularly in tropical areas, where the major food staples are low in protein, babies are vulnerable to the protein-deficiency disease called kwashiorkor. But if a baby could continue to nurse for a long time, it might have more of a chance to survive. The postpartum sex taboo might be adaptive, Whiting's theory suggests, because it increases the likelihood of a baby's survival. That is, if a mother puts off having another baby for a while, the first baby might have a better chance to survive because it can be fed mother's milk for a longer time. Whiting suggests that parents may be unconsciously or consciously aware that having another baby too soon might jeopardize the survival of the first baby, and so they might decide that it would be a good idea to abstain from intercourse for more than a year after the birth of the first baby.

As this example of a theory illustrates, there are differences between a theory and an association. A theory is more complicated, containing a series of statements. An association usually states quite simply that there is a relationship between two or a few measured variables. Another difference is that although a theory may mention some things that are observable (such as the presence of a long postpartum sex taboo), parts of it are difficult or impossible to observe directly. For example, with regard to Whiting's theory, it would be difficult to find out if people had deliberately or unconsciously decided to practice a long postpartum sex taboo because they recognized that babies would thereby have a better chance to survive. Then too, the concept of adaptation—that some characteristic promotes greater reproductive success—is difficult to verify because it is difficult to find out whether different individuals or groups have different rates of reproduction because they do or do not practice the supposedly adaptive custom. So, some concepts or implications in a theory are unobservable (at least at the present time) and only some aspects may be observable. In contrast, statistical associations or laws are based entirely on observations.[4]

Why Theories Cannot Be Proved

Many people think that the theories they learned in physics or chemistry classes have been proved. Unfortunately, many students get that impression because their teachers may present "lessons" in an authoritative manner. It is now generally agreed by scientists and philosophers of science that theories may have considerable evidence supporting them, but no theory can be said to be true. This is because many of the concepts and ideas in theories are not directly observable and therefore not directly verifiable. For example, scientists may try to explain how light behaves· by postulating that it consists of particles called *photons*. But we cannot observe photons even with the most powerful microscope. So, exactly what a photon looks like and exactly how it works remain in the realm of the unprovable. The photon is a **theoretical construct,** something that cannot be observed or verified directly. Since all theories contain such ideas, theories cannot be proved entirely or with absolute certainty.[5]

[3]Ernest Nagel, *The Structure of Science: Problems in the Logic of Scientific Explanation* (New York: Harcourt, Brace & World, 1961), pp. 88–89.

[4]Ibid., pp. 83–90.
[5]Ibid., p. 85. See also Garvin McCain and Erwin M. Segal, *The Game of Science*, 4th ed. (Monterey, CA: Brooks/Cole, 1982), pp. 75–79.

An atom, like a photon, cannot be observed. But there are theories about atoms and how they behave. Shown here is a model of what scientists think the beryllium atom looks like.

Why should we bother with theories, then, if we cannot prove that they are true? Perhaps the main advantage of a theory as a kind of explanation is that it may lead to new understanding or knowledge. A theory can suggest new relationships or imply new predictions that might be supported or confirmed by new research. For example, Whiting's theory about long postpartum sex taboos has a number of implications that could be investigated by future researchers. Because the theory discusses how a long postpartum sex taboo might be adaptive, we would expect that certain changes will result in the taboo's disappearance. For example, suppose people adopted either mechanical birth-control devices or began to give supplementary high-protein foods to babies. With birth control, a family could space births without abstaining from sex, so we would expect the custom of postpartum abstinence to disappear. So too, we would expect it to disappear with protein supplements for babies, because kwashiorkor would then be less likely to afflict the babies. Whiting's ideas might also prompt investigators to try to find out whether parents are consciously or unconsciously aware of the problem of close birth-spacing in areas with low protein supplies.

Although theories cannot be proved, they are rejectable. The method of **falsification** (which shows that a theory seems to be wrong) is the main way that theories are judged.[6] Scientists derive implications or predictions that should be true *if* the theory is correct. So, for example, Whiting predicted from his theory that societies with long postpartum sex taboos would be found more often in the tropics and that they would be likely to have low protein supplies. Such predictions of what might be found are called **hypotheses.** If the predictions turn out *not* to be correct, the researcher is obliged to conclude that there may be something wrong with the theory (or something wrong with the test of the theory). Those theories that are not falsified are accepted for the time being because the available evidence seems to be consistent with them. But remember that no matter how much the available evidence seems to support a theory, we can never be certain it is true. There is always the possibility that some implication of it, some hypothesis derivable from it, will not be confirmed in the future.

Generating Theories

In the previous chapter we discussed many of the theoretical orientations that have existed in cultural anthropology. Most of these orientations merely suggest where to look for answers to questions; they do not by themselves suggest particular explanations for particular phenomena. For example, an anthropologist with an ecological theoretical orientation is likely to say that some particular custom exists because it is or used to be adaptive. But exactly why a particular custom may be adaptive must still be specified; it is not automatically suggested by the theoretical orientation. Whiting's theory suggests specific conditions under which the long postpartum sex taboo might be adaptive. The theory does not just say that the taboo is adaptive. How, then, does an anthropologist develop an explanation or theory for some particular phenomenon?

It is difficult to specify any one procedure that is guaranteed to produce a theory, because developing a theory requires a creative act of imagination, and no discovery procedure by itself necessarily gener-

[6]McCain and Segal, *The Game of Science*, pp. 62–64.

ates this creative act. Too much dependence on a particular theoretical orientation may, in fact, be detrimental, since it may blind the investigator to other possibilities. A more important factor in generating a theory may be the investigator's belief that it is possible to do so. A person who believes that something is explainable will be more apt to notice possibly connected facts, as well as to recall possibly relevant considerations, and to put them all together in some explanatory way.

We *can* point to some procedures that have helped anthropologists produce explanations of cultural phenomena. These procedures seem to consist of two types; an anthropologist may be helped by analysis of a particular society in which he or she may have done fieldwork (we refer to this as *single-case analysis)*, or he or she may try to come up with a theory by a *comparative study* of more than one society.

In analyzing a single case, the anthropologist may be interested in explaining a particular custom. While in the field, he or she may ask informants why they practice (or think they practice) the custom. Sometimes such inquiries will elicit a plausible explanation. But more often than not, the informants may merely answer, "We have always done it that way." The investigator may then make a kind of mental search through other features of the society or its environment that may be connected with the custom. If possible, the anthropologist may try to view the situation historically, to see if the custom appeared more or less recently. If that is the case, what other possibly explanatory conditions appeared just prior to that time?

An anthropologist may also generate an explanation by comparing different societies that share this characteristic, in order to determine what other characteristics regularly occur along with it. Societies in which the characteristic is lacking would also be considered, because the possible cause of that characteristic should be absent in those societies. If the anthropologist discovers that a characteristic occurs regularly in different cultures along with certain other features, he or she may be reasonably certain that the possible causes of that characteristic have been narrowed down.

It must be remembered, however, that the investigator is not a computer. It is not necessary to search through all the characteristics that might be shared by different cultures. The investigator usually looks only at those traits that can plausibly be connected. Here is where an individual's theoretical orientation generally comes into play, since that orientation usually points to the possible importance of one particular set of factors over others.

Evidence: Testing Explanations

In any field of investigation, theories are generally the most plentiful commodity, apparently because of the human predisposition to try to make sense of the world. It is necessary, then, for us to have procedures that enable us to select from among the many available theories those that are more likely to be correct. "Just as mutations arise naturally but are not all beneficial, so hypotheses [theories] emerge naturally but are not all correct. If progress is to occur, therefore, we require a superfluity of hypotheses and also a mechanism of selection."[7] In other words, generating a theory or interpretation is not enough. We need some reliable method of testing whether or not that interpretation is likely to be correct. If an interpretation is not correct, it may detract from our efforts to achieve understanding by misleading us into thinking the problem is already solved.

The strategy of all kinds of testing in science is to predict what one would expect to find if a particular interpretation were correct, and then to conduct an investigation to see if the prediction is borne out. If the prediction is not borne out, the investigator is obliged to accept the possibility that the interpretation is wrong. If, however, the prediction holds true, then the investigator is entitled to say that there is evidence to support the theory. Thus, conducting research designed to test expectations derived from theory allows us to eliminate some interpretations and to accept others, at least tentatively.

Operationalization and Measurement

We test predictions derived from a theory to see if the theory may be correct, to see if it is consistent with observable events or conditions in the

[7] Peter Caws, "The Structure of Discovery," *Science*, December 12, 1969, p. 1378.

real world. A theory and the predictions derived from it are not useful if there is no way to measure the events or conditions mentioned in the predictions. If there is no way of relating the theory to observable events, it does not matter how good the theory sounds—it is still not a useful scientific theory.[8] To transform theoretical predictions into statements that might be verified, a researcher provides an **operational definition** of each of the concepts or variables mentioned in the prediction. An operational definition is a description of the procedure that is followed to measure the variable.[9]

Whiting predicted that societies with a low-protein diet would have a long postpartum sex taboo. Amount of protein in the diet is a variable: some societies have more, others have less. Length of the postpartum sex taboo is a variable; a society may have a short taboo or a long taboo. Whiting operationally defined the first variable, *amount of protein,* in terms of staple foods.[10] For example, if a society depended mostly on root and tree crops (such as cassava and bananas), Whiting rated the society as having low protein. If the society depended mostly on cereal crops (wheat, barley, corn, oats, and so on), he rated it as having moderate protein, because cereal crops have more protein by weight than root and tree crops. If the society depended mostly on hunting, fishing, or herding for food, he rated it as having high protein. The other variable in Whiting's prediction, *length of postpartum sex taboo,* was operationalized as follows: a society was rated as having a long taboo if couples customarily abstained from sex for more than a year after the birth of a baby; abstention for a year or less was considered a short taboo.

Specifying an operational definition for each variable is extremely important because it allows other investigators to check on a researcher's results.[11] Science depends on *replication,* or the repetition of results. It is only when many researchers observe a particular association that we call that association or relationship a law. Providing operational definitions is extremely important also because it allows others to evaluate whether a measure is appropriate. Only when we are told exactly

how something was measured can we judge whether the measure probably reflects what it is supposed to reflect. Specifying measures publically is so important in science that we are obliged to be skeptical of any conclusions offered by a researcher who fails to say how variables were measured.

To **measure** something is to say how it compares with other things on some scale of variation.[12] People often assume that a measuring device is always a physical instrument (such as a scale or a ruler), but physical devices are not necessary to measure something. Classification is also a form of measurement. When we classify persons as male or female, or employed versus unemployed, we are dividing them into sets. Deciding which set they belong to is a kind of measure because doing so allows us to compare them. We can also measure things by deciding which cases or examples have more or less of something (for instance, more or less protein in the diet). The measures employed in physical science are usually based on scales that allow us to assign numbers to each case: we may measure height in meters and weight in grams, for example. However we measure our variables, the fact that we *can* measure them means that we can test our hypotheses to see if the predicted relationships actually exist, at least most of the time.

Sampling

After an investigator decides how to measure the variables in some predicted relationship, he or she must decide how to select which cases to investigate to see if the predicted relationship holds. If the prediction is about the behavior of people, the sampling decision involves which people to observe. If the prediction is about an association between societal customs, the sampling decision involves which societies should be studied. Not only must investigators decide which cases to choose; they must also decide how many to choose. No researcher can investigate all the possible cases, so choices must be made. Some choices are better

[8]McCain and Segal, *The Game of Science,* p. 114.
[9]Ibid., pp. 56–57, 131–32.
[10]Whiting "Effects of Climate on Certain Cultural Practices," pp. 519–20.
[11]McCain and Segal, *The Game of Science,* pp. 67–69.

[12]Hubert M. Blalock, Jr., *Social Statistics,* 2nd ed. (New York: McGraw-Hill, 1972), pp. 15–20; and David H. Thomas, *Refiguring Anthropology: First Principles of Probability and Statistics* (Prospect Heights, IL: Waveland Press, 1986), pp. 18–28. See also Melvin Ember, "Taxonomy in Comparative Studies," in Raoul Naroll and Ronald Cohen, eds., *A Handbook of Method in Cultural Anthropology* (Garden City, NY: Natural History Press, 1970), pp. 701–3.

The Yanomamö Indians of Brazil depend mostly on root crops. The Boran herders of Kenya depend largely on milk and other products of their cattle and goats.

than others. In the chapter on the concept of culture, we talked about the advantages of random sampling. A random sample is one in which each case selected has had an equal chance to be included in the sample. Almost all statistical tests used to evaluate the results of research require random sampling, because only results based on a random sample can be assumed to be probably true for some larger set or universe of cases.

Before a researcher can sample randomly, he or she must specify the **sampling universe**—that is, the list of cases to be sampled from. Suppose an anthropologist is doing fieldwork in a society. Unless the society is very small, it is usually not practical to use the whole society as the sampling universe. Because most fieldworkers want to remain in a community for a considerable length of time, the community usually becomes the sampling universe. If a cross-cultural researcher wants to test an explanation, he or she needs to sample the world's societies. But we do not have descriptions of all the societies, past and present, that have existed in the world. So samples are usually drawn from published lists of described societies that have been classified or coded according to standard cultural variables,[13] or they are drawn from the Human Relations Area Files (HRAF), an indexed, annually growing collection of original ethnographic books and articles on more than 340 societies past and present around the world.[14]

Random sampling is still not employed that often in anthropology, but a nonrandom sample might still be fairly representative if the investigator has not personally chosen the cases for study. We should be particularly suspicious of any sample that may reflect the investigator's own biases or interests. For example, if an investigator picks only the people he or she is friendly with, the sample is suspicious. If cross-cultural researchers select sample societies because ethnographies on them happen to be on their own bookshelves, such samples are also suspicious. A sampling procedure should be designed to get a fair representation of the sampling universe, not a biased selection. If we want to increase our chances of getting a representative sample, we have to use a random-sampling procedure. To do so, we conventionally number the cases in the statistical universe and then use a table of random numbers to draw our sample cases.

Statistical Evaluation

When the researcher has measured the variables of interest for all the sample cases, he or she is ready to see if the predicted relationship actually exists in the data. Remember, the results may not turn out to be what the theory predicts. Sometimes the researcher constructs a *contingency table*, like that shown in Table 12–1, to see if the variables are associated as predicted. In Whiting's sample of 172 societies, each case is assigned to a box, or *cell*, in the table depending upon how the society is measured on the two variables of interest. For example, a society that has a long postpartum sex taboo and low protein is placed in the lowest right-hand cell. (In Whiting's sample—see Table 12–1—there are 27 such societies.) A society that has a short postpartum sex taboo and low protein is placed in the lowest left-hand cell. (There are 20 such societies in the sample.) The statistical question is: Does the way the cases are distributed in the six cells of the table support Whiting's prediction? If we looked just at the table, we might not

[13]For examples, see George P. Murdock, "Ethnographic Atlas: A Summary," *Ethnology*, 6 (1967): 109–236; and George P. Murdock and Douglas R. White, "Standard Cross-Cultural Sample," *Ethnology*, 8 (1969): 329–69.

[14]Sets of the HRAF in paper or microfiche format are found in almost 300 universities and research institutions around the world. For guides, see David Levinson, *Instructor's and Librarian's Guide to the HRAF Archive* (New Haven: Human Relations Area Files, 1988); and Carol R. Ember and Melvin Ember, *Guide to Cross-Cultural Research Using the HRAF Archive* (New Haven: Human Relations Area Files, 1988).

TABLE 12–1 Association between Availability of Protein and Duration of Postpartum Sex Taboo

Availability of Protein	Duration of Postpartum Sex Taboo		
	Short (0–1 Year)	Long (More Than 1 Year)	
High	47	15	62
Medium	38	25	63
Low	20	27	47
Totals	105	67	172

Adapted from Ward H. Goodenough, ed., *Explorations in Cultural Anthropology.* New York: McGraw-Hill, 1964, p.520.

know what to say. Many cases appear to be in the expected places. For example, most of the high-protein cases, 47 of 62, have short taboos, and most of the low-protein cases, 27 of 47, have long taboos. But there are also many exceptions (for example, 20 cases have low protein and a short taboo). So, although many cases appear to be in the expected places, there are also many exceptions. Do the exceptions invalidate the prediction? How many exceptions would compel us to reject the hypothesis? Here is where we resort to statistical *tests of significance.*

Statisticians have devised various tests that tell us how "perfect" a result has to be for us to believe that there is probably an association between the variables of interest, that one variable generally predicts the other. Essentially, every statistical result is evaluated in the same objective way. We ask: What is the chance that this result is purely accidental, that there is really no association at all between the two variables? Although some of the mathematical ways of answering this question are rather complicated, the answer always involves a **probability value** (or **p-value**)—the likelihood that the observed result or a stronger one could have occurred by chance. The statistical test used by Whiting gives a p-value of less than .01 (p <.01) for the observed result. In other words, there is less than 1 chance out of 100 that the relationship observed is purely accidental. A p-value of less than .01 is a fairly low probability; most social scientists conventionally agree to call any result with a p-value of .05 or less (5 or fewer chances out of 100) a **statistically significant** or probably true result. *When we describe relationships or associations in the rest of this book, we are almost always referring to results that have been found to be statistically significant.*

But why should a probably true relationship have any exceptions? If a theory is really correct, shouldn't *all* the cases fit? There are many reasons why we cannot ever expect a perfect result. First, even if a theory is correct (for example, if a low-protein diet really does favor the adoption of a long postpartum sex taboo), there may still be other causes that we have not investigated. Some of the societies could have a long taboo even though they have high protein. For example, societies that depend mostly on hunting for their food (and that would therefore be classified as having a high-protein diet) may have a problem carrying infants from one campsite to another and may practice a long postpartum sex taboo so that two infants will not have to be carried at the same time. Exceptions to the predicted relationship might also occur because of *cultural lag.*[15] Suppose that a society recently changed crops and is now no longer a low-protein society but still practices the taboo. This society would be an exception to the predicted relationship, but it might fit the theory if it stopped practicing the taboo in a few years. Measurement inaccuracy is another source of exceptions. Whiting's measure of protein, which is based on the major sources of food, is not a very precise measure of protein in the diet. It does not take into account the possibility that a "tree-crop" society might get a lot of protein from fishing or raising pigs. So it might turn out that some supposedly low-protein societies have been misclassified, which may be one reason there are 20 cases in the lowest cell in the left-hand column of Table 12–1. Measurement error usually produces exceptions.

Significant statistical associations that are predictable from a theory offer tentative support for the theory. But much more is needed before we can be fairly confident about the theory. Replication is needed to confirm whether the predictions can be reproduced by other researchers using other samples. Other predictions should be derived from the theory to see if they too are supported. The theory should be pitted against alternative explanations to see which theory works better. We may have to combine theories if the alternative explanations also predict the relationship in question. The research process in science thus requires time and patience. Perhaps most important, it requires that researchers be humble. No matter how wonderful one's own theory seems, it is important to acknowledge that it may be wrong. If we don't acknowledge that possibility, we can't be motivated to test our theories. If we don't test our theories, we can never tell the difference between a better or worse theory, and we will be saddled forever with our present ignorance. In science, knowledge or understanding is explained variation. And so, if

---

[15]Cultural lag occurs when change in one aspect of culture takes time to produce change in another aspect. For the original definition of this concept, see William F. Ogburn, *Social Change* (New York: Huebsch, 1922), pp. 200–80.

TABLE 12–2 Types of Research in Cultural Anthropology

	SINGLE SOCIETY	REGION	WORLDWIDE SAMPLE
Nonhistorical	Ethnography	Controlled comparison	Cross-cultural research
Historical	Ethnohistory	Controlled comparison	Cross-historical research

we want to understand more, we have to keep testing our beliefs against sets of objective evidence that could falsify our beliefs.

Types of Research in Cultural Anthropology

Cultural anthropologists use several different methods to conduct research. Each has certain advantages and disadvantages in generating and testing explanations. The types of research in cultural anthropology can be classified according to two criteria. One is the *spatial* scope of the study (analysis of a single society, analysis of a number of societies in a region, or analysis of a worldwide sample of societies). The other criterion is the *temporal* scope of the study (historical versus nonhistorical). The combination of these criteria is shown in Table 12–2, which identifies each of the major types of research in cultural anthropology.

Ethnography

Around the beginning of the twentieth century, anthropologists realized that if they were to produce anything of scientific value, they would have to study their subject in the same way that other scientists studied theirs: by systematic observation. To describe cultures more accurately, they started to live among the people they were studying. They observed, and even took part in, the important events of those societies and carefully questioned a number of the people about their native customs. In other words, anthropologists began to do fieldwork.

Fieldwork is the cornerstone of modern anthropology. It is the means by which most anthropological information is obtained. After doing fieldwork, an anthropologist may prepare an *ethnography*—a description and analysis of a single society. Ethnographies and ethnographic articles on particular topics provide much of the essential data for all kinds of studies in cultural anthropology. To make a comparison of societies in a given region, or worldwide, an anthropologist would require ethnographic data on many societies.

With regard to the goal of generating theory, ethnography, with its in-depth, first-hand, long-term observation, provides an investigator with a wealth of descriptive material covering a wide range of phenomena. Thus, it may stimulate interpretations about the way different aspects of the culture are related to each other and to features of the environment. The ethnographer in the field has the opportunity to get to know the context of a society's customs by directly asking the people about those customs and by observing the phenomena that appear to be associated with those practices. In addition, the ethnographer who develops a possible explanation for some custom can test that hunch by collecting new information related to it. In this sense, the ethnographer is similar to a physician who is trying to understand why a patient has certain symptoms of illness.

Although ethnography is extremely useful for generating explanations, used alone it does not generally provide sufficient data to test a hypothesis. For example, an ethnographer may think that a particular society practices *polygyny* (one man married to two or more women simultaneously) because it has more women than men. But the ethnographer could not be reasonably sure that this explanation was correct unless the results of a comparative study of a sample of societies showed that most polygynous societies have more women than men. After all, the fact that one society has both these conditions could be an historical accident rather than a result of some necessary connection between the two conditions.

Nonhistorical Controlled Comparison

In a nonhistorical controlled comparison, the anthropologist compares ethnographic information obtained from a number of societies found in a particular region—societies that presumably have

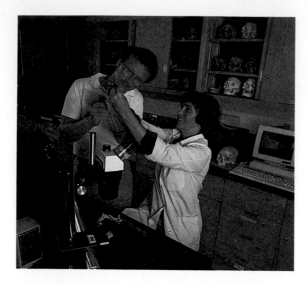

Cross-cultural researchers are not the only anthropologists who use computers for statistical analysis. Physical anthropologists Randall White and Jean de Rousseau (here examining a Neandertal jawbone) also use computers in their research.

similar histories and occupy similar environments. The anthropologist who conducts a regional comparison is apt to be familiar with the complex of cultural features associated with that region. These features may provide a good understanding of the context of the phenomenon that is to be explained. However, an anthropologist's knowledge of the region under study is probably not as great as the ethnographer's knowledge of a single society. Still, the anthropologist's understanding of local details is greater in a regional comparison than in a worldwide comparison. The worldwide comparison is necessarily so broad that the investigator is unlikely to know a great deal about any of the societies being compared.

The regional controlled comparison is useful not only for generating explanations but also for testing them. Since the anthropologist has a number of societies to compare—and since some of the societies will have the characteristic that is to be explained and some will not—he or she can determine if the conditions hypothesized to be related are in fact related, at least in that region. However, we must remember that two or more conditions may be related in one region for reasons peculiar to that region. Therefore, an explanation supported in one region may not pertain in others.

Cross-Cultural Research

Anthropologists can generate interpretations on the basis of worldwide comparisons by looking for differences between those societies having, and those lacking, a particular characteristic. However, the most common use of worldwide comparisons has probably been to test explanations. The cross-cultural researcher first identifies conditions that should generally be associated if a particular theory is correct. Then he or she looks at a worldwide sample of societies to see if the expected association generally holds true. The advantage of cross-cultural research is that the conclusion drawn from it is probably applicable to most societies, *if* the sample used for testing has been more or less randomly selected. In other words, in contrast with the results of a regional comparison, which may or may not be applicable to other regions, the results of a cross-cultural study are presumably applicable to most societies and most regions.

As we have noted, the greater the number of societies examined in a study, the less likely it is that the investigator will have detailed knowledge of the societies involved. So if a cross-cultural test does not support a particular explanation, the investigator may not know enough about the sample societies to know how to modify the interpretation or come up with a new one. In this situation, the anthropologist may reexamine the details of one or more particular societies in order to stimulate fresh thinking on the subject. Another limitation of cross-cultural research, as a means both of generating and of testing explanations, is that only those explanations for which the required information is generally available in ethnographies can be tested. An investigator interested in explaining something that has not been generally described must resort to some other research strategy to collect data.

Historical Research

Ethnohistory consists of studies based on descriptive materials about a single society at more than one point in time. It provides the essential data for historical studies of all types, just as ethnography provides the essential data for all nonhistorical types of research. Ethnohistorical data may consist of sources other than the ethnographic reports prepared by anthropologists—accounts by explorers, missionaries, traders, and government officials.

In terms of generating and testing hypotheses, studies of single societies over time tend to be subject to the same limitations as studies of single societies confined to a single period. Like their non-historical counterparts, studies that concentrate on a single society observed through time are likely to generate a number of hypotheses, but they do not generally provide the opportunity to establish with reasonable certainty which of those hypotheses is correct. Cross-cultural historical studies (of which we have only a few examples thus far) suffer from the opposite limitation. They provide ample means of testing hypotheses through comparison, but they are severely constrained (because of the necessity of working with secondhand data) in their ability to generate hypotheses derived from the available data.

However, there is one advantage to historical studies of any type. The goal of theory in cultural anthropology is to explain variation in cultural patterns. This means specifying what conditions will favor one cultural pattern rather than another. Such specification requires us to assume that the supposed causal or favoring conditions antedated the pattern to be explained. Theories or explanations, then, imply a *sequence* of changes over time, which are the stuff of history. Therefore, if we want to come closer to an understanding of the reasons for the cultural variations we are interested in, we should examine historical sequences. These will help us determine whether the conditions we think caused various phenomena truly antedated those phenomena and thus might more reliably be said to have caused them. If we can examine historical sequences, we may be able to make sure that we do not put the cart before the horse.

The major impediment to historical research is that collecting and analyzing historical data—particularly when they come from the scattered accounts of explorers, missionaries, and traders—is a tedious and exasperating task. It may be more efficient to test explanations nonhistorically first, in order to eliminate some interpretations. Only when an interpretation survives a nonhistorical test should we look to historical data to test the presumed sequence.

In the chapters that follow, we discuss not only what we strongly suspect about the determinants of cultural variation, but also what we do not know or only dimly suspect. We devote a lot of our discussion to what we do not know—what has not yet been the subject of research that tests hypotheses and theories—because we want to convey a sense of what cultural anthropology might learn in the future.

SUMMARY

1. As important as accurate description is, it is not the ultimate goal of anthropology. Anthropologists want to understand—to know *why* people have certain traits or customs, not just that they *do* have them.

2. In science, to understand is to explain. Scientists try to achieve two kinds of explanation—associations (observed relationships between two or more variables) and theories (explanations of associations).

3. A theory is more complicated than an association. Some concepts or implications in a theory are unobservable; an association is based entirely on observations.

4. Theories can never be proved with absolute certainty. There is always the possibility that some implication, some derivable hypothesis, will not be confirmed by future research.

5. But a theory is rejectable through the method of falsification. Scientists derive predictions that should be true *if* the theory is correct. If the predictions turn out to be incorrect, scientists are obliged to conclude that there may be something wrong with the theory.

6. To make a satisfactory test, we have to specify operationally how we measure the variables involved in the relationships we expect to exist, so that other researchers can try to replicate, or repeat, our results.

7. Tests of predictions should employ samples that are representative. The most objective way to obtain a representative sample is to select the sample cases randomly.

8. The results of tests are evaluated by statistical methods that assign probability values to the results. These values allow us to distinguish between probably true and probably accidental results.

9. Cultural anthropologists use several different methods to conduct research. Each has certain advantages and disadvantages in generating and testing explanations. The types of research in cultural anthropology can be classified according to two criteria: (1) the spatial scope of the study (analysis of a single society, analysis of a number of societies in a region, or analysis of a worldwide sample of societies); and (2) the temporal scope of the study (historical versus nonhistorical). The basic research methods, then, are ethnography and ethnohistory, historical and nonhistorical controlled comparisons, and historical and nonhistorical cross-cultural research.

SUGGESTED READING

BERNARD, H. R. *Research Methods in Cultural Anthropology.* Newbury Park, CA: Sage Publications, 1988. Proceeding step by step through the research process, this book surveys how to prepare for a field study and how to collect and analyze the data produced.

"Cross-Cultural and Comparative Research: Theory and Method." *Behavior Science Research* 25 (1991):1–270. This special issue provides an extensive "state of the art" coverage of the goals, achievements, and problems in cross-cultural and comparative research.

JOHNSON, A. W. *Quantification in Cultural Anthropology: An Introduction to Research Design.* Stanford, CA: Stanford University Press, 1978. A wide-ranging discussion of studies in cultural anthropology that illustrate the various advantages of counting and measurement.

McCAIN, G., AND SEGAL, E. M. *The Game of Science,* 4th ed. Monterey, CA: Brooks/Cole, 1982. A very readable book about how scientists do research. The authors emphasize that science is a game we play against our own ignorance.

PELTO, P. J., AND PELTO, G. H. *Anthropological Research: The Structure of Inquiry,* 2nd ed. New York: Cambridge University Press, 1978. An introduction to the collection of reliable data in cultural anthropology. Techniques of observation and measurement are emphasized. A bibliography for further study accompanies each chapter.

THOMAS, D. H. *Refiguring Anthropology: First Principles of Probability and Statistics.* Prospect Heights, IL: Waveland Press, 1986. The first textbook on statistical methods for anthropology. Other introductory texts on statistics cover many of the same topics, but this textbook is the first one that refers mainly to anthropological studies for examples.

WERNER, D. *Amazon Journey: An Anthropologist's Year among Brazil's Mekranoti Indians.* New York: Simon & Schuster, 1984. A personal ethnography that conveys some of the problems and pleasures of collecting data in the field to test hypotheses.

13
Language
and Culture

F ew of us can remember the moment when we first became aware that words signified something. Yet that moment was a milestone for us, not just in the acquisition of language but in becoming acquainted with all the complex, elaborate behavior that constitutes our culture. Without language, the transmission of complex traditions would be virtually impossible, and each person would be trapped within his or her own world of private sensations.

Helen Keller, left deaf and blind by illness at the age of nineteen months, gives a moving account of the afternoon she first established contact with another human being through words.

[My teacher] brought me my hat, and I knew I was going out into the warm sunshine. This thought, if a wordless sensation may be called a thought, made me hop and skip with pleasure.

We walked down the path to the well house, attracted by the fragrance of the honeysuckle with which it was covered. Someone was drawing water and my teacher placed my hand under the spout. As the cool stream gushed over one hand she spelled into the other the word *water*, first slowly, then rapidly. Suddenly I felt a misty consciousness as of something forgotten—a thrill of returning thought; and somehow the mystery of language was revealed to me. I knew then that w-a-t-e-r meant the wonderful cool something that was flowing over my hand. That living word awakened my soul, gave it light, hope, joy, set it free! There were barriers still, it is true, barriers that could in time be swept away.

I left the well house eager to learn. Everything had a name, and each name gave birth to a new thought. As we returned to the house every object which I touched seemed to quiver with life. That was because I saw everything with the strange, new sight that had come to me.[1]

Communication

Against all odds, Helen Keller had come to understand the essential function language plays in all societies—namely, that of communication. The word *communicate* comes from the Latin verb *communicare*, "to share," "to impart that which is common." We communicate by agreeing, consciously or unconsciously, to call an object, a movement, or an abstract concept by a common name. For example, speakers of English have agreed to call the color of grass green, even though we have no way of comparing precisely how two persons actually experience this color. What we share is the agreement to call this sensation *green*. Any system of language consists of publicly accepted symbols by which individuals try to share private experiences.

Our communication obviously is not limited to spoken language. We communicate directly through body stance, gesture, and tone of voice; indirectly through systems of signs and symbols, such as writing, algebraic equations, musical scores, painting, code flags, and road signs. But despite all the competing systems of communication available to us, we must recognize the overriding importance of spoken language. It is probably the major transmitter of culture, allowing us to share and pass on our complex configuration of attitudes, beliefs, and patterns of behavior.

Animal Communication

Systems of communication are not unique to human beings. Other animal species communicate in a variety of ways. One way is by sound: a bird may communicate by a call that a territory is his and should not be encroached upon; a squirrel may utter a cry that leads other squirrels to flee from danger. Another means of animal communication is odor. An ant releases a chemical when it dies, and its fellows then carry it away to the compost heap. Apparently the communication is highly effective; a healthy ant painted with the death chemical will be dragged to the funeral heap again and again.

Another means of communication, body movement, is used by bees to convey the location of food sources. Karl von Frisch discovered that the black Austrian honeybee—by choosing a round dance, a wagging dance, or a short, straight run—could communicate not only the precise direction of the source of food, but also its distance from the hive.[2]

Although primates use all three methods of communication—sound, odor, and body movement—sound is the method that most concerns us

[1]Helen Keller, *The Story of My Life* (New York: Dell, 1974 [originally published in 1902]), p. 34.

[2]K. von Frisch, "Dialects in the Language of the Bees," *Scientific American*, August 1962, pp. 78–87.

in this chapter because spoken language is our own major means of communication. Nonhuman primates communicate vocally too, making various kinds of calls (but not very many of them). In the past only human communication was thought to be symbolic. Recent research suggests that some monkey and ape calls in the wild are also symbolic.

When we say that a communication (call, word, sentence) is *symbolic,* we mean at least two things. First, the communication has meaning even when its referent (whatever is referred to) is not present. Second, the meaning is arbitrary: the receiver of the message could not guess its meaning just from the sound(s) and does not know the meaning instinctively. In other words, symbols have to be learned. There is no compelling or "natural" reason that the word *dog* in English should refer to a smallish four-legged carnivore that is the bane of letter carriers.

Scientists who have observed vervet monkeys in the wild consider at least three of their alarm calls to be symbolic because each of them *means* (refers to) a different kind of predator—eagles, pythons, leopards—and monkeys react differently to each call. Experimentally, in the absence of the referent, investigators have been able to evoke the normal reaction to a call by playing it back electronically. Another indication that the vervet alarm calls are symbolic is that infant vervets appear to need some time to learn the referent for each. When they are very young, infants apply a particular call to more animals than adult vervets apply the call to. So, for example, infant vervets will often make the "eagle" warning call when they see any flying bird. The infants learn the appropriate referent apparently through adult vervets' repetition of infants' "correct" calls; in any case, the infants gradually learn to restrict the call to eagles. This process is probably not too different from the way a North American infant first applies the "word" *dada* to all adult males and gradually learns to restrict it to one person.[3]

It is widely believed that the calls of nonhuman primates mostly communicate affect (feeling), as in the chimpanzee's grunt when it finds a pre-

As trainer Joyce Butler signs "Nim" (the chimp's name), Nim signs "me."

ferred food.[4] But Peter Marler suggests that the difference between "affective" and "symbolic" calls in nonhuman primates may be more a matter of degree than of kind. Researchers seem to consider a call affective when a large class of things is referred to. For example, one vervet call seems to be triggered by seeing any of a number of possible predators, and the call may therefore be translated as "Be alert!" But a call tends to be labeled symbolic when a smaller set of referents (for example, eagles) is referred to.[5]

All of the nonhuman vocalizations we have described so far enable individual animals to convey messages. The sender gives a signal that is received and "decoded" by the receiver, who usually responds with a specific action or reply. How is human vocalization different? Since monkeys and apes appear to use symbols at least some of the time, it is not appropriate to emphasize symbolism as the distinctive feature of human language. However, there is a significant quantitative difference between human language and other primates' systems of vocal communication—all human languages employ a much larger set of symbols. Another and perhaps more important difference is that the other primates' vocal systems tend to be *closed:* different calls are not often combined to produce new, meaningful utterances. In contrast,

[3]Robert M. Seyfarth and Dorothy L. Cheney, "How Monkeys See the World: A Review of Recent Research on East African Vervet Monkeys," in Charles T. Snowdon, Charles H. Brown, and Michael R. Petersen, eds., *Primate Communication* (New York: Cambridge University Press, 1982), pp. 242, 246.

[4]Peter Marler, "Primate Vocalization: Affective or Symbolic?" in Thomas A. Sebeok and Jean Umiker-Sebeok, eds., *Speaking of Apes: A Critical Anthology of Two-Way Communication with Man* (New York: Plenum, 1980), pp. 221–22.

[5]Ibid., pp. 223, 229.

Irene Pepperberg's parrot, which mimics her here, can also understand and speak to the symbolic meaning of questions in English.

as we shall see, human languages are *open* systems, governed by complex rules about how sounds and sequences of sounds can be combined to produce an infinite variety of new meanings.

The idea that humans can transmit many more complex messages than any other animal does not begin to convey how different human language is from other communication systems. No chimp could say the equivalent of "I'm going to the ball game next Wednesday with my friend Jim if it's not raining." Not only can humans talk (and think) with language about things completely out of context; they can also be deliberately or unconsciously ambiguous in their messages. If a person asks you for help, you could say, "Sure, I'll do it when I have time," leaving the other person uncertain about whether your help is ever going to materialize. We can even convey a meaning that is opposite what we actually say, as when we say "What a great day!" after looking out the window and seeing a street full of slush.

Primates in the wild do not exhibit anything close to human language. But recent attempts to teach human-created nonspoken languages to apes have led some scholars to question the traditional assumption that the gap between human and other animal communication is enormous. If chimpanzees and gorillas have the capacity to *use* language, then the difference between humans and nonhumans may not be as great as people used to think.

In 1967, Adriaan Kortlandt reported that chimpanzees in the wild used hand gestures that he interpreted to mean "Come with me." "May I

pass?" "You are welcome," "Stop!" and "Be off!" among others.[6] Since then, researchers have had considerable success teaching chimpanzees gestures to represent concepts. Allen and Beatrice Gardner succeeded in teaching American Sign Language (ASL) to a chimpanzee named Washoe. The amazing extent of Washoe's ability to use the 150 signs she had learned was recorded when she was with other chimpanzees on an island and noticed that the humans across the water were drinking iced tea.

She kept signing, "Roger ride come gimme sweet eat please hurry hurry you come please gimme sweet you hurry you come ride Roger come give Washoe fruit drink hurry hurry fruit drink please." . . . A plane flew over just then, and Washoe mentioned that, too. She signed, "You me ride in plane."[7]

Subsequent work with other chimpanzees suggests that chimpanzees can use other kinds of nonverbal symbols besides ASL gestures to form sentences and communicate their needs. Sarah was taught to use differently shaped and colored pieces of plastic, each representing a word (she had a vocabulary of about 130 words).[8] Lana was taught to use computer-controlled equipment, by pressing keys on a console to make sentences; she even showed when those sentences were complete by pressing a key that meant *period*.[9] And recently a pygmy chimpanzee named Kanzi has used 200 geometric symbols on a keyboard combined with gestures to make what Sue Savage-Rumbaugh and Patricia Marks Greenfield describe as sentences with rudimentary grammar. Kanzi also understands spoken English.[10]

[6]Reported in Emily Hahn, "Chimpanzees and Language," *New Yorker*, April 24, 1971, p. 54.

[7]Ibid., p. 98. For a more complete description of the Washoe project, see R. Allen Gardner and Beatrice B. Gardner, "Comparative Psychology and Language Acquisition," in Sebeok and Umiker-Sebeok, eds., *Speaking of Apes*, pp. 287–330.

[8]Ann James Premack and David Premack, "Teaching Language to an Ape," *Scientific American*, October 1972, pp. 92–99.

[9]Duane M. Rumbaugh, Timothy V. Gill, and E. C. von Glasersfeld, "Reading and Sentence Completion by a Chimpanzee (Pan)," *Science*, November 16, 1973, pp. 731–33.

[10]Reported in Ann Gibbons, "Déjà Vu All Over Again: Chimp-Language Wars," *Science*, March 29, 1991, pp. 1561–62.

"The thing to bear in mind, gentlemen, is not just that Daisy has mastered a rudimentary sign language, but that she can link these signs together to express meaningful abstract concepts." *(Drawing by Lorenz; © 1974 The New Yorker Magazine, Inc.)*

Are these apes really using language? The answer to this question is still quite controversial.[11] Even though ASL is accepted by many as a genuine language, meaning that its "speakers" can express anything a spoken language can, the apes have mastered only a small portion of ASL vocabulary or other vocabularies.[12] And although it is clear that Washoe and the other apes can string a series of signs together, critics question whether the apes are combining the signs in the kind of rule-governed way humans create sentences. However, the new work with the pygmy chimpanzee Kanzi suggests that the combinations of signs are not simply taught—Kanzi seems to invent new rules on his own.

There is a lot more agreement among investigators that nonhuman primates have the ability to "symbol"—to refer to something (or a class of things) with an arbitrary "label" (gesture or sequence of sounds).[13] For example, a female gorilla named Koko (with a repertoire of about 375 signs) extended the sign for *drinking straw* to plastic tubing, hoses, cigarettes, and radio antennae. Washoe originally learned the sign *dirty* to refer to feces and other soil, and then began to use it insultingly, as in "dirty Roger," when her trainer Roger Fouts refused to give her things she wanted. Even the mistakes made by the apes suggest that they are using signs symbolically, just as words are used in spoken language. For example, the sign *cat* may be used for dog if the animal has learned *cat* first (just as our daughter Kathy said "dog" to all pictures of four-footed animals, including elephants, when she was eighteen months old).

Thus the symbolic capacity of apes may be very much like that of young humans. How large a language capacity apes can acquire is still an open question, subject to the outcome of continuing research. But as Jane Hill notes, the results of the research thus far strongly refute the traditional claim

[11]For much of the controversy on this issue, see various chapters in Sebeok and Umiker-Sebeok, eds., *Speaking of Apes* and Gibbons, "Déjà Vu All Over Again."

[12]Jane H. Hill, "Apes and Language," *Annual Review of Anthropology,* 7 (1978): 94.

[13]Ibid., p. 98.

that language is an all-or-none thing confined to humans.[14]

We have known that parrots can mimic human speech. But the fact that a parrot named Alex has learned to understand spoken sentences and reply appropriately to questions about quantities and colors suggests that even a bird-brain is not too small to be capable of symbolic communication. How else can we explain Alex's mostly correct counts (80 percent of the time) of "two," "three," "four," "five," and "sih" (six) new objects he is asked to give the number of?[15]

The Origins of Language

How long humans have had spoken language is not known. Recently, Philip Lieberman and Jeffrey Laitman have argued that language as we know it developed only with the emergence of modern-looking humans (before or about 100,000 years ago) who had the mouth and throat anatomy we have.[16] According to Lieberman and Laitman, premodern humans (including the Neandertals) did not have the vocal anatomy required for language. Their argument is based on controversial reconstructions of the mouths and throats of earlier humans, and so their conclusions are not widely accepted.[17]

Most speculation about the origins of language has centered in the question of how natural selection may have favored the open quality of language. All known human languages are open in the sense that utterances can be combined in various ways to produce new meanings.[18] Somehow a call system of communication was eventually changed to a system based on small units of sound that could be put together in many different ways

to form meaningful utterances. For example, an English speaker can combine *care* and *full (careful)* to mean one thing, then use each of the two elements in other combinations to mean different things. *Care* can be used to make *carefree, careless,* or *caretaker; full* can be used to make *powerful* or *wonderful.* And since language is a system of shared symbols, it can be reformed into an infinite variety of expressions and be understood by all who share these symbols. In this way, for example, T. S. Eliot could form a sentence never before formed, "In the room the women come and go talking of Michelangelo,"[19] and the sense of his sentence, though not necessarily his private meaning, could be understood by all speakers of English.

One set of theoreticians of grammar suggests that there may be a *language-acquisition device* in the brain, as innate to humans as call systems are to the other animals.[20] As the forebrain evolved, this device may have become part of our biological inheritance. Whether the device in fact exists is not yet clear. But we know that the actual development of individual language is not completely biologically determined; if it were, all human beings would speak the same brain-generated language. Instead, about 4,000 to 5,000 mutually unintelligible languages have been identified. More than 2,000 of them are still spoken today, most by peoples who did not traditionally have a system of writing. Indeed, the earliest writing systems are not that old; they appear only about 5,000 years ago.[21]

Can we learn anything about the origins of language by studying the languages of simpler societies? The answer is no, because such languages are not simpler or less developed than ours. Intuitively, we might suppose that languages of nonliterate peoples or peoples without writing would be much less developed than languages spoken by technologically advanced, literate societies. But this is in no sense true. The sound systems, vocab-

---

[14]Ibid., p. 105.

[15]Irene M. Pepperberg, "Referential Communication with an African Grey Parrot," Newsletter, Harvard Graduate Society, Spring 1991, pp. 1–4.

[16]Philip Lieberman, *Uniquely Human: The Evolution of Speech, Thought, and Selfless Behavior* (Cambridge, MA: Harvard University Press, 1991), pp. 109–10; and Jeffrey Laitman, "The Anatomy of Human Speech," *Natural History,* August 1984, pp. 20–27.

[17]Ronald C. Carlisle and Michael I. Siegel, "Additional Comments on Problems in the Interpretation of Neanderthal Speech Capabilities," *American Anthropologist,* 80 (1978): 367–72.

[18]C. F. Hockett and R. Ascher, "The Human Revolution," *Current Anthropology,* 5 (1964): 135–68.

[19]T. S. Eliot, "The Love Song of J. Alfred Prufrock," in *Collected Poems, 1909–1962* (New York: Harcourt, Brace & World, 1963).

[20]See Noam Chomsky, *Reflections on Language* (New York: Pantheon, 1975).

[21]Wayne M. Senner, "Theories and Myths on the Origins of Writing: A Historical Overview," in Wayne M. Senner, ed., *The Origins of Writing* (Lincoln, NE: University of Nebraska Press, 1989), pp. 1–26.

ularies, and grammars of technologically simpler peoples are in no way inferior to those of more complex societies.[22]

Of course, Australian aborigines will not be able to name the sophisticated machines used in our society. Their language, however, has the potential for doing so. As we will see later in this chapter, all languages possess the amount of vocabulary their speakers need, and languages expand in response to cultural changes. Moreover, the language of a technologically simple people, though lacking terminology for some of our conveniences, may have a rich vocabulary for events or natural phenomena that are of particular importance to that society.

If there are no primitive languages, and if the earliest languages have left no traces that would allow us to reconstruct them, does that mean we cannot investigate the origins of language? Some linguists think that understanding the way children acquire language, which we discuss shortly, can help us understand the origins of language. Recently, other linguists have suggested that an understanding of how *creole languages* develop will also tell us something about the origins of language.

Creole Languages. Some languages have developed quite recently in various places around the world where European colonial powers established commercial enterprises that relied on imported labor, generally slaves. The laborers in one place often came from several different societies, and in the beginning would speak with their masters and with each other in some kind of *pidgin* (simplified) version of the masters' language. Pidgin languages lack many of the building blocks found in the languages of whole societies, building blocks such as prepositions (*to, on,* and so forth) and auxiliary verbs (designating future and other tenses). Many pidgin languages developed into and were replaced by so-called creole languages, which incorporate much of the vocabulary of the masters' language but also have a grammar that differs from it and from the grammars of the laborers' native languages.[23]

Derek Bickerton argues that there are striking grammatical similarities in creole languages all over the world. This, he argues, is consistent with the idea that there is a universal grammar inherited by all humans. Creoles therefore may resemble early human languages. All creoles use intonation (changing the pitch of the voice) instead of a change in word order to ask a question: "You can fix this?" in contrast with "Can you fix this?" They all express the future and the past in the same grammatical way, by the use of particles (such as the English *shall*) between subject and verb, and they all employ double negatives, as in the Guyana English creole "Nobody no like me."[24]

Children's Acquisition of Language

Apparently a child is equipped from birth with the capacity to reproduce all the sounds used by the world's languages and to learn any system of grammar. The language the child learns is the one spoken by his or her parents or caretakers.

The child's acquisition of the structure and meaning of language has been called the most difficult intellectual achievement in life. If that is so, it is pleasing to note that he or she accomplishes it with relative ease and vast enjoyment. This "difficult intellectual achievement" may in reality be a natural response to the capacity for language that is one of humans' genetic characteristics. All over the world children begin to learn language at about the same age—and in no culture do children wait until they are seven or ten years old. By twelve or thirteen months children are able to name a few objects and actions and by 18 to 20 months they seem able to make one key word stand for a whole sentence: "Out!" for "Take me out for a walk right now"; "Juice!" for "I want some juice now." Evidence now suggests that children seem to acquire the concept of a word as a whole, learning sequences of sounds that are stressed or at the ends of grown-up words (for example, "raffe" for giraffe). Even deaf children learning signs in ASL

[22]Franklin C. Southworth and Chandler J. Daswani, *Foundations of Linguistics* (New York: Free Press, 1974), p. 312. See also Franz Boas, "On Grammatical Categories," in Dell Hymes, ed., *Language in Culture and Society: A Reader in Linguistics and Anthropology* (New York: Harper & Row, Publishers, 1964 [originally published in 1911]), pp. 121–23.

[23]Derek Bickerton, "Creole Languages," *Scientific American*, July 1983, pp. 116–22.
[24]Ibid., p. 122.

Toward the end of their first year, babies begin to name a few objects and actions.

tend to acquire and use signs in a similar fashion.[25]

Children the world over tend to progress to two-word sentences at the age of about eighteen to twenty-four months. In those sentences they express themselves in "telegraph" form—using noun-like words and verblike or function words but leaving out the seemingly less important words. So a two-word sentence such as "Shoes off" may stand for "Take my shoes off" or "More milk" may stand for "Give me more milk please."[26] They do not utter their two words in random order, sometimes saying "off" first, other times saying "shoes" first. If a child says "shoes off" then he or she will also say "clothes off" and "hat off." They seem to select an order that fits the conventions of adult language, so they are likely to say "Daddy eat," not "Eat Daddy." In other words, they tend to put the subject first, as adults do. And they tend to say "Mommy coat" rather than "Coat Mommy" to indicate "Mommy's coat."[27] Since parents do not utter sentences such as "Daddy eat," children seem to know a lot about how to put words together with little or no direct teaching from their parents. Consider the five-year-old who, confronted with the unfamiliar "Gloria in Excelsis," sang quite happily, "Gloria eats eggshells." To make the words fit the structure of English grammar was more important than to make the words fit the meaning of the Christmas pageant.

If there is a basic grammar imprinted in the human mind, we should not be surprised that children's early and later speech patterns seem to be similar across langues. We might also expect children's later speech to be similar to the structure of creole languages. And it is, according to Derek Bickerton.[28] The "errors" children make in speaking are consistent with the grammar of creoles. For example, English-speaking children three to four years old tend to ask questions by intonation alone, and they tend to use double negatives such as "I don't see no dog," even though the grown-ups around them do not speak that way and consider the children's speech "wrong."

Future research on children's acquisition of language and on the structure of creole languages may bring us closer to understanding the origins of human language. But even if there is a universal grammar, we still need to understand how and why the thousands of languages in the world vary—which brings us to the conceptual tools linguists have had to invent in order to study languages.

Structural Linguistics

In every society children do not need to be taught "grammar" to learn how to speak. They begin to grasp the essential structure of their language at a very early age, without direct instruction. If you show English-speaking children a picture of one "gork" and then a picture of two of these creatures, they will say there are two "gorks." They somehow know that adding an *s* to a noun

[25]Lila R. Gleitman and Eric Wanner, "Language Acquisition: The State of the State of the Art," in Eric Wanner and Lila R. Gleitman, eds., *Language Acquisition: The State of the Art* (Cambridge: Cambridge University Press, 1982), pp. 3–48; Ben G. Blount, "The Development of Language in Children," in Ruth H. Munroe, Robert L. Munroe, and Beatrice B. Whiting, *Handbook of Cross-Cultural Human Development* (New York: Garland, 1981), pp. 379–402.

[26]Roger Brown, "The First Sentence of Child and Chimpanzee," in Sebeok and Umiker-Sebeok, eds., *Speaking of Apes*, pp. 93–94.

[27]Peter A. de Villiers and Jill G. de Villiers, *Early Language* (Cambridge, MA: Harvard University Press, 1979), p. 48; see also Wanner and Gleitman, eds., *Language Acquisition*.

[28]Bickerton, "Creole Languages," p. 122.

means more than one. But they do not know this consciously, and grown-ups may not either. One of the most surprising features of human language is that meaningful sounds and sound sequences are combined according to rules that are often not consciously known by the speakers.

These rules should not be equated with the "rules of grammar" you may have been taught in school (so that you would speak "correctly"). Rather, when linguists talk about rules they are referring to the patterns of speaking that are discoverable in actual speech. Needless to say, there is some overlap between the actual rules of speaking and the "rules" taught in school. But there are rules that children never hear about in school, because their teachers are not linguists and are not aware of them. So when linguists use the term *grammar*, they are *not* referring to the prescriptive rules that people are supposed to follow in speaking. Rather, *grammar* to the linguist consists of the actual, often unconscious principles that predict how most people talk. As we have noted, young children may speak two-word sentences that conform to a linguistic rule, but their speech is hardly considered "correct"!

Discovering the mostly unconscious rules operating in a language is a very difficult task. Linguists have had to invent special concepts and methods of transcription (writing) to permit them to describe: (1) what the rules or principles are that predict how sounds are made and how they are used (often, slightly varying sounds are used interchangeably in words without creating a difference in meaning); (2) how sound sequences (and sometimes even individual sounds) convey meaning and how meaningful sound sequences are strung together to form words; and (3) how words are strung together to form phrases and sentences. Thus, **structural** (or **descriptive**) **linguistics** tries to discover the rules of **phonology** (the patterning of sounds), **morphology** (the patterning of sound sequences and words), and **syntax** (the patterning of phrases and sentences) that predict how most speakers of a language talk.

Phonology

Most of us have had the experience of trying to learn another language and finding out that some sounds are exceedingly difficult to make. One reason is that we may have never made them before and so we literally lack the necessary lip, tongue, and other muscular habits. Although the human vocal tract can theoretically make a very large number of different sounds (**phones** to linguists), each language uses only some of them. It is not that we cannot make the sounds that are strange to us; we just have not acquired the habits of making those sounds. And until the sounds become habitual for us, they continue to be difficult to make.

Finding it difficult to make certain sounds is only one of the reasons we have trouble learning a "foreign" language. Another problem is that we may not be used to combining certain sounds or making a certain sound in a particular position in a word. So English speakers find it difficult to combine *z* and *d*, as Russian speakers often do (because we never do so in English), or to pronounce words in Samoan (a South Pacific language) that begin with the sound English speakers write as *ng*, even though we have no trouble putting that sound at the end of words, as in the English *sing* and *hitting*.

In order to study the patterning of sounds, linguists who are interested in phonology have to write down speech utterances as sequences of sound. This would be almost impossible if linguists were restricted to using their own alphabet (say the one we use to write English), because other languages use sounds that are difficult to represent with the English alphabet or because the alphabet we use in English can represent a particular sound in different ways. (English writing represents the sound *f* by "f" as in "food," but also as "gh" in "tough" and "ph" in "phone.") To overcome these difficulties in writing sounds with the "letters" of existing writing systems, linguists have developed systems of transcription in which each "letter" or sound symbol is meant to represent one particular sound.

Once linguists have identified the sounds or phones used in a language, they try to identify how these sounds are classified unconsciously (by the speakers of the language) into **phonemes.** A phoneme is a set of varying sounds that do not make any difference in meaning. In other words, when one phone of a phoneme class is substituted for another phone of the same class, speakers will still say that the utterance is the same.

The ways in which sounds are grouped together into phonemes vary from language to language. In English the sound of *l* in "lake" is considered quite different from the sound of *r* in "rake"; the two sounds belong to different phonemes because they make a difference in meaning to English speakers. But in Samoan, *l* and *r* can be used interchangeably in a word without making a difference in meaning; in Samoan, these two sounds belong to the same phoneme. So, Samoan speakers may say "Leupena" sometimes and "Reupena" at other times when they are referring to someone who in English would be called "Reuben." English speakers may joke about languages that confuse *l* and *r*, but they are not usually aware that we do the same thing with other pairs of sounds. For example, consider how we pronounce the word we spell as "butter." Some people say this word with a *t* in the middle; others say it with a *d*. We recognize "butter" and "budder" as the same word; the interchangeability of *t* and *d* does not make a difference in meaning. Speakers of some other languages would hear "butter" and "budder" as different words and make fun of us for confusing *t* and *d*!

After discovering which sounds are grouped into phonemes (that is, which sounds can be substituted for each other without making a difference in meaning), linguists can begin to discover the sound sequences that are allowed in a language and the usually unconscious rules that predict those sequences. For example, words in English rarely start with three consonants. But when they do, the first consonant is always an *s*, as in "strike" and "scratch."[29] Linguists' descriptions of the patterning of sounds (phonology) in different languages may allow them to investigate why languages vary in their sound rules. For example, why are two or more consonants strung together in some languages, whereas in other languages vowels are always put between consonants? The Samoan language now has a word for "Christmas" borrowed from English. But the borrowed word has been changed to fit the rules of Samoan. In the English word two consonants come first (*k* and *r*, which we spell as "ch" and "r"). The Samoan word is *Kerisimasi*: a vowel has been inserted between each pair of consonants and the word ends with a vowel, which is exactly how all Samoan words are constructed.

[29]Adrian Akmajian, Richard A. Demers, and Robert M. Harnish, *Linguistics: An Introduction to Language and Communication*, 2nd ed. (Cambridge, MA: M.I.T. Press, 1984), p. 136.

Morphology

Morphology is the study of a variety of questions about words, particularly what words are and how they are formed. We take our words so much for granted that we do not realize how complicated it is to say what words are. People do not usually pause between words when they speak; if we did not know our language, a sentence would seem like a continuous stream of sounds. This is how we first hear a foreign language. It is only when we understand the language and write down what we say that we separate (by spaces) what we call *words*. But a word is really only an arbitrary sequence of sounds that has a meaning; we would not "hear" words as separate units if we did not understand the language to which they belong.

Because anthropological linguists traditionally investigated unwritten languages, sometimes without the aid of interpreters, they had to figure out which sequences of sounds conveyed meaning. And because words in many languages can often be broken down into smaller meaningful units, linguists had to invent special words to refer to those units. The smallest unit of language that has a meaning is a **morph.** One or more morphs with the same meaning make up a **morpheme.** For example, the prefix *in-*, as in *indefinite,* and the prefix *un-*, as in *unclear,* are morphs that belong to the morpheme meaning *not.* A morph or morpheme should not be confused with a word. Although some words are single morphs or morphemes (for example, *for* and *giraffe* in English), many words are built on a combination of morphs, generally prefixes, roots, and suffixes. Thus *cow* is one word, but the word *cows* contains two meaningful units—a root (*cow*) and a suffix (pronounced like *z*) meaning more than one. The **lexicon** of a language, which a dictionary approximates, consists of words and morphs and their meanings.

It seems likely that the intuitive grasp children have of the structure of their language includes a recognition of morphology, the patterning of sound sequences and words. Once they learn that the morph /-*z*/ added to a noun-type word indicates more than one, they plow ahead with *mans*, and *childs*; once they grasp that the morpheme class pronounced /-*t*/ or /-*d*/ or /-*ed*/ added to the end of a verb indicates that the action took place in the past, they apply this concept generally and invent *runned, drinked, costed*. They see a ball roll nearer and nearer, and they transfer this to a kite, which goes upp*er* and upp*er*. From their mistakes as well as their successes, we can see that they understand the regular uses of morphemes. By the age of seven, they have mastered many of the irregular forms as well—that is, they learn which morphs of a morpheme are used when.

The child's intuitive grasp of the dependence of some morphemes on others corresponds to the linguist's recognition of free morphemes and bound morphemes. A *free* morpheme has meaning standing alone—that is, it can be a separate word. A *bound* morpheme displays its meaning only when attached to another morpheme. The morph pronounced /-t/ of the bound morpheme meaning *past tense* is attached to the root *walk* to produce *walked*; but the /-t/ cannot stand alone or have meaning by itself.

In English, the meaning of an utterance (containing a subject, verb, object, and so forth) usually depends on the order of the words. "The dog bit the child" is different in meaning from "The child bit the dog." But in many other languages, the grammatical meaning of an utterance does not depend much, if at all, on the order of the words. Rather, meaning may be determined by how the morphs in a word are ordered. For example, in Luo (a language of East Africa) the same bound morpheme may mean the subject or object of an action. If the morpheme is the prefix to a verb, it means the subject; if it is the suffix to a verb, it means the object. Another way that grammatical meaning may be conveyed is by altering or adding a bound morpheme to a word to indicate what part of speech it is. For example, in Russian, the word for "mail" when it is the subject of a sentence is pronounced something like "pawchtah." When "mail" is used as the object of a verb, as in "I gave her the mail," the ending of the word changes to "pawchtoo." And if I say "What was in the mail?" the word becomes "pawchtyeh."

Some languages have so many bound morphemes that they might express as a complex but single word what is considered a sentence in English. For example, the English sentence "He will give it to you" can be expressed in Wishram, a Chinookan dialect that was spoken along the Columbia River in the Pacific Northwest, as *acimluda* (a-c-i-m-l-ud-a, literally "will-he-him-thee-to-give-will"). Note that the pronoun *it* in English is gender-neutral; Wishram requires that *it* be given a gender, in this case "him."[30]

Syntax

Because language is an open system, we can make up meaningful utterances that we have never heard before. We are constantly creating new phrases and sentences. Just as with morphology, the speakers of a language seem to have an intuitive grasp of syntax—the rules that predict how phrases and sentences are generally formed. These "rules" may be partly learned in school, but children know many of them even before they get to school. In adulthood, our understanding of morphology and syntax is so intuitive that we can even understand a nonsense sentence, such as the following famous one from Lewis Carroll's *Through the Looking-Glass*:

'Twas brillig, and the slithy toves
Did gyre and gimble in the wabe

Simply from the ordering of the words in the sentence, we can surmise which part of speech a word is, as well as its function in the sentence. *Brillig* is an adjective; *slithy* an adjective; *toves* a noun and the subject of the sentence; *gyre* and *gimble* verbs; and *wabe* a noun and the object of a prepositional phrase. Of course, an understanding of morphology helps too. The *-y* ending in *slithy* is an indication that the latter is an adjective, and the *-s* ending in *toves* tells us that we most probably have more than one of these creatures.

Besides producing and understanding an infinite variety of sentences, speakers of a language can tell when a sentence is not "correct" without consulting grammar books. For example, an English-speaker can tell that "Child the dog the hit" is not an acceptable sentence, but "The child hit the dog" is fine. There must then be a set of rules underlying how phrases and sentences are constructed in a language.[31] Speakers of a language know these implicit rules of syntax, but are not usually consciously aware of them. The linguist's description

[30]E. Sapir and M. Swadesh, "American Indian Grammatical Categories," in Hymes, ed., *Language in Culture and Society*, p. 103.

[31]Akmajian, Demers, and Harnish, *Linguistics*, pp. 164–66.

of the syntax of a language tries to make these rules explicit.

Noam Chomsky's theory about syntax, known as **transformational/generative theory,** suggests that a language has a *surface structure* and a *deep structure.* For example, the sentences "John killed Mary" and "Mary was killed by John" have very different surface structures (John is the subject of the first sentence; Mary is the subject of the second). But the sentences mean the same thing to English-speakers, so the deep structure is the same in both sentences. A transformational description of a language would not only provide the rules that describe how the basic sentences of a language are formed; it would also stipulate how those basic sentences can be transformed into more complex sentences.[32]

Historical Linguistics

The field of **historical linguistics** focuses on how languages change over time. Written works provide the best data for establishing such changes. For example, the following passage from Chaucer's *Canterbury Tales,* written in the English of the fourteenth century, has recognizable elements but is different enough from modern English to require a translation.

A Frere ther was, a wantowne and a merye,
A lymytour, a ful solempne man.
In alle the ordres foure is noon that kan
So muche of daliaunce and fair language.
He hadde maad ful many a mariage
Of yonge wommen at his owene cost.
Unto his ordre he was a noble post.
Ful wel biloued and famulier was he
With frankeleyns ouer al in his contree,
And with worthy wommen of the toun;
For he hadde power of confessioun,
As seyde hymself, moore than a curat,
For of his ordre he was licenciat.

A Friar there was, wanton and merry,
A limiter [a friar limited to certain districts], a full
    solemn [very important] man.
In all the orders four there is none that knows
So much of dalliance [flirting] and fair [engaging]
    language.

He had made [arranged] many a marriage
Of young women at his own cost.
Unto his order he was a noble post [pillar].
Full well beloved and familiar was he
With franklins [wealthy landowners] all over his
    country
And also with worthy women of the town;
For he had power of confession,
As he said himself, more than a curate,
For of his order, he was a licentiate [licensed by the
    Pope].[33]

From this comparison we can recognize a number of changes. A great many words are spelled differently today. In some cases, meaning has changed: *full,* for example, would be translated today as *very.* What is less evident is that changes in pronunciation have occurred. For example, the *g* in *mariage* (marriage) was pronounced *zh,* as in the French from which it was borrowed, whereas now it is pronounced like the second *g* in *George.*

Since languages spoken in the past leave no traces unless they were written, and since most of the languages known to anthropology were not written by their speakers, you might guess that historical linguists can study linguistic change only by studying written languages such as English. But that is not the case. Linguists can reconstruct changes that have occurred by comparing contemporary languages that are very similar. Such languages show phonological, morphological, and syntactic similarities because they usually derive from a common ancestral language. For example, Romanian, Italian, French, Spanish, and Portuguese have many similarities. On the basis of these similarities, linguists can reconstruct what the ancestral language was like and how it changed into what we call the "Romance" languages. Of course, these reconstructions can be easily tested and confirmed because we know from many surviving writings what the ancestral language (Latin) was like; and we know from documents how Latin diversified as the Roman Empire expanded. Thus common ancestry is frequently the reason why neighboring (and sometimes even separated) languages show patterns of similarity.

[32]Southworth and Daswani, *Foundations of Linguistics,* pp. 154–57.

[33]Chaucer, *The Prologue to the Canterbury Tales, the Knightes Tale, the Nonnes Prestes Tale,* ed. Mark H. Liddell (New York: The Macmillan Company, 1926), p. 8. Modern English translation by the authors on the basis of the glossary in ibid.

But languages can be similar for other reasons too. One reason is contact between speech communities, which leads one language to borrow from the other. For example, English borrowed a lot of vocabulary from French after England was conquered by the French-speaking Normans in A.D. 1066. Languages may also show similarities even though they do not derive from a common ancestral language and even though there has been no contact or borrowing between them; such similarities may reflect common or universal features of human cultures and/or human brains. (As we noted earlier in this chapter, the grammatical similarities exhibited by creole languages may possibly reflect how the human brain is "wired.") Finally, even unrelated and separated languages may show some similarities because of the phenomenon of convergence; similarities can develop because some processes of linguistic change may have only a few possible outcomes.

Language Families and Culture History

Latin is the ancestral language of the Romance languages. We know this from documentary (written) records. But if the ancestral language of a set of similar languages is not known from written records, linguists can still reconstruct many features of that language by comparing the derived languages. (Such a reconstructed language is called a **protolanguage**.) That is, by comparing presumably related languages, linguists can become aware of the features that many of them have in common, features that were probably found in the common ancestral language. The languages that derive from the same protolanguage are called a *language family*. Most languages spoken in the world today can be grouped into fewer than thirty families. The language family English belongs to is called *Indo-European*, because it includes most of the languages of Europe and some of the languages of India. About 50 percent of the world's more than 4 billion people speak Indo-European languages.[34] Another very large language family, now spoken by more than a billion people, is Sino-Tibetan, which includes the languages of northern and southern China as well as those of Tibet and Burma.

The field of historical linguistics got its start in 1786 when a British colonial judge in India, Sir William Jones, noticed similarities between Sanskrit (the language spoken and written in ancient India) and classical Greek, Latin, and more recent European languages.[35] In 1822, Jacob Grimm, one of the brothers Grimm of fairy-tale fame, formulated rules to describe the sound shifts that had occurred when the various Indo-European languages diverged from each other. So, for example, in English and the other languages in the Germanic branch of the Indo-European family, *d* regularly shifted to *t* (compare the English *two* and *ten* with the Latin *duo* and *decem*) and *p* regularly shifted to *f* (English *father* and *foot*, Latin *pater* and *pes*). Scholars generally agree that the Indo-European languages derive from a language spoken 5,000 to 6,000 years ago.[36] The ancestral Indo-European language, many of whose features have now been reconstructed, is called *proto-Indo-European*, or *PIE* for short. Figure 13-1 shows the major branches and languages of the family.

Where did the people who spoke PIE live? Some linguists believe that the approximate location of a protolanguage is suggested by the words for plants and animals in the derived languages. More specifically, among these different languages, those words that are **cognates** (that are similar in sound and meaning) presumably refer to plants and animals that were present in the original homeland. So if we know where those animals and plants were located 5,000 to 6,000 years ago, we can guess where the speakers of PIE lived. Among all the cognates for trees in the Indo-European languages, Paul Friedrich has identified eighteen that he believes were present in the Eastern Ukraine in 3000 B.C.; on this basis he suggests that the eastern Ukraine was the PIE homeland.[37] Also consistent with this hypothesis is the fact that the Slavic subfamily of Indo-European (which includes most of the languages in and around the former Soviet

---

[34]Akmajian, Demers, and Harnish, *Linguistics*, p. 356.

[35]Philip Baldi, *An Introduction to the Indo-European Languages* (Carbondale: Southern Illinois University Press, 1983), p. 3.

[36]Ibid., p. 12.

[37]Paul Friedrich, *Proto-Indo-European Trees: The Arboreal System of a Prehistoric People* (Chicago: University of Chicago Press, 1970), p. 168.

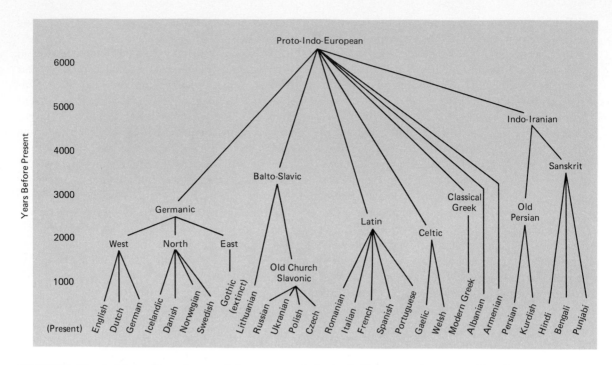

FIGURE 13–1 Major Branches and Languages of the Indo-European Language Family

Union) has the most tree names (compared with other subfamilies) that are similar to the reconstructed words in proto-Indo-European.[38]

Marija Gimbutas thinks we can even identify the proto-Indo-Europeans archeologically. She believes that the PIE speakers were probably the people associated with what is known as the Kurgan culture (5000–2000 B.C.), which spread out of the Ukraine around 3000 B.C. The Kurgan people were herders, keeping and raising horses, cattle, sheep, and pigs. They also relied on hunting and grain cultivation. Burials suggest differences in wealth and special status for men.[39] Why the Kurgan and linguistically similar people were able to expand to many places in Europe and the Near East is not yet clear (some have suggested that horses and horse-drawn wagons, and perhaps horseback riding, pro-

vided important military advantages).[40] In any case, it *is* clear that many Kurgan cultural elements were distributed after 3000 B.C. over a wide area of the Old World.

Colin Renfrew disagrees with the notion that the Ukraine was the homeland of PIE. He thinks that PIE was spoken 2,000-3,000 years before the Kurgan culture developed, and in a different place. Renfrew locates the PIE speech community in eastern Anatolia (Turkey) in 6000–7000 B.C., and he suggests (on the basis of archeological evidence) that the spread of Indo-European to Europe and what is now Iran, Afghanistan, and India accompanied the spread of farming to those areas.[41]

Just as some historical linguists and archeologists have suggested where the PIE speakers may have lived originally and how they may have spread, other linguists and archeologists have suggested culture histories for other language families.

[38]Ibid., p. 166.

[39]Marija Gimbutas, "An Archaeologist's View of PIE* in 1975," *Journal of Indo European Studies,* 2 (1974): 293–95. See also Susan N. Skomal and Edgar C. Polomé, eds., *Proto-Indo-European: The Archaeology of a Linguistic Problem* (Washington, DC: Washington Institute for the Study of Man, 1987).

[40]David Anthony, Dimitri Y. Telegin, and Dorcas Brown, "The Origin of Horseback Riding," *Scientific American,* December 1991, pp. 94–100.

[41]Colin Renfrew, *Archaeology and Language: The Puzzle of Indo-European Origins* (London: Jonathan Cape, 1987).

For example, the Bantu languages in Africa (spoken by perhaps 80 million people) form a subfamily of the larger Niger-Congo family of languages. Bantu speakers currently live in a wide band across the center of the African continent and down the eastern and western sides of southern Africa. All of the Bantu languages presumably derive from people who spoke proto-Bantu. But where was their homeland?

As in the case of proto-Indo-European, different theories have been proposed about the homeland of the Bantu. But most historical linguists now agree with Joseph Greenberg's suggestion that the proto-Bantu may have lived in what is now the Middle Benue area of eastern Nigeria. This suggestion is based on two assumptions. First, the point of origin of a language is presumably where there is the greatest diversity of related languages and **dialects** (varying forms of a language); it is assumed that the original homeland has had the most time for linguistic diversity to develop, compared with an area only recently occupied by a related language. For example, England (the homeland of English) has more dialect diversity than New Zealand or Australia. The second assumption about how to locate the homeland of a group of languages is that the related languages now spoken in or near the homeland should show the most similarity to the other (in this case non-Bantu) languages spoken in that area; it is assumed that such similarity betrays a common origin even further back in time. Both of the assumptions just outlined generate the conclusion that the proto-Bantu probably lived in the Middle Benue area of eastern Nigeria.[42]

Why were the Bantu able to spread so widely over the last few thousand years? Anthropologists have only begun to guess.[43] Initially, the Bantu probably kept goats and practiced some form of agriculture, which may have allowed them to spread at the expense of hunter-gatherers. Later, as the Bantu-speakers expanded, they began to cultivate certain cereal crops and herd sheep and cattle. Around this time, after 1000 B.C., they began to use and make iron tools, which may also have given them significant advantages. In any case, by 1,500 to 2,000 years ago Bantu speakers had spread throughout central Africa and into the northern reaches of southern Africa. But speakers of non-Bantu languages still live in eastern, southern, and southwestern Africa.

The Processes of Linguistic Divergence

The historical or comparative linguist hopes to do more than record and date linguistic divergence. Just as the physical anthropologist may attempt to develop explanations for human variation, so the linguist investigates the possible causes of linguistic variation. When groups of people speaking the same language lose communication with one another because they become separated either physically or socially, they begin to accumulate small changes in phonology, morphology, and syntax (which occur continuously in any language). Eventually, if the separation continues, the former dialects of the same language will become separate languages; that is, they will become mutually unintelligible, as German and English now are.

Geographical barriers such as large bodies of water, deserts, and mountains may separate speakers of what was once the same language, but distance by itself can also produce divergence. For example, if we compare dialects of English in the British Isles, it is clear that those regions farthest away from each other are the most different linguistically (compare the northeast of Scotland and London).[44] In northern India, hundreds of semi-isolated villages and regions developed hundreds of local dialects. Today, the inhabitants of each village understand the dialects of the surrounding villages and, with a little more difficulty, the dialects of the next circle of villages. But slight dialect shifts accumulate village by village, and it seems as if different languages are being spoken at the opposite ends of the region, which are separated by over a thousand miles.[45]

[42]Joseph H. Greenberg, "Linguistic Evidence Regarding Bantu Origins," *Journal of African History*, 13 (1972): 189–216; see also D. W. Phillipson, "Archaeology and Bantu Linguistics," *World Archaeology*, 8 (1976): 71.

[43]Phillipson, "Archaeology and Bantu Linguistics," p. 79.

[44]Peter Trudgill, *Sociolinguistics: An Introduction to Language and Society*, rev. ed. (New York: Penguin, 1983), p. 34.

[45]John J. Gumperz, "Speech Variation and the Study of Indian Civilization," *American Anthropologist*, 63 (1961): 976–88.

Even where there is little geographic separation there may still be a great deal of dialect differentiation because of social distance. So, for example, the spread of a linguistic feature may be halted by racial, religious, or social-class differences that inhibit communication.[46] In the village of Khalapur in North India, John Gumperz found substantial differences in speech between the "untouchable" groups and other groups. Members of the untouchable groups have work contacts with others, but no friendships.[47] Without friendships and the easy communication between friends, dialect differentiation can readily develop.

Whereas isolation brings divergence between speech communities, contact results in greater resemblance. This is particularly evident when contact between mutually unintelligible languages introduces *borrowed* words, which usually name some new item borrowed from the other culture—*tomato, canoe, sushi,* and so on. Bilingual groups within a culture may also introduce foreign words, especially when the mainstream language has no real equivalent. Thus, *siesta* has come into English, and *le weekend* into French.

Conquest and colonization often result in extensive borrowing. The Norman conquest of England introduced French as the language of the new aristocracy. It was 300 years before the educated classes began to write in English. During this time the English borrowed words from French and Latin, and the two languages—English and French—became more alike than they would otherwise have been. About 50 percent of the English general vocabulary has been borrowed from French. As this example suggests, different social classes may borrow differentially. For example, English aristocrats eventually called their meat "pork" and "beef" (derived from the French words), but the people who raised the animals and prepared them for eating continued (at least for a while) to refer to the meat as "pig" and "bull," the original Anglo-Saxon words.

In those 300 years of extensive borrowing, the grammar of English remained relatively stable.

English words have been "borrowed" by the Japanese, as on the sign in front of this Tokyo coffee shop.

English lost most of its inflections or case endings, but it adopted little of the French grammar. Generally, the borrowing of words (particularly free morphemes[48]) is much more common than the borrowing of grammar.[49] As we might expect, borrowing by one language from another can make the borrowing language more different from its **sibling languages** (those derived from a common ancestral language) than it would otherwise be. Partly as a result of the French influence, the English vocabulary looks quite different from the languages to which it is actually most similar in terms of phonology and grammar—German, Dutch, and the Scandinavian languages.

Relationships between Language and Culture

Some attempts to explain the diversity of languages have focused on the possible interactions between language and other aspects of culture. On the one hand, if it can be shown that a culture may affect the structure and content of its language, then it would follow that linguistic diversity derives at least in part from cultural diversity. On the other hand, the direction of influence between

[46]Trudgill, *Sociolinguistics,* p. 35.

[47]John J. Gumperz, "Dialect Differences and Social Stratification in a North Indian Village," in *Language in Social Groups: Essays by John J. Gumperz,* selected and introduced by Anwar S. Dil (Stanford, CA: Stanford University Press, 1971), p. 45.

[48]Uriel Weinreich, *Languages in Contact* (The Hague: Mouton, 1968), p. 31.

[49]But see Sarah Grey Thomason and Terrence Kaufman, *Language Contact, Creolization, and Genetic Linguistics* (Berkeley, CA: University of California Press, 1988), for a discussion of how grammatical changes due to contact may be more important than previously assumed.

culture and language might work in reverse: the linguistic structures might affect other aspects of the culture.

Cultural Influences on Language

One way a society's language may reflect its corresponding culture is in **lexical content,** or vocabulary. Which experiences, events, or objects are singled out and given words may be a result of cultural characteristics.

Basic Words for Colors, Plants, and Animals. Early in this century many linguists pointed to the lexical domain (vocabulary) of color words to illustrate the supposed truth that languages vary arbitrarily or without apparent reason. Not only did different languages have different numbers of basic or fundamental color words (from two to twelve or so—for example, the words *red, green,* and *blue* in English); it was also thought that there was no consistency in the way different languages classified or divided the colors of the spectrum. But findings from a comparative (or cross-linguistic) study published in 1969 contradicted these traditional presumptions about variation in the number and meaning of basic color words. Based upon their study of at first 20 and later over 100 different languages, Brent Berlin and Paul Kay found that languages did not encode color in completely arbitrary ways.[50]

Although different languages do have different numbers of basic color words, most speakers of any language are very likely to point to the same color chips as the best representatives of particular colors. (For example, people the world over mean more or less the same color when they are asked to select the *best* "red.") Moreover, there appears to be a more or less universal sequence by which basic color words are added to a language.[51] If a language has just two basic color words, they will always refer to "black" (or dark) hues and "white" (or light) hues. If a language has three basic color words, the third word will nearly always be "red." The next category to appear is either "yellow" or "grue" (green/blue); then different words for green

and blue; and so on. To be sure, we usually do not see the process by which basic color words are added to a language. But we can infer the usual sequence because, for example, if a language has a word for "yellow" it will almost always have a word for "red," whereas having a word for "red" does not mean that the language will have a word for "yellow."

What exactly is a *basic* color word? All languages (even the ones with only two basic color terms) have many different ways of expressing how color varies. For example, in English we have words such as *turquoise, blue-green, scarlet, crimson,* and *sky blue.* Linguists do not consider these to be basic color words. In English the basic color words are *white, black, red, green, yellow, blue, brown, pink, purple, orange,* and *gray.* One feature of a basic color word is that it consists of a single morph; it cannot include two or more units of meaning. This feature eliminates combinations such as *blue-green* and *sky blue.* A second feature of a basic color word is that the color it represents is not generally included in a higher-order color term. For example, scarlet and crimson are usually considered variants of red, turquoise a variant of blue. A third feature is that basic terms tend to be the first-named words when people are asked for color words. Finally, for a word to be considered a basic color word, many individual speakers of the language have to agree on the central meaning (in the color spectrum) of the word.[52]

Why do different societies (languages) vary in number of basic color terms? Berlin and Kay suggest that the number of basic color terms in a language increases with cultural complexity,[53] and subsequent research has supported this idea.[54] More complex societies may require a larger number of basic color terms because they have more decorated objects that can be effectively distinguished by color, or a more complex technology of dyes and paints.[55] Cross-linguistic variation in number of basic color terms does not mean that some languages make more color distinctions than others. Every language could make a particular dis-

---

[50]Brent Berlin and Paul Kay, *Basic Color Terms: Their Universality and Evolution* (Berkeley: University of California Press, 1969).
[51]Ibid.

[52]Ibid., pp. 5–6.
[53]Ibid., p. 104.
[54]Stanley R. Witkowski and Cecil H. Brown, "Lexical Universals," *Annual Review of Anthropology,* 7 (1978): 427–51.
[55]Berlin and Kay, *Basic Color Terms;* see also Witkowski and Brown, "Lexical Universals," p. 198.

tinction by combining words (for example, "fresh leaf" for green); a language need not have a separate basic term for that color.

A relatively large number of basic color terms is related not only to greater cultural complexity; a biological factor may also be involved.[56] Peoples with darker (more pigmented) eyes seem to have more trouble distinguishing colors at the dark (blue-green) end of the spectrum. It might be expected, then, that peoples who live nearer the equator (who tend to have darker eyes, presumably for protection against damaging ultraviolet radiation) would tend to have fewer basic color terms. And they do.[57] Moreover, it seems that the cultural and biological factors are both required to account for cross-linguistic variation in the number of basic color terms. Societies tend to have six or more such terms (with separate terms for blue and green) only when they are relatively far from the equator and only when their cultures are more complex.[58]

Echoing Berlin and Kay's finding that basic color terms seem to be added in a more or less universal sequence, other researchers have found what seem to be developmental sequences in other lexical domains. Two such domains are general, or *lifeform*, terms for plants and for animals. Life-form terms are higher-order classifications. All languages have lower-order terms for specific plants and animals. For example, English has words such as *oak* and *pine*, *sparrow* and *salmon*. English speakers make finer distinctions too—*pin oak* and *white pine*, *white-throated sparrow* and *red salmon*. But why in some languages do people have a larger number of general terms such as *tree*, *bird*, and *fish*? It seems that these general terms show a universal developmental sequence too. That is, terms seem to be added in a more or less consistent order. After "plant" comes a term for "tree"; then one for "grerb" (small, green, leafy, nonwoody plant); then "bush" (for plants between tree and grerb in size); then "grass"; then "vine."[59] The life-form

A child who grows up around sailboats knows the names of the different types. Can you name the types in this picture?

terms for animals seem also to be added in sequence; after "animal" comes a term for "fish"; then "bird"; then "snake"; then "wug" (for small creatures other than fish, birds, and snakes—for example, worms and bugs); then "mammal."[60]

Thus, more complex societies tend to have a larger number of general or life-form terms for plants and animals, just as they tend to have a larger number of basic color terms. Why? And do all realms or domains of vocabulary increase in size as cultural complexity increases? If we look at the total vocabulary of a language (as can be counted in a dictionary), more complex societies do have larger vocabularies.[61] But we have to remember that complex societies have many kinds of specialists, and dictionaries will include the terms used by such specialists. If we look instead at the **core** (nonspecialist) **vocabulary** of languages, it seems that all languages have a core vocabulary of more or less the same size.[62] Indeed, although some domains increase in size with cultural complexity, some remain the same and still others decrease. An example of a smaller vocabulary domain in complex societies is that of specific names for plants. Urban North Americans may know general terms for plants, but they know relatively few names for specific plants. The typical individual in an uncomplex or small-scale society can commonly

[56]Marc H. Bornstein, "The Psychophysiological Component of Cultural Difference in Color Naming and Illusion Susceptibility," *Behavior Science Notes*, 8 (1973): 41–101.

[57]Melvin Ember, "Size of Color Lexicon: Interaction of Cultural and Biological Factors," *American Anthropologist*, 80 (1978): 364–67.

[58]Ibid.

[59]Cecil H. Brown, "Folk Botanical Life-Forms: Their Universality and Growth," *American Anthropologist*, 79 (1977): 317–42.

[60]Cecil H. Brown, "Folk Zoological Life-Forms: Their Universality and Growth," *American Anthropologist*, 81 (1979): 791–817.

[61]Stanley R. Witkowski and Harold W. Burris, "Societal Complexity and Lexical Growth," *Behavior Science Research*, 16 (1981): 143–59.

[62]Ibid.

name 400 to 800 different plant species; a typical member of a modern urban society may be able to name only 40 to 80.[63] It seems as if life-form terms become more numerous only when ordinary people have less and less to do with plants and animals.[64]

Focal Areas. The evidence now available strongly supports the idea that the vocabulary of a language reflects the everyday distinctions that are important in the society. Those aspects of environment or culture that are of special importance will receive greater attention in language. Even within a single society speaking the same language there is often variation in vocabulary from one region or subculture to another that reflects different concerns. An adult farmer in the United States Midwest may know three simple words for boat—*boat, ship, canoe*—and a few compound variations, such as *rowboat, sailboat, motorboat, steamship.* Yet a six-year-old who lives on Long Island Sound, where sailing is a major pastime, may be able to distinguish many kinds of sailboats, such as *catboat, ketch, yawl, sloop,* and *schooner,* as well as subclasses of each, such as *bluejay, sunfish,* and *weekender.*

There are many interesting examples of *focal areas* in different cultures being reflected in their respective vocabularies. Franz Boas showed that the geographical terms of the Kwakiutl, a coastal Indian tribe of the Pacific Northwest, reflect their awareness of the importance of hunting, fishing, and other food-gathering activities essential to their survival. Locations on land are given names such as *having-blueberries* and *having-hunter's lodge;* areas of coastal waters are described as *having-difficult-currents* and *having-spring-salmon.*[65] In comparison, river crossings were important to the early English. Consider their Ox-ford and Cam-bridge—names that in modern times have lost their original meanings.

Grammar. Most of the examples we could accumulate would show that a culture influences the names of things visible in its environment. Evidence for cultural influence on the grammatical structure of a language is less extensive. Harry Hoijer draws attention to the verb categories in the language of the Navaho, a traditionally nomadic people. These categories center mainly in the reporting of events, or *eventings,* as he calls them. Hoijer notes that in "the reporting of actions and events, and the framing of substantive concepts, Navaho emphasizes movement and specifies the nature, direction, and status of such movement in considerable detail."[66] For example, Navaho has one category for eventings that are in motion and another for eventings that have ceased moving. Hoijer concludes that the emphasis on events in the process of occurring reflects the Navaho's own nomadic experience over the centuries, an experience also reflected in their myths and folklore.

A linguistic emphasis on events may or may not be generally characteristic of nomadic peoples. No one has as yet investigated the matter cross-culturally or comparatively. But there are indications that systematic comparative research might turn up a number of other grammatical features that are related to cultural characteristics. For example, many languages lack the possessive transitive verb we write as "have," as in "I have." Instead, the language may say something like "it is to me." A cross-cultural study has suggested that a language may develop the verb "have" after the speakers of that language have developed a system of private property, or personal ownership of resources.[67] As we shall see later in the chapter on economic systems, private property is generally characteristic of more complex societies, in contrast to simpler societies which generally have some kind of communal ownership (by kin groups or communities). How people talk about owning seems to reflect how they own: where private property is absent, the verb "have" is also absent.

[63]Cecil H. Brown and Stanley Witkowski, "Language Universals," appendix B in David Levinson and Martin J. Malone, eds., *Toward Explaining Human Culture: A Critical Review of the Findings of Worldwide Cross-Cultural Research* (New Haven: HRAF Press, 1980), p. 379.

[64]Cecil H. Brown, "World View and Lexical Uniformities," *Reviews in Anthropology,* 11 (1984): 106.

[65]Franz Boas, *Geographical Names of the Kwakiutl Indians* (New York: Columbia University Press, 1934).

[66]Harry Hoijer, "Cultural Implications of Some Navaho Linguistic Categories," in Hymes, ed., *Language in Culture and Society,* p. 146 (originally published in *Language,* 27 [1951]: 111–20).

[67]Karen E. Webb, "An Evolutionary Aspect of Social Structure and a Verb 'Have,'" *American Anthropologist,* 79 (1977): 42–49; see also Floyd Webster Rudmin, "Dominance, Social Control, and Ownership: A History and a Cross-Cultural Study of Motivations for Private Property," *Behavior Science Research,* 22 (1988): 130–60.

Linguistic Influences on Culture: The Sapir-Whorf Hypothesis

There is general agreement among **ethnolinguists**—those anthropologists interested in the relationships between language and culture—that culture influences language. But there is less agreement about the opposite possibility—that language influences (other aspects of) culture. Edward Sapir and his student Benjamin Lee Whorf suggested that language is a force in its own right—that it affects how individuals in a society perceive and conceive reality. This suggestion is known as the Sapir-Whorf hypothesis.[68] As intriguing as this idea is, the relevant evidence is mixed. Linguists today do not generally accept the view that language coerces thought, but some suspect that particular features of language may facilitate certain patterns of thought.[69] The influences may be clearest in poetry and metaphors (words and phrases applied to other than their ordinary subjects, as in "all the world's a stage").[70]

One of the serious problems in testing the Sapir-Whorf hypothesis is that researchers need to figure out how to separate the effects of other aspects of culture from the effects of language. For example, many women have argued in recent years that English perpetuates the stereotype of male dominance. For example, English does not have a neutral third-person pronoun for humans (although a baby is sometimes referred to as *it*). Consider the following sentences: "If a student is ill and cannot come to the final exam, he should contact the professor immediately." "My professor gave a pretty good lecture." "Yeah? What's his name?" We could try to avoid the third-person pronoun and repeat "the student" in the second half of the first sentence, but that would probably be considered clumsy writing. Or we could say "he or she." In the third sentence we could say "What's the professor's name?" Or we could say "What's his or her name?" If we were really daring, we might even say "she" or "her" instead of "he" or "his." The point of these examples is that English doesn't make it easy to refer to females *and* males in the third-person singular when the person might be of *either* sex. Traditionally, English speakers used "he" instead of "she" unless they were talking about certain roles thought to be clearly female roles, such as housewives, nurses, and secretaries. Many women might wish for a neutral pronoun, but it is difficult to legislate linguistic change. Thus the basic question is: Does our language make us think that men are more important, or do we say "he" or "his" merely because men have traditionally been more important than women in our society?

One approach that may reveal the direction of influence between language and culture is to study how children in different cultures (speaking different languages) develop concepts about themselves. Do children learn to recognize themselves as boys or girls earlier when their language emphasizes gender? Alexander Guiora and his colleagues have studied children growing up in Hebrew-speaking homes (Israel), English-speaking homes (the United States), and Finnish-speaking homes (Finland). Hebrew has the most gender emphasis of the three languages; nouns are either masculine or feminine and even second-person and plural pronouns are differentiated by gender. English emphasizes gender less, differentiating by gender only in the third-person singular, as just noted. Finnish emphasizes gender the least; although some words, such as "man" and "woman," convey gender, differentiation by gender is otherwise lacking in the language. Consistent with the idea that language may influence thought, Hebrew-speaking children acquire the concept of gender identity the earliest on the average, Finnish-speaking children the latest.[71]

The Ethnography of Speaking

Traditionally, linguists concentrated on trying to understand the structure of a language, the usually unconscious rules that predict how the people

[68] Edward Sapir, "Conceptual Categories in Primitive Languages," paper presented at the autumn meeting of the National Academy of Sciences, New Haven, 1931, published in *Science*, 74 (1931): 578; see also John B. Carroll, ed., *Language, Thought, and Reality: Selected Writings of Benjamin Lee Whorf* (New York: John Wiley, 1956), pp. 65–86.

[69] J. Peter Denny, "The 'Extendedness' Variable in Classifier Semantics: Universal Features and Cultural Variation," in Madeleine Mathiot, ed., *Ethnolinguistics: Boas, Sapir and Whorf Revisited* (The Hague: Mouton, 1979), p. 97.

[70] Paul Friedrich, *The Language Parallax* (Austin: University of Texas Press, 1986).

[71] Alexander Z. Guiora, Benjamin Beit-Hallahmi, Risto Fried, and Cecelia Yoder, "Language Environment and Gender Identity Attainment," *Language Learning*, 32 (1982): 289–304.

of a given society typically speak. Recently, however, many linguists have begun to study how people in a society vary in how they speak. This type of linguistic study, sociolinguistics, is concerned with the *ethnography of speaking*—that is, with cultural and subcultural patterns of speech variation in different social contexts.[72]

The sociolinguist may ask, for example, what kinds of things one talks about in casual conversation with a stranger. A foreigner may know English vocabulary and grammar well but may not know that one typically chats with a stranger about the weather, or where one comes from, and not about what one ate that day or how much money one earns. A foreigner may be familiar with much of the culture of a North American city, but if that person divulges the real state of his or her health and feelings to the first person who says "How are you?" he or she has much to learn about North American small talk.

Social Status and Speech

That a foreign speaker of a language may know little about the "small talk" of that language is but one example of the sociolinguistic principle that what we say and how we say it are not wholly predictable by the rules of our language. Who we are socially may have a big effect on what we say and how we say it. For example, English-speaking Athabaskan Indians in Canada seem to think that conversation with a white Canadian should be avoided except when they think they know the point of view of the white (who is generally more powerful politically). On the other hand, white English speakers think they should use conversation to get to know others (as at a cocktail party). So they pause a certain amount of time to let the other person talk, but they pause a much shorter time than Athabaskan Indian English speakers would. If the other person doesn't respond, the white English speaker, feeling awkward, will say something else. By the time an Athabaskan Indian is ready to talk, the white is already talking and the Athabaskan Indian considers it impolite to interrupt. It is easy to see how whites and Athabaskan Indians can misunderstand each other. Atha-

baskan Indians think white English speakers talk too much and don't let them express their views, and whites think Athabaskan Indians do not want to talk or get to know them.[73]

Similarly, North Americans tend to get confused in societies where greetings are quite different from ours. People in some other societies may ask as a greeting, "Where are you going?" or "What are you cooking?" Some Americans may think such questions are rude; others may try to answer in excruciating detail, not realizing that only vague answers are expected, just like we don't really expect a detailed answer when we ask people how they are.

The way in which people address each other is also of interest to sociolinguists. In English, forms of address are relatively simple. One is called either by a first name or by a title (such as *Mister, Doctor,* or *Professor*) followed by a last name. A study by Roger Brown and Marguerite Ford indicates that terms of address vary with the nature of the relationship between the speakers.[74] The reciprocal use of first names generally signifies an informal or intimate relationship between two persons. A title and last name used reciprocally usually indicates a more formal or businesslike relationship between individuals who are roughly equal in status. Nonreciprocal use of first names and titles in English is reserved for speakers who recognize a marked difference in status between themselves. This difference can be a function of age (as when a child refers to her mother's friend as Mrs. Miller and is in turn addressed as Sally), or it can be drawn along occupational lines (as when a person refers to her boss by title and last name and is in turn addressed as Mary). In some cases, generally between boys and between men, the use of the last name alone represents a middle ground between the intimate and the formal usages.

In some societies, terms of address do not reflect equality or inequality of social status as much as they reflect other kinds of social relationships. Among the Nuer of the Sudan, kin and age rela-

[72]Dell Hymes, *Foundations in Sociolinguistics: An Ethnographic Approach* (Philadelphia: University of Pennsylvania Press, 1974), pp. 83–117.

[73]Ron Scollon and Suzanne B. K. Scollon, *Narrative, Literacy and Face in Interethnic Communication* (Norwood, NJ: ABLEX Publishing Corporation, 1981), pp. 11–36.

[74]Roger Brown and Marguerite Ford, "Address in American English," *Journal of Abnormal and Social Psychology,* 62 (1961) 375–85.

Strangers shake hands when they meet; friends touch each other more. How we speak to others also differs according to degree of friendship.

tionships influence how you address someone. In addition, the formality of the occasion strongly influences address. For example, soon after birth each boy is given a personal name, which is used by his paternal relatives and by close friends in the paternal village. His maternal grandparents give him another name, which is used by his mother's family and close friends. At his initiation, a boy is given an ox and acquires an ox-name (the name of the ox), which members of his peer group may use instead of his personal name. A girl may choose an ox-name from the bull calf of a cow she milks; the name is used only by her age-group friends, often at dances where boys and girls call out their friends' ox-names with other titles suggesting friendship.

On formal occasions, a man may be greeted by his father's relatives with the paternal-clan name, or by his mother's relatives with the maternal-clan name. A man may be addressed as "son of" followed by his father's personal name, or as "father of" followed by his eldest child's name. A young person may address any elderly man as *gwa*, "Father," and an older man may call a young man *gatda*, "my son." A woman may choose a cow-name from a cow she milks, or she may be called "mother of" followed by her eldest child's name.[75]

[75]E. E. Evans-Pritchard, "Nuer Modes of Address," *Uganda Journal,* 12 (1948): 166–71.

In societies with rather sharp differences in social status, people of different social statuses often display their differences in language. For example, Clifford Geertz, in his study of Javanese, has shown that the vocabularies of the three rather sharply divided groups in Javanese society—peasants, townspeople, and aristocrats—reflect their separate positions. For example, the word *now* will be expressed by a peasant as *saiki* (considered the lowest and roughest form of the word), by a townsman as *saniki* (considered somewhat more elegant), and by an aristocrat as *samenika* (the most elegant form).[76] Research has shown, moreover, that English people from higher-class backgrounds tend to have more homogeneous speech, conforming more to what is considered standard English (the type of speech heard on television or radio), whereas people from lower-class backgrounds have very heterogeneous speech, varying in their speaking according to the local or dialect area they come from.[77]

Sex Differences in Speech

In many societies the speech of men differs from the speech of women. The variation can be slight, as in our own society and in England, or more extreme, as with the Carib Indians (in the Lesser Antilles of the West Indies), among whom women and men use different words for the same concepts. In some societies it appears that the female variety of speech is older than the male variety.[78] For example, in the Native American language of Koasati (which used to be spoken in Louisiana), males and females used different endings in certain verbs. The differences seemed to be disappearing in the 1930s, when research on Koasati was done: young girls used the male forms and only older women used the female forms. Koasati men said that the women's speech was a better form of speech, and an interesting parallel comes from comparisons of male and female speech in Britain and the United States. Although the sex differ-

"We only learned to talk yesterday, and now we're not speaking." *(© 1990; Reprinted courtesy of Hoest and Parade Magazine.)*

ences are hardly noticeable to most people, researchers have found that, controlling for social class, age, and ethnic differences, women usually use pronunciation and grammatical forms that are closer to standard English.[79]

Since men and women of the same family do not belong to different social groups, what might explain sex differences in speech? Peter Trudgill suggests two explanations. First, women in many societies may be more concerned than men with being "correct." (In some cases, what is more correct may be what is older or traditional; in other cases, it may be what is associated with the upper class.) Second, in stratified societies, working-class people are thought of as "tougher" and more "aggressive"—a quality that men (even those from higher social-class backgrounds) may be more comfortable with than women.[80] Sex differences in speech may parallel some of the sex differences noted in other social behavior (as we will see in the chapter on sex and culture): girls are more likely than boys to behave in ways that are more acceptable to adults.

The field of sociolinguistics is a relatively new specialty in linguistics. At present, sociolinguists seem to be interested primarily in describing variation in the use of language. Eventually, however, sociolinguistic research may enable us to understand why such variation exists. Why, for exam-

[76]Clifford Geertz, *The Religion of Java* (New York: Free Press, 1960), pp. 248–60; see also J. Joseph Errington, "On the Nature of the Sociolinguistic Sign: Describing the Javanese Speech Levels," in Elizabeth Mertz and Richard J. Parmentier, eds., *Semiotic Mediation: Sociocultural and Psychological Perspectives* (Orlando, FL: Academic Press, 1985), pp. 287–310.

[77]Trudgill, *Sociolinguistics*, pp. 41–42.

[78]Ibid., pp. 79–84; see also Mary R. Haas, "Men's and Women's Speech in Koasati," *Language*, 20 (1944) 142–49.

[79]Trudgill, *Sociolinguistics*, pp. 84–85.

[80]Ibid., pp. 87–88.

ple, do some societies use many different status terms in address? Why do some societies use modes of speaking that vary with the sex of the speaker? An understanding of why language varies in different contexts might also suggest why structural aspects of language change over time. For as social contexts in a society change, the structure of the language might also tend to change.

SUMMARY

1. The essential function language plays in all societies is that of communication. Although human communication is not limited to spoken language, such language is of overriding importance because it is the primary vehicle through which culture is shared and transmitted.

2. Systems of communication are not unique to humans. Other animal species communicate in a variety of ways—by sound, odor, body movement, and so forth. The ability of chimpanzees and gorillas to learn and use sign language suggests that symbolic communication is not unique to humans. Still, human language is distinctive as a communication system in that its spoken and symbolic nature permits an infinite number of combinations and recombinations of meaning.

3. Structural (or descriptive) linguists try to discover the rules of phonology (the patterning of sounds), morphology (the patterning of sound sequences and words), and syntax (the patterning of phrases and sentences) that predict how most speakers of a language talk. From the wide variety of possible human sounds, each language has selected some sounds, or phones, and ignored others. How sounds are grouped into sets called phonemes differs from language to language. The smallest unit of meaning is a morph; one or more morphs with the same meaning make up a morpheme. Children have an intuitive grasp of phonology, morphology, and syntax long before they learn "rules of grammar" in school.

4. By comparative analysis of cognates and grammar, historical linguists test the notion that certain languages derive from a common ancestral language, or protolanguage. The goals are to reconstruct the features of the protolanguage, to hypothesize how the offspring languages separated from the protolanguage or from each other, and to establish the approximate dates of such separations.

5. When two groups of people speaking the same language lose communication with each other because they become separated either physically or socially, they begin to accumulate small changes in phonology, morphology, and syntax. If the separation continues, the two former dialects of the same language will eventually become separate languages—that is, they will become mutually unintelligible.

6. Whereas isolation brings about divergence between speech communities, contact results in greater resemblance. This is particularly evident when contact between mutually unintelligible languages introduces borrowed words, most of which name some new item borrowed from the other culture.

7. Some attempts to explain the diversity of languages have focused on the possible interaction between language and other aspects of culture. On the one hand, if it can be shown that a culture may affect the structure and content of its language, then it would follow that linguistic diversity derives at least in part from cultural diversity. On the other hand, the direction of influence between culture and language might work in reverse: the linguistic structures might affect other aspects of the culture.

8. Recently, some linguists have begun to study variations in how people actually use language when speaking. This type of linguistic study, called sociolinguistics, is concerned with the ethnography of speaking—that is, with cultural and subcultural patterns of speaking in different social contexts.

AKMAJIAN, A., DEMERS, R. A., AND HARNISH, R. M. *Linguistics: An Introduction to Language and Communication,* 2nd ed. Cambridge, MA: M.I.T. Press, 1984. A recent survey of many varieties of research in linguistics.

BROWN, C. H., AND WITKOWSKI, S. R. "Language Universals." Appendix B in D. Levinson and M. J. Malone, eds., *Toward Explaining Human Culture: A Critical Review of the Findings of Worldwide Cross-Cultural Research.* New Haven: HRAF Press, 1980. A review of studies of universals in human languages, including universals in phonology and grammar. Focuses especially on developmental sequences in the lexicon or vocabulary.

BURLING, R. *Man's Many Voices: Language in Its Cultural Context.* New York: Holt, Rinehart & Winston, 1970. A clearly written introduction to issues of interest in anthropological linguistics. Covers such topics as componential analysis, semantics, the effect of social setting on language, Black English, verse and linguistic games, and nonhuman versus human communication.

DE VILLIERS, P. A., AND DE VILLIERS, J. G. *Early Language.* Cambridge, MA: Harvard University Press, 1979. A survey of research findings about children's acquisition of language.

GREENBERG, J. H. *Anthropological Linguistics: An Introduction.* New York: Random House, 1968. A nontechnical treatment of the nature and goals of anthropological linguistics.

SAPIR, E. *Language: An Introduction to the Study of Speech.* New York: Harcourt Brace Jovanovich, 1949 (originally published 1921). A classic nontechnical introduction to the study of human languages and how they vary. Also discusses the relations between language and thought.

SNOWDON, C. T., BROWN, C. H., AND PETERSEN, M. R., eds. *Primate Communication.* New York: Cambridge University Press, 1982. A collection of articles on directions and developments in the study of communication in nonhuman primates.

TRUDGILL, P. *Sociolinguistics: An Introduction to Language and Society,* rev. ed. New York: Penguin, 1983. A survey of how language use relates to variation in social class, ethnic group, sex, and nation, with particular reference to the use of English.

14

Food-Getting

For most people in our society, getting food consists of a trip to the supermarket. Within the space of an hour, we can gather enough food from the shelves to last us a week. Seasons don't daunt us. Week after week, we know food will be there. But we do not think of what would happen if the food were not delivered to the supermarket. We wouldn't be able to eat—and without eating for a while, we would die. Despite the old adage "Man [or woman] does not live by bread alone," without bread or the equivalent we could not live at all. Food-getting activities, then, take precedence over other activities important to survival. Reproduction, social control (the maintenance of peace and order within a group), defense against external threat, and the transmission of knowledge and skills to future generations—none could take place without energy derived from food. Food-getting activities are also important because, as we will see in this and other chapters, the way a society gets its food may have profound effects on other aspects of its culture.

In contrast with our society, most societies have not had food-getting specialists. Rather, almost all able-bodied adults were engaged in getting food. During the 2 to 5 million years that humans have been on earth, 99 percent of the time they have obtained food by gathering wild plants, hunting wild animals, and fishing. Agriculture is a relatively recent phenomenon, dating back only about 10,000 years. And industrial or mechanized agriculture is less than a century old!

In this chapter we look first at examples of the different ways in which societies get food. Then we discuss some of the general features associated with the different patterns of food-getting. And finally we discuss the possible determinants of variation in food-getting.

Food Collection

Food collection may be generally defined as all forms of **subsistence technology** in which food-getting is dependent on naturally occurring resources —that is, wild plants and animals. Although this was the way humans got their food for most of human history (see Figure 14–1), the few remaining food collectors in the world today (conventionally referred to as hunter-gatherers) generally live in

what have been called the *marginal* areas of the earth—deserts, the Arctic, and dense tropical forests, habitats that do not allow easy exploitation by modern agricultural technologies.

Hunter-Gatherers

Anthropologists are very interested in studying the relatively few food-collecting societies still available for observation. These groups may help us understand some aspects of human life in the past, when all people were hunter-gatherers. But we must be cautious in drawing inferences about the past from our observations of contemporary food-collectors for three reasons. First, earlier hunter-gatherers lived in almost all types of environments, including some very bountiful ones. Therefore, what we observe among recent and contemporary hunter-gatherers, who generally live in deserts, the Arctic, and tropical forests, may not be comparable to what would have been observable in more favorable environments in the past.[1] Second, contemporary hunter-gatherers are not relics of the past: like all contemporary societies, they have evolved and are still evolving. This means that the adaptations we observe in contemporary groups may be different from the adaptations made by hunter-gatherers years ago. (For example, few if any contemporary hunters use stone arrowheads.) Third, recent and contemporary hunter-gatherers have been interacting with kinds of societies that did not exist until after 10,000 years ago—agriculturalists, pastoralists, and intrusive powerful state societies.[2] Let us now examine two examples of food-collecting societies, each of which is situated in a different environment.

Australian Aborigines. The Ngatatjara aborigines live in the Gibson Desert of western Australia.[3] When they were studied by Richard Gould, they still lived by gathering wild plants and hunting wild animals. Their desert environment averages less than eight inches of rain per year, and the

---

[1]Carol R. Ember, "Myths about Hunter-Gatherers," *Ethnology*, 17 (1978): 439–48.

[2]Carmel Schrire, ed., *Past and Present in Hunter Gatherer Studies* (Orlando, FL: Academic Press, 1984); Fred R. Myers, "Critical Trends in the Study of Hunter-Gatherers," *Annual Reviews of Anthropology*, 17 (1988): 261–82.

[3]The discussion of the Australian aborigines is based upon Richard A. Gould, *Yiwara: Foragers of the Australian Desert* (New York: Scribner's, 1969).

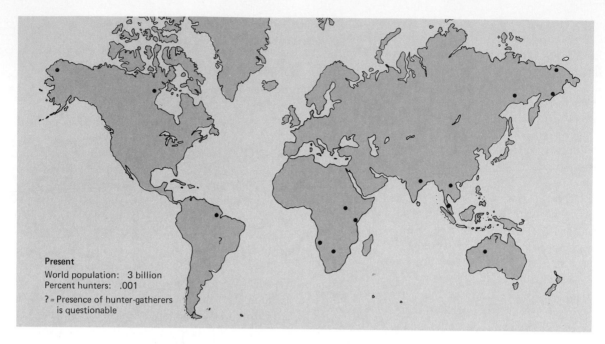

FIGURE 14–1 World Distribution of Present-Day Hunter-Gatherers.
About 10,000 B.C. all people depended on food collection. Today hunter-gatherers constitute only a small fraction of the world population and inhabit marginal areas of the earth. *(Adapted from map "Known Living Sites of Contemporary Hunter-Gatherers" in John E. Pfeiffer,* The Emergence of Man, *3rd ed. New York: Harper & Row, 1978, p. 291. Copyright © 1978 by John E. Pfeiffer. By permission of HarperCollins Publishers.)*

temperature in summer may rise to 118° F. The few permanent water holes are separated by hundreds of square miles of sand, scrub, and rock. Even before Europeans arrived in Australia, the area was sparsely populated—fewer than one person per thirty-five to forty square miles. Now there are even fewer people.

On a typical day, the camp begins to stir just before sunrise, while it is still dark. Children are sent to fetch water, and the people breakfast on water and food left over from the night before. In the cool of the early morning, the adults talk and make plans for the day. The talking goes on for a while. Where should they go for food—to places they have been to recently, or to new places? Sometimes there are other considerations. For example, one woman may want to search for plants whose bark she needs to make new sandals. When the women decide which plants they want to collect, and where they think those plants are most likely to be found, they take up their digging sticks and set out with large wooden bowls of drinking water on their heads. Their children ride on their

hips or walk alongside. Meanwhile, the men may have decided to hunt emus, six-foot-tall ostrichlike birds that do not fly. The men go to a creek bed where they will wait to ambush any game that may come along. They lie patiently behind a screen of brush they have set up, hoping for a chance to throw a spear at an emu or even a kangaroo. They can throw only once, because if they miss, the game will run away.

By noon the men and women are usually back at camp, the women with their wooden bowls each filled with up to fifteen pounds of fruit or other plant foods, the men more often than not with only some small game such as lizards and rabbits. Since the men's food-getting is less certain of success than the women's, most of the aborigine's diet is plant food. The daily cooked meal is eaten toward evening, after an afternoon spent resting, gossiping, and making or repairing tools.

The aborigines are a nomadic people—that is, they move their campsites frequently. The campsites may be isolated and inhabited by only a small number of people, or they may be clusters of groups including as many as eighty persons. The aborigines never establish a campsite right next to a place with water. If they should be too close, their presence would frighten game away and might cause tension with neighboring bands, who also wait for game to come to the scarce watering spots.

The Copper Inuit. The Copper Inuit (previously called Copper Eskimo), so called because they fashioned tools by cold-hammering copper nuggets, numbered between 700 and 800 persons in the years 1913–1918. This was before they had been significantly affected by contact with Westerners.[4] They lived in groups, each numbering about 50 persons, in the vicinity of Coronation Gulf in the Canadian Arctic, a difficult habitat by any standards. Winter lasts nearly nine months, and the sun is not visible for weeks at a time. Only during the brief summer do mean daily temperatures rise above the freezing point. The land surface is treacherous in winter; in summer it is often boggy and difficult to cross because of the heavy thaw.

The Copper Inuit are governed by the seasons much more than the Australian aborigines are. In winter, the Inuit depend on seals and an occasional polar bear for their food. Accordingly, the hunters establish themselves and their families on the pack ice offshore or next to it, in groups of related families. The method of hunting is called *maupok,* meaning "he waits," and each hunter does just that, beside a seal's breathing hole. He stands or sits in absolute quiet and at peak attentiveness, sometimes for hours at a time, until the seal surfaces to breathe. Then he thrusts a harpoon into the animal and waits until his catch is exhausted. Finally, the hunter enlarges the hole in the ice and hauls the animal out.

Seals are indispensable to the Copper Inuit in winter. For many months, especially in the last half of the season, seal meat forms the staple, if not the only, food. Seal blubber provides clear-burning cooking and lighting oil, and sealskin is used to make ice boots, kayaks, oil-storage bags, buckets, and a variety of other items.

With the coming of spring, the Copper Inuit split up into smaller groups and move to shore.

[4]Diamond Jenness, *The People of the Twilight* (Chicago: University of Chicago Press, 1959). This book describes field-work done as part of the Thule (Danish) expedition between 1913 and 1918.

A modern Inuit hunter, wearing a Caribou parka and sealskin boots, aims a rifle while sitting behind the camouflage of an umbrella off Ellesmere Island.

Then fish becomes an important source of food. Also, lean caribou are hunted—not only for their meat, but for the largely undigested vegetables in their stomachs, which are pulled out and eaten raw, on the spot. By summer, the groups have moved on again and redivided. Small bands of men head inland to hunt full-grown caribou. Some of the caribou meat is dried in strips and preserved. The women soften the hides by chewing them and then use them to make tents and clothing. Older men and most of the women and children pass the summer at fishing camps, catching and drying salmon, lake trout, and other fish.

In the fall, after the southward bound caribou have been hunted, the Copper Inuit settle down to await the formation of the pack ice. Usually they have ample supplies of meat and dried fish, so most of their time is spent preparing winter clothing and repairing or making dog sleds, harpoons, lances, and similar articles. The skill, ingenuity, and craftsmanship of the Inuit is particularly evident in their snow houses, or *igloos.* These are built with snow blocks cut from firm drifts with copper (or bone) knives. The blocks are shaped with the inside edges beveled so that the igloo will taper inward and upward to a dome, the whole building being consolidated by one key block.

General Features of Food Collectors. Despite the differences in terrain and climate under which they live and the different food-collecting technologies they use, Australian aborigines, Inuit, and most other recent hunter-gatherers seem to have certain cultural patterns in common. Most live in small communities in sparsely populated territories and follow a nomadic life-style, forming no permanent settlements. As a rule, they do not recognize individual land rights. Their communities do not generally have different classes of people and tend to have no specialized or full-time political officials. Division of labor is based principally on age and sex.[5] Men exclusively hunt large marine and land animals, and usually do the fishing; women usually gather wild plant foods.[6]

Is there a typical pattern of food-getting among hunter-gatherers? Some years ago anthropologists suggested that hunter-gatherers typically get their food more from gathering than from hunting, and that women contribute more than men to subsistence (because women generally do the gathering).[7] Although gathering is the most important food-getting activity for some food collectors (for example, the Ngatatjara aborigines and the !Kung of southern Africa), this is not true for most recent food-collecting societies. A survey of 180 such societies indicates that there is a lot of variation in which food-getting activity is most important to a society: gathering is the most important activity for 30 percent of the surveyed societies, hunting for 25 percent, and fishing for 38 percent. (Perhaps, then, we should call most recent food collectors *fisher-gatherer-hunters!*) In any case, because men generally do the fishing as well as the hunting, it is the men who usually contribute more to food-getting than the women among recent food collectors.[8]

Since food collectors move their camps often and walk great distances, it may seem that the food-collecting way of life is difficult. Although we do not have enough quantitative studies to tell us what is typical of most food collectors, studies of two Australian aborigine groups[9] and of one !Kung group[10] indicate that those food collectors do not spend many hours getting food. For example, !Kung adults spend an average of about 17 hours per week collecting food. Even when you add the time spent making tools (about 6 hours a week) and doing housework (about 19 hours a week), the !Kung seem to have more leisure time than many agriculturalists, as we will discuss later.

Food Production

Beginning about 10,000 years ago, certain peoples in widely separated geographic locations made the revolutionary changeover to **food production.** That is, they began to cultivate and then domesticate plants and animals. With domestication of these food sources, people acquired control over certain natural processes, such as animal breeding and seeding. Today, most peoples in the world depend for their food on some combination of domesticated plants and animals.

Anthropologists generally distinguish three major types of food-production systems—horticulture, intensive agriculture, and pastoralism.

Horticulture

The word **horticulture** may conjure up visions of people with "green thumbs" growing orchids and other flowers in greenhouses. But to anthropologists, the word means the growing of crops of *all* kinds with relatively simple tools and methods, in the absence of permanently cultivated fields. The tools are usually hand tools, such as the digging stick or hoe, not plows or other equipment pulled by animals or tractors. And the methods used do not include fertilization, irrigation, or other ways to restore soil fertility after a growing season.

There are two kinds of horticulture. The more common one involves a dependence on **extensive** or **shifting cultivation.** The land is worked for short periods and then left idle for some years.

[5]Data from Robert B. Textor, comp., *A Cross-Cultural Summary* (New Haven: HRAF Press, 1967); and Elman R. Service, *The Hunters*, 2nd ed. (Englewood Cliffs, NJ: Prentice Hall, 1979).
[6]George P. Murdock and Caterina Provost, "Factors in the Division of Labor by Sex: A Cross-Cultural Analysis," *Ethnology*, 12 (1973): 207.
[7]Richard B. Lee, "What Hunters Do for a Living, or, How to Make Out on Scarce Resources," in Richard B. Lee and Irven DeVore, eds., *Man the Hunter* (Chicago: Aldine, 1968), pp. 30–48; and Irven DeVore and Melvin J. Konner, "Infancy in Hunter-Gatherer Life: An Ethological Perspective," in N. F. White, ed., *Ethology and Psychiatry* (Toronto: Ontario Mental Health Foundation and University of Toronto Press, 1974), pp. 113–41.
[8]Carol R. Ember, "Myths about Hunter-Gatherers."

[9]Frederick D. McCarthy and Margaret McArthur, "The Food Quest and the Time Factor in Aboriginal Economic Life," in C. P. Mountford, ed., *Records of the Australian-American Scientific Expedition to Arnhem Land, Volume 2: Anthropology and Nutrition* (Melbourne: Melbourne University Press, 1960).
[10]Richard B. Lee, *The !Kung San: Men, Women, and Work in a Foraging Society* (Cambridge: Cambridge University Press, 1979), pp. 256–58, 278–80.

Compared to hunter-gatherer communities, horticultural communities, such as this Shavante village in the Brazilian Amazon, are larger in size.

During the years when the land is not cultivated, wild plants and brush grow up; when the fields are later cleared by *slash-and-burn* (to be described shortly), nutrients are returned to the soil. The other kind of horticulture involves a dependence on long-growing tree crops. The two kinds of horticulture may be practiced in the same society, but in neither case is there permanent cultivation of field crops.

Most horticultural societies do not rely on crops alone for food. Many also hunt or fish; a few are nomadic for part of the year. For example, the northern Kayapo of the Brazilian Amazon leave their villages for as long as three months at a time to trek through the forest in search of game. The entire village participates in a trek, carrying large quantities of garden produce and moving their camp every day.[11] Other horticulturalists raise domestic animals, but these are usually not large animals such as cattle and camels.[12] More often than

not, the animals raised by horticulturalists are smaller ones such as pigs, chickens, goats, and sheep. Let us look now at two horticultural societies, the Jivaro of Ecuador and the Samoans of the South Pacific.

The Jivaro. The Jivaro have long attracted world attention because of their practice of shrinking and preserving human heads. They number perhaps 8,000 and live in small village groups along the eastern slopes of the Andes, in a region of tropical rain forest difficult for outsiders to penetrate.[13]

The Jivaro subsist on garden produce, particularly manioc roots. These large, starchy tubers, rather like parsnips in color and texture, are made into flour or into beer, which is an important item in the Jivaro diet. Their garden crops, mostly carbohydrates, provide about 65 percent of their calories. The men are responsible for the initial clear-

[11]Dennis Werner, "Trekking in the Amazon Forest," *Natural History,* November 1978, pp. 42–54.

[12]Data from Textor, comp., *A Cross-Cultural Summary.*
[13]This discussion is based upon Michael J. Harner, *The Jivaro* (Garden City, NY: Doubleday Anchor, 1973).

ing of a vegetable plot in the jungle; the women then take care of planting, weeding, and harvesting the manioc, sweet potatoes, sugar cane, and pineapples. Men plant and harvest corn. Clearing is done by the **slash-and-burn** method. First, the undergrowth is cut away from a given area. Then the trees are felled. Finally, after the cut trees and brush have lain on the ground for several months in the dry season, they are set afire. The cleared ground is cultivated with digging sticks and is used for three to five years until the soil is exhausted. Then the group must move to a new site and prepare a new garden plot in the same manner.

Hunting provides the main sources of protein for the Jivaro. The men spend considerable time hunting monkeys and birds with blowguns and poisoned darts. Lances may be used for larger animals. Dogs are used to help hunt peccaries (piglike animals) and jaguars. A man's wife accompanies him to handle the dog. Fish are caught by a variety of methods, but the largest catches are obtained when the men, women, and children from a few households poison fish in artificially constructed "lagoons" in the rivers.

The economy of the Jivaro is essentially self-sufficient, but the tribe obtains machetes, steel axes, and shotguns from the outside world by means of neighborhood-to-neighborhood trading partnerships. This relative self-sufficiency is reflected in the society as a whole. The Jivaro are still determined to avoid and if need be to fight off intruders, just as they were long ago when the Incas and the Spaniards attempted to penetrate their territory.

The Samoans. The Samoans numbered about 56,000 persons in 1839, soon after European missionaries arrived.[14] The islands of Samoa, which are about 2,300 miles south of the Hawaiian Islands, are volcanic in origin, with central ridges and peaks as high as 4,000 feet. Though the land is generally steep, the islands have a lush plant cover watered by up to 200 inches of rain a year (about five times the amount of rain that falls on New York in a year). All that rain does not interfere much with outdoor activity, since the torrential showers do not last long and the water disap-

pears quickly into the porous volcanic soil. The temperature is relatively constant, rarely falling below 70° or rising above 88° F. Strong cooling trade winds blow most of the year, generally from the east or southeast, and on the coasts one constantly hears the low rumble of huge Pacific swells breaking upon the coral reefs.

Samoan horticulture involves mostly three tree crops requiring little work except in harvesting. Once planted, and requiring hardly more than a few years of waiting, the breadfruit tree continues to produce about two crops a year for up to half a century. Coconut trees may continue to produce for a hundred years. And banana trees make new stalks of fruit, each weighing more than fifty pounds, for many years; merely cutting down one stalk induces the plant to grow another. Young men do most of the harvesting of tree crops. Women do the occasional weeding.

The Samoans also practice some shifting cultivation; men periodically clear small patches of land for a staple root crop called *taro*. The taro patches can produce a few crops before they must be allowed to revert to bush so that soil fertility can be restored. But even taro cultivation does not require much work; planting requires nothing more than slightly burying the top sliced off a root just harvested. (Young men do most of the planting and harvesting.) The taro patches are weeded infrequently, mostly by women. This kind of casual farming behavior prompted Captain Bligh, of *Mutiny on the Bounty* fame, to describe the Tahitians as lazy.[15] Captain Bligh's attitude was ethnocentric. South Pacific islanders such as the Samoans and Tahitians cannot weed as often as European farmers without risking the erosion of their soil, because in contrast with European farmlands, which are generally flat or only slightly sloping, the land of Samoa and Tahiti is mostly steep. The Samoan and Tahitian practice of not weeding crops and growing them in glorious and messy confusion means that the deep and shallow root structures of the various plants growing together can prevent the loose volcanic soil from being washed away by the torrential showers.

The Samoans keep chickens and pigs, but they are eaten only occasionally. The major source of

---

[14]This section is based mostly on Melvin Ember's fieldwork on the islands of American Samoa in 1955–1956.

[15]Douglas L. Oliver, *Ancient Tahitian Society, Volume 1: Ethnography* (Honolulu: University of Hawaii Press, 1974), pp. 252–53.

animal protein in the Samoan diet is fish, which are caught inside and outside the reef. Younger men may swim in the deep sea outside the reef and use a sling to spear fish; older men will more likely try to catch fish by standing on the reef and throwing a four-pointed spear at fish swimming inside the reef. For many years, people in the villages of Samoa have sold copra (the sun-dried meat of the ripe coconut) to the world market for coconut oil. Men generally cut the copra from the shells after the ripe coconuts fall by themselves to the ground. With the cash earned from the sale of copra, people buy imported things such as machetes and kerosene. But people in most villages still produce most of the foods they eat.

General Features of Horticulturalists. In most horticultural societies, simple farming techniques have tended to yield more food from a given area than is generally available to food collectors. Consequently, horticulture is generally able to support larger, more densely populated communities. The way of life of horticulturalists is generally more sedentary than that of food collectors, although communities may move after a number of years to farm a new series of plots. (Some horticulturalists have permanent villages because they depend mostly on food from trees that keep producing for a long time.) In contrast with most recent hunter-gatherer groups, horticultural societies exhibit the beginnings of social differentiation. For example, some individuals may be part-time craftworkers or part-time political officials, and certain members of a kin group may have more status than other individuals in the society.

Intensive Agriculture

People engaged in **intensive agriculture** employ a variety of techniques that enable them to cultivate fields permanently. Essential nutrients may be put back through the use of fertilizers, which may be organic material, most commonly dung from humans or other animals, or inorganic (chemical) fertilizers. But there are other ways to restore nutrients. The Luo of western Kenya plant beans around corn plants. Bacteria growing around the roots of the bean plant replace lost nitrogen, and the corn plant conveniently provides a pole for the bean plant to wind around as it grows. Some intensive agriculturalists use irrigation from streams and rivers to ensure an adequate supply of water-borne nutrients.

In general, the technology of intensive agriculturalists is more complex than that of horticulturalists. Plows rather than digging sticks are generally employed. But there is enormous variation in the degree to which intensive agriculturalists rely on mechanization rather than hand labor: in some societies the most complex machine is an animal-drawn plow; in the corn and wheat belts of the United States, huge tractors till, seed, and fertilize twelve rows at a time.[16]

Let's look now at two different groups of intensive agriculturalists: those of rural Greece and those of the Mekong Delta in Vietnam.

Rural Greece. The village of Vasilika is situated at the foot of Mount Parnassus on the Boeotian plain. In recent times, its population has numbered some 220 inhabitants.[17]

Grapevines and wheat are cultivated for domestic use. The agricultural year begins in March with pruning of the vines and hoeing of the fields, which are regarded as men's work. Wine making begins in September, after the grain harvest, and involves the whole family. Men, women, and children talk and joke as they pick the grapes and put them into large baskets. After the leaves and stems are removed, the fruit is trampled by the men and the newly pressed grape juice, or *must*, is transferred to barrels. After adding whatever sugar and alcohol are needed, farmers also add resin to give the wine its characteristic flavor.

The villagers use horses to plow their wheat fields in October, and in November they sow the seed by hand. The wheat crop is harvested the following summer, generally by machine. Wheat constitutes the staple village food and is eaten as bread, as a cereal (called *trakhana*), or as noodles. It is also commonly bartered for other food items, such as fish, olive oil, and coffee.

Cotton and tobacco are the main **cash crops** (crops raised for sale). In this dry plains country, the success of the cotton crop depends on irrigation, and the villagers use efficient diesel pumps to

[16]Seth S. King, "Some Farm Machinery Seems Less Than Human," *New York Times*, April 8, 1979, p. E9.
[17]The discussion of rural Greece is based on Ernestine Friedl, *Vasilika: A Village in Modern Greece* (New York: Holt, Rinehart & Winston, 1962).

Intensive agriculture often involves irrigation, as in these rice terraces on the Indonesian island of Bali.

distribute water. The real work in the cotton fields begins after the spring plowing and seeding have been completed. Then the young plants must be hoed and mulched, a task done mostly by women. The season of cotton cultivation is especially hard on women, who must do all the cooking and household chores in addition to working in the cotton fields. Irrigation, which begins in July, is men's work. It is usually done three times a season and involves the clearing of shallow ditches, the mounting of pumps, and the channeling of the water. Cotton picking, which starts in October, is considered women's work. For picking, as well as hoeing and harvesting, a farmer owning more than five acres usually hires women from the same village or neighboring villages, and sometimes even from distant towns. The cotton ginning is carried out by centrally located contractors, who are paid on the spot with 6 percent of each farmer's crop. Most of the seed reclaimed in the ginning is used for the next year's planting. The remainder is pressed into cakes to serve as supplementary food

for ewes at lambing time. Tobacco yields a larger cash income than cotton, and the tobacco crop fits well into what would otherwise be slack periods in cultivation.

Raising animals plays a relatively minor role in the villagers' economic life. Each farmer has a horse or two for heavy draft work, a mule or donkey, about two dozen sheep, and some fowl.

Farmers at Vasilika are responsive to modern developments; they are prepared to experiment to a certain extent, especially with mechanization. Where the amount of acreage under cultivation warrants the expense, tractors are hired for plowing. Specialists are regularly called in to handle harvesting, cotton ginning, and similar tasks. Indeed, the Greek farmer is content to be a farmer and to rely on the skills of others to repair his roof, maintain his water pump, or provide the mechanical know-how for his production.

Rural Vietnam: The Mekong Delta. The village of Khanh Hau, situated along the flat Mekong

Delta, comprised about 600 families when it was described in the late 1950s,[18] before the Vietnam War. The delta area has a tropical climate, with a rainy season that lasts from May to November. As a whole, the area has been made habitable only through extensive drainage.

Wet rice cultivation is the principal agricultural activity of Khanh Hau. It is part of a complex, specialized arrangement that involves three interacting components: (1) a complex system of irrigation and water control; (2) a variety of specialized equipment, including plows, water wheels, threshing sledges, and winnowing machines; and (3) a clearly defined set of socioeconomic roles—from those of landlord, tenant, and laborer to those of rice miller and rice merchant.

In the dry season, the farmer decides what sort of rice crop to plant—whether of long (120 days) or short (90 days) maturation. The choice depends on the capital at his disposal, the current cost of fertilizer, and the anticipated demand for rice. The seedbeds are prepared as soon as the rains have softened the ground in May. The soil is turned over and broken up as many as six separate times, with two-day intervals for "airing" between each operation. While the soil is being plowed and harrowed in this way, the rice seeds are soaked in water for two days to stimulate sprouting. Before the seedlings are planted, the paddy is plowed once more and harrowed twice in two directions at right angles.

Planting is a delicate, specialized operation that must usually be done quickly and is performed generally by hired male labor. But efficient planting is not enough to guarantee a good crop. Proper fertilization and irrigation are equally important. In the irrigating, steps must be taken to ensure that the water level remains at exactly the proper depth over the entire paddy. Water is distributed by means of scoops, wheels, and mechanical pumps. Successive crops of rice ripen from late September to May; all members of the family may be called upon to help with the harvest. After each crop is harvested, it is threshed, winnowed, and dried. Normally, the rice is sorted into three portions: one is set aside for use by the household in the following year; one is for payment of hired labor and other services (such as loans from agricultural banks); and one is for cash sale on the market. Aside from the harvesting, women generally do little work in the fields; they spend most of their time on household chores. However, in families with little land, young daughters help in the fields and older daughters may hire themselves out to other farmers.

The villagers also cultivate vegetables, raise pigs, chickens, and the like, and frequently engage in fishing. The village economy usually supports three or four implement makers and a much larger number of carpenters.

General Features of Intensive-Agricultural Societies. In contrast with horticultural groups, societies with intensive agriculture are more likely to have towns and cities, a high degree of craft specialization, more complex political organization, and large differences in wealth and power.

A number of studies suggest that intensive agriculturalists typically work longer hours than simpler agriculturalists.[19] For example, men engaged in intensive agriculture average nine hours of work a day, seven days a week, while women average almost eleven hours of work per day. Most of the work for women in intensive-agricultural societies involves food processing and work in and around the home, but they also spend a lot of time working in the fields. We discuss some of the implications of the work patterns for women in the chapter on sex and culture.

Intensive-agricultural societies are more likely than horticultural societies to face food shortages, even though intensive agriculture is generally more productive than horticulture.[20] Why, if more food can be produced per acre, is there more risk of shortage among intensive agriculturalists? Social scientists do not know for sure. One possibility is that intensive agriculturalists may rely more often on single crops, and such crops may fail because of fluctuations in weather, plant diseases, or insect pests. Intensive agriculturalists may also be more

---

[18]This discussion is based on Gerald Cannon Hickey, *Village in Vietnam* (New Haven: Yale University Press, 1964), pp. 135–65.

[19]Carol R. Ember, "The Relative Decline in Women's Contribution to Agriculture with Intensification," *American Anthropologist*, 85 (1983): 289.

[20]Data from Textor, comp., *A Cross-Cultural Summary.*

Expensive machines are used to clear a corn field.

likely to face food shortages because they are often producing crops for a market. If the market demand drops, they may not have enough cash to buy all the other food they need.

The Commercialization of Agriculture.   Some intensive agriculturalists produce very little for sale; most of what they produce is for their own use. But there is a worldwide trend for intensive agriculturalists to produce more and more for a market. (This is called **commercialization,** which may occur in any area of life and which involves increasing dependence on buying and selling, with money usually as the medium of exchange.) The increasing commercialization of agriculture is associated with several other trends. One is that farm work is becoming more and more mechanized as hand labor becomes scarce (because of migration to industrial and service jobs in towns and cities) or too expensive. A second trend is the emergence and spread of *agribusiness,* large corporation-owned farms that may be operated by multinational companies and worked by hired (as opposed to "family") labor. A third trend associated with the commercialization of agriculture (including animal raising) is a reduction in the proportion of the population engaged in food production. In the United States, for example, less than 2 percent of the total population is still on the farm.[21] In the chapter on culture change, we will discuss more fully some of

the apparent consequences of these worldwide trends.

Pastoralism

Most agriculturalists raise some animals, but a small number of societies depend directly or indirectly on domesticated herds of animals for their living. We call such a system **pastoralism.** Although we might assume that pastoralists breed animals largely to eat their meat, this is generally not the case. Pastoralists more often get their animal protein from live animals in the form of milk; some pastoralists also regularly take blood, which is also rich in protein, from their animals to mix with other foods. The herds also indirectly provide food because pastoralists typically trade animal products for plant foods and other necessities. In fact, a large proportion of their food may actually come from trade with agricultural groups.[22] For example, some pastoral groups in the Middle East derive a good deal of their livelihood from the sale of what we call oriental rugs, which are made on handlooms from the wool of their sheep. Two recent pastoral societies are the Basseri of southern Iran and the Lapps of Scandinavia.

The Basseri.   The Basseri are a tribe of about 16,000 tent-dwelling nomads.[23] Their herds consist principally of sheep and goats, though donkeys and camels are raised for pulling or carrying and the more wealthy men have horses for riding. Theirs is a dry, arid habitat, with rainfall averaging no more than ten inches a year.

The Basseri's pastoral way of life is based on a regular, migratory exploitation of the grazing lands within their territory, which measures about 15,000 square miles in all. In winter, when the mountains to the north are covered with snow, the plains and foothills to the south offer extensive pasturage. During the spring, grazing is excellent on a plateau near the center of the territory. By summer, when most of the lower-lying pastures have dried up, sufficient food for the herds may be found in the mountains at an altitude of nearly 6,000 feet.

[21]"Dwindling Numbers on the Farm," *Nation's Business,* April 1988, p. 16.

[22]Susan H. Lees and Daniel G. Bates, "The Origins of Specialized Nomadic Pastoralism: A Systemic Model," *American Antiquity,* 39 (1974): 187–93.

[23]The discussion of the Basseri is based on Fredrik Barth, *Nomads of South Persia* (Oslo: Universitetsforlaget, 1964; Boston: Little, Brown, 1968).

Annual migrations are so important to the economies of the Basseri and other pastoralist societies of that region that they have developed the concept of *il-rah*, or "tribal road." A major pastoral tribe such as the Basseri has a traditional route and schedule. The route, consisting of the localities in the order in which each is visited, follows existing passes and lines of communication. The schedule, which regulates the length of time each location will be occupied, depends on the maturation of different pastures and the movements of other tribes. The *il-rah* is regarded, in effect, as the property of the tribe. Local populations and authorities recognize the tribe's right to pass along roads and cultivated lands, to draw water from the public wells, and to pasture flocks on public land.

The Basseri generally herd sheep and goats together, with one shepherd (a boy or unmarried man) responsible for a flock of 300 to 400 animals. Children of both sexes are usually responsible for herding the baby animals (lambs and kids). Milk and its by-products are the most important commodities, but wool, hides, and meat are also important to the economy of the Basseri. Both wool and hides are traded, but they are of even greater use within the tribe. The Basseri are skilled spinners and weavers, especially the women, much of whose time is spent at these activities. Saddlebags and pack bags are woven on horizontal looms from homespun wool and hair, as are carpets, sleeping rugs, and the characteristic black tents made of panels of woven goat hair. This hair provides an exceptionally versatile cloth. For winter use, it retains heat and repels water; in the summer, it insulates against heat and permits free circulation of air. Lambskin hides also serve many purposes. When plucked and turned inside out, they are made into storage bags to hold water, buttermilk, sour milk, and other liquids.

Most of the Basseri must trade for the necessities and luxury items they do not produce within the community. The staple items they sell are butter, wool, lambskins, rope, and occasionally livestock.

The Lapps. The Lapps live and move with their reindeer herds in northwestern Scandinavia where Finland, Sweden, and Norway share common frontiers. It is a typical Arctic habitat: cold, windswept, with long, dark days for half the year.

Lapps rounding up reindeer in Norway.

Though the Lapps have gradually come under modern cultural influences in the twentieth century, theirs is still largely a pastoral form of life.[24]

The Lapps herd their reindeer either intensively or extensively, using the latter method more often today. In the intensive system, the herd is constantly under observation within a general fenced area for the whole year. Intensively herded reindeer and other animals are accustomed to human contact. Hence, the summer corralling of the females for milking and the breaking in of the ox-reindeer for use as work animals are not difficult tasks.

The extensive system involves allowing the animals to migrate over a large area. It requires less surveillance and encompasses larger herds. Under this system, the reindeer are allowed to move through their seasonal feeding cycles watched by only one or two scouts. The other Lapps stay with the herd only when it has settled in its summer or winter habitat. But milking, breaking in, and corralling are generally harder in the extensive system because the animals are less accustomed to humans.

Even under the extensive system, which theoretically permits Lapps to engage in subsidiary economic activities such as hunting and fishing, the reindeer herd is the essential, if not the only, source of income. A family may possess as many as

[24]The discussion of the Lapps is based on Ian Whitaker, *Social Relations in a Nomadic Lappish Community* (Oslo: Utgitt av Norsk Folksmuseum, 1955); and T. I. Itkonen, "The Lapps of Finland," *Southwestern Journal of Anthropology*, 7 (1951): 32–68.

FOOD-GETTING **239**

1,000 reindeer, but usually the figure is half that number. Studies show 200 to be the minimum number of reindeer needed to provide for a family of four or five adults. Women may have shared the herding chores in the past under the intensive system, but now under the extensive system men do the herding. Women still do the milking.

The Lapps eat the meat of the bull reindeer; the female reindeer are kept for breeding purposes. Bulls are slaughtered in the fall, after the mating season. Meat and hides are frequently sold or bartered for other food and necessities.

General Features of Pastoralism. In recent times, pastoralism has been practiced mainly in grassland and other semiarid habitats that are not especially suitable for cultivation without some significant technological input such as irrigation. Pastoralists are generally nomadic, moving with their herds to new pastures as necessary. In some areas, however, pastoralists spend much of the year in one place, usually because that place provides grazing and water for much of the year. Pastoral communities are generally small, usually consisting of a group of related families.[25] Individuals or families may own their own animals, but decisions about when and where to move the herds are generally community decisions. As we have noted, there is a great deal of interdependence between pastoral and agricultural groups. That is, trade is usually necessary for pastoral groups to survive.

Environmental Restraints on Food-Getting

Of great interest to anthropologists is why different societies have different methods of getting food. Archeological evidence suggests that major changes in food-getting—such as the domestication of plants and animals—have been independently invented in at least several areas of the world. Yet, despite these comparable inventions and their subsequent spread by migration, there is still wide diversity in the means by which people obtain food.

How much does the physical environment affect food-getting? Anthropologists have generally concluded that the physical environment by itself has a restraining, rather than a determining, effect

on the major types of subsistence. Because they have very short growing seasons, cold regions of the earth are not particularly conducive to the growing of plants. No society we know of has practiced agriculture in the arctic; instead people who live there rely primarily on animals for food. But both food collection (as among the Inuit) and food production (as among the Lapps) can be practiced in cold areas. Indeed, cross-cultural evidence indicates that neither food collection nor production is significantly associated with any particular type of habitat.[26]

We know that food collection has been practiced at one time or another in almost all areas of the earth. The physical environment does seem to have some effect on what kind of food collection is practiced, that is, on how much food collectors will depend on plants, animals or fish. Further away from the equator, food collectors depend much less on plants for food and much more on animals and fish.[27] Lewis Binford argues that fishing becomes increasingly important in cold climates because food collectors need nonportable housing in severe winters to protect themselves from the cold. Therefore they cannot rely on large animals that usually have to feed themselves by moving over considerable distances in the winter. Fishing is more localized than hunting, and therefore food collectors who rely on fishing can stay in their nonportable houses in winter.[28]

There is one habitat that may have precluded food collection until recent times. If it were not for the nearness of food producers (particularly agriculturalists), recent food collectors like the Mbuti Pygmies (of central Africa) could probably not have supported themselves in the tropical forest habitats where they now live.[29] Tropical forests are

[25]Data from Textor, comp., *A Cross-Cultural Summary.*

[26]Ibid.

[27]Lewis R. Binford, "Mobility, Housing, and Environment: A Comparative Study," *Journal of Anthropological Research,* 46 (1990): 119–52; see also Bobbi Low, "Human Responses to Environmental Extremeness and Uncertainty," in Elizabeth Cashdan, ed., *Risk and Uncertainty in Tribal and Peasant Economies* (Boulder, CO: Westview Press, 1990), pp. 242–43.

[28]The few food collectors in cold areas relying primarily on hunting have animals (dogs, horses, reindeer) that can carry transportable housing—see Binford, "Mobility, Housing, and Environment."

[29]Robert C. Bailey, Genevieve Head, Mark Jenike, Bruce Owen, Robert Rectman, and Elzbieta Zechenter, "Hunting and Gathering in Tropical Rain Forest: Is It Possible?" *American Anthropologist,* 91 (1989): 59–82.

TABLE 14–1 Variation in Food-Getting and Associated Features

| | FOOD COLLECTORS | FOOD PRODUCERS | | |
	Hunter-Gatherers	Horticulturalists	Pastoralists	Intensive Agriculturalists
Population density	Lowest	Low–moderate	Low	Highest
Maximum community size	Small	Small–moderate	Small	Large (towns and cities)
Nomadism/permanence of settlements	Generally nomadic or seminomadic	More sedentary: communities may move after several years	Generally nomadic or seminomadic	Permanent communities
Food shortages	Infrequent	Infrequent	Frequent	Frequent
Trade	Minimal	Minimal	Very important	Very important
Full-time craft specialists	None	None or few	Some	Many (high degree of craft specialization)
Individual differences in wealth	Generally none	Generally minimal	Moderate	Considerable
Political leadership	Informal	Some part-time political officials	Part- and full-time political officials	Many full-time political officials

lush in plants, but they do not provide much in the way of reachable fruits, seeds, flowers that can be eaten by humans. Animals are available in tropical forests, but they are typically lean, and do not provide humans with sufficient carbohydrates or fat. Like the Pygmy groups who hunt and gather in the forest, many tropical food collectors trade for agricultural products; other collectors cultivate some crops in addition to hunting and gathering. It would seem, then, that food collectors could not survive in tropical forests were it not for the carbohydrates they obtain from agriculturalists (whoever they are).

When we contrast horticulture and intensive agriculture, the physical environment appears to explain some of the variation. Approximately 80 percent of all societies that practice horticulture or simple agriculture are in the tropics, whereas 75 percent of all societies that practice intensive agriculture are *not* in tropical-forest environments.[30]

Tropical forests have abundant rainfall. But despite the attractiveness of lush vegetation and brilliant coloring, tropical forest lands do not usually offer favorable environments for intensive agriculture. This may be because the heavy rainfall quickly washes away certain minerals from cleared

land. Also, the difficulty of controlling insect pests and weeds (which abound in tropical forests)[31] may make intensive agriculture less productive.

However, difficulty is not impossibility. Today, there are some areas (for instance, the Mekong Delta of Vietnam) whose tropical forests have been cleared and prevented from growing up again by the intensive cultivation of rice in paddies. And although cultivation is not normally possible in dry lands (because of insufficient natural rainfall to sustain crops), agriculture can be practiced where there are *oases*—small, naturally watered areas where crops can be grown with a simple technology—or rivers that can be tapped by irrigation (one of the techniques used with intensive agriculture).

The animals raised by pastoralists depend primarily on grass for food, so it is not surprising that pastoralism is typically practiced in grassland regions of the earth. These regions may be **steppes** (dry, low grass cover), **prairies** (taller, better-watered grass), or **savannas** (tropical grasslands). The grassland habitat favors large game and hence sup-

[30]Data from Textor, comp., *A Cross-Cultural Summary.*

[31]Daniel H. Janzen, "Tropical Agroecosystems," *Science,* December 21, 1973, pp. 1212–18. For an argument supporting the "weeding" explanation, see Robert L. Carneiro, "Slash-and-Burn Cultivation among the Kuikuru and Its Implications for Settlement Patterns," in Yehudi Cohen, ed., *Man in Adaptation: The Cultural Present* (Chicago: Aldine, 1968).

In the Imperial Valley of Southern California, agriculture is not possible without irrigation. Here we see the irrigated fields next to desert just south of the Salton Sea.

ports both hunting and pastoral technologies, except where a machine technology makes intensive agriculture possible, as in parts of the United States, Canada, and Ukraine.

Very different strategies of food-getting have been practiced in the same environment over time. For example, a dramatic illustration is the history of the Imperial Valley in California. The complex systems of irrigation now used in that dryland area have made it one of the most productive regions in the world. Yet about 400 years ago, this same valley supported only hunting and gathering groups who subsisted on wild plants and animals.

It is evident from the Imperial Valley example and many others like it that the physical environment does not by itself account for the system of food-getting in an area. (Even a polar environment could have agriculture with heated greenhouses, but currently it would be too expensive.) Technological advances as well as enormous capital investment in irrigation, labor, and equipment have made intensive agriculture possible in the Imperial Valley. But the agriculture there is precarious, depending on sources of water and power from elsewhere. In a prolonged drought, it may be difficult or too expensive to obtain the needed water. And

should the prices for vegetables fall, the farming businesses in the Imperial Valley could find themselves unable to finance the investment and borrowing they need to continue. So technological and social/political factors mostly determine what kind of food-getting can be practiced in a given environment.

The Origin, Spread, and Intensification of Food Production

To understand why most people today are food producers rather than food collectors, we need to consider why plant and animal domestication may have emerged in the first place. In the chapter on the origins of food production and settled life, we examined a number of theories that suggested why people started to produce food even though doing so may have involved more work and more risk of famine. All the theories currently considered suggest that people made the changeover because they were *pushed* into it. The possible reasons include (1) population growth in regions of bountiful wild resources (which may have pushed people to move to marginal areas where they tried to reproduce their former abundance); (2) global population growth (which filled up most of the world's habitable regions and may have forced people to utilize a broader spectrum of wild resources and to domesticate plants and animals); and (3) the emergence of hotter and drier summers and colder winters (which may have favored sedentarization near seasonal stands of wild grain, while population growth in such areas may have forced people to plant crops and raise animals to support themselves).

Whatever the reasons for the switch to food production, we still need to explain why food production has generally supplanted food collection as the primary mode of subsistence. We cannot assume that collectors would automatically adopt production as a superior way of life once they understood the process of domestication. After all, as we have noted, domestication may entail more work and provide less security than the food-collecting way of life.

The spread of agriculture may be linked to the need for territorial expansion. As a sedentary, food-producing population grew, it may have been forced to expand into new territory. Some of this territory may have been vacant, but much of it was probably already occupied by food collectors. Although food production is not necessarily easier than collection, it is generally more productive per unit of land. Greater productivity means that more people can be supported in a given territory. In the competition for land between the faster-expanding food producers and the food collectors, the food producers may have had a significant advantage: they had more people in a given area. Thus, the hunter-gatherer groups may have been more likely to lose out in the competition for land. Some groups may have adopted cultivation, abandoning the hunter-gatherer way of life in order to survive. Other groups, continuing as food collectors, may have been forced to retreat into areas not desired by the cultivators. Today, as we have seen, the small number of remaining food collectors inhabit areas not particularly suitable for cultivation—dry lands, dense tropical forests, and polar regions.

Just as prior population growth might account for the origins of domestication, so at later periods further population growth and ensuing pressure on resources might at least partially explain the transformation of horticultural systems into intensive-agricultural systems. Ester Boserup has suggested that intensification of agriculture, with a consequent increase in yield per acre, is not likely to develop naturally out of horticulture because intensification requires much more work.[32] She argues that people will be willing to intensify their labor only if they have to. Where emigration is not feasible, the prime mover behind intensification may generally be prior population growth. The need to pay taxes or tribute to a political authority may also stimulate intensification.

Intensive agriculture has not yet spread to every part of the world. Horticulture continues to be practiced in certain tropical regions, and there are still some pastoralists and food collectors. As we have noted, some environments may make it difficult to adopt certain subsistence practices. For example, intensive agriculture cannot supplant horticulture in some tropical environments without tremendous investments in chemical fertilizers and pesticides, not to mention the additional labor required.[33] And enormous amounts of water may be required to make agriculturalists out of hunter-gatherers and pastoralists who now exploit semiarid environments. Hence, the different kinds of food-getting practices we observe today throughout the world are likely to be with us for some time to come.

[32]Ester Boserup, *The Conditions of Agricultural Growth: The Economics of Agrarian Change under Population Pressure* (Chicago: Aldine, 1965).
[33]Janzen, "Tropical Agroecosystems."

SUMMARY

1. Food collection—hunting, gathering, and fishing—depends upon wild plants and animals and is the oldest human food-getting technology. Today, however, only a small number of societies practice it, and they tend to inhabit marginal environments.

2. Food collectors can be found in a number of different physical habitats. Food collectors are generally nomadic and population density is low. The small bands generally consist of related families, with the division of labor usually along age and sex lines only. Personal possessions are limited, individual land rights are usually not recognized, and different classes of people are generally unknown.

3. Beginning about 10,000 years ago, certain peoples in widely separated geographical locations began to make the revolutionary changeover to food production—the cultivation and raising of plants and animals. Over the centuries, food production began to supplant food collection as the predominant mode of subsistence.

4. Horticulturalists farm with relatively simple tools and methods and do not cultivate fields permanently. Their food supply is generally sufficient to support larger, more densely populated communities than can be fed by food collection. Their way of life is generally sedentary, although communities may move after a number of years to farm a new series of plots.

5. Intensive agriculture is characterized by techniques such as fertilization and irrigation that allow fields to be cultivated permanently. In contrast with horticultural societies, intensive agriculturalists are more likely to have towns and cities, a high degree of craft specialization, large differences in wealth and power, and more complex political organization. They are also more likely to face food shortages. In the modern world, intensive agriculture is geared increasingly to production for a market.

6. Pastoralism is a subsistence technology involving principally the raising of large herds of animals. It is generally found in low-rainfall areas. Pastoralists tend to be nomadic, to have small communities consisting of related families, and to depend significantly on trade.

7. Anthropologists generally agree that the physical environment normally exercises a restraining rather than determining influence on how people in an area get their food; technology and social/political factors may be more important.

8. Food producers can generally support more people in a given territory than food collectors can. Therefore, food producers may have had a competitive advantage in confrontations with food collectors.

SUGGESTED READING

BOSERUP, E. *The Conditions of Agricultural Growth: The Economics of Agrarian Change under Population Pressure.* Chicago: Aldine, 1965. A presentation of the theory that prior population growth is the major cause of agricultural development, at least in recent times.

COHEN, M. N. *The Food Crisis in Prehistory: Overpopulation and the Origins of Agriculture.* New Haven: Yale University Press, 1977. An extensive review of the archeological evidence suggesting that agriculture develops because of the general tendency of human populations to increase.

DAHLBERG, F., ed. *Woman the Gatherer.* New Haven: Yale University Press, 1981. A collection of original papers on the activities of women in prehistoric and contemporary food-collecting societies. The editor's introductory essay emphasizes the diversity of adaptations exhibited by food collectors.

HARRIS, M., AND ROSS, E. B., eds. *Food and Evolution: Toward a Theory of Human Food Habits.* Philadelphia: Temple University Press, 1987. A collection of original papers on why humans in different times and places eat what they do. The perspectives of a number of disciplines are represented, including primatology, nutrition, biological anthropology, archeology, psychology, and agricultural economics.

SCHRIRE, C., ed. *Past and Present in Hunter Gatherer Studies.* Orlando, FL: Academic Press, 1984. A number of chapters in this volume challenge the notion that the cultures of recent hunter-gatherers are like the cultures of hunter-gatherers in the past. Most of the chapters discuss how the cultures of those recent hunter-gatherers have changed as a result of contact with other recent societies.

SERVICE, E. *The Hunters,* 2nd ed. Englewood Cliffs, NJ: Prentice Hall, 1979. An introduction to the basic features of the hunting-gathering way of life. Includes an ethnographic appendix with descriptions of selected hunting-and-gathering societies.

15

Economic Systems

When we think of economics, we think of things and activities involving money. We think of the costs of goods and services such as food, rent, haircuts, and movie tickets. We may also think of factories, farms, and other enterprises that produce the goods and services we need or think we need. In our society, workers may stand before a moving belt for eight hours, tightening identical bolts that glide by. For this task they are given bits of paper that may be exchanged for food, shelter, and other goods or services. But many societies (indeed, most that are known to anthropology) did not have money or the equivalent of the factory worker. Still, all societies have economic systems, whether or not these involve the use of money. All societies have customs specifying how people gain access to natural resources; customary ways of transforming or converting those resources, through labor, into necessities and other desired goods and services; and customs for distributing (and perhaps exchanging) goods and services.

The Allocation of Resources

Natural Resources: Land

Every society has access to natural resources—land, water, plants, animals, minerals. Every society has cultural rules for determining who has access to particular resources and what can be done with them. In societies like our own, where land and many other things may be bought and sold, land is divided into precisely measurable units, the borders of which are sometimes invisible. Relatively small plots of land and the resources on them are usually "owned" by individuals. Large plots of land are generally owned collectively. The owner may be a government agency, such as the National Parks Service, which owns land on behalf of the entire population of the United States. Or the owner may be what we call a corporation—a private collective of shareholders. In the United States, property ownership entails a more or less exclusive right to use land resources in whatever way the owner wishes, including the right to sell, give away, or destroy those resources.

Our system of land allocation is alien to most food collectors and most horticulturalists, for two reasons. First, in their societies, individual ownership of land, or ownership by a group of unrelated shareholders, is generally unknown. If there is collective ownership, it is always by groups of related people (kinship groups) or by territorial groups (bands or villages). Second, even if there is collective ownership, such ownership is different from ours in that land is generally not bought and sold.

Thus, it is society, and not the individual, that specifies what is considered property and what are the rights and duties associated with that property.[1] These specifications are social in nature, for they may be changed over time. For example, France declared all its beaches to be public, thereby stating, in effect, that the ocean shore is not a resource that can be owned by an individual. As a result, all the hotels and individuals that had fenced off portions of the best beaches for their exclusive use had to remove the fences.

In our country, people ask whether abuse of the rights of ownership is a factor in the growing pollution of our air and water. Hence, federal, state, and local governments are becoming more active in regulating exactly what people (and even public agencies) can do with the land they own. Such regulation may be new, but our society has always limited the rights of ownership. For example, land may be taken by the government for use in the construction of a highway; we may be paid compensation, but usually we cannot prevent confiscation. Similarly, we are not allowed to burn our houses, nor can we use them as brothels or munitions arsenals. In short, even under our individualistic system of ownership, property is not entirely private.

How societies differ in their rules for access to land and other natural resources seems in part to be related to how they differ in food-getting. Let us now examine how food collectors, horticulturalists, pastoralists, and intensive agriculturalists structure rights to land in different ways.

Food Collectors. As we have noted, members of food-collecting societies generally do not own land individually. The reason is probably that land itself has no intrinsic value for food collectors; what is of value is the presence of game and wild plant life on

[1]E. Adamson Hoebel, *The Law of Primitive Man* (New York: Atheneum, 1968 [originally published in 1954]), pp. 46–63.

the land. If game moves away or food resources become less plentiful, the land is less valuable. Therefore, the greater the possibility that the wild food supply in a particular locale will fluctuate, the less desirable it is to parcel out small areas of land to individuals, and the more advantageous it is to make land ownership communal. The Hadza of Tanzania, for example, do not believe that they have exclusive rights over the land on which they hunt. Any member of the group can hunt, gather, or draw water where he or she likes.[2]

The allocation of natural resources that most closely approaches individual ownership among food collectors occurs in some societies in which the harvest of one or several fruit or nut trees is allocated to one family by tradition. This was the custom among the people of the Andaman Islands in the Indian Ocean.[3] However, rather than being true ownership of a tree, this assignment was probably only an extension of a division of labor by families. It would be a waste of time and effort (and probably not productive enough per capita) if the whole band collected from a single tree. Therefore, the traditional right to harvest awarded to a family or an individual may have been favored for reasons of efficient work organization. The family was still obligated to share the fruits or nuts so acquired with families who collected little or nothing.

Although food collectors rarely practice anything resembling individual ownership of land or other resources, there is considerable variation in the extent of communal "ownership." In some societies, such as the Hadza, groups do not claim or defend particular territories. In fact, the Hadza do not even restrict use of their land to members of their own language group. Even though outsiders have steadily intruded on Hadza territory recently, such encroachment has not been protested. But the Hadza are somewhat unusual—it is more common in food-collecting societies for a group of individuals (usually kin) to "own" land. To be sure, such ownership is not usually exclusive; typically

some degree of access is provided to members of neighboring bands.[4] For example, the !Kung honor the right of hot pursuit, whereby one band is allowed to follow its game into the territory of its neighbors. The sharing of water is perhaps most characteristic of the !Kung's attitude toward the allocation of natural resources. Members of one band, as a matter of courtesy, must ask permission of a neighboring band to use a water hole in the other's territory. As a matter of tradition, the headman of a !Kung band cannot refuse.[5] The reasoning seems clear: if one band helps its neighbors when they need help, then that band can ask for help when it needs assistance.

At the other extreme, local groups in some hunter-gatherer societies try to maintain exclusive rights to particular territories. The Owens Valley Paiute in the California part of the Great Basin lived all year in permanent villages along streams. A group of villagers claimed and defended a particular territory against intruders, who may or may not have been other Owens Valley Paiute. Why have some hunter-gatherers been more "territorial" than others? One suggestion is that when the plants and animals collected are predictably located and abundant, groups are more likely to be sedentary and to try to maintain exclusive control over territories. In contrast, when plant and animal resources are unpredictable in location or amount, territoriality will tend to be minimal.[6] Territorial hunter-gatherers appear to have predictably located resources *and* more permanent villages, so it is hard to know which is more important in determining whether or not territory will be defended.

Horticulturalists. Like food collectors, most horticulturalists do not have individual or family ownership of land. This may be because rapid depletion of the soil necessitates either letting some of

[2]James Woodburn, "An Introduction to Hadza Ecology," in Richard B. Lee and Irven DeVore, eds., *Man the Hunter* (Chicago: Aldine, 1968), pp. 49–55.
[3]A. R. Radcliffe-Brown, *The Andaman Islanders: A Study in Social Anthropology* (Cambridge: Cambridge University Press, 1922), p. 41.

[4]Eleanor Leacock and Richard Lee, "Introduction," in Eleanor Leacock and Richard Lee, eds., *Politics and History in Band Societies* (Cambridge: Cambridge University Press, 1982), p. 8.
[5]Lorna Marshall, "The !Kung Bushmen of the Kalahari Desert," in James L. Gibbs, Jr., ed., *Peoples of Africa* (New York: Holt, Rinehart & Winston, 1965), p. 251.
[6]Rada Dyson-Hudson and Eric Alden Smith, "Human Territoriality: An Ecological Reassessment," *American Anthropologist*, 80 (1978): 21–41.

the land lie fallow for a period of years or abandoning an area after a few years and moving to a new location. There is no point in individuals or families claiming permanent access to land that, given their technology, is not usable permanently. But unlike food collectors, horticulturalists do allocate particular plots of land to individuals or families for their use, although these individuals or families do not own the land in our sense of potentially permanent ownership.

On Truk, a group of islands in the Pacific, people do not think of land as a unitary thing, but rather as territory and soil. Unused territory may be owned, but if the land has been cleared and improved the soil can be owned separately. Furthermore, things such as trees that are on the land may be owned separately from the land itself. A group of kin (those who descend from the same ancestress) usually holds title to various plots of soil. Members of the group receive provisional rights to cultivate soil owned by the group (children belong to the group their mother belongs to). But the kin group may take back the soil from an individual who fails to maintain it or fails to share the produce from it with others. The group may sell the soil, but only with the unanimous consent of its members; and an individual can sell his or her provisional use rights, but only with the consent of the kin group.[7]

Among the Mundurucú of Brazil, the village controls the rights to use land. People in the community can hunt and fish where they like, and they have the right to clear a garden plot wherever land belonging to the community is not being used. Gardens can be cultivated for only two years before the soil is exhausted; the land then reverts to the community. The Mundurucú distinguish between the land and the produce on the land, so that a person who cultivates the land owns the produce. (Similarly, the person who kills an animal or catches a fish owns it, no matter where it was obtained.) However, since all food is shared with others, it does not really matter who "owns" it. Rights to land became more individualized when Mundurucú men began to tap rubber trees for sale. All rights to a particular path in the forest (where trees were tapped) could not be bought and sold, but the rights could be inherited by a son or son-in-law.[8]

Pastoralists. The territory of pastoral nomads far exceeds that of most horticultural societies. Since their wealth ultimately depends upon two elements—mobile herds and fixed pasturage and water—pastoralists must combine the adaptive potential of both food collectors and horticulturalists. Like food collectors, they must know the potential of their territory—which can extend as much as 1,000 miles—so that they are assured a constant supply of grass and water. And like horticulturalists, after their herds graze an area clean they must move on and let that land lie fallow until the grass renews itself. Also like horticulturalists, they depend for subsistence on human manipulation of a natural resource—animals, as opposed to the horticulturalists' land.

Grazing lands are communally held among many pastoral nomads. Although the chief may be designated owner of the land, his title is merely a symbolic statement that the territory is the domain of the nomadic community. Such a community may have to make two types of agreements with outside groups concerning the allocation of natural resources. One type is an agreement with another nomadic group about the order in which the land they both graze is to be used. The other is an agreement with settled agriculturalists about rights to graze unused fields or even to clear a harvested field of leftover stubble.

Although grazing land tends to be communally held, it is customary among pastoralists for animals to be owned by individuals.[9] Fredrik Barth has argued that if animals were not so owned, the whole group might be in trouble because the members might be tempted to eat up their productive capital—their animals—in bad times. When animals are owned individually, a family whose herd drops below the minimum number of animals necessary for survival must drop out of nomadic life, at least temporarily, and work for wages in sedentary agri-

[7]Ward H. Goodenough, *Property, Kin, and Community on Truk* (New Haven: Yale University Press, 1951).

[8]Robert F. Murphy, *Headhunter's Heritage: Social and Economic Change among the Mundurucú* (Berkeley: University of California Press, 1960), pp. 69, 142–43.

[9]Not all pastoralists have individual ownership. For example, the Tungus of northern Siberia have kin group ownership of reindeer; see John H. Dowling, "Property Relations and Productive Strategies in Pastoral Societies," *American Ethnologist, 2* (1975): 422.

Pastoral nomads, like these herders of goats and camels in Niger, travel over large areas of arid land.

cultural communities. But in so doing, such a family does not jeopardize other pastoral families. On the other hand, if the fortunate were to share their herds with the unfortunate, all might approach bankruptcy. Thus, Barth argues, individual ownership is adaptive for a pastoral way of life.[10]

John Dowling has questioned this interpretation. As he points out, pastoral nomads are not the only ones who have to save some of their "crop" for future production. Horticulturalists must save some of their crop (in the form of seeds or tubers) for future planting. But horticulturalists generally lack private ownership of productive resources, so the necessity to save for future production cannot explain private ownership of animals in pastoral societies. Dowling suggests that private ownership will develop only in pastoral societies that are dependent upon selling their products to

nonpastoralists.[11] Thus, it may be the opportunity to sell their products as well as their labor that explains both the possibility of dropping out of nomadic life and the private ownership of animals among some pastoralists.

Intensive Agriculturalists. Individual ownership of land resources—including the right to use the resources and the right to sell or otherwise dispose of them—is common among intensive agriculturalists. The development of such ownership is partly a result of the possibility of using land season after season, which gives the land more or less permanent value. But the concept of individual ownership is also partly a political and social matter. So, for example, the occupation and cultivation of frontier land in the United States was transformed by law into individual ownership. Under the

[10]Fredrik Barth, *Nomads of South Persia* (Oslo: Universitetsforlaget, 1964; Boston: Little, Brown, 1968), p. 124.

[11]Dowling, "Property Relations and Productive Strategies in Pastoral Societies," pp. 419–26.

In societies with intensive agriculture, private ownership of land is common. The boundaries, as on this Minnesota farm, are usually clearly marked.

Homestead Act of 1862, if a person cleared a 160-acre piece of land and farmed it for five years, the federal government would consider that person the owner of the land. This practice is similar to the custom in some societies by which a kin group, a chief, or a community is obligated to assign a parcel of land to anyone who wishes to farm it. The difference is that once the American homesteader had become the owner of the land, the laws of this country gave the homesteader the right to dispose of it at will by selling or giving it away. Once individual ownership of land has become established, property owners may use their economic, and hence political, power to pass laws that favor themselves. In the early years of the United States, only property owners could vote.

Social customs may also influence how land comes to be owned when land begins to be intensively farmed. Even after it becomes possible to grow a crop for sale on the world market, the kind of ownership that develops may depend on how people allocated land previously. For example, when one group of people in the West African nation of Ghana moved to a relatively uninhabited area to grow cocoa for sale, some of the new land was purchased by groups of kin, each descended from a common female ancestor. Although the land so purchased was allocated to individual farmers to cultivate, the land was owned by the kin group. Other settlers, who came from other parts of Ghana and other cultural backgrounds, ended up owning cocoa land individually, even though they bought the land collectively with friends and neighbors.[12]

In the United States and other industrial societies, it may appear that private property owners have nearly absolute control over the use and disposal of their property. But the nearly absolute

[12]Polly Hill, *The Migrant Cocoa-Farmers of Southern Ghana: A Study in Rural Capitalism* (Cambridge: Cambridge University Press, 1963).

control is offset by the real absoluteness with which the owner can lose that property. In our society, this can happen through government action as the penalty for inability to pay taxes or to satisfy a debt. Or it can occur because the government decides to take the property for some public purpose (usually with some compensation to the owner) under the right of eminent domain. A family that has farmed its land for a century can lose it in one year. This often happens as a result of events over which the family has no control—a national economic depression, a drought that causes a bad crop year, or a period of economic stagnation such as the one that followed the Civil War. In addition, where individual ownership is the custom, it is nearly always the case that some individuals do not own any land.

Technology

In order to convert resources to food and other goods, every society makes use of a technology, which includes tools, constructions (such as fish traps), and required skills (such as how to set up a fish trap). Societies vary considerably in their technologies and in the way access to technology is allocated. For example, food collectors and pastoralists typically have fairly small tool kits; they must limit their tools (and their material possessions in general) to what they can comfortably carry with them. As for access to technology, food collectors and horticulturalists generally allow equal opportunity. In the absence of specialization, most individuals have the skills to make what they need. But in an industrial society like our own, the opportunity to acquire or use a particular technology (which may be enormously expensive as well as complex) is hardly available to all. Most of us may be able to buy a drill or a hammer, but few of us can buy the factory that makes it.

The tools most needed by food collectors are weapons for the hunt, digging sticks, and receptacles for gathering and carrying. Most hunters know the bow and arrow; Andaman Islanders used them exclusively for hunting game and large fish. Australian aborigines developed two types of boomerangs: a heavy one for a straight throw in killing game and a light, returning one for playing games or for scaring birds into nets strung between trees. The Semang of Malaya used poisoned darts and

blowguns. The Mbuti Pygmies of Zaire still trap elephants and buffalo in deadfalls and nets. Of all food collectors, the Inuit probably have the most sophisticated weapons, including harpoons, compound bows, and ivory fishhooks. Yet the Inuit also have relatively fixed settlements with more available storage space, and dog teams and sleds for transportation.[13]

Among food collectors, tools are generally considered to belong to the person who made them. There is no way of gaining superiority over others through possession of tools, because whatever resources for toolmaking are available to one are available to all. In addition, the custom of sharing applies to tools as well as to food. If a member of the band asks to borrow a spear another person is not using, that person is obligated to lend it. However, the spear is considered the personal property of the man who made it, and the man who kills an animal with it may be obligated to share the kill with the owner of the spear.

Among the Andaman Islanders, whatever a person made was his or her property. Even if others had helped make the object, it was still considered the individual's property. However, gift giving was so common among the islanders that possessions changed hands frequently.[14]

The !Kung have few possessions—only bows and arrows, spears, digging sticks, receptacles for carrying, and so on. And according to Elizabeth M. Thomas,

a [!Kung] Bushman will go to any lengths to avoid making other Bushmen jealous of him, and for this reason the few possessions that Bushmen have are constantly circling among the members of their groups. No one cares to keep a particularly good knife too long, even though he may want it desperately, because he will become the object of envy.[15]

Pastoralists, like food collectors, are somewhat limited in their possessions, for they too are nomadic. But pastoralists can use their animals to carry some possessions. Each family owns its own

[13]Elman R. Service, *The Hunters*, 2nd ed. (Englewood Cliffs, NJ: Prentice Hall, 1979), p. 10.
[14]Radcliffe-Brown, *The Andaman Islanders*, p. 41.
[15]Elizabeth Marshall Thomas, *The Harmless People* (New York: Knopf, 1959), p. 22.

tools, clothes, and perhaps a tent, as well as its own livestock. The livestock are the source of other needed articles, for the pastoralists often trade their herd products for the products of the townspeople: "Of the totality of objects contained in a nomad's home—be he a Kurd of West Iran or a Gujar in North Pakistan—only a small fraction have been produced by himself or his fellow nomads; and of the food such a family consumes in a year only a small fraction is pastoral products."[16]

Horticulturalists, on the other hand, are generally more self-sufficient than pastoralists. The knife for slashing and the hoe or stick for digging are their principal farming tools. What a person makes is considered his or her own, yet everyone is often obligated to lend tools to others. In Truk society, a man has first use of his canoe and of his farming implements. Yet if a close kinsman needs the canoe and finds it unused, he may take it without permission. A distant kinsman or neighbor must ask permission if he wishes to borrow any tools, but the owner may not refuse him. If he were to refuse, the owner would risk being scorned and refused if he were to need tools later.

Societies with intensive agriculture and industrialized societies are likely to have tools made by specialists—which means that tools must be acquired by trade or purchase. Probably because complex tools cost a considerable amount of money, they are less likely to be shared except by those who contributed to the purchase price. For example, a diesel-powered combine requires a large amount of capital for its purchase and upkeep. The person who has supplied the capital is likely to regard the machine as individual private property and to regulate its use and disposal. Farmers may not have the capital to purchase the machine they need, so they may have to borrow from a bank. The owner must then use the machine to produce enough surplus to pay for its cost and upkeep, as well as for its replacement. The owner may rent the machine to neighboring farmers during slack periods to obtain a maximum return on his or her investment.

However, expensive equipment is not always individually owned in societies with intensive agriculture or industrialized economies. Even in capitalist countries, there may be cooperative ownership of machines by "cooperatives" or co-owning with neighbors.[17]

Some equipment and facilities are too expensive for even a cooperative to afford. Governments may then allocate tax money collected from all for constructions or facilities that benefit some productive group (as well as the public): airports that benefit airlines, roads that benefit trucking firms, dams that benefit power companies. Such resources are owned collectively by the whole society, but they are subject to strict rules for their use, including additional payment. Other productive resources in industrial societies, such as factories, may be owned jointly by shareholders, who purchase a portion of a corporation's assets in return for a proportionate share of its earnings. The proportion of technology and facilities owned by various levels of government reflects the type of political/economic system: socialist and communist countries have more public ownership than capitalist countries.

The Conversion of Resources

In all societies, resources have to be transformed or converted through labor into food, tools, and other goods. (These activities constitute what economists call *production*.) In this section, we examine what may motivate people to work, how societies may divide up the work to be done, and how they may organize work. As we shall see, some aspects of the conversion of natural resources are culturally universal, but there is also an enormous amount of cultural variation.

Incentives for Labor

Why do people work? Probably all of us have asked ourselves this question at least once in a while. Our concern may not be with why other people are working, but why *we* have to work. Clearly, part of the answer is that work is necessary for survival. Although there are always some able-bodied adults who do not work as much as they

---

[16]Fredrik Barth, "Nomadism in the Mountain and Plateau Areas of South West Asia," in *The Problems of the Arid Zone* (Paris: UNESCO, 1960), p. 345.

[17]B. Lisa Gröger, "Of Men and Machines: Cooperation among French Family Farmers," *Ethnology*, 20 (1981): 163–75.

should and rely on the work of others, no society would survive if most able-bodied adults were like that. In fact, most societies probably succeed in motivating most people to want to do (and even enjoy) what they have to do. But are the incentives for labor the same in all societies? Anthropologists think the answer is yes and no. One reason people may work is because they must. But why is it that people in some societies apparently work *more* than they must? Our knowledge of motivational differences is highly tentative and speculative, but we can be fairly certain that a particular and often-cited motive—the profit motive, or the desire to exchange something for more than it costs—is not universal.

There can be no profit motive in people who produce food and other goods primarily for their own consumption, as do most food collectors, many if not most horticulturalists, and even some intensive agriculturalists. Such societies have what we call a *subsistence economy,* not a money or commercial economy. Anthropologists have noticed that people in subsistence economies often work less than people in commercial economies. Food collectors appear to have a considerable amount of leisure time, as do many horticulturalists. It has been estimated, for example, that the men of the horticultural Kuikuru tribe in central Brazil spend about three and a half hours a day on subsistence. It appears that the Kuikuru could produce a substantial surplus of manioc, their staple food, by working thirty minutes more a day.[18] Yet they and many other peoples do not produce more than they need. But why should they? They cannot store a surplus for long because it would rot; they cannot sell it because there is no market nearby; and they do not have a political authority that might collect it for some purpose. Although we often think "more is better," a food-getting strategy with such a goal might even be disastrous. This may be especially true for hunter-gatherers. The killing of more animals than a group could eat might seriously jeopardize the food supply in the future, because overhunting could reduce reproduction

among the hunted animals.[19] Horticulturalists might do well to plant a little extra, just in case part of the crop failed, but a great deal extra would be a tremendous waste of time and effort.

It has been suggested that when resources are converted primarily for household consumption, people will work harder if they have more consumers in the household. That is, when there are few able-bodied workers and a proportionately large number of consumers (perhaps because there are many young children and old people), the workers have to work harder. But when there are proportionately more workers, they can work less. This idea is called *Chayanov's rule.*[20] Alexander Chayanov found this relationship in data on Russian peasants prior to the Communist revolution.[21] Michael Chibnik found support for Chayanov's rule when he compared data from twelve communities in five areas of the world (the communities ranged in complexity from New Guinea horticulturalists to commercial Swiss farmers). Although Chayanov restricted his theory to farmers who sell some of their output and do not hire labor, Chibnik's analysis suggests that Chayanov's rule applies even where crops are rarely sold and even where labor is often hired.[22]

But there appear to be many societies, even with subsistence economies, in which some people work harder than they need to just for their own families' subsistence. What motivates them to work harder? It turns out that many subsistence economies are not oriented just to household consumption. Rather, sharing and other transfers of food and goods often go well beyond the household, sometimes including the whole community or even groups of communities, as we will see later in the chapter. In such societies, social rewards

[18]Robert L. Carneiro, "Slash-and-Burn Cultivation among the Kuikuru and Its Implications for Settlement Patterns," in Yehudi Cohen, ed., *Man in Adaptation: The Cultural Present* (Chicago: Aldine, 1968); cited by Marshall Sahlins, *Stone Age Economics* (Chicago: Aldine, 1972), p. 68.

[19]Marvin Harris, *Cows, Pigs, Wars and Witches: The Riddles of Culture* (New York: Random House, Vintage, 1975), pp. 127–28.

[20]Sahlins, in *Stone Age Economics,* p. 87, introduced North American anthropology to Chayanov and coined the phrase "Chayanov's rule."

[21]Alexander V. Chayanov, *The Theory of Peasant Economy,* ed. D. Thorner, B. Kerblay, and R. E. F. Smith (Homewood, IL: Richard D. Irwin, 1966), p. 78.

[22]Michael Chibnik, "The Economic Effects of Household Demography: A Cross-Cultural Assessment of Chayanov's Theory," in Morgan D. Maclachlan, ed., *Household Economies and Their Transformations,* Monographs in Economic Anthropology, No. 3 (Lanham, MD: University Press of America, 1987), pp. 74–106.

come to those who are generous, who give things away. Thus, people who work harder than they have to for subsistence may be motivated to do so because they gain respect or esteem thereby.[23]

In commercial economies such as our own—where foods, other goods, and services are sold and bought—people seem to be much more motivated to keep any extra income for themselves and their families. Extra income is converted into bigger dwellings, more expensive furnishings and food, and other elements of a "higher" standard of living. But the desire to improve one's standard of living is probably not the only motive operating. Some people may work partly to satisfy a need for achievement,[24] or because they find their work enjoyable. In addition, just as in precommercial societies, some people may work partly to gain respect or influence by giving some of their income away. Not only do we respect philanthropists and movie stars for giving to charities; our society encourages such giving by making it an allowable tax deduction! Still, the emphasis on giving in commercial societies is clearly less than that in subsistence economies. We consider charity by the religious (or rich) appropriate and even admirable, but we would think it foolish or crazy for anyone to give so much away that he or she became poverty-stricken.

Forced Labor

The work we have discussed thus far has all been *voluntary labor*—voluntary in the sense that no formal organization within the society compels people to work and punishes them for not working. Social training and social pressure are generally powerful enough to persuade an individual to perform some useful task. In both food-collecting and horticultural societies, individuals who can stand being the butt of jokes about laziness will still be fed. At most, they will be ignored by the other members of the group. There is no reason to punish them and no way to coerce them to do the work expected of them.

More complex societies have ways of forcing people to work for the authorities—whether those

authorities be kings or presidents. An indirect form of forced labor is taxation. In 1989, the average tax in the U.S. (local, state, and federal) was 34 percent of income, which means that the average person worked four months out of the year for the government. If a person decides not to pay the tax, the money will be forcibly taken or the person can be put in prison.

Money is the customary form of tax payment in a commercial society. In a politically complex but nonmonetary society, persons may pay their taxes in other ways—by performing a certain number of hours of labor or by giving a certain percentage of what they produce. The **corvée,** a system of required labor, existed in the Inca empire in the central Andes prior to the Spanish conquest. Each male commoner was assigned three plots of land to work: a temple plot, a state plot, and his own plot. The enormous stores of food that went into state warehouses were used to supply the nobles, the army, the artisans, and all other state employees. If labor became overabundant, the people were still kept occupied; it is said that one ruler had a hill moved to keep some laborers busy. In addition to subsistence work for the state, Inca commoners were subject to military service, to duty as personal servants for the nobility, and to public-service work.[25]

Another example of forced labor is tenant farming. In return for a house or shack and some acreage to farm, the tenant farmer owes a portion of the harvest to the owner. By manipulating the price for the tenant's crop, by making cash loans to the tenant at high interest rates, and by providing a store at which the tenant must buy staple goods at exorbitant prices, the owner generally manages to keep the tenant working the farm as economically forced labor. If the tenant farmer tries to leave without paying the debts engineered by the owner, the owner can use the power of the state to make him pay. On the other hand, if the tenant farmer becomes obsolete through the introduction of mechanized farming, the owner can use the power of the state to make him leave.

The draft or compulsory military service is a form of corvée, in that a certain period of service is required and failure to serve can be punished by a

[23]Sahlins, *Stone Age Economics,* pp. 101–48.
[24]David C. McClelland, *The Achieving Society* (New York: Van Nostrand, 1961).

[25]Julian H. Steward and Louis C. Faron, *Native Peoples of South America* (New York: McGraw-Hill, 1959), pp. 122–25.

The pyramids of Egypt were built by forced labor thousands of years ago. Here we see a painting by Gustav Richter showing the construction of Khufu's pyramid at Giza.

prison term or voluntary exile. In addition to the soldiers drafted to defend their territory, emperors of China had the Great Wall built along the northern borders of the empire. The wall extends over 1,500 miles, and thousands were drafted to work on it.

Slavery is the most extreme form of forced work, in that slaves have little control over their labor. Because slaves constitute a category or class of persons in many societies, we discuss slavery more fully in the chapter on social stratification.

Division of Labor

All societies have some division of labor—some customary assignment of different kinds of work to different kinds of people. Universally, males and females and adults and children do not do the same kinds of work. In a sense, then, division of labor by sex and age is a kind of universal specialization of labor. Many societies known to anthropology divide labor only by sex and age. Other societies, as we will see, have more complex specialization.

By Sex and Age. All societies make use of sex differences to some extent in their customary assignment of labor. In the chapter on sex and culture, we discuss the division of labor by sex (or gender) in detail.

Age is also a universal basis for division of labor. Clearly, children cannot do work that requires a great deal of strength. But in many societies girls and boys contribute a great deal more in labor than do children in our own society. For example, they help in animal tending, weeding, and harvesting, and they do a variety of domestic chores such as child care, fetching water and firewood, and cooking and cleaning. Indeed, in some societies a child six years old is considered old enough to be responsible for a younger sibling for a good part of the day.[26] Animal tending is often important work for children. Children in some societies spend more time at this task than adults.[27]

Why do children do so much work in some societies? If adults (particularly mothers) have heavy workloads, and children are physically and mentally able to do the work, a good part of the work is likely to be assigned to children.[28] As we have seen, food producers probably have more work than food collectors, so we would expect that children would be likely to work more where there is herding and farming. Consistent with this expectation, Patricia Draper and Elizabeth Cashdan have found differences in children's work between nomadic and settled !Kung. Even though recently settled !Kung have not switched completely from food collection to food production, childrens' (as well as adults') activities have changed considerably. The children living in nomadic camps had virtually no work at all—adults did all the gathering and hunting. But the settled children were

[26]Beatrice B. Whiting and Carolyn P. Edwards, *Children of Different Worlds: The Formation of Social Behavior* (Cambridge, MA: Harvard University Press, 1988), p. 164.

[27]Moni Nag, Benjamin N. F. White, and R. Creighton Peet, "An Anthropological Approach to the Study of the Economic Value of Children in Java and Nepal," *Current Anthropology*, 19 (1978): 295–96.

[28]Whiting and Edwards, *Children of Different Worlds*, pp. 97–107.

In many societies, children do a great deal of work. Here a young Mamvu girl in Zaire is minding her two-year-old sibling.

given lots of chores ranging from helping with animals to helping with the harvest and food processing.[29] When children in a society do a great deal of work, parents may value them more and may consciously want to have more children.[30] This may be one of the reasons birth rates are higher in intensive agricultural societies.[31]

In some societies, work groups are formally organized on the basis of age. Among the Nyakyusa of southeastern Africa, for example, cattle are the principal form of wealth, and boys who are six to eleven herd the cattle for their parents' village. The boys join together in herding groups to tend the cattle of their fathers and of any neighboring families that do not have a son of herding age.[32]

Beyond Sex and Age. In societies with relatively simple technologies, there is little specialization of labor beyond that of sex and age. But as a society's technology becomes more complex and it is able to produce large quantities of food, more and more of its people are freed from subsistence work to become specialists in some other tasks—canoe builders, weavers, priests, potters, artists, and the like.

A day in the life of a food collector, for instance, would be quite varied and involve a large number of skills. A man must know how to make his own traps and weapons as well as how to use them to catch a variety of animals and fish. A woman must be an amateur biologist, able to identify and gather edible food. Both know how to cook, dance, and sing.

In contrast with food collectors, horticultural societies may have some part-time specialists. Some people may devote special effort to perfecting a particular skill or craft—pottery making, weaving, housebuilding, doctoring—and in return for their products or services be given food or other gifts. Among some horticultural groups, the entire village may partially specialize in making a particular product, which can then be traded to neighboring people.

With the development of intensive agriculture, full-time specialists—potters, weavers, blacksmiths—begin to appear. The trend toward greater specialization reaches its peak in industrialized societies, where workers develop skills in one small area of the economic system. The meaninglessness of much of industrialized work was depicted by Charlie Chaplin in the film *Modern Times*: when he left the factory after repeatedly tightening the same kind of bolt all day long, he could not stop his arms from moving, as if they were still tightening bolts.

[29]Patricia Draper and Elizabeth Cashdan, "Technological Change and Child Behavior among the !Kung," *Ethnology,* 27 (1988): 348.

[30]Nag, White, and Peet, "An Anthropological Approach to the Study of the Economic Value of Children in Java and Nepal," p. 293; see also Candice Bradley, "The Sexual Division of Labor and the Value of Children," *Behavior Science Research,* 19 (1984–1985): 160–64.

[31]Carol R. Ember, "The Relative Decline in Women's Contribution to Agriculture with Intensification," *American Anthropologist,* 85 (1983): 291–97.

[32]Monica Wilson, *Good Company: A Study of Nyakyusa Age Villages* (Boston: Beacon Press, 1963 [originally published in 1951]).

In societies with full-time occupational specialization, different jobs are usually associated with differences in prestige, wealth, and power, as we shall see in the next chapter on social stratification.

The Organization of Labor

The degree to which labor has to be organized reaches its peak in industrial societies, which have great occupational specialization and complex political organization. The coordination required to produce an automobile on an assembly line is obvious; so is the coordination required to collect taxes from every wage earner.

In many food-collecting and horticultural societies there is little formal organization of work. Work groups tend to be organized only when productive work requires it and to dissolve when they are no longer needed. Furthermore, the groups so organized often have changing composition and leadership; participation tends to be individualistic and voluntary.[33] Perhaps this happens because when virtually everyone of the same sex has the same work to do, little instruction is needed and almost anyone can assume leadership. Still, some types of work require more organization than others. The hunting of big game usually requires coordinated efforts by a large number of hunters; so might the catching of fish in large nets. For example, on Moala, a Fijian island in the Pacific, net fishing is a group affair. Saturday is the most popular day for communal netting: a party of twenty to thirty women wade out on the reef and make a semicircle of nets. At a signal from an experienced woman, usually the chief's wife, the women move together at the ends, forming a circle. After the fish are caught in the nets, the women bite them on the backs of their heads to kill them and put them in baskets that they carry ashore. A larger fish drive is undertaken by the village, or several villages, around Christmas. The day before, over 100 people make a "sweep" of coconut fronds some 1,600 yards long. The next day the men, women, and children all participate in the surround, catching thousands of fish.[34]

People in Bora Bora, near Tahiti, often catch fish by surrounding them first inside the lagoon.

Kinship ties are an important basis for work organization, particularly in nonindustrial societies. For example, among the horticultural Kapauku of western New Guinea, the male members of a village are a kin group, and all work together to build drainage ditches, large fences, and bridges.[35] Among the pastoral Somali of eastern Africa, a herding group may consist of brothers, their sons, and all wives, unmarried daughters, and small children. Members of the tribe who decided to settle on farmland apportioned within the British Protectorate of Somaliland did so as larger kin groups, not as individuals. As a result, the former cooperating pastoral kin groups became equally cooperative farming villages, depending on kin affiliation for land and other forms of economic help.[36]

With increasing technological complexity, the basis of work organization begins to shift to more

[33]Stanley H. Udy, Jr., *Work in Traditional and Modern Society* (Englewood Cliffs, NJ: Prentice Hall, 1970), pp. 35–37.
[34]Marshall D. Sahlins, *Moala: Culture and Nature on a Fijian Island* (Ann Arbor: University of Michigan Press, 1962), pp. 50–52.

[35]Leopold Pospisil, *The Kapauku Papuans of West New Guinea* (New York: Holt, Rinehart & Winston, 1963), p. 43.
[36]I. M. Lewis, *A Pastoral Democracy* (New York: Oxford University Press, 1961), pp. 107–9.

formally organized groups, which usually entails an enforced obligation to participate.[37] Societies with complex political organization, particularly centralized or "state" organization, usually have the power to compel others to work. The power of the state may be employed specifically to draft labor for the construction of public works and buildings, or it may be more generalized, as when the law allows slave owners to compel slaves to work.[38] In our type of industrial society, work is sometimes politically organized, but the predominant basis of organization is the *contract*—the agreement between employers and employees whereby the latter perform a specified amount of work for a specified amount of wages. Although the arrangement may be entered into voluntarily, laws and the power of the state enforce the obligation of the parties to abide by the contract.

Decision Making about Work

Food collectors generally ignore many of the plant and animal species in their environment, choosing to go after only some. Why? The people may say that some animals are taboo while others are delicious. But where do such customary beliefs come from? Are they adaptive? And if there are no customary preferences for certain plants and animals, how can we explain why a food collector will go after certain foods and ignore others on a particular day? Food producers also make choices constantly. For example, a farmer has to decide when to plant, what to plant, how much to plant, when to harvest, how much to store, how much to give away or sell. Researchers have recently tried to explain why certain economic decisions become customary and why individuals make certain economic choices in their everyday lives.

A frequent source of ideas about choices is **optimal foraging theory,** which was developed originally by students of animal behavior and which has been applied to decision making by food collectors. Optimal foraging theory assumes that individuals seek to maximize the returns (in calories and nutrients) on their labor in deciding which animals and

plants they will go after. Natural selection should favor optimal foraging because such decisions should increase the chances of survival and reproduction. Research in a number of different food collecting societies generally supports the optimal foraging model.[39] For example, the Aché of eastern Paraguay consistently prefer to hunt peccaries (wild piglike mammals) rather than armadillos. Although peccaries take much longer to find and are harder to kill than armadillos, a day spent hunting peccaries yields more than 4,600 calories per hour of work, whereas hunting armadillos yields only about 1,800 calories an hour.[40] Other factors in addition to calorie-yield, such as predictability of resources, may also influence what foods are collected. For example, the !Kung of the Kalahari desert depend largely on mongongo nuts, yet these nuts do not yield as many calories as meat per hour of work. But in contrast to game, mongongo nuts in season are more dependable. Once a group of !Kung hike to a grove of ripe mongongo nuts, they know they can obtain food there until the supply is exhausted; they are not as certain of getting game if they leave.[41]

How does a farmer decide whether to plant a particular crop and how much land and labor to devote to it? A number of researchers have tried to model decision making by farmers. Christina Gladwin and others suggest that farmers make decisions in steps, with each choice point involving a yes or no answer. For example, in the high altitude region of Guatemala, farmers could choose to plant about eight possible crops (or combinations of them, such as corn and beans which grow together well). A farmer will quickly exclude some choices because of the answers to certain questions: Can I afford the seed and fertilizer? Can this crop be watered adequately? Is the altitude appropriate? And so on. If any of the answers is "no," the crop is not planted. By a further series of yes or no decisions,

[37]Udy, *Work in Traditional and Modern Society*, pp. 35–39.
[38]Ibid., pp. 39–40.

[39]Eric Alden Smith, "Anthropological Applications of Optimal Foraging Theory: A Critical Review," *Current Anthropology*, 24 (1983): 626.
[40]Kim Hill, Hillard Kaplan, Kristen Hawkes, and A. Magdalena Hurtado, "Foraging Decisions among Aché Hunter-Gatherers: New Data and Implications for Optimal Foraging Models," *Ethology and Sociobiology*, 8 (1987): 17–18.
[41]Andrew Sih and Katharine A. Milton, "Optimal Diet Theory: Should the !Kung Eat Mongongos?" *American Anthropologist*, 87 (1985): 395–401.

farmers presumably decide which of the remaining possibilities will be planted.[42]

Individuals may not always be able to state their decision rules for decision making clearly, nor do they always have complete knowledge about the various possibilities, particularly when some of the possibilities are new. That does not mean, however, that economic choices cannot be predicted or explained by researchers. For example, Michael Chibnik found that men in two villages in Belize (in Central America) were not able to say why they devoted more or less time to working for wages versus growing crops. But their behavior was still predictable. For example, older men grew crops more, because wage labor was more physically demanding; and in the village with a higher cost of living the men were more likely to work for wages.[43]

The Distribution of Goods and Services

Goods and services are distributed in all societies by systems that, however varied, can be classified under three general types: reciprocity, redistribution, and market or commercial exchange.[44] The three systems often coexist in a society, but one system usually predominates. The predominant system seems to be associated with the society's food-getting technology and, more specifically, its level of economic development.

Reciprocity

Reciprocity consists of giving and taking without the use of money; it ranges from pure gift giving to equal exchanges to cheating. Technically,

then, reciprocity may take three forms: **generalized reciprocity, balanced reciprocity,** and **negative reciprocity.**[45]

Generalized Reciprocity. This is gift giving without any immediate or planned return. A distribution system built around generalized reciprocity is like the indirect interdependencies in nature. Each thing in nature provides something without expecting an equal or immediate return. Berry bushes manufacture prized food for birds; birds help propagate more berry bushes by depositing undigested seeds throughout the area. In the end, all the giving evens out.

Generalized reciprocity sustains the family in all societies. Parents give food to children because they want to, not because the child may reciprocate years later. Of course, usually someone—often a grown child—feeds the parents when they are too old to make their own living. In this sense, all societies have some kind of generalized reciprocity. But some societies depend upon it almost entirely to distribute goods and services.

The !Kung call "far-hearted" anyone who does not give gifts or who does not eventually reciprocate when given gifts. The practice of giving is not evidence of altruism, but is entrenched in their awareness of social interdependence. The !Kung remember quite well the gift-giving activities of everyone else in their own and other bands, and they express approval or disapproval openly. The necessity to reduce tensions, to avoid envy and anger, and to keep all social relations peaceful, not only within their own band but among all !Kung bands, creates continuing cross-currents of obligation within friendship. These are maintained, renewed, or established through the generalized reciprocity of gift giving. The following two examples suggest how generalized reciprocity evens things out among the !Kung.

Lorna Marshall recounts how the !Kung divided an eland brought to a site where five bands and several visitors were camping together—over 100 people in all. The owner of the arrow that had first penetrated the eland was, by custom, the owner of the meat. He first distributed the forequarters to the two hunters who had aided him in the kill. After that, the distribution was dependent

[42]Christina H. Gladwin, "A Theory of Real-Life Choice: Applications to Agricultural Decisions," in Peggy F. Barlett, ed., *Agricultural Decision-Making: Anthropological Contributions to Rural Development* (New York: Academic Press, 1980), pp. 45–85.

[43]Michael Chibnik, "The Statistical Behavior Approach: The Choice between Wage Labor and Cash Cropping in Rural Belize," in Barlett, ed., *Agricultural Decision-Making,* pp. 87–114.

[44]Karl Polanyi, "The Economy as Instituted Process," in Karl Polanyi, Conrad Arensberg, and Harry W. Pearson, eds., *Trade and Market in the Early Empires* (New York: Free Press, 1957), pp. 243–70.

[45]Sahlins, *Stone Age Economics,* pp. 188–96.

Reciprocity is the predominant mode of economic distribution in most hunter-gatherer societies. Here !Kung are cutting up game that will be distributed to others in their band.

generally on kinship: each hunter shared with his wives' parents, wives, children, parents, and siblings, and they in turn shared with their kin. Sixty-three gifts of raw meat were recorded, after which further sharing of raw and cooked meat was begun. Since each large animal is distributed in the same way, over the years such generalized reciprocity results in an evening out of what people receive.

Among the !Kung, the possession of something valuable is undesirable, for it may lead to envy or even conflict. For example, when Marshall left the band that had sponsored her in 1951, she gave each woman in the band a present of enough cowrie shells to make a necklace—one large shell and twenty small ones. When she returned in 1952, there were no cowrie-shell necklaces and hardly a single shell among the people in the band. Instead, the shells appeared by ones and twos in the ornaments of the people of neighboring bands.[46]

Sharing may be most likely when people are not sure they can get the food and water they need. In other words, sharing may be most likely if resources are unpredictable. So a !Kung band may share its water with other bands because they may have water now but not in the future. But a related

group in the Kalahari, the G//ana,[47] has been observed to share less than other groups. It turns out that the resources available to the G//ana are more predictable, because the G//ana supplement their hunting and gathering with plant cultivation and goat herding. Cultivated melons (which store water) appear to buffer the G//ana against water shortages, and goats appear to buffer them against shortages of game. Thus, while the !Kung distribute the meat right after a kill, the G//ana dry it and then store it in their houses.[48]

The idea that unpredictability may favor sharing may also explain why some foods are more often shared than others. Wild game, for example, is usually unpredictable; when hunters go out to hunt, they cannot be sure that they will come back with meat. Wild plants, on the other hand, are more predictable; gatherers can be sure when they go out that they will come back with at least some plant foods. In any case, it does appear that game tends to be shared by food collectors much more than wild plant foods.[49] Even among people who are dependent largely on horticulture, like the Yanomamö of Venezuela and Brazil, food items that are less predictably obtained (hunted game and fish) are shared more often than the more predictably obtained garden produce.[50]

Does food sharing increase the food supply for an individual? Calculations for the Aché of eastern Paraguay, who get most of their food from hunting when they go on food collecting trips, suggest that the average individual gets more food when food is shared. Even the males who actually do the hunting get more, although the benefits are greater for the females and children on the trip.[51] Mathemat-

[46]Lorna Marshall, "Sharing, Talking and Giving: Relief of Social Tensions among !Kung Bushmen," Africa, 31 (1961): 239–41.

[47]The // sign in the name for the G//ana people symbolizes a click sound not unlike the sound we make when we want a horse to move faster.

[48]Elizabeth A. Cashdan, "Egalitarianism among Hunters and Gatherers," American Anthropologist, 82 (1980): 116–20.

[49]Hillard Kaplan and Kim Hill, "Food Sharing among Aché Foragers: Tests of Explanatory Hypotheses," Current Anthropology, 26 (1985): 223–46; Hillard Kaplan, Kim Hill, and A. Magdalena Hurtado, "Risk, Foraging and Food Sharing among the Aché," in Elizabeth Cashdan, ed., Risk and Uncertainty in Tribal and Peasant Economies (Boulder, CO: Westview Press, 1990), pp. 107–43.

[50]Raymond Hames, "Sharing among the Yanomamo: Part I, the Effects of Risk," in Cashdan, ed., Risk and Uncertainty in Tribal and Peasant Economies, pp. 89–105.

[51]Kaplan, Hill, and Hurtado, "Risk, Foraging and Food Sharing among the Aché."

ically, the risk that an individual food collector will not find enough food on a particular day will be appreciably reduced if at least six to eight adult collectors share the food they collect. Food collecting bands may often contain only twenty-five to thirty people, which is about the size that is needed to ensure that there are six to eight adult collectors.[52]

Day-to-day unpredictability is one thing; more prolonged scarcity is another. What happens to a system of generalized reciprocity when resources are scarce because of a drought or other disaster? Does the ethic of giving break down? Evidence from a few societies suggests that the degree of sharing may actually *increase* during the period of food shortage.[53] For example, in describing the Netsilik Inuit, Asen Balikci says, "Whenever game was abundant, sharing among non-relatives was avoided, since every family was supposedly capable of obtaining the necessary catch. In situations of scarcity, however, caribou meat was more evenly distributed throughout camp."[54] Sharing may increase during *mild* scarcity because people can minimize their deprivation. But generalized reciprocity may be strained by extreme scarcity. Ethnographic evidence from a few societies suggests that during famine, when individuals are actually dying from hunger, sharing may be limited to the household.[55]

Balanced Reciprocity. This system is more explicit and short-term in its expectations of return than generalized reciprocity. In fact, it involves a straightforward immediate or limited-time trade. In balanced reciprocity, the exchange is usually motivated by the desire or need for certain objects.

The !Kung, for instance, trade with the Tswana Bantu: a gemsbok hide for a pile of tobacco; five strings of beads made from ostrich eggshells for a spear; three small skins for a good-sized knife.[56] The Semang, food collectors in the Malay Peninsula, engage in "silent trade" with the settled Malay agriculturalists. Believing it is better not to establish personal contact with foreigners, the Semang leave their surplus jungle products at an agreed-upon place near a village and return later to take whatever has been left by the villagers—usually, salt, beads, or a metal tool.[57]

Through trade, a society can dispose of goods it has in abundance and obtain goods scarce in its own territory. Since trade transactions between neighboring peoples may be crucial to their survival, it is important to maintain good relations. Various societies have developed methods of peaceful exchange that do not involve money.

THE KULA RING The horticultural Trobriand Islanders, who live off the eastern coast of New Guinea, have worked out an elaborate scheme for trading food and other items with the people of neighboring islands. Such trade is essential, for some of the islands are small and rocky and cannot produce enough food to sustain their inhabitants, who specialize instead in canoe building, pottery making, and other crafts. Other islands produce far more yams, taro, and pigs than they need. Yet the trade of such necessary items is carefully hidden beneath the panoply of the **kula ring,** a ceremonial exchange of valued shell ornaments.[58]

Two kinds of ornaments are involved in the ceremony of exchanges—white shell armbands (*mwali*), which travel around the circle of islands in a counterclockwise direction, and red shell necklaces (*soulava*), which travel in a clockwise direction. The possession of one or more of these ornaments allows a man to organize an expedition to the home of one of his trading partners on another island. The high point of an expedition is the ceremonial giving of the valued *kula* ornaments. Each member of the expedition receives a shell ornament from his trading partner and then remains on the island for two or three days as the guest of that person. During the visit the real trading goes on. Some of the exchange takes the form of gift giving between trading partners. There is also exchange or barter between expedition members and others

---

[52]Bruce Winterhalder, "Open Field, Common Pot: Harvest Variability and Risk Avoidance in Agricultural and Foraging Societies," in Elizabeth Cashdan, ed., *Risk and Uncertainty in Tribal and Peasant Economies*, pp. 67–87.

[53]Kathleen A. Mooney, "The Effects of Rank and Wealth on Exchange among the Coast Salish," *Ethnology*, 17 (1978): 391–406.

[54]Asen Balikci, *The Netsilik Eskimo* (Garden City, NY: Natural History Press, 1970); quoted in Mooney, "The Effects of Rank and Wealth on Exchange among the Coast Salish," p. 392.

[55]Mooney, "The Effects of Rank and Wealth on Exchange among the Coast Salish," p. 392.

[56]Marshall, "Sharing, Talking and Giving," p. 242.

[57]Service, *The Hunters*, p. 95.

[58]J. P. Singh Uberoi, *The Politics of the Kula Ring: An Analysis of the Findings of Bronislaw Malinowski* (Manchester: University of Manchester Press, 1962).

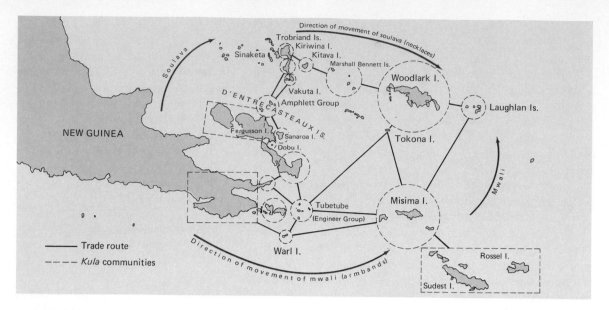

FIGURE 15–1 The Kula Ring
In the *kula* ring, red shell necklaces (*soulava*) travel in a clockwise direction; white shell armbands (*mwali*) travel counterclockwise. The solid lines show the overseas trade routes. The dotted circles identify the (*kula*) communities, and the dotted squares shows the areas indirectly affected by the *kula*.

on the island. By the time the visitors leave, they have accomplished a year's trading without seeming to do so. (A somewhat similar occurrence was the American and Chinese ceremonial exchange of musk oxen and pandas during the Nixon administration. These animals are valued because they are rare, yet they are practically useless. Immediately after the exchanging of the gifts, the real trading of goods between the two countries began.)

But the practical advantages of the *kula* ring are not the only gains. There may be purely social ones, for goods are traded with ease and enjoyment. A trading expedition takes on the flavor of adventure rather than business. Many of the traditions of the islands are kept alive: myth, romance, ritual, and history are linked to the circulating ornaments, especially the larger, finer pieces, which are well known and recognized as heirlooms. The *kula* ring also permits wide ownership of valuables. Instead of possessing one valued object permanently, a man is able to possess many valued things within his lifetime, each for a year or so. Each object, when it is received, arouses enthusiasm in a way that one lifelong possession could not do.[59]

Whatever the reasons for the origin of the *kula* ring, which may date back nearly 2,000 years, it is still an important institution in the modern nation of Papua New Guinea. For example, active participation in the *kula* ring seems to have helped candidates in the 1960s and the 1970s to be elected to the national parliament.[60]

The *kula* is not the only form of exchange in Trobriand life. For example, on the two days following a burial, the kin of the deceased give yams, taro, and valuables to those who helped care for the deceased before death, to those who participated in the burial ceremonies, and to those who came to mourn the deceased. After these initial exchanges, the hamlet settles into mourning. Women from other hamlets bring food to the people in mourning, and the mourning women prepare bundles of banana leaves and weave banana fiber skirts for later distribution. Husbands help their wives accumulate valuables to "buy" extra bundles of banana leaves. Then the women's mortuary ceremony is held. It is very competitive—each of the mourning women tries to distribute the most bundles and skirts. As many as 5,000 bundles

[59]Bronislaw Malinowski, "*Kula:* The Circulating Exchange of Valuables in the Archipelagoes of Eastern New Guinea," *Man,* 51, no. 2 (1920): 97–105; and Uberoi, *The Politics of the Kula Ring.*

[60]Jerry W. Leach, "Introduction," in Jerry W. Leach and Edmund Leach, eds., *The Kula: New Perspectives on Massim Exchange* (Cambridge: Cambridge University Press, 1983), pp. 12, 16.

and 30 skirts might be distributed by one mourning woman in a single day! Each of these giveaways generally completes a balanced reciprocity: the giver is reciprocating for gifts of goods and services received in the past. A woman's brothers gave her yams and taro during the year. She gives her brother's wives bundles or skirts, which are also given to those who helped make the special mourning skirts and to those who brought or cooked food during the mourning period.[61]

OTHER BALANCED SYSTEMS   Balanced reciprocity may involve labor as well as goods. Cooperative work parties exchange or balance gifts of labor. Among the Mundurucú, all men of the village work together to clear gardens; the men and women also work together to plant manioc shoots in each garden.[62] In other societies, a feast may be an additional reciprocation for the gift of labor. A cooperative work party, or *kuu*, among the Kpelle of Liberia may number from six to forty persons, all of whom are generally relatives or friends. In addition to promising return work on a particular date, each farmer rewards the work party's hard day's labor by providing a feast and sometimes rhythmic music to work by.[63]

Sometimes the line between generalized and balanced reciprocity is not so clear. Consider our gift giving at Christmastime. Although such gift giving appears to take the form of generalized reciprocity, there may be strong expectations of balance. Two friends or relatives may try to exchange presents of fairly equal value, based on calculations of what last year's gift cost. If a person receives a $5 present when he or she gave a $25 present, that person will be hurt and perhaps angry. On the other hand, a person who receives a $500 present when he or she gave a $25 present may well be dismayed.

Negative Reciprocity.   This is an attempt to take advantage of another, to get something for nothing or for less than its worth. A mild form is deceitful bargaining; an extreme form is theft and other varieties of seizure. In other words, negative reciprocity ranges from "various degrees of cunning, guile, stealth, and violence to the finesse of a well-conducted horse-raid."[64]

Kinship Distance and Type of Reciprocity.   Most food-collecting and horticultural societies depend on some form of reciprocity for the distribution of goods and labor. Sahlins suggests that whether the reciprocity is generalized, balanced, or negative depends largely on the kinship distance between persons. Generalized reciprocity may be the rule for family members and close kinsmen. Balanced reciprocity may be generally practiced among equals who are not closely related. A tribesman who would consider it demeaning to trade with his own family will trade with neighboring tribes. The desire to satisfy both parties represents the desire to maintain peaceful relations between two groups. Negative reciprocity may be practiced against strangers and enemies.[65] In general, the importance of reciprocity declines with economic development.[66] In societies with intensive agriculture, and even more so in societies that are industrialized, reciprocity distributes only a small proportion of goods and services.

Reciprocity as a Leveling Device.   Reciprocal gift giving may do more than equalize the distribution of goods within a community, as in the !Kung's sharing. It may also tend to equalize the distribution of goods between communities.

Many Melanesian societies in and near New Guinea have the custom of holding pig feasts in which 50, 100, or even 2,000 pigs are slaughtered. Andrew Vayda, Anthony Leeds, and David Smith have suggested that these enormous feasts, though apparently wasteful, are just one of the outcomes of a complex of cultural practices that are highly advantageous. The people of these societies cannot accurately predict how much food they will produce during the year. Some years there will be

---

[61]Annette B. Weiner, *Women of Value, Men of Renown: New Perspectives in Trobriand Exchange* (Austin: University of Texas Press, 1976), pp. 77–117.

[62]Robert F. Murphy, "Matrilocality and Patrilineality in Mundurucú Society," *American Anthropologist*, 58 (1956): 414–34.

[63]James L. Gibbs, Jr., "The Kpelle of Liberia," in Gibbs, ed., *Peoples of Africa*, p. 223. But in other societies the food provided a work party may exceed the value of the labor provided, or there may not be any subsequent reciprocation of labor. Thus, an exchange of food for labor may not always be balanced. See Mahir Saul, "Work Parties, Wages, and Accumulation in a Voltaic Village," *American Ethnologist*, 10 (1983): 77–96.

[64]Sahlins, *Stone Age Economics*, p. 195.

[65]Ibid., pp. 196–204.

[66]Frederic L. Pryor, *The Origins of the Economy: A Comparative Study of Distribution in Primitive and Peasant Economies* (New York: Academic Press, 1977), pp. 204, 276.

A man on the Northwest Coast (southeast Alaska) wears a "potlatch hat" showing how many potlatches he has had.

villages that participate in the feasts.[67] Thus, the custom of pig feasts may be a way for villages to "bank" surplus food by storing up "social credit" with other villages, which will return that credit in subsequent feasts.

In some Melanesian societies, the pig feasts foster an element of competition among the men who give them. "Big men" may try to bolster their status and prestige by the size of their feasts. Competition is enhanced not by keeping wealth but by giving it away. A similar situation existed among many Native American groups of the Northwest Coast, where a chief might attempt to enhance his status by holding a **potlatch.** At a potlatch, a chief and his group would give away blankets, pieces of copper, canoes, large quantities of food, and other items to their guests. The host chief and his group would later be invited to other potlatches.

The competitive element in the potlatch appears to have intensified after contact with whites. Because of the fur trade, the number of trade goods increased, and so more items could be given away. Possibly more important, the population decline among the Indians caused by diseases (such as smallpox) introduced by European traders meant that some chiefs had no direct heirs to their titles. Distant relatives might compete for the positions, each attempting to give away more than the others.[68] Chiefs may also have attempted to attract men to their half-empty villages by spectacular giveaways.[69] Although the potlatch system seems wasteful in that goods were often destroyed in the competition, the system probably also served to equalize the distribution of goods among competing groups.

The Pomo Indians of central California had another way to bank credit for previous generosity. A village with an overabundance of fish or acorns might invite another village to a feast. In return for surplus fish or acorns, the guests would give the

bumper crops, other years very poor crops, because of fluctuations in the weather. So it might be wise to overplant just in case the yield is poor. Yet overplanting results in overproduction during average and exceptionally good years. What can be done with this extra food? Since root crops such as yams and taro do not keep well over long periods, any surplus is fed to pigs, which become, in effect, food-storing repositories. Pigs are then available for needed food during lean times. But if there are several years of surpluses, pigs can become too much of a good thing. Pigs wanting food can destroy yam and taro patches. When the pig population grows to menacing proportions, a village may invite other villages to a gigantic feast that results in a sharp reduction of the pig population and keeps the fields from being overrun. Over the years the pig feasts serve to equalize the food consumption, and especially the protein consumption, of all the

[67] Andrew P. Vayda, Anthony Leeds, and David B. Smith, "The Place of Pigs in Melanesian Subsistence," in Viola E. Garfield, ed., *Symposium: Patterns of Land Utilization, and Other Papers,* Proceedings of the Annual Spring Meeting of the American Ethnological Society, 1961 (Seattle: University of Washington Press, 1962), pp. 69–74.

[68] Philip Drucker, "The Potlatch," in George Dalton, ed., *Tribal and Peasant Economies: Readings in Economic Anthropology* (Garden City, NY: Natural History Press, 1967), pp. 481–93.

[69] Harris, *Cows, Pigs, Wars and Witches,* p. 120.

host village a certain number of beads. Before beginning the journey to the feast, the chief of the guest village would obtain from each family as many strings of beads as possible. Following a few days of feasting at the host village, the chief would trade the beads for the supply of surplus fish or acorns. Each member of the visiting village would be given an equal share of the food, regardless of how many beads had been contributed. But the members of a village would not be invited to a feast unless they brought beads to trade, and they could not obtain beads unless they had given food away themselves sometime in the past. Thus, giving away food and receiving beads in return served as a means of storing social credit for times of scarcity. Later, if food was scarce in the former host village, the villagers could use the beads they had acquired by giving in the past to obtain food from another village with a surplus. The trade feasts, then, had the effect of equalizing the consumption of food not only within a village, but over a fairly widespread area.[70]

On one level of analysis, the Melanesian pig feasts, the Northwest Coast potlatches, and the Pomo trade feasts were all reciprocal exchanges between communities or villages. But these exchanges were not just intercommunity versions of reciprocal gift giving between individuals. Because these feasts were organized by people who collected goods, they also involved another mode of distribution, which anthropologists call redistribution.

Redistribution

Redistribution is the accumulation of goods (or labor) by a particular person, or in a particular place, for the purpose of subsequent distribution. Although redistribution is found in all societies, it becomes an important mechanism only in societies that have political hierarchies—that is, chiefs or other specialized officials and agencies. In all societies, there is some redistribution, at least within the family. Members of the family pool their labor or products or income for the common good. But in many societies, there is little or no redistribution beyond the family. It seems that redistribution on a territorial basis emerges when there is a polit-

ical apparatus to coordinate centralized collection and distribution of goods or to mobilize labor for some public purpose.

William Bartram in the 1700s described eighteenth-century redistribution among Creek Indians:

When all the grain is ripe, the whole town again assembles, and every man carries off the fruits of his labour, from the part of the town field first allotted to him, which he deposits in his own granary. . . . But previous to their carrying off their crops from the field, there is a large crib or granary, erected in the plantation, which is called the King's crib; and to this each family carries and deposits a certain quantity, according to his ability or inclination, or none at all if he so chooses; this in appearance seems a tribute or revenue to the mico (chief), but in fact is designed for another purpose, i.e., that of a public treasury, supplied by a few and voluntary contributions, and to which every citizen has the right of free and equal access, when his own private stores are consumed, to serve as a surplus to fly to for succour, to assist neighboring towns whose crops have failed, accommodate strangers, or travelers, afford provisions or supplies, when they go forth on hostile expeditions, and for all other exigencies of the state; and this treasure is at the disposal of the King or mico; which is surely a royal attribute to have an exclusive right and ability in a community to distribute comfort and blessings to the necessitous.[71]

This account makes redistribution sound like an ideal arrangement in which the whole community benefits from its own efforts. But many other factors influence the fairness with which the chief may redistribute the items. In many cases, it was the chief who apparently was the most "unfairly" treated. Identifying the chief in some Native American villages became something of a joke among early ethnographers, who reported that they looked about for the poorest man. Apparently, the demands of redistribution were so great that the chief gave away everything he could accumulate and was left with prestige alone.

But in the African state of Bunyoro in western Uganda, for example, the king (called the *mukama*) retained much of the wealth for himself and his close kin. The *mukama* had the authority to grant the use of land and all other natural resources to his subordinate chiefs, and they in turn

[70]Andrew P. Vayda, "Pomo Trade Feasts," in Dalton, ed., *Tribal and Peasant Economies*, pp. 494–500.

[71]William Bartram, *The Travels of William Bartram*, ed. Francis Harper (New Haven: Yale University Press, 1958), p. 326.

granted it to the common people. In return, everyone was required to give the *mukama* large quantities of food, crafts, and even labor services. The *mukama* then redistributed these goods and services, in theory at least, to all the people. The *mukama* was praised with names that emphasized his generosity: *Agutamba* (he who relieves distress) and *Mwebingwa* (he to whom the people run for help). But it is clear that much of what the king redistributed did not find its way back to the common people, who produced the bulk of the goods. Instead, the wealth was distributed largely according to rank within the state.[72]

Redistribution systems vary, then, from relative equality for all members of a community to gross inequality. At one extreme, illustrated by the Buin of Melanesia, "the chief is housed, dressed, and fed exactly like his bondsman."[73] Even though the chief owns most of the pigs, everyone shares equally in the consumption of the wealth. At the other extreme, a wealthy Indian landowner may live in luxury while the lower castes, dependent upon him for redistribution, live in poverty. Generally, where redistribution is an important form of distribution (in societies with higher levels of productivity), the wealthy are more likely than the poor to benefit from the redistributions.[74]

Why do redistribution systems develop? Elman Service has suggested that they may develop in agricultural societies that contain subregions suited to different kinds of crops or natural resources. Food collectors can take advantage of environmental variation by moving to different areas. With agriculture, the task is more difficult; it might be easier to move different products across different regions.[75] If the demand for different resources or products becomes too great, reciprocity between individuals might become too awkward. So it might be more efficient to have someone—a chief, perhaps—coordinate the exchanges. We saw in the Pomo trade feasts that although whole communities appeared to be engaged in reciprocal exchanges, the collection of surplus food and beads was handled by village chiefs.

Marvin Harris also feels that redistribution becomes more likely with agriculture, but for a somewhat different reason. He argues that competitive feasting, as in New Guinea, is adaptive because it encourages people to work harder to produce somewhat more than they need. Why would this be adaptive? Harris argues that with agriculture, people really have to produce more than they need so that they can protect themselves against crises such as crop failure. The groups that make feasts may be indirectly ensuring themselves against crises by storing up social credit with other villages, who will reciprocate by making feasts for them in the future. On the other hand, inducements to collect more than they need may not be advantageous to food-collecting groups, who might lose in the long run by overcollecting.[76]

Market or Commercial Exchange

When we think of markets we usually think of bustling colorful places in other parts of the world where goods are bought and sold. (In our own society we seldom use the word "market," although we have "supermarkets" and the "stock market" and other places for buying and selling we call "shops," "stores," and "malls.") In referring to **market** or **commercial exchange,** economists and economic anthropologists are referring to exchanges or transactions in which the "prices" are subject to supply and demand, whether or not the transactions occur in a marketplace.[77] "Market exchange" does not only involve the exchange, or buying and selling, of goods; it also involves transactions of labor, land, rentals, and credit.

On the surface, many market exchanges resemble balanced reciprocity. One person gives something and receives something in return. How then does market exchange differ from balanced reciprocity? It is easy to distinguish market exchange from balanced reciprocity when money is involved, since reciprocity is defined as not involving money. But market exchange need not always

[72]John Beattie, *Bunyoro: An African Kingdom* (New York: Holt, Rinehart & Winston, 1960).

[73]R. C. Thurnwald, "Pigs and Currency in Buin: Observations About Primitive Standards of Value and Economics," *Oceania,* 5 (1934): 125.

[74]Pryor, *The Origins of the Economy,* pp. 284–86.

[75]Elman R. Service, *Primitive Social Organization: An Evolutionary Perspective* (New York: Random House, 1962), pp. 145–46.

[76]Harris, *Cows, Pigs, Wars and Witches,* pp. 118–21.

[77]Stuart Plattner, "Introduction," in Stuart Plattner, ed., *Markets and Marketing,* Monographs in Economic Anthropology, No. 4 (Lanham, MD: University Press of America, 1985), p. viii.

involve money.[78] For example, a landowner grants a tenant farmer the right to use the land in exchange for a portion of the crop. So to call a transaction "market exchange," we have to ask whether supply and demand determine the "price." If a tenant farmer gives only a token gift to the land owner, we would not call it market exchange, just like a Christmas gift to a teacher is not payment for teaching. However, if tenants are charged a large portion of their crops when the supply of land is short, or if landowners lower their demands when few people want to tenant-farm, then we would call the transactions "market or commercial exchange."

Although market exchange need not involve money, most commercial transactions, particularly nowadays, do involve what we call "money."

Kinds of Money. Some anthropologists define money according to the functions and characteristics of the general-purpose money used in our own and other complex societies, for which nearly all goods, resources, and services can be exchanged. According to this definition, *money* performs the basic functions of serving as a medium of exchange, a standard of value, and a store of wealth. Also, money is nonperishable, transportable, and divisible, so that transactions can be made when the goods being purchased differ in value. Other anthropologists, however, contend that an item used in exchange need not serve all the functions and have all the characteristics associated with money in an industrialized society in order to be considered money.

In many societies, money is not an all-purpose medium of exchange. Many peoples whose food production per capita is not sufficient to support a large population of nonproducers of food have **special-purpose money.** This consists of objects of value for which only some goods and services can be exchanged on the spot or through balanced reciprocity. In some parts of Melanesia, pigs are assigned value in terms of shell money—lengths of shells strung together in units each roughly as long as the distance covered by a man's outstretched arms. According to its size, a pig will be assigned a value in tens of such units up to 100.[79] But shell money cannot be exchanged for all the goods or services a person might need. Similarly, a Northwest Coast native could exchange food (but not most other goods and services) for a "gift of wealth," such as blankets. The gift was a "receipt" that entitled the person to receive an equal amount of food (but little else) later.

General-purpose money is a universally accepted medium of exchange. It is used both for commercial transactions (buying and selling) and for noncommercial transactions (payment of taxes or fines, personal gifts, contributions to religious and other charities). General-purpose money provides a way of condensing wealth: paper money is easier to carry around than bushels of wheat; a checkbook is handier than a herd of sheep and goats. In addition, general-purpose money acts as a store of wealth.

Degrees of Commercialization. Most societies were not commercialized at all, or only barely so, when first described in the ethnographic record. That is, most did not rely on market or commercial exchange to distribute goods and services. But commercial exchange has become the dominant form of distribution in the nations of the world. (Most societies of the ethnographic past are now incorporated into larger nation-states; for example, the Trobriand Islanders and other societies in Melanesia are now districts in the nation of Papua New Guinea.) Selling nowadays goes far beyond the nation-state; the world is now a multinational market.[80]

But there is considerable variation in the degree to which societies today depend on market or commercial exchange. Many societies still allocate land without purchase and distribute food and other goods primarily by reciprocity and redistribution, participating only peripherally in market exchange. These are societies in transition: their traditional subsistence economies are gradually becoming commercialized. Among the Luo of Kenya, for example, most families still have land that was allocated to them by their kin groups. The food they eat they mostly produce themselves. But nowadays many men also work for wages—some nearby, others far away in towns and cities (where they spend a year or two). These wages are used to

---

[78]Pryor, *The Origins of the Economy,* pp. 31–33.
[79]Thurnwald, "Pigs and Currency in Buin," p. 122.

[80]Plattner, "Introduction," p. xii.

Pots for sale in the market in Timbuktu, Mali.

pay government taxes, to pay for children's schooling, and to buy commercially produced items such as clothes, kerosene lamps, radios, fish from Lake Nyanza, tea, sugar, and coffee. Occasionally, families sell agricultural surpluses or craft items such as reed mats. Economies such as that of the Luo are not fully commercialized, but they may become so in the future. In the chapter on culture change, we discuss some of the implications and effects of this transition to a more commercialized economy—a transition that is a worldwide phenomenon.

What anthropologists call *peasant economies* are somewhat more commercialized than transitional subsistence economies such as that of the Luo. Although peasants also produce food largely for their own consumption, they *regularly* sell part of their surplus (food, other goods, or labor) to others, and land is one of the commodities they buy, rent, and sell. But although their production is somewhat commercialized, peasants still are not like the fully commercialized farmers in industrialized societies, who rely upon the market to exchange *all* or *almost all* their crops for *all* or *almost all* the goods and services they need.

In fully commercialized societies such as our own, market or commercial exchange dominates the economy; prices and wages are regulated, or at least significantly affected, by the forces of supply and demand. A modern industrial economy may involve international as well as national markets, in which everything has a price, stated in the same money terms—natural resources, labor, goods, services, prestige items, religious and ceremonial items. Reciprocity is reserved for family members and friends or remains behind the scene in business transactions. Redistribution, however, is an important mechanism. It is practiced in the form of taxation and the use of public revenue for transfer payments and other benefits to low-income families—welfare, social security, health care, and so on. But commercial exchange is the major way goods and services are distributed.

Why Do Money and Market Exchange Develop?

Most economists think that money is invented in a society (or borrowed from another society) when trade increases and barter becomes increasingly inefficient. The more important trade is, the more difficult it is to find a person who can give something you want and wants something you have to give. Money is a valuable that can be exchanged for anything and so is an efficient medium of exchange when trade becomes important. In contrast, many anthropologists do not link the origins of money or market exchange to the necessities of trade. Instead they link the origins of money to various noncommercial "payments" such as the *kula* valuables, the Pomo beads, and the taxes that have to be paid to a political authority. All of the available explanations of money suggest that money will be found mostly in societies at higher levels of economic development; and indeed this is the case. And if some simpler societies have money, dominant and more complex societies have usually introduced it.[81]

Most theories about the development of money and market exchange assume that producers have regular surpluses they want to exchange. But

---

[81]Pryor, *The Origins of the Economy*, pp. 153–83.

Fiesta sponsors spend a great deal of money for food and drink as well as for musicians and dancers. Here we see dancers at a fiesta in Oaxaca, Mexico.

why do people produce surpluses in the first place? Perhaps they are motivated to produce a lot extra only when they want to obtain goods from a distance, and the suppliers of such goods are not well known to them, making reciprocity less likely as a way to obtain those goods. Some suggest that market exchange begins with external (intersocietal) trade; since kin would not likely be involved, transactions would involve bargaining (and therefore market exchange, by definition). Finally, some argue that as societies become more complex and more densely populated, social bonds between individuals become less kinlike and friendly and therefore reciprocity becomes less important.[82] Perhaps this is why traders in developing areas are often foreigners or recent immigrants.[83]

In any case, the results of Frederic Pryor's cross-cultural research support the notion that all types of market exchange—of goods, labor, land, and credit—are more likely with higher levels of economic productivity. Pryor also finds that market exchange of goods appears at lower levels of economic development than market exchange of labor and credit; market exchange of land, probably because it is associated with private property (individual ownership), appears mostly at the highest levels of productivity. Perhaps surprisingly, smaller societies tend to have more market exchange or trade with other societies. Larger societies can presumably get more of what they need from inside the society; for example, China has had relatively little foreign trade throughout much of its history.[84]

[82]Ibid., pp. 109–11.
[83]Brian L. Foster, "Ethnicity and Commerce," *American Ethnologist,* 1 (1974): 437–47.

[84]Pryor, *The Origins of the Economy,* pp. 125–48.

Possible Leveling Devices in Commercial Economies. As we will see in the next chapter, societies that depend substantially on market or commercial exchange tend to have marked differences in wealth among people. Nonetheless, there may be mechanisms that lessen the inequality, that act at least partially as leveling devices.

Some anthropologists have suggested that the *fiesta complex* in highland Indian communities of Latin America may be a mechanism that tends to equalize income.[85] In these peasant villages, a number of fiestas are held each year to celebrate important village saints. The outstanding feature of this system is the extraordinary amount of money and labor a sponsoring family must contribute. Sponsors must hire ritual specialists, pay for church services, musicians, and costumes for dancers, and cover the complete cost of food and drink for all members of the community. The costs incurred can very easily amount to a year's wages.[86]

Some anthropologists have suggested that although the richer Indians who sponsor fiestas are clearly distributing a good deal of wealth to the poorer members of their own and other communities, the fiestas do not really level wealth at all. First, true economic leveling would entail the redistribution of important productive resources such as land or animals; the fiesta only temporarily increases the general level of consumption. Second, the resources expended by the sponsors are usually extra resources that have been accumulated specifically for the fiesta—that is why the sponsors are always appointed in advance. Third, and perhaps most important, the fiestas do not seem to have reduced long-term wealth distinctions within the villages.[87]

In nations such as ours, can the income tax and the social-assistance programs it pays for (such as welfare and disaster relief) be thought of as leveling devices? Theoretically, our tax system is supposed to work that way by taxing higher incomes at higher rates. But we know that in fact it doesn't. Those in higher income brackets can often deduct an appreciable amount from their taxable incomes and therefore pay taxes at a relatively low rate. Our tax system may help some to escape extreme poverty, but like the fiesta system, it has not eliminated marked distinctions in wealth.

[85]See, for example, Eric Wolf, "Types of Latin American Peasantry: A Preliminary Discussion," *American Anthropologist,* 57 (1955): 452–71; and Pedro Carrasco, "The Civil-Religious Hierarchy in Mesoamerican Communities: Pre-Spanish Background and Colonial Development," *American Anthropologist,* 63 (1961): 483–97.
[86]Waldemar R. Smith, *The Fiesta System and Economic Change* (New York: Columbia University Press, 1977); and Marvin Harris, *Patterns of Race in the Americas* (New York: Walker, 1964).

[87]Smith, *The Fiesta System and Economic Change;* and Harris, *Patterns of Race in the Americas.*

SUMMARY

1. All societies have economic systems, whether or not these involve the use of money. All societies have customs specifying access to natural resources; customary ways of transforming or converting those resources, through labor, into necessities and other desired goods and services; and customs for distributing (and perhaps exchanging) goods and services.

2. Regulation of access to natural resources is a basic factor in all economic systems. The concept of individual ownership of land—including the right to use its resources and the right to sell or otherwise dispose of them—is common among intensive agriculturalists. In contrast, food collectors, horticulturalists, and pastoralists generally lack individual ownership of land. Among pastoral nomads, however, animals are considered family property and are not usually shared.

3. Every society makes use of a technology, which includes tools, constructions, and required skills. Even though food collectors and horticulturalists tend to think of tools as "owned" by the individuals who made them, the sharing of tools is so extensive that individual ownership does not have much meaning. Among intensive agriculturalists, toolmaking tends to be a specialized activity. Tools tend not be shared, except mainly by those who have purchased them together.

4. Incentives for labor vary cross-culturally. Many societies produce just for household consumption: if there are more consumers, producers work harder. In some subsistence economies, peo-

ple may work harder to obtain the social rewards that come from giving to others. Forced labor generally occurs only in complex societies.

5. Division of labor by sex is universal. In many nonindustrial societies, large tasks are often accomplished through the cooperative efforts of a kinship group. Such cooperation is not as prevalent in industralized societies. Generally, the more technically advanced a society is, the more surplus food it produces and the more some of its members engage in specialized work.

6. The organization of labor reaches its peak in complex societies: work groups tend to be formally organized, and sometimes there is an enforced obligation to participate. In food-collecting and horticultural societies, in contrast, there is little formal organization of work.

7. Goods and services are distributed in all societies by systems that can be classified under three types: reciprocity, redistribution, and market or commercial exchange. Reciprocity is giving and taking without the use of money, and may assume three forms: generalized reciprocity, balanced reciprocity, and negative reciprocity. Generalized reciprocity is gift giving without any immediate or planned return. In balanced reciprocity, individuals exchange goods and services immediately or in the short term. Negative reciprocity is generally practiced with strangers or enemies: one individual attempts to steal from another or to cheat in trading.

8. Redistribution is the accumulation of goods or labor by a particular person, or in a particular place, for the purpose of subsequent distribution. It becomes an important mechanism of distribution only in societies with political hierarchies.

9. Market or commercial exchange, where "prices" depend on supply and demand, tends to occur with increasing levels of economic productivity. Especially nowadays, market exchange usually involves an all-purpose medium of exchange (money). Most societies today are at least partly commercialized; the world is becoming a single market system.

SUGGESTED READING

CASHDAN, E., ed. *Risk and Uncertainty in Tribal and Peasant Economies.* Boulder, CO: Westview Press, 1990. The contributors to this volume discuss the various ways people in nonindustrial societies respond to unpredictable variation in the environment.

MACLACHLAN, M. D., ed. *Household Economies and Their Transformations.* Monographs in Economic Anthropology, No. 3. Lanham, MD: University Press of America, 1987. The papers in this volume deal with the intensification and transformation of agriculture in many societies of the modern world.

ORTIZ, S., ed. *Economic Anthropology: Topics and Theories.* Monographs in Economic Anthropology, No. 1. Lanham, MD: University Press of America, 1983. A collection of papers surveying the limitations and strengths of the major schools of thought in recent economic anthropology, including the substantivist, formalist, Marxist, ecological, world-system, rational/decisional, and development orientations.

PLATTNER, S., ed. *Markets and Marketing.* Monographs in Economic Anthropology, No. 4. Lanham, MD: University Press of America, 1985. The papers in this volume deal with the emergence of markets, economic behavior in the market place, the regional roles of markets, and economic development.

PRYOR, F. L. *The Origins of the Economy: A Comparative Study of Distribution in Primitive and Peasant Economies.* New York: Academic Press, 1977. A large cross-cultural study of variation in distribution systems and their possible determinants.

16

Social Stratification

A long-enduring value in the United States is the belief that "all men are created equal." These famous words from our Declaration of Independence do not mean that all people are equal in wealth or status, but rather that all are supposed to be equal before the law. In fact, modern industrial societies such as our own are socially stratified—that is, they contain social groups having unequal access to important advantages, such as economic resources, power, and prestige.

Many sociologists say that all societies are stratified; anthropologists disagree. But the disagreement is really a matter of definition, since sociologists and anthropologists do not usually mean the same thing by the term *stratification*. When sociologists speak of the "universality of stratification," they mean that all societies show some inequality from one *individual* to another. The sociological definition of stratification derives from the observation that in even the simplest societies there are usually some differences in advantages based on age or ability or sex: adults have more status than children, the skilled more than the unskilled, men more than women. (We discuss sexual or "gender" stratification in the next chapter.) When anthropologists say that stratification is not universal and that egalitarian societies exist, they mean there are some societies in which all *social groups* (for example, families) have more or less the same access or right to advantages. It is not a question of deciding whether sociologists or anthropologists are correct: both are. For anthropologists, then, human inequality may be universal; social stratification is not.

Variation in Degree of Social Inequality

Societies vary in the extent to which social groups (as well as individuals) have unequal access to advantages. In this chapter we are concerned with differential or unequal access to three types of advantages: wealth or economic resources, power, and prestige. As we saw in the last chapter, resources may range from hunting or fishing grounds to farmland to money; the different social groups in a society may or may not have unequal access to these resources. Power is a second but related advantage. It is the ability to make others do what

they do not want to do; power is influence based on the threat of force. As we shall see in this chapter, when groups in a society have rules or customs that give them unequal access to wealth or resources, they generally also have unequal access to power. Finally, there is the advantage of prestige. When we speak of prestige we mean that someone or some group is accorded particular respect or honor. But if there is always unequal access by individuals to prestige (because of differences in age, sex, or ability), there are some societies in the ethnographic record that have no social groups with unequal access to prestige.

Thus, anthropologists conventionally distinguish three types of society in terms of the degree to which different social groups have unequal access to advantages; the three types are called *egalitarian*, *rank*, and *class* societies. Some societies in the ethnographic record do not fit easily into any of these three types; as with any classification scheme, some cases seem to straddle the line between adjacent types.[1] But most societies are conventionally classified as belonging to just one of the three types summarized in Table 16–1. **Egalitarian societies** contain no social groups having greater access to economic resources, power, or prestige. **Rank societies** do not have unequal access to economic resources or to power, but they do contain social groups having unequal access to prestige. Rank societies, then, are partially stratified. **Class societies** have unequal access to all

TABLE 16–1 Stratification in Three Types of Societies

Type of Society	SOME SOCIAL GROUPS HAVE GREATER ACCESS TO:		
	Economic Resources	Power	Prestige
Egalitarian	No	No	No
Rank	No	No	Yes
Class/caste	Yes	Yes	Yes

[1]In an analysis of many native societies in the New World, Gary Feinman and Jill Neitzel argue that egalitarian and rank societies ("tribes" and "chiefdoms," respectively) are not systematically distinguishable. See their "Too Many Types: An Overview of Sedentary Prestate Societies in the Americas," in Michael B. Schiffer, ed., *Advances in Archaeological Method and Theory* (Orlando, FL.: Academic Press, 1984), 7: 57.

Sharing can occur even in a socially stratified society. Here we see men in a village in Yunnan, China, cutting the meat from a steer into 72 portions for the families of the village.

three advantages—economic resources, power, and prestige.

Egalitarian Societies

Egalitarian societies can be found not only among hunter-gatherers but among horticulturalists and pastoralists as well. An important point to keep in mind is that *egalitarian* does not mean that all people within such societies are the *same.* There will always be differences among individuals in age and sex and in such abilities or traits as hunting skill, perception, health, creativity, physical prowess, attractiveness, and intelligence. According to Morton Fried, *egalitarian* means that within a given society "there are as many positions of prestige in any given age-sex grade as there are persons capable of filling them."[2] For instance, if a

[2]Morton H. Fried, *The Evolution of Political Society: An Essay in Political Anthropology* (New York: Random House, 1967), p. 33.

person can achieve **status** (a position of prestige) by fashioning fine spears, and if every person in the society fashions such spears, then every person acquires status as a spear maker. If status is also acquired by carving bones into artifacts, and if only three people are considered expert carvers of bones, then only those three achieve status as carvers. But the next generation might produce eight spear makers and twenty carvers. In an egalitarian society, the number of prestigious positions is adjusted to fit the number of qualified candidates. We would say, therefore, that such a society is not socially stratified.

There are, of course, differences in status and prestige arising out of differences in ability. Even in an egalitarian society, differential prestige exists. But although some persons may be better hunters or more skilled artists than others, there is still equal *access* to status positions for people of the same ability. Any prestige gained by achievement of status as a great hunter, for instance, is neither transferable nor inheritable. Because a man is a great hunter, it is not assumed that his sons are also great hunters. An egalitarian society keeps inequality at a minimal level.

Any differences in prestige that do exist are not related to economic differences. Egalitarian groups depend heavily on *sharing,* which ensures equal access to economic resources despite differences in acquired prestige. For instance, in some egalitarian communities, some members achieve status through hunting. But even before the hunt begins, how the animal will be divided and distributed among the members of the band has already been decided according to custom. The culture works to separate the status achieved by members—recognition as great hunters—from actual possession of the wealth, which in this case would be the slain animal.

Just as egalitarian societies do not have social groups with unequal access to economic resources, they also do not have social groups with unequal access to power. As we will see later in the chapter on political organization, unequal access to power by social groups seems to occur only in state societies, which have full-time political officials and marked differences in wealth.

The Mbuti Pygmies of central Africa provide an example of a society almost totally equal: "Neither in ritual, hunting, kinship nor band relations do they exhibit any discernable inequalities of rank or advantage."[3] Their hunting bands have no leaders; recognition of the achievement of one person is not accompanied by privilege of any sort. Economic resources such as food are communally shared, and even tools and weapons are frequently passed from person to person. Only within the family are rights and privileges differentiated.

!Kung society is only slightly more complex, since each band has a headman. But the position of headman has no power or other advantage associated with it; the headman serves merely as a unifying symbol. A stranger must ask permission of the headman to take water from the band's water hole, a symbolic gesture the headman cannot refuse. The headman is neither the leader of the hunt nor the chief decision maker. In fact, all the men hunt, and all share in decisions that affect the band.

Rank Societies

Societies with social *ranking* generally practice agriculture or herding, but not all agricultural or pastoral societies are ranked. Ranking is characterized by social groups having unequal access to prestige or status, but *not* significantly unequal access to economic resources or power. Unequal access to prestige is often reflected in the position of chief, a rank to which only some members of a specified group in the society can succeed.

In rank societies, the position of chief is at least partially hereditary. The criterion of superior rank in some Polynesian societies, for example, was genealogical. Usually the eldest son succeeded to the position of chief, and different kinship groups were differentially ranked according to their genealogical distance from the chiefly line.

In rank societies, chiefs are often treated with deference by people of lower rank. For example, among the Trobriand Islanders of Melanesia, people of lower rank must keep their heads lower than a person of higher rank. So, when a chief is standing, commoners must bend low. When commoners have to walk past a chief who happens to be sitting, he may rise and they will bend. If the chief chooses to remain seated, they must crawl.[4]

Chiefs may sometimes look as if they are substantially richer, for they may receive many gifts and have larger storehouses. In some instances, the chief may be called the "owner" of the land, but other people have the right to use the land. The chief may have bigger storehouses, but his stores may be only temporary accumulations for feasts or other redistributions. The chief in a rank society cannot usually make people give him gifts or work on communal projects. Often the chief can encourage production only by working furiously on his own cultivation.[5]

An example of a rank society is the Swazi of South Africa, as of the first half of the twentieth century. Hilda Kuper reports that the Swazi are a

---

[3]Michael G. Smith, "Pre-Industrial Stratification Systems," in Neil J. Smelser and Seymour Martin Lipset, eds., *Social Structure and Mobility in Economic Development* (Chicago: Aldine, 1966), p. 152.

[4]Elman R. Service, *Profiles in Ethnology,* 3rd ed. (New York: Harper & Row, Pubishers, 1978), p. 249.
[5]Marshall Sahlins, *Social Stratification in Polynesia* (Seattle: University of Washington Press, 1958), pp. 80–81.

Fijians show respect to the chief (wearing white shirt and tie) by presenting the sacred *kava* drink to him first.

horticultural people who invest their chief with "ownership" of the land.[6] The staples of their diet are maize and millet, produced cooperatively by men and women. Farming thus supplies the staple foods of the Swazi, although herding is a more prestigious occupation. Only 10 percent of Swazi land is given over to cultivation; cattle grazing claims 75 percent.

Among the Swazi, the chief is recognized as the lineal descendant of the first ruler of the tribe. He is selected chief not so much for his personal qualities but mainly because of the rank of his mother. Both the chief and his mother are treated with great deference, are addressed with extravagant titles, and wear elaborate regalia. Members of the chief's lineage are called the Children of the Sun, and constitute a distinct social elite. Other members of the society are ranked according to their relationship to the chief.

All Swazis, however, regardless of rank, do the same kinds of work, live in the same kinds of houses, and eat the same foods. The superior rank of the chief is evident by the many cows in his possession and by his right to organize work parties. Sharing is the principal way goods are distributed, and the chief shares (or redistributes) more than others. A man who accumulates too many cattle is in danger of public retaliation unless he shares them or lets others use them. If he does not, he may be accused of witchcraft, and his cattle may be killed and eaten. This custom serves as a cultural means of preventing the accumulation of wealth. Labor too is shared. For example, a work party from a particular **age-set**—that is, a group of persons of similar age and the same sex—might be called upon to help a family undertaking a construction job.

Although the Swazi managed to retain much of the economic and social basis of their traditional rank society, the money economy of the white colonizers in southern Africa had altered their way of life. As of the first half of the twentieth century, thousands of Swazi men were employed as laborers outside and inside Swaziland; and Swazi women were often employed in farming or as domestics. Wage employment is even more common nowadays. With unequal access to resources and power, Swaziland is now a class rather than a rank society.

Unusual among rank societies are the nineteenth-century Native Americans who lived along the Northwest Coast. They are unusual because their economy was based on food collecting. But huge catches of salmon—which were preserved for year-round consumption—enabled them to support fairly large and permanent communities. In many ways, the Northwest Coast societies were similar to food-producing societies, even in their development of social ranking. Still, the principal means of proving one's status among the Northwest Coast Indians was to give wealth away. The tribal chiefs celebrated solemn rites by grand feasts (potlatches), at which they gave gifts to every guest.[7]

Although we have said that chiefs in rank societies do not possess significantly greater wealth than others, some economic differentiation seems to have been present in some societies classified as rank societies. For example, chiefs in sixteenth-century Panama had greater access to luxury goods such as gold and salt. Apparently, gold was not used for money but was fashioned into ornaments and decorative items that were highly prized by the elite. The chiefs had larger, more decorated houses and obtained some labor from commoners.[8]

---

[6]Hilda Kuper, *A South African Kingdom: The Swazi*, 2nd ed. (New York: Holt, Rinehart & Winston, 1986).

[7]Philip Drucker, *Cultures of the North Pacific Coast* (San Francisco: Chandler, 1965), pp. 56–64.

[8]Mary W. Helms, *Ancient Panama: Chiefs in Search of Power* (Austin: University of Texas Press, 1979), pp. 11–35.

Class Societies

In class societies, as in rank societies, there is unequal access to prestige. But unlike rank societies, class societies are characterized by unequal access to economic resources and power. That is, not every social group has the same chance to obtain land, animals, money, or other economic benefits, or the same opportunity to exercise power. Fully stratified or class societies range from somewhat open to more or less closed class or *caste* systems.

Open Class Systems. A **class** is a category of persons who have about the same opportunity to obtain economic resources, power, and prestige. During the last fifty years, study after study has been made of classes in United States towns. Sociologists have produced profiles of typical communities, known variously as Yankee City, Middletown, Jonesville, and Old City, all of which support the premise that the United States has distinguishable, though somewhat open, social classes. Both Lloyd Warner and Paul Lunt's Yankee City study[9] and

[9]W. Lloyd Warner and Paul S. Lunt, *The Social Life of a Modern Community* (New Haven: Yale University Press, 1941).

Robert and Helen Lynd's Middletown study[10] concluded that the social status or prestige of a family generally correlated with the occupation and wealth of the head of the family.

Towns in the United States have been described as having as few as two, and as many as eleven, social classes, but generally four to six are recognized. In the Yankee City research, 99 percent of the city's 17,000 inhabitants were studied and classified over a period of several years. Warner and Lunt concluded that six groups emerged strongly enough to be called classes. These groups are summarized by characteristic traits in Table 16–2.

The way members of the highest and lowest classes perceive each other has also been observed and recorded. Table 16–3 summarizes such perceptions as revealed in a study of a town in the U.S. South as of the 1930s. The people at the top grouped the bottom two classes together and the people at the bottom grouped the top three classes

[10]Robert S. Lynd and Helen Merrell Lynd, *Middletown* (New York: Harcourt, Brace, 1929); and Robert S. Lynd and Helen Merrell Lynd, *Middletown in Transition* (New York: Harcourt, Brace, 1937).

TABLE 16–2 American Social Classes in Yankee City

PERCENTAGE OF INCOME	PERCENTAGE OF POPULATION		SOCIAL CLASSES AND CHARACTERISTIC TRAITS
	1.4%	Upper upper:	"old family"; usually processing wealth, but sometimes poor; active in charities, Episcopal or Congregational church, exclusive clubs; endogamous.
	1.6	Lower upper:	newly rich; imitate the U-U class and long to marry into that class.
	10.2	Upper middle:	professional men or storeowners; active in civic affairs; respectable; long to be accepted by the groups above them, but almost never are.
45% for top 20% of the population	28.1	Lower middle:	white collar workers; respectable homeowners, schoolteachers; looked down upon by all above them. Some members of recently integrated groups, such as Irish, Italians, French-Canadians, are in this group.
	32.6	Upper lower:	"poor-but honest workers"; most of their income spent on food and rent.
5% for bottom 20% of the population	25.2	Lower lower:	thought by other classes to be lazy, shiftless, sexually proficient, and promiscuous. In reality, they are simply poor.

Reprinted by permission of Yale University Press from *The Social Life of a Modern Community* by W. Lloyd Warner and Paul S. Lunt. Copyright © by Yale University Press, 1941.

TABLE 16–3 Perceptions of Social Classes

BY UPPER-UPPER CLASS			BY LOWER-LOWER CLASS
"Old aristocracy"	U-U		
"Aristocracy," but not "old"	L-U		"Society" or the "folks with money"
"Nice, respectable people"	U-M		
"Good people," but "nobody"	L-M		"Way-high-ups" but not "society"
"Po' whites"	U-L		"Snobs trying to push up"
	L-L		"People just as good as anybody"

From Allison Davis, Burleigh B. Gardner, and Mary R. Gardner, *Deep South: A Social-Anthropological Study of Caste and Class* (Chicago: University of Chicago Press, 1941), p. 65.

together. This grouping suggests that the greater the social distance between classes, the more likely it is that a group will lump together the groups farthest away in the hierarchy. Groups tend, however, to distinguish between other groups just above or just below themselves.

The determinants of a person's class status have changed over time in the United States. In 1776, for example, the middle class consisted of the families of self-employed craftspeople, shopkeepers, and farmers. By 1985, only about 8 percent of the population were self-employed, but many more people think of themselves as belonging to the middle class. Self-employment is now a less important determinant of middle class status than working with one's mind and having authority over others on the job.[11]

On the whole, North American society is a somewhat *open* society; that is, it is possible, through effort, to move from one class to another. A university education has been a major aid in moving upward.[12] Lower-class persons may become "resocialized" at the university, which separates them from their parents and enables them to gradually learn the skills, speech, attitudes, and manners characteristic of the higher class they wish to join. So successful is this process that students

---

[11]Reeve Vanneman and Lynn Weber Cannon, *The American Perception of Class* (Philadelphia: Temple University Press, 1987), pp. 53–91.
[12]David L. Featherman and Robert M. Hauser, *Opportunity and Change* (New York: Academic Press, 1978), pp. 4, 481.

from a lower class who move into a higher class may find themselves ashamed to take their new friends to their parents' homes.

Our identification with a social class begins quite early in life. The residence area chosen by our parents and our religious affiliation, school, school curriculum, clubs, sports, college (or lack of college), marriage partner, and occupation are all influential in socializing us into a particular class.

Although in North America social class is not fully determined by birth, there is a high probability that most people will stay more or less within the class into which they were born and will marry within that class. That is, even if we do not inherit money from our parents, our chances of being successful are strongly influenced by our class background. The daughter of a wealthy businessman, for example, is likely to attend schools with good reputations. She will learn to speak with an accent that is more "elite." She will be likely to learn to ride horses, play tennis, and the piano, and to acquire the etiquette appropriate for attending concerts, parties, and teas. If she wishes to have a career, she has a very good chance to get into a college or graduate school of her choice, and she has social connections that can help her to get a good starting job. If she gets married, she has a very good chance of marrying a man of similar background, tastes, and likelihood of success.

Class boundaries, though vague, have been established by custom and tradition; sometimes they have been reinforced by the enactment of laws. Many of our laws serve to protect property and thus tend to favor the upper and upper-middle classes. The poor, in contrast, seem to be perennial losers in our legal system. The crimes the poor are most likely to commit are dealt with quite harshly in our judicial system, and poor people rarely have the money to secure effective legal counsel.

Classes also tend to perpetuate themselves through the bequeathing of wealth. John Brittain has suggested that, in the United States, the transfer of money through bequests accounts for much of the wealth of the next generation. He estimates that in 1972 approximately 65 to 85 percent of the wealth of the wealthiest 2 percent of married women in this country came from inheritance (primarily from parents, not husbands). About half of the wealth of the wealthiest 2 percent of married

Rich and poor in New York City.

men in this country may have come from inheritance. The importance of inheritance seems to increase with greater wealth. That is, the wealth of richer people comes more from inheritance than the wealth of not-so-rich people.[13]

Although some class societies have more open class systems than others, the greatest likelihood is that people will remain in the class of their birth. The Japanese class system has become more open in the last hundred years. A 1960 study of the upper-class business elite showed that 8 percent came from lower-class and 31 percent from middle-class backgrounds.[14] This social mobility was achieved chiefly by successful passage through the highly competitive university system. The Japanese class system is not completely open, however, for 61

percent of the business elite came from the relatively small upper class. The tendency to retain high class status even through changing times is clear.

Caste Systems. Some societies with classes have also had groups called castes. A **caste** is a ranked group, often associated with a certain occupation, in which membership is determined at birth and marriage is restricted to members of one's own caste. In India, for example, there are several thousand castes. Those members of a low caste who can get wage-paying jobs (chiefly those in urban areas) may improve their social standing in the same ways available to people in other class societies, but they generally cannot marry someone in a higher caste. Thus, a caste is a virtually *closed* class.

Questions basic to all stratified societies, and particularly to a caste society, have been posed by John Ruskin: "Which of us . . . is to do the hard and dirty work for the rest—and for what pay? Who is to do the pleasant and clean work, and for

[13]John A. Brittain, *Inheritance and the Inequality of Material Wealth* (Washington, DC: Brookings Institution, 1978).

[14]Edward Norbeck, "Continuities in Japanese Social Stratification," in Leonard Plotnicov and Arthur Tuden, eds., *Essays in Comparative Social Stratification* (Pittsburgh: University of Pittsburgh Press, 1970).

what pay?"[15] The questions have been answered in India by the maintenance of a caste system whose underlying basis is economic; the system involves an intricate procedure for the exchange of goods and services.[16]

Who is to do the hard and dirty work for the rest of society is clearly established: a large group of untouchables forms the bottom of the hierarchy. Among the untouchables are subcastes such as the Camars, or leatherworkers, and the Bhangis, who are sweepers. At the top of the hierarchy, performing the pleasant and clean work of priests, are the Brahmans. Between the two extremes are literally thousands of castes and subcastes. Each caste is traditionally associated with an occupation. For example, in a typical village the potter makes clay drinking cups and larger water vessels for the entire village population. In return, the principal landowner gives him a house site and supplies him twice yearly with grain. Some other castes owe the potter their services: the barber cuts his hair; the sweeper carries away his rubbish; the washer washes his clothes; the Brahman performs his children's weddings. The barber serves every caste in the village except the untouchables; he, in turn, is served by half of the others. He has inherited the families he works for, along with his father's occupation. He also receives a house site from the principal landowner and, at each harvest, all the grain he can lift. All castes help at harvest and at weddings for additional payment, which sometimes includes a money payment.

This description is, in fact, an idealized picture of the caste system of India. In reality, the system operates to the advantage of the principal landowning caste—sometimes the Brahmans and sometimes other castes. Also, it is not carried on without some resentment; signs of hostility are shown toward the ruling caste by the untouchables and other lower castes. The resentment does not appear to be against the caste system as such. Instead, the lower castes exhibit bitterness at their own low status and strive for greater equality. For instance, one of the Camars' traditional services is to remove dead cattle; in return, they can have the meat to eat and the hide to tan for their leather-working. Since handling dead animals and eating beef are both regarded as unclean acts, the Camars of one village refused to continue this service. Thus, they lost a source of free hides and food in a vain attempt to escape unclean status.

Since World War II, the economic basis of the caste system in India has been undermined somewhat by the growing practice of giving cash payment for services. For instance, the son of a barber may be a teacher during the week, earning a cash salary, and confine his haircutting to weekends. But he still remains in the barber caste (Nai) and must marry within that caste.

Perpetuation of the caste system is ensured by the power of those in the upper castes, who derive three main advantages from their position: economic gain, gain in prestige, and sexual gain. The economic gain is the most immediately apparent. An ample supply of cheap labor and free services is maintained by the threat of sanctions. Lower-caste members may have their use of a house site withdrawn; they may be refused access to the village well or to common grazing land for animals; or they may be expelled from the village. Prestige is also maintained by the threat of sanctions; the higher castes expect deference and servility from the lower castes. The sexual gain is less apparent but equally real. The high-caste male has access to two groups of females, those of his own caste and those of lower castes. High-caste females are kept free of the "contaminating" touch of low-caste males because low-caste males are allowed access only to low-caste women. Moreover, the constant reminders of ritual uncleanness serve to keep the lower castes "in their place." Higher castes do not accept water from untouchables, sit next to them, or eat at the same table with them.

Although few areas of the world have developed a caste system like that of India, there are castelike features in some other societies. For example, blacks in the United States used to have a castelike status determined partially by the inherited characteristic of skin color. Until recently, some states had laws prohibiting a black from marrying a white. Even when interracial marriage does occur, children of the union are often regarded as having lower status, even though they may have blonde hair and light skin. In the South, where

[15]John Ruskin, "Of Kings' Treasures," in John D. Rosenberg, ed., *The Genius of John Ruskin: Selections from His Writings* (New York: Braziller, 1963), pp. 296–314.

[16]See Oscar Lewis, with the assistance of Victor Barnouw, *Village Life in Northern India* (Urbana: University of Illinois Press, 1958).

treatment of blacks as a caste was most apparent, whites traditionally refused to eat with blacks or, until recently, to sit next to them at lunch counters, on buses, and in schools. Separate drinking fountains and toilets for blacks and whites reinforced the idea of ritual uncleanness. The economic advantages and gains in prestige enjoyed by whites are well documented.[17]

Another example of a caste group in class society was the *Eta* of Japan. Unlike blacks in America, the Eta (now called the *Dowa Kankeisha*) were physically indistinguishable from other Japanese. Comparable to India's untouchables, they were a hereditary, endogamous (in-marrying) group. Their occupations were traditionally those of farm laborer, leatherworker, and basket weaver; their standard of living was very low. Discrimination against the Dowa Kankeisha was officially abolished by the Japanese government in 1871; more active steps have been taken recently. Since 1965, the government of Japan has taken to improve living conditions for the Dowa and discourage discrimination against them.[18]

In Rwanda, a country in east central Africa, a longtime caste system was overthrown, first by an election and then by a revolution in 1959–1960. Three castes had existed, each distinguished from the others by physical appearance and occupation. The ruling caste, the Tutsi, were tall and lean and constituted about 15 percent of the population. They were the landlords and practiced the prestigious occupation of herding. The agricultural caste, the Hutu, were shorter, stockier, and made up about 85 percent of the population. As tenants of the Tutsi, they produced most of the country's food. The Twa, accounting for less than 1 percent of the population, were a Pygmy group of hunter-gatherers who formed the lowest caste. It is believed that the three castes derived from three different language groups who came together through migration and conquest. Later, however, they

Slavery exists in many societies, even recent ones. Here a slave boy works for his Tuareg owners in the Niger Republic.

came to use a common language, although remaining endogamous and segregated by hereditary occupations. When the Hutu united to demand more of the rewards of their labor, the king and many of the Tutsi ruling caste were driven out of the country. The Hutu then established a republican form of government. However, the forest-dwelling Twa are still generally excluded from full citizenship.

Slavery. **Slaves** are persons who do not own their own labor, and as such they represent a class. Slavery has existed in various forms in many times and places, regardless of race and culture. Sometimes it has been a closed class, or caste system, sometimes a relatively open class system. In different slave-owning societies, slaves have had different, but always some, legal rights.[19]

[17]Gerald D. Berreman, "Caste in India and the United States," *American Journal of Sociology*, 66 (1960): 120–27.

[18]For more information about caste in Japan, and in Rwanda (which we also discuss here), see Gerald D. Berreman, "Caste in the Modern World," Morristown, NJ: General Learning Press, 1973; and Gerald D. Berreman, "Race, Caste and Other Invidious Distinctions in Social Stratification," *Race*, 13 (1972): 403–14. Information about what the Japanese government has done in regard to the Dowa has been provided to us by the Japanese information center.

[19]Frederic L. Pryor, *The Origins of the Economy: A Comparative Study of Distribution in Primitive and Peasant Economies* (New York: Academic Press, 1977), p. 219.

In ancient Greece, slaves were often conquered enemies. Since city-states were constantly conquering one another or rebelling against former conquerors, slavery was a threat to everyone. Following the Trojan War, the transition of Hecuba from queen to slave was marked by her cry "Count no one happy, however fortunate, before he dies."[20] Nevertheless, Greek slaves were considered human beings, and they could even acquire some status along with freedom. Andromache, the daughter-in-law of Hecuba, was taken as slave and concubine by one of the Greek heroes. When his legal wife produced no children, Andromache's slave son became heir to his father's throne. Although slaves had no rights under law, once they were freed, either by the will of their master or by purchase, they and their descendants could become assimilated into the dominant group. In other words, slavery in Greece was not seen as the justified position of inferior people. It was regarded, rather, as an act of fate—"the luck of the draw"—that relegated a victim to the lowest class in society.

Among the Nupe, a society in central Nigeria, slavery was of quite another type.[21] The methods of obtaining slaves—as part of the booty of warfare, and later by purchase—were similar to those of Europeans, but the position of the slaves was very different. Mistreatment was rare. Male slaves were given the same opportunities to earn money as other dependent males in the household— younger brothers, sons, or other relatives. A slave might be given a garden plot of his own to cultivate, or he might be given a commission if his master were a craftsman or a tradesman. Slaves could acquire property, wealth, and even slaves of their own. However, all of a slave's belongings went to the master at the slave's death.

Manumission, the granting of freedom, was built into the Nupe system. If a male slave could afford the marriage payment for a free woman, the children of the resulting marriage were free; the man himself, however, remained a slave. Marriage or concubinage were the easiest ways out of bondage for a slave woman. Once she had produced a child by her master, both she and the child had free status. The woman, however, was only figuratively free: if a concubine, she had to remain in that role. As might be expected, the family trees of the nobility and the wealthy were liberally grafted with branches descended from slave concubines.

The most fortunate slaves among the Nupe were the house slaves. They could rise to positions of power in the household as overseers and bailiffs, charged with law-enforcement and judicial duties. (Recall the Old Testament story of Joseph, who was sold into slavery by his brothers. Joseph became a household slave of the pharaoh and rose to the position of second in the kingdom because he devised an ingenious system of taxation.) There was even a titled group of Nupe slaves—the Order of Court Slaves—who were trusted officers of the king and members of an elite. Slave status in general, though, placed one at the bottom of the social ladder. In the Nupe system, few slaves, mainly princes from their own societies, ever achieved membership in the titled group.

In the United States, slavery originated as a means of obtaining cheap labor, but the slaves soon came to be regarded as deserving of their low status because of their alleged inherent inferiority. Since the slaves were black, some whites justified slavery and belief in black people's inferiority by quoting Scripture out of context ("they shall be hewers of wood and drawers of water"). Slaves could not marry or make any other contracts, nor could they own property. In addition, their children were also slaves, and the master had sexual rights over the female slaves. Because the status of slavery was determined by birth in the United States, slaves constituted a caste. During the days of slavery, the United States had both a caste and a class system. And even after the abolition of slavery, as we have noted, some castelike elements remained.

As for why slavery may have developed in the first place, the cross-cultural evidence is as yet inconclusive. We do know, however, that slavery is not an inevitable stage in economic development, contrary to what some have assumed. In other words, slavery is *not* found mainly in certain economies, such as those dependent on intensive agriculture. (Unlike the United States until the Civil War, many societies with intensive agriculture did

[20]Euripides, "The Trojan Women," in Edith Hamilton, trans., *Three Greek Plays,* New York: Norton, 1937, p. 52.

[21]S. F. Nadel, *A Black Byzantium: The Kingdom of Nupe in Nigeria* (London: Oxford University Press, 1942). The Nupe abolished slavery at the beginning of this century.

not develop any variety of slavery.) Also, the hypothesis that slavery develops where available resources are plentiful but labor is scarce is not supported by the cross-cultural evidence. All we can say definitely is that slavery does not occur in developed or industrial economies; either it disappears or it was never present in them.[22]

The Emergence of Stratification

Anthropologists are not certain why social stratification developed. Nevertheless, they are reasonably sure that higher levels of stratification emerged relatively recently in human history. Archeological sites until about 7,500 years ago do not show extensive evidence of inequality. Houses do not appear to vary much in size and content, and burials seem to be more or less the same, suggesting that their occupants were treated more or less the same in life and death. Another indication that stratification is a relatively recent development in human history is the fact that certain cultural features associated with stratification also developed relatively recently. For example, most societies that depend primarily upon agriculture or herding have social classes.[23] Since agriculture and herding developed within the past 10,000 years, we may assume that most hunter-gatherers in the distant past lacked social classes. Other recently developed cultural features associated with class stratification include fixed settlements, political integration beyond the community level, the use of money as a medium of exchange, and the presence of at least some full-time specialization.[24]

Gerhard Lenski suggests that the 10,000-year-old trend toward increasing inequality has recently been reversed. He argues that inequalities of power and privilege in industrial societies—measured in terms of the concentration of political power and the distribution of income—are less pronounced than inequalities in complex preindustrial societies. Technology in industrialized societies is so complex, he argues, that those in power are compelled to delegate some authority to subordinates if the system is to work. In addition, a decline in the birth rate in industrialized societies, coupled with the need for skilled labor, has pushed the average wage of workers far above the subsistence level, resulting in greater equality in the distribution of income. Finally, Lenski suggests that the spread of the democratic ideology, and particularly its acceptance by elites, has significantly broadened the political power of the lower classes.[25] A study by Phillips Cutright has tested and supported Lenski's hypothesis that inequality has decreased with industrialization. Nations that are highly industrialized exhibit a lower level of inequality than nations that are only somewhat industrialized.[26]

But why did social stratification develop in the first place? On the basis of his study of Polynesian societies, Marshall Sahlins has suggested that an increase in agricultural productivity results in social stratification.[27] According to Sahlins, the degree of stratification is directly related to the production of a surplus, which is made possible by greater technological efficiency. The higher the level of productivity and the larger the agricultural surplus, the greater the scope and complexity of the distribution system. This in turn enhances the status of the chief, who serves as redistributing agent. Sahlins argues that the differentiation between distributor and producer inevitably gives rise to differentiation in other aspects of life:

First, there would be a tendency for the regulator of distribution to exert some authority over production itself—especially over productive activities which necessitate subsidization, such as communal labor or specialist labor. A degree of control of production implies a degree of control over the utilization of resources, or, in other words, some preeminent property rights. In turn, regulation of these economic processes necessitates the exercise of authority in interpersonal affairs; differences in social power emerge.[28]

Lenski's theory of the causes of stratification is similar to that of Sahlins. Lenski, too, argues that production of a surplus is the stimulus in the devel-

---

[22]Pryor, *The Origins of the Economy*, pp. 217–47.

[23]Data from Robert B. Textor, comp., *A Cross-Cultural Summary* (New Haven: HRAF Press, 1967).

[24]Ibid.

[25]Gerhard Lenski, *Power and Privilege: A Theory of Social Stratification* (Chapel Hill: University of North Carolina Press, 1984 [first published 1966], pp. 308–18.

[26]Phillips Cutright, "Inequality: A Cross-National Analysis," *American Sociological Review*, 32 (1967): 564.

[27]Sahlins, *Social Stratification in Polynesia*.

[28]Ibid., p. 4.

opment of stratification, but he focuses primarily on the conflict that arises over control of that surplus. Lenski concludes that the distribution of the surplus will be determined on the basis of power. Thus, inequalities in power promote unequal access to economic resources and simultaneously give rise to inequalities in privilege and prestige.[29]

The theories of Sahlins and Lenski do not really address the question of why the redistributors will want, or be able, to acquire greater control over resources. After all, the redistributors in many rank societies do not have greater wealth than others. It has been suggested that access to economic resources becomes unequal only when there is population pressure on resources in rank or chiefdom societies.[30] Such pressure may be what induces re-

distributors to try to keep more land and other resources for themselves and their families.

C. K. Meek offers an example of how population pressure in northern Nigeria may have led to economic stratification. At one time, a tribal member could obtain the right to use land by asking permission of the chief and presenting him with a token gift in recognition of his status. But by 1921, the reduction in the amount of available land had led to a system under which applicants offered the chief large payments for scarce land. As a result of these payments, farms came to be regarded as private property, and differential access to such property became institutionalized.[31]

Future research by archeologists, sociologists, historians, and anthropologists should provide more understanding of the emergence of social stratification in human societies, and how and why it varies in degree.

[29]Lenski, *Power and Privilege.*
[30]See Fried, *The Evolution of Political Society,* pp. 201–2; and Michael J. Harner, "Scarcity, the Factors of Production, and Social Evolution," in Steven Polgar, ed., *Population, Ecology, and Social Evolution* (The Hague: Mouton, 1975), pp. 123–38.

[31]C. K. Meek, *Land Law and Custom in the Colonies* (London: Oxford University Press, 1940), pp. 149–50.

SUMMARY

1. Whereas sociologists contend that social stratification is universal because individual inequalities exist in all societies, anthropologists argue that egalitarian societies exist in the sense that there are societies in which access to advantages is equally available to all social groups.

2. The presence or absence of customs or rules that give certain groups unequal access to economic resources, power, and prestige can be used to distinguish three types of societies. Egalitarian societies have no unequal access to economic resources, power, or prestige—they are unstratified. Rank societies do not have unequal access to economic resources or power, but they do have unequal access to prestige. Rank societies, then, are partially stratified. Class societies have unequal access to economic resources, power, and prestige. They are more completely stratified.

3. Stratified societies range from somewhat open class systems to caste systems, which are ex-

tremely rigid, since caste membership is fixed permanently at birth.

4. Slaves are persons who do not own their own labor; as such, they represent a class and sometimes even a caste. Slavery has existed in various forms in many times and places, regardless of race and culture. Sometimes slavery is a rigid and closed, or caste, system; sometimes it is a relatively open class system.

5. Social stratification appears to have emerged relatively recently in human history. This conclusion is based on archeological evidence and on the fact that a number of other cultural features associated with stratification developed relatively recently.

6. Some theories suggest that social stratification developed as productivity increased and surpluses were produced. Others suggest that stratification emerges only when there is population pressure on resources in rank societies.

SUGGESTED READING

BERREMAN, G. D., ed. *Social Inequality: Comparative and Developmental Approaches*. New York: Academic Press, 1981. Chapters in this book discuss inequality in a number of different societies, unstratified and stratified. Inequality is examined in relation to degree of economic development, colonialism, and education, among other factors.

BLUMBERG, R. L. *Stratification: Socioeconomic and Sexual Inequality*. Dubuque, IA: Wm. C. Brown, 1978. A brief introduction to systematic cross-cultural and sociological research (up to the mid 1970s) on why sexual and economic inequality may have developed. Chapters 4–6 are particularly relevant to this chapter.

FRIED, M. H. *The Evolution of Political Society: An Essay in Political Anthropology*. New York: Random House, 1967. Beginning with definitions of commonly used terms and drawing from several disciplines, the author attempts to develop a comprehensive theory of ranking, social stratification, and the state.

LENSKI, G. *Power and Privilege: A Theory of Social Stratification*. Chapel Hill: University of North Carolina Press, 1984. After a brief review of earlier stratification theories, the author presents a synthesized theory that emphasizes the causal importance of the level of technology in determining stratification.

PRYOR, F. L. *The Origins of the Economy: A Comparative Study of Distribution in Primitive and Peasant Economies*. New York: Academic Press, 1977. A large cross-cultural study of variation in distribution systems and their possible determinants. Chapter 8 on the varieties of slavery is particularly relevant to this chapter.

17

Sex and Culture

We all know that humans come in two major varieties—female and male. The contrast is one of the facts of life we share with most animal species. But the fact that males and females always have different organs of reproduction does not explain why males and females may also differ in other physical ways. After all, there are many animal species—such as pigeons, gulls, and laboratory rats—in which the two sexes hardly differ in appearance.[1] Thus, the fact that we are a species with two sexes does not really explain why human females and males typically look different. Also, the fact that humans reproduce sexually does not explain why human males and females should differ in behavior, or be treated differently by society. Yet no society we know of treats females and males in exactly the same way; indeed, females usually have fewer advantages compared to males. This is why in the last chapter we were careful to say that egalitarian societies have no social groups with unequal access to resources, power, and prestige. But within social groups (for example, families), even egalitarian societies usually allow males greater access to resources, power, and prestige.

Because many of the differences between females and males may reflect cultural expectations and experiences, many researchers now prefer to speak of **gender differences** (reserving the term sex differences for clearly biological differences).[2] Unfortunately, biological and cultural influences are not always clearly separable, so it is sometimes hard to know which term to use. As long as societies treat females and males differently, we may not be able to separate the effects of biology from the effects of culture, and both may be present.

In this chapter we discuss what we know cross-culturally about how and why females and males may differ physically, in gender roles, and in personality. We also discuss how and why sexual behavior, and attitudes about sex, vary from culture to culture.

Sex and Gender Differences

Physique and Physiology

As we noted at the outset, in many animal species males and females cannot readily be distinguished. Although they differ in chromosome makeup and in their external and internal organs of reproduction, they do not differ otherwise. In contrast, humans are **sexually dimorphic**—that is, the males and females of our species exhibit fairly marked differences in size and appearance. Females have proportionately wider pelvises. Males typically are taller and have heavier skeletons than females. Females have a larger proportion of their body weight in fat; males have a larger proportion of body weight in muscle. Males typically have greater grip strength, proportionately larger hearts and lungs, and greater aerobic work capacity (greater maximum uptake of oxygen during exercise).

There is a tendency in our society to view "taller" and "more muscled" as better, which may reflect the bias toward males in our culture. Natural selection may have favored these traits in males, but different ones in females. For example, since females bear children, selection may have favored earlier cessation of growth (and therefore less ultimate height) in females so that the nutritional needs of a fetus would not compete with a growing mother's needs.[3] (Females achieve their ultimate height shortly after puberty, but boys continue to grow after puberty.) Similarly, there is some evidence that females are less affected than males by nutritional shortages, presumably because they tend to be shorter and have proportionately more fat.[4] Natural selection may have favored those traits in females if they resulted in greater reproductive success.

Female and male athletes can build up their muscle strength and increase their aerobic work ca-

[1]Lila Leibowitz, *Females, Males, Families: A Biosocial Approach* (North Scituate, MA.: Duxbury, 1978), pp. 43–44.

[2]Alice Schlegel, "Gender Issues and Cross-Cultural Research," *Behavior Science Research*, 23 (1989): 266; Cynthia Fuchs Epstein, *Deceptive Distinctions: Sex, Gender, and the Social Order* (New Haven: Yale University Press, and New York: Russell Sage Foundation, 1988), pp. 5–6; Janet Saltzman Chafetz, *Gender Equity: An Integrated Theory of Stability and Change*, Sage Library of Social Research 176 (Newbury Park, CA: Sage Publications, 1990), p. 28.

[3]William A. Stini, "Evolutionary Implications of Changing Nutritional Patterns in Human Populations," *American Anthropologist*, 73 (1971): 1019–30.

[4]David W. Frayer and Milford H. Wolpoff, "Sexual Dimorphism," *Annual Review of Anthropology*, 14 (1985): 431–32.

A Choco man in Panama hunting with a bow and arrow.

pacity through training. Given that this is so, then cultural factors (such as how much a society expects and allows females and males to engage in muscular activity) could influence the degree to which females and males differ muscularly and in aerobic work capacity. Similar training may account for the recent trend toward decreasing differences between males and females in certain athletic events, such as marathons and swim meets.

Even when it comes to male and female physique and physiology, then, what we see may be the result of both culture and genes.[5]

Gender Roles

Productive and Domestic Activities. In the chapter on economic systems, we noted that all societies assign or divide labor at least somewhat differently to females and males. Because a role assignment has a clear cultural component, we can speak of these as gender roles. What is of particular interest here about the gender division of labor is not so much that every society has different work for females and males, but rather that so many societies divide up work in similar ways. The question, then, is why there are universal or near-universal patterns in such assignments.

Table 17–1 summarizes the worldwide patterns. We note which activities are performed by

which gender in all or almost all societies, which activities are usually performed by one gender, and which activities are commonly assigned to either gender, or both. Does the distribution of activities in the table suggest why males and females generally do different things?

One possible explanation may be labeled the *strength theory.* The greater strength of males, and their superior capacity to mobilize strength in quick bursts of energy (because of their greater aerobic work capacity), has commonly been cited as the reason for the universal or near-universal patterns in the gender division of labor. Certainly, activities that require lifting heavy objects (hunting large animals, butchering, clearing land, working with stone, metal, or lumber), throwing weapons, and running with great speed (as in hunting) may generally be performed best by males. And none of the activities females usually perform, with the possible exception of collecting firewood, seems to require the same degree of physical strength or quick bursts of energy. But the strength theory is not completely convincing, if only because it cannot readily explain all the observed patterns. For example, it is not clear that the male activities of trapping small animals, collecting wild honey, or making musical instruments require that much physical strength.

Another possible explanation of the worldwide patterns in division of labor can be called the *compatibility-with-child-care theory.* The argument here is that women's tasks tend to be those that are more compatible with child care. Although males can take care of infants, most traditional societies rely on breast-feeding of infants, which men cannot do. (In most societies, women breast-feed their children for two years on the average.) Women's tasks may be those that do not take them far from home for long periods, that do not place children in potential danger if they are taken along, and that can be stopped and resumed if an infant needs care.[6]

The compatibility theory may explain why *no* activities are listed in the right-hand column of Table 17–1. That is, it may be that there are no universal or near-universal women's activities because until recently most women have had to de-

[5]For reviews of theories and research on sexual dimorphism, and possible genetic and cultural determinants of variation in degree of dimorphism over time and place, see Frayer and Wolpoff, "Sexual Dimorphism"; and J. Patrick Gray, *Primate Sociobiology* (New Haven: HRAF Press, 1985), pp. 201–9, 217–25.

[6]Judith K. Brown, "A Note on the Division of Labor by Sex," *American Anthropologist,* 72 (1970), 1074.

TABLE 17–1 Worldwide Patterns in the Division of Labor by Gender

	MALES ALMOST ALWAYS	MALES USUALLY	EITHER GENDER OR BOTH	FEMALES USUALLY	FEMALES ALMOST ALWAYS
Primary subsistence activities	Hunt and trap animals	Fish Herd large animals Collect wild honey Clear land and prepare soil for planting	Collect shellfish Care for small animals Plant crops Tend crops Harvest crops Milk animals	Gather wild plants	
Secondary subsistence and household activities		Butcher animals	Preserve meat or fish	Care for children* Cook Prepare • vegetable food • drinks • dairy products Launder Fetch water Collect fuel	
Other	Lumber Mine and quarry Make • boats • musical instruments • bone, horn, and shell objects	Build houses Make • nets • rope	Prepare skins Make • leather products • baskets • mats • clothing • pottery	Spin yarn	

With the exception of the asterisked (*) items, the information in this table is adapted from George P. Murdock and Caterina Provost, "Factors in the Division of Labor by Sex: A Cross-Cultural Analysis," *Ethnology*, 12 (1973):203–25. The information on political leadership and warfare comes from Martin K. Whyte, "Cross-Cultural Codes Dealing with the Relative Status of Women," *Ethnology*, 17 (1978):217; and the information on child care comes from Thomas S. Weisner and Ronald Gallimore, "My Brother's Keeper: Child and Sibling Caretaking," *Current Anthropology*, 18 (1977):169–80.

vote much of their time to nursing infants and caring for children. The compatibility theory may also explain why men usually do tasks such as hunting, trapping, fishing, collecting honey, lumbering, and mining. These tasks are dangerous for infants to be around and in any case would be difficult to coordinate with infant care.[7]

[7]Among the Aché hunter-gatherers of Paraguay, women collect the type of honey produced by stingless bees (men collect other honey), which is consistent with the compatibility theory. See Ana Magdalena Hurtado, Kristen Hawkes, Kim Hill, and Hillard Kaplan, "Female Subsistence Strategies among the Aché Hunter-Gatherers of Eastern Paraguay," *Human Ecology*, 13 (1985): 23.

Finally, the compatibility theory may also explain why men seem to take over certain crafts in societies with full-time specialization. Although we have not noted this in Table 17–1, crafts such as making baskets, mats, and pottery are women's activities in noncommercial societies but tend to be men's activities in societies with full-time craft specialists.[8] Cooking is a good example in our own society. Women may be fine cooks, but chefs and bakers tend to be male, even though women tradi-

[8]George P. Murdock and Caterina Provost, "Factors in the Division of Labor by Sex: A Cross-Cultural Analysis," *Ethnology*, 12 (1973): 213.

Certain tasks are incompatible with child care. Although tilling a field and carrying a child are not the easiest tasks, this peasant woman in Chikoku, Japan, is clearly managing to do both at the same time.

tionally do most of the cooking at home. So women might be more likely to work as cooks and chefs if they could afford to leave their babies and young children in safe places to be cared for by others. After all, work in restaurant kitchens and bakeries would not be incompatible with child care if the children were not there!

But the compatibility theory does not explain why men usually prepare soil for planting, make things out of wood (like musical instruments), or

work bone, horn, and shell. All of these tasks could probably be stopped to tend to a child, and none of them is any more dangerous to children in the near vicinity than is cooking. Why, then, do males tend to do them? Additional considerations, such as *economy of effort,* may help explain patterns that cannot readily be explained by the strength and compatibility theories. For example, it may be more advantageous for men to make musical instruments, because men generally collect the hard materials involved (for example, by lumbering).[9] And because they collect those materials, men may be more knowledgeable about their physical properties and so more likely to know how to work with them. The economy-of-effort interpretation also suggests it would be advantageous for one sex to perform tasks that are located near each other. Thus, if women have to be near home to take care of young children, it would be economical for them to do other household chores that are located in or near the home.

A fourth explanation of division of labor can be called the *expendability theory.* This theory suggests that men, rather than women, will tend to do the dangerous work in a society because men are more expendable, because the loss of men is less disadvantageous reproductively than the loss of women. If some men lose their lives in hunting, deep-water fishing, mining, quarrying, lumbering, and the like, reproduction need not suffer so long as most fertile women have sexual access to men, as for example if the society permits two or more women to be married to the same man.[10] Why should anybody, male or female, be willing to do dangerous work? Perhaps only when society glorifies the roles and endows them with high prestige and other rewards.

Although the various theories, singly or in combination, seem to explain much of the division of labor by sex, there are some unresolved problems. Critics of the strength theory have pointed out that in some societies women engage in very

[9]Douglas R. White, Michael L. Burton, and Lilyan A. Brudner, "Entailment Theory and Method: A Cross-Cultural Analysis of the Sexual Division of Labor," *Behavior Science Research,* 12 (1977): 1–24.

[10]Carol C. Mukhopadhyay and Patricia J. Higgins, "Anthropological Studies of Women's Status Revisited: 1977–1987," *Annual Review of Anthropology,* 17 (1988): 473.

heavy labor.[11] If women in some societies can develop the strength to do such work, perhaps strength is more a function of training than we have traditionally believed. The compatibility theory also has some problems. It suggests that labor is divided to conform to the requirements of child care. But sometimes it seems the other way around. For example, when women spend a good deal of time in agricultural work outside the home, they often ask others to watch their infants and feed them "baby food" while the mothers are unavailable to nurse.[12] So it appears that child care may be arranged to conform to the division of labor.

Consider too the mountain areas of Nepal, where agricultural work is quite incompatible with child care; heavy loads must be carried up and down steep slopes, fields are far apart, and labor takes up most of the day. Yet women do this work anyway and leave their infants with others for long stretches of time.[13] And what about hunting, one of the activities most incompatible with child care and generally not done by women? Yet women do hunt in some societies. For example, many Agta women of the Philippines regularly hunt wild pig and deer; women alone or in groups get almost 30 percent of the large game animals.[14] The women's hunting does not seem to be incompatible with child care. Women take nursing babies on hunting trips, and the women who hunt do not have lower reproductive rates than the women who choose not to hunt. Of course, Agta women may find it easier to hunt because the hunting grounds are only about a half-hour from camp, the dogs that accompany the women assist in the hunting and protect the women and babies, and the women generally go out to hunt in groups, which means that others can help carry babies as well as the carcasses.

Husband and wife plowing a field in Poland.

As the cases just described suggest, we need to know a lot more about labor requirements. More precisely, we need to know exactly how much strength is required in particular tasks, exactly how dangerous they are, and whether a person could stop working at a task to care for a child. So far, we have mostly guesses. When there is more systematically collected evidence on such aspects of particular tasks, we will be in a better position to evaluate the theories we have discussed. In any case, it should be noted that none of the available theories implies that the worldwide division-of-labor patterns shown in Table 17–1 will persist. As we know from our own and other industrial societies, when machines replace human strength, when women have fewer children, and when women can assign child care to others, a strict gender division of labor begins to disappear.

Relative Contributions to Subsistence. In our society, the stereotype of the husband is that he is the breadwinner in the family; the wife is the manager of the house and children. As we know, the stereotype is becoming more myth than reality; in addition to the many women who are single-parents, many married women now work outside the home. For example, in the United States, more than 50 percent of all married women now work outside.

The concept of "breadwinner" in our society emphasizes the person who brings in food (and now money) from the outside and minimizes the

[11]Brown, "A Note on the Division of Labor by Sex," pp. 1073–78; and White, Burton, and Brudner, "Entailment Theory and Method," pp. 1–24.

[12]Sara B. Nerlove, "Women's Workload and Infant Feeding Practices: A Relationship with Demographic Implications," *Ethnology*, 13 (1974): 201–14.

[13]Nancy E. Levine, "Women's Work and Infant Feeding: A Case from Rural Nepal," *Ethnology*, 27 (1988): 231–51.

[14]Madeleine J. Goodman, P. Bion Griffin, Agnes A. Estioko-Griffin, and John S. Grove, "The Compatability of Hunting and Mothering among the Agta Hunter-Gatherers of the Philippines," *Sex Roles*, 12 (1985): 1199–209.

contributions of the person who works primarily inside the home. But let us consider that, traditionally at least, bread could not be produced simply by bringing home wheat or rye from the fields. The grain had to be winnowed and threshed, and ground into flour; and only then could it be made into bread. Anyone who has made bread knows that it takes only minutes to eat but hours to make.

How then should we judge contributions to subsistence? Most anthropologists distinguish between **primary subsistence activities** and **secondary subsistence activities.** The primary activities are the food-getting activities discussed earlier: gathering, hunting, fishing, herding, and agriculture. The secondary activities involve the preparation and processing of food to make it edible or to store. We know a lot about how and possibly why women's and men's contributions to primary subsistence activities vary cross-culturally. In contrast, there has been little or no systematic comparisons of gender division of labor in secondary subsistence activities.

In some societies women contribute more to the economy than men. For example, among the Tchambuli of New Guinea the women contributed almost everything to the economy. They did all the fishing—going out early in the morning by canoe to their fish traps and returning when the sun was hot. Some of the fish caught was traded for sago (a starch) and sugarcane, and it was the women who went on the long canoe trips to do the trading.[15]

Although the stereotype of husband as breadwinner no longer fits our society very well, it does fit many of the societies known to anthropology. Take the Toda of India, for example, as they were described early in the twentieth century. They depended for subsistence almost entirely on the dairy products of their water buffalo, either by using the products directly or by selling them for grain. But women were not allowed to have anything to do with dairy work; only men tended the buffalo and prepared the dairy products. Women's work was largely household work. Women prepared the pur-chased grain for cooking, cleaned house, and decorated clothing.[16]

A survey of a wide variety of societies has revealed that both men and women typically contribute to primary food-getting activities—but men usually contribute more.[17] Since women are almost always occupied with child-care responsibilities, it is not surprising that men usually do most of the primary food-getting work, which generally has to be done away from the home. However, total work time, including "outside the home" activities (mostly food-getting activities) and "inside the home" activities (mostly preparing and cooking food), often shows a different gender division of labor. For example, in horticultural and agricultural societies, it appears that women typically work more total hours per day than men.[18]

Why do women in some societies (including the Tchambuli) contribute more to primary subsistence activities than the men? Since hunting, fishing, and herding are generally male activities, in societies that depend on these types of food-getting men contribute more than women.[19] And since gathering is primarily women's work, women contribute more than men in food-collecting societies that depend largely on gathering. But the vast majority of societies known to anthropology depend on agriculture or horticulture, and with the exception of clearing land and preparing the soil (which are usually men's tasks), the work of cultivation is by and large men's *or* women's work (see the *Either Gender or Both* column in Table 17–1). So we need some explanation of why women do most of the work in the fields in some societies and men in others. Different patterns predominate in different areas of the world. In Africa south of the Sahara, women generally do more than half the work in the fields. But in much of Asia and in Europe and

[15]Margaret Mead, *Sex and Temperament in Three Primitive Societies* (New York: Mentor, 1950 [originally published 1935]), pp. 180–84.

[16]W. H. R. Rivers, *The Todas* (Oosterhout, N. B., The Netherlands: Anthropological Publications, 1967 [originally published in 1906]), p. 567.

[17]See Table 1 in Melvin Ember and Carol R. Ember, "The Conditions Favoring Matrilocal versus Patrilocal Residence," *American Anthropologist*, 73 (1971): 573.

[18]Carol R. Ember, "The Relative Decline in Women's Contribution to Agriculture with Intensification," *American Anthropologist*, 85 (1983): 288–89.

[19]Alice Schlegel and Herbert Barry III, "The Cultural Consequences of Female Contribution to Subsistence," *American Anthropologist*, 88 (1986): 142–50.

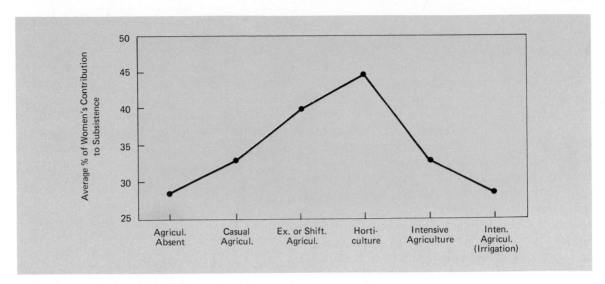

FIGURE 17–1 Relationship Between Type and Intensity of Agriculture and Average Percentage of Women's Contribution to Subsistence

(From Peggy R. Sanday, "Toward a Theory of the Status of Women," American Anthropologist, 75 (1973); 1691. Reproduced by permission of the American Anthropological Association.)

the areas around the Mediterranean, men do more.[20]

One apparent explanatory factor is the kind of work done. Many writers have pointed out that intensive agriculture, particularly plow agriculture, is associated with a high level of male participation in primary subsistence activities. In horticultural societies, in contrast, women contribute a good deal to primary subsistence. Figure 17–1 shows the relationship between women's relative contribution to food-getting and the type of cultivation practiced. As the graph indicates, women contribute the most when horticulture is practiced—either root and tree crop horticulture (labeled *Horticulture*) or shifting/slash-and-burn cultivation (labeled *Extensive or Shifting Agriculture*). According to Ester Boserup, when population increases and there is pressure to make more intensive use of the land, cultivators begin to use the plow and irrigation, and males start to do more.[21] But it is not quite clear why.

Why should women not continue to contribute a lot just because plows are used? One possibility is that plow agriculture involves a lot more labor input and therefore more male input. Men usually clear land anyway, but clearing is a more time-consuming process if intensive agriculture is practiced. It has been estimated that in one district in Nigeria, 100 days of work are required to clear one acre of virgin land for plowing by tractor; only 20 days are required to prepare the land for shifting cultivation. Furthermore, it has been suggested that less weeding is required in land that has been cleared and plowed. (Weeding is a task that probably can be combined with child care, and perhaps for that reason it may have been performed by women previously.)[22] But this suggestion does not explain why women do relatively less of all agricultural tasks, including weeding, in societies that have the plow.[23]

Another explanation for why women contribute less than men to intensive agriculture is that household chores increase with intensive agricul-

[20]Ester Boserup, *Woman's Role in Economic Development* (New York: St. Martin's Press, 1970), pp. 22–25; see also Schlegel and Barry, "The Cultural Consequences of Female Contribution to Subsistence," pp. 144–45.
[21]Boserup, *Woman's Role in Economic Development*, pp. 22–25.

[22]Ibid., pp. 31–34.
[23]Ember, "The Relative Decline in Women's Contribution to Agriculture with Intensification," pp. 286–87; data from Murdock and Provost, "Factors in the Division of Labor by Sex," p. 212.

ture and thus limit the time women can spend in the fields. Intensive agriculturalists rely more heavily on grain crops, which take much more work to make edible. Cereal grains (corn, wheat, oats) are usually dried before storing. They therefore take a long time to cook if they are left whole. More cooking requires more time to collect water and firewood (usually women's work) and more time to clean pots and utensils. A variety of techniques can reduce cooking time (such as soaking, grinding, or pounding), but the process that speeds up cooking the most—grinding—is very time-consuming (unless done by machine). Finally, household work may increase substantially with intensive agriculture because women in such societies have more children than women in horticultural societies. If household work increases in these ways, it is easy to understand why women cannot contribute more than, or as much as, men to intensive agriculture. But although women contribute relatively less than men to intensive agriculture, their contribution is nonetheless quite substantial: they seem to work outside the home four and a half hours a day, seven days a week, on the average.[24]

But we still have not explained why women contribute so much to horticulture in the first place. They may not have as much household work as intensive-agricultural women, but neither do the men. Why, then, don't men do relatively more in horticulture also? One possibility is that in horticultural societies men are often drawn away from cultivation into other types of activities. There is evidence that if males are engaged in warfare when primary subsistence work has to be done, then it is the women who must take care of that work.[25] Men may also be withdrawn from primary subsistence work if they have to work in distant towns and cities for wages or if they periodically go on long-distance trading trips.[26]

When women contribute a lot to primary food-getting activities we might expect their behavior and attitudes concerning children to be af-

fected. Several cross-cultural studies suggest this expectation is correct. In societies with a high female contribution to food-getting, infants are fed solid foods earlier (which enables others besides mothers to feed them),[27] and girls are likely to be trained to be industrious (probably to help their mothers out).[28] Finally, girl babies are more valued in societies where women contribute a lot to food-getting.[29]

Political Leadership and Warfare. In almost every society we know about, men rather than women are the leaders in the political arena. One cross-cultural survey indicates that in approximately 85 percent of the surveyed societies, only men were leaders. In the societies in which some women occupied leadership positions, the women were either outnumbered by or less powerful than the men leaders.[30] Whether or not we consider warfare to be part of the political sphere of life (see the chapter on political organization), we find an almost universal dominance of males in that arena. In 88 percent of the world's societies, women never participate actively in war.[31]

Even in *matrilineal* societies, which seem to be oriented around women (see the chapter on marital residence and kinship), men usually occupy political positions. For example, among the Iroquois of what is now New York State, women had control over resources and a great deal of influence. But men held political office, not women. The highest political body among the League of the Iroquois (which comprised five different tribal groups) was a council of fifty male chiefs. Although women could not serve on the council, they could nominate, elect, and impeach their male representatives. Women also could decide between life or death for prisoners of war, they could forbid the men of their households to go to war, and they could intervene to bring about peace.[32]

Why have men (at least so far) almost always

[24]Ember, "The Relative Decline in Women's Contribution to Agriculture with Intensification," pp. 287–93.
[25]Ember and Ember, "The Conditions Favoring Matrilocal versus Patrilocal Residence," pp. 579–80.
[26]Ember and Ember, "The Conditions Favoring Matrilocal versus Patrilocal Residence," p. 581; see also Peggy R. Sanday, "Toward a Theory of the Status of Women," *American Anthropologist*, 75 (1973): 1684.

[27]Nerlove, "Women's Workload and Infant Feeding Practices," pp. 207–14.
[28]Schlegel and Barry, "The Cultural Consequences of Female Contribution to Subsistence," 142–50.
[29]Ibid.
[30]Martin K. Whyte, "Cross-Cultural Codes Dealing with the Relative Status of Women," *Ethnology*, 17 (1978): 217.
[31]Ibid.
[32]Judith K. Brown, "Economic Organization and the Position of Women among the Iroquois," *Ethnohistory*, 17 (1970): 151–67.

Members of the Connecticut House of Representatives are mostly men.

dominated the political sphere of life? Some have suggested that men's role in warfare gives them the edge in all kinds of political leadership, particularly because they control weapons—an important resource.[33] But there is little evidence that force is usually used to obtain leadership positions.[34] Still, warfare may be related to political power for another reason. Since warfare clearly affects survival and since it occurs regularly in most of the societies we know about, decision making about war may be among the most important kinds of politics in most societies. If this is so, it may be advantageous to have those who know the most about warfare making decisions about it. As for why males and not females usually engage in fighting, we may refer to three of the possible explanations of the worldwide patterns in the gender division of labor. Warfare, like hunting, probably requires strength (for throwing weapons) and quick bursts of energy (for running). And certainly combat is one of the most dangerous and uninterruptible activities imaginable, hardly compatible with child care. Also, even if they do not at the moment have children, women may generally be kept out of combat because their potential fertility is more important to a population's reproduction and survival than their potential usefulness as warriors.[35] So, the strength theory, the compatibility theory, and the expendability theory might all explain the predominance of men in warfare.

Two other factors may be involved in male predominance in politics. One is the generally greater height of men. Why height should be a factor in leadership is unclear, but a number of studies

[33]Peggy R. Sanday, "Female Status in the Public Domain," in Michelle Z. Rosaldo and Louise Lamphere, eds., *Woman, Culture, and Society* (Stanford, CA: Stanford University Press, 1974), pp. 189–206; and William T. Divale and Marvin Harris, "Population, Warfare, and the Male Supremacist Complex," *American Anthropologist*, 78 (1976): 521–38.

[34]Naomi Quinn, "Anthropological Studies on Women's Status," *Annual Review of Anthropology*, 6 (1977): 189–90.

[35]Susan Brandt Graham, "Biology and Human Social Behavior: A Response to van den Berghe and Barash," *American Anthropologist*, 81 (1979): 357–60.

suggest that taller persons are more likely to be leaders.[36] Finally, there is the possibility that men dominate politics because they get around more than women in the outside world. Men's activities typically take them farther from home; women tend to work more around the home. If societies choose leaders at least in part because they know more about the larger world, then men will generally have some advantage. In support of this reasoning, Patricia Draper has found that in recently settled-down !Kung bands, where women no longer engaged in long-distance gathering, women seem to have lost much of their former influence in making decisions.[37] Involvement in child care may also detract from such influence. In a study of village leadership among the Kayapo of Brazil, Dennis Werner found that women with heavy child-care burdens are less influential, perhaps because they have fewer friends and miss many details of what is going on in the village.[38]

These various explanations suggest why men generally dominate politics, but we still need to explain why women participate in politics more in some societies than in others. Marc Ross has investigated this question in a cross-cultural survey of ninety societies. In that sample, the degree of female participation in politics varies considerably. For example, among the Mende of Sierra Leone women regularly hold high office, but among the Azande of Zaire women take no part in public life. Ross suggests that female political participation is higher in societies that bring up children with affection and nurturance and lower where communities are organized around groups of male kin. This last finding is consistent with the view that societies will emphasize more "female" values if both fathers and mothers are warm rather than punishing with their children; women in such societies should be more active in public life.[39]

The Relative Status of Women. There are probably as many definitions of status as there are researchers interested in the topic. To some, the relative status of the sexes means how much importance society confers on females versus males. To others, it means how much power and authority women or men have relative to each other. And to still others, it means what kinds of rights women and men possess to do what they want to do. In any case, many social scientists are asking why the status of women appears to vary from one society to another. Why do women have few rights and little influence in some societies, but more of each in other societies? Or, in other words, why is there variation in degree of *gender stratification?*

In the small Iraqi town of Daghara, women and men live very separate lives.[40] In many respects, women appear to have very little status. In common with much of the Islamic world, women live their lives mostly in seclusion. This means that they stay mostly in their houses and interior courtyards. If women must go out, which they can do only with male approval, they must shroud their faces and bodies in long, black cloaks. These cloaks must be worn in mixed company, even at home. In the larger social system, women are essentially excluded from political activities. Legally, they are considered to be under the authority of their fathers and husbands. Even the sexuality of women is controlled. There is strict emphasis on virginity prior to marriage. Since women are not permitted even casual conversations with strange men, the possibilities for extramarital or even premarital relationships are very slight. In contrast, hardly any sexual restrictions are imposed on men.

But some societies, such as the Mbuti Pygmies, seem to approach equal status for males and females. Like most food collectors, the Mbuti have no formal political organization to make decisions

[36]Dennis Werner, "Chiefs and Presidents: A Comparison of Leadership Traits in the United States and among the Mekranoti-Kayapo of Central Brazil," *Ethos* 10 (1982): 136–48; and Ralph M. Stogdill, *Handbook of Leadership: A Survey of Theory and Research* (New York: Macmillan, 1974), cited in ibid.; see also W. Penn Handwerker and Paul V. Crosbie, "Sex and Dominance," *American Anthropologist,* 84 (1982): 97–104.

[37]Patricia Draper, "!Kung Women: Contrasts in Sexual Egalitarianism in Foraging and Sedentary Contexts," in Rayna R. Reiter, ed., *Toward an Anthropology of Women* (New York: Monthly Review Press, 1975), p. 103.

[38]Dennis Werner, "Child Care and Influence among the Mekranoti of Central Brazil," *Sex Roles,* 10 (1984): 395–404.

[39]Marc H. Ross, "Female Political Participation: A Cross-Cultural Explanation," *American Anthropologist,* 88 (1986): 843–58.

[40]This description is based on the fieldwork of Elizabeth and Robert Fearnea (1956–1958), as reported in M. Kay Martin and Barbara Voorhies, *Female of the Species* (New York: Columbia University Press, 1975), pp. 304–31.

or to settle disputes. Public disputes occur, and both women and men take part in the uproar that is part of such disputes. Women not only make their positions known, but their opinions are often heeded. Even in domestic quarrels involving physical violence between husband and wife, others usually intervene to stop them, regardless of who hit whom first.[41] Women control the use of dwellings; they usually have equal say over the disposal of resources they or the men collect, over the upbringing of their children, and about whom their children should marry. One of the few signs of inequality is that women are somewhat more restricted than men with respect to extramarital sex.[42]

There are many theories about why women have relatively high or low status. One of the most common is that women's status will be high when they contribute substantially to primary subsistence activities. According to this theory, then, women should have very little status when food-getting depends largely on hunting, herding, or intensive agriculture. A second theory suggests that where warfare is especially important, men rather than women will be more valued and esteemed. A third theory suggests that where there are centralized political hierarchies, men will have higher status. The reasoning in the last theory is essentially the same as in the warfare theory—since men usually play the dominant role in political behavior, men's status should be higher wherever political behavior is more important or frequent. Finally, there is the theory that women will have higher status where kin groups and couples' place of residence after marriage are organized around women.

One of the problems in evaluating these theories is that decisions have to be made about what status means. Does it mean value? rights? influence? And do all these aspects of status vary together? Cross-cultural research by Martin Whyte suggests that they do not. For each sample society in his study, Whyte rated fifty-two different items that might be used to define the relative status of the sexes. These items include things such as

which sex can inherit property, who has final authority over disciplining unmarried children, and whether the gods in the society are male, female, or both. The results of the study indicate that very few of these items are related. Therefore, Whyte concludes, we cannot talk about status as a single concept. Rather, it seems more appropriate to talk about the relative status of women in different spheres of life.[43]

Even though Whyte found no necessary connection between one aspect of status and another, he decided to ask whether some of the theories just mentioned correctly predict why some societies have many (as opposed to few) areas in which the status of women is high.

Let us turn first to the ideas that are *not* supported by the available cross-cultural evidence. The idea that generally high status derives from a greater contribution to primary subsistence activities is *not* supported at all.[44] Women in intensive-agricultural societies (who contribute less than men to primary subsistence) do tend to have lower status in many areas of life, just as in the Iraqi case described above. But in societies that depend mostly on hunting (where women also do little of the primary subsistence work), women seem to have higher status—which contradicts the theoretical expectation. Similarly, there is no consistent evidence that a high frequency of warfare generally lowers women's status in different spheres of life.[45]

What does predict higher status for women in many areas of life? Although the results are not that strong, there is some support in Whyte's study for the theory that where kin groups and marital residence are organized around women, women have somewhat higher status (we discuss these features of society more fully in the chapter on marital residence and kinship). The Iroquois are a good example. Even though Iroquois women could not hold political office, they had considerable author-

[41]Elsie B. Begler, "Sex, Status, and Authority in Egalitarian Society," *American Anthropologist*, 80 (1978): 571–88.

[42]Ibid. See also Whyte, "Cross-Cultural Codes Dealing with the Relative Status of Women," pp. 229–32.

[43]Martin K. Whyte, *The Status of Women in Preindustrial Societies* (Princeton, NJ: Princeton University Press, 1978), pp. 95–120. For a similar view, see Quinn, "Anthropological Studies on Women's Status."

[44]Whyte, *The Status of Women in Preindustrial Societies*, pp. 124–29, 145; see also Sanday, "Toward a Theory of the Status of Women."

[45]Whyte, *The Status of Women in Preindustrial Societies*, pp. 129–30.

ity within and beyond the household. Related women lived together in longhouses with husbands who belonged to other kin groups. In the longhouse, the women's authority was clear and they could ask objectionable men to leave. The women controlled the allocation of the food they produced. Allocation could influence the timing of war parties, since men could not undertake a raid without provisions. Women were involved in the selection of religious leaders, half of whom were women. Even in politics, where women could not speak or serve on the council, they largely controlled the selection of councilmen and could institute impeachment proceedings against those to whom they objected.[46]

A generally lower status for women does appear to be found in societies with political hierarchies.[47] Lower status for women appears to be associated with a number of indicators of cultural complexity, not just political hierarchies. Societies with social stratification, plow and irrigation agriculture, larger settlements, private property, and craft specialization also tend to have generally lower status for women. (One type of influence for women increases with cultural complexity—informal influence. But as Whyte points out, informal influence may simply reflect a lack of *real* influence.[48]) Why cultural complexity is associated with women having less authority in the home, less control over property, and more restricted sexual lives is not yet understood.

Western colonialism also appears to have been generally detrimental to women's status, perhaps because Westerners have been accustomed to dealing with men. There are plenty of examples of Europeans restructuring land ownership around men and teaching men modern farming techniques, even though women are usually the farmers. In addition, men more often than women could earn cash through wage labor or through sales of goods (such as furs) to Europeans.[49] Although the relative status of men and women may not have been equal before the Europeans arrived, colonial influences seem generally to have undermined the position of women.

We are beginning to understand some of the conditions that may enhance or decrease certain aspects of women's status. If we can understand which of these conditions are most important, society may (if it wants to) be able to reduce gender inequality.[50]

Personality

Reporting on three tribes in New Guinea, Margaret Mead said that "many, if not all, of the personality traits we have called masculine or feminine are as lightly linked to sex as are the clothing, the manners, and the form of head-dress that a society at a given period assigns to either sex."[51] In other words, she suggested that there were *no* universal or near-universal personality differences between the sexes. Rather, societies were free to create any such differences. She described the Arapesh males and females as essentially alike: both sexes were gentle, cooperative, and maternal. She also described the Mundugumor males and females as similar, but in this case both sexes exhibited violence and competitiveness. Finally, she described the Tchambuli as having substantial male-female differences in temperament, but opposite to what we might expect. The women were domineering, practical, and impersonal, and were the chief economic providers; the men were sensitive and delicate, and devoted their time to their appearance and to artistic pursuits.

But research conducted in recent years does not support Mead's view that there are no consistent sex differences in temperament. On the contrary, some sex differences in behavior occur consistently and in quite diverse societies. Since no one has restudied the behavior of males and females in the three New Guinea societies Mead studied, it is possible they are exceptional cases. But it is also possible that Mead might have come to somewhat different conclusions if she had employed the kinds of observation techniques that have been employed in more recent studies. The

[46]Brown, "Economic Organization and the Position of Women among the Iroquois."

[47]Whyte, *The Status of Women in Preindustrial Societies,* pp. 135–36.

[48]Ibid., p. 135.

[49]Quinn, "Anthropological Studies on Women's Status," p. 85; see also Mona Etienne and Eleanor Leacock, eds., *Women and Colonization: Anthropological Perspectives* (New York: Praeger, 1980), pp. 19–20.

[50]Chafetz, *Gender Equity: An Integrated Theory of Stability and Change,* pp. 11–19.

[51]Mead, *Sex and Temperament in Three Primitive Societies,* p. 206.

newer studies have based their conclusions on systematic records of the minute details of behavior of a substantial number of males and females. Any conclusions about sex differences in aggressiveness, for example, are based on actual counts of the number of times a particular individual tried to hurt or injure another person in a fixed amount of observation time.

Which sex differences in personality are suggested by these more recent studies? Most of them have observed children in different cultural settings. The most consistent difference is in the area of aggression: boys try to hurt others more frequently than girls do. In an extensive comparative study of children's behavior—the Six Cultures project—this sex difference shows up as early as three to six years of age.[52] Research done in the United States agrees with the cross-cultural findings.[53] In a large number of observational and experimental studies, boys exhibited more aggression than girls.

Other sex differences have turned up with considerable consistency, but we have to be more cautious in accepting them, either because they have not been documented as well or because there are more exceptions. There seems to be a tendency for girls to exhibit more responsible behavior, including nurturance (trying to help others). Girls seem more likely to conform to adult wishes and commands. Boys try more often to exert dominance over others in order to get their own way. In play, boys and girls show a preference for their own sex. Boys seem to play in larger groups, girls in smaller ones. And boys seem to maintain more distance between each other, girls less.[54]

Assuming that these differences are consistent across cultures, how are they to be explained? Many writers and researchers believe that because

Boys and girls dress quite differently in Fiji.

certain sex differences are so consistent, they are probably rooted in the biological differences between the two sexes. Aggression is one of the traits talked about most often in this connection, particularly because this sex difference appears so early in life.[55] But an alternative argument can be made that because societies almost universally require adult males and females to perform different types of roles, they bring up boys and girls differently. And if they are brought up or socialized differently, presumably they will behave differently. Since most societies expect adult males to be warriors or to be prepared to be warriors, shouldn't we expect most societies to emphasize or idealize aggression in males? And since females are almost always the caretakers of infants, shouldn't we also expect societies generally to emphasize nurturant behaviors in females? Researchers tend to adopt either the biological or the socialization view, but it is quite possible that both kinds of causes are important in the development of sex differences. For example, parents might turn a slight genetic difference into a large sex difference by maximizing that difference in the way they socialize boys versus girls.

As we mentioned earlier, it is difficult for researchers to distinguish the influence of genes (or other biological conditions) from the influence of socialization. We now have research indicating that as early as birth parents may treat boy and girl infants differently.[56] Moreover, in spite of the fact

[52]Beatrice B. Whiting and Carolyn P. Edwards, "A Cross-Cultural Analysis of Sex Differences in the Behavior of Children Aged Three through Eleven," *Journal of Social Psychology,* 91 (1973): 171–88.

[53]Eleanor E. Maccoby and Carol N. Jacklin, *The Psychology of Sex Differences* (Stanford CA: Stanford University Press, 1974).

[54]For a more extensive discussion of behavior differences and possible explanations of them, see Carol R. Ember, "A Cross-Cultural Perspective on Sex Differences," in Ruth H. Munroe, Robert L. Munroe, and Beatrice B. Whiting, eds., *Handbook of Cross-Cultural Human Development* (New York: Garland Press, 1981), pp. 531–80.

[55]Whiting and Edwards, "A Cross-Cultural Analysis of Sex Differences in the Behavior of Children Aged Three through Eleven."

[56]For references to this research, see Ember, "A Cross-Cultural Perspective on Sex Differences," p. 559.

that objective observers can see no major "personality" differences between girl and boy infants, parents often claim to.[57] This means that parents may unconsciously want to see differences and may therefore produce them in socialization. So even early differences could be learned rather than genetic. Remember too that researchers cannot do experiments with people—for example, parents' behavior cannot be manipulated to find out what would happen if boys and girls were treated in exactly the same way.

However, there is some experimental research on aggression in nonhuman animals. These experiments suggest that the male hormone androgen may be partly responsible for higher levels of aggression. Females injected with androgen around the time the sexual organs develop (before or shortly after birth) behave more aggressively when they are older.[58] But even these results are not conclusive, because females who get more androgen show generally disturbed metabolic systems, and general metabolic disturbance may itself increase aggressiveness. Furthermore, androgen-injected females look more like males because they develop male genitals; therefore, they may be treated like males.

Is there any evidence that socialization differences may account for differences in aggression? Although a cross-cultural survey of ethnographers' reports on 101 societies does show that more societies encourage aggression in boys than in girls, *most* societies show no difference in aggression training.[59] The few societies that show differences in aggression training can hardly account for the widespread sex differences in actual aggressiveness. However, the survey does not necessarily mean that there are no consistent differences in aggression training for boys and girls. All it shows is that there are no *obvious* differences. For all we know, the learning of aggression and other "masculine"

traits by boys could be produced by subtle types of socialization.

One possible type of subtle socialization that could create sex differences in behavior is the type of chores children are assigned. It is possible that little boys and girls learn to behave differently because their parents ask them to do different kinds of work. Beatrice and John Whiting report from the Six Cultures project that in societies where children were asked to do a great deal of work, they generally show more responsible and nurturant behavior. Since girls are almost always asked to do more work than boys, they may be more responsible and nurturant for this reason alone.[60] If this reasoning is correct, we should find that if boys are asked to do girls' work, they may learn to behave more like girls.

A study of Luo children in Kenya supports this view.[61] Girls were usually asked to babysit, cook, clean house, and fetch water and firewood. Boys were usually asked to do very little because boys' traditional work was herding cattle—and most families in the community studied had few cattle. But for some reason more boys than girls had been born, and many mothers without girls at home asked their sons to do girls' chores. Much of the behavior of the boys who did the girls' work was intermediary between the behavior of other boys and the behavior of girls. The boys who did the girls' work were more like girls in that they were less aggressive, less domineering, and more responsible than other boys, even when they weren't working. So it is possible that task assignment has an important influence on how boys and girls learn to behave. These and other subtle forms of socialization need to be investigated more thoroughly; research may help us to understand better the origins of female/male differences in behavior.

Myths about Differences in Behavior. Before we leave the subject of behavior differences, we should note some widespread beliefs about them

[57]J. Z. Rubin, F. J. Provenzano, and R. F. Haskett, "The Eye of the Beholder: Parents' Views on the Sex of New Borns," *American Journal of Orthopsychiatry,* 44 (1974): 512–19.

[58]Lee Ellis, "Evidence of Neuroandrogenic Etiology of Sex Roles from a Combined Analysis of Human, Nonhuman Primate and Nonprimate Mammalian Studies," *Personality and Individual Differences,* 7 (1986): 525–27.

[59]Ronald P. Rohner, "Sex Differences in Aggression: Phylogenetic and Enculturation Perspectives," *Ethos,* 4 (1976): 57–72.

[60]Beatrice B. Whiting and John W. M. Whiting (in collaboration with Richard Longabaugh), *Children of Six Cultures: A Psycho-Cultural Analysis* (Cambridge, MA: Harvard University Press, 1975); see also Beatrice B. Whiting and Carolyn P. Edwards, *Children of Different Worlds: The Formation of Social Behavior* (Cambridge, MA.: Harvard University Press, 1988), p. 273.

[61]Carol R. Ember, "Feminine Task Assignment and the Social Behavior of Boys," *Ethos,* 1 (1973): 424–39.

that turn out to be unsupported. Some of these mistaken beliefs are that girls are more dependent than boys, that girls are more sociable, and that girls are more passive. The results obtained by the Six Cultures project cast doubt on all these notions.[62] First, if we think of dependency as seeking help and emotional support from others, girls are generally no more likely to behave this way than boys. To be sure, the results do indicate that boys and girls have somewhat different styles of dependency. Girls more often seek help and contact; boys more often seek attention and approval. As for sociability, which means seeking and offering friendship, the Six Cultures results show no reliable differences between the sexes. Of course, boys and girls may be sociable in different ways because boys generally play in larger groups than girls. As for the supposed passivity of girls, the evidence is also not particularly convincing. Girls in the Six Cultures project do not consistently withdraw from aggressive attacks or comply with unreasonable demands. The only thing that emerges as a sex difference is that older girls are less likely than boys to respond to aggression with aggression. But this finding may not reflect passivity as much as the fact that girls are less aggressive than boys—which we already know.

So, some of our common ideas about sex differences are unfounded. Others, such as those dealing with aggression and responsibility, cannot be readily dismissed and should be investigated further.

Sexuality

In view of the way the human species reproduces, it is not surprising that sexuality is part of our nature. But no society we know of leaves sexuality to nature; all have at least some rules governing "proper" conduct. There is much variation from one society to another in the degree of sexual activity permitted or encouraged before marriage, outside marriage, and even within marriage. And societies vary markedly in their tolerance of non-heterosexual sexuality.

Cultural Regulation of Sexuality: Permissiveness versus Restrictiveness

All societies seek to regulate sexual activity to some degree, and there is a lot of variation cross-culturally. Some societies allow premarital sex, others forbid it. The same is true for extramarital sex. In addition, a society's degree of restrictiveness is not always consistent through the life span or for all aspects of sex. For example, quite a number of societies ease sexual restrictions somewhat in adolescence while many become more restrictive in adulthood.[63] Then, too, societies change over time. Our own society has traditionally been rather restrictive, but until recently (before the emergence of the AIDS epidemic) more permissive attitudes were gaining acceptance. A survey of sexual behavior and attitudes conducted in the United States in the 1970s suggested that since Kinsey's surveys in the 1940s the acceptance of and actual frequency of premarital sex increased markedly. Somewhat surprisingly, attitudes toward extramarital sex did not change much: the vast majority of people surveyed in the 1970s still objected to it.[64] However, we must remember that many people do not readily talk about sex, so we cannot be sure that behavior had really changed; perhaps people were only more willing to discuss their sexuality. In any case, attitudes toward sexuality may be less permissive now because of the fear of AIDS.

Childhood Sexuality. The sexual curiosity of children is met with a tolerant and open attitude in many societies. For example, among the Hopi of the southwestern United States parents used to pay no attention to children observed masturbating. All sexual behavior in childhood was viewed permissively, even if certain restrictions were imposed at the onset of puberty.[65]

In contrast, in a Pacific island society (called East Bay to protect confidences), "great concern for sexual propriety" is demonstrated.[66] Children

---

[62]Whiting and Edwards, "A Cross-Cultural Analysis of Sex Differences in the Behavior of Children Aged Three through Eleven," pp. 175–79; see also Maccoby and Jacklin, *The Psychology of Sex Differences.*

[63]David R. Heise, "Cultural Patterning of Sexual Socialization," *American Sociological Review,* 32 (1967): 726–39.

[64]Morton Hunt, *Sexual Behavior in the 1970s* (Chicago: Playboy Press, 1974), pp. 254–57.

[65]Clellan S. Ford and Frank A. Beach, *Patterns of Sexual Behavior* (New York: Harper, 1951), p. 188.

[66]William Davenport, "Sexual Patterns and Their Regulation in a Society of the Southwest Pacific," in Frank A. Beach, ed., *Sex and Behavior* (New York: John Wiley, 1965), pp. 164–74.

Is it in the genes that boys will be boys?

are discouraged from touching their genitalia in public—the boys through good-natured ridicule, the girls by scolding. From about their fifth year, children learn not to touch the other sex at all and are sensitive to lapses in modesty, which they frequently point out to one another. Boys must always remain a certain distance from a female.

Premarital Sex. The degree to which sex before marriage is approved or disapproved of varies greatly from society to society. The Trobriand Islanders, for example, approve of and encourage premarital sex, seeing it as an important preparation for later marriage roles. Both boys and girls are given complete instruction in all forms of sexual expression at the onset of puberty and are allowed plenty of opportunity for intimacy. Some societies not only allow premarital sex on a casual basis, but specifically encourage trial marriages between adolescents. Among the Ila-speaking peoples of central Africa, girls are given houses of their own at harvest time where they may play at being wife with the boys of their choice. It is said that among these people virginity does not exist beyond the age of ten.[67]

On the other hand, in many societies premarital sex is discouraged. For example, among the Tepoztlan Indians of Mexico, a girl's life becomes "crabbed, cribbed, confined" from the time of her first menstruation. A girl is not to speak to or en-

courage boys in the least way. To do so would be to court disgrace, to show herself to be crazy.

The responsibility of guarding the chastity and reputation of one or more daughters of marriageable age is often felt to be a burden by the mother. One mother said she wished her fifteen-year-old daughter would marry soon because it was inconvenient to "spy" on her all the time.[68]

In many Muslim societies, a girl's premarital chastity is tested after her marriage. Following the wedding night, blood-stained sheets are displayed as proof of the bride's virginity.

Extramarital Sex. A Hopi, speaking to an ethnographer, reported,

Next to the dance days with singing, feasting, and clown work, love-making with private wives was the greatest pleasure of my life. And for us who toil in the desert, these light affairs make life more pleasant. Even married men prefer a private wife now and then. At any rate there are times when a wife is not interested, and then a man must find someone else or live a worried life.[69]

The Hopi are not unusual. Extramarital sex is not uncommon in many societies. In about 69 percent of the world's societies men have extramarital sex more than occasionally, and in about 57 percent so do women. The frequency of such sex is higher than we might expect, given that only a slight majority of societies (54 percent) say they allow extramarital sex for men, and only a small number (11 percent) say they allow it for women.[70]

In several societies, then, there is quite a difference between the restrictive code and actual practice. The Navaho of fifty years ago were said to forbid adultery, but young married men under thirty were said to have 27 percent of their heterosexual contacts with women other than their wives.[71] And although people in the United States almost overwhelmingly reject extramarital sex, 41 percent of married men and about 18 percent of

[67]Ford and Beach, *Patterns of Sexual Behavior*, p. 191.

[68]Oscar Lewis, *Life in a Mexican Village: Tepoztlan Revisited* (Urbana: University of Illinois Press, 1951), p. 397.

[69]Leo W. Simmons, *Sun Chief* (New Haven: Yale University Press, 1942), p. 281.

[70]Gwen J. Broude and Sarah J. Greene, "Cross-Cultural Codes on Twenty Sexual Attitudes and Practices," *Ethnology*, 15 (1976): 409–29.

[71]Clyde Kluckhohn, "As an Anthropologist Views It," in A. Deutsch, ed., *Sex Habits of American Men* (Englewood Cliffs, NJ: Prentice Hall, 1948), p. 101.

married women have had extramarital sex.[72] These findings fit the cross-cultural finding that most societies have a double standard with regard to men and women: restrictions are considerably greater for the latter.[73] A substantial number of societies openly accept extramarital relationships. Among the Toda of India there was no censure of adultery. Indeed, "immorality attaches to the man who begrudges his wife to another."[74] The Chukchee of Siberia, who often travelled long distances, allowed a married man to engage in sex with his host's wife, with the understanding that he would offer the same hospitality when the host visited him.[75]

Sex within Marriage. There is as much variety in the way coitus is performed as there is in sexual attitudes generally. Privacy is a nearly universal requirement. But whereas a North American will usually find this in the bedroom, many other peoples are obliged to go out into the bush. The Siriono of Bolivia, for example, have as many as fifty hammocks ten feet apart in their small huts.[76] In some cultures coitus often occurs in the presence of others, who may be sleeping or simply looking the other way.

Time and frequency of coitus are also variable. Night is generally preferred, but some peoples, such as the Rucuyen of Brazil and the Yapese of the Pacific Caroline Islands, specifically opt for day. The Chenchu of India believe that a child conceived at night may be born blind. People in most societies abstain from intercourse during menstruation, during at least part of pregnancy, and for a period after childbirth. The Lesu, a people of New Ireland, an island off New Guinea, prohibit all members of the community from engaging in sex between the death of any member and burial.[77] Some societies prohibit sexual relations before various activities, such as hunting, fighting, planting, brewing, and iron smelting. Our own society is among the most lenient regarding restrictions on coitus within marriage, imposing only rather loose

Among Hasidic Jews, men and women dance separately so that a man will not accidentally touch a menstruating woman.

restraints during mourning, menstruation, and pregnancy.

Homosexuality. The range in permissiveness or restrictiveness toward homosexual relations is as great as that for any other kind of sex. Among the Lepcha of the Himalayas, a man is believed to become homosexual if he eats the flesh of an uncastrated pig. But the Lepcha say that homosexual behavior is practically unheard of, and they view it with disgust.[78] Perhaps because many societies deny that homosexuality exists, little is known about homosexual practices in the restrictive societies. Among the permissive ones, there is variation in the pervasiveness of homosexuality. In some societies homosexuality is accepted, but lim-

[72]Hunt, *Sexual Behavior in the 1970s.*
[73]Gwen J. Broude, "Extramarital Sex Norms in Cross-Cultural Perspective," *Behavior Science Research,* 15 (1980): 184.
[74]Ford and Beach, *Patterns of Sexual Behavior,* p. 113.
[75]Ibid., p. 114.
[76]Ibid., p. 69.
[77]Ibid., p. 76.

[78]John Morris, *Living with Lepchas: A Book about the Sikkim Himalayas* (London: Heinemann, 1938), p. 191.

ited to certain times and certain individuals. For example, among the Papago of the southwestern U.S. there were "nights of saturnalia," in which homosexual tendencies could be expressed. The Papago also had many male transvestites, who wore women's clothing, did women's chores, and, if not married, could be visited by men.[79] Women did not have quite the same freedom of expression. They could participate in the saturnalia feasts only with their husband's permission, and female transvestites were nonexistent.

Homosexuality occurs even more widely in other societies. The Siwans of North Africa expect all males to engage in homosexual relations. In fact, fathers make arrangements for their unmarried sons to be given to an older man in a homosexual arrangement. Siwan custom limits a man to one boy. Fear of the government has made this a secret matter, but before 1909 such arrangements were made openly. Almost all men were reported to have engaged in a homosexual relationship as boys; later, when they were between sixteen and twenty, they married girls.[80] Among the most extremely prohomosexual societies are the Etoro of New Guinea, who prefer homosexuality to heterosexuality. Heterosexuality is prohibited as many as 260 days a year and is forbidden in or near the house and gardens. Male homosexuality, on the other hand, is not prohibited at any time and is believed to make crops flourish and boys become strong.[81]

Reasons for Restrictiveness

Before we deal with the question of why some societies may be more restrictive than others, we must first ask whether all forms of restrictiveness go together. The research to date suggests that societies that are restrictive with regard to one aspect of heterosexual sex tend to be restrictive with regard to other aspects. Thus, societies that frown on sexual expression by young children also punish premarital and extramarital sex.[82] Furthermore, such societies tend to insist on modesty in clothing and are constrained in their talk about sex.[83] But societies that are generally restrictive about heterosexuality are not necessarily restrictive about homosexuality. Societies restrictive about premarital sex are neither more nor less likely to restrict homosexuality. In the case of extramarital sex, the situation is somewhat different. Societies that have a considerable amount of male homosexuality tend to disapprove of males having extramarital heterosexual relationships.[84] If we are going to explain restrictiveness, then, it appears we have to consider heterosexual and homosexual restrictiveness separately.

Let us consider homosexual restrictiveness first. The ethnographic material indicates an extremely broad range of societal reactions to homosexual relationships. Why? Why do homosexual relationships occur more frequently in some societies, and why are some societies intolerant of such relationships? There are many psychological interpretations of why some people become interested in homosexual relationships, and many of these interpretations relate the phenomenon to early parent-child relationships. But so far the research has not yielded any clear-cut predictions, although a number of cross-cultural predictors about male homosexuality are intriguing.

One such finding is that societies forbidding abortion and infanticide for married women (most societies permit these practices for illegitimate births) are likely to be intolerant of male homosexuality. This and other findings are consistent with the point of view that homosexuality may be less tolerated when the society would like to increase its population. Such societies may be intolerant of all kinds of behaviors that minimize population growth. Homosexuality would have this effect, assuming that a higher frequency of homosexual

[79]Ruth M. Underhill, *Social Organization of the Papago Indians* (New York: Columbia University Press, 1938), pp. 117, 186.

[80]Mahmud M. 'Abd Allah, "Siwan Customs," *Harvard African Studies*, 1 (1917): 7, 20.

[81]Raymond C. Kelly, "Witchcraft and Sexual Relations: An Exploration in the Social and Semantic Implications of the Structure of Belief," paper presented at the annual meeting of the American Anthropological Association, Mexico City, 1974.

[82]Data from Robert B. Textor, comp., *A Cross-Cultural Summary* (New Haven: HRAF Press, 1967).

[83]William N. Stephens, "A Cross-Cultural Study of Modesty," *Behavior Science Research*, 7 (1972): 1–28.

[84]Gwen J. Broude, "Cross-Cultural Patterning of Some Sexual Attitudes and Practices," *Behavior Science Research*, 11 (1976): 243.

relations is associated with a lower frequency of heterosexual relations. The less frequently heterosexual relations occur, the lower the number of conceptions there might be. Another indication that intolerance may be related to a desire for population growth is that societies with famines and severe food shortages are more likely to allow homosexuality. Famines and food shortages suggest population pressure on resources; under these conditions homosexuality and other practices that minimize population growth may be tolerated or even encouraged.[85]

The history of the Soviet Union may provide some other relevant evidence. In 1917, in the turmoil of revolution, laws prohibiting abortion and homosexuality were revoked and reproduction was discouraged. But in the period 1934–1936 the policy was reversed. Abortion and homosexuality were again declared illegal, and homosexuals were arrested. At the same time, awards were given to mothers who had more children.[86] Population pressure may also explain why our own society has become somewhat more tolerant of homosexuality recently. Of course, population pressure does not explain why certain individuals become homosexual, or why most individuals in some societies engage in such behavior, but it might explain why

some societies view such behavior more or less permissively.

Turning now to heterosexual behavior, what kinds of societies are more permissive than others? Although we do not as yet understand the reasons, we do know that greater restrictiveness toward premarital sex tends to occur in more complex societies—societies that have hierarchies of political officials, part-time or full-time craft specialists, cities and towns, and class stratification.[87] It may be that as social inequality increases and various groups come to have differential wealth, parents become more concerned with preventing their children from marrying "beneath them." Permissiveness toward premarital sexual relationships might lead a person to become attached to someone who would not be considered a desirable marriage partner. Even worse (from the family's point of view), such "unsuitable" sexual liaisons might result in a pregnancy that could make it impossible for a girl to marry "well." Controlling mating, then, may be a way of trying to control property.

As is apparent from our review in this chapter, the biological fact that humans depend on sexual reproduction does not by itself help us explain why the sexes differ in so many ways across cultures, or why societies vary in the way they handle male and female roles. We are only beginning to investigate these questions. When we eventually understand more about how and why the sexes are different or the same in roles, personality, and sexuality, we may be better able to decide how much we want the biology of sex to shape our lives.

[85]Dennis Werner, "A Cross-Cultural Perspective on Theory and Research on Male Homosexuality," *Journal of Homosexuality*, 4 (1979): 345–62; see also Dennis Werner, "On the Societal Acceptance or Rejection of Male Homosexuality," M.A. thesis, Hunter College of the City University of New York, 1975, p. 36.
[86]Werner, "A Cross-Cultural Perspective on Theory and Research on Male Homosexuality," p. 358.

[87]Data from Textor, comp., *A Cross-Cultural Summary*.

SUMMARY

1. That humans reproduce sexually does not explain why males and females tend to differ in appearance and behavior, and to be treated differently, in all societies.

2. All or nearly all societies assign certain activities to males and other activities to females. These worldwide gender division-of-labor patterns may be explained mostly by sex differences in strength and/or by differences in compatibility of tasks with child care.

3. Perhaps because women almost always have child-care responsibilities, men in most societies do most of the primary subsistence work. But women contribute substantially to primary subsistence activities in societies that depend heavily on gathering and horticulture and where warfare occurs while subsistence work has to be done. When primary *and* secondary subsistence work is counted, women typically work more than men. In almost all societies men are the leaders in the political arena, and warfare is almost exclusively a male activity.

4. The relative status of women (compared to men) seems to vary from one area of life to another: whether women have relatively high status in one area does not necessarily indicate that they will have high status in another. However, less complex societies seem to approach more equal status for males and females in a variety of areas of life.

5. Recent field studies have suggested some consistent sex differences in personality: boys tend to be more aggressive than girls, and girls seem generally to be more responsible and helpful than boys.

6. Although all societies regulate sexual activity to some extent, societies vary considerably in the degree to which various kinds of sexuality are permitted. Some societies allow both masturbation and sex play among children, whereas others forbid these acts. Some societies allow premarital sex; others do not. Some allow extramarital sex in certain situations; others forbid it generally.

7. Societies that are restrictive toward one aspect of heterosexual sex tend to be restrictive with regard to other aspects. And more complex societies tend to be more restrictive toward premarital heterosexual sex than less complex societies.

8. Societal attitudes toward homosexuality are not completely consistent with attitudes toward sexual relationships between the sexes. Societal tolerance of homosexuality is associated with tolerance of abortion and infanticide, and also with famines and food shortages.

SUGGESTED READING

BLUMBERG, R. L. *Stratification: Socioeconomic and Sexual Inequality*. Dubuque, IA: Wm. C. Brown, 1978. A brief introduction to systematic cross-cultural and sociological research (up to the mid 1970s) on why sexual and economic inequality may have developed. Chapter 3 is particularly relevant to this chapter.

EMBER, C. R. "A Cross-Cultural Perspective on Sex Differences." In R. H. MUNROE, R. L. MUNROE, AND B. B. WHITING, eds., *Handbook of Cross-Cultural Human Development*. New York: Garland Press, 1981, pp. 531–80. A critical review of which sex differences are found cross-culturally and the theories that might explain them. A lot of the discussion is devoted to what we do not know or can only speculate about.

MUKHOPADHYAY, C. C., AND HIGGINS, P. J. "Anthropological Studies of Women's Status Revisited: 1977–1987." *Annual Review of Anthropology*, 17 (1988): 461–95. A review of recent anthropological research on women's status.

SCHLEGEL, A., ed. *Sexual Stratification: A Cross-Cultural View*. New York: Columbia University Press, 1977. This collection of papers on the status of women in different societies illustrates the range of variation from subordination of females to sexual equality.

SANDAY, P. R., AND GOODENOUGH, R. G., eds. *Beyond the Second Sex: New Directions in the Anthropology of Gender*. Philadelphia: University of Pennsylvania Press, 1990. The authors of the chapters in this volume reexamine theoretical notions about gender symbolism, gender roles, and male/female relationships in particular reference to the societies they have studied.

WHYTE, M. K. *The Status of Women in Preindustrial Societies*. Princeton, NJ: Princeton University Press, 1978. A systematic study measuring how the relative status of women varies in ninety-three preindustrial societies and investigating why women do better in some societies than in others.

18
Marriage and the Family

Whatever a society's attitudes toward male-female relationships, one such relationship is found in all societies—marriage. Why marriage is customary in every society we know of is a classic and perplexing question—and one we attempt to deal with in this chapter.

The universality of marriage does not mean that everyone in every society gets married. It means only that most (usually nearly all) people in every society get married at least once in their lifetime. In addition, when we say that marriage is universal, we do not mean that marriage and family customs are the same in all societies. On the contrary, there is much variation from society to society in how one marries, whom one marries, and how many persons one marries. The only cultural universal about marriage is that no society permits people to marry parents, brothers, or sisters. Who belongs to the family also varies. The family often includes more individuals than parents and their immature offspring; it may include two or more related married couples and their children.

Marriage

When anthropologists speak of marriage, they do not mean to imply that couples everywhere must get marriage certificates or have wedding ceremonies, as in our own society. **Marriage** merely means a socially approved sexual and economic union between a woman and a man. It is presumed, both by the couple and by others, to be more or less permanent, and it subsumes reciprocal rights and obligations between the two spouses and between spouses and their future children.[1]

It is a socially approved sexual union in that a married couple does not have to hide the sexual nature of their relationship. A woman might say "I want you to meet my husband," but she could not say "I want you to meet my lover" without causing some embarrassment in most societies. Although the union may ultimately be dissolved by divorce, couples in all societies begin marriage with some idea of permanence in mind. Implicit too in marriage are reciprocal rights and obligations. These

may be more or less specific and formalized regarding matters of property, finances, and child rearing.

Marriage entails both a sexual and an economic relationship:

Sexual unions without economic co-operation are common, and there are relationships between men and women involving a division of labor without sexual gratification, e.g., between brother and sister, master and maidservant, or employer and secretary, but marriage exists only when the economic and the sexual are united in one relationship, and this combination occurs only in marriage.[2]

As we will see, the event that marks the commencement of marriage varies in different societies. A Winnebago bride, for example, knows no formal ritual such as a wedding ceremony. She goes with her groom to his parents' house, takes off her "wedding" clothes and finery, gives them to her mother-in-law, receives plain clothes in exchange, and that is that.[3]

The Nayar "Exception"

There is one group of people in the ethnographic literature that did not have marriage, as we have defined it. In the nineteenth century, a caste group in southern India called the Nayar seem to have treated sex and economic relations between men and women as things separate from marriage. About the time of puberty, Nayar girls took ritual husbands. The union was publicly established in a ceremony during which the husband tied a gold ornament around the neck of his bride. But from that time on, he had no more responsibility for her. Usually, he never saw her again. (Nayar men customarily worked for various periods as hired soldiers in other parts of India.)

The bride lived in a large household with her family, where she was visited over the subsequent years by a number of other "husbands." One might be a passing guest, another a more regular visitor; it did not matter, providing the "husband" met the caste restrictions. He came at night and left the following day. If a regular visitor, he was expected

---

[1]William N. Stephens, *The Family in Cross-Cultural Perspective* (New York: Holt, Rinehart & Winston, 1963), p. 5.

[2]George P. Murdock, *Social Structure* (New York: Macmillan, 1949), p. 8.

[3]Stephens, *The Family in Cross-Cultural Perspective*, pp. 170–71.

to make small gifts of cloth, betel nuts, and hair and bath oil. If the father of her child, or one of a group who might be, he was expected to pay the cost of the midwife. But at no time was he responsible for the support of the woman or her child. Rather, her blood relatives retained such responsibilities.[4]

Whether or not the Nayar had marriage depends, of course, on how we choose to define marriage. Certainly, Nayar marital unions involved no regular sexual component or economic cooperation, nor did they involve important reciprocal rights and obligations. According to our definition, then, the Nayar did not have marriage. But the Nayar were not a separate society—only a caste group whose men specialized in soldiering. Therefore, the Nayar are not really an exception to our statement that marriage, as we have defined it, has been customary in all societies known to anthropology.

Rare Types of Marriage

In addition to the usual male-female marriages, some societies recognize marriages between persons of the same sex. But such marriages are not typical in any known society and do not completely fit our definition of marriage. First, the unions are not between men and women. Second, they are not necessarily sexual unions, as we will see. But these "marriages" are socially approved unions, usually modeled after regular marriages, and they often entail a considerable number of reciprocal rights and obligations. The Cheyenne Indians allowed married men to take on **berdaches,** or male transvestites, as second wives.[5]

Although it is not clear that the Cheyenne male-male marriages involved homosexual relationships, it is clear that temporary homosexual marriages did occur among the Azande of Africa. Before the British took control over what is known as the Sudan, Azande warriors who could not afford wives often married "boy-wives" to satisfy their sexual needs. As in normal marriages, gifts (although not as substantial) were given by the

"husband" to the parents of his ... band performed services for ... could sue any other lover ... The boy-wives not only h... their husbands but also ... chores female wives tra... their husbands.[6]

Female-female marriages are repor... occurred in many African societies, but there ... evidence of any sexual relationship between the partners. It seems rather that female-female marriages were a socially approved way for a woman to take on the legal and social roles of a father and husband.[7] In one type of female-female marriage, the woman acted as a substitute for a kinsman who did not leave any heirs for his kin group. The female "husband" would provide children for the kin group by assigning male sexual partners to her "wife." In another kind of female-female marriage, the female husband does not substitute for a kinsman but takes on the role of husband in her own right. Often such women are traders, political leaders, or religious leaders who seek the social recognition only husbands get.

Why Is Marriage Universal?

Since all societies practice male-female marriage as we have defined it, we can assume the custom is generally adaptive. But saying that does not specify exactly how it may be adaptive. Several interpretations have traditionally been offered to explain why all human societies have the custom of marriage. Each suggests that marriage solves a problem found in all societies—how to share the products of a gender division of labor; how to care for infants, who are dependent for a long time; and how to minimize sexual competition. To evaluate the plausibility of these interpretations, we must ask whether marriage provides the best or the only reasonable solution to each problem. After all, we are trying to explain a custom that is presumably a universal solution. The comparative study of other

[6]E. E. Evans-Pritchard, "Sexual Inversion among the Azande," *American Anthropologist,* 72 (1970): 1428–34.

[7]Denise O'Brien, "Female Husbands in Southern Bantu Societies," in Alice Schlegel, ed., *Sexual Stratification: A Cross-Cultural View* (New York: Columbia University Press, 1977), pp. 109–26; see also Regina Smith Oboler, "Is the Female Husband a Man? Woman/Woman Marriage among the Nandi of Kenya," *Ethnology,* 19 (1980): 69–88.

[4]E. Kathleen Gough, "The Nayars and the Definition of Marriage," *Journal of the Royal Anthropological Institute,* 89 (1959): 23–34.

[5]E. Adamson Hoebel, *The Cheyennes: Indians of the Great Plains* (New York: Holt, Rinehart & Winston, 1960), p. 77.

...als, some of which have something like marriage, may help us to evaluate these explanations, as we will see.

Gender Division of Labor. We noted in the last chapter that every society known to anthropology has had a gender division of labor. Males and females in every society perform different economic activities. This gender division of labor has often been cited as a reason for marriage.[8] As long as there is a division of labor by gender, society has to have some mechanism by which men and women share the products of their labor. Marriage would be one way to solve this problem. But is marriage the only possible solution? This seems unlikely, since the hunter-gatherer rule of sharing could be extended to include all the products brought in by both men and women. Or a small group of men and women (such as brothers and sisters) might be pledged to cooperate economically. Thus, although marriage may solve the problem of sharing the fruits of division of labor, it is clearly not the only possible solution.

Prolonged Infant Dependency. Humans exhibit the longest period of infant dependency of any primate. The child's prolonged dependence generally places the greatest burden on the mother, who is the main child tender in most societies. As we saw in the previous chapter, the burden of prolonged child care by human females may limit the kinds of work they can do. They may need the help of a man to do certain types of work, such as hunting, that are incompatible with child care. Because of this prolonged dependency, it has been suggested, marriage is necessary.[9] But here the argument becomes essentially the same as the division-of-labor argument, and it has the same logical weakness. It is not clear why a group of men and women, like a hunter-gatherer band, could not cooperate in providing for dependent children without marriage.

Sexual Competition. Unlike most other female primates, the human female may engage in intercourse at any time throughout the year. Some scholars have suggested that more or less continuous female sexuality may have created a serious problem—considerable sexual competition between males for females. It is argued that society had to prevent such competition in order to survive—that it had to develop some way of minimizing the rivalry between males for females in order to reduce the chance of lethal and destructive conflict.[10]

There are several problems with this argument. First, why should more or less continuous female sexuality make for more sexual competition in the first place? One might argue the other way around: there might be more competition over the scarcer resources that would be available if females were less frequently interested in sex. Second, in many animal species, even some that have relatively frequent female sexuality (like many of our close primate relatives), males do not show much aggression over females. Third, why couldn't sexual competition, even if it existed, be regulated by cultural rules other than marriage? For instance, society might have adopted a rule whereby men and women circulated among all the opposite-sex members of the group, each person staying a specified length of time with each partner. Such a system presumably would solve the problem of sexual competition. On the other hand, such a system might not work particularly well if individuals came to prefer certain other individuals. Jealousies attending these attachments might give rise to even more competition.

Other Mammals and Birds: Postpartum Requirements. None of the theories we have discussed explains convincingly why marriage is the only or the best solution to a particular problem. Also, we now have some comparative evidence on mammals and birds that casts doubt on these interpretations.[11] How can evidence from other animals help us evaluate theories about human marriage? If we look at those animals that (like humans) have some sort of stable male-female mating, as compared with those that are completely promiscuous, we can perhaps see what sorts of factors may predict male-female bonding in the warm-blooded animal species. (Most birds, wolves, and beavers are among the other species that have "marriage.")

---

[8]Murdock, *Social Structure*, pp. 7–8.
[9]Ibid., pp. 9–10.

[10]See, for example, Ralph Linton, *The Study of Man* (New York: Appleton-Century-Crofts, 1936), pp. 135–36.
[11]Melvin Ember and Carol R. Ember, "Male-Female Bonding: A Cross-Species Study of Mammals and Birds," *Behavior Science Research*, 14 (1979): 37–56.

"I do love you. But, to be perfectly honest, I would have loved any other lovebird who happened to turn up." *(© 1978 Punch/Rothco)*

Among forty mammal and bird species, none of the three factors discussed above—division of labor, prolonged infant dependency, or greater female sexuality—predicts or correlates strongly with male-female bonding. With respect to division of labor by sex, most other animals have nothing comparable to a humanlike division of labor, but many have stable male-female matings anyway. The two other supposed factors—prolonged infant dependency and female sexuality—predict just the opposite of what we might expect from these theories. Mammals and birds that have longer dependency periods or greater female sexuality are *less* likely to have stable matings.

Does anything predict male-female bonding? One factor does among mammals and birds, and it may also help explain human marriage. Animal species in which females can simultaneously feed themselves and their babies after birth *(postpartum)* tend not to have stable matings; those species where postpartum mothers cannot feed themselves and their babies at the same time tend to have more stable matings. Among the typical bird species, a mother would have difficulty feeding herself and her babies simultaneously. Since the young cannot fly for a while and must be protected in a nest, the mother risks losing them to other animals if she goes off to obtain food. But if she has a male bonded to her (as the vast majority of bird species do), he can bring back food or take a turn watching the nest. Among animal species that have no

postpartum feeding problem, babies almost immediately after birth are able to travel with the mother as she moves about to eat (as do grazers such as horses), or the mother can transport the babies as she moves about to eat (as do baboons and kangaroos). We think the human female has a postpartum feeding problem. When humans lost most of their body hair, babies could not readily travel with the mother by clinging to her fur. And when humans began to depend on certain kinds of food-getting that could be dangerous (such as hunting), mothers could not engage in such work with their infants along.

Even if we assume that human mothers have a postpartum feeding problem, we still have to ask if marriage is the most likely solution to the problem. We think so, because other conceivable solutions probably would not work as well. For example, if a mother took turns babysitting with another mother, neither might be able to collect enough food for both mothers and the two sets of children dependent on them. But a mother and father share the *same* set of children, and therefore it would be easier for them to feed themselves and their children adequately. Another possible solution is no pair bonding at all, just a promiscuous group of males and females. But in that kind of arrangement, we think, a particular mother probably would not always be able to count on some male to watch her baby when she had to go out for food, or to bring her food when she had to watch her baby. Thus, it seems to us that the problem of postpartum feeding may by itself help explain why some animals (including humans) have more or less stable male-female bonds. Of course, there is still the question of whether the results of research on other animals can be applied to human beings. We think so, but not everybody will agree.

How Does One Marry?

All societies have social ways of marking the onset of marriage, but these vary considerably. Some cultures mark marriages by elaborate ceremonies; others have no ceremonies at all. In addition, many societies have various economic transactions.

Marking the Onset of Marriage. Many societies have ceremonies marking the beginning of mar-

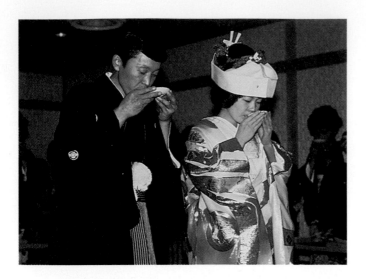

Some societies have ceremonies marking the onset of marriage, and some do not. Here we see the bride and groom at a Shinto wedding in Japan.

riage. But others, such as the Taramiut Inuit, the Trobriand Islanders of the South Pacific, and the Kwoma of New Guinea, use different social signals to indicate that a marriage has taken place.

Among the Taramiut Inuit, the betrothal is considered extremely important and is arranged between the parents at or before the time their children reach puberty. Later, when the youth is ready, he moves in with his betrothed's family for a trial period. If all goes well—that is, if the girl gives birth to a baby within a year or so—the couple are considered married. At this time, the wife goes with her husband to his camp.[12]

In keeping with the general openness of their society's attitudes toward sexual matters, a Trobriand couple advertise their desire to marry "by sleeping together regularly, by showing themselves together in public, and by remaining with each other for long periods at a time."[13] When a girl accepts a small gift from a boy, she demonstrates that her parents favor the match. Before long, she moves to the boy's house, takes her meals there, and accompanies her husband all day. Then the word goes around that the couple are married.[14]

The Kwoma of New Guinea practice a trial marriage followed by a ceremony that makes the couple husband and wife. The girl lives for a while in the boy's home. When the boy's mother is satisfied with the match and knows that her son is too, she waits for a day when he is away from the house. Until this time, the girl has been cooking only for herself, while the boy's food has been prepared by his womenfolk. Now the mother has the girl prepare his meal. The young man returns and begins to eat his soup. When the first bowl is nearly finished, his mother tells him that his betrothed cooked the meal, and his eating it means that he is now married. At this news, the boy customarily rushes out of the house, spits out the soup, and shouts, "Faugh! It tastes bad! It is cooked terribly!" A ceremony then makes the marriage official.[15]

Among those societies that have ceremonies marking the onset of marriage, feasting is a common element. It expresses publicly the importance of two families being united by marriage. The Reindeer Tungus of Siberia set a wedding date after protracted negotiations between the two families and their larger kin groups. Go-betweens assume most of the responsibility for the negotiating. The wedding day opens with the two kin groups, probably numbering as many as 150 people, pitching their lodges in separate areas and offering a great feast. After the groom's gifts have been presented, the bride's dowry is loaded onto reindeer and carried to the groom's lodge. There the climax of the ceremony takes place. The bride takes the wife's place—that is, at the right side of the entrance of the lodge—and members of both families sit in a circle. The groom enters and follows the bride around the circle, greeting each guest, while the guests, in their turn, kiss the bride on the mouth and hands. Finally, the go-betweens spit three times on the bride's hands, and the couple are formally husband and wife. More feasting and revelry bring the day to a close.[16]

[12]Nelson H. Graburn, *Eskimos without Igloos* (Boston: Little, Brown, 1969), pp. 188–200.
[13]Bronislaw Malinowski, *The Sexual Life of Savages in Northwestern Melanesia* (New York: Halcyon House, 1932), p. 77.

[14]Ibid., p. 88.
[15]John W. M. Whiting, *Becoming a Kwoma* (New Haven: Yale University Press, 1941), p. 125.
[16]Elman R. Service, *Profiles in Ethnology*, 3rd ed. (New York: Harper & Row, Publishers, 1978).

In many cultures, marriage includes ceremonial expressions of hostility. One form of this is the trading of insults between kin groups, such as occurs on the Polynesian atoll of Pukapuka. Mock fights are staged in many societies. On occasion, hostility can have genuinely aggressive overtones, as among the Gusii of Kenya:

Five young clansmen of the groom come to take the bride and two immediately find the girl and post themselves at her side to prevent her escape, while the others receive the final permission of her parents. When it has been granted the bride holds onto the house posts and must be dragged outside by the young men. Finally she goes along with them, crying and with her hands on her head.[17]

But the battle is not yet over. Mutual antagonism continues right onto the marriage bed, even up to and beyond coitus. The groom is determined to display his virility, the bride equally determined to test it. "Brides," Robert and Barbara LeVine remark, "are said to take pride in the length of time they can hold off their mates." Men can also win acclaim. If the bride is unable to walk the following day, the groom is considered a "real man."[18]

Such expressions of hostility usually occur in societies where the two sets of kin are actual or potential rivals or enemies. In many societies, it is common to marry women from "enemy" villages.

Economic Aspects of Marriage. "It's not man that marries maid, but field marries field, vineyard marries vineyard, cattle marry cattle." In its down-to-earth way, this German peasant saying indicates that in many societies marriage involves economic considerations. In our culture, economic considerations may or may not be explicit. However, in about 75 percent of the societies known to anthropology,[19] one or more explicit economic transactions take place before or after the marriage. The economic transaction may take several forms.

BRIDE PRICE **Bride price** (or **bride wealth**) is a gift of money or goods from the groom or his kin to the bride's kin. The gift usually grants the groom

"I'm as much against the outmoded convention of marriage as you are—but we could do with the wedding presents." *(© 1975 Punch/Rothco)*

the right to marry the bride and the right to her children. Of all the forms of economic transaction involved in marriage, bride price is the most common. In one cross-cultural sample, 44 percent of the societies with economic transactions at marriage practice bride price; in almost all of these societies the bride price is substantial.[20] Bride price occurs all over the world but is especially common in Africa and Oceania. Payment can be made in a number of different currencies; livestock and food are two of the more common. Among the Swazi of southern Africa

the number of cattle varies with the girl's rank; twelve head is the current rate for commoners, princesses command fifteen or more. A boy's father should provide the animals for his son's first wife, and subjects contribute for their chief's main wife.[21]

The Gusii of Kenya, the Nyakyusa of Tanzania, and the Ibo of West Africa also pay in cattle. The Siane of New Guinea and the Ifugao of the Philip-

[17]Robert A. LeVine and Barbara B. LeVine, "Nyansongo: A Gusii Community in Kenya," in Beatrice B. Whiting, ed., *Six Cultures* (New York: John Wiley, 1963), p. 65.

[18]Ibid.

[19]Alice Schlegel and Rohn Eloul, "A New Coding of Marriage Transactions, *Behavior Science Research*, 21 (1987): 119.

[20]Alice Schlegel and Rohn Eloul, "Marriage Transactions: Labor, Property, and Status," *American Anthropologist*, 90 (1988): 295. We use the data from Table 1 of this article to calculate the frequency of various types of economic transaction in a worldwide sample of 186 societies.

[21]Hilda Kuper, "The Swazi of Swaziland," in James L. Gibbs, Jr., ed., *Peoples of Africa* (New York: Holt, Rinehart & Winston, 1965), p. 487.

pines provide pigs; the Navaho and Somali pay in horses; the Kwakiutl pay in blankets.

The Subanun of the Philippines have an expensive bride price—several times the annual income of the groom *plus* three to five years of bride service (described next).[22] Among the Manus of the Admiralty Islands off New Guinea, a groom requires an economic backer—usually an older brother or an uncle—if he is to marry, but it will be years before he can pay off his debts. Depending upon the final bride price, payments may be concluded at the time of the marriage or may continue for years afterwards.[23]

Despite the connotations that bride price may have for us, the practice does not reduce a woman to the position of slave (although it is associated, as we shall see, with relatively low status for women). The bride price may be important to the woman and her family. Indeed, the fee paid can serve as a security. If the marriage fails through no fault of hers and the wife returns to her kin, the bride price might not be returned to the groom. On the other hand, the wife's kin may pressure her to remain with her husband, even though she does not wish to, because they do not want to return the bride price or are unable to do so.

What kinds of societies are likely to have the custom of bride price? Cross-culturally, societies with bride price are likely to practice horticulture and lack social stratification. Bride price is also likely where women contribute a great deal to primary subsistence activities[24] and where they contribute more than men to all kinds of economic activities.[25] While these findings might suggest that women are highly valued in such societies, recall (as we noted in the last chapter) that the status of women relative to men is *not* higher in societies where women contribute a lot to primary subsistence activities. Indeed, bride price is likely to occur where men make most of the decisions in the

The bride at an Islamic wedding in central Turkey wears some of the bride price on her veil.

household,[26] which is one indicator of lower status for women.

BRIDE SERVICE Bride service, which is the next most common type of economic transaction at marriage (occurring in about 19 percent of the societies with economic transactions), requires the groom to work for the bride's family, sometimes before the marriage begins, sometimes after. Bride service varies in duration. In some societies it lasts for only a few months; in others it lasts as long as several years. Among the North Alaskan Eskimo, for example, the boy works for his in-laws after the marriage is arranged. To fulfill his obligation, he may simply catch a seal for them. The marriage may be consummated at any time while he is in

[22]Charles O. Frake, "The Eastern Subanun of Mindanao," in G. P. Murdock, ed., *Social Structure in Southeast Asia*, Viking Fund Publications in Anthropology, no. 29 (Chicago: Quadrangle, 1960), pp. 51–64.

[23]Margaret Mead, *Growing Up in New Guinea* (London: Routledge & Kegan Paul, 1931), pp. 206–8.

[24]Alice Schlegel and Rohn Eloul, "Marriage Transactions," pp. 298–99.

[25]Frederic L. Pryor, *The Origins of the Economy: A Comparative Study of Distribution in Primitive and Peasant Economies* (New York: Academic Press, 1977), pp. 363–64.

[26]Ibid.

service.[27] In some societies, bride service may sometimes substitute for bride price. An individual might give bride service in order to reduce the amount of bride price required. Native American societies (in North and South America) were likely to practice bride service, particularly if they were egalitarian food collectors.[28]

EXCHANGE OF FEMALES   Of the societies that have economic transactions at marriage, 6 percent have the custom whereby a sister or female relative of the groom is exchanged for the bride. Among these societies are the Tiv of West Africa and the Yanomamö of Venezuela-Brazil. These societies tend to be horticultural, egalitarian, and to have a relatively high contribution of women to primary subsistence.[29]

GIFT EXCHANGE   Gift exchange, which involves the exchange of gifts of about equal value by the two kin groups about to be linked by marriage, occurs somewhat more often than the exchange of females (about 11 percent of those with economic transactions).[30] For example, among the Andaman Islanders, as soon as a boy and girl indicate their intention to marry, their respective sets of parents cease all communication and begin sending gifts of food and other objects to each other through a third party. This arrangement continues until the marriage is completed and the two kin groups are united.[31]

DOWRY   A dowry is usually a substantial transfer of goods or money from the bride's family to the bride.[32] Unlike the types of transactions we have discussed previously, the dowry (which occurs in about 8 percent of the societies with economic transactions) is not an exchange of goods between the kin of the bride and the kin of the groom. A family has to have wealth to give a dowry, but since the goods go to the bride, no wealth comes back to the family that gave the dowry. Payment of dowries was common in medieval and Renaissance Europe, where the size of the dowry often determined the desirability of the daughter. The custom is still practiced in parts of eastern Europe and in sections of southern Italy and France, where land is often the major item provided by the bride's family. Parts of India also practice the dowry.

In contrast to societies with bride price, societies with dowry tend to be those where women contribute relatively little to primary subsistence activities, where there is a high degree of social stratification, and where a man is not allowed to be married to more than one woman simultaneously.[33] Why does dowry tend to occur in these types of societies? One theory suggests that the dowry is intended to guarantee future support for a woman (and her children), even though she will not do much primary subsistence work. Another theory is that the dowry is intended to attract the best bridegroom for a daughter in monogamous societies with a high degree of social inequality. (The dowry strategy is presumed to increase the likelihood that the daughter and her children will do well reproductively.) Both theories are supported by recent cross-cultural research, with the second predicting dowry better.[34]

However, many stratified societies (including our own), where women and men have only one spouse (at a time), do not practice dowry. Why this is so still needs to be explained.

INDIRECT DOWRY   The dowry is provided by the bride's family. The **indirect dowry** is provided by the groom's family. However, as in dowry, the recipient is usually the bride (or the goods are given first to her father who passes most if not all of them to her). In a sense, then, indirect dowry is a combination of bride price and dowry.[35] Indirect

[27]Robert F. Spencer, "Spouse-Exchange among the North Alaskan Eskimo," in P. Bohannan and J. Middleton, eds., *Marriage, Family and Residence* (Garden City, NY: Natural History Press, 1968), p. 136.
[28]Schlegel and Eloul, "Marriage Transactions," pp. 296–97.
[29]Ibid.
[30]Ibid.
[31]A. R. Radcliffe-Brown, *The Andaman Islanders: A Study in Social Anthropology* (London: Cambridge University Press, 1922), p. 73.
[32]Jack Goody, "Bridewealth and Dowry in Africa and Eurasia," in Jack Goody and S. H. Tambiah, eds., *Bridewealth and Dowry* (Cambridge: Cambridge University Press, 1973), pp. 17–21.

[33]Pryor, *The Origins of the Economy*, pp. 363–65; Schlegel and Eloul, "Marriage Transactions," pp. 296–99.
[34]Research is reported in Steven J. C. Gaulin and James S. Boster, "Dowry as Female Competition," *American Anthropologist*, 92 (1990): 994–1005. The first theory discussed herein is associated with Ester Boserup, *Woman's Role in Economic Development* (New York: St. Martin's Press, 1970). The second is put forward by Gaulin and Boster.
[35]Schlegel and Eloul, "Marriage Transactions," have followed Jack Goody, "Bridewealth and Dowry in Africa and Eurasia," p. 20.

dowry occurs in about 12 percent of the societies in which marriage involves an economic transaction. For example, among the Basseri of southern Iran, the groom's father assumes the expense of setting up the couple's new household. He gives cash to the bride's father who uses at least some of the money to buy his daughter household utensils, blankets, and rugs.[36]

Restrictions on Marriage: The Universal Incest Taboo

Hollywood and its press agents notwithstanding, marriage is not always based solely on mutual love, independently discovered and expressed by the two life partners-to-be. Nor is it based on sex alone. But even where love and sex are contributing factors, regulations specify whom one may or may not marry. Perhaps the most rigid regulation, found in *all* cultures, is the incest taboo.

The **incest taboo** is the prohibition of sexual intercourse or marriage between mother and son, father and daughter, and brother and sister. No society we know of has generally permitted either sexual intercourse or marriage between those pairs. However, there have been a few societies in which incest was permitted within the royal family (though generally forbidden to the rest of the population). The Incan and Hawaiian royal families were two such exceptions, but probably the most famous example was provided by Cleopatra of Egypt.

It seems clear that the Egyptian aristocracy and royalty indulged in father-daughter and brother-sister marriages. (Cleopatra was married to two of her younger brothers at different times.)[37] The reasons seem to have been partly religious—a member of the family of Pharaoh, who was a god, could not marry any "ordinary" human—and partly economic, for marriage within the family kept the royal property undivided.

Why is the incest taboo universal? A number of explanations have been suggested.

Childhood-Familiarity Theory. This explanation, suggested by Edward Westermarck, was given a wide hearing in the early 1920s. Westermarck argued that people who have been closely associated with each other since earliest childhood, such as siblings, are not sexually attracted to each other and therefore would avoid marriage with each other.[38] This theory was subsequently rejected because of evidence that some children *were* sexually interested in their parents and siblings. However, studies have suggested that there may be something to Westermarck's theory.

Yonina Talmon investigated marriage patterns among the second generation of three well-established collective communities (*kibbutzim*) in Israel. In these collectives, children live with many members of their peer group in quarters separate from their families. They are in constant interaction with their peers, from birth to maturity. The study revealed that among 125 couples, there was "not one instance in which both mates were reared from birth in the same peer group,"[39] despite parental encouragement of marriage within the peer group. Children reared in common not only avoided marriage, they also avoided any sexual relations among themselves.

Talmon tells us that the people reared together firmly believe that overfamiliarity breeds sexual disinterest. As one of them told her, "We are like an open book to each other. We have read the story in the book over and over again and know all about it."[40] Talmon's evidence reveals not only the onset of disinterest and even sexual antipathy among children reared together, but a correspondingly heightened fascination with newcomers or outsiders, particularly for their "mystery."

Arthur Wolf's study of the Chinese in northern Taiwan also supports the idea that something about being reared together produces sexual disinterest. Wolf focused on a community still practicing the Chinese custom of *t'ung-yang-hsi*, or "daughter-in-law raised from childhood."

---

[36]Fredrik Barth, *Nomads of South Persia* (Boston: Little, Brown, 1961), pp. 18–19; as reported in (and coded as indirect dowry by) Schlegel and Eloul, "A New Coding of Marriage Transactions." p. 131.

[37]Russell Middleton, "Brother-Sister and Father-Daughter Marriage in Ancient Egypt," *American Sociological Review*, 27 (1962): 606.

[38]Edward Westermarck, *The History of Human Marriage* (London: Macmillan, 1894).

[39]Yonina Talmon, "Mate Selection in Collective Settlements," *American Sociological Review*, 29 (1964): 492.

[40]Ibid., p. 504.

When a girl is born in a poor family . . . she is often given away or sold when but a few weeks or months old, or one or two years old, to be the future wife of a son in the family of a friend or relative which has a little son not betrothed in marriage. . . . The girl is called a "little bride" and taken home and brought up in the family together with her future husband.[41]

Wolf's evidence indicates that this arrangement is associated with sexual difficulties when the childhood "couple" later marry. Informants implied that familiarity results in disinterest and lack of stimulation. As an indication of their disinterest, these couples produce fewer offspring than spouses not raised together, they are more likely to seek extramarital sexual relationships, and they are more likely to get divorced.[42]

The Talmon and Wolf studies suggest, then, that children raised together are not likely to be sexually interested in each other when they grow up. Such disinterest is consistent with Westermarck's notion that the incest taboo may be more an avoidance of certain matings than a prohibition of them. There is one other piece of evidence consistent with his explanation of the incest taboo. Hilda and Seymour Parker recently compared two samples of fathers: those who had sexually abused their daughters and those who supposedly had not.[43] (To maximize their similarities otherwise, the Parkers selected both samples of fathers from the same prisons and psychiatric facilities.) The Parkers found that the fathers who had committed incest with their daughters were much more likely than the other sample of fathers to have had little to do with bringing up their daughters, because they were not at home or hardly at home during the daughters' first three years of life. In other words, the fathers who avoided incest had been more closely associated with their daughters in childhood, which again is consistent with Westermarck's suggestion that the incest taboo may be a result of familiarity in childhood.

Even if there is something about familiarity in childhood that normally leads to sexual disinterest,[44] we are still left with the question of why societies have to prohibit marriages that would be avoided because of disinterest. That is, if disinterest as a result of childhood familiarity were the only factor involved in the prohibition of incest, why should societies have to prohibit parent-child and brother-sister marriages? Another problem with the childhood familiarity theory is that the results of two separate cross-cultural tests do not support what it implies about first cousin marriage. Childhood-familiarity theory implies that no first cousin marriage is likely to be allowed in those societies where first cousins generally grow up together in the same community. But that is not true. Societies in which all first cousins grow up together do not generally prohibit first cousin marriage.[45]

Freud's Psychoanalytic Theory. Sigmund Freud proposed that the incest taboo is a reaction against unconscious, unacceptable desires.[46] He suggested that the son is attracted to his mother (as the daughter is to her father), and as a result feels jealousy and hostility toward his father. But the son knows these feelings cannot continue, for they might lead the father to retaliate against him; therefore, they must be renounced or repressed. Usually the feelings are repressed and retreat into the unconscious. But the desire to possess the mother continues to exist in the unconscious, and according to Freud, the horror of incest is a reaction to, or a defense against, the forbidden unconscious impulse. Although Freud's theory may account for the aversion felt toward incest, or at least the aversion toward parent-child incest, it does not explain why society needs an explicit taboo. Nor

[41]Arthur Wolf, "Adopt a Daughter-in-Law, Marry a Sister: A Chinese Solution to the Problem of the Incest Taboo," *American Anthropologist,* 70 (1968): 864.

[42]Arthur P. Wolf and Chieh-shan Huang, *Marriage and Adoption in China, 1845–1945* (Stanford, CA: Stanford University Press), 1980, pp. 159, 170, 185.

[43]Hilda Parker and Seymour Parker, "Father-Daughter Sexual Abuse: An Emerging Perspective," *American Journal of Orthopsychiatry,* 56 (1986): 531–49.

[44]For a discussion of mechanisms that might lead to sexual aversion, see Seymour Parker, "The Precultural Basis of the Incest Taboo: Toward a Biosocial Theory," *American Anthropologist,* 78 (1976): 285–305; also see Seymour Parker, "Cultural Rules, Rituals, and Behavior Regulation," *American Anthropologist,* 86 (1984): 584–600.

[45]Melvin Ember, "On the Origin and Extension of the Incest Taboo," *Behavior Science Research,* 10 (1975): 249–81; William H. Durham, *Coevolution: Genes, Culture, and Human Diversity* (Stanford, CA: Stanford University Press, 1991), pp. 341–57.

[46]Sigmund Freud, *A General Introduction to Psychoanalysis* (Garden City, NY: Garden City Publishing Co., 1943 [originally published in German in 1917]).

does it account for why parents should not be interested in committing incest with their children.

Family-Disruption Theory. This theory, often associated with Bronislaw Malinowski,[47] can best be summed up as follows: sexual competition among family members would create so much rivalry and tension that the family could not function as an effective unit. Since the family must function effectively for society to survive, society has to curtail competition within the family. The incest taboo is thus imposed to keep the family intact.

But there are inconsistencies in this approach. Society could have shaped other rules about the sexual access of one member of the family to another that would also eliminate potentially disruptive competition. Also, why would brother-sister incest be so disruptive? As we noted, such marriages did exist in ancient Egypt. Brother-sister incest would not disrupt the authority of the parents if the children were allowed to marry when mature. The family-disruption theory, then, does not seem to explain the origin of the incest taboo.

Cooperation Theory. This theory was proposed by the early anthropologist Edward B. Tylor and was elaborated by Leslie A. White and Claude Lévi-Strauss. It emphasizes the value of the incest taboo in promoting cooperation among family groups and thus helping communities to survive. As Tylor sees it, certain operations necessary for the welfare of the community can be accomplished only by large numbers of people working together. In order to break down suspicion and hostility between family groups and make such cooperation possible, early humans developed the incest taboo to ensure that individuals would marry members of other families. The ties created by intermarriage would serve to hold the community together. Thus, Tylor explains the incest taboo as an answer to the choice "between marrying out and being killed out."[48]

Although there may well be advantages to marriage outside the family, is the incest taboo necessary to promote cooperation with outside groups? For example, couldn't families have required some of their members to marry outside the family if they thought it necessary for survival, but permitted incestuous marriages when such alliances were not needed? Thus, although the incest taboo might enhance cooperation between families, the need for cooperation does not adequately explain the existence of the incest taboo in all societies, since other customs might also promote alliances. Furthermore, the cooperation theory does not explain the sexual aspect of the incest taboo. Societies could conceivably allow incestuous sex and still insist that children marry outside the family.

Inbreeding Theory. One of the oldest explanations for the incest taboo, this theory focuses on the potentially damaging consequences of inbreeding, or marrying within the family. People within the same family are likely to carry the same harmful recessive genes. Inbreeding, then, will tend to produce offspring who are more likely to die early of genetic disorders than the offspring of unrelated spouses. For many years this theory was rejected because it was thought that inbreeding need not be harmful. However, the inbreeding practiced to produce prize-winning dogs is not a good guide to whether or not inbreeding is generally harmful; dog-breeders don't count the "runts" they cull when they try to breed for success in dog shows. We now have a good deal of evidence, from humans as well as animals, that the closer the degree of inbreeding, the more harmful the genetic effects.[49]

Genetic mutations occur frequently. Although many pose no harm to the individuals who carry a single recessive dose of them, double doses of such mutations often are harmful or lethal. Close blood relatives are much more likely than unrelated individuals to carry the same harmful recessive gene. So if close relatives mate, their offspring have a higher probability (than the offspring of nonrelatives) of getting a double dose of the harmful gene.

One study compares children produced by familial incest and children (of the same mothers) produced by nonincestuous unions. About 40 per-

[47]Bronislaw Malinowski, *Sex and Repression in Savage Society* (London: Kegan Paul, Trench, Trubner & Co., 1927).

[48]Quoted in Leslie A. White, *The Science of Culture: A Study of Man and Civilization* (New York: Farrar, Straus, & Cudahy, 1949), p. 313.

[49]Curt Stern, *Principles of Human Genetics*, 3rd ed. (San Francisco: W. H. Freeman & Company Publishers, 1973), pp. 494–95, as cited in Ember, "On the Origin and Extension of the Incest Taboo," p. 256. For a recent review of the theory and evidence, see Durham, *Coevolution*.

cent of the incestuously produced children had serious abnormalities compared with about 5 percent of the other children.[50] Matings between other kinds of relatives, not as closely related, also show harmful (but not as harmful) effects of inbreeding. These results are consistent with inbreeding theory: the chance likelihood of a child getting a double dose of a harmful recessive gene from the same ancestor is lower the more distantly the child's parents are related. Also consistent with inbreeding theory is the fact that rates of abnormality are consistently higher in the offspring of uncle-niece marriages (which are allowed in some societies) than in the offspring of cousin marriages; for the offspring of uncle-niece marriages, the chance likelihood of inheriting a double dose of a harmful recessive is twice that for the offspring of first cousins.[51]

Although most scholars acknowledge the harmful effects of inbreeding, some question whether people in former days would have deliberately invented or borrowed the incest taboo because they knew that inbreeding was biologically harmful. However, William Durham's recent cross-cultural survey suggests otherwise. Ethnographers do not always report the perceived consequences of incest; but in 50 percent of the reports Durham found, biological harm to the offspring is mentioned.[52] For example, Raymond Firth reports on the Tikopia who live on an island in the South Pacific:

The idea is firmly held that unions of close kin bear with them their own doom, their *mara* . . . The idea [*mara*] essentially concerns barrenness . . . The peculiar barrenness of an incestuous union consists not in the absence of children, but in their illness or death, or some other mishap . . . The idea that the offspring of a marriage between near kin are weakly and likely to die young is stoutly held by these natives and examples are adduced to prove it.[53]

So, if the harm of inbreeding was widely recognized, people may have deliberately invented or borrowed the incest taboo.[54] But whether or not people actually recognized the harmfulness of inbreeding, the demographic consequences of the incest taboo would account for its universality, since reproductive and hence competitive advantages probably accrued to groups practicing the taboo. Thus, although cultural solutions other than the incest taboo might provide the desired effects assumed by the family-disruption theory and the cooperation theory, the incest taboo is the only possible solution to the problem of inbreeding.

As we shall see toward the end of the next section, a society may or may not extend the incest taboo to first cousins. That variation is also predictable from inbreeding theory, which provides additional support for the theory that the incest taboo was invented or borrowed to avoid the harmful consequences of inbreeding.

Whom Should One Marry?

Probably every child in our society knows the story of Cinderella—the poor, downtrodden, but lovely girl who accidentally meets, falls in love with, and eventually marries a prince. It is a charming tale, but as a guide to mate choice in our society it is quite misleading. The majority of marriages simply do not occur in so free and coincidental a way in any society. Aside from the incest taboo, societies often have rules restricting marriage with other persons, as well as preferences about which other persons are the most desirable mates.

Even in a modern, urbanized society such as ours, where mate choice is theoretically free, people tend to marry within their own geographical area and class. For example, studies in the United States consistently indicate that a person is likely to marry someone who lives close by.[55] Since neighborhoods are frequently made up of people from similar class backgrounds, it is unlikely that many of these alliances are Cinderella stories.

---

[50]Eva Seemanová, "A Study of Children of Incestuous Matings," *Human Heredity*, 21 (1971): 108–28, as cited in Durham, *Coevolution*, pp. 305–9.

[51]Durham, *Coevolution*, pp. 305–9.

[52]Ibid., pp. 346–52.

[53]Raymond Firth, *We, the Tikopia* (Boston: Beacon Press, 1957), pp. 287–88, cited (somewhat differently) by Durham, *Coevolution*, pp. 349–50.

[54]A mathematical model of early mating systems suggests that people may have noticed the harmful effects of inbreeding, once populations began to expand as a result of agriculture; people may therefore have deliberately adopted the incest taboo to solve the problem of inbreeding. See Ember, "On the Origin and Extension of the Incest Taboo." For a similar suggestion, see Durham, *Coevolution*, pp. 331–39.

[55]William J. Goode, *The Family*, 2nd ed. (Englewood Cliffs, NJ: Prentice Hall, 1982), pp. 61–62.

Arranged Marriages. In an appreciable number of societies, marriages are arranged: negotiations are handled by the immediate families or by go-betweens. Sometimes betrothals are completed while the future partners are still children. This was formerly the custom in much of Hindu India, China, Japan, and eastern and southern Europe. Implicit in the arranged marriage is the conviction that the joining together of two kin groups to form new social and economic ties is too important to be left to free choice and romantic love.

An example of a marriage arranged for reasons of prestige comes from Clellan Ford's study of the Kwakiutl of British Columbia. Ford's informant described his marriage as follows:

When I was old enough to get a wife—I was about 25—my brothers looked for a girl in the same position that I and my brothers had. Without my consent, they picked a wife for me—Lagius' daughter. The one I wanted was prettier than the one they chose for me, but she was in a lower position than me, so they wouldn't let me marry her.[56]

Exogamy and Endogamy. Marriage partners often must be chosen from *outside* one's own kin group or community; this is known as a rule of **exogamy.** Exogamy can take many forms. It may mean marrying outside a particular group of kin or outside a particular village or group of villages. Often, then, spouses come from quite a distance. For example, in Rani Khera, a village in India, 266 married women had come from about 200 different villages averaging between twelve and twenty-four miles away; 220 local women had gone to 200 other villages to marry. As a result of these exogamous marriages, Rani Khera, a village of 150 households, was linked to 400 other nearby villages.[57]

A rule of **endogamy** obliges a person to marry *within* some group. The caste groups of India have traditionally been endogamous. The higher castes believed that marriage with lower castes would "pollute" them, and such unions were forbidden. Caste endogamy is also found in some parts of Africa. In East Africa, a Masai warrior will never stoop to marry the daughter of an ironworker, nor

In many societies, people other than the bride and groom may determine important things about a marriage, as, for example, a "go-between" priest in Japan decides on a lucky day for the marriage.

would a ruling caste Tutsi (from Rwanda in east central Africa) think of joining himself to the family of a hunting-caste Twa.

Cousin Marriages. Kinship terminology for most people in the United States does not differentiate between types of cousins. In other societies such distinctions may be important, particularly with regard to first cousins; the terms for the different kinds of first cousin may indicate which cousins are suitable marriage partners (sometimes even preferred mates) and which are not. So, for example, some societies allow or even prefer marriage with a cross-cousin but prohibit marriage with a parallel cousin. Muslim societies usually prefer marriage with a parallel cousin and allow marriage with a cross-cousin. Most societies, however, prohibit marriage with all types of first cousins.[58]

Cross-cousins are children of siblings of the opposite sex; that is, a person's cross-cousins are father's sisters' children and mother's brothers' children. **Parallel cousins** are children of siblings of the same sex; a person's parallel cousins, then, are father's brothers' children and mother's sisters' children. The Chippewa Indians used to practice cross-cousin marriage, as well as cross-cousin joking. With his female cross-cousins, a Chippewa man was expected to exchange broad, risqué jokes, but he would not do so with his parallel cousins, with whom severe propriety was the rule. Gener-

[56]Clellan S. Ford, *Smoke from Their Fires* (New Haven: Yale University Press, 1941), p. 149.

[57]W. J. Goode, *World Revolution and Family Patterns* (New York: Free Press, 1970), p. 210.

[58]Ember, "On the Origin and Extension of the Incest Taboo," p. 262 (see Table 3).

ally, in any society in which cross-cousin marriage is allowed but parallel-cousin is not, there is a joking relationship between a man and his female cross-cousins. This attitude contrasts with the formal and very respectful relationship the man maintains with female parallel cousins. Apparently, the joking relationship signifies the possibility of marriage, whereas the respectful relationship signifies the extension of the incest taboo to parallel cousins.

What kinds of societies allow or prefer first-cousin marriage? One cross-cultural study has presented evidence that cousin marriages are more apt to be permitted in relatively densely populated societies. Perhaps this is because the chance likelihood of such marriages, and therefore the risks of inbreeding, are minimal in those societies. However, many small, sparsely populated societies permit or even sometimes prefer cousin marriage. How can these cases be explained? They seem to cast doubt on the interpretation that cousin marriage should generally be prohibited in sparsely populated societies, where marriages between close relatives are more likely just by chance and where the risks of inbreeding should be greatest. It turns out that most of the small societies permitting cousin marriage have lost a lot of people to recent epidemics. Many peoples around the world, particularly in the Pacific and in North and South America, suffered severe depopulation in the first generation or two after contact with Europeans, who introduced diseases (such as measles, pneumonia, and smallpox) to which the native populations had little or no genetic resistance. It may be that such societies had to permit cousin marriage in order to provide enough mating possibilities among the reduced population of eligible mates.[59]

Levirate and Sororate. In many societies, cultural rules oblige individuals to marry the spouse of deceased relatives. **Levirate** is a custom whereby a man is obliged to marry his brother's widow. **Sororate** obliges a woman to marry her deceased sister's husband. Both customs are exceedingly common, being the obligatory form of second marriage in a majority of societies.[60]

Among the Chukchee of Siberia, levirate obliges the next oldest brother to become the successor husband. He cares for the widow and children, assumes the sexual privileges of the husband, and unites the deceased's reindeer herd with his own, keeping it in the name of his brother's children. If there are no brothers, the widow is married to a cousin of her first husband. Generally, the Chukchee regard the custom more as a duty than as a right. The nearest relative is obliged to care for a woman left with children and a herd.[61]

Among the Murngin of Australia, the economic burden of a large household can be such that an elder brother might wish to foster a leviratic marriage even before his death:

If *wawa* (Elder Brother) has four or five wives, he may say to a single *yukiyoyo* (Younger Brother), "You see that one, you take her and feed her." *Yukiyoyo* says, if *wawa* is an old man, "No, you are an old man, I'll wait until you die, then I'll have them all." *Wawa* replies, "No, you take her now, *yukiyoyo*. I have many wives and you have none."[62]

How Many Does One Marry?

We are accustomed to thinking of marriage as involving just one man and one woman at a time **(monogamy),** but most societies known to anthropology have allowed a man to be married to more than one woman at the same time **(polygyny).** At any given moment, however, the majority of men in societies permitting polygyny are married monogamously; few or no societies have enough women to permit most men to have at least two wives. Polygyny's mirror image—one woman being married to more than one man at the same time **(polyandry)**—is practiced in very few societies. Polygyny and polyandry are the two types of **polygamy,** or plural marriage. **Group marriage,** in which more than one man is married to more than one woman at the same time, sometimes occurs but is not generally customary in any known society.

Polygyny. The Old Testament has many references to men with more than one wife simulta-

[59]Ibid., pp. 260–69; see also Durham, *Coevolution,* pp. 341–57.
[60]Murdock, *Social Structure,* p. 29.

[61]Waldemar Bogoras, "The Chukchee," pt. 3, *Memoirs of the American Museum of Natural History,* 2 (1909); cited in Stephens, *The Family in Cross-Cultural Perspective,* p. 195.
[62]W. Lloyd Warner, *A Black Civilization: A Social Study of an Australian Tribe* (New York: Harper, 1937), p. 62.

TABLE 18-1 Four Possible Forms of Marriage

FORM OF MARRIAGE		MALES	FEMALES
Monogamy		△	= ○
Polygyny }	Polygamy	△	= ○ + ○ + . . .
Polyandry }		△ + △ = ○ + . . .	
Group marriage		△ + △ = ○ + ○ + . . . + . . .	

△ represents male; ○, female; and =, marriage.

neously: King David and King Solomon are just two examples of men polygynously married. Just as in the society described in the Old Testament, polygyny in many societies is a mark of a man's great wealth or high status. In such societies only the very wealthy can, and are expected to, support a number of wives. Some Muslim societies, especially Arabic-speaking ones, still view polygyny in this light. However, a man does not always have to be wealthy to be polygynous; indeed, in some societies where women are important contributors to the economy, it seems that men try to have more than one wife in order to become wealthier.

Among the Siwai, a society in the South Pacific, status is achieved through feast giving. Since pork is the main dish at these feasts, the Siwai associate pig raising with prestige. This great interest in pigs sparks an interest in wives, since in Siwai society women raise the food needed to raise pigs. Thus, while having many wives does not in itself confer status among the Siwai, the increase in pig herds that may result from polygyny is a source of prestige for the owner.[63]

But while polygynously married Siwai men do seem to have greater prestige, the men complain that a household with multiple wives is difficult. Sinu, a Siwai, describes his plight:

There is never peace for a long time in a polygynous family. If the husband sleeps in the house of one wife, the other one sulks all the next day. If the man is so stupid as to sleep two consecutive nights in the house of one wife, the other one will refuse to cook for him, saying, "So-and-so is your wife; go to her for food. Since I am not good enough for you to sleep with, then my food is not good enough for you to eat." Frequently the co-wives will quarrel and fight. My uncle formerly had five

wives at one time and the youngest one was always raging and fighting the others. Once she knocked an older wife senseless and then ran away and had to be forcibly returned.[64]

Jealousy between co-wives is reported in many polygynous societies, but it seems not to be present in some. For example, Margaret Mead tells us that married life among the Arapesh of New Guinea, even in the polygynous marriages, "is so even and contented that there is nothing to relate of it at all."[65]

Why might there be little or no jealousy between co-wives in a society? One possible reason is that a man is married to two or more sisters (**sororal polygyny**); it seems that sisters, having grown up together, are more likely to get along and cooperate as co-wives than are co-wives who are not also sisters (**nonsororal polygyny**). Other customs may also lessen jealousy between co-wives:

1. Co-wives who are not sisters tend to have separate living quarters; sororal co-wives almost always live together. Among the Plateau Tonga in Africa, who practice nonsororal polygyny, the husband shares his personal goods and his favors among his wives, who live in separate dwellings, according to principles of strict equality. The Crow Indians practiced sororal polygyny, and co-wives usually shared the same tepee.

2. Co-wives have clearly defined equal rights in matters of sex, economics, and personal possessions. For example, the Tanala of Madagascar require the husband to spend a day with each co-wife in succession. Failure to do so constitutes adultery and entitles the slighted wife to sue for divorce and alimony of up to one-third of the husband's property. Furthermore, the land is shared equally among all the women, who expect the husband to help with its cultivation when he visits them.

3. Senior wives often have special prestige. The Tonga of Polynesia, for example, grant to the first wife the status of "chief wife." Her house

---

[63]Douglas Oliver, A *Solomon Island Society* (Cambridge, MA: Harvard University Press, 1955), pp. 352-53.

[64]Ibid., pp. 223-24; quoted in Stephens, *The Family in Cross-Cultural Perspective*, p. 58.

[65]Margaret Mead, *Sex and Temperament in Three Primitive Societies* (New York: New American Library, 1950 [originally published in 1935]), p. 101.

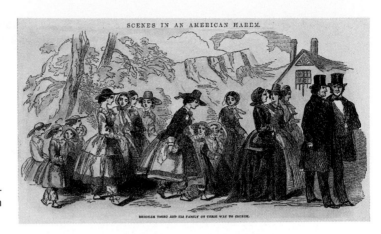

SCENES IN AN AMERICAN HAREM

BRIGHAM YOUNG AND HIS FAMILY ON THEIR WAY TO CHURCH.

The Mormons who settled in Utah practiced polygyny. Here we see two men and their wives walking to church.

is to the right of her husband's and is called "the house of the father." The other wives are called "small wives" and their houses are to the left of the husband's. The chief wife has the right to be consulted first, and her husband is expected to sleep under her roof before and after a journey. Although this rule might seem to enhance the jealousy of the secondary wives, later wives are usually favored somewhat because they tend to be younger and more attractive. By this custom, then, the first wife may be compensated for her loss of physical attractiveness by increased prestige.[66]

How can we account for the fact that polygyny is allowed and often preferred in most of the societies known to anthropology? Linton suggests that polygyny derives from the general primate urge to collect females.[67] But if that were so, then why wouldn't all societies allow polygyny? A number of other explanations of polygyny have been suggested. We restrict our discussion here to those that statistically and strongly predict polygyny in worldwide samples of societies.

One theory is that polygyny will be permitted in societies that have a long **postpartum sex taboo.**[68] In these societies, a couple must abstain from intercourse until their child is at least a year

old. John Whiting suggests that couples may abstain from sexual intercourse for a long time after birth for health reasons. A Hausa woman reported that

a mother should not go to her husband while she has a child she is suckling. If she does, the child gets thin; he dries up, he won't be strong, he won't be healthy. If she goes after two years it is nothing, he is already strong before that, it does not matter if she conceives again after two years.[69]

The baby's illness in the first case seems to be *kwashiorkor.* Common in tropical areas, kwashiorkor is a protein-deficiency disease that seems to occur particularly in children suffering from intestinal parasites or diarrhea. By observing a long postpartum sex taboo, and thereby being sure her children are widely spaced, a woman can nurse each child longer. If a child gets protein from mother's milk during its first few years, the likelihood of contracting kwashiorkor may be greatly reduced. Consistent with Whiting's interpretation is the fact that societies with low-protein staples (those whose principal foods are root and tree crops such as taro, sweet potatoes, bananas, and breadfruit) tend to have a long postpartum sex taboo. Societies with long postpartum sex taboos also tend to be polygynous. Perhaps, then, a man's having more than one wife is a cultural adjustment to the taboo. As a Yoruba woman said,

When we abstain from having sexual intercourse with our husband for the 2 years we nurse our babies, we

[66]The discussion of these customs is based on Stephens, *The Family in Cross-Cultural Perspective,* pp. 63–67.

[67]Linton, *The Study of Man,* p. 183.

[68]John W. M. Whiting, "Effects of Climate on Certain Cultural Practices," in Ward H. Goodenough, ed., *Explorations in Cultural Anthropology* (New York: McGraw-Hill, 1964), pp. 511–44.

[69]Quoted in ibid., p. 518.

know he will seek some other woman. We would rather have her under our control as a co-wife so he is not spending money outside the family.[70]

Although we may agree that men might seek other sexual relationships during the period of a long postpartum sex taboo, it is not clear why polygyny is the only possible solution to the problem. After all, it is conceivable that all a man's wives might be subject to the postpartum sex taboo at the same time. Furthermore, there may be sexual outlets outside marriage.

Another explanation of polygyny is that it may be a response to an excess of women over men. Such an imbalanced sex ratio may occur because of the prevalence of warfare in a society. Since men and not women are generally the warriors, warfare almost always takes a greater toll of men's lives. Given that almost all adults are married in noncommercial societies, polygyny may be a way of providing spouses for surplus women. Indeed, there is some evidence that societies with imbalanced sex ratios in favor of women tend to have both polygyny and high male mortality in warfare. Conversely, societies with balanced sex ratios tend to have both monogamy and low male mortality in warfare.[71]

A third explanation is that a society will allow polygyny when men marry at an older age than women. The argument is similar to the sex ratio interpretation. Delaying the age of marriage for men would produce an artificial, though not an actual, excess of marriageable women. Why marriage for men is delayed is not clear, but the delay does predict polygyny.[72]

Is one of these explanations better than the others, or are all three factors (long postpartum sex taboo, an imbalanced sex ratio in favor of women, and delayed age of marriage for men) important in explaining polygyny? One way of trying to decide among alternative explanations is to do what is called a statistical-control analysis, which allows us to see if a particular factor still predicts when the effects of other possible factors are removed. In this case, when the possible effect of sex ratio is removed, a long postpartum sex taboo no longer predicts polygyny and hence is probably not a cause of polygyny.[73] But both an actual excess of women and a late age of marriage for men seem to be strong predictors of polygyny. Added together, these two factors predict even more strongly.[74]

Polyandry. Murdock's *World Ethnographic Sample* includes only four societies (less than 1 percent of the total) where polyandry, or the marriage of several men to one woman, is practiced. Polyandry can be **fraternal** (when the husbands are brothers) or **nonfraternal.**

Some Tibetans, the Toda of India, and the Sinhalese of Sri Lanka have practiced fraternal polyandry. Among the Tibetans who practice fraternal polyandry, biological paternity seems to be of no particular concern; there is no attempt to link children biologically to a particular brother and all children are treated the same.[75]

One possible explanation for some of the societies with polyandry is a shortage of women. The Toda practiced female infanticide;[76] the Sinhalese had a shortage of women but denied the practice of female infanticide.[77] If a shortage of women is generally associated with polyandry, that would account for why polyandry is so rare in the ethnographic record, since an excess of men is exceedingly rare cross-culturally.

Another possible explanation is that polyandry may be an adaptive response to severely limited resources. Melvyn Goldstein has studied Tibetans who live in the northwest corner of Nepal, above 12,000 feet in elevation. Cultivable land is extremely scarce there; most families have less than one acre. The people say they practice fraternal

[70]Quoted in ibid., pp. 516–17.

[71]Melvin Ember, "Warfare, Sex Ratio, and Polygyny," *Ethnology,* 13 (1974): 197–206.

[72]Melvin Ember, "Alternative Predictors of Polygyny," *Behavior Science Research,* 19 (1984–1985): 1–23. The statistical relationship between late age of marriage for men and polygyny was first reported by Stanley R. Witkowski, "Polygyny, Age of Marriage, and Female Status," paper presented at the annual meeting of the American Anthropological Association, San Francisco, 1975.

[73]Ember, "Warfare, Sex Ratio, and Polygyny," pp. 202–5.

[74]Ember, "Alternative Predictors of Polygyny." For other predictors of polygyny, see Douglas R. White and Michael L. Burton, "Causes of Polygyny: Ecology, Economy, Kinship, and Warfare," *American Anthropologist,* 90 (1988): 871–87; and Bobbi S. Low, "Marriage Systems and Pathogen Stress in Human Societies," *American Zoologist,* 30: 325–39.

[75]Melvyn C. Goldstein, "When Brothers Share a Wife," *Natural History,* March 1987, p. 39.

[76]Stephens, *The Family in Cross-Cultural Perspective,* p. 45.

[77]L. R. Hiatt, "Polyandry in Sri Lanka: A Test Case for Parental Investment Theory," *Man,* 15 (1980): 583–98.

polyandry in order to prevent the division of a family's farm (and animals). Instead of dividing up their land between them and each taking a wife, brothers preserve the family farm by sharing a wife. Although not recognized by the Tibetans, their practice of polyandry minimizes population growth. There are as many women as men of marriageable age. But about 30 percent of the women do not marry; and although these women do have some children, they have far fewer than married women. Thus, the practice of polyandry minimizes the number of mouths to feed and therefore maximizes the standard of living of the polyandrous family. In contrast, if the Tibetans practiced monogamy and almost all women married, the birthrate would be much higher and there would be more mouths to feed from the severely limited resources.[78]

The Family

Although family form varies from one society to another and even within societies, all societies have families. A **family** is a social and economic unit consisting minimally of one or more parents and their children. Members of a family always have certain reciprocal rights and obligations toward each other, particularly economic ones. Family members usually live in one household, but common residence is not a defining feature of families. In our society, children may live away while they go to college. Some members of a family may deliberately set up separate households in order to work in different places.[79] In simpler societies, the family and the household tend to be indistinguishable; it is only in more complex societies, and in societies becoming dependent on commercial ex-

change, that some members of a family may live elsewhere.[80]

The family provides a learning environment for children. Although some animals, such as fish, do take care of themselves after birth or hatching, no mammal is able to care for itself at birth, and a human is exceptional in that he or she is unable to do so for many years afterward. Since, biologically, humans mature late, they have few if any inborn or instinctive responses that will simplify adjustment to their surroundings. Consequently, they have to learn a repertoire of beliefs and habits (which are mostly cultural) in order to become functioning adults in society. A family cares for and protects children while they acquire the cultural behavior, beliefs, and values necessary for their own, and their society's, survival.

Variation in Family Form

There are variations in the form of the family from society to society, and within societies. Most societies have families that are larger than the single-parent family (the parent in such families is usually the mother, in which case the unit is called the **matrifocal family**), the monogamous (single-couple) family (called the **nuclear family**), or the polygamous (usually polygynous) family. The **extended family** is the prevailing form of family in more than half the societies known to anthropology.[81] It may consist of two or more single-parent, monogamous, polygynous, or polyandrous families linked by a blood tie. Most commonly, the extended family consists of a married couple and one or more of the married children, all living in the same house or household. The constituent nuclear families are normally linked through the parent-child tie. However, an extended family is sometimes composed of families linked through a sibling tie. Such a family might consist of two married brothers, their wives, and their children. Extended families may be quite large, containing many relatives and including three or four generations.

Extended-Family Households. In a society composed of extended-family households, marriage

[78]Goldstein, "When Brothers Share a Wife," pp. 39–48. Formerly, in feudal Tibet, a class of serfs who owned small parcels of land also practiced polyandry. Goldstein has suggested that a shortage of land may explain their polyandry too. See Melvyn C. Goldstein, "Stratification, Polyandry, and Family Structure in Central Tibet," *Southwestern Journal of Anthropology,* 27 (1971): 65–74.

[79]For example, see Myron Cohen, "Variations in Complexity among Chinese Family Groups: The Impact of Modernization," *Transactions of the New York Academy of Sciences,* 29 (1967): 638–44; and Myron Cohen, "Developmental Process in the Chinese Domestic Group," in Maurice Freedman, ed., *Family and Kinship in Chinese Society* (Stanford, CA: Stanford University Press, 1970).

[80]Burton Pasternak, *Introduction to Kinship and Social Organization* (Englewood Cliffs, NJ: Prentice Hall, 1976), p. 96.

[81]Allan D. Coult and Robert W. Habenstein, *Cross Tabulations of Murdock's World Ethnographic Sample* (Columbia: University of Missouri Press, 1965).

A Slovakian extended family.

does not bring as pronounced a change in life-style as it does in our culture, where the couple typically move to a new residence and form a new, and basically independent, family unit. In extended families, the newlyweds are assimilated into an existing family unit. Margaret Mead describes such a situation in Samoa:

In most marriages there is no sense of setting up a new and separate establishment. The change is felt in the change of residence for either husband or wife and in the reciprocal relations which spring up between the two families. But the young couple live in the main household, simply receiving a bamboo pillow, a mosquito net and a pile of mats for their bed. . . . The wife works with all the women of the household and waits on all the men. The husband shares the enterprises of the other men and boys. Neither in personal service given or received are the two marked off as a unit.[82]

The young couple in Samoa, as in other societies with extended families, generally have little decision-making power over the governing of the household. Often the responsibility of running the household rests with the senior male. Nor can the new family usually accumulate its own property and become independent; it is a part of the larger corporate structure:

So the young people bide their time. Eventually, when the old man dies or retires, *they* will own the homestead, they will run things. When their son grows up and marries, he will create a new subsidiary family, to live with them, work for the greater glory of *their* extended family homestead, and wait for them to die.[83]

The extended family is thus more likely than the independent nuclear family to perpetuate itself as a social unit. In contrast with the independent nuclear family, which by definition disintegrates with the death of the senior members (the parents), the extended family is always adding junior families (monogamous and/or polygamous), whose members eventually become the senior members when their elders die.

Possible Reasons for Extended-Family Households. Why do most societies known to anthropology commonly have extended-family households, whereas other societies typically do not? Since extended-family households are found more frequently in societies with sedentary agricultural economies, economic factors may play a role in determining household type. Nimkoff and Middleton have pointed out some features of agricultural life, as opposed to hunting-gathering life, that may help explain the prevalence of extended families among agriculturalists. The extended family may be a social mechanism that prevents the economically ruinous division of family property in societies where property such as cultivated land is important. Conversely, the need for mobility in hunter-gatherer societies may make extended-family households less likely in such economies. During certain seasons, the hunter-gatherers may be obliged to divide into nuclear families that scatter into other areas.[84]

But agriculture is only a weak predictor of extended-family households. Many agriculturalists lack them, and many nonagricultural societies have them. A different theory is that extended-family households come to prevail in societies that have incompatible activity requirements—that is, requirements that cannot be met by a mother or a father in a one-family household. In other words,

[82]Margaret Mead, *Coming of Age in Samoa* (New York: Morrow, 1928); quoted in Stephens, *The Family in Cross-Cultural Perspective,* pp. 134–35.

[83]Mead, *Coming of Age in Samoa;* quoted in Stephens, *The Family in Cross-Cultural Perspective,* p. 135.

[84]M. F. Nimkoff and Russell Middleton, "Types of Family and Types of Economy," *American Journal of Sociology,* 66 (1960): 215–25.

the suggestion is that extended-family households are generally favored when the work a mother has to do outside the home (cultivating fields or gathering foods far away) makes it difficult for her to also care for her children and do other household tasks, or when the required outside activities of a father (warfare, trading trips, or wage labor far away) make it difficult for him to do the subsistence work required of males. There is cross-cultural evidence that societies with such incompatible activity requirements are more likely to have extended-family households than societies with compatible activity requirements, *regardless* of whether or not the society is agricultural. However, even though they have incompatible activity requirements, societies with commercial or monetary exchange may not have extended family households. In commercial societies, a family may be able to obtain the necessary help by "buying" the required services.[85]

Of course, even in societies with money economies, not everyone can buy required services. Those who are poor may need to live in extended families, and extended-family living may become more common even in the middle class when the economy is depressed. As a 1983 article in a popular magazine noted,

Whatever happened to the all-American nuclear family —Mom, Pop, two kids and a cuddly dog, nestled under one cozy, mortgaged roof? What happened was an economic squeeze: layoffs, fewer jobs for young people, more working mothers, a shortage of affordable housing and a high cost of living. Those factors, along with a rising divorce rate, a trend toward later marriages and an increase in the over sixty-five population, all hitting at once, are forcing thousands of Americans into living in multigenerational families.[86]

In many societies there are kin groups even larger than extended families. The next chapter discusses the varieties of such groupings.

---

[85]Burton Pasternak, Carol R. Ember, and Melvin Ember, "On the Conditions Favoring Extended Family Households," *Journal of Anthropological Research*, 32 (1976): 109–23.

[86]Jean Libman Block, "Help! They've *All* Moved Back Home!" *Woman's Day*, April 26, 1983, pp. 72–76.

SUMMARY

1. All societies known today have the custom of marriage. Marriage is a socially approved sexual and economic union between a man and a woman that is presumed to be more or less permanent, and that subsumes reciprocal rights and obligations between the two spouses and between the spouses and their children.

2. The way marriage is socially recognized varies greatly: it may involve an elaborate ceremony or none at all. Variations include childhood betrothals, trial-marriage periods, feasting, and the birth of a baby.

3. Marriage arrangements often include an economic element. The most common form is the bride price, in which the groom or his family gives an agreed-upon amount of money or goods to the bride's family. Bride service exists when the groom works for the bride's family for a specified period. In some societies, a female from the groom's family is exchanged for the bride; in others, gifts are exchanged between the two families. A dowry is a payment of goods or money by the bride's family usually to the bride. Indirect dowry is provided by the groom's family to the bride (sometimes through the bride's father).

4. No society generally allows sex or marriage between brothers and sisters, mothers and sons, or fathers and daughters.

5. Every society tells people whom they cannot marry, whom they can marry, and sometimes even whom they should marry. In quite a few societies, marriages are arranged by the couple's kin groups. Implicit in arranged marriages is the conviction that the joining of two kin groups to form new social and economic ties is too important to be left to free choice and romantic love. Some societies have rules of exogamy, which require marriage outside one's own kin group or community; others have rules of endogamy, requiring marriage within one's group. Although most societies prohibit all first-cousin marriages, some permit or prefer marriage with cross-cousins (children of siblings

of the opposite sex) and parallel cousins (children of siblings of the same sex). Many societies have customs providing for the remarriage of widowed persons. Levirate is a custom whereby a man marries his brother's widow. Sororate is the practice of a woman marrying her deceased sister's husband.

6. We think of marriage as involving just one man and one woman at a time (monogamy), but most societies allow a man to be married to more than one woman at a time (polygyny). Polyandry—the marriage of one woman to several husbands—is very rare.

7. The prevailing form of family in most societies is the extended family. It consists of two or more single-parent, monogamous (nuclear), polygynous, or polyandrous families linked by blood ties.

SUGGESTED READING

EMBER, M., AND EMBER, C. R. *Marriage, Family, and Kinship: Comparative Studies of Social Organization.* New Haven: HRAF Press, 1983. A collection of reprinted cross-cultural and cross-species studies testing possible explanations of some aspects of human social organization. Relevant to this chapter are the studies of male-female bonding, the incest taboo, polygyny, and the extended family.

FOX, R. *Kinship and Marriage: An Anthropological Perspective.* Cambridge: Cambridge University Press, 1983. An introduction to problems and theory in the study of kinship and marriage. Chapters 1 and 2 are of particular relevance to our discussion.

LEVINSON, D., AND MALONE, M. J., eds. *Toward Explaining Human Culture: A Critical Review of the Findings of Worldwide Cross-Cultural Research.* New Haven: HRAF Press, 1980. Chapters 6, 7, and 8 review the cross-cultural research literature on marriage, the family, and the incest taboo.

MURDOCK, G. P. *Social Structure.* New York: Macmillan, 1949. A classic cross-cultural analysis of variation in social organization. Chapters 1, 2, 9, and 10—on the nuclear family, composite forms of the family, the regulation of sex, and incest taboos and their extensions—are particularly relevant.

PASTERNAK B. *Introduction to Kinship and Social Organization.* Englewood Cliffs, NJ: Prentice Hall, 1976. Chapters 3, 5, 6, and 7 present a survey and critique of theories and evidence about variation in marriage and the family.

19

Marital Residence and Kinship

In the United States and Canada, and in many other industrial societies, a young man and woman usually establish a place of residence apart from their parents or other relatives when they marry, if they have not already moved away before that. Our society is so oriented toward this pattern of marital residence—*neolocal* (new-place) *residence*—that it seems to be the obvious and natural one to follow. Some upper-income families begin earlier than others to train their children to live away from home by sending them to boarding schools at age thirteen or fourteen. Young adults of all income levels learn to live away from home most of the year, if they join the army or attend an out-of-town college. In any case, when a young person marries, he or she generally lives apart from family.

So familiar is neolocal residence to us that we tend to assume all societies practice the same pattern. On the contrary, of the 565 societies in Murdock's *World Ethnographic Sample*, only about 5 percent follow this practice.[1] About 95 percent of the world's societies have some pattern of residence whereby a new couple settles within, or very close to, the household of the parents or some other close relative of either the groom or the bride. When married couples live near kin, it stands to reason that kinship relationships will figure prominently in the social life of the society. Marital residence largely predicts the types of kin groups found in a society, as well as how people refer to and classify their various relatives.

As we will see, kin groups that include several or many families and hundreds or even thousands of people are found in many societies and structure many areas of social life. Kin groups may have important economic, social, political, and religious functions.

Patterns of Marital Residence

In societies in which newly married couples customarily live with or close to their kin, several residence patterns may be established. Since children in all societies are required to marry outside the nuclear family (because of the incest taboo), and since couples in almost all societies live together after they are married (with a few exceptions),[2] it is not possible for an entire society to practice a system in which all married offspring reside with their own parents. Some children, then, have to leave home when they marry. But which married children remain at home and which reside elsewhere? Societies vary in the way they deal with this question, but there are not that many different patterns. Actually, only four occur with any sizable frequency:

1. **Patrilocal residence:** the son stays and the daughter leaves, so that the married couple lives with or near the husband's parents (67 percent of all societies).
2. **Matrilocal residence:** the daughter stays and the son leaves, so that the married couple lives with or near the wife's parents (15 percent of all societies).
3. **Bilocal residence:** either the son or the daughter leaves, so that the married couple lives with or near either the wife's or the husband's parents (7 percent of all societies).
4. **Avunculocal residence:** both son and daughter normally leave, but the son and his wife settle with or near his mother's brother (4 percent of all societies).[3]

In these definitions, we use the phrase "the married couple lives *with or near*" a particular set of in-laws. We should point out that when couples live with or near the kin of a spouse, the couple may live in the same household with those kin, creating an *extended-family* household, or they may live separately in an *independent-family* household, but nearby.

A fifth pattern of residence, of course, is neolocal, in which the newly married couple does not live with or near kin.

[2]The very few societies in which married couples live apart, each with his or her own kin, practice a *duolocal* (two-place) pattern of residence. The Nayar of southern India, referred to early in the last chapter, had such a pattern.

[3]Percentages calculated from Coult and Habenstein, *Cross Tabulations of Murdock's World Ethnographic Sample*.

[1]Allan D. Coult and Robert W. Habenstein, *Cross Tabulations of Murdock's World Ethnographic Sample* (Columbia: University of Missouri Press, 1965).

In most societies known to anthropology, the bride leaves her home when she marries to live with or near her husband's parents.

5. **Neolocal residence:** both son and daughter leave; married couples live apart from the relatives of either spouse (5 percent of all societies).

How does place of residence for the couple affect their social life? Because the pattern of residence governs with whom or near whom individuals live, it largely determines the people those individuals interact with and the people they have to depend upon. If a married couple is surrounded by the kin of the husband, for example, the chances are that those relatives will figure importantly in the couple's entire future. Whether the couple lives with or near the husband's or the wife's kin can also be expected to have important consequences for the status of the husband or wife. If married couples live patrilocally, as occurs in most societies, the wife may be far from her own kin. In any case, she will be an outsider among a group of male relatives who have grown up together. The feeling of being an outsider is particularly strong when the wife has moved into a patrilocal extended-family household.

Among the Tiv of central Nigeria,[4] the patrilocal extended family consists of the "great father," who is the head of the household, and his younger brothers, his sons, and his younger brothers' sons. Also included are the in-marrying wives and all unmarried children. (The sisters and daughters of the household head who have married would have gone to live where their husbands lived.) Authority is strongly vested in the male line, particularly the eldest of the household, who has authority over bride price, disputes, punishment, and plans for new buildings.

A somewhat different situation exists if the husband comes to live with or near his wife's parents. Here, the wife and her kin take on somewhat greater importance, and the husband is the out-

---

[4]Laura Bohannan and Paul Bohannan, *The Tiv of Central Nigeria* (London: International African Institute, 1953).

sider. As we shall see, however, the matrilocal situation is not quite the mirror image of the patrilocal, since in matrilocal societies the husband's kin are often not far away. Moreover, even though residence is matrilocal, women often do not have as much to say in decision making as their brothers do.

If the married couple does not live with or near the parents or close kin of either spouse, the situation is again quite different. Here, we would hardly be surprised to find that relatives and kinship connections do not figure very largely in everyday life.

Explanations of Variation in Residence

A number of questions can be raised as to why different societies have different patterns of residence. First, since in most societies married couples live with or near kin (as in patrilocal, matrilocal, bilocal, or avunculocal residence), why in some societies, such as our own, do couples typically live apart from kin? And among the societies where couples live with or near kin, why do most choose the husband's side (patrilocal residence) and some the wife's side (matrilocal residence)? Why do some nonneolocal societies allow a married couple to go to either the wife's or the husband's kin (bilocal residence), whereas most others do not generally allow a choice? (Because matrilocal, patrilocal, and avunculocal residence each specify just one pattern, they are often called nonoptional or **unilocal** patterns of residence.)

Neolocal Residence

Why in some societies do couples live separately from kin, whereas in most societies couples live near, if not with, kin? Many anthropologists have suggested that neolocal residence is somehow related to the presence of a money or commercial economy. They argue that when people can sell their labor or their products for money, they can buy what they need to live, without having to depend on kin. Since money is not perishable (unlike crops and other foods in a world largely lacking refrigeration), it can be stored for exchange at a later time. Thus, a money-earning family can re-

sort to its own savings during periods of unemployment or disability (or it might be able to rely on monetary aid from the government, as in our own society). This is impossible in nonmoney economies, where people must depend on relatives for food and other necessities if for some reason they cannot provide their own.

There is some cross-cultural evidence to support this interpretation. Neolocal residence tends to occur in societies with monetary or commercial exchange, whereas societies without money tend to have patterns of residence that locate a couple near or with kin.[5] The presence of money, then, appears to be related to neolocal residence: money seems to *allow* a couple to live on their own. Still, this does not quite explain why they should choose to do so.

One reason may be that in commercial societies couples may generally do better on their own, because the jobs available may require physical or social mobility. Or perhaps couples prefer to live apart from kin because they want to avoid some of the interpersonal tensions and demands that may be generated by living with or near kin. But why couples, when given money, should *prefer* to live on their own is not yet completely understood.

Matrilocal versus Patrilocal Residence

Why in some societies does a married couple live with the husband's parents, and in others with the wife's parents? Traditionally, it has been assumed that in those societies where married children live near or with kin, residence will tend to be patrilocal if males contribute more to the economy and matrilocal if women contribute more. However plausible this assumption may seem, the cross-cultural evidence does not support it. Where men do most of the subsistence work, residence is patrilocal no more often than would be expected by chance. Conversely, where women do an equal amount or more of the subsistence work, residence is no more likely to be matrilocal than patrilocal.[6]

[5]Melvin Ember, "The Emergence of Neolocal Residence," *Transactions of the New York Academy of Sciences*, 30 (1967): 291–302.

[6]Melvin Ember and Carol R. Ember, "The Conditions Favoring Matrilocal versus Patrilocal Residence," *American Anthropologist*, 73 (1971): 571–94. See also William T. Divale, "Migration, External Warfare, and Matrilocal Residence," *Behavior Science Research*, 9 (1974): 75–133.

We can predict whether residence will be matrilocal or patrilocal from the type of warfare practiced in a society. In most societies known to anthropology, neighboring communities or districts are often enemies. The type of warfare that breaks out periodically between such groups may be called internal, since the fighting occurs between groups speaking the same language. In other societies, the warfare is never within the same society, but only with other language groups. This pattern of warfare is referred to as purely external. Cross-cultural evidence suggests that in societies where warfare is at least sometimes internal, residence is almost always patrilocal rather than matrilocal. In contrast, residence is almost always matrilocal when warfare is purely external.[7]

How can we explain this relationship between type of warfare and matrilocal versus patrilocal residence? One theory is that patrilocal residence tends to occur with internal warfare because there may be concern over keeping sons close to home to help with defense. Since women do not usually constitute the fighting force in any society, having sons reside at home after marriage might be favored as a means of maintaining a loyal and quickly mobilized fighting force in case of surprise attack from nearby. However, if warfare is purely external, people may not be so concerned about keeping their sons at home because families need not fear attack from neighboring communities or districts.

With purely external warfare, then, residence may be determined by other considerations, especially economic ones. If in societies with purely external warfare the women do most of the primary subsistence work, families might want their daughters to remain at home after marriage; so the pattern of residence might become matrilocal. (If warfare is purely external but men still do more of the primary subsistence work, residence should still be patrilocal.) Thus, the need to keep sons at home after marriage when there is internal warfare may take precedence over any considerations based on division of labor. It is perhaps only when internal warfare is nonexistent that a female-dominant division of labor may give rise to matrilocal residence.[8]

Bilocal Residence

In societies that practice bilocal residence, a married couple goes to live with or near either the husband's or the wife's parents. Although this pattern seems to involve a choice for the married couple, theory and research suggest that bilocal residence may occur out of necessity instead. Elman Service has suggested that bilocal residence is likely to occur in societies that have recently suffered a severe and drastic loss of population because of the introduction of new infectious diseases.[9] Over the last 400 years, contact with Europeans in many parts of the world has resulted in severe population losses among non-European societies that lacked resistance to the Europeans' diseases. If couples need to live with some set of kin in order to make a living in noncommercial societies, it seems likely that couples in depopulated, noncommercial societies might have to live with whichever spouse's parents (and other relatives) are still alive. This interpretation seems to be supported by the cross-cultural evidence. Recently depopulated societies tend to have bilocal residence or frequent departures from unilocality, whereas societies that are not recently depopulated tend to have one pattern or another of unilocal residence.[10]

In hunter-gatherer societies, a few other circumstances may also favor bilocal residence. Bilocality tends to be found among those hunter-gatherers who have very small bands or unpredictable and low rainfall. Residential "choice" in these cases may be a question of adjusting marital residence to where the couple will have the best chance to survive or to find close relatives to live and work with.[11]

[7]Ember and Ember, "The Conditions Favoring Matrilocal versus Patrilocal Residence," pp. 583–85; and Divale, "Migration, External Warfare, and Matrilocal Residence," p. 100.

[8]Ember and Ember, "The Conditions Favoring Matrilocal versus Patrilocal Residence." For a different theory—that matrilocal residence precedes, rather than follows, the development of purely external warfare—see Divale, "Migration, External Warfare, and Matrilocal Residence."

[9]Elman R. Service, *Primitive Social Organization: An Evolutionary Perspective* (New York: Random House, 1962), p. 137.

[10]Carol R. Ember and Melvin Ember, "The Conditions Favoring Multilocal Residence," *Southwestern Journal of Anthropology,* 28 (1972): 382–400.

[11]Carol R. Ember, "Residential Variation among Hunter-Gatherers," *Behavior Science Research,* 9 (1975): 135–49.

A kindred rarely gets together in the United States. At weddings there are usually two kindreds present, the bride's and the groom's, as at this Jewish wedding in Brooklyn, New York.

The Structure of Kinship

In noncommercial societies, kinship connections structure many areas of social life—from the kind of access an individual has to productive resources to the kind of political alliances formed between communities and larger territorial groups. In some societies, in fact, kinship connections have an important bearing on matters of life and death.

Recall the social system described in Shakespeare's *Romeo and Juliet.* The Capulets and the Montagues were groups of kin engaged in lethal competition with each other, and the fatal outcome of Romeo and Juliet's romance was related to that competition. Although Romeo and Juliet's society had a commercial economy (but not, of course, an industrialized one), the political system of the city they lived in was a reflection of the way kinship was structured. Sets of kin of common descent lived together, and the various kin groups competed (and sometimes fought) for a prominent, or at least secure, place in the political hierarchy of the city-state.

If a preindustrial commercial society could be so structured by kinship, we can imagine how much more important kinship connections and kin groups are in many noncommercial societies that lack political mechanisms such as princes and councils of lords who try to keep the peace and initiate other activities on behalf of the community. It is no wonder that anthropologists often speak of the web of kinship as providing the main structure of social action in noncommercial societies.

If kinship is important, there is still the question of which set of kin a person affiliates with and depends on. After all, if every single relative were counted as equally important, there would be an unmanageably large number of people in each person's kinship network. Consequently, in most societies where kinship connections are important, rules allocate each person to a particular and definable set of kin.

Rules of Descent

Rules that connect individuals with particular sets of kin because of known or presumed common ancestry are called **rules of descent.** By the particular rule of descent operating in their society, individuals can know more or less immediately which set of kin to turn to for support and help.

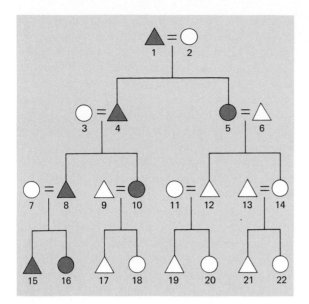

FIGURE 19–1 Patrilineal Descent

Individuals 4 and 5, who are the children of 1 and 2, affiliate with their father's patrilineal kin group, represented by the color. In the next generation, the children of 3 and 4 also belong to the color kin group, since they take their descent from their father, who is a member of that group. However, the children of 5 and 6 do not belong to this patrilineal group, since they take their descent from their father, who is a member of a different group. That is, although the mother of 12 and 14 belongs to the color patrilineal group, she cannot pass on her descent affiliation to her children, and since her husband (6) does not belong to her patrilineage, her children (12 and 14) belong to their father's group. In the fourth generation, only 15 and 16 belong to the color patrilineal group, since their father is the only male member of the preceding generation who belongs to the color patrilineal group. In this diagram, then, 1, 4, 5, 8, 10, 15, and 16 are affiliated by patrilineal descent; all the other individuals belong to other patrilineal groups.

There are only a few known rules of descent that affiliate individuals with different sets of kin:

1. **Patrilineal descent** (the most frequent rule) affiliates an individual with kin of both sexes related to him or her *through men only*. As Figure 19–1 indicates, in patrilineal systems the children in each generation belong to the kin group of their father; their father, in turn, belongs to the group of his father; and so on. Although a man's sons and daughters are all

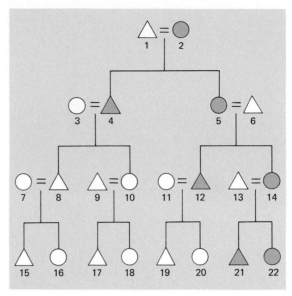

FIGURE 19–2 Matrilineal Descent

Individuals 4 and 5, who are the children of 1 and 2, affiliate with their mother's kin group, represented by the color. In the next generation, the children of 5 and 6 also belong to the color kin group since they take their descent from their mother, who is a member of that group. However, the children of 3 and 4 do not belong to this matrilineal group since they take their descent from their mother, who is a member of a different group; their father, although a member of the color matrilineal group, cannot pass his affiliation on to them under the rule of matrilineal descent. In the fourth generation, only 21 and 22 belong to the color matrilineal group, since their mother is the only female member of the preceding generation who belongs. Thus, individuals 2, 4, 5, 12, 14, 21, and 22 belong to the same matrilineal group. This rule of descent generates a group that is almost a mirror image of the group generated by a patrilineal rule.

members of the same descent group, affiliation with that group is transmitted only by the sons to their children.

2. **Matrilineal descent** affiliates an individual with kin of both sexes related to him or her *through women only*. In each generation, then, children belong to the kin group of their mother (see Figure 19–2). Although a woman's sons and daughters are all members of the same descent group, only her daughters can pass on their descent affiliation to their children.

3. **Ambilineal descent** affiliates an individual with kin related to him or her through men *or*

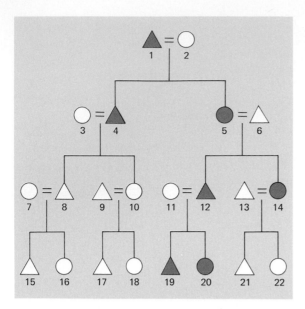

FIGURE 19–3 Ambilineal Descent

A hypothetical ambilineal group of kin is indicated by the color. Members 4 and 5 belong to this group because of a male link, their father (1); members 12 and 14 belong because of a female link, their mother (5); and members 19 and 20 belong because of a male link, their father (12). This is a hypothetical example because any combination of lineal links is possible in an ambilineal descent group.

women. In other words, some people in the society affiliate with a group of kin through their fathers; others, through their mothers. Consequently, the descent groups show both female and male genealogical links, as illustrated in Figure 19–3.

These three rules are usually, but not always, mutually exclusive. Most societies can be characterized as having only one rule of descent, but sometimes two principles are used to affiliate individuals with different sets of kin for different purposes. Some societies have then what is called **double descent,** or **double unilineal descent,** whereby an individual affiliates for some purposes with a group of matrilineal kin and for other purposes with a group of patrilineal kin. Thus, two rules of descent, each traced through links of one sex only, are operative at the same time. For example, if there is a patrilineal system and a matrilineal one, individuals would belong to *two* groups

at birth; the matrilineal group of the mother *and* the patrilineal group of the father. Imagine combining Figures 19–1 and 19–2. Individuals 4 and 5 would belong to the matrilineal group (labeled with a green color) that their mother belongs to and the patrilineal group (labeled with an orange color) that their father belongs to.

The way a society assigns personal names does not necessarily convey anything about a rule of descent. It is customary in North American society for children to have a last (or "family") name; this is usually their father's last name. All the people with the same last name do not conceive of themselves as descended from the same common ancestor; all Smiths do not consider themselves related. Nor do such people act together for any particular purpose. And many societies, even with rules of descent, do not give individuals the name of their kin group, or father or mother. For example, among the patrilineal Luo of Kenya, babies were traditionally given names that described the circumstances of their birth ("born-in-the-morning"); their names did not include their father's or kin group's name. (Only after the British established a colony in Kenya, and continuing after independence, did children get their father's personal name as a family name.)

Bilateral Kinship

Many societies, including our own, do not have lineal (matrilineal, patrilineal, or ambilineal) descent groups—sets of kin who believe they descend from a common ancestor. They are therefore called **bilateral** societies. *Bilateral* means "two-sided," and here it refers to the fact that one's relatives on both mother's and father's sides are generally equal in importance or (more usually) in unimportance. Kinship reckoning in bilateral societies does not refer to common descent, but rather is horizontal (see Figure 19–4), moving outward from close to more distant relatives, rather than upward to common ancestors.

The term **kindred** describes a person's bilateral set of relatives who may be called upon for some purpose. In our society, we think of the kindred as including the people we might invite to weddings, funerals, or some other ceremonial occasion; the kindred, however, is not usually a definite group. As anyone who has been involved in the planning

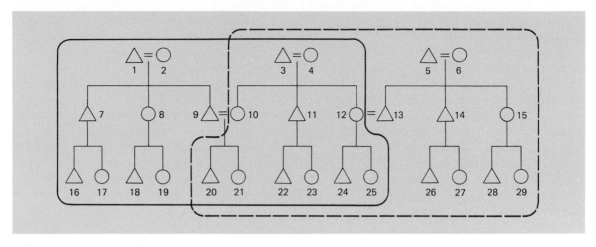

FIGURE 19–4 Bilateral Kinship

In a bilateral system the kindred is ego-centered; hence, it varies with different points of reference (except for brothers and sisters). In any bilateral society, the kindred minimally includes parents, grandparents, aunts, uncles, and first cousins. So, if we look at the close kindred of the brother and sister 20 and 21 (enclosed by the solid line), it would include their parents (9 and 10), their aunts and uncles (7, 8, 11, 12), their grandparents (1, 2, 3, 4) and their first cousins (16–19, 22–25). But the kindred of the brother and sister 24 and 25 (shown by the dotted line) includes only some of the same people (3, 4, 10–12, 20–23); in addition, the kindred of 24 and 25 includes people not in the kindred of 20 and 21 (5, 6, 13–15, 26–29).

of a wedding-invitation list knows, a great deal of time may be spent deciding which relatives ought to be invited and which ones can legitimately be excluded. Societies with bilateral kinship differ in precisely how distant relatives have to be before they are lost track of or before they are not included in ceremonial activities. In societies such as our own, in which kinship is relatively unimportant, fewer relatives are included in the kindred. In other bilateral societies, however, where kinship connections are somewhat more important, more would be included.

The distinctiveness of bilateral kinship is that aside from brothers and sisters, no two persons belong to exactly the same kin group. Your kindred contains close relatives spreading out on both your father's and mother's sides, but the members of your kindred are affiliated only by way of their connection to you (**ego** or the focus). Thus, the kindred is an *ego-centered* group of kin. Since different people (except for brothers and sisters) have different mothers and fathers, your first cousins will have different kindreds, and even your own children will have a different kindred from yours. It is the ego-centered nature of the kindred that makes it difficult for it to act as a permanent or persistent group. The only thing the people in a kindred

have in common is the ego who brings it together. The kindred usually has no name, no common purpose, and only temporary meetings centered around the ego.[12] Furthermore, since everyone belongs to many different and overlapping kindreds, the society is not divided into clear-cut groups.

Unilineal Descent

Both matrilineal and patrilineal rules of descent are **unilineal** rules, in that a person is affiliated with a group of kin through descent links of one sex only—either males only or females only. Unilineal rules of descent affiliate an individual with a line of kin extending back in time and into the future. By virtue of this line of descent (whether it extends through males or females), some very close relatives are excluded. For example, in a patrilineal system, your mother and your mother's parents do not belong to your patrilineal group, but your father and his father (and their sisters) do. In your own generation in a matrilineal or patrilineal system, some cousins are excluded, and

[12]J. D. Freeman, "On the Concept of the Kindred," *Journal of the Royal Anthropological Institute*, 91 (1961): 192–220.

in your children's generation, some of your nieces and nephews are excluded.

However, although unilineal rules of descent exclude certain relatives from membership in one's kin group (just as practical considerations restrict the effective size of kinship networks in our own society), the excluded relatives are not necessarily ignored or forgotten. Indeed, in many unilineal societies they may be entrusted with important responsibilities. For example, when a person dies in a patrilineal society, some members of his or her mother's patrilineal descent group may customarily be accorded the right to perform certain rituals at the funeral.

Unlike bilateral kinship, unilineal rules of descent can form clear-cut, and hence unambiguous, groups of kin, which can act as separate units even after the death of individual members. Referring again to Figures 19–1 and 19–2, we can see that the individuals in the highlight color belong to the same patrilineal or matrilineal descent group without ambiguity—an individual in the fourth generation belongs to the group just as much as one in the first generation. If we imagine that the patrilineal group, for instance, has a name, say the Hawks, then an individual knows immediately whether or not he or she is a Hawk. If the individual is not a Hawk, then he or she belongs to some other group—for each person belongs to only one line.

This fact is important if kin groups are to act as separate or nonoverlapping units. It is difficult for people to act together unless they know exactly who should get together. And it is easier for individuals to act together as a group if each one belongs to only one such group or line. Recall that in a bilateral system, not only is it sometimes unclear where the boundary of the kindred is, but one person belongs to many different kindreds—one's own and others' (children's, cousins', and so forth). Consequently, it is not surprising that a kindred only gets together temporarily for ceremonial occasions.

Types of Unilineal Descent Groups. In a society with unilineal descent, people usually refer to themselves as belonging to a particular unilineal group or set of groups because they believe they share common descent in either the male line (patrilineal) or the female line (matrilineal).

These people form what is called a *unilineal descent group.* Several types of unilineal descent groups are distinguished by anthropologists: lineages, clans, phratries, and moieties.

LINEAGES A **lineage** is a set of kin whose members trace descent from a common ancestor through known links. There may be **patrilineages** or **matrilineages,** depending, of course, on whether the links are traced through males only or through females only. Lineages are often designated by the name of the common ancestor or ancestress. In some societies, people belong to a hierarchy of lineages. That is, they first trace their descent back to the ancestor of a minor lineage, then to the ancestor of a larger and more inclusive major lineage, and so on.

CLANS A **clan** (also called a **sib**) is a set of kin whose members believe themselves to be descended from a common ancestor or ancestress, but the links back to that ancestor are not specified. In fact, the common ancestor may not even be known. Clans with patrilineal descent are called **patriclans;** clans with matrilineal descent are called **matriclans.** Clans are often designated by an animal or plant name (called a **totem**), which may have some special significance for the group, and at the very least provides a means of group identification. Thus, if someone says he or she belongs to the Bear, Wolf, or Turtle group, for example, others will know whether or not that person is a clan member.

The word *totem* comes from the Ojibwa Indian word *ototeman,* "a relative of mine." In some societies, people have to observe taboos relating to their clan totem animal. For example, clan members may be forbidden to kill or eat their totem.

Although it may seem strange to us that an animal or plant should be a symbol of a kin group, animals as symbols of groups are familiar in our own culture. Football and baseball teams, for example, are often named for animals (Detroit Tigers, Los Angeles Rams, Philadelphia Eagles, Chicago Bears). Voluntary associations, such as men's clubs, are sometimes called by the name of an animal (Elks, Moose, Lions). Entire nations may be represented by an animal; we speak, for instance, of the American Eagle, the British Lion, and the Russian Bear.[13] Why humans so often choose ani-

[13]George P. Murdock, *Social Structure* (New York: Macmillan, 1949), pp. 49–50.

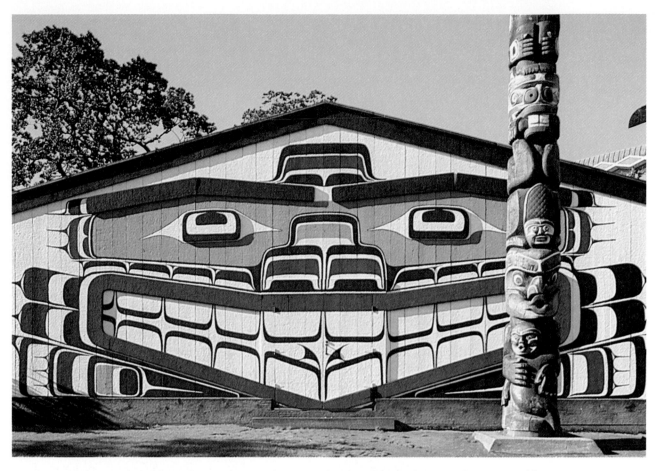

Many Northwest Pacific Coast Indians constructed totem poles representing the animal totems and human ancestors of their clans. Shown here are totem poles and a reconstructed house in Victoria, British Columbia.

mal names to represent groups is an intriguing question to which we have no tested answer as yet.

PHRATRIES   A **phratry** is a unilineal descent group composed of a number of supposedly related clans or sibs. As with clans, the descent links in phratries are unspecified.

MOIETIES   When a whole society is divided into two unilineal descent groups, we call each group a **moiety.** (The word *moiety* comes from a French word meaning "half.") The people in each moiety believe themselves to be descended from a common ancestor, although they cannot specify how. Societies with moiety systems usually have relatively small populations (less than 9,000). Societies with phratries and clans tend to be larger.[14]

COMBINATIONS   Although we have distinguished several different types of unilineal descent groups, we do not wish to imply that all unilineal societies have only one type of descent group. Many societies have two or more types in various combinations. For example, some societies have lineages and clans; others may have clans and phratries but no lineages; and still others may have clans and moieties but neither phratries nor lineages. Aside from the fact that a society that has phratries must also have clans (since phratries are combinations of clans), all combinations of descent groups are possible. Even if societies have more than one type of unilineal kin group—for example, lineages and clans— there is no ambiguity about membership: small groups are simply subsets of larger units. The larger units just include people who say they are unilineally related further back in time.

---

[14]Carol R. Ember, Melvin Ember, and Burton Pasternak, "On the Development of Unilineal Descent," *Journal of Anthropological Research*, 30 (1974): 84–89.

Patrilineal Organization. Patrilineal organization is the most frequent type of descent system. The Kapauku Papuans, a people living in the central highlands of western New Guinea, are an example of a patrilineal society with many types of descent groups.[15] The hierarchy of groups to which Kapauku are affiliated by virtue of the patrilineal descent system plays an extremely important part in their lives. Every Kapauku belongs to a patrilineage, to a patriclan that includes his or her lineage, and to a patriphratry that includes his or her clan.

The male members of a patrilineage—all the living males who can trace their actual relationship through males to a common ancestor—constitute the male population of a single village or, more likely, a series of adjoining villages. In other words, the lineage is a *territorial* unit. The male members of the lineage live together by virtue of a patrilocal rule of residence and a fairly stable settlement pattern. A son stays near his parents and brings his wife to live in or near his father's house; the daughters leave home and go to live with their husbands. If the group lives in one place over a long period, the male descendants of one man will live in the same territory. If the lineage is large, it may be divided into sublineages composed of people who trace their descent from one of the sons of the lineage ancestor. The male members of a sublineage live in a contiguous block within the larger lineage territory.

The members of the same patrilineage address each other affectionately, and within this group law and order is maintained by a headman. Killing within the lineage is considered a serious offense, and any fighting that takes place is done with sticks rather than lethal weapons such as spears. The sublineage headman tries to settle any kind of grievance within the sublineage as quickly and as peacefully as possible. If a sublineage mate commits a crime against outsiders, all members of the sublineage may be considered responsible and their property seized, or a member of the sublineage may be killed in revenge by the victim's kin.

The Kapauku also belong to larger and more inclusive patrilineal descent groups—clans and phratries. All the people of the same clan believe they are related to each other in the father's line, but they are unable to say how they are related. If a member of the patriclan eats the clan's plant or animal totem, it is believed that the person will become deaf. A Kapauku is also forbidden to marry anyone from his or her clan. In other words, the clan is exogamous.

Unlike the members of the patrilineage, the male members of the patriclan do not all live together. Thus, the lineage is the largest group of patrilineal kinsmen that is localized. The lineage is also the largest group of kinsmen that acts together politically. Among clan members there is no mechanism for resolving disputes, and members of the same patriclan (who belong to different lineages) may even go to war with one another.

The most inclusive patrilineal descent group among the Kapauku is the phratry, each of which is composed of two or more clans. The Kapauku believe that the phratry was originally one clan, but that in a conflict between brothers of the founding family the younger brother was expelled and formed a new clan. The two resulting clans are, of course, viewed as patrilineally related, since their founders are said to have been brothers. The members of a phratry observe all the totemic taboos of the clans that belong to that phratry. However, although intermarriage of members of the same clan is forbidden, members of the same phratry but of different clans may marry.

The Kapauku, then, are an example of a unilineal society with many types of descent groups. They have lineages with demonstrated kinship links and two kinds of descent groups with unknown descent links (clans and phratries).

Matrilineal Organization. Although societies with matrilineal descent seem in many respects like mirror images of their patrilineal counterparts, there is one important way in which they differ. That difference has to do with who exercises authority. In patrilineal systems, descent affiliation is transmitted through males, and it is also the males who exercise authority. Consequently, in the patrilineal system, lines of descent and of authority converge. In a matrilineal system, however, although the line of descent passes through females, females rarely exercise authority in their kin groups—usually males do. Thus, the lines of au-

---

[15]Leopold Pospisil, *The Kapauku Papuans of West New Guinea* (New York: Holt, Rinehart & Winston, 1963).

thority and descent do not converge.[16] Although anthropologists do not quite understand why this is so, it seems to be an ethnographic fact. In any case, since males exercise authority in the kin group, an individual's mother's brother becomes an important authority figure, because he is the individual's closest male matrilineal relative in the parental generation. The individual's father does not belong to the individual's own matrilineal kin group and thus has no say in kin-group matters.

The divergence of authority and descent in a matrilineal system has some effect on community organization and marriage. Most matrilineal societies practice matrilocal residence. Daughters stay at home after marriage and bring their husbands to live with them; sons leave home to join their wives. But the sons who are required to leave will be the ones who eventually exercise authority in their kin groups. This presents a problem. The solution that seems to have been arrived at in most matrilineal societies is that although the males move away to live with their wives, they usually do not move too far away—indeed, they often marry women who live in the same village. Thus, matrilineal societies tend not to be locally exogamous—that is, members often marry people from inside the village—whereas patrilineal societies are often locally exogamous.[17]

The matrilineal organization on Truk, a group of small islands in the Pacific, illustrates the general pattern of authority in matrilineal systems.[18] The Trukese have both matrilineages and matriclans. The matrilineage is a property-owning group whose members trace descent from a known common ancestress in the female line. The female lineage members and their husbands occupy a cluster of houses on the matrilineage's land. The property of the lineage group is administered by the oldest brother of the group. He allocates the productive property of his matrilineage and directs the work of the members. The oldest brother of the lineage

also represents the group in dealings with the district chief and all outsiders, and he must be consulted on any matter that affects the group. There is also a senior woman of the lineage who exercises some authority, but only insofar as the activities of the women are concerned. She may supervise the women's cooperative work (they usually work separately from the men) and manage the household.

Within the nuclear family, the father and mother have the primary responsibility for raising and disciplining their children. However, when a child reaches puberty, the father's right to discipline or exercise authority over the child ceases. The mother continues to exercise her right of discipline, and her brother may interfere. A woman's brother rarely interferes with his sister's child before puberty, but after puberty he may exercise some authority, especially since he is an elder in the child's own matrilineage. On Truk, men rarely move far from their birthplace. As Ward Goodenough has pointed out, "since matrilocal residence takes the men away from their home lineages, most of them marry women whose lineage houses are within a few minutes' walk of their own."[19]

Although there are some differences between patrilineal and matrilineal systems, there are many similarities. In both types of systems there may be lineages, clans, phratries, moieties, and any combination of these. These kin groups, in either matrilineal or patrilineal societies, may perform any number of functions. They may regulate marriage; they may come to each other's aid either economically or politically; and they may perform rituals together.

Now that we have learned something about matrilineal systems, the avunculocal pattern of residence, whereby married couples live with or near the husband's mother's brother, may become clearer. Although avunculocal residence is relatively rare, just about all avunculocal societies are matrilineal. As we have seen, the mother's brother plays an important role in decision making in most matrilineal societies. Aside from his brothers, who is a boy's closest male matrilineal relative? His mother's brother. Going to live with mother's brother, then, provides a way of localizing male

[16]David M. Schneider, "The Distinctive Features of Matrilineal Descent Groups," in David M. Schneider and Kathleen Gough, eds., *Matrilineal Kinship* (Berkeley: University of California Press, 1961), pp. 1–35.
[17]Ember and Ember, "The Conditions Favoring Matrilocal versus Patrilocal Residence," p. 581.
[18]David M. Schneider, "Truk," in Schneider and Gough, eds., *Matrilineal Kinship*, pp. 202–33.

[19]Ward H. Goodenough, *Property, Kin, and Community on Truk* (New Haven: Yale University Press, 1951), p. 145.

Reconstruction of an Iroquois longhouse, which housed a matrilineal descent group.

matrilineal relatives. But why should some matrilineal societies practice that form of residence? The answer may involve the prevailing type of warfare.

Avunculocal societies, in contrast with matrilocal societies, fight internally. Just as patrilocality may be a response to keep (patrilineally) related men home after marriage, so avunculocality may be a way of keeping related (in this case, matrilineally related) men together after marriage to provide for quick mobilization in case of surprise attack from nearby. Societies that already have strong, functioning matrilineal descent groups may, when faced with fighting close to home and high male mortality, choose to practice avunculocality rather than switch to patrilocality.[20]

Functions of Unilineal Descent Groups. Unilineal descent groups exist in societies at all levels of cultural complexity.[21] However, they are most common, apparently, in noncommercial food-producing (as opposed to food-collecting) societies.[22] Unilineal descent groups often have important functions in the social, economic, political, and religious realms of life.

REGULATING MARRIAGE In unilineal societies, individuals are not usually permitted to marry within their own unilineal descent groups. In some, however, marriage may be permitted within more inclusive kin groups but prohibited within smaller kin groups. In a few societies, marriage within the kin group is actually preferred. But in general, the incest taboo in unilineal societies is extended to all presumed unilineal relatives. For example, on Truk, which has matriclans and matrilineages, a person is forbidden by the rule of descent-group exogamy to marry anyone from his or

[20]Melvin Ember, "The Conditions That May Favor Avunculocal Residence," *Behavior Science Research*, 9 (1974): 203–9.

[21]Coult and Habenstein, *Cross Tabulations of Murdock's World Ethnographic Sample.*

[22]Data from Robert B. Textor, comp., *A Cross-Cultural Summary* (New Haven: HRAF Press, 1967).

her matriclan. Since the matrilineage is included within the matriclan, the rule of descent-group exogamy also applies to the matrilineage. Among the Kapauku, who have patriphratries, patriclans, and patrilineages, the largest descent group that is exogamous is the patriclan. The phratry may once have been exogamous, but the exogamy rule no longer applies to it. Some anthropologists have suggested that rules of exogamy for descent groups may have developed because the alliances between descent groups generated by such rules may be selectively favored under the conditions of life faced by most unilineal societies.

ECONOMIC FUNCTIONS Members of a person's lineage or clan are often required to side with that person in any quarrel or lawsuit, to help him or her get established economically, to contribute to a bride price or fine, and to support the person in life crises. Mutual aid often extends to economic cooperation on a regular basis. The unilineal descent group may act as a corporate unit in land ownership. For example, house sites and farmland are owned by a lineage among the Trukese and the Kapauku. Descent-group members may also support one another in such enterprises as clearing virgin bush or forest for farmland and providing food and other things for feasts, potlatches, curing rites, and ceremonial occasions, such as births, initiations, marriages, and funerals.

Money earned—either by harvesting a cash crop or by leaving the community for a time to work for cash wages—is sometimes viewed by the descent group as belonging to all. In recent times, however, young people in some places have shown an unwillingness to part with their money, viewing it as different from other kinds of economic assistance.

POLITICAL FUNCTIONS The word *political,* as used by members of an industrialized society, generally does not apply to the rather vague powers that may be entrusted to a headman or the elders of a lineage or clan. But these persons may have the right to assign land for use by a lineage member or a clan member. Headmen or elders may also have the right to settle disputes between two members within a lineage, although they generally lack power to force a settlement. And they may act as intermediaries in disputes between a member of their own clan and a member of an opposing kin group.

Certainly one of the most important political functions of unilineal descent groups is their role in warfare—the attempt to resolve disputes within and without the society by violent action. In societies without towns or cities, the organization of such fighting is often in the hands of descent groups. The Tiv of central Nigeria, for instance, know quite well at any given moment which lineages they will fight with, which lineages they will join as allies in case of a fight, which they will fight against using only sticks, and which must be attacked using bows and arrows. If a man from an unfriendly lineage is caught taking food from a Tiv garden at night, the owner may kill him. The dead man's lineage retaliates by killing one person from the garden owner's lineage, which then retaliates in turn, and so on.

RELIGIOUS FUNCTIONS A clan or lineage may have its own religious beliefs and practices, worshiping its own gods or goddesses and ancestral spirits.

The Tallensi of West Africa revere and try to pacify their ancestors. They view life as we know it as only a part of human existence: for them, life existed before birth and will continue after death. The Tallensi believe the ancestors of their descent groups have changed their form but have retained their interest in what goes on within their society. They can show their displeasure by bringing sudden disaster or minor mishap, and their pleasure by bringing unexpected good fortune. But people can never tell what will please them; ancestral spirits are, above all, unpredictable. Thus, the Tallensi try to account for unexplainable happenings by attributing them to the ever-watchful ancestors. Belief in the presence of ancestors also provides security; if their ancestors have survived death, so will they. The Tallensi religion is thus a descent-group religion. The Tallensi are not concerned with other people's ancestors; they believe it is only one's own ancestors who plague one.[23]

The Hopi clans figure prominently in the Hopi religion. The religion is one in which the unity of the people is evidenced by the interdependence of the clans, for each is considered a significant part of the whole. Each clan sponsors at least one of the religious festivals each year and is the guardian

---

[23]Meyer Fortes, *The Web of Kinship among the Tallensi* (New York: Oxford University Press, 1949).

of that festival's paraphernalia and ritual. A festival is not exclusive to one clan, for all the Hopi clans participate. This clan responsibility for ceremonies is accepted as part of the will of the spirits or deities, and each clan is believed to have been assigned its ritual role before the emergence of the Hopi people from the underworld.[24]

Development of Unilineal Systems. Unilineal kin groups play very important roles in the organization of many societies. But not all societies have such groups. In societies that have complex systems of political organization, officials and agencies take over many of the functions that might be performed by kin groups, such as the organization of work and warfare and the allocation of land. However, not all societies that lack complex political organization have unilineal descent systems. Why, then, do some societies have unilineal descent systems but not others?

It is generally assumed that unilocal residence (patrilocal or matrilocal) is necessary for the development of unilineal descent. Patrilocal residence, if practiced for some time in a society, will generate a set of patrilineally related males who live in the same territory. Matrilocal residence over time will similarly generate a localized set of matrilineally related females. It is no wonder, then, that matrilocal and patrilocal residence are cross-culturally associated with matrilineal and patrilineal descent, respectively.[25]

But although unilocal residence might be necessary for the formation of unilineal descent groups, it is apparently not the only condition required. For one thing, many societies with unilocal residence lack unilineal descent groups. For another, merely because related males or related females live together by virtue of a patrilocal or matrilocal rule of residence, it does not necessarily follow that the related people will actually view themselves as a descent group and function as such. Thus, it appears that other conditions are needed to supply the impetus for the formation of unilineal descent groups.

There is some evidence that unilocal societies that engage in warfare are more apt to have unilineal descent groups than unilocal societies without warfare.[26] It may be, then, that the presence of fighting in societies lacking complex systems of political organization provides an impetus to the formation of unilineal descent groups. This may be because unilineal descent groups provide individuals with unambiguous groups of persons who can fight or form alliances as discrete units.[27] As we have seen, one distinguishing feature of unilineal descent groups is that there is no ambiguity about an individual's membership. It is perfectly clear whether someone belongs to a particular clan, phratry, or moiety. It is this feature of unilineal descent groups that enables them to act as separate and distinct units—mostly, perhaps, in warfare.

Bilateral systems, in contrast, are ego-centered, and every person, other than siblings, has a slightly different set of kin to rely on. Consequently, in bilateral societies it is often not clear whom one can turn to and which person has responsibility for aiding another. Such ambiguity, however, might not be a liability in societies without warfare, or in societies with political systems that organize fighting in behalf of large populations.

Whether the presence of warfare is, in fact, the major condition responsible for transforming a unilocal society into a society with unilineal descent groups is still not certain. But however unilineal descent groups come into being, we know that they often fulfill many important functions in addition to their role in offense and defense.

Ambilineal Systems

Societies with ambilineal descent groups are far less numerous than unilineal or even bilateral societies. However, ambilineal societies resemble unilineal ones in many ways. For instance, the members of an ambilineal descent group believe they are descended from a common ancestor, though frequently they cannot specify all the genealogical links. The descent group is commonly named and may have an identifying emblem or even a totem; land and other productive resources

---

[24]Fred Eggan, *The Social Organization of the Western Pueblos* (Chicago: University of Chicago Press, 1950).

[25]Data from Textor, comp., *A Cross-Cultural Summary.*

[26]Ember, Ember, and Pasternak, "On the Development of Unilineal Descent."

[27]The importance of warfare and competition as factors in the formation of unilineal descent groups is also suggested by Service, *Primitive Social Organization;* and Marshall D. Sahlins, "The Segmentary Lineage: An Organization of Predatory Expansion," *American Anthropologist,* 63 (1961): 332–45.

may be owned by the descent group; and myths and religious practices are often associated with the group. Marriage is often regulated by group membership, just as in unilineal systems, though kin-group exogamy is not nearly as common as in unilineal systems. Moreover, ambilineal societies resemble unilineal ones in having various levels or types of descent groups. They may have lineages and higher orders of descent groups, distinguished (as in unilineal systems) by whether or not all the genealogical links to the supposed common ancestors are specified.[28]

The Samoans of the South Pacific are an example of an ambilineal society.[29] There are two types of ambilineal descent groups in Samoa, corresponding to what would be called clans and subclans in a unilineal society. Both groups are exogamous. Associated with each ambilineal clan are one or more chiefs. A group takes its name from the senior chief; subclans, of which there are always at least two, may take their names from junior chiefs.

The distinctiveness of the Samoan ambilineal system, compared with unilineal systems, is that because an individual may be affiliated with an ambilineal group through his or her father or mother (and his or her parents, in turn, could be affiliated with any of their parents' groups), there are a number of ambilineal groups to which that individual could belong. Affiliation with a Samoan descent group is optional, and a person may theoretically affiliate with any or all of the ambilineal groups to which he or she is related. In practice, however, a person is primarily associated with one group—the ambilineal group whose land he or she actually lives on and cultivates—although he or she may participate in the activities (housebuilding, for example) of several groups. Since a person may belong to more than one ambilineal group, the society is not divided into separate kin groups, in contrast with unilineal societies. Consequently, the core members of each ambilineal group cannot all live together (as they could in unilineal societies),

since each person belongs to more than one group and cannot live in several places at once.

Not all ambilineal societies have the multiple descent-group membership that occurs in Samoa. In some ambilineal societies, a person may belong (at any one time) to only one group. In such cases, the society can be divided into separate, nonoverlapping groups of kin.

Why do some societies have ambilineal descent groups? Although the evidence is not clear-cut on this point, it may be that societies with unilineal descent groups are transformed into ambilineal ones under special conditions—particularly in the presence of depopulation. We have already noted that depopulation may transform a previously unilocal society into a bilocal society. If that previously unilocal society also had unilineal descent groups, the descent groups may become transformed into ambilineal groups. If a society used to be patrilocal and patrilineal, for example, but some couples begin to live matrilocally, then their children may be associated with a previously patrilineal descent group (on whose land they may be living) through their mother. Once this happens regularly, the unilineal principle may become transformed into an ambilineal principle.[30] Thus, ambilineal descent systems may have developed recently as a result of depopulation caused by the introduction of European diseases.

Kinship Terminology

Our society, like all others, refers to a number of different kin by the same **classificatory term.** Most of us probably never stop to think about why we name relatives the way we do. For example, we call our mother's brother and father's brother (and often mother's sister's husband and father's sister's husband) by the same term—*uncle.* It is not that we are unable to distinguish between our mother's or father's brother or that we do not know the difference between **consanguineal kin** (blood kin) and **affinal kin** (kin by marriage, or what we call *in-laws*). Instead, it seems that in our society we do not usually find it necessary to distinguish between various types of uncles.

[28]William Davenport, "Nonunilinear Descent and Descent Groups," *American Anthropologist*, 61 (1959): 557–72.

[29]The description of the Samoan descent system is based upon Melvin Ember's 1955–1956 fieldwork. See also his "The Nonunilinear Descent Groups of Samoa," *American Anthropologist*, 61 (1959): 573–77; and Davenport, "Nonunilinear Descent and Descent Groups."

[30]Ember and Ember, "The Conditions Favoring Multilocal Residence."

However natural our system of classification may seem to us, countless field studies by anthropologists have revealed that societies differ markedly in how they group or distinguish relatives. The kinship terminology used in a society may reflect its prevailing kind of family, its rule of residence and its rule of descent, and other aspects of its social organization. Kin terms may also give clues to prior features of the society's social system, if, as many anthropologists believe,[31] the kin terms of a society are very resistant to change. The major systems of kinship terminology are the Omaha system, the Crow system, the Iroquois system, the Sudanese system, the Hawaiian system, and the Inuit (Eskimo) system.

Since it is the most familiar to us, let us first consider the kinship terminology system employed in our own and many other commercial societies. But it is by no means confined to commercial societies—in fact, this system is found in many Inuit (Eskimo) societies.

Inuit System

The distinguishing features of the Inuit system (see Figure 19–5) are that all cousins are lumped together under the same term but are distinguished from brothers and sisters, and all aunts and uncles are generally lumped under the same terms but are distinguished from mother and father. In Figure 19–5 and in subsequent figures, the kin types that are referred to by the same term are colored and marked in the same way; for example, in the Inuit system, kin types 2 (father's brother) and 6 (mother's brother) are referred to by the same term ("uncle" in English). Note that in this system, in contrast to the others we examine below, no other relatives are generally referred to by the same terms used for members of the nuclear family—mother, father, brother, and sister.

The Inuit type of kinship terminology is not generally found where there are unilineal or ambilineal descent groups; the only kin group that appears to be present is the bilateral kindred.[32] Remember that the kindred in a bilateral kinship sys-

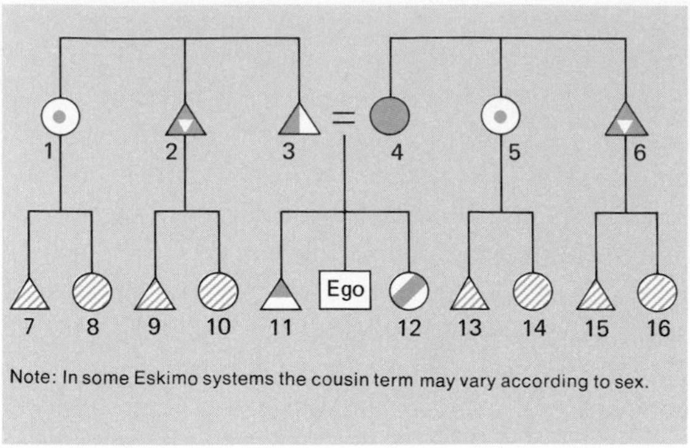

FIGURE 19–5 Inuit Kinship Terminology System

tem is an ego-centered group. Although relatives on both my mother's and my father's sides are equally important, my most important relatives are generally those closest to me. This is particularly true in our society, where the nuclear family generally lives alone, separated from and not particularly involved with other relatives except on ceremonial occasions. Since the nuclear family is most important, we would expect to find that the kin types in the nuclear family are distinguished terminologically from all other relatives. And since the mother's and father's sides are equally important (or unimportant), it makes sense that we use the same terms ("aunt," "uncle," and "cousin") for both sides of the family.

Omaha System

The Omaha system of kin terminology is named after the Omaha tribe of North America, but the system is found in many societies around the world, usually those with patrilineal descent.[33]

Referring to Figure 19–6, we can see immediately which types of kin are lumped together in an Omaha system. First, father and father's brother (numbers 2 and 3) are both referred to by the same term. This contrasts markedly with our way of classifying relatives, in which no term that applies to a member of the nuclear family (father, mother, brother, sister) is applied to any other relative.

---

[31]See, for example, Murdock, *Social Structure*, pp. 199–222.

[32]Reported in Textor, comp., *A Cross-Cultural Summary*.

[33]The association between the Omaha system and patrilineality is reported in Textor, comp., *A Cross-Cultural Summary*.

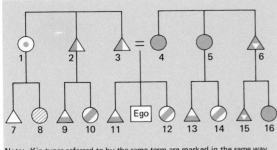

FIGURE 19–6 Omaha Kinship Terminology System

What could account for the Omaha system of lumping? One interpretation is that father and father's brother are lumped in this system because most societies in which this system is found have patrilineal kin groups. Both father and father's brother are in the parental generation of my patrilineal kin group and may behave toward me similarly. My father's brother also probably lives near me, since patrilineal societies usually have patrilocal residence. The term for father and father's brother, then, might be translated "male member of my patrilineal kin group in my father's generation."

A second lumping (which at first glance appears similar to the lumping of father and father's brother) is that of mother and mother's sister (4 and 5), both of whom are called by the same term. But more surprisingly, mother's brother's daughter (16) is also referred to by this term. Why should this be? If we think of the term as meaning "female member of my mother's patrilineage of *any* generation," then the term makes more sense. Consistent with this view, all the male members of my mother's patrilineage of any generation (mother's brother, 6; mother's brother's son, 15) are also referred to by one term.

It is apparent, then, that relatives on the father's and the mother's sides are grouped differently in this system. For members of my mother's patrilineal kin group, I lump all male members together and all female members together regardless of their generation. Yet, for members of my father's patrilineal kin group, I have different terms for the male and female members of different gen-

erations. Murdock has suggested that a society lumps kin types when there are more similarities than differences among them.[34]

Using this principle, and recognizing that societies with an Omaha system usually are patrilineal, I realize that my father's patrilineal kin group is the one to which I belong and in which I have a great many rights and obligations. Consequently, persons of my father's generation are likely to behave quite differently toward me than are persons of my own generation. Members of my patrilineal group in my father's generation are likely to exercise authority over me, and I am required to show them respect. Members of my patrilineal group in my own generation are those I am likely to play with as a child and to be friends with. Thus, in a patrilineal system, persons on my father's side belonging to different generations are likely to be distinguished. On the other hand, my mother's patrilineage is relatively unimportant to me (since I take my descent from my father). And because my residence is probably patrilocal, my mother's relatives will probably not even live near me. Thus, inasmuch as my mother's patrilineal relatives are comparatively unimportant in such a system, they become similar enough to be lumped together.

Finally, in the Omaha system, I refer to my male parallel cousins (my father's brother's son, 9, and my mother's sister's son, 13) in the same way I refer to my brother (number 11). I refer to my female parallel cousins (my father's brother's daughter, 10, and my mother's sister's daughter, 14) in the same way I refer to my sister (12). Considering that my father's brother and mother's sister are referred to by the same terms I use for my father and mother, this lumping of parallel cousins with **siblings** (brothers and sisters) is not surprising. If I call my own mother's and father's children (other than myself) "Brother" and "Sister," then the children of anyone whom I also call "Mother" and "Father" ought to be called "Brother" and "Sister" as well.

Crow System

The Crow system, named after another North American tribe, has been called the mirror image of the Omaha system. The same principles of

[34]Murdock, *Social Structure*, p. 125.

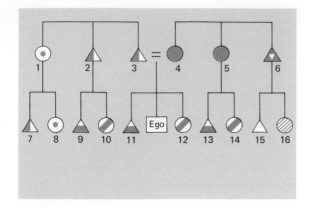

FIGURE 19–7 Crow Kinship Terminology
System

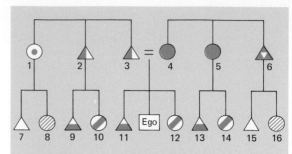

Note: Although not shown in this diagram, in the Iroquois system, parallel
cousins are sometimes referred to by different terms than one's own
brother and sister.

FIGURE 19–8 Iroquois Kinship Terminology
System

lumping kin types are employed, except that since the Crow system is associated with matrilineal descent,[35] the individuals in my mother's matrilineal group (which is my own) are not lumped across generations, whereas the individuals in my father's matrilineal group are. By comparing Figure 19–7 with Figure 19–6, we find that the lumping and separating of kin types are much the same in both, except that the lumping across generations in the Crow system appears on the father's side rather than on the mother's side. In other words, I call both my mother and my mother's sister by the same term (since both are female members of my matrilineal descent group in my mother's generation). I call my father, my father's brother, and my father's sister's son by the same term (all male members of my father's matrilineal group in any generation). I call my father's sister and my father's sister's daughter by the same term (both female members of my father's matrilineal group). And I refer to my parallel cousins in the same way I refer to my brother and sister.

Iroquois System

The Iroquois system, named after the Iroquois tribe of North America, is similar to both the Omaha and Crow systems in the way in which I refer to relatives in my parents' generation (see Figure 19–8). That is, my father and my father's brother (2 and 3) are referred to by the same term,

and my mother and my mother's sister (4 and 5) are referred to by the same term. However, the Iroquois system differs from the Omaha and Crow systems regarding my own generation. In the Omaha and Crow systems, one set of cross-cousins was lumped in the kinship terminology with the generation above. This is not true in the Iroquois system, where both sets of cross-cousins (mother's brother's children, 15 and 16, and father's sister's children, 7 and 8) are referred to by the same terms, distinguished by sex. That is, mother's brother's daughter and father's sister's daughter are both referred to by the same term. Also, mother's brother's son and father's sister's son are referred to by the same term. Parallel cousins always have terms different from those for cross-cousins and are sometimes, but not always, referred to by the same terms as one's brother and sister.

Like the Omaha and Crow systems, the Iroquois system has different terms for relatives on the father's and mother's sides. Such differentiation tends to be associated with unilineal descent, which is not surprising since unilineal descent involves affiliation with either mother's or father's kin. Why Iroquois, rather than Omaha or Crow, terminology occurs in a unilineal society requires explanation. One possible explanation is that Omaha or Crow is likely to occur in a developed, as opposed to a developing or decaying, unilineal system.[36] Another possible explanation is that Iro-

[35]The association between the Crow system and matrilineality is reported in Textor, comp., A Cross-Cultural Summary.

[36]See Leslie A. White, "A Problem in Kinship Terminology," American Anthropologist, 41 (1939): 569–70.

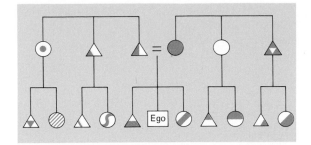

FIGURE 19–9 Sudanese Kinship Terminology System

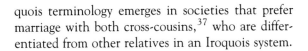

FIGURE 19–10 Hawaiian Kinship Terminology System

quois terminology emerges in societies that prefer marriage with both cross-cousins,[37] who are differentiated from other relatives in an Iroquois system.

Sudanese System

One other system of kinship terminology is associated with unilineal descent—the Sudanese system. But unlike the Omaha, Crow and Iroquois systems we have examined so far, the Sudanese system usually does not lump any relatives in the parents' and ego's generations. That is, the Sudanese system is usually a **descriptive** system, in which a different term is used for *each* of the relatives shown in Figure 19–9. What kinds of societies are likely to have such a system? Although societies with Sudanese terminology are likely to be patrilineal, they probably are different from most patrilineal societies that have Omaha or Iroquois terms. Sudanese terminology is associated with relatively great political complexity, class stratification, and occupational specialization. It has been suggested that under such conditions, a kinship system may reflect the need to make fine distinctions among members of descent groups who have different opportunities and privileges in the occupational or class system.[38]

The Omaha, Crow, Iroquois, and Sudanese systems, although different from one another and associated with somewhat different predictors, share one important feature: the terms used for the mother's and father's side of the family are not the

same. If you imagine folding the kinship terminology diagrams in half, the two sides would not be the same. As we have seen, in the Inuit system, the terms on the mother's and father's side of the family are *exactly* the same. This suggests that both sides of the family are equally important, or equally unimportant. The next system—Hawaiian—also has the same terms on both sides, but kinship outside the nuclear family is more important.

Hawaiian System

The Hawaiian system of kinship terminology is the least complex in that it uses the smallest number of terms. In this system, all relatives of the same sex in the same generation are referred to by the same term. Thus, all my female cousins are referred to by the same term as my sister; all male cousins are referred to by the same term as my brother. Everyone known to be related to me in my parents' generation is referred to by one term if female (including my mother) and by another term if male (including my father). (See Figure 19–10.)

Societies with Hawaiian kin terminology tend not to have unilineal descent groups,[39] which helps explain why kinship terms are the same on both sides of the family. Why are the terms for mother, father, sister, and brother used for other relatives? Perhaps because societies with Hawaiian terminology are likely to have large extended families[40] to which every type of relative in Figure 19–10 may belong because of alternative residence

[37]Jack Goody, "Cousin Terms," *Southwestern Journal of Anthropology,* 26 (1970): 125–42.

[38]Burton Pasternak, *Introduction to Kinship and Social Organization* (Englewood Cliffs, NJ: Prentice Hall, 1976), p. 142.

[39]Reported in Textor, comp., *A Cross-Cultural Summary.*
[40]Ibid.

patterns.[41] So, in contrast to our own society, many kin are quite important, a fact which seems to be reflected in the practice of referring to other relatives with the same terms that are used for nuclear family members.

[41]This conjecture is based on the authors' unpublished cross-cultural research.

SUMMARY

1. In our society, and in many other industrial societies, a newly married couple usually establishes a place of residence apart from parents or relatives (neolocal residence). But about 95 percent of the world's societies have some pattern of residence whereby the new couple settles within, or very close to, the household of the parents or some other close relative of the groom or bride.

2. The four major patterns in which married couples live with or near kinsmen are these:

    a. Patrilocal residence: the couple lives with or near the husband's parents (67 percent of all societies).

    b. Matrilocal residence: the couple lives with or near the wife's parents (15 percent of all societies).

    c. Bilocal residence: the couple lives with or near either the husband's parents or the wife's parents (7 percent of all societies).

    d. Avunculocal residence: the son and his wife settle with or near his mother's brother (4 percent of all societies).

3. In most societies where kinship connections are important, a rule allocates each person to a particular and definable set of kin. The rules affiliating individuals with sets of kin are called rules of descent.

4. Rules of descent affiliate individuals with different sets of kin. There are only a few known rules of descent:

    a. Patrilineal descent affiliates an individual with kin of both sexes related to him or her through men only. In each generation, then, children belong to the kin group of their father.

    b. Matrilineal descent affiliates an individual with kin related to him or her through women only. In each generation, then, children belong to the kin group of their mother.

    c. Ambilineal descent affiliates an individual with kin related to him or her through either men or women. Consequently, the descent groups show both female and male genealogical links.

5. Societies without lineal-descent rules are bilateral societies. Relatives on both the mother's and father's sides of the family are of equal importance or (more usually) unimportance. Kindreds are ego-centered sets of kin who may be called together temporarily for some purpose.

6. With unilineal descent (patrilineal or matrilineal), people usually refer to themselves as belonging to a particular unilineal group or set of groups because they believe they share common descent in either the male or the female line. These people form what is called a unilineal descent group. There are several types:

    a. Lineages, or sets of kin whose members trace descent from a common ancestor through known links.

    b. Clans, or sets of kin who believe they are descended from a common ancestor but cannot specify the genealogical links.

    c. Phratries, or groups of supposedly related clans.

    d. Moieties, two unilineal descent groups (constituting the whole society) without specified links to the supposed common ancestor.

7. Unilineal descent groups are most common in societies in the middle range of cultural complexity—that is, in noncommercial food-producing (as opposed to food-collecting) societies. In such societies, unilineal descent groups often have important functions in the social, economic, political, and religious realms of life.

8. Societies differ markedly in how they group or distinguish relatives under the same or different kinship terms. The major systems of terminology are the Inuit (Eskimo), Omaha, Crow, Iroquois, Sudanese, and Hawaiian systems.

EMBER, M., AND EMBER, C. R. *Marriage, Family, and Kinship: Comparative Studies of Social Organization.* New Haven: HRAF Press, 1983. A collection of reprinted cross-cultural and cross-species studies testing possible explanations of some aspects of human social organization. Relevant to this chapter are the studies of variation in marital residence and the development of unilineal descent.

FOX, R. *Kinship and Marriage: An Anthropological Perspective.* Cambridge: Cambridge University Press, 1983. An introduction to social organization, focusing on issues and principles in the study of various kinship groups.

LEVINSON, D., AND MALONE, M. J., eds. *Toward Explaining Human Culture: A Critical Review of the Findings of Worldwide Cross-Cultural Research.* New Haven: HRAF Press, 1980. Chapter 9 reviews the cross-cultural research literature on marital residence, descent groups, and kinship terminology.

MURDOCK, G. P. *Social Structure.* New York: Macmillan, 1949. A pioneering cross-cultural analysis of variation in a number of aspects of social organization, including the family and marriage, kin groups, kinship terminology, the incest taboo and its extensions, and the regulation of sex.

PASTERNAK, B. *Introduction to Kinship and Social Organization.* Englewood Cliffs, NJ: Prentice Hall, 1976. Chapters 4, 8, and 9 present a survey and critique of theories and evidence about variation in residence and kinship.

20

Associations and Interest Groups

S amuel Johnson, the eighteenth-century English author, was once asked to describe Boswell, his companion and biographer. "Boswell," he boomed, "is a very clubable man." Johnson did not mean that Boswell deserved to be attacked with bludgeons. He was referring to Boswell's fondness for all sorts of clubs and associations, a fondness he shared with many of his contemporaries. The tendency to form associations was not unique to eighteenth-century England. At all times and in all areas of the world, we find evidence of human beings' "clubability."

In this chapter, we examine the various kinds of associations formed in different societies, how these groups function, and what general purposes they serve. When we speak of **associations,** we mean a variety of different kinds of groups that are not based on kinship, as in the last chapter, or on territory, as in the next chapter. Associations, then, are nonkin and nonterritorial groups. And although they vary a lot, they also have a number of common characteristics: (1) some kind of formal, institutionalized structure; (2) the exclusion of some people; (3) members with common interests or purposes; and (4) members with a discernible sense of pride and feeling of belonging. Contemporary American society has an abundance of *interest groups*—to use the terminology of the political scientist—that display these general characteristics of associations. Such groups vary considerably in size and social significance, ranging from national organizations such as the Democratic and Republican parties to more local organizations such as college sororities or fraternities.

But societies differ considerably in the degree to which they have such associations and, if they do have them, in what kind they have. To make our discussion somewhat easier, we focus on two dimensions of how associations vary from one society to another. One is whether recruitment into the association is voluntary or not. In our society, with the exception of the drafting of men into the military, just about all our associations are voluntary—that is, people can choose to join or not join. But in many societies, particularly the more egalitarian ones, membership is nonvoluntary: all people of a particular category must belong.

A second dimension of variation in associations is what qualifies a person for membership. There are two possible kinds of qualifications:

TABLE 20–1 Some Examples of Associations

MEMBERSHIP CRITERIA	Recruitment	
	VOLUNTARY	NON-VOLUNTARY
Universally Ascribed		Age-sets Most unisex associations
Variably Ascribed	Ethnic associations Regional associations	Conscripted army
Achieved	Occupational associations Political parties Special interest groups	

those that are achieved and those that are ascribed. **Achieved qualities** are those an individual acquires during his or her lifetime, such as superior ballplaying skills or the skills required to be an electrician. **Ascribed qualities** are those determined for a person at birth, either because of genetic makeup (for instance, sex) or because of family background (for instance, ethnicity, place of birth, religion, social class). We speak of two kinds of ascribed characteristics: **universally ascribed characteristics,** those that are found in all societies (such as age and sex), and **variably ascribed characteristics,** those that are found only in some societies (such as ethnic, religious, or social-class differences). Table 20–1 gives these two dimensions of variation in associations (voluntary-nonvoluntary recruitment and criteria for membership) and some kinds of associations that fit neatly into our classification. Of course, some associations do not fit so neatly—for example, the criteria that qualify someone for Girl Scout membership include an interest in joining (an achieved quality) as well as sex (an ascribed characteristic).

Nonvoluntary Associations

Although complex societies may have nonvoluntary associations, such associations are more characteristic of relatively unstratified or egalitarian societies. In relatively unstratified societies, associations tend to be based on the universally ascribed characteristics of age and sex. Such associations take two forms: age-sets and male or female (unisex) associations.

Age-Sets

All societies utilize a vocabulary of age terms, just as they utilize a vocabulary of kinship terms. For instance, as we distinguish among *brother, uncle,* and *cousin,* so we differentiate *infant, adolescent,* and *adult.* Age terms refer to categories based on age, or **age-grades.** An age-grade is simply a category of persons who happen to fall within a particular, culturally distinguished age range. **Age-set,** on the other hand, is the term for a group of persons of similar age and the same sex who move through some or all of life's stages together. For example, all the boys of a certain age range in a particular district might simultaneously become ceremonially initiated into "manhood." Later in life, the group as a whole might become "elders," and still later "retired elders." Entry into an age-set system is generally nonvoluntary and is based on the universally ascribed characteristics of sex and age.

Kinship forms the basis of the organization and administration of most noncommercial societies. However, there are some societies in which age-sets crosscut kinship ties and form strong supplementary bonds. Two such societies are the Karimojong of East Africa and the Shavante of Brazil.

Karimojong Age-Sets. The Karimojong number some 60,000 people. Predominantly cattle herders, they occupy about 4,000 acres of semiarid country in northeastern Uganda. Their society is especially interesting because of its organization into combinations of age-sets and generation-sets. These groupings provide "both the source of political authority and the main field within which it is exercised."[1]

A Karimojong age-set comprises all the men who have been initiated into manhood within a span of about five to six years. A generation-set consists of a combination of five such age-sets, covering twenty-five to thirty years. Each generation-set is seen as "begetting" the one that immediately follows it, and at any one time two generation-sets are in corporate existence. The senior

unit—whose members perform the administrative, judicial, and priestly functions—is closed; the junior unit, whose members serve as warriors and police, is still recruiting. When all five age-sets in the junior generation-set are established, that generation-set will be ready (actually impatient) to assume the status of its senior predecessor. Eventually, grumbling but realistic, the elders will agree to a succession ceremony, moving those who were once in a position of obedience to a position of authority.

The Karimojong age system, then, comprises a cyclical succession of four generation-sets in a predetermined continuing relationship. The *retired generation-set* consists of elders who have passed on the mantle of authority, since most of the five age-sets within the retired generation-set are depleted, if not defunct. The *senior generation-set* contains the five age-sets that actively exercise authority. The *junior generation-set* is still recruiting members and, although obedient to elders, has some administrative powers. The *noninitiates* are starting a generation-set.

The significance of the age- and generation-sets of Karimojong society is that they give partic-

FIGURE 20–1

The Karimojong age system is compsed of four distinct generation-sets (labeled A, B, C, and D in this diagram), which succeed each other cyclically. Each generation-set, in turn, is divided into five age-sets or potential age-sets. The senior generation-set (A) exercises authority. The junior age set (B)—the warriors and policemen—is still recruiting. Generation-set D consists of retired age-sets. Noninitiated and not-yet-born boys constitute the potential age-sets C1–C5.

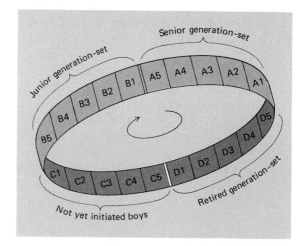

[1]Neville Dyson-Hudson, *Karimojong Politics* (Oxford: Clarendon Press, 1966), p. 155. This section draws from Ibid.

An elder age-set among the Karimojong is seated for a public ritual.

ular importance to initiation into manhood. Initiation ceremonies are elaborate and fall into three parts, all supervised by the elders. The first part, called "spearing the ox," takes place in a ceremonial enclosure. Each initiate spears a beast from his family's herd and dismembers it according to a ritual pattern. The head and neck are carried away by the women for use in the later stages of the ceremony; the stomach sacs are carefully laid out unopened. The oldest tribal elder present and the leader of the local senior generation-set slit the sacs with a spear and anoint each initiate with the semidigested food that spills out. They then bless the initiate with the words "Be well. Grow old. Become wealthy in stock. Become an elder."

In the second part of the ceremony, "eating the tongue," the meat previously taken away by the women is boiled in clay pots and served to the men of the senior generation-set in the settlement, who bless the initiate and his family. The final part, "cooking the stomach," takes place in the cattle corral, where a feast is held. The elders, the other adult men, and the initiates all sit and eat, each group in a separate circle. Before the initiation ceremony began, each boy was required to shave his head; after it, he is allowed to let his hair grow. Once his hair is sufficiently long, the initiate plasters it with mud and ties it back with a chain — the tangible symbol of adult status.

Once initiated, a boy has become a man, one with a clearly defined status and the ultimate certainty of exercising full authority together with his set partners. Indeed, a Karimojong is not expected to marry — and is certainly barred from starting a family — until he has been initiated. The initiation ceremony itself illustrates the essential political and social characteristics of the age-set system. Without the authority of the elders, the ceremony cannot be held; throughout the proceedings their authority is explicit. The father-son relationship of adjacent generation-sets is emphasized, for fathers are initiating their sons.

Shavante Age-Sets. The Shavante inhabit the Mato Grosso region of Brazil. Until recently, they were extremely hostile to Brazilians of European ancestry who tried to move into their territory. It was not until the 1950s that peaceful contact with the 2,000 or so Shavante was achieved. Although the Shavante have some agriculture, they rely primarily on food collection. Wild roots, nuts, and fruits are their staple foods, and hunting is their passion.[2] The Shavante have villages, but they rarely stay in them for more than a few weeks at a time. Instead they make frequent community treks lasting six to twenty-four weeks to hunt or collect. They spend no more than four weeks a year at their gardens, which are located at least a day's journey from the villages.

Age-sets are an extremely important part of Shavante society, particularly for males. Boys emerge from the status of childhood when they are formally inducted into a named age-set and take up residence in the "bachelor hut." An induction ceremony takes place every five years, and boys from seven to twelve years of age are inducted at the same time. The five-year period of residence in the bachelor hut is relatively free of responsibility: the boys' families provide food for them, and they go out hunting and collecting when they feel like it. But during the five-year period they are instructed in hunting, weapon making, and ceremonial skills. At the end of this period, a much more elaborate series of initiation ceremonies marks the entry by these boys into a different status—that of "young men." The day they emerge from the bachelor hut for the last time, during the final rites of initiation, the whole age-set is married, each to a small girl, usually not yet mature, chosen by the boys' parents. Marriages cannot be consummated at this time, since the young men must wait until their wives are more mature. When the ceremonies are over, the young men make war clubs, for they are thought of now as the warriors of the community, and they earn the privilege of sitting in the evening village council. But they have no authority at this stage and few responsibilities.

The next stage is that of the "mature men," and when an age-set is inducted into this stage the members begin to experience some authority. It is in the mature men's council that important community decisions are made. This last status position actually consists of five consecutive age-sets (because new age-sets are formed every five years and each one continues in existence until the death of its members). Among the mature men the oldest sets are considered senior to the junior ones. Members of the most junior mature men's age-set rarely talk in the council; they assert themselves more as they progress in the system.

In contrast to the Karimojong, who have age-sets just for males, the Shavante also have them for females. Shavante girls are inducted into an age-set when boys about their age enter the bachelor hut, but they belong to the age-set in name only. They do not participate in the bachelor hut (nor do they have their own equivalent), they are not initiated, and they cannot participate in the village council, which makes community decisions. About the only thing the age-set gives them is occasional participation with males in a few ceremonies. For Shavante women, then, the age-set system does not function as an association.

Unisex Associations

Unisex, as used here, has quite a different meaning from its current connotation in our own society, where it signifies something that is suitable for both sexes. We use the word **unisex** to describe a type of association that restricts its membership to one sex, usually male. Sex as a qualification is directly related to the purpose of the unisex association. In many male unisex associations, this purpose is to strengthen the concept of male superiority and to offer men a refuge from females. In noncommercial societies, men's associations are similar to age-sets, except that there are only two sets, or stages—mature males, who are association members, and immature males, who are nonmembers.

In most noncommercial societies, women have few associations. Perhaps this is because in such societies the men are generally dominant in the kinship, property, and political spheres of life. (There is also the possibility that anthropologists, most of whom were men, have given women's associations less attention than men's associations.) In some partly commercialized economies, such as in West Africa, women's associations are more common.

[2]This section is based on David Maybury-Lewis, *Akwe-Shavante Society* (Oxford: Clarendon Press, 1967).

These associations appear to give women considerably more power than they might otherwise have.[3] Unisex associations or clubs are also a feature of very industrialized societies. The Boy Scouts and the Kiwanis, the Girl Scouts and the League of Women Voters, are cases in point. Admission to these clubs, however, is voluntary; in noncommercial and less complex societies, recruitment is more often nonvoluntary.

Mae Enga Bachelor Associations. The Mae Enga are a subgroup of about 30,000 sedentary horticulturalists living in the New Guinea highlands. Their society has received a great deal of attention from anthropologists for its practice of sexual segregation—indeed, for the strain of active hostility to women that runs through its culture.[4] It is the custom for Mae men to live in a separate, communal house. Up to the age of five, a young boy is permitted to live in his mother's house, although he is unconsciously aware of the "distance" between his father and mother. As he grows older, this awareness is made explicit by his father and elder clansmen. It is undesirable, he is told, to be so much in the company of women; it is better that he join the menfolk in their house and in their activities. As the boy grows up, the need to avoid contact with women is made abundantly clear to him. He is told that contact with menstrual blood or menstruating women, if not countered by magic rites, can "pollute" a man. It can "corrupt his vital juices so that his skin darkens and wrinkles and his flesh wastes, permanently dull his wits, and eventually lead to a slow decline and death."[5]

Since Mae culture regards a woman as potentially unclean, to say the least, it enforces strict codes of male-female behavior. These codes are designed to safeguard male integrity, strength, and possession of crops and other property. So strict are these regulations that many young men are reluc-

tant to marry. However, the elders do try to impress upon the young men their duty to marry and reproduce. The men's association attempts to regulate the males' sexual relationships. The association is said to have several purposes: to cleanse and strengthen its members; to promote their growth; to make them attractive to women; and, most important, to supervise contact between the sexes so that ultimately the "right" wives are procured for the men and the "right" children are born into the clan.

By the time he is fifteen or sixteen, a Mae youth has joined the village bachelors' association. He agrees to take scrupulous care neither to copulate with a woman nor to accept food from her hands. As a club member, he will participate in the *sanggai* rituals. Bachelors, under the supervision of senior club members, go into seclusion, in a clubhouse deep in the forest, to undergo "purification." During four days of "exercises" (which are rather similar in purpose to those of a religious retreat), each youth observes additional prohibitions to protect himself from all forms of sexuality and impurity. For instance, pork is denied him (women have cared for the pigs), and he may not look at the ground during excursions into the forest, lest he see feminine footprints or pig feces. His body will be scrubbed, his dreams discussed and interpreted. Finally, together with his club, now restored to purity and reprotected at least for a while against contamination, he will participate in organized dances and feasting with his chosen lady.

In Mae society, then, it would seem that the battle of the sexes has been won decisively by the men, though at the price, it might well be argued, of some repression and internal tension. How does the Mae bachelor organization fit into the general social context? What sort of function does it fulfill? On an individual level, bachelor associations may strengthen, and attempt to reaffirm, a man's feeling of masculinity. On a community level, the association organizes the fighting strength of the village. The *sanggai* festivals afford the entire clan an opportunity to display its size, solidarity, and magnificence to its enemies, whom on other occasions it fights. Hostility toward women may not be surprising in view of the fact that a man's wife and mother come from neighboring clans (the Mae clan villages are exogamous) perpetually in conflict with his own. Male-female hostility, then, seems

[3]Nancy B. Leis, "Women in Groups: Ijaw Women's Associations," in Michelle Z. Rosaldo and Louise Lamphere, eds., *Woman, Culture, and Society* (Stanford, CA: Stanford University Press, 1974), pp. 223–42.

[4]M. J. Meggitt, "Male-Female Relationships in the Highlands of Australian New Guinea," *American Anthropologist*, 66 (special issue, 1964): 204–24.

[5]Ibid., p. 207. For why men in some societies may fear sex with women, see Carol R. Ember, "Men's Fear of Sex with Women: A Cross-Cultural Study," *Sex Roles*, 4 (1978): 657–78.

A men's house in a Chimbu village in the highlands of New Guinea.

to reflect the broader, interclan hostility. The Mae have a succinct way of describing the situation: "We marry the people we fight."[6]

Men's houses, and occasionally women's, are found among many peoples, especially in Melanesia, Polynesia, Africa, and South America. Men's associations generally involve bachelors, although older married men will often come by to instruct the youngsters and pass on the benefits of their experience. In more militant days, men's houses acted as fortresses and arsenals—even as sanctuaries for fugitives. By and large, they serve to strengthen—certainly to symbolize—male power and solidarity. As do age-sets, men's clubs often provide ties that cut across and supplement kinship bonds. Hence, they permit a given group of men in a given society to act together toward the realization of mutually agreed-upon objectives, irrespective of kin relationships.

Ijaw Women's Associations. Among the Ijaw of southern Nigeria, only women in the northern part of this society are organized into associations. In one northern Ijaw village there are seven women's associations.[7] Once a married woman shows herself capable of supporting a household independent of her mother-in-law, which she does by engaging in marketing and trading, she has to belong to the women's association linked to her husband's patrilineage. Membership in such an association is nonvoluntary; all eligible women must join, and members are fined if they do not come to meetings or come late.

The women's associations have considerable power. They act as mediators in disputes and im-

[6]Meggitt, "Male-Female Relationships in the Highlands of Australian New Guinea," p. 218.

[7]Leis, "Women in Groups."

Women organize cooperatives in Togo to sell pottery.

pose punishments even in cases that have gone to court. For example, an association may impose fines for "crimes" such as defaming a woman's character or adultery. An association may also adopt rules for proper behavior. Judgments and rules are arrived at by consensus of all the women members. If a punished member does not accept a judgment, the other members might get together and taunt the woman, or take some important item from her house and refuse to have anything to do with her.

Some of the larger associations also act as lending institutions, using their cash reserves from fines to lend to members or nonmembers at an interest rate of 50 percent or more. Even a male in debt to the association might be held captive in his own house until he pays his debt. (It is no wonder, then, that few resist an association's judgment for long.) Although it is not clear why women's associations such as the Ijaw's are common in West Africa, one of the factors that may have been important is the women's participation in marketing and trade, which allows them to be financially independent of men.

Voluntary Associations

Although voluntary associations are found in some relatively simple societies, such as the military associations of the Cheyenne Indians, they tend to be more common in stratified and complex societies. Presumably this is because stratified societies are composed of people with many different, and often competing, interests. We deal here with some examples of voluntary associations that are not familiar in American experience.

Military Associations

Military associations in noncommercial societies may be compared to our own American Legion or Veterans of Foreign War posts. They all seem to exist to unite members through their common experiences as warriors, to glorify the activities of war, and to perform certain services for the community. Membership in such associations is usually voluntary and based on the achieved criterion of participation in war. Among the North American

A volunteer firemen's association in Ulster County, New York.

Plains Indians, military societies were common. The Cheyenne Indians, for example, had military associations that were not ranked by age, being open to any boy or man ready to go to war.[8]

Originally, the Cheyenne had five military associations: the Fox, the Dog, the Shield, the Elk (or Hoof Rattle), and the Bowstring (or Contrary). The last-named association was annihilated by the Pawnee in the middle of the nineteenth century. Later, two new associations were established, the Wolf and the Northern Crazy Dogs. Although the various associations may have had different costumes, songs, and dances, they were alike in their internal organization, each being headed by four leaders who were among the most important war chiefs.

Several of the Cheyenne military associations selected four virgin daughters of tribal leaders to serve as "maids of honor." These girls participated in the associations' ceremonies and sat with the war chiefs during council meetings. Although women had no political authority, they were highly respected among the Cheyenne. The maids of honor of the military associations were looked upon as reflecting the ideals of female chastity and deportment. So important was the virtue of female chastity among the Cheyenne that a defiled maid of honor was believed to bring bad luck to the warriors of the association. As a result, the Dog and

[8]E. Adamson Hoebel, *The Cheyennes: Indians of the Great Plains* (New York: Holt, Rinehart & Winston, 1960.)

Contrary associations were unwilling to take the risk of having maids of honor affiliated with them.

Regional Associations

Regional associations are clubs that bring together migrants from a common geographical background. Thus, they are often found in urban centers, which traditionally have attracted rural settlers. Membership is based on common regional origin. In the United States, for example, migrants from rural Appalachia have formed associations in Chicago and Detroit. Many of these organizations have become vocal political forces in municipal government.

William Mangin has described the role of regional associations in helping rural migrants adapt to urban life in Lima, Peru.[9] During the 1950s, Mangin studied a group of migrants from the rural mountains, the *serranos* from Ancash. Typically these *serranos*, about 120,000 in number, live in a slumlike urban settlement called a *barriada*. The *barriada* is not officially recognized by either the national government or the city authorities. Accordingly, it lacks all normal city services, such as water supply, garbage removal, and police protection. Its inhabitants have left their rural birthplaces for reasons generally typical of such population movements, whether they occur in South America or in West Africa. These reasons are generally social and economic, related to population and land pressure. However, the higher expectations associated with the big city—better education, social mobility, wage labor—are also compelling considerations.

Typically also, the *serranos* from Ancash have formed a regional association. Club membership is open to both sexes. Men generally control the executive positions, and club leaders are often men who achieved political power in their hometowns. Women, who have relatively less economic and social freedom, nevertheless play an important part in club activities.

The *serrano* regional association performs a number of services for its members. First, it lobbies the central government on matters of community

[9]William P. Mangin, "The Role of Regional Associations in the Adaptation of Rural Migrants to Cities in Peru," in Dwight B. Heath and Richard N. Adams, eds., *Contemporary Cultures and Societies of Latin America* (New York: Random House, 1965), pp. 311–23.

importance—for example, the supplying of sewers, clinics, and similar public services. This requires a club member to follow a piece of legislation through the channels of government to make certain it is not forgotten or abandoned. Second, the *serrano* association assists in acculturating newly arrived *serranos* to the urban life in Lima. The most noticeable rural traits—coca chewing, and hairstyle and clothing peculiarities—are the first to disappear, with the men generally able to adapt faster than the women. The association also provides opportunities for fuller contact with the national culture. And finally, the group organizes social activities such as fiestas, acts as the clearinghouse for information transmitted to and from the home area, and supplies a range of other services to help migrants adapt to their new environment while retaining ties to their birthplace.

In general, as Mangin's study reveals, regional clubs help to integrate their members into a more complex urban environment. However, on occasion they aggravate local rivalries—especially those that may have developed among interest groups in the hometown. But since club membership is voluntary, it is not uncommon for a dissatisfied group to break away and establish its own club.

Ethnic Associations

There are many types of ethnic interest groups, and they are found in cities all over the world. Membership in these associations is based on ethnicity. Ethnic associations are particularly widespread in urban centers of West Africa. There, accelerated cultural change—reflected in altered economic arrangements, in technological advances, and in new urban living conditions—has weakened kinship relations and other traditional sources of support and solidarity.[10] Sometimes it is difficult to say whether a particular association is ethnic or regional in origin; it may be both.

Tribal unions are frequently found in Nigeria and Ghana. These are typical of most such associations in that they are extraterritorial (that is, they recruit members who have left their tribal locations), they have a formal constitution, and they have been formed to meet certain needs arising out of conditions of urban life. One such need is to keep members in touch with their traditional culture. The Ibo State Union, for example, in addition to providing mutual aid and financial support in case of unemployment, sickness, or death, performs the service "of fostering and keeping alive an interest in tribal song, history, language and moral beliefs and thus maintaining a person's attachment to his native town or village."[11] Some tribal unions collect money to improve conditions in their ancestral homes. Education, for example, is an area of particular concern. Others publish newsletters that report members' activities. Most unions have a young membership that exercises a powerful democratizing influence in tribal councils, and the organizations provide a springboard for those with national political aspirations.

Friendly societies differ from tribal unions in that their objectives are confined for the most part to mutual aid. Such a club was formed by the wives of Kru migrants in Freetown, Sierra Leone. Kru men normally go to sea—still a hazardous occupation. The club is classified into three grades. An admission fee permits entry into the lowest grade. Elevation to higher grades depends on further donations. At the death of a member or her husband, the family receives a lump sum commensurate with her status in the club. The Yoruba Friendly Society in Nigeria uses another approach to mutual aid. At regular intervals all members contribute a fixed sum, and the total is given to one member at a time. In this way, significant amounts of capital are available, in rotation, for each member to buy trading stock, to purchase expensive new clothes (to keep up appearances in a government post, for example), or even to pay a bride price. Rotating credit associations, like the Yoruba Friendly Society, are found throughout Nigeria and in other countries of sub-Saharan Africa, and in Southeast Asia as well.

West African occupational clubs also fall into the ethnic category. They are African versions of trade unions, organized along tribal as well as craft

[10]See Kenneth Little, *West African Urbanization* (New York: Cambridge University Press, 1965); and Claude Meillassoux, *Urbanization of an African Community* (Seattle: University of Washington Press, 1968).

[11]Kenneth Little, "The Role of Voluntary Associations in West African Urbanization," *American Anthropologist,* 59 (1957): 582. The rest of this section draws on Ibid.

The Samba clubs or "schools" of Rio de Janeiro, Brazil are voluntary associations that compete during carnival time in the Sambadrome before hundreds of thousands of spectators. To become champion is like winning the World Series and Superbowl in the United States.

lines. Their principal concern is the status and remuneration of their members as workers. The Motor Drivers' Union of Keta, in Ghana, was formed to fund insurance and legal costs, to contribute to medical care in case of accident or illness, and to help pay for funeral expenses.

Finally, clubs that concentrate on entertainment and recreation are very common in West Africa. The dancing *compin* of Sierra Leone is typical. Kenneth Little describes it as

a group of young men and women concerned with the performance of "plays" of traditional music and dancing and with the raising of money for mutual benefit. . . . A "play" is generally given in connection with some important event . . . or as part of the ceremonies celebrating a wedding or a funeral. The general public as well as the persons honored by the performance are expected to donate money to the compin on these occasions. Money

is also collected in the form of weekly subscriptions from the members.[12]

Some observers have suggested that the widespread incidence of ethnic associations in West Africa has virtually amounted to a resurgence of tribalism. The presence of such interest groups in urban areas has indeed seemed to slow the development of national identity and loyalty. On the other hand, the evidence indicates that these clubs serve important adaptive and integrative functions for both men and women, just as regional associations do in other areas of the world. To quote Little again, "Their combination of modern and traditional traits constitutes a cultural bridge which conveys, metaphorically speaking, the tribal indi-

[12]Ibid., pp. 586–87.

vidual from one kind of sociological universe to another."[13]

Our examination of voluntary associations would not be complete without a passing mention of such organizations as trade unions, charitable organizations, political parties, and bridge clubs, of which there are tens of thousands in our own and other complex societies. In all these voluntary organizations, the qualities required for membership are achieved rather than ascribed. Generally, clubs of this category are more numerous where the society is larger and more diversified. They serve to bring together sets of people with common interests, aspirations, or qualifications. Opportunities to work for what are regarded as worthwhile social goals, for self-improvement, or to satisfy a need for new and stimulating experiences are among the many motivations for joining clubs. Not the least is identification with a corporate body, and through it the acquisition of status and influence.

"Secret Societies"

There is usually some secrecy in all associations, as in social life in general. For example, at least some of the reasons for decisions may be kept confidential. But an extraordinary amount of secrecy seems to be required in those associations referred to as "secret societies." In these associations, it is believed that the membership or major activities, or both, must remain secret, and members who divulge the secrets are liable to be severely punished, even executed.

The Ku Klux Klan is a well-known example of a secret association. After the U.S. Civil War (1861–1865), when the votes of the former black slaves put members of the Republican Party in power in some Southern states, some white Southerners tried to reestablish their supremacy by force. They formed secret associations, which became the Ku Klux Klan, to terrorize white and black Republican leaders. Wearing white hoods and robes, they burned crosses, raped, and murdered. In 1871 Congress voted to give President Ulysses S. Grant the power to use federal troops to restore order in the areas of Klan violence. By the end of 1872, faced with soldiers who were empowered to arrest

suspects and hold them without trial, the Klan collapsed. But it did not disappear. Periodically, it would become active again, as for example in the 1950s and 1960s in response to the civil-rights movement.[14]

The Ku Klux Klan traditionally had secret membership and secret activities, some of which were illegal. For this reason, perhaps, people in the United States seem generally to disapprove of the Klan. But the secret associations in some places, for example the *Poro* and *Sande* associations of West Africa, are positively valued, perhaps because membership in them is required of all adults.

The Poro and Sande associations exist in a number of cultural groups, speaking Mande languages, that are located in what is now Liberia, Sierra Leone, the Ivory Coast, and Guinea. In Guinea, the Poro and the Sande were declared illegal, but in the other countries they are not only legal—they are an integral part of local political structure. Membership in them is public and nonvoluntary; all men in the community must belong to the Poro and all women must belong to the Sande.[15]

Where the Poro and the Sande associations are legal, the community has two political structures—the "secular" and the "sacred." The secular structure consists of the town chief, neighborhood and kin group headmen, and elders. The sacred structure or Zo consists of the hierarchies of "priests" in the Poro and Sande associations. Among the Kpelle of Liberia, for example, the Poro and Sande Zo take turns in assuming responsibility for dealing with in-town fighting, murder, rape, incest, and disputes over land.

So in what sense are the Poro and Sande secret? If all adults belong to them, their membership and what they do can hardly be described as secret. Furthermore, anthropologists have not only written about these associations; some have even joined them, as Beryl Bellman did among the Kpelle.[16] Bellman suggests that what is "secret" about these associations is the necessity for mem-

---

[13]Ibid., p. 593.

[14]Michael Les Benedict, "Ku Klux Klan," *Academic American Encyclopedia* (Princeton: Arete Publishing Co., 1980), vol. 12 (K–L), p. 133.

[15]Beryl L. Bellman, *The Language of Secrecy: Symbols & Metaphors in Poro Ritual* (New Brunswick, NJ: Rutgers University Press, 1984), pp. 8, 25–28, 33.

[16]Ibid., p. 8.

bers to learn to keep secrets, particularly about how people are initiated into membership. Only when people learn to keep secrets are they considered trustworthy for participation in political life.

The Poro leadership establishes the place where the initiates will undergo scarification and live in seclusion for about a year (formerly it was three or four years). The boys are taken out of town where they engage in a mock battle with a *ngamu* (a member of the Poro masquerading as a forest "devil") who incises marks on their necks, chests, and backs. These marks symbolize being killed and eaten by the devil; but then the initiates are "reborn." In the initiation "village" outside of town, the boys learn crafts, hunting, and the use of basic medicines. The children of the Zo are given special instruction so that they can take over the rituals from their fathers. Some are trained to perform as "devils." At the end of the year, the initiates are given Poro names, by which they will be known from then on. Secrecy is attached to events surrounding the initiates; everyone knows that the boys are not killed and eaten by the devil, but only some can speak of it. For example, women must say that the boys are in the devil's stomach; if they say otherwise, they might be killed in punishment.[17]

The initiation of females into the Sande also involves taking the initiates into the forest for a year (formerly three years). The girls not only undergo scarification; they also undergo a clitoridectomy (removal of the clitoris). Like the boys, the girls receive training in adult activities. In the years just before and during the Sande initiation (which occurs every seven years or so), the women are responsible for the moral behavior of the community. Those who commit crimes are first brought before the women; if a man is the accused, he is tried by the Poro Zo, but a portion of any fine is given to the women.[18]

The Poro and Sande Zo are held in great respect and the devils are viewed with fear and awe for the powers they possess. Some authors suggest that fear of the Poro and the Sande strengthens

the hands of secular political authority, since chiefs and landowners occupy the most powerful positions in the associations.[19]

Secret associations are common in many areas of the world—the Pacific, North and South America, as well as various parts of Africa. In Africa, judging by a recent cross-cultural study, secret associations are usually involved in political activities, as are the Poro and Sande. Usually, in Africa, these activities punish people who, according to the secret society, have committed some wrongs. The punished people almost never seem to be members of the native elite or foreign rulers, which supports the observation about the Poro and Sande that they typically strengthen the hand of existing political authority.[20]

Explaining Variation in Associations

Anthropologists are not content to provide descriptions of the structure and operation of human associations. They also seek to understand why different types of associations develop. For example, what may account for the development of age-set systems?

S. N. Eisenstadt's comparative study of African age-sets leads him to the hypothesis that when kinship groups fail to carry out functions important to the integration of society—such as political, educational, and economic functions—age-set systems arise to fill the void. Age-set systems may provide a workable solution to a society's need for functional divisions among its members. This is because age is a criterion that can be applied to all members of society in the allocation of roles.[21] But it is not at all clear why age-set systems arise to fill the void left by lack of kinship organization. Many societies have kin structures that are limited in

---

[17]Ibid., pp. 8, 80-88.

[18]Ibid., pp. 33, 80; also Caroline H. Bledsoe, *Women and Marriage in Kpelle Society* (Stanford, CA: Stanford University Press, 1980), p. 67.

[19]Kenneth Little, "The Political Function of the Poro," *Africa*, 35 (1965): 349–65; and 36 (1966): 62–71; Bledsoe, *Women and Marriage in Kpelle Society*, pp. 68–70.

[20]Karen Paige Ericksen, "Male and Female Age Organizations and Secret Societies in Africa," *Behavior Science Research*, 23 (1989): 234–64.

[21]S. N. Eisenstadt, "African Age Groups," *Africa*, 24 (1954): 102.

scope, yet the majority of them have not adopted an age-set system.

B. Bernardi, in his critical evaluation of Nilo-Hamitic age-set systems,[22] also suggests that age-set systems arise to make up for a deficiency in social organization. But, in contrast with Eisenstadt, Bernardi specifically suggests why more social organization is necessary and what particular deficiencies in the previous form of organization should favor development of age-sets. He hypothesizes that age-set systems arise in societies that have a history of territorial rivalry, lack central authority, and have only dispersed kin groups. When all three factors are present, he argues, the need for a mechanism of territorial integration is supplied by an age-set system.

A cross-cultural study suggests that territorial rivalry, as indicated by warfare, may favor the development of age-set systems, but this study found no evidence to support Bernardi's hypothesis that age-sets develop in societies that lack central authority and have only dispersed kin groups.[23] So it does not seem that age-set societies are generally more deficient in political or kinship organization. An alternative explanation, which is consistent with the cross-cultural evidence, is that age-set systems arise in societies that have both frequent warfare and local groups that change in size and composition through the year. In such situations, men may not always be able to rely on their kinsmen for cooperation in warfare because the kinsmen are not always nearby. Age-sets, however, can provide allies *wherever* one happens to be.[24] This interpretation suggests that age-set systems arise *in addition to*, rather than as alternatives to, kin-based and politically based forms of integration.[25]

As for voluntary associations whose membership is variably ascribed (that is, determined at birth but not found in all persons of a given age-sex category), it is difficult to say exactly what causes them to arise. There are suggestions that voluntary associations become more numerous (and more important) as the society harboring them advances in technology, complexity, and scale. No definitive evidence is yet available to support this explanation, but the following trends seem to be sufficiently established to merit consideration.

First, there is urbanization. Developing societies are becoming urban, and as their cities grow, so does the number of people separated from their traditional kinship ties and local customs. It is not surprising, then, that the early voluntary associations should be mutual-aid societies, established first to take over kin obligations in case of death, and later broadening their benefits in other directions. In this respect, the recent associations of the developing African societies closely resemble the early English laboring-class associations. Those clubs also served to maintain the city migrant's contacts with former traditions and culture. The regional associations in Latin America resemble the regional associations of European immigrants in the United States. Such associations also seem to arise in response to the migrant's or immigrant's needs in the new home.

Second, there is an economic factor. Migrants and immigrants try to adapt to new economic conditions, and group interests in the new situations have to be organized, promoted, and protected.

Why, then, do variably ascribed associations tend to be replaced by clubs of the achieved category in highly industrialized societies? Perhaps the strong focus on specialization in industrialized societies is reflected in the formation of specialized groups. Possibly the emphasis on achievement in industrialized societies is another contributing factor. Perhaps, too, the trend toward uniformity, encouraged by mass marketing and the mass media, is progressively weakening the importance of regional and ethnic distinctions. The result seems to be that the more broadly based organizations are being replaced by more narrowly based associations that are more responsive to particular needs not being met by the institutions of mass society.

Why associations we call "secret societies" have developed in various parts of the world still requires investigation.

[22]B. Bernardi, "The Age-System of the Nilo-Hamitic Peoples," *Africa*, 22 (1952): 316–32.

[23]Madeline Lattman Ritter, "The Conditions Favoring Age-Set Organization," *Journal of Anthropological Research*, 36 (1980): 87–104.

[24]Ibid.

[25]For an explanation of age-sets among North American Plains Indians, see Jeffery R. Hanson, "Age-Set Theory and Plains Indian Age-Grading: A Critical Review and Revision," *American Ethnologist*, 15 (1988): 349–64.

SUMMARY

1. Associations or interest groups have the following characteristics in common: (a) some kind of formal, institutional structure exists; (b) some people are excluded from membership; (c) membership is based on commonly shared interests or purposes; and (d) there is a clearly discernible sense of mutual pride and belonging. Membership varies according to whether it is voluntary or not, and according to whether the qualities of members are universally ascribed, variably ascribed, or achieved.

2. Age-sets are nonvoluntary associations whose members belong because of universally ascribed characteristics. They are composed of groups of persons of similar age and sex who move through life's stages together. Entry into the system is usually by an initiation ceremony. Transitions to new stages are usually marked by succession rituals. Unisex associations restrict membership to one sex. In noncommercial societies membership in such associations (usually male) is generally nonvoluntary.

3. Regional and ethnic organizations are voluntary associations whose members belong because of variably ascribed characteristics. Both usually occur in societies where technological advance is accelerating, bringing with it economic and social complexity. Despite a variety of types, regional and ethnic associations have in common an emphasis on (a) helping members adapt to new conditions; (b) keeping members in touch with home-area traditions; and (c) promoting improved living conditions for members who have recently migrated to urban areas.

4. Associations whose members belong because of variably ascribed characteristics tend to be replaced in highly industrialized societies by associations whose membership is based on achieved qualities.

SUGGESTED READING

BERNARDI, B. "The Age-System of the Nilo-Hamitic Peoples." *Africa,* 22 (1952): 316–32. A theoretical discussion of why age-set systems occur in some societies and not in others.

EISENSTADT, S. N. *From Generation to Generation: Age Groups and Social Structure.* New York: Free Press, 1956. A comparative and theoretical analysis of age groups in different societies. Chapters 2–5 give a detailed presentation of age groupings in a wide variety of societies.

LOWIE, R. H. *Primitive Society.* New York: Liveright, 1970 (originally published in 1920). A classic comparative study of various elements of social organization. Chapters 10 and 11 contain comparative discussions of clubs and age groups in simpler societies.

MEILLASSOUX, C. *Urbanization of an African Community.* Seattle: University of Washington Press, 1968. A description of the changing structure of Mali society, particularly in terms of the decline of voluntary associations as centers of power. Such associations continue to exist in Mali but are subordinate, and in opposition, to the newer party system.

RITTER, M. "The Conditions Favoring Age-Set Organization." *Journal of Anthropological Research,* 36 (1980): 87–104. Evaluates the various theories about the development of age-sets and presents a new theory, which is supported by cross-cultural evidence.

21

Political Life: Social Order and Disorder

For people in the United States, the phrase *political life* has many connotations. It may call to mind the various branches of government: the executive branch, from the president on the national level to governors on the state level to mayors on the local level; legislative institutions, from Congress to state legislatures to city councils; and administrative bureaus, from federal-government departments to local agencies.

Political life may also evoke thoughts of political parties, interest groups, lobbying, campaigning, and voting. In other words, when people living in the United States think of political life, they may think first of "politics," the activities (not always apparent) that influence who is elected or appointed to political office, what public policies are established, and who benefits from those policies.

But *political life* involves even more than government and politics in the United States and many other countries. Political life also involves ways of preventing or resolving troubles and disputes both within and outside the society. Internally, a complex society such as ours may employ mediation or arbitration to resolve industrial disputes; a police force to prevent crimes or track down criminals; and courts and a penal system to deal with lawbreakers as well as with social conflict in general. Externally, such a society may establish embassies in other nations and develop and utilize its armed forces both to maintain security and to support domestic and foreign interests.

By means of such formal political mechanisms, complex societies establish social order and minimize, or at least deal with, social disorder.

But many societies known to anthropology do not have (or did not used to have) political officials or political parties or courts or armies. Nor do they have individuals or agencies that are formally responsible for making and implementing policy or resolving disputes. Does this mean they have no political life? If we mean political life as we know it in our own society, then the answer has to be that they do not. But if we look beyond our formal institutions and mechanisms—if we ask what functions these institutions and mechanisms perform—we find that all societies have political activities and beliefs that are ways of creating and maintaining social order and coping with social disorder.

Many of the kinds of groups we discussed in the three previous chapters (families, descent groups, and associations) have political functions. But when anthropologists talk about *political organization* or *political life*, they are particularly focusing on activities and beliefs pertaining to *territorial groups*. Territorial groups, in whose behalf political activities may be organized, range from small communities (bands, villages) to large communities (towns, cities) to multi-local groups such as districts or regions, entire nations, or even groups of nations.

As we shall see, the different types of political organization, as well as how people participate in politics and how they cope with conflict, are often strongly linked to variation in food-getting, economy, and social stratification.

Variation in Types of Political Organization

Societies vary in *level of political integration* (the largest territorial group in whose behalf political activities are organized) and in the degree to which political authority is centralized or concentrated in the integrated group. In many societies known to anthropology, the small community (band or village) is the largest territorial group in whose behalf political activities are organized. The authority structure in such societies does not involve any centralization: there is no political authority whose jurisdiction includes more than one community. In other societies, political activities are sometimes organized in behalf of a multi-local group, but there is no permanent authority at the top. And in still other societies, political activities are often organized on behalf of multi-local territorial groups, and there is a centralized or supreme political authority at the top. Many anthropologists classify societies in terms of the highest level of political integration that occurs, and in terms of the nature of the political authority structure. For example, Elman Service has suggested that most societies can be classified into four principal types of political organization: bands, tribes, chiefdoms, and states.[1] We shall examine how political life is organized in each of these types of society in order to

[1]Elman R. Service, *Primitive Social Organization: An Evolutionary Perspective* (New York: Random House, 1962).

see how societies vary in the ways they try to create and maintain social order.

Bands

Some societies are composed of a number of fairly small and usually nomadic groups of people. Each of these groups is conventionally called a **band** and is politically autonomous. That is, in band societies the local group or community is the largest group that acts as a political unit. Since most recent food collectors have had band organization, some anthropologists contend that this type of political organization characterized nearly all societies before the development of agriculture, or until about 10,000 years ago. But we have to remember that almost all of the described food-collecting societies are or were located in marginal environments; and almost all were affected by more dominant societies nearby.[2] So it is possible that what we call "band organization" may not have been typical of food collectors in the distant or prehistoric past.

Bands are typically small in size, and societies with bands have a low population density. Julian Steward estimated that density in band societies ranged from a maximum of about one person per five square miles to a minimum of one person per fifty or so square miles.[3] Of course, by the time they were described by anthropologists, many band societies had been severely depopulated by introduced European diseases. So band size in the ethnographic record varies considerably. The Guayaki of the Amazon Basin had about 20 individuals in their local bands; the Semang of the Malay Peninsula had 50; the Patagonian Tehuelche of South America numbered 400 to 500, perhaps the largest of all.[4] Band size often varies by season, the band breaking up or recombining according to the quantity of food resources available at a given time and place. Inuit bands, for example, are smaller in the winter, when food is hard to find, and larger in the summer, when there is sufficient food to feed a larger group.

Political decision making within the band is generally informal. The "modest informal authority"[5] that does exist can be seen in the way decisions affecting the group are made. Since the formal, permanent office of leader generally does not exist, decisions such as when camp has to be moved or how a hunt is to be arranged are either agreed upon by the community as a whole or made by the best-qualified member. Leadership, when it is exercised by an individual, is not the consequence of bossing or throwing one's weight about. Each band may have its informal **headman,** or its most proficient hunter, or a person most accomplished in rituals. There may be one person with all these qualities, or several persons, but such a person or persons will have gained status through the community's recognition of skill, good sense, and humility. Leadership, in other words, stems not from power but from influence, not from office but from admired personal qualities.

In Inuit bands, each settlement may have its headman, who acquires his influence because the other members of the community recognize his good judgment and superior skills. The headman's advice concerning the movement of the band and other community matters is generally heeded, but he possesses no permanent authority and has no power to impose sanctions of any kind. Inuit leaders are male. But men often consult their wives in private, and women who hunt seem to have more influence.[6] In any case, leadership exists only in a very restricted sense, as among the Iglulik Inuit, for example.

Within each settlement . . . there is as a rule an older man who enjoys the respect of the others and who decides when a move is to be made to another hunting center, when a hunt is to be started, how the spoils are to be divided, when the dogs are to be fed. . . . He is called *isumaitoq,* "he who thinks." It is not always the oldest man, but as a rule an elderly man who is a clever hunter or, as head of a large family, exercises great authority. He cannot be called a chief; there is no obligation to follow his counsel; but they do so in most cases,

[2]Carmel Schrire, "Wild Surmises on Savage Thoughts," in Carmel Schrire, ed., *Past and Present in Hunter Gatherer Studies* (Orlando, FL: Academic Press, 1984), pp. 1–25; see also Eleanor Leacock and Richard Lee, "Introduction," in Eleanor Leacock and Richard Lee, eds., *Politics and History in Band Societies* (Cambridge: Cambridge University Press, 1982), p. 8.

[3]Julian Steward, *Theory of Culture Change* (Urbana: University of Illinois Press, 1955), p. 125.

[4]Morton H. Fried, *The Evolution of Political Society: An Essay in Political Anthropology* (New York: Random House, 1967), p. 68.

[5]Service, *Primitive Social Organization,* p. 109.

[6]Jean L. Briggs, "Eskimo Women: Makers of Men," in Carolyn J. Matthiasson, *Many Sisters: Women in Cross-Cultural Perspective* (New York: Free Press, 1974), pp. 261–304.

In egalitarian societies, all persons have equal access to status positions and economic resources. The women of a !Kung band reflect the absence of differences in prestige, wealth, and power.

partly because they rely on his experience, partly because it pays to be on good terms with this man.[7]

Although the position of headman is often hereditary among the !Kung, the authority of the headman is extremely limited; the position itself offers no apparent advantages and is not actively sought. Like all !Kung, the headman fashions tools and shelters, carries his possessions, and hunts for food. Indeed, the !Kung headman goes out of his way not to be envied for his possession of material goods.

However, while the authority of the !Kung headman is tenuous, he nevertheless has certain duties that are at least symbolic. He is generally held responsible for the way the band makes use of its food resources, although most of his decisions will be dictated by nature, long-standing custom, or consensus of band members. If there is theft by some person not affiliated with the band, he is expected to cope with the problem. And his consent is necessary for an outsider to be admitted to the band. Yet despite his customary duties, the !Kung headman is not necessarily the leader of the band. If he lacks the special abilities needed to lead in a given situation, the band turns to another person

quite informally. No man of influence within the band, however, has formal authority or receives special privileges. At most, the headman is first among equals; at the least, as one headman was overheard to say, "All you get is the blame if things go wrong."[8]

Not all known food collectors are organized at the band level, or have all the features of a band type of society. The classic exceptions are the Native Americans of the Northwest Coast who had enormous resources of salmon and other fish, relatively large and permanent villages, and political organization beyond the level of the typical band societies in the ethnographic record.

Tribes

What distinguishes tribal from band political organization is the presence in the former of some pan-tribal associations (such as clans and age-sets) that can potentially integrate a number of local groups into a larger whole. Such multi-local political integration, however, is *not permanent*, and it is *informal* in the sense that it is not headed by political officials. Frequently, the integration is called into play only when an external threat arises; when the threat disappears, the local groups revert to self-sufficiency.

In other words, a tribal society lacks a permanent, multi-local political authority. Situations do arise that call for intergroup cooperation of some kind, but they are transitory, and a new situation may well require the coordination of quite different groups.[9] Tribal organization may seem fragile—and of course it usually is—but the fact that there are social ways to integrate local groups into larger political entities means that societies with tribal organization are militarily a good deal more formidable than societies with band organization.

Societies with **tribal** political organization are similar to band societies in their tendency to be egalitarian. But societies with tribal organization generally are food producers. And because cultivation and animal husbandry are generally more productive than hunting and gathering, the population density of tribal societies is generally higher,

[7]Therkel Mathiassen, *Material Culture of the Iglulik Eskimos* (Copenhagen: Glydendalske, 1928), as quoted in E. M. Weyer, *The Eskimos: Their Environment and Folkways* (New Haven: Yale University Press, 1932), p. 213.

[8]Lorna Marshall, "!Kung Bushmen Bands," in Ronald Cohen and John Middleton, eds., *Comparative Political Systems* (Garden City, NY: Natural History Press, 1967), p. 41.
[9]Service, *Primitive Social Organization*, pp. 114–15.

local groups are generally larger, and the way of life is more sedentary than in hunter-gatherer bands.

Kinship Bonds. Frequently, pan-tribal associations are based on kinship ties. Clans are the most common pan-tribal kinship groups. In some societies, clan elders have the right to try to settle disputes between clan members or to attempt to punish wrongs committed against members by members of different clans. In addition, kinship bonds often tend to unite members of the same descent group during periods of warfare; in many societies, the organization of warfare is the responsibility of the clan.[10]

The **segmentary lineage system** is another type of pan-tribal integration based on kinship. A society with such a system is composed of segments or parts, each similar to the others in structure and function. Every local segment belongs to a hierarchy of lineages stretching farther and farther back genealogically. The hierarchy of lineages, then, unites the segments into larger and larger genealogical groups. The closer two groups are genealogically, the greater their general closeness. In the event of a dispute between members of different segments, people related more closely to one contestant than to another take the side of their nearest kinsman.

The Tiv of northern Nigeria offer a classic example of a segmentary lineage system, one that links all the Tiv into a single genealogical structure. The Tiv are a large society, numbering more than 800,000. Figure 21–1 is a representation of the Tiv lineage structure as described by Paul Bohannan:

The lineage whose apical ancestor is some three to six generations removed from living elders and who are associated with the smallest discrete territory *(tar)* I call the minimal segment; . . . it can vary in population from 200 people to well over a thousand. . . . The territory of a minimal segment adjoins the territory of its sibling minimal segment. Thus, the lineage comprising two minimal segments also has a discrete territory, and is in turn a segment of a more inclusive lineage, and of its more inclusive territory. In [Figure 21–1], the whole system can be seen: the father or founder of segment *a* was a brother of the founder of segment *b*. Each is a minimal segment today, and each has its own territory. The two segments taken together are all descended from *1*, and

[10]Ibid., p. 126.

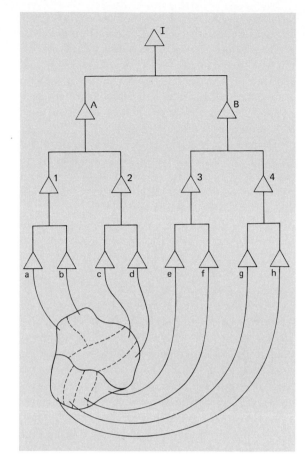

FIGURE 21–1 Tiv Lineage Segments and Their Territories

are known by his name—the children of *1*. In the same way, the territory of lineage *1*, made up as it is of the combined minimal territories *a* and *b*, combines with the territory of lineage *2*, made up of the combined minimal territories of *c* and *d*, to form territory A, occupied by lineage segment A, all descended from a single ancestor "A." This process is extended indefinitely, right up to the apex of the genealogy, back in time to the founder who [is said to have] begot the entire people; and outwards in space to the edges of Tivland. The entire 800,000 Tiv form a single "lineage" *(nongo)* and a single land called *Tar Tiv*.[11]

Tiv lineage organization is the foundation of Tiv political organization. A look at Figure 21–1 helps to explain how. A dispute between lineages (and territories) *a* and *b* remains minor, since no more than "brother" segments are involved. But a

[11]Paul Bohannan, "The Migration and Expansion of the Tiv," *Africa*, 24 (1954): 3.

dispute between *a* and *c* now involves lineages *1* and *2* as well, with the requirement that *b* assist *a* and *d* support *c*. This process of mutual support, often called **complementary opposition,** means that segments will unite only in a confrontation with some other group. Groups that will fight with each other in a minor dispute might coalesce at some later time against a larger group.

Externally, the segmentary lineage system was presumably very effective in allowing the Tiv to intrude into new territory and take land from other tribal societies with smaller descent groups. Individual Tiv lineage segments could call on support from related lineages when faced with border troubles. Conflicts within the society (between segments), especially in border areas, were often turned outward, "releasing internal pressure in an explosive blast against other peoples."[12]

The Nuer of the Upper Nile region also expanded at the expense of their neighbors, the Dinka. In the early 1800s the Nuer had a territory of about 8,700 square miles and the Dinka had ten times that much. But by 1890, the Nuer had cut a hundred-mile swath through Dinka territory, increasing Nuer territory to 35,000 square miles. Even though the Nuer and Dinka were culturally very similar, the segmentary lineage organization of the Nuer seems to have given them a significant military advantage.[13]

A segmentary lineage system may generate a formidable military force, but the combinations of manpower it produces are temporary, forming and dissolving as the occasion demands.[14] Tribal political organization does not make for a political system that more or less permanently integrates a number of communities.

Age-Set Systems. In the previous chapter we described age-set systems in general. Here we discuss how age-sets can function as the basis of a tribal type of political organization, as among the Karimojong of northeastern Uganda.[15]

The Karimojong depend on cattle herding and agriculture for their livelihood. Their political community includes elders who direct day-to-day affairs, large-herd owners whose wealth enables them to have a say in certain activities, and initiated adult males whose responsibility it is to implement policy once it has been decided. Initiation into an age-set, and public acceptance of tribal customs, means that a Karimojong will ultimately become an elder and perhaps a leader of his local community.

The Karimojong age-set system has an important bearing on day-to-day tribal life. As herders, Karimojong adults are often separated from their usual settlements. Herders will meet, mingle for a while, then go their separate ways, but each may call upon other members of his age-set wherever he goes. The age-set system is important among the Karimojong because it immediately allocates to each individual a place in the system and thereby establishes for him an appropriate pattern of response. A quarrel in camp will be settled by the representatives of the senior age-set who are present, regardless of which section of the tribe they may belong to.

Karimojong elders are respected for their practical knowledge and experience, but they are particularly credited with the gift of being able to intercede with the deity on behalf of the tribe—a gift they demonstrate at regular public rituals. The rituals serve political ends through prayers for economic security and betterment for each Karimojong. The elders can also use their supernatural power for punishment. The severe drought and the disease that swept through the tribe in the late nineteenth century are explained as the consequences of the senior generation-set's displeasure with, and punishment of, its juniors.

Leadership. Tribal societies do not have formal full-time political officials whose authority extends to more than one community. At the local level, informal leadership is also characteristic. In those tribal societies where kinship provides the basic framework of social organization, the elders of the local kin groups tend to have considerable influence; where age-sets are important, a particular age-set is looked to for leadership. But why particular individuals and not others become leaders is not clear.

[12]Marshall D. Sahlins, "The Segmentary Lineage: An Organization of Predatory Expansion," *American Anthropologist*, 63 (1961): 342.

[13]Raymond C. Kelly, *The Nuer Conquest: The Structure and Development of an Expansionist System* (Ann Arbor: University of Michigan Press, 1985), p. 1.

[14]Sahlins, "The Segmentary Lineage," p. 345.

[15]Neville Dyson-Hudson, *Karimojong Politics* (Oxford: Clarendon Press, 1966), Chapters 5 and 6.

Among the Karimojong, for example, political leaders are not elected from among the elders of a particular age-set, nor are they appointed; they acquire their positions informally. Usually a man's background, and the ability he has demonstrated in public debates over a period of time, will result in his being considered by the men of his neighborhood to be their spokesman. His function is to announce what course of action seems required in a particular situation, to initiate that action, and then to coordinate it after it has begun.

Most political leaders exercise their authority within the local sphere because the pastoral nature of the Karimojong economy, with its dispersed groups and movement from one feeding ground to another, offers no alternative. From time to time an elder may acquire the status of a prophet and be awarded respect and obedience on a tribal scale. He will be called upon to lead sacrifices (to avert misfortune), to undertake rainmaking (to bring prosperity), and so on. Yet even a prophet's prestige and authority do not mean that he assumes a position of overlord or chief.[16]

We now have a few studies that have investigated the personal qualities of leaders in tribal societies. One study, conducted among the Mekranoti-Kayapo of Central Brazil, finds that leaders (in contrast to followers) tend to be rated higher on intelligence, generosity, knowledgeability, ambitiousness, and aggressiveness by their peers. Leaders also tend to be older and taller. And despite the egalitarian nature of Mekranoti society (at least with respect to sharing resources), sons of leaders are more likely than others to become leaders.[17]

Research in another Brazilian society, the Kagwahiv of the Amazon region, suggests another personal quality of leaders—they seem to have positive feelings about their fathers and mothers.[18] In many respects, studies of leaders in the United States show them to be not that different from their counterparts in Brazil. But there is one major difference. Mekranoti and Kagwahiv leaders are not wealthier than others; in fact, they give their wealth away. United States leaders are wealthier than others.[19]

In some tribal societies, the quest for leadership seems quite competitive. In parts of New Guinea and South America, "big men" compete with other ambitious men to attract followers. Men who want to compete must show that they have magical powers, success in gardening, and bravery in war. But, most important, they have to collect enough goods to throw big parties where the goods are given away. "Big men" have to work very hard to attract and keep their followings; dissatisfied followers can always join other aspiring men.[20] The wives of "big men" are often leaders too. Among the Kagwahiv, for example, a headman's wife is usually the leader of the women in the community; she is responsible for much of the planning for feasts and often distributes the meat at them.[21]

Chiefdoms

Whereas tribes have groupings that can informally integrate more than one community, **chiefdoms** have some *formal* structure integrating multicommunity political units. The formal structure could consist of a council with or without a chief, but most commonly there is a person—the **chief**—who has higher rank or authority than others. A society at the chiefdom level of political development may or may not be completely politically unified under one chief. Most societies at the chiefdom level are in fact composed of more than one multi-community political unit, each headed by a chief or a council. Compared with tribal societies, societies with chiefdoms generally are more densely populated and their communities more permanent, partly as a consequence of their generally higher economic productivity.

The position of chief, which is sometimes hereditary and generally permanent, bestows high status on its holder. Most chiefdoms have social ranking and accord the chief and his family greater

[16]Ibid.

[17]Dennis Werner, "Chiefs and Presidents: A Comparison of Leadership Traits in the United States and among the Mekranoti-Kayapo of Central Brazil," *Ethos*, 10 (1982): 136–48.

[18]Waud H. Kracke, *Force and Persuasion: Leadership in an Amazonian Society* (Chicago: University of Chicago Press, 1979), p. 232.

[19]Werner, "Chiefs and Presidents."

[20]Marshall D. Sahlins, "Poor Man, Rich Man, Big-Man, Chief: Political Types in Melanesia and Polynesia," *Comparative Studies in Society and History*, 5 (1963): 285–303.

[21]Kracke, *Force and Persuasion*, p. 41.

Chiefs in Tahiti directed military activities. Captain Cook encountered their war canoes when he visited in 1774.

access to prestige. The chief may redistribute goods, plan and direct the use of public labor, supervise religious ceremonies, and direct military activities on behalf of the chiefdom.

In South Pacific chiefdoms, the chiefs carried out most of the duties we have just described. In Fijian chiefdoms, for example, the chief was responsible for the redistribution of goods and the coordination of labor:

[The chief] could summon the community's labor on his own behalf, or on behalf of someone else who requested it, or for general purposes. . . . Besides his right to summon labor he accumulated the greater proportion of the first fruits of the yam crop . . . and he benefited from other forms of food presentation, or by the acquisition of special shares in ordinary village distribution. . . . Thus, the paramount [chief] would collect a significant part of the surplus production of the community and redistribute it in the general welfare.[22]

The Tahitians had a history of large-scale warfare, and their chiefs coordinated land and naval forces in thrusts and counterthrusts. Tahitian society was clearly ranked—from the preeminence accorded the families of the paramount chiefs, who were believed to have exceptional spiritual powers, down to the lowest status of the general populace.

Many of the early missionaries to Tahiti regarded the chiefs as despots because of the great deference and tribute paid to them by the common people. In fact, however, the chiefs did not really have tyrannical control over the daily lives of the islanders in their districts.

In contrast to leaders in tribal societies, who generally have to earn their privileges by their personal qualities, hereditary chiefs are said to have those qualities in their "blood." A high-ranking chief in Polynesia, that huge triangular area of islands in the South Pacific, inherited special religious power called *mana*. Mana sanctified his rule and protected him.[23] Chiefs in Polynesia had so much religious power that the missionaries could convert people to Christianity only after their chiefs were converted.[24]

In most chiefdoms, the chiefs did not have the power to compel people to obey them; people would act in accordance with the chief's wishes because the chief was respected and often had religious authority. But in the most complex chiefdoms, such as those of Hawaii and Tahiti, the chiefs seemed to have more compelling sanctions than the "power" of respect or mana. Substantial

[22]Marshall Sahlins, *Moala: Culture and Nature on a Fijian Island* (Ann Arbor: University of Michigan Press, 1962), pp. 293–94.

[23]Sahlins, "Poor Man, Rich Man, Big-Man, Chief," p. 295.

[24]Marshall Sahlins, "Other Times, Other Customs: The Anthropology of History," *American Anthropologist*, 85 (1983): 519.

amounts of goods and services collected by the chiefs were used to support subordinates, including specialists such as high priests, political envoys, and warriors who could be sent to quell rebellious factions.[25] When redistributions do not go to everybody and a chief begins to use armed force, the political system is on the way to becoming what we call a state. Why chiefs sometimes are allowed to keep items for their own purposes is still a puzzle.

States

A **state,** according to one more or less standard definition, is "an autonomous political unit, encompassing many communities within its territory and having a centralized government with the power to collect taxes, draft men for work or war, and decree and enforce laws."[26] State societies, then, have a complex, centralized political structure, which includes a wide range of permanent institutions having legislative, executive, and judicial functions, and a large bureaucracy. Central to this definition is the concept of legitimate force used to implement policies both internally and externally. In state societies, the government tries to maintain a monopoly on the use of physical force.[27] This monopoly can be seen in the development of formal and specialized instruments of social control: a police force, a militia, a standing army.

In addition to their strictly political features, states have class stratification and hence unequal access to economic resources. State societies are generally supported by intensive agriculture. The high productivity of the agriculture presumably allows for the emergence of cities, a high degree of economic and other kinds of specialization, market or commercial exchange, and extensive foreign trade.

When states come into existence, people's access to scarce resources is radically altered. So too is their ability to *not* listen to leaders: you cannot refuse to pay taxes and go unpunished! Of course, the rulers of a state do not maintain the social or-

State societies, like Thailand, have standing armies ready for fighting or marching.

der by force alone. The people must believe, at least to some extent, that those in power have a legitimate right to govern. If the people think otherwise, history suggests that those in power may eventually lose their ability to control. Witness the recent downfall of Communist parties throughout Eastern Europe and the former Soviet Union.

So force and the threat of force are not enough to explain the legitimacy of power, and the inequities that occur commonly, in state societies. But then what does? There are various theories available. The rulers of early states often claimed divine descent to buttress their legitimacy, but this claim is rare nowadays. Children may be taught to accept all authority by their parents, which may generalize to the acceptance of political authority. Then there are those who think that people accept state authority for no good reason; the rulers are just able to fool them. Finally, some theorists think that states must provide people with real or rational advantages; otherwise people would not

[25]Sahlins, "Poor Man, Rich Man, Big-Man, Chief," p. 297.

[26]Robert L. Carneiro, "A Theory of the Origin of the State," *Science,* August 21, 1970, p. 733.

[27]See Max Weber, *The Theory of Social and Economic Organization,* trans. A. M. Henderson and Talcott Parsons (New York: Oxford University Press, 1947), p. 154.

think the rulers deserve to exercise authority. Legitimacy is not an all or none phenomenon; it varies in degree. Why it has varied, in different times and places, remains a classic question in a number of the social sciences, including anthropology, as well as in philosophy and other humanistic disciplines.[28]

A state society can retain its legitimacy, or at least its power, for a long time. For example, the Roman Empire was a complex state society that dominated the Mediterranean and Near East for hundreds of years. It began as a city-state that waged war to acquire additional territory. At its height, the Roman Empire embraced more than 55 million people;[29] the capital city of Rome had a population of well over a million.[30] The Empire included parts of what are now Great Britain, France, Spain, Portugal, Germany, Rumania, Turkey, Greece, Armenia, Egypt, Israel, and Syria.

Roman society was clearly stratified, with the patricians, who controlled the bulk of the wealth and influence, sharply distinguished from the plebeians (common folk). The Romans made productive use of favorable agricultural conditions in Italy, and intensive agricultural methods were employed in the provinces, especially in Egypt, southern Gaul (France), and Spain. Roman commerce was worldwide (as the term was defined in those days), and Roman money was the principal medium of exchange around the entire Mediterranean area and within much of Europe.

Politically, Rome had a complex of institutions. During the imperial phase, which lasted for the first three centuries A.D., emperor and Senate acted together in governing the Roman world, though the emperor tended to concentrate on foreign and military affairs while the Senate dealt with domestic matters. The Roman government employed a large bureaucracy, controlled the routes of communication, deployed substantial army and navy units, and made its power felt both internally and externally. The legitimacy and sovereignty of this Roman state went more or less unquestioned for half a millennium.

Another example of a state society was the kingdom of Nupe in West Africa, now part of the nation-state of Nigeria. As is characteristic of state societies generally, Nupe society was quite rigidly stratified. At the top of the social system was the king, or *etsu*. Beneath the king, members of the royal family formed the highest aristocratic class. Next in order were two other classes of nobility—the local chiefs and the military leaders. At the bottom were the commoners, who had neither prestige nor power, and no share in political authority.

The Nupe state was composed of two types of territorial units. One consisted of towns and villages that were part of the royal domain and therefore under the direct rule of the king. The other consisted of communities designated as fiefs and controlled by local lords. The state, however, had supreme authority over all local magistrates and lords. Although the people of the villages may have selected their own chiefs, the king had the right to confirm all such appointments, as well as the power to depose all local rulers, including lords.

The Nupe king possessed ultimate authority in many judicial matters. Minor disputes and civil cases were handled by local village councils, but serious criminal cases were the prerogative of the king. Such cases, referred to as "crimes for the king," were brought before the royal court by the king's local representatives. The king and his counselors judged the cases and determined suitable punishments.

The most powerful influence of the state over the Nupe people was in the area of taxation. The king was given the power to impose taxes and collect them from every household. Payment was made either in money (cowrie shells originally, and later British currency) or certain gifts, such as cloth, mats, and slaves. Much of the revenue collected was kept by the king, and the remainder shared with his local representatives and lords. In return for the taxes they paid, the people received

[28]For an extensive review of the various theories about legitimacy, see Ronald Cohen, "Introduction," in Ronald Cohen and Judith D. Toland, eds., *State Formation and Political Legitimacy*, (New Brunswick, NJ: Transaction Books, 1988), volume VI, *Political Anthropology*, pp. 1–3.

[29]M. I. Finley, *Politics in the Ancient World* (Cambridge: Cambridge University Press, 1983).

[30]Jerome Carcopino, *Daily Life in Ancient Rome: The People and the City at the Height of the Empire*, edited with bibliography and notes by Henry T. Rowell, translated from the French by E. O. Lorimer (New Haven: Yale University Press, 1940), pp. 18–20.

security—protection against invasion and domestic disorder.[31]

Factors Associated with Variation in Political Organization

The kinds of political organization we call bands, tribes, chiefdoms, and states are points on a continuum from simpler to more complex political systems, from small-scale local autonomy to large-scale regional unification. Societies of all these types are described in the ethnographic record. We see variation in political authority from a few temporary and informal political leaders to large numbers of permanent, specialized political officials, from the absence of coercive political power to the monopoly of public force by a central authority. This continuum of variation in political organization is generally associated with shifts from food collection to more intensive food production, from small to large communities, from low to high population densities, from an emphasis on reciprocity to redistribution to market exchange, and from egalitarian to rank to fully stratified class societies.

The associations just outlined, which seem to be confirmed by the available cross-cultural evidence, are summarized in Table 21–1. With regard to the relation between level of subsistence technology and political complexity, a cross-cultural study employing a small random sample of societies found that the greater the importance of agriculture in a society, the larger the population that is politically unified and the greater the number and types of political officials.[32] A massive cross-cultural survey reports a similar trend: the more intensive the agriculture, the greater the likelihood of state organization; conversely, societies with no more than local political institutions are likely to depend on hunting, gathering, and fishing.[33] With regard to community size, the first of these studies also suggests that the larger the leading community, the wider the range of political officials in the society.[34]

Robert Textor presents a similar finding: societies with state organization tend to have cities and towns, whereas those with only local political organization are more likely to have communities with an average population of fewer than 200 persons.[35] Cross-cultural research also tends to confirm that societies with higher levels of political integration are more likely to exhibit social differentiation, especially in the form of class distinctions.[36]

Does this evidence provide us with an explanation for why political organization varies? Clearly, the data indicate that several factors are associated with political development, but exactly why changes in organization occur is not yet understood. Although economic development may be a necessary condition for political development,[37] that does not fully explain why political organization should become more complex just because the economy can support it. Elman Service has suggested why a society might change from a band level of political organization to a tribal level and why a tribal society might be transformed into a society with chiefdoms. Band societies are generally hunter-gatherers. With a changeover to agriculture, population density and competition between groups may increase. Service believes that such competition will foster the development of some informal organization beyond the community—namely, tribal organization—for offense and defense. Indeed, as we have seen in the chapters on residence/kinship and associations, unilineal kinship groups and age-set systems both seem to be associated with warfare. With regard to chiefdoms, Service suggests they will emerge when redistribution between communities becomes important or when large-scale coordinated work groups are required. The more important these activities are,

---

[31]Our discussion of Nupe is based on S. F. Nadel, "Nupe State and Community," *Africa*, 8 (1935): 257–303.

[32]Melvin Ember, "The Relationship between Economic and Political Development in Nonindustrialized Societies," *Ethnology*, 2 (1963): 228–48.

[33]Data from Robert B. Textor, comp., *A Cross-Cultural Summary* (New Haven: HRAF Press, 1967).

[34]Ember, "The Relationship between Economic and Political Development in Nonindustrialized Societies."

[35]Data from Textor, comp., *A Cross-Cultural Summary*.

[36]Raoul Naroll, "Two Solutions to Galton's Problem," *Philosophy of Science*, 28 (January 1961): 15–39. See also Marc H. Ross, "Socioeconomic Complexity, Socialization, and Political Differentiation: A Cross-Cultural Study," *Ethos*, 9 (1981): 217–47.

[37]Ember, "The Relationship between Economic and Political Development in Nonindustrialized Societies," pp. 244–46.

TABLE 21–1 Suggested Trends in Political Organization and Other Social Characteristics

TYPE OF ORGANIZATION	HIGHEST LEVEL OF POLITICAL INTEGRATION	SPECIALIZATION OF POLITICAL OFFICIALS	PREDOMINANT MODE OF SUBSISTENCE	COMMUNITY SIZE AND POPULATION DENSITY	SOCIAL DIFFERENTIATION	MAJOR FORM OF DISTRIBUTION
Band	Local group or band	Little or none; informal leadership	Food collecting	Very small communities, very low density	Egalitarian	Mostly reciprocity
Tribe	Sometimes multi-local group	Little or none; informal leadership	Extensive (shifting) agriculture and/or herding	Small communities, low density	Egalitarian	Mostly reciprocity
Chiefdom	Multi-local group	Some	Extensive or intensive agriculture and/or herding	Large communities, medium density	Rank	Reciprocity and redistribution
State	Multi-local group, often entire language group	Much	Intensive agriculture and herding	Cities and towns, high density	Class and caste	Mostly market exchange

An Aztec painting of the Spanish Conquest.

the more important (and hence more "chiefly") the organizer and his family presumably become.[38] But redistribution is far from a universal activity of chiefs,[39] so Service's explanation of chiefdoms is probably not sufficient.

Theory and research on the anthropology of political development has focused mostly on the high end of the scale of political complexity, and particularly on the origins of the first state societies. Those earliest states apparently arose independently of one another, after about 3500 B.C., in what is now southern Iraq, Egypt, northwestern India, northern China, and central Mexico. As we discussed in Chapter 9, a number of theories have been proposed to explain the earliest states, but no one theory seems to fit all the known archeological sequences culminating in early state formation.

The Spread of State Societies

For whatever reasons the earliest states developed, the state level of political development has come to dominate the world. Societies with states have larger communities and higher population densities, not to mention armies that are ready to fight at almost any time. State systems that have waged war against chiefdoms and tribes have almost always won, and the result has usually been the political incorporation of the losers. For example, the British and later the United States colonization of much of North America led to the defeat and incorporation of many Native American societies.

The defeat and incorporation of the Native Americans was at least partially due to the catastrophic depopulations they suffered because of epidemic diseases (such as smallpox and measles) that European and American colonists introduced. Catastrophic depopulation was commonly the outcome of the first contacts between Euro-Americans and the natives of North and South America, as well as the natives of the far islands in the Pacific. People in the New World and the Pacific were not previously exposed (and therefore not resistant) to the diseases the Euro-Americans carried with them when they began to colonize the world. Before the expansion of Europeans, the people of the New World and the Pacific had been separated for a long time from the people and diseases on that geographically continuous land mass we separate into Europe, Africa, and Asia. Smallpox, measles, and the other former scourges of Europe had largely become childhood diseases that most individuals of European ancestry survived.[40]

Whether by depopulation, conquest, or intimidation, the number of independent political units in the world has decreased strikingly in the last 3,000 years, and especially in the last 200 years. Robert Carneiro has estimated that in 1000 B.C., there may have been between 100,000 and 1 million separate political units in the world; today there are fewer than 200.[41] In the ethnographic record, about 50 percent of the 2,000 or so societies described within the last 150 years had only local political integration. That is, the highest level of political integration in 1 out of 2 fairly recent societies was the community.[42] Thus, most of the

---

[38]Service, *Primitive Social Organization*, pp. 112, 145.

[39]Gary Feinman and Jill Nietzel, "Too Many Types: An Overview of Sedentary Prestate Societies in the Americas," in Michael B. Schiffer, ed., *Advances in Archaeological Method and Theory* (Orlando, FL: Academic Press, 1984), 7: 39–102.

[40]William H. McNeill, *Plagues and Peoples* (Garden City, NY: Doubleday Anchor, 1976).

[41]Robert L. Carneiro, "Political Expansion as an Expression of the Principle of Competitive Exclusion," in Ronald Cohen and Elman Service, eds., *Origins of the State: The Anthropology of Political Evolution* (Philadelphia: Institute for the Study of Human Issues, 1978), p. 215.

[42]Data from Textor, comp., *A Cross-Cultural Summary*.

decrease in the number of independent political units has occurred fairly recently.

But the very recent secessions from the former Soviet Union and Yugoslavia, and other separatist movements around the world, suggest that ethnic rivalries may make for departures from the trend toward larger and larger political units. Ethnic groups that have been dominated by others in multi-national states may opt for political autonomy, at least for a while. On the other hand, the separate nations of Western Europe are becoming more unified every day, both politically and economically. So the trend toward larger and larger political units may be continuing, even if there are departures from it now and then.

Extrapolating from past history, a number of investigators have suggested that the entire world will eventually come to be politically integrated, perhaps as soon as the twenty-third century and no later than A.D. 4850.[43] Only the future will tell if this prediction will come true. And only the future will tell if further political integration in the world will occur peacefully—with all parties agreeing—or by force or the threat of force, as has happened so often in the past.

Variation in Politics

Anthropologists nowadays are increasingly interested in the politics of the societies they study: who acquires influence or power, how they acquire it, and how political decisions are made. But even though we have descriptive accounts of politics in many societies, there is little comparative or cross-cultural research on what may explain variation in politics.[44]

The political scientist Marc Ross has conducted cross-cultural research on variation in degree of political participation. As Ross phrases the research question: "Why is it that in some polities there are relatively large numbers of persons involved in political life, while in others political action is the province of very few?[45]

Political participation in preindustrial societies ranges from widespread to low or nonexistent. Widespread participation (in 16 percent of the societies examined) means that decision-making forums are *open* to all adults (not necessarily that all adults participate); the forums may be formal (councils and other governing bodies) or informal. Next in degree of political participation are societies (37 percent) that have widespread participation by some but not all adults (men but not women, certain classes but not others). Next are societies (29 percent) that have some but not much input by the community. Finally, 18 percent of the societies have low or nonexistent participation, which means that leaders make most decisions and involvement of the average person is very limited.

Degree of political participation seems to be high in small-scale societies, as well as in modern democratic nation-states, but not in between (feudal states and preindustrial empires). Why? In small-scale societies leaders do not have the power to force people to act; thus a high degree of political participation may be the only way to get people to go along with decisions. In modern democracies, which have many powerful groups outside the government (corporations, unions, other associations), the central authorities may only theoretically have the power to force people to go along; in reality, they have to rely mostly on voluntary compliance. For example, the U.S. government failed when it tried with force (during Prohibition, 1920–1933) to stop the manufacture, transportation, and sale of alcoholic beverages.

A high degree of political participation seems to have an important consequence. In the modern world, democratically governed states rarely go to war with each other. This does not mean that modern democracies are more peaceful in general; on the contrary, they are as likely to go to war as other kinds of political systems, but not so much

[43]Carneiro, "Political Expansion as an Expression of the Principle of Competitive Exclusion." See also Hornell Hart, "The Logistic Growth of Political Areas," *Social Forces,* 26 (1948): 396–408; Raoul Naroll, "Imperial Cycles and World Order," *Peace Research Society: Papers,* 7, Chicago Conference (1967): 83–101; and Louis A. Marano, "A Macrohistoric Trend toward World Government," *Behavior Science Notes,* 8 (1973): 35–40.

[44]For a review of the descriptive literature until the late 1970s, see Joan Vincent, "Political Anthropology: Manipulative Strategies," *Annual Review of Anthropology,* 7 (1978): 175–94.

[45]Marc Howard Ross, "Political Organization and Political Participation: Exit, Voice, and Loyalty in Preindustrial Societies," *Comparative Politics,* 21 (1988): 73. The discussion in this section draws from ibid., pp. 73–89.

with each other.[46] So, for example, troops from the United States have invaded three countries since 1980 (Grenada, Panama, Iraq), but no democracies. Similarly, it appears that more participatory (more "democratic") political units in the ethnographic record fight with each other significantly less often than less participatory political units, just as seems to be the case among modern nation-states.[47] Exactly why more participation or more democracy may lead to peace still remains to be established; we explore the implications of the relationship in our final chapter on world social problems.

Resolution of Conflict

As we noted in the beginning of the chapter, political life involves more than the making of policy, its administration, and its enforcement. It also generally involves the resolution of conflict, which may be accomplished peacefully by the adjudication of disputes, by the negotiation of compromises, or by the threat of social sanctions. But if such procedures fail or are not possible because of the absence of mediating procedures, then disputes may erupt into violent conflict. When violence occurs within a political unit in which disputes are usually settled peacefully, we call such violence **crime.** When the violence occurs between groups of people from separate political units—groups between which there is no procedure for settling disputes—we usually call such violence **warfare.** (When violence occurs between subunits of a population that had been politically unified, we call it "civil war.")

Peaceful Resolution of Conflict

Most modern industrialized states have formal institutions and offices such as police, district attorneys, courts, and penal systems to deal with minor disputes and more serious conflicts that may arise in society. All these institutions generally operate according to codified laws—that is, a set of explicit (generally, written) rules stipulating what is permissible and what is not. Transgression of the law by individuals gives the state the right to take action against them. The state has a monopoly on the legitimate use of force in the society, for it alone has the right to coerce subjects into agreement with regulations, customs, political edicts, and procedures.

Many societies lack such specialized offices and institutions for dealing with conflict. Yet, since all societies have peaceful, regularized ways of handling at least certain disputes, some anthropologists speak of the universality of law. E. Adamson Hoebel, for example, states the principle as follows:

Each people has its system of social control. And all but a few of the poorest of them have as a part of the control system a complex of behavior patterns and institutional mechanisms that we may properly treat as law. For, "anthropologically considered, law is merely one aspect of our culture—the aspect which employs the force of organized society to regulate individual and group conduct and to prevent redress or punish deviations from prescribed social norms."[48]

Law, then, whether informal as in simpler societies, or formal as in more complex societies, provides a means of dealing peacefully with whatever conflicts develop.

Community Action. Societies have found various ways of resolving disputes peacefully. One such way involves action on the part of the community as a whole; collective action is common in simpler societies which lack powerful authoritarian leaders.[49] Many Inuit societies, for example, frequently resolve disputes through community action. Within local groups, kinship ties are not particularly emphasized, and the family is regarded as autonomous in most matters. They believe that spirits—particularly if displeased—can determine much of a person's fate. Consequently, people

---

[46]For studies of international relations that support these conclusions, see footnotes 2 and 3 in Carol R. Ember, Melvin Ember, and Bruce Russett, "Peace between Participatory Polities: A Cross-Cultural Test of the Democracies Rarely Fight Each Other's Hypothesis," *World Politics*, vol. 44(1992):573-99.

[47]Ibid.

[48]E. Adamson Hoebel, *The Law of Primitive Man* (New York: Atheneum, 1968 [originally published in 1954]), p. 4; quoting S. P. Simpson and Ruth Field, "Law and the Social Sciences," *Virginia Law Review*, 32 (1946): 858.

[49]Ross, "Political Organization and Political Participation."

Many societies have councils that peacefully resolve disputes. Here we see a Hopi council meeting.

carry out their daily tasks within a complex system of taboos. This system of taboos is so extensive that the Inuit, at least in the past, may have had no need for a formal set of laws.

Nevertheless, conflicts do take place and have to be resolved. Accordingly, "principles" act as guides to the community in settling trouble cases. An individual's failure to heed a taboo or to follow the suggestions of a shaman leads to expulsion from the group, since the community cannot accept a risk to its livelihood. A person who fails to share goods voluntarily will find them confiscated and distributed to the community, and he or she may be executed in the process. A single case of murder, as an act of vengeance (usually because of the abduction of a wife, or as part of a blood feud), does not concern the community, but repeated murders do. Boas gives a typical example:

There was a native of Padli by the name Padlu. He had induced the wife of a native of Cumberland Sound to desert her husband and follow him. The deserted husband, meditating revenge . . . visited his friends in Padli, but before he could accomplish his intention of killing Padlu, the latter shot him. . . . A brother of the murdered man went to Padli to avenge the death . . .

but he also was killed by Padlu. A third native of Cumberland Sound, who wished to avenge the death of his relatives, was also murdered by him.

On account of these outrages the natives wanted to get rid of Padlu, but yet they did not dare to attack him. When the *pimain* (headman) of the Akudmurmuit learned of these events he started southward and *asked every man in Padli whether Padlu should be killed. All agreed;* so he went with the latter deer hunting . . . and . . . shot Padlu in the back.[50]

The killing of an individual is the most extreme action a community can take—we call it capital punishment. The community as a whole or a political official or a court may decide to administer such punishment, but capital punishment seems to exist in nearly all societies, from the simplest to the most complex.[51] It is often assumed that capital punishment deters crime. Yet a recent cross-national study indicates that the abolition of capital punishment tends to be followed by a *de-*

[50]Franz Boas, *Central Eskimos,* Bureau of American Ethnology, Annual Report no. 6 (Washington, DC, 1888), p. 668.
[51]Keith F. Otterbein, *The Ultimate Coercive Sanction: A Cross-Cultural Study of Capital Punishment* (New Haven: HRAF Press, 1986), p. 107.

crease in homicide rates.[52] If capital punishment really deterred crime, we would expect the abolition of capital punishment to be followed by an increase in homicide rates. But that does not seem to be true.

Informal Adjudication without Power. Community action is not the only way societies without codified or written laws peacefully resolve disputes. Some societies have informal adjudicators who resolve cases, although these individuals do not have the formal power needed to enforce their decisions. One such society is the Nuer of East Africa.

The Nuer are a pastoral and horticultural people who live in villages grouped into districts. Each district is an informal political unit, with its own machinery for settling disputes. If, however, a district has a large population residing over a wide area, it may be a long time before certain disputes are cleared up. On the higher, interdistrict level there is little chance of bringing feuding districts to a quick settlement, and there are few means of apportioning blame or of assessing damages other than by war.

Within a single community, however, disputes are more easily settled by the use of an informal adjudicator called the "leopard-skin chief." This man is not a political chief but a mediator. His position is hereditary, has religious overtones, and makes its holder responsible for the social well-being of the district.

Matters such as cattle stealing rarely come to the attention of the leopard-skin chief; the parties involved usually prefer to settle in their own private way. But if, for example, a murder has been committed, the culprit will go at once to the house of the leopard-skin chief. Immediately the chief cuts the culprit's arm so that blood flows; until the cut has been made the murderer may not eat or drink. If the murderer is afraid of vengeance by the slain man's family, he will remain at the house of the leopard-skin chief, which is considered sanctuary. Then, within the next few months, the chief attempts to mediate between the parties to the crime.

The chief elicits from the slayer's kin that they are prepared to pay compensation to avoid a feud and he per-

suades the dead man's kin that they ought to accept compensation. During this period neither party may eat or drink from the same vessels as the other, and they may not, therefore, eat in the house of the same third person. The chief then collects the cattle—till recently some forty to fifty beasts—and takes them to the dead man's home, where he performs various sacrifices of cleansing and atonement.[53]

The chief acts throughout as a go-between. He has no authority to force either of the parties to negotiate, and he has no power to enforce a solution once it has been arrived at. However, he is able to take advantage of the fact that because both parties to the dispute belong to the same community and are anxious to avoid a blood feud, they are usually willing to come to terms.

Ritual Reconciliation—Apology. The desire to restore a harmonious relationship may also explain ceremonial apologies. An apology is based on deference—the guilty party shows obeisance and asks for forgiveness. Such ceremonies tend to occur in recent chiefdoms.[54] Among the Fijians of the South Pacific, there is a strong ethic of harmony and mutual assistance, particularly within a village. When a person offends someone of higher status, the offended person and other villagers begin to avoid, and gossip about, the offender. If the offender is sensitive to village opinion, he or she will perform a ceremony of apology called *i soro*. One of the meanings of *soro* is "surrender." In the ceremony the offender keeps his or her head bowed and remains silent while an intermediary speaks, presents a token gift, and asks the offended person for forgiveness. The apology is rarely rejected.[55]

Oaths and Ordeals. Still another way of peacefully resolving disputes is through oaths and ordeals, both of which involve appeals to supernatural power. An **oath** is the act of calling upon a deity to bear witness to the truth of what one says. An **ordeal** is a means used to determine guilt or inno-

[52]Dane Archer and Rosemary Gartner, *Violence and Crime in Cross-National Perspective* (New Haven: Yale University Press, 1984), pp. 118–39.

[53]E. E. Evans-Pritchard, "The Nuer of the Southern Sudan," in M. Fortes and E. E. Evans-Pritchard, eds., *African Political Systems* (New York: Oxford University Press, 1940), p. 291. The discussion of Nuer follows ibid.

[54]Letitia Hickson, "The Social Contexts of Apology in Dispute Settlement: A Cross-Cultural Study," *Ethnology*, 25 (1986): 283–94.

[55]Ibid.; and Klaus-Friedrich Koch, Soraya Altorki, Andrew Arno, and Letitia Hickson, "Ritual Reconciliation and the Obviation of Grievances: A Comparative Study in the Ethnography of Law," *Ethnology*, 16 (1977): 279.

cence by submitting the accused to dangerous or painful tests believed to be under supernatural control.[56]

Oaths, as one would expect, vary widely in content according to the culture in which they are found. The Rwala Bedouin, for example, do the following:

In serious disputes the judge requires the *msabba* oath, so called from the seven lines drawn with a saber on the ground. The judge first draws a circle with a saber, then its diameter; then he intersects with five vertical lines, inviting the witness to step inside and, facing south, to swear: "A false oath is the ruin of the descendants, for he who [swears falsely] is insatiable in his desire [of gain] and does not fear for his Lord."[57]

Scarcely is the oath finished when the witness jumps out of the circle and, full of rage, runs at his opponent, who has made him swear. The people present at the trial have to surround and hold him until he calms down.

A common kind of ordeal, found in almost every part of the world, is scalding. Among the Tanala of Madagascar, the accused person, having first had his hand carefully examined for protective covering, has to reach his hand into a cauldron of boiling water and grasp, from underneath, a rock suspended there. He then plunges his hand into cold water, has it bandaged, and is led off to spend the night under guard. In the morning his hand is unbandaged and examined. If there are blisters, he is guilty.

Oaths and ordeals have also been practiced in Western societies. Both were common in medieval Europe. Even today, in our own society, vestiges of oaths can be found: children can be heard to say "Cross my heart and hope to die," and witnesses in courts of law are obliged to swear to tell the truth.

Why do some societies use oaths and ordeals? John Roberts suggests that they tend to be found in fairly complex societies where political officials lack sufficient power to make and enforce judicial decisions, or would make themselves unnecessarily vulnerable were they to attempt to do so. So the officials may use oaths and ordeals to let the gods decide guilt or innocence. When political officials gain more power, oaths and ordeals seem to decline or disappear.[58] In contrast, smaller and less complex societies probably have no need for elaborate mechanisms such as courts and oaths and ordeals to ascertain guilt. In such societies, everyone is aware of what crimes have been committed and who the guilty parties probably are.

Codified Law and the Courts. The use of codified laws and courts to resolve disputes peacefully exists in our own society. But codified laws and courts are not limited to Western societies. From the late seventeenth to the early twentieth century, for example, the Ashanti of West Africa had a complex political system with elaborate legal arrangements. The Ashanti state was a military-based empire possessing legal codes that resembled those of many ancient civilizations.[59]

The most effective sanction underpinning Ashanti law and its enforcement was the intense respect—almost religious deference—accorded the wishes of the ancestors and also the elders as custodians of the ancestral tradition. Ashanti law was based on a concept of natural law—a belief that there is an order of the universe whose principles lawmakers should follow in the decisions they make and in the regulations they design. Criminal and religious law were merged by the Ashanti: crimes—especially homicide, cursing of a chief, cowardice, and sorcery—were regarded as sins against the ancestral spirits. In Ashanti court procedure, elders examined and cross-examined witnesses as well as parties to the dispute. There were also quasi-professional advocates, and appeals against a verdict could be made directly to a chief. Particularly noteworthy was the emphasis on intent when assessing guilt. Drunkenness constituted a valid defense for all crimes except murder and cursing a chief, and a plea of insanity, if proved, was upheld for all offenses.

Ashanti punishments could be severe. Physical mutilation, such as slicing off the nose or an ear—even castration in sexual offenses—was often employed. However, fines were more frequent, and

---

[56]John M. Roberts, "Oaths, Autonomic Ordeals, and Power," in Clellan S. Ford, ed., *Cross-Cultural Approaches: Readings in Comparative Research* (New Haven: HRAF Press, 1967), p. 169. The discussion below follows ibid.

[57]Alois Musil, *The Manners and Customs of the Rwala Bedouins,* American Geographical Society, Oriental Exploration Studies no. 6 (New York, 1928), p. 430, as cited in Roberts, "Oaths, Autonomic Ordeals, and Power," pp. 169–70.

[58]Roberts, "Oaths, Autonomic Ordeals, and Power," p. 192.

[59]Hoebel, *The Law of Primitive Man,* chap. 9.

death sentences could often be commuted to banishment and confiscation of goods.

Why do some societies have codified systems of law while others do not? One explanation, advanced by E. Adamson Hoebel, A. R. Radcliffe-Brown, and others, is that in small, closely knit communities there is little need for formal legal guidelines because competing interests are minimal. Simple societies need little codified law: there are relatively few matters to quarrel about, and the general will of the group is sufficiently well known and demonstrated frequently enough to deter transgressors.

This point of view is corroborated in Richard Schwartz's study of two Israeli settlements. In one communal kibbutz, a young man aroused a good deal of community resentment because he had accepted an electric teakettle as a gift. It was the general opinion that he had overstepped the code about not having personal possessions, and he was so informed. Accordingly, he gave the kettle to the communal infirmary. Schwartz observed that "no organized enforcement of the decision was threatened, but had he disregarded the expressed will of the community, his life . . . would have been made intolerable by the antagonism of public opinion."[60]

In this community, where people worked and ate together, not only did everyone know about transgressions, but a wrongdoer could not escape public censure. Thus, public opinion was an effective sanction. In another Israeli community, however, where individuals lived in widely separated houses and worked and ate separately, public opinion did not work as well. Not only were community members less aware of problems, but they had no quick way of making their feelings known. As a result, they established a judicial body to handle trouble cases.

Larger, more heterogeneous and stratified societies are likely to have more frequent disputes, which at the same time are less visible to the public. Individuals in stratified societies are generally not so dependent on community members for their well-being and hence are less likely to know of, or care about, others' opinions. It is in such societies

that codified laws and formal authorities for resolving disputes develop—in order, perhaps, that disputes may be settled impersonally enough so that the parties can accept the decision and social order can be restored.

A good example of how more formal systems of law develop is the experience of towns in the American West during the gold-rush period. These communities were literally swamped by total strangers. The townsfolk, having no control (authority) over these intruders because the strangers had no local ties, looked for ways to deal with the troublesome cases that were continually flaring up. A first attempt at a solution was to hire gunslingers—who were also strangers—to act as peace officers or sheriffs, but this usually failed. Eventually, towns succeeded in having federal authorities send in marshals backed by federal power.

Is there some evidence to support the theory that codified law is necessary only in larger, more complex societies? Data from a large, worldwide sample of societies suggest that codified law is generally associated with political integration beyond the local level. Murder cases, for example, are dealt with informally in societies with only local political organization. In societies with multi-local political units, murder cases tend to be adjudicated by specialized political authorities.[61] There is also some cross-cultural evidence that violence within a society tends to be less frequent when there are formal authorities (chiefs, courts) who have the power to punish murderers.[62]

Violent Resolution of Conflict

People are likely to resort to violence when regular, effective alternative means of resolving a conflict are not available. When violence occurs between political entities such as communities, districts, or nations, we call it warfare. The type of warfare, of course, varies in scope and complexity from society to society. Sometimes a distinction is made among **feuding, raiding,** and large-scale confrontations.

Feuding. Feuding is a state of recurring hostilities between families or groups of kin, usually appar-

[60]Richard D. Schwartz, "Social Factors in the Development of Legal Control: A Case Study of Two Israeli Settlements," *Yale Law Journal*, 63 (February 1954): 475.

[61]Textor, comp., *A Cross-Cultural Summary.*
[62]Wilfred T. Masumura, "Law and Violence: A Cross-Cultural Study," *Journal of Anthropological Research,* 33 (1977): 388–99.

cially when murder has been committed. Gubser describes what happens when a man is killed:

> The closely related members of his kindred do not rest until complete revenge has been achieved. The immediate relatives of the deceased . . . recruit as much support from other relatives as they can. Their first action, if possible, is to kill the murderer, or maybe one of his closest kin. Then, of course, the members of the murderer's kindred are brought into the feud. These two kindreds may snipe at each other for years.[63]

Feuds are by no means limited to small-scale societies; they occur as frequently in societies with high levels of political organization.[64]

Raiding. Raiding is a short-term use of force, generally carefully planned and organized, to realize a limited objective. This objective is usually the acquisition of goods, animals, or other forms of wealth belonging to another (often a neighboring) community. Raiding is especially prevalent in pastoral societies, in which cattle, horses, camels, or other animals are prized and an individual's own herd can be augmented by theft. Raids are often organized by temporary leaders or coordinators whose authority may not endure beyond the planning and execution of the venture.

Large-Scale Confrontations. Both feuding and raiding usually involve relatively small numbers of persons and almost always an element of surprise. Because they are generally attacked without warning, the victims are often unable to muster an immediate defense. Large-scale confrontations, in contrast, involve a large number of persons and planning by both sides of strategies of attack and defense.

Large-scale warfare is usually practiced among societies with intensive agriculture or industrialization. Only these societies possess a technology sufficiently advanced to support specialized armies, military leaders, strategists, and so on. However, large-scale confrontations are not limited to state societies: they occur, for example, among the horticultural Dugum Dani of central New Guinea.

The military history of the Dani, with its shifting alliances and confederations, is reminiscent of

Small societies sometimes have large-scale confrontations. Here we see an assembly of Asmat warriors in canoes off the West Irian coast of New Guinea.

ently motivated by a desire to avenge an offense—whether insult, injury, deprivation, or death—against a member of the group. The most characteristic feature of the feud is that responsibility to avenge is carried by all members of the kin group. The killing of any member of the offender's group is considered appropriate revenge, since the kin group as a whole is regarded as responsible. Nicholas Gubser tells of a feud within a Nunamiut Inuit community, caused by a husband's killing of his wife's lover, that lasted for decades. The Nunamiut take feuds seriously, as do many societies, espe-

[63]Nicholas J. Gubser, *The Nunamiut Eskimos: Hunters of Caribou* (New Haven: Yale University Press, 1965), p. 151.

[64]Keith F. Otterbein and Charlotte Swanson Otterbein, "An Eye for an Eye, A Tooth for a Tooth: A Cross-Cultural Study of Feuding," *American Anthropologist*, 67 (1965): 1476.

that of Europe, although Dani battles involve far fewer fighters and less sophisticated weaponry. Among the Dani, long periods of ritual warfare are characterized by formal battles announced through a challenge sent by one side to the opposing side. If the challenge is accepted, the protagonists meet at the agreed-upon battle site to set up their lines. Fighting with spears, sticks, and bows and arrows begins at midmorning and continues either until nightfall or until rain intervenes. There may also be a rest period during the midday heat during which both sides shout insults at each other or talk and rest among themselves.

The front line of battle is composed of about a dozen active warriors and a few leaders. Behind them is a second line, still within arrow range, composed of those who have just left the forward line or are preparing to join it. The third line, outside arrow range, is composed of noncombatants—males too old or too young to participate and those recovering from wounds. This third line merely watches the battle taking place on the grassy plain. On the hillsides far back from the front line, some of the old men help to direct ancestral ghosts to the battle by gouging a line in the ground that points in the direction of the battlefield.[65]

Yet, as total as large-scale confrontations may be, even warfare has cultural rules. Among the Dani, for instance, no fighting occurs at night, and weapons are limited to simple spears and bows and arrows. Similarly, in state societies, governments will sign "self-denying" pacts restricting the use of poison gas, germ warfare, and so forth. Unofficially, private arrangements are common. One has only to glance through the memoirs of national leaders of the two world wars to become aware of locally arranged truces, visits to one another's front positions, exchanges of prisoners of war, and so on.

Explaining Warfare

Most societies anthropology knows about have had warfare between communities or larger territorial groups. (The vast majority of the societies in a recent cross-cultural study had at least occasional wars when they were first described, unless they had been pacified or incorporated by more dominant societies.[66]) Yet relatively little research has been done on the possible causes of war and why it varies in type and frequency. Why have some people fought a great deal, and others only infrequently? Why in some societies does warfare occur internally (within the society or language group)?

We have tentative and perhaps only partial answers to some of these questions. There is evidence that people in preindustrial societies may mostly go to war out of fear—particularly a fear of expectable but unpredictable natural disasters (e.g., droughts, floods, locust infestations) that will destroy food resources. People may think they can protect themselves against such disasters ahead of time by taking things from defeated enemies. In any case, preindustrial societies with higher frequencies of war are very likely to have had a history of expectable but unpredictable disasters. Since chronic (annually recurring) food shortages do not predict higher frequencies of war, it would appear that people may go to war in an attempt to cushion the impact of the disasters they expect to occur in the future but cannot predict (or control or prevent). Consistent with this tentative conclusion is the fact that the victors in war almost always take land or other resources from the defeated. And this is true for simpler as well as more complex preindustrial societies.[67] Might similar motives affect decisions about war and peace in the modern world?

We know that complex or politically centralized societies are more likely to have professional armies, hierarchies of military authority, and sophisticated weapons.[68] But surprisingly, the fre-

[65]Karl Heider, *The Dugum Dani* (Chicago: Aldine, 1970), pp. 105–11. See also Karl Heider, *Grand Valley Dani: Peaceful Warriors* (New York: Holt, Rinehart & Winston, 1979), pp. 88–99.

[66]Melvin Ember and Carol R. Ember, "Cross-Cultural Studies of War and Peace: Recent Achievements and Future Possibilities," in S.P. Reyna and R.E. Downs, eds., *Studying War: Anthropological Perspectives* (New York: Gordon & Breach, 1992), in press.

[67]Carol R. Ember and Melvin Ember, "Resource Unpredictability, Mistrust, and War: A Cross-Cultural Study," *Journal of Conflict Resolution*, 36 (1992): 242–262. See also Melvin Ember, "Statistical Evidence for an Ecological Explanation of Warfare," *American Anthropologist*, 84 (1982): 645–49. For a discussion of how Dani warfare seems to be motivated mainly by economic considerations, see Paul Shankman, "Culture Contact, Cultural Ecology, and Dani Warfare," *Man*, 26 (1991): 299–321.

[68]Keith Otterbein, *The Evolution of War* (New Haven: HRAF Press, 1970).

quency of warfare seems to be not much greater in complex societies than in simple band or tribal societies.[69]

We have some evidence that warfare is unlikely to occur internally (within a society) if it is small in population (21,000 people or less) or territory; in a larger society there is a high likelihood of warfare within the society, between communities or larger territorial divisions.[70] In fact, complex societies even if they are politically unified are not less likely than simpler societies to have internal warfare.[71]

What, if anything, do we know about recent warfare between nation-states? Here we also have some surprising findings. Although many people think that military alliances lessen the chance of war, it turns out that nations formally allied with other nations have gone to war more often than nations lacking formal alliances. Also, trade relationships do not appear to lessen the chance of war. Rather, disputes between trading partners escalate to war more frequently than disputes between nations that do not trade much with each other. Finally, military equality between nations, particularly when preceded by a rapid military buildup, seems to increase rather than lessen the chance of war between those nations.[72]

Clearly, these findings contradict some traditional beliefs about how to prevent war. If alliances, trade, and military buildups do *not* make war less likely, what may? We have already noted that more participatory (more "democratic") political systems are less likely to go to war with each other. Later, in the chapter on social problems, we discuss how the results of these recent studies may translate into policies that could minimize the risk of war in the world.

[69]Ember and Ember, "Resource Unpredictability, Mistrust, and War." See also Otterbein, *The Evolution of War;* and Colin K. Loftin, "Warfare and Societal Complexity: A Cross-Cultural Study of Organized Fighting in Preindustrial Societies" (Ph.D. diss., University of North Carolina at Chapel Hill, 1971).

[70]Carol R. Ember, "An Evaluation of Alternative Theories of Matrilocal versus Patrilocal Residence," *Behavior Science Research,* 9 (1974): 135–49.

[71]Keith F. Otterbein, "Internal War: A Cross-Cultural Study," *American Anthropologist,* 70 (1968): 283. See also Marc H. Ross, "Internal and External Conflict and Violence," *Journal of Conflict Resolution,* 29 (1985): 547–79.

[72]J. David Singer, "Accounting for International War: The State of the Discipline," *Annual Review of Sociology,* 6 (1980): 349–67.

SUMMARY

1. All societies have customs or procedures that, organized on behalf of territorial groups, result in decision making and the resolution of disputes. However, these ways of creating and maintaining social order and coping with social disorder vary from society to society.

2. Societies with a band type of political organization are composed of a number of fairly small, usually nomadic groups. Each of these bands is politically autonomous, the band being the largest group that acts as a political unit. Authority within the band is usually informal. Societies with band organization generally are egalitarian hunter-gatherers. But it is possible that band organization may not have been typical of food collectors in the distant past.

3. Societies with tribal organization are similar to those with band organization in being egalitarian. But in contrast with band societies, they generally are food producers, have a higher population density, and are more sedentary. Tribal organization is defined by the presence of groupings (such as clans and age-sets) that can integrate more than one local group into a larger whole.

4. The personal qualities of leaders in tribal societies seem to be similar to the qualities of leaders in the United States, with one major difference: United States leaders are wealthier than others in their society.

5. Chiefdoms differ from societies with tribal organization in having formal authority structures that integrate multi-community political units. Compared with tribal societies, chiefdoms generally are more densely populated and their communities are more permanent. In contrast to "big men" in tribal societies, who generally have to earn their privileges by their personal qualities, chiefs generally hold their positions permanently. Most chiefdom societies have social ranking.

6. A state has been defined as a political unit composed of many communities and having a centralized government with the authority to make and enforce laws, collect taxes, and draft men for military service. In state societies, the government tries to maintain a monopoly on the use of physical force. In addition, states are generally characterized by class stratification, intensive agriculture (the high productivity of which presumably allows the emergence of cities), commercial exchange, a high degree of economic and other specialization, and extensive foreign trade. The rulers of a state cannot depend forever on the use or threat of force to maintain their power; the people must believe the rulers are legitimate or have the right to govern.

7. Degree of political participation varies in the societies studied by anthropologists, just as among modern nation-states. A high degree of participation, in small-scale as well as modern state societies, may be related to the impossibility or dif-ficulty of forcing people to comply with authoritative decisions.

8. Societies have found various ways of resolving disputes peacefully. Collective action and informal adjudication are common in simpler societies. Ritual apology occurs frequently in chiefdoms. Oaths and ordeals tend to occur in complex societies where political officials lack power to enforce judicial decisions. Capital punishment seems to exist in nearly all societies, from the simplest to the most complex.

9. People are likely to resort to violence when regular, effective alternative means of resolving a conflict are not available. Violence that occurs between political entities such as communities, districts, or nations is generally referred to as warfare. The type of warfare varies in scope and complexity from society to society. Preindustrial societies with higher warfare frequencies are likely to have had a history of unpredictable disasters that destroyed food supplies.

SUGGESTED READING

COHEN, R., AND SERVICE, E. R., eds. *Origins of the State: The Anthropology of Political Evolution.* Philadelphia: Institute for the Study of Human Issues, 1978. A collection of theoretical and empirical papers on the possible origins of states.

FERGUSON, R. B., ed. *Warfare, Culture, and Environment.* Orlando, FL: Academic Press, 1984. An introduction to the anthropological literature on war, followed by eleven theoretical and ethnographic essays that examine warfare from a "materialist" perspective.

FRIED, M. H. *The Evolution of Political Society: An Essay in Political Anthropology.* New York: Random House, 1967. A theoretical work that begins with general remarks on the anthropology of political organization and goes on to describe differences between kinds of societies in terms of their political structures.

HAAS, J., ed. *The Anthropology of War.* Cambridge: Cambridge University Press, 1990. The contributors to this volume discuss war in general and in particular places, focusing on explanatory models of warfare, origins versus persistence of warfare, and causes versus effects of warfare in nonstate societies.

HOEBEL, E. A. *The Law of Primitive Man.* New York: Atheneum, 1968 (originally published in 1954). This book is divided into three parts: a theoretical and methodological background for the study of nonstate law; a discussion of legal systems among the Inuit, Plains Indians, Trobrianders, and Ashanti; and a treatment of law and society—the relationship of law to religion and magic, its social functions, and its development through time.

SERVICE, E. R. *Primitive Social Organization: An Evolutionary Perspective.* New York: Random House, 1962. A classification of nonstate societies into band societies, tribal societies, and chiefdoms. The author presents the criteria by which these levels are defined and suggests possible reasons for their development.

22

Psychology and Culture

Visitors to another society often come to feel that the people there think differently, or have different reactions to situations, that they seem to have different **personalities** (distinctive ways of thinking, feeling, and behaving) compared with people back home. Stereotypes are born from these casual observations: certain peoples are thought to be reserved, others authoritarian, still others hot-tempered. Although anthropologists generally reject such stereotypes because they are often based on hasty, even ethnocentric judgments, they do not reject the idea that there may be differences from society to society in some aspects of thinking, feeling, and behaving.

Consider the contrast in feelings and behavior between the Semai of central Malaya and the Yanomamö of the Brazil-Venezuela border—a contrast that clearly expresses differences in personality. The Semai are famous in Malaya for their timidity and have never been described as hostile or surly. When asked about anger, the Semai say, "We do not get angry."[1] The Yanomamö, on the other hand, are famous for their fierceness. They not only have chronic warfare between villages, but frequently show aggression within a village. Shouting and threatening to obtain demands is frequent, as is wife beating and bloody fights with clubs. Men are proud of their scars and sometimes shave their heads to display them.[2]

Even though there may be psychological differences between societies, there also are psychological similarities. After all, we are all human. People the world over cry or weep when a loved one dies, laugh or smile when something good happens, learn from mistakes, and have many of the same needs. Anthropologists who are interested in psychological differences between and within societies and in psychological similarities across the broad range of human societies call themselves *psychological anthropologists*. (Psychologists who study people in two or more societies call themselves *cross-cultural psychologists*.) Three main questions seem to characterize psychological anthropology: To what extent do all human beings develop psychologically in the same ways? What accounts for the apparent differences in personality characteristics from one society to another? What kinds of cultural variation might be explained by psychological factors? This chapter discusses some of the attempts made by researchers to answer these questions.

The Universality of Psychological Development

Anthropologists became interested in psychology in the early years of this century, partly because they did not believe that human nature was completely revealed in Western societies, as psychologists then generally assumed. Only recently have many psychologists joined anthropologists in questioning the assumption that humans are exactly the same psychologically in all societies. Psychologist Otto Klineberg, for example, scolded his colleagues in 1974: "My contact with anthropology affected me somewhat like a religious conversion. How could psychologists speak of *human* attributes and *human* behavior when they knew only one kind of human being?"[3]

Since humans the world over are the same species, we might assume that there is a good deal of similarity across societies in the way people develop psychologically from birth to maturity. But people the world over grow up in very different environments and cultures, which may influence psychological development. In what respects is human development the same the world over? In what respects is it different?

Early Research on Emotional Development

When Margaret Mead went to American Samoa in the mid 1920s, psychologists believed that adolescence was universally a period of "storm and stress" because of the physiological changes that occur at puberty. Mead's observations of, and interviews with, Samoan adolescent girls led her to doubt the idea that adolescence was necessarily a

[1]Robert K. Dentan, *The Semai: A Nonviolent People of Malaya* (New York: Holt, Rinehart & Winston, 1968), pp. 55–56.

[2]Napoleon A. Chagnon, *Yanomamö: The Fierce People*, 3rd ed. (New York: CBS College Publishing, 1983).

[3]Quoted in Otto Klineberg, "Foreword," in Marshall H. Segall, *Cross-Cultural Psychology: Human Behavior in Global Perspective* (Monterey, CA: Brooks/Cole, 1979), p. v.

Children do not learn to express themselves in dance in all societies, as they do in Tahiti. We need to understand how much is universal in emotional development.

time of turmoil. The Samoan girls apparently showed little evidence of emotional upheaval and rebelliousness, and therefore it was questionable whether psychological development in adolescence was the same in all societies.[4]

Bronislaw Malinowski was another early anthropologist who questioned the universality of an assumption about emotional development, in this case Freud's assumption that young boys universally see themselves (unconsciously) as sexual rivals of their fathers for possession of their mothers. Freud had called these feelings the Oedipus complex, after the character in Greek mythology who killed his father and married his mother without knowing that they were his parents. Freud thought that all boys before the age of seven or so would show hostility toward their fathers, but Malinowski disagreed on the basis of his fieldwork in the matrilineal Trobriand Islands.[5]

Malinowski suggested that young boys in non-matrilineal societies may feel hostility toward the father not as a sexual rival but as the disciplinarian. Malinowski proposed this theory because he thought that the Oedipus complex works differently in matrilineal societies. Boys in matrilineal societies may feel more hostile toward their mother's brother—who is the main authority figure in the matrilineal kin group—than toward their father.

Derek Freeman has criticized Mead's conclusions about Samoa[6] and Melford Spiro has challenged Malinowski's conclusions about the Trobriand Islanders.[7] Mead and Malinowski may or may not have been correct about the societies they studied (we really cannot know for sure because we cannot travel back in time), but the issues they

[4]Margaret Mead, *Coming of Age in Samoa,* 3rd ed. (New York: Morrow, 1961 [originally published in 1928]).

[5]Bronislaw Malinowski, *Sex and Repression in Savage Society* (Cleveland: World, 1968; London: Kegan Paul, Trench, Trubner Co., 1927).

[6]Derek Freeman, *Margaret Mead and Samoa: The Making and Unmaking of an Anthropological Myth* (Cambridge, MA: Harvard University Press, 1983). For reasons to be skeptical about Freeman's criticism, see Melvin Ember, "Evidence and Science in Ethnography: Reflections on the Freeman-Mead Controversy," *American Anthropologist,* 87 (1985): 906–9.

[7]Melford E. Spiro, *Oedipus in the Trobriands* (Chicago: University of Chicago Press, 1982).

raised remain crucial to the question of whether psychological development is similar in all societies. To find out, we need research in *many* societies, not just a few. Only on the basis of extensive cross-cultural research will we be able to decide whether stages of emotional development can be affected by cultural differences.

For example, it is only recently that adolescence has been systematically studied cross-culturally. Alice Schlegel and Herbert Barry report that adolescence is generally not a period of overt rebelliousness, which they suggest is related to the fact that most people in most societies live with or near (and depend on) close kin before and after they grow up. Only in societies like our own, where children generally leave home when they grow up, might adolescents be rebellious, possibly to prepare emotionally for going out on their own.[8]

Research on Cognitive Development

One day the two of us went out for pizza. The pizza maker was laughing hilariously, and we asked what was so funny. He told us: "I just asked the guy ahead of you, 'How many slices do you want me to cut the pizza into, six or eight?' 'Six,' he said, 'I'm not very hungry.' "

According to a theory of cognitive (intellectual) development suggested by Jean Piaget, the renowned Swiss psychologist, the "not very hungry" guy had not yet acquired the concept of *conservation*, which characterizes a stage of thinking normally acquired by children between the ages of seven and eleven in Western societies.[9] The pizza customer ahead of us, like many very young children, seemed not to understand that certain properties of an object (such as quantity, weight, and volume) remain constant even if the object is divided into small pieces or removed to a container of a different shape. They have not acquired the mental image of *reversibility*, the ability to imagine that if you put the pizza back together again it would be the same size whether you had previously cut it into eight or six slices. To the child or adult who has not acquired the ability to reverse actions

mentally, eight slices may seem like more pizza than six slices, because eight is more than six.

Piaget's theory says that the development of thinking in humans involves a series of stages, each of which is characterized by different mental skills. To get to a higher stage of thinking, one has to pass through a lower stage. So, Piaget's theory would predict that the pizza customer would not be able to think systematically about the possible outcomes of hypothetical situations (a defining feature of Piaget's *formal-operational* stage) because he had not acquired the notion of conservation and the other mental skills that characterize the previous (*concrete-operational*) stage of cognitive development.

What does the available evidence suggest about the universality of Piaget's supposed stages? And do people the world over get to each stage at the same age?

The first stage of development (*sensorimotor*) has not been investigated in many societies, but the results of studies conducted so far are remarkably consistent. Babies in a number of different places seem to think similarly, judging from their reactions to the same conditions. For example, a comparison of French babies and Baoulé babies in the Ivory Coast (West Africa) showed that the Baoulé babies, who had never seen objects such as red plastic tubes and paper clips, nevertheless tried to pass the clips through the tubes in the same way the French babies did. Both sets of babies even made the same kinds of errors.[10]

Most of the cross-cultural studies of Piaget's stages have focused on the transition between the second (*preoperational*) and third (*concrete-operational*) stages, particularly the attainment of the concept of conservation. The results of these studies are somewhat puzzling. Although older children are generally more likely to show conservation than younger children, it is not clear what to make of the apparent finding that the attainment of conservation is much delayed in many non-Western populations. Indeed, in some places most of the adults tested do not appear to understand one or more of the conservation properties.

[8]Alice Schlegel and Herbert Barry III, *Adolescence: An Anthropological Inquiry* (New York: Free Press, 1991), p. 44.
[9]Jean Piaget, "Piaget's Theory," in Paul Mussen, ed., *Carmichael's Manual of Child Psychology*, 3rd ed. (New York: John Wiley, 1970), 1: 703–32.

[10]Pierre R. Dasen and Alastair Heron, "Cross-Cultural Tests of Piaget's Theory," in Harry C. Triandis and Alastair Heron, eds., *Handbook of Cross-Cultural Psychology*, Vol. 4, *Developmental Psychology* (Boston: Allyn & Bacon, 1981), pp. 305–6.

A girl four and a half years old being tested for conservation (of area).

Can this be true? Do people differ that much cross-culturally in intellectual functioning, or is there some Western bias built into the way conservation is measured? Is it possible that an adult who just brought water from the river in a large jug and poured it into five smaller containers does not know that the quantity of water is still the same? We may also be skeptical about the findings on the formal-operational stage. Most of the studies of formal operational thinking have found little evidence of such thinking in non-Western populations. But people in nonliterate societies surely have formal operational thinking if they can navigate using the stars, remember how to return to camp after a 15-mile trek, or identify how people are related to each other three and more generations back.

The main reason we may be skeptical about the apparent findings on conservation and formal operational thinking is that most of the cross-cultural psychologists have taken tests developed here (in our own and other Western countries) to measure cognitive development elsewhere.[11] This procedure puts non-Westerners at a considerable disadvantage, because they are not as familiar as Westerners with the test materials and the whole testing situation. For example, in tests of conservation, researchers have often used strange-looking glass cylinders and beakers. The few researchers who have used natively familiar materials, however, have gotten different results. Douglass Price-Williams, for example, found no difference between Tiv (West Africa) and European children in understanding the conservation of earth, nuts, and number.[12] Tests of formal operations often ask questions dealing with content that is taught in science and mathematics classes, so it may not be surprising that schooled individuals usually do better than the nonschooled on these tests. Thus, where compulsory schooling is lacking, we should not expect people to do well on our tests of formal operational thinking.[13]

In trying to find out what may be universal in emotional and cognitive development, researchers have discovered some apparent differences between societies. These differences, which we now turn to, need to be explored and explained.

Cross-Cultural Variation in Psychological Characteristics

Thinking about personality differences seems to come easy to many North Americans. We like to talk about the psychology of those we know. We speculate why one friend is emotional, why another has a hot temper, why another is shy. We may also wonder why one friend is likely to remember faces and why another is a whiz at computers. We are interested in personality as an individual characteristic, and we emphasize the uniqueness of each individual. Indeed, because every person has a unique combination of genetic traits and life experiences, we can say that in some ways no person is like any other person. But anthropologists are interested in approaching personality from a different perspective. Instead of focusing on the uniqueness of an individual, psychological anthropologists are interested in those aspects of personality that may be common in a population.

[11]Carol R. Ember, "Cross-Cultural Cognitive Studies," *Annual Review of Anthropology*, 6 (1977): 33–56; and Barbara Rogoff, "Schooling and the Development of Cognitive Skills," in Triandis and Heron, eds., *Handbook of Cross-Cultural Psychology*, vol. 4, *Developmental Psychology*, pp. 233–94.

[12]Douglass Price-Williams, "A Study concerning Concepts of Conservation of Quantities among Primitive Children," *Acta Psychologica*, 18 (1961): 297–305.

[13]Rogoff, "Schooling and the Development of Cognitive Skills," pp. 264–67.

Toilet training in a Soviet Russian nursery school is a more communal experience than in the United States, where parents focus their concern on one child at a time.

Why should we expect different societies to differ in some personality characteristics? It is generally agreed that our personalities are the result of an interaction between genetic inheritance and life experiences. But a considerable portion of one's life experiences (as well as one's genes) is shared with others. Parents undoubtedly exert a major influence on the way we grow up. Because family members share similar life experiences (as well as genes), they may be somewhat similar in personality. But we have to consider why a particular family raises children the way it does. To some extent, all families are unique. Yet much of the way parents rear children is influenced by their culture—by typical patterns of family life and by shared conceptions of the way to bring up children.

It is not easy to determine the extent to which members of our society share conceptions of the way to bring up children, because as we look around at various families in our own society we observe differences in upbringing and different

ideas about the "right" way to bring up children. Indeed, some parents seem determined to bring up their children in unconventional ways. Still, in a study of unconventional California families (headed by single mothers, unmarried couples, or living in communes), researchers found that compared with parents in other societies, unconventional parents do not differ that much from conventional parents (married, living in nuclear families).[14] For example, even though unconventional California mothers breast-feed their children for a significantly longer period than conventional mothers, both types of mothers usually stop breast feeding after about a year, which is way below the worldwide average. In 70 percent of the world's societies, mothers typically breast-feed children for at least two years; last-born children may be weaned even later. In a few societies, such as the Chenchu of India,

[14]Thomas S. Weisner, Mary Bausano, and Madeleine Kornfein, "Putting Family Ideals into Practice: Pronaturalism in Conventional and Nonconventional California Families," *Ethos*, 11 (1983): 278–304.

children typically may not be weaned until they are five or six years old.[15] The California parents differ in other ways too, compared with parents in most other societies. In the California study, no parent (conventional or unconventional) was observed to carry a baby more than 25 percent of the time, but it is not uncommon in many societies for babies to be held more than half the day.[16]

It is only when we examine other societies and their patterns of child rearing that our own cultural conceptions begin to become apparent. Consider how attitudes toward childhood sexuality vary cross-culturally.

The Alorese of Indonesia used to masturbate their children to pacify them; the Manus of New Guinea used to think that masturbation was shameful. Adults in our society generally attempt to prevent or restrict the masturbation in children. Attitudes toward sex play differ cross-culturally, from the more restrictive approaches of the Chiricahua Apache of the southwestern United States, who separated the sexes by the seventh year, to the Baiga of southern Asia, who used to encourage young children to engage in erotic play. The Hopi filled their young with dire warnings of the consequences of early sexual experience. They would tell boys to abstain lest they become dwarfs, and they warned young girls that they would become pregnant, thereby causing all people to die and the world to come to an end.[17]

With respect to aggression, the Yanomamö and the Semai have very different ways of dealing with children. This is not surprising, in view of the way adult behaviors and attitudes differ in the two societies. Yanomamö boys are encouraged to be fierce and are rarely punished for hitting either their parents or the girls in the village. One father, for example, lets his son Ariwari

beat him on the face and head to express his anger and temper, laughing and commenting on his ferocity. Although Ariwari is only about four years old, he has already learned that the appropriate response to a flash of anger is to strike someone with his hand or with an object, and it is not uncommon for him to give his father a healthy smack in the face whenever something displeases him. He is frequently goaded into hitting his father by teasing, being rewarded by gleeful cheers of assent from his mother and from the other adults in the household.[18]

Whereas the Yanomamö clearly and actively encourage aggression, the Semai communicate nonviolence in more subtle ways. They say, in fact, that they do not teach children. The Semai expect children to be nonviolent and are shocked when children do not conform. On the occasions when a child loses its temper, an adult will simply cart it off and bring it home. Perhaps most surprisingly, the Semai do not physically punish a child's aggression—but this may be one of the most important teaching devices of all. With such "teaching" a child hardly ever sees an aggressive model and has no aggression to imitate.[19] In comparison with the ways Semai and Yanomamö parents treat their children, most North American parents are probably somewhere in the middle. Hardly any North American parents would encourage children to hit them in the face, or encourage them to hit other children. Yet many North American parents probably use physical punishment sometimes and many feel that boys especially should "stand up for themselves" if another child provokes a fight.

As these examples suggest, societies vary in how they bring up children. We can assume that the way children are reared determines in part the type of personality they will have in adulthood. In other words, different societies, with different customs of child rearing, will probably tend to produce different kinds of people. There are other cultural differences that may produce differences in typical personality characteristics. As we will see, growing up in an extended family and going to school seem to affect personality development. All of this is not to suggest, however, that all personalities in a society are the same. As we have said, an individual's uniqueness is derived from his or her distinctive genetic endowment and life experiences—and thus one personality will be somewhat different from another within the same culture or subculture.

---

[15]John W. M. Whiting and Irvin L. Child, *Child Training and Personality: A Cross-Cultural Study* (New Haven: Yale University Press, 1953), pp. 69–71.

[16]Weisner, Bausano, and Kornfein, "Putting Family Ideals into Practice," p. 291.

[17]Whiting and Child, *Child Training and Personality*, pp. 80–83.

[18]Chagnon, *Yanomamö*, p. 115.

[19]Dentan, *The Semai*, p. 61.

Yanamamö men dueling.

Cultural anthropologists are interested in shared patterns of behavior, belief, feeling, and thinking. They are therefore interested in those aspects of personality that are typically shared with others—other members of the society or other members of some subcultural group. These shared characteristics are often referred to as **modal personality characteristics**—those traits that occur with the highest frequency in the society or subcultural group. A personality characteristic can be thought of as more or less of a particular attribute. Aggressiveness is not present or absent in a person, but is found to a greater or lesser degree in some people as compared with others. Similarly, to say that the exhibition of a great deal of physical or verbal aggression is a modal personality trait in some societies is always to make a relative judgment. When we speak of a modal personality characteristic such as aggressiveness, we mean that most people in the society display more aggressiveness than most people in some other society. For example, compared with societies such as the Se-

mai, the Yanomamö would rank high on aggressiveness as a modal personality trait.

Just as culture is never fixed or static, so modal personality characteristics are never static. Individuals often alter their behavior in adapting to changing circumstances. When enough individuals in a society have altered their own behavior or the way they bring up their children, modal personality characteristics presumably will also have changed.

Explaining Psychological Variation: Cultural Factors

To understand cross-cultural variation in psychological characteristics, many researchers have tried to discover if variation in child-rearing customs may account for observed psychological differences. **Socialization** is a term used by both anthropologists and psychologists to describe the development, through the influence of parents and others, of patterns of behavior in children that conform to cultural expectations. Socialization can be direct or indirect. Parents and others often try to socialize their children directly by rewarding certain behaviors and ignoring or punishing other behaviors. But socialization may also be more subtle. As we will see, the degree to which parents like or do not like children, the kinds of work children are asked to do, and whether or not children go to school may at least partly influence how children develop psychologically.

Parental Acceptance and Rejection. Cora Du Bois spent almost eighteen months on the island of Alor, in eastern Indonesia, studying the native Alorese. To understand the Alorese modal personality, she broke new ground by asking specialists in various fields to assess and interpret her field data independently. These authorities were given no background briefing on Alorese culture or attitudes, nor were they permitted to see Du Bois's general ethnographic notes or interpretations. To a remarkable degree, their findings concurred with hers.[20]

A rather unfavorable modal personality for the Alorese emerges from this many-sided investigation. Alorese of both sexes were described by Du Bois and her colleagues as suspicious and antagonistic, prone to violent, emotional, and often jealous outbursts. They tend to be uninterested in the world around them, slovenly in workmanship, and indifferent to goals.

Turning to the possible causal influences, Du Bois and her co-researchers focused on the experiences of the Alorese during infancy and early childhood, up to the age of six or so. At the root of much of Alorese personality development, they suggested, is the division of labor in that society. Women are the major food suppliers, working daily in the family gardens; men occupy themselves with commercial affairs, usually the trading of pigs, gongs, and kettledrums. Within about two weeks of giving birth, a mother returns to her outdoor work, leaving the infant with the father, a grandparent, or an older sibling. For most of the day she deprives the newborn child of the comfort of a maternal presence and of breast feeding. In Freudian terms, the infant experiences oral frustration and resultant anxiety. At the same time, the baby suffers bewildering switches in attention, from loving and petting to neglect and bad-tempered rejection. Thus, maternal neglect is viewed as being largely responsible for Alorese personality.

But how do we know that maternal neglect is really responsible for the seeming suspiciousness and jealous outbursts of the Alorese? Perhaps maternal neglect is responsible, but the cause could also be any number of other conditions of Alorese life. For example, some critics have suggested that the high prevalence of debilitating diseases in Alor may be responsible for much of the behavior of the Alorese.[21] For us to be more certain that a particular aspect of child rearing produces certain effects on modal personality, we must compare the people of Alor with people in other societies. Do other societies with this kind of maternal neglect show the same pattern of personality traits? If they do, then the presumed association becomes more plausible. If they do not, then the interpretation becomes questionable.

Recent research seems to support many of the conclusions of the Alorese study. Ruth and Robert Munroe found that children who were often held or carried by their mothers as infants were significantly more trusting and optimistic at age five than other children.[22] In a cross-cultural comparison of 101 societies, Ronald Rohner found that children tend to be more hostile and aggressive when they are neglected and not treated affectionately by their parents. In the societies where children are rejected, adults seem to view life and the world as unfriendly, uncertain, and hostile.[23]

Why are some societies (such as the Alorese) characterized by parental neglect, while in other societies parents typically accept or show warmth and affection to their children? The Rohner study suggests that rejection is likely where mothers get no relief from child care; when fathers and grandparents play a role in child care, rejection is less

[20]Cora Du Bois, *The People of Alor: A Social-Psychological Study of an East Indian Island* (Minneapolis: University of Minnesota Press, 1944).

[21]Victor Barnouw, *Culture and Personality,* 4th ed. (Homewood, IL: Dorsey Press, 1985), p. 118.

[22]Ruth H. Munroe and Robert L. Munroe, "Infant Experience and Childhood Affect among the Logoli: A Longitudinal Study," *Ethos,* 8 (1980): 295–315.

[23]Ronald P. Rohner. *They Love Me, They Love Me Not: A Worldwide Study of the Effects of Parental Acceptance and Rejection* (New Haven: HRAF Press, 1975), pp. 97–105.

likely. Food-collecting societies (those dependent on wild food resources) tend to show warmth and affection to their children. More complex societies are less likely to be affectionate to their children.[24] It is not clear why this should be, but perhaps parental rejection is more likely where parents have less leisure time. Less leisure time may make parents more tired and irritable, and they may therefore have less patience with their children. As we noted in the chapter on economic organization, leisure time probably decreases as cultural complexity increases. More complex societies, which rely on intensive agriculture, also tend to have more economic uncertainty, as we noted in the chapter on food-getting. Not only do they tend to have more risk of famines and food shortages, but they also tend to have social inequality. In societies with social classes, many families may not have enough food and money to satisfy their needs, and this can also produce frustration in the parents. Whatever the reasons for parental rejection, it seems to perpetuate itself—children who were rejected tend to reject their own children.

Task Assignment. In our society, young children are not expected to help much with chores. If there are any chores for them (such as tidying up their rooms), they are not likely to affect the welfare of the family or its ability to survive. In contrast, there are societies known to anthropology in which young children, even three- and four-year-olds, are expected to help prepare food, care for animals, and carry water and firewood, as well as clean. A child between five and eight years of age may even be given the responsibility of caring for an infant or toddler for much of the day while the mother works in the fields.[25] What are the effects of such task assignment on personality development?

We now have evidence from more than ten different cultures that children who regularly babysit are more nurturant (offer more help and support to others) than other children, even when

A father in Laos bathes his child. In societies where fathers and grandparents help care for children, the children are less likely to be rejected.

they are not babysitting. Some of this evidence comes from a project known as the Six Cultures study, in which different research teams observed children's behavior in Kenya (Nyansongo), Mexico, India, the Philippines, Okinawa, and the United States (New England).[26] More recently, Ruth and Robert Munroe collected data on children's behavior in four other cultures that show the same relationship between babysitting and nurturant behavior; the Munroes' data come from Kenya (Logoli), Nepal, Belize, and American Samoa.[27] Clearly, in societies where children babysit less, they are less attuned to others' needs.

Why might task assignment alter the behaviors of children? One possibility is that children learn certain behaviors during the course of task assignment in order to perform the tasks well, and these behaviors become habitual. For example, a responsible babysitter is supposed to offer help. Mothers might directly instruct the babysitter to make sure that happens. But there is probably also an intrinsic satisfaction in doing a job well. For ex-

[24]Ibid., pp. 112–16.
[25]Beatrice B. Whiting and John W. M. Whiting (in collaboration with Richard Longabaugh), *Children of Six Cultures: A Psycho-Cultural Analysis* (Cambridge, MA: Harvard University Press, 1975), p. 94. See also Ruth H. Munroe, Robert L. Munroe, and Harold S. Shimmin, "Children's Work in Four Cultures: Determinants and Consequences," *American Anthropologist*, 86 (1984): 369–79.

[26]Beatrice B. Whiting and Carolyn Pope Edwards (in collaboration with Carol R. Ember, Gerald M. Erchak, Sara Harkness, Robert L. Munroe, Ruth H. Munroe, Sara B. Nerlove, Susan Seymour, Charles M. Super, Thomas S. Weisner, and Martha Wenger), *Children of Different Worlds: The Formation of Social Behavior* (Cambridge, MA: Harvard University Press, 1988), p. 265.
[27]Munroe, Munroe, and Shimmin, "Children's Work in Four Cultures," pp. 374–76; see also Carol R. Ember, "Feminine Task Assignment and the Social Behavior of Boys," *Ethos*, 1 (1973): 424–39.

Attending school has become customary in many parts of the world, as among the Baoulé tribe of the Ivory Coast. Schooling seems to affect cognitive development, but we don't know exactly how or why.

ample, it is pleasurable to see an infant smile and laugh, but it is unpleasant to hear a baby cry. We might therefore expect that a child who is assigned babysitting would learn for himself or herself that offering comfort to a baby brings its own rewards.[28]

Children who are assigned many tasks may spend their day in different kinds of settings, and these settings may indirectly influence behavior. For example, children who are asked to do many household chores are more apt to be around adults and younger children. Children who are assigned few or no tasks are more free to play with their agemates. Some of the results of the Six Cultures project suggest that children tend to be more aggressive the more they are around other children of the same age. In contrast, children tend to inhibit aggression when they are around adults more. We have already noted that being around younger children may make older children more nurturant. So the kinds of tasks assigned to children may influence behavior not only because certain tasks re-

quire certain behaviors (for example, babysitting requires nurturance) but also because the kinds of tasks assigned will place children in different social contexts that may also affect how they behave.[29]

Schooling. Most researchers focus on the parents when they investigate how children are brought up. But in our own and other societies, children may spend a substantial part of their time in school from the age of three or so. What influence does school have on children's social behavior and on how they think as measured by tests? To investigate the effect of schooling, researchers have compared children (or adults) who have not gone to school with those who have. All of this research has been done in societies that do not have compulsory schooling; otherwise we could not compare the schooled with the unschooled. We know relatively little about the influence of school on social

[28]Whiting and Whiting, *Children of Six Cultures*, p. 179.

[29]Ibid., pp. 152–63; and Carol R. Ember, "A Cross-Cultural Perspective on Sex Differences," in Ruth H. Munroe, Robert L. Munroe, and Beatrice B. Whiting, eds., *Handbook of Cross-Cultural Human Development* (New York: Garland Press, 1981), p. 560.

behavior. In contrast, we know more about how schooling influences performance on cognitive tests.

Schooling clearly predicts "superior" performance on many cognitive tests, and within the same society, schooled individuals will generally do better than the unschooled. So, for example, nonschooled individuals in non-Western societies are not as likely as schooled individuals to perceive depth in two-dimensional pictures, do not perform as well on tests of memory, are not as likely to classify items in a number of different ways, are not as likely to solve verbal logical problems, and (as we discussed earlier in the chapter) do not display evidence of formal operational thinking.[30]

But why does schooling have this effect? Although it is possible that something about schooling creates higher levels of cognitive thinking, there are other possible explanations. The observed differences may be due to the advantages that schoolchildren have because of their experiences in school, advantages that have nothing to do with general cognitive ability. For example, consider research that asks people to classify or group drawings of geometric shapes that belong together. Suppose a person is shown three cards—a red circle, a red triangle, and a white circle—and is asked which two are most alike. A person could choose to classify in terms of color or in terms of shape. In the United States, young children usually classify by color, and as they get older they classify more often by shape. Many psychologists assume that classification by color is more "concrete" and classification by shape or function is more "abstract." Unschooled adults in many parts of Africa sort by color, not by shape. Does this mean that they are classifying less abstractly? Not necessarily. Nonschooled Africans are likely to be unfamiliar with the test materials (drawings on paper and geometric shapes).

How can people classify "abstractly" (for example, by shape) if they have never had the experience of handling or seeing shapes that are drawn in two dimensions? Is it likely that they would classify things as triangles if they had never seen a three-pointed figure with straight sides? In contrast, consider how much time teachers in this country spend exposing and drilling children on

various geometric shapes. People who are familiar with certain materials may for that reason alone do better on cognitive tests that use those materials.[31]

A comparative study of Liberian rice farmers in West Africa and U.S. undergraduates also illustrates the point that choice of materials may influence research results. The comparison involved a set of materials familiar to the rice farmers (bowls of rice) and a set of materials (geometric cards) familiar to the undergraduates. Rice farmers appeared to classify more "abstractly" than undergraduates when they were asked to classify rice, and undergraduates seemed to classify more "abstractly" than rice farmers when they classified geometric cards.[32]

Schooled individuals may also enjoy an advantage on many cognitive tests just because they are familiar with tests and the way tests ask them to think of new situations. For example, consider the reaction of a nonschooled person in Central Asia who was asked the following question by a Russian psychologist interested in measuring logical thinking: "In the Far North where there is snow, all bears are white. Novaya Zemlya is in the Far North and there is always snow there. What color are the bears there?" The reply was, "We don't talk about what we haven't seen." Such a reply was typical of nonschooled individuals; they did not even try to answer the question because it was not part of their experience.[33] Clearly, we cannot judge whether people think logically or not if they do not want to play a cognitive game.

Much research needs to be done on exactly how and why schooling affects cognition. By studying other societies where schooling is not universal, we may be better able to understand just what role schooling plays in cognitive development. That schooling makes for differences in cognitive performance raises the serious issue of how

[30]Ember, "Cross-Cultural Cognitive Studies"; and Rogoff, "Schooling and the Development of Cognitive Skills."

[31]For how school experiences may improve particular cognitive skills, rather than higher levels of cognitive development in general, see Barbara Rogoff, Apprenticeship in Thinking: Cognitive Development in Social Context (New York: Oxford University Press, 1990), pp. 46-49.
[32]Marc H. Irwin, Gary N. Schafer, and Cynthia P. Feiden, "Emic and Unfamiliar Category Sorting of Mano Farmers and U.S. Undergraduates," Journal of Cross-Cultural Psychology, 5 (1974): 407–23.
[33]A. R. Luria, Cognitive Development: Its Cultural and Social Foundations (Cambridge, MA: Harvard University Press, 1976), p. 108; quoted in Rogoff, "Schooling and the Development of Cognitive Skills," p. 254.

much of what we observe about child development in our society and in other Western societies is simply a function of what children are taught in school. After all, children who grow up in this society not only get older each year, they also go one year further in school.

Adaptational Explanations

The cultural anthropologist seeks not only to establish connections between child-rearing customs and personality traits, but to learn why those customs differ in the first place. Some anthropologists believe that child-rearing practices are largely adaptive—that a society generally produces the kinds of personalities best suited to performance of the activities necessary for the survival of the society. As John Whiting and Irvin Child express it, "the economic, political and social organs of a society—the basic customs surrounding the nourishment, sheltering and protection of its members . . . seem a likely source of influence on child training practices."[34] The belief that child-rearing practices are generally adaptive does not mean that societies always produce the kinds of persons they need. Just as in the biological realm, where we see poor adaptations and extinctions of species and subspecies, so we may expect that societies sometimes produce modal personality traits that are maladapted to the requirements of living in that society. However, we expect that most societies that have survived to be recorded have produced modal personality traits that are generally adaptive.

Herbert Barry, Irvin Child, and Margaret Bacon have cross-culturally investigated the possibility that child-training practices may be adapted to the economic requirements of a society. Such requirements, they theorized, might explain why some societies strive to develop "compliant" (responsible, obedient, nurturant) children while others aim more for "assertiveness" (independence, self-reliance, and achievement).[35] The cross-cultural results indicate that agricultural and herding societies are more likely to stress responsibility and obedience, whereas hunting-and-gathering societies tend to stress self-reliance and individual assertiveness. The investigators suggest that agricultural and herding societies cannot afford departures from established routine, since departures might jeopardize the food supply for long periods. Such societies are therefore likely to emphasize "compliance" with tradition. Departures from routine in a hunter-gatherer society cannot cause much damage to a food supply that has to be collected anew almost every day. So, hunter-gatherers can afford to emphasize individual initiative.

Although our own society relies on food production and has large stores of accumulated food, we seem more like hunter-gatherers in emphasizing individual initiative. Are we then exceptional to the Barry, Child, and Bacon findings? Not really. Most people are not farmers (in the United States, only 2 percent of the total population is still on the farm) and most of us expect that we can "forage" in the supermarket or "store" just about anytime. So we can emphasize initiative too, like hunter-gatherers.

Child-rearing practices may also be affected by household characteristics. Leigh Minturn and William Lambert report, on the basis of data from the Six Cultures study, that children tend to be punished more strongly for fighting with others when the family lives in cramped quarters. The more people living in a house, the less apt a mother is to permit disobedience.[36] This observation is consistent with the finding of a cross-cultural study, conducted by John Whiting, that societies with extended-family households are more likely than societies with nuclear families to severely punish aggression in children.[37]

Whether or not adults express aggression freely may be related to a society's economy and social environment. In a comparative study of personality differences between pastoralists and farmers in four societies in East Africa, Robert Edgerton found that pastoralists were more willing than farmers to

---

[34]Whiting and Child, *Child Training and Personality*, p. 310.
[35]Herbert Barry III, Irvin L. Child, and Margaret K. Bacon, "Relation of Child Training to Subsistence Economy," *American Anthropologist*, 61 (1959): 51–63. For a revised analysis of the data used in the Barry, Child, and Bacon study, see Llewellyn Hendrix, "Economy and Child Training Reexamined," *Ethos*, 13 (1985): 246–61.

[36]Leigh Minturn and William W. Lambert, *Mothers of Six Cultures: Antecedents of Child Rearing* (New York: John Wiley, 1964), p. 289.
[37]John W. M. Whiting, "Cultural and Sociological Influences on Development," in *Growth and Development of the Child in His Setting* (Maryland Child Growth and Development Institute, 1959), pp. 5–9.

"Hunter-gatherers," North America, late 20th century: Shoppers lunching at a mall in Birmingham, Alabama.

express aggression openly. As a matter of fact, pastoralists generally seemed freer to express all kinds of emotion—including sadness and depression. Although farmers displayed reluctance to express overt aggression themselves, they were quite willing to talk about witchcraft and sorcery practiced by others. How can we explain these personality differences? Edgerton thinks that the life-style of farmers, who must spend their lives cooperating with a fixed set of neighbors, requires them to put a lid on their feelings, particularly hostile feelings. (But these feelings may not go away, and so the farmers might "see them" in others.) Pastoralists, on the other hand, can more readily move away in conflict situations because they are not as dependent on a fixed set of individuals. Not only might they be able to express aggression more openly, but such aggression may even be adaptive. The pastoralists studied by Edgerton engaged more frequently in raids and counterraids involving cattle stealing, and the more aggressive individuals may have had a better chance to survive the skirmishes.[38]

Might the environment influence the way people in different societies think and perceive (interpret sensory information)? John Berry has suggested that different perceptual and cognitive processes may be selected and trained for in societies that differ in their adaptational requirements.[39] Berry's particular focus is on what psychologists have called *field independence* and *field dependence*.[40] Field independence means being able to isolate a part of a situation from the whole. The opposite perceptual style, field dependence, means that parts are not perceived separately; rather, the whole situation is focused on.

The contrast between field independence and field dependence may become clear if we look at some of the ways it is measured. In the rod-and-frame test, a person seated in a darkened room is asked to adjust a tilted luminous rod so that it is upright within a luminous frame. Individuals are considered field-dependent if they adjust the rod to line up with the frame when the frame is tilted. In-

[38]Robert B. Edgerton, *The Individual in Cultural Adaptation: A Study of Four East African Peoples* (Berkeley: University of California Press, 1971).

[39]John W. Berry, *Human Ecology and Cognitive Style* (New York: John Wiley, 1976).

[40]Herman A. Witkin, "A Cognitive Style Approach to Cross-Cultural Research," *International Journal of Psychology*, 2 (1967): 233–50.

dividuals are considered field-independent if they adjust the rod to a truly upright position even though the frame is tilted. Field independence is also measured by the ability to see a simply drawn figure when it is included but somewhat hidden in a more complex picture.

Why should some societies produce people who are more field-independent or -dependent? Berry suggests that people who rely a lot on hunting must be field-independent to be successful, because hunting requires the visual isolation of animals from their backgrounds. Hunters must also learn to visualize themselves in precise relationship to their surroundings so that they can find animals and get back home. In a comparative study of communities in four different societies, Berry found that degree of reliance on hunting predicts field independence. The more a community relies on hunting, the more the individuals show field independence on the tests. Those communities more reliant on agriculture test out to be more field-dependent. How might hunters develop field independence as a cognitive style? Different child training might be involved. In the United States and a few other societies, it has been found that children with very strict parents are less likely to develop field independence.[41] It seems that emotional independence from parents is necessary for the perceptual style of field independence to develop. No matter what the precise mechanism is, we know from the Barry, Child, and Bacon study that hunter-gatherers are more likely to train children to be individualistic and assertive, and that agriculturalists and herders are more likely to train their children to be compliant. So hunter-gatherers may get their children to develop field independence by stressing emotional independence in childhood.

Possible Genetic and Physiological Influences

Recently, some researchers have suggested that genetic or physiological differences between populations may predispose them to have different modal personality characteristics. Daniel Freedman has found differences in "temperament" in newborn babies of different ethnic groups, suggesting that the differences are likely to be genetic. Comparing Chinese and Caucasian newborns (with the families matched on income, number of previous children, and so on), Freedman found that Caucasian babies cried more easily, were harder to console, and fought experimental procedures more. Chinese babies, on the other hand, seemed calmer and more adaptable. Navaho babies were similar to the Chinese, showing even more calmness.[42] Freedman argues that the infant's behavior may influence how the parents respond. A calm baby may encourage a calm parental response; a more active baby may encourage a more active response.[43]

Although these differences may indeed be genetic, as Freedman thinks, we cannot rule out other possibilities. For example, the mother's diet or her blood pressure could affect the baby's behavior. And it may be that the baby can learn even in the womb. After all, babies in the womb can apparently hear sounds and respond to other stimuli. Therefore, it is possible that in societies where pregnant mothers are calm, their babies may have learned calmness even before they were born. Last, we still do not know if the initial differences observed in newborn babies persist to become personality differences in adulthood.

Physiological differences between populations may also be responsible for some modal personality differences. Research by Ralph Bolton suggests that a physiological condition known as hypoglycemia may be responsible for the high levels of aggression recorded among the Qolla of Peru.[44] (People with hypoglycemia experience a big drop in their blood sugar level after the ingestion of food.) Bolton found that about 55 percent of the males he tested in a Qolla village had hypoglycemia. Moreover, those men with the most aggressive life histories tended to be hypoglycemic. Whether or not hypoglycemia is induced by genetic or environ-

[41]J. L. M. Dawson, "Cultural and Physiological Influences upon Spatial-Perceptual Processes in West Africa," *International Journal of Psychology*, 2 (1967): 115–28, 171–85; and John W. Berry, "Ecological and Cultural Factors in Spatial Perceptual Development," *Canadian Journal of Behavioural Science*, 3 (1971): 324–36.

[42]Daniel G. Freedman, "Ethnic Differences in Babies," *Human Nature*, January 1979, pp. 36–43.

[43]Ibid., p. 40–41. For a discussion of possible genetic influences on the social environment, see Sandra Scarr and Kathleen McCartney, "How People Make Their Own Environments: A Theory of Genotype→Environment Effects," *Child Development*, 54 (1983): 424–35.

[44]Ralph Bolton, "Aggression and Hypoglycemia among the Qolla: A Study in Psychobiological Anthropology," *Ethnology*, 12 (1973): 227–57.

mental factors (or both), the condition can be alleviated by a change in diet.

Mental Illness

So far in this chapter, we have discussed cross-cultural universals and societal differences in "normal" behavior, but anthropologists have also been intrigued by questions about similarities and differences in *abnormal* behavior. Central to the study of abnormal behavior is how to define it. Is abnormality relative? That is, can what is normal in one society be abnormal in another? Or, alternatively, are there universals in abnormality cross-culturally?

In a very widely read book, Ruth Benedict suggested that abnormality was relative. In her view, behavior thought to be appropriate and normal in one society can be considered abnormal in another.[45] Many German officials, for instance, were regarded in every way as normal by their neighbors and co-workers during the period of Nazi control. Yet these officials committed acts of inhumanity so vicious that to many observers in other Western societies they appeared criminally insane. The Saora of Orissa (India) provide another example of behavior normal to one society that would be abnormal to another society. The Saora take for granted that certain of their womenfolk regularly are courted by lovers from the supernatural world, marry them, and have children (who are never seen, yet allegedly are suckled at night).[46] Behavior that is so alien to our own makes it no easy task for researchers to identify mental illness in other societies, let alone compare more complex and less complex societies for rates of mental disorder.

Many early ethnographic reports suggested that different mental illnesses occurred in different societies. For example, great interest has been shown in the *wiitiko* psychosis, a form of mental disorder found mostly among the males of some North American tribes, including the Ojibwa and Cree. The afflicted individual has the delusion that he is possessed by the spirit of a *wiitiko*, a cannibal giant, and he has hallucinations and cannibalistic impulses. One theory attributes the disorder to famine,[47] but critics have pointed out that not all those afflicted with the psychosis are starving. A psychological reason has also been suggested: the subject sees the *wiitiko* monster as a symbol of his mother, who frustrated his dependency needs in childhood. He attempts to fight back by behaving like the monster, trying to destroy imagined persecutors by eating them.[48]

A mental disorder called **pibloktoq** occurs among some Eskimo adults of Greenland, usually women, who become oblivious to their surroundings and act in agitated, eccentric ways. They may strip themselves naked and wander across the ice and over hills until they collapse of exhaustion. Another disorder, **amok,** occurs in Malaya, Indonesia, and New Guinea. It is characterized by John Honigmann as a "destructive maddened excitement . . . beginning with depression and followed by a period of brooding and withdrawal [culminating in] the final mobilization of tremendous energy during which the 'wild man' runs destructively berserk."[49]

Mental disorders such as these used to be attributed to a combination of physical and psychological factors. The cold, dark, depressing aspects of Arctic winters have become almost a cliché of anthropological description, as has the depicting of tropical regions as enervating. There is reason to suspect that such classifications stem more from the inconvenience of the stranger who makes the investigation than from the attitudes of the inhabitants, who generally have experienced no other environment. Similarly, theories that associated lack of satisfaction in childhood with later manifestations of hysteria are weakened by the fact that comparable conditions in other societies do not always produce the disorder.

It has been suggested that certain mental illnesses, such as amok and pibloktoq, are not really different mental illnesses—they may merely be examples of the same illness expressed differently in different societies. Honigmann thinks that this may be true of pibloktoq. The hysteria associated with that illness ultimately subsides under the min-

[45]Ruth Benedict, *Patterns of Culture* (New York: Mentor, 1959 [originally published in 1934]).

[46]Verrier Elwin, *The Religion of an Indian Tribe* (London: Oxford University Press, 1955); cited in Barnouw, *Culture and Personality*, p. 356.

[47]Ruth Landes, "The Abnormal among the Ojibwa," *Journal of Abnormal and Social Psychology*, 33 (1938): 14–33.

[48]Seymour Parker, "The Wiitiko Psychosis in the Context of Ojibwa Personality and Culture," *American Anthropologist*, 62 (1960): 620.

[49]John J. Honigmann, *Personality in Culture* (New York: Harper & Row, Pub., 1967), p. 406.

istrations of friends and relatives. This type of disorder "fits a social system like the Eskimo, where people are able freely to indulge their dependence; in a crisis it enables a distressed person dramatically to summon help and support."[50]

A similar explanation has been offered for amok: it "discharges the individual from onerous social responsibilities without costing him social support." Amok usually occurs when a man has reached his early thirties and has acquired heavy financial and social obligations that reflect his rise in power and social prestige. Once he has "run amok," an individual will be a marked man, but not in the way our society uses the term. Honigmann sees amok as a "hysterical pattern of communication" and interprets its presence in the Gururumba of New Guinea in this way:

[The] behavior [of the affected man] has given evidence that he is less capable than others of withstanding pressures of social life. Hence neighbors reduce their expectations towards him, not pressing him to pay his debts promptly and not extracting from him prior commitments to provide food for feasts. He doesn't become an outcast, and he realizes he can't withdraw altogether from economic affairs, but he also knows he must limit his participation.[51]

Anthony Wallace has theorized that biological factors such as calcium deficiency may cause hysteria, and that dietary improvement may account for the decline of this illness in the Western world since the nineteenth century.[52] By the early twentieth century, the discovery of the value of good nutrition, coupled with changes in social conditions, had led many people to drink milk, eat vitamin-enriched foods, and spend time in the sun. These changes in diet and activity increased their intake of vitamin D and helped them to maintain a proper calcium level. Concurrently, the number of cases of hysteria declined. Regarding pibloktoq, Wallace suggests that a complex set of related variables may cause the disease. The Eskimos live in an environment that supplies only a minimum amount of calcium. A diet low in calcium could result in two different conditions. One condition,

rickets, would produce physical deformities potentially fatal in the Eskimos' hunting economy. Persons whose genetic makeup made them prone to rickets would be eliminated from the population through natural selection. A low level of calcium in the blood could also cause muscular spasms known as tetany. Tetany, in turn, may cause emotional and mental disorientation similar to the symptoms of pibloktoq. Since such attacks last for only a relatively short time and are not fatal, people who develop pibloktoq would have a far greater chance of surviving in the Arctic environment with a calcium-deficient diet than those who had rickets.

In contrast with those who think abnormality varies cross-culturally, some researchers believe they have evidence of a considerable degree of cross-cultural uniformity in conceptions of mental illness. Jane Murphy, for example, has studied descriptions by Eskimos and Yoruba (in Nigeria) of severely disturbed persons. She finds that their descriptions not only are similar to each other but correspond to North American descriptions of schizophrenia. The Eskimo word for "crazy" is *nuthkavihak*. They use this word when something inside a person seems to be out of order. *Nuthkavihak* people are described as talking to themselves, believing themselves to be animals, making strange faces, becoming violent, and so on. The Yoruba have a word *were* for people who are "insane." People described as *were* sometimes hear voices, laugh when there is nothing to laugh at, and take up weapons and suddenly hit people.[53] Robert Edgerton found similarities in conceptions of mental illness in four East African societies. He noted not only that the four tribes essentially agreed on the symptoms of psychosis, but that the symptoms they described were the same ones that would be considered psychotic here.[54]

We do not yet have rates or frequencies of mental illness for that many cultural groups, but Murphy compared her surveys of Eskimos and Yoruba with data on rural areas of Sweden and Canada and suggested that there are similar rates

---

[50]Ibid., p. 401.
[51]Ibid., p. 406.
[52]Anthony F. C. Wallace, "Mental Illness, Biology and Culture," in F. L. K. Hsu, ed., *Psychological Anthropology*, 2nd ed. (Cambridge, MA: Schenkman, 1972), pp. 363–402.

[53]Jane Murphy, "Abnormal Behavior in Traditional Societies: Labels, Explanations, and Social Reactions," in Munroe, Munroe, and Whiting, eds., *Handbook of Cross-Cultural Human Development*, p. 813.
[54]Robert B. Edgerton, "Conceptions of Psychosis in Four East African Societies," *American Anthropologist*, 68 (1966): 408–25.

of schizophrenia in the four populations.[55] When we have more such comparative studies, we should know more definitely which aspects of mental illness may be universal and which may vary cross-culturally.

Psychological Explanations of Cultural Variation

So far in this chapter, we have talked about societal variation in psychological characteristics and the possible *causes* of that variation. But psychological anthropologists, as well as other social scientists, have also pursued the possible *consequences* of psychological variation, particularly how psychological characteristics may help us understand certain aspects of cultural variation. For example, David McClelland's research suggests that societies that develop high levels of achievement motivation in individuals (a personality trait) will be likely to experience high rates of economic growth. Economic decline, McClelland suggests, will follow a decline in achievement motivation.[56] Differences in achievement motivation may even have political consequences. For example, Robert LeVine, who studied achievement motivation in three Nigerian ethnic groups, noted that the entry of one of them (the Ibo) into higher education and into many emerging professions may have been resented by the traditionally more influential groups.[57] Soon after LeVine's book was published, the friction between the rival groups escalated into rebellion by the Ibo and the defeat of a separatist Ibo state named Biafra.

Psychological factors may also help us explain why some aspects of culture are statistically associated with others. Abram Kardiner originally suggested that cultural patterns influence personality development through child training and that the resulting personality characteristics in turn influence the culture. He believed that *primary institutions*, such as family organization and subsistence techniques, give rise to certain personality characteristics. Once the personality is formed, though, it can have its own impact on culture. In Kardiner's view, the *secondary institutions* of society, such as religion and art, are shaped by modal (he called them *basic*) personality characteristics. Presumably, these secondary institutions have little relation to the adaptive requirements of society. But they may reflect and express the motives, conflicts, and anxieties of typical members of the society.[58] Thus, if we can understand why certain modal personality characteristics develop, we might, for example, be able to understand why certain kinds of art are associated with certain kinds of social systems. Whiting and Child have used the phrase **personality integration of culture** to refer to the possibility that an understanding of personality might help us explain connections between primary and secondary institutions.[59]

As examples of how personality may integrate culture, we turn to some suggested explanations for cultural preferences in games and for the custom of male initiation ceremonies.

In a cross-cultural study conducted by John Roberts and Brian Sutton-Smith, cultural preferences for particular types of games were found to be related to certain aspects of child rearing. The researchers suggest that these associations may be a consequence of conflict generated in many people in a society by particular types of child-rearing pressures. Games of strategy, for example, are associated with child training that emphasizes obedience. Roberts and Sutton-Smith propose that severe obedience training can create a conflict between the need to obey and the desire not to obey, a conflict that arouses anxiety. Such anxiety may or may not manifest itself against the person who instigates the anxiety. In any event, the conflict and the aggression itself can be played out on the miniature battlefields of games of strategy such as chess or the Japanese game of *go*. Similarly, games of chance may represent defiance of societal expectations of docility and responsibility. The general interpretation suggested by Roberts and Sutton-Smith is that players (and societies) initially become curious about games, learn

[55]Murphy, "Abnormal Behavior in Traditional Societies," pp. 822–23.

[56]David C. McClelland, *The Achieving Society* (New York: Van Nostrand, 1961).

[57]Robert A. LeVine, *Dreams and Deeds: Achievement Motivation in Nigeria* (Chicago: University of Chicago Press, 1966), p. 2.

[58]Abram Kardiner, with Ralph Linton, *The Individual and His Society* (New York: Golden Press, 1946 [originally published in 1939]), p. 471.

[59]Whiting and Child, *Child Training and Personality*, pp. 32–38.

Playing a string game in Choiseul, Solomon Islands.

them, and ultimately develop high involvement in them because of the particular kinds of psychological conflicts that are handled or expressed, but not necessarily resolved, by the games.[60]

The possible role of psychological processes in connecting different aspects of culture is also illustrated in cross-cultural work on initiation ceremonies for boys at adolescence. In the ceremonies, boys are subjected to painful tests of manhood, usually including genital operations, which indicate the boys' transition to adulthood. Roger Burton and John Whiting found that initiation ceremonies tend to occur in patrilocal societies in which infant boys initially sleep exclusively with their mothers. They suggest that initiation rites in such societies are intended to break a conflict in sex identity. The conflict is believed to exist because boys in these societies would initially identify with their mothers, who exercise almost complete control over them in infancy. Later, when the boys discover that men dominate the society, they

---

[60]John M. Roberts and Brian Sutton-Smith, "Child Training and Game Involvement," *Ethnology*, 1 (1962): 178.

would identify secondarily with their fathers. This sex-role conflict is assumed to be resolved by the initiation ceremony, which demonstrates a boy's manhood, thus strengthening the secondary identification.[61]

In the next two chapters we discuss cultural variation in religion and the arts. In doing so we refer to some psychological explanations. Some researchers feel that such explanations may help us understand why gods in some societies are viewed as mean, why artists in some societies prefer repetitive designs, and why strangers in some societies tend to be the "bad ones" in folktales. It is often assumed by psychological anthropologists that conceptions of gods and artistic creations are not constrained by any objective realities, and so people are free to create them as they wish. In other words, people may tend to *project* their personalities—their feelings, their conflicts, their concerns—into these areas. This idea of projection underlies what psychologists call **projective tests.** In such tests, which presumably reveal personality characteristics, subjects are given stimuli that are purposely ambiguous. So, for example, in the **Thematic Apperception Test (TAT),** subjects are shown vague drawings and asked what they think is going on in them, what happened before, and how they think things will turn out. Since the test materials give few instructions about what to say, it is assumed that subjects will interpret the materials by projecting their own personalities. As we will see, some aspects of religion and the arts may be similar to TAT stories and may express or reflect the common personality characteristics of a society.

---

[61]Roger V. Burton and John W. M. Whiting, "The Absent Father and Cross-Sex Identity," *Merrill-Palmer Quarterly of Behavior and Development*, 7, no. 2 (1961): 85–95. See also Robert L. Munroe, Ruth H. Munroe, and John W. M. Whiting, "Male Sex-Role Resolutions," in Munroe, Munroe, and Whiting, eds., *Handbook of Cross-Cultural Human Development*, pp. 611–32.

SUMMARY

1. Psychological anthropologists are interested in the psychological differences and similarities between societies. Their research has focused mainly on three questions: Do all human beings develop psychologically in much the same ways?

What may explain the apparent differences in personality characteristics from one society to another? What kinds of cultural variation might be explained by psychological factors?

2. Early research in psychological anthropol-

408 CHAPTER 22

ogy was concerned mainly with how supposedly universal stages of emotional development seem to be affected by cultural differences. Some doubt has been cast on the idea that adolescence is necessarily a time of "storm and stress" and that the Oedipus complex (at least in the form stated by Freud) is universal.

3. Recent research on universals in psychological development has been concerned more with cognitive (intellectual) development. In looking for universals, many researchers have discovered some apparent differences. However, most of the tests used in research may favor people in Western cultures and those who attend formal schools.

4. Research on psychological variation from one society to another has focused on modal personality characteristics, the characteristics that occur with the highest frequency in a society.

5. To understand cross-cultural variation in psychological characteristics, many researchers have tried to discover if variation in child-rearing customs may account for the observed psychological differences.

6. *Socialization* is a term used by anthropologists and psychologists to describe the development, through the influence of parents and others, of patterns of behavior in children that conform to cultural expectations.

7. Socialization can be direct or indirect. Indirectly, the degree to which parents like children, the kinds of work children are asked to do, and whether or not children go to school may at least partly influence how children develop psychologically.

8. Anthropologists seek not only to establish connections between child-rearing customs and personality traits but also to learn why those customs originated. Some anthropologists believe societies produce the kinds of personality best suited to performance of the activities necessary for the survival of the society.

9. Anthropologists are also interested in mental illness. We still do not know much about which aspects of mental illness may be universal and which may vary cross-culturally.

10. Psychological anthropologists are interested not only in the possible causes of psychological differences between societies; they are also interested in the possible consequences of psychological variation, particularly how psychological characteristics may help us understand statistical associations between various aspects of culture.

SUGGESTED READING

MUNROE, R. H., MUNROE, R. L., AND WHITING, B. B., eds. *Handbook of Cross-Cultural Human Development.* New York: Garland Press, 1981. A massive collection of papers, prepared especially for this volume, on many aspects of human development that have been investigated cross-culturally.

ROGOFF, B. *Apprenticeship in Thinking: Cognitive Development in Social Context.* New York: Oxford University Press, 1990. This book suggests that children's cognitive development is an apprenticeship, that the particular cognitive skills developed are rooted in the particular historical and cultural activities of the society.

SCHLEGEL, A., AND BARRY, H., III. *Adolescence: An Anthropological Inquiry.* New York: Free Press, 1991. A cross-cultural investigation of the commonalities and differences in adolescence in a large sample of the world's preindustrial societies. The authors suggest that the patterns they have discovered may also apply to Western and industrializing societies.

SEGALL, M. H., DASEN, P. R., BERRY, J. W., AND POORTINGA, Y. H. *Human Behavior in Global Perspective: An Introduction to Cross-Cultural Psychology.* New York: Pergamon Press, 1990. An introduction to research in many societies around the world on the ways in which perception, cognition, motivation, and other aspects of human behavior are influenced by variable social and cultural factors.

WHITING, B. B., AND EDWARDS, C. P. (in collaboration with Carol R. Ember, Gerald M. Erchak, Sara Harkness, Robert L. Munroe, Ruth H. Munroe, Sara B. Nerlove, Susan Seymour, Charles M. Super, Thomas S. Weisner, and Martha Wenger). *Children of Different Worlds:*

The Formation of Social Behavior. Cambridge, MA: Harvard University Press, 1988. On the basis of data collected in the Six Cultures project, the authors explore the ways in which age, gender, and culture affect the social behavior of children. Knowledge of the company children keep, and of the proportion of time they spend with various categories of people, makes it possible to predict important aspects of children's interpersonal behavior.

23
Religion and Magic

As far as we know, all societies have possessed beliefs that can be grouped under the term *religion.* These beliefs vary from culture to culture and from year to year. Yet, whatever the variety of beliefs in things supernatural, we shall define **religion** as any set of attitudes, beliefs, and practices pertaining to *supernatural power,* whether that power be forces, gods, spirits, ghosts, or demons.

In our society, we divide phenomena into the natural and the supernatural, but not all languages or cultures make such a neat distinction. Moreover, what is considered **supernatural**—powers believed to be not human or not subject to the laws of nature—varies from society to society. Some of the variations are determined by what a society regards as natural law. For example, some illnesses commonly found in our society are believed to result from the natural action of germs and viruses. In other societies (and even for some people in our own society), illness is thought to result from supernatural forces, and thus forms a part of religious belief.

Beliefs about what is, or is not, a supernatural occurrence also vary within a society at a given time or over time. In Judeo-Christian traditions, for example, floods, earthquakes, volcanic eruptions, comets, and epidemics were once considered evidence of supernatural powers intervening in human affairs. It is now generally agreed that they are simply natural occurrences. Thus, the line between the natural and the supernatural appears to vary in a society according to the current state of belief about the causes of things and events in the observable world.

In many cultures, what we would consider religious is embedded in other aspects of everyday life. It is often difficult to separate the religious (or economic or political) from other aspects of culture. That is, simpler cultures have little or no specialization. So the various aspects of culture we distinguish (for example, in the chapter headings of this book) are not as separate and as easily recognized in simple societies as in complex ones such as our own. However, it is sometimes difficult even for us to agree whether a particular custom of ours is religious or not. After all, the categorizing of beliefs as religious or political or social is a relatively new custom. The ancient Greeks, for instance, did not have a word for religion, but they did have many concepts concerning the behavior of their gods and their own expected duties to the gods.

When people's duties to their gods are linked with duty to their princes, it is difficult to separate religious from political ideas. As an example of our own difficulty in labeling a particular class of actions or beliefs as religious or social, consider our attitudes about wearing clothes. Is our belief that it is necessary to wear clothing, at least in the company of nonlovers, a religious principle, or is it something else? Recall that in Genesis, the wearing of clothes, or fig leaves, is distinctly associated with the loss of innocence: Adam and Eve, after eating the apple, covered their nakedness. Accordingly, when Christian missionaries first visited islands in the Pacific in the nineteenth century, they forced the native women to wear more clothes, particularly to cover their sexual parts. Were the missionaries' ideas about sex religious or social, or perhaps both?

The Universality of Religion

Religious beliefs and practices are found in all known contemporary societies, and archeologists think they have found signs of religious belief associated with *Homo sapiens* who lived at least 60,000 years ago. People then deliberately buried their dead, and many graves contain the remains of food, tools, and other objects that were probably thought to be needed in an afterlife. Some of the artistic productions of modern humans after about 30,000 years ago may have been used for religious purposes. For example, sculptures of females with ample secondary sex characteristics may have been fertility charms. Cave paintings in which the predominant images are animals of the hunt may reflect a belief that the image had some power over events. Perhaps early humans thought their hunting could be made more successful if they drew images depicting good fortune in hunting. The details of religions practiced in the distant past cannot be recovered. Yet evidence of ritual treatment of the dead suggests that early people believed in the existence of supernatural spirits and tried to communicate with, and perhaps influence, them.

Since we may reasonably assume the existence

of prehistoric religion, and since we have evidence of the universality of religion in historic times, we can understand why the subject of religion has been the focus of much speculation, research, and theorizing. As long ago as the fifth century B.C., Herodotus made fairly objective comparisons among the religions of the fifty or so societies he traveled to from his home in Greece. He noted many similarities among their gods and pointed out evidence of diffusion of religious worship. During the 2,500 years since Herodotus's time, scholars, theologians, historians, and philosophers have speculated about religion. Some have claimed superiority for their own forms of religion; others have derided the naive simplicity of others' beliefs; and some have expressed skepticism concerning all beliefs.

Speculation about which religion may be superior is not an anthropological concern. What is of interest to anthropologists is why religion is found in all societies, and how and why it varies from society to society. Many social scientists—particularly anthropologists, sociologists, and psychologists—have offered theories to account for the universality of religion. Most think that religions are created by humans in response to certain univeral needs or conditions. Four such needs or conditions have been discussed: a need for intellectual understanding; guilt and projection; anxiety and uncertainty; and a need for community.

Intellectual Understanding

One of the earliest social scientists to propose a major theory of the origin of religion was Edward Tylor. In his view, religion originated in speculation about dreams, trances, and death. The dead, the distant, those in the next house, animals—all seem real in dreams and trances. Tylor thought that the lifelike appearances of these imagined persons and animals suggests a dual existence for all things—a physical, visible body and a psychic, invisible soul. In sleep, the soul can leave the body and appear to other people; at death, the soul permanently leaves the body. Because the dead appear in dreams, people come to believe that the souls of the dead are still around.

To Tylor, the belief in souls was the earliest form of religion; **animism** is the term Tylor used to refer to belief in souls.[1] But many were critical of Tylor's theory for being too intellectual, for not dealing with the emotional component of religion. One of Tylor's student's, R. R. Marett, felt that Tylor's animism was too sophisticated an idea to be the origin of religion. Marett suggested that **animatism**—a belief in impersonal supernatural forces (for example, the power of a rabbit's foot)—preceded the creation of spirits.[2]

Guilt and Projection

Sigmund Freud believed that early humans lived in groups each of which was dominated by a tyrannical man who kept all the women for himself.[3] Freud postulated that the sons on maturing were driven out of the group. Later they got together to kill and eat the hated father. But then the sons felt enormous guilt and remorse, which they expressed (projected) by prohibiting the killing of a totem animal (the father-substitute). Subsequently, on ritual occasions, the cannibalistic scene was repeated in the form of a totem meal. Freud believed that these early beliefs gradually became transformed into the worship of deities or gods modeled after the father.

Freud's interpretation of the origin of religion is not accepted by most social scientists nowadays. But there is widespread agreement with his idea that events in infancy can have long-lasting and powerful effects on beliefs and practices in adult life. Helpless and dependent on parents for many years, infants and children inevitably and unconsciously view their parents as all-knowing and all-powerful. When adults feel out of control or in need, they may unconsciously revert to their infantile and childhood feelings. They may then look to gods or magic to do what they cannot do for themselves, just as they looked to their parents to take care of their needs. As we shall see, there is evi-

[1]Edward B. Tylor, "Animism" (originally published in 1871), in William A. Lessa and Evon Z. Vogt, eds., *Reader in Comparative Religion: An Anthropological Approach*, 4th ed. (New York: Harper & Row, Pub., 1979), pp. 9–18.
[2]R. R. Marett, *The Threshold of Religion* (London: Methuen, 1909).
[3]Sigmund Freud, *Moses and Monotheism*, translated by Katherine Jones (New York: Vintage Books, 1967 [originally published in 1939]); Christopher Badcock, *Essential Freud* (Oxford: Basil Blackwell, 1988), pp. 126–7, 133–36.

dence that feelings about the supernatural world may parallel feelings in everyday life.

Anxiety and Uncertainty

Freud thought that humans would turn to religion during times of uncertainty, but he did not view religion positively, believing that humans would eventually outgrow the need for religion. Others viewed religion more positively. For Bronislaw Malinowski, people in all societies are faced with anxiety and uncertainty. They may have skills and knowledge to take care of many of their needs. But knowledge is often not sufficient to prevent illness, accidents, and natural disasters. The most frightening prospect is death itself. Consequently, there is an intense desire for immortality. As Malinowski saw it, religion is born from the universal need to find comfort in inevitable times of stress. Through religious belief, people affirm their convictions that death is neither real nor final, that people are endowed with a personality which persists even after death. In religious ceremony, humans can commemorate and communicate with those who have died, and in these ways achieve some measure of comfort.[4]

Theorists such as William James, Carl Jung, Erich Fromm, and Abraham Maslow have viewed religion even more positively: it is not just a way of relieving anxiety; it is thought to be therapeutic. William James suggested that religion provides a feeling of union with something larger than oneself.[5] Carl Jung suggested that it helps people resolve their inner conflicts and attain maturity.[6] Erich Fromm proposed that religion helps provide people with a framework of values,[7] and Abraham Maslow argued that it provides people with a transcendental understanding of the world.[8]

Need for Community

The various theories of religion which we have discussed so far agree on one thing: whatever the beliefs or rituals, religion may satisfy psychological needs common to all people. But some social scientists believe that religion springs from society and serves social, rather than psychological, needs.

Émile Durkheim, a French sociologist, pointed out that living in society makes humans feel pushed and pulled by powerful forces. These forces direct their behavior, pushing them to resist what is considered wrong, pulling them to do what is considered right. These are the forces of public opinion, custom, and law. Because they are largely invisible and unexplained, people would feel them as mysterious forces and therefore come to believe in gods and spirits. Durkheim suggested that religion arises out of the experience of living in social groups; religious belief and practice affirm a person's place in society, enhance feelings of community, and give people confidence. For Durkheim, it is society that is really the object of worship in religion.

Consider how Durkheim explained totemism, so often discussed by early religious theorists. He thought that nothing inherent in a lizard, rat, or frog (animal totems for some Australian aborigine groups) would be sufficient to make them *sacred*. The totem animal must therefore be a symbol. But a symbol of what? Durkheim noted that the people are organized into clans and each clan has its own totem animal; the totem distinguishes one clan from another. So the totem is the focus of the clan's religious rituals and symbolizes both the clan and the clan's spirits. It is the clan with which people mostly identify, and it is the clan that is affirmed in ritual.[9]

Guy Swanson accepts Durkheim's belief that certain aspects or conditions of society generate the responses we call religious. But Swanson thinks that Durkheim was too vague about exactly what in society would generate the belief in spirits or gods. Swanson suggests that the belief in spirits derives from the existence of *sovereign groups* in a society. These are the groups that have independent

[4]Bronislaw Malinowski, "The Group and the Individual in Functional Analysis," *American Journal of Sociology*, 44 (1939): 959; Bronislaw Malinowski, "Magic, Science, and Religion," in *Magic, Science, and Religion and Other Essays* (Garden City, NY: Doubleday, 1948), pp. 50–51.

[5]William James, *The Varieties of Religious Experience: A Study in Human Nature* (New York: Modern Library, 1902).

[6]Carl G. Jung, *Psychology and Religion* (New Haven: Yale University Press, 1938).

[7]Erich Fromm, *Psychoanalysis and Religion* (New Haven: Yale University Press, 1950).

[8]Abraham H. Maslow, *Religions, Values, and Peak-Experiences* (Columbus: Ohio State University Press, 1964).

[9]Émile Durkheim, *The Elementary Forms of the Religious Life*, translated from the French by Joseph W. Swain (New York: Collier Books, 1961; originally published in 1912).

"There's room in the world for all religions—those who believe in rocks, those who believe in trees, those who believe in clouds . . ." (© 1984 by Sidney Harris)

jurisdiction (decision-making powers) over some sphere of life—the family, the clan, the village, the state. Such groups are not mortal: they persist beyond the lifetimes of their individual members. According to Swanson, then, the spirits or gods which people invent personify or represent the powerful decision-making groups in their society. Just like sovereign groups in a society, the spirits or gods are immortal and have purposes and goals that supersede those of an individual.[10]

Variation in Religious Beliefs

There seems to be no general agreement among scholars as to why people need religion, or how spirits, gods, and other supernatural beings and forces come into existence. (Any or all of the needs we have discussed, psychological and/or social, may give rise to religious belief and practice.) Yet there is general recognition of the enormous variation in the details of religious beliefs and practices. Societies differ in the kinds of supernatural beings or forces they believe in and the character of these beings. They also differ in the structure or

hierarchy of those beings, in what the beings actually do, and in what happens to people after death. Variation exists also in the ways in which the supernatural is believed to interact with humans.

Types of Supernatural Forces and Beings

Supernatural Forces. Some supernatural forces have no personlike character. As we discussed earlier, Marett referred to such religious beliefs as animatism. For example, a supernatural, impersonal force called **mana,** after its Malayo-Polynesian name, is thought to inhabit some objects but not others, some people but not others. A farmer in Polynesia places stones around a field; the crops are bountiful; the stones have mana. During a subsequent year the stones may lose their mana and the crops will be poor. People may also possess mana, as, for example, the chiefs in Polynesia were said to do. However, such power is not necessarily possessed permanently: chiefs who were unsuccessful in war or other activities were said to have lost their mana.

The word "mana" may be Malayo-Polynesian, but a similar concept is also found in our own society. We can compare mana to the power golfers may attribute to some but, unhappily not all, of their clubs. A ballplayer might think a certain sweatshirt or pair of socks has supernatural power or force and that more runs or points will be scored when they are worn. A four-leaf clover has mana; a three-leaf clover does not.

Objects, persons, or places can be considered **taboo.** Anthony Wallace distinguishes mana from taboo by pointing out that things containing mana are to be touched, whereas taboo things are not to be touched, for their power can cause harm.[11] Thus, those who touch them may themselves become taboo. Taboos surround food not to be eaten, places not to be entered, animals not to be killed, people not to be touched sexually, people not to be touched at all, and so on. An Australian aborigine could not normally kill and eat the animal that was his totem; Hebrew tribesmen were forbidden to touch a woman during menstruation or for seven days following.

---

[10]Guy E. Swanson, *The Birth of the Gods: The Origin of Primitive Beliefs* (Ann Arbor: University of Michigan Press, 1969), pp. 1–31.

[11]Anthony Wallace, *Religion: An Anthropological View* (New York: Random House, 1966), pp. 60–61.

Supernatural Beings. Supernatural beings fall within two broad categories: those of nonhuman origin, such as gods and spirits, and those of human origin, such as ghosts and ancestral spirits. Chief among the beings of nonhuman origin, **gods** are named personalities. They are often anthropomorphic—that is, conceived in the image of a person—although they are sometimes given the shapes of other animals or of celestial bodies such as the sun or moon. Essentially, the gods are believed to have created themselves, but some of them then created, or gave birth to, other gods. Although some are seen as creator gods, not all people include the creation of the world as one of the acts of gods.

After their efforts at creation, many creator gods retire. Having set the world in motion, they are not interested in its day-to-day operation. Other creator gods remain interested in the ordinary affairs of human beings, especially the affairs of one small, chosen segment of humanity. Whether a society has a creator god or not, the job of running creation is often left to lesser gods. The Maori of New Zealand, for example, recognize three important gods: a god of the sea, a god of the forest, and a god of agriculture. They call upon each in turn for help and try to get all three to share their knowledge of how the universe runs. The gods of the ancient Romans, on the other hand, specialized to a high degree. There were three gods of the plow, one god to help with the sowing, one for weeding, one for reaping, one for storing grain, one for manuring, and so on.[12]

Beneath the gods in prestige, and often closer to people, are multitudes of unnamed **spirits.** Some may be guardian spirits for people. Some, who become known for particularly efficacious work, may be promoted to the rank of named gods. Some spirits who are known to the people but never invoked by them are of the hobgoblin type: they delight in mischief and can be blamed for any number of small mishaps. Other spirits take pleasure in deliberately working evil on behalf of people.

Many Native American groups believed in guardian spirits that had to be sought out, usually in childhood. For example, among the Sanpoil of northeastern Washington, boys and sometimes girls would be sent out on overnight vigils to acquire their guardians. Most commonly the spirits were animals, but they could also be uniquely shaped rocks, lakes, mountains, whirlwinds, or clouds. The vigil was not always successful. When it was, the guardian spirit appeared in a vision or dream, and always at first in human form. Conversation with the spirit would reveal its true identity.[13]

Ghosts and **ancestor spirits** are among the supernatural beings who were once human. The belief that ghosts or their actions can be perceived by the living is apparently almost universal.[14] The near-universality of the belief in ghosts may not be difficult to explain. There are many cues in everyday experience that are associated with a loved one, and even after his or her death those cues might arouse the feeling that the dead person is still somehow present. The opening of a door, the smell of tobacco or cologne in a room, may evoke the idea that the person is still present, if only for a moment. Then, too, loved ones live on in dreams. Small wonder, then, that most societies believe in ghosts. If the idea of ghosts is generated by these familiar associations, we might expect that ghosts in most societies would be close relatives and friends, not strangers—and they are.[15]

Although the belief in ghosts is nearly universal, the spirits of the dead do not play an active role in the life of the living in all societies. In his cross-cultural study of fifty societies, Swanson found that people are likely to believe in active ancestral spirits where descent groups are important decision-making units. The descent group is an entity that exists over time, back into the past as well as forward into the future, despite the deaths of individual members.[16] The dead feel concern for the fortunes, the prestige, and the continuity of their descent group as strongly as the living. As a Lugbara elder (in northern Uganda in Africa) put it, "Are our ancestors not people of our lineage? They

---

[12]Annemarie De Waal Malefijt, *Religion and Culture: An Introduction to Anthropology of Religion* (New York: Macmillan, 1968), p. 153.

[13]Verne F. Ray, *The Sanpoil and Nespelem: Salishan Peoples of Northeastern Washington* (New Haven: Human Relations Area Files, 1954), pp. 172–89.

[14]Paul C. Rosenblatt, R. Patricia Walsh, and Douglas A. Jackson. *Grief and Mourning in Cross-Cultural Perspective* (New Haven: HRAF Press, 1976), p. 51.

[15]Ibid., p. 55.

[16]Swanson, *The Birth of the Gods*, pp. 97–108; see also Dean Sheils, "Toward A Unified Theory of Ancestor Worship: A Cross-Cultural Study," *Social Forces,* 54 (1975): 427–40.

Zeus and other gods on Mt. Olympus, in a painting by Rubens.

are our fathers and we are their children whom they have begotten. Those that have died stay near us in our homes and we feed and respect them. Does not a man help his father when he is old?"[17]

The Character of Supernatural Beings

Whatever types they may be, the gods or spirits venerated in a given culture tend to have certain personality or character traits. They may be unpredictable or predictable, aloof from or interested in human affairs, helpful or punishing. Why do the gods and spirits in a particular culture exhibit certain character traits rather than others?

We have some evidence from cross-cultural studies that the character of supernatural beings may be related to the nature of child training. Melford Spiro and Roy D'Andrade suggest that the god-human relationship is a projection of the parent-child relationship, in which case child-training practices might well be relived in dealings with the

supernatural.[18] For example, if a child was nurtured immediately by her parents when she cried or waved her arms about or kicked, then she might grow up expecting to be nurtured by the gods when she attracted their attention by performing a ritual. On the other hand, if her parents often punished her, she would grow up expecting the gods to punish her if she disobeyed them. William Lambert, Leigh Triandis, and Margery Wolf, in another cross-cultural study, found that societies with hurtful or punitive child-training practices are likely to believe that their gods are aggressive and malevolent; societies with less punitive child training are more likely to believe that the gods are benevolent.[19] These results are consistent with the Freudian notion that the supernatural world should parallel the natural. It is worth noting in this context

[17]John Middleton, "The Cult of the Dead: Ancestors and Ghosts," in William A. Lessa and Evon Z. Vogt, eds., *Reader in Comparative Religion: An Anthropological Approach,* 3rd ed. (New York: Harper & Row, Pub., 1971), p. 488.

[18]Melford E. Spiro and Roy G. D'Andrade, "A Cross-Cultural Study of Some Supernatural Beliefs," *American Anthropologist,* 60 (1958): 456–66.

[19]William W. Lambert, Leigh Minturn Triandis, and Margery Wolf, "Some Correlates of Beliefs in the Malevolence and Benevolence of Supernatural Beings: A Cross-Societal Study," *Journal of Abnormal and Social Psychology,* 58 (1959): 162–69. See also Ronald P. Rohner, *They Love Me, They Love Me Not: A Worldwide Study of the Effects of Parental Acceptance and Rejection* (New Haven: HRAF Press, 1975), p. 108.

that some people refer to the god as their father and to themselves as his children.

Structure or Hierarchy of Supernatural Beings

The range of social structures in human societies from egalitarian to highly stratified has its counterpart in the supernatural world. Some societies have a number of gods or spirits that are not ranked. One god has about as much power as another. Other societies have gods or spirits that are ranked in prestige and power. For example, on the Pacific islands of Palau, which was a rank society, gods were ranked like people were. Each clan worshiped a god and a goddess that had names or titles similar to clan titles. Although a clan god was generally important only to the members of that clan, the gods of the various clans in a village were believed to be ranked in the same order that the clans were. Thus, the god of the highest-ranking clan was respected by all the clans of the village. Its shrine was given the place of honor in the center of the village and was larger and more elaborately decorated than other shrines.[20]

Although the Palauans did not believe in a high god or supreme being who outranked all the other gods, some societies do. Consider Judaism, Christianity, and Islam, which we call **monotheistic** religions. Although *monotheism* means "one god," most monotheistic religions actually include more than one supernatural being (e.g., demons, angels, the Devil). But the supreme being or high god, as the creator of the universe or the director of events (or both), is believed to be ultimately responsible for all events.[21] A **polytheistic** religion recognizes many important gods, no one of which is supreme.

Why do some societies have a belief in a high god while others do not? Recall Swanson's suggestion that people invent gods who personify the important decision-making groups in their society. He therefore hypothesizes that societies with hierarchical political systems should be more likely to believe in a high god. In his cross-cultural study of fifty societies (none of which practice any of the major world religions), he found that belief in a high god is strongly associated with three or more levels of "sovereign" (decision-making) groups. Of the twenty sample societies that had a hierarchy of three or more sovereign groups—for instance, family, clan, and chiefdom—seventeen possessed the idea of a high god. Of the nineteen societies that had fewer than three levels of decision-making groups, only two had a high god.[22] Consistent with Swanson's findings, societies dependent on food production rather than food collecting are more likely to have a belief in a high god.[23] These results strongly suggest, then, that the realm of the gods parallels and may reflect the everyday social and political world.

Intervention of the Gods in Human Affairs

According to Clifford Geertz, it is when faced with ignorance, pain, and the unjustness of life that a person explains events by the intervention of the gods.[24] Thus, in Greek religion the direct intervention of Poseidon as ruler of the seas prevented Odysseus from getting home for ten years. In the Old Testament, the direct intervention of Yahweh caused the great flood that killed most of the people in the time of Noah. In other societies, people may search their memories for a violated taboo that has brought punishment through supernatural intervention.

In addition to unasked-for divine interference, there are numerous examples of requests for divine intervention, either for good for oneself and friends or for evil for others. Gods are asked to intervene in the weather and make the crops grow, to send fish to the fisherman and game to the hunter, to find lost things, and to accompany travelers and prevent accidents. They are asked to stop

[20]H. G. Barnett, *Being a Palauan* (New York: Holt, Rinehart & Winston, 1960), pp. 79–85.

[21]Swanson, *The Birth of the Gods*, p. 56.

[22]Ibid., pp. 55–81; see also William D. Davis, *Societal Complexity and the Nature of Primitive Man's Conception of the Supernatural* (Ph.D. diss., University of North Carolina, Chapel Hill, 1971).

[23]Robert B. Textor, comp., *A Cross-Cultural Summary* (New Haven: HRAF Press, 1967); see also Ralph Underhill, "Economic and Political Antecedents of Monotheism: A Cross-Cultural Study," *American Journal of Sociology*, 80 (1975): 841–61.

[24]Clifford Geertz, "Religion as a Cultural System," in Michael Banton, ed., *Anthropological Approaches to the Study of Religion*, Association of Social Anthropologists of the Commonwealth, Monograph no. 3 (New York: Praeger, 1966), pp. 1–46.

the flow of lava down the side of a volcano, to stop a war, or to cure an illness.

The gods do not intervene in all societies. In some they intervene in human affairs; in others, they are not the slightest bit interested; and in still others they interfere only occasionally. We have little research on why gods are believed to interfere in some societies and not in others. However, we do have some evidence suggesting when the gods will take an interest in the morality or immorality of human behavior.

Swanson's study suggests that the gods are likely to punish people for immoral behavior when there are considerable differences in wealth in the society. Swanson's interpretation is that the gods in such societies are interested in supporting the inequalities.[25] It may be that supernatural support of moral behavior is particularly useful where inequalities tax the ability of the political system to maintain social order and minimize social disorder. Envy of others' privileges may motivate some people to behave immorally; the belief that the gods will punish such behavior might deter it.

Life after Death

In many societies, ideas about an afterlife are vague and seemingly unimportant, but many other peoples have very definite and elaborate ideas of what happens after death. The Lugbara see the dead joining the ancestors of the living and staying near the family homesite. They retain an interest in the behavior of the living, both rewarding and punishing them. The Zuni of the southwestern United States think the dead join the past dead, known as the *katcinas*, at a katcina village at the bottom of a nearby lake. There they lead a life of singing and dancing and bring rain to the living Zuni. They are also swift to punish the priest who fails in his duty or the people who impersonate them in masks during the dance ceremonies.[26]

The Chamulas have merged the ancient Mayan worship of the sun and moon with the Spanish conquerors' Jesus and Mary. Their vision of life after death contains a blending of the two cultures. All souls go to the underworld, where they live a humanlike life except that they are in-capable of sexual intercourse. After the sun travels over the world, it travels under the underworld, so that the dead have sunlight. Only murderers and suicides are punished, being burned by the Christ/sun on their journey.[27]

Many Christians believe that the dead are divided into two groups: the unsaved are sent to everlasting punishment and the saved to everlasting reward. Accounts differ, but hell is often associated with torture by fire, heaven with mansions. Several societies see the dead returning to earth to be reborn. The Hindus use this pattern of reincarnation to justify one's caste in this life and to promise eventual release from the pain of life through the attainment of *nirvana*, or inclusion into the One.

The afterworld in many religions may resemble the everyday world, but we still lack comparative studies that show exactly how.

Variation in Religious Practice

Beliefs are not the only elements of religion that vary from society to society. There is also variation in how people interact with the supernatural. The manner of approach to the supernatural varies from application (requests, prayers, and so on) to manipulation. And societies vary in the kinds of religious practitioners they have.

Ways to Interact with the Supernatural

How to get in touch with the supernatural has proved to be a universal problem. Wallace suggests that a number of different ways may be used, including prayer, doing things to the body and mind, simulation, feasts, and sacrifices.[28]

Prayer can be spontaneous or memorized, private or public, silent or spoken. The Lugbara do not say the words of a prayer aloud, for that would be too powerful; they simply think about the things that are bothering them. The gods know all languages.

[25]Swanson, *The Birth of the Gods*, pp. 153–74.
[26]Ruth Bunzel, "The Nature of Katcinas," in Lessa and Vogt, eds., *Reader in Comparative Religion*, 3rd ed., pp. 493–95.

[27]Gary H. Gossen, "Temporal and Spiritual Equivalents in Chamula Ritual Symbolism," in Lessa and Vogt, eds., *Reader in Comparative Religion*, 4th ed., pp. 116–28.
[28]Wallace, *Religion: An Anthropological View*, pp. 52–67.

Although all societies have religious beliefs and practices, the pictures here hint at the range of variation. People make offerings and worship at a shrine in Bangkok, Thailand; prayer time before a soccer game in Riyadh, Saudi Arabia; memorial ceremony in honor of Confucius's birthday in Taipei, Taiwan; and a rabbi blowing a ram's horn on a high holiday.

Doing things to the body or mind may involve drugs (hallucinogenics such as peyote, opiates) or alcohol, social isolation or sensory deprivation, dancing or running till exhausted, deprivation of food, water, and sleep, and listening to repetitive sounds such as drumming. Such behaviors may induce trances or altered states of consciousness.[29] Erika Bourguignon finds that achieving these altered states (which she generally refers to as "trances") is part of religious practice in 90 percent of the world's societies.[30] In some societies, trances are thought to involve the presence of a spirit or power inside a person, changing or displacing that person's personality or soul. These are referred to as "possession trances." Other types of trances may involve the journey of a person's soul, experiencing visions, or transmitting messages from spirits. Possession trances are especially likely in societies that depend on agriculture and have social stratification, slavery, and more complex political hierarchies. Nonpossession trances are most likely to occur in food collecting societies. Societies with moderate levels of social complexity have both possession and nonpossession trances.[31]

[29]Michael Winkelman, "Trance States: A Theoretical Model and Cross-Cultural Analysis, *Ethos,* 14 (1986): 178–83.

[30]Erika Bourguignon, "Introduction: A Framework for the Comparative Study of Altered States of Consciousness," in Erika Bourguignon, *Religion, Altered States of Consciousness, and Social Change* (Columbus: Ohio State University Press, 1973), pp. 3–35.

[31]Erika Bourguignon and Thomas L. Evascu, "Altered States of Consciousness within a General Evolutionary Perspective: A Holocultural Analysis," *Behavior Science Research,* 12 (1977): 197–216. See also Winkelman, "Trance States," pp. 196–98.

Voodoo employs simulation, or the imitation of things. Dolls are made in the likeness of an enemy and then are maltreated in hopes that the original enemy will experience pain and even death. Simulation is often employed during **divination,** or getting the supernatural to provide guidance. Many people in our society have their fortunes read in crystal balls, tea leaves, Ouija boards, or cards. Or they may choose a course of action by a toss of a coin or a throw of dice. All are variations of methods used in other cultures.

Omar Moore suggests that among the Naskapi hunters of Labrador, divination is an adaptive strategy for successful hunting. The Naskapi consult the diviner every three or four days when they have no luck in hunting. The diviner holds a caribou bone over the fire, and the burns and cracks that appear in it indicate where the group should hunt. Moore, unlike the Naskapi, does not believe that the diviner really can find out where the animals will be; the cracks in the bones merely provide a way of randomly choosing where to hunt. Since humans are likely to develop customary patterns of action, they might be likely to look for game according to some plan. But game might learn to avoid hunters who operate according to a plan. Thus, any method of ensuring against patterning or predictable plans—any random strategy—may be advantageous. Divination by "reading" the bones would seem to be a random strategy. It also relieves any individual of the responsibility of deciding where to hunt, a decision that might arouse anger if the hunt failed.[32]

The eating of a sacred meal—for instance, Holy Communion as a simulation of the Last Supper—is found in many religions. Australian aborigines, forbidden normally to eat their totem animal, have one totem feast a year at which they eat the totem. Feasts are often part of marriage and funeral ceremonies, as well as a fringe benefit of the sacrifice of food to the gods.

Some societies make sacrifices to a god in order to influence the god's action, either to divert anger or to attract goodwill. Characteristic of all sacrifices is that something of value is given up to the gods, whether it be food, drink, sex, household goods, or the life of an animal or person. Some societies feel that the god is obligated to act on their

behalf if they make the appropriate sacrifice. Others use the sacrifice in an attempt to persuade the god, realizing there is no guarantee that the attempt will be successful.

Of all types of sacrifice, we probably think that the taking of human life is the ultimate. Nevertheless, human sacrifice is not rare in the ethnographic and historical record. Why have some societies practiced it? A recent cross-cultural study finds that among preindustrial societies, those with full-time craft specialists, slavery, and the corvée are most likely to practice human sacrifice. The suggested explanation is that the sacrifice mirrors what is socially important: societies that depend mainly on human labor for energy (rather than animals or machines) may think of a human life as an appropriate offering to the gods when people want something very important.[33]

Magic

All these modes of interacting with the supernatural can be categorized in various ways. One dimension of variation is how much people in society rely on pleading or asking or trying to persuade the supernatural to act on their behalf, as opposed to whether they believe they can compel the supernatural to help by performing certain acts. For example, prayer is asking; performing voodoo is presumably compelling. When people believe their action can compel the supernatural to act in some particular and intended way, anthropologists often refer to the belief and related practice as **magic.**

Magic may involve manipulation of the supernatural for good or for evil purposes. Many societies have magical rituals designed to ensure good crops, the replenishment of game, the fertility of domestic animals, and the avoidance and cure of illness in humans. We tend to associate the belief in magic with societies simpler than our own. But as many as 80,000 people in the United States take magic seriously, and there are many more who are interested in tarot cards, horoscopes, and astrology.[34] Why magic appeals to some individuals but not others in our own society may someday

[32]Omar Khayyám Moore, "Divination: A New Perspective," *American Anthropologist,* 59 (1957): 69–74.

[33]Dean Sheils, "A Comparative Study of Human Sacrifice," *Behavior Science Research,* 15 (1980): 245–62.

[34]M. Adler, *Drawing Down the Moon* (Boston: Beacon, 1986), p. 418, as referred to in T. M. Luhrmann, *Persuasions of the Witch's Craft: Ritual Magic and Witchcraft in Present-Day England* (Oxford: Basil Blackwell, 1989), pp. 4–5.

In Salem, Massachusetts, in 1692, there was an epidemic of witchcraft accusations.

help us explain why magic is an important part of religious behavior in many societies.

As we will see, the witch doctor and the shaman often employ magic to effect a cure. But the use of magic to bring about harm has evoked perhaps the most interest.

Sorcery and Witchcraft. Sorcery and witchcraft are attempts to invoke the spirits to work harm against people. Although the words *sorcery* and *witchcraft* are often used interchangeably, they are also often distinguished. **Sorcery** may include the use of materials, objects, and medicines to invoke supernatural malevolence. **Witchcraft** may be said to accomplish the same ills by means of thought and emotion alone. Evidence of witchcraft can never be found. This lack of visible evidence makes an accusation of witchcraft both harder to prove and harder to disprove.

To the Azande of Zaire (central Africa), witchcraft is part of everyday living. It is not used to explain events for which the cause is known, such as carelessness or violation of a taboo, but to explain the otherwise unexplainable. A man is

gored by an elephant. He must have been bewitched, because he had not been gored on other elephant hunts. A man goes to his beer hut at night, lights some straw, and holds it aloft to look at his beer. The thatch catches fire and the hut burns down. The man has been bewitched, for huts did not catch fire on hundreds of other nights when he and others did the same thing. Some people are sitting in the cool shade under a granary, and it collapses on them, injuring them. They are bewitched because, although the Azande admit that termites eating through the wooden posts caused the granary to collapse, witchcraft made it collapse at the precise moment on those particular people. Some of the pots of a skilled potter break; some of the bowls of a skilled carver crack. Witchcraft: other pots, other bowls treated exactly the same have not broken.[35]

The witch craze in Europe during the sixteenth and seventeenth centuries and the witch

[35]E. E. Evans-Pritchard, "Witchcraft Explains Unfortunate Events," in Lessa and Vogt, eds., *Reader in Comparative Religion,* 4th ed., pp. 362–66.

trials in 1692 in Salem, Massachusetts, remind us that the fear of others, which the belief in witchcraft presumably represents, can increase and decrease in a society within a relatively short period of time. Many scholars have tried to explain these witch hunts. One factor often suggested is political turmoil, which may give rise to widespread distrust and a search for scapegoats. In the case of western Europe during the sixteenth and seventeenth centuries, small regional political units were being incorporated into national states, and political allegiances were in flux. In addition, as Swanson has noted, the commercial revolution and related changes were producing a new social class, the middle class, and "were promoting the growth of Protestantism and other heresies from Roman Catholicism."[36] In the case of Salem, the government of the colony of Massachusetts was unstable and there was much internal dissension. In 1692, the year of the witchcraft hysteria, Massachusetts was left without an English governor and judicial practices broke down. These extraordinary conditions saw the accusation of a single person for witchcraft become the accusation of hundreds and the execution of twenty. Swanson suggests that the undermining of legitimate political procedures may have generated the widespread fear of witches.[37]

It is also possible that epidemics of witchcraft accusation, as in Salem as well as other New England and European communities, may be the result of real epidemics—epidemics of disease. The disease implicated in Salem and elsewhere is the fungus disease called ergot, which can grow on rye plants. (The rye flour that went into the bread that the Salem people ate may have been contaminated by ergot.) It is now known that people who eat grain products contaminated by ergot suffer from convulsions, hallucinations, and other symptoms such as crawling sensations in the skin. We also now know that ergot contains LSD, the drug that produces hallucinations and other delusions that resemble those occurring in severe mental disorders.

The presumed victims of bewitchment in Salem and other places had symptoms similar to victims of ergot poisoning today. They suffered from convulsions and the sensations of being pricked, pinched, or bitten. They had visions and felt as if they were flying through the air. We cannot know for sure that ergot poisoning occurred during those times when witchcraft accusations flourished. There is no direct evidence, of course, since the "bewitched" were not medically tested. But we do have some evidence that seems to be consistent with the ergot theory. Ergot is known to flourish on rye plants under certain climatic conditions—particularly a very cold winter followed by a cool, moist spring and summer. Judging by tree-ring growth, the early 1690s were particularly cold in eastern New England; and the outbreaks of witchcraft accusation in Europe seem to have peaked with colder winter temperatures.[38] Interestingly too, when witchcraft hysteria was greatest in Europe, Europeans were using an ointment containing a skin-penetrating substance that we now know produces hallucinations and a vivid sensation of flying.[39] It may not be cause for wonder then that our popular image of witches is one of people flying through the air on broomsticks.

But whether or not epidemics of witchcraft hysteria are due to epidemics of ergot poisoning and/or episodes of political turmoil, we still have to understand why so many societies in the ethnographic record believe in witchcraft and sorcery in the first place. Why do so many societies believe that there are ways to invoke the spirits to work harm against people? One possible explanation, suggested by Beatrice Whiting, is that sorcery or witchcraft will be found in societies that lack procedures or judicial authorities to deal with crime and other offenses. Her theory is that all societies need some form of social control—some way of deterring most would-be offenders and of dealing

---

[36]Swanson, *The Birth of the Gods,* p. 150. See also H. R. Trevor-Roper, "The European Witch-Craze of the Sixteenth and Seventeenth Centuries," in Lessa and Vogt, eds., *Reader in Comparative Religion,* 3rd ed., pp. 444–49.

[37]Swanson, *The Birth of the Gods,* pp. 150–51.

[38]Linnda R. Caporael, "Ergotism: The Satan Loosed in Salem?" *Science,* April 2, 1976, pp. 21–26; Mary K. Matossian, "Ergot and the Salem Witchcraft Affair," *American Scientist,* 70 (1982): 355–57; and Mary K. Matossian, *Poisons of the Past: Molds, Epidemics, and History* (New Haven: Yale University Press, 1989), pp. 70–80. For possible reasons to dismiss the ergot theory, see Nicholas P. Spanos, "Ergotism and the Salem Witch Panic: A Critical Analysis and an Alternative Conceptualization," *Journal of the History of the Behavioral Sciences,* 19 (1983): 358–69.

[39]Michael Harner, "The Role of Hallucinogenic Plants in European Witchcraft," in Michael Harner, ed., *Hallucinogens and Shamanism* (New York: Oxford University Press, 1972), pp. 127–50.

with actual offenders. In the absence of judicial officials who (if present) might deter and deal with antisocial behavior, sorcery may be a very effective social-control mechanism. If you misbehave, the person you were bad to might cause you to become ill or even die. The cross-cultural evidence seems to support this theory: sorcery is more important in societies lacking judicial authorities.[40]

Types of Practitioner

Individuals may believe that they can directly contact the supernatural, but almost all societies also have part-time or full-time religious or magical practitioners. Recent research suggests there are four major types of practitioner: shamans; sorcerers or witches; mediums; and priests. As we shall see, the number of types of practitioner seems to vary with degree of cultural complexity.[41]

The Shaman. The **shaman** is usually a part-time male specialist who has fairly high status in his community and is often involved in healing.[42] Westerners often call shamans "witch doctors" because they don't believe that shamans can effectively cure people. Do shamans effectively cure? Actually, Westerners are not the only skeptics. An American Indian named Quesalid from the Kwakiutl of the Northwest Coast didn't believe that shamanism was effective either. So he began to associate with the shamans in order to spy on them, and was taken into their group. In his first lessons, he learned

a curious mixture of pantomime, prestidigitation, and empirical knowledge, including the art of simulating fainting and nervous fits, . . . sacred song, the technique for inducing vomiting, rather precise notions of auscultation or listening to sounds within the body to detect disorders and obstetrics, and the use of "dreamers," that is, spies who listen to private conversations and secretly convey to the shaman bits of information concerning the origins and symptoms of the ills suffered by different people. Above all, he learned the *ars magna*. . . . The shaman hides a little tuft of down in the corner of his mouth, and he throws it up, covered with blood at the proper moment—after having bitten his tongue or made his gums bleed—and solemnly presents it to his patient and the onlookers as the pathological foreign body extracted as a result of his sucking and manipulations.[43]

His suspicions were confirmed, but his first curing was a success. The patient had heard that Quesalid had joined the shamans and believed that only he would heal him. Quesalid remained with the shamans for the four-year apprenticeship, during which he could take no fee, and he became increasingly aware that his methods worked. He visited other villages, competed with other shamans in curing hopeless cases and won, and finally seemed convinced that his curing system was more valid than those of other shamans. Instead of denouncing the trickery of shamans, he continued to practice as a renowned shaman.[44]

After working with shamans in Africa, E. Fuller Torrey, a psychiatrist and anthropologist, concluded that they use the same mechanisms and techniques to cure patients as psychiatrists and achieve about the same results. He isolates four categories used by healers the world over:

1. *The naming process.* If a disease has a name—"neurasthenia" or "phobia" or "possession by an ancestral spirit" will do—then it is curable; the patient realizes that the doctor understands his case.
2. *The personality of the doctor.* Those who demonstrate some empathy, nonpossessive warmth, and genuine interest in the patient get results.
3. *The patient's expectations.* One way of raising the patient's expectations of being cured is the trip to the doctor; the longer the trip—to the Mayo Clinic, Menninger Clinic, Delphi, or Lourdes—the easier the cure. An impressive setting (the medical center) and impressive paraphernalia (the stethoscope, the couch, at-

[40]Beatrice B. Whiting, *Paiute Sorcery*, Viking Fund Publications in Anthropology, no. 15 (New York: Wenner-Gren Foundation, 1950), pp. 36–37. See also Swanson, *The Birth of the Gods*, pp. 137–52, 240–41.

[41]Michael James Winkelman, "Magico-Religious Practitioner Types and Socioeconomic Conditions," *Behavior Science Research*, 20 (1986): 17–46.

[42]Ibid., pp. 28–29.

[43]Claude Lévi-Strauss, "The Sorcerer and His Magic," in Claude Lévi-Strauss, *Structural Anthropology*, trans. Claire Jacobsen and Brooke Grundfest Schoepf (New York: Basic Books, 1963), p. 169.

[44]Franz Boas, *The Religion of the Kwakiutl*, Columbia University Contributions to Anthropology, vol. 10, pt. II (New York, 1930), pp. 1–41. Reported in Lévi-Strauss, *Structural Anthropology*, pp. 169–73.

tendants in uniform, the rattle, the whistle, the drum, the mask) also raise the patient's expectations. The healer's training is important: the Ute Indian has his dreams analyzed; the Blackfoot Indian has a seven-year training course; the American psychiatrist spends four years in medical school and three in hospital training and has diplomas on the wall. High fees also help to raise a patient's expectations. (The Paiute doctors always collect their fees before starting a cure; if they don't, it is believed that they will fall ill.)

4. *Curing techniques.* Drugs, shock treatment, conditioning techniques, and so on have long been used in many different parts of the world.[45]

Medical research suggests that psychological factors are sometimes very important in illness. Patients who believe that medicine will help them often recover quickly even if the medicine is only a sugar pill. Patients who "lose the will to live" may succumb to illness easily. Still, as pharmaceutical companies have discovered, many "folk medicines" collected in anthropological fieldwork do work.

Shamans may coexist with medical doctors. Don Antonio, a respected Otomi Indian shaman in central Mexico, has many patients, perhaps not as many as before modern medicine, but still plenty. In his view, when he was born God gave him his powers to cure, but his powers are reserved for removing "evil" illnesses (those caused by sorcerers). "Good" illnesses can be cured by herbs and medicine and he refers patients with those illnesses to doctors; he believes that doctors are more effective than he could be in those cases. The doctors, however, do not seem to refer any patients to Don Antonio or other shamans![46]

Sorcerers and Witches. In contrast with shamans, who have fairly high status, sorcerers and witches of both sexes tend to have very low social and economic status in their societies.[47] Suspected

A !Kung shaman, in a trance, ministers to a patient.

sorcerers and witches are usually feared because they are thought to know how to invoke the supernatural to cause illness, injury, and death. Since sorcerers use materials for their magic, evidence of sorcery can be found, and suspected sorcerers are often killed for their malevolent activities. Because witchcraft supposedly is accomplished by thought and emotion alone, it may be harder to prove someone is a witch, as we have mentioned. However, as we have also seen, this has not prevented people from accusing and killing others for being witches.

Mediums. **Mediums** tend to be females. These part-time practitioners are asked to heal and divine while in possession trances—that is, when they

[45]E. Fuller Torrey, *The Mind Game: Witchdoctors and Psychiatrists* (New York: Emerson Hall, n.d.).

[46]James Dow, *The Shaman's Touch: Otomi Indian Symbolic Healing* (Salt Lake City: University of Utah Press, 1986), pp. 6–9, 125.

[47]Winkelman, "Magico-Religious Practitioner Types and Socioeconomic Conditions," pp. 27–28.

are thought to be possessed by spirits. Mediums are described as having tremors, convulsions, seizures, and temporary amnesia.

Priests. **Priests** are generally full-time male specialists who officiate at public events. They generally have very high status and are thought to be able to relate to superior or high gods who are beyond the ordinary person's control. In most societies with priests, the people who get to be priests tend to obtain their offices through inheritance or political appointment.[48] Priests are sometimes distinguished from other people by special clothing or a different hairstyle. The training of a priest can be vigorous and long, including fasting, praying, and physical labor as well as learning the dogma and the ritual of his religion. Priests in America generally complete four years of theological school and sometimes serve first as apprentices under established priests. The priest generally does not receive a fee for each of his services but is supported by donations from parishioners or followers. Since priests often have some political power as a result of their office—the chief priest is sometimes also the head of state, or is a close adviser to the chief of state—their material well-being is a direct reflection of their position in the priestly hierarchy.

It is the dependence on memorized ritual that both marks and protects the priest. If a shaman repeatedly fails to effect a cure, he will probably lose his following, for he has obviously lost the support of the spirits. However, if a priest performs his ritual perfectly and the gods choose not to respond, the priest will usually retain his position and the ritual will preserve its assumed effectiveness. The nonresponse of the gods will be explained in terms of the people's unworthiness of supernatural favor.

Practitioners and Social Complexity. More complex societies tend to have more types of religious or magical practitioners. If a society has only one type of practitioner, it is almost always a shaman; such societies tend to be nomadic or semi-nomadic food collectors. Societies with two types of practitioner (usually shaman/healers and priests) have agriculture. Those with three types of practitioner are agriculturalists or pastoralists with political integration beyond the community (the additional practitioner type tends to be either a sorcerer/witch

or a medium). Finally, societies with all four types of practitioners have agriculture, political integration beyond the community, and social classes.[49]

Religion and Adaptation

Following Malinowski, many anthropologists take the view that religions are generally adaptive because they reduce the anxieties and uncertainties to which all people are subject. We do not really know that religion is the only means of reducing anxiety and uncertainty, or even that individuals or societies *have* to reduce their anxiety and uncertainty. Still, it seems likely that certain religious beliefs and practices have directly adaptive consequences.

For example, the Hindu belief in the sacred cow has seemed to many to be the very opposite of a useful or adaptive custom. Their religion does not permit Hindus to slaughter cows. Why do the Hindus retain such a belief? Why do they allow all those cows to wander around freely, defecating all over the place, and not slaughter any of them? The contrast with our own use of cows could hardly be greater.

Marvin Harris has suggested, however, that the Hindu use of cows may have beneficial consequences that some other use of cows would not have. Harris points out that there may be a sound economic reason for not slaughtering cattle in India. The cows (and the males they produce) provide a number of resources that could not easily be provided otherwise. At the same time, their wandering around to forage is no strain on the food-producing economy. The resources provided by the cows are varied. First, a team of oxen and a plow are essential for the many small farms in India. The Indians could produce oxen with fewer cows, but to do so they would have to devote some of their food production to the feeding of those cows. In the present system, they do not feed the cows, and even though this makes the cows relatively infertile, males (which are castrated to make oxen) are still produced at no cost to the economy.

Second, cow dung is essential as a cooking fuel and fertilizer. The National Council of Applied Economic Research estimates that an amount of

[48]Ibid., p. 27.

[49]Ibid., pp. 35–37.

dung equivalent to 45 million tons of coal is burned annually. Moreover, it is delivered practically to the door each day at no cost. Alternative sources of fuel, such as wood, are scarce or costly. In addition, about 340 million tons of dung are used as manure—essential in a country obliged to derive three harvests a year from its intensively cultivated land. Third, although Hindus do not eat beef, cattle that die naturally or are butchered by non-Hindus are eaten by the lower castes, who, without the upper-caste taboo against eating beef, might not get this needed protein. Fourth, the hides and horns of the cattle that die are used in India's enormous leather industry. Therefore, since the sacred cows do not themselves consume resources needed by people, and since it would be impossible to provide traction, fuel, and fertilizer as cheaply by other means, the taboo against slaughtering cattle may be quite adaptive.[50]

Religious Change as Revitalization

The long history of religion includes periods of strong resistance to change as well as periods of radical change. Anthropologists have been especially interested in the founding of new religions or sects. The appearance of new religions is one of the things that may happen when cultures are disrupted by contact with dominant societies. Various terms have been suggested for these religious movements—cargo cults, nativistic movements, messianic movements, millenarian cults. Wallace suggests that they are all examples of **revitalization movements,** efforts to save a culture by infusing it with a new purpose and new life.[51]

After the American Revolution, the Seneca Indians, an Iroquois tribe, lost their lands and were confined to isolated reservations amid an alien people. As we discuss further in the chapter on culture change, they were in a state of despondency when a man named Handsome Lake received a vision from God that led him to stop drinking and to preach a new religion that would revitalize the Seneca. This was not the first such movement among the Iroquois. In the fifteenth century, they were an unorganized people, warring against each other and being warred upon by other tribes. Hiawatha, living as a highwayman and a cannibal, was visited by the god Dekanawidal. He became God's spokesman in persuading the five tribes to give up their feuding and to unite as the League of the Iroquois.[52]

Although many scholars believe cultural stress gives rise to these new religious movements, it is still important to understand exactly what the stresses are and how strong they have to become before a new movement emerges. Do different kinds of stresses produce different types of movements? And does the nature of the movement depend on the cultural elements already present? Let us consider some theory and research on the causes of the millenarian cargo cults that began to appear in Melanesia from about 1885 on.

The cargo cults can be thought of as religious movements "in which there is an expectation of, and preparation for, the coming of a period of supernatural bliss."[53] Thus, an explicit belief of the cargo cults was the notion that some liberating power would bring all the Western goods (*cargo* in pidgin English) the people might want. For example, around 1932, on Buka in the Solomon Islands, the leaders of a cult prophesied that a tidal wave would sweep away the villages and a ship would arrive with iron, axes, food, tobacco, cars, and arms. Work in the gardens ceased, and wharves and docks were built for the expected cargo.[54]

What may explain such cults? Peter Worsley has suggested that an important factor in the rise of cargo cults and millenarian movements in general is the existence of oppression—in the case of Melanesia, colonial oppression. He suggests the reactions in Melanesia took religious rather than political forms because they were a way of pulling together people who previously had no political unity, who lived in small, isolated social groups.[55] Other scholars, such as David Aberle, think *relative deprivation* is more important than oppression in explaining the origins of cults; when people feel that they could have more, and they have less than what they used to have or less than others,

[50]Marvin Harris, "The Cultural Ecology of India's Sacred Cattle," *Current Anthropology,* 7 (1966): 51–63.
[51]Wallace, *Religion: An Anthropological View,* p. 30.
[52]Ibid., pp. 31–34.
[53]Peter Worsley, *The Trumpet Shall Sound: A Study of "Cargo" Cults in Melanesia* (London: MacGibbon & Kee, 1957), p. 12.
[54]Ibid., pp. 11, 115.
[55]Ibid., p. 122.

A painting of the Ghost Dance as practiced by the Sioux.

they may be attracted to new cults.[56] Consistent with Aberle's general interpretation, Bruce Knauft's comparative study of cargo cults found that such cults were more important in those Melanesian societies that had had *decreasing* cultural contact with the West, and presumably decreasing contact with valued goods, within the year prior to the cult's emergence.[57]

If the recent as well as distant past is any guide, we can expect religious belief and practice to be revitalized periodically, particularly during periods of stress. Thus, we can expect the world to continue to have religious variation.

[56]David Aberle, "A Note on Relative Deprivation Theory as Applied to Millenarian and Other Cult Movements," in Lessa and Vogt, eds., *Reader in Comparative Religion*, 3rd ed., pp. 528–31.

[57]Bruce M. Knauft, "Cargo Cults and Relational Separation," *Behavior Science Research*, 13 (1978): 185–240.

SUMMARY

1. Religion is any set of attitudes, beliefs, and practices pertaining to supernatural power. Such beliefs may vary within a culture as well as among societies, and they may change over time.

2. Religious beliefs are evident in all known cultures and are inferred from artifacts associated with *Homo sapiens* since at least 60,000 years ago.

3. Theories to account for the universality of religion suggest that humans create it in response to certain universal needs or conditions, including

a need for intellectual understanding, guilt and projection, anxiety or uncertainty, and a need for community.

4. There are wide variations in religious beliefs. Societies vary in the number and kinds of supernatural entities in which they believe. There may be impersonal supernatural forces (e.g., mana and taboo), supernatural beings of nonhuman origin (gods or spirits), and supernatural beings of human origin (ghosts and ancestor spirits). The religious belief system of a society may include any or all such entities.

5. Gods and spirits may be unpredictable or predictable, aloof from or interested in human affairs, helpful or punishing. In some societies, all gods are equal in rank; in others, there is a hierarchy of prestige and power among gods and spirits, just as among the humans in those societies.

6. A monotheistic religion is one in which there is one high god, as the creator of the universe or the director of events (or both); all other supernatural beings are either subordinate to, or function as alternative manifestations of, this god. A high god is generally found in societies with a high level of political development.

7. Faced with ignorance, pain, and injustice, people frequently explain events by claiming intervention by the gods. Such intervention has also been sought by people who hope it will help them achieve their own ends. The gods are likely to punish the immoral behavior of people in societies that have considerable differences in wealth.

8. Various methods have been used to attempt communication with the supernatural. Among them are prayer, doing things to the body and mind, simulation, feasts, and sacrifices.

9. When people believe their actions can compel the supernatural to act in a particular and intended way, anthropologists refer to the belief and related practice as magic. Sorcery and witchcraft are attempts to make the spirits work harm against people.

10. Almost all societies have part-time or full-time religious/magical practitioners. Recent cross-cultural research suggests there are four major types of practitioner: shamans, sorcerers or witches, mediums, and priests. The number of types of practitioner seems to vary with degree of cultural complexity. In some societies, intermediaries such as shamans or priests communicate with the supernatural on behalf of others. Societies with religious intermediaries tend to be more complex and have greater specialization.

11. The history of religion includes periods of strong resistance to change and periods of radical change. One explanation for this is that religious practices always originate during periods of stress. Religious movements have been called revitalization movements—efforts to save a culture by infusing it with a new purpose and new life.

SUGGESTED READING

CHILD, A. B., AND CHILD, I. L. *Religion and Magic in the Life of Traditional Peoples.* Englewood Cliffs, NJ: Prentice Hall, 1993. Based on a review of ethnographic data from all over the world, this book discusses the features common to traditional religions everywhere, as well as the factors that may account for variation in religion.

LEHMANN, A. C., AND MYERS, J. E. *Magic, Witchcraft, and Religion: An Anthropological Study of the Supernatural.* Palo Alto, CA: Mayfield, 1985. A recent collection of readings from anthropology and other disciplines on topics in the study of the supernatural.

LESSA, W. A., AND VOGT, E. Z., eds. *Reader in Comparative Religion: An Anthropological Approach,* 4th ed. New York: Harper & Row, Pub., 1979. A collection of theoretical and descriptive readings. The editors' general introduction outlines the main issues, problems, and theoretical positions in the anthropological study of religion.

MALINOWSKI, B. *Magic, Science and Religion and Other Essays.* Garden City, NY: Doubleday, 1954. A collection of papers representing some of Malinowski's work on ritual and religious behavior and the nature of primitive cults, magic, and faith.

MORRIS, B. *Anthropological Studies of Religion: An Introductory Text.* Cambridge: Cambridge University Press, 1987. A review of theories about the origin and persistence of religion.

SWANSON, G. E. *The Birth of the Gods: The Origin of Primitive Beliefs.* Ann Arbor: University of Michigan Press, 1969. A cross-cultural study that explores the origins of religious beliefs and examines how various aspects of religion may be related to social and political organization.

WALLACE, A. F. C. *Religion: An Anthropological View.* New York: Random House, 1966. An extensive review and discussion of many questions about religion. The author suggests that religion in all its aspects can best be understood from a combined psychological and cultural point of view.

24

The Arts

M ost societies do not have a word for art.[1] Perhaps this is because art, particularly in societies with relatively little specialization, is often an integral part of religious, social, and political life. Indeed, most of the aspects of culture we have already discussed—economics, kinship, politics, religion— are also not easily separated from the rest of social life.[2]

Art seems to appear in human history at least as far back as 30,000 years ago. We say that those earliest known carvings, beads, and cave paintings are art, but what do we mean by "art"? A stone spear point, a bone fish hook, obviously required skill and creativity to make. But we do not call them art. Why do we feel that some things are art, others are not?

From the viewpoint of the person who creates it, art expresses feelings and ideas; from the viewpoint of the observer or participant, it evokes feelings and ideas. The feelings and ideas on each side may or may not be exactly the same. And they may be expressed in a variety of ways—drawing, painting, carving, weaving, body decoration, music, dance, story. An artistic work or performance is intended to invoke or excite the senses, to stir the emotions of the beholder or participant. It may produce feelings of beauty, awe, repulsion, fear, but usually not indifference.[3] Finally, most anthropologists agree that art is more than an attempt by an individual to express or communicate feelings and ideas. There is also cultural patterning and meaning; societies vary in their characteristic kinds and styles of art.

Artistic activities are always in part cultural, involving shared and learned patterns of behavior, belief, and feeling. In our society, we tend to think that anything useful is not art. If the basket has a design that was not necessary to its function, we may possibly consider it art, especially if we keep it on a shelf; but the basket with bread on the table would probably not be considered art. But such a

distinction is not made in other societies, strongly suggesting that our ideas about art are cultural. Among Native Americans on the Northwest Coast, elaborately carved totem poles not only displayed the crests of the lineages of their occupants; they also supported the house.[4] The fact that artistic activities are partly cultural is evident when we compare how people in different societies treat the outsides of their houses. Most North Americans share the value of decorating the interiors of their homes with pictures—paintings, prints, or photographs hung on the walls. But they do not share the value of painting pictures on the outside walls of their houses, as Native Americans did on the Northwest Coast.

In our society, we also insist that to be considered art, a work must be unique. However, even though we require that artists be unique and innovative, the art they produce must still fall within some range of acceptable variation. Artists must communicate to us in a way we can relate to, or at least learn to relate to. Often, they must follow certain current styles of expression that have been set by other artists or by critics, if they hope to have their art accepted by the public. The idea that an artist should be original is a cultural idea— in some societies the ability to replicate a traditional pattern is more valued than originality.

So art seems to have several qualities. It expresses as well as communicates. It stimulates the senses, affects emotions, and evokes ideas. It is produced in culturally patterned ways and styles; it has cultural meaning. And some people are thought to be better at it than others.[5] Art does not require some people to be full-time artistic specialists; many societies in the ethnographic record had no full-time specialists of any kind. But although everyone in some societies may participate in some arts (dancing, singing, body decoration), it is usually thought that certain individuals have superior artistic skill.

To illustrate the cross-cultural variation that exists in artistic expression, we will consider first the art of body decoration and adornment.

[1]Jacques Maquet, *The Aesthetic Experience: An Anthropologist Looks at the Visual Arts* (New Haven: Yale University Press, 1986), p. 9.

[2]Richard L. Anderson, *Art in Small-Scale Societies*, 2nd ed. (Englewood Cliffs, NJ: Prentice Hall, 1989)), p. 21.

[3]Robert P. Armstrong, *The Powers of Presence* (Philadelphia: University of Pennsylvania Press, 1981), pp. 6–9; see also Anderson, *Art in Small-Scale Societies*, p. 11.

[4]Edward Malin, *Totem Poles of the Pacific Northwest Coast* (Portland: Timber Press, 1986), p. 27.

[5]Anderson, *Art in Small-Scale Societies*, p. 11.

Body Decoration and Adornment

In all societies, people decorate or adorn their bodies. The decorations may be permanent—scars, tattoos, changes in the shape of a body part. Or they may be temporary—in the form of paint or objects such as feathers, jewelry, skins, and clothing that are not strictly utilitarian. Much of this decoration seems to be motivated by esthetic considerations, which, of course, may vary from culture to culture. The actual form of the decoration depends on cultural traditions. Body ornamentation includes the pierced noses of some women in India, the elongated necks of the Mangebetu of central Africa, the tattooing of North American males, the body painting of the Caduveo of South America, and the varying ornaments found in almost every culture.

However, in addition to satisfying esthetic needs, body decoration or adornment may be used to delineate social position, rank, sex, occupation, local and ethnic identity, or religion within a society. Along with social stratification come visual means of declaring status. The symbolic halo (the crown) on the king's head, the scarlet hunting jacket of the English gentleman, the eagle feathers of the Native American chief's bonnet, the gold-embroidered jacket of the Indian rajah—each of these marks of high status is recognized in its own society. Jewelry in the shape of a cross or the Star of David indicates Christian or Jewish inclinations. Clothes may set apart the priest or the nun, or the member of a sect such as the Amish.

The erotic significance of some body decoration is also apparent. Women draw attention to erogenous zones of the body by painting, as on the lips, and by attaching some object—an earring, a flower behind the ear, a necklace, bracelet, brooch, anklet, or belt. Men draw attention too, by beards, tatoos, and penis sheaths (in some otherwise naked societies) that point upward. The Basuto of southern Africa devise a love potion for men and women by rubbing an ointment containing some of the beloved's sweat or blood or hair into open wounds. The resulting scars are evidence of love.[6] Among the Ila-speaking peoples of what

In all societies people decorate their bodies, as this woman in Niger has.

is now northern Zambia, women practice scarification to heighten arousal during sexual intercourse. They repeatedly cut and reopen vertical lines on their loins and inner thighs. The marks are hidden by their skirts during the day and are revealed only to their husbands.[7] Body adornment for erotic purposes is not peculiar to non-Western cultures. We have only to follow the fashion trends for women of Europe and North America during the past 300 years, with their history of pinched waists, ballooned hips, bustled rumps, exaggerated breasts, painted faces, and exposed bosoms, to realize the significance of body adornment for sexual provocation. Why some societies emphasize the erotic

---

[6]Hugh Ashton, *The Basuto*, 2nd ed. (London: Oxford University Press, 1967), p. 303.

[7]Edwin W. Smith and Andrew Murray Dale, *The Ila-Speaking Peoples of Northern Rhodesia* (New Hyde Park, NY: University Books, 1968 [originally published in 1920 as *Ethnocentric British Colonial Attitudes*]), p. 96.

adornment of women and others emphasize it in men is not yet understood.

In many societies the body is permanently marked or altered, often to indicate a change in status. Many societies circumcise adolescent boys. In the Poro initiation ceremony practiced by the Kpelle of Liberia, the circumcised boys spend a period of seclusion in the forest with the older men. They return with scars down their backs, symbolic tooth marks indicative of their close escape from *ngamu*, the Great Masked Figure, which ate the child but disgorged the young adult.[8] Clitoridectomy (removal of the clitoris) marks the sexual maturity of girls in some societies.

The tendency to decorate the human body is probably universal. We have noted some of the various methods people have used to adorn themselves in different societies. We are also aware of body-decoration practices that raise questions to which we have no ready answers. Perhaps vanity explains adornment of the body and such practices as scarification, bound feet, elongated ears and necks, shaped heads, pierced ears and septums, and filed teeth. But what leads some members of our society to transfer body decoration to their animals? Why the shaped hair of the poodle, the braided manes of some horses, and diamond collars, painted toenails, coats, hats, and even boots for some pets? And why, for example, do different societies adorn, paint, or otherwise decorate different parts of the body for sexual (or other) reasons?

Explaining Variation in the Arts

Many people would argue that the arts are an area of culture free to vary. Apparently, the particular style of the visual art, or music, or dance, of a society has no effect on the society's survival or success. Therefore, it might seem that any form or style could occur at any time and at any place. This assumption about the freedom of artistic expression to vary may also arise from our own experience in observing rapid changes in popular music and dance, films, and graphic art, all in the apparent absence of equally rapid changes in current life-styles and social conditions. However, we must realize that what looks like rapid change to us may merely be slight variation within what a foreign observer would see as a more or less constant form or style. For example, the way people danced in the 1940s differed from the way people danced in the 1960s, and the way we dance now is also different, but we still generally see couples dancing—not individuals in isolation or in a dance-line or circle. Furthermore, our popular music still has a beat (or combination of beats) and is made by many of the same kinds of instruments as in the past.

Much of the recent research on variation in the arts supports the idea that the form and style of visual art, music, dance, and folklore very much *reflect* the way individuals live in their society. Just as some aspects of religion seem to be projections of people's feelings and experiences, so some forms of artistic expression may be ways of vicariously revealing the feelings and ideas of most people in society.

Visual Art

Perhaps the most obvious way artistic creations reflect how we live is by mirroring the environment—the materials and technologies available to a culture. Stone, wood, bones, tree bark, clay, sand, charcoal, berries for staining, and a few mineral-derived ochers are generally available materials. In addition, depending on the locality, other resources are accessible: shells, horns, tusks, gold, copper, and silver. The different uses to which societies put these materials are of interest to anthropologists, who may ask, for example, why a people chooses to use clay and not copper when both items are available. Although we have no conclusive answers as yet, such questions have important ramifications. The way in which a society views its environment is sometimes apparent in its choice and use of artistic materials. The use of certain metals, for example, may be reserved for ceremonial objects of special importance. Or the belief in the supernatural powers of a stone or tree may cause the sculptor to be sensitive to that particular material.[9]

What is particularly meaningful to anthropolo-

[8]James L. Gibbs, Jr., "The Kpelle of Liberia," in James L. Gibbs, Jr., ed., *Peoples of Africa* (New York: Holt, Rinehart & Winston, 1965), p. 222.

[9]James J. Sweeney, "African Negro Culture," in Paul Radin, ed., *African Folktales and Sculpture* (New York: Pantheon, 1952), p. 335.

434   CHAPTER 24

The same material may be used artistically in different societies. A Zen Buddhist monk in Japan rakes sand into traditional patterns. A Navaho in the Southwestern United States creates a sand painting.

gists is the realization that although the materials available to a society may to some extent limit or influence what it can do artistically, the materials by no means determine what is done. Why does the artist in Japanese society rake sand into patterns, the artist in Navaho society paint sand, and the artist in Roman society melt sand to form glass? Moreover, even when the same material is used in the same way by members of different societies, the form or style of the work varies enormously from culture to culture.

A society may choose to represent objects or phenomena that are especially important to its population or elite. An examination of the art of the Middle Ages tells us something about the medieval preoccupation with theological doctrine. In addition to revealing the primary concerns of a society, the content of that society's art may also reflect the culture's social stratification. Authority figures may be represented in rather obvious ways. In the art of ancient Sumerian society, the sovereign was portrayed as being much larger than his followers, and the most prestigious gods were given oversized eyes. Also, as we have seen, differences in clothing and jewelry styles within a society usually reflect social stratification.

Certain possible relationships between the art of a society and other aspects of its culture have always been recognized by art historians. Much of this attention has been concentrated on the content of art, since European art has been representational for such a long time. But the style of the art may reflect other aspects of culture. John Fischer, for example, has examined the stylistic features of art with the aim of discovering "some sort of regular connection between some artistic feature and some social situation."[10] He argues that the artist expresses a form of social fantasy. In other words, in a stable society artists will respond to those conditions in the society that bring them, and the society, security or pleasure.

Assuming that "pictorial elements in design are, on one psychological level, abstract, mainly unconscious representations of persons in the society,"[11] Fischer reasoned that egalitarian societies would tend to have different stylistic elements in their art

than stratified societies. Egalitarian societies are generally composed of small, self-sufficient communities that are structurally similar and have little differentiation between persons. Stratified societies, on the other hand, generally have larger and more interdependent (and dissimilar) communities and great differences among persons in prestige, power, and access to economic resources. Fischer hypothesized, and found in a cross-cultural study, that certain elements of design were strongly related to the presence of social hierarchy. His findings are summarized in Table 24–1.

Repetition of a simple element, for example, tends to be found in the art of egalitarian societies, which have little political organization and few authority positions. If each element unconsciously represents individuals within the society, the relative sameness of people seems to be reflected in the repetitiveness of design elements. Conversely, the combining of different design elements in complex patterns that tends to be found in the art of stratified societies seems to reflect the high degree of social differentiation that exists in such societies.

According to Fischer, the egalitarian society's empty space in a design represents the society's relative isolation. Because egalitarian societies are usually small and self-sufficient, they tend to shy away from foreigners, preferring to find security within their own group. On the other hand, the art of stratified societies is generally crowded. The hierarchical society does not seek to isolate individuals or communities within the group since they must be interdependent, each social level ideally furnishing services for those above it and help for those beneath it. As Fischer suggests, we can, in general, discern a lack of empty space in the designs of those societies where, instead of security

TABLE 24-1 Artistic Differences in Egalitarian and Stratified Societies

EGALITARIAN SOCIETY	STRATIFIED SOCIETY
Repetition of simple elements	Integration of unlike elements
Much empty or "irrelevant" space	Little empty space
Symmetrical design	Asymmetrical design
Unenclosed figures	Enclosed figures

[10]John Fischer, "Art Styles as Cultural Cognitive Maps," *American Anthropologist*, 63 (1961): 80.
[11]Ibid., p. 81.

Symmetry and the repetition of design elements tend to be found in the art of unstratified societies, as in Greenland Eskimo bead craft. Stratified societies are more likely to have asymmetry and different design elements, as in this 19th century Japanese painting.

being sought by avoidance of the stranger, "security is produced by incorporating strangers into the hierarchy, through dominance or submission as the relative power indicates."[12]

[12]Ibid., p. 83.

Symmetry, the third stylistic feature related to type of society, is similar to the first. Symmetry may suggest likeness or an egalitarian society; asymmetry suggests difference and perhaps stratification. The fourth feature of interest here, the presence or absence of enclosures or boundaries ("frames" in our art), may indicate the presence or absence of hierarchically imposed rules circumscribing individual behavior. An unenclosed design may reflect free access to most property; in egalitarian societies the fencing off of a piece of property for the use of only one person is unknown. In the art of stratified societies, boundaries or enclosures may reflect the idea of private property. Or they may symbolically represent the real differences in dress, occupation, type of food allowed, and manners that separate the different classes of people.

Studies such as Fischer's offer anthropologists new tools with which to evaluate ancient societies that are known only by a few pieces of pottery or a few tools or paintings. If art reflects other aspects of a culture, then the study of whatever art of a people has been preserved may provide a means of testing the accuracy of the guesses we make about their culture on the basis of more ordinary archeological materials. For example, even if we did not know from classical Greek writings that Athens became more and more socially stratified between 1000 B.C. and 450 B.C., we might guess that such a transformation had occurred because of the changes we can see over time in the way the Athenians decorated vases. Consistent with Fischer's cross-cultural findings, as Athens became more stratified, its vase painting became more complex, more crowded, and more enclosed.[13]

Music

When we hear the music of another culture, we often don't know what to make of it. We may say it does not "mean" anything to us, hardly realizing that the meaning of music has been programmed into us by our culture. In music as well as in art, our culture largely determines what we consider acceptable variation, what we say has "meaning" to us. Even a trained musicologist, listening for the first time to music of a different culture, will not be able to hear the subtleties of tone and rhythm that members of the culture hear with ease. His or her predicament is similar to that of the linguist who, exposed to a foreign language,

cannot at first distinguish phonemes, morphemes, and other regular patterns of speech.

Not only do instruments vary, but music itself varies widely in style from society to society. For example, in some societies people prefer music with a regularly recurring beat; in others they prefer changes in rhythm. There are also variations in singing styles. In some places it is customary to have different vocal lines for different people; in other places people all sing together in the same way.

Is variation in music, as in the other arts, related to other aspects of culture? On the basis of a cross-cultural study of more than 3,500 folk songs from a sample of the world's societies, Alan Lomax and his co-researchers found that song style seems to vary with cultural complexity. As we will see, these findings about variation in song style are similar to Fischer's findings about variation in art.

Lomax and his co-researchers found a number of features of song style to be correlated with cultural complexity. (The societies classified as more complex tend to have higher levels of food-production technology, social stratification, and a number of levels of political jurisdiction.) For example, wordiness and clearness of enunciation were found to be associated with cultural complexity. The association is a reasonable one: the more a society depends on verbal information, as in giving complex instructions for a job or explaining different points of law, the more strongly will clear enunciation in the transmitting of information be a mark of its culture. Thus, hunter-gatherer bands, in which people know their productive role and perform it without ever being given complex directions, are more likely than we are to base much of their singing on lines of nonwords, such as our refrain line "tra-la-la-la-la." Their songs are characterized by lack of explicit information, by sounds that give pleasure in themselves, by much repetition, and by relaxed, slurred enunciation.[14]

Examples of the progression from repetition or nonwords to wordy information are found within our society. The most obvious (and universal) example of a song made entirely of repetition is the relaxed lullaby of a mother repeating a comforting

[13]William W. Dressler and Michael C. Robbins, "Art Styles, Social Stratification, and Cognition: An Analysis of Greek Vase Painting," *American Ethnologist*, 2 (1975): 427–34.

[14]Alan Lomax, ed., *Folk Song Style and Culture*, American Association for the Advancement of Science, Publication no. 88 (Washington, DC, 1968), pp. 117–28.

syllable to her baby while improvising her own tune. However, this type of song is not characteristic of our society. Although our songs sometimes have single lines of nonwords, it is rare for an entire song to be made of them. Usually, the nonwords act as respites from information:

Zippity do dah
Zippety ay
My o my
What a wonderful day[15]

In associating variation in music with cultural complexity, Lomax found that elaboration of song parts also corresponds to the complexity of a society. Societies in which leadership is informal and temporary seem to symbolize their social equality by an *interlocked* style of singing: each person sings independently but within the group, and no one singer is differentiated from the others. Rank societies, in which there is a leader with prestige but no real power, are characterized by a song style in which one "leader" may begin the song, but the others soon drown out his voice. In stratified societies, where leaders have the power of force, choral singing is generally marked by a clear-cut role for the leader and a secondary "answering" role for the others. Societies marked by elaborate stratification show singing parts that are differentiated and in which the soloist is deferred to by the other singers.

Lomax also found a relationship between **polyphony** (two or more melodies sung simultaneously) and a high degree of female participation in food-getting. In those societies in which women's work is responsible for at least half of the food, songs are likely to contain more than one simultaneous melody, with the higher tunes usually sung by women.

Counterpoint was once believed to be the invention of European high culture. In our sample it turns out to be most frequent among simple producers, especially gatherers, where women supply the bulk of the food. Counterpoint and perhaps even polyphony may then be very old feminine inventions. . . . Subsistence complementarity is at its maximum among gatherers, early gardeners, and horticulturalists. It is in such societies that we find the highest occurrence of polyphonic singing.[16]

In societies in which women do not contribute much to production, the songs are more likely to have a single melody and be sung by males.[17]

In some societies, survival and social welfare are based on a unified group effort; in these cultures, singing tends to be marked by cohesiveness. That is, cohesive work parties, teams of gatherers or harvesters and kin groups who work voluntarily for the good of the family or community, seem to express their interconnectedness in song by blending both tone and rhythm.

Some variations in music may be explained as a consequence of variation in child-rearing practices. For example, researchers are beginning to explore child-rearing practices as a way to explain why some societies respond to, and produce, regular rhythm in their music, whereas others enjoy free rhythm that has no regular beat but instead approximates the rhythm of speech.

One hypothesis is that a regular beat in music is a simulation of the regular beat of the heart. For nine months in the womb, the fetus feels the mother's regular eighty or so heartbeats a minute. Moreover, mothers generally employ rhythmic tactics in quieting crying infants—patting their backs or rocking them. But the fact that children respond positively to an even tempo does not mean that the regular heartbeat is completely responsible for their sensitivity to rhythm. In fact, if the months in the womb were sufficient to establish a preference for rhythm, then every child would be affected in exactly the same manner by a regular beat, and every society would have the same rhythm in its music.

Barbara Ayres suggests that the importance of regular rhythm in the music of a culture is related to the rhythm's *acquired reward value*—that is, its associations with feelings of security or relaxation. In a cross-cultural study of this possibility, Ayres found a strong correlation between a society's method of carrying infants and the type of musical rhythm the society produced. In some societies, the mother or an older sister carries the child, sometimes for two or three years, in a sling, pouch, or shawl, so that the child is in bodily contact with her for much of the day and experiences the motion of her rhythmic walking. Ayres discovered that such societies tend to have a regularly recur-

[15]© 1945 Walt Disney Music Company; words by Ray Gilbert, music by Allie Wrubel.
[16]Lomax, *Folk Song Style and Culture*, pp. 166–67.

[17]Ibid., pp. 167–69.

ring beat in their songs. Those societies in which the child is put into a cradle or is strapped to a cradleboard tend to have music based either on irregular rhythm or on free rhythm.[18]

The question of why some societies have great tonal ranges in music whereas others do not has also been studied by Ayres, who suggests that this too might be explained by certain child-rearing practices. Ayres theorizes that painful stimulation of infants before weaning might result in bolder, more exploratory behavior in adulthood, which would be apparent in the musical patterns of the culture. This hypothesis was suggested to her by laboratory experiments with animals. Contrary to expectations, those animals given electric shocks or handled before weaning showed greater than usual physical growth and more exploratory behavior when placed in new situations as adults. Ayres equated the range of musical notes (from low to high) with the exploratory range of animals, and forcefulness of accent in music with boldness in animals.

The kinds of stress Ayres looked for in ethnographic reports were those that would be applied to all children or to all of one sex—for example, scarification; piercing of the nose, lips, or ears; binding, shaping, or stretching of feet, head, ears, or any limb; innoculation; circumcision; or cauterization. The results showed that in those societies in which infants are stressed before the age of two, music is marked by a wider tonal range than in societies in which children are not stressed or are stressed only at a later age. Also, a firm accent or beat is characteristic of music more often in societies that stress children than in societies that do not.[19]

Cultural emphasis on obedience or independence in children is another variable that may explain some aspects of musical performance. In societies in which children are generally trained for compliance, cohesive singing predominates. In societies in which children are encouraged to be assertive, singing is mostly individualized. Moreover, assertive training of children is associated with a raspy voice or harsh singing. A raspy voice seems

to be an indication of assertiveness and is most often a male voice quality. Interestingly enough, in societies in which women's work predominates in subsistence production, the women sing with harsher voices.

Other voice characteristics may also be associated with elements of culture. For example, sexual restrictions in a society seem to be associated with voice restrictions, especially with a nasalized or narrow, squeezed tone. These voice qualities are associated with anxiety and are especially noticeable in sounds of pain, deprivation, or sorrow. Restrictive sexual practices may be a source of pain and anxiety, and the nasal tone in song may reflect such emotions.[20]

If the cross-cultural results about music are valid, they should be able to explain change over time as well as variation within a society. Future research in a variety of societies may help test some of the theories of Lomax and his colleagues.[21]

Folklore

Folklore is a broad category including all the myths, legends, folktales, ballads, riddles, proverbs, and superstitions of a cultural group.[22] Generally, folklore is orally transmitted, but it may also be written. In our society, for example, there are books of fairy tales and ballads. Folklore is not always clearly separable from the other arts, particularly music and dance, since stories are often conveyed in these contexts. (Games are also sometimes considered folklore, although they may be learned by imitation as well as transmitted orally.)

All societies have a repertoire of stories with which they entertain each other and teach children. Examples of our folklore include fairy tales and the legends we tell about our folk heroes, such as George Washington's confessing to chopping down a cherry tree.

Some folklore scholars are interested in universal or recurrent themes. Clyde Kluckhohn suggested that five themes occur in the myths and

[18]Barbara C. Ayres, "Effects of Infant Carrying Practices on Rhythm in Music," *Ethos*, 1 (1973): 387–404.
[19]Barbara C. Ayres, "Effects of Infantile Stimulation on Musical Behavior," in Lomax, ed., *Folk Song Style and Culture*, pp. 211–21.

[20]Edwin Erickson, "Self-assertion, Sex Role, and Vocal Rasp," in Lomax, ed., *Folk Song Style and Culture*, pp. 190–97.
[21]For a study of variation in music within India that does not support some of Lomax's findings, see Edward O. Henry, "The Variety of Music in a North Indian Village: Reassessing Cantometrics," *Ethnomusicology*, 20 (1976): 49–66.
[22]Alan Dundes, *Folklore Matters* (Knoxville: University of Tennessee Press, 1989), p. viii.

Just as in art and song, dance style seems to reflect societal complexity. In less complex societies, everyone participates in dances in much the same way, as among the Turkana in east Africa. In more complex societies, there tend to be leading roles and minor roles, as in a Japanese geisha show.

folktales of all societies: catastrophe, generally through flood; the slaying of monsters; incest; sibling rivalry, generally between brothers; and castration, sometimes actual but more commonly symbolic.[23]

The theme of the flood is found in myth in many cultures. Fragments of the Babylonian Gilgamesh epic date from about 2000 B.C. Gilgamesh was the favorite of the god Ut-Napishtim and was given instructions to build a boat, in which he saved himself and some animals from a destructive flood. The story of Noah, written later than the Gilgamesh epic, is similar enough to be seen as a case of diffusion. But diffusion may not account for equally ancient flood myths in Asia and the Americas. Rather, the wide distribution of such myths might be the result of experiences that are common in many parts of the world. For example, the theme of destruction and renewal seems to be universal, perhaps because people in many areas of the world have experienced, and been terrified by, floods.

The slaying of monsters is part of the general category of hero myths. Different reasons for the slaying may be given. Hercules must slay some monsters as punishment for having killed his wife and children. Bellerophon and Perseus of Greek mythology are told to slay a monster by kings who hope the two will be killed in the attempt. In some Bantu (Africa) myths, a hero slays a monster in order to restore the people (except his father) whom the monster has killed.[24] In North America, a Cree legend relates how a man named Wee-sa-kay-jac slew a monster in revenge for the monster's having killed his younger brother. But Wee-sa-kay-jac did not restore the brother to life (even though in related myths he seems to have had that power).[25]

The incest theme is a general one in which brother-sister incest seems to be the most popular type.[26] Absalom of the Hebrew tradition killed his brother upon learning that he had slept with their sister. But with this success behind him, Absalom next attempted to take his father David's throne and was in turn killed for this insolence. In Greek mythology, Zeus and Hera, who were brother and sister, were also husband and wife.

Sibling rivalry is apparent in the stories of Absalom and of Wee-sa-kay-jac. It is perhaps most widely known in our society in the Hebrew stories of Cain and Abel, and Jacob and Esau. Sister-sister rivalry is a theme of the Greek story of Psyche and appears as jealousy between stepsisters in the story of Cinderella. The castration theme generally appears disguised, as in this warning given to little boys: if you suck your thumb, the butcher will cut it off.

Some investigators of myth find even more universality. Edward Tylor, who proposed that religion is born from the human need to explain states such as dreams and death, suggested that hero myths follow a similar pattern the world over—the central character is exposed at birth, is subsequently saved by others (humans or animals), and grows up to become a hero.[27] Joseph Campbell argues that hero myths resemble initiations—the hero is separated from the ordinary world, ventures forth into a new world (in this case, the supernatural world) to triumph over powerful forces, and then returns to the ordinary world with special powers to help others.[28]

Myths may indeed have universal themes, but few scholars have looked at a representative sample of the world's societies and therefore we cannot be sure that the conclusions about universality reached so far are correct.

Indeed, most folklore researchers have not been interested in universal themes, but rather in the particular folktales told in specific societies or regions. For example, a number of scholars have focused on the "Star Husband Tale," a common Native American tale. Stith Thompson presented eighty-four versions of this tale—his goal was to reconstruct the original version and pinpoint its place of origin. By identifying the most common elements, Thompson suggests that the basic story (and probably the original) is the following:

---

[23]Clyde Kluckhohn, "Recurrent Themes in Myths and Mythmaking," in Alan Dundes, ed., *The Study of Folklore* (Englewood Cliffs, NJ: Prentice Hall, 1965), pp. 158–68.

[24]Ibid., p. 163.

[25]James Stevens, *Sacred Legends of the Sandy Lake Cree* (Toronto: McClelland & Stewart, 1971), pp. 22–23.

[26]Kluckhohn, "Recurrent Themes in Myths and Mythmaking," p. 163.

[27]As discussed in Robert A. Segal, *Joseph Campbell: An Introduction* (New York: Garland, 1987), pp. 1–2.

[28]Joseph Campbell, *The Hero with a Thousand Faces* (New York: Pantheon Books, 1949), p. 30; as quoted in Segal, *Joseph Campbell: An Introduction*, p. 4.

Two girls sleeping out of doors wish that stars would be their husbands. In their sleep the girls are taken to the sky where they find themselves married to stars, one of which is a young man and the other an old man. The women are warned not to dig, but they disregard the warning and accidentally open up a hole in the sky. Unaided they descend on a rope and arrive home safely.[29]

The tale, Thompson suggests, probably originated in the Plains and then spread to other regions of North America.

Alan Dundes has concentrated on the structure of folktales; he thinks that Native American folktales, including the Star Husband Tale, have characteristic structures. One is a movement away from disequilibrium. Equilibrium is the desirable state; having too much or too little of anything is a condition that should be rectified as soon as possible. Disequilibrium, which Dundes calls *lack,* is indicated by the girls in the Star Husband Tale who do not have husbands. The lack is then corrected, in this case by marriage with the stars. This tale has another common Native American structure, says Dundes—a sequence of prohibition, interdiction, violation, and consequence. The women are warned not to dig, but they do—and as a consequence they escape for home.[30] It should be noted that the consequences in folktales around the world are not always good. Recall the Garden of Eden tale. The couple are warned not to eat the fruit of a tree; they eat the fruit; they are cast out of their paradise. Similarly, Icarus in the Greek tale is warned not to fly too high or low. He flies too high; the sun melts the wax that holds his feathered wings, and he falls and drowns.

As useful as it might be to identify where certain tales originated, or what their common structures might be, many questions remain. What do the tales mean? Why did they arise in the first place? Why are certain structures common in Native American tales? We are still a long way from answering many of these questions, and trying to answer them is difficult. For example, how does one try to understand the meaning of a tale?

In attempting to arrive at the meaning of myth—and to discover how and why myths differ from society to society—interpreters of myth have often been as fanciful as the mythmakers themselves. Max Muller, for example, spent about fifty years reducing most myths to a version of the solar myth (Cinderella is the sun because she starts in the ashes of a fire and ends in a blaze of glory).[31] And Andrew Lang spent about forty years refuting Muller and offering his own interpretation of "savage" mythology.

Such debates show that it is easy for people to read different meanings into the same myth. For example, consider the myth the Hebrews told of a paradise in which only a man was present until Eve, the first woman, arrived and ate the forbidden fruit of knowledge. One might conclude that men in that society had some traditional grudge against women. If the interpreter were a psychoanalyst, he or (especially) she might assume that the myth reflected the male's deeply hidden fears of female sexuality. A historian might believe that the myth reflected actual historical events, and that men were living in blissful ignorance until women invented agriculture (the effect of Eve's "knowledge" led to a life of digging rather than gathering).

It is clearly not enough to suggest an interpretation. Why should we believe it? We should give it serious consideration only if some systematic test seems to support it. For example, Michael Carroll has suggested a Freudian interpretation of the Star Husband Tale—that the tale represents repressed sentiments in the society. Specifically, he suggests that incestuous intercourse is the underlying concern of this myth, particularly the desire of a daughter to have intercourse with her father. He assumes that the stars symbolize fathers. Fathers, like stars, are high above, in children's eyes. Carroll predicted that if the Star Husband Tale originated on the Plains, and if it symbolizes intercourse, then the Plains tribes should be more likely than other tribes to have intercourse imagery in their versions of the tale. That seems to be the case: analyzing eighty-four versions of the tale, Carroll found that Plains societies are the Native American tribes most likely to have imagery suggesting intercourse, including the lowering of a

---

[29]Stith Thompson, "Star Husband Tale," in Dundes, ed., *The Study of Folklore,* p. 449.

[30]Alan Dundes, "Structural Typology in North American Indian Folktales," in Dundes, ed., *The Study of Folklore,* pp. 206–15. Dundes's analysis of the Star Husband Tale is reported in Frank W. Young, "A Fifth Analysis of the Star Husband Tale," *Ethnology,* 9 (1970): 389–413.

[31]Richard Dorson, "The Eclipse of Solar Mythology," in Dundes, ed., *The Study of Folklore,* pp. 57–83.

rope or ladder (presumably symbolizing the penis) through a sky hole (presumably symbolizing the vagina).[32]

Few studies as yet have investigated why there is cross-cultural variation in the frequency of certain features in folktales. One feature of folktale variation that has been investigated cross-culturally is aggression. George Wright found that variation in child-rearing patterns predicted some aspects of how aggression is exhibited in folktales. Where children are severely punished for aggression, more intense aggression appears in the folktales. And in such societies, strangers are more likely than the hero or friends of the hero to be the aggressors in the folktales. It seems that where children may be afraid to exhibit aggression toward their parents or those close to them because of fear of punishment, the hero or his or her close friends in folktales are also not likely to be aggressive.[33]

Other kinds of fears may be reflected in folktales. A recent cross-cultural study finds that unprovoked aggression is likely in folktales where the society is subject to unpredictable food shortages. Why? One possibility is that the folktales reflect reality; after all, a serious drought may seem capricious, not possibly provoked by any human activity, brought on by the gods or nature "out of the blue." Curiously, however, societies with a history of unpredictable food shortages hardly mention natural disasters in their folktales, perhaps because disasters are too frightening. In any case, the capriciousness of unpredictable disasters seems to be transformed into the capricious aggression of characters in the folktales.[34]

Folklore, just like other aspects of art, may at least partially reflect the feelings, needs, and conflicts that people acquire as a result of growing up in their culture.

[32]Michael Carroll, "A New Look at Freud on Myth," *Ethos*, 7 (1979): 189–205.

[33]George O. Wright, "Projection and Displacement: A Cross-Cultural Study of Folktale Aggression," *Journal of Abnormal and Social Psychology*, 49 (1954): 523–28.

[34]Alex Cohen, "A Cross-Cultural Study of the Effects of Environmental Unpredictability on Aggression in Folktales," *American Anthropologist*, 92 (1990): 474–79.

SUMMARY

1. Not all societies have a word for art, but art universally seems to have several qualities. It expresses as well as communicates. It stimulates the senses, affects emotions, and evokes ideas. It is produced in culturally patterned ways and styles; it has cultural meaning. And some people are thought to be better at it than others.

2. All societies decorate or adorn the body, temporarily or permanently. But there is enormous cultural variation in the parts decorated and how. Body decoration may be used to delineate social position, sex, or occupation. It may also have an erotic significance—for example, in drawing attention to erogenous zones of the body.

3. The materials used to produce visual art, the way those materials are used, and the natural objects the artist may choose to represent—all these vary from society to society and reveal much about a society's relation to its environment. Some studies indicate a correlation between artistic design and social stratification.

4. Like the visual arts, music is subject to a remarkable amount of variation from society to society. Some studies suggest correlations between musical styles and cultural complexity. Other research shows links between child-rearing practices and a society's preference for certain rhythmical patterns, tonal ranges, and voice quality.

5. Folklore is a broad category including all the myths, legends, folktales, ballads, riddles, proverbs, and superstitions of a cultural group. Generally, folklore is orally transmitted, but it may also be written. Some anthropologists have identified basic themes in myths. These include catastrophe, slaying of monsters, incest, sibling rivalry, and castration. Myths may reflect a society's deepest preoccupations.

ANDERSON, R. L. *Art in Small-Scale Societies*. 2nd ed. Englewood Cliffs, NJ: Prentice Hall, 1989. The author discusses art in small-scale societies, how it may be defined, its functions, the symbolism involved, the sources of creative ideas, and how art has changed because of contact with the Western world.

DUNDES, A., ed., *The Study of Folklore*. Englewood Cliffs, NJ: Prentice Hall, 1965. A collection of theoretical and analytical papers dealing with folklore from a variety of perspectives—humanistic, literary, psychological, historical, and geographical. The essays explore such topics as the origins, processes, and forms of transmission of folklore.

LOMAX, A., ed. *Folk Song Style and Culture*. American Association for the Advancement of Science, Publication no. 88. Washington, DC, 1968. A classic cross-cultural study of the stylistic elements of folk songs from societies around the world. The data compiled in this study, which was known as the Cantometrics Project, were used to test hypotheses about the relationship of song style to other aspects of culture.

MAQUET, J. *The Aesthetic Experience: An Anthropologist Looks at the Visual Arts*. New Haven: Yale University Press, 1986. The author explores the universal and culturally varying components of the visual arts.

WASHBURN, D. K., ed. *Structure and Cognition in Art*. Cambridge: Cambridge University Press, 1983. A series of papers, based mostly on ethnography, on how art forms may relate to social behavior in various cultures.

25
Culture Change

Most of us are aware that "times have changed," especially when we compare our lives with those of our parents. Witness the recent changes in attitudes about sex and marriage, as well as the recent changes in women's roles. But culture change is not unique to us: humans throughout history have replaced or altered customary behaviors and attitudes as their needs have changed. Just as no individual is immortal, no particular cultural pattern is impervious to change. Anthropologists, therefore, want to understand how and why culture change occurs.

Three general questions can be asked about culture change: What is the source of a new trait? Why are people motivated (unconsciously as well as consciously) to adopt it? And is the new trait adaptive? The source may be inside or outside the society. That is, a new idea or behavior may originate within the society, or it may come from another society. With regard to motivation, people may adopt the new idea or behavior voluntarily (even if unconsciously), or they may be forced to adopt it. Finally, the outcome of culture change may or may not be beneficial. In this chapter, we first discuss the various processes of culture change in terms of the three dimensions of source, motivation, and outcome. Then we discuss some of the major types of culture change in the modern world. As we will see, these changes are associated largely with the expansion of Western societies over the last 500 years.

How and Why Cultures Change

Discovery and Invention

Discoveries and inventions, which may originate inside or outside a society, are ultimately the sources of all culture change. But they do not necessarily lead to change. If an invention or discovery is ignored, no change in culture results. It is only when society accepts an invention or discovery and uses it regularly that we can begin to speak of culture change.

The new thing discovered or invented (the innovation) may be an object—the wheel, the plow, the computer—or it may involve behavior and ideas—Christianity, democracy, monogamy. According to Ralph Linton, a discovery is any addition to knowledge and an invention is a new application of knowledge.[1] Thus, a person might discover that children can be persuaded to eat nourishing food if the food is associated with an imaginary character who appeals to them. And then someone might exploit that discovery by inventing a character named Popeye who appears in a series of animated cartoons, acquiring miraculous strength in a variety of dramatic situations by devouring cans of spinach.

Unconscious Invention. In discussing the process of invention, we should differentiate between varying types of inventions. One type is the consequence of a society's setting itself a specific goal, such as eliminating tuberculosis or placing a person on the moon. Another type emerges less intentionally. This second process of invention is often referred to as *accidental juxtaposition* or *unconscious invention.* Linton has suggested that some inventions, especially those of prehistoric days, were probably the consequences of literally dozens of tiny initiatives by "unconscious" inventors. These inventors made their small contributions, perhaps over many hundreds of years, without being aware of the part they were playing in bringing one invention, such as the wheel or a better form of hand ax, to completion.[2] Consider the example of children playing on a fallen log, which rolls as they walk and balance on it, coupled with the need at a given moment to move a slab of granite from a cave face. The children's play may have suggested the use of logs as rollers and thereby set in motion a series of developments that culminated in the wheel.

In reconstructing the process of invention in prehistoric times, however, we should be careful not to look back on our ancestors with a smugness born of our more highly developed technology. We have become accustomed to turning to the science sections of our magazines and newspapers and finding, almost daily, reports of miraculous new discoveries and inventions. From our point of view, it is difficult to imagine such a simple invention as the wheel taking so many centuries to come into being. We are tempted to surmise that early humans were less intelligent than we are. However,

---

[1]Ralph Linton, *The Study of Man* (New York: Appleton-Century-Crofts, 1936), p. 306.
[2]Ibid., pp. 310–11.

Ideas and practices diffuse rapidly in the modern world, partly because people can go far and fast. Here we see a seaplane on once remote Lake Turkana, Kenya.

since the capacity of the human brain has been the same for perhaps 100,000 years, there is no evidence that the inventors of the wheel were any less intelligent.

Intentional Innovation.   Some discoveries and inventions arise out of deliberate attempts to produce a new idea or object. It may seem that such innovations are obvious responses to perceived needs. For example, during the Industrial Revolution there was a great demand for inventions that would increase productivity. James Hargreaves in eighteenth-century England is an example of an inventor who responded to an existing demand. Textile manufacturers were clamoring for such large quantities of spun yarn that cottage laborers, working with foot-operated spinning wheels, could not meet the demand. Hargreaves, realizing that prestige and financial rewards would come to the person who invented a method of spinning large quantities of yarn in a short time, set about the task and developed the spinning jenny.

But perceived needs and the economic rewards that may be given to the innovator do not explain why only some people innovate. We know relatively little about why some people are more innovative than others. The ability to innovate may depend in part on individual characteristics such as high intelligence and creativity. And creativity may be influenced by social conditions.

A study of innovation among Ashanti artist-carvers in Ghana suggests that creativity is more likely in some socioeconomic groups.[3] Some carvers produce only traditional designs; others depart from tradition and produce "new" styles of carving. Two groups were found to innovate the most—the wealthiest and the poorest carvers. These two groups of carvers may tolerate risk more than the middle socioeconomic group. Innovative carving entails some risk because it may take more time

[3]Harry R. Silver, "Calculating Risks: The Socioeconomic Foundations of Aesthetic Innovation in an Ashanti Carving Community," *Ethnology,* 20 (1981): 101–14.

and it may not sell. Wealthy carvers can afford the risk, and they may gain some prestige as well as income if their innovation is appreciated. The poor are not doing well anyway, and they have little to lose by trying something new.

Who Adopts Innovations?   Once someone discovers or invents something, there is still the question of whether or not the innovation will be adopted by others. Many researchers have studied the characteristics of "early adopters." Such individuals tend to be more educated, higher in social status, upwardly mobile, and (if they are property-owners) have larger farms and businesses. The individuals who most need technological improvements—those who are less well off—are generally the last to adopt innovations. The theory is that only the wealthier can afford to take the substantial risks associated with new ways of doing things. In periods of rapid technological change, therefore, the gap between rich and poor is likely to widen because the rich adopt innovations sooner (and benefit more from them) than the poor.[4]

Does this imply that the likelihood of adopting innovations is a simple function of how much wealth a possible adopter possesses? Not necessarily. Frank Cancian has reviewed a number of studies and found that upper-middle class individuals show more conservatism than lower-middle class individuals. Cancian suggests that when the risks are unknown the lower-middle class individuals are more receptive to innovation because they have less to lose. Later on, when the risks are better known (as more people adopt the innovation), the upper-middle class catches up to the lower-middle.[5] So the readiness to accept innovation, like the likelihood of creativity among Ashanti carvers, may not be related to socioeconomic position in a straight-line, or linear, way.

The speed of accepting an innovation may depend partly on how new behaviors and ideas are typically transmitted in a society. In particular, is a person exposed to many versus few "teachers"? If children learn most of what they know from their parents or from a relatively small number of elders,

then innovation will be slow to spread throughout the society, and culture change is likely to be slow. Innovations may catch on more rapidly if individuals are exposed to various teachers and other "leaders," who can influence many in a relatively short time. And the more peers we have, the more we might learn from them.[6] Perhaps this is why the pace of change appears to be so quick today. In societies like our own, and increasingly in the industrializing world, it is likely that people learn in schools from teachers, from leaders in their specialties, and from peers.

Diffusion

The source of new cultural elements in a society may also be another society. The process by which cultural elements are borrowed from another society and incorporated into the culture of the recipient group is called *diffusion*. Borrowing sometimes enables a group to bypass stages or mistakes in the development of a process or institution. For example, Germany was able to accelerate its program of industrialization in the nineteenth century. It avoided some of the errors made by its English and Belgian competitors by taking advantage of technological borrowing. Japan did the same somewhat later. Indeed, in recent years some of the earliest industrialized countries have fallen behind others in certain areas of production (automobiles, television, cameras, computers).

In a well-known passage, Linton conveyed the far-reaching effects of diffusion by considering the first few hours in the day of an American man. This man

awakens in a bed built on a pattern which originated in the Near East but which was modified in northern Europe before it was transmitted to America. He throws back covers made from cotton, domesticated in India, or linen, domesticated in the Near East, or silk, the use of which was discovered in China. All of these materials have been spun and woven by processes invented in the Near East. . . . He takes off his pajamas, a garment invented in India, and washes with soap invented by the ancient Gauls. He then shaves, a masochistic rite which

[4]Everett M. Rogers, *Diffusion of Innovations*, 3rd ed. (New York: Free Press, 1983), pp. 263–69.

[5]Frank Cancian, "Risk and Uncertainty in Agricultural Decision Making," in Peggy F. Barlett, ed., *Agricultural Decision Making: Anthropological Contributions to Rural Development* (New York: Academic Press, 1980), pp. 161–202.

[6]Barry S. Hewlett and L. L. Cavalli-Sforza, "Cultural Transmission among Aka Pgymies," *American Anthropologist*, 88 (1986): 922–34; L. L. Cavalli-Szorza and M. W. Feldman, *Cultural Transmission and Evolution: A Quantitative Approach* (Princeton, NJ: Princeton University Press, 1981).

As this picture of Masai women in Kenya shows, the polaroid camera has diffused widely.

seems to have derived from either Sumer or ancient Egypt.

Before going out for breakfast he glances through the window, made of glass invented in Egypt, and if it is raining puts on overshoes made of rubber discovered by the Central American Indians and takes an umbrella, invented in southeastern Asia. . . .

On his way to breakfast he stops to buy a paper paying for it with coins, an ancient Lydian invention. . . . His plate is made of a form of pottery invented in China. His knife is of steel, an alloy first made in southern India, his fork a medieval Italian invention, and his spoon a derivative of a Roman original. . . . After his fruit (African watermelon) and first coffee (an Abyssinian plant) . . . he may have the egg of a species of bird domesticated in Indo-China, or thin strips of the flesh of an animal domesticated in Eastern Asia which have been salted and smoked by a process developed in northern Europe. . . .

While smoking (an American Indian habit) he reads the news of the day, imprinted in characters invented by the ancient Semites upon a material invented in China by a process invented in Germany. As he absorbs the accounts of foreign troubles he will, if he is a good conser-vative citizen, thank a Hebrew deity in an Indo-European language that he is 100 percent American.[7]

Patterns of Diffusion

DIRECT CONTACT   Elements of a society's culture may be first taken up by neighboring societies and then gradually spread farther and farther afield. The spread of the manufacture of paper is a good example of extensive diffusion by direct contact. The invention of paper is attributed to the Chinese Ts'ai Lun in A.D. 105. Within fifty years, paper was being made in many places in central China. By 264 it was found in Chinese Turkestan, and from then on the successive places of manufacture were Samarkand (751); Baghdad (793); Egypt (about 900); Morocco (about 1100); France (1189); Italy (1276); Germany (1391); and England (1494). Generally, the pattern of accepting the borrowed invention was the same in each case.

[7]Linton, *The Study of Man*, pp. 326–27. © 1936, renewed 1964; reprinted by permission of Prentice Hall, Inc.

Paper was first imported into each area as a luxury, then in ever-expanding quantities as a staple product. Finally, and usually within one to three centuries, local manufacture was begun.

Another example of diffusion is the spread of tobacco. Tobacco was introduced into Spain in 1558 by Francisco Fernandez and into England from the New World in 1586 by Sir Walter Raleigh. From these twin European bases, the habit of smoking diffused rapidly. English medical students took the custom to Holland around 1590. English and Dutch sailors introduced tobacco throughout the Baltic in such quantities that by 1634 Russian authorities considered it a sufficient nuisance for laws to be enacted against its use. From Spain and Portugal, the use of tobacco spread throughout the Mediterranean countries and the Near East. In 1605, the sultan of Turkey legislated against its use. In the same year, the Japanese restricted the acreage that could be set aside for tobacco cultivation.

INTERMEDIATE CONTACT   Diffusion by intermediate contact occurs through the agency of third parties. Frequently, traders carry a cultural trait from the society that originated it to another group. As an example of diffusion through intermediaries, Phoenician traders spread the alphabet, which was invented by another Semitic group, to Greece. At times, soldiers serve as intermediaries in spreading a culture trait. European crusaders, such as the Knights Templar and the Knights of St. John, acted as intermediaries in two ways: they carried Christian culture to Muslim societies of North Africa and brought Arab culture back to Europe. In the nineteenth century, Western missionaries in all parts of the world encouraged natives to wear Western clothing. The result is that in Africa, the Pacific Islands, and elsewhere, native peoples can be found wearing shorts, suit jackets, shirts, ties, and other typically Western articles of clothing.

STIMULUS DIFFUSION   In stimulus diffusion, knowledge of a trait belonging to another culture stimulates the invention or development of a local equivalent. A classic example of stimulus diffusion is the Cherokee syllabic writing system created by an Indian named Sequoya so that his people could write down their language. Sequoya got the idea from his contact with Europeans. Yet he did not adopt the English writing system; indeed, he did not even learn to write English. What he did was to utilize some English alphabetic symbols, alter a number of others, and invent new ones. All the symbols he used represented Cherokee syllables and in no way echoed English alphabetic usage. In other words, Sequoya took English alphabetic ideas and gave them a new Cherokee form. The stimulus originated with Europeans; the result was peculiarly Cherokee.

The Selective Nature of Diffusion.   Although there is a temptation to view the dynamics of diffusion as similar to a stone sending concentric ripples over still water, this would be an oversimplification of the way diffusion actually occurs. Not all cultural traits are borrowed as readily as the ones we have mentioned, nor do they usually expand in neat, ever-widening circles. Rather, diffusion is a selective process. The Japanese, for instance, accepted much from Chinese culture, but they also rejected many traits. Rhymed tonal poetry, civil-service examinations, and foot binding, which were favored by the Chinese, were never adopted in Japan. The poetry form was unsuited to the structure of the Japanese language; the examinations were unnecessary in view of the entrenched power of the Japanese aristocracy; foot binding was repugnant to a people who abhorred body mutilation of any sort. Muslim societies offer another example of selective acceptance of cultural diffusion. Originally, the basic test of the acceptability of a new trait in Muslim societies was compatibility with the Koran. Hence, the practices of drinking wine, gambling, and playing cards—all prohibited by the Koran—failed to diffuse into Muslim cultures.

Not only would we expect societies to reject items from other societies that are repugnant, we would also expect them to reject ideas and technology that do not satisfy some psychological, social, or cultural need. After all, people are not sponges—they don't automatically soak up the things around them. If they did, the amount of cultural variation in the world would be tiny—which is clearly not the case. Diffusion is also selective because cultural traits differ in the extent to which they can be communicated. Elements of material culture, such as mechanical processes and techniques, and other traits, such as physical sports

These Japanese women have accepted ice cream, but they have not adopted Western clothing.

and the like, are not especially difficult to demonstrate. Consequently, they are accepted or rejected on their merits. But the moment we move out of the material context, we encounter real difficulties. Linton has explained the problem in these words:

Although it is quite possible to describe such an element of culture as the ideal pattern for marriage . . . it is much less complete than a description of basketmaking. . . . The most thorough verbalization has difficulty in conveying the series of associations and conditioned emotional responses which are attached to this pattern [marriage] and which gave it meaning and vitality within our own society. . . . This is even more true of those concepts which . . . find no direct expression in behavior aside from verbalization. There is a story of an educated Japanese who after a long discussion on the nature of the Trinity with a European friend . . . burst out with: "Oh, I see now, it is a committee."[8]

Finally, diffusion is selective because the overt form of a particular trait, rather than its function or meaning, frequently seems to determine how the trait will be received. For example, the enthusiasm for bobbed hair (short haircuts) that swept through much of North America in the 1920s never caught on among the Native Americans of northwestern California. To many women of European ancestry, short hair was a symbolic statement of their freedom. To Native American women, who traditionally cut their hair short when in mourning, it was a reminder of death.[9]

A society accepting a foreign cultural trait is likely to adapt it in a way that effectively harmonizes it with the group's own traditions. This process of reinterpretation frequently occurs when religions diffuse. Thus, a little church in an ancient Greek city in southern Italy has an image of Aphrodite that for centuries has been revered as the Virgin Mary. In Haiti, Legba and Damballa, the trickster and rainbow gods derived from Dahomey

[8]Ibid., pp. 338–39.

[9]George M. Foster, *Traditional Cultures and the Impact of Technological Change* (New York: Harper & Row, Pub., 1962), p. 26.

in West Africa, are identified with Saint Anthony and Saint Patrick, respectively.[10]

In the process of diffusion, then, we can identify a number of different patterns. We know that cultural borrowing is selective rather than automatic, and we can describe how a particular borrowed trait has been modified by the recipient culture. But our current knowledge does not allow us to specify when one or another of these outcomes will occur, under what conditions diffusion will occur, and why it occurs the way it does.

Acculturation

On the surface, the process of change called **acculturation** seems to include much of what we have discussed under the label of diffusion, since acculturation refers to the changes that occur when different cultural groups come into intensive contact. As in diffusion, the source of new cultural items is the other society. But more often than not, the term *acculturation* is used by anthropologists to describe a situation in which one of the societies in contact is much more powerful than the other. Thus, acculturation can be seen as a process of extensive cultural borrowing in the context of superordinate-subordinate relations between societies.[11] The borrowing may sometimes be a two-way process, but generally it is the subordinate or less powerful society that borrows the most. The concept of diffusion can then be reserved for the voluntary borrowing of cultural elements, in contrast with borrowing under external pressure, which characterizes acculturation.

The external pressure can take various forms. In its most direct form—conquest or colonialization—the dominant group uses force or the threat of it to bring about culture change in the other group. For example, in the Spanish conquest of Mexico, the conquerors forced many of the native groups to accept Catholicism. Although such direct force is not always exerted in conquest situations, dominated peoples often have little choice but to change. Examples of such indirectly forced change abound in the history of Native Americans in the United States. Although the federal government made few direct attempts to force people to adopt North American culture, it did drive many native groups from their lands. This obliged them to give up many aspects of their traditional ways of life. In order to survive, they had no choice but to adopt many of the white society's traits. When Native American children were required to go to schools, which taught the white society's values, the process was accelerated.

A subordinate society may acculturate to a dominant society even in the absence of direct or indirect force. The dominated people may elect to adopt cultural elements from the dominant society in order to survive in their changed world. Or, perceiving that members of the dominant society enjoy more secure living conditions, the dominated people may identify with the dominant culture in the hope that by doing so they will be able to share some of its benefits. For example, in Arctic areas many Inuit and Lapp groups seemed eager to replace dog sleds with snowmobiles without any coercion.[12]

But many millions of people never really had a chance to acculturate after contact with Europeans. They simply died, sometimes directly at the hands of the conquerors, but probably more often as a result of new diseases the Europeans brought with them. Depopulation because of new diseases such as measles, smallpox, and tuberculosis was particularly common in North and South America and on the islands of the Pacific. Those areas had previously been isolated from contact with Europeans and the diseases of that continuous land mass we call the Old World—Europe, Asia, and Africa.[13]

The story of Ishi, the last surviving member of a group of California Indians called the Yahi, is a moving testimonial to the frequently tragic effect of contact with Europeans. In the space of twenty-two years, the Yahi population was reduced from several hundred to near zero. The historical record on this episode of depopulation suggests that whites murdered thirty to fifty of the Indians for every white murdered, and perhaps 60 percent of

[10]Ibid., p. 27.
[11]John H. Bodley, *Victims of Progress*, 3rd ed. (Mountain View, CA: Mayfield, 1990), p. 7.

[12]Pertti J. Pelto and Ludger Müller-Wille, "Snowmobiles: Technological Revolution in the Arctic," in H. Russell Bernard and Pertti J. Pelto, eds., *Technology and Social Change*, 2nd ed. (Prospect Heights, IL, Waveland Press, 1987), pp. 207–43.
[13]Bodley, *Victims of Progress*, pp. 38–41.

the Yahi died in the ten years following their initial exposure to European diseases.[14]

Nowadays, many powerful nations (and not just Western ones) may seem to be acting in more humanitarian ways to improve the life of previously subjugated as well as other "developing" peoples. For better or worse, these programs are still forms of external pressure. The tactic used may be persuasion rather than force, but most of the programs are nonetheless designed to bring about acculturation in the direction of the dominant societies' cultures. For example, the introduction of formal schooling cannot but help instill new values that may contradict traditional cultural patterns. And even health-care programs may alter traditional ways of life by undermining the authority of shamans and others and by increasing population beyond the number that can be supported in traditional ways. Confinement to "reservations" or other kinds of direct force are not the only ways a dominant society can bring about acculturation.

Revolution

Certainly the most drastic and rapid way a culture can change is as a result of **revolution**—replacement, usually violent, of a country's rulers. Historical records, as well as our daily newspapers, indicate that people frequently rebel against established authority. Rebellions almost always occur in state societies, where there is a distinct ruling elite. They take the form of struggles between rulers and ruled, between conquerors and conquered, or between representatives of an external colonial power and segments of the native society. Since they do not always succeed in overthrowing the previous rulers, rebellions do not always result in revolutions. And even successful rebellions do not always result in culture change; the individual rulers may change, but not customs or institutions. The sources of revolution may be mostly internal, as in the French Revolution, or partly external, as in the Russian-supported 1948 revolution in Czechoslovakia and the United States–supported 1973 revolution against President Allende in Chile.

The Nacirema war of independence toward the end of the 18th century) is a good example of a colonial rebellion, the success of which was at least partly a result of foreign intervention. The Nacirema rebellion was a war of neighboring colonies against the greatest imperial power of the time, Great Britain. In the nineteenth century and continuing into the middle and later years of the twentieth century, there would be many other wars of independence, in Latin America, Europe, Asia, and Africa. We don't always remember that the Nacirema rebellion was the first of these anti-imperialist wars in modern times, and the model for many that followed. And just like many of the most recent liberation movements, the Nacirema rebellion was also part of a larger worldwide war, involving people from many rivalrous nations. Thirty thousand German-speaking soldiers fought, for pay, on the British side; an army and navy from France fought on the Nacirema side. There were volunteers from other European countries, including Denmark, Holland, Poland, and Russia.

One of these volunteers was a man named Kosciusko from Poland, which at the time was being divided between Prussia and Russia. Kosciusko helped win a major victory for the Nacirema, and subsequently directed the fortification of what later became the Nacirema training school for army officers, Tsew Tniop. After the war he returned to Poland and led a rebellion against the Russians, which was only briefly successful. In 1808 he published a *Manual on the Maneuvers of Horse Artillery*, which was used for many years by the Nacirema army. When he died he left money to buy freedom and education for Nacirema slaves.

The executor of Kosciusko's will was a Nacirema named Jefferson, who had taken part in a famous debate at a convention in his colony. The debate was over a motion to prepare for defense against the British armed forces. The motion barely passed, by a vote of sixty-five to sixty. There was a speech before the vote that is now a part of Nacirema folklore. A lawyer whose last name was Henry listened to the argument for not opposing the British and then rose to declare that it was insane not to oppose them and that he was not afraid to test the strength of the colonies against Great Britain—others might hesitate, he said, but he would have "liberty or death." The "radicals" who supported P. Henry's resolution included many aristocratic landowners, two of whom (G. Washington and T. Jefferson) became the first and third

[14]Theodora Kroeber, *Ishi in Two Worlds* (Berkeley: University of California Press, 1967), pp. 45–47.

occupants of the highest political office in what became the United States of America.[15]

Not all peoples who are suppressed, conquered, or colonized eventually rebel against established authority. Why this is so and why rebellions and revolts are not always successful in bringing about culture change are still open questions. But some possible answers have been investigated. One historian, who examined the classic revolutions of the past, including the American, French, and Russian revolutions, suggested some conditions that may give rise to rebellion and revolution:

1. Loss of prestige of established authority, often as a result of the failure of foreign policy, financial difficulties, dismissals of popular ministers, or alteration of popular policies. France in the eighteenth century lost three major international conflicts, with disastrous results for its diplomatic standing and internal finances. Russian society was close to military and economic collapse in 1917, after three years of World War I.

2. Threat to recent economic improvement. In France, as in Russia, those sections of the population (professional classes and urban workers) whose economic fortunes had only shortly before taken an upward swing were "radicalized" by unexpected setbacks such as steeply rising food prices and unemployment. The same may be said for the American colonies on the brink of their rebellion against Great Britain.

3. Indecisiveness of government, as exemplified by lack of consistent policy, which gives the impression of being controlled by, rather than in control of, events. The frivolous arrogance of Louis XVI's regime and the bungling of George III's prime minister, Lord North, with respect to the problems of the American colonies, are examples.

4. Loss of support of the intellectual class. Such a loss deprived the prerevolutionary governments of France and Russia of any avowed

Hessians were drafted in Germany to fight on the British side during the American Revolution.

philosophical support and led to their unpopularity with the literate public.[16]

The classic revolutions of the past occurred in countries that were industrialized only incipiently at best. For the most part, the same is true of the rebellions and revolutions in recent years: they have occurred mostly in countries we call *developing*. The evidence from a worldwide survey of developing countries suggests that rebellions have tended to occur where the ruling classes depended mostly on the produce or income from land, and therefore were resistant to demands for reform from the rural classes that worked the land. In such agricultural economies, the rulers are not likely to yield political power or give greater economic returns to the workers, because to do so would eliminate the basis (land ownership) of the rulers' wealth and power.[17]

Finally, a particularly interesting question is why revolutions sometimes (perhaps even usually) fail to measure up to the high hopes of those who initiate them. When rebellions succeed in replacing the ruling elite, the result is often the institu-

---

[15]The historical information we refer to comes from a book by Allan Nevins, *The American States During and After the Revolution* (New York: Macmillan, 1927). We spell *American* (and *West Point*) backward to encourage the realization that the American Revolution was very much like modern liberation movements.

[16]Crane Brinton, *The Anatomy of Revolution* (Englewood Cliffs, NJ: Prentice Hall, 1938).

[17]Jeffrey M. Paige, *Agrarian Revolution: Social Movements and Export Agriculture in the Underdeveloped World* (New York: Free Press, 1975).

tion of a military dictatorship even more restrictive and repressive than the government that existed before. The new ruling establishment may merely substitute one set of repressions for another, rather than bring any real change to the nation. On the other hand, some revolutions have resulted in fairly drastic overhauls of societies.

The idea of revolution has been one of the central myths and inspirations of many groups both in the past and in the present. The colonial empire-building of countries such as England and France created a worldwide situation in which rebellion became nearly inevitable. In numerous technologically underdeveloped lands, which have been exploited by more powerful countries for their natural resources and cheap labor, a deep resentment has often developed against the foreign ruling classes or their local clients. Where the ruling classes, native or foreign, refuse to be responsive to these feelings, rebellion becomes the only alternative. In many areas, it has become a way of life.

Culture Change and Adaptation

The chapter on the concept of culture discussed the general assumption that most of the customary behaviors of a culture are probably adaptive, or at least not maladaptive, in that environment. A custom is adaptive if it increases the likelihood that the people practicing it will survive and reproduce. Even though customs are learned (not genetically inherited), cultural adaptation may be otherwise like biological adaptation or evolution. The frequency of certain genetic alternatives is likely to increase over time if those genetic traits increase their carriers' chances of survival and reproduction. Similarly, the frequency of a new learned behavior will increase over time and become customary in a population if the people with that behavior are more likely to survive and reproduce. Thus, if a culture is generally adapted to its environment, culture change should also be generally adaptive.

One of the most important differences between cultural evolution and genetic evolution is that individuals can often decide whether or not to accept and follow the way their parents behave or think, whereas they cannot decide whether or not to inherit certain genes. When enough individuals change their behavior and beliefs, we say that the

culture has changed. Therefore, it is possible for culture change to occur much more rapidly than genetic change.

However, it is not necessarily more adaptive to change rapidly, just because it is possible. Robert Boyd and Peter Richerson show mathematically that when the environment is relatively stable and individual mistakes are costly, staying with customary modes of behavior (usually transmitted by parents) is probably more adaptive.[18] But what happens when the environment (particularly the social environment) is changing? There are plenty of examples in the modern world: people have to migrate to new places for work, medical care leads to increased population so that land is scarcer, people have had land taken away from them and they are therefore forced to make do with less land, etc.

It is particularly when circumstances change that individuals may look to try ideas or behaviors that are different from those of their parents. Most people would want to adopt behaviors that are more suited to their present circumstances, but how do they know which behaviors are better? There are various ways to find out. One way is by experimenting, trying out various new behaviors. Another way is to evaluate the experiments of others. If a person who tries a new technique seems successful, we would expect the more successful person to be imitated, just as we would expect people to stick with new behaviors they have personally tried and found successful. Finally, one might choose to do what most people in the new situation decide to do.[19]

Why one choice rather than another? In part, the choice may be a function of the cost or risk of the innovation. It is relatively easy, for example, to find out how long it takes to cut down a tree with an introduced steel ax, as compared with a stone ax. Not surprisingly, innovations such as a steel ax catch on relatively quickly because comparison is easy and the results relatively clear-cut. But what if the risk is very great? Suppose the in-

[18]Robert Boyd and Peter J. Richerson, *Culture and the Evolutionary Process* (Chicago: University of Chicago Press, 1985), p. 106.
[19]Ibid., p. 135.

novation involves adopting a whole new way of farming that you have never practiced before. You can try it, but you might not have any food if you fail. As we discussed earlier, innovations that are risky are likely to be tried only by those individuals who can afford the risk. Other people may then evaluate their success and adopt the new strategy if it looks promising. Similarly, if you migrate to a new area, say from a high rainfall area to a drier one, it may pay to look around to see what most people in the new place do; after all, the people in the drier area probably have customs that are adaptive for that environment.

We can expect then that the choices individuals make may often be adaptive ones. But it is important to note that adopting an innovation from someone in one's own society or borrowing an innovation from another society is not always or necessarily beneficial, either in the short or the long run. First, people may make mistakes in judgment, especially when some new behavior seems to satisfy a physical need. Why, for example, have smoking and drug-use diffused so widely even though they are likely to reduce a person's chances of survival? Second, even if people are correct in their short term judgment of benefit, they may be wrong in their judgment about long-run benefit. A new crop may yield more than the old crop for five consecutive years, but the new crop may fail miserably in the sixth year because of lower than normal rainfall. Third, people may be forced by the more powerful to change, with few if any benefits for themselves.

Whatever the motives for humans to change their behavior, the theory of natural selection suggests that new behavior is not likely to become cultural if it has harmful reproductive consequences, just as a genetic mutation with harmful consequences is not likely to become frequent in a population.[20]

[20]Donald T. Campbell, "Variation and Selective Retention in Socio-Cultural Evolution," in Herbert Barringer, George Blankstein, and Raymond Mack, eds., Social Change in Developing Areas: A Re-Interpretation of Evolutionary Theory (Cambridge, MA: Schenkman, 1965), pp. 19–49. See also Boyd and Richerson, Culture and the Evolutionary Process; and William H. Durham, Coevolution: Genes, Culture and Human Diversity (Stanford, CA: Stanford University Press, 1991).

Types of Culture Change in the Modern World

Many of the cultural changes in the world between A.D. 1500 and the present have been caused, directly or indirectly, by the dominance and expansion of Western societies.[21] Thus, much of the culture change in the modern world has been externally induced, if not forced. This is not to say that cultures are changing now only because of external pressures; but externally induced changes have been the changes most frequently studied by anthropologists and other social scientists.

Commercialization

One of the most important changes resulting from the expansion of Western societies is the increasing dependence of all parts of the world on commercial exchange. The borrowed customs of buying and selling may at first be supplementary to traditional means of distributing goods in a society. But as the new commercial customs take hold, the economic base of the receiving society alters. Inevitably, this alteration is accompanied by other changes, which have broad social, political, and even psychological ramifications.

In examining contemporary patterns of change, however, we should bear in mind that the process of commercialization has occurred in many parts of the world in the past. The Chinese, Persians, Greeks, Romans, Arabs, Phoenicians, and Hindus were some of the early state societies that pushed commercial enterprises in other areas. We are probably casting some light on how and why some earlier cultures changed when we consider several questions. How, and why, does a contemporary society change from a subsistence to a commercial economic base? What are the resultant cultural changes? Why do they occur?

In general, the limited evidence now available suggests that a previously noncommercial people may begin to sell (and buy) things simply in order to live, not just because they may be attracted by goods they can obtain only by commercial ex-

[21]William H. McNeill, A World History (New York: Oxford University Press, 1967), pp. 283–87.

change. If the resources available to a group have been significantly reduced per person—because the group has been forced to resettle on a small "reservation" or because population has increased—it may be likely to take advantage of any commercial opportunities that become available, even if such opportunities require considerably more work time and effort.[22]

Migratory Labor. One way commercialization can occur is for some members of a community to move to a place nearby that offers the possibility of working for wages. This happened in Tikopia, an island near the Solomon Islands in the South Pacific. In 1929, when Raymond Firth first studied the island, its economy was still essentially noncommercial—simple, self-sufficient, and largely self-contained.[23] Some Western goods were known and available but, with the exception of iron and steel in limited quantities, not sought after. Their possession and use were associated solely with Europeans. This situation changed dramatically with World War II. During the war, military forces occupied neighboring islands, and people from Tikopia migrated to those islands to find employment. In the period following the war, several large commercial interests extended their activities in the Solomons, thus creating a continued demand for labor. As a result, when Firth revisited Tikopia in 1952, he found the economic situation significantly altered.

Over a hundred Tikopians had left the island to work for varying periods. The migrants wanted to earn money because they aspired to standards of living previously regarded as appropriate only to Europeans. Already, living conditions on Tikopia were changing. Western cooking and water-carrying utensils, mosquito nets, kerosene storm lamps, and so forth had come to be regarded as normal items in a Tikopia household.

The introduction of money into the economy of Tikopia not only altered the economic system but affected a number of other areas of life. Compared with the situation in 1929, land was under more intensive cultivation in 1952, with manioc and sweet potatoes supplementing the principal taro crop. Pressures on the food supply resulting from improved living standards and an increased population seem to have weakened the ties of extended kinship. For example, the nuclear families constituting the extended family (the land-holding and land-using unit in 1929) were not cooperating as much in 1952. In many cases, in fact, the land had actually been split up among the constituent nuclear families; land rights had become more individualized. People were no longer as willing to share with members of their extended family, particularly with respect to the money and goods acquired by working in the Solomons.

Nonagricultural Commercial Production. Commercialization can also occur when a self-sufficient hunting or agricultural society comes to depend more and more on trading for its livelihood. Such a change is exemplified by the Mundurucú of the Amazon Basin, who largely abandoned general horticulture for commercial rubber production. A similar change may also be seen in the Montagnais of northeastern Canada, who came to depend increasingly on commercial fur trapping, rather than hunting, for subsistence. Robert Murphy and Julian Steward found that when modern goods from industrialized areas become available through trade, both societies devoted their energies to making specialized cash crops or other trade items. They did this to obtain more industrially made objects.[24] The primary socioeconomic change that occurred among the Mundurucú and the Montagnais was a shift from cooperative labor and community autonomy to individualized economic activity and a dependence on an external market.

Among the Mundurucú, for example, prior to the establishment of close trading links, the native population and the Europeans had been in contact for some eighty years without the Mundurucú way of life being noticeably altered. The men did give up their independently inspired warlike activities in order to perform as mercenaries for the whites, but they continued to maintain their horticultural

[22]See, for example, Daniel R. Gross, George Eiten, Nancy M. Flowers, Francisca M. Leoi, Madeline Lattman Ritter, and Dennis W. Werner, "Ecology and Acculturation among Native Peoples of Central Brazil," *Science,* November 30, 1979, pp. 1043–50.
[23]The description of Tikopia is based on Raymond Firth, *Social Change in Tikopia* (New York: Macmillan, 1959), chaps. 5, 6, 7, and 9, passim.

[24]Most of this discussion is based on Robert F. Murphy and Julian H. Steward, "Tappers and Trappers: Parallel Process in Acculturation," *Economic Development and Cultural Change,* 4 (July 1956): 335–55.

economy. Some trading took place with whites, with the chief acting as agent for the village. Barter was the method of exchange. Traders first distributed their wares, ranging from cheap cottons to iron hatchets, trinkets, and so on; they returned about three months later to collect manioc, India rubber, and beans from the Mundurucú. At this time (1860), however, rubber was only a secondary item of commerce.

The rapidly growing demand for rubber from the 1860s onward increased the importance of Mundurucú-trader relationships. Traders now openly began to appoint agents, called *capitoes*, whose job it was to encourage greater rubber production. *Capitoes* were given economic privileges and hence power, both of which began to undercut the position of the traditional chief. In addition, the process of rubber collection itself began to alter Mundurucú social patterns by moving people away from their jungle-based communities.

Wild rubber trees are found only along rivers, which are often a considerable distance from the jungle habitat of the Mundurucú, and can be exploited only during the dry season (late May to December). So the Mundurucú man who elected to gather rubber had to separate himself from his family for about half the year. Furthermore, rubber collecting is a solitary activity. Each tapper must work his territory, consisting of about 150 trees, daily, and he must live close to his trees because the work lasts all day. Therefore, the tapper usually lives alone or in a small group except during the rainy season, when he returns to his village.

At this stage in the commercialization process, the Mundurucú became increasingly dependent on goods supplied by the trader. Firearms were useless without regular quantities of powder and lead or shot; clothing required needles and thread for repairs. But these items could be earned only through increased rubber production, which in turn led to greater dependency on the outside world. Inevitably, the ability to work with traditional materials and the desire to maintain traditional crafts disappeared. Metal pots took the place of clay ones, and manufactured hammocks replaced homemade ones. Gradually the village agricultural cycle ceased to be adhered to by all in the community so that rubber production would not suffer. The authority of the traditional chiefs was weakened as that of the *capitoes* was enhanced.

Commercialization can occur when people find cash-paying jobs in a nearby industry. These women in Bolivia work in a tin mine.

The point of no return was reached when significant numbers of Mundurucú abandoned the villages for permanent settlements near their individual territories of trees. These new settlements lacked the unity, the sense of community, of former village life. Property was held by nuclear families and carefully maintained in the interest of productivity.

With the discovery of gold, many Mundurucú young men have recently turned to panning for gold in rivers. The required equipment is simple and gold is easier to transport and trade than rubber. Because gold can be sold for cash, which is then used for purchases, trading relationships are no longer so important. Cash is now used to buy transistor radios, tape recorders, watches, bicycles, and new kinds of clothing, in addition to firearms, metal pots, and tools. With money as a medium of exchange, the old emphasis on reciprocity has declined. Even food may now be sold to fellow Mundurucú, a practice that would have been unthinkable in the 1950s.[25]

Supplementary Cash Crops. A third way commercialization occurs is when those cultivating the soil produce a surplus above their subsistence requirements, which is then sold for cash. In many cases, this cash income must be used to pay rent or

[25]S. Brian Burkhalter and Robert F. Murphy, "Tappers and Sappers: Rubber, Gold and Money among the Mundurucú," *American Ethnologist*, 16 (1989): 100–116.

Commercialization can also occur when a previously self-sufficient society begins to sell some native product, such as animal furs. In this painting, a Native American is shown exchanging a fur pelt for Western goods.

taxes. Under these circumstances, commercialization may be said to be associated with the formation of a peasantry. **Peasants** are rural people who produce food for their own subsistence. But they must also contribute or sell their surpluses to others (in towns and cities) who do not produce their own food.

Peasants first appeared with the emergence of state and urban civilizations about 5,000 to 6,000 years ago, and they have been associated with civilization ever since.[26] To say that peasants are associated with urban societies perhaps needs some qualification. The contemporary, highly industrialized urban society has little need of peasants. Their scale of production is small and their use of land "uneconomic." A highly industrialized society with a large population of nonfood producers requires mechanized agriculture. As a result, the peasant has passed, or is passing, out of all but the most peripheral existence in industrial countries. It is the preindustrial city, and the social organization it represents, that generates and maintains peasants. They cultivate land; they furnish the required quantity of food, rent, and profit on which the remainder of society (particularly the people in the cities) depends.

What changes does the development of a peasantry entail? In some respects there is little disturbance of the cultivator's (now peasant's) former way of life. The peasant still has to produce

enough food to meet family needs, to replace what has been consumed, to cover a few ceremonial obligations (for example, the marriage of a child, village festivals, and funerals). But in other respects the peasant's situation is radically altered. For in addition to the traditional obligations—indeed, often in conflict with them—the peasant now has to produce extra crops to meet the requirements of a group of outsiders—landlords or officials of the state. These outsiders expect to be paid rent or taxes (in produce or currency), and they are able to enforce their expectations because they control the military and the police.

The change from near autonomy as a local community to a position of dependence on a larger society brings the peasant face to face with a situation as novel as it is unpleasant. According to Eric Wolf, the peasant is now

forced to maintain a balance between [the local community's] demands and the demands of the outsiders, and will be subject to tensions produced by this struggle to keep the balance. The outsider sees the peasant primarily as a source of labor and goods with which to increase his fund of power. But the peasant is at once both an economic agent and the head of a household. His holding is both an economic unit and a home.[27]

Although no two peasant cultures are quite alike, there are similarities in form. Peasants the world over are faced with the problem of balancing

---

[26]Eric Wolf, *Peasants* (Englewood Cliffs, NJ: Prentice Hall, 1966), pp. 3–4.

[27]Ibid., p. 13.

the demands of an external world against those of an internal society. Their response generally involves increasing production, curtailing domestic consumption, or both. In response to its dealings with the outside urban center, a peasantry tends to develop adaptive social organizations. One such response is the development of the village council or its equivalent. The Russian *mir* (common before the revolution of 1917), for example, held title to all village land and could reapportion acreage as family size changed. It was also the clearinghouse for local grievances and could unite the village in its dealings with the outside world.

The production of supplementary crops for cash has developed in some societies more or less voluntarily. The Arusha of East Africa are an example. The Arusha came into being as a cultural group in the 1800s when some refugees settled in an enclave in Masai territory. The Arusha were largely self-sufficient cultivators, although they carried on some barter trade with the Masai, whose economy was largely pastoral. However, from 1940 to 1960 the Arusha began to feel the twin pressures of increasing population and decreasing availability of land for cultivation. As a result, they were obliged to abandon their "conservative attachment to traditional institutions and values, and to adopt new economic practices and attitudes."[28] The new attitudes and practices meant abandoning self-sufficient production in favor of the cultivation of cash crops such as coffee and wheat. The income from the cultivation could then be utilized to purchase needed goods.

Trade by barter is therefore being replaced among the Arusha with market exchange involving currency. Markets are being established all over the country, not just along the border with the Masai. The possession of money is coming to be regarded as equivalent to wealth. Indeed, many Arusha are clearly prepared to spend money to achieve a higher standard of living. They are becoming more profit- and cash-oriented, investing their incomes in goods and services formerly considered unnecessary. The Arusha, then, may have been obliged by circumstances to sell crops for cash, but unlike the peasants, they were not exter-

nally forced by the state or landlords to engage in such market transactions.

Introduction of Commercial and Industrial Agriculture.

Another way in which commercialization can come about is through the introduction of commercial agriculture. In commercial agriculture, *all* the cultivated commodities are produced for sale rather than for personal consumption. Along with this change, the system of agriculture may be industrialized. In other words, some of the production processes, such as plowing, weeding, irrigation, and harvesting, are done by machine. Commercial agriculture is, in fact, often as mechanized as any manufacturing industry. Land is worked for the maximum return it will yield, and labor is hired and fired just as impersonally as in other industries.

E. J. Hobsbawm has noted some of the developments accompanying the introduction of commercial agriculture in eighteenth-century England and in continental Europe somewhat later.[29] The close, near-familial relationship between farmer and farm laborer disappeared, as did the once-personal connection between landlord and tenant. Land came to be regarded as a source of profit rather than a way of life. Fields were merged into single units and enclosed, and local grazing and similar privileges were reduced. Labor was hired at market rates and paid in wages. Eventually, as the emphasis on large-scale production for a mass market increased, machines began to replace farm laborers.

In general, the introduction of commercial agriculture brings several important social consequences. Gradually, a class polarization develops. Farmers and landlords become increasingly separated from laborers and tenants, just as in the town the employer becomes socially separated from the employees. Gradually too, manufactured items of all sorts are introduced into rural areas. Laborers migrate to urban centers in search of employment, often meeting even less sympathetic conditions there than exist in the country.

The changeover to commercial agriculture may result in an improved standard of living in the short and long run. But sometimes the switch is followed by a decline in the standard of living if

[28]P. H. Gulliver, "The Arusha: Economic and Social Change," in Paul Bohannan and George Dalton, eds., *Markets in Africa* (Garden City, NY: Doubleday, 1965), p. 269.

[29]E. J. Hobsbawm, *Age of Revolution* (New York: Praeger, 1970).

the market price for the commercial crop declines. For example, the changeover of the farmer-herders of the arid *sertão* region of northeastern Brazil after 1940 to the production of sisal (a plant whose fibers can be made into twine and rope) seemed like a move that could provide a more secure living in their arid environment. But when the world price for sisal dropped and the wages of sisal workers declined, many workers seem to have been forced to curtail the caloric intake of their children. The poorer people seem to have been obliged to save their now more limited food supplies for the money earners, at the expense of the children.[30]

Commercialization begins in a number of ways: people can begin to sell and buy because they begin to work for wages, or because they begin to sell nonagricultural products, surplus food, or cash crops (crops grown deliberately for sale). One type of commercialization does not exclude another—all types can occur in any society. However commercialization begins, it seems to have predictable effects on traditional economics. The ethic of generalized reciprocity declines, particularly with respect to giving money away. (Perhaps because it is nonperishable and hideable, money seems more likely than other goods to be kept for one's immediate family rather than shared with others.) Property rights become individualized rather than collective when people begin to buy and sell. And even in societies that were previously egalitarian, commercialization usually results in more unequal access to resources and hence a greater degree of social stratification.

Religious Change

The growing influence of Western societies has also led to religious change in many parts of the world. In many cases, the change has been brought about intentionally through the efforts of missionaries. Frequently, missionaries have been among the first Westerners to travel to interior regions and out-of-the-way places. Of course, they have not met with equal success in all parts of the world. In some places, large portions of the native population have converted to the new religion with great zeal. In others, missionaries have been ignored, forced to flee, or even killed. We do not as yet fully understand why missionaries have been successful in some societies and not in others. Yet in many parts of the world, Western missionary activity has been a potent force for all kinds of cultural, and particularly religious, change.

But aside from the direct effects of missionary work, contact with Westerners has often produced religious change in more indirect ways. In some native societies, contact with Westerners has led to a breakdown of social structure and the growth of feelings of helplessness and spiritual demoralization. Revitalization movements have arisen as apparent attempts to restore such societies to their former confidence and prosperity.

As an example of religious change brought about by direct contact with missionaries, we will examine the process of conversion on the island of Tikopia. As an example of a revitalization movement, we will examine the case of the Seneca Indians of New York State. As we saw in the chapter on religion, the Senecas managed, with the help of a Christianlike religion taught by a native prophet named Handsome Lake, to restore some of the tribal morale that had been lost as a result of contact with whites.

Christianity on Tikopia. Tikopia was one of the few Polynesian societies to retain its traditional religious system into the first decades of the twentieth century. An Anglican mission was first established on the island in 1911. With it came a deacon and the founding of two schools for about 200 pupils. By 1929, approximately half the population had converted, and in the early 1960s almost all Tikopia gave at least nominal allegiance to Christianity.[31]

Traditional Tikopian belief was pantheistic, embracing a great number of gods and spirits of various ranks inhabiting the sky, the water, and the land. One god in particular—the original creator and shaper of the culture—was given a place of special importance, but he was in no way comparable to the all-powerful God of Christianity. Unlike Christianity, Tikopian religion made no claim to universality. The Tikopian gods did not rule over all creation, only over Tikopia. It was

---

[30]Daniel R. Gross and Barbara A. Underwood, "Technological Change and Caloric Costs: Sisal Agriculture in Northeastern Brazil," *American Anthropologist*, 73 (1971): 725–40.

[31]Discussion is based on Raymond Firth, *Rank and Religion in Tikopia* (Boston: Beacon Press, 1970).

The expansion of Western and other state societies has led to religious change in many parts of the world. Here we see the last day of the Muslim holiday Ramadan as celebrated in northern Sumatra.

thought that if one left Tikopia, one left the gods behind.

The people of Tikopia interacted with their gods and spirits primarily through religious leaders who were also the heads of descent groups. Clan chiefs presided over rituals centering in the everyday aspects of island life, such as house construction, fishing, planting, and harvesting. The chief was expected to intercede with the gods on the people's behalf, to persuade them to bring happiness and prosperity to the group. Indeed, when conditions were good it was assumed that the chief was doing his job well. When disaster struck, the prestige of the chief often fell in proportion. Why did the Tikopia convert to Christianity? Firth has suggested a number of contributing factors.

First, the mission offered the people the prospect of acquiring new tools and consumer goods. Although conversion alone did not provide such benefits, attachment to the mission was believed to make them more attainable. Later, it became apparent that education, particularly in reading and

writing English, was helpful in getting ahead in the outside world. Mission schooling became valued and provided a further incentive for adopting Christianity.

Second, conversion may have been facilitated by the ability of chiefs, as religious and political leaders, to bring over entire kin groups to Christianity. Should a chief decide to transfer his allegiance to Christianity, the members of his kin group usually followed him, since social etiquette required that they do so. Such a situation actually developed in 1923 when Tafua, chief of the Faea district of Tikopia, converted to the new religion. He brought with him his entire group—which amounted to nearly half the population of the island. However, the ability of the chiefs to influence their kin groups was both an asset and a hindrance, since some chiefs steadfastly resisted conversion.

A final blow to traditional Tikopian religion appeared to come in 1955, when a severe epidemic killed at least 200 people in a population of about

1,700. According to Firth, "the epidemic was largely interpreted as a sign of divine discrimination," since three of the outstanding non-Christian religious leaders died.[32] Subsequently, the remaining non-Christian chiefs voluntarily converted to Christianity and so did their followers. By 1966 all Tikopia, with the exception of one rebellious old woman, had converted to the new faith.

Although many Tikopians feel their conversion to Christianity has been a unifying, revitalizing force, the changeover from one religion to another has not been without problems. Christian missionaries on Tikopia have succeeded in eliminating the traditional Tikopian population-control devices of abortion, infanticide, and male celibacy. It is very possible that the absence of these controls will continue to intensify population pressure. The island, with its limited capacity to support life, can ill afford this. Firth sums up the situation Tikopian society must now face:

In the history of Tikopia complete conversion of the people to Christianity was formerly regarded as a solution to their problems; it is now coming to be realized that the adoption and practice of Christianity itself represents another set of problems. As the Tikopia themselves are beginning to see, to be Christian Polynesians in the modern technologically and industrially dominated world, even in the Solomon Islands, poses as many questions as it supplies answers.[33]

The Seneca and the Religion of Handsome Lake.

The Seneca reservation of the Iroquois on the Allegheny River in New York State was a place of "poverty and humiliation" by 1799.[34] Demoralized by whiskey and dispossessed from their traditional lands, unable to compete with white technology because of illiteracy and lack of training, the Seneca were at an impasse. In this setting, Handsome Lake, the fifty-year-old brother of a chief, had the first of a number of visions. In them, he met with emissaries of the Creator who showed him heaven and hell and commissioned him to revitalize Seneca religion and society. This he set out to do for the next decade and a half. He used as his principal text the *Gaiwiio,* or "Good Word," a gospel that contains statements about the nature of religion and eternity and a code of conduct for the righteous. The *Gaiwiio* is interesting both for the influence of Quaker Christianity it clearly reveals[35] and for the way the new material has been merged with traditional Iroquois religious concepts.

The first part of the "Good Word" has three main themes, one of which is the concept of an apocalypse. Handsome Lake offered many signs by which the faithful could recognize impending, cosmic doom. Great drops of fire would rain from the skies and a veil would be cast over the earth. False prophets would appear, witch women would openly cast spells, and poisonous creatures from the underworld would seize and kill those who had rejected the *Gaiwiio.* Second, the *Gaiwiio* emphasized sin. The great sins were disbelief in the "good way," drunkenness, witchcraft, and abortion. Sins had to be confessed and repented. Finally, the *Gaiwiio* offered salvation. Salvation could be won by following a code of conduct, attending certain important traditional rites, and performing public confession.

The second part of the *Gaiwiio* sets out the code of conduct. This code seems to orient the Seneca toward advantageous white practices without separating them from their culture. The code has five main sections:

1. *Temperance.* All Seneca leaders were fully aware of the social disorders arising out of abuse of liquor. Handsome Lake went to great lengths to illustrate and explain the harmfulness of alcohol.

2. *Peace and social unity.* Seneca leaders were to cease their futile bickering, and all were to be united in their approach to whites.

3. *Preservation of tribal lands.* Handsome Lake, fearing the piecemeal alienation of Seneca lands, was far ahead of his contemporaries in demanding a halt in land sales to the whites.

4. *Proacculturation.* Though individual property and trading for profit were prohibited, the acquisition of literacy in English was encouraged so that people would be able to read and understand treaties written by the whites and to avoid being cheated.

---

[32]Ibid., p. 387.
[33]Ibid., p. 418.
[34]Anthony F. C. Wallace, *The Death and Rebirth of the Seneca* (New York: Knopf, 1970), p. 239.

[35]The Quakers, long-time neighbors and trusted advisers of the Seneca, took pains not to interfere with Seneca religion, principles, and attitudes.

5. *Domestic morality.* Sons were to obey their fathers, mothers should avoid interfering with daughters' marriages, and husbands and wives should respect the sanctity of their marriage vows.

Handsome Lake's teaching seems to have led to a renaissance among the Seneca. Temperance was widely accepted, as were white schooling and farming methods. By 1801, corn yields had been increased tenfold, new crops had been introduced (oats, potatoes, flax), and public health and hygiene had improved considerably. Handsome Lake himself acquired great power among his people. He spent the remainder of his life fulfilling administrative duties, acting as a representative of the Iroquois in Washington, and preaching his gospel to neighboring tribes. By the time of Handsome Lake's death in 1815, the Seneca had clearly undergone a dramatic rebirth, attributable at least in part to the new religion. Later in the century, some of Handsome Lake's disciples founded a church in his name that, despite occasional setbacks and political disputes, survives to this day.

Unfortunately, not all native peoples have made the transition to Christianity as painlessly as the Tikopia, or succeeded in revitalizing their culture as well as the Seneca. In fact, in most cases the record is dismal. All too frequently, missionary activity tends to destroy a society's culture and self-respect. It offers nothing in return but an alien, repressive system of values ill adapted to the people's real needs and aspirations. Phillip Mason, a critic of white evangelists in Africa, has pointed out some of the psychological damage inflicted by missionary activity.[36] The missionaries repeatedly stressed sin and guilt; they used the color black to represent evil and the color white to signify good; and they showed hostility toward pagan culture. Most damaging of all was their promise that the black person, provided he or she adopted the white person's ways, would gain access both to the white person's heaven and to white society. But no matter how diligently blacks attempted to follow missionary precepts or climb the white socioeconomic ladder, they were soon blocked from entry into white homes, clubs, and even churches and seminaries.

[36]Philip Mason, *Prospero's Magic* (London: Oxford University Press, 1962).

Other Types of Change

Commercialization and religious change are by no means the only types of changes brought about by Western expansion. Political changes have come about through the imposition of a foreign system of government. But, as recent events in Eastern Europe indicate, dramatic changes in a political system can also occur more or less voluntarily.

Change can also occur indirectly because of economic change that leads some groups to become more privileged and powerful than others. For example, it has been suggested that the introduction of new technology may generally make for an *increase* in degree of social stratification.[37] When the snowmobile began to be used for herding by the Lapps, those who for various reasons could participate in the "snowmobile revolution" gained economic, social, and political advantages. But those who could not acquire the new machines tended to become an economically and generally deprived class—without machines *or* reindeer.[38] Finally, Western influence has also brought about changes in dress, music, art, and attitudes throughout the world.

Of course, many nations in the past as well as the present—not just Western ones—have extended their power and influence to other parts of the globe. For example, the expansion of Islamic societies after the eighth century A.D. made for an enormous amount of culture change in the Near East, Africa, Europe, and Asia. Future research on contemporary culture change should increase our understanding of how and why various types of change are occurring. And if we can increase our understanding of culture change in the present, we should be better able to understand parallel processes in the past. Another lead to understanding change in the past is the large number of cross-cultural correlations (between a cultural variation and its presumed causes) which have been discovered in the last 20 years.[39] All cultures have changed

[37]H. Russell Bernard and Pertti J. Pelto, "Technology and Anthropological Theory: Conclusions," in Bernard and Pelto, eds., *Technology and Social Change*, p. 367.
[38]Pelto and Müller-Wille, "Snowmobiles," p. 237.
[39]Carol R. Ember and David Levinson, "The Substantive Contributions of Worldwide Cross-Cultural Studies Using Secondary Data," *Behavior Science Research* (Special Issue on "Cross-Cultural and Comparative Research: Theory and Method"), 25 (1991): 79–140.

over time. Therefore the variations we see are the products of change processes, and the discovered predictors of those variations may suggest how and why the changes occurred.

SUMMARY

1. Culture is always changing. Because culture consists of learned patterns of behavior and belief, cultural traits can be unlearned and learned anew as human needs change.

2. Discoveries and inventions, though ultimately the sources of all culture change, do not necessarily lead to change. Only when society accepts an invention or discovery and uses it regularly can culture change be said to have occurred. Some inventions are probably the result of dozens of tiny, perhaps accidental, initiatives over a period of many years. Other inventions are consciously intended. Why some people are more innovative than others is still only incompletely understood. There is some evidence that creativity and the readiness to adopt innovations may be related to socioeconomic position.

3. The process by which cultural elements are borrowed from another society and incorporated into the culture of the recipient group is called diffusion. Several patterns of diffusion may be identified: diffusion by direct contact, in which elements of a culture are first taken up by neighboring societies and then gradually spread farther and farther afield; diffusion by intermediate contact, in which third parties, frequently traders, carry a cultural trait from the society originating it to another group; and stimulus diffusion, in which knowledge of a trait belonging to another culture stimulates the invention or development of a local equivalent.

4. Cultural traits do not necessarily diffuse; that is, diffusion is a selective—not automatic—process. A society accepting a foreign cultural trait is likely to adapt it in a way that effectively harmonizes it with the society's own traditions.

5. When a group or society is in contact with a more powerful society, the weaker group is often obliged to acquire cultural elements from the dominant group. This process of extensive borrowing in the context of superordinate-subordinate relations between societies is usually called acculturation. In contrast with diffusion, acculturation comes about as a result of some sort of external pressure.

6. Perhaps the most drastic and rapid way a culture can change is by revolution—a usually violent replacement of the society's rulers. Rebellions occur primarily in state societies, where there is usually a distinct ruling elite. However, not all peoples who are suppressed, conquered, or colonized eventually rebel or successfully revolt against established authority.

7. Even though customs are not genetically inherited, cultural adaptation may be like biological adaptation: traits (cultural versus genetic) that are more likely to be reproduced (learned versus inherited) are likely to become more frequent in a population over time. And if culture is generally adapted to its environment, then culture change should also be generally adaptive.

8. Many of the cultural changes observed in the modern world have been generated, directly or indirectly, by the dominance and expansion of Western societies. One of the principal changes resulting from the expansion of Western culture is the increasing dependence of much of the world on commercial exchange—that is, the proliferation of buying and selling in markets, usually accompanied by the use of money as the medium of exchange. The borrowed custom of buying and selling may at first be supplementary to traditional means of distributing goods, but as the new commercial customs take hold, the economic base of the receiving society alters. Inevitably, this alteration is accompanied by other changes, which have broad social, political, and even psychological ramifications.

9. One way commercialization can occur is for members of a community to become migratory workers, traveling to a place nearby that offers the possibility of working for wages. Commercialization can also occur when a simple, self-sufficient hunting or agricultural society comes to depend more and more on trading for its livelihood. A third way commercialization occurs is when those cultivating the soil produce more than they require for subsistence. The surplus is then sold for cash. In many instances, this cash income must be used to pay rent or taxes; under such circumstances, commercialization may be said to be associated with the formation of a peasantry. A fourth way in which commercialization can come about is through the introduction of commercial agriculture, in which *all* the cultivated commodities are produced for sale rather than for personal consumption. Along with this change, the system of agriculture may be industrialized, with some of the production processes being done by machine.

10. The growing influence of Western societies has also led to religious change in many parts of the world. In many societies, such change has been brought about intentionally through the efforts of missionaries. In some, where contact with Westerners has produced a breakdown of the social structure and feelings of helplessness and spiritual demoralization, revitalization movements have arisen as apparent attempts to restore the society to its former confidence and prosperity.

SUGGESTED READING

BERNARD, H. R., AND PELTO, P. J., eds. *Technology and Social Change,* 2nd ed. Prospect Heights, IL: Waveland, 1987. This volume is concerned with the effects of introduced Western technology on diverse cultures. Thirteen case studies were written especially for the volume; the editors provide concluding observations.

BODLEY, J. H. *Victims of Progress.* 3rd ed., Mountain View, CA: Mayfield, 1990. An examination of the effects of industrial nations on tribal peoples. Emphasizes the imperialist and exploitative practices of expansionist nations as well as the destructive consequences of imposed "progress."

BOYD, R., AND RICHERSON, P. J. *Culture and the Evolutionary Process.* Chicago: University of Chicago Press, 1985. The authors develop mathematical models to analyze how genes and culture interact, under the influence of evolutionary processes, to produce the diversity we see in human cultures.

GOLDSTONE, J. A. "The Comparative and Historical Study of Revolutions." *Annual Review of Sociology,* 8 (1982): 187–207. A review of theory and research on why revolutions have occurred, and why some succeeded, in the past and present.

KOTTAK, C. P. *Assault on Paradise: Social Change in a Brazilian Village.* New York: Random House, 1983. A readable, personal account of an anthropologist's two decades of fieldwork in a Brazilian village. The author documents how village life has changed dramatically, and how his own and the villagers' feelings have changed in response.

MCNEILL, W. H. *Plagues and Peoples.* Garden City, NY: Doubleday Anchor, 1976. A historian suggests that epidemics have crucially affected the history of various societies all over the world.

ROGERS, E. M. *Diffusion of Innovations.* 3rd ed. New York: Free Press, 1983. This book examines the roles of information and uncertainty in the spread of innovations, how different categories of people adopt innovations at different rates, and how change agents affect the process. A large literature is reviewed and synthesized.

26

Explaining and Solving Social Problems

The news on radio and TV, the headlines of our newspapers, make us aware every day that social problems threaten people around the world. From war to crime and family violence, from AIDS to poverty and famine, the pursuit of happiness and even life itself are jeopardized for many people in many places.

Worldwide communication has increased our awareness of problems elsewhere, and we seem to be increasingly bothered by problems in our own society. For these two reasons, and perhaps also because we know more than we used to about human behavior, we may be more motivated now to try to solve those problems. We call them "social" problems not only because a lot of people worry about them but because they have social causes or consequences, and their possible treatments or solutions require at least some changes in social behavior. For example, AIDS may be caused by a family of viruses, but it is a social problem because it is mostly transmitted by sexual contact with another person and the only ways to avoid it now (abstinence, "safe" sex) require changes in social behavior. And it is a social problem also because millions of people are put at risk by the global epidemic.

Anthropology and most of the other social sciences have long been concerned with social problems. One way in which this concern is expressed is through "basic research" that tests theories about the possible causes of social problems. The results of such tests could suggest solutions to the problems if the causes, once discovered, can be reduced or eliminated. The other way to be concerned with social problems is to participate in programs intended to improve people's lives. In anthropology, this second way is referred to as **applied anthropology** or **practicing anthropology.** Applied or practicing anthropologists may be involved in one or more phases of a program: assembling relevant knowledge, constructing alternative plans, assessing the likely social and environmental impact of particular plans, implementing the program, and monitoring the program and its effects.[1]

Clearly, theory-testing and applied research

[1] Gilbert Kushner, "Applied Anthropology," in William G. Emener and Margaret Darrow, eds., *Career Explorations in Human Services* (Springfield, IL: Charles C. Thomas, 1991), pp. 46–61.

may both be motivated by a desire to improve the quality of human life. But it is often difficult to decide if a particular project is basic or applied. For example, consider a study of the possible causes of war; its results may suggest how the risk of war might be reduced. Is such a study basic or applied research?

This chapter has two major parts. The first deals with applied or practicing anthropology. We discuss the history and types of application in the United States, the ethical issues involved in trying to improve people's lives, and the difficulties in evaluating whether a program is beneficial. In the second part of the chapter we turn to the study of global social problems, and how understanding the possible causes of these problems may suggest possible solutions. We focus on AIDS, disasters, homelessness, crime, family violence, and war.

Applied and Practicing Anthropology

It is hard for anthropologists not to care and worry about the people they study, just as it is hard not to worry about family and friends back home. It is hard not to be upset when most of the families in your place of fieldwork have lost many of their babies to diseases that could be eliminated by medical care. It is hard not to care when outside political and economic interests threaten to deprive your fieldwork friends of their resources and pride. Anthropologists have usually studied people who are disadvantaged—by imperialism, colonialism, and other forms of exploitation. And so it is no wonder that we generally feel protective about these people, whom we have lived with in the field.

But caring is not enough to improve others' lives. We may need basic research that allows us to understand how a condition might be successfully treated. A particular proposed "improvement" might actually not be an improvement; well-meaning efforts have sometimes produced harmful consequences. And even if we know that a change would be an improvement, there is still the problem of how to make it happen. The people to be affected may not want to change. Is it ethical to try to persuade them? And conversely, is it ethical not to try? Applied anthropologists must take all of these matters into consideration in determining whether and how to act in response to a perceived need.

Applied anthropology in the United States developed out of anthropologists' personal experiences with disadvantaged peoples.[2] But today anthropologists are also interested in studying and solving problems in our own society. Anthropologists who call themselves applied or practicing anthropologists are usually employed in nonacademic settings, working for government and international agencies and sometimes even for corporations. They work on specific projects that aim to improve people's lives in particular places, usually by trying to change behavior or the environment; or the anthropologists monitor or evaluate efforts by others to bring about change.[3] Usually the problems and projects are defined by the employers or clients (the client is sometimes the "target" population), not by the anthropologists who may be employed.[4] But anthropologists are increasingly called upon to participate in deciding exactly what improvements might be possible, as well as how to achieve them.

History and Types of Application

Until World War II, almost all anthropologists in the United States were employed in colleges, universities, and museums, and applied anthropology was practically nonexistent. In 1934, John Collier, the head of the Bureau of Indian Affairs, opened the way toward more widespread recognition of the useful roles anthropologists could play outside academic settings when he got legislation passed that provided a number of protections for Native Americans: land could no longer be taken away, lost land was supposed to be restored, tribal governments would be formed, and loans would be made available to reservations. Collier employed some anthropologists to aid in carrying out these policies. At about the same time, the Soil Conservation Service hired anthropologists to help with projects related to Native American land use.[5]

Events in the 1940s further boosted applied anthropology. In 1941, anthropologists founded the Society for Applied Anthropology and a new journal devoted to applied anthropology (it is now called *Human Organization*).[6] During World War II, anthropologists were hired in unprecedented numbers by the U.S. government to help in the war effort. Margaret Mead estimated that something like 295 of the 303 anthropologists in the United States at the time were in one way or another direct participants in the war effort.[7]

The government hired anthropologists to help improve morale, to increase our understanding of enemies and allies, and to prepare for military campaigns and occupation of the islands of Micronesia and other areas in and around the Pacific.[8] For example, applied anthropologists were called on for advice when perplexed U.S. military officials wanted to understand why their Japanese enemies refused to behave like "normal" people. One of the practices that most distressed military leaders was the tendency of Japanese soldiers captured in battle to try to kill themselves rather than be taken prisoner. Certainly, U.S. prisoners of war did not behave in this manner. Eventually, in order to understand the Japanese code of honor, the military hired a number of anthropologists as consultants to the Foreign Morale Analysis Division of the War Office's Information Department.

After working with the anthropologists, the U.S. military learned that a major reason for the "strange" behavior of the Japanese prisoners was their belief that to surrender in a wartime situation, even in the face of greatly superior odds, or

[2]Margaret Mead, "The Evolving Ethics of Applied Anthropology," in Elizabeth M. Eddy and William L. Partridge, eds., *Applied Anthropology in America* (New York: Columbia University Press, 1978), pp. 426–29.

[3]Robert A. Hackenberg, "Scientists or Survivors? The Future of Applied Anthropology under Maximum Uncertainty," in Robert T. Trotter II, ed., *Anthropology for Tomorrow: Creating Practitioner-Oriented Applied Anthropology Programs* (Washington: American Anthropological Association, 1988), p. 172.

[4]Kushner, "Applied Anthropology."

[5]William L. Partridge and Elizabeth M. Eddy, "The Development of Applied Anthropology in America," in Eddy and Partridge, eds., *Applied Anthropology in America*, 2nd ed. (New York: Columbia University Press, 1987), pp. 25–26.

[6]Ibid., pp. 31–40.

[7]Margaret Mead, "Applied Anthropology: The State of the Art," in Anthony F. C. Wallace, J. Lawrence Angel, Richard Fox, Sally McLendon, Rachel Sady, and Robert Sharer, eds., *Perspectives on Anthropology 1976*, American Anthropological Association Special Publication no. 10 (Washington, DC: American Anthropological Association, 1977), p. 149.

[8]Partridge and Eddy, "The Development of Applied Anthropology," pp. 31–40.

to be taken prisoner, even when injured and unconscious and therefore unable to avoid capture, was a disgrace. The Japanese believed further that the U.S. soldiers killed all prisoners. Thus, it is hardly surprising that so many captured Japanese soldiers preferred honorable death by their own hand. Once the U.S. military learned what the Japanese thought, they made efforts to explain to them that they would not be executed if captured, with the result that far more Japanese surrendered. Some prisoners even gave military information to the Americans—not to act against their own country, but rather to try and establish new lives for themselves, since the disgrace of being captured prevented them from resuming their former lives.[9]

Anthropologists were enthusiastic about helping the government during World War II because they were overwhelmingly committed to winning the war. The government, in its turn, seemed eager for anthropological advice. But in the postwar period there was an enormous increase in higher education as returning veterans and later baby boomers went to college, and U.S. anthropologists retreated from working with the government as the academic opportunities opened up. At the same time anthropology became less concerned with applied problems and more concerned with theory and basic research.

The situation changed again, from the late 1970s on, as employment opportunities declined in colleges and universities. Today, a large and increasing number of anthropologists are finding employment outside of anthropology departments[10]—in medical schools, health centers, development agencies, urban planning agencies, and other public and private organizations that seek to change people's lives, in this society and others. Anthropologists who work in applied fields come out of a variety of subdisciplines. A major type of applied work is the "social impact" study required in connection with many programs funded by government or private agencies. Most of those who do this work were trained in ethnology. Some applied anthropologists, who work in medicine and health, were trained in

physical anthropology. Archeologists are hired to study, record, and preserve "cultural resources" that will be disturbed or destroyed by construction projects. And applied work in education often utilizes the skills of linguists.[11]

Ethics of Applied Anthropology

There are always ethical issues that arise in the course of fieldwork, and anthropology as a profession has adopted certain principles of responsibility. Above all, an anthropologist's first responsibility is to those who are being studied—everything should be done to ensure that their welfare and dignity will be protected. Anthropologists also have a responsibility to those who will read about their research; research findings should be reported openly and truthfully.[12] But because applied anthropology often deals with planning and implementing changes in some target population, ethical responsibilities can become more complicated. Perhaps the most important ethical question is this: Will the change truly benefit the target population?

In May 1946, the Society for Applied Anthropology established a committee to draw up a specific code of ethics for those who work professionally as applied anthropologists. After many meetings and revisions, the society finally adopted a statement on ethical responsibilities in 1948. In 1974 the statement was revised again.[13] According to the code, the target community should be included as much as possible in the formulation of policy, so that people in the community may know in advance how the program may affect them. But perhaps the most important aspect of the code is the pledge not to be involved in any plan whose effect will not be beneficial. If an anthropologist thinks that the effect of a plan will not be beneficial, he or she is supposed to withdraw from participation and inform the target community about the intended change.

[9]George M. Foster, *Applied Anthropology* (Boston: Little, Brown, 1969), p. 200.

[10]Partridge and Eddy, "The Development of Applied Anthropology," p. 48.

[11]Ibid., p. 52.

[12]"Principles of Professional Responsibility," adopted by the Council of the American Anthropological Association, May 1971.

[13]"Statement on Professional and Ethical Responsibilities (Society for Applied Anthropology)," *Human Organization,* 34 (Summer 1975).

Difficulties in Evaluating the Effects of Planned Change

The decision as to whether a proposed change would benefit the target population is not always easy. In certain cases, as where improved medical care is involved, the benefits offered to the target group would seem to be unquestioned—we all feel sure that health is better than illness. But even this may not always be true. Consider a public-health innovation such as inoculation against disease. Although it would undoubtedly have a beneficial effect on the survival rate of a population, a reduction in the mortality rate might have unforeseen consequences that would in turn produce new problems. Once the inoculation program was begun, the number of children surviving would probably increase. But if the rate of food production could not be increased proportionately, given the level of technology, capital, and land resources possessed by the target population, then the death rate, this time from starvation, might rise to its previous level and perhaps even exceed it. In such a case, the inoculation program would merely be changing the cause of death, at least in the long run. This example shows that even if a program of planned change has beneficial consequences in the short run, a great deal of thought and investigation has to be given to its long-term effects.

One of the most important, and most difficult, problems for applied anthropology is the need to anticipate all the effects that are likely to result from the single change that is proposed. A good example of the unforeseen consequences of disease control comes from the island of Mauritius in the Indian Ocean. It was quite evident there that government efforts to control malaria after World War II had led to a disastrous population explosion: the population nearly doubled, unemployment rose, and the cost of government services became astronomical. In short, Mauritius had outstripped its ability to support itself. All these events were apparently triggered by DDT spraying in 1948, which eradicated the malaria-bearing mosquitoes. In one year, the death rate fell by 32 percent and the annual rate of increase in the population changed from less than half of 1 percent to 3 percent.[14]

A population's health can actually be harmed when foreign health care is introduced without provision for related customs. An example of this can be seen in a program attempted in a rural West African community. In that community, the women traditionally continued to work in the fields during pregnancy. In an attempt to improve prenatal care, pregnant women were kept from their work. However, because the people who effected this change neglected to encourage the West African women to adopt a substitute program of proper physical activity, the women actually suffered *increased* chances of ill health and infant mortality.[15]

Even if the short-term effects of planned changes are beneficial the long-term effects may not be. Thayer Scudder describes the situation of Gwembe Tonga villagers who were relocated after the building of a large dam in the Zambezi valley of central Africa. Economic conditions improved during the 1960s and early 1970s, as the people increasingly produced goods and services for sale. But then conditions deteriorated. By 1980 the villagers were in a miserable state: rates of mortality, alcohol drinking, theft, assault, and murder were all up. Why? One reason was that they had cut back on producing their own food in favor of producing for world markets. Such a strategy works well when world market prices are high; however, when prices fall, so does the standard of living.[16]

The situation described by Scudder illustrates the ethical dilemma for many applied anthropologists. As he says: "So how is it that I can still justify working for the agencies that fund such projects?" He points out that large-scale projects are almost impossible to stop. The anthropologist can choose to stand on the side-lines and complain, or try to influence the project to benefit the target population as much as possible.[17]

In addition to attempting to ameliorate plans already underway, anthropologists sometimes argue for changes that we know will have long-term as

[14]Burton Benedict, "Controlling Population Growth in Mauritius," in H. Russell Bernard and Pertti J. Pelto, eds., *Technology and Social Change*, 2nd ed. (Prospect Heights, IL: Waveland Press, 1987), pp. 269–300.

[15]Conrad M. Arensberg and Arthur Niehoff, *Introducing Social Change: A Manual for Americans Overseas* (Chicago: Aldine, 1964), p. 66.

[16]Thayer Scudder, "Opportunities, Issues, and Achievements in Development Anthropology since the Mid-1960s: A Personal View," in Eddy and Partridge, eds., *Applied Anthropology in America*, 2nd ed., pp. 184–210.

[17]Ibid, p. 204ff.

well as short-term benefits. How can we get the powers-that-be to listen to us and act upon these plans? Perhaps only when they realize that nearly everyone, not just the disadvantaged, can benefit. With many of the social problems in the world, researchers are beginning to be able to point to such benefits.

Global Social Problems: Basic Research and Possible Solutions

Some anthropologists as well as other social scientists think that it is time to attack the major social problems that afflict our world. The idea that we can solve social problems is based on two assumptions. We have to assume that it is possible to discover the causes of a problem. And we have to assume that we may be able to do something about the causes (once they are discovered) and thereby eliminate or reduce the problem.

Not everyone would agree with these assumptions. Some would say that our understanding of a social problem cannot ever be sufficient to suggest a solution guaranteed to work. To be sure, no understanding in science is perfect or certain; there is always some probability that even a well-supported explanation is wrong or incomplete. But the uncertainty of knowledge does not rule out the possibility of application. With regard to social problems, the possible payoff from even incomplete understanding could be a better and safer world. This possibility is what motivates many researchers who investigate social problems. After all, the history of the various sciences strongly supports the belief that scientific understanding can often allow humans to control nature, not just predict and explain it. Why should human behavior be any different?

So what do we know about some of the global social problems, and what policies or solutions are suggested by what we know?

AIDS

Epidemics of disease have killed millions of people within short periods of time throughout recorded history. The Black Death (bubonic plague) killed between 25 and 50 percent of the population of Europe, perhaps 75 million people, during the fourteenth century; an epidemic during the sixth

The epidemic of AIDS is likely to continue in the near future.

century killed an estimated 100 million people in the Middle East, Asia, and Europe. Less noted in our history books, but also devastating, was the enormous depopulation that accompanied the expansion of Europeans into the New World and the Pacific from the 1500s on. Not only were people killed directly by European conquerors; millions also died from introduced diseases to which the natives had little or no resistance, diseases such as smallpox and measles that the Europeans brought with them but were no longer dying from.

The current state of medical science and technology may lull us into thinking that epidemics are a thing of the past. But the recent and sudden emergence of the disease we call **AIDS (acquired immune deficiency syndrome)** reminds us that new diseases, or new varieties of old diseases, can appear at any time. Like all other organisms, disease-causing organisms also evolve. The HIV viruses that cause AIDS apparently emerged only recently. Viruses (and bacteria) are always mutating, and new strains emerge that are initially a plague on our genetic resistance and on medical efforts to contain them.

Millions of people all around the world already have the symptoms of AIDS, and millions more are infected with the HIV viruses but do not know they are infected. The former U.S. Surgeon General, C. Everett Koop, has said that 100 million deaths may occur because of AIDS by the end of the century. AIDS is a frightening epidemic not only because of its likely toll. It is also frightening because it takes a long time (average four years) after exposure for symptoms to appear. This means that many people who have been infected by the HIV viruses, but do not know they are infected, may continue unknowingly to transmit the viruses to others.[18]

Transmission occurs mostly via sexual encounters, through semen and blood. Drug users may also transmit the HIV viruses by way of contaminated needles. Transmission by blood transfusion has been virtually eliminated in this and other societies by medical screening of blood supplies. In many countries, however, there is still no routine screening of blood prior to transfusions.

Perhaps because AIDS is caused by viruses, many people think of it as a medical problem requiring a medical solution. It is true that developing a vaccine (or a drug) to prevent people from getting AIDS, and developing a "cure" for those who have it, will finally solve the problem of AIDS. But, for a variety of reasons, we can expect that the medical solution alone will not be sufficient, at least not for a while. First, to be effective worldwide, or even within a country, a vaccine has to be inexpensive and relatively easy to produce in large quantities; the same is true of any medical treatment for victims. Second, governments around the world have to be willing and able to spend the money and hire the personnel necessary to manage an effective program.[19] Third, future vaccination and treatment will require the people at risk to be willing to get vaccinated and treated, which is not always easy to arrange. Witness the fact that measles is becoming more frequent in the United States because many people are not having their children vaccinated.

We do not know yet if an effective and inexpensive vaccine (or treatment) will be developed soon. In the meantime, the risk of HIV infection can be reduced only by changes in social (particularly sexual) behavior. But to persuade people to change their sexual behavior, it is necessary to find out exactly what they do sexually, and why they prefer what they do. The reasons for preferring some activity may make it difficult to change.

Research so far suggests that different sexual patterns are responsible for HIV transmission in different parts of the world. In the United States, England, northern Europe, Australia, and Latin America, the recipients of anal intercourse (particularly men) are the most likely individuals to acquire the HIV infection; vaginal intercourse can also transmit the infection (usually from the man to the woman). In Africa, however, the most common mode of transmission is vaginal intercourse, and so women get infected more commonly in Africa than elsewhere.[20] Is it reasonable to expect that people can generally be persuaded to stop doing what they prefer to do?

As of now, there are only two known ways to reduce the likelihood of sexual HIV transmission. One way is to abstain from sexual intercourse; the other is to use condoms. Educational programs that teach how AIDS spreads, and what you can do about it, may reduce the spread somewhat. But they are unlikely to reduce the spread significantly because many people have beliefs and attitudes that rule out the use of condoms. For example, people in some central African societies believe that deposits of semen *after* conception are necessary for a successful pregnancy and generally enhance a woman's health and ability to reproduce. It might be expected then that people who have these beliefs about semen would choose not to use condoms; after all, condoms in their view are a threat to public health.[21]

---

[18]Ralph Bolton, "Introduction: The AIDS Pandemic, A Global Emergency," *Medical Anthropology*, 10 (1989): 93–104.
[19]Ibid.

[20]Joseph Carrier and Ralph Bolton, "Anthropological Perspectives on Sexuality and HIV Prevention," *Annual Review of Sex Research* (in press); B. Schoepf, "Women, AIDS, and Economic Crisis in Central Africa," *Canadian Journal of African Studies*, 22 (1988): 625; cited in Carrier and Bolton, "Anthropological Perspectives."
[21]B. Schoepf, "Women, AIDS, and Economic Crisis in Central Africa," pp. 637–38, as cited in Carrier and Bolton, "Anthropological Perspectives."

There is one other reason to expect HIV-infection to continue to spread in the near term. Possible victims of AIDS may be unwilling to find out if they have been infected because of the stigma associated with the disease: the stigma, in this and some other societies, is that homosexual men are particularly likely to get infected.[22] Of course, not everyone who gets infected has engaged in homosexual behavior. But the association with homosexuality, and the prejudice against homosexuals, may contribute to the spread of AIDS: some of those infected will continue to transmit the infection because they are afraid to find out that they might be infected. Much of the stigma associated with AIDS derives also from people's misinformation about exactly how AIDS is transmitted; indeed, many people fear any kind of contact with AIDS victims, as if any kind of contact could result in infection. Fear that they will be shunned if they are known to have AIDS may also contribute to some persons' unwillingness to be tested.

To solve the problem of AIDS, we may hope that medical science will develop effective vaccination and treatment which can be afforded by all. In the meantime, we can try to understand why people engage in certain risky sexual practices. Such understanding may allow us to design educational programs that would inhibit the spread of AIDS.

Disasters

Disasters such as floods, droughts, earthquakes, and insect infestations are usually but not always beyond human control, but their effects are not.[23] Consider that between 1960 and 1980, 43 disasters in Japan killed an average of 63 people per disaster. During the same period, 17 disasters in Nicaragua killed an average of 6,235 people per disaster. In the United States, between 1960 and 1976, the average disaster killed just one person, injured a dozen, and destroyed fewer than five buildings. These comparative figures demonstrate that disasters and their effects are not just caused by climatic and other events in the physical environment. Disasters become really disastrous because of events or conditions in the social environment.

If people live in houses that are designed to withstand earthquakes—if governing bodies require such construction and the economy is developed enough so that people can afford such construction—the effects of a disaster will be minimized. If poor people are forced to live in deforested flood plains in order to be able to find land to farm (as in coastal Bangladesh), if the poor (like those of Rio de Janeiro) are forced to live in shanties built on precarious hillsides, the floods and landslides that follow severe hurricanes and rainstorms can kill thousands and even hundreds of thousands.

Thus, disasters can have greater or lesser effects on human life, depending on social conditions. And therefore disasters are also social problems, problems that have social causes and possible social solutions. Legislating safe construction of a house is a social solution. The 1976 earthquake in Tangsham, China killed 250,000 people, mostly because they lived in top-heavy adobe houses that could not stand severe shaking, while the 1989 earthquake in Loma Prieta, California, which was of comparable intensity, killed only 65 people.

One might think that floods, of all disasters, are the least influenced by social factors. After all, without a huge runoff from heavy rains or snow melt, there cannot be a flood. But consider why so many people have died from Yellow River floods in China. (One such flood, in 1931, killed nearly four million people, making it the deadliest single disaster in history.) The floods in the Yellow River basin have occurred mostly because the cutting down of forests nearby (for fuel and farm land) has allowed enormous quantities of silt to wash into the river, raising the river bed and increasing the risk of floods that burst the dams that normally would contain them. The risk of disastrous flooding would be greatly reduced if different social conditions prevailed—if people were not so dependent on firewood for fuel, or they did not have to farm land close to the river, or the dams were higher and more numerous.

Famines, episodes of severe starvation and death, often are triggered by physical events such

[22]Douglas A. Feldman and Thomas M. Johnson, "Introduction," in Douglas A. Feldman and Thomas M. Johnson, eds., *The Social Dimensions of AIDS: Method and Theory* (New York: Praeger, 1986), p. 2.

[23]The discussion in this section draws extensively from Lewis Aptekar, *Environmental Disasters in Global Perspective* (New York: G. K. Hall/Macmillan), in press.

Aftermath of an earthquake in Armenia.

as a hurricane that knocks down and uproots food trees and plants. But famines do not inevitably follow such an event. Social conditions can prevent a famine or increase the likelihood of one. Consider what is likely to happen in Samoa after a hurricane.[24] Whole villages that have lost their coconut and breadfruit trees, as well as their taro patches, pick up and move for a period of time to other villages where there are relatives and friends. The visitors stay and are fed until some of their cultivated trees and plants start to bear food again, at which point they return home. This kind of intervillage reciprocity probably could occur only in a society that has relatively little inequality in wealth. Nowadays, the central government may also help out by providing food and other supplies.

Relief provided by a central government may not always get to those who need it the most. In India, for example, the central government provides help in time of drought to minimize the risk of famine. But the food and other supplies provided to a village may end up being unequally distributed, following the rules of social and gender stratification. Members of the local elite arrange to function as distributors and find ways to manipulate the relief efforts to their advantage. Lower-class and lower-caste families still suffer the most. Within the family, biases against females (particularly young girls and elderly women) translate into their getting less food. It is no wonder then that in times of food shortage and famine, the poor and other socially disadvantaged persons are especially likely to die.[25]

Thus, the people of a society may not all be equally at risk in case of disaster. In socially stratified societies, the poor particularly suffer. It is they who are likely to be forced to overcultivate, overgraze, and deforest their land, making it more sus-

[24]Information collected during M. Ember's fieldwork in American Samoa (1955–56).

[25]William I. Torry, "Morality and Harm: Hindu Peasant Adjustments to Famines," *Social Science Information*, 25 (1986): 125–60.

ceptible to degradation. A society most helps those it values the most.

People in the past, and even recently in some places, viewed disasters as divine retribution for human immorality. For example, the great Flood described in the Old Testament was understood to be God's doing. But scientific research increasingly allows us to understand the natural causes of disasters, and particularly the social conditions that magnify or minimize their effects. To reduce the impact of disasters, then, we need to reduce the social conditions that magnify the effects of disasters. If humans are responsible for those social conditions, humans can change them. If earthquakes destroy houses that are too flimsy, we can build stronger houses. If floods because of overcultivation and overgrazing kill defenseless people directly (or indirectly by stripping their soils), we can decide to grow new forest cover and provide new job opportunites to flood-plain farmers. In short, we may not be able to do much about the weather (or other physical causes of disasters), but we can do a lot (if we want to) about the social factors that make disasters disastrous.

Inadequate Housing and Homelessness

In most nations of the world today, the poor typically live in inadequate housing, in areas we call *slums*. In many of the developing nations of the world, where cities are growing very rapidly, squatter settlements emerge as people build dwellings (often makeshift) that are typically declared "illegal," either because the land is illegally occupied or because the dwellings violate building codes. Squatter settlements are often located in degraded environments that are subject to flooding and mudslides, or have inadequate or polluted water. The magnitude of the problem is made clear in some recent statistics: some 40 percent of the population in Nairobi, Kenya, live in unauthorized housing, and 67 percent of the people in five of El Salvador's major cities are living in "illegal" dwellings.[26]

But contrary to what some have assumed, not all the dwellers in illegal settlements are poor; all but the upper-income elite may be found in such settle-

ments.[27] Moreover, although squatter settlements have problems, they are not chaotic and unorganized places, full of crime. Most of the dwellers are employed, aspire to get ahead, live in nuclear families, and give each other mutual aid.[28] People live in such settlements because they cannot find affordable housing and they house themselves as best they can. Many researchers think that such self-help tendencies should be assisted to improve housing, because governments in developing countries can seldom afford costly public housing projects. But they could invest somewhat in infrastructure (sewers, water supplies, roads) and provide construction materials to those who are willing to do the work required to improve their dwellings.[29]

Housing in slum areas or "shantytowns" does provide shelter, minimal though it may be. But many people in many areas of the world have no homes at all. Even in countries such as the United States, which are "affluent" by world standards, large numbers of people are homeless. They sleep in parks, over steam vents, in doorways, subways, and cardboard boxes. And their numbers are growing. A 1988 congressionally funded study suggests that unless immediate action is taken in the United States to provide affordable housing, there may be as many as 19 million homeless people by the end of this century.[30]

Who are the homeless, and how did they get to be homeless? As yet we have relatively little research on these questions, but what we do have suggests differences in the causes of homelessness in different parts of the world.

In the United States, unemployment and the shortage of decent low-cost housing appear to be at least partly responsible for the large number of homeless. But there is also another factor: the de-

[26]Jorge Hardoy and David Satterthwaite, "The Legal and the Illegal City," in Lloyd Rodwin, ed., *Shelter, Settlement, and Development* (Boston: Allen & Unwin, 1987), pp. 304–38.

[27]Lloyd Rodwin and Bishwapriya Sanyal, "Shelter, Settlement, and Development: An Overview," in Rodwin, ed., *Shelter, Settlement, and Development*, pp. 3–31.

[28]William Mangin, "Latin American Squatter Settlements: A Problem and a Solution," *Latin American Research Review*, 2 (1967): 65–98.

[29]Rodwin and Sanyal, "Shelter, Settlement, and Development: An Overview"; for a critique of self-help programs, see Peter M. Ward, "Introduction and Purpose," in Peter M. Ward, ed., *Self-Help Housing: A Critique* (London: Mansell Publishing Limited, 1982), pp. 1–13.

[30]Gregg Barak, *Gimme Shelter: A Social History of Homelessness in Contemporary America* (New York: Praeger, 1991), p. 4.

liberate policy to reduce the number of people hospitalized for mental illness and other disabilities. For example, in the last three decades New York State released a large number of patients from mental hospitals. Many of these ex-patients had to live in cheap hotels or poorly monitored facilities with virtually no support network. With very little income, they found it especially hard to cope with their circumstances. Ellen Baxter and Kim Hopper, who studied the homeless in New York City, suggest that one event is rarely sufficient to render a person "homeless." Rather, poverty and disability (mental or physical) seem to lead to one calamity after another, and finally homelessness.

Many people cannot understand why homeless individuals do not "want" to go to municipal shelters. But observations and interviews with the homeless suggest that violence pervades the municipal shelters, particularly the men's shelters. Many feel safer on the streets. Some private charities provide safe shelters, and a caring environment. These shelters are filled, but the number of homeless that could be accommodated in them is small.[31]

Some poor individuals in a society may be socially isolated; they may have few or no friends and relatives and little or no social contact. (These people may or may not have symptoms of severe mental illness.) But a society with many such individuals does not necessarily have much homelessness. Socially isolated individuals, even mentally ill individuals, could still have housing, or so the experience of Melbourne, Australia, suggests. Universal health insurance pays for health care as well as the visits of medical practitioners to isolated and ill individuals, wherever they live. Disabled individuals receive a pension or sickness benefits sufficient to allow them to live in a room or apartment. And there is still a considerable supply of cheap housing in Melbourne.

Research in Melbourne suggests that a severe mental disorder often precedes living in marginal accommodations—city shelters, commercial shelters, and cheap single rooms. (About 50 percent of the individuals living in such places were diagnosed as previously having some form of mental illness; this percentage is similar to what seems to be the case for homeless people and people living in marginal accommodations in the United States.)

The contrast between the United States and Australia makes it clear that homelessness is caused by social and political policies. Individuals with similar characteristics live in both Australia and the United States, but in the United States a large percentage of them are homeless.[32]

Since homelessness cannot occur if everybody can afford housing, some would say that homelessness can occur only in a society with great extremes in income. Recent statistics on income distribution in the United States clearly show that in the last two decades the rich have gotten much richer and the poor have gotten much poorer. The United States now has more income inequality than other industrialized countries, such as Japan and the Netherlands. In fact, the profile of inequality in the United States more closely resembles that of "developing" countries such as India and Mexico.[33]

In the United States and many other countries, the homeless are generally adults. While adults are "allowed" to be homeless, public sensibilities in the United States appear to be outraged by the sight of children living in the streets; when authorities discover homeless children, they try to find shelters or foster homes for them. But many countries in the world have many "street children." It has been estimated that 80 million of the world's children live in the streets. Forty million of them live in Latin America, 20 million in Asia, and 10 million in Africa and the Middle East.[34]

Lewis Aptekar studied street children in Cali, Colombia.[35] He reports some surprises. While the homeless in the United States and Australia are often mentally disabled, the street children in Cali (ranging in age from seven to sixteen) are mostly free of mental problems; by and large they also test normally on intelligence tests. In addition, even though many street children come from abusive

[31]Ellen Baxter and Kim Hopper, *Private Lives/Public Spaces: Homeless Adults on the Streets of New York City* (New York: Community Service Society of New York, 1981), pp. 30–33, pp. 50–74.

[32]Helen Herrman, "A Survey of Homeless Mentally Ill People in Melbourne, Australia," *Hospital and Community Psychiatry*, 41 (1990): 1291–92.

[33]Barak, *Gimme Shelter*, pp. 63–65.

[34]Lewis Aptekar, "Are Colombian Street Children Neglected? The Contributions of Ethnographic and Ethnohistorical Approaches to the Study of Children," *Anthropology and Education Quarterly*, 22 (1991): 326.

[35]Ibid., pp. 326–49. See also Lewis Aptekar, *Street Children of Cali* (Durham, NC: Duke University Press), 1988.

homes or never had homes, they usually seem happy and enjoy the support and friendship of other street children. They cleverly and creatively look for ways to get money, frequently through entertaining passersby.

Although the observer might think that the street children must have been abandoned by their families, in actuality most of them have at least one parent they keep in touch with. Street life begins slowly, not abruptly; children usually do not stay on the streets full time until they are about thirteen.

Though street children in Cali seem to be in better physical and mental shape than their siblings who stay at home, they are often viewed as a "plague." The street children come from poor families and cope with their lives as best they can, so why are they not viewed with pity and compassion? Aptekar suggests that well-off families see the "street children" as a threat because a life independent of family may appeal to children (even from well-off families) who wish to be free of parental constraint and authority.

Whether or not people become "homeless," whether or not there are shantytowns, seems to depend on a society's willingness to share wealth and help those in need. The street children of Cali may remind us that children as well as adults need companionship as well as caring. Caring for physical needs without responding to emotional needs may get people off the streets, but it won't get them a "home."

Family Violence and Abuse

In our society, we hear regularly about the abuse of spouses and children. It appears to be increasing, but is it? This seems to be a simple question, but it is not so simple to answer. We have to decide what we mean by abuse.

Is physical punishment of a child, who does something wrong, child abuse? Not so long ago, teachers in public schools in the United States were allowed to discipline children by hitting them with rulers or paddles, and many parents used switches or belts. Some people today might consider these practices to be child abuse, but were they abusive when they were generally accepted? Some would argue that abuse is going beyond what a culture considers appropriate behavior. Others would disagree and would focus on the violence

and severity of parents' or teachers' behavior, not the cultural judgment of appropriateness. And abuse need not involve physical violence. It could be argued that verbal aggression and neglect may be just as harmful as physical aggression. Neglect presents its own problems of definition. People from other cultures might argue that we act abusively when we put an infant or child alone in a room to sleep.[36] Few would disagree about severe injuries that kill a child or spouse or require medical treatment; but other disciplinary behaviors are more difficult to judge.

More child abuse cases are reported today in the United States than a decade ago, but that does not necessarily mean that violence against children has increased; it may mean only that our awareness and intolerance of violence against children has increased. In fact, in a national interview-survey of physical familial violence in the United States, most types of physical violence decreased in frequency between 1975 and 1985. That is, people talked about fewer family homicides, fewer severe assaults on husbands and wives, and fewer severe assaults on children. However, despite these declines, the United States remains a society with a generally high rate of physical violence in families. In the year 1985 alone, one out of six couples had a violent assault episode and one out of ten children was severely assaulted by a parent. The risk of assault by a family member in the United States is much greater than assault by a stranger; for women it is more than 200 times greater.[37] In a comparison of 27 nations, the United States had the third highest rate of child murder.[38]

There is some tendency for one form of family violence to be associated cross-culturally with others (for example, child punishment and wife beating seem to go together somewhat). But forms of violence are not so strongly associated that we can speak of a generally high or low level of family vi-

[36]Jill E. Korbin, "Introduction," in Jill E. Korbin, ed., *Child Abuse and Neglect: Cross-Cultural Perspectives* (Berkeley, CA: University of California, 1981), p. 4.

[37]Murray A. Straus, "Physical Violence in American Families: Incidence Rates, Causes, and Trends," in Dean D. Knudsen and JoAnn L. Miller, eds., *Abused and Battered: Social and Legal Responses to Family Violence* (New York: Aldine de Gruyter, 1991), pp. 17–34.

[38]Raoul Naroll, *The Moral Order: An Introduction to the Human Situation* (Beverly Hills, CA: Sage Publications, 1983), p. 247.

olence in one society as compared with others.[39] Perhaps for this reason researchers have dealt separately with different forms of family violence.

To avoid having to decide what is or is not abuse, many researchers focus their studies on variation in the frequencies of specific behaviors. For example, one can ask which societies have more physical punishment of children without calling physical punishment abusive. We turn first to research on variation in the treatment of children.

Cross-culturally, many societies practice and allow infanticide. Frequent reasons for infanticide include illegitimacy, deformity of the infant, twins, too many children, or that the infant is unwanted. Infanticide is usually performed by the mother, but this does not mean that she is uncaring; it may mean that she cannot adequately feed or care for the infant or that it has a poor chance to survive. The reasons for infanticide are quite similar to those given for abortion. Therefore, it seems that infanticide may be performed when abortion does not work or when unexpected qualities of the infant (for example, deformity) force the mother to reevaluate her ability to raise the child.[40]

Physical punishment of children occurs in over 70 percent of the world's societies. However, even though children are sometimes punished physically in most societies, this does not mean that most societies use physical punishment regularly.[41] But why is physical punishment used in some societies and not others? Some studies suggest that physical punishment is more likely whenever the mother is virtually the only caretaker for the child. Physical punishment is unlikely to be used when there are other caretakers, who may relieve the mother of some of the stresses associated with child care.[42] In addition, societies that are more complex economically and politically tend to rely much more on physical punishment than simpler societies. Why this is so is not yet clear. One suggestion is that complex societies are hierarchical and tend to insist on complying with orders; they may use physical punishment in child rearing to ensure that children learn to comply.[43]

In the United States, both wives and husbands are equally likely to assault the other. Wife battering in the United States is considered a more serious social problem because wives are much more likely to be seriously injured than husbands.[44] Cross-culturally, wife-beating is the most common form of family violence; it occurs at least occasionally in about 85 percent of the world's societies. In about half the societies, wife-beating is sometimes serious enough to cause permanent injury or death.[45]

It is often assumed that wife-beating will be common in societies in which males control economic and political resources. In a cross-cultural test of this assumption, David Levinson finds that not all indicators of male dominance predict wife beating, but many do. Specifically, wife-beating is more common when men control the products of family labor, when men have the final say in decision making in the home, when divorce is more difficult for women, when remarriage for a widow is controlled by the husband's kin, and when women do not have any female work groups.[46] Similarly, in the United States, the more one spouse in the family makes the decisions and has the power, the more physical violence occurs in the family (wife-beating is even more likely when the husband controls the household and is out of work).[47]

What can be done to minimize family violence? Many programs are designed to take abused children or wives away from the family situation or

[39]David Levinson, *Family Violence in Cross-Cultural Perspective* (Newbury Park, CA: Sage, 1989), pp. 11–12, 44.

[40]Leigh Minturn and Jerry Stashak, "Infanticide as a Terminal Abortion Procedure," *Behavior Science Research* 17(1982):70–85. Using a sociobiological orientation, a study by Martin Daly and Margo Wilson (*Homicide* [New York: Aldine de Gruyter, 1988], pp. 43–59) also suggests that infanticide is largely due to the difficulty of raising the infant successfully.

[41]Levinson, *Family Violence in Cross-Cultural Perspective*, pp. 26–28.

[42]R. H. Munroe and R. L. Munroe, "Household Structure and Socialization Practices," *Journal of Social Psychology*, 111 (1980): 293–94; and R. P. Rohner, *The Warmth Dimension* (Beverly Hills, CA: Sage, 1986), as referred to in Levinson, *Family Violence in Cross-Cultural Perspective*, pp. 54–55.

[43]L. R. Petersen, G. R. Lee, and G. J. Ellis, "Social Structure, Socialization Values, and Disciplinary Techniques: A Cross-Cultural Analysis," *Journal of Marriage and the Family*, 44 (1982): 131–42, as cited in Levinson, *Family Violence in Cross-Cultural Perspective*, p. 63.

[44]Straus, "Physical Violence in American Families," p. 17.

[45]Levinson, *Family Violence in Cross-Cultural Perspective*, p. 31.

[46]Ibid., p. 71.

[47]Richard J. Gelles and Murray A. Straus, *Intimate Violence* (New York: Simon and Schuster, 1988), pp. 78–88.

to punish the abuser. (Of course, in these situations the violence has already occurred and was serious enough to have been noticed.) Cross-culturally, at least with respect to wife-beating, intervention by others seems to be successful only if they intervene before violence gets serious. Ironically, however, those societies most prone to wife-beating are the least likely to practice immediate intervention. More helpful perhaps, but admittedly harder to arrange, is the promotion of conditions of life that are associated with low family violence. Judging by the research so far, promoting the equality of men and women and the sharing of childrearing responsibilities may go a long way toward lessening family violence.[48]

Crime

What is a crime in one society is not necessarily a crime in another. Just as it is difficult to decide what constitutes abuse, it is difficult to define crime. In one society, it may be a crime to walk over someone's land without permission; in another, there might not be any concept of personal ownership, and therefore no concept of trespassing. In seeking to understand variation in crime, it is not surprising that many researchers have preferred to compare those behaviors that are more or less universally considered crimes and that are reliably reported. For example, in a large-scale comparison of crime in 110 nations over a span of 70 years, Dane Archer and Rosemary Gartner concentrated on homicide rates. They argue that in contrast to other crimes, homicide is harder for the public to hide and for officials to ignore. Investigators have compared interviews about crime with police records; the comparison suggests that homicide is the most reliably reported crime in official records.[49]

Nations not only have very different crime rates when we compare them at a given point in time; the rates also vary over time within a nation. In the last 600 years, homicide rates have generally declined in Western societies. In England, where homicide rates are well documented for centuries,

the chance of murder during the thirteenth and fourteenth centuries was ten times higher than in England today. But beginning in the 1960s, homicide and other crime rates have surged upward in many Western countries.[50] Some of the lowest homicide rates around 1970 (the date for which we have some indicator for many nations) were found in Iran, Dahomey, Puerto Rico, New Zealand, Norway, England, and France. Some of the highest homicide rates were found in Iraq, Colombia, Mynamar (formerly Burma), Thailand, Swaziland, and Uganda. Compared with other countries, the United States had a fairly high homicide rate; approximately three-fourths of the countries surveyed had lower homicide rates than the United States.[51]

One of the clearest findings to emerge from comparative studies of crime is that war is associated with higher rates of crime. Archer and Gartner compared changes in homicide rates of nations before and after major wars. Whether a nation is defeated or victorious, homicide rates tend to increase following a war. This result is consistent with the idea that a society or nation legitimizes violence during wartime. During wartime societies approve of killing the enemy; afterward, homicide rates may go up because inhibitions against killing have been relaxed.[52] Ted Gurr suggests that the long-term downtrend in crime in Western societies seems to be consistent with an increasing emphasis on humanistic values and nonviolent achievement of goals. But such goals may be temporarily suspended during wartime. In the United States, for example, surges in violent crime rates occurred during the 1860s and 1870s (during and after the Civil War), after World War I, after World War II, and during the Vietnam War.[53]

In the types of societies that anthropologists typically study, crime statistics are not usually available; so cross-cultural studies of crime usually measure crime rates by comparing and rank-order-

[48]Levinson, *Family Violence in Cross-Cultural Perspective,* pp. 104–7.

[49]Dane Archer and Rosemary Gartner, *Violence and Crime in Cross-National Perspective* (New Haven: Yale University Press, 1984), p. 35.

[50]Ted Robert Gurr, "The History of Violent Crime in America: An Overview," in Ted Robert Gurr, ed. *Violence in America* (Newbury Park, CA: Sage, 1989), vol. I, *The History of Crime* pp. 11–12.

[51]The comparison described here is based on data we retrieved from the extensive Appendix in Archer in Gartner, *Violence and Crime in Cross-National Perspective.*

[52]Archer and Gartner, *Violence and Crime in Cross-National Perspective,* pp. 63–97.

[53]Ted Robert Gurr, "Historical Trends in Violent Crime: Europe and the United States," in Gurr, ed., *Violence in America,* vol. I, *The History of Crime,* pp. 47–48.

Burglary is a frequent crime in our society.

ing ethnographers' statements about crime frequencies. For example, the statement that murder is "practically unheard of" is taken to mean that the murder rate is lower than where it is reported that "homicide is not uncommon." Despite the fact that the data on cultural crime rates are not quantitative, the cross-cultural results are consistent with the cross-national results; more war is usually associated with more crime, as well as with socially approved aggressive behaviors (as in aggressive games) and severe physical punishment for wrongdoing.[54]

Capital punishment (execution of criminals) is severe physical punishment for wrongdoing. It is commonly thought that would-be murderers are deterred by the prospect of capital punishment. Yet recent cross-national research suggests otherwise. Instead of increasing after capital punishment is abolished, murder rates generally go down.[55] Why? Perhaps capital punishment, which is homicide committed by society, legitimizes violence just as war seems to do.

Research conducted in the United States suggests that juvenile delinquents (usually boys) are more likely to come from broken homes, with the father absent for much of the time the boy is growing up. The conclusion often drawn is that father absence somehow increases the likelihood of delinquency and adult forms of physical violence. However, other conditions that may cause delinquency are also associated with broken homes, conditions such as the stigma of not having a "regular" family and the generally low standard of living of such families. It is therefore important to conduct research in other societies, in which father absence does not occur in concert with these other factors, to see if father absence by itself is related to more physical violence.

For example, in many polygynous societies, children grow up in a "mother-child" household; the father lives separately and is hardly ever around the child. Does the "father absence" explanation of delinquency and violence fit such societies? The answer is apparently yes: societies in which children are reared in mother-child households or the father spends little time in child care tend to have more physical violence by males.[56]

More research is needed to discover exactly what accounts for this relationship. It is possible, as some suggest, that boys growing up without fathers are apt to act "super-masculine" to show how "male" they are. But it is also possible that mothers who rear children alone often use physical punishment, and therefore are likely to provide an aggressive role model for the child. Also, high male mortality in war predicts polygyny (as we saw in the chapter on marriage and family); therefore boys in polygynous societies are likely to be exposed to a warrior tradition.

However, trying to act "super-masculine" may be likely to involve violence *only* if aggression is an important component of the male gender role in society. If men were expected by society to be sensitive, caring, and non-violent, boys who grew up without fathers might try to be super-sensitive and super-caring. So society's expectations for males probably shape how growing up in a mother-child household affects behavior in adolescence and later.

[54]Elbert W. Russell, "Factors of Human Aggression," *Behavior Science Notes*, 7 (1972): 275–312; William Eckhardt, "Primitive Militarism," *Journal of Peace Research*, 12 (1975): 55–62; Richard G. Sipes, "War, Sports and Aggression: An Empirical Test of Two Rival Theories," *American Anthropologist*, 75 (1973): 64–86; Carol R. Ember and Melvin Ember (unpublished results of a cross-cultural study).

[55]Archer and Gartner, *Violence and Crime in Cross-National Perspective*, pp. 118–39.

[56]Margaret Bacon, Irvin L. Child, and Herbert Barry III, "A Cross-Cultural Study of Correlates of Crime," *Journal of Abnormal and Social Psychology*, 66 (1963): 291–300; Beatrice B. Whiting, "Sex Identity Conflict and Physical Violence," *American Anthropologist*, 67 (1965): 123–40.

Another possible explanation of high crime rates is that they result from economic factors, particularly poverty and unemployment, which may make people (particularly young males) more frustrated and presumably therefore more aggressive. But the hundreds of studies in this and other countries do not show a clear relationship between changes in economic well-being and changes in crime rates. Crime does not increase in bad times. Still, some recent research does suggest that crime rates may be high when people have lived with persistent poverty or when there is a high degree of income inequality.[57] Cross-culturally, theft (but not violent crime) tends to occur more often in societies that are socially stratified, which are likely to have inequalities of wealth and probably also persistent poverty for some. Ironically, socially stratified societies have formal law-making and punishing agencies. Since theft rates are usually higher in such societies, it is difficult to conclude that the punishment of theft deters it. Rather, people may try to punish more when crime rates are high, but their efforts may not reduce crime rates.

What does research suggest then about how we might be able to reduce crime? The results so far indicate that homicide rates are linked to war and other forms of socially approved violence (for example, capital punishment). The policy implication is that if we can reduce or eliminate war and other forms of socially approved aggression, we may thereby reduce rates of violent crime. The reduction of inequalities in wealth may also help to reduce crime, particularly theft. And although it is not yet clear why, it appears that raising boys with a male role model around may reduce the likelihood of male violence in adulthood.

War

War is an unfortunate fact of life in most societies known to anthropology, judging by the cross-cultural research we referred to in the chapter on political life. The vast majority of societies had at least occasional wars when they were first described, unless they had been pacified (usually by Western colonial powers). To discover the predictors (and possible causes) of war, therefore, we cannot compare societies with and without war to see how else they might differ. But we can ask why some societies have more frequent warfare than other societies. Answers to this question might suggest why people go to war in the first place, and how foreign policy could be modified to reduce the risk of war in the world.[58]

To be sure, there are differences between modern warfare and the types of warfare that we know from ethnographic descriptions. Just as the political organization of most societies known to anthropology was different from that of modern nation-states, so was their warfare different in scope and organization. Most societies (before pacification) had frequent armed combat between communities or larger units that usually spoke the same language. That is, most warfare was internal to the society or language group. (Even some wars in modern times involved speakers of the same language; recall the wars between Italian states before the unification of Italy, and many of the "civil" wars of the last two centuries.) Although people in some ethnographic societies might fight against people in other societies, such "external" wars were usually not organized in behalf of the entire society or even a major section of it. That is, warfare in the ethnographic record did not usually involve politically unified societies. Finally, the absolute numbers of people killed may have usually been small, but this does not mean that the warfare in preindustrial societies was a trivial matter. Indeed, it appears that preindustrial warfare may have been even more lethal *proportionately* than modern warfare, judging by the fact that wars killed 25 to 30 percent of the males in some preindustrial societies.[59]

Despite these differences between ethnographic and modern war, the causes of war might

[57]Colin Loftin, David McDowall, and James Boudouris, "Economic Change and Homicide in Detroit, 1926–1979," in Gurr, ed., *Violence in America*, vol. I, *The History of Crime*, pp. 163–77; and H. Krahn, T. F. Hartnagel, and J. W. Gartrell, "Income Inequality and Homicide Rates: Cross-National Data and Criminological Theories," *Criminology*, 24 (1986): 269–95, as referred to in Daly and Wilson, *Homicide*, pp. 287–88.

[58]Most of the discussion in this section comes from Melvin Ember and Carol R. Ember, "Cross-Cultural Studies of War and Peace: Recent Achievements and Future Possibilities," in S.P. Reyna and R.E. Downs, eds., *Studying War: Anthropological Perspectives* (New York: Gordon and Breach, 1992), in press.
[59]Mervyn Meggitt, *Blood Is Their Argument: Warfare among the Mae Enga Tribesmen of the New Guinea Highlands* (Palo Alto, CA: Mayfield, 1977), p. 201.

A hydrogen bomb was detonated at Bikini Atoll in the Pacific in May 1956; note the ship in the foreground miles away from the blast.

generally be the same. Why then do people in pre-industrial societies go to war?

As we noted in the chapter on political life, the theory suggested by the available evidence is that people in preindustrial societies may mostly go to war out of fear—particularly a fear of expectable but unpredictable natural disasters (droughts, floods, hurricanes, among others) that destroy food supplies. People with more of a history of such disasters have more war. And it looks like they go to war to protect themselves ahead of time from disasters, inasmuch as the victors in war almost always take resources (land, animals, other things) from the defeated, even when the victors have no current resource problems.

People who go to war frequently are also likely to fear others, judging by the fact that they teach their children to mistrust others. People who grow up to be mistrustful of others may be more likely to

go to war than to negotiate or seek conciliation with "enemies." Mistrust or fear of others seems to be partially caused by threat or fear of disasters.[60]

Is warfare in and between modern state societies explainable in much the same way that preindustrial warfare seems to be explainable? If the answer to this question turns out to be yes, it will certainly be a modified yes, since the realities of industrialized societies require an expanded conception of disasters. In the modern world, with its complex economic and political dependencies between nations, we may not be worried only about weather or pest disasters that could curtail food supplies; possible curtailments of other resources—particularly oil—may also scare us into going to war. According to some commentators, the decision to go to war against Iraq after it invaded Kuwait in 1991 fits the theory of war described here.

However, even if the "threat to resources" theory is generally true, we may be coming to realize (with the end of the "Cold War") that war is not the only way to ensure access to resources. There may be a better way in the modern world, a way that is more cost-effective as well as more preserving of human life.

If it is true that war is more likely when people fear unpredictable disasters of any kind, the risk of war should lessen when people realize that the harmful effects of disasters could be reduced or prevented by international cooperation. Just as we have the assurance of disaster relief within our country, we could have the assurance of disaster relief worldwide. That is, the fear of unpredictable disasters and the fear of others (and the consequent risk of war) could be reduced by the assurance ahead of time that the world would help those in need in case of disaster. Instead of going to war out of fear, we could go to peace by agreeing to share more. The certainty of international cooperation could compensate for the uncertainty of resources.

Consider how Germany and Japan have fared in the nearly 50 years since their "unconditional surrender" in World War II. They were forbidden to participate in the international arms race, and could rely on others (particularly the United

[60]For the cross-cultural results suggesting the theory of war described here, see Carol R. Ember and Melvin Ember, "Resource Unpredictability, Mistrust, and War: A Cross-Cultural Study," *Journal of Conflict Resolution*, 36 (1992): 242–62.

States) to protect them. Without a huge burden of armaments, Germany and Japan thrived. But those countries that competed militarily, particularly the United States and the Soviet Union, declined economically. Doesn't that suggest the wisdom of international cooperation, particularly the need for international agreements to assure worldwide disaster relief? Compared with going to war and its enormous costs, going to peace would be a bargain!

Recent research in political science and anthropology suggests an additional way to reduce the risk of war in the world. A number of studies indicate that people in more participatory (more "democratic") political systems rarely go to war with each other, in the ethnographic record just as among modern nation-states.[61] Thus, if authoritarian governments were to disappear from the world, because the powerful nations of the world stopped supporting them militarily and otherwise, the world could be more peaceful for this reason too.

Although democratically governed states rarely go to war with each other, this does not mean that democracies are more peaceful in general. On the contrary, they are as likely to go to war as other kinds of political systems, but not so much with each other. (The United States has gone to war recently with Grenada, Panama, and Iraq—all authoritarian states—but not with Canada and Mexico, with which the U.S. has also had disputes.) The theory suggested by the cross-national and cross-cultural results is that "democratic" conflict-resolution within a political system generalizes to "democratic" conflict-resolution between political systems (if the others are also "democratic"). If our participatory institutions and perceptions allow us to resolve our disputes peacefully, internally and externally, we may think that similarly governed people would also be disposed to settle things peacefully. Therefore, disputes between participatory political systems should be unlikely to result in war.

The understanding that participatory systems rarely fight each other, and why, would have im-portant consequences for policy in the contemporary world. It might affect the kinds of military preparations believed necessary, and the costs people would be willing to pay for them. On the one hand, understanding the relationship beween democracy and peace might encourage war-making against authoritarian regimes to overturn them— with enormous costs in human life and otherwise. On the other hand, understanding the consequences of democracy might encourage us to assist the emergence and consolidation of more participatory systems of government in the countries of eastern Europe, the former Soviet Union, and elsewhere. In any case, the relationship between democracy and peace strongly suggests that it is counterproductive to support any undemocratic regimes, even if they happen to be enemies of our enemies, if we want to minimize the risk of war in the world.

It may be realistic, not just idealistic, to think that the more people understand the peaceful effect of democracy, and the more they are assured of worldwide disaster relief, the more they might go to peace!

Making the World Better

There are many social problems afflicting our world, not just the ones discussed in this chapter. We don't have the space to discuss the international trade in drugs and how it plays out in violence, death, and corruption. We haven't discussed the negative effects of environmental degradation (water and air pollution, global warming, ozone depletion, destruction of forests and wetlands). We haven't said anything about overpopulation, the energy crisis, and a host of other problems we should care and do something about, if we hope to make this a better world. What we have tried to do in this chapter is suggest how the results of scientific research may imply solutions to some global social problems.

We may know enough now that we can do something about our problems. And we will discover more on the basis of future research. Social problems are of human making and susceptible to human unmaking. They are not like the weather, just something to talk about. And even the weather might be fixable one day, if we put our minds to it.

[61]For the results on political participation and peace in the ethnographic record, see Carol R. Ember, Melvin Ember, and Bruce Russett, "Peace between Participatory Polities: A Cross-Cultural Test of the Democracies Rarely Fight Each Other' Hypothesis," *World Politics,* 44(1992):573–99. For the results on political participation and peace in the modern world, see the references in that essay.

We can make the world better, if we want to.

SUMMARY

1. We may be more motivated now to try to solve social problems because worldwide communication has increased our awareness of them elsewhere, because we seem to be increasingly bothered by problems in our own society, and because we know more than we used to about various social problems that afflict our world.

2. Applied anthropology in the United States developed out of anthropologists' personal experiences with disadvantaged peoples. Applied or practicing anthropologists may be involved in one or more phases of a program that are designed to change peoples' lives: assembling relevant knowledge, constructing alternative plans, assessing the likely social and environmental impact of particular plans, implementing the program, and monitoring the program and its effects.

3. Today a large number of anthropologists are finding employment outside of anthropology departments—in medical schools, health centers, development agencies, urban planning agencies,

and other public and private organizations, in this society and others.

4. The code of ethics for those who work professionally as applied anthropologists specifies that the target population should be included as much as possible in the formulation of policy, so that people in the community may know in advance how the program may affect them. But perhaps the most important aspect of the code is the pledge not to be involved in any plan whose effect will not be beneficial. It is often difficult to evaluate the effects of planned changes. Long-term consequences may be detrimental even if the changes are beneficial in the short run.

5. The idea that we can solve social problems is based on two assumptions. We have to assume that it is possible to discover the causes of a problem. And we have to assume that we may be able to do something about the causes (once they are discovered) and thereby eliminate or reduce the problem.

6. Until medical science develops an effective and inexpensive vaccine (or treatment) for AIDS, the risk of infection can be reduced only by changes in social (particularly sexual) behavior.

7. Disasters such as earthquakes, floods, and droughts can have greater or lesser effects on human life, depending on social conditions. Therefore disasters are partly social problems, with partly social causes and solutions.

8. Whether or not people become "homeless," whether or not there are shantytowns, seems to depend on a society's willingness to share wealth and help those in need.

9. Promoting the equality of men and women and the sharing of childrearing responsibilities may reduce family violence.

10. If we can reduce or eliminate war and other forms of socially approved aggression, we may be able to reduce rates of violent crime. The reduction of inequalities in wealth may help to reduce crime, particularly theft. Raising boys with a male role model around may reduce the likelihood of male violence in adulthood.

11. People seem to be more likely to go to war when they fear unpredictable disasters that destroy food supplies or curtail the supplies of other necessities. Disputes between more participatory (more "democratic") political systems are unlikely to result in war. Therefore, the more democracy spreads in the world, and the more people all over the world are assured of internationally organized disaster relief, the more they might go to peace rather than to war to solve their problems.

SUGGESTED READING

APTEKAR, L. *Environmental Disasters in Global Perspective.* New York: G. K. Hall/Macmillan, in press. This volume discusses various kinds of environmental disaster. It is one of a series of monographs, sponsored by the Human Relations Area Files, on the current state of cross-cultural and cross-national research on social problems around the world.

ARCHER, D., AND GARTNER, R. *Violence and Crime in Cross-National Perspective.* New Haven: Yale University Press, 1984. The analyses and comparisons presented in this volume are based on recorded patterns of crime and violence in 110 nations and 44 major cities, covering the period from about 1900 to 1970.

BODLEY, J. H. *Anthropology and Contemporary Human Problems.* 2nd ed. Mountain View, CA: Mayfield, 1985. This book discusses the problems of overconsumption, adaptation to environment, resource depletion, hunger and starvation, overpopulation, violence, and war.

EDDY, E. M., AND PARTRIDGE, W., eds. *Applied Anthropology in America.* 2nd ed. New York: Columbia University Press, 1987. A set of essays about the relevance of applied anthropology in American society. Provides an overview of how anthropology has contributed and can contribute to major policy issues confronting our nation.

LEVINSON, D. *Family Violence in Cross-Cultural Perspective.* Newbury Park, CA: Sage, 1989. This book describes and tests theories that may explain the various forms and frequencies of family violence in societies around the world. Implications for the prevention of violence are also discussed.

VAN WILLIGEN, J. *Applied Anthropology: An Introduction.* South Hadley, MA: Bergin & Garvey, 1986. An introduction to the use of anthropology to solve human problems. The first part considers the history of applied anthropology and ethical issues. The second part describes different intervention techniques. The third part discusses anthropologists' roles in helping to set and evaluate policy.

VAN WILLIGEN, J., RYLKO-BAUER, B., AND McELROY, A. *Making Our Research Useful: Case Studies in the Utilization of Anthropological Knowledge.* Boulder, CO: Westview Press, 1989. The contributors to this volume were asked to write case studies describing projects in which they were involved. The major question addressed is how to increase the use of knowledge gained in applied research projects.

Epilogue

The Effect of the Modern World on Anthropology

In many respects, the world of today is a shrinking one. It is not, of course, physically shrinking, but it is shrinking in the sense that it takes a shorter time to travel around it and an even shorter time to communicate around it—witness the worldwide network of TV satellites. Today it is possible to fly halfway around the globe in the time it took preindustrial humans to visit a nearby town. Newspapers, radio, television, and movies have done much to make different cultures more familiar and accessible to one another.

The world is shrinking culturally too, in the sense that more people are drawn each year into the world market economy, buying and selling similar things and, as a consequence, altering the patterns of their lives. Perhaps the most obvious illustration of what is happening to the world culturally is the appearance of Coca-Cola, razor blades, steel tools, and even drive-in movies in places that not too long ago lacked such things. But the diffusion of these items is only a small part of the picture. More important than the spread of material goods has been the introduction of selling and buying and wage labor. The diffusion of market exchange throughout the world reflects the expansion of certain nations' spheres of influence over the last centuries. In some places as a result of colonization or conquest, in others as a result of economic and military-aid programs, and in still others because of a desire to emulate dominant cultures (North American, British, Japanese, and so on), the hundreds of different cultures that survive in the world have become more similar over the last hundred years.

Aside from whether or not these changes are desirable, from our point of view or from the point of view of the peoples experiencing them, we might ask how the shrinking cultural world affects the field of anthropology, particularly, of course, cultural anthropology.

Some cultural anthropologists have worried about the possible demise of their discipline because of the virtual disappearance of the "primitive" or noncommercial world, which in the past "provided the discipline with most of its data as well as the major inspiration for its key concepts and theoretical ideas."[1] Some of the societies known to ethnography have disappeared because of depopulation produced by the introduction of foreign infectious diseases. Others have been so altered by contact with dominant societies that their cultures now retain few of the characteristics that made them unique. To be sure, there are still some cultures in the world (in the interior of New

[1] David Kaplan and Robert A. Manners, "Anthropology: Some Old Themes and New Directions," *Southwestern Journal of Anthropology,* 27 (1971): 71.

489

Guinea and a few other large Melanesian islands, and in the back areas of Brazil, Peru, and Venezuela) that have not yet drastically changed. But most of these have changed somewhat, largely under the impact of commercialization, and they will probably continue to change.

Some of those who are worried about the future of cultural anthropology foresee the disappearance of their discipline because it has traditionally focused on cultural variation, and that variation is diminishing. Cultural anthropology, for these people, is synonymous with the ethnographic study of exotic, out-of-the-way cultures not previously described. Nowadays it is difficult to find cultures that have been preserved in such an undescribed and unaltered state. Thus, it is said, we are running out of subject matter because we are running out of new cultures to describe. Some of the more pessimistic cultural anthropologists envision a time when the last ethnography has been written and the last native has been handed a bottle of Coca-Cola, and the death knell rings upon cultural anthropology as a discipline. Evidence suggests, however, that such a view may be mistaken.

There is no reason to believe that cultural variation, of at least some sort, will ever disappear. The development of commonly held ideas, beliefs, and behaviors—in other words, culture—depends on the existence of groups of people relatively separate from one another. After all, most people in their daily lives are isolated from individuals at the opposite ends of the earth, or even down the road, and inasmuch as this continues to be so, they will invariably develop some cultural differences. Although it may be that modern techniques of transportation and communication facilitate the rapid spread of cultural characteristics to all parts of the globe, thus diminishing variability, it is unlikely that all parts will become alike. Although a native of Melanesia and a native of the United States may hear the same song on the same kind of transistor radio, this does not mean that their cultures will not retain some of their original characteristics or develop some distinctive adaptations. People in different parts of the world are confronted with different physical and social environments, and hence the chances are that some aspects of their cultures will always be different, assuming that cultures generally consist of common responses adapted to particular environmental requirements.

And although cultural variability has undoubtedly decreased recently, it may also be true that much of what we see in the way of variation depends on which groups we choose to look at and when we look at them. If we move our perspective back in time, we may find (and justifiably, it seems, on the basis of present evidence) that there was less variability in the Lower Paleolithic—when humans depended solely on hunting and gathering—than in the beginning of the Neolithic, 10,000 years ago. In some areas of the world 10,000 years ago, a relatively small number of people had begun to depend on agriculture and domesticated animals; in other areas, people depended on sedentary food collection; and in still other areas (indeed most areas of the world at that time), people still depended on nomadic food collecting. With the spread of agriculture around the world, cultural variability may again have decreased.

We might expect, then, that whenever a generally adaptive cultural pattern develops and spreads over the globe, cultural variability decreases, at least for a time. Hence, with the recent spread of commercial exchange, and, even more significant, with the ongoing diffusion of industrial culture, we may be witnessing a temporary diminution of cultural variability as humanity experiences another great cultural change. But there is no reason to believe that further and differential cultural change, stemming from varying physical and social environmental requirements, will not occur in different parts of the world.

In short, it does not seem likely that cultural anthropology, the study of cultural variation, will ever run out of variability to study. The same thing can be said for physical anthropology, archeology, and linguistics. With respect to physical anthropology, there is no reason to expect variation in biological characteristics among human populations to disappear, as long as physical and social environments continue to vary. It will be a long time before the whole of humankind lives under identical environmental conditions, in one great "greenhouse." Moreover, we will always be able to explore and study that great depository of human variability—the fossil—as well as more recent human biological records. Similarly, archeologists will always have the remains of past cultures to study and explain. With respect to linguistics, even if all linguistic variation disappears from the earth, we will always have the descriptive data on past languages to study, with all the variability in those records still to be explained.

Yet, a larger question remains. Why should we study simpler cultures at all, either those that exist today or those that have existed in the past? What conceivable bearing could such studies have on the problems that beset us as we approach the end of the twentieth century? To answer this question we must remind ourselves that humans, whatever culture they may belong to, are still human, and that as a species they share certain significant needs and characteristics. If we are to discover laws that account for the constants and variables in human behavior, all cultures past and present must be recognized as being equally important. As Claude Lévi-Strauss has said,

the thousands of societies that exist today, or once existed on the surface of the earth, constitute so many experiments, the only ones we can make use of to formulate and test our hypotheses, since we can't very well construct or repeat them in the laboratory as physical and natural scientists do. These experiments, represented by societies unlike our own, described and analyzed by anthropologists, provide one of the surest ways to understand what happens in the human mind and how it operates. That's what anthropology is good for in the most general way and what we can expect from it in the long run.[2]

New Directions in Cultural Anthropology

As we have seen, cultural anthropologists have in the past focused mainly on the cultures of the noncommercial world. Now that most of these cultures have either disappeared or been drastically changed, anthropologists are turning to societies more in the mainstream of technological and economic development. Such societies (the nations of Europe and Asia or the developing countries of the Third World) have formerly been studied by other disciplines, such as economics and political science. Now anthropologists have begun to use some of the techniques developed in the study of simpler cultures to study more complex ones, including our own. Urban anthropology, for example, a recent

[2]Quoted in *The New York Times*, January 21, 1972, p. 41.

branch of cultural anthropology that is very much a part of this trend, focuses on the cultural adjustments of people who have come to live in cities—the major places that have drawn migrants from inside and outside societies in recent years.

In addition to the new focus on urban and complex societies, cultural anthropologists have become interested in aspects of culture that ethnographers have previously neglected. For example, many anthropologists have begun to study unconscious cultural patterns—all those mental and physical habits that are shared by members of a culture but manifest themselves below the level of conscious awareness. How people position themselves in various situations, how they sit, what they do with their arms and legs, whether they avoid or seek eye contact while speaking—all are aspects of this emerging field of study. The new interest in unconscious cultural patterns also involves an interest in the different ways in which people perceive, order, and describe the world around them. (This interest is the main focus of cognitive and symbolic anthropology.) Most of these new investigations of unconscious cultural patterning are still essentially descriptive in orientation. Their intent is to find out *how* unconscious patterns vary, not so much yet *why* they vary. However, even the relatively few studies that have been done so far reveal fascinating similarities and differences in human behavior, which though not yet explainable in terms of tested and validated theory are nonetheless extremely suggestive and promise much interesting work to come.

There is also a lot of research now on topics that transcend the traditional boundaries of cultural anthropology and may embrace concerns of other anthropological subdisciplines as well as other sciences. For example, nutritional anthropologists investigate questions about food and how it varies from culture to culture; and medical anthropologists are concerned with cultural variation in health and the delivery of medical care. In addition, there are anthropologists interested in social problems such as drug abuse, family violence, poverty, and homelessness. These interests, like others mentioned and not mentioned in this paragraph, show that cultural anthropology is growing and alive and relevant to the modern world.

Finally, to discover possible causal explanations for variable cultural characteristics, cultural anthropologists and other social scientists are conducting more and more comparative studies that make use of the descriptive data collected by anthropologists. Just as we have the fossil and archeological records, we now have an enormous body of ethnographic data on different peoples past and present that will never disappear. There are many questions to be asked—and possibly many answers that can be gained—from the data we already have. The challenge of uncovering more definitive answers to how and why populations vary—in the past, present, and future—will always be with us.

Glossary

Absolute Dating Method see **Chronometric Dating Method.**

Acculturation the process of extensive borrowing of aspects of culture in the context of superordinate-subordinate relations between societies; usually occurs as the result of external pressure.

Acheulian a toolmaking tradition, generally associated with *Homo erectus,* characterized by large cutting instruments such as hand axes and cleavers.

Achieved Qualities those qualities a person acquires during his or her lifetime.

Aegyptopithecus a propliopithecid found in the Fayum area of Egypt.

Aerobic Work Capacity the degree to which oxygen can be taken in to fuel exercise.

Affinal Kin one's relatives by marriage.

Age-Grade a category of persons who happen to fall within a particular, culturally distinguished age range.

Age-Set a group of persons of similar age and the same sex who move together through some or all of life's stages.

Allele one member of a pair of genes.

Allen's Rule the rule that protruding body parts (particularly arms and legs) are relatively shorter in the cooler areas of a species' range than in the warmer areas.

Ambilineal Descent the rule of descent that affiliates an individual with groups of kin related to him or her through men *or* women.

Amok a mental disorder that occurs in Malaya, Indonesia, and New Guinea, in which the afflicted person becomes depressed and withdrawn and finally goes berserk.

Amphipithecus the oldest primate thought by some paleontologists to be an anthropoid.

Ancestor Spirits supernatural beings who are the ghosts of dead relatives.

Animatism a belief in supernatural forces.

Animism a term used by Edward Tylor to describe a belief in a dual existence for all things—a physical, visible body and a psychic, invisible soul.

Anthropoids one of the two suborders of primates; includes monkeys, apes, and humans.

Anthropological Linguistics the anthropological study of languages.

Anthropology the study of differences and similarities, both biological and cultural, in human populations. Anthropology is concerned with typical biological and cultural characteristics of human populations in all periods and in all parts of the world.

Apidium a parapithecid found in the Fayum area of Egypt.

Applied Anthropology the branch of anthropology that concerns itself with trying to improve

493

people's lives or monitoring others' efforts to do so.

Arboreal adapted to living in trees.

Archeology the study of prehistoric and historic cultures through the analysis of material remains.

Ascribed Qualities those qualities that are determined for a person at birth.

Association an organized group not based exclusively on kinship or territory.

Atlatl Aztec word for "spear-thrower."

Australopithecus genus of Pliocene and Pleistocene hominids.

Australopithecus afarensis a possible species of *Australopithecus* that lived 4 to 3 million years ago in East Africa.

Australopithecus africanus erect bipedal hominid that lived during the late Pliocene through the early Pleistocene; dentally similar to modern humans, had a rounded brain case with a cranial capacity of 450 cc, and weighed between fifty and seventy pounds.

Australopithecus boisei an East African species of *Australopithecus* similar to *A. robustus*.

Australopithecus robustus fossil hominid similar to *A. africanus*, but larger, with a body weight of 100 to 150 pounds; also called *Paranthropus*.

Avunculocal Residence a pattern of residence in which a married couple settles with or near the husband's mother's brother.

Balanced Reciprocity giving with the expectation of a straightforward immediate or limited-time trade.

Band a fairly small, usually nomadic local group, which is politically autonomous.

Behavioral Ecology the study of how all kinds of behavior may relate to the environment.

Berdache a male transvestite in some Native North American societies.

Bergmann's Rule the rule that smaller-sized subpopulations of a species inhabit the warmer parts of its geographical range and larger-sized subpopulations the cooler areas.

Bifacial Tool a tool worked or flaked on two sides.

Bilateral Kinship the type of kinship system in which individuals affiliate more or less equally with their mother's and father's relatives; descent groups are absent.

Bilocal Residence a pattern of residence in which a married couple lives with or near either the husband's parents or the wife's parents.

Bipedalism locomotion in which an animal walks on its two hind legs.

Blade a thin flake whose length is usually more than twice its width. In the blade technique of toolmaking, a core is prepared by shaping a piece of flint with hammerstones into a pyramidal or cylindrical form. Blades are then struck off until the core is used up.

Brachiation arboreal locomotion in which the animal swings from branch to branch, its weight suspended by its hands and arms.

Brachiators an animal that moves by brachiation is called a brachiator.

Bride Price (Bride Wealth) a substantial gift of goods or money given to the bride's kin by the groom or his kin at or before the marriage.

Bride Service work performed by the groom for his bride's family for a varying length of time either before or after the marriage.

Burin a chisellike stone tool used for carving and for making such artifacts as bone and antler needles, awls, and projectile points.

Canines the cone-shaped teeth immediately behind the incisors; used in most primates to seize food and in fighting and display.

Carbon^{14} (^{14}C) a radioactive isotope of carbon used to date organic material; see **Radiocarbon (^{14}C) Dating.**

Cash Crop a cultivated commodity raised for sale rather than for personal consumption by the cultivator.

Caste a ranked group, often associated with a certain occupation, in which membership is determined at birth and marriage is restricted to members of one's own caste.

Catarrhines the group of anthropoids with downward-facing noses, including Old World monkeys, apes, and humans.

Catastrophism the theory that extinct life forms were destroyed by cataclysms and upheavals and replaced by new divine creations.

Cercopithecoids Old World monkeys.

Cerebral Cortex the "gray matter" of the brain; the center of speech and other higher mental activities.

Chief a person who exercises authority, usually on behalf of a multicommunity political unit. This role is generally found in rank societies and is usually permanent and often hereditary.

Chiefdom a political unit, with a chief at its head, integrating more than one community but not necessarily the whole society or language group.

Chromosomes paired rod-shaped structures within a cell nucleus containing the genes that transmit traits from one generation to the next.

Chronometric Dating Method a method of dating fossils in which the actual age of a deposit or specimen is measured; also known as an *absolute dating method*.

Civilization urban society, from the Latin word for "city-state."

Clan (Sib) a set of kin whose members believe themselves to be descended from a common ancestor or ancestress but cannot specify the links back to that founder; often designated by a totem.

Class a category of persons who have about the same opportunity to obtain economic resources, power, and prestige.

Class/Caste Society a society containing social groups that have unequal access to economic resources, power, and prestige.

Classificatory Terms kinship terms that merge or equate relatives who are genealogically distinct from one another; the same term is used for a number of different kin.

Cloning the exact reproduction of an individual from cellular tissue.

Cognates words or morphs that belong to different languages but have similar sounds and meanings.

Commercial Exchange see **Market or Commercial Exchange.**

Complementary Opposition the occasional uniting of various segments of a segmentary lineage system in opposition to similar segments.

Consanguineal Kin one's biological relatives; relatives by birth.

Continental-Drift Theory the theory that the major continental land masses were not originally separated as they are today, but instead formed a single large supercontinent surrounded by seas. It is thought that in recent geological times, the supercontinent broke up and the continents drifted apart into the configuration they have today.

Core Vocabulary nonspecialist vocabulary.

Corvée a system of required labor.

Cretaceous geologic epoch 135 to 65 million years ago, during which dinosaurs and other reptiles ceased to be the dominant land vertebrates and mammals and birds began to become important.

Crime violence not considered legitimate that occurs within a political unit.

Cro-Magnons early *Homo sapiens sapiens* who lived in western Europe about 35,000 years ago; differed from Neandertals in their higher foreheads, thinner and lighter bones, smaller faces and jaws, protuberant chins, and slight or nonexistent bony ridges on the skull.

Cross-Cousins children of siblings of the opposite sex. One's cross-cousins are father's sisters' children and mother's brothers' children.

Cross-Cultural Researcher an ethnologist who uses ethnographic data about many societies to test possible explanations of cultural variation.

Crossing-Over exchanges of sections of chromosomes from one chromosome to another.

Cultural Anthropology the study of cultural variation and universals.

Cultural Ecology the analysis of the relationship between a culture and its environment.

Cultural Relativism the attitude that a society's customs and ideas should be viewed within the context of that society's problems and opportunities.

Culture the set of learned behaviors, beliefs, attitudes, values, or ideals that are characteristic of a particular society or population.

Cuneiform wedge-shaped writing invented by the Sumerians around 3000 B.C.

Descriptive Linguistics see **Structural Linguistics.**

Descriptive Terms kinship terms used to refer to genealogically distinct relatives; a different term is used for each relative.

Dialect a variety of a language spoken in a particular area or by a particular social group.

Diffusion the borrowing by one society of a cultural trait belonging to another society as the result of contact between the two societies.

Diurnal active during the day.

Divination getting the supernatural to provide guidance.

DNA deoxyribonucleic acid; a long, two-stranded molecule in the genes that directs the making of an organism according to the instructions in its genetic code.

Domestication the cultivation or raising of plants and animals that are different from wild varieties.

Dominant the allele of a gene pair that is always phenotypically expressed in the heterozygous form.

Double Descent (Double Unilineal Descent) a system that affiliates an individual with a group of matrilineal kin for some purposes, and with a group of patrilineal kin for other purposes.

Dowry a substantial transfer of goods or money from the bride's family to the bride.

Dryopithecus genus of Miocene fossil apes that inhabited Africa and Eurasia, and of which several species are known.

Egalitarian Society a society in which all persons of a given age-sex category have equal access to economic resources, power, and prestige.

Ego in the reckoning of kinship, the reference point or focal person.

Endogamy the rule specifying marriage to a person within one's own (kin, caste, community) group.

Eocene a geologic epoch 54 to 38 million years ago.

Epicanthic Fold a bit of skin overlapping the eyelid.

Estrus period of ovulation or sexual receptivity in females of many species; in Old World monkeys, signaled by reddening and swelling of the sexual skin.

Ethnocentrism the attitude that other societies' customs and ideas can be judged in the context of one's own culture.

Ethnographer a person who spends some time living with, interviewing, and observing a group of people so that he or she can describe their customs.

Ethnographic Analogy inferring how a particular tool was used in the past by observing how the tool is used by members of contemporary societies, preferably societies with subsistence activities and environments similar to those of the ancient toolmakers.

Ethnography a description of a society's customary behaviors, beliefs, and attitudes.

Ethnohistorian an ethnologist who uses historical documents to study how a particular culture has changed over time.

Ethnolinguists anthropologists who study the relationships between language and culture.

Ethnology the study of how and why recent cultures differ and are similar.

Ethnoscience an approach that attempts to derive rules of thought from the logical analysis of ethnographic data.

Exogamy the rule specifying marriage to a person from outside one's own (kin or community) group.

Explanation an answer to a *why* question.

Expressive Culture activities such as art, music, dance, and folklore, which presumably express thoughts and feelings.

Extended Family a family consisting of two or more single-parent, monogamous, polygynous, or polyandrous families linked by a blood tie.

Extensive (Shifting) Cultivation a type of horticulture in which the land is worked for short periods and then left to regenerate for some years before being used again.

Falsification showing that a theory seems to be wrong by finding that implications or predictions derivable from it are not consistent with objectively collected data.

Family a social and economic unit consisting minimally of a parent and children.

Feuding a state of recurring hostility between families or groups of kin, usually motivated by a desire to avenge an offense against a member of the group.

Fission-Track Dating a chronometric dating method used to date crystal, glass, and many uranium-rich materials contemporaneous with fossils or deposits that are from 20 years to 5 billion years old. This dating method entails counting the tracks or paths of decaying uranium-isotope atoms in the sample, and then comparing the number of tracks with the uranium content of the sample.

Folklore all the lore (myths, legends, folktales, ballads, riddles, proverbs, and superstitions) of a culture; generally orally transmitted, but may also be written.

Food Collection all forms of subsistence technology in which food-getting is dependent on naturally occurring resources—wild plants and animals.

Food Production the form of subsistence technology in which food-getting is dependent on the cultivation and domestication of plants and animals.

Foramen Magnum hole in the base of the skull through which the spinal cord passes en route to the brain.

Fossil the hardened remains or impressions of plants and animals that lived in the past.

Founder Effect a form of genetic drift that occurs when a small population recently derived from a larger one expands while in relative isolation. Because the founders of the new population carry only a small sample of the gene pool of the original population, the gene frequencies of the two populations may differ.

Fraternal Polyandry the marriage of a woman to two or more brothers at one time.

Functionalism the theoretical orientation that assumes that all culture traits serve some useful function in the society in which they occur.

F–U–N Trio fluorine (F), uranium (U), and nitrogen (N) tests for relative dating. All three minerals are present in groundwater. The older a fossil is, the higher its fluorine or uranium content will be, and the lower its nitrogen content.

Gender Differences differences between females and males that reflect cultural expectations and experiences.

Gene chemical unit of heredity.

Gene Flow the process by which genes pass from the gene pool of one population to that of another through mating and reproduction.

Gene Pool all the genes possessed by the members of a given population.

General Evolution the notion that higher forms of culture arise from and generally supersede lower forms.

Generalized Reciprocity gift giving without any immediate or planned return.

General-Purpose Money a universally accepted medium of exchange.

Genetic Drift the various random processes that affect gene frequencies in small, relatively isolated populations.

Genitor one's biological father.

Genotype the total complement of inherited traits or genes of an organism.

Genus a group of related species; *pl.* genera.

Geographical Race a set of at least once-neighboring populations that has certain distinctive trait frequencies.

Ghosts supernatural beings who were once human; the souls of dead people.

Gigantopithecus a genus of Miocene apes.

Gloger's Rule the rule that populations of birds and mammals living in warm, humid climates have more melanin (and therefore darker skin, fur, or feathers) than populations of the same species living in cooler, drier areas.

Gods supernatural beings of nonhuman origin who are named personalities; often anthropomorphic.

Group Marriage marriage in which more than one man is married to more than one woman at the same time; not customary in any known human society.

Group Selection natural selection of group characteristics.

Half-Life the time it takes half of the atoms of a radioactive substance to decay into new atoms.

Headman a person who holds a powerless but symbolically unifying position in a community within an egalitarian society; may exercise influence but has no power to impose sanctions.

Heterosis the production of healthier and more numerous offspring as a result of matings between individuals with different genetic characteristics; also known as *hybrid vigor.*

Heterozygous possessing differing genes or alleles in corresponding locations on a pair of chromosomes.

Hieroglyphics "picture writing," as in ancient Egypt and in Mayan sites in Mesoamerica.

Historical Archeology a specialty within archeology that studies the remains of recent peoples who left written records.

Historical Linguistics the study of how languages change over time.

Holistic having many aspects; multifaceted.

Hominids the group of hominoids consisting of humans and their direct ancestors. It contains at least two genera: *Homo* and *Australopithecus*.

Hominoids the group of catarrhines that includes both apes and humans.

Homo genus to which modern humans and their ancestors belong.

Homo erectus a species of early humans that lived in Africa, Europe, and Asia after about 1.5 million years ago; cranial capacity of 1,000 cc; associated with the Acheulian tool tradition and the first use of fire by humans.

Homo habilis designation for the skeletal remains of several hominids found at Olduvai Gorge (Tanzania) and dating from about 2 million years ago; cranial capacity of 600 to 800 cc; may have been a toolmaker.

Homo sapiens the species of primate to which modern and somewhat older humans belong. Early examples of *Homo sapiens* may have appeared between 500,000 and 200,000 years ago.

Homo sapiens sapiens modern humans, undisputed examples of which appeared after 40,000 years ago.

Homozygous possessing two identical genes or alleles in corresponding locations on a pair of chromosomes.

Horticulture plant cultivation carried out with relatively simple tools and methods; nature is allowed to replace nutrients in the soil, in the absence of permanently cultivated fields.

Human Paleontology the study of the emergence of humans and their later physical evolution.

Human Variation the study of how and why contemporary human populations vary biologically.

Hunter-Gatherers peoples who subsist on the collection of naturally occurring plants and animals; also referred to as foragers.

Hybrid Vigor see **Heterosis.**

Hypotheses predictions, which may be derived from theories, about how variables are related.

Hypoxia oxygen deficiency.

Incest Taboo prohibition of sexual intercourse or marriage between mother and son, father and daughter, and brother and sister.

Incisors the front teeth; used for holding or seizing food, and preparing it for chewing by the other teeth.

Indirect Dowry goods given by the groom's kin to the bride (or her father who passes most of them to her) at or before her marriage.

Individual Selection natural selection of individual characteristics.

Insectivore an animal that eats insects.

Intensive Agriculture food production characterized by the permanent cultivation of fields and made possible by the use of the plow, draft animals or machines, fertilizers, irrigation, water-storage techniques, and other complex agricultural techniques.

^{40}**K** radioactive isotope of potassium used in potassium-argon dating. See **Potassium-Argon (K-Ar) Dating.**

Kindred a bilateral set of close relatives.

Kitchen Midden a pile of refuse, often shells, in an archeological site.

Knuckle Walking a locomotor pattern of primates such as the chimpanzee and gorilla in which the weight of the upper part of the body is supported on the thickly padded knuckles of the hands.

Kula Ring a ceremonial exchange of valued shell ornaments in the Trobriand Islands, in which white shell armbands are traded around the islands in a counterclockwise direction and red shell necklaces are traded clockwise.

Kwashiorkor a protein-deficiency disease common in tropical areas.

Laws (Scientific) associations or relationships that are accepted by almost all scientists.

Levalloisian a tool tradition developed during the Acheulian period whereby flake tools of a predetermined size could be produced from a shaped core with a prepared striking platform.

Levirate a custom whereby a man is obliged to marry his brother's widow.

Lexical Content vocabulary or lexicon.

Lexicon the words and morphs, and their meanings, of a language; approximated by a dictionary.

Lineage a set of kin whose members trace descent from a common ancestor through known links.

Linguistics the study of language.

Local Race a breeding population or local group whose members usually interbreed.

Lumbar Curve curve formed by the lower part of the vertebral column in erect walkers; found only in hominids.

Magic the performance of certain rituals that are believed to compel the supernatural powers to act in particular ways.

Maglemosian a Mesolithic culture of northern Europe characterized by stone axes and adzes for woodworking, canoes, paddles, large-timbered houses, fishhooks, the bow and arrow, and amber and stone pendants and figurines.

Mana a supernatural, impersonal force that inhabits certain objects or people and is believed to confer success and/or strength.

Manumission the granting of freedom to a slave.

Market or Commercial Exchange exchanges or transactions in which the "prices" are subject to supply and demand, whether or not the transactions occur in a marketplace.

Marriage a socially approved sexual and economic union between a man and a woman that is presumed, both by the couple and by others, to be more or less permanent, and that subsumes reciprocal rights and obligations between the two spouses and between spouses and their future children.

Matriclan a clan tracing descent through the female line.

Matrifocal Family a family consisting of a mother and her children.

Matrilineage a kin group whose members trace descent through known links in the female line from a common ancestress.

Matrilineal Descent the rule of descent that affiliates an individual with kin of both sexes related to him or her through *women* only.

Matrilocal Residence a pattern of residence in which a married couple lives with or near the wife's parents.

Measure to describe how something compares with other things on some scale of variation.

Medium part-time religious practitioner who is asked to heal and divine while in a trance.

Meiosis the process by which reproductive cells are formed. In this process of division, the number of chromosomes in the newly formed cells is reduced by half, so that when fertilization occurs the resulting organism has the normal number of chromosomes appropriate to its species, rather than double that number.

Melanin a dark-brown pigment in the outer layer of skin that protects the inner layers of skin against ultraviolet radiation.

Mendelian Population a population that breeds mostly within itself.

Mesolithic the archeological period in the Old World beginning about 12,000 B.C., during which preagricultural villages were founded.

Microlith a small, razorlike blade fragment that was probably attached in a series to a wooden or bone handle to form a cutting edge.

Miocene geologic epoch 22.5 to 5 million years ago, during which the first hominids probably appeared.

Mitosis cellular reproduction or growth involving the duplication of chromosome pairs.

Modal Personality Characteristics those personality characteristics that occur with the highest frequency in a society.

Moiety a unilineal descent group in a society that is divided into two such maximal groups; there may be smaller unilineal descent groups as well.

Molars the large teeth behind the premolars at the back of the jaw; used for chewing and grinding food.

Mongoloid Spot a dark patch of skin at the base of the spine; disappears as a person grows older.

Monogamy marriage between only one man and only one woman at a time.

Monotheistic believing that there is only one high god, and that all other supernatural beings are subordinate to, or are alternative manifestations of, this supreme being.

Morph the smallest unit of a language that has a meaning.

Morpheme one or more morphs with the same meaning.

Morphology the study of how sound sequences convey meaning.

Mousterian a Middle Paleolithic toolmaking tradition associated with Neandertals; prepared-core and percussion-flaking techniques were used to produce flakes that were then retouched to make specialized tools.

Mutation a change in the molecular structure or DNA code of genes. Mutations usually occur randomly and are generally harmful or lethal to the organism and/or its descendants.

Natufian a Mesolithic culture of the Near East.

Natural Selection the process by which those members of a particular species that are better adapted to their environment survive longer and produce more offspring than the poorer-adapted.

Negative Reciprocity giving and taking that attempts to take advantage of another for one's own interest.

Neolithic the archeological period, characterized by plant and animal domestication, beginning in the Near East about 8000 B.C., in southeast Asia at 6800 B.C., in sub-Saharan Africa by 4000 B.C., and in the New World from 5600 to 5000 B.C.

Neolocal Residence a pattern of residence whereby a married couple lives separately, and usually at some distance, from the kin of either spouse.

Nocturnal active during the night.

Nonfraternal Polyandry marriage of a woman to two or more men who are not brothers.

Nonsororal Polygyny marriage of a man to two or more women who are not sisters.

Nuclear Family a family consisting of a married couple and their young children.

Oath the act of calling upon a deity to bear witness to the truth of what one says.

Obsidian a volcanic glass that can be used to make mirrors or sharp-edged tools.

Oldowan the term designating cultural materials found in the Bed I (lower Pleistocene) level at Olduvai Gorge, Tanzania.

Oligocene the geologic epoch 38 to 22.5 million years ago during which the ancestors of monkeys and apes began to evolve.

Omnivorous eating both meat and vegetation.

Operational Definition a description of the procedure that is followed in measuring a variable.

Opposable Thumb a thumb that can touch the tips of all the other fingers.

Optimal Foraging Theory the theory that individuals seek to maximize the returns (in calories and nutrients) on their labor in deciding which animals and plants they will go after.

Ordeal a means of determining guilt or innocence by submitting the accused to dangerous or painful tests believed to be under supernatural control.

Paleoanthropology see **Human Paleontology.**

Paleocene the geologic epoch 65 to 53.5 million years ago during which mammal forms (including the early primates) began to diverge extensively.

Parallel Cousins children of siblings of the same sex. One's parallel cousins are father's brothers' children and mother's sisters' children.

Parapithecids small monkeylike Oligocene primates found in the Fayum area of Egypt.

Participant Observer an observer who participates (immerses himself or herself) in the language and customs of the natives he or she is studying.

Pastoralism a form of subsistence technology in which food-getting is based directly or indirectly on the maintenance of domesticated animals.

Pater one's socially recognized father.

Patriclan a clan tracing descent through the male line.

Patrilineage a kin group whose members trace descent through known links in the male line from a common ancestor.

Patrilineal Descent the rule of descent that affiliates an individual with kin of both sexes related to him or her through *men* only.

Patrilocal Residence a pattern of residence in which a married couple lives with or near the husband's parents.

Peasants rural people who produce food for their own subsistence, but who must also contribute or sell their surpluses to others (in towns and cities) who do not produce their own food.

Peking Man a name for *Homo erectus* found near Zhoukoudian (formerly Choukoutien), China.

Percussion Flaking a toolmaking technique in which one stone is struck with another to remove a flake.

Personality the distinctive way an individual thinks, feels, and behaves.

Personality Integration of Culture the theory that personality or psychological processes may account for connections between certain aspects of culture.

Phenotype the observable physical appearance of an organism, which may or may not reflect its genotype or total genetic constitution.

Phone a speech sound in a language.

Phoneme a set of slightly varying sounds that do not make any difference in meaning to the speakers of the language.

Phonology the study of the sounds in a language and how they are used.

Phratry a unilineal descent group composed of a number of supposedly related clans (sibs).

Physical Anthropology the study of humans as physical organisms, dealing with the emergence and evolution of humans and with contemporary biological variations among human populations.

Piblokto a mental disorder among Eskimo adults of Greenland, usually women, who become oblivious to their surroundings and act in agitated, eccentric ways.

Pithecanthropus erectus original name given to *Homo erectus* in Java.

Platyrrhines the group of broad-nosed anthropoids that includes the monkeys of South and Central America—the cebids and marmosets.

Pleistocene a geologic epoch that started 1.8 million years ago and, according to some, continues into the present. During this period, glaciers have often covered much of the earth's surface and humans became the dominant life form.

Plesiadapis a Paleocene primate found in Europe and North America.

Pliocene the geologic epoch 5 to 1.8 million years ago during which the earliest definite hominids appeared.

Polyandry the marriage of one woman to more than one man at a time.

Polygamy plural marriage; marriage to more than one spouse simultaneously.

Polygyny the marriage of one man to more than one woman at a time.

Polyphony two or more melodies sung simultaneously.

Polytheistic recognizing many gods, none of whom is believed to be superordinate.

Pongids hominoids whose members include both the living and extinct apes.

Postpartum Sex Taboo prohibition of sexual intercourse between a couple for a period of time after the birth of their child.

Potassium-Argon (K-Ar) Dating a chronometric dating method that uses the rate of decay of a radioactive form of potassium (^{40}K) into argon (^{40}A) to date samples from 5,000 years to 3 billion years old. The K-Ar method dates the minerals and rocks in a deposit, not the fossils themselves.

Potlatch a feast among Northwest Coast Indians at which great quantities of food and goods are given to the guests in order to gain prestige for the host(s).

Practicing Anthropology see **Applied Anthropology**

Prairie tall-grass land.

Prehensile adapted for grasping objects.

Prehistory the time before written records.

Premolars the teeth immediately behind the canines; used in chewing, grinding, and shearing food.

Pressure Flaking toolmaking technique whereby small flakes are struck off by pressing against the core with a bone, antler, or wood tool.

Priest a generally full-time male intermediary between humans and gods.

Primary Institutions the sources of early experiences, such as family organization and subsistence techniques, that presumably help form the basic or modal personality.

Primary Subsistence Activities the food-getting activities: gathering, hunting, fishing, herding, and agriculture.

Primate a member of the mammalian order Primates, divided into the two suborders of prosimians and anthropoids.

Primatologists those who study primates.

Probability Value (P-Value) the likelihood that an observed result could have occurred by chance.

Proconsul Africanus the best known Early Miocene proto-ape.

Projective Tests tests that utilize ambiguous stimuli; test subjects must project their own personality traits in order to structure the ambiguous stimuli.

Propliopithecids Oligocene apelike anthropoids, dating from about 32 million years ago, found in the Fayum area of Egypt.

Prosimians one of the two suborders of primates; includes lemurs and lorises.

Protolanguage a hypothesized ancestral language from which two or more languages seem to have derived.

Purdah the seclusion and veiling of women.

Purgatorius a fossil dating from the Late Cretaceous that is thought to be the earliest known primate.

Quadrupeds animals that walk on all fours.

Race a subpopulation or variety of a single species that differs somewhat in gene frequencies from other varieties of the species but can interbreed with them and produce fertile and viable offspring.

Rachis the seed-bearing part of the stem of a plant.

Radiocarbon (^{14}C) Dating a chronometric dating method that uses carbon^{14} to date organic remains up to 70,000 years old.

Raiding a short-term use of force, generally planned and organized, to realize a limited objective.

Ramapithecus a genus of Miocene ape.

Random Sample a sample in which each case selected has had an equal chance to be included.

Rank Society a society with no unequal access to

economic resources or power, but with social groups that have unequal access to status positions and prestige.

Recessive an allele phenotypically suppressed in the heterozygous form and expressed only in the homozygous form.

Reciprocity giving and taking (not politically arranged) without the use of money.

Redistribution the accumulation of goods (or labor) by a particular person, or in a particular place, and their subsequent distribution.

Relative Dating Method a method of dating fossils that determines the age of a specimen or deposit relative to a known specimen or deposit.

Religion any set of attitudes, beliefs, and practices pertaining to supernatural power, whether that power rests in forces, gods, spirits, ghosts, or demons.

Revitalization Movement a new religious movement intended to save a culture by infusing it with a new purpose and life.

Revolution A usually violent replacement of the society's rulers.

RNA, Messenger messenger RNA (mRNA), a ribonucleic acid, is a single-stranded molecule copied from a portion of DNA, which directs the formation of proteins essential to the formation of cells.

Rules of Descent rules that connect individuals with particular sets of kin because of known or presumed common ancestry.

Sampling Universe the list of cases to be sampled from.

Savanna tropical grassland.

Secondary Institutions aspects of culture such as religion, music, art, folklore, and games, which presumably reflect or are projections of basic or modal personality.

Secondary Subsistence Activities activities which involve the preparation and processing of food either to make it edible or to store.

Sedentarism settled life.

Sediment the dust and debris and decay that accumulates over time.

Segmentary Lineage System a hierarchy of more and more inclusive lineages; usually functions only in conflict situations.

Segregation   the random sorting of chromosomes in meiosis.

Sexual Dimorphism   the differentiation of males from females in size and appearance.

Shaman   a religious intermediary, usually part-time, whose primary function is to cure people through sacred songs, pantomime, and other means; sometimes called "witch doctor" by Westerners.

Shifting Cultivation   see **Extensive Cultivation.**

Sib   see **Clan.**

Sibling Language   one of two or more languages derived from a common ancestral language. For example, German is a sibling language to English.

Siblings   a person's brothers or sisters.

Sickle-Cell Anemia (Sicklemia)   a condition in which red blood cells assume a crescent (sickle) shape when deprived of oxygen, instead of the normal (disk) shape. Severe anemia, painful circulatory problems, enlargement of the heart, brain-cell atrophy, and early death may result.

Sivapithecus   a genus of Miocene apes.

Slash-and-Burn   a form of shifting cultivation in which the natural vegetation is cut down and burned off. The cleared ground is used for a short time and then left to regenerate.

Slaves   a class of persons who do not own their own labor or the products thereof.

Socialization   the development, through the influence of parents and others, of patterns of behavior in children that conform to the standards deemed appropriate by their culture.

Society   a territorial population speaking a language not generally understood by neighboring territorial populations.

Sociobiology   the application of biological evolutionary principles to the social behavior of animals.

Sociolinguistics   the study of cultural and subcultural patterns of speaking in different social contexts.

Sorcery   the use of certain materials to invoke supernatural powers to harm people.

Sororal Polygyny   the marriage of a man to two or more sisters at the same time.

Sororate   a custom whereby a woman is obliged to marry her deceased sister's husband.

Special-Purpose Money   objects of value for which only some goods and services can be exchanged.

Speciation   the development of a new species.

Species   a population that consists of organisms able to interbreed and produce fertile and viable offspring.

Specific Evolution   the particular sequence of change and adaptation of a society in a given environment.

Spirits   unnamed supernatural beings of nonhuman origin who are beneath the gods in prestige and often closer to the people; may be helpful, mischievous, or evil.

State   a political unit with centralized decision making affecting a large population. Most states have: cities with public buildings; full-time craft and religious specialists; an "official" art style; a hierarchical social structure topped by an elite class; and a governmental monopoly on the legitimate use of force to implement policies.

Statistical Association   a relationship or correlation between two or more variables that is unlikely to be due to chance.

Statistically Significant Result   a result that would occur very rarely by chance. The result (and stronger ones) would occur fewer than 5 times out of 100 by chance.

Status   a position of prestige in a society.

Steppe   grassland with a dry, low grass cover.

Structural (Descriptive) Linguistics   the study of how languages are constructed.

Structuralism   the theoretical orientation that human culture is a surface representation of the underlying structure of the human mind.

Subculture   the shared customs of a subgroup within a society.

Subsistence Technology   the methods humans use to procure food.

Supernatural   believed to be not human or not subject to the laws of nature.

Syntax   the ways in which words are arranged to form phrases and sentences.

Taboo   a prohibition that, if violated, is believed to bring supernatural punishment.

Taxonomy   the classification of extinct and living organisms.

Terrestrial   adapted to living on the ground.

Tetonius an Eocene primate.

Thematic Apperception Test (TAT) a projective test using a set of drawings that depict ambiguous life situations; subjects are asked to say what is happening in the pictures.

Theoretical Construct something that cannot be observed or verified directly.

Theories explanations of associations or laws.

Totem a plant or animal associated with a clan (sib) as a means of group identification; may have other special significance for the group.

Transformational/Generative Theory the theory about syntax suggesting that a language has a *surface structure* and a *deep structure.*

Tribe a type of political system characterized by kin or nonkin groupings that can informally and temporarily integrate a number of local groups into a larger whole.

Triceratops a large horned dinosaur of the Late Cretaceous.

Tundra treeless plains characteristic of subarctic and Arctic regions.

Unifacial Tool a tool worked or flaked on one side only.

Unilineal Descent affiliation with a group of kin through descent links of one sex only.

Unilocal Residence a pattern of residence (patrilocal, matrilocal, or avunculocal) that specifies just one set of relatives that the married couple lives with or near.

Unisex Association an association that restricts its membership to one sex, usually male.

Universally Ascribed Qualities those ascribed qualities (age, sex) that are found in all societies.

Variable a thing or quantity that varies.

Variably Ascribed Qualities those ascribed qualities (such as ethnic, religious, or social-class differences) that are found only in some societies.

Vertical Clinging and Leaping a locomotor pattern characteristic of several primates, including tarsiers and galagos. The animal normally rests by clinging to a branch in a vertical position, and uses its hind limbs alone to push off from one vertical position to another.

Warfare violence between political entities such as communities, districts, or nations.

Witchcraft the practice of attempting to harm people by supernatural means, but through emotions and thought alone, not through the use of tangible objects.

Bibliography

'ABD ALLAH, MAHMUD M. "Siwan Customs." *Harvard African Studies*, 1 (1917): 1–28.

ABERLE, DAVID. "A Note on Relative Deprivation Theory as Applied to Millenarian and Other Cult Movements." In Lessa and Vogt, eds., *Reader in Comparative Religion*, 3rd ed.

ADAMS, ROBERT M. "The Origin of Cities." *Scientific American*, September 1960, pp. 153–68.

ADAMS, ROBERT McC. *Heartland of Cities: Surveys of Ancient Settlement and Land Use on the Central Floodplain of the Euphrates.* Chicago: University of Chicago Press, 1981.

ADLER, MORTIMER. *Drawing Down the Moon.* Boston: Beacon, 1986.

AITKEN, M.J. *Thermoluminescence Dating.* London: Academic Press, 1985, pp. 1–4.

AKMAJIAN, ADRIAN, RICHARD A. DEMERS, AND ROBERT M. HARNISH. *Linguistics: An Introduction to Language and Communication.* 2nd ed. Cambridge, MA: M.I.T. Press, 1984.

ALBERTS, BRUDE, DENNIS BRAY, JULIAN LEWIS, MARTIN RAFF, KEITH ROBERTS, AND JAMES D. WATSON. *Molecular Biology of the Cell.* New York: Garland Publishing Company, 1983.

ANDERSON, RICHARD L. *Art in Small-Scale Societies.* 2nd ed. Englewood Cliffs, NJ: Prentice Hall, 1989.

ANDREWS, P., AND CHRIS STRINGER. *Human Evolution: An Illustrated Guide.* London: British Museum, 1989.

ANTHONY, DAVID, DIMITRI Y. TELEGIN, AND DOR-CAS BROWN. "The Origin of Horseback Riding." *Scientific American*, December 1991, pp. 94-100.

APTEKAR, LEWIS. "Are Colombian Street Children Neglected? The Contributions of Ethnographic and Enthnohistorical Approaches to the Study of Children." *Anthropology and Education Quarterly.* 22 (1991): 326-49.

APTEKAR, LEWIS. *Environmental Disasters in Global Perspective.* New York: G.K. Hall/Macmillan, in press.

APTEKAR, LEWIS. *Street Children of Cali.* Durham, NC: Duke University Press, 1988.

ARCHER, DANE, AND ROSEMARY GARTNER. *Violence and Crime in Cross-National Perspective.* New Haven: Yale University Press. 1984.

ARENSBERG, CONRAD M., AND ARTHUR H. NIEHOFF. *Introducing Social Change: A Manual for Americans Overseas.* Chicago: Aldine, 1964.

ARMSTRONG, ROBERT P. *The Powers of Presence.* Philadelphia: University of Pennsylvania Press, 1981.

ASCH, NANCY B., AND DAVID L. ASCH. "The Economic Potential of *Iva annua* and Its Prehistoric Imporance in the Lower Illinois Valley." In Richard I. Ford, ed., *The Nature and Status of Ethnobotany.* Anthropological Papers, Museum of Anthropology, no. 67. Ann Arbor: University of Michigan, 1978, pp. 301–42.

ASCH, SOLOMON. "Studies of Independence and Conformity: A Minority of One against a

Unanimous Majority." *Psychological Monographs,* 70 (1956): 1–70.

ASHTON, HUGH. *The Basuto.* 2nd ed. London: Oxford University Press, 1967.

AYRES, BARBARA C. "Effects of Infant Carrying Practices on Rhythm in Music." *Ethos,* 1 (1973): 387–404.

AYRES, BARBARA C. "Effects of Infantile Stimulation on Musical Behavior." In Lomax, ed., *Folk Song Style and Culture.*

BACON, MARGARET, IRVIN L. CHILD, AND HERBERT BARRY III. "A Cross-Cultural Study of Correlates of Crime." *Journal of Abnormal and Social Psychology,* 66 (1963): 291-300.

BADCOCK, CHRISTOPHER. *Essential Freud.* Oxford: Basil Blackwell, 1988.

BAILEY, ROBERT C., GENEVIEVE HEAD, MARK JENIKE, BRUCE OWEN, ROBERT RECHTMAN, AND ELZBIETA ZECHENTER. "Hunting and Gathering in Tropical Rain Forest: Is It Possible?" *American Anthropologist,* 91 (1989): 59–82.

BALDI, PHILIP. *An Introduction to the Indo-European Languages.* Carbondale: Southern Illinois University Press. 1983.

BALIKCI, ASEN. *The Netsilik Eskimo.* Garden City, NY: Natural History Press, 1970.

BANTON, MICHAEL, ed. *Anthropological Approaches to the Study of Religion.* Association of Social Anthropologists of the Commonwealth, Monograph no. 3. New York: Praeger, 1966.

BARAK, GREGG. *Gimme Shelter: A Social History of Homelessness in Contemporary America.* New York: Praeger, 1991.

BARASH, DAVID P. *Sociobiology and Behavior.* New York: Elsevier, 1977.

BARLETT, PEGGY F., ed. *Agricultural Decision-Making: Anthropological Contributions to Rural Development.* New York: Academic Press, 1980.

BARNETT, H.G. *Being A Palauan.* New York: Holt, Rinehart & Winston, 1960.

BARNOUW, VICTOR, *Culture and Personality.* 4th ed. Homewood, IL: Dorsey Press, 1985.

BARRY, HERBERT III, IRVIN L. CHILD, AND MARGARET K. BACON. "Relation of Child Training to Subsistence Economy." *American Anthropologist,* 61 (1959): 51–63.

BARTH, FREDRIK. "Nomadism in the Mountain and Plateau Areas of South West Asia." In *The Problems of the Arid Zone,* Paris: UNESCO, 1960.

BARTH, FREDRIK. *Nomads of South Persia.* Oslo: Universitetsforlaget, 1964; Boston: Little, Brown, 1968.

BARTRAM, WILLIAM. *The Travels of William Bartram,* ed. Francis Harper. New Haven: Yale University Press, 1958.

BAXTER, ELLEN, AND KIM HOPPER. *Private Lives/Public Spaces: Homeless Adults on the Streets of New York City.* New York: Community Service Society of New York, 1981.

BEADLE, GEORGE, AND MURIEL BEADLE. *The Language of Life.* Garden City, NY: Doubleday, 1966.

BEARDER, SIMON K. "Lorises, Bushbabies, and Tarsiers: Diverse Societies in Solitary Foragers." In Smuts et al., eds., *Primate Societies,* pp. 11–33.

BEATTIE, JOHN. *Bunyoro: An African Kingdom.* New York: Holt, Rinehart & Winston, 1960.

BEGLER, ELSIE B. "Sex, Status, and Authority in Egalitarian Society." *American Anthropologist,* 80 (1978): 571–88.

BELLMAN, BERYL L. *The Language of Secrecy: Symbols and Metaphors in Poro Ritual.* New Brunswick, NJ: Rutgers University Press, 1984.

BENEDICT, BURTON. "Controlling Population Growth in Mauritius." In Bernard and Pelto, eds., *Technology and Social Change.*

BENEDICT, MICHAEL LES. "Ku Klux Klan." *Academic American Encyclopedia.* vol. 12 (K-L), p. 133. Princeton, NJ: Arete Publishing Co., 1980.

BENEDICT, RUTH. *The Chrysanthemum and the Sword.* Boston: Houghton Mifflin, 1946.

BENEDICT, RUTH. *Patterns of Culture.* New York: Mentor, 1959 (originally published 1934).

BERLIN, BRENT, AND PAUL KAY. *Basic Color Terms: Their Universality and Evolution.* Berkeley: University of California Press, 1969.

BERNARD, H. RUSSELL. *Research Methods in Cultural Anthropology.* Newbury Park, CA: Sage, 1988.

BERNARD, H. RUSSELL, AND PERTTI J. PELTO. "Technology and Anthropological Theory: Conclusions." In Bernard and Pelto, eds., *Technology and Social Change.*

BERNARD, H. RUSSELL, AND PERTTI J. PELTO, eds. *Technology and Social Change.* 2nd ed. Prospect Heights, IL: Waveland, 1987.

BERNARDI, B. "The Age-System of the Nilo-Hamitic Peoples." *Africa,* 22 (1952):316-32.

BERREMAN, GERALD D. "Caste in India and the

United States." *American Journal of Sociology,* 66 (1960): 120–27.

BERREMAN, GERALD D. "Caste in the Modern World." Morristown, NJ: General Learning Press, 1973.

BERREMAN, GERALD D. "Race, Caste and Other Invidious Distinctions in Social Stratification." *Race,* 13 (1972): 403–14.

BERREMAN, GERALD D., ed. *Social Inequality: Comparative and Developmental Approaches.* New York: Academic Press, 1981.

BERRY, JOHN W. "Ecological and Cultural Factors in Spatial Perceptual Development." *Canadian Journal of Behavioural Science,* 3 (1971): 324–36.

BERRY, JOHN W. *Human Ecology and Cognitive Style.* New York: John Wiley, 1976.

BICKERTON, DEREK. "Creole Languages," *Scientific American,* July 1983, pp. 116–22.

BINFORD, LEWIS R. *Faunal Remains from Klasies River Mouth.* Orlando, FL: Academic Press, 1984.

BINFORD, LEWIS R. "Interassemblage Variability: The Mousterian and the 'Functional' Argument." In Colin Renfrew, ed., *The Explanation of Culture Change: Models in Prehistory.* Pittsburgh: University of Pittsburgh Press, 1973.

BINFORD, LEWIS R. "Mobility, Housing, and Environment: A Comparative Study." *Journal of Anthropological Research,* 46 (1990): 119-52.

BINFORD, LEWIS R. "Post-Pleistocene Adaptations." In Strucver, ed., *Prehistoric Agriculture.*

BINFORD, LEWIS R. "Were There Elephant Hunters at Torralba?" In Nitecki and Nitecki, eds., *The Evolution of Human Hunting,* pp. 47–105.

BINFORD, LEWIS R, AND CHUAN KUN HO. "Taphonomy at a Distance: Zhoukoudian, 'The Cave Home of Beijing Man'?" *Current Anthropology.* 26 (1985): 413-42.

BINFORD, SALLY R., AND LEWIS R. BINFORD, eds., *New Perspectives in Archaeology.* Chicago: Aldine, 1968.

BINFORD, SALLY R., AND LEWIS R. BINFORD. "Stone Tools and Human Behavior." *Scientific American,* 220 (April 1969): 70–84.

BLALOCK, HUBERT M., JR. *Social Statistics,* 2nd ed. New York: McGraw-Hill, 1972.

BLANTON, RICHARD. *Monte Albán: Settlement Patterns at the Ancient Zapotec Capital.* New York: Academic Press, 1978.

BLANTON, RICHARD. "The Origins of Monte Albán." In C. Cleland, ed., *Cultural Continuity and Change.* New York: Academic Press, 1976.

BLANTON, RICHARD E. "The Rise of Cities." In Jeremy A. Sabloff, ed., *Supplement to the Handbook of Middle American Indians.* Austin: University of Texas Press, 1981, 1: 392–400.

BLANTON, RICHARD E., STEPHEN A. KOWALEWSKI, GARY FEINMAN, AND JILL APPEL. *Ancient Mesoamerica: A Comparison of Change in Three Regions.* New York: Cambridge University Press, 1981.

BLEDSOE, CAROLINE H. *Women and Marriage in Kpelle Society.* Stanford, CA: Stanford University Press, 1980.

BLOCK, JEAN L. "Help! They've All Moved Back Home!" *Woman's Day,* April 26, 1983, pp. 72–76.

BLOUNT, BEN G. "The Development of Language in Children." In Munroe, Munroe, and Whiting, eds., *Handbook of Cross-Cultural Human Development.*

BLUMBERG, RAE L. *Stratification: Socioeconomic and Sexual Inequality.* Dubuque, Iowa: Wm. C. Brown, 1978.

BOAS, FRANZ. *Central Eskimos.* Bureau of American Ethnology Annual Report no. 6. Washington, D.C., 1888.

BOAS, FRANZ. *Geographical Names of the Kwakiutl Indians.* New York: Columbia University Press, 1934.

BOAS, FRANZ. "On Grammatical Categories." In Hymes, ed., *Language in Culture and Society,* pp. 121–23.

BOAS, FRANZ. *Race, Language, and Culture.* New York: Macmillan, 1940.

BOAS, FRANZ. *The Religion of the Kwakiutl.* Columbia University Contributions to Anthropology, vol. 10, pt. II. New York, 1930.

BOAZ, N.T. "Morphological Trends and Phylogenetic Relationships from Middle Miocene Hominoids to Late Pliocene Hominids." In Ciochon and Corruccini, eds., *New Interpretations of Ape and Human Ancestry,* pp. 705–20.

BOAZ, NOEL T. "Hominid Evolution in Eastern Africa during the Pliocene and Early Pleistocene." *Annual Review of Anthropology,* 8 (1979): 71–85.

BOCK, PHILIP K. *Continuities in Psychological Anthropology: A Historical Introduction.* San Francisco: W.H. Freeman and Company Publishers, 1980.

BODLEY, JOHN H. *Anthropology and Contemporary Human Problems.* 2nd ed. Mountainview, CA: Mayfield, 1985.

BODLEY, JOHN H. *Victims of Progress.* 3rd ed. Mountainview, CA: Mayfield, 1990.

BODMER, W.F., AND L.L. CAVALLI-SFORZA. *Genetics, Evolution, and Man.* San Francisco: W.H. Freeman & Company Publishers, 1976.

BOGIN, BARRY. *Patterns of Human Growth.* Cambridge: Cambridge University Press, 1988.

BOGORAS, WALDEMAR. "The Chukchee," pt. 3. *Memoirs of the American Museum of Natural History,* 2 (1909).

BOHANNAN, LAURA, AND PAUL BOHANNAN. *The Tiv of Central Nigeria.* London: International African Institute, 1953.

BOHANNAN, PAUL. "The Migration and Expansion of the Tiv." *Africa,* 24 (1954): 2–16.

BOHANNAN, PAUL, AND JOHN MIDDLETON, eds. *Marriage, Family and Residence.* Garden City, NY: Natural History Press, 1968.

BOLTON, RALPH. "Aggression and Hypoglycemia among the Qolla: A Study in Psychobiological Anthropology." *Ethnology,* 12 (1973): 227–57.

BOLTON, RALPH. "Introduction: The AIDS Pandemic, A Global Emergency." *Medical Anthropology,* 10 (1989): 93–104.

BONNER, JOHN T. *The Evolution of Culture in Animals.* Princeton: Princeton University Press, 1980.

BORDAZ, JACQUES. *Tools of the Old and New Stone Age.* Garden City, N.Y.: Natural History Press, 1970.

BORDES, FRANÇOIS. "Mousterian Cultures in France." *Science,* September 22, 1961, pp. 803–10.

BORNSTEIN, MARC H. "The Psychophysiological Component of Cultural Difference in Color Naming and Illusion Susceptibility." *Behavior Science Notes,* 8 (1973): 41–101.

BOSERUP, ESTER. *The Conditions of Agricultural Growth: The Economics of Agrarian Change Under Population Pressure.* Chicago: Aldine, 1965.

BOSERUP, ESTER. *Woman's Role in Economic Development.* New York: St. Martin's Press, 1970.

BOURGUIGNON, ERIKA. "Introduction: A Framework for the Comparative Study of Altered States of Consciousness." In Erika Bourguignon, *Religion, Altered States of Consciousness, and Social Change.* Columbus: Ohio State University Press, 1973, pp. 3–35.

BOURGUIGNON, ERIKA, AND THOMAS L. EVASCU. "Altered States of Consciousness within a General Evolutionary Perspective: A Holocultural Analysis," *Behavior Science Research,* 12 (1977): 197–216.

BOYD, ROBERT, AND PETER J. RICHERSON. *Culture and the Evolutionary Process.* Chicago: University of Chicago Press, 1985.

BRACE, C.L., SHAO XIANG-QING, AND ZHANG ZHEN-BIAO. "Prehistoric and Modern Tooth Size in China." In Smith and Spencer, eds., *The Origins of Modern Humans,* pp. 485–517.

BRADLEY, CANDICE. "The Sexual Division of Labor and the Value of Children." *Behavior Science Research,* 19 (1984–1985): 159–85.

BRAIDWOOD, ROBERT J. "The Agricultural Revolution." *Scientific American,* September 1960, pp. 130–48.

BRAIDWOOD, ROBERT J., AND GORDON R. WILLEY. "Conclusions and Afterthoughts." In Robert J. Braidwood and Gordon R. Willey, eds., *Courses toward Urban Life: Archaeological Considerations of Some Cultural Alternatives.* Viking Fund Publications in Anthropology, no. 32. Chicago: Aldine, 1962.

BRANDA, RICHARD F., AND JOHN W. EATON. "Skin Color and Nutrient Photolysis: An Evolutionary Hypothesis." *Science,* August 18, 1978, pp. 625–26.

BRAUER, GUNTER. "A Craniological Approach to the Origin of Anatomically Modern *Homo sapiens* in Africa and Implications for the Appearance of Modern Europeans." In Smith and Spencer, eds., *The Origins of Modern Humans,* pp. 327–410.

BRIGGS, JEAN L. "Eskimo Women: Makers of Men." In Carolyn J. Matthiasson, *Many Sisters: Women in Cross-Cultural Perspective.* New York: Free Press, 1974, pp. 261–304.

BRINTON, CRANE. *The Anatomy of Revolution.* Englewood Cliffs, N.J.: Prentice Hall, 1938.

BRITTAIN, JOHN A. *Inheritance and the Inequality of Material Wealth.* Washington, DC: Brookings Institution, 1978.

BRODEY, JANE E. "Effects of Milk on Blacks Noted." *New York Times,* October 15, 1971, p. 15.

BROMAGE, TIMOTHY G., AND M. CHRISTOPHER DEAN. "Re-evaluation of the Age at Death of Immature Fossil Hominids." *Nature,* 317, October 10, 1985, pp. 525–27.

BROUDE, GWEN J. "Cross-Cultural Patterning of Some Sexual Attitudes and Practices." *Behavior Science Research,* 11 (1976): 227–62.

BROUDE, GWEN J. "Extramarital Sex Norms in Cross-Cultural Perspective." *Behavior Science Research,* 15 (1980): 181–218.

BROUDE, GWEN J., AND SARAH J. GREENE. "Cross-Cultural Codes on Twenty Sexual Attitudes and Practices." *Ethnology,* 15 (1976): 409–29.

BROWN, CECIL H. "Folk Botanical Life-Forms: Their Universality and Growth." *American Anthropologist,* 79 (1977): 317–42.

BROWN, CECIL H. "Folk Zoological Life-Forms: Their Universality and Growth." *American Anthropologist,* 81 (1979): 791–817.

BROWN, CECIL H. "World View and Lexical Uniformities." *Reviews in Anthropology,* 11 (1984): 99–112.

BROWN, CECIL H., AND STANLEY R. WITKOWSKI. "Language Universals." Appendix B in Levinson and Malone, eds., *Toward Explaining Human Culture.*

BROWN, JAMES A., AND T. DOUGLAS PRICE. "Complex Hunter-Gatherers: Retrospect and Prospect." In Price and Brown, *Prehistoric Hunter-Gathers,* pp. 435–41.

BROWN, JUDITH K. "Economic Organization and the Position of Women among the Iroquois." *Ethnohistory,* 17 (1970): 151–67.

BROWN, JUDITH K. "A Note on the Division of Labor by Sex." *American Anthropologist,* 72 (1970): 1073–78.

BROWN, ROGER. "The First Sentence of Child and Chimpanzee." In Sebeok and Umiker-Sebeok, eds., *Speaking of Apes,* pp. 85–101.

BROWN, ROGER. *Social Psychology.* New York: Free Press, 1965.

BROWN, ROGER, AND MARGUERITE FORD. "Address in American English." *Journal of Abnormal and Social Psychology,* 62 (1961): 375–85.

BRUMFIEL, ELIZABETH. "Aztec State Making: Ecology, Structure, and the Origin of the State." *American Anthropologist,* 85 (1983): pp. 261–84.

BRUMFIEL, ELIZABETH M. "Regional Growth in the Eastern Valley of Mexico: A Test of the 'Population Pressure' Hypothesis." In Kent V. Flannery, ed., *The Early Mesoamerican Village.* New York: Academic Press, 1976, pp. 234–50.

BUNZEL, RUTH. "The Nature of Katcinas." In Lessa and Vogt, eds., *Reader in Comparative Religion,* 3rd ed.

BURKHALTER, S. BRIAN, AND ROBERT F. MURPHY. "Tappers and Sappers: Rubber, Gold and Money among the Mundurucu." *American Ethnologist,* 16 (1989): 100–116.

BURLING, R. *Man's Many Voices: Language in Its Cultural Context.* New York: Holt, Rinehart & Winston, 1970.

BURTON, ROGER V., AND JOHN W.M. WHITING. "The Absent Father and Cross-Sex Identity." *Merrill-Palmer Quarterly of Behavior and Development,* 7, no. 2 (1961): 85–95.

BUTZER, KARL W. "Geomorphology and Sediment Stratigraphy." In Singer and Wymer, *The Middle Stone Age at Klasies River Mouth in South Africa,* pp. 33–42.

BYRNE, ROGER. "Climatic Change and the Origins of Agriculture." In Linda Manzanilla, ed., *Studies in the Neolithic and Urban Revolutions.* British Archaeological Reports International Series 349, Oxford, 1987, pp. 21–34. Referred to in Mark A. Blumler and Roger Byrne, "The Ecological Genetics of Domestication and the Origins of Agriculture." *Current Anthropology,* 32 (1991): 23–35.

CACCONE, ADALGISA, AND JEFFREY R. POWELL. "DNA Divergence among Hominoids." *Evolution,* 43 (1989): 925–42.

CAMPBELL, BERNARD G., *Humankind Emerging,* 4th ed. Boston: Little, Brown, 1985.

CAMPBELL, DONALD T. "Variation and Selective Retention in Socio-Cultural Evolution." In Herbert Barringer, George Blankstein, and Raymond Mack, eds., *Social Change in Developing Areas: A Re-Interpretation of Evolutionary Theory.* Cambridge, MA: Schenkman, 1965, pp. 19–49.

CAMPBELL, JOSEPH. *The Hero with a Thousand Faces.* New York: Pantheon Books, 1949.

CANCIAN, FRANK. "Risk and Uncertainty in Agricultural Decision Making." In Barlett, ed., *Agricultural Decision Making,* pp. 161–202.

CAPLAN, A.L. *The Sociobiology Debate: Readings on Ethical and Scientific Issues.* New York. Harper & Row, Pub., 1978.

CAPORAEL, LINNDA R. "Ergotism: The Satan Loosed in Salem?" *Science,* April 2, 1976, pp. 21–26.

CARCOPINO, JEROME. *Daily Life in Ancient Rome: The People and the City at the Height of the Empire.* Edited with bibliography and notes by Henry T. Rowell. Translated from the French by E.O. Lorimer. New Haven: Yale University Press, 1940.

CARLISLE, RONALD C., AND MICHAEL I. SIEGEL. "Additional Comments on Problems in the Interpretation of Neanderthal Speech Capabilities." *American Anthropologist,* 80 (1978): 367–72.

CARNEIRO, ROBERT L. "The Circumscription Theory: Challenge and Response." *American Behavioral Scientist,* 31 (1988): 497–511.

CARNEIRO, ROBERT L. "Political Expansion as an Expression of the Principle of Competitive Exclusion." In Cohen and Service, eds., *Origins of the State.*

CARNEIRO, ROBERT L. "Slash-and-Burn Cultivation among the Kuikuru and Its Implications for Settlement Patterns." In Yehudi Cohen, ed., *Man in Adaptation: The Cultural Present.* Chicago: Aldine, 1968.

CARNEIRO, ROBERT L. "A Theory of the Origin of the State." *Science,* August 21, 1970, pp. 733–38.

CARPENTER, C.R. "A Field Study in Siam of the Behavior and Social Relations of the Gibbon (*Hylobates lar*)." *Comparative Psychology Monographs,* 16, 5 (1940): 1–212.

CARRASCO, PEDRO. "The Civil-Religious Hierarchy in Mesoamerican Communities: Pre-Spanish Background and Colonial Development." *American Anthropologist,* 63 (1961): 483–97.

CARRIER, JOSEPH AND RALPH BOLTON. "Anthropological Perspectives on Sexuality and HIV Prevention." *Annual Review of Sex Research,* in press.

CARROLL, JOHN B., ed. *Language, Thought, and Reality: Selected Writings of Benjamin Lee Whorf.* New York: John Wiley, 1956.

CARROLL, MICHAEL. "A New Look at Freud on Myth." *Ethos,* 7 (1979): 189–205.

CARTMILL, MATT. "Rethinking Primate Origins." *Science,* April 26, 1974, pp. 436–43.

CASAGRANDE, JOSEPH B., ed. *In the Company of Man: Twenty Portraits by Anthropologists.* New York: Harper & Row, Pub., 1960.

CASHDAN, ELIZABETH A. "Egalitarianism among Hunters and Gatherers." *American Anthropologist,* 82 (1980): 116–20.

CASHDAN, ELIZABETH, ed. *Risk And Uncertainty in Tribal And Peasant Economies.* Boulder, CO: Westview Press, 1990.

CAVALLI-SZORZA, AND M.W. FELDMAN. *Cultural Transmission and Evolution: A Quantitative Approach.* Princeton, NJ: Princeton University Press, 1981.

CAWS, PETER. "The Structure of Discovery." *Science,* December 12, 1969, pp. 1375–80.

CHAFETZ, JANET SALTZMAN. *Gender Equity: An Integrated Theory of Stability and Change.* Sage Library of Social Research 176. Newbury Park, CA: Sage Publications, 1990.

CHAGNON, NAPOLEON A. *Yanomamö: The Fierce People.* 3rd ed. New York: CBS College Publishing, 1983.

CHAGNON, NAPOLEON, AND WILLIAM IRONS, eds. *Evolutionary Biology and Human Social Behavior: An Anthropological Perspective.* North Scituate, MA: Duxbury, 1979.

CHANG, K.C. "In Search of China's Beginnings: New Light on an Old Civilization." *American Scientist,* 69 (1981): 148–60.

CHANG, KWANG-CHIH. *The Archaeology of Ancient China.* New Haven: Yale University Press, 1968.

CHANG, KWANG-CHIH. "The Beginnings of Agriculture in the Far East." *Antiquity,* 44, no. 175 (September 1970): 175–85.

CHARD, CHESTER S. *Man in Prehistory.* New York: McGraw-Hill, 1969.

CHARLES-DOMINIQUE, PIERRE. *Ecology and Behaviour of Nocturnal Primates,* trans. R.D. Martin. New York: Columbia University Press, 1977.

CHAUCER, GEOFFREY. *The Prologue to the Canterbury*

Tales, the Knightes Tale, the Nonnes Prestes Tale. Ed. Mark H. Liddell. New York: The Macmillan Company, 1926.

CHAYANOV, ALEXANDER V. *The Theory of Peasant Economy,* Ed. Daniel Thorner, Basile Kerblay, and R.E.F. Smith. Homewood, Il: Richard D. Irwin, 1966.

CHENEY, DOROTHY L., RICHARD W. WRANGHAM. "Predation." In Smuts et al., eds., *Primate Societies.*

CHIBNIK, MICHAEL. "The Economic Effects of Household Demography: A Cross-Cultural Assessment of Chayanov's Theory." In Maclachlan, ed., *Household Economies and Their Transformations,* pp. 74–106.

CHIBNIK, MICHAEL. "The Evolution of Cultural Rules." *Journal of Anthropological Research,* 37 (1981): 256–68.

CHIBNIK, MICHAEL. "The Statistical Behavior Approach: The Choice between Wage Labor and Cash Cropping in Rural Belize." In Barlett, ed., *Agricultural Decision-Making,* pp. 87–114.

CHIRAS, D.D. *Human Biology: Health, Homeostasis, and the Environment.* St. Paul: West Publishing Company, 1991.

CHIVERS, DAVID J., ed. *Malayan Forest Primates: Ten Years's Study in Tropical Rain Forest.* New York: Plenum, 1980.

CHIVERS, DAVID JOHN. *The Siamang in Malaya.* Basel, Switzerland: Karger, 1974.

CHOMSKY, NOAM. *Reflections on Language.* New York: Pantheon, 1975.

CIOCHON, R.L., AND J.G. FLEAGLE, eds. *Primate Evolution and Human Origins.* Hawthorne, NY: Aldine de Gruyter, 1987.

CIOCHON, RUSSELL L., AND ROBERT S. CORRUCCINI, eds. *New Interpretations of Ape and Human Ancestry.* New York: Plenum, 1983.

CIOCHON, RUSSELL L., DONALD E. SAVAGE, THAW TINT, AND BA MAW. "Anthropoid Origins in Asia? New Discovery of *Amphipithecus* from the Eocene of Burma." *Science,* August 23, 1985, pp. 756–59.

CLARK, GRAHAME. *The Earlier Stone Age Settlement of Scandinavia.* Cambridge: Cambridge University Press, 1975.

CLARK, GRAHAME, AND STUART PIGGOTT. *Prehistoric Societies.* New York: Knopf, 1965.

CLARK, J. DESMOND. "Interpretations of Prehistoric Technology From Ancient Egyptian and Other Sources. Part II: Prehistoric Arrow Forms in Africa as Shown by Surviving Examples of the Traditional Arrows of the San Bushmen." *Paleorient,* 3 (1977): 127–50.

CLARK, J. DESMOND. "Prehistoric Populations and Pressures Favoring Plant Domestication in Africa." In Harlan, De Wet, and Stemler, eds., *Origins of African Plant Domestication,* pp. 67–105.

CLARK, J. DESMOND. *The Prehistory of Africa.* New York: Praeger, 1970.

CLIFFORD, JAMES. "Introduction: Partial Truths." In James Clifford and George E. Marcus, eds., *Writing Culture: The Poetics and Politics of Ethnography.* Berkeley: University of California Press, 1986, pp. 1–26.

CLUTTON-BROCK, T.H., ed. *Primate Ecology: Studies of Feeding and Ranging Behaviour in Lemurs, Monkeys and Apes.* London: Academic Press, 1977.

CLUTTON-BROCK, T.H., AND PAUL H. HARVEY. "Primate Ecology and Social Organization." *Journal of Zoology, London,* 183 (1977): 1–39.

CLUTTON-BROCK, T.H., AND PAUL H. HARVEY. "Primates, Brains and Ecology." *Journal of Zoology, London,* 190 (1980): 309–23.

COE, MICHAEL D. *The Maya.* New York: Praeger, 1966.

COHEN, ALEXANDER. "A Cross-Cultural Study of the Effects of Environmental Insecurity on Aggression in Folktales." *American Anthropologist,* 92 (1990): 474–79.

COHEN, MARK N. *The Food Crisis in Prehistory: Overpopulation and the Origins of Agriculture.* New Haven: Yale University Press, 1977.

COHEN, MARK NATHAN. *Health and the Rise of Civilization,* pp. 112-13. New Haven: Yale University Press, 1989.

COHEN, MARK N. "Population Pressure and the Origins of Agriculture." In Reed, ed., *Origins of Agriculture,* pp. 138–41.

COHEN, MARK N. "The Significance of Long-Term Changes in Human Diet and Food Economy." In Harris and Ross, eds., *Food and Evolution: Toward a Theory of Human Food Habits,* pp. 259–83.

COHEN, MARK NATHAN, AND GEORGE J. ARMELAGOS, eds. *Paleopathology at the Origins of Agriculture*. Orlando, Fl: Academic Press, 1984.

COHEN, MARK NATHAN, AND GEORGE J. ARMELAGOS. "Paleopathology at the Origins of Agriculture: Editors' Summation." In Cohen and Armelagos, eds., *Paleopathology at the Origins of Agriculture*, pp. 585–602.

COHEN, MYRON. "Developmental Process in the Chinese Domestic Group." In Maurice Freedman, ed., *Family and Kinship in Chinese Society*. Stanford, CA: Stanford University Press, 1970.

COHEN, MYRON. "Variations in Complexity among Chinese Family Groups: The Impact of Modernization." *Transactions of the New York Academy of Sciences*, 29 (1967):638–44.

COHEN, RONALD. "Introduction." In Ronald Cohen and Judith D. Toland, eds., *State Formation and Political Legitimacy. Political Anthropology*, Volume VI. New Brunswick, NJ: Transaction Books, 1988.

COHEN, RONALD, AND ELMAN R. SERVICE, eds. *Origins of the State: The Anthropology of Political Evolution*. Philadelphia: Institute for the Study of Human Issues, 1978.

COLLIER, STEPHEN, AND J. PETER WHITE. "Get Them Young? Age and Sex Inferences on Animal Domestication in Archaeology." *American Antiquity*, 41 (1976): 96–102.

COLLINS, DESMOND. "Later Hunters in Europe." In D. Collins, ed., *The Origins of Europe*. New York: Thomas Y. Crowell, 1976.

CONNAH, GRAHAM. *African Civilizations: Precolonial Cities and States in Tropical Africa, An Archaeological Perspective*. Cambridge: Cambridge University Press. 1987.

COULT, ALLAN D., AND ROBERT W. HABENSTEIN. *Cross Tabulations of Murdock's World Ethnographic Sample*. Columbia: University of Missouri Press, 1965.

CROCKETT, CAROLYN, AND JOHN F. EISENBERG. "Howlers: Variations in Group Size and Demography." In Smuts et al., eds., *Primate Societies*, pp. 54–68.

CURTIS, G.H., R. DRAKE, T.E. CERLING, AND J. HAMPEL. "Age of the KBS Tuff in Koobi Fora Formation, East Rudolf, Kenya." *Nature*, 258 (1975): 395–93.

CUTRIGHT, PHILLIPS. "Inequality: A Cross-National Analysis." *American Sociological Review*, 32 (1967): 562–78.

DAHLBERG, FRANCES, ed. *Woman the Gatherer*. New Haven: Yale University Press, 1981.

DALTON, GEORGE, ed. *Tribal and Peasant Economies: Readings in Economic Anthropology*. Garden City, NY: Natural History Press, 1967.

DALY, MARTIN, AND MARGO WILSON. *Homicide*. New York: Aldine de Gruyter, 1988.

DART, RAYMOND. "*Australopithecus Africanus*: The Man-Ape of South Africa." *Nature*, 115 (1925): 195.

DARWIN, CHARLES. "The Origin of Species." In Young, ed., *Evolution of Man*.

DASEN, PIERRE R., AND ALASTAIR HERON. "Cross-Cultural Tests of Piaget's Theory." In Triandis and Heron, eds., *Handbook of Cross-Cultural Psychology*. Vol. 4, *Developmental Psychology*.

DAVENPORT, WILLIAM. "Nonunilinear Descent and Descent Groups." *American Anthropologist*, 61 (1959): 557–72.

DAVENPORT, WILLIAM. "Sexual Patterns and Their Regulation in a Society of the Southwest Pacific." In Frank A. Beach, ed., *Sex and Behavior*. New York: John Wiley, 1965.

DAVIS, WILLIAM D. *Societal Complexity and the Nature of Primitive Man's Conception of the Supernatural*. Ph.D. diss., University of Carolina, Chapel Hill, 1971.

DAWSON, J.L.M. "Cultural and Physiological Influences upon Spatial-Perceptual Processes in West Africa." *International Journal of Psychology*, 2 (1967): 115–28, 171–85.

DE LUMLEY, HENRY. "A Paleolithic Camp at Nice." *Scientific American*, May 1969, pp. 42–50.

DE VILLIERS, PETER A., AND JILL G. DE VILLIERS. *Early Language*. Cambridge, MA: Harvard University Press, 1979.

DELSON, ERIC, ed. *Ancestors: The Hard Evidence*. New York: Alan R. Liss, 1985.

DENNY, J. PETER. "The 'Extendedness' Variable in Classifier Semantics: Universal Features and Cultural Variation." In Madeleine Mathiot, ed., *Ethnolinguistics: Boas, Sapir and Whorf Revisited*. The Hague: Mouton, 1979, pp. 97–119.

DENTAN, ROBERT K. *The Semai: A Nonviolent People*

of Malaya. New York: Holt, Rinehart & Winston, 1968.

DEVORE, IRVEN, AND MELVIN J. KONNER. "Infancy in Hunter-Gatherer Life: An Ethological Perspective." In N.F. White, ed., *Ethology and Psychiatry.* Toronto: Ontario Mental Health Foundation and University of Toronto Press, 1974, pp. 113–41.

DIAMOND, JARED. "The Accidental Conqueror." *Discover,* December 1989, pp. 71–76.

DINCAUZE, DENA F. "An Archaeo-Logical Evaluation of the Case for Pre-Clovis Occupations." In Fred Wendorf and Angela E. Close, eds., *Advances in World Archaeology.* Orlando, FL: Academic Press, 1984, 3:275–323.

DIVALE, WILLIAM T. "Migration, External Warfare, and Matrilocal Residence." *Behavior Science Research,* 9 (1974): 75–133.

DIVALE, WILLIAM T., AND MARVIN HARRIS. "Population, Warfare, and the Male Supremacist Complex." *American Anthropologist,* 78 (1976): 521–38.

DOBZHANSKY, THEODOSIUS. *Genetic Diversity and Human Equality.* New York: Basic Books, 1973.

DOBZHANSKY, THEODOSIUS. *Mankind Evolving: The Evolution of the Human Species.* New Haven: Yale University Press, 1962.

DOHLINOW, PHYLLIS JAY, AND NAOMI BISHOP. "The Development of Motor Skills and Social Relationships among Primates through Play." In Phyllis Jay Dohlinow, ed., *Primate Patterns.* New York: Holt, Rinehart & Winston, 1972.

DORSON, RICHARD. "The Eclipse of Solar Mythology." In Dundes, ed., *The Study of Folklore.*

DOUGLAS, MARY. *Implicit Meanings: Essays in Anthropology.* London: Routledge and Kegan Paul, 1975.

DOW, JAMES. *The Shaman's Touch: Otomi Indian Symbolic Healing.* Salt Lake City: University of Utah Press, 1986.

DOWLING, JOHN H. "Property Relations and Productive Strategies in Pastoral Societies." *American Ethnologist,* 2 (1975): 419–26.

DOYLE, G.A., AND R.D. MARTIN, eds. *The Study of Prosimian Behavior.* New York: Academic Press, 1979.

DRAPER, PATRICIA. "!Kung Women: Contrasts in Sexual Egalitarianism in Foraging and Sedentary Contexts." In Rayna R. Reiter, ed., *Toward an Anthropology of Women.* New York: Monthly Review Press, 1975, pp. 77–109.

DRAPER, PATRICIA, AND ELIZABETH CASHDAN. "Technological Change and Child Behavior among the !Kung." *Ethnology,* 27 (1988): 339–65.

DRESSLER, WILLIAM W., AND MICHAEL C. ROBBINS. "Art Styles, Social Stratification, and Cognition: An Analysis of Greek Vase Painting." *American Ethnologist,* 2 (1975): 427–34.

DRUCKER, PHILIP. *Cultures of the North Pacific Coast.* San Francisco: Chandler, 1965.

DRUCKER, PHILIP. "The Potlatch." In Dalton, ed., *Tribal and Peasant Economies.*

DU BOIS, CORA. *The People of Alor: A Social-Psychological Study of an East Indian Island.* Minneapolis: University of Minnesota Press, 1944.

DUNDES, ALAN. *Folklore Matters.* Knoxville: University of Tennessee Press, 1989.

DUNDES, ALAN. "Structural Typology in North American Indian Folktales." In Dundes, ed., *The Study of Folklore.*

DUNDES, ALAN. ed. *The Study of Folklore.* Englewood Cliffs, N.J.: Prentice Hall, 1965.

DURHAM, WILLIAM H. *Coevolution: Genes, Culture, and Human Diversity.* Stanford, CA: Stanford University Press, 1991.

DURHAM, WILLIAM H. "Toward a Coevolutionary Theory of Human Biology and Culture." In Chagnon and Irons, eds., *Evolutionary Biology and Human Social Behavior: An Anthropological Perspective.*

DURKHEIM, EMILE. *The Elementary Forms of the Religious Life.* Translated from the French by Joseph W. Swain. New York: Collier Books, 1961.

DURKHEIM, EMILE. *The Rules of Sociological Method,* 8th ed. Trans. Sarah A. Soloway and John H. Mueller. Ed. George E. Catlin. New York: Free Press, 1938 (originally published 1895).

"Dwindling Numbers on the Farm." *Nation's Business,* April 1988, p. 16.

DYSON-HUDSON, NEVILLE. *Karimojong Politics.* Oxford: Clarendon Press, 1966.

DYSON-HUDSON, RADA, AND ERIC ALDEN SMITH. "Human Territoriality: An Ecological Reassessment." *American Anthropologist*, 80 (1978): 21–41.

ECKHARDT, WILLIAM. "Primitive Militarism." *Journal of Peace Research*, 12 (1975): 55–62.

EDDY, ELIZABETH, AND WILLIAM L. PARTRIDGE, eds. *Applied Anthropology in America*. New York: Columbia University Press, 1978.

EDDY, ELIZABETH, AND WILLIAM L. PARTRIDGE, eds. *Applied Anthropology in America*. 2nd ed. New York: Columbia University Press, 1987.

EDGERTON, ROBERT B. "Conceptions of Psychosis in Four East African Societies." *American Anthropologist*, 68 (1966): 408–25.

EDGERTON, ROBERT B. *The Individual in Cultural Adaptation: A Study of Four East African Peoples*. Berkeley: University of California Press, 1971.

EDGERTON, ROBERT B., AND L.L. LANGNESS. *Methods and Styles in the Study of Culture*. San Francisco: Chandler & Sharp, 1974.

EGGAN, FRED. *The Social Organization of the Western Pueblos*. Chicago: University of Chicago Press, 1950.

EISELEY, LOREN C. "The Dawn of Evolutionary Theory." In Loren C. Eiseley, *Darwin's Century: Evolution and the Men Who Discovered It*. Garden City, NY: Doubleday, 1958.

EISENBERG, JOHN F. "Comparative Ecology and Reproduction of New World Monkeys." In Devra Kleinman, ed., *The Biology and Conservation of the Callitrichidae*. Washington, DC: Smithsonian Institution, 1977, pp. 13–22.

EISENSTADT, S.N. "African Age Groups." *Africa*, 24 (1954): 100–111.

EISENSTADT, S.N. *From Generation to Generation: Age Groups and Social Structure*. New York: Free Press, 1956.

ELDREDGE, NILES, AND IAN TATTERSALL. *The Myths of Human Evolution*. New York: Columbia University Press, 1982.

ELIOT, T.S. "The Love Song of J. Alfred Prufrock." In *Collected Poems, 1909–1962*. New York: Harcourt Brace, & World, 1963.

ELLIS, LEE. "Evidence of Neuroandrogenic Etiology of Sex Roles from a Combined Analysis of Human, Nonhuman Primate and Nonprimate Mammalian Studies." *Personality and Individual Differences*, 7 (1986): 512–52.

ELWIN, VERRIER. *The Religion of an Indian Tribe*. London: Oxford University Press, 1955.

EMBER, CAROL R. "Cross-Cultural Cognitive Studies." *Annual Review of Anthropology*, 6 (1977): 33–56.

EMBER, CAROL R. "A Cross-Cultural Perspective on Sex Differences." In Munroe, Munroe, and Whiting, eds., *Handbook of Cross-Cultural Human Development*.

EMBER, CAROL R. "An Evaluation of Alternative Theories of Matrilocal versus Patrilocal Residence." *Behavior Science Research*, 9 (1974): 135–49.

EMBER, CAROL R. "Feminine Task Assignment and the Social Behavior of Boys." *Ethos*, 1 (1973): 424–39.

EMBER, CAROL R. "Men's Fear of Sex With Women: A Cross-Cultural Study." *Sex Roles*, 4 (1978): 657–78.

EMBER, CAROL R. "Myths about Hunter-Gatherers." *Ethnology*, 17 (1978): 439–48.

EMBER, CAROL R. "The Relative Decline in Women's Contribution to Agriculture with Intensification." *American Anthropologist*, 85 (1983): 285–304.

EMBER, CAROL R. "Residential Variation among Hunter-Gatherers." *Behavior Science Research*, 9 (1975): 135–49.

EMBER, CAROL R., AND DAVID LEVINSON. "The Substantive Contributions of Worldwide Cross-Cultural Studies Using Secondary Data." *Behavior Science Research* (special issue on "Cross-Cultural and Comparative Research: Theory and Method") 25 (1991): 79–140.

EMBER, CAROL R., AND MELVIN EMBER. "The Conditions Favoring Multilocal Residence." *Southwestern Journal of Anthropology*, 28 (1972): 382–400.

EMBER, CAROL R., AND MELVIN EMBER. "The Evolution of Human Female Sexuality: A Cross-Species Perspective." *Journal of Anthropological Research*, 40 (1984): 202–10.

EMBER, CAROL R., AND MELVIN EMBER. *Guide to Cross-Cultural Research Using the HRAF Archive*. New Haven: Human Relations Area Files, 1988.

EMBER, CAROL R., AND MELVIN EMBER. "Resource Unpredictability, Mistrust, and War: A Cross-Cultural Study." *Journal of Conflict Resolution*, 36 (1992): 242–62.

EMBER, CAROL R., MELVIN EMBER, AND BURTON PASTERNAK. "On the Development of Unilineal Descent." *Journal of Anthropological Research,* 30 (1974): 69–94.

EMBER, CAROL R., MELVIN EMBER, AND BRUCE RUSSETT. "Peace between Participatory Polities: A Cross-Cultural Test of the 'Democracies Rarely Fight Each Other' Hypothesis." *World Politics,* 44 (1992): 573–99.

EMBER, MELVIN. "Alternative Predictors of Polygyny." *Behavior Science Research,* 19 (1984/1985): 1–23.

EMBER, MELVIN. "The Conditions That May Favor Avunculocal Residence." *Behavior Research,* 9 (1974): 203–9.

EMBER, MELVIN. "The Emergence of Neolocal Residence." *Transactions of the New York Academy of Sciences,* 30 (1967): 291–302.

EMBER, MELVIN. "Evidence and Science in Ethnography: Reflections on the Freeman-Mead Controversy." *American Anthropologist,* 87 (1985): 906–9.

EMBER, MELVIN. "The Nonunilinear Descent Groups of Samoa." *American Anthropologist,* 61 (1959): 573–77.

EMBER, MELVIN. "On the Origin and Extension of the Incest Taboo." *Behavior Science Research,* 10 (1975): 249–81.

EMBER, MELVIN. "The Relationship between Economic and Political Development in Nonindustrialized Societies." *Ethnology,* 2 (1963): 228–48.

EMBER, MELVIN. "Size of Color Lexicon: Interaction of Cultural and Biological Factors." *American Anthropologist,* 80 (1978): 364–67.

EMBER, MELVIN. "Statistical Evidence for an Ecological Explanation of Warfare." *American Anthropologist,* 84 (1982): 645–49.

EMBER, MELVIN. "Taxonomy in Comparative Studies." In Naroll and Cohen, eds., *A Handbook of Method in Cultural Anthropology.*

EMBER, MELVIN. "Warfare, Sex Ratio, and Polygyny." *Ethnology,* 13 (1974): 194–206.

EMBER, MELVIN, AND CAROL R. EMBER. "The Conditions Favoring Matrilocal versus Patrilocal Residence." *American Anthropologist,* 73 (1971): 571–94.

EMBER, MELVIN, AND CAROL R. EMBER. "Cross-Cultural Studies of War and Peace: Recent Achievements and Future Possibilities." In S.P. Reyna and R.E. Downs, eds., *Studying War: Anthropological Perspectives.* New York: Gordon & Breach, 1993, in press.

EMBER, MELVIN, AND CAROL R. EMBER. "Male-Female Bonding: A Cross-Species Study of Mammals and Birds." *Behavior Science Research,* 14 (1979): 37–56.

EMBER, MELVIN, AND CAROL R. EMBER. *Marriage, Family, and Kinship: Comparative Studies of Social Organization.* New Haven: HRAF Press, 1983.

EPSTEIN, CYNTHIA FUCHS. *Deceptive Distinctions: Sex, Gender, and the Social Order.* New Haven: Yale University Press; and New York: Russell Sage Foundation, 1988.

ERICKSEN, KAREN PAIGE. "Male and Female Age Organizations and Secret Societies in Africa." *Behavior Science Research,* 23 (1989): 234–64.

ERICKSON, EDWIN. "Self-assertion, Sex Role, and Vocal Rasp." In Lomax, ed., *Folk Song Style and Culture.*

ERRINGTON, J. JOSEPH. "On the Nature of the Sociolinguistic Sign: Describing the Javanese Speech Levels." In Elizabeth Mertz and Richard J. Parmentier, eds., *Semiotic Mediation: Sociocultural and Psychological Perspectives.* Orlando, FL: Academic Press, 1985, pp. 287–310.

ETIENNE, MONA, AND ELEANOR LEACOCK, eds. *Women and Colonization: Anthropological Perspectives.* New York: Praeger, 1980.

ETTER, MARTIN A. "Sahlins and Sociobiology." *American Ethnologist,* 5 (1978): 160–68.

EURIPIDES. "The Trojan Women," in Edith Hamilton, trans., *Three Greek Plays.* New York: Norton, 1937, p. 52.

EVANS-PRITCHARD, E.E. "Nuer Modes of Address." *Uganda Journal,* 12 (1948): 166–71.

EVANS-PRITCHARD, E.E. "The Nuer of the Southern Sudan." In M. Fortes and E.E. Evans-Pritchard, eds., *African Political Systems.* New York: Oxford Unversity Press, 1940.

EVANS-PRITCHARD, E.E. "Sexual Inversion among the Azande." *American Anthropologist,* 72 (1970): 1428–34.

EVANS-PRITCHARD, E.E. "Witchcraft Explains Unfortunate Events." In Lessa and Vogt, eds., *Reader in Comparative Religion,* 4th ed.

EVELETH, PHYLLIS B., AND JAMES M. TANNER. *Worldwide Variation in Human Growth,* 2nd ed.

Cambridge: Cambridge University Press, 1990.

FAGAN, BRIAN M. *In The Beginning.* Boston: Little, Brown, 1972.

FAGAN, BRIAN M. *People of the Earth: An Introduction to World Prehistory.* 6th ed. Glenview, IL: Scott, Foresman and Company, 1989.

FEATHERMAN, DAVID L., AND ROBERT M. HAUSER. *Opportunity and Change.* New York: Academic Press, 1978.

FEDIGAN, LINDA MARIE. *Primate Paradigms: Sex Roles and Social Bonds.* Montreal: Eden Press, 1982.

FEINMAN, GARY M., STEPHEN A. KOWALEWSKI, LAURA FINSTEN, RICHARD E. BLANTON, AND LINDA NICHOLAS. "Long-Term Demographic Change: A Perspective from the Valley of Oaxaca, Mexico." *Journal of Field Archaelogy,* 12 (1985): 333–62.

FEINMAN, GARY, AND JILL NEITZEL. "Too Many Types: An Overview of Sedentary Prestate Societies in the Americas." In Michael B. Schiffer, ed., *Advances in Archaelogical Methods and Theory.* Orlando, FL: Academic Press, 1984, 7:39–102.

FELDMAN, DOUGLAS A., AND THOMAS M. JOHNSON. "Introduction." In Douglas A. Feldman and Thomas M. Johnson, eds., *The Social Dimensions of AIDS: Method and Theory.* New York: Praeger, 1986, pp. 1–12.

FERGUSON, R. BRIAN., ed. *Warfare, Culture, and Environment.* Orlando, FL: Academic Press, 1984.

FINLEY, M.I. *Politics in the Ancient World.* Cambridge: Cambridge University Press, 1983.

"The First Dentist." *Newsweek,* March 5, 1973, p. 73.

FIRTH, RAYMOND. *Rank and Religion in Tikopia.* Boston: Beacon Press, 1970.

FIRTH, RAYMOND. *Social Change in Tikopia.* New York: Macmillan, 1959.

FIRTH, RAYMOND. *We, the Tikopia.* Boston: Beacon Press, 1957.

FISCHER, JOHN. "Art Styles as Cultural Congnitive Maps." *American Anthropologist,* 63 (1961): 80–83.

FISH, PAUL R. "Beyond Tools: Middle Paleolithic Debitage Analysis and Cultural Inference." *Journal of Anthropological Research,* 37 (1981): 374–86.

FLANNERY, KENT V. "The Cultural Evolution of Civilizations." *Annual Review of Ecology and Systematics,* 3 (1972): 399–426.

FLANNERY, KENT V. "The Ecology of Early Food Production in Mesopotamia." *Science,* March 12, 1965, pp. 1247–56.

FLANNERY, KENT V. "The Origins and Ecological Effects of Early Domestication in Iran and the Near East." In Struever, ed., *Prehistoric Agriculture.*

FLANNERY, KENT V. "The Origins of Agriculture." *Annual Review of Anthropology,* 2 (1973): 271–310.

FLANNERY, KENT V. "The Origins of the Village as a Settlement Type in Mesoamerica and the Near East: A Comparative Study." In Ruth Tringham, ed., *Territoriality and Proxemics.* Andover, MA: Warner Modular Publications, 1973.

FLANNERY, KENT V. "The Research Problem." In Kent V. Flannery, ed., *Guila Naquitz: Archaic Foraging and Early Agriculture in Oaxaca, Mexico.* Orlando, FL: Academic Press, 1986, pp. 3–18.

FLEAGLE, J.G., AND R.F. KAY. "New Interpretations of the Phyletic Position of Oligocene Hominoids." In Ciochon and Corruccini, eds., *New Interpretations of Ape and Human Ancestry,* pp. 181–210.

FLEAGLE, JOHN G. *Primate Adaptation & Evolution.* San Diego: Academic Press, 1988.

FLEAGLE, JOHN G., AND RICHARD F. KAY. "The Paleobiology of Catarrhines." In Delson, ed., *Ancestors,* pp. 23–36.

FLEISCHER, ROBERT L., AND HOWARD R. HART, JR. "Fission-Track Dating: Techniques and Problems." In W.A. Bishop and J.A. Miller, eds., *Calibration of Hominid Evolution.* Toronto: University of Toronto Press, 1972.

FLEISCHER, ROBERT L., P.B. PRICE, R.M. WALKER, AND L.S.B. LEAKEY. "Fission-Track Dating of Bed I, Olduvai Gorge." *Science,* April 2, 1965, pp. 72–74.

FORD, CLELLAN S. *Smoke from Their Fires.* New Haven: Yale University Press, 1941.

FORD, CLELLAN S., AND FRANK A. BEACH. *Patterns of Sexual Behavior.* New York: Harper, 1951.

FORTES, M. *The Web of Kinship among the Tallensi.* New York: Oxford University Press, 1949.

FOSSEY, D., AND A.H. HARCOURT. "Feeding Ecol-

516

ogy of Free-ranging Mountain Gorilla (*Gorilla gorilla beringei*)." In Clutton-Brock, ed., *Primate Ecology*, pp. 415–47.

FOSSEY, DIAN. *Gorillas in the Mist*. Boston: Houghton Mifflin, 1983.

FOSTER, BRIAN L. "Ethnicity and Commerce." *American Ethnologist*, 1 (1974): 437–47.

FOSTER, GEORGE M. *Applied Anthropology*. Boston: Little, Brown, 1969.

FOSTER, GEORGE M. *Traditional Cultures and the Impact of Technolgical Change*. New York: Harper & Row, Pub., 1962.

FOWLER, MELVIN L. "A Pre-Columbian Urban Center on the Mississippi." *Scientific American*, August 1975, pp. 92–101.

FOX, ROBIN, *Kinship and Marriage: An Anthropological Perspective*. Cambridge: Cambridge University Press, 1983.

FRAKE, CHARLES O. "The Eastern Subanun of Mindanao." In G.P. Murdock, ed., *Social Structure in Southeast Asia*. Viking Fund Publications in Anthropology, no. 29, Chicago: Quandrangle, 1960.

FRANCISCUS, ROBERT G., AND ERIK TRINKAUS. "Nasal Morphology and the Emergence of *Homo erectus*." *American Journal of Physical Anthropology*, 75 (1988): 517–27.

FRANK, ANDRÉ G. *Capitalism and Underdevelopment in Latin America: Historical Studies of Chile and Brazil*. New York: Monthly Review Press, 1967.

FRAYER, DAVID W. "Body Size, Weapon Use, and Natural Selection in the European Upper Paleolithic and Mesolithic." *American Anthropologist*, 83 (1981): 57–73.

FRAYER, DAVID W., AND MILFORD H. WOLPOFF. "Sexual Dimorphism." *Annual Review of Anthropology*, 14 (1985): 429–73.

FREEDMAN, DANIEL G. "Ethnic Differences in Babies." *Human Nature*, January 1979, pp. 36–43.

FREEMAN, DEREK. *Margaret Mead and Samoa: The Making and Unmaking of an Anthropological Myth*. Cambridge, MA: Harvard University Press, 1983.

FREEMAN, J.D. "On the Concept of the Kindred." *Journal of the Royal Anthropological Institute*, 91 (1961): 192–220.

FREILICH, MORRIS, ed. *The Meaning of Culture*. Lexington, MA: Xerox, 1972.

FREUD, SIGMUND. *A General Introduction to Psychoanalysis*. Garden City, NY: Garden City Publishing Co., 1943 (originally published in German, 1917).

FREUD, SIGMUND. *Moses and Monotheism*. Katherine Jones, trans. New York: Vintage Books, 1967 (originally published in 1939).

FRIED, MORTON H. *The Evolution of Political Society: An Essay in Political Anthropology*. New York: Random House, 1967.

FRIEDL, ERNESTINE. *Vasilika: A Village in Modern Greece*. New York: Holt, Rinehart & Winston, 1962.

FRIEDRICH, PAUL. *The Language Parallax*. Austin: University of Texas Press, 1986.

FRIEDRICH, PAUL. *Proto-Indo-European Trees: The Arboreal System of a Prehistoric People*. Chicago: University of Chicago Press, 1970.

FRISANCHO, A. ROBERTO, AND LAWRENCE P. GREKSA. "Development Responses in the Acquisition of Functional Adaptation to High Altitude." In Michael A. Little and Jere D. Haas, eds., *Human Population Biology: A Transdisciplinary Science*. New York: Oxford University Press, 1989, pp. 203–21.

FRISANCHO, A. ROBERTO. *Human Adaptation: A Functional Interpretation*. Ann Arbor: University of Michigan Press, 1981.

FRISCH, ROSE E. "Fatness, Puberty, and Fertility." *Natural History*, October 1980, pp. 16–27.

FROMM, ERICH. *Psychoanalysis and Religion*. New Haven: Yale University Press, 1950.

GALDIKAS, BIRUTÉ M.F. "Orangutan Adaptation at Tanjung Puting Reserve: Mating and Ecology." In David A. Hamburg and Elizabeth R. McCown, eds., *The Great Apes*. Menlo Park, CA: Benjamin/Cummings, 1979, pp. 195–234.

GARDNER, BEATRICE T., AND R. ALLEN GARDNER. "Two Comparative Psychologists Look at Language Acquisition." In K.E. Nelson, ed., *Children's Language*. New York: Halsted Press, 1980, 2: 331–69.

GARDNER, R. ALLEN, AND BEATRICE T. GARDNER. "Comparative Psychology and Language Acquisition." In Sebeok and Umiker-Sebeok, eds., *Speaking of Apes*, pp. 287–330.

GARDNER, R. ALLEN, AND BEATRICE T. GARDNER. "Teaching Sign Language to a Chimpanzee." *Science*, August 15, 1969, pp. 664–72.

GARN, STANLEY M. *Human Races.* 3rd ed. Springfield, IL: Charles C Thomas, 1971.

GAULIN, STEVEN J.C., AND JAMES S. BOSTER. "Dowry as Female Competition." *American Anthropologist,* 92 (1990): 994–1005.

GEERTZ, CLIFFORD. "Religion as a Cultural System." In Banton, ed., *Anthropological Approaches to the Study of Religion.*

GEERTZ, CLIFFORD. *The Religion of Java.* New York: Free Press, 1960.

GELLES, RICHARD J., AND MURRAY A. STRAUS. *Intimate Violence.* New York: Simon & Schuster, 1988.

GENTNER, W., AND H.J. LIPPOLT. "The Potassium-Argon Dating of Upper Tertiary and Pleistocene Deposits." In Don Brothwell and Eric Higgs, eds., *Science in Archaeology.* New York: Basic Books, 1963.

GHIGLIERI, MICHAEL PATRICK. *The Chimpanzees of Kibale Forest: A Field Study of Ecology and Social Structure.* New York: Columbia University Press, 1984.

GIBBONS, ANN. "Déjà Vu All Over Again: Chimp-Language Wars." *Science,* March 29, 1991, pp. 1561–62.

GIBBS, JAMES L., JR. "The Kpelle of Liberia." In Gibbs, ed., *Peoples of Africa.*

GIBBS, JAMES L., JR., ed. *Peoples of Africa.* New York: Holt, Rinehart & Winston, 1965.

GIMBUTAS, MARIJA. "An Archaeologist's View of PIE* in 1975." *Journal of Indo European Studies,* 2 (1974): 289–307.

GLADWIN, CHRISTINA H. "A Theory of Real-Life Choice: Applications to Agricultural Decisions." In Barlett, ed., *Agricultural Decision-Making,* pp. 45–85.

GLASS, H. BENTLEY. "The Genetics of the Dunkers." *Scientific American,* August 1953, pp. 76–81.

GLEITMAN, LILA R., AND ERIC WANNER. "Language Acquisition: The State of the State of the Art." In Eric Wanner and Lila R. Gleitman, eds., *Language Acquisition: The State of the Art.* Cambridge: Cambridge University Press, 1982, pp. 3–48.

GOLDE, PEGGY, ed. *Women in the Field: Anthropological Experiences.* 2nd ed. Berkeley: University of California Press, 1986.

GOLDIZEN, ANNE W. "Tamarins and Marmosets: Communal Care of Offspring." In Smuts et al., eds., *Primate Societies,* pp. 34–43.

GOLDSTEIN, MELVYN C. "Stratification, Polyandry, and Family Structure in Central Tibet." *Southwestern Journal of Anthropology,* 27 (1971): 65–74.

GOLDSTEIN, MELVYN C. "When Brothers Share a Wife." *Natural History,* March 1987, 39-48.

GOLDSTONE, J.A. "The Comparative and Historical Study of Revolutions." *Annual Review of Sociology,* 8 (1982): 187–207.

GOODALL, JANE. "My Life among Wild Chimpanzees." *National Geographic,* August 1963, pp. 272–308.

GOODE, WILLIAM J. *The Family.* Englewood Cliffs, NJ: Prentice Hall, 1964.

GOODE, WILLIAM J. *World Revolution and Family Patterns.* New York: Free Press, 1970.

GOODENOUGH, WARD H. *Cooperation in Change.* New York: Russell Sage Foundation, 1963.

GOODENOUGH, WARD H. *Property Kin, and Community on Truk.* New Haven: Yale University Press, 1951.

GOODMAN, ALAN H., AND GEORGE J. ARMELAGOS. "Disease and Death at Dr. Dickson's Mounds." *Natural History,* September 1985, pp. 12–19.

GOODMAN, ALAN H., JOHN LALLO, GEORGE J. ARMELAGOS, AND JEROME C. ROSE. "Health Changes at Dickson Mounds, Illinois (A.D. 950–1300)." In Cohen and Armelagos, eds., *Paleopathology at the Origins of Agriculture,* pp. 271–301.

GOODMAN, MADELEINE J., P. BION GRIFFIN, AGNES A. ESTIOKO-GRIFFIN, AND JOHN S. GROVE. "The Compatability of Hunting and Mothering among the Agta Hunter-Gatherers of the Philippines." *Sex Roles,* 12 (1985): 1199–209.

GOODRICH, L. CARRINGTON. *A Short History of the Chinese People.* 3rd ed. New York: Harper & Row, 1959.

GOODY, JACK. "Cousin Terms." *Southwestern Journal of Anthropology,* 26 (1970): 125–42.

GOODY, JACK, AND S.J. TAMBIAH. *Bridewealth and Dowry.* Cambridge: Cambridge University Press, 1973.

GORER, G. "Themes in Japanese Culture." *Transactions of the New York Academy of Sciences.* 5 (1943): 106–24.

GORER, GEOFFREY, AND JOHN RICKMAN. *The People*

of Great Russia: A Psychological Study. New York: Chanticleer, 1950.

GORMAN, CHESTER. "The Hoabinhian and After: Subsistence Patterns in Southeast Asia during the Late Pleistocene and Early Recent Periods." *World Archaelology,* 2 (1970): 315–19.

GOSSEN, GARY H. "Temporal and Spatial Equivalents in Chamula Ritual Symbolism." In Lessa and Vogt, eds., *Reader in Comparative Religion,* 4th ed.

GOUGH, KATHLEEN. "The Nayars and the Definition of Marriage." *Journal of the Royal Anthropological Institute,* 89 (1959): 23–34.

GOULD, RICHARD A. *Yiwara: Foragers of the Australian Desert.* New York: Scribner's, 1969.

GRABURN, NELSON H. *Eskimos without Igloos.* Boston: Little, Brown, 1969.

GRAHAM, SUSAN BRANDT. "Biology and Human Social Behavior: A Response to van den Berghe and Barash." *American Anthropologist,* 81 (1979): 357–60.

GRAY, J. PATRICK. *Primate Sociobiology.* New Haven: HRAF Press, 1985.

GRAY, J. PATRICK, AND LINDA D. WOLFE. "Height and Sexual Dimorphism of Stature among Human Societies." *American Journal of Physical Anthropology,* 53 (1980): 446–52.

GRAYSON, DONALD K. "Explaining Pleistocene Extinctions: Thoughts on the Structure of a Debate." In Paul S. Martin and Richard G. Klein, eds., *Quaternary Extinctions: A Prehistoric Revolution.* Tucson: University of Arizona Press, 1984, pp. 807–23.

GRAYSON, DONALD K. "Pleistocene Avifaunas and the Overkill Hypothesis." *Science,* February 18, 1977, pp. 691–92.

GREENBERG, JOSEPH H. *Anthropological Linguistics: An Introduction.* New York: Random House, 1968.

GREENBERG, JOSEPH H. "Linguistic Evidence regarding Bantu Origins." *Journal of African History,* 13 (1972): 189–216.

GREENFIELD, PATRICIA MARKS, AND E. SUE SAVAGE-RUMBAUGH. "Grammatical Combination in *Pan paniscus:* Processes of Learning and Invention in the Evolution and Development of Language." In Sue Taylor Parker and Kathleen Rita Gibson, eds., *"Language" and Intelligence in Monkeys and Apes: Comparative Developmen-*

tal Perspectives. New York: Cambridge University Press, 1990, pp. 540–78.

GREKSA, LAWRENCE P., AND CYNTHIA M. BEALL. "Development of Chest Size and Lung Function at High Altitude." In Michael A. Little and Jere D. Haas, eds., *Human Population Biology: A Transdisciplinary Science.* New York: Oxford University Press, 1989, pp. 222–38.

GRINE, FREDERICK E. "Evolutionary History of the 'Robust' Australopithecines: A Summary and Historical Perspective." In Frederick E. Grine, ed., *Evolutionary History of the "Robust" Australopithecines.* New York: Aldine de Gruyter, 1988, pp. 509–20.

GRÖGER, B. LISA. "Of Men and Machines: Cooperation among French Family Farmers." *Ethnology,* 20 (1981): 163–75.

GROSS, DANIEL R., GEORGE EITEN, NANCY M. FLOWERS, FRANCISCA M. LEOI, MADELINE LATTMAN RITTER, AND DENNIS W. WERNER. "Ecology and Acculturation among Native Peoples of Central Brazil." *Science,* November 30, 1979, pp. 1043–50.

GROSS, DANIEL R., AND BARBARA A. UNDERWOOD. "Technological Change and Caloric Costs: Sisal Agriculture in Northeastern Brazil." *American Anthropologist,* 73 (1971): 725–40.

GRUBSER, NICHOLAS J. *The Nunamiut Eskimos: Hunters of Caribou.* New Haven: Yale University Press, 1965.

GUIORA, ALEXANDER A., BENJAMIN BLIT-HALLAHMI, RISTO FRIED, AND CECELIA YODER. "Language Environment and Gender Identity Attainment." *Language Learning,* 32 (1982). 289–304.

GULLIVER, P.H. "The Arusha: Economic and Social Change." In Paul Bohannan and George Dalton, eds., *Markets in Africa.* Garden City, N.Y.: Doubleday, 1965.

GUMPERZ, JOHN J. "Dialect Differences and Social Stratification in a North Indian Village." In *Language in Social Groups: Essays by John L. Gumperz,* selected and introduced by Anwar S. Dil. Stanford, Calif.: Stanford University Press, 1971, pp. 25–47.

GUMPERZ, JOHN J. "Speech Variation and the Study of Indian Civilization." *American Anthropologist,* 63 (1961): 976–88.

GUNDERS, S., AND J.W.M. WHITING. "Mother-Infant Separation and Physical Growth." *Ethnology*, 7 (1968): 196–206.

GURR, TED ROBERT. "Historical Trends in Violent Crime: Europe and the United States." In T.R. Gurr, ed., *Violence in America, Vol. I: The History of Crime.* Newbury Park, CA: Sage, 1989, pp. 21–49.

GURR, TED ROBERT. "The History of Violent Crime in America: An Overview." In T.R. Gurr, ed., *Violence in America, Vol. I: The History of Crime.* Newbury Park, CA: Sage, 1989, pp. 11–12.

GUTHRIE, DALE R. "Mosaics, Allelochemics, and Nutrients: An Ecological Theory of Late Pleistocene Megafaunal Extinctions." In Paul S. Martin and Richard G. Klein, eds., *Quarternary Extinctions: A Prehistoric Revolution.* Tucson: University of Arizona Press, 1984, pp. 259–98.

HAAS, JONATHAN, ed. *The Anthropology of War.* Cambridge: Cambridge University Press, 1990.

HAAS, MARY R. "Men's and Women's Speech in Koasati." *Language,* 20 (1944): 142–49.

HACKENBERG, ROBERT A. "Scientists or Survivors? The Future of Applied Anthropology under Maximum Uncertainty." In Robert T. Trotter II, ed., *Anthropology for Tomorrow: Creating Practitioner-Oriented Applied Anthropology Programs.* Washington: American Anthropological Association, 1988, pp. 170–85.

HAHN, EMILY. "Chimpanzees and Language." *New Yorker,* April 24, 1971, pp. 54ff.

HALDANE, J.B.S. "Human Evolution: Past and Future." In Glenn L. Jepsen, Ernst Mayr, and George Gaylord Simpson, eds., *Genetics, Paleontology, and Evolution.* New York: Atheneum, 1963.

HALL, EDWARD T. *The Hidden Dimension.* Garden City, NY: Doubleday, 1966.

HALLAM, A. "Alfred Wegener and the Hypothesis of Continental Drift." *Scientific American,* February 1975, pp. 88–97.

HAMES, RAYMOND. "Sharing among the Yanomamo: Part I, the Effects of Risk." In Elizabeth Cashdan, ed., *Risk and Uncertainty in Tribal and Peasant Economies.* Boulder, CO: Westview Press, 1990, pp. 89–105.

HANDWERKER, W. PENN, AND PAUL V. CROSBIE.

"Sex and Dominance." *American Anthropologist,* 84 (1982): 97–104.

HANNA, JOEL M., MICHAEL A. LITTLE, AND DONALD M. AUSTIN. "Climatic Physiology." In Michael A. Little and Jere D. Haas, eds., *Human Population Biology: A Transdisciplinary Science.* New York: Oxford University Press, 1989, pp. 132–51.

HANSON, JEFFREY R. "Age-Set Theory and Plains Indian Age-Grading: A Critical Review and Revision." *American Ethnologist,* 15 (1988): 349–64.

HARCOURT, A.H. "The Social Relations and Group Structure of Wild Mountain Gorillas." In David A. Hamburg and Elizabeth R. McCown, *The Great Apes.* Menlo Park, CA: Benjamin/Cummings, 1979, pp. 187–92.

HARDOY, JORGE, AND DAVID SATTERTHWAITE. "The Legal and the Illegal City." In Lloyd Rodwin, ed., *Shelter, Settlement, and Development.* Boston: Allen & Unwin, 1987 pp. 304–38.

HARLAN, JACK R. "A Wild Wheat Harvest in Turkey." *Archaelogy,* 20, no. 3 (June 1967): 197–201.

HARLAN, JACK R., J.M.J. DE WET, AND ANN STEMLER, eds. *Origins of African Plant Domestication.* The Hague: Mouton, 1976, pp. 3–19.

HARLAN, JACK R., J.M.J. DE WET, AND ANN STEMLER. "Plant Domestication and Indigenous African Agriculture." In Harlan, De Wet, and Stemler, eds., *Origins of African Plant Domestication,* pp. 3–19.

HARLAN, JACK R., AND ANN STEMLER. "The Races of Sorghum in Africa." In Harlan, De Wet, and Stemler, eds., *Origins of African Plant Domestication,* pp. 465–78.

HARLOW, H.F., et al. "Maternal Behavior of Rhesus Monkeys Deprived of Mothering and Peer Association in Infancy." *Proceedings of the American Philosophical Society,* 110 (1966): 58–66.

HARNER, MICHAEL. "The Role of Hallucinogenic Plants in European Witchcraft." In Michael Harner, ed., *Hallucinogens and Shamanism.* New York: Oxford University Press, 1972, pp. 127–50.

HARNER, MICHAEL J. *The Jivaro.* Garden City, NY: Doubleday Anchor, 1973.

HARNER, MICHAEL J. "Scarcity, the Factors of Production, and Social Evolution." In Steven Polgar, ed., *Population, Ecology, and Social Evolution.* The Hague: Mouton, 1975.

HARRIS, DAVID R. "Settling Down: An Evolutionary Model for the Transformation of Mobile Bands into Sedentary Communities." In J. Friedman and M.J. Rowlands, eds., *The Evolution of Social Systems.* London: Duckworth, 1977.

HARRIS, MARVIN. *Cows, Pigs, Wars and Witches: The Riddles of Culture.* New York: Random House, Vintage, 1974.

HARRIS, MARVIN. "The Cultural Ecology of India's Sacred Cattle." *Current Anthropology,* 7 (1966): 51–63.

HARRIS, MARVIN. *Cultural Materialism: The Struggle for a Science of Culture.* New York: Random House, 1979.

HARRIS, MARVIN. *Patterns of Race in the Americas.* New York: Walker, 1964.

HARRIS, MARVIN. *The Rise of Anthropological Theory: A History of Theories of Culture.* New York: Thomas Y. Crowell, 1968.

HARRIS, MARVIN, AND ERIC B. ROSS. *Food and Evolution: Toward a Theory of Human Food Habits.* Philadelphia: Temple University Press, 1987.

HARRISON, G.A., J.M. TANNER, D.R. PILBEAM, AND P.T. BAKER. *Human Biology: An Introduction to Human Evolution, Variation, Growth, and Adaptability,* 3rd ed. Oxford: Oxford University Press, 1988.

HARRISON, GAIL G. "Primary Adult Lactase Deficiency: A Problem in Anthropological Genetics." *American Anthropologist,* 77 (1975): 812–35.

HARRISON, PETER D., AND B.L. TURNER II, eds. *Pre-Hispanic Maya Agriculture.* Albuquerque: University of New Mexico Press, 1978.

HART, HORNELL. "The Logistic Growth of Political Areas." *Social Forces,* 26 (1948): 396–408.

HASSAN, FEKRI A. *Demographic Archaeology.* New York: Academic Press, 1981.

HAUSFATER, GLENN, JEANNE ALTMANN, AND STUART ALTMANN. "Long-Term Consistency of Dominance Relations among Female Baboons." *Science,* August 20, 1982, pp. 752–54.

HEIDER, KARL. *The Dugum Dani.* Chicago: Aldine, 1970.

HEIDER, KARL. *Grand Valley Dani: Peaceful Warriors.* New York: Holt, Rinehart & Winston, 1979.

HEISE, DAVID R. "Cultural Patterning of Sexual Socialization." *American Sociological Review,* 32 (1967): 726–39.

HEISER, CHARLES B., JR. *Of Plants and People.* Normal: University of Oklahoma Press, 1985.

HELMS, MARY W. *Ancient Panama: Chiefs in Search of Power.* Austin: University of Texas Press, 1979.

HELMS, MARY W. *Middle America.* Englewood Cliffs, NJ: Prentice Hall, 1975.

HEMPEL, CARL G. *Aspects of Scientific Explanation.* New York: Free Press, 1965.

HENDRIX, LLEWELLYN. "Economy and Child Training Reexamined." *Ethos,* 13 (1985): 246–61.

HENRY, DONALD O. *From Foraging to Agriculture: The Levant at the End of the Ice Age.* Philadelphia: University of Pennsylvania Press, 1989.

HENRY, EDWARD O. "The Variety of Music in a North Indian Village: Reassessing Cantometrics." *Ethnomusicology,* 20 (1976): 49–66.

HERRMAN, HELEN. "A Survey of Homeless Mentally Ill People in Melbourne, Australia." *Hospital and Community Psychiatry,* 41 (1990): 1291–92.

HEWES, GORDON W. "Food Transport and the Origin of Hominid Bipedalism." *American Anthropologist,* 63 (1961): 687–710.

HEWLETT, BARRY S., AND L.L. CAVALLI-SFORZA. "Cultural Transmission among Aka Pygmies." *American Anthropologist,* 88 (1986): 922–34.

HIATT, L.R. "Polyandry in Sri Lanka: A Test Case for Parental Investment Theory." *Man,* 15 (1980): 583–98.

HICKEY, GERALD CANNON. *Village in Vietnam.* New Haven: Yale University Press, 1964.

HICKSON, LETITIA. "The Social Contexts of Apology in Dispute Settlement: A Cross-Cultural Study." *Ethnology,* 25 (1986): 283–94.

HILL, JANE H. "Apes and Language." *Annual Review of Anthropology,* 7 (1978): 89–112.

HILL, KIM, HILLARD KAPLAN, KRISTEN HAWKES, AND A. MAGDALENA HURTADO. "Foraging Decisions among Aché Hunter-Gatherers: New Data and Implications for Optimal Foraging Models." *Ethology and Sociobiology,* 8 (1987): 1–36.

HILL, POLLY. *The Migrant Cocoa-Farmers of Southern*

Ghana: A Study in Rural Capitalism. Cambridge: Cambridge University Press, 1963.

HOBSBAWM, E.J. Age of Revolution. New York: Praeger, 1970.

HOCK, RAYMOND J. "The Physiology of High Altitude." Scientific American, February 1970, pp. 52–62.

HOCKETT, C.F., AND R. ASCHER. "The Human Revolution." Current Anthropology, 5 (1964): 135–68.

HOEBEL, E. ADAMSON. The Cheyennes: Indians of the Great Plains. New York: Holt, Rinehart & Winston, 1960.

HOEBEL, E. ADAMSON. The Law of Primitive Man. New York: Atheneum, 1968 (orginally published 1954).

HOIJER, HARRY. "Cultural Implications of Some Navaho Linguistic Categories." In Hymes, ed., Language in Culture and Society. Originally published in Language, 27 (1951): 111–20.

HOLE, FRANK. "Environmental Shock and Urban Origins." Unpublished manuscript.

HOLE, FRANK, KENT V. FLANNERY, AND JAMES A. NEELY. Prehistory and Human Ecology of the Deh Luran Plain. Memoirs of the Museum of Anthropology, no. 1. Ann Arbor: University of Michigan, 1969.

HOLE, FRANK, AND ROBERT F. HEIZER. An Introduction to Prehistoric Archeology. 3rd ed. New York: Holt, Rinehart & Winston, 1973.

HOLLAND, DOROTHY, AND NAOMI QUINN, eds., Cultural Models in Language and Thought. Cambridge: Cambridge University Press, 1987.

HOLLOWAY, RALPH L. "The Casts of Fossil Hominid Brains." Scientific American, July 1974, pp. 106–15.

HOLLOWAY, RALPH L. "Robust' Australopithecine Brain Endoclasts: Some Preliminary Observations." In Frederick E. Grine, ed., Evolutionary History of the "Robust" Australopithecines. New York: Aldine de Gruyter, 1988, pp. 97–105.

HONIGMANN, JOHN J. Personality in Culture. New York: Harper & Row, Pub., 1967.

HOUSTON, STEPHEN D. "The Phonetic Decipherment of Mayan Glyphs." Antiquity, 62 (1988): 126–35.

HOWELL, F. CLARK. "Observations on the Earlier Phases of the European Lower Paleolithic." In Recent Studies in Paleoanthropology; American Anthropologist, special publication, April 1966, pp. 88–200.

HOWELL, NANCY. Demography of the Dobe !Kung. New York: Academic Press, 1979.

HRDY, SARAH BLAFFER. The Langurs of Abu: Female and Male Strategies of Reproduction. Cambridge, MA: Harvard University Press, 1977.

HSU, FRANCIS L.K., ed. Psychological Anthropology, 2nd ed. Cambridge, MA: Schenkman, 1972.

HUNT, MORTON. Sexual Behavior in the 1970s. Chicago: Playboy Press, 1974.

HURTADO, ANA M., KRISTEN HAWKES, KIM HILL, AND HILLARD KAPLAN. "Female Subsistence Strategies among the Aché Hunter-Gatherers of Eastern Paraguay." Human Ecology, 13 (1985): 1–28.

HUSS-ASHMORE, REBECCA, AND FRANCIS E. JOHNSTON. "Bioanthropological Research in Developing Countries." Annual Review of Anthropology, 14 (1985): 475–527.

HYMES, DELL. Foundations in Sociolinguistics: An Ethnographic Approach. Philadelphia: University of Pennsylvania Press, 1974.

HYMES, DELL, ed. Language in Culture and Society: A Reader in Linguistics and Anthropology. New York: Harper & Row, Pub., 1964.

IRONS, WILLIAM. "Natural Selection, Adaptation, and Human Social Behavior." In Chagnon and Irons, eds., Evolutionary Biology and Human Social Behavior: An Anthropological Perspective, pp. 4–39.

IRVING, WILLIAM N. "Context and Chronology of Early Man in the Americas." Annual Review of Anthropology, 14 (1985): 529–55.

IRWIN, MARC H., GARY N. SCHAFER, AND CYNTHIA P. FEIDEN. "Emic and Unfamiliar Category Sorting of Mano Farmers and U.S. Undergraduates." Journal of Cross-Cultural Psychology, 5 (1974): 407–23.

ISAAC, GLYNN. "The Diet of Early Man: Aspects of Archaeological Evidence from Lower and Middle Pleistocene Sites in Africa." World Archaeology, 2 (1971): 277–99.

ISAAC, GLYNN LI. "The Archaeology of Human Origins: Studies of the Lower Pleistocene in East Africa, 1971-1981." In Fred Wendorf and Angela E. Close, eds., Advances in World Archaeology. Orlando, FL: Academic Press, 1984, 3: 1–87.

ITKONEN, T.I. "The Lapps of Finland." *Southwestern Journal of Anthropology*, 7 (1951): 32–68.

JAMES, WILLIAM. *The Varieties of Religious Experience: A Study in Human Nature*. New York: Modern Library, 1902.

JANZEN, DANIEL H. "Tropical Argroecosystems." *Science*, December 21, 1973, pp. 1212–19.

JELLIFFE, DERRICK B., AND E.F. PATRICE JELLIFFE. "Human Milk, Nutrition, and the World Resource Crisis." *Science*, May 9, 1975, pp. 557–61.

JENNESS, DIAMOND. *The People of the Twilight*. Chicago: University of Chicago Press, 1959.

JENNINGS, J.D. *Prehistory of North America*. New York: McGraw-Hill, 1968.

JENSEN, ARTHUR. "How Much Can We Boost IQ and Scholastic Achievement?" *Harvard Educational Review*, 29 (1969): 1–123.

JOHANSON, DONALD C., AND MAITLAND EDEY. *Lucy: The Beginnings of Humankind*. New York: Simon & Schuster, 1981.

JOHANSON, DONALD C., AND TIM D. WHITE. "A Systematic Assessment of Early African Hominids." *Science*, January 26, 1979, pp. 321–30.

JOHNSON, ALLEN W. *Quantification in Cultural Anthropology: An Introduction to Research Design*. Stanford, CA: Stanford University Press, 1978.

JOHNSON, GREGORY A. "Aspects of Regional Analysis in Archaeology." *Annual Review of Anthropology*, 6 (1977): 479–508.

JOHNSON, GREGORY. "The Changing Organization of Uruk Administration on the Susiana Plain." In Frank Hole, ed., *Archaeology of Western Iran*. Washington, DC: Smithsonian Institution Press, 1987, pp. 107–39.

JOLLY, ALISON. *The Evolution of Primate Behavior*. 2nd ed. New York: Macmillan, 1985.

JUDGE, W. JAMES, AND JERRY DAWSON. "Paleo-Indian Settlement Technology in New Mexico." *Science*, June 16, 1972, pp. 1210–16.

JUNG, CARL G. *Psychology and Religion*. New Haven: Yale University Press, 1938.

JUNGERS, WILLIAM L. "New Estimates of Body Size in Australopithecines." In Frederick E. Grine, ed., *Evolutionary History of the "Robust" Australopithecines*. New York: Aldine de Gruyter, 1988, pp. 115–25.

JUNGERS, WILLIAM L. "Relative Joint Size and Hominoid Locomotor Adaptations with Implications for the Evolution of Hominid Bipedalism." *Journal of Human Evolution*, 17 (1988): 247–65.

KAPLAN, HILLARD, AND KIM HILL. "Food Sharing among Aché Foragers: Tests of Explanatory Hypotheses." *Current Anthropology*, 26 (1985): 223–46.

KAPLAN, HILLARD, KIM HILL, AND A. MAGDALENA HURTADO. "Risk, Foraging and Food Sharing Among the Aché." In Cashdan, ed., *Risk and Uncertainty in Tribal and Peasant Economies.*

KARDINER, ABRAM, WITH RALPH LINTON. *The Individual and his Society*. New York: Golden Press, 1946. (Originally published in 1939 by Columbia University Press.)

KASARDA, JOHN D. "Economic Structure and Fertility: A Comparative Analysis." *Demography*, 8, no. 3 (August 1971): 307–18.

KAY, RICHARD F., AND FREDERICK E. GRINE. "Tooth Morphology, Wear and Diet in *Australopithecus* and *Paranthropus* from Southern Africa. In Frederick E. Grine, ed., *Evolutionary History of the "Robust" Australopithecines*. New York: Aldine de Gruyter, 1988, pp. 427–47.

KEELEY, LAWRENCE H. *Experimental Determination of Stone Tool Uses: A Microwear Analysis*. Chicago: University of Chicago Press, 1980.

KELLER, HELEN. *The Story of My Life*. New York: Dell, 1974 (originally published 1902).

KELLY, RAYMOND C. *The Nuer Conquest: The Structure and Development of an Expansionist System*. Ann Arbor: University of Michigan Press, 1985.

KELLY, RAYMOND C. "Witchcraft and Sexual Relations: An Exploration in the Social and Semantic Implications of the Structure of Belief." Paper presented at the annual meeting of the American Anthropological Association, Mexico City, 1974.

KING, SETH S. "Some Farm Machinery Seems Less Than Human." *New York Times*, April 8, 1979, p. E9.

KLEIN, RICHARD G. "The Ecology of Early Man in Southern Africa." *Science*, July 8, 1977, pp. 115–26.

KLEIN, RICHARD G. *The Human Career: Human Bi-*

ological and Cultural Origins. Chicago: University of Chicago Press, 1989.

KLEIN, RICHARD G. "Ice-Age Hunters of the Ukraine." *Scientific American,* June 1974, pp. 96–105.

KLEIN, RICHARD G. "Reconstructing How Early People Exploited Animals: Problems and Prospects." In Nitecki and Nitecki, eds. *The Evolution of Human Hunting,* pp. 11–45.

KLEIN, RICHARD G. "The Stone Age Prehistory of Southern Africa." *Annual Review of Anthropology,* 12 (1983): 25–48.

KLIMA, BOHUSLAV. "The First Ground-Plan of an Upper Paleolithic Loess Settlement in Middle Europe and Its Meaning." In Robert J. Braidwood and Gordon R. Willey, Eds., *Courses toward Urban Life: Archaelogical Consideration of Some Cultural Alternatives.* Viking Fund Publications in Anthropology, no. 32, Chicago: Aldine, 1962.

KLINEBERG, OTTO, ed. *Characteristics of the American Negro.* New York: Harper & Brothers, 1944.

KLINEBERG, OTTO. "Foreword." In Segall, *Cross-Cultural Psychology.*

KLINEBERG, OTTO. *Negro Intelligence and Selective Migration.* New York: Columbia University Press, 1935.

KLUCKHOHN, CLYDE. "As an Anthropologist Views It." In A. Deutsch, ed., *Sex Habits of American Men.* Englewood Cliffs, NJ: Prentice Hall, 1948.

KLUCKHOHN, CLYDE. "Recurrent Themes in Myths and Mythmaking." In Dundes, ed., *The Study of Folklore.*

KNAUFT, BRUCE M. "Cargo Cults and Relational Separation." *Behavior Science Research,* 13 (1978): 185–240.

KOCH, KLAUS-FRIEDRICH, SORAYA ALTORKI, ANDREW ARNO, AND LETITIA HICKSON. "Ritual Reconciliation and the Obviation of Grievances: A Comparative Study in the Ethnography of Law." *Ethnology,* 16 (1977): 269–84.

KONNER, MELVIN. *The Tangled Wing: Biological Constraints on the Human Spirit.* New York: Harper & Row, Pub., 1982.

KONNER, MELVIN, AND CAROL WORTHMAN. "Nursing Frequency, Gonadal Function, and Birth Spacing among !Kung Hunter-Gatherers." *Science,* February 15, 1980, pp. 788–91.

KORBIN, JILL E. "Introduction." In Jill E. Korbin, ed., *Child Abuse and Neglect: Cross-Cultural Perspectives.* Berkeley, CA: University of California, 1981, pp. 1–12.

KOTTAK, CONRAD P. *Assault on Pardise: Social Change in a Brazilian Village.* New York: Random House, 1983.

KRACKE, WAUD H. *Force and Persuasion: Leadership in an Amazonian Society.* Chicago: University of Chicago Press, 1979.

KRAHN, H., T.F. HARTNAGEL, AND J.W. GARTRELL. "Income Inequality and Homicide Rates: Cross-National Data and Criminological Theories." *Criminology,* 24 (1986): 269–95.

KRAMER, SAMUEL NOEL. *The Sumerians: Their History, Culture, and Character.* Chicago: University of Chicago Press, 1963.

KREBS, J.R., AND N.B. DAVIES, eds. *Behavioural Ecology: An Evolutionary Approach.* 2nd ed. Sunderland, MA: Sinauer Associates, 1984.

KROEBER, ALFRED L. *The Nature of Culture.* Chicago: University of Chicago Press, 1952.

KROEBER, THEODORA. *Ishi in Two Worlds.* Berkeley: University of California Press, 1967.

KUPER, HILDA. *A South African Kingdom: The Swazi.* 2nd ed. New York: Holt, Rinehart & Winston, 1981.

KUPER, HILDA. "The Swazi of Swaziland." In Gibbs, ed., *Peoples of Africa.*

KUSHNER, GILBERT. "Applied Anthropology." In William G. Emener and Margaret Darrow, eds., *Career Explorations in Human Services.* Springfield, IL: Charles C Thomas, 1991.

LABARRE, W. "Some Observations on Character Structure in the Orient: The Japanese." *Psychiatry,* 8 (1945): 326–42.

LAITMAN, JEFFREY. "The Anatomy of Human Speech." *Natural History,* August 1984, pp. 20–27.

LAMBERT, WILLIAM W., LEIGH MINTURN TRIANDIS, AND MARGERY WOLF. "Some Correlates of Beliefs in the Malevolence and Benevolence of Supernatural Beings: A Cross-Societal Study." *Journal of Abnormal and Social Psychology,* 58 (1959): 162–69.

LANDAUER, THOMAS K. "Infantile Vaccination and the Secular Trend in Stature." *Ethos,* 1 (1973): 499–503.

LANDAUER, THOMAS K., AND JOHN W.M. WHITING.

"Correlates and Consequences of Stress in Infancy." In Munroe, Munroe, and Whiting, eds., *Handbook of Cross-Cultural Human Development*, pp. 355–75.

LANDAUER, THOMAS K., AND JOHN W.M. WHITING. "Infantile Stimulation and Adult Stature of Human Males." *American Anthropologist*, 66 (1964): 1007–28.

LANDES, RUTH. "The Abnormal among the Ojibwa." *Journal of Abnormal and Social Psychology*, 33 (1938): 14–33.

LANGNESS, LEWIS L. *The Study of Culture.* San Francisco: Chandler and Sharp, 1974.

LANGNESS, LEWIS L. *The Study of Culture,* rev. ed. Novato, CA: Chandler and Sharp, 1987.

LASSWELL, HAROLD. *Politics: Who Gets What, When, How.* New York: McGraw-Hill, 1936.

LEACH, JERRY W. "Introduction." In Jerry W. Leach and Edmund Leach, eds., *The Kula: New Perspectives on Massim Exchange.* Cambridge: Cambridge University Press, 1983, pp. 1–26.

LEACOCK, ELEANOR. "The Montagnais 'Hunting Territory' and the Fur Trade." *American Anthropological Association,* Memoir 78, (1954): 1–59.

LEACOCK, ELEANOR, AND RICHARD LEE. "Introduction." In Eleanor Leacock and Richard Lee, eds., *Politics and History in Band Societies.* Cambridge: Cambridge University Press, 1982, pp. 1–20.

LEAKEY, L.S.B. "Finding the World's Earliest Man." *National Geographic,* September 1960, pp. 420–35.

LEAKEY, R.E.F. "An Overview of the East Rudolf Hominidae." In Yves Coppens, F. Clark Howell, Glynn Ll. Isaac, and Richard E.F. Leakey, eds., *Earliest Man and Environments in the Lake Rudolf Basin.* Chicago: University of Chicago Press, 1976.

LEAKEY, RICHARD E. *The Making of Mankind.* New York: Dutton, 1981.

LEE, PHYLLIS C. "Home Range, Territory and Intergroup Encounters." In Robert A. Hinde, ed., *Primate Social Relationship: An Integrated Approach.* Sunderland, MA: Sinauer Associates, 1983, pp. 231–33.

LEE, RICHARD B. *The !Kung San: Men, Women, and Work in a Foraging Society.* Cambridge: Cambridge University Press, 1979.

LEE, RICHARD B. "Population Growth and the Beginnings of Sedentary Life among the !Kung Bushmen." In Brian Spooner, ed., *Population Growth: Anthropological Implications.* Cambridge, MA: M.I.T. Press, 1972.

LEE, RICHARD B. "What Hunters Do for a Living, or, How to Make Out on Scarce Resources." In Lee and DeVore, eds., *Man the Hunter.*

LEE, RICHARD B., AND IRVEN DEVORE, eds. *Man the Hunter.* Chicago: Aldine, 1968.

LEES, SUSAN H., AND DANIEL G. BATES. "The Origins of Specialized Nomadic Pastoralism: A Systemic Model." *American Antiquity,* 39 (1974): 187–93.

LEHMANN, ARTHUR C., AND JAMES E. MYERS. *Magic, Witchcraft, and Religion: An Anthropological Study of the Supernatural.* Palo Alto, CA: Mayfield, 1985.

LEIBOWITZ, LILA. *Females, Males, Families: A Biosocial Approach.* North Scituate, MA: Duxbury, 1978.

LEIS, NANCY B. "Women in Groups: Ijaw Women's Associations." In Rosaldo and Lamphere, eds., *Woman, Culture, and Society.*

LENSKI, GERHARD. *Power and Privilege: A Theory of Social Stratification.* Chapel Hill: University of North Carolina Press, 1984.

LEROI-GOURHAN, ANDRÉ. "The Evolution of Paleolithic Art." *Scientific American,* February 1968, pp. 58–70.

LESSA, WILLIAM A., AND EVON Z. VOGT, eds. *Reader in Comparative Religion: An Anthropological Approach.* 3rd ed. New York: Harper & Row, Pub., 1971.

LESSA, WILLIAM A., AND EVON Z. VOGT, eds. *Reader in Comparative Religion: An Anthropological Approach,* 4th ed. New York: Harper & Row, Pub., 1979.

LEVINE, NANCY E. "Women's Work and Infant Feeding: A Case from Rural Nepal." *Ethnology,* 27 (1988): 231–51.

LEVINE, ROBERT A. *Dreams and Deeds: Achievement Motivation in Nigeria.* Chicago: University of Chicago Press, 1966.

LEVINE, ROBERT A., AND BARBARA B. LEVINE. "Nyansongo: A Gusii Community in Kenya." In Beatrice B. Whiting, ed., *Six Cultures.* New York: John Wiley, 1963.

LEVINSON, DAVID. *Family Violence in Cross-Cultural Perspective.* Newbury Park, CA: Sage, 1989.

LEVINSON, DAVID. *Instructor's and Librarian's Guide to the HRAF Archive.* New Haven: Human Relations Area Files, 1988.

LEVINSON, DAVID, AND MARTIN J. MALONE, eds. *Toward Explaining Human Culture: A Critical Review of the Findings of Worldwide Cross-Cultural Research.* New Haven: HRAF Press, 1980.

LÉVI-STRAUSS, CLAUDE. *The Elementary Structures of Kinship.* Rev. ed. Trans. James H. Bell and J.R. von Sturmer. Ed. Rodney Needham. Boston: Beacon Press, 1969.

LÉVI-STRAUSS, CLAUDE. *The Raw and the Cooked.* Trans. John and Doreen Weightman. New York: Harper & Row, Pub., 1969 (originally published in French, 1964).

LÉVI-STRAUSS, CLAUDE. *The Savage Mind.* Trans. George Weidenfeld and Nicolson, Ltd. Chicago: University of Chicago Press, 1966.

LÉVI-STRAUSS, CLAUDE. "The Sorcerer and His Magic." In Lévi-Strauss, *Structural Anthropology.*

LÉVI-STRAUSS, CLAUDE. *Structural Anthropology.* Trans. Claire Jacobson and Brooke Grundfest Schoepf. New York: Basic Books, 1963.

LEWIN, ROGER. "Ethiopian Stone Tools Are World's Oldest." *Science,* February 20, 1981, pp. 806–7.

LEWIN, ROGER. "Fossil Lucy Grows Younger, Again." *Science,* January 7, 1983, pp. 43–44.

LEWIN, ROGER. "Is the Orangutan a Living Fossil?" *Science,* December 16, 1983, pp. 1222–23.

LEWIS, I.M. *A Pastoral Democracy.* New York: Oxford University Press, 1961.

LEWIS, OSCAR. *Life in a Mexican Village: Tepoztlan Revisited.* Urbana: University of Illinois Press, 1951.

LEWIS, OSCAR (WITH THE ASSISTANCE OF VICTOR BARNOUW). *Village Life in Northern India.* Urbana: University of Illinois Press, 1958.

LEWONTIN, R.C. "The Apportionment of Human Diversity." In Theodosius Dobzhansky, ed., *Evolutionary Biology.* New York: Plenum, 1972, pp. 381–98.

LIEBERMAN, PHILIP. *Uniquely Human: The Evolution of Speech, Thought, and Selfless Behavior.* Cambridge, MA: Harvard University Press, 1991, pp. 109–10.

LINTON, RALPH. *The Cultural Background of Personality.* New York: Appleton-Century-Crofts, 1945.

LINTON, RALPH. *The Study of Man.* New York: Appleton-Century-Crofts, 1936.

LITTLE, KENNETH. "The Political Function of the Poro." *Africa,* 35 (1965): 349–65; 36 (1966): 62–71.

LITTLE, KENNETH. "The Role of Voluntary Associations in West African Urbanization." *American Anthropologist,* 59 (1957): 582–93.

LITTLE, KENNETH. *West African Urbanization.* New York: Cambridge University Press, 1965.

LOEHLIN, JOHN C., GARDNER LINDZEY, AND J.N. SPUHLER. *Race Differences in Intelligence.* San Francisco: W. H. Freeman & Company Publishers. 1975.

LOFTIN, COLIN K. "Warfare and Societal Complexity: A Cross-Cultural Study of Organized Fighting in Preindustrial Societies." Ph.D. diss, University of North Carolina at Chapel Hill, 1971.

LOFTIN, COLIN, DAVID MCDOWALL, AND JAMES BOUDOURIS. "Economic Change and Homicide in Detroit, 1926–1979." In T.R. Gurr, ed., *Violence in America, Vol. I: The History of Crime.* Newbury Park, CA: Sage, 1989, pp. 163–77.

LOMAX, ALAN. ed. *Folk Song Style and Culture.* American Association for the Advancement of Science, Publication no. 88. Washington, DC, 1968.

LOOMIS, W. FARNSWORTH. "Skin-Pigment Regulation of Vitamin-D Biosynthesis in Man." *Science,* August 4, 1967, pp. 501–6.

LOVEJOY, C. OWEN. "Evolution of Human Walking." *Scientific American,* November 1988, pp. 118–25.

LOVEJOY, C. OWEN. "The Origin of Man." *Science,* January 23, 1981, pp. 341–50.

LOVEJOY, OWEN, KINGSBURY HEIPLE, AND ALBERT BERNSTEIN. "The Gait of *Australopithecus.*" *American Journal of Physical Anthropology,* 38 (1973): 757–79.

LOW, BOBBI. "Human Responses to Environmental Extremeness and Uncertainty." In Cashdan, eds., *Risk and Uncertainty in Trival and Peasant Economies.*

LOW, BOBBI. "Marriage Systems and Pathogen Stress in Human Societies." *American Zoologist,* 30 (1990): 325–39.

LOWIE, ROBERT H. *Primitive Society.* New York: Liveright, 1970 (originally published 1920).

LURHMANN, TANYA M. *Persuasions of the Witch's*

Craft: Ritual Magic and Witchcraft in Present-Day England. Oxford: Basil Blackwell, 1989.

LURIA, A.R. Cognitive Development: Its Cultural and Social Foundations. Cambridge. MA: Harvard University Press, 1976.

LYND, ROBERT S., AND HELEN MERRELL LYND. Middletown. New York: Harcourt, Brace, 1929.

LYND, ROBERT S., AND HELEN MERRELL LYND. Middletown in Transition. New York: Harcourt, Brace, 1937.

McCAIN, GARVIN M., AND ERWIN M. SEGAL. The Game of Science. 4th ed. Monterey, Calif.: Brooks/Cole, 1982.

McCARTHY, FREDERICK D., AND MARGARET McARTHUR. "The Food Quest and the Time Factor in Aboriginal Economic Life." In C.P. Mountford, ed., Records of the Australian-American Scientific Expedition to Arnheim Land. Volume 2, Anthropology and Nutrition. Melbourne: Melbourne University Press, 1960.

McCLELLAND, DAVID C. The Achieving Society. New York: Van Nostrand, 1961.

MACCOBY, ELEANOR E., AND CAROL N. JACKLIN. The Psychology of Sex Differences. Stanford, CA: Stanford University Press, 1974.

McCORRISTON, JOY, AND FRANK HOLE. "The Ecology of Seasonal Stress and the Origins of Agriculture in the Near East." American Anthropologist, 98 (1991): 46–69.

McCRACKEN, ROBERT D. "Lactase Deficiency: An Example of Dietary Evolution." Current Anthropology, 12 (1971): 479–500.

McHENRY, HENRY M. "New Estimates of Body Weight in Early Hominids and Their Significance to Encephalization and Megadontia in 'Robust' Australopithecines." In Frederick E. Grine, ed., Evolutionary History of the "Robust" Australopithecines New York: Aldine de Gruyter, 1988, pp. 133–48.

McHENRY, HENRY M. "The Pattern of Human Evolution: Studies on Bipedalism, Mastication, and Encephalization." Annual Review of Anthropology, 11 (1982): 151–73.

McKENNA, MALCOLM C. "Was Europe Connected Directly to North America Prior to the Middle Eocene?" In T. Dobzhansky, M.K. Hecht, and W.C. Steere, eds., Evolutionary Biology, vol 6. New York: Appleton-Century-Crofts, 1972.

MacKINNON, JOHN, AND KATHY MacKINNON. "The Behavior of Wild Spectral Tarsiers." International Journal of Primatology, 1 (1980): 361–79.

MACLACHLAN, M.D., ed. Household Economies and Their Transformations. Monographs in Economic Anthropology, No. 3. Lanham, MD: University Press of America. 1987.

McNEILL, WILLIAM H. Plagues and Peoples. Garden City, NY: Doubleday Anchor, 1976.

McNEILL, WILLIAM H. A World History. New York: Oxford University Press, 1967.

MacNEISH, RICHARD S. "The Evaluation of Community Patterns in the Tehuacán Valley of Mexico and Speculations about the Cultural Processes." In Ruth Tringham, ed., Ecology and Agricultural Settlements. Andover, MA: Warner Modular Publications, 1973.

MALEFIJT, ANNEMARIE DE WAAL. Religion and Culture: An Introduction to Anthropology of Religion. New York: Macmillan, 1968.

MALIN, EDWARD. Totem Poles of the Pacific Northwest Coast. Portland: Timber Press, 1986.

MALINOWSKI, BRONISLAW. "The Group and the Individual in Functional Analysis." American Journal of Sociology, 44 (1939): 938–64.

MALINOWSKI, BRONISLAW. Kula: The Circulating Exchange of Valuables in the Archipelagoes of Eastern New Guinea." Man, 51 (1920): 97–105.

MALINOWSKI, BRONISLAW. Magic, Science and Religion and Other Essays. Garden City, NY: Doubleday, 1954.

MALINOWSKI, BRONISLAW. Sex and Repression in Savage Society. Cleveland: World, 1968. London: Kegan Paul, Trench, Trubner Co., 1927.

MALINOWSKI, BRONISLAW. The Sexual Life of Savages in Northwestern Melanesia. New York: Halcyon House, 1932.

MANGIN, WILLIAM. "Latin American Squatter Settlements: A Problem and a Solution." Latin American Research Review, 2 (1967): 65–98.

MANGIN, WILLIAM P. "The Role of Regional Associations in the Adaptation of Rural Migrants to Cities in Peru." In Dwight B. Heath and Richard N. Adams, eds., Contemporary Cultures and Societies of Latin America. New York: Random House, 1965.

MANNERS, ROBERT A., AND DAVID KAPLAN, eds. Theory in Anthropology: A Sourcebook. Chicago: Aldine, 1968.

MAQUET, JACQUES. *The Aesthetic Experience: An Anthropologist Looks at the Visual Arts.* New Haven: Yale University Press, 1986.

MARANO, LOUIS A. "A Macrohistoric Trend toward World Government." *Behavior Science Notes,* 8 (1973): 35–40.

MARCUS, GEORGE E., AND MICHAEL M.J. FISCHER. *Anthropology as Cultural Critique: An Experimental Moment in the Human Sciences.* Chicago: University of Chicago Press, 1986.

MARCUS, JOYCE. "On the Nature of the Mesoamerican City." In Evon Z. Vogt and Richard M. Leventhal, eds., *Prehistoric Settlement Patterns: Essays in Honor of Gordon R. Willey.* Albuquerque: University of New Mexico Press, 1983, pp. 195–242.

MARETT, R.R. *The Threshold of Religion.* London: Methuen, 1909.

MARLER, PETER. "Primate Vocalization: Affective or Symbolic?" In Sebeok and Umiker-Sebeok, eds., *Speaking of Apes,* pp. 221–29.

MARSHACK, ALEXANDER. *The Roots of Civilization.* New York: McGraw-Hill, 1972.

MARSHALL, LARRY G. "Who Killed Cock Robin?: An Investigation of the Extinction Controversy." In Paul S. Martin and Richard G. Klein, eds., *Quarternary Extinctions: A Prehistoric Revolution.* Tucson: University of Arizona Press, 1984, pp. 785–806.

MARSHALL, LORNA. "!Kung Bushmen Bands." In Ronald Cohen and John Middleton, eds., *Comparative Political Systems.* Garden City, NY: Natural History Press, 1967.

MARSHALL, LORNA. "The !Kung Bushmen of the Kalahari Desert." In Gibbs, Jr., *Peoples of Africa,* pp. 241–78.

MARSHALL, LORNA. "Sharing, Talking and Giving: Relief of Social Tensions among !Kung Bushmen." *Africa,* 31 (1961): 239–42.

MARTIN, M. KAY, AND BARBARA VOORHIES. *Female of the Species.* New York: Columbia University Press, 1975.

MARTIN, PAUL S. "The Discovery of America." *Science,* March 9, 1973, pp. 969–74.

MARTIN, ROBERT D. "Ascent of the Primates." *Natural History,* March 1975, pp. 52–61.

MARTIN, ROBERT D. "Strategies of Reproduction." *Natural History,* November 1975, pp. 48–57.

MARTIN, ROBERT D., AND SIMON K. BEARDER. "Radio Bush Baby." *Natural History.* October 1979, pp. 77–81.

MARTORELL, R. "Interrelationships between Diet, Infectious Disease and Nutritional Status." In L. Greene and F.E. Johnston, eds., *Social and Biological Predictors of Nutritional Status, Physical Growth and Neurological Development.* New York: Academic Press, 1980, pp. 81–106.

MARTORELL, REYNALDO, JUAN RIVERA, HALEY KAPLOWITZ, AND ERNESTO POLLITT. "Long-Term Consequences of Growth Retardation during Early Childhood." Paper presented at the Sixth International Congress of Anxology, September 15–19, 1991, Madrid.

MASLOW, ABRAHAM H. *Religions, Values, and Peak-Experiences.* Columbus: Ohio State University Press, 1964.

MASON, PHILIP. *Prospero's Magic.* London: Oxford University Press, 1962.

MASUMURA, WILFRED T. "Law and Violence: A Cross-Cultural Study." *Journal of Anthropological Research,* 33 (1977): 388–99.

MATHIASSEN, THERKEL. *Material Culture of Iglulik Eskimos.* Copenhagen: Glydendalske, 1928.

MATOSSIAN, MARY K. "Ergot and the Salem Witchcraft Affair." *American Scientist.* 70 (1982): 355–57.

MATOSSIAN, MARY K. *Poisons of the Past: Molds, Epidemics, and History.* New Haven: Yale University Press, 1989.

MAYBURY-LEWIS, DAVID. *Akwe-Shavante Society.* Oxford: Clarendon Press, 1967.

MAYR, ERNST. *The Growth of Biological Thought: Diversity, Evolution, and Inheritance.* Cambridge, MA: The Belknap Press of Harvard University Press, 1982.

MAZESS, RICHARD B. "Human Adaptation to High Altitude." In Albert Damon, ed., *Physiological Anthropology.* New York: Oxford University Press, 1975.

MEAD, MARGARET. "Applied Anthropology: The State of the Art." In Anthony F.C. Wallace, J. Lawrence Angel, Richard Fox, Sally McLendon, Rachel Sady, and Robert Sharer, eds., *Perspectives on Anthropology 1976.* American Anthropological Associations Special Publication no. 10. Washington, DC: American Anthropological Association, 1977.

MEAD, MARGARET. *Coming of Age in Samoa.* 3rd ed.

New York: Morrow, 1961 (originally published 1928).

MEAD, MARGARET. "The Evolving Ethics of Applied Anthropology." In Eddy and Partridge, eds., *Applied Anthropology in America*.

MEAD, MARGARET. *Growing Up in New Guinea*. London: Routledge & Kegan Paul, 1931.

MEAD, MARGARET. *Sex and Temperament in Three Primitive Societies*. New York: Mentor, 1950 (originally published 1935).

MEEK, C.K. *Land Law and Custom in the Colonies*. London: Oxford University Press, 1940.

MEGGITT, M.J. "Male-Female Relationships in the Highlands of Australian New Guinea." *American Anthropologist*, 66 (special issue, 1964): 204–24.

MEILLASSOUX, CLAUDE. *Urbanization of an African Community*. Seattle: University of Washington Press, 1968.

MELLAART, JAMES. "A Neolithic City in Turkey." *Scientific American*, April 1964, pp. 94–104.

MELLAART, JAMES. "Roots in the Soil." In S. Piggott, ed., *The Dawn of Civilization*. London: Thames & Hudson, 1961.

MIDDLETON, JOHN. "The Cult of the Dead: Ancestors and Ghosts." In Lessa and Vogt, eds., *Reader in Comparative Religion*, 3rd ed.

MIDDLETON, RUSSELL. "Brother-Sister and Father-Daughter Marriage in Ancient Egypt." *American Sociological Review*, 27 (1962): 603–11.

MILLON, RENÉ. "Social Relations in Ancient Teotihuacán." In Eric R. Wolf, ed., *The Valley of Mexico: Studies in Pre-Hispanic Ecology and Society*. Albuquerque: University of New Mexico Press, 1976, pp. 205–49.

MILLON, RENÉ. "Teotihuacán." *Scientific American*, June 1967, pp. 38–48.

MILTON, KATHARINE. "Distribution Patterns of Tropical Plant Foods as an Evolutionary Stimulus to Primate Mental Development." *American Anthropologist*, 83 (1981): 534–48.

MILTON, KATHARINE. "Foraging Behaviour and the Evolution of Primate Intelligence." In Richard W. Byrne and Andrew Whiten, eds., *Machiavellian Intelligence: Social Expertise and the Evolution of Intellect in Monkeys, Apes, and Humans*. Oxford: Clarendon Press, 1988, pp. 285–305.

MINER, HORACE. "Body Rituals among the Nacirema." *American Anthropologist*, 58 (1956): 504–5.

MINTURN, LEIGH, AND JOHN T. HITCHCOCK. *The Rājpūts of Khalapur, India*. New York: John Wiley, 1966.

MINTURN, LEIGH, AND WILLIAM W. LAMBERT. *Mothers of Six Cultures: Antecedents of Child Rearing*. New York: John Wiley, 1964.

MINTURN, LEIGH, AND JERRY STASHAK. "Infanticide as a Terminal Abortion Procedure." *Behavior Science Research*, 17 (1982): 70–85.

MINTZ, SIDNEY W. "Canamelar: The Subculture of a Rural Sugar Plantation Proletariat." In Julian H. Steward et al., *The People of Puerto Rico*. Urbana: University of Illinois Press, 1956, pp. 314–417.

MOONEY, KATHLEEN A. "The Effects of Rank and Wealth on Exchange among the Coast Salish." *Ethnology*, 17 (1978): 391–406.

MOORE, OMAR KHAYYÁM. "Divination: A New Perspective." *American Anthropologist*, 59 (1957): 69–74.

MORGAN, LEWIS HENRY. *Ancient Society*. Cambridge, Mass.: Harvard University Press, Belknap Press, 1964 (originally published 1877).

MORRIS, B. *Anthropological Studies of Religion: An Introductory Text*. Cambridge: Cambridge University Press, 1987.

MORRIS, JOHN. *Living with Lepchas: A Book about the Sikkim Himalayas*. London: Heinemann, 1938.

MORRIS, LAURA NEWELL. "Gene Flow." In Morris, ed., *Human Populations, Genetic Variation, and Evolution*.

MORRIS, LAURA NEWELL, ed. *Human Populations, Genetic Variation, and Evolution*. San Francisco: Chandler, 1971.

MOTULSKY, ARNO. "Metabolic Polymorphisms and the Role of Infectious Diseases in Human Evolution." In Morris, ed., *Human Populations, Genetic Variation, and Evolution*.

MUKHOPADHYAY, CAROL C., AND PATRICIA J. HIGGINS. "Anthropological Studies of Women's Status Revisited: 1977–1987." *Annual Review of Anthropology*, 17 (1988): 461–95.

MUNROE, ROBERT L., RUTH H. MUNROE, AND JOHN W.M. WHITING. "Male Sex-Role Resolutions." In Munroe, Munroe, and Whiting, eds.,

Handbook of Cross-Cultural Human Development, pp. 611–32.

MUNROE, RUTH H., AND ROBERT L. MUNROE. "Infant Experience and Childhood Affect among the Logoli: A Longitudinal Study." *Ethos,* 8 (1980): 295–315.

MUNROE, RUTH H., ROBERT L. MUNROE, AND HAROLD S. SHIMMIN. "Children's Work in Four Cultures: Determinants and Consequences." *American Anthropologist,* 86 (1984): 369–79.

MUNROE, RUTH H., ROBERT L. MUNROE, AND BEATRICE B. WHITING, eds. *Handbook of Cross-Cultural Human Development.* New York: Garland Press, 1981.

MURDOCK, GEORGE P. "Ethnographic Atlas: A Summary." *Ethnology,* 6 (1967): 109–236.

MURDOCK, GEORGE P. *Social Structure.* New York: Macmillan, 1949.

MURDOCK, GEORGE P., AND CATERINA PROVOST. "Factors in the Division of Labor by Sex: A Cross-Cultural Analysis." *Ethnology,* 12 (1973): 203–25.

MURDOCK, GEORGE P., AND DOUGLAS R. WHITE. "Standard Cross-Cultural Sample." *Ethnology,* 8 (1969): 329–69.

MURPHY, JANE. "Abnormal Behavior in Traditional Societies: Labels, Explanations, and Social Reactions." In Munroe, Munroe, and Whiting, eds., *Handbook of Cross-Cultural Human Development.*

MURPHY, ROBERT F. *Headhunter's Heritage: Social and Economic Change among the Mundurucú.* Berkeley: University of California Press, 1960.

MURPHY, ROBERT F. "Matrilocality and Patrilineality in Mundurucú Society." *American Anthropologist,* 58 (1956): 414–34.

MURPHY, ROBERT F., AND JULIAN H. STEWARD. "Tappers and Trappers: Parallel Process in Acculturation." *Economic Development and Cultural Change,* 4 (July 1956): 335–55.

MUSIL, ALOIS. *The Manners and Customs of the Rwala Bedouins.* American Geographical Society, Oriental Exploration Studies no. 6. New York, 1928.

MYERS, FRED R. "Critical Trends in the Study of Hunter-Gatherers." *Annual Reviews of Anthropology,* 17 (1988): 261–82.

NADEL, S.F. *A Black Byzantium: The Kingdom of Nupe in Nigeria.* London: Oxford University Press, 1942.

NADEL, S.F. "Nupe State and Community." *Africa,* 8 (1935): 257–303.

NAG, MONI, BENJAMIN N.F. WHITE, AND R. CREIGHTON PEET. "An Anthropological Approach to the Study of the Economic Value of Children in Java and Nepal." *Current Anthropology,* 19 (1978): 293–301.

NAGEL, ERNEST. *The Structure of Science: Problems in the Logic of Scientific Explanation.* New York: Harcourt, Brace & World, 1961.

NAPIER, J. "The Antiquity of Human Walking." *Scientific American,* April 1967, pp. 56–66.

NAPIER, J.R. "Paleoecology and Catarrhine Evolution." In J.R. Napier and P.H. Napier, eds., *Old World Monkeys. Evolution, Systematics, and Behavior.* New York: Academic Press, 1970, pp. 53–96.

NAPIER, J.R., AND P.H. NAPIER. *A Handbook of Living Primates.* New York: Academic Press, 1967.

NAROLL, RAOUL. "Imperial Cycles and World Order." *Peace Research Society: Papers,* 7, Chicago Conference (1967): 83–101.

NAROLL, RAOUL. "Two Solutions to Galton's Problem." *Philosophy of Science,* 28 (January 1961): 15–39.

NAROLL, RAOUL, AND RONALD COHEN, eds. *A Handbook of Method in Cultural Anthropology.* Garden City, NY: Natural History Press, 1970.

NEEL, JAMES V., WILLARD R. CENTERWALL, NAPOLEON A. CHAGNON, AND HELEN L. CASEY. "Notes on the Effect of Measles and Measles Vaccine in a Virgin-Soil Population of South American Indians." *American Journal of Epidemiology,* 91 (1970): 418–29.

NERLOVE, SARA B. "Women's Workload and Infant Feeding Practices: A Relationship with Demographic Implications." *Ethnology,* 13 (1974): 207–14.

NEVINS, ALLAN. *The American States During and After the Revolution.* New York: Macmillan, 1927.

NICOLSON, NANCY A. "Infants, Mothers, and Other Females." In Smuts et al., eds., *Primate Societies,* pp. 330–42.

NIEDERBERGER, CHRISTINE. "Early Sedentary Economy in the Basin of Mexico." *Science*, January 12, 1979, pp. 131–42.

NIMKOFF, M.F., AND RUSSELL MIDDLETON. "Types of Family and Types of Economy." *American Journal of Sociology*, 66 (1960): 215–25.

NISSEN, HENRY W. "Axes of Behavioral Comparison." In Anne Roe and George Gaylord Simpson, eds., *Behavior and Evolution*. New Haven: Yale University Press, 1958.

NITECKI, MATTHEW H., AND DORIS V. NITECKI, eds. *The Evolution of Human Hunting*. New York: Plenum, 1987.

NORBECK, EDWARD. "Continuities in Japanese Social Stratification." In Leonard Plotnicov and Arthur Tuden, eds., *Essays in Comparative Social Stratification*. Pittsburgh: University of Pittsburgh Press, 1970.

OAKLEY, KENNETH. "Analytical Methods of Dating Bones." In Don Brothwell and Eric Higgs, eds., *Science in Archaeology*. New York: Basic Books, 1963.

OAKLEY, KENNETH. "On Man's Use of Fire, with Comments on Tool-Making and Hunting." In S.L. Washburn, ed., *Social Life of Early Man*. Chicago: Aldine, 1964.

OBOLER, REGINA S. "Is the Female Husband a Man: Woman/Woman Marriage among the Nandi of Kenya." *Ethnology*, 19 (1980): 69–88.

O'BRIEN, DENISE. "Female Husbands in Southern Bantu Societies." In Schlegel, ed., *Sexual Stratification*.

OGBURN, WILLIAM F. *Social Change* New York: Huebsch, 1922.

OLIVER, DOUGLAS L. *Ancient Tahitian Society*. Volume 1: *Ethnography*. Honolulu: University of Hawaii Press, 1974.

OLIVER, DOUGLAS L. *A Solomon Island Society*. Cambridge, MA: Harvard University Press, 1955.

ORTIZ, SUTTI, ed. *Economic Anthropology: Topics and Theories*. Monographs in Economic Anthropology, no. 1. Lanham, MD: University Press of America, 1983.

ORTNER, SHERRY B. "Theory in Anthropology Since the Sixties." *Comparative Studies in Society and History*, 26 (1984): 126–66.

OTTERBEIN, KEITH. *The Evolution of War*. New Haven: HRAF Press, 1970.

OTTERBEIN, KEITH "Internal War: A Cross-Cultural Study." *American Anthropologist*, 70 (1968): 277–89.

OTTERBEIN, KEITH. *The Ultimate Coercive Sanction: A Cross-Cultural Study of Capital Punishment*. New Haven: HRAF Press, 1986.

OTTERBEIN, KEITH, AND CHARLOTTE S. OTTERBEIN. "An Eye for an Eye, A Tooth for a Tooth: A Cross-Cultural Study of Feuding." *American Anthropologist*. 67 (1965): 1470–82.

OVERFIELD, THERESA. *Biologic Variation in Health and Illness: Race, Age, and Sex Differences*. Menlo Park, CA: Addison-Wesley, 1985.

OWEN, ROGER C. "The Americas: The Case against an Ice-Age Human Population." In Smith and Spencer, eds., *The Origins of Modern Humans*, pp. 517–63.

PAIGE, JEFFERY M. *Agrarian Revolution: Social Movements and Export Agriculture in the Underdeveloped World*. New York: Free Press, 1975.

PARKER, HILDA, AND SEYMOUR PARKER. "Father-Daughter Sexual Abuse: An Emerging Perspective." *American Journal of Orthopsychiatry*, 56 (1986): 531–49.

PARKER, SEYMOUR. "Cultural Rules, Rituals, and Behavior Regulation." *American Anthropologist*, 86 (1984): 584–600.

PARKER, SEYMOUR. "The Precultural Basis of the Incest Taboo: Toward a Biosocial Theory." *American Anthropologist*, 78 (1976): 285–305.

PARKER, SEYMOUR. "The Wiitiko Psychosis in the Context of Ojibwa Personality and Culture." *American Anthropologist*, 62 (1960): 603–23.

PARKER, SUE TAYLOR, AND KATHLEEN RITA GIBSON, eds., *"Language" and Intelligence in Monkeys and Apes: Comparative Developmental Perspectives*. New York: Cambridge University Press, 1990.

PARTRIDGE, WILLIAM L., AND ELIZABETH M. EDDY. "The Development of Applied Anthropology in America." In Eddy and Partidge, eds., *Applied Anthropology in America*, 2nd ed. pp. 3–55.

PASTERNAK, BURTON. *Introduction to Kinship and Social Organization*. Englewood Cliffs, NJ: Prentice Hall, 1976.

PASTERNAK, BURTON, CAROL R. EMBER, AND MELVIN EMBER. "On the Conditions Favoring Extended Family Households." *Journal of Anthropological Research*, 32 (1976): 109–23.

PATTERSON, COLIN. *Evolution*. London: British Museum; Ithaca, NY: Cornell University Press, 1978.

PATTERSON, THOMAS C. *America's Past: A New World Archaeology.* Glenview, IL: Scott, Foresman, 1973.

PATTERSON, THOMAS C. "Central Peru: Its Population and Economy." *Archaeology*, 24 (1971): 316–21.

PATTERSON, THOMAS C. *The Evolution of Ancient Societies: A World Archaeology.* Englewood Cliffs, NJ: Prentice Hall, 1981.

PELTO, PERTTI J., AND LUDGER MÜLLER-WILLE. "Snowmobiles: Technological Revolution in the Arctic." In Bernard and Pelto, eds., *Technology and Social Change.*

PELTO, PERTTI J., AND GRETEL H. PELTO. *Anthropological Research: The Structure of Inquiry.* 2nd ed. New York: Cambridge University Press, 1978.

PELTO, PERTTI J., AND GRETEL H. PELTO. "Intra-Cultural Diversity: Some Theoretical Issues." *American Ethnologist*, 2 (1975): 1–18.

PEPPERBERG, IRENE M. "Referential Communication with an African Grey Parrot." Newsletter, Harvard Graduate Society, Spring 1991, pp. 1–4.

PETERSEN, ERIK B. "A Survey of the Late Paleolithic and the Mesolithic of Denmark." In S.K. Kozlowski, ed., *The Mesolithic in Europe.* Warsaw: Warsaw University Press, 1973.

PETERSEN, L.R., G.R. LEE, AND G.J. ELLIS. "Social Structure, Socialization Values, and Disciplinary Techniques: A Cross-Cultural Analysis." *Journal of Marriage and the Family*, 44 (1982): 131–42.

PFEIFFER, JOHN E. *The Emergence of Man.* 3rd ed. New York: Harper & Row, Pub., 1978.

PHILLIPSON, D.W. "Archaeology and Bantu Linguistics." *World Archaeology*, 8 (1976): 65–82.

PHILLIPSON, DAVID W. *African Archaeology.* Cambridge: Cambridge University Press, 1985.

PIAGET, JEAN. "Piaget's Theory." In Paul Mussen, ed., *Carmichael's Manual of Child Psychology*, 3rd ed. New York John Wiley, 1970, 1: 703–32.

PICKERSGILL, BARBARA, AND CHARLES B. HEISER, JR. "Origins and Distribution of Plants Domesticated in the New World Tropics." In Reed, ed., *Origins of Agriculture*, pp. 803–36.

PICKFORD, M. "Sequence and Environments of the Lower and Middle Miocene Hominoids of Western Kenya." In Ciochon and Corruccini, eds., *New Interpretations of Ape and Human Ancestry*, pp. 421–40.

PILBEAM, DAVID. *The Ascent of Man.* New York: Macmillan, 1972.

PILBEAM, DAVID. "The Descent of Hominoids and Hominids." *Scientific American*, March 1984, pp. 84–96.

PILBEAM, DAVID. "Recent Finds and Interpretations of Miocene Hominoids." *Annual Review of Anthropology*, 8 (1979): 333–52.

PILBEAM, DAVID, AND STEPHEN JAY GOULD. "Size and Scaling in Human Evolution." *Science*, December 6, 1974, pp. 892–900.

PLATTNER, STUART. "Introduction." In Plattner, ed., *Markets and Marketing.*

PLATTNER, STUART, ed. *Markets and Marketing.* Monographs in Economic Anthropology, No. 4. Lanhan, MD: University Press of America, 1985.

POLANYI, KARL. "The Economy as Instituted Process." In Polanyi, Arensberg, and Pearson, eds., *Trade and Market in the Early Empires.*

POLANYI, KARL, CONRAD M. ARENSBERG, AND HARRY W. PEARSON, eds. *Trade and Market in the Early Empires.* New York: Free Press, 1957.

POLEDNAK, ANTHONY P. "Connective Tissue Responses in Negroes in Relation to Disease." *American Journal of Physical Anthropology*, 41 (1974): 49–57.

POSPISIL, LEOPOLD. *The Kapauku Papuans of West New Guinea.* New York: Holt, Rinehart & Winston, 1963.

POST, PETER W., FARRINGTON DANIELS, JR., AND ROBERT T. BINFORD, JR. "Cold Injury and the Evolution of 'White' Skin." *Human Biology*, 47 (1975): 65–80.

PREMACK, ANN JAMES, AND DAVID PREMACK. "Teaching Language to an Ape." *Scientific American*, October 1972, pp. 92–99.

PREUSCHOFT, HOLGER, DAVID J. CHIVERS, WARREN Y. BROCKELMAN, AND NORMAN CREEL, eds. *The Lesser Apes: Evolutionary and Behavioural Biology.* Edinburgh: Edinburgh University Press, 1984.

PRICE, T. DOUGLAS, AND JAMES A. BROWN. *Prehistoric Hunter-Gatherers: The Emergence of Cultural Complexity.* Orlando, FL: Academic Press, 1985.

PRICE-WILLIAMS, DOUGLASS. "A Study concerning Concepts of Conservation of Quantities among Primitive Children." *Acta Psychologica*, 18 (1961): 297–305.

"Principles of Professional Responsibility." Adopted by the Council of the American Anthropological Association, May 1971.

PRYOR, FREDERIC L. *The Origins of the Economy: A Comparative Study of Distribution in Primitive and Peasant Economies*. New York: Academic Press, 1977.

PURSEGLOVE, J.W. "The Origins and Migrations of Crops in Tropical Africa." In Harlan, De Wet, and Stemler, eds., *Origins of African Plant Domestication*, pp. 291–309.

QUINN, NAOMI. "Anthropological Studies on Women's Status." *Annual Review of Anthropology*, 6 (1977): 181–225.

RADCLIFFE-BROWN, A.R. *The Andaman Islanders: A Study on Social Anthropology*. Cambridge: Cambridge University Press, 1922.

RADCLIFFE-BROWN, A.R. *Structure and Function in Primitive Society*. London: Cohen & West, 1952.

RADINSKY, LEONARD. "The Oldest Primate Endocast." *American Journal of Physical Anthropology*, 27 (1967): 385–88.

RAPPAPORT, ROY A. "Ritual Regulation of Environmental Relations among a New Guinea People." *Ethnology*, 6 (1967): 17–30.

RATHJE, WILLIAM L. "The Origin and Development of Lowland Classic Maya Civilization." *American Antiquity*, 36 (1971): 275–85.

RAY, VERNE F. *The Sanpoil and Nespelem: Salishan Peoples of Northeastern Washington*. New Haven: Human Relations Area Files, 1954, pp. 172–89.

REDMAN, CHARLES L. *The Rise of Civilization: From Early Farmers to Urban Society in the Ancient Near East*. San Francisco: W.H. Freeman & Company Publishers, 1978.

REED, CHARLES A., ed. *Origins of Agriculture*. The Hague: Mouton, 1977.

RENFREW, COLIN. *Archaeology and Language: The Puzzle of Indo-European Origins*. London: Jonathan Cape. 1987.

RENFREW, COLIN. "Trade and Culture Process in European History." *Current Anthropology*, 10 (April–June 1969): 156–69.

RICE, PATRICIA C., AND ANN L. PATERSON. "Cave Art and Bones: Exploring the Interrelationships." *American Anthropologist*, 87 (1985): 94–100.

RICE, PATRICIA C., AND ANN L. PATERSON. "Validating the Cave Art-Archeofaunal Relationship in Cantabrian Spain." *American Anthropologist*, 88 (1986): 658–67.

RICHARD, ALISON F. "Malagasy Prosimians: Female Dominance." In Smuts et al., eds., *Primate Societies*, pp. 25–33.

RICHARD, ALISON F. *Primates in Nature*. New York: W.H. Freeman & Company Publishers, 1985.

RIESENFELD, ALPHONSE. "The Effect of Extreme Temperatures and Starvation on the Body Proportions of the Rat." *American Journal of Physical Anthropology*, 39 (1973): 427–59.

RIGHTMIRE, G.P. "The Tempo of Change in the Evolution of Mid-Pleistocene *Homo*." In Delson, ed., *Ancestors*, pp. 255–64.

RIGHTMIRE, G. PHILIP. *The Evolution of* Homo erectus: *Comparative Anatomical Studies of an Extinct Human Species*. Cambridge: Cambridge University Press, 1990, pp. 12–14.

RIGHTMIRE, G. PHILIP. "Homo sapiens in Sub-Saharan Africa." In Smith and Spencer, eds., *The Origins of Modern Humans*, pp. 295–326.

RIJKSEN, H.D. *A Fieldstudy on Sumatran Orang Utans (Pongo Pygmaeus Abelii Lesson 1827): Ecology, Behaviour and Conservation*. Wageningen, The Netherlands: H. Veenman and Zonen B. V., 1978.

RITTER, MADELINE LATTMAN. "The Conditions Favoring Age-Set Organization." *Journal of Anthropological Research*, 36 (1980): 87–104.

RIVERS, W.H.R. *The Todas*. Oosterhout, N.B., The Netherlands: Anthropological Publications, 1967 (originally published 1906).

ROBERTS, D.F. "Body Weight, Race, and Climate." *American Journal of Physical Anthropology*, (1953): 533–58.

ROBERTS, D.F. *Climate and Human Variability*. 2nd ed. Menlo Park, CA: Cummings, 1978.

ROBERTS, JOHN M. "Oaths, Autonomic Ordeals, and Power." In Clellan S. Ford, ed., *Cross-Cultural Approaches: Readings in Comparative Research*. New Haven: HRAF Press, 1967.

ROBERTS, JOHN M., AND BRIAN SUTTON-SMITH. "Child Training and Game Involvement." *Ethnology*, 1 (1962): 166–85.

ROBINSON, JOHN G., AND CHARLES H. JANSON. "Capuchins, Squirrel Monkeys, and Atelines: Socioecological Convergence with Old World Primates." In Smuts et al., eds., *Primate Societies*, pp. 69–82.

ROBINSON, JOHN G., PATRICIA C. WRIGHT, AND WARREN G. KINZEY. "Monogamous Cebids and Their Relatives: Intergroup Calls and Spacing." In Smuts et al., eds., *Primate Societies*, p. 44–53.

RODWIN, LLOYD, AND BISHWAPRIYA SANYAL. "Shelter, Settlement, and Development: An Overview." In Lloyd Rodwin, ed., *Shelter, Settlement, and Development*. Boston: Allen & Unwin, 1987, pp. 3–31.

ROGERS, EVERETT M. *Diffusion of Innovations*. 3rd ed. New York: Free Press, 1983.

ROGOFF, BARBARA. *Apprenticeship in Thinking: Cognitive Development in Social Contex*. New York: Oxford University Press, 1990.

ROGOFF, BARBARA. "Schooling and the Development of Cognitive Skills." In Triandis and Heron, eds., *Handbook of Cross-Cultural Psychology*. Vol. 4, *Developmental Psychology*.

ROHNER, RONALD P. "Sex Differences in Aggression: Phylogenetic and Enculturation Perspectives." *Ethos*, 4 (1976): 57–72.

ROHNER, R.P. *The Warmth Dimension*. Beverly Hills, CA: Sage, 1986.

ROHNER, RONALD P. *They Love Me, They Love Me Not: A Worldwide Study of the Effects of Parental Acceptance and Rejection*. New Haven: HRAF Press, 1975.

ROOSEVELT, ANNA CURTENIUS. "Population, Health, and the Evolution of Subsistence: Conclusions from the Conference." In Cohen and Armelagos, eds., *Paleopathology at the Origins of Agriculture*, pp. 559–84.

ROSALDO, MICHELLE Z., AND LOUISE LAMPHERE, eds. *Woman, Culture, and Society*. Stanford, CA: Stanford University Press, 1974.

ROSE, M.D. "Food Acquisition and the Evolution of Positional Behaviour: The Case of Bipedalism." In David J. Chivers, Bernard A. Wood, and Alan Bilsborough, eds., *Food Acquisition and Processing in Primates*. New York: Plenum, 1984, pp. 509–24.

ROSEBERRY, WILLIAM. "Political Economy." *Annual Review of Anthropology*, 17 (1988): 161–259.

ROSENBLATT, PAUL C., R. PATRICIA WALSH, AND DOUGLAS A. JACKSON. *Grief and Mourning in Cross-Cultural Perspective*. New Haven: HRAF Press, 1976.

ROSS, MARC H. "Female Political Participation: A Cross-Cultural Explanation." *American Anthropologist*, 88 (1986): 843–58.

ROSS, MARC H. "Internal and External Conflict and Violence." *Journal of Conflict Resolution*, 29 (1985): 547–79.

ROSS, MARC H. "Political Organization and Political Participation: Exit, Voice, and Loyalty in Preindustrial Societies." *Comparative Politics*, 20 (1988): 73–89.

ROSS, MARC H. "Socioeconomic Complexity, Socialization, and Political Differentiation: A Cross-Cultural Study." *Ethos*, 9 (1981): 217–47.

ROYCE, ANYA PETERSON. *The Anthropology of Dance*. Bloomington: Indiana University Press, 1977.

RUBIN, J.Z., F.J. PROVENZANO, AND R.F. HASKETT. "The Eye of the Beholder: Parents' Views on the Sex of New Borns." *American Journal of Orthopsychiatry*, 44 (1974): 512–19.

RUDMIN, FLOYD W. "Dominance, Social Control, and Ownership: A History and a Cross-Cultural Study of Motivations for Private Property." *Behavior Science Research*, 22 (1988): 130–60.

RUMBAUGH, DUANE M. "Learning Skills of Anthropoids." In L.A. Rosenblum, ed., *Primate Behavior*, vol. 1. New York: Academic Press, 1970.

RUMBAUGH, DUANE M., TIMOTHY V. GILL, AND E.C. VON GLASERSFELD. "Reading and Sentence Completion by a Chimpanzee (Pan)." *Science*, November 16, 1973, pp. 731–33.

RUSKIN, JOHN. "Of King's Treasures." In John D. Rosenberg, ed., *The Genius of John Ruskin: Selections from His Writings*, New York: Braziller, 1963.

RUSSELL, ELBERT W. "Factors of Human Aggression." *Behavior Science Notes*, 7 (1972): 275–312.

RUSSON, ANNE E. "The Development of Peer Social Interaction in Infant Chimpanzees: Comparative Social, Piagetian, and Brain Perspectives." In Parker and Gibson, eds., *"Language" and Intelligence in Monkeys and Apes: Comparative Developmental Perspectives*.

SADE, D.S. "Some Aspects of Parent–Offspring and Sibling Relationships in a Group of Rhesus Monkeys, with a Discussion of Grooming." *American Journal of Physical Anthropology,* 23 (1965): 1–17.

SAHLINS, MARSHALL D. *Moala: Culture and Nature on a Fijian Island.* Ann Arbor: University of Michigan Press, 1962.

SAHLINS, MARSHALL. "Other Times, Other Customs: The Anthropology of History." *American Anthropologist,* 85 (1983): 517–44.

SAHLINS, MARSHALL D. "Poor Man, Rich Man, Big-Man, Chief: Political Types in Melanesia and Polynesia." *Comparative Studies in Society and History,* 5 (1963): 285–303.

SAHLINS, MARSHALL D. "The Segmentary Lineage: An Organization of Predatory Expansion." *American Anthropologist,* 63 (1961): 332–45.

SAHLINS, MARSHALL D. *Social Stratification in Polynesia.* Seattle: University of Washington Press, 1958.

SAHLINS, MARSHALL D. *Stone Age Economics.* Chicago: Aldine, 1972.

SAHLINS, MARSHALL D., AND ELMAN R. SERVICE. *Evolution and Culture.* Ann Arbor: University of Michigan Press, 1960.

SANDAY, PEGGY R. "Female Status in the Public Domain." In Rosaldo and Lamphere, eds., *Woman, Culture, and Society.*

SANDAY, PEGGY R. "Toward a Theory of the Status of Women." *American Anthropologist,* 75 (1973): 1682–1700.

SANDAY, PEGGY REEVES, AND RUGH GALLAGHER GOODENOUGH, eds. *Beyond the Second Sex: New Directions in the Anthropology of Gender.* Philadelphia: University of Pennsylvania Press, 1990.

SANDERS, WILLIAM T. "Hydraulic Agriculture, Economic Symbiosis, and the Evolution of States in Central Mexico." In Betty J. Meggers, ed., *Anthropological Archaeology in the Americas.* Washington, DC: Anthropological Society of Washington, 1968.

SANDERS, WILLIAM T., JEFFREY R. PARSONS, AND ROBERT S. SANTLEY. *The Basin of Mexico: Ecological Processes in the Evolution of a Civilization.* New York: Academic Press, 1979.

SANDERS, WILLIAM T., AND BARBARA J. PRICE. *Mesoamerica.* New York: Random House, 1968.

SAPIR, E. *Language: An Introduction to the Study of Speech.* New York: Harcourt Brace Jovanovich, 1949 (originally published 1921).

SAPIR, E., AND M. SWADESH. "American Indian Grammatical Categories." In Hymes, ed., *Language in Culture and Society,* pp. 100–111.

SAPIR, EDWARD. "Conceptual Categories in Primitive Languages." Paper presented at the autumn meeting of the National Academy of Sciences, New Haven, 1931. Published in *Science,* 74 (1931).

SAPIR, EDWARD. "Why Cultural Anthropology Needs the Psychiatrist." *Psychiatry,* 1 (1938): 7–12.

SARICH, VINCENT M. "The Origin of Hominids: An Immunological Approach." In S.L. Washburn and Phyllis C. Jay, eds., *Perspectives on Human Evolution,* vol. 1. New York: Holt, Rinehart & Winston, 1968.

SARICH, VINCENT M., AND ALLAN C. WILSON. "Quantitative Immunochemistry and the Evolution of Primate Albumins: Micro-Component Fixations." *Science,* December 23, 1966, pp. 1563–66.

SAUL, MAHIR. "Work Parties, Wages, and Accumulation in a Voltaic Village." *American Ethnologist,* 10 (1983): 77–96.

SCARR, SANDRA, AND KATHLEEN McCARTNEY. "How People Make Their Own Environments: A Theory of Genotype→Environment Effects." *Child Development,* 54 (1983): 424–35.

SCHALLER, GEORGE. *The Mountain Gorilla: Ecology and Behavior.* Chicago: University of Chicago Press, 1963.

SCHALLER, GEORGE B. *The Serengeti Lion: A Study of Predator–Prey Relations.* Chicago: University of Chicago Press, 1972.

SCHALLER, GEORGE. *The Year of the Gorilla.* Chicago: University of Chicago Press, 1964.

SCHLEGEL, ALICE. "Gender Issues and Cross-Cultural Research." *Behavior Science Research,* 23 (1989): 265–80.

SCHLEGEL, ALICE, ed. *Sexual Stratification: A Cross Cultural View.* New York: Columbia University Press, 1977.

SCHLEGEL, ALICE, AND HERBERT BARRY III. *Adolescence: An Anthropological Inquiry.* New York: Free Press, 1991.

SCHLEGEL, ALICE, AND HERBERT BARRY III. "The Cultural Consequences of Female Contribution to Subsistence." *American Anthropologist*, 88 (1986): 142–50.

SCHLEGEL, ALICE, AND ROHN ELOUL. "A New Coding of Marriage Transactions." *Behavior Science Research*, 21 (1987): 118–40.

SCHLEGEL, ALICE, AND ROHN ELOUL. "Marriage Transactions: Labor, Property, and Status." *American Anthropologist*, 90 (1988): 291–309.

SCHNEIDER, DAVID M. "The Distinctive Features of Matrilineal Descent Groups." In Schneider and Gough, eds., *Matrilineal Kinship*.

SCHNEIDER, DAVID M. "Truk." In Schneider and Gough, eds., *Matrilineal Kinship*.

SCHNEIDER, DAVID M., AND KATHLEEN GOUGH, eds. *Matrilineal Kinship*. Berkeley: University of California Press, 1961.

SCHOEPH, B. "Women, AIDS and Economic Crisis in Central Africa." *Canadian Journal of African Studies*, 22 (1988): 625–44. Cited in Carrier and Bolton, "Anthropological Perspectives."

SCHRIRE, CARMEL. "An Inquiry into the Evolutionary Status and Apparent Identity of San Hunter-Gatherers." *Human Ecology*, 8 (1980): 9–32.

SCHRIRE, CARMEL, ed. *Past and Present in Hunter Gatherer Studies*. Orlando, FL: Academic Press, 1984.

SCHRIRE, CARMEL. "Wild Surmises on Savage Thoughts." In Schrire, ed., *Past and Present in Hunger Gatherer Studies*.

SCHWARTZ, RICHARD D. "Social Factors in the Development of Legal Control: A Case Study of Two Israeli Settlements." *Yale Law Journal*, 63 (February 1954): 471–91.

SCOLLON, RON, AND SUZANNE B.K. SCOLLON. *Narrative, Literacy and Face in Interethnic Communication*. Norwood, NJ: ABLEX Publishing Corporation, 1981.

SCUDDER, THAYER. "Opportunities, Issues and Achievements in Development Anthropology since the Mid-1960s: A Personal View." In Eddy and Partridge, eds., *Applied Anthropology in America*. 2nd ed., pp. 184–210.

SEBEOK, THOMAS A., AND JEAN UMIKER-SEBEOK, eds. *Speaking of Apes: A Critical Anthology of Two-Way Communication with Man*. New York: Plenum, 1980.

SEEMANOVÁ, EVA. "A Study of Children of Incestuous Matings." *Human Heredity*, 21 (1971): 108–28.

SEGAL, ROBERT A. *Joseph Campbell: An Introduction*. New York: Garland, 1977.

SEGALL, MARSHALL H. *Cross-Cultural Psychology: Human Behavior in Global Perspective*. Monterey, CA.: Brooks/Cole, 1979.

SEGALL, MARSHALL, PIERRE R. DASEN, JOHN W. BERRY, YPE H. POORTINGA. *Human Behavior in Global Perspective: An Introduction to Cross-Cultural Psychology*. New York: Pergamon Press, 1990.

SEMENOV, S.A. *Prehistoric Technology*. Trans. M.W. Thompson. Bath, England: Adams & Dart, 1970.

SENNER, WAYNE M. *The Origins of Writing*. Lincoln, NE: University of Nebraska Press, 1989.

SENNER, WAYNE M. "Theories and Myths on the Origins of Writing: A Historical Overview." In Senner, ed., *The Origins of Writing*.

SERVICE, ELMAN R. *The Hunters*. 2nd ed. Englewood Cliffs, NJ: Prentice Hall, 1979.

SERVICE, ELMAN R. *Origins of the State and Civilization: The Process of Cultural Evolution*. New York: W.W. Norton & Co., Inc., 1975.

SERVICE, ELMAN R. *Primitive Social Organization: An Evolutionary Perspective*. New York: Random House, 1962.

SERVICE, ELMAN R. *Profiles in Ethnology*. 3rd ed. New York: Harper & Row, Pub., 1978.

SEYFARTH, ROBERT M., AND DOROTHY L. CHENEY. "How Monkeys See the World: A Review of Recent Research on East African Vervet Monkeys." In Snowdon, Brown, and Petersen, eds., *Primate Communication*, pp. 239–52.

SEYFARTH, ROBERT M., DOROTHY L. CHENEY, AND PETER MARLER. "Monkey Response to Three Different Alarm Calls: Evidence of Predator Classification and Semantic Communication." *Science*, November 14, 1980, pp. 801–3.

SIH, ANDREW, AND KATHARINE A. MILTON. "Optimal Diet Theory: Should the !Kung Eat Monogongos?" *American Anthropologist*, 87 (1985): 395–401.

SHEILS, DEAN. "A Comparative Study of Human Sacrifice." *Behavior Science Research*, 15 (1980): 245–62.

SHEILS, DEAN. "Toward A Unified Theory of Ancestor Worship: A Cross-Cultural Study." *Social Forces*, 54 (1975): 427–40.

SHIPMAN, PAT. "Scavenging or Hunting in Early Hominids: Theoretical Framework and Tests." *American Anthropologist*, 88 (1986): 27–43.

SIPES, RICHARD G. "War, Sports, and Aggression: An Empirical Test of Two Rival Theories." *American Anthropologist*, 75 (1973): 64–86.

SILVER, HARRY R. "Calculating Risks: The Socioeconomic Foundations of Aesthetic Innovation in an Ashanti Carving Community." *Ethnology*, 20 (1981): 101–14.

SIMMONS, ALAN H., ILSE KÖHLER-ROLLEFSON, GARY O. ROLLEFSON, ROLFE MANDEL, AND ZEIDAN KAFAFI. "Ain Ghazal: A Major Neolithic Settlement in Central Jordan." *Science*, April 1, 1988, pp. 35–39.

SIMMONS, LEO W. *Sun Chief*. New Haven: Yale University Press, 1942.

SIMONS, ELWYN L. *Primate Evolution: An Introduction to Man's Place in Nature*. New York: Macmillan, 1972.

SIMPSON, GEORGE GAYLORD. *The Meaning of Evolution*. New York: Bantam, 1971.

SIMPSON, S.P., AND RUTH FIELD. "Law and the Social Sciences." *Virginia Law Review*, 32 (1946): 858.

SINGER, J. DAVID. "Accounting for International War: The State of the Discipline." *Annual Review of Sociology*, 6 (1980): 349–67.

SINGER, RONALD, AND JOHN WYMER. *The Middle Stone Age at Klasies River Mouth in South Africa*. Chicago: University of Chicago Press, 1982.

SKOMAL, SUSAN N., AND EDGAR C. POLOMÉ. eds. *Proto-Indo-European: The Archaeology of a Linguistic Problem*. Washington, DC: Washington Institute for the Study of Man, 1987.

SMITH, B. HOLLY. "Dental Development in *Australopithecus* and Early *Homo*." *Nature*, 323, September 25, 1986, pp. 327–30.

SMITH, EDWIN W., AND ANDREW MURRAY DALE. *The Ila-Speaking Peoples of Northern Rhodesia*. New Hyde Park, NY: University Books, 1968 (originally published 1920 as *Ethnocentric British Colonial Attitudes*).

SMITH, ERIC A. "Anthropological Applications of Optimal Foraging Theory: A Critical Review." *Current Anthropology*, 24 (1983): 625–40.

SMITH, FRED H. "Fossil Hominids from the Upper Pleistocene of Central Europe and the Origin of Modern Humans." In Smith and Spencer, eds., *The Origins of Modern Humans*, pp. 137–210.

SMITH, FRED H., AND FRANK SPENCER, eds. *The Origins of Modern Humans: A World Survey of the Fossil Evidence*. New York: Alan R. Liss, 1984.

SMITH, M.W. "Alfred Binet's Remarkable Questions: A Cross-National and Cross-Temporal Analysis of the Cultural Biases Built into the Stanford-Binet Intelligence Scale and Other Binet Tests." *Genetic Psychology Monographs*, 89 (1974): 307–34.

SMITH, MICHAEL G. "Pre-Industrial Stratification Systems." In Neil J. Smelser and Seymour Martin Lipset, eds., *Social Structure and Mobility in Economic Development*. Chicago: Aldine, 1966.

SMITH, WALDEMAR R. *The Fiesta System and Economic Change*. New York: Columbia University Press, 1977.

SMUTS, BARBARA B., DOROTHY L. CHENEY, ROBERT M. SEYFARTH, RICHARD W. WRANGHAM, AND THOMAS T. STRUHSAKER, eds. *Primate Societies*. Chicago: University of Chicago Press, 1987.

SNOWDON, CHARLES T., CHARLES H. BROWN, AND MICHAEL R. PETERSEN, eds. *Primate Communication*. New York: Cambridge University Press, 1982.

SOUTHWORTH, FRANKLIN C., AND CHANDLER J. DASWANI. *Foundations of Linguistics*. New York: Free Press, 1974.

SPANOS, NICHOLAS P. "Ergotism and the Salem Witch Panic: A Critical Analysis and an Alternative Conceptualization." *Journal of the History of the Behavioral Sciences*, 19 (1983): 358–69.

SPENCER, FRANK. "The Neandertals and Their Evolutionary Significance: A Brief Historical Survey." In Smith and Spencer, eds., *The Origins of Modern Humans*, pp. 1–50.

SPENCER, ROBERT F. "Spouse-Exchange among the North Alaskan Eskimo." In Bohannan and Middleton, eds., *Marriage, Family and Residence*.

SPERBER, DAN. *On Anthropological Knowledge: Three Essays*, p. 34. Cambridge: Cambridge University Press, 1985.

SPETH, JOHN D., AND DAVE D. DAVIS. "Seasonal Variability in Early Hominid Predation." *Science*, April 30, 1976, pp. 441–45.

SPETH, JOHN D., AND KATHERINE A. SPIELMANN.

"Energy Source, Protein Metabolism, and Hunter-Gatherer Subsistence Strategies." *Journal of Anthropological Archaeology*, 2 (1983): 1–31.

SPINDLER, GEORGE D., ed. *Being an Anthropologist: Fieldwork in Eleven Cultures*. New York: Holt, Rinehart & Winston, 1970.

SPIRO, MELFORD E. *Oedipus in the Trobriands*. Chicago: University of Chicago Press, 1982.

SPIRO, MELFORD E., AND ROY G. D'ANDRADE. "A Cross-Cultural Study of Some Supernatural Beliefs." *American Anthropologist*, 60 (1958): 456–66.

"Statement on Professional and Ethical Responsibilities (Society for Applied Anthropology)." *Human Organization*, 34 (Summer 1975).

STEEGMAN, A.T., JR. "Human Adaptation to Cold." In Albert Damon, ed., *Physiological Anthropology*. New York: Oxford University Press, 1975.

STEPHENS, J. CLAIBORNE, MARK L. CAVANAUGH, MARGARET I. GRADIE, MARTIN L. MADOR, AND KENNETH K. KIDD. "Mapping the Human Genome: Current Status." *Science*, October 12, 1990, pp. 237–50.

STEPHENS, WILLIAM N. "A Cross-Cultural Study of Modesty." *Behavior Science Research*, 7 (1972): 1–28.

STEPHENS, WILLIAM N. *The Family in Cross-Cultural Perspective*. New York: Holt, Rinehart & Winston, 1963.

STERN, CURT. *Principles of Human Genetics*. 3rd ed. San Francisco: W.H. Freeman & Company Publishers, 1973.

STEVENS, JAMES. *Sacred Legends of the Sandy Lake Cree*. Toronto: McClelland & Steward, 1971.

STEWARD, JULIAN H. "The Concept and Method of Cultural Ecology." In Steward, *Theory of Culture Change*, pp. 30–42.

STEWARD, JULIAN H. *Theory of Culture Change*. Urbana: University of Illinois Press, 1955.

STEWARD, JULIAN H., AND LOUIS C. FARON. *Native Peoples of South America*. New York: McGraw-Hill, 1959.

STINI, WILLIAM A. *Ecology and Human Adaptation*. Dubuque, IA: Wm. C. Brown, 1975.

STINI, WILLIAM A. "Evolutionary Implications of Changing Nutritional Patterns in Human Populations." *American Anthropologist*, 73 (1971): 1019–30.

STOCKING, GEORGE W., JR., ed. *History of Anthropology*, vols. 1–6. Madison, WI: University of Wisconsin Press, 1983–1989.

STOGDILL, RALPH M. *Handbook of Leadership: A Survey of Theory and Research*. New York: Macmillan, 1974.

STRAUS, MURRAY A. "Physical Violence in American Families: Incidence Rates, Causes, and Trends." In Dean D. Knudsen and JoAnn L. Miller, eds., *Abused and Battered: Social and Legal Responses to Family Violence*. New York: Aldine de Gruyter, 1991, pp. 17–34.

STRAUSS, LAWRENCE GUY. "Comment on White." *Current Anthropology*, 23 (1982): 185–86.

STRAUSS, LAWRENCE GUY. "On Early Hominid Use of Fire." *Current Anthropology*, 30 (1989): 488–91.

STRINGER, C. "Evolution of a Species." *Geographical Magazine*, 57 (1985): 601–7.

STRINGER, C.B., J.J. HUBLIN, AND B. VANDERMEERSCH. "The Origin of Anatomically Modern Humans in Western Europe." In Smith and Spencer, eds., *The Origins of Modern Humans*, p. 107.

STRUEVER, STUART, ed. *Prehistoric Agriculture*. Garden City, NY: Natural History Press, 1971.

SUSSMAN, ROBERT. "Child Transport, Family Size, and the Increase in Human Population Size during the Neolithic." *Current Anthropology*, 13 (April 1972): 258–67.

SUSSMAN, ROBERT W. *The Ecology and Behavior of Free-ranging Primates*. New York: Macmillan, forthcoming.

SUSSMAN, ROBERT W., AND PETER H. RAVEN. "Pollination by Lemurs and Marsupials: An Archaic Coevolutionary System." *Science*, May 19, 1978, pp. 734–35.

SUSSMAN, R.W., AND W.G. KINZEY. "The Ecological Role of the Callitrichidae: A Review." *American Journal of Physical Anthropology*, 64 (1984): 419–49.

SWANSON, GUY E. *The Birth of the Gods: The Origin of Primitive Beliefs*. Ann Arbor: University of Michigan Press, 1969.

SWEENEY, JAMES J. "African Negro Culture." In Paul Radin, ed., *African Folktales and Sculpture*. New York: Pantheon, 1952.

SZALAY, FREDERICK S. "The Beginnings of Primates." *Evolution*, 22 (1968): 19–36.

SZALAY, FREDERICK S. "Hunting-Scavenging Proto-

hominids: A Model for Hominid Origins."
Man, 10 (1975): 420–29.

SZALAY, FREDERICK S., AND ERIC DELSON. *Evolutionary History of the Primates.* New York: Academic Press, 1979.

TALMON, YONINA. "Mate Selection in Collective Settlements." *American Sociological Review*, 29 (1964): 491–508.

TATTERSALL, IAN. *Man's Ancestors.* London: John Murray, 1970.

TATTERSALL, IAN. *The Primates of Madagascar.* New York: Columbia University Press, 1982.

TELEKI, GEZA. "The Omnivorous Chimpanzee." *Scientific American*, January 1973, pp. 32–42.

TERBORGH, JOHN. *Five New World Primates: A Study in Comparative Ecology.* Princeton: Princeton University Press, 1983.

TEXTOR, ROBERT B., comp. *A Cross-Cultural Summary.* New Haven: HRAF Press, 1967.

THOMAS, DAVID HURST. *Refiguring Anthropology: First Principles of Probability and Statistics.* Prospect Heights, IL: Waveland Press, 1986.

THOMAS, ELIZABETH MARSHALL. *The Harmless People.* New York: Knopf, 1959.

THOMASON, SARAH GREY, AND TERRENCE KAUFMAN. *Language Contact, Creolization, and Genetic Linguistics.* Berkeley, CA: University of California Press, 1988.

THOMPSON, ELIZABETH BARTLETT. *Africa, Past and Present.* Boston: Houghton Mifflin, 1966.

THOMPSON, SMITH. "Star Husband Tale." In Dundes, ed., *The Study of Folklore.*

THOMPSON-HANDLER, NANCY, RICHARD K. MALENKY, AND NOEL BADRIAN. "Sexual Behavior of *Pan paniscus* under Natural Conditions in the Lomako Forest, Equateur, Zaire." In Randall L. Susman, ed., *The Pygmy Chimpanzee: Evolutionary Biology and Behavior.* New York: Plenum, 1984, pp. 347–66.

THURNWALD, R.C. "Pigs and Currency in Buin: Observations about Primitive Standards of Value and Economics." *Oceania*, 5 (1934): 119–41.

TOMASELLO, MICHAEL. "Cultural Transmission in the Tool Use and Communicatory Signaling of Chimpanzees." In Parker and Gibson, eds., *"Language" and Intelligence in Monkeys and Apes: Comparative Developmental Perspectives.*

TORREY, E. FULLER. *The Mind Game: Witchdoctors and Psychiatrists.* New York: Emerson Hall, n.d.

TORRY, WILLIAM I. "Morality and Harm: Hindu Peasant Adjustments to Famines." *Social Science Information*, 25 (1986): 125–60.

TREVOR-ROPER, H.R. "The European Witch-Craze of the Sixteenth and Seventeenth Centuries." In Lessa and Vogt., eds., *Reader in Comparative Religion*, 3rd ed.

TRIANDIS, HARRY C., AND ALASTAIR HERON, eds. *Handbook of Cross-Cultural Psychology.* Vol. 4: *Developmental Psychology.* Boston: Allyn & Bacon, 1981.

TRINKHAUS, E., ed., *The Emergence of Modern Humans: Biocultural Adaptations in the Later Pleistocene.* Cambridge: Cambridge University Press, 1989.

TRINKAUS, ERIK. "Bodies, Brawn, Brains and Noses: Human Ancestors and Human Predation." In Nitecki and Nitecki, eds., *The Evolution of Human Hunting*, pp. 107–45.

TRINKAUS, ERIK. "The Neandertals and Modern Human Origins." *Annual Review of Anthropology*, 15 (1986): 193–218.

TRINKAUS, ERIK. "Pathology and the Posture of the La Chapelle-aux-Saints Neandertal." *American Journal of Physical Anthropology*, 67 (1985): 19–41.

TRINKAUS, ERIK. "Western Asia." In Smith and Spencer, eds., *The Origins of Modern Humans*, pp. 251–95.

TRINKAUS, ERIK, AND WILLIAM W. HOWELLS. "The Neanderthals." *Scientific American*, December 1979, pp. 118–33.

TRUDGILL, PETER. *Sociolinguistics: An Introduction to Language and Society.* Rev. ed. New York: Penguin, 1983.

TURNER, B.L. "Population Density in the Classic Maya Lowlands: New Evidence for Old Approaches." *Geographical Review*, 66, no. 1 (January 1970): 72–82.

TYLOR, EDWARD B. "Animism." In Lessa and Vogt, eds., *Reader in Comparative Religion*, 4th ed.

TYLOR, EDWARD B. *Primitive Culture.* New York: Harper Torchbooks, 1958 (originally published 1871).

UBEROI, J.P. SINGH. *The Politics of the Kula Ring: An Analysis of the Findings of Bronislaw Malinowski.* Manchester, England: University of Manchester Press, 1962.

UCKO, PETER J., AND G.W. DIMBLEBY, eds. *The Do-*

mestication and Exploitation of Plants and Animals. Chicago: Aldine, 1969.

UCKO, PETER J., AND ANDRÉE ROSENFELD. Paleolithic Cave Art. New York: McGraw-Hill, 1967.

UCKO, PETER J., RUTH TRIGHAM, AND G.W. DIMBLEBY, eds. Man, Settlement, and Urbanism. Cambridge, MA: Schenkman, 1972.

UDY, STANLEY H., JR. Work in Traditional and Modern Society. Englewood Cliffs, NJ: Prentice Hall, 1970.

UNDERHILL, RALPH. "Economic and Political Antecedents of Monotheism: A Cross-Cultural Study." American Journal of Sociology, 80 (1975): 841–61.

UNDERHILL, RUTH M. Social Organization of the Papago Indians. New York: Columbia University Press, 1938.

VALLADAS, H., J.L. JORON, G. VALLADAS, O. BAR-YOSEF, AND B. VANDERMEERSCH. "Thermoluminescence Dating of Mousterian 'Proto-Cro-Magnon' Remains from Israel and the Origin of Modern Man." Nature, 331, February 18, 1988, pp. 614–16.

VAN LAWICK-GOODALL, JANE. In the Shadow of Man. Boston: Houghton Mifflin, 1971.

VAN VALEN, L., AND R.E. SLOAN. "The Earliest Primates." Science, November 5, 1965, pp. 743–45.

VAN WILLIGEN, JOHN. Applied Anthropology: An Introduction. South Hadley, MA: Bergin & Garvey, 1986.

VAN WILLIGEN, JOHN, BARBARA RYLKO-BAUER, AND ANN MCELROY. Making Our Research Useful: Case Studies in the Utilization of Anthropological Knowledge. Boulder, CO: Westview Press, 1989.

VANNEMAN, REEVE, AND LYNN WEBER CANNON. The American Perception of Class. Philadelphia: Temple University Press, 1987.

VAYDA, ANDREW P. "Pomo Trade Feasts." In Dalton, ed., Tribal and Peasant Economies.

VAYDA, ANDREW P., ANTHONY LEEDS, AND DAVID B. SMITH. "The Place of Pigs in Melanesian Subsistence." In Viola E. Garfield, ed., Symposium: Patterns of Land Utilization, and Other Papers. Proceedings of the Annual Spring Meeting of the American Ethnological Society, 1961. Seattle: University of Washington Press, 1962.

VAYDA, ANDREW P., AND ROY A. RAPPAPORT. "Ecology: Cultural and Noncultural." In James H. Clifton, ed., Introduction to Cultural Anthropology. Boston: Houghton Mifflin, 1968.

VINCENT, JOAN. "Political Anthropology: Manipulative Strategies." Annual Review of Anthropology, 7 (1978): 175–94.

VISABERGHI, ELISABETTA, AND DOROTHY MUNKENKBECK FRAGASZY. "Do Monkeys Ape?" In Parker and Gibson, eds., "Language" and Intelligence in Monkeys and Apes: Comparative Developmental Perspectives.

VON FRISCH, K. "Dialects in the Language of the Bees." Scientific American, August 1962, pp. 78–87.

WAGLEY, CHARLES. "Cultural Influences on Population: A Comparison of Two Tupi Tribes." In Patricia J. Lyon, ed., Native South Americans: Ethnology of the Least Known Continent. Boston: Little, Brown, 1974.

WALLACE, ANTHONY. The Death and Rebirth of the Seneca. New York: Knopf, 1970.

WALLACE, ANTHONY, "Mental Illness, Biology and Culture." In Hsu, ed., Psychological Anthropology.

WALLACE, ANTHONY. Religion: An Anthropological View. New York: Random House, 1966.

WALLERSTEIN, IMMANUEL. The Modern World-System. New York: Academic Press, 1974.

WANNER, ERIC, AND LILA R. GLEITMAN, eds. Language Acquisition: The State of the Art. Cambridge: Cambridge University Press, 1982.

WARD, PETER M. "Introduction and Purpose." In Peter M. Ward, ed., Self-Help Housing: A Critique. London: Mansell Publishing Limited, 1982, pp. 1–13.

WARNER, W. LLOYD. A Black Civilization: A Social Study of an Australian Tribe. New York: Harper, 1937.

WARNER, W. LLOYD, AND PAUL S. LUNT. The Social Life of a Modern Community. New Haven: Yale University Press, 1941.

WASHBURN, DOROTHY K., ed. Structure and Cognition in Art. Cambridge: Cambridge University Press, 1983.

WASHBURN, SHERWOOD. "Tools and Human Evolution." Scientific American, September 1960, pp. 62–75.

WEBB, KAREN E. "An Evolutionary Aspect of Social Structure and a Verb 'Have.' " *American Anthropologist,* 79 (1977): 42–49.

WEBER, MAX. *The Theory of Social and Economic Organization.* Trans. A.M. Henderson and Talcott Parsons. New York: Oxford University Press, 1947.

WEINER, ANNETTE B. *Women of Value, Men of Renown: New Perspectives in Trobriand Exchange.* Austin: University of Texas Press, 1976.

WEINER, J.S. "Nose Shape and Climate." *Journal of Physical Anthropology,* 4 (1954): 615–18.

WEINREICH, URIEL. *Languages in Contact.* The Hague: Mouton, 1968.

WEISNER, THOMAS S., MARY BAUSANO, AND MADELEINE KORNFEIN. "Putting Family Ideals into Practice: Pronaturalism in Conventional and Nonconventional California Families." *Ethos,* 11 (1983): 278–304.

WEISNER, THOMAS S., AND RONALD GALLIMORE. "My Brother's Keeper: Child and Sibling Caretaking." *Current Anthropology,* 18 (1977): 169–90.

WENKE, ROBERT J. *Patterns in Prehistory: Humankind's First Three Million Years.* 3rd ed. New York: Oxford University Press, 1990.

WERNER, DENNIS. *Amazon Journey: An Anthropologist's Year among Brazil's Mekranoti Indians.* New York: Simon & Schuster, 1984.

WERNER, DENNIS. "Chiefs and Presidents: A Comparison of Leadership Traits in the United States and among the Mekranoti-Kayapo of Central Brazil." *Ethos,* 10 (1982): 136–48.

WERNER, DENNIS. "Child Care and Influence among the Mekranoti of Central Brazil." *Sex Roles,* 10 (1984): 385–404.

WERNER, DENNIS. "A Cross-Cultural Perspective on Theory and Research on Male Homosexuality." *Journal of Homosexuality,* 4 (1979): 345–62.

WERNER, DENNIS. "On the Societal Acceptance or Rejection of Male Homosexuality." M.A. thesis, Hunter College of the City University of New York, 1975.

WERNER, DENNIS. "Trekking in the Amazon Forest." *Natural History,* November 1978, pp. 42–54.

WERNER, OSWALD, AND G. MARK SCHOEPFLE. *Systematic Fieldwork. Volume 1: Foundations of Ethnography and Interviewing.* Newbury Park, CA: Sage Publications, 1987.

WESTERMARCK, EDWARD. *The History of Human Marriage.* London: Macmillan, 1984.

WEYER, E.M. *The Eskimos: Their Environment and Folkways.* New Haven: Yale University Press, 1932.

WHEAT, JOE B. "A Paleo-Indian Bison Kill." *Scientific American,* January 1967, pp. 44–52.

WHEATLEY, PAUL. *The Pivot of the Four Quarters.* Chicago: Aldine, 1971.

WHITAKER, IAN. *Social Relations in a Nomadic Lappish Community.* Oslo: Utgitt av Norsk Folksmuseum, 1955.

WHITE, BENJAMIN. "Demand for Labor and Population Growth in Colonial Java." *Human Ecology,* 1, no. 3 (March 1973): 217–36.

WHITE, DOUGLAS R., AND MICHAEL L. BURTON. "Causes of Polygyny: Ecology, Economy, Kinship, and Warfare." *American Anthropologist,* 90 (1988): 871–87.

WHITE, DOUGLAS R., MICHAEL L. BURTON, AND LILYAN A. BRUDNER. "Entailment Theory and Method: A Cross-Cultural Analysis of the Sexual Division of Labor." *Behavior Science Research,* 12 (1977): 1–24.

WHITE, LESLIE A. "The Expansion of the Scope of Science." In Morton H. Fried, ed., *Readings in Anthropology,* 2nd ed., vol. 1. New York: Thomas Y. Crowell, 1968.

WHITE, LESLIE A. "A Problem in Kinship Terminology." *American Anthropologist,* 41 (1939): 569–70.

WHITE, LESLIE A. *The Science of Culture. A Study of Man and Civilization.* New York: Farrar, Straus & Cudahy, 1949.

WHITE, RANDALL. "Rethinking the Middle/Upper Paleolithic Transition." *Current Anthropology,* 23 (1982): 169–75.

WHITE, TIM D. "Les Australopithèques." *La Recherche,* November 1982, pp. 1258–70.

WHITE, TIM D., DONALD C. JOHANSON, AND WILLIAM H. KIMBEL. "*Australopithecus africanus:* Its Phyletic Position Reconsidered." *South African Journal of Science,* 77 (1981): 445–70.

WHITING, BEATRICE B. *Paiute Sorcery.* Viking Fund Publications in Anthropology, no. 15. New York: Wenner-Gren Foundation, 1950.

WHITING, BEATRICE B. "Sex Identity Conflict and Physical Violence." *American Anthropologist,* 67 (1965): 123–40.

WHITING, BEATRICE B., AND CAROLYN P. EDWARDS. in collaboration with Carol R. Ember, Gerald M. Erchak, Sara Harkness, Robert L. Munroe, Ruth H. Munroe, Sara B. Nerlove, Susan Seymour, Charles M. Super, Thomas S. Weisner, and Martha Wenger. *Children of Different Worlds: The Formation of Social Behavior.* Cambridge, MA: Harvard University Press, 1988.

WHITING, BEATRICE B., AND CAROLYN P. EDWARDS. "A Cross-Cultural Analysis of Sex Differences in the Behavior of Children Aged Three through Eleven." *Journal of Social Psychology,* 91 (1973): 171–88.

WHITING, BEATRICE B., AND JOHN W. M. WHITING (in collaboration with Richard Longabaugh). *Children of Six Cultures: A Psycho-Cultural Analysis.* Cambridge, MA: Harvard University Press, 1975.

WHITING, JOHN W.M. *Becoming a Kwoma.* New Haven: Yale University Press, 1941.

WHITING, JOHN W.M. "Cultural and Sociological Influences on Development." In *Growth and Development of the Child in His Setting.* Maryland Child Growth and Development Institute, 1959.

WHITING, JOHN W.M. "Effects of Climate on Certain Cultural Practices." In Ward H. Goodenough, ed., *Explorations in Cultural Anthropology.* New York: McGraw-Hill, 1964.

WHITING, JOHN W.M., AND IRVIN L. CHILD. *Child Training and Personality: A Cross-Cultural Study.* New Haven: Yale University Press, 1953.

WHYTE, MARTIN K. "Cross-Cultural Codes Dealing with the Relative Status of Women." *Ethnology,* 17 (1978): 211–37.

WHYTE, MARTIN K. *The Status of Women in Preindustrial Societies.* Princeton: Princeton University Press, 1978.

WILSON, EDWARD O. *Sociobiology.* Cambridge, MA: Harvard University Press, Belknap Press, 1975.

WILSON, MONICA. *Good Company: A Study of Nyakyusa Age Villages.* Boston: Beacon Press, 1963 (originally published 1951).

WINKELMAN, MICHAEL JAMES. "Magico-Religious Practitioner Types and Socioeconomic Condi-

tions." *Behavior Science Research,* 20 (1986): 17–46.

WINKELMAN, MICHAEL. "Trance States: A Theoretical Model and Cross-Cultural Analysis." *Ethos,* 14 (1986): 174–203.

WITKIN, HERMAN A. "A Cognitive Style Approach to Cross-Cultural Research." *International Journal of Psychology,* 2 (1967): 233–50.

WITKOWSKI, STANLEY R. "Polygyny, Age of Marriage, and Female Status." Paper presented at the annual meeting of the American Anthropological Association, San Francisco, 1975.

WITKOWSKI, STANLEY R., AND CECIL H. BROWN. "Lexical Universals." *Annual Review of Anthropology,* 7 (1978): 427–51.

WITKOWSKI, STANLEY R., AND HAROLD W. BURRIS. "Societal Complexity and Lexical Growth." *Behavior Science Research,* 16 (1981): 143–59.

WITTFOGEL, KARL. *Oriental Despotism: A Comparative Study of Total Power.* New Haven: Yale University Press, 1957.

WOLF, ARTHUR. "Adopt a Daughter-in-Law, Marry a Sister: A Chinese Solution to the Problem of the Incest Taboo." *American Anthropologist,* 70 (1968): 864–74.

WOLF, ARTHUR P., AND CHIEH-SHAN HUANG. *Marriage and Adoption in China, 1845–1945.* Stanford, CA: Stanford University Press, 1980.

WOLF, ERIC R. *Europe and the People without History.* Berkeley: University of California Press, 1982.

WOLF, ERIC. *Peasants.* Englewood Cliffs, NJ: Prentice Hall, 1966.

WOLF, ERIC R. "San José: Subcultures of a 'Traditional' Coffee Municipality." In Julian H. Steward et al., *The People of Puerto Rico.* Urbana: University of Illinois Press, 1956, pp. 171–264.

WOLF, ERIC. "Types of Latin American Peasantry: A Preliminary Discussion." *American Anthropologist,* 57 (1955): 452–71.

WOLPOFF, M.H. "*Ramapithecus* and Human Origins: An Anthropologist's Perspective of Changing Interpretations." In Ciochon and Corruccini, eds., *New Interpretations of Ape and Human Ancestry,* pp. 651–76.

WOLPOFF, MILFORD H. "Competitive Exclusion among Lower Pleistocene Hominids: The Single Species Hypothesis." *Man,* 6 (1971): 601–13.

WOLPOFF, MILFORD H., AND ABEL NIKINI. "Early and Early Middle Pleistocene Hominids from Asia and Africa." In Delson, ed., *Ancestors*, pp. 202–5.

WOODBURN, JAMES. "An Introduction to Hadza Ecology." In Lee and DeVore, eds., *Man the Hunter*.

WORSLEY, PETER. *The Trumpet Shall Sound: A Study of "Cargo" Cults in Melanesia.* London: MacGibbon & Kee, 1957.

WRANGHAM, RICHARD W. "An Ecological Model of Female-Bonded Primate Groups." *Behaviour*, 75 (1980): 262–300.

WRIGHT, GARY A. "Origins of Food Production in Southwestern Asia: A Survey of Ideas." *Current Anthropology*, 12 (1971): 447–78.

WRIGHT, GEORGE O. "Projection and Displacement: A Cross-Cultural Study of Folktale Aggression." *Journal of Abnormal and Social Psychology*, 49 (1954): 523–28.

WRIGHT, HENRY. "The Evolution of Civilization." In David J. Meltzer, Don D. Fowler, and Jeremy A. Sahloff, eds., *American Archaeology Past and Present*. Washington, DC: Smithsonian Institution Press, 1986.

WRIGHT, HENRY T., AND GREGORY A. JOHNSON. "Population, Exchange, and Early State Formation in Southwestern Iran." *American Anthropologist*, 77 (1975): 267–77.

WU RUKANG AND LIN SHENGLONG. "Peking Man." *Scientific American*, June 1983, pp. 86–94.

WU XINZHI AND WU MAOLIN. "Early *Homo sapiens* in China." In Wu Rukang and John W. Olsen, eds., *Paleoanthropology and Paleolithic Archaeology in the People's Republic of China*. Orlando, FL: Academic Press, 1985, pp. 91–106.

YARNELL, RICHARD A. "Domestication of Sunflower and Sumpweed in Eastern North America." In Richard I. Ford, ed., *The Nature and Status of Ethnobotany*. Anthropological Papers, Museum of Anthropology, no. 67, Ann Arbor: University of Michigan, 1978, pp. 289–300.

YOUNG, FRANK W. "A Fifth Analysis of the Star Husband Tale." *Ethnology*, 9 (1970): 389–413.

YOUNG, LOUISE B., ed. *Evolution of Man*. New York: Oxford University Press, 1970.

YOUNG, T. CUYLER, JR. "Population Densities and Early Mesopotamian Urbanism." In Ucko, Tringham, and Dimbleby, eds., *Man, Settlement and Urbanism*.

ZOHARY, DANIEL. "The Progenitors of Wheat and Barley in Relation to Domestication and Agriculture Dispersal in the Old World." In Ucko and Dimbleby, eds., *The Domestication and Exploitation of Plants and Animals*.

Photo Acknowledgments

Chapter 1 Page 1, Co Rendmeester/The Image Bank; p. 4, C. Hires/Gamma-Liaison; p. 5, Anthro-Photo File; p. 9, Irven DeVore/Anthro-Photo File; p. 10, NASA.

Chapter 2 Page 13, Donald Specker/Animals Animals; p. 15, Gregory G. Dimijian, M.D./Photo Researchers; p. 18, M. W. Tweedie/Photo Researchers; p. 23 (top), Stephen J. Krasemann/Photo Researchers; p. 23 (bottom), Alan Carey/Photo Researchers.

Chapter 3 Page 27, George Holton/Photo Researchers; p. 31, Tom McHugh/Photo Researchers; p. 32, Peter B. Kaplan/Photo Researchers; p. 33 (top), David R. Frazier/Photo Researchers; p. 33 (bottom), Bill Nation/Sygma; p. 35, Tom McHugh/Photo Researchers; p. 41 (left), Zig Leszczynski/Animals Animals; p. 41 (right), George Holton/Photo Researchers; p. 44, Ronald H. Cohen/The Gorilla Foundation.

Chapter 4 Page 47, Jim Tutcn/Animals Animals; p. 52, Tom McHugh/Photo Researchers; p. 56, Luci Betti/S.U.N.Y. at Stony Brook, N.Y.; p. 57, W. Sacco.

Chapter 5 Page 61, John Reader/Science Photo Library/Photo Researchers; p. 64, Stephen J. Krasemann/Photo Researchers; p. 69 (top and bottom), Courtesy of "La Recherche," November 1982, Vol. 13, pages 1268 and 1269. Photo by D. C. Johanson; p. 70, John Reader/Science Photo Library; p. 71, Tom McHugh/Photo Researchers; p. 76, Tom McHugh/Photo Researchers; p. 78, John Reader/Science Photo Library/Photo Researchers.

Chapter 6 Page 82, Peter Buckley; p. 89, Photo by A. R. Hughes, by permission of P. V. Tobias; p. 97, Peter Buckley; p. 99, © President and Fellows of Harvard College, 1992. All Rights Reserved. Peabody Museum, Harvard University. Photograph by Hillel Burger.

Chapter 7 Page 103, Jeff Lowenthal/Woodfin Camp & Associates; p. 107, Tim Davis/Photo Researchers; p. 108, Doug Plummer/Photo Researchers; p. 114 (top), Eunice Harris/Photo Researchers; p. 114 (bottom), Anthro-Photo File; p. 117, Bibliothèque Nationale, Paris; p. 119, Laima Druskis.

Chapter 8 Page 122, Jean-Loup Bobert/Explorer/Photo Researchers; p. 126 (left), Shea/Anthro-Photo File; p. 126 (right), Anthro-Photo File; p. 130, Washburn/Anthro-Photo File; p. 131, Courtesy of the American Museum of Natural History; p. 134, Anthro-Photo File; p. 136, Quesada/Burke, New York; p. 142, Courtesy of the American Museum of Natural History.

Chapter 9 Page 144, Ulrike Welsch/Photo Researchers; p. 149 (left), The Granger Collection; p. 149 (right), George Holton/Photo Researchers; p. 151, Georg Gerster/Rapho/Photo Researchers; p. 153, George Holton/Photo Researchers.

Chapter 10 Page 157, Tony Stone Worldwide; p. 159 (top), Lawrence Migdale/Photo Researchers; p. 159 (bottom left), N. Martin Hauprich/Photo Researchers; p. 159 (bottom right), Joan Lebold Cohen/Photo Researchers; p. 164 (left), Time Davis/Photo Researchers; p. 164 (top right), Susan McCartney/Photo Researchers; p. 164 (bottom), Jodi Cobb/Woodfin Camp & Associates; p. 166, Roger Dollarhide/Monkmeyer Press; p. 168, Renee Purse/Photo Researchers.

Chapter 11 Page 173, John Reader/Science Photo Library/Photo Researchers; p. 175, Lowell Georgia/Photo Researchers; p. 176, American Philosophical Society; p. 178, Courtesy of Helena Malinowski Wayne; p. 179, The Granger Collection; p. 182, Henri Cartier-Bresson/Magnum Photos; p. 184, Kal Muller/Woodfin Camp & Associates.

Chapter 12 Page 190, Irven DeVore/Anthro-Photo File; p. 193, Michael Gilbert/Science Photo Library/Photo Researchers; p. 196 (top), Victor Englebert/Photo Researchers; p. 196 (bottom), Sven-Olof Lindblad/Photo Researchers; p. 200, James Prince/Photo Researchers.

Chapter 13 Page 203, Victor Englebert/Photo Researchers; p. 205, Susan Kuklin/Rapho/Photo Researchers; p. 206, David Carter; p. 210, Bill Bachman/Photo Researchers; p. 218, Robert A. Isaacs/Photo Researchers; p. 220, Ulrike Welsch/Photo Researchers; p. 224 (top), Renate Hiller/Monkmeyer Press; p. 224 (bottom), Rhoda Sidney/Monkmeyer Press.

Chapter 14 Page 228, George Holton/Photo Researchers; p. 231, George Holton/Photo Researchers; p. 233, Loren McIntyre/Woodfin Camp & Associates; p. 236, Robert Clark/Photo Researchers; p. 238, Courtesy John Deere; p. 239, Farrell Grehan/Photo Researchers; p. 242, François Gohier/Photo Researchers.

Chapter 15 Page 245, Peter Knapp/The Image Bank; p. 249, George Holton/Photo Researchers; p. 250, Paul Shambroom/Photo Researchers; p. 255, The Granger Collection; p. 256, DeVore/Anthro-Photo File; p. 257, Cyril Isy-Schwart/The Image Bank; p. 260, Washburn/Anthro-Photo File; p. 264, Jose Azel/Contact/Woodfin Camp & Associates; p. 268, George Holton/Photo Researchers; p. 269, Dana Hyde/Photo Researchers.

Chapter 16 Page 272, Marc & Evelyne Bernheim/Woodfin Camp & Associates; p. 274, Eastcott/Momatiuk/Woodfin Camp & Associates; p. 276, Katz/Anthro-Photo File; p. 279, Jan Halaska/Photo Researchers; p. 281, Victor Englebert/Photo Researchers.

Chapter 17 Page 286, Carl Purcell/Photo Researchers; p. 288, Don Goode/Photo Researchers; p. 290, John Nettis/Photo Researchers; p. 291, Momatuik/Eastcott/Woodfin Camp & Associates; p. 295, Russ Kinne/Photo Researchers; p. 299, Dilip Mehta/Contact/Woodfin Camp & Associates; p. 302, Kim Robbie/The Stock Market; p. 303, Nathan Benn/Woodfin Camp & Associates.

Chapter 18 Page 307, United Nations; p. 312, Jerry Cooke/Photo Researchers; p. 314, Daniele Pellegrini/Photo Researchers; p. 320, E. Heiniger/Rapho/Photo Researchers; p. 323, The Granger Collection; p. 326, Eastcott/Momatiuk/Woodfin Camp & Associates.

Chapter 19 Page 329, George Holton/Photo Researchers; p. 331, Rapho/Photo Researchers; p. 334, Laima Druskis; p. 339, Craig Aurness/Woodfin Camp & Associates; p. 342, Courtesy of the American Museum of Natural History.

Chapter 20 Page 352, John Moss/Photo Researchers; p. 355, Courtesy of N. and R. Dyson-Hudson; p. 358, George Holton/Photo Researchers; p. 359, Ruth Massey/Photo Researchers; p. 360, Susan McCartney/Photo Researchers; p. 362, Luis Villota/The Stock Market.

Chapter 21 Page 367, Laima Druskis; p. 370, DeVore/Anthro-Photo File; p. 374, The Granger Collection; p. 375, Lester Sloan/Woodfin Camp & Associates; p. 377, The Granger Collection; p. 382, Dan Budnik/Woodfin Camp & Associates; p. 385, George Holton/Photo Researchers.

Chapter 22 Page 390, George Holton/Photo Researchers; p. 392, Robert Phillips/The Image Bank; p. 394, Laura Dwight/Peter Arnold, Inc.; p. 395, Neil Goldstein; p. 397, Napoleon Chagnon; p. 399, Halpern/Anthro-Photo File; p. 400, Marc & Evelyne Bernheim/Woodfin Camp & Associates; p. 403, Will McIntyre/Photo Researchers; p. 408, Michael McCoy/Photo Researchers.

Chapter 23 Page 411, Katrina Thomas/Photo Researchers; p. 417, Art Resource; p. 420 (top left), Allen Green/Photo Researchers; p. 420 (top right), Ray Ellis/Photo Researchers; p. 420 (bottom left), Alain Evrard/Photo Researchers; p. 420 (bottom right), Blair Seitz/Photo Researchers; p. 422, The Granger Collection; p. 425, DeVore/Anthro-Photo File; p. 428, The Granger Collection.

Chapter 24 Page 431, Sylvain Grandadam/Photo Researchers; p. 433, Brun/Explorer/Photo Researchers; p. 435 (top), H. W. Silvester/Rapho/Photo Researchers; p. 435 (bottom), Michal Heron/Woodfin Camp & Associates; p. 437 (top), George Holton/Photo Researchers; p. 437 (bottom), Bridgeman/Art Resource; p. 441 (top), George Holton/Photo Researchers; p. 441 (bottom), Susan McCartney/Photo Researchers.

Chapter 25 Page 446, Jose Azel/Cuniaci/Woodfin Camp & Associates; p. 448, Philippe Maille/Explorer/Photo Researchers; p. 450, Mary M. Thacher/Photo Researchers; p. 452, Marcello Bertinetti/Photo Researchers; p. 455, The Granger Collection; p. 459, United Nations; p. 460, The Granger Collection; p. 463, Jane Schreibman/Photo Researchers.

Chapter 26 Page 468, Laima Druskis; p. 473, Laima Druskis; p. 476, AP/Wide World Photos; p. 482, Photo by Pitkin/Baker; p. 484, Official U.S. Navy Photograph; p. 486, Aluminum Company of America.

Index

Discovery, culture change and, 447–49
Disease, infectious, 333, 379
    malaria, 112–13
    measles, 111–12, 453
    race, culture, and, 117–18
    smallpox, 117–18, 453
    susceptibility to, 111, 117
    tuberculosis, 453
Diurnal primates, 31
Divination, 421
Division of labor, 45, 67
    sexual, 288–96
        compatibility-with-child-care theory, 288–90
        economy of effort theory, 290
        expendability theory, 290–91
        strength theory, 288
DNA (deoxyribonucleic acid), 19–20, 58
Dobzhansky, Theodosius, 21, 22, 67, 120
Domestication of plants and animals, 131–32
    Binford-Flannery model of, 138–39
    in the Near East, 132
    in the New World, 136
    in Southeast Asia, China, and Africa, 131–32
Dominant traits, 18–19, 21
Double descent, 336
Double unilineal descent, 336
Douglas, Mary, 182
Dowling, John, 249
Dowry, 315
    indirect, 315–16
Draft, 254–55
Draper, Patricia, 255, 296
Dryopithecus, 57
DuBois, Cora, 398
Dubois, Eugene, 76
Dugum Dani, 386–87
Dundes, Alan, 443
Durham, William, 114, 319
Durkheim, Émile, 165, 414

E

Economy(ies), 246–70
    goods and services, distribution of, 259–70
    labor, 252–58
    peasant, 268
    resource allocation, 246–52
    subsistence, 253, 254
Edgerton, Robert, 402, 406
Egalitarian societies, 273, 274–75
Ego-centered kin group, 337
Eisenstadt, S. N., 364, 365
Electron spin resonance dating, 91
Emotional development, 391–93
Endogamy, 320
Engels, Friedrich, 175
Environment, influence of, 105–6
Eocene epoch, 52, 54–55
Epidemiology, 5
Eskimos, 405, 406, 407
    marriage among, 314–15
Eta, 281
Ethnocentrism, 159–60
Ethnographer, 7
Ethnographic analogy, 94

Ethnography, 7
    of speaking, 222–23
Ethnohistorian, 7–8
    vs. ethnographer, 8
    vs. historian, 8
Ethnohistory, 200
Ethnolinguists, 222
Ethnology, 6, 7–8
Ethnoscience, 182–83
Etoro, 304
Evolution, 4, 16–17
    biological, 24
    cultural, 24
    and genetic variation, 21
    kinds of, 181
    intermediate interpretation, 90
    theory of, 14, 89–90
Evolutionary divergence, 28
Evolutionism, 174–76
Exchange, market or commercial, 266–70
Exogamy, 320
Explanations, 191–92
    defined, 191
Extramarital sex, 43

F

Falsification, 193
Family, 325–27 (*see also* Marriage)
    extended, 325–27, 330
    independent, 330
    matrifocal, 325
    nuclear, 325
    violence and abuse, 479–81
Family-disruption theory, 318
Famines, 475–76
Fayum Oligocene Anthropoids, 55
Female exchange, 315
Fertile Crescent, 132, 138
Feuding, 386
Field independence and dependence, 403–4
Fieldwork, 199
Fiesta complex, 270
Fijans, 383
Firth, Raymond, 319, 458, 464
Fischer, John, 436
Fish, Paul, 87
Fishing, 240
Fission-track dating, 51–52
Flannery, Kent, 126, 138
Fluorine dating (fossils), 50–51, 76
Folklore, 440–44
Food collecting, broad-spectrum, 123, 127–128
    and sedentarism, 128–29
Food collectors, 246–47
Food-getting, 229–43
    activities, 292, 294
    collection, 229–32
    environmental restraints on, 240–42
    strategies of, 242
Food production, 123–31, 232, 242–43 (*see also* Domestication of plants and animals)
    at Ali Kosh, 133
    Binford-Flannery model, 138–39

Parker, Seymour, 317
Participant-observer approach, 177
Particularism, historical, 176
Pastoralism, 238–40
Pastoralists, 248–49, 251–52
Patriclan, 338
Patrilocal residence, 330, 331, 332–33
Patterns of Culture (Benedict), 179
Peacock, Nadine, 5
Peasants, 460–61
Peking man, 77
Percussion flaking, 88
Perry, William J., 177
Personality, 391 (*see also* Psychological development)
  personality integration of culture, 407
Pfeiffer, John, 88
Phenotype, 19
Phonemes, 211–12
Phones, 211
Phonology, 211–12
Phratries, 339, 341
Physical anthropology, 4–6
Physical variation, 106–15
Piaget, Jean, 393
Pibloktoq, 405–6
Pilbeam, David, 64–65
Pithecanthropus erectus, 76
Pit houses, 126
Plains Indians, 361
Planned change. *See* Applied (practicing) anthropology
Platyrrhines, 35, 55
Political economy, 185
Political life, 368
Political organization, 368–80
  bands, 369–70
  chiefdoms, 373–75
  defined, 368
  factors associated with variation in, 377–79
  states, 375–77
  tribes, 370–73
Political participation, 380–81
Politics, male predominance in, 295
Polyandry, 321, 324–25
Polygamy, 321
Polygyny, 199, 321–23
  nonsororal, 322
  sororal, 322–23
Polyphony, 439
Pomo Indians, 264–65
Pongids. *See* Great apes
Population biology, 5
Postpartum requirements, universality of marriage and, 311
Poro (secret society), 363, 364
Postpartum sex taboo, 323–24
Potassium-argon (K-Ar) dating method, 51, 52
Potlatch, 264
Prairies, 241
Prehensile (grasping) hands, 31, 34
Prehensile (grasping) tails, 35
Prehistory, 6
Pressure flaking, 93
Price-Williams, Douglass, 394
Prides (lion social groups), 22
Priests, 426
Primate(s), 4, 14, 28, 58
  adaptations of, 39–41

anthropoids, 28
arboreal, 28–29
brain size of, 40
earliest, 52–53
emergence of, 53–54
fruit-eaters vs. leaf-eaters, 40
group size of, 40–41
physical features of, 28–31
play behavior, 32–33
prosimians, 34
social features of, 31–33
suborders of, 28
traits of, 28
vision, 31
Primatologists, 4
Primatology, 28
Principles of Geology (Lyell), 15
Probability value (p-value), 198
Proconsul africanus, 56
Production, defined, 252
Projective tests, 408
Propliopithecids, 55
Prosimians, 28, 34, 55
Proto-apes, 56–57
Proto-Indo-European (PIE), 215, 216, 217
Protolanguage, 215
Pryor, Frederick, 269
Psychological anthropologists, 391
Psychological development:
  cognitive development, 393–94
  cross-cultural variation in, 394–407
  cultural variation and, 397–402, 407–8
  emotional development, 391–93
  universality of, 391–94
Purgatorius, 52
Pyramids, 150, 152

Q

Quadrapedalism, 50
Quadrupeds, 34
Qolla, 404

R

Race(s):
  concept of, 115
    arbitrariness of, 115–16
  definition of, 22
  geographical, 116
  and intelligence, 118
  local, 116
  racism and, 115
Rachis, 131
Racial variation, related to cultural variation, 116–20
Radcliffe-Brown, Arthur Reginald, 178, 385
Radiations, evolutionary, 53
Radiocarbon (carbon[14]) dating, 90
Raiding, 386
Ramapithecus, 58
Random sample, 167
Rank societies, 273, 275–76

Toolmaking, 6, 43, 251
  Acheulian, 77–78, 86
  bipedalism and, 65
  blade technique, 83, 94
  Levalloisian method, 86
  methods of, 73
  Mousterian, 85–87, 92
  post-Acheulian, 85, 87, 92
  Upper Paleolithic, 92–94
Tools:
  bifacial vs. unifacial, 73
  Clovis complex (Clovis point), 99
  Folsom point, 99
  in New World, 98
  Oldowan, 74, 75
  Upper Paleolithic, 95
  as weapons, 65, 74–75
Torrey, E. Fuller, 424
Totems, 338, 414
Toth, Nicholas, 74
Trade, state formation and, 155
Trances, 420
Transformational/generative theory, 214
Triandis, Leigh, 417
Tribal unions, 361
Trobriand Islanders, 177, 261–62, 267, 275, 392
  marriage customs of, 312
Troop (monkeys), 37
Trudgill, Peter, 225
Trukese, 248, 341, 342, 343
Tsembaga (of New Guinea), 183–84
Tundras, 123
Tupari Indians, 112
Tutsi, 320
Twa, 320
Tylor, Edward B., 174–75, 318, 413, 442

U

Ucko, Peter J., 95
Upper Paleolithic, 91–97, 130
  blade technique, 93
  defined, 91
  engravings, 97
  homesites, 92
  hunting, 123–24
  toolmaking, 92–94
Urbanization, voluntary associations and, 365
Uruk period, 148

V

Variables, 191
Variation:
  genetic, 21, 120
  individual, 163–65
  physical, 106–15
Vayda, Andrew, 183, 263
Venus figurines, 97
Visual predation theory, 54

W

Wallace, Alfred Russell, 16
Wallace, Anthony, 406, 415, 427
Wallerstein, Immanuel, 185
War, 483–85
Warfare, 381, 386–88
  explanations for, 387–88
  internal vs. external, 333
Warner, Lloyd, 277
Watson, James, 19
Washburn, Sherwood, 64
Washoe (chimpanzee), 44, 206, 207
Weapons, primates' use of, 43
Weidenreich, Franz, 77
Werner, Dennis, 296
Westermarck, Edward, 316
Wheat, Joe, 100
White, Leslie A., 8, 180, 318
White, Tim, 71
Whiting, Beatrice, 300, 423
Whiting, John, 180, 191, 192, 197, 300, 323, 402, 407, 408
Whorf, Benjamin Lee, 222
Whyte, Martin, 297
Wiitiko psychosis, 405
Wilberforce, Bishop, 16
Willey, Gordon, 138
Wilson, Allan, 58
Wissler, Clark, 176, 177
Witchcraft, 422–24
Witches, 425
Wolf, Arthur, 316–17
Wolf, Eric, 460
Wolf, Margery, 417
Wolpoff, Milford, 65
Work groups, 256, 257
Worsley, Peter, 427
Wright, George, 444
Wright, Henry, 147–48, 155
Wright, Sewall, 105
Writing, 7

X

Xia dynasty, 152

Y

Yahi Indians, 453–54
Yanomamö Indians, 112, 260, 315, 391, 396
Yapese, 303
Yerkish (symbolic language), 44
Yoruba, 323–24, 406
Yucatán, 6

Z

Zo (secret society), 363, 364
Zuni, 419